American Legal History

385-410
459-492   411-58   495-535
535-40   515-32
655-75

535-40

385-492
495 - 540
655 - 75

The North West Ordinance 1787 America

Prigg v. Pennsylvania 1842 Pennsylvania

Dred Scott v. Sanford 1857 Missouri

Civil Rights Act 1866 ← 14th Amendment

Slaughtehouse Cases 1873

Civil Rights Act 1875

People v sWeeT 1925

Korematsu v. United States 1944 California

Brown v. Board of Ed 1954 Kansas

Civil rights Act 1964

AMERICAN LEGAL HISTORY

Cases and Materials

◆

Third Edition

KERMIT L. HALL
Utah State University

PAUL FINKELMAN
University of Tulsa College of Law

JAMES W. ELY, Jr.
Vanderbilt University

New York   Oxford
OXFORD UNIVERSITY PRESS
2005

Oxford University Press

Oxford   New York
Auckland   Bangkok   Buenos Aires   Cape Town   Chennai
Dar es Salaam   Delhi   Hong Kong   Istanbul   Karachi   Kolkata
Kuala Lumpur   Madrid   Melbourne   Mexico City   Mumbai   Nairobi
São Paulo   Shanghai   Taipei   Tokyo   Toronto

Copyright © 1991, 1996, 2005 by Oxford University Press, Inc.

Published by Oxford University Press, Inc.
198 Madison Avenue, New York, New York 10016
www.oup.com

Oxford is a registered trademark of Oxford University Press

Library of Congress Cataloging-in-Publication Data
Hall, Kermit L.
    American legal history : cases and materials / Kermit L. Hall, Paul Finkelman, James W. Ely.—3rd ed.
        p. cm.
    Includes bibliographical references and index.
    ISBN 0-19-516224-2 (cloth : alk. paper)—ISBN 0-19-516225-0 (pbk. : alk. paper)
    1. Law—United States—History—Cases.   I. Finkelman, Paul, 1949–   II. Ely, James W., 1938–   III. Title.

KF352.A7H35 2004
349.73—dc22   2004046501

Printing number: 9 8 7 6 5 4 3 2 1

Printed in the United States of America
on acid-free paper

We dedicate this book to our mentors and friends
who have taught us so much over the years

John Hope Franklin
Harold M. Hyman
Stanley N. Katz
Stanley I. Kutler
Paul L. Murphy
William M. Wiecek

Contents

Chapter 2: Law in a Republican Revolution, 1760–1815   78

Chapter 4: Slavery, the Civil War, Reconstruction, and Segregation   215

Chapter 7: Total War, Civil Liberties, and Civil Rights   411

Chapter 8: The Rise of Legal Liberalism, Economic Reform, and the New Deal, 1900–1945   459

Chapter 10: Law and the Economy in Modern America   571

Preface

When we wrote the first edition of *American Legal History: Cases and Materials* in 1990, legal history was still a relatively new and emerging field. A growing number of law schools and some history departments offered courses, albeit sporadically, in the history of private law and legal institutions. When law was studied in its historical context, the emphasis was almost always on public law generally and the work of the Supreme Court specifically. Courses in either constitutional history or, in political science departments and law schools, its twin, constitutional law, were the closest brush that most undergraduates and law students had with the nation's legal past. The history of American law was often a reprise on major Supreme Court cases and the justices who delivered them. Today, however, American legal history has become a mature field, with many professors in law schools and history departments teaching courses and producing scholarship in the field. Thanks in part to a more expansive and scholarly approach to legal education in law schools and to the impact of social history on the undergraduate history curriculum, American legal history is now taught at almost every law school and in a good number of history departments. And it is increasingly taught with an eye to merging rather than separating themes of private and public law development.

This new edition of *American Legal History* reflects the growing interest in the field. The book is much longer than the first and second editions. We have added new material, especially on the law of property and in the modern period. We have expanded our coverage of colonial America. We have taken into account new developments in law and tried to put into greater context the legal challenges that will confront us in the twenty-first century.

This book is designed to serve undergraduate and graduate courses in history and political science while fitting comfortably in legal history courses taught in law schools. However, in many ways, we departed from the usual structure of both law school casebooks and traditional documentary collections used in history and political science courses. We have made a particular effort to meet the needs of instructors and students, whatever their academic discipline, by including extensive headnotes that place documents in their historical context. We have excluded perplexing questions and small-change notecases that overwhelm many law school casebooks. We have also provided excerpts of cases that are longer than those typically found in documentary collections and many law school casebooks. Finally, we have used materials from secondary sources, such as articles from law reviews and journals, only sparingly. Our goal is to let the documents of legal history speak for themselves.

Because we take an expansive view of American legal culture, we have included materials not usually found in casebooks, such as speeches, government reports, lengthy excerpts from statutes, and works of philosophy. These kinds of documents, we believe, help to fit legal change with social, economic, and political developments. In short, our approach stresses the tension inherent in our legal system between law as a technical subject with its own internal logic and law as a scheme of social choice responsive to a host of political, social, and economic pressures.

We have chosen documents that illustrate important developments in legal history or that exemplify a particular direction of legal change. This approach reflects the reality of legal history. Legal change is often marked not by a great case and a great precedent, but by a series of incremental developments that gradually lead to a new consensus within the legal community and often society as a whole. In this way, legal history at the state level is not like the history of the federal Constitution, where a change of justices on the United States Supreme Court has resulted in dramatic changes in constitutional law.

We, of course, recognize that the federal government, whether through the Supreme Court, Congress, or the presidency, has been a powerful engine of legal change. But we also believe that an important ingredient in our legal history has been the changed importance of each within our legal system. For example, the nineteenth-century Supreme Court often ratified legal developments that had begun at the state level; the early-twentieth-century Court often stymied legal change; and the post–Depression era Supreme Court has often been in the vanguard of legal change. Since the Civil War, the nature of American federalism has shifted from a state-oriented system to one centered on the national government.

Since the 1930s the Supreme Court and Congress have done much to promote social change through the law. Indeed, when one views the history of American law, as we do, as the unfolding of social choices through the legal process, then the modern High Court and its justices, as well as Congress, take on considerable importance. For these reasons, our later chapters have far more material dealing with the national government—the Court, Congress, and even the presidency—than do the earlier ones.

Throughout this book, we have sought to provide opportunities to understand the interaction of public and private law developments. We believe, on balance, that the traditional distinction between legal and constitutional history has been often misleading, invariably artificial, and frequently irrelevant. Public and private law are best viewed as reciprocal and reinforcing phenomena. Changes in private and public law evolved from decisions by state courts and the lower federal courts, as well as from laws passed by state legislatures. Because these changes took place within the American federal system, legal developments were necessarily incremental, local, and seldom simultaneous throughout the country. Nevertheless, legal change did spread, usually reaching most, if not all, states. Many of these changes were also part of our constitutional history. To illustrate: the steamboat monopoly granted to Robert R. Livingston and Robert Fulton in New York, which had the blessing of that state's highest court, and the subsequent development of the Erie Canal in New York were probably as important to the growth of American commerce, and the development of the Constitution's commerce clause, as Chief Justice Marshall's landmark opinion in *Gibbons* v. *Ogden* (1824). In some areas of law, such as torts, state legislative policy making and state court decisions have always predominated. In the modern era, however, in areas such as civil liberties and civil rights, decisions by the Supreme Court have not only initiated new paths in the law, but also instantly nationalized them as well. Desegregation, reapportionment, and the legal recognition of personal autonomy and a right to privacy are well-known examples of the impact of the nation's highest court on law and public policy. They have also been, of course, highly controversial, since Americans have disagreed not only about the substance of these changes, but also about whether the Court's role in bringing them about has been appropriate.

We have combined the organizational principles of both history and law in this volume. Most law school casebooks are arranged topically, as is most legal education itself. This topical approach is even true for the study of constitutional law, which is the most historical course of the traditional law school curriculum. Historical studies, however, are usually organized chronologically to show change over time. We have embraced this approach, not only because we have, after all, fashioned a book of history, but also because we believe that the best way to understand the important changes in American law is to appreciate the constancy of much of our legal culture from its English origins to the present. Our goal is to display legal developments in their historical context.

While we have organized the book chronologically, we have also retained thematic and topical coherence. Thus many subjects—such as torts, property, the law of race relations, marriage and the family, and contracts—reappear throughout the volume. This arrangement makes it possible to follow legal developments in many fields over the course of three and a half centuries. The organization of this book, therefore, reflects our abiding belief that legal history can contribute to both an undergraduate's study of the American past and a law student's grasp of the legal system.

When we published the first edition of this book, we expressed the hope that our colleagues would step forward with suggestions, criticisms, and comments. Many did, and we thank them at the end of this preface. Library staffs at the Utah State University, the University of Tulsa College of Law, and the Vanderbilt University Law School were particularly helpful for this revision. In our other editions we had the assistance of librarians at the University of Florida, the Brooklyn Law School, the Syracuse University College of Law, the Ohio State University, the Chicago-Kent College of Law, and Virginia Tech as well as the staffs of the University of Pittsburgh Law Library, the Albany Law School Library, and the Broome County Supreme Court Library.

Research assistants and clerical staff have shared the more mundane aspects of documentary collection and editing. Over the years we have been aided by the following students, many of whom have gone on to become professors and scholars in their own right. We thank Tracey Kort Roesle, Steven Prescott, Eric Rise, Elizabeth Monroe, Steve Noll, Mica McKinney, Neil Abercrombie, Colleen Grzeskowiak, Bill Karchner, Valerie Cross, Degna P. Levister, Elayna Nacci, and Jordan Tamagi. Over the years a number of administrative assistants, reference librarians, and clerical staff have helped us. We especially thank Phyllis A. Hall, Rose Ernstrom, Diane Barnett, and Teresa Denton at Utah State University; Rita Langford and Melanie Nelson at the University of Tulsa College of Law; and Janet Hirt, Emily Urban, Stephen Jordan, and Janelle Steele at the Vanderbilt University Law School.

We also wish to thank a variety of colleagues and friends whose help was essential to the making of this book and its revision. They include John Arthur, Gordon Bakken, Michal Belknap, Martin H. Belsky, Jon W. Bruce, George Butler, Robert Cottrol, Michael Kent Curtis, Davison Douglas, Lawrence Friedman, Don Gifford, Stephen Gottlieb, Peter Hoffer, Tim Huebner, John Johnson, Stanley N. Katz, Judy Lauer, Jenni Parrish, Robert Rasmussen, Judith Schafer, Melvin Urofsky, Michael Vandenbergh, Bertram Wyatt-Brown, and Jamil Zainaldin.

Finally, we owe a special thanks to William M. Wiecek, a great friend who was a co-editor on the first two editions of this book. Much of the structure and content of this volume was shaped by Bill's enormous knowledge, wisdom, and scholarly standards.

Our colleagues and spouses have patiently borne the sacrifices of time forced on them. Peter Coveney at Oxford University Press threw his enthusiastic support behind this edition and has helped us throughout the project. He is both a great editor and a great friend.

The dedication of this book acknowledges our teachers, the proverbial giants on whose shoulders we attempt to stand. American legal history owes an incalculable debt to their wisdom and teaching. The three of us are the richer for their friendship, encouragement, and good counsel.

Logan, Utah   K.L.H.
Tulsa, Oklahoma   P.F.
Nashville, Tennessee   J.W.E., Jr.

American Legal History

→ 1 ←

Law in the Morning of America: The Beginnings of American Law, to 1760

In his famous book *The Common Law* (1881), Oliver Wendell Holmes, Jr. (who later became a U.S. Supreme Court justice) concluded that "the life of the law has not been logic; it has been experience." He observed that "the felt necessities of the times, the prevalent moral and political theories," and "intuitions of public policy, avowed or unconscious" have been central to the development of American law.

The development of law in early America illustrates the wisdom of Holmes's observation. The English who came to America brought a well-developed legal culture with them. Their cultural "baggage" included English statutes, case law, and common law, as well as local rules, customs, and usages. They came from a legalistic society, and some of the early leaders, like John Winthrop of the Massachusetts Bay Colony, had legal training and experience. But new conditions and changed social circumstances led, almost immediately, to both subtle and dramatic legal changes. Colonial law was a dynamic as it blended the inherited English legal culture with new rules that were necessary for a new environment. In addition, some colonists brought with them ideas about law that were quite distinct from what existed in England. Quakers in Pennsylvania, for example, firmly believed that law should be merciful, and thus they consciously rejected the huge number of English laws that provided for capital punishment.

English inhabitants of the mainland colonies, even those who were born in the New World, did not think of themselves as "Americans" until the last third of the eighteenth century. Rather, they considered themselves English people who happened to be living outside of Great Britain but within the Empire. They therefore regarded themselves as heirs of the English constitutional tradition, especially those parts of it that guaranteed individual liberty. Yet, even as they stressed their "rights as Englishmen," these settlers discovered that New World conditions both required and allowed for an alteration of English ways.

Some English Protestant thought emphasized both the individual and the community. It thus laid a foundation for the prominent place of individualism in American law, giving American legal institutions, both public and private, a strong bent toward protecting the rights of the individual. At the same time, the communitarian element of Protestant theology— especially among the Puritans and Quakers—suggested a role for law in protecting the community. American law has never been exclusively individualistic in its emphasis. Community needs, rather than those of the individual, were particularly important in the early period when English Americans felt themselves beset on all sides by hostile peoples: Catholic Spaniards to the south, Catholic French to the north, Indians everywhere, and enslaved Africans in their midst. This feeling produced a fortress mentality that used law to fortify the community.

Although Americans thought of themselves as English people, the very act of creating new societies provided both the opportunity and the necessity for inventing or adapting legal institutions appropriate to the New World environment. For example, legal institutions that supported the established church in England, such as canon law and its ecclesiastical courts, were unsuited to the new colonies. The religious dissenters in New England and Pennsylvania rejected all church hierarchy, and the Anglican Church never became the established church in these places. Even where Anglicans predominated, like Virginia and Georgia, the lack of an educated clergy—or sometimes any clergy at all—made it impossible for church courts to successfully cross the Atlantic. In the religiously heterogeneous colonies, like Rhode Island, New York, New Jersey, and South Carolina, adoption of canon law was both impractical and irrelevant. Instead, these colonies, along with Pennsylvania, pioneered in creating governments that tolerated religious diversity. The emergence of religious toleration in the colonies was an adaptation to conditions unique to the New World.

Americans ultimately created a legal order based on older traditions and ideas, but which in the end was significantly different. They accomplished this without having to crawl out from underneath centuries of legal tradition and custom found in Europe. Americans often selected out of the English heritage only those legal elements that met their needs. Rhode Island's 1663 charter, for example, limited conformity to those English laws suited to the "nature and constitution of the place and people there."[1] In 1833 Justice Joseph Story summed up this tradition in his book *Commentaries on the Constitution*, noting that the colonists "did not carry over with them all the laws of England when they migrated hither, for many of them must, from the nature of the case, be wholly inapplicable to their situation, and inconsistent with their comfort and property." Rather they brought "with them all the laws applicable to their situation, and not repugnant to the local and political circumstances, in which they are placed."[2] Americans created their legal order in a spirit of eclectic opportunism, drawing from various sources of law and devising new rules of law when they found nothing suitable in existing systems.

While never fully free to reject all English laws they did not like, or adopt all new rules they wanted, Americans were less constrained than their English cousins in molding laws to fit their society's needs. Consequently, American law was easier to reform and more instrumentalist in its development than British law.

Americans did not develop their laws unthinkingly or reflexively. On the contrary, they displayed a remarkable sophistication in thinking about the governance of their societies. In addition to English common law and statutes, they drew freely from a variety of legal sources, including Roman law, local English law and customs, contemporary justice-of-the-peace manuals, and some biblical law (especially in the early seventeenth century). Similarly, they turned to various sources for political theory including the writings of Montesquieu, James Harrington, and John Locke. Thus, by the eve of the Revolution, Americans had developed a political philosophy to support the choices they made about the directions of their legal development. Eventually, they reaffirmed their commitment to the English common law as the foundation of their legal order, but it was the common law stripped of unsuitable doctrines. Americans regarded the common law as a guarantor of personal liberty, not merely as a system for regulation of property, inheritance, and private disputes. Thus conceived, the common law became a foundation of republican liberty after the American Revolution.

Early American law contained within itself the basis of the legal and constitutional order of the post-Revolutionary states and nation. During the colonial period, American law incorporated some essentials of what we today call the rule of law, including concepts of higher law, limited government, separation of powers, an independent judiciary, due process of law, and consent as the basis of legal obligation. Legal development in the colonial period anticipated much of what later became American constitutionalism. Law, as historian Arthur Bestor has observed, both molds people and the way they think as much as it is molded by them.[3] So it was with law in America's morning. We have become the people that we are today in part because of the laws that we adopted, borrowed, and created in the early English settlements.

THE ENGLISH HERITAGE AND MAGNA CHARTA

American law traces its beginning to the landmarks of English constitutional development. The earliest and most revered of these was Magna Charta. The "great charter" began as an agreement between King John I and the leading barons of England. On June 15, 1215, the barons surrounded the king on Runnymede Island and forced him to sign the document. Much of the document's sixty-three chapters dealt with property, inheritance, and feudal obligations. But a number of significant provisions were directed at the fair administration of law, fundamental justice, and basic rights.

Magna Charta
1215

Magna Charta was ostensibly designed to protect the barons and their property from the king. However, the language of the document was more open-ended and ultimately became available to "all free men of our realm." More than half a millennium later, many of its provisions had evolved into important constitutional provisions and legal principles in the United States. For example, Chapter 17, requiring that lawsuits "not follow the royal court around," evolved into the provision in Article III, Section 2, of the United States Constitution, requiring that Congress fix the places where courts would meet. Similarly, Chapter 18 can be seen as the ancestor of the grand jury. Chapters 20 and 21 of the Magna Charta, providing that fines be "in proportion to the degree of" the offense, led to the ban on excessive fines found in the Eighth Amendment to the Constitution. Chapter 35 is the ancestor of the provision in Article I, Section 8 of the Constitution that authorizes Congress to "fix the Standard of Weights and Measures." Chapter 39 is the source of modern procedural and substantive due process. Magna Charta's law-of-the-land phrasing appears in many of the early American state constitutions and, together with the concept of due process, is at the core of modern concepts of the fair administration of justice and the protection of fundamental liberties. Magna

Charta contains many key concepts of American law, such as the idea that the government cannot take private property without compensation, the notion that no one can "sell" justice, and the commitment to maintain a legal system based on "law of the land."

John, by the grace of God, king of England, lord of Ireland, duke of Normandy and Aquitaine, and count of Anjou, to the archbishop, bishops, abbots, earls, barons, justiciaries, foresters, sheriffs, stewards, servants, and to all his bailiffs and liege subjects, greetings.

1. In the first place we have granted to God, and by this our present charter confirmed for us and our heirs forever that the English Church shall be free, and shall have her rights entire, and her liberties inviolate; and we will that it be thus observed; . . . We have also granted to all freemen of our kingdom, for us and our heirs forever, all the underwritten liberties, to be had and held by them and their heirs, of us and our heirs forever.

◆ ◆ ◆

17. Common pleas [trial courts] shall not follow our court [that is the "Royal Court"], but shall be held in some fixed place.

18. Inquests of novel disseisin, of mort d'ancestor, and of darrein presentment shall not be held elsewhere than in their own county courts, and that in manner following; We, or, if we should be out of the realm, our chief justiciar, will send two justiciaries through every county four times a year, who shall alone with four knights of the county chosen by the county, hold the said assizes in the county court, on the day and in the place of meeting of that court.

◆ ◆ ◆

20. A freeman shall not be amerced for a slight offense, except in accordance with the degree of the offense; and for a grave offense he shall be amerced in accordance with the gravity of the offense, yet saving always his "contentment"; and a merchant in the same way, saving his "merchandise"; and a villein shall be amerced in the same way, saving his "wainage" if they have fallen into our mercy: and none of the aforesaid amercements shall be imposed except by the oath of honest men of the neighborhood.

21. Earls and barons shall not be amerced except through their peers, and only in accordance with the degree of the offense.

◆ ◆ ◆

28. No constable or other bailiff of ours shall take corn or other provisions from anyone without immediately tendering money therefor, unless he can have postponement thereof by permission of the seller.

◆ ◆ ◆

30. No sheriff or bailiff of ours, or other person, shall take the horses or carts of any freeman for transport duty, against the will of the said freeman.

31. Neither we nor our bailiffs shall take, for our castles or for any other work of ours, wood which is not ours, against the will of the owner of that wood.

◆ ◆ ◆

35. Let there be one measure of wine throughout our whole realm; and one measure of ale; and one measure of corn, to wit, "the London quarter"; and one width of cloth (whether dyed, or russet, or "halberget"), to wit, two ells within the selvedges; of weights also let it be as of measures.

◆ ◆ ◆

38. No bailiff for the future shall, upon his own unsupported complaint, put anyone to his "law," without credible witnesses brought for this purposes.

39. No freemen shall be taken or imprisoned or disseised or exiled or in any way destroyed, nor will we go upon him nor send upon him, except by the lawful judgment of his peers or by the law of the land.

40. To no one will we sell, to no one will we refuse or delay, right or justice.

◆ ◆ ◆

45. We will appoint as justices, constables, sheriffs, or bailiffs only such as know the law of the realm and mean to observe it well.

◆ ◆ ◆

63. Wherefore we will and firmly order that the English Church be free, and that the men in our kingdom have and hold all the aforesaid liberties, rights, and concessions, well and peaceably, freely and quietly, fully and wholly, for themselves and their heirs, of us and our heirs, in all respects and in all places forever, as is aforesaid.

Note: Due Process and the Law of the Land

Two parliamentary enactments of the late Middle Ages explicitly extended some of the benefits of Magna Charta beyond the nobility to all subjects of the realm. An act of 1346 provided that "every Man may be free to sue for and defend his Right in our Courts and elsewhere, according to the Law" (20 Edw. III, c. 4). A law passed in 1354 introduced the phrase "due process of law" for the first time into English law and declared that "no Man, of what Estate or Condition that he be, shall be put out of Land or Tenement, nor taken, nor imprisoned, nor put to Death, without being brought in answer by due Process of Law" (28 Edw. III, c. 3). American courts in the nineteenth and twentieth centuries were to hold that the phrases "law of the land" and "due process of law" were equivalent. The notion of "due process" would eventually emerge as a driving force in the expansion of legal rights for all Americans.

Note: The Reformation and Tudor England

Until 1531 Roman Catholicism was the official, or "established," church for England. As the Protestant Reformation swept northern and parts of central Europe, King Henry VIII of England remained a staunch Catholic. In 1521 the pope declared Henry to be a "Defender of the Faith" after the English king wrote a small book attacking Martin Luther's writings. However, in 1527 the pope rejected Henry's request for an annulment of his marriage to Catherine of Aragon, his Spanish wife. Henry responded by initiating what is known as the English Reformation. He broke away from the Catholic faith and in 1531 became head of the newly created Church of England (also known as the Anglican Church), which became the official religion of his nation. The king of England was now the head of the church, which increased its popularity within the realm—no longer would England be subject to the rulings and decisions of a foreign potentate. In addition, Henry distributed or sold vast amounts of church lands, thus giving many of England's elite a financial stake in the religion. The new church abolished priestly celibacy, which gained Henry support among many of the clergy, and most English clerics easily made the transition to the new faith. While most Englishmen and women were happy to abandon Catholicism, some thought the English Reformation had not gone far enough. English followers of the Swiss theologian John Calvin wanted to further reform, or "purify," the Church and were thus called Puritans. These dissenters argued for the abolition of the church hierarchy, including bishops and archbishops, and demanded a less elaborate form of worship.

Henry generally tolerated these dissenters but never supported their goals. His successor, King Edward VI, was far more sympathetic to the Puritans, but his short reign (1547–1553) prevented any fundamental changes in the new church. Edward's early death put his oldest sister, Mary, on the throne. Queen Mary (r. 1553–1558) was the daughter of Henry's first wife, Catherine of Aragon; like her mother, Mary was a practicing Catholic and as such wanted to bring England back under the authority of the pope. Queen Mary brutally persecuted Protestant leaders, especially Puritans, ordering many to be burned at the stake. The reign of "Bloody Mary," as she was known, was mercifully brief. But its impact on subsequent constitutional developments was profound. The deaths of the Marian martyrs, burned at the stake at Smithfield, were alive in the historical memory of many eighteenth-century Americans. This left them with a profound fear of tyranny and for many Americans an equally strong fear of the Catholic Church.

Mary's death led to the reign of her younger sister Elizabeth—"Good Queen Bess" as she would be known. Under Elizabeth I (r. 1558–1603), the people of England enjoyed growing prosperity and, by the standards of the era, remarkable freedom. Elizabeth did not tolerate open dissent—political or religious—but she also claimed that she did not seek "windows into men's souls" and thus did nothing to persecute Puritans and other Protestant dissenters as long as they quietly practiced their faith and did not challenge her reign. Under Elizabeth, England experienced a cultural golden age, exemplified by the writing of William Shakespeare and Christopher Marlowe. In 1585 the first English settlement in the New World was attempted at Roanoke Island, off the coast of present-day North Carolina. Meanwhile, the defeat of the Spanish Armada in 1588 made England a world power and set the stage for successful English settlements two decades later.

At the death of Elizabeth in 1603, England turned to her cousin, King James VI of Scotland, who moved south to become King James I of England. James was far more autocratic than Elizabeth, and his harassment of religious dissenters led some to move to Holland and later to America, where in 1620 they created the Plymouth Colony. Even before this, in 1607, England established its first successful New World settlement, Jamestown, which was the first town of the Virginia Colony.

THE VIRGINIA COLONY

The Virginia Colony was organized as a joint stock company, but unlike a modern corporation, the charter for the corporation came directly from the king. The goals of the Crown were partially idealistic and religious, as the king hoped the colony would lead to the conversion of the "heathen" Indians. The investors (known as "adventurers of the company") bought stock in hopes of making a profit. None of these goals and hopes were ever realized. Relations with the Indians were more murderous than religious, and the colony constantly lost money and was initially an economic and political failure. It was also a great human fiasco, with a huge death rate for the colonists and violent, often murderous relations with the local Indians. In 1611 the stockholders in London sent Sir Thomas Dale to Virginia with men, supplies, and orders to impose a legal order based on the notion that as deputy governor he should "proceed rather as Chauncelor then a judge, rather uppon the naturall right and equity then upon the nicenes and letter of the lawe."[4] Instead he imposed a set of laws that were more military than civilian. While it may be unfair to blame Dale for these rules, since others in the Virginia Company were involved in their drafting and implementation, they are remembered as "Dale's Laws." The attempts to impose this harsh rule through Dale's Laws succeeded only in alienating settlers. The charter was revoked in 1624 and a royal governor was appointed. By this time, however, three developments within the colony would have a long-term impact on American legal history.

In 1617 Virginians began to plant tobacco as a cash crop. This would set the stage for the development of a plantation economy and bring great wealth to Virginia's planter elite. In 1619 Virginia's landowners established the House of Burgesses—the first representative legislature in the New World. The experience in lawmaking over the next 150 years would prepare Virginians and other Americans for self-government after the Revolution. Ironically, in the same year that an elected legislature arrived in Virginia, the first Africans also arrived. These blacks were treated as indentured servants, but within a generation Virginia would become committed to a slave-based economy in which race would become a marker of servitude and legal inferiority.

Dale's Laws
1611

Dale's Laws contained eighty-eight separately numbered provisions, divided into two sections. The first section, dealing with laws "Divine" and "Morall," contained thirty-seven separate provisions, although many dealt with multiple topics. The laws were designed to regulate economic, political, and religious life in the colony, as well as to prevent settlers from leaving without permission. The second part, not printed here, contained fifty-one separate provisions dealing with laws "Martiall." These provisions contained numerous punishments of whipping or death for soldiers in Virginia who violated the rules for their behavior. Dale's Laws are most notable for their harsh punishments, including boring a hole in the tongue of an offender with a needle, cutting off ears, branding, whipping, and numerous capital punishments for relatively minor offenses. For example, death penalties were enforced for taking any amount of food while weeding gardens or crops—indeed, eating a single grape while tending to the vines owned by the colony was punishable by death, as was privately trading with any ships that came to Virginia or killing a chicken (even one's own) without permission of the authorities. Denying any doctrine of the Church of England, "blasphem[ing] Gods holy name," or a third conviction for failure to attend church were also punishable by death. Many of these punishments were carried out. One man who stole a few pints of oatmeal "had a needle thrust through his tongue and was then chained to a tree until he starved."[5] Punishment under the laws for running away to the Indians was particularly savage. One Englishman recorded punishments ordered by the governor in 1612 against some men who had gone to live with the Indians and then been recaptured: "Some he appointed to be hanged Some burned Some to be broken upon wheles, others to be staked and some to be shott to death."[6]

LAWES DIVINE, MORALL AND MARTIALL, &C.

Articles, Lawes, and Orders, Divine, Politique, and Martiall for the Colony in Virginea: first established by Sir Thomas Gates Knight, Lieutenant Generall, the 24. of May 1610. exemplified and approved by the Right Honourable Sir Thomas West Knight, Lord Lawair, Lord Governour and Captaine Generall the 12. of June 1610. Againe exemplified and enlarged by Sir Thomas Dale Knight, Marshall, and Deputie Governour, the 22. of June. 1611.

Whereas his Majestie like himselfe a most zealous Prince hath in his owne Realmes a principall care of true Religion, and reverence to God, and hath alwaies strictly commaunded his Generals and Governours, with all his forces wheresoever, to let their waies be like his ends, for the glorie of God.

And forasmuch as no good service can be performed, or warre well managed, where militarie discipline is not observed, and militarie discipline cannot be kept, where the rules or chiefe parts thereof, be not certainly set downe, and generally knowne, I have (with the advise and counsell of Sir Thomas Gates Knight, Lieutenant Generall) adhered unto the lawes divine, and orders politique, and martiall of his Lordship (the same exemplified) an addition of such others, as I have found either the necessitie of the present State of the Colonie to require, or the infancie, and weaknesse of the body thereof, as yet able to digest, and doe now publish them to all persons in the Colonie, that they may as well take knowledge of the Lawes themselves, as of the penaltie and punishment, which without partialitie shall be inflicted upon the breakers of the same.

♦ ♦ ♦

2. That no man speake impiously or maliciously, against the holy and blessed Trinitie, or any of the three persons, that is to say, against God the Father, God the Son, and God the holy Ghost, or against the knowne Articles of the Christian faith, upon paine of death.

3. That no man blaspheme Gods holy name upon paine of death, or use unlawful oathes, taking the name of God in vaine, curse, or banne, upon paine of severe punishment for the first offence so committed, and for the second, to have a bodkin thrust through his tongue, and if he continue the blaspheming of Gods holy name, for the third time so offending, he shall be brought to a martiall court, and there receive censure of death for his offence.

4. No man shall use any traiterous words against his Majesties Person, or royall authority upon paine of death.

5. No man shall speake any word, or do any act, which may tend to the derision, or despight of Gods holy word upon paine of death: Nor shall any man unworthily demeane himselfe unto any Preacher, or Minister of the same,

but generally hold them in all reverent regard, and dutiful intreatie, otherwise he the offender shall openly be whipt three times, and ask publike forgivenesse in the assembly of the congregation three several Saboth daies.

6. Everie man and woman duly twice a day upon the first Towling of the Bell shall upon the working daies repaire unto the Church, to hear divine Service upon pain of losing his or her dayes allowance for the first omission, for the second to be whipt, and for the third to be condemned to the Gallies for six Moneths. Likewise no man or woman shall dare to violate or breake the Sabboth by any gaming, publique, or private abroad, or at home, but duly sanctifie and observe the same, both himselfe and his familie, by preparing themselves at home with private prayer, that they may be the better fitted for the publique, according to the commandements of God, and the orders of our Church, as also every man and woman shall repaire in the morning to the divine service, and Sermons preached upon the Saboth day, and in the afternoon to divine service, and Catechising, upon paine for the first fault to lose their provision, and allowance for the whole weeke following, for the second to lose the said allowance, and also to be whipt, and for the third to suffer death.

♦ ♦ ♦

8. He that upon pretended malice, shall murther or take away the life of any man, shall bee punished with death.

9. No man shal commit the horrible, and detestable sins of Sodomie upon pain of death; & he or she that can be lawfully convict of Adultery shall be punished with death. No man shall ravish or force any woman, maid or Indian, or other, upon pain of death, and know ye that he or shee, that shall commit fornication, and evident proofe made thereof, for their first fault shall be whipt, for their second they shall be whipt, and for their third shall be whipt three times a weeke for one month, and aske publique forgivenesse in the Assembly of the Congregation.

10. No man shall bee found guilty of Sacriledge, which is a Trespasse as well committed in violating and abusing any sacred ministry, duty or office of the Church, irreverently,

or prophanely, as by beeing a Church robber, to filch, steale or carry away any thing out of the Church appertaining thereunto, or unto any holy, and consecrated place, to the divine Service of God, which no man should doe upon paine of death: likewise he that shall rob the store of any commodities therein, of what quality soever, whether provisions of victuals, or of Arms, Trucking stuffe, Apparrell, Linnen, or Wollen, Hose or Shooes, Hats or Caps, Instruments or Tooles of Steeles, Iron, &c. or shall rob from his fellow souldier, or neighbour, any thing that is his, victuals, apparell, household stuffe, toole, or what necessary else soever, by water or land, out of boate, house, or knapsack, shall bee punished with death.

11. Hee that shall take an oath untruly, or beare false witnesse in any cause, or against any man whatsoever, shall be punished with death.

12. No manner of person whatsoever, shall dare to detract, slaunder, calumniate, or utter unseemely, and unfitting speeches, either against his Majesties Honourable Councell for this Colony, resident in England, or against the Committies, Assistants unto the said Councell, or against the zealous indeavors, & intentions of the whole body of Adventurers for this pious and Christian Plantation, or against any publique booke, or bookes, which by their mature advise, and grave wisedomes, shall be thought fit, to be set foorth and publisht, for the advancement of the good of this Colony, and the felicity thereof, upon paine for the first time so offending, to bee whipt three severall times, and upon his knees to acknowledge his offence and to aske forgivenesse upon the Saboth day in the assembly of the congregation, and for the second time so offending to be condemned to the Galley for three yeares, and for the third time so offending to be punished with death.

◆　◆　◆

14. No man shall give any disgracefull words, or commit any act to the disgrace of any person in this Colonie, or any part thereof, upon paine of being tied head and feete together, upon the guard everie night for the space of one moneth, besides to bee publikely disgraced himselfe, and be made uncapable ever after to

possesse any place, or execute any office in this imployment.

15. No man of what condition soever shall barter, trucke, or trade with the Indians, except he be thereunto appointed by lawful authority, upon paine of death.

16. No man shall rifle or dispoile, by force or violence, take away any thing from any Indian comming to trade, or otherwise, upon paine of death.

17. No Cape Marchant, or Provant Master, or Munition Master, or Truck Master, or keeper of any store, shall at any time imbezzell, sell, or give away any thing under his Charge to any Favorite . . . upon paine of death.

◆　◆　◆

19. There shall no Capttain, Master, Marriner, saylor, or any else of what quality or condition soever, belonging to any Ship or Ships, at this time remaining, or which shall hereafter arrive within this our River, bargaine, buy, truck, or trade with any one member in this Colony, man, woman, or child, for any toole or instrument of iron, steel or what else, whether appertaining to Smith Carpenter, Joyner, Shipwright, or any manuall occupation, or handicraft man whatsoever, resident within our Colonie, nor shall they buy or bargaine, for any apparell, linnen, or wollen, householdstuffe, bedde, bedding, sheete towels, napkins, brasse, pewter, or such like, eyther for ready money, or provisions, nor shall they exchange their provisions, of what quality soever, whether Butter, Cheese, Bisket, meal, Oatmele, Aquavite, oyle, Bacon, any kind of Spice, or such like, for any such aforesaid instruments, or tooles, Apparell, or householdstuffe, at any time, or so long as they shall here remain, from the date of these presents upon paine of losse of their wages in England, confiscation and forfeiture of such their monies and provisions, and upon peril beside of such corporall punishment as shall be inflicted upon them by verdict and censure of a martiall Court: Nor shall any officer, souldier, or Trades man, or any else of what sort soever, members of this Colony, dare to sell any such Toole, or instruments, necessary and usefull, for the businesse of the Colonie, or trucke, sell, exchange, or give away his apparell, or household

stuffe of what sort soever, unto any such Sea-
man, either for money, or any such foresaid provisions, upon paine of 3 times severall whipping, for the one offender, and the other upon
perill of incurring censure, whether of disgrace,
or addition of such punishment, as shall bee
thought fit by a Court martiall.

20. Whereas sometimes heeretofore the
covetous and wide affections of some greedy
and ill disposed Seamen, Saylers, and Marriners, laying hold upon the advantage of the
present necessity, under which the Colony
sometimes suffered, have sold unto our people,
provisions of Meale, Oatmeale, Bisket, Butter,
Cheese &c, at unreasonable rates, and prises unconscionable: for avoiding the like to bee now
put in practise, there shall no Captain, Master,
Marriner, or Saylor, or what Officer else belonging to any ship, or shippes, now within our
river, or heereafter which shall arrive, shall dare
to bargaine, exchange, barter, truck, trade, or
sell, upon paine of death, unto any one Land-
man member of this present Colony, any provisions of what kind soever, above the determined valuations, and prises, set downe and
proclaimed, and sent therefore unto each of
your severall ships, to bee fixed uppon your
Maine mast, to the intent that want of due notice, and ignorance in this case, be no excuse,
or plea, for any one offender herein.

21. Sithence we are not to bee a little care-
full, and our young Cattell, & Breeders may be
cherished, that by the preservation, and increase
of them, the Colony heere may receive in due
time assured and great benefite, and the adventurers at home may be eased of so great a burthen, by sending unto us yeerely supplies of this
kinde, which now heere for a while, carefully
attended, may turne their supplies unto us into
provisions of other qualities, when of these wee
shall be able to subsist our selves, and which
wee may in short time, be powerful enough to
doe, if we wil according to our owne knowledge of what is good for our selves, forbeare to
work into our owne wants, againe, by over hasty
destroying, and devouring the stocks, apu authors of so profitable succeeding a Commodity,
as increase of Cattel, Kine, Hogges, Goates,
Poultrie &c. must of necessity bee granted, in
every common mans judgement, to render unto

us: Now know yee therefore, these promises
carefully considered, that it is our will and pleasure, that every one, of what quality or condition soever hee bee, in this present Colony, to
take due notice of this our Edict, whereby wee
do strictly charge and command, that no man
shall dare to kill, or destroy any Bull, Cow,
Calfe, Mare, Horse, Colt, Goate, Swine, Cocke,
Henne, Chicken, Dogge, Turkie, or any tame
Cattel, or Poultry, of what condition soever;
whether his owne, or appertaining to another
man, without leave from the Generall, upon
paine of death in the Principall, and in the ac-
cessary, burning in the Hand, and losse of his
eares, and unto the concealer of the same foure
and twenty houres whipping, with addition of
further punishment, as shall be thought fitte by
the censure, and verdict of a Martiall Court.

22. Ther shall no man or woman, Laun-
derer or Launderesse, dare to wash any un-
cleane Linnen, drive bucks, or throw out the
water or suds of fowle cloathes, in the open
streete, within the Pallizadoes, or within forty
foote of the same, nor rench, and make cleane,
any kettle, pot, or pan, or such like vessell
within twenty foote of the olde well, or new
Pumpe: nor shall any one aforesaid, within lesse
than a quarter of one mile from the Pallizadoes,
dare to doe the necessities of nature, since by
thse unmanly, slothfull, and loathsome immod-
esties, the whole Fort may bee choaked, and
poisoned with ill aires, and so corrupt (as in all
reason cannot but much infect the same) and
this shall they take notice of, and avoide, upon
paine of whipping and further punishment, as
shall be thought meete, by the censure of a martiall Court.

23. No man shall imbezzell, lose, or willingly breake, or fraudulently make away, either
Spade, Shovell, Hatchet, Axe, Mattocke, or
other toole or instrument uppon paine of
whipping.

◆   ◆   ◆

25. Every man shall have an especiall and
due care, to keepe his house sweete and cleane,
as also so much of the streete, as lieth before
his door, and especially he shall so provide,
and set his bedstead whereon he lieth, that it
may stand three foote at least from the ground,

as he will answere the contrarie at a martiall Court.

♦ ♦ ♦

28. No souldier or tradesman, but shall be readie, both in the morning, & in the afternoone, upon the beating of the Drum, to goe out unto his worke, nor shall hee return home, or from his worke, before the Drum beate againe, and the officer appointed for that businesse, bring him of, upon perill for the first fault to lie upon the Guard head and heeles together all night, for the second time so faulting to be whipt, and for the third time so offending to be condemned to the Gallies for a yeare.

29. No man or woman, (upon paine of death) shall runne away from the Colonie, to Powhathan, or any savage Weroance else whatsoever.

30. He that shall conspire any thing against the person of the Lord Governour, and Captaine Generall, against the Lieutenant Generall, or against the Marshall, or against any publike service commaunded by them, for the dignitie, and advancement of the good of the Colony, shall be punished with death: and he that shall have knowledge of any such pretended act of disloyalty of treason, and shall not reveale the same unto his Captaine, or unto the Governour of that fort or towne wherein he is, within the space of one houre, shall for the concealing of the same after that time, be not onely held an accessory, but alike culpalbe as the principall traitor or conspirer, and for the same likewise he shall suffer death.

31. What man or woman soever, shall rob any garden, publike or private, being set to weed the same, or wilfully pluck up therin any roote, herbe, or flower, to spoile and wast or steale the same, or robbe any vineyard, or gather up the grapes, or steale any eares of the corne growing, whether in the ground belonging to the same fort or towne where he dwelleth, or in any other, shall be punished with death.

♦ ♦ ♦

33. There is not one man nor woman in this Colonie now present, or hereafter to arrive, but shall give up an account of his and their faith, and religion, and repaire unto the Minis-

ter, that by his conference with them, hee may understand, and gather, whether heretofore they have beene sufficiently instructed, and catechised in the principles and grounds of Religion . . . if they shal refuse so to repaire unto him, and he the Minister give notice thereof unto the Governour, or that chiefe officer of that towne or fort, wherein he or she, the parties so offending shall remaine, the Governour shall cause the offender for his first time of refusall to be whipt, for the second time to be whipt twice, and to acknowledge his fault upon the Saboth day, in the assembly of the congregation, and for the third time to be whipt every day until he hath made the same acknowledgement, and asked forgivenesse for the same, and shall repaire unto the Minster, to be further instructed as aforesaid: and upon the Saboth when the Minister shall catechise, and of him demaund any question concerning his faith and knowledge, he shall not refuse to make answere upon the same perill.

♦ ♦ ♦

35. No Captaine, Master, or Mariner, of what condition soever, shall depart or carry out of our river, any Ship, Barke, Gally, Pinnace &c. Roaders belonging to the Colonie, either now therein, or hither arriving, without leave and commission from the Generall or chiefe Commaunder of the Colonie upon paine of death.

36. No man or woman whatsoever, members of this Colonie shall sell or give unto any Captaine, Marriner, Master, or Sailer, &c. any commoditie of this countrey, of what quality soever, to be transported out of the Colonie, for his or their owne private uses, upon paine of death.

37. . . . All such Bakers as are appointed to bake bread, or what else, either for the store to be given out in generall, or for any one in particular, shall not steale nor imbezzell, loose, or defraud any man of his due and proper weight and measure, nor use any dishonest and deceitfull tricke to make the bread weigh heavier, or make it coarser upon purpose to keepe backe any part or measure of the flower or meale committed unto him, nor aske, take, or detaine any one loafe more or lesse for his hire

or paines for so baking, since whilst he who delivered unto him such meale or flower, being to attend the businesse of the Colonie, such baker or bakers are imposed upon no other service or duties, but onely so to bake for such as do worke, and this shall hee take notice of, upon paine for the first time offending herein of losing his eares, and for the second time to be condemned a yeare to the Gallies, and for the third time offending, to be condemned to the Gallies for three yeares.

All such cookes as are appointed to seeth, bake or dresse any manner of way, flesh, fish, or what else, of what kind soever, either for the generall company, or for any private man, shall not make lesse, or cut away any part or parcel of such flesh, fish, &c. Nor detaine or demaund any part or parcell, as allowance or hire for his so dressing the same, since as aforesaid of the baker, hee or they such Cooke or Cookes, exempted from other publike works abroad, are to attend such seething and dressing of such publike flesh, fish, or other provisions of what kinde soever, as their service and duties expected from them by the Colony, and this shall they take notice of, upon paine for the first time offending herein, of losing his eares, and for the second time to be condemned a yeare to the Gallies: and for the third time offending to be condemned to the Gallies for three yeares.

All fishermen, dressers of Sturgeon or such like appointed to fish, or to cure the said Sturgeon for the use of the Colonie, shall give a just and true account of all such fish as they shall take by day or night, of what kinde soever, the same to bring unto the Governour: As also of all such kegges of Sturgeon or Caviare as they shall prepare and cure upon perill for the first time offending heerein, of loosing his eares, and for the second time to be condemned a yeare to the Gallies, and for the third time offending, to be condemned to the Gallies for three yeares.

Every Minister or Preacher shall every Sabboth day before Catechising, read all these lawes and ordinances, publikely in the assembly of the congregation upon paine of his entertainment checkt for that weeke.

THE BEGINNINGS OF CONSTITUTIONALISM IN AMERICA

Throughout the American experience, the polestar of public law has been the concept of "constitutionalism," a vague and comprehensive catchword embracing the ideals of limited government, the rule of law, and the various structural devices that achieve the substantive content of republican government in America. The origins of constitutionalism long predated the Revolution and the creation of the American Republic. They derived partly from the way that we think about the sources of law, and partly from the way that Americans structured the governments of their societies.

The concepts first developed most clearly in two religiously based colonies: Plymouth and Massachusetts Bay. Both were settled by Calvinist Protestants who believed that the English Reformation of Henry VIII had not gone far enough. As one Puritan minister put it, in breaking with the Roman church, King Henry had lopped off the "head" of Catholicism (the pope), but left the "body" intact by maintaining bishops, elaborate ritual, and a top-down practice in which the people were more the recipients of religion than participants in it. The Puritans and the Separatists differed in one fundamental way. The Puritans believed that the Church of England could be reformed—purified—and so they were willing to worship in the Anglican Church while in England, in addition to holding their own meetings and services; the Separatists considered the English church to be beyond redemption, and thus had separated themselves from it. On other matters, these groups were similar. Most important, they believed that churches, and the larger society, should be organized on the basis of a compact between the members. Compact theory and practice, as exemplified in the Mayflower

Compact of 1620, was a basic element of constitutionalism. So was representative government, a logical derivative of social covenants.

Another central constitutional principle of American culture has been the conflict between governmental power and individual liberty. Americans confronted this dualism from the outset, especially in Massachusetts. Neither the Puritans nor the Separatists believed in religious freedom; they wanted to be free to worship as they wished but did not have any interest in extending such liberties or rights to others. They stressed the need for conformity within their community.

John Winthrop, a founder and longtime leader of the Massachusetts Bay Colony, addressed the issue in his lay sermon aboard the ship *Arbella* in 1629 just before the Puritans landed in Massachusetts. Here Winthrop coined the endlessly captivating image of America as a "city upon a hill." Winthrop emphasized the primacy of community over individual interests. Roger Williams, a learned and enormously well-liked Puritan minister who arrived in Massachusetts Bay just a short time after Winthrop, quickly rejected Puritan and Separatist orthodoxy. He ultimately espoused an altogether different approach to governance, condemning government efforts to coerce religious belief and practice. Ultimately he became the founder of the Rhode Island Colony, which allowed virtually unlimited religious free exercise and did not have an established church. Between them, Winthrop and Williams defined the polar opposites of power and liberty that have remained in tension throughout our political history. The Laws and Liberties of Massachusetts (1648) provided a sophisticated official affirmation of the sources of governmental authority and underscored the growing belief in America that law should be published and accessible to the people. They also illustrate the variety of ways in which the Puritans attempted to merge a "Bible commonwealth" with the everyday needs of their society.

Constitutionalism also derived from the structuring of colonial government, which took different forms. The covenants of Plymouth embodied compact theory in its purest form. A variant was the liberal and democratic order established in Rhode Island under the influence of Roger Williams. Emigration to the New World languished during the English Civil War and Protectorate but resumed vigorously after the restoration of the monarchy in 1661. The charters and compacts of the Restoration period embody many innovations in the forms and principles of government, such as the bizarre and abortive experiments in John Locke's Fundamental Constitutions of Carolina, the liberal and democratizing approaches of William Penn in his Frames of Government for Pennsylvania, and the do-it-yourself innovations in guarantees for personal liberty in New York's Charter of Libertyes (1683). All attest to the robust experimentation in a constitutional form of government that characterized America's first century.

The Mayflower Compact
1620

The Pilgrims who settled in Plymouth, Massachusetts, were Calvinist Protestants known as Separatists because they had broken with the Church of England, which they believed was inherently corrupt and beyond redemption. In England such beliefs and practices led to harassment and persecution. Their move to America benefited the Crown by getting these trou-

blesome people out of England while further securing England's tenuous beachhead on the North American continent. It allowed the Separatists to practice their religion undisturbed, although in a strange land far from the world in which they had always lived. Thus, the Crown authorized them to settle in the northern part of the Virginia Colony. However, their ship, The Mayflower, *landed hundreds of miles north of where it was supposed to arrive. The captain was anxious to return to England before the winter set in, and so the Pilgrims landed at Plymouth Bay, in what is today Massachusetts. Lacking legal authority to settle where they had landed—the Crown had specifically allowed them to move to Virginia—the Pilgrims drafted the Mayflower Compact to give themselves permission to land where they wanted.*

This brief document is in effect a contract or an agreement between the settlers and illustrates how the notion of a compact influenced the earliest settlers of New England. It also represented an effort by the Pilgrim leadership of the Plymouth Colony to control the non-Pilgrims who were among the settlers. The Mayflower Compact is commonly considered to be America's first constitution.

In the Name of God, Amen. We, whose names are underwritten, the Loyal Subjects of our dread Sovereign Lord King James, by the Grace of God, of Great Britain, France, and Ireland, King, Defender of the Faith, &c. Having undertaken for the Glory of God, and Advancement of the Christian Faith, and the Honour of our King and Country, a Voyage to plant the first Colony in northern Parts of Virginia; Do by these Presents, solemnly and mutually, in the Presence of God and one another covenant and combine ourselves together into a civil Body Politick, for our better Ordering and Preservation, and Furtherance of the Ends aforesaid: And by Virtue hereof do enact, constitute, and frame, such just and equal Laws, Ordinances, Acts, Constitutions, and Offices, from time to time, as shall be thought most meet and convenient for the general good of the Colony; unto which we promise all due Submission and Obedience.

JOHN WINTHROP
"A Model of Christian Charity"
1629

At the beginning of colonization in the early seventeenth century, English settlers aspired to an organic unity in the societies they were creating. One basis of this hope was the social compact, or covenant, uniting all members of a society through the bond of an agreement that constituted them as a body politic. This thinking was particularly congenial to Puritans, for whom covenant already occupied a central place in their religious faith. From the organic bond created by compact flowed a utopian vision of America as a "city upon a hill." John Winthrop drew these themes together in his shipboard sermon on the Arbella *in 1629, in a masterly fusion of theological and secular concepts blazing with the inner vision of prophecy.*

For the work we have in hand, it is by mutual consent through a special overruling providence and a more than an ordinary approbation of the churches of Christ, to seek out a place of cohabitation and consortship, under a due form of government both civil and ecclesiastical. In such cases as this, the care of the public must oversway all private respects by which not only conscience but mere civil policy doth bind us; for it is a true rule that particular estates cannot subsist in the ruin of the public.

♦ ♦ ♦

Thus stands the cause between God and us: we are entered into covenant with Him for this work; we have taken out a commission, the Lord hath given us leave to draw our own articles. We have professed to enterprise these actions upon these and these ends; we have hereupon besought Him of favor and blessing. Now if the Lord shall please to hear us and bring us in peace to the place we desire, then hath He ratified this covenant and sealed our Commission [and] will expect a strict performance of the articles contained in it. But if we shall neglect the observation of these articles which are the ends we have propounded, and dissembling with our God, shall fall to embrace this present world and prosecute our carnal intentions, seeking great things for ourselves and our posterity, the Lord will surely break out in wrath against us, be revenged of such a perjured people, and make us know the price of the breach of such a covenant.

Now the only way to avoid this ship-wreck and to provide for our posterity is to follow the counsel of Micah: to do justly, to love mercy, to walk humbly with our God. For this end, we must be knit together in this work as one man. We must entertain each other in brotherly affection; we must be willing to abridge ourselves of our superfluities for the supply of others' necessities; we must uphold a familiar commerce together in all meekness, gentleness, patience and liberality. We must delight in each other, make others' conditions our own, rejoice together, mourn together, labor and suffer together: always having before our eyes our commission and community in the work, our community as members of the same body. So shall we keep the unity of the spirit in the bond of peace, the Lord will be our God and delight to dwell among us, as His own people, and will command a blessing upon us in all our ways.

♦ ♦ ♦

For we must consider that we shall be as a city upon a hill, the eyes of all people are upon us. So that if we shall deal falsely with our God in this work we have undertaken, and so cause him to withdraw His present help from us, we shall be made a story and a by-word through the world.

Note: Roger Williams and Religious Liberty

The unity demanded by Winthrop dissolved quickly in Massachusetts. In the realm of political theory, a principal enemy of that unity was the tension between the need for powerful government and the demand for individual liberty. In the 1630s the colony expelled Anne Hutchinson for blasphemy, although her real offense was her outspoken views on religion and her willingness to challenge the male-dominated religious and political hierarchy. An even greater threat to the Puritan establishment came from Roger Williams, a profoundly smart and sensitive man who seems to have been well liked even by those who wanted to expel him from the community.

Williams came to Massachusetts Bay as a Puritan minister but quickly drifted into Separatism, having concluded that the Church of England was in fact beyond redemption or purification. His restless and brilliant mind was not limited to narrow issues of church governance. He questioned the right of the settlers to live on Indian lands and the right of the King to give those lands to the settlers; he believed the settlers should buy the land from the native inhabitants. He also challenged the right of the government to use the cross on the English flag, arguing that the Crown had no right to appropriate the symbol of Christ for its own use. To the horror of people like Winthrop, William cut St. George's Cross out of an

English flag. Williams even objected to the laws requiring mandatory church attendance. He saw no reason to pray next to people who were only in church to avoid a fine. In 1635 the authorities in Massachusetts Bay, convinced that Williams jeopardized the very existence of the colony, ordered that he be banished from the colony. Before they could send him back to England, however, he escaped to Narragansett Bay, where local Indians took him in. In 1636 he purchased land from the Indians and began the colony of Rhode Island, which, unlike all other colonies, had no established church. The two documents that follow illustrate the ideas that Williams developed that led to a theory of religious toleration. The first, "The Bloudy Tenent of Persecution for Cause of Conscience" (1644), was directed at the authorities in Massachusetts Bay who had banished him. The second is a short but succinct statement on religious toleration he made later in life.

Roger Williams was certainly not typical of his time and place, and his call for religious freedom should not be taken as representative of American thought in the seventeenth century. Yet Williams prefigures later trends in American thinking about public law, particularly the relationship between church and state in a secular, pluralistic society. He was ahead of his time in his ideas about popular sovereignty.

ROGER WILLIAMS

"The Bloudy Tenent of Persecution for Cause of Conscience"
1644

Williams wrote this tract in response to a tract written by the leading ministers in Massachusetts, entitled "A Model of Church and Civil Power." Here Williams powerfully argues for the separation of both.

All Civill States with their Officers of justice in their respective constitutions and administrations are proved essentially Civill, and therefore not Judges, Governours or Defendours of the Spiritual or Christian state and Worship.

Sixthly, It is the will and command of God that (since the coming of his Sonne the Lord Jesus) a permission of the most Paganish, Jewish, Turkish, or Antichristian consciences and worships, bee granted to all men in all Nations and Countries: and they are onely to bee fought against with that Sword which is only (in Soule matters) able to conquer, to wit, the Sword of Gods Spirit, the Word of God.

♦   ♦   ♦

Eighthly, God requireth not an uniformity of Religion to be inacted and inforced in any civil state, which inforced uniformity (sooner or later) is the greatest occasion of civill Warre, ravishing of conscience, persecution of Christ

Jesus in his servents, and of the hypocrisie and destruction of millions of souls.

Ninthly, In holding an inforced uniformity of Religion in a Civill State, wee must necessarily disclaime our desires and hopes of the Jewes conversion to Christ.

Tenthly, An inforced uniformity of Religion throughout a Nation or civill State, confounds the Civill and Religious, denies the principles of Christianity and civility, and that Jesus Christ is come in the Flesh.

Eleventhly, the Permission of other consciences and worships then a state professeth, only can (according to God) procure a firme and lasting peace, (good assurance being taken according to the wisedome of the civill state for uniformity of civill obedience from all sorts).

Twelfthly, lastly, true civility and Christianity may both flourish in a state or Kingdome, notwithstanding the permission of divers and contrary consciences, either of Jew or Gentile.

. . . [T]he proper meanes whereby the Civill Power may and should attaine its end, are onely Political, and principally these Five.

First the erecting and establishing what forme of Civill Government may seeme in wisedome most meet, according to generall rules of the Word, and state of the people.

Secondly, the making, publishing, and establishing of wholesome Civil Laws, not only such as concern Civill Justice, but also the free passage of true Religion: for, outward Civill Peace ariseth and is maintained from them both, from the latter as well as the former:

Civill peace cannot stand intire, where Religion is corrupted, . . . And yet such Lawes, though conversant about Religion, may still be counted Civill Lawes, as on the contrary, an Oath doth still remaine Religious, though conversant about Civill matters.

Thirdly, Election and appointment of Civill officers, to see execution of those Lawes.

Fourthly, Civill Punishments and Rewards, of Trangressors and Observers of these Lawes.

Fifthly, Taking up Armes against the Enemies of Civill Peace.

♦ ♦ ♦

So that the Magistrates, as Magistrates, have no power of setting up the Forme of Church Government, electing Church officers, punishing with Church censures, but to see that the Church doth her duty herein. And on the other side, the Churches as Churches, have no power (though as members of the Commonweale they may have power) of erecting or altering formes of Civill Government, electing of Civill officers, inflicting Civill punishments (no, not on persons excommunicate) as by deposing Magistrates from their Civill Authoritie, or withdrawing the hearts of the people against them, to their Lawes, no more then to discharge wives, or children, or servants, from due obedience to their husbands, parents, or masters: or by taking up armes against their Magistrates, though he persecute them for Conscience: for though members of Churches who are publique officers also of the Civill State, may suppresse by force the violent of Usurpers, as Jehoiada did Athaliah, yet this they doe not as members of the Church, but as officers of the Civill State.

♦ ♦ ♦

First, whereas they say, that the Civill Power may erect and establish what forme of civill Government may seem in wisdom most meet, I acknowledge the proposition to be most true, both in itself, and also considered with the end of it, that a civill Government is an Ordinance of God, to conserve the civill peace of people so farre as concernes their Bodes and Goods, as formerly hath been said.

But from this Grant I infer, (as before hath been touched) that the Soveraigne, originall, and foundation of civill power lies in the people, (whom they must needs meane by the civill power distinct from the Government set up.) And if so, that a People may erect and establish what forme of Government seemes to them most meete for their civill condition: It is evident that such Governments as are by them erected and established, have no more power, nor for no longer time, then the civill power or people consenting and agreeing shall betrust them with. This is cleere not only in Reason, but in the experience of all commonweales, where the people are not deprived of their naturall freedome by the power of Tyrants.

Roger Williams to the Town of Providence
1655

In this short letter to the town of Providence, Rhode Island, Williams denies that he favors absolute religious liberty, noting in the letter his opposition to exempting people from their civic obligations on the basis of religious claims. At the same time, he reiterates the need to let all people worship as they please.

[Providence, January, 1654–5.]

That ever I should speak or write a tittle, that tends to such an infinite liberty of conscience, is a mistake, and which I have ever disclaimed and abhorred. To prevent such mistakes, I shall at present only propose this case: There goes many a ship to sea, with many hundred souls in one ship, whose weal and woe is common, and is a true picture of a commonwealth, or a human combination or society. It hath fallen out sometimes, that both papists and protestants, Jews and Turks, may be embarked in one ship; upon which supposal I affirm, that all the liberty of conscience, that ever I pleaded for, turns upon these two hinges—that none of the papists, protestants, Jews, or Turks, be forced to come to the ship's prayers or worship, nor compelled from their own particular prayers or worship, if they practice any. I further add, that I never denied, that notwithstanding this liberty, the commander of this ship ought to command the ship's course, yea, and also command that justice, peace and sobriety, be kept and practiced, both among the seamen and all the passengers. If any of the seamen refuse to perform their services, or passengers to pay their freight; if any refuse to help, in person or purse, towards the common charges or defence; if any refuse to obey the common laws and orders of the ship, concerning their common peace or preservation; if any shall mutiny and rise up against their commanders and officers; if any should preach or write that there ought to be no commanders or officers, because all are equal in Christ, therefore no masters nor officers, no law nor orders, nor corrections nor punishments;—I say, I never denied, but in such cases, whatever is pretended, the commander or commanders may judge, resist, compel and punish such transgressors, according to their deserts and merits. This if seriously and honestly minded, may, if it so please the Father of lights, let in some light to such as willingly shut not their eyes.

I remain studious of your common peace and liberty.

Roger Williams

The Laws and Liberties of Massachusetts
1648

This justification for the origins of government would be a significant document in any age. But considering that it was written less than thirty years after the founding of the Massachusetts Bay Colony, its sophistication and maturity are extraordinary. Seldom has a legislative drafting committee composed so cogent a statement of political philosophy, encompassing the ideals of the community and an articulate theory of imputed consent. The purpose of the Laws and Liberties contrasts sharply with those in Virginia's first code, Dale's Laws.

To Our Beloved Brethren and Neighbours the Inhabitants of the Massachusetts, the Governour, Assistants and Deputies assembled in the Generall Court of that Jurisdiction with grace and peace in our Lord Jesus Christ

THE BOOK OF THE GENERAL LAWES AND LIBERTYES CONCERNING &C

So soon as God had set up Politicall Government among his people Israel he gave them a body of lawes for judgement both in civil and criminal causes. These mere breif and fundamental principles, yet withall so full and comprehensive as out of them clear deductions were to be drawne to all particular cases in future times. For a Common-wealth without lawes is like a Ship without rigging and steeradge. Nor is it sufficient to have principles or fundamentalls, but these are to be drawn out into so many of their deductions as the time and condition of that people may have use of. And it is very unsafe & injurious to the body of the people to put them to learn their duty and libertie from generall rules, nor is it enough to have lawes except they be also just. Therefore among other priviledges which the Lord bestowed upon his peculiar people, these he calls them specially to consider of, that God was neerer to them and their lawes were more righteous then other nations. God was sayd to be amongst them or neer to them because of his Ordnances established by himselfe, and their lawes righteous because himselfe was their Law-giver: yet in the comparison are implyed two things, first that other nations had somthing of God's presence amongst them. Secondly that there was also some what of equitie in their lawes, for it pleased the Father (upon the Covenant of Redemption with his Son) to restore so much of his Image to lost man as whereby all nations are disposed to worship God, and to advance righteousnes: which appears in that of the Apostle Rom. I. 21. They knew God &c: and in the 2. 14. They did by nature the things conteined in the law of God. But the nations corrupting his Ordinances (both of Religion, and Justice) God withdrew his presence from them proportionably whereby they were given up to abominable lusts Rom. 2. 21. Whereas if they had walked according to the light & law of nature they might have been preserved from such moral evils and might have injoyed a common blessing in all their natural and civil Ordinances: now, if it might have been so with the nations who were so much strangers to the Covenant of Grace, what advantage have they who have interest in this Covenant, and may injoye the special presence of God in the puritie and native simplicitie of all his Ordinances by which he is so neer to his owne people. This hath been no small priviledge, and advantage to us in New England that our Churches, and civil State have been planted, and growne up (like two twinnes) together like that of Israel in the wildernes by which wee were put in minde (and had opportunitie put into our hands) not only to gather our Churches, and set up the Ordinaces of Christ Jesus in them according to the Apostolick patterne by such light as the Lord graciously afforded us: but also withall to frame our civil Politie, and lawes according to the rules of his most holy word whereby each do help and strengthen other (the Churches the civil Authoritie, and the civil Authoritie the Churches) and so both prosper the better without such amulation, and contention for priviledges or priority as have proved the misery (if not ruine) of both in some other places.

♦ ♦ ♦

The . . . present Volume, we have not published it as a perfect body of laws sufficient to carry on the Government established for future times, nor could it be expected that we should promise such a thing. For if it be no disparagement to the wisedome of that High Court of Parliament in England that in four hundred years they could not so compile their lawes, and regulate proceedings in Courts of justice &c: but that they had still new work to do of the same kinde almost every Parliament: there can be no just cause to blame a poor Colonie (being unfurnished of Lawyers and Statesmen) that in eighteen years hath produced no more, nor better rules for a good, and setled Government then this Book holds forth. . . .

These Lawes which were made successively in divers former years, we have reduced under severall heads in an alphabeticall method, that so they might the more readilye be found, & that the divers lawes concerning one matter being placed together the scope and intent of the whole and of every of them might the more easily be apprehended . . . wherin (upon every occasion) you might readily see the rule which you ought to walke by. . . .

You have called us from amongst the rest of our Bretheren and given us power to make these laws: we must now call upon you to see them executed: remembring that old & true proverb, The execution of the law is the life of the law. If one sort of you viz: non-Freemen should object that you had no hand in calling us to this worke, and therfore think yourselvs not bound to obedience &c. Wee answer that a subsequent, or implicit consent is of like force in this case, as an expresse precedent power: for in putting your persons and estates into the protection and way of subsistance held forth and exercised within this Jurisdiction, you doe tacitly submit to this Government and to all the wholesome lawes therof. . . .

If any of you meet with some law that seemes not to tend to your particular benefit, you must consider that lawes are made with respect to the whole people, and not to each particular person: and obedience to them must be yeilded with respect to the common welfare, not to thy private advantage, and as thou yeildest obedience to the law for common good, but to thy dis-advantage: so another must observe some other law for thy good, though to his own damage; thus must we be content to bear one anothers burden and so fullfill the Law of Christ.

That distinction which is put between the Lawes of God and the lawes of men, becomes a snare to many as it is mis-applied in the ordering of their obedience to civil Authoritie; for when the Authoritie is of God and that in way of an Ordinance Rom. 13. I. and when the administration of it is according to deductions, and rules gathered from the word of God, and the clear light of nature in civil nations, surely there is no humane law that tendeth to common good (according to those principles) but the same is mediately a law of God, and that in way of an Ordinance which all are to submit unto and that for conscience sake. Rom. 13. 5.

◆ ◆ ◆

Forasmuch as the free fruition of such Liberties, Immunities, priviledges as humanitie, civilitie & christianity call for as due to everie man in his place, & proportion, without impeachment & infringement hath ever been, & ever will be the tranquility & stability of Churches & Comon-wealths; & the deniall or deprivall therof the disturbance, if not ruine of both:

It is therefore ordered by this Court, & Authority therof, That no mans life shall be taken away; no mans honour or good name shall be stayned; no mans person shal be arrested, restrained, bannished, dismembred nor any wayes punished; no man shall be deprived of his wife or children; no mans goods or estate shal be taken away from him; nor any wayes indamaged under colour of Law or countenance of Authoritie unles it be by the vertue or equity of some espresse law of the Country warranting

the same established by a General Court & sufficiently published; or in case of the defect of a law in any particular case by the word of God. And in capital cases, or in cases excomunicate, condemned or other, shall have full power and libertie to make their Wills & Testaments & other lawfull Alienations of their lands and estates.

◆ ◆ ◆

Ana-Baptists

Forasmuch as experience hath plentifully & often proved that since the first arising of the Ana-baptists about a hundred years past they have been the Incendiaries of Commonwealths & the Infectors of persons in main matters of Religion, & the Troublers of Churches in most places where they have been, & that they who have held the baptizing of Infants unlawful, have usually held other errors or heresies together therwith (though as hereticks use to doe they have concealed the same untill they espied a fit advantage and opportunity to vent them by way of question or scruple) and wheras divers of this kinde have since our coming into New-England appeared amongst ourselvs, some wherof as others before them have denied the Ordinance of Magistracy, and the law fulnes of making warre, others the lawfulness of Magistrates, and their Inspection into any breach of the first Table: which opinions if conived at by us are like to be increased among us & so necessarily bring guilt upon us, infection, & trouble to the Churches & hazard to the whole Commonwealth:

It is therefore orderd by this Court & Authoritie therof, that if any person or persons within this Jurisdiction shall either openly condemn or oppose the baptizing of Infants, or goe about secretely to seduce others from the approbation or use therof, or shal purposely depart the Congregation at the administration of that Ordinance; or shal deny the Ordinance of Magistry, or their lawfull right or authoritie to make war, or to punish the outward breaches of the first Table, and shall appear to the Court willfully and obstinately to continue therin, after due meanes of conviction, everie such person or persons shall be sentenced to Banishment.

◆ ◆ ◆

Bond-Slavery

It is ordered by this Court and authoritie therof, that there shall never be any bond-slavery, villenage or captivitie amongst us; unlesse it be lawfull captives, taken in just warrs, and such strangers as willingly sell themselves, or are solde to us: and such shall have the libertyes and christian usages which the law of God established in Israell concerning such persons doth morally require, provided, this exempts none from servitude who shall be judged thereto by Authoritie.

Burglarie and Theft

Forasmuch as many persons of late years have been, and are apt to be injurious to the goods and lives of others, notwithstanding all care and meanes to prevent and punish the same; . . .

It is therefore ordered by this Court and Authoritie therof that if any person shall commit Burglarie by breaking up any dwelling house, or shall rob any person in the field, or high wayes; such a person so offending shall for the first offence be branded on the forehead with the letter (B) If he shall offend in the same kinde the second time, he shall be branded as before and also be severally whipped: and if he shall fall into the like offence the third time he shall be put to death, as being incorrigible. And if any person shal commit such Burglarie, or rob in the fields or house on the Lords day besides the former punishments, he shal for the first offence have one of his ears cut off. And for the second offence in the same kinde he shal loose his other ear in the same maner. And if he fall into the same offence a third time he shal be put to death if it appear to the Court he did it presumptously.

For the prevention of Pilfring and Theft, it is ordered by this Court and Authoritie therof; that if any person shal be taken or known to rob any orchard or garden, that shall hurt, or steal away any grafts or fruit trees, fruits, linnen, woollen, or any other goods left out in orchards, gardens, backsides, or any other place in house or fields: or shall steal any wood or other goods from the water-side, from mens doors, or yards; he shall forfeit treble damage to the owners therof. And if they be children, or servants that shall trespasse heerin, if their parents or masters will not pay the penaltie before expressed, they shal be openly whipped. And forasmuch as many times it so falls out that small thefts and other offences of a criminall nature, are committed both by English & Indian, in townes remote from any prison, or other fit place to which such malefactors may be committed till the next Court, it is therfore heerby ordered; that any Magistrate upon complaint made to him may hear, and upon due proof determin any small offences of the aforesayed nature, according to the laws heer established, and give warrant to the Constable of that town where the offender lives to levie the same: provided the damage or fine exceed not fourty shillings: provided also it shall be lawfull for either partie to appeal to the next Court to be holden in that Jurisdiction, giving sufficient caution to prosecute the same to effect at the said Court. And everie Magistrate shall make return yearly to the Court of Jurisdiction, wherin he liveth of what cases he hath so ended. And also the Constables of all such fines as they have received. And where the offender hath nothing to satisfie such Magistrate may punish by stocks, or whipping as the cause shall deserve, not exceeding ten stripes. It is also ordered that all servants & workmen imbeazling the goods of their masters, or such as set them on work that make restitution and be lyable to all lawes & penalties as other men.

Capital Lawes

1. If any man after legal conviction shall *have or worship* any other God, but the *Lord God*: he shall be put to death. Exod. 22. 20. Deut. 13. 6. & 10. Deut. 17. 2. 6.

2. If any man or woman be a *witch*, that is, hath or consulteth with a familiar spirit, they shall be put to death. Exod. 22. 18. Levit. 20. 27. Deut. 18. 10. 11.

3. If any person within this Jurisdiction whether Christian or Pagan shall wittingly and willingly presume to *blaspheme* the holy Name

of God, Father, Son or Holy-Ghost, with direct, expresse, presumptuous, or high-handed blasphemy, either by wilfull or obstinate denying the true God, or his Creation, or Government of the world: or shall curse God in like manner, or reproach the holy Religion of God as if it were but a politick device to keep ignorant men in awe; or shal utter any other kinde of Blasphemy of the like nature & degree they shall be put to death. Levit. 24, 15. 16.

4. If any person shall commit any wilfull *murther*, which is Man slaughter, committed upon premeditate malice, hatred, or crueltie not in a mans necessary and just defence, nor by meer casualty against his will, he shall be put to death. Exod. 21. 12. 13. Numb. 35. 31.

5. If any person slayeth another suddenly in his *anger*, or *cruelty* of passion, he shall be put to death. Levit. 24. 17. Numb. 35. 20. 21.

6. If any person shall slay another through guile, either by *poysoning*, or other such develish practice, he shall be put to death. Exod. 21. 14.

7. If any man or woman shall *lye with any beast*, or bruit creature, by carnall copulation; they shall surely be put to death: and the beast shall be slain, & buried, and not eaten. Lev. 20, 15. 16.

8. If any man *lyeth with man-kinde* as he lieth with a woman, both of them have committed abomination, they both shal surely be put to death: unles the one partie were forced (or be under fourteen years of age in which case he shall be seveerly punished). Levit. 20. 13.

9. If any person commit *adulterie* with a married, or espoused wife; the Adulterer & Adulteresse shal surely be put to death. Lev. 20. 19. & 18. 20. Deu. 22. 23. 27.

10. If any man *stealeth a man*, or Mankinde, he shall surely be put to death. Exodus 21. 16.

11. If any man rise up by *false-witnes* wittingly, and of purpose to take away any mans life: he shal be put to death. Deut. 19. 16. 18. 16.

12. If any man shall *conspire*, and attempt any Invasion, Insurrection, or publick Rebellion against our Common-Wealth: or shall indeavour to surprize any Town, or Townes, Fort, or Forts therin; or shall treacherously, & persidiously attempt the Alteration and Subversion of our frame of Politie, or Government fundamentally he shall be put to death. Numb. 16. 2 Sam. 3. 2 Sam. 18. 2 Sam. 20.

13. If any child, or children, above sixteen years old, and of sufficient understanding, shall *curse*, or *smite* their natural *father*, or *mother*; he or they shall be put to death: unles it can be sufficiently testified that the Parents have been very unchristianly negligent in the eduction of such children; or so provoked them by extream, and cruel correction; that they have been forced therunto to preserve themselves from death or maiming. Exod. 21. 17. Lev. 20. 9. Exod. 21. 15.

14. If a man have a stubborn or *rebellious son*, of sufficient years & uderstanding (viz) sixteen years of age, which will not obey the voice of his Father, or the voice of his Mother, and that when they have chastened him will not harken unto them: then shal his Father & Mother being his natural parets, lay hold on him, & bring him to the Magistrates assembled in Court & testifie unto them that their Son is stubborn & rebellious & will not obey their voice and chastisement, but lives in sundry notorious crimes, such a son shal be put to death. Deut. 21. 20. 21.

15. If any man shal *ravish* any maid or single woman, comitting carnal copulation with her by force, against her own will; that is above the age of ten years he shal be punished either with death, or with some other greivous punishmet according to circumstances as the Judges, or General court shal determin.

♦ ♦ ♦

Fornication

It is ordered by this Court and Authoritie therof, That if any man shall commit Fornication with any single woman, they shall be punished either by enjoyning to Marriage, or Fine, or corporall punishment, or all or any of these as the Judges in the courts of Assistants shall appoint most agreeable to the word of God. And this Order to continue till the Court take further order.

Gaming

Upon complaint of great disorder by the use of the game called Shuffle-board, in houses of common entertainment, wherby much pretious time is spent unfruitfully and much wast of wine and beer occasioned, it is therfore ordered and enacted by the Authoritie of this Court;

That no person shall henceforth use the said game of Shuffle-board in any such house, nor in any other house used as common for such purpose, upon payn for every Keeper of such house to forfeit for every such offence twenty shillings: and for every person playing at the said game in any such house, to forfeit for everie such offence five shillings: Nor shall any person at any time play or game for any monie, or mony-worth upon penalty of forfeiting treble the value therof: one half to the partie informing, the other half to the Treasurie. And any Magistrate may hear and determin any offence against this Law.

Heresie

Although no humane power be Lord over the Faith & Consciences of men, and therfore may not constrein them to beleive or professe against their Consciences: yet because such as bring in damnable heresies, tending to the subversion of the Christian Faith, and destruction of the soules of men, ought duly to be restreined from such notorious impiety, it is therfore ordered and decreed by this Court;

That if any Christian within this Jurisdiction shall go about to subvert and destroy the christian Faith and Religion, by broaching or mainteining any damnable heresie; as denying the immortalitie of the Soul, or the resurrection of the body, or any sin to be repented of in the Regenerate, or any evil done by the outward man to be accounted sin: or denying that Christ gave himself a Ransom for our sins, or shal affirm that wee are not justified by his Death and Righteousnes, but by the perfection of our own works; or shall deny the moralitie of the fourth commandement, or shall indeavour to seduce others to any the herisies aforementioned, everie such person continuing obstinate therin after due means of conviction shal be sentenced to Banishment.

Idlenes

It is ordered by this Court and Authoritie therof, that no person, Housholder or other shall spend his time idlely or unproffitably under pain of such punishment as the Court of Assistants or County Court shall think meet to inflict. And for this end it is ordered that the Constable of everie place shall use speciall care and diligence to take knowledge of offenders in this kinde, especially of common coasters, unproffitable fowlers and tobacco takers, and present the same unto the two next Assistants, who shall have power to hear and determin the cause, or transfer it to the next Court.

Jesuits

This Court taking into consideration the great wars, combustions and divisions which are this day in Europe: and that the same are observed to be raysed and fomented chiefly by the secret underminings, and solicitations of those of the Jesuiticall Order, men brought up and devoted to the religion and court of Rome; which hath occasioned divers States to expell them their territories; for prevention wherof among our selves, It is ordered and enacted by Authoritie of this Court,

That no Jesuit, or spiritual or ecclesiastical person (as they are termed) ordained by the authoritie of the Pope, or Sea of Rome shall henceforth at any time repair to, or come within this Jurisdiction: And if any person shal give just cause of suspicion that he is one of such Societie or Order he shall be brought before some of the Magistrates, and if he cannot free himselfe of such suspicion he shall be committed to prison, or bound over to the next Court of Assistants, to be tryed and proceeded with by Ba§ishment or otherwise as the Court shall see cause: and if any person so banished shall be taken the second time within this Jurisdiction upon lawfull tryall and conviction he shall be put to death. Provided this Law shall not extend to any such Jesuit, spiritual or ecclesiasticall person as shall be cast upon our shoars, by shipwrack or other accident, so as he continue no longer then till he may have opportunitie of passage for his departure; nor to any such as shall come in company with any Messenger hither upon publick occasions, or any Merchant or Master of any ship, belonging to any place not in emnitie with the State of England, or our selves, so as they depart again with the same

Messenger, Master of Merchant, and behave themselves in-offensively during their aboad heer.

In-keepers, Tippling, Drunkenes

Forasmuch as there is a necessary use of houses of common entertainment in every Common-wealth, and of such as retail wine, beer and vict-uals; yet because there are so many abuses of that lawfull libertie, both by persons entertain-ing and persons entertained, there is also need of strict Laws and Rules to regulate such an em-ployment: It is therefore ordered by this Court and Authoritie thereof;

That no person or persons shall at any time under any pretence or colour whatsoever un-dertake to be a common Victuailer, Keeper of a Cooks shop or house for common entertain-ment, Taverner, or publick seller of wine, ale, beer or strongwater (by re-tale) nor shall any sell wine privatly in his house or out of doors by a lesse quantitie or under a quarter cask: without approbation of the selected Townsmen and Licence of the Shire Court where they dwell: upon pain of forfeiture of five pounds for everie such offence, or imprisonment at pleasure of the Court, where satisfaction can-not be had.

And every person so licenced for common entertainment shall have some inoffensive Signe obvious for strangers direction, and such as have no such Signe after three months so li-cenced from time to time shall lose their li-cence: and others allowed in their stead. And any licenced person that selleth beer shall not sell any above two-pence the ale-quart: upon penaltie of three shillings four pence for everie such offence. And it is permitted to any that will to sell beer out of doors at a pennie the ale-quart and under.

Neither shall any such licenced person aforesaid suffer any to be drunken, or drink ex-cessively viz: above half a pinte of wine for one person at one time; or to continue tippling above the space of half an hour, or at unreasonable times, or after nine of the clock at night in, or about any of their houses on penaltie of five shillings for everie such offence.

And everie person found drunken viz: so that he be thereby bereaved or disabled in the use of his understanding, appearing in his speech or gesture in any of the said houses or elsewhere shall forfeit ten shillings. And for ex-cessive drinking three shillings four pence. And for continuing above half an hour tippling two shillings six pence. And for tippling at unrea-sonable times, or after nine a clock at night five shillings: for everie offence in these particulars being lawfully convict thereof. . . .

Provided notwithstanding such licenced persons may entertain sea-faring men, or land travellers in the night-season, when they come first on shore, or from their journy for their nec-essarie refreshment, or when they prepare for their voyage or journie the next day early; so there be no disorder among them; and also Strangers, Lodgers or other persons in an or-derly way may continue in such houses of com-mon entertainment during meal times, or upon lawfull busines what time their occasions shall require.

♦   ♦   ♦

And if any person offend in drunkenes, ex-cessive or long drinking the second time they shall pay double Fines. And if they fall into the same offence the third time they shall pay tre-ble Fines. And if the parties be not able to pay the Fines then he that is found drunk shall be punished by whipping to the number of ten stripes: and he that offends in excessive or long drinking shall be put into the stocks for three hours when the weather may not hazzard his life or lims. And if they offend the fourth time they shall be imprisoned until they put in two sufficient Sureties for their good behaviour.

♦   ♦   ♦

Lying

Whereas truth in words as well as in actions is required of all men, especially of Chistians who are the professed Servants of the God to Truth; and wheras all lying is contrary to truth, and some sorts of lyes are not only sinfull (as all lyes are) but also pernicious to the Public-weal, and injurious to particular persons; it is therfore ordered by this Court and Authoritie therof,

That everie person of the age of discretion (which is accounted fourteen years) who shall wittingly and willingly make, or publish any Lye which may be pernicious to the publick weal, or tending to the damage or injurie of any particular person, or with intent to deceive and abuse the people with false news or reports: and the same duly proved in any Court or before any one Magistrate (who hath heerby power graunted to hear, and determin all offences against this Law) such person shall be fined for the first offence ten shillings, or if the partie be unable to pay the same then to be set in the stocks so long as the said Court or Magistrate shall appoint, in some open place, not exceeding two hours. For the second offence in that kinde wherof any shall be legally convicted the sum of twenty shillings, or be whipped upon the naked body not exceeding ten stripes. And for the third offence that way fourty shillings, or if the partie be unable to pay, then to be whipped with more stripes, not exceeding fifteen. And if yet any shall offend in like kinde, and be legally convicted therof, such person, male or female, shall be fined ten shillings a time more then formerly: or if the partie so offending be unable to pay, then to be whipped with five, or six more stripes then formerly not exceeding fourty at any time.

◆ ◆ ◆

Masters, Servants, Labourers

1. It is ordered by this Court and the Authoritie therof, that no servant, either man or maid shall either give, sell or truck any commoditie whatsoever without licence from their Masters, during the time of their service under pain of Fine, or corporal punishment at the discretion of the Court as the offence shall deserve.

2. And that all workmen shall work the whole day allowing convenient time for food and rest.

3. It is also ordered that when any servants shall run from their masters . . . it shall be lawfull for the next Magistrate, or the Constable and two of the chief Inhabitants where no Magistrate is to presse men and boats or pinnaces at the publick charge to pursue such persons by Sea or Land and ring them back by force of Arms.

4. It is also ordered by the Authoritie aforesaid, that the Free-men of everie town may from time to time as occasion shall require agree amongst themselves about the prizes, and rates of all workmens labours and servants wages. And everie person inhabiting in any town, whether workman, labourer or servant shall be bound to the same rates which the said Freemen, or the greater part shall binde themselves unto: and whosoever shall exceed those rates so agreed shall be punished by the discretion of the Court of that Shire, according to the qualitie and measure of the offence.

◆ ◆ ◆

6. It is ordered, and by this Court declared, that if any servant shall flee from the tyrannie and crueltie of his, or her Master to the house of any Freeman of the same town, they shall be there protected and susteined till due order be taken for their releif.

◆ ◆ ◆

8. And that if any man smite out the eye, or tooth of his man-servant, or maid-servant; or otherwise maim, or much disfigure them (unles it be by meer casualtie) he shall let them goe free from his service, and shall allow such farther recompence as the Court shall adjudge him.

◆ ◆ ◆

Suits, Vexatious Suits

It is ordered and decreed, and by this Court declared; that in all Cases where it appears to the Court that the Plaintiffe hath willingly & wittingly done wrong to the Defendant in commencing and prosecuting any Action, Suit, Complaint or Indictment in his own name or in the name of others, he shall pay treble damages to the partie greived, and be fined fourty shillings to the Common Treasurie.

Swyne

It is ordered by this Court, and by the Authoritie therof; that every *Township* within this Jurisdiction shall henceforth have power, and are heerby required from time to time to make Orders for preventing all harms by swine in corn, meadow, pastures and gardens; as also to impose penalties according to their best discretion: and to appoint one of their Inhabitants by *War-*

rent under the hands of the Select-men, or the Constable where no Select-men are, to levie all such Fines and Penalties by them in that case imposed (if the Town neglect it).

♦ ♦ ♦

Tobacco

This Court finding that since the repealing of the former Laws against Tobacco, the same is more abused then before doth therfore order,

That no man shall take any *tobacco* within twenty poles of any house, or so neer as may indanger the same, or neer any Barn, corn, or hay-cock as may occasion the fyring therof, upon pain of ten shillings for everie such offence, besides full recompence of all damages done by means therof. Nor shall any take *tobacco* in any Inne or common Victualing-house, except in a private room there, so as neither the Master of the said house nor any other Guests there shall take offence therat, which if any doe, then such person shall forthwith for-

bear, upon pain of two shillings sixpence for everie such offence. And for all Fines incurred by this Law, one half part shall be to the Informer the other to the poor of the town where the offence is done.

Torture

It is ordered, decreed, and by this Court declared; that no man shall be forced by torture to confesse any crime against himselfe or any other, unles it be in some Capital case, where he is first fully convicted by clear and sufficient evidence to be guilty. After which, if the Case be of that nature that it is very apparent there be other Conspirators or Confoederates with him; then he may be tortured, yet not with such tortures as be barbarous and inhumane.

And that no man shall be beaten with above fourty stripes for one Fact at one time. Nor shall any man be punished with whipping, except he have not othewise to answer the Law, unles his crime be very shamefull, and his course of life vitious and *profligate*.

The Rhode Island Patent
1643

Because the English Civil War had already begun, this patent was issued by Parliament, not the king. It accordingly has several remarkably advanced features: the settlers themselves constituted the corporation and were endowed with full powers of self-government; the principle of majoritarianism was explicitly recognized; and the patent was issued on the application of the settlers, who were then free to set up any "Form of Civil Government" that suited them. These progressive features were appropriate to this settlement of religiously independent settlers. Because the patent did not provide for appointment of the governor by the Crown, proprietor, or company in England, Rhode Island (like Connecticut) became an autonomous quasi-commonwealth. The more conservative neighbors called it "the licentious republic," in part because it allowed full religious liberty for all people, had no established church, and had an expansive right of suffrage that was not tied to religious belief. The founder of the colony, Roger Williams, insisted on purchasing land from local Indians, which set the stage for peaceful white–Indian relations until Rhode Island was dragged into King Philip's War in 1675.

And whereas there is a Tract of Land in the Continent of America aforesaid, called by the Name of the Narraganset Bay; . . .

And whereas the said English, have repre-

sented their Desire to the said Earl, and Commissioners to have their hopeful beginnings approved and confirmed by granting unto them a free Charter of Civil Incorporation and Government: that they may order and govern their Plantation in such a Manner as to maintain Justice and peace, both among themselves and towards all Men with whom they shall have to do. . . .

[We do] by the Authority of the aforesaid Ordinance of the Lords and Commons give, grant and confirm to the aforesaid Inhabitants of the Towns of Providence, Portsmouth and Newport, a free and absolute Charter of Incorporation to be known by the Name of the Incorporation of Providence Plantations, in the Narraganset-Bay, in New-England.—Together with full Power and Authority to rule themselves, and such others as shall hereafter inhabit within any Part of the said Tract of land, by such a Form of Civil Government, as by voluntary consent of all, or the greater Part of them, they shall find most suitable to their Estate and Condition: and, for that End, to make and ordain such Civil Laws and Constitutions, and to inflict such punishments upon Transgressors, and for Execution therefor so to place, and displace Officers of Justice, as they, or the greater Part of them, shall by free Consent agree unto. Provided nevertheless, that the said Laws, Constitutions, and Punishments, for the Civil Government of the said Plantations be conformable to the Laws of England so far as the Nature and Constitution of the place will admit.

Note: England's Civil War

England's constitutional struggles in the seventeenth century shaped how Americans thought about law and fundamental liberties. The Stuart monarchs insisted that the king was superior to the laws and was himself the lawgiver; in the words of Lord Chancellor Ellesmere in *Calvin's* Case (1608), "The monarch is the law; the king is the law speaking." Opposed to these absolutist pretensions was an idea originally expressed by Henry de Bracton in the thirteenth century: the king is under God and under the law. Sir Edward Coke, chief justice of the Court of Common Pleas in the early seventeenth century and one of England's greatest legal minds, warmly promoted this idea.

Tensions developed between the Stuart monarchs and successive Parliaments over constitutional questions involving the raising of taxes. The Crown's growing need for revenue to finance foreign military campaigns and to subdue the rebellious Scots confronted the stubborn determination of parliamentarians to establish parliamentary prerogatives and limit the king's attempts to govern without the consent of Parliament. The oppression of Protestant dissenters, especially under Charles I, further exacerbated the growing crisis. Even people who were comfortable with the Anglican Church were appalled by the sometimes savage punishments meted out under Charles. These struggles led to a crisis in English society in the 1630s, and then the English Civil War (1642–1649), which resulted in the complete triumph of the supporters of Parliament. The victors tried King Charles I for treason and beheaded him in 1649.

This led to a unique period in English history, the republican Commonwealth, known as the Protectorate after the accession of Oliver Cromwell as Lord Protector in 1653. Puritan theological and political belief enjoyed a short-lived ascendancy during the Commonwealth, while more radical and democratic ideas surfaced. After Cromwell's death, Parliament restored the monarchy, placing Charles II, son of Charles I, on the throne in 1660.

THE POST-RESTORATION COLONIAL GOVERNMENTS

The upheavals of the Civil War and Commonwealth temporarily halted most emigration from England and the process of chartering colonies. With the return of domestic peace in 1660, both resumed vigorously. After the restoration, King Charles II granted colonial charters to proprietors—individuals of groups of men—who in effect owned all the land in the colony and had enormous political power over the colony. The goals of the proprietors differed dramatically. William Penn wanted to create a haven for religious dissidents, particularly Quakers, and had no interest in personal gain; the eight proprietors of the Carolina Colony—rich and politically connected members of he nobility—hoped to increase their already considerable wealth. The proprietors in both places drafted their own documents for the governance of their colonies. The following excerpts illustrate three widely variant forms that American experimentation in government making took. The first, the fantastic Fundamental Constitutions of Carolina, penned by John Locke, has an almost science-fiction air about it. The second, William Penn's 1682 draft of his Frame of Government, is a more realistic yet liberal attempt by a much different kind of proprietor to provide a paternalistic constitution. The third model for government, the Charter of Libertyes, was written by colonists in New York but never went into effect because the king vetoed it at the request of his brother, James, Duke of York, who soon became King James II. This proposed frame of government illustrates the growing demands for self-government and protection of the rights among the colonists. A century later, the colonists would be in a position to back up such demands with political organization and military force.

The Fundamental Constitutions of Carolina
1669

The Fundamental Constitutions of Carolina is an exotic document, far outside the main-stream of American constitutional development. The document illustrates the desire of the South Carolina proprietors to replicate English society, led by a hierarchy of landed, hered-itary nobility. This was a fantasy that could never have been transplanted to the mainland colonies, but it suggested a proprietary attitude reflective of the noble elite or Restoration England. This document was written by John Locke, the Enlightenment philosopher most noted for his assertions of the rights of all men and his theories that undermined the legiti-macy of the monarchy. However, Locke prepared the Fundamental Constitutions for the eight proprietors—which included a lord, a duke, and two earls and a future earl (who was then a baron)—who were among the most powerful men in England. Securities for slavery sat cheek by jowl with guarantees of religious freedom and civil liberty. On the heels of twenty years of civil war, caused to a great extent by religious dissent and oppression, Locke's doc-ument wisely provided religious liberty for all colonists. Reflecting the growing importance of slavery to the New World economy—and the African slave trade to the English economy—the Fundamental Constitutions specifically protected the rights of the colonists to own slaves. All versions of the Fundamental Constitutions were drafted by John Locke, then in the ser-vice of one of the proprietors, Baron Anthony Ashley Cooper, the Chancellor of the Exche-quer, who later became the First Earl of Shaftesbury; the one excerpted here dates from 1669.

Our sovereign Lord The King having, out of his Royal Grace and Bounty, granted unto us the Province of Carolina, with all the Royalties, Proprieties, Jurisdictions, and Privileges of a

County Palatine, as large and ample as the County Palatine of Durham, with other great Privileges; for the better settlement of the Government of the said Place, and establishing the Interest of the Lords Proprietor with Equality, and without Confusion; and that the Government of this Province may be made most agreeable to the Monarchy under which we live, and of which this Province is a part; and that we may avoid erecting a numerous Democracy: we the Lords and Proprietors of the Province aforesaid, have agreed to this following Form of Government, to be perpetually established amongst us, unto which we do oblige our selves, our Heirs and Successors, in the most binding ways that can be devised.

1. The eldest of the Lords Proprietors shall be Palatine; and upon the Decease of the Palatine, the eldest of the seven surviving Proprietors shall always succeed him.

♦ ♦ ♦

3. The whole Province shall be divided into Counties; each County shall consist of eight Seigniories, eight Baronies, and four Precincts; each Precinct shall consist of six Colonies.

♦ ♦ ♦

9. There shall be just as many Landgraves as there are Counties, and twice as many Caciques, and no more. These shall be the hereditary Nobility of the Province, and, by right of their Dignity, be Members of Parliament. Each Landgrave shall have four Baronies, and each Cacique two Baronies, hereditarily and unalterably annexed to and settled upon the said dignity.

♦ ♦ ♦

71. There shall be a Parliament, consisting of the Proprietors, or their Deputies, the Landgraves and Caciques, and one Freeholder out of every Precinct, to be chosen by the Freeholders of the said Precinct respectively. They shall Sit all together in one Room, and have every Member one vote.

♦ ♦ ♦

97. But since the Natives of that Place, who will be concerned in our Plantation, are utterly Strangers to Christianity, whose Idolatry, Ignorance, or Mistake gives us no right to expel or use them ill; and those who remove from other Parts to Plant there will unavoidably be of different Opinions concerning Matters of Religion, the liberty whereof they will expect to have allowed them, and it will not be reasonable for us, on this account, to keep them out; that Civil Peace may be maintained amidst the diversity of Opinions, and our Agreement and Compact with all Men may be duly and faithfully observed, the violations whereof, upon what pretence soever, cannot be without great offence to Almighty God, and great scandal to the true Religion, which we profess; and also, that Jews, Heathens, and other Dissenters from the purity of Christian Religion may not be scared and kept at a distance from it, but, by having an opportunity of acquainting themselves with the truth and reasonableness of its Doctrines, and the peaceableness and inoffensiveness of its Professors, may, by good usage and persuasion, and all those convincing Methods of gentleness and meekness suitable to the Rules and Design of the Gospel, be won over to embrace and unfeignedly receive the Truth: Therefore, any seven or more Persons agreeing in any religion, shall constitute a church or profession, to which they shall give some name, to distinguish it from others.

♦ ♦ ♦

107. Since Charity obliges us to wish well to the Souls of all Men and Religion ought to alter nothing any Man's Civil Estate or Right, it shall be lawful for Slaves, as well as others, to Enter themselves and be of what church or Profession [of religion] any of them shall think best, and thereof be as fully Members as any Freeman. But yet, no Slave shall hereby be exempted from that Civil Dominion his Master has over him, but be in all other things in the same State and Condition he was in before.

♦ ♦ ♦

110. Every Freeman of Carolina shall have absolute Power and Authority over his Negro Slaves, of what Opinion or Religion soever.

WILLIAM PENN

First Frame of Government
1682

William Penn's preface to the Frame of Government that he provided for Pennsylvania in 1682 not only displayed his benign spirit but also contained several ideas congenial to Americans in the ensuing century, such as the concept of balancing forces in government and the central place of popular virtue in sustaining the constitutions of free governments.

I know what is said by the several admirers of monarchy, aristocracy and democracy, which are the rule of one, a few, and many, and are the three common ideas of government, when men discourse on the subject. But I chuse to solve the controversy with this small distinction, and it belongs to all three: Any government is free to the people under it (whatever be the frame) where the laws rule, and the people are a party to those laws, and more than this is tyranny, oligarchy, or confusion.

♦ ♦ ♦

Governments, like clocks, go from the motion men give them; and as governments are made and moved by men, so by them they are ruined too. Wherefore governments rather depend upon men, than men upon governments. Let men bee good, and the government cannot be bad; if it be ill, they will cure it. But, if men be bad, let the government be never so good, they will endeavor to warp and spoil it to their turn.

I know some say, let us have good laws, and no matter for the men that execute them: but let them consider, that though good laws do well, good men do better: for good laws may want good men, and be abolished or evaded by ill men: but good men will never want good laws, nor suffer ill ones. It is true, good laws have some awe upon ill ministers, but that is where they have not power to escape or abolish them, and the people are generally wise and good: but a loose and depraved people (which is the question) love laws and an administration like themselves. That, therefore, which makes a good constitution, must keep it, viz: men of wisdom and virtue, qualities, that because they descend not with worldly inheritances, must be carefully propagated by a virtuous education of youth; for which after ages will owe more to the care and prudence of founders, and the successive magistracy, than to their parents, for their private patrimonies.

♦ ♦ ♦

But, next to the power of necessity (which is a solicitor, that will take no denial) this induced me to a compliance, that we have (with reverence to God, and good conscience to men) to the best of our skill contrived and composed to the frame and laws of this government, to the great end of all government, viz: To support power in reverence with the people and to secure the people from the abuse of power; that they may be free by their just obedience, and the magistrates honourable, for their administration: for liberty without obedience is confusion, and obedience without liberty is slavery. To carry this evenness is partly owing to the constitution, and partly to the magistracy: where either of these fail, government will be subject to convulsions; but where both are wanting, it must be totally subverted; then where both meet, the government is like to endure. Which I humbly pray and hope God will please to make the lot of this Pensilvania. Amen.

William Penn

The New-York Charter of Libertyes
1683

The Charter of Libertyes contained liberal guarantees for the liberty of the colonists, significantly including those most basic elements of the ancient constitution—Magna Charta's Chapter 39, and the petit and grand juries. Note too these forward-looking provisions: a primitive homestead exemption, the forerunner of the Third Amendment, and the security of dower. The provision for religious toleration was inevitable in a province as heterogeneous as New York; the only surprise is that religious establishments survived at all, albeit in an enfeebled state. This statute ("Charter" is a misnomer) never became law; it was vetoed by the king. But it is suggestive of innate liberal inclinations that were released by the Glorious Revolution in the colonies.

For the better Establishing the Government of this province of New Yorke and that Justice and Right may be Equally done to all persons within the same

Bee It Enacted by The Governour Councell and Representatives now in Generall Assembly mett and assembled and by the authority of the same.

That the Supreme Legislative Authority under his Majesty and Royall Highnesse James Duke of Yorke Albany &c Lord Proprietor of the said province shall forever be and reside in a Governour, Councell, and the people mett in Generall Assembly.

That The Exercise of the Chiefe Magistracy and Administracon of the Government over the said province shall bee in the said Governour assisted by a Councell with whose advice and Consent or with at least four of them he is to rule and Governe the same according to the Lawes thereof.

♦ ♦ ♦

That Noe freeman shall be taken and imprisoned or be disseized of his ffreehold or Libertye or ffree Customes or be outlawed or Exiled or any other ways destroyed nor shall be passed upon adjudged or condemned But by the Lawfull Judgment of his peers and by the Law of this province. Justice nor Right shall be neither sold denyed or deferred to any man within this province.

That Noe aid, Tax, Tallage, Assessment, Custome, Loane, Benevolence or Imposicon whatsoever shall be layed assessed imposed or levyed on any of his Majestyes Subjects within this province or their Estates upon any manner of Colour or pretence but by the act and Consent of the Governour Councell and Representatives of that people in Generall Assembly mett and Assembled.

That noe Man of what Estate or Condicon soever shall be putt out of his Lands or Tenements, nor taken, nor imprisoned, nor disherited, nor banished nor any wayes distroyed without being brought to Answere by due Course of Law.

That a freeman shall not be amerced for a small fault, but after the manner of his fault and for a great fault after the Greatness thereof Saveing to him his freehold, And a husbandman saveing to him his Wainage and a merchant likewise saveing to him his merchandize. And none of the said Amerciaments shall be assessed but by the oath of twelve honest and Lawfull men of the Vicinage provided the faults and misdemeanours be not in Contempt of Courts of Judicature.

All Tryalls shall be by the verdict of twelve men, and as neer as may be peers or Equalls And of the neighbourhood and in the County Shire or Division where the fact Shall arise or grow Whether the Same be by Indictment Informacon Declaracon or otherwise against the person Offender or Defendant.

That In all Cases Capitall or Criminall there shall be a grand Inquest who shall first present the offence and then twelve men of the neighborhood to try the Offender who after his plea to the Indictment shall be allowed his reasonable Challenges.

That In all Cases whatsoever Bayle by sufficient Suretyes shall be allowed and taken unless for treason or felony plainly and specially Expressed and menconed in the Warrant of Committment provided Alwayes that nothing herein contained shall Extend to discharge out of prison upon bayle any person taken in Execucon for debts or otherwise legally sentenced by the Judgment of any of the Courts of Record within the province.

That Noe ffreeman shall be compelled to receive any Marriners or Souldiers into his house and there suffere them to Sojourne against their willes provided Alwayes it be not in time of Actuall Warr within this province.

That Noe Commissions for proceeding by Marshall Law against any of his Majestyes Subjects within this province shall issue forth to any person or persons whatsoever Least by Colour of them any of his Majestyes Subjects bee destroyed or putt to death Except all such officers persons and Soldiers in pay throughout the Government.

♦ ♦ ♦

That Noe Estate of a feme Covert shall be sold or conveyed But by Deed acknowledged by her in Some Court of Record the Woman being secretly Examined if She doth it freely without threats or Compulsion of her husband.

♦ ♦ ♦

That a Widdow after the death of her husband shall have her Dower And shall and may tarry in the Chiefe house of her husband forty dayes after the death of her husband within which forty days her Dower shall be assigned her And for her Dower shall be assigned unto her the third part of all the Lands of her husband dureing Coverture, Except she were endowed of Lesse before Marriage.

♦ ♦ ♦

That Noe person or persons which professe ffaith in God by Jesus Christ Shall at any time be any wayes molested punished disquited or called in Question for any Difference in opinion or Matter of Religious Concernment, who doe not actually disturb the Civill peace of the province, But that all and Every such person or persons may from time to time and at all times freely have and fully enjoy his or their Judgments or Consciencyes in matters of Religion throughout all the province, they behaving themselves peaceably and quietly and not useing this Liberty to Lycentiousnesse nor to the civill Injury or outward disturbance of others.

THE GLORIOUS REVOLUTION

The restoration of the monarchy did not resolve underlying constitutional conflicts, however. Charles II (r. 1660–1685), and especially his brother and successor, King James II (r. 1685–1689), learned little from their father's unhappy reign, treason trial, and execution. Both were arbitrary monarchs who tried to resurrect the concept of the divine rights of kings. During their reigns persistent conflicts arose between Parliament and the Crown. The Habeas Corpus Act of 1679 provided a statutory basis for issuance of that guarantee of the subject's liberty, but a more comprehensive resolution of the threat posed by royal assertions of power was still needed. Supporters of parliamentary power (now called Whigs) were dismayed when Charles's brother, James II, succeeded him to the throne in 1685. King James II was also the head of the Church of England. But privately he was in fact a Roman Catholic and hoped to reinstate the Roman church as the official faith of England as well as establish a more arbitrary royal rule without the necessity of turning to Parliament. In effect, he wanted to roll back more than a century of English political development. One step along this route was his attempt to issue a royal "indulgence" to remove disabilities that Parliament had imposed on Roman Catholics and dissenters. From a modern perspective this seems like a progressive and admirable plan. But James's reasons for this were hardly progressive. His goal was to appoint Catholic military officers who would then help him use the army to maintain his increasingly arbitrary rule. Furthermore, he tried to force the Church of England to participate in this project by ordering the church officials to read (and endorse) his indulgence at church services. The very idea of issuing the indulgence, which would suspend an act of Parliament, threatened the power of the elected legislature, while the substance of the indulgence threatened the Church of England and the common understanding of the basis of political order in England. In 1688, facing unified resistance, James fled the kingdom and Parliament offered the throne to his Protestant daughter, Mary, and her husband, William, Prince of Orange. The Glorious Revolution finally settled the constitutional struggles of the seventeenth century in favor of Parliament, secured the Protestant Reformation, and buried absolutist pretensions. Many of these results were explicitly ratified by Parliament in the Bill of Rights of 1689.

Note: The Case of the Seven Bishops (1688)

The Case of the Seven Bishops demonstrated the threat to fundamental liberties posed by Stuart absolutism. The trial involved constitutional questions over the right to petition and to free speech and over the Crown's attempts to use seditious libel prosecutions to suppress criticism of the government. In order to appoint Catholic military officers, who would presumably support his increasing authoritarian regime, James II issued the Declaration of Indulgence in 1687 and ordered that it be read in all churches of the realm. The indulgence, as already noted, purported to suspend an act of Parliament and allow the appointment of Catholics and Protestant dissenters to military and political offices. Seven Anglican bishops privately petitioned the king to be relieved from this requirement, partly because of the threat it posed to the security of the Reformation and the place of the established church, and partly because they believed it to be an unconstitutional exercise by the king of the power of dispensation. That is, the king was taking it upon himself, without any constitutional warrant, to disregard a law passed by Parliament. Indeed, in 1662 and 1672 Parliament had declared it illegal for the king to act in this way. King James II received the bishops' petition, but upon reading its contents he tore it up and chased the bishops out of his chamber. The next day copies of the petition appeared all over London. Since the petition of the bishops condemned the actions of the king, James properly understood that the publication and distribution of the petition undermined his ability to govern. As such it violated the existing law of seditious libel, which in effect is the crime of embarrassing or denouncing the government.

Papacy and absolutism were of course at the heart of the controversy, but in the Case of the Seven Bishops, they were complicated by the two other constitutional issues: the right of subjects to petition the king and the reach of the common-law crime of seditious libel as a means of suppressing political opposition. In the trial of the bishops, the chief justice of King's Bench instructed the jury that "anything that shall disturb the government or make mischief and a stir among the people" constitutes seditious libel. Elaborating on this position, Justice Allybone wrote:

> I think, in the first place, that no man can take upon him to write against the actual exercise of the government unless he have leave from the government, but he makes a libel, be what he writes true or false. . . . Then, I lay down this for my next posi-

tion: that no private man can take upon him to write concerning the government at all. For what has any private man to do with the government, if his interest be not stirred or shaken? . . . When I intrude myself into other men's business that does not concern my particular interest, I am a libeler. . . . Now then, let us consider further, whether, if I will take upon me to contradict the government, any specious pretence that I shall put upon it shall . . . give it a better denomination. And truly I think it is the worse because it comes in a better dress . . . ; so that, whether it be in the form of a supplication or an address or a petition, if it be what it ought not to be, let us call it by its true name . . . —it is a libel. . . . Then, gentlemen, consider what this petition is. This is a petition relating to something that was done and ordered by the government. Whether the reasons of the petition be true or false, I will not examine that now; nor will I examine the prerogative of the crown; but only take notice that this relates to the acts of the government. . . . And shall or ought anybody to come and impeach that as illegal which the government has done? Truly, in my opinion, I do not think he should or ought; for by this rule may every act of the government be shaken when there is not a parliament . . . sitting.

Two of the judges disagreed with this view, even though it was the settled law. The bishops themselves did not attempt to change the law but simply argued that they had not released the petition that circulated around London and implied that it was not the same one they had given the king. The jury accepted these claims at face value and acquitted the bishops, to wild popular acclaim. Shortly thereafter, James II was forced to leave the country and Parliament invited his daughter, Mary, and her Dutch husband, Prince William of Orange, to take the English throne.

The popular and political vindication of the bishops did not resolve any of the legal issues raised in their case, though. These included the following: Do subjects have a right to petition the king or Parliament, and, if so, may any conditions be imposed on that right? Can persons be criminally prosecuted for criticizing the government or its policies? Is truth a defense in a prosecution for seditious libel? How far may a jury disregard the instructions of a court in a criminal prosecution? Can the jury determine for itself whether a law should be disregarded on the grounds that it is unconstitutional? Many of these issues were raised a generation later in the colony of New York in *Zenger's Case* (1735), excerpted later in this chapter.

The English Bill of Rights
1689

This document, the first fruit of the Glorious Revolution, set forth the liberties of the subject that the parliamentary party had demanded for most of the seventeenth century. It also set out rules for limiting the political power of the monarch. Thus it was a specific rejection of the claims by the Stuart kings of royal absolutism. The English Bill of Rights is also a direct forerunner of the American Bill of Rights and the limitations on the executive branch that would be written into the U.S. Constitution a century later.

And thereupon the said lords spiritual and temporal, and commons, pursuant to their respective letters and elections, being now assembled in a full and free representative of this nation, taking into their most serious consideration the best means for attaining the ends aforesaid, do in the first place (as their ancestors in like case have usually done) for the vindicating and asserting their ancient rights and liberties, declare:

1. That the pretended power of suspending laws, or the execution of laws, by regal authority, without consent of parliament, is illegal.

2. That the pretended power of dispensing of laws, or the execution of laws, by regal authority, as it hath been assumed and exercised of late, is illegal.

3. That the commission for erecting the late court of commissioners for ecclesiastical causes, and all other commissions and courts of like nature are illegal and pernicious.

4. That levying money for or to the use of the crown, by pretence of prerogative, without grant of parliament, for longer time, or in other manner than the same is or shall be granted, is illegal.

5. That it is the right of the subjects to petition the King, and all committments and prosecutions for such petitioning are illegal.

6. That the raising or keeping a standing army within the kingdom in time of peace, unless it is with consent of parliament, is against law.

7. That the subjects which are protestants, may have arms for their defence suitable to their conditions, and as allowed by law.

8. That election of members of parliament ought to be free.

9. That the freedom of speech, and debates or proceedings in parliament, ought not to be impeached or questioned in any court or place out of parliament.

10. That excessive bail ought not to be required, nor excessive fines imposed; nor cruel and unusual punishments inflicted.

♦ ♦ ♦

13. And that for redress of all grievances, and for the amending strengthening and preserving of the laws, parliaments ought to be held frequently.

JOHN LOCKE

"Second Treatise of Civil Government"
1690

John Locke, writing during the Glorious Revolution, summed up the principles for which the Whigs contended, providing a basis for modern theories of democratic government. A century later, Americans of the Revolutionary generation, familiar with his writings, regarded them as a synopsis of the constitutional principles vindicated in the Glorious Revolution. Although other writers, notably Baron de Montesquieu and William Blackstone, were also influential and sometimes more frequently cited in American Revolutionary debates, Locke's eloquent summation of liberal constitutional principles seemed to hold up to Americans a mirror of the ideas of their own Revolution.

Man being born, as has been proved, with a Title to perfect Freedom, and an uncontrouled enjoyment of all the Rights and Priviledges of the Law of Nature, equally with any other Man, or Number of Men in the World, hath by Nature a Power, not only to preserve his Property, that is, his Life, Liberty and Estate, against the Injuries and Attempts of other Men; but to judge of, and punish the breaches of that Law in others, as he is perswaded the Offence deserves. . . .

Whenever, therefore, any number of men are so united into one society as to quit every one his executive power of the law of nature and to resign it to the public, there and there only is a political or civil society. And this is done wherever any number of men, in the state of nature, enter into society to make one people, one body politic, under one supreme government, or else when any one joins himself to, and incorporates with any government already made; for thereby he authorizes the society or, which is all one, the legislative thereof to make laws for him as the public good of the society shall require, to the execution whereof his own assistance, as to his own decrees, is due. And this puts men out of a state of nature into that of a commonwealth by setting up a judge on early, with authority to determine all the controversies and redress the injuries that may happen to any member of the commonwealth, which judge is the legislative or magistrates appointed by it. . . .

Men being, as has been said, by nature all free, equal, and independent, no one can be put out of this estate and subjected to the political power of another without his own consent. The only way whereby any one divests himself of his natural liberty and puts on the bonds of civil society is by agreeing with other men to join and unite into a community for their comfortable, safe, and peaceable living one amongst another, in a secure enjoyment of their properties and a greater security against any that are not of it. This any number of men may do, because it injures not the freedom of the rest; they are left as they were in the liberty of the state of nature. When any number of men have so consented to make one community or government, they are thereby presently incorporated and make one body politic wherein the majority have a right to act and conclude the rest. . . .

The great and chief end, therefore, of men's uniting into commonwealths and putting themselves under government is the preservation of their property. To which in the state of nature there are many things wanting.

First there wants an established, settled, known law, received and allowed by common consent to be the standard of right and wrong and the common measure to decide all controversies between them; for though the law of nature be plain and intelligible to all rational creatures, yet men, being biased by their interests as well as ignorant for want of studying it, are not apt to allow of it as a law binding to them in the application of it to their particular cases.

Secondly, in the state of nature there wants a known and indifferent judge with authority to determine all differences according to the established law; for every one in that state being both judge and executioner of the law of nature, men being partial to themselves, passion and revenge is very apt to carry them too far and with too much heat in their own cases, as well as negligence and unconcernedness to make them too remiss in other men's.

Thirdly, in the state of nature there often wants power to go back and support the sentence when right, and to give it due execution. They who by any injustice offend will seldom fail, where they are able, by force, to make good their injustice; such resistance many times makes the punishment dangerous and frequently destructive to those who attempt it.

◆ ◆ ◆

But though Men when they enter into Society, give up the Equality, Liberty, and Executive Power they had in the State of Nature, into the hands of the Society, to be so far disposed of by the Legislative, as the good of the Society shall require; yet it being only with an intention in every one the better to preserve himself his Liberty and Property; (For no rational Creature can be supposed to change his condition with an intention to be worse) the power of the Society, or Legislative constituted by them, can never be suppos'd to extend farther than the common good; but is obliged to secure every ones Property by providing against those three defects above-mentioned, that made the State of Nature so unsafe and uneasie. And so whoever has the Legislative or Supream Power of any Common-wealth, is bound to govern by establish'd standing Laws, promulgated and known to the People, and not by Extemporary Decrees; by indifferent and upright Judges, who are to decide Controversies by those Laws; and to employ the force of the Community at home, only in the Execution of such Laws, or abroad to prevent or redress Foreign Injuries, and secure the Community from Inroads and Invasion. And all this to be directed to no end, but the Peace, Safety, and publick good of the People.

◆ ◆ ◆

These are the bounds which the trust that is put in them by the society and the law of God and nature have set to the legislative power of every commonwealth, in all forms of government:

First, they are to govern by promulgated established laws, not to be varied in particular cases, but to have one rule for rich and poor, for the favorite at court and the countryman at plough.

Secondly, these laws ought to be designed for no other end ultimately but the good of the people.

Thirdly, they must not raise taxes on the property of the people without the consent of the people, given by themselves or their deputies. And this properly concerns only such governments where the legislative is always in being, or at least where the people have not reserved any part of the legislative to deputies to be from time to time chosen by themselves.

Though in a Constituted Commonwealth, standing upon its own Basis, and acting according to its own Nature, that is, acting for the preservation of the Community, there can be but one Supream Power, which is the Legislative, to which all the rest are and must be subordinate, yet the Legislative being only a Fiduciary Power to act for certain ends, there remains still in the People a Supream Power to remove or alter the Legislative, when they find the Legislative act contrary to the trust reposed in them. For all Power given with trust for the attaining an end, being limited by that end, whenever that end is manifestly neglected, or opposed, the trust must necessarily be forfeited, and the Power devolve into the hands of those that gave it, who may place it anew where they shall think best for their safety and security.

THE SOURCES OF LAW IN AMERICA

American lawyers have sometimes claimed that the common law was the only body of English law that Americans drew on for their own law, that it was adopted early in the period of English settlement, and that its reception was both inevitable and noncontroversial. Some judges still make such assertions. Yet, each of these assumptions is wrong.

More than half a century ago, the legal historian Julius Goebel speculated that it would have been unlikely that the settlers of New England would have replicated the common law— "as absurd as to expect that they would establish a religious system on the principles of the Anglican Church."[7] Rather, he suggested, in creating their new legal order they would have drawn on the body of law most familiar to them: English local and customary law of the sort found in the borough customals and in the practice of the manorial and county courts. Subsequent scholarship has confirmed Goebel's conjecture. The result was a heterogeneous body of law, "a layman's version of English legal institutions," as Daniel Boorstin called it.[8]

In New York during the proprietary period (1664–1684), at least five separate bodies of law and judicial systems prevailed: Dutch civil law, which was based on Roman law; the "Bible codes" of the Connecticut immigrants in Westchester County and on Long Island, reaffirmed in the Duke's Laws of 1665; the laws enforced in the manorial courts on Long Island and up the Hudson River valley; the new statutes enacted by the colonial legislature; and the common law, which was fully applied to New York in the legal reforms of 1691. But until it did, the common law met vigorous competition from its rivals. A Dutch resident of Dutchess County expressed his contempt for the new system, declaring that he "valued no English law no more than a Turd."[9]

American law was composed in unequal parts of vaguely and inaccurately remembered fragments of common law, local law, Mosaic law (in most of New England and in parts of Long Island), and Roman law. Colonial law was also constantly changing to adapt to the circumstances and physical geography of the New World. To further complicate the picture, the colonies borrowed from one another's laws extensively yet with great selectivity, choosing only those elements of law suited to their local conditions.

The English common law was a part of American law, of course, however imperfectly it may have been understood and received before 1700. So were parliamentary statutes enacted before the settlement of a particular colony. Subsequent statutes were not part of a colony's laws unless explicitly made applicable to it. New England presents a special case, however. Although the common law was eventually received there after the American Revolution, Massachusetts resisted the extension of English law before the 1690s. John Winthrop insolently proclaimed that "our allegiance binds us not to the laws of England any longer than while we live in England, for the laws of the Parliament of England reach no further, nor do the king's writs under the great seal go any further."[10] In 1678, the General Court of Massachusetts Bay objected to the Navigation Acts, insisting that "the lawes of England are bounded within the fower [four] seas, and doe not reach America."[11] John Adams, writing in 1776 as "Novanglus," reiterated that viewpoint: "Our ancestors were entitled to the common law of England when they emigrated; that is, to just so much of it as they pleased to adopt, and no more. They were not bound or obliged to submit to it, unless they chose."[12]

Note: Reception of the Common Law

The common law was eventually received in all American jurisdictions, including refractory New England, by the nineteenth century. The beginnings of reception may be found in the charters to companies and proprietors granted by the Stuart monarchs in the early seventeenth century. Most of these charters insisted that any laws enacted by the colonists for their own governance must conform to the legal culture of the mother country. The Massachusetts Charter of 1629 declared that the leaders of the colony "from tyme to tyme" were empowered "to make Lawes and Ordinances for the Good and Welfare of the saide Company, and the Government and ordering of the saide Lande and Plantation, and the People inhabiting and to inhabite the same" as long as "such Lawes and Ordinances be not contrarire or repugnanat to the Lawes and Statuts of this our Realme of England." A subsequent clause in the charter empowered the magistrates of the colony to "ordeine, and establishe all Manner of wholesome and reasonable Orders, Lawes, Statutes, and Ordinances, Directions, and Instructions, not contrairie to the Lawes of this our Realme of England."[13] Similarly, the charter of New Plymouth authorized legislation, "provided that the said lawes and orders be not repugnante to the lawes of Englande."[14] The Maryland Charter granted lawmaking powers to the new government, provided that "the said Ordinances be consonant to Reason and be not repugnant nor contrary, but (so far as conveniently may be done) agreeable to the Laws, Statutes, or Rights of our Kingdom of England: And so that the same Ordinances do not, in any Sort, extend to oblige, bind, charge, or take away the Right or Interest of any Person or Persons, of, or in Member, Life, Freehold, Goods or Chattels."[15]

Such provisions were the first step on the road to the reception of the common law in America, as well as to the transference of English libertarian traditions, such as the principles derived from Magna Charta. Viewed by the Crown at the time as a means of controlling distant settlements, the conformity clauses came to be seen by Americans in the next century as an assurance that the settlers enjoyed the same rights and liberties as English people who had never left the realm. At the same time, these provisions allowed for vast experimentation in lawmaking, and indeed through these powers the colonies developed their own laws on a variety of topics, including inheritance, water rights, land usage, and personal rights, including the development of slavery.

William Blackstone on Reception
1765

Long before Americans began to think seriously about the transit of English law, English judges and lawyers had begun to work out the basis for a theory of reception of their legal systems. This was not surprising, since the English had become active colonizers in the sixteenth century and had had to confront the practical problems of legal administration for places like Ireland even earlier. After a century of development, the English theory of reception was summed up by William Blackstone, the magisterial commentator on English laws, in his four-volume treatise, Commentaries on the Laws of England *(1765).*

Besides these adjacent islands, our more distant plantations in America, and elsewhere, are also in some respect subject to the English laws. Plantations or colonies, in distant countries, are either such where the lands are claimed by right of occupancy only by finding them desert and uncultivated, and peopling them from the mother-country; or where, when already cultivated, they have been either gained by conquest, or ceded to us by treaties. And both these rights are founded upon the law of nature, or at least upon that of nations. But there is a difference between these two species of colonies, with respect to the laws by which they are bound. For it hath been held that if an uninhabited country be discovered and planted by English subjects, all the English laws then in being, which are the birthright of every subject, are immediately there in force. But this must be understood with very many and very great restrictions. Such colonists carry with them only so much of the English law as is applicable to their own situation and the condition of an infant colony; such, for instance, as the general rules of inheritance, and of protection from personal injuries. The artificial refinements and distinctions incident to the property of a great and commercial people, the laws of police and revenue, (such especially as are enforced by penalties,) the mode of maintenance for the established clergy, the jurisdic-

tion of spiritual courts, and a multitude of other provisions, are neither necessary nor convenient for them, and therefore are not in force. What shall be admitted and what rejected, at what times, and under what restrictions, must, in case of dispute, be decided in the first instance by their own provincial judicature, subject to the revision and control of the king in council: the whole of their constitution being also liable to be new-modelled and reformed by the general superintending power of the legislature in the mother-country. But in conquered or ceded countries, that have already laws of their own, the king may indeed alter and change those laws; but till he does actually change them, the ancient laws of the country remain, unless such as are against the law of God, as in the case of an infidel country. Our American plantations are principally of this latter sort, being obtained in the last century either by right of conquest and driving out the natives (with what natural justice I shall not at present inquire), or by treaties. And therefore the common law of England, as such, has no allowance or authority there; they being no part of the mother-country, but distinct (though dependent) dominions. They are subject, however, to the control of the parliament; though (like Ireland, Man, and the rest) not bound by any acts of parliament, unless particularly named.

Giddings v. Brown
1657

The process of reception of English law may be glimpsed in this precocious opinion in a case involving a challenge to a compelled assessment, levied to support the maintenance of a town's minister. This opinion demonstrates that ideas we associate with the nineteenth century, such as rudimentary forms of substantive due process and the rule of law, were current in the seventeenth century. Judge Symonds's opinion emphasizes the primacy of fundamental law, seen in both a religious and a secular sense.

[Court of Assistants for Essex County, Massachusetts, per Samuel Symonds, Assistant:]

I understand this to be about a fundamentall law, and that a fundamentall law properly so called. It is such a law as that God and nature have given to a people. So that it is in the trust of their governors in highest place and others, to preserve, but not in their power to take away from them. Of which sort are these, viz.

1. Election of the supreame governours.

2. That every subject shall and may enjoy what he hath a civell right or title unto, soe as it cannot be taken from him by way of gift or loan, to the use or to be made the right or property of another man, without his owne free consent.

3. That such lawes (though called libertyes) yet more properly they may be called rights, and in this sense this may be added as a third fundamentall law, . . .

First, This may be given as a reason, that it is against a fundamentall law in nature to be compelled to pay that which others doe give. For then no man hath any certaynty or right to what he hath, if it be in the power of others (by pretence of authority or without) to give it away (when in their prudence they conceive it to be for the benefit of the owner soe to doe) without his owne consent.

Secondly, This to me is some strengthening to induce my apprehension in this case, viz. That not withstanding in England, it cannot be denied, but that mens estates were sometymes unduly taken from them: Some by force, some by fraud, some by sinister wresting of evidence, yea, and sometimes of law itselfe as about knighthood-money, shipmoney, &c. yet I dare say, if search be made into histories, lawyers bookes of reports, records &c. it cannot be made to appeare that in the most exorbitant times any man hath had his estate taken from him as by the gift of others, under colour of lawe, or countenance of authority. Noe, noe, lawyers would have blushed to have given such a construction of lawes; and suddenly their faces would have waxed pale. For the Kinge would have beene too wise to have owned the plea. And what would all wise men have said for such taking away the greatest outward right or liberty from them? For it may be understood, that benevolencies, incouraging gratuities, leaves, or privy seales, were not required by law, or by pretence of lawe, but desired as by favour. However they were obtained by illegall and tyranicall meanes, as was apprehended.

♦   ♦   ♦

See Sir Henry Finch, recorder of London, in his first booke of lawe, page 74, having ended his rules about native fundamentall lawes, he saith in the next page, Therefore lawes positive doe lose their force and are noe lawes at all, which are directly contrary to the former viz. native or fundamentall.

♦   ♦   ♦

But now to answer some objections that may be made to the case in hande.

Objection. Suppose it be true what is expressed, and granted that he were a strange man that should deny the same in the generall: Yet, notwithstanding, it hindereth not that a towne (when and as often as they thinke good, in their prudence) may doe it for good ends, and soe (in speciall cases) it may lawfully be done in the particular, upon the lawe made page the 9th, that every inhabitant shall contribute to all charges in church and commonwealth (whereof he doth or may receive a benefitt) else he shall be strayned.

Answer. I conceive that it is an extreame dishonour cast upon the generall court, to make such a construction of their positive laws as doth infringe the fundamentall law of mine and thine: for it must needs be voyd, if it should indeed be necessarily construed against the right or liberty of the subject. But the law in its true sense is good.

LAW AND COLONIAL SOCIETY

Law permeated the lives and institutions of early Americans, just as it does in our society today. It regulated their behavior and their social relations, even the most intimate, in ways that we would find unacceptable in our time. Women, children, and other persons who did not enjoy full legal and political capacity labored under disabilities imposed by law. In addition, the spirit of paternalism permeated such laws. Blacks, both slaves and free, were much more severely regulated, and almost nothing of a benign paternalist nature can be found in the early laws of slavery and race. In the more hierarchical society of early America, law attempted to police the boundaries between the classes with far greater rigor than it does in our time.

The criminal law of colonial America served numerous purposes, as it still does. Among these were economic regulation, maintenance of order (especially for purposes of encouraging economic growth), policing morality, and, above all, social control. When thinking about criminal law in America before the Civil War, it is necessary to remember that prisons were nonexistent before independence; jails or lockups were often little more than some convenient attic, basement, or even a cave; police forces existed only in the form of a rural constabulary and a rudimentary watch force in some cities; and law enforcement was much more a private citizen's responsibility than it is today.

MORALITY AND COLONIAL LAW

The colonists brought with them notions of morality that could lead to public repentance, shaming, whippings, or even executions for immoral behavior. In 1627, Virginia authorities ordered that "John Phillips & Joan White for their offence in committing fornication whereby the Joan hath had a bastard, shall be w[h]ipped at ye Post at James Citty & receaue [receive] 40 stripes a piece. And further that . . . they may be separated and not suffered to come together." When class entered the picture, however, the results might be different. In 1670 Mary Jones and Mary Hewes accused their master of raping them. But at his trial he was cleared and the court "ordered that the said Mary Hewes and Mary Jones being his servts. Are ordred to double there tyme they have been from him." Class and race may have affected the punishments. In 1640 the Virginia court pronounced the following opinions: "Whereas Robert Sweat, hath begotten with child a negro woman servant belonging unto Lieutenant Sheppard, the court hath therefore ordered that the said negro woman shall be whipped at the whipping post and the said Sweat shall tomorrow in the forenoon do public penance for his offence at James city church at the time of devine service according to the laws of England in that case p[ro]vided.[16] Such punishments were common in the colonies for nonmarital sex, although often the parties, rather than being separated, were forced to marry. More dramatic violations of the moral codes of the period led to harsher sentences.

"A Horrible Case of Beastiality"
Plymouth Colony
1642

The New England colonies were known for even harsher punishments for morality. The following story, taken from the diary of governor William Bradford, was not unique. Others in New England and elsewhere suffered extreme penalties for the greatest violations of colonial moral codes. What makes this case so remarkable is the details Bradford offers and his analysis of why this crime took place. Bradford was the longtime governor of the Plymouth Colony, and his diary is considered one of the first important works of American literature.

Marvelous it may be to see and consider how some kind of wickedness did grow and break forth here, in a land where the same was so much witnessed against and so narrowly looked unto, and severely punished when it was known, as in no place more, or so much, that I have known or heard of; insomuch that they have been somewhat censured even by moderate and good men for their severity in punishments. And yet all this could not suppress the breaking out of sundry notorious sins (as this year, besides other, gives us too many sad precedents and instances), especially drunkenness and uncleanness. Not only incontinency between persons unmarried, for which many both men and women have been punished sharply enough, but some married persons also. But that which is worse, even sodomy and buggery (things fearful to name) have broke forth in this land oftener than once.

1. I say it may justly be marveled at and cause us to fear and tremble at the consideration of our corrupt natures, which are so hardly bridled, subdued and mortified; nay, cannot by any other means but the powerful work and grace of God's Spirit. But (besides this) one reason may be that the Devil may carry a greater spite against the churches of Christ and the gospel here, by how much the more they endeavour to preserve holiness and purity amongst them and strictly punisheth the contrary when it ariseth either in church or commonwealth; that he might cast a blemish and stain upon them in the eyes of [the] world, who use to be rash in judgment. I would rather think thus, than that Satan hathmore power in these heathen lands, as some have thought, than in more Christian nations, especially over God's servants in them.

2. Another reason may be, that it may be in this case as it is with waters when their streams are stopped or dammed up. When they get passage they flow with more violence and make more noise and disturbance than when they are suffered to run quietly in their own channels; so wickedness being here more stopped by strict laws, and the same more nearly looked unto so as it cannot run in a common road of liberty as it would and is inclined, it searches everywhere and at last breaks out where it gets vent.

3. A third reason may be, here (as I am verily persuaded) is not more evils in this kind, nor nothing near so many by proportion as in other places; but they are here more discovered and seen and made public by due search, inquisition and due punishment; for the churches look narrowly to, their members, and the magistrates over all, more strictly than in other places. Besides, here the people are but few in comparison of other places which are full and populous and lie hid, as it were, in a wood or thicket and many horrible evils by that means are never seen nor known; whereas here they are, as it were, brought into the light and set in the plain field, or rather on a hill, made conspicuous to the view of all. But to proceed.

♦ ♦ ♦

And after the time of the writing of these things befell a very sad accident of the like foul nature in this government, this very year, which

I shall now relate. There was a youth whose name was Thomas Granger. He was servant to an honest man of Duxbury, being about 16 or 17 years of age. (His father and mother lived at the same time at Scituate.) He was this year detected of buggery, and indicted for the same, with a mare, a cow, two goats, five sheep, two calves and a turkey. Horrible it is to mention, but the truth of the history requires it. He was first discovered by one that accidentally saw his lewd practice towards the mare. (I forbear particulars.) Being upon it examined and committed, in the end he not only confessed the fact with that beast at that time, but sundry times before and at several times with all the rest of the forenamed in his indictment. And this his free confession was not only in private to the magistrates (though at first he strived to deny it) but to sundry, both ministers and others; and afterwards, upon his indictment, to the whole Court and jury; and confirmed it at his execution. And whereas some of the sheep could not so well be known by his description of them, others with them were brought before him and he declared which were they and which were not. And accordingly he was cast by the jury and condemned, and after executed about the 8th of September, 1642. A very sad spectacle it was. For first the mare and then the cow and the rest of the lesser cattle were killed before his face, according to the law, Leviticus xx.15; and then he himself was executed. The cattle were all cast into a great and large pit that was digged of purpose for them, and no use made of any part of them.

Upon the examination of this person and also of a former that had made some sodomitical attempts upon another, it being demanded of them how they came first to the knowledge and practice of such wickedness, the one confessed he had long used it in old England; and this youth last spoken of said he was taught it by another that had heard of such things from some in England when he was there, and they kept cattle together. By which it appears how one wicked person may infect many, and what care all ought to have what servants they bring into their families.

But it may be demanded how came it to pass that so many wicked persons and profane people should so quickly come over into this land and mix themselves amongst them? Seeing it was religious men that began the work and they came for religion's sake? I confess this may be marveled at, at least in time to come, when the reasons thereof should not be known; and the more because here was so many hardships and wants met withal. I shall therefore endeavour to give some answer hereunto.

1. And first, according to that in the gospel, it is ever to be remembered that where the Lord begins to sow good seed, there the envious man will endeavour to sow tares.

2. Men being to come over into a wilderness, in which much labour and service was to be done about building and planting, etc., such as wanted help in that respect, when they could not have such as they would, were glad to take such as they could; and so, many untoward servants, sundry of them proved, that were thus brought over, both men and women-kind who, when their times were expired, became families of themselves, which gave increase hereunto.

3. Another and a main reason hereof was that men, finding so many godly disposed persons willing to come into these parts, some began to make a trade of it, to transport passengers and their goods, and hired ships for that end. And then, to make up their freight and advance their profit, cared not who the persons were, so they had money to pay them. And by this means the country became pestered with many unworthy persons who, being come over, crept into one place or other.

4. Again, the Lord's blessing usually following His people as well in outward as spiritual things (though afflictions be mixed withal) do make many to adhere to the People of God, as many followed Christ for the loaves' sake (John vi.26) and a "mixed multitude" came into the wilderness with the People of God out of Egypt of old (Exodus xii.38). So also there were sent by their friends, some under hope that they would be made better; others that they might be eased of such burthens, and they kept from shame at home, that would necessarily follow their dissolute courses. And thus, by one means or other, in 20 years' time it is a question whether the greater part be not grown the worser?

MARRIAGE, WOMEN, AND THE FAMILY

William Blackstone on Women
in the Eyes of the Law
1765

Blackstone summed up the legal status of married women at common law in his passages on the husband–wife relationship, which the lawyers of the time called "coverture." (Blackstone himself explains the etymology of this "law-french" word in the following passages.) Like the law of slavery, the legal subordination of women strikes the late-twentieth-century mind as shocking; yet Blackstone and his contemporaries regarded it as part of the natural order of things—indeed, as a consequence of natural law.

By marriage, the husband and wife are one person in law: that is, the very being or legal existence of the woman is suspended during the marriage, or at least is incorporated and consolidated into that of the husband: under whose wing, protection, and cover, she performs everything; and is therefore called in our law-french a femme covert; . . . [she] is said to be covert-baron, or under the protection and influence of her husband, her baron, or lord; and her condition during her marriage is called her coverture. Upon this principle, of an union of person in husband and wife, depend almost all the legal rights, duties and disabilities, that either of them acquire by the marriage. I speak not at present of the rights of property, but of such as are merely personal.

♦ ♦ ♦

If the wife be injured in her person or property, she can bring no action for redress without her husband's concurrence, and in his name, as well as her owne: neither can she be sued, without making the husband a defendant.

♦ ♦ ♦

But though our law in general considers man and wife as one person, yet there are some instances in which she is separately considered; as inferior to him, and acting by his compulsion. And therefore all deeds executed and acts done, by her, during her coverture, are void, or at least voidable; except it be a fine, or the like matter of record, in which case she must be solely and secretly examined, to learn if her act be voluntary. She cannot by will devise lands to her husband, unless under special circumstances; for at the time of making it she is supposed to be under his coercion. And in some felonies, and other inferior crimes, committed by her, through constraint of her husband, the law excuses her: but this extends not to treason or murder.

The husband also (by the old law) might give his wife moderate correction. For as he is to answer for her misbehaviour, the law thought it reasonable to intrust him with this power of restraining her, by domestic chastisement, in the same moderation that a man is allowed to correct his servants or children; for whom the master or parent is also liable in some cases to answer. But this power of correction was confined within reasonable bounds, and the husband was prohibited from using any violence to his wife. . . . The civil law gave the husband the same, or a larger authority over his wife. . . . But, with us, in the politer reign of Charles the Second, this power of correction began to be doubted: and a wife may now have security of the peace against her husband; or in return, a husband against his wife. Yet the lower rank of people, who were always fond of the old common law, still claim and exert their ancient privilege: and the courts of law still permit a husband to restrain a wife of her liberty, in case of any gross misbehaviour.

These are the chief legal effects of marriage during the coverture; upon which we may observe, that even the disabilities, which the wife lies under, are for the most part intended for her protection and benefit. So great a favorite is the female sex of the laws of England.

Note: Women and the Law in the Colonial Era

In the light of modern scholarship, Blackstone's generalizations may be too broad, even facile, as applied to the American colonies. American law concerning the rights and status of women before independence was much more diverse than Blackstone's summation would suggest—which is to be expected, since he was writing on the law of the mother country and seldom deigned to take notice of colonial law.

Historians today are divided on the question of how well married American women fared under the law, compared with their English sisters. Richard B. Morris's pioneering work, *Studies in the History of American Law,* originally published in 1930, presented a benign, optimistic view of women's condition:

> The new legal rights which married women acquired to a greater or lesser degree throughout the colonies evolved out of the revised concept of the institution of marriage which resulted from the Protestant Revolution and out of the different economic and social conditions of colonial America. . . . (1) The courts clearly recognized the right of both the husband and the wife to the consortium of the other spouse, and to that end enjoined compulsory cohabitation upon couples whose mutual indifference had led to their separation, and ordered wife-deserters to return home. (2) The courts throughout the colonies took practical steps to compel recreant husbands to support their wives and children, and, in the south, an action for alimony independent of the suit for judicial separation was frequently brought. (3) The married woman was protected from the personal abuse, the cruelty, and the improper conduct exercised toward her by her husband. This attitude of humane paternalism over marriage was without precedent at common law. . . .
>
> These frequent testimonial practices, in which little or no deference was shown to restrictions existing under the common-law system, render the additional service of illustrating the extent to which the married woman in the American colonies had achieved emancipation in the law.[17]

But seventeenth- and eighteenth-century American society was too complex for such generalizations to sustain validity outside a specific time and place. Recent work, specifically focusing on the question of women's legal status from the seventeenth through the nineteenth centuries, has been skeptical of claims for a liberalized legal status of women. Marylynn Salmon's study *Women and the Law of Property in Early America* reached the following conclusions, suggesting that Blackstone's generalizations came closer to describing the reality of colonial practice than Morris thought:

> My inquiry into the property rights of American women revealed above all else a picture of their enforced dependence, both before and after the Revolution. Single women functioned on a legal par with men in property rights (although they did not enjoy the political rights associated with property ownership in early American society), but wives exercised only a truncated proprietary capacity. No colony or state allowed married women, or femes coverts, as lawmakers termed them, the legal ability to act independently with regard to property. Only under certain circumstances, at particular times, in precise ways, could a wife exercise even lim-

ited control over the family estate, including what she contributed to it. Under property law, the male head of household held the power to manage his own property as well as his wife's.[18]

There is considerable, although scattered, evidence to support Morris's view. One example is a 1718 Pennsylvania statute conferring the special legal status of "feme-sole traders" on married women who conducted businesses during their husbands' extended absence. The act recited the reasons for its necessity, before enumerating the specially conferred legal capacities enjoyed by the women to whom it applied.

An Act Concerning Feme-Sole Traders
1718

Whereas It often happens that mariners and others, whose circumstances as well as vocations oblige them to go to sea, leave their wives in a way of shop-keeping: and such of them as are industrious, and take due care to pay the merchants they gain so much credit with, as to be well supplied with shop-goods from time to time, whereby they get a competent maintenance for themselves and children, and have been enabled to discharge considerable debts left unpaid by their husbands at their going away; but some of those husbands, having so far lost sight of their duty to their wives and tender children, that their affections are turned to those, who, in all probability, will put them upon measures, not only to waste what they may get abroad, but misapply such effects as they leave in this province: For preventing whereof, and to the end that the estates belonging to such absent husbands may be secured for the maintenance of their wives and children, and that the goods and effects which such wives acquire, or are entrusted to sell in their husband's absence, may be preserved for satisfying of those who so entrust them, That where any mariners or others are gone, or hereafter shall go, to sea, leaving their wives at shop-keeping, or to work for their livelihood at any other trade in this province, all such wives shall be deemed adjudged and taken, and are hereby declared to be, as feme-sole traders, and shall have ability, and are by this act enabled, to sue and be sued, plead and be impleaded, at law, in any court or courts of this province, during their husbands' natural lives, without naming their husbands in such suits, pleas or actions: And when judgments are given against such wives for any debts contracted, or sums of money due from them, since their husbands left them, executions shall be awarded against the goods and chattels in the possession of such wives, or in the hands or possession of others in trust for them.[19]

Widows of New York and Taxes

A letter to the editor—the editor in this case being none other than John Peter Zenger—from a group of New York women hinted at underlying economic circumstances that provided the necessary social and economic preconditions for some liberalization of women's status.

Mr. Zenger,

We, the widows of this city, have had a Meeting, and as our case is something Deplorable, we beg you will give it Place in your Weekly Journal, that we may be Relieved, It is as follows. We are the House keepers, Pay our

Taxes, carry on Trade, and most of us are she Merchants, and as we in some measure contribute to the Support of Government, we ought to be Intitled to some of the Sweets of it; but we find ourselves entirely neglected, while the Husbands that live in our Neighborhood are daily invited to Dine at Court; we have the Vanity to think we can be full as Entertaining, and make as brave a Defence in Case of an Invasion and Perhaps not turn Taile as soon as some of them.[20]

CHILDREN, APPRENTICESHIP, EDUCATION

The local governments of colonial America intervened drastically into the internal affairs of families, supervising the welfare of children and, in cases of suspected neglect, placing them with masters in a system known as binding-out. American legislation on the subject derived from the Elizabethan Poor Law of 1601.[21] The system of apprenticeship was widely used both as a means of providing for orphaned children and for training children up to a trade. Naturally, almost all the children bound out were of poor parents; the more affluent were able to make their own arrangements. In this sense, apprenticeship served as an instrument of social control. It was also a means of providing for some rudimentary but compulsory education. New England was unusual in even considering, much less aspiring to, universal public education.

Virginia Apprenticeship Statute
1646

Whereas sundry laws and statutes by act of parliament established, have with great wisdome ordained, for the better educating of youth in honest and profitable trades and manufactures, as also to avoyd sloath and idleness wherewith such young children are easily corrupted, as also for reliefe of such parents whose poverty extends not give them breeding, That the justices of the peace should at their discretion, bind out children to tradesmen or husbandmen to be brought up in some good and lawfull calling, And whereas God almighty, among many his other blessings, hath vouchsafed increase of children to this collony, who now are multiplied to a considerable number, who if instructed in good and lawfull trades may much improve the honor and reputation of the country, and noe lesse their owne good and theire parents comfort: But forasmuch as for the most part the parents, either through fond indulgence or perverse obstinacy, are most averse and unwilling to parte with their children, Be it therefore inacted by authoritie of this Grand Assembly, according to the aforesayd laudable custom in the kingdom of England, That the commissioners of the several countyes respectively do, at their discretion, make choice of two children in each county of the age of eight or seven years at the least, either male or female, which are to be sent up to James Citty between this and June next to be imployed in the public flax houses under such master and mistresse as shall be there appointed, In carding, knitting and spinning &c. And that the said children be furnished from the said county with sixe barrells of come, two coverletts, or one rugg and one blankett: One bed, one wooden bowle or tray, two pewter spoons, a sow shote of six months old, two laying hens, with convenient apparell both linen and woollen, with hose and shooes. And for the better provision of howseing for the said children, It is inacted, That there be two houses built by the first of April next of forty foot long apiece with good and substantial timber, The houses to be twenty foot broad apiece, eight foot high in the pitche and a stack of brick chimneys standing in the midst of each house, and that they be lofted with sawne boards and made with convenient partitions, And it is further thought fitt that the commissioners have caution not to take up any children but from such parents who by reason of their poverty are disabled to maintaine and educate them.

Children's Education in Plymouth
1685

Forasmuch as the good Education of Children and Youth is of singular use and benefit to any Commonwealth; and whereas many Parents and Masters either through an over respect to their own Occasions and Business, or not duely considering the good of their Children and Servants, have too much neglected their duties in their Education whilst they are young and capable of Learning.

It is Ordered: That the Select men of every Town, shall have a vigilant Eye from time to time over their Brethen and Neighbours, to see that all Parents and Masters do duely endeavour by themselves or others to teach their Children and Servants as they grow capable, so much Learning as through the blessing of God they may attain; at least to be able duely to read the Scriptures, and other profitable Books Printed in the English Tongue; and the knowledge of the Capital Laws; and in some competent measure, the main Grounds and Principles of Christian Religion, necessary to Salvation; by causing them to learn some orthodox Catechisime without book, or otherwayes instructing them, as they may be able to give a due answer to such plain and ordinary questions as may by them or others be propounded to them concerning the same. And

further that all Parents and Masters do breed and bring up their Children and Apprentices in some honest lawful Calling and Imployment, that may be profitable for themselves and the Country. And if after Warning and Admonition given by any of the Select Men unto such Parents or Masters, they shall still remain negligent in their duty, in any of the particulars aforementioned, whereby Children or Servants may be in danger to grow Barbarous, Rude and Stubborn, and so to prove Pests instead of Blessings to the Country; That then a Fine of ten shillings shall be Levyed on the Goods of such Negligent Parent or Master to the Towns use, except extream poverty call for a Mitigation of the Fine. And if in three Months after that, there be no due care taken, and continued for the Education of such Children and Apprentices as aforesaid, then a Fine of twenty shillings to be Levyed on such Delinquents to the Towns use; except as aforesaid. And lastly, if in three Months after that their be no Reformation of the said Neglect, then the Select Men, with the Advice of two Magistrates shall put such Children to Apprentice; Boyes till they come to twenty one, and Girls eighteen years of Age, where they may be Educated according to the Rules of this Order.

WHITE INDENTURED SERVITUDE

Black slaves were not the only unfree people in colonial America. Many whites, too, were held in an unfree status known as indentured servitude. Comparison of slavery with servitude suggests at first glance that the latter was less oppressive. Servants served for only a term of years (usually four to seven); slaves remained slaves for life. The status of servants did not extend to their children (except to babies born to servant girls, and that for only a limited period); slave mothers passed on slave status to their children. Statutory law required that servants be taught to read; it forbade teaching slaves their letters. But servitude was in practice a less benign institution than it might appear. Social historians estimate that in the seventeenth century, only one in ten white indentured servants survived to become a property-owning free person; the rest died in servitude or, if they survived, emerged as day laborers or hired farmhands. Thus the adult servant, especially in the seventeenth century, was in many ways closer in status to a slave than he or she was to a juvenile apprentice.

In re Wm. Wootton and John Bradye
1640

Servants were harshly treated, especially in the seventeenth-century South, and they often ran away. Since the early colonies often depended on indentured labor, the authorities dealt harshly with runaways. Typical is this report of a case in Virginia, decided in October 1640.

The Court had ordered that Wm. Wootton and *John Bradye* as principall actors and contivers in a most dangerous conspiracy by attempting to run out of the country and Inticing divers others to be actors int eh said conspiracy to be whipt. from the gallows to the Court door and that said *Bradye* shall be Branded with an Iron in the shoulder, and *Wotton* in the forehead each of them to serve the Colony seven years, the service due from the said *Wotton* to the said Mr. *Sanderson* being first performed, each of thme to work in Irons during the time of the said censure for the rest of the said . . . servants (*viz*) *John Winchester, Wm. Drummer[,] Robt. Rouse* and *Robt. Mosely* to be whipt only as also *Margarett Beard*, and that the masters of the said servants shall pay the fees due from the servants to the sheriffs and the servants shall make good the same,at the Expiration of their time by a years service apiece to their said masters and that none of them shall be released from their Irons without order from this Board.[22]

South Carolina Servant Regulations
1761

The following document, a selection from an eighteenth-century justice-of-the-peace manual for the province of South Carolina, recapitulates the statutory basis of servitude, as seen in 1761.

Where any person or persons are imported into this province without being under indenture or contract, and are unable or unwilling to pay for their passages, it shall be lawful for the importer or importers of such person or persons, before any one of his Majesty's justices of the peace within this province, to take an indenture or indentures executed under the hand and seal of such person or persons, in consideration of such passage money, to serve the said importer or his assigns five years, from the arrival of such person or persons in this province, if he or she at the time of such arrival is of the age of sixteen years or upwards; and to serve until the age of twenty-one years, if such person or persons, at his or her arrival is under the age of sixteen years; which indenture or indentures shall be as binding and effectual in law as if the same had been exe-cuted before the arrival of such person or persons in this province. . . .

If any servant or servants shall lay violent hands on, beat or strike his, her or their master, mistress or overseer, and be convicted thereof by confession, or evidence of his fellow servant or otherwise, before any two justices of the peace in this province, the said justices are required and authorized to order such servant to serve his or her master or mistress, or their assigns, without any wages, for any time not exceeding six months after his or her time by indenture or otherwise is expired, or to order such corporal punishment to be inflicted on such servant, by the hands of a constable or some other white person, not exceeding twenty-one stripes, as the said justices shall in their discretion think fitting, according to the nature of the crime.

Any servant or servants unlawfully absenting from his, her or their master, mistress or overseer, shall for every such day's absence serve a week, and so in proportion for a longer or shorter time, provided the whole servitude for such absence does not exceed two years, over and above the time any such servant was to serve by indenture or otherwise, and shall also satisfy his, her or their master or mistress for all such charges as shall be laid out and expended for taking up, whipping and bringing home such servant, by a further and additional servitude, provided the whole time of such additional servitude does not exceed one year after the expiration of the first servitude.

♦ ♦ ♦

Every master or mistress shall provide and allow his or her servant or servants, sufficient diet, cloathing and lodging, and shall not exceed the bounds of moderation in correcting them beyond the merit of their offences; and it is lawful for any servant, upon any master or mistress, or overseer, by order or consent of any such master or mistress denying and not providing sufficient meat, drink, lodging and cloathing, or who shall unreasonably burthen them beyond their strength with labour, or debar them of their necessary rest and sleep, or excessively beat or abuse them to repair to any one of his Majesty's justices, there to make his, her or their complaint. And if the said justice shall find by lawful proof that the said servant's complaint is just, he is impowered and required, under the penalty of Five Pounds proclamation-money, by warrant under his hand and seal directed to the next constable, to levy and distrain the goods and chattels of such master or mistress, any sum not exceeding Four Pounds proclamation-money, to be disposed of for the use of the poor of the parish where such offence is committed. And for the second offence, any two justices of the peace are authorised and required, under the penalty of Five Pounds procla-

mation-money each, by instrument in writing under their hands and seals, to make an order directed to any constable to sell and dispose of the remaining time of service of such servant to any other white person, for such money as can be got for the same, to be paid to the church-wardens of the parish where the offence is committed, for the use of the poor.

♦ ♦ ♦

No servant or servants whatsoever shall travel by land or water above two miles from the place of his, her or their residence, without a note under the hand of his, her or their master or mistress, or overseer, expressing a permission for such servants so travelling. And if such servant or servants be found two miles from the place of his or their residence, they shall be deemed and taken as fugitive servants, and shall suffer such penalties and punishments as are provided against run-away servants.

♦ ♦ ♦

In all cases where a man is punishable by a fine, a servant shall receive corporal punishment; (that is to say) for every Twenty Shillings proclamation-money fine nine lashes, and so many such several punishments as there are pounds severally included in the fine. Provided the whole doth not exceed thirty-nine lashes.

♦ ♦ ♦

Every man-servant shall, at the expiration of his servitude, have allowed and given to him, one new hat, a good coat and breeches, either of jersey or broad cloth, two new shirts of coarse white linen, one new pair of shoes and stockings. And all women servants, at the expiration of their servitude, shall have allowed and given them, a waistcoat and petticoat of new half thicks or coarse plains, two new shifts of white linen, a new pair of shoes and stockings, a blue apron, and two caps of white linen.

SLAVERY

The origins of slavery in America are murky. At the time Europeans throughout the New World had been enslaving Africans for more than a century. But slavery was unknown in

England and there was no legal structure to support it in the colonies. Thus, when the first Africans arrived in Virginia, in 1619, they were treated as indentured servants—the only system of unfree labor that the English understood—and some of these first Africans eventually became free. English settlers from the start were conscious of differences between themselves and the Africans, although they defined this difference not in terms of race, as we do today—black and white—but in terms of culture and religion—Englishmen or Christians versus savages or pagans. Race consciousness as we know it in modern times was not present at the beginning but developed later. Indeed, in 1624 a black man named John Phillip was allowed to testify in a lawsuit involving white litigants, because, as the court noted, Phillip was "a negro Christened in *England 12* yeers since."[23]

By the 1640s Virginians had begun to enslave blacks, developing law in a haphazard way. However, by the 1660s Virginia was clearly committed to slavery. The early cases[24] and statutes[25] give us a hint of the way in which the colonists used law to create a system of bondage in America. These cases illustrate that in the early years, Virginians were unsure of how to treat blacks. They also illustrate the way in which the colonists made other distinctions, based on ethnicity and social status.

In re John Punch
McIlwaine 466
July 9, 1640

Whereas Hugh Gwyn hath . . . Brought back from *Maryland* three servants formerly run away from the said *Gwyn, the court doth therefore order* that the said three servants shall receive the punishment of whipping and to have thirty stripes apiece one called *Victor, a dutchman,* the other a *Scotchman* called *James Gregory,* shall first serve out their times with their master according to their Indentures, and one whole year apiece after the time of their service is Expired. . . . [a]nd after that service to their said master is Expired to serve the colony for three whole years apiece, and that the third being a negro named *John Punch* shall serve his said master or his assigns for the time of his natural Life here or elsewhere.

In re Emanuel
McIlwaine 467
July 22, 1640

Capt Wm Pierce Esqr [complained] that six of his servants and a negro of Mr *Reginolds* has plotted to run away unto the *Dutch* . . . [they had] taken the skiff of the said Capt Wm Pierce their master, and corn powder and shot and guns . . . the Court . . . did order that *Christopher Miller* a *dutchman* (a prince agent in the business) should receive the punishment of whipping and to have thirty stripes, and to be burnt in the cheek with the letter R and work with a shakle on his leg for one whole year, and longer if said master, shall see cause and after his full time of service is Expired with his said master to serve the colony for seven whole years, and the said *Peter Wilcocke* to receive thirty stripes and to be Burnt in the cheek with the letter R and . . . to serve the colony for three years . . . *Richd Cookson* . . . to serve the colony for two years and a half . . . *Rich^d* Hill to remain upon his good behaviour until the next offence . . .

Andrew Noxe to receive thirty stripes . . . *John Williams* a *dutchman* and a Chirugeon . . . to serve the colony for seven years, and *Emanuel* the Negro to receive thirty stripes and to be burnt in the cheek with the letter R. and to work in shakle one year or more as his master shall see cause. . . .

Re Mulatto
McIlwaine 504
March 1656

Mulatto held to be a slave and appeal taken.

Re Edward Mozingo
McIlwaine 316
October 1672

Whereas . . . *Edward Mozingo* a Negro man had been and was an apprentice by Indenture . . . and that by Computation his terme of Servitude for Twenty Eight yeares is now Expired . . . *It* *is Ajudged by this Court* that the said Edw: *Mozingo* be and Remayne free to all Intents and purposes by order of This Court [.]

Moore v. *Light*
McIlwaine 354
October 1673

Whereas Andrew Moore A Servant Negro to Mr *Geo: Light* . . . [came] into this County but for five yeare, *It is Thereof order[e]d* that the Said *Moore* bee free from his said master, and that the Said Mr *Light* pay him Corne and Clothes According to the custome of the Country and four hundred Pounds tob[acc]o & Caske for his service Done him Since he was free, and pay Costs[.]

Against Runaway Servants
Act XVI, March 1657–1658
(1 Hening 440)

Whereas there are divers loyteringe runnawaies in this countrey who very often absent themselves from their masters service . . . Bee it *therefore enacted* . . . that all runnawayes . . . shall be liable to make satisfaction by service at the end of their times by indenture vizt. double the time of service so neglected and in some cases more . . . [for] the second time or oftener . . . they shall be branded in the shoulder with the letter R. and alsoe double their time of service neglected.

How Long Servants Without Indentures Shall Serve
Act XVIII, March 1657–1658
(1 Hening 441–42)

Whereas divers controversies have risen between masters and servants being brought into this collonie without indentures or convenants to testifie their agreements, whereby masters and servants have been often prejudiced . . . [therefore] such persons as shall be imported, haveing no indenture or covenant, either men or women, if they be above sixteen "Years old shall serve four yeers, If under fifteen to serve till hee or shee shall be one and twenty yeers of age, and the courts to be judges of their ages.

An Act for the Dutch and All Other Strangers for Tradeing to This Place
Act XVI, March 1659–1660
(1 Hening 540)

Whereas the restriction of trade hath appeared to be the greatest impediment to the advance of the estimation and value of our present only commodity tobacco, *Bee* it *enacted* . . . That the Dutch and all strangers of what Xpian nation soever in amity with the people of England shall have free liberty to trade with us, for all allowable comodities . . . *Provided* they give bond and pay the impost of tenn shillings per hogshead laid upon all tobacco exported to any fforreigne dominions . . . *Allwaies provided,* That if the said Dutch or other forreigners shall import any negro slaves, They the said Dutch or others shall, for the tobacco really produced by the sale of the said negro, pay only the impost of two shillings per hogshead, the like being paid by our owne nation.

Run-aways
Act CII, March 1661–1662
(2 Hening 116–17)

Bee it therefore enacted that all runaways . . . shalbe lyable to make satisfaction by service . . . double their times of service soe neglected and if the time of their running away was in the crop or the charge of recovering them extraordinary the court shall lymitt a longer time of service . . . and in case any English servant shall run away in company of any negroes who are incapable of making satisfaction by addition of a time, *it is enacted* that the English soe running away in the company with them shall at the time of service to their owne masters expired, serve the masters of the said negroes for their absence soe long as they should have done by this act if they had not beene slaves, every christian in company serving his proportion; and if the negroes be lost or dye in such time of their being run away, the christian servants in company with them shall by proportion among them, either pay fower [four] thousand five hundred pounds of tobacco and caske or fower [four] yeares service for every negroe soe lost or dead.

Negro Womens Children to Serve According to the Condition of the Mother
Act XII, December 1662
(2 Hening 170)

Whereas some doubts have arrisen whether children got by Englishmen upon a negro women should be slave or ffree, Be it therefore enacted . . . that all children borne in this country shall be held bond or free only according to the condition of the mother, *And* that if any christian shall committ ffornication with a negro man or women, hee or shee soe offending shall pay double the ffines imposed by the former act.

An Act Declaring that Baptisme of Slaves Doth Not Exempt Them from Bondage
Act II, September 1667
(2 Hening 260)

Whereas some doubts have arisin whether children that are slaves by birth, and by the charity and piety of their owners made pertakers of the blessed sacrament of baptisme, should by vertue of their baptisme be made ffree; *It is enacted* . . . that the conferring of baptisme doth not alter the condition of the person as to his bondage or ffreedome; that diverse masters, ffreed from this doubt, may more carefully endeavour the propagation of christianity by permitting . . . slaves . . . to be admitted to that sacrament.

Act Act About the Casuall Killing of Slaves
Act I, October 1669
(2 Hening 270)

Whereas the only law in force for the punishment of refractory servants resisting their master, mistris or overseer cannot be inflicted upon negroes, nor the obstinacy of many of them by other than violent meanes supprest, *Be it enacted* . . . *if* any slave resist his master . . . and by the extremity of the correction should chance to die, that his death shall not be accompted ffelony, but the master . . . be acquit from molestation, since it cannot be presumed that prepensed malice . . . should induce any man to destroy his owne estate.

An Act for Preventing Negro Insurrections
Act X, June 1680
(2 Hening 481)

Whereas the frequent meeting of considerable numbers of negroe slaves under pretence of feasts and burialls is judged of dangerous consequence . . . *Bee it enacted* . . . *it* shall not be lawfull for any negroe or other slave to carry or arme himselfe with any club, staffe, gunn, sword or any other weapon of defence or offence, nor to goe or depart from of his masters ground without a certificate from his master, mistris or overseer, . . . if any negroe or other slave shall presume to lift up his hand in opposition against any christian, . . . (he shall] receive thirty lashes on his bare back well laid on. *And . . . if* any negroe or other slave shall absent himself from his masters service and lye hid and lurking in obscure places, comitting injuries to the inhabitants, and shall resist any . . . lawfull authority . . . it shalbe lawfull . . . to kill the said negroe or slave . . . .

The Germantown Protest Against Slavery
1688

This is the first known public objection to slaveholding and the slave trade in the British mainland colonies of North America. It was adopted by a group of German Mennonite settlers in Pennsylvania and foreshadowed ideas concerning slavery that were to become dominant among the Quakers during the eighteenth century. While wholly moral and religious in content, the Germantown protest came to have legal and constitutional implications, demonstrating Americans' facility in translating extralegal concerns into constitutional discourse.

These are the reasons why we are against the traffic of men-body, as followeth: Is there any that would be done or handled at this manner? viz., to be sold or made a slave for all the time of his life? How fearful and faint-hearted are many at sea, when they see a strange vessel, being afraid it should be a Turk and they should be taken, and sold for slaves into Turkey. Now, what is this better done, than Turks do? Yea, rather it is worse for them, which say they are Christians: for we hear that the most part of such negers are brought hither against their will and consent, and that many of them are stolen. Now, though they are black, we cannot conceive there is more liberty to have them slaves as it is to have other white ones. There is a saying, that we should do to all men like as we will be done ourselves; making no difference of what generation, descent, or colour they are. And those who steal or rob men, and those who buy or purchase them are they not all alike? Here is liberty of conscience, which is right and reasonable: here ought to be likewise liberty of the body except of evil-doers, which is another case. But to bring men thither, or to rob and sell them against their will, we stand against. In Europe there are many oppressed for conscience sake: and here there are those oppressed which are of a black colour. And we who know that men must not commit adultery—some do com-mitt adultery in others, separating wives from their husbands and giving them to others: and some sell the children of these poor creatures to other men. Ah! do consider well this thing, you who do it, if you would be done at this manner—and if it is done according to Christianity! You surpass Holland and Germany in this thing. This makes an ill report in all those countries of Europe, where they hear of [it], that the Quakers do here handel men as they handel there the cattle. And for that reason some have no mind or inclination to come hither. And who shall maintain this your cause, or plead for it? Truly, we cannot do so, except you shall inform us better hereof, viz.: that Christians have liberty to practice these things. Pray, what thing in the world can be done worse towards us, than if men should rob or steal us away, and sell us for slaves to strange countries; separating husbands from their wives and children. Being now this is not done in the manner we would be done; therefore, we contradict, and are against this traffic of men-body. And we who profess that it is not lawful to steal, must, likewise, avoid to purchase such things as are stolen, but rather help to stop this robbing and stealing, if possible. And such men ought to be delivered out of the hands of the robbers, and set free as in Europe. Then is Pennsylvania to have a good report, instead, it hath now a bad one, for this sake, in other countries; Especially whereas the Europeans are desirous to know in what manner the Quakers do rule in their province: and most of them do look upon us with an envious eye. But if this is done well, what shall we say is done evil?

If once these slaves (which they say are so wicked and stubborn men,) should join themselves—fight for their freedom, and handel their masters and mistresses, as they did handel them before; will these masters and mistresses take the sword at hand and war against these poor slaves, like, as we are able to believe, some will not refuse to do? Or have these poor negers not as much right to fight for their freedom, as you have to keep them slaves?

Now consider well this thing, if it is good or bad. And in case you find it to be good to handel these blacks in that manner, we desire and require you hereby lovingly that you may inform us herein, which at this time never was done, viz., that Christians have such a liberty to do so. To the end we shall be satisfied on this point, and satisfy likewise our good friends and acquaintances in our native country, to whom it is a terror, or fearful thing, that men should be handelled so in Pennsylvania.

South Carolina Slave Code
1740

This codification of statutory laws relating to slaves was the most comprehensive of the pre-Revolutionary period. Its provisions established the fundamental characteristics of slavery in the mainland colonies and set forth a comprehensive regulation of blacks' and whites' behavior in a slave society. The substance of this code permeated the laws of the slave states until the Civil War. South Carolina adopted this code a year after the Stono rebellion, in which at least twenty whites and perhaps one hundred slaves died. This was the most bloody slave rebellion in the colonial period. This statute reflects the need to control slaves, who by this time outnumbered whites two to one in South Carolina.

AN ACT FOR THE BETTER ORDERING AND GOVERNING [OF] NEGROES AND OTHER SLAVES IN THIS PROVINCE

Whereas in his majesty's plantations in America, slavery has been introduced and allowed; and the people commonly called negroes, Indians, mulatos and mestizos have [been] deemed absolute slaves, and the subjects of property in the hands of particular persons the extent of whose power over slaves ought to be settled and limited by positive laws so that the slaves may be kept in due subjection and obedience, and the owners and other persons having the care and government of slaves, may be restrained from exercising too great rigour and cruelty over them; and that the public peace and order of this Province may be preserved: Be it enacted, that all negroes, Indians (free Indians in amity with this government, and negroes, mulatos and mestizos who are now free excepted) mulatos or mestizos who now are or shall hereafter be in this Province, and all their issue and offspring born or to be born, shall be and they are hereby declared to be and remain for ever herafter absolute slaves, and shall follow the condition of the mother; and shall be deemed, . . . taken, reputed and adjudged in law to be chattels personal in the hands of their owners and possessors and their executors, administrators and assigns to all intents, constructions and purposes whatsoever, Provided that if any negro Indian mulato, or mestizo shall claim his or her freedom, it shall and may be lawful for such negro, Indian, mulato, or mestizo, or any person or persons whatsoever, on his or her behalf to apply to the justices of his Majesty's court of common pleas by petition or motion, either during the sitting of the said court, or before any of the justices of the same court at any time in the vacation. And the said court or any of the justices thereof, shall and they are hereby fully impowered to admit any person so applying, to be guardian for any negro, Indian, mulato or mestizo, claiming his, her or their freedom, and such guardians shall be enabled, intitled and capable in law to bring an action of trespass, in the nature of ravishment of ward against any person who shall claim property in, or who shall be in possession of any such negro, Indian, mulato or mestizo.

♦ ♦ ♦

Provided that in any action or suit to be brought in pursuance of the direction of this act the burthen of the proof shall lay upon the plaintiff, and it shall be always presumed, that every negro, Indian, mulato, and mestizo, is a slave unless the contrary can be made appear (the Indians in amity with this government excepted) in which case the burden of the proof shall lie on the defendant.

♦ ♦ ♦

III. And for the better keeping slaves in due order and subjection: be it further enacted that no person whatsoever, shall permit or suffer any slave under his or their care or management, and who lives, or is employed in Charlestown, or any other town in this Province to go out of the limits of the said town, or any such slave, who lives in the country to go out of the plantation to which such slave belongs, or in which plantation such slave is usually employed, without a letter subscribed and directed, or a ticket in the words following.

♦ ♦ ♦

V. If any slave who shall be out of the house or plantation where such slave shall live or shall be usually employed, or without some white person in company with such slave, shall refuse to submit or to undergo the examination of any white person, it shall be lawful for any such white Person to pursue, apprehend and moderately correct such slave; and if such slave

shall assault and strike such white person, such slave may be lawfully killed.

♦ ♦ ♦

IX. And whereas natural justice forbids, that any person of what condition soever should be condemned unheard, and the order of civil government requires that for the due and equal administration of justice, some convenient method and form of trial should be established, Be it therefore enacted, that all crimes and offences which shall be committed by slaves in this Province and for which capital punishment shall or lawfully may be inflicted, shall be heard, examined, tried, adjudged, and finally determined by any 2 justices assigned to keep the peace, and any number of freeholders not less than 3 or more than 5 in the county where the offence shall be committed and can be most conveniently assembled; either of which justices, on complaint made or information received of any such offence committed by a slave, shall commit the offender to the safe custody of the constable of the parish where such offence shall be committed, and shall without delay by warrant under his hand and seal, call to his assistance, and request any one of the nearest justices of the peace to associate with him; and shall by the same warrant summon such a number of the neighbouring freeholders as aforesaid, to assemble and meet together with the said justices, at a certain day and place not exceeding 3 days after the apprehending of such slave or slaves: and the justices and freeholders being so assembled, shall cause the slave accused or charged, to be brought before them, and shall hear the accusations which shall be brought against such slave, and his or her defence, and shall proceed to the examination of witnesses, and other evidence, and finally hear and determine the matter brought before them, in the most summary and expeditious manner; and in case the offender shall be convicted of any crime for which by law the offender ought to suffer death, the said justices shall give judgment, and award and cause execution of their sentence to be done, by inflicting such manner of death, and at such time as the said justices, by and with the consent of the freeholders shall direct, and which they shall judge will be most effectual to deter others from offending in the like manner.

♦ ♦ ♦

[XVI.] Be it therefore enacted, that the several crimes and offences hereinafter particularly enumerated, are hereby declared to be felony without the benefit of the clergy, That is to say, If any slave, free negro, mulatto, Indian, or mestizo, shall willfully and maliciously burn or destroy any stack of rice, corn or other grain, of the product, growth or manufacture of this Province; or shall willfully and maliciously set fire to, bur or destroy any tar kiln, barrels of pitch, tar, turpentine or rosin, or any other of the goods or commodities of the growth, produce or manufacture of this Province; or shall feloniously steal, take or carry away any slave, being the property of another, with intent to carry such slave out of this Province; or shall willfully and maliciously poison, or administer any poison to any person, free man, woman, servant or slave; every such slave, free negro, mulatto, Indian (except as before excepted) and mestizo, shall suffer death as a felon.

XVII. Any slave who shall be guilty of homicide of any sort, upon any white person, except by misadventure or in defence of his master or other person under whose care and government such slave shall be, shall upon conviction thereof as aforesaid, suffer death. And every slave who shall raise or attempt to raise an insurrection in this Province, or shall endeavor to delude or entice any slave to run away and leave this Province; every such slave and slaves, and his and their accomplices, aiders and abettors, shall upon conviction as aforesaid suffer death. Provided always, That it shall and may be lawful to and for the justices who shall pronounce sentence against such slaves, and by and with the advice and consent of the freeholders as aforesaid, if several slaves shall receive sentence at one time, to mitigate and alter the sentence of any slave other than such as shall be convicted of the homicide of a white person, who they shall think may deserve mercy, and may inflict such corporal punishment (other than death) on any such slave, as they in their discretion shall think fit, any thing herein contained to the contrary thereof in any wise notwithstanding. Provided, That one or more of the said slaves who shall be

convicted of the crimes or offences aforesaid, where several are concerned, shall be executed for example, to deter others from offending in the like kind.

♦ ♦ ♦

XXXIII. And whereas several owners of slaves do suffer their slaves to go and work where they please, upon condition of paying to their owners certain sums of money agreed upon between the owner and slave; which practice occasioned such slaves to pilfer and steal to raise money for their owners, as well as to maintain themselves in drunkenness and evil courses; for prevention of which practices for the future, Be it enacted, that no owner, master or mistress of any slave, after the passing of this act, shall permit or suffer any of his, her or their slaves to go and work out of their respective houses or families, without a ticket in writing under pain of forfeiting the sum of current money, for every such offence.

♦ ♦ ♦

XXXVI. And for that as it is absolutely necessary to the safety of this Province, that all due care be taken to restrain the wanderings and meetings of negroes and other slaves, at all times, and more especially on Saturday nights, Sundays and other holidays, and the using and carrying wooden swords, and other mischievous and dangerous weapons, or using and keeping of drums, horns, or other loud instruments, which may call together or give sign or notice to one another of their wicked designs and purposes; and that all masters, overseers and others may be enjoined diligently and carefully to prevent the same, Be it enacted, that it shall be lawfull for all masters, overseers and other persons whomsoever, to apprehend and take up any negro or other slave that shall be found out of the plantation of his or their master or owner, at any time, especially on Saturday nights, Sundays or other holidays, not being on lawful business, and with a letter from their master or a ticket, or not having a white person with them, and the said negro or other slave or slaves correct by a moderate whipping.

XXXVII. And whereas cruelty is not only highly unbecoming those who profess themselves Christians, but is odious in the eyes of all men who have any sense of virtue or humanity; therefore to restrain and prevent barbarity being exercised toward slaves, Be it enacted, That if any person or persons whosoever, shall willfully murder his own slave, or the slave of another person, every such person shall upon conviction thereof, forfeit and pay the sum of £700 current money, and shall be rendered, and is hereby declared altogether and forever incapable of holding, exercising, enjoying or receiving the profits of any office, place or employment civil or military within this Province: . . . And if any person shall on a sudden heat or passion, or by undue correction, kill his own slave or the slave of any person, he shall forfeit the sum of £350 current money, And in case any person or persons shall wilfully cut out the tongue, put out the eye, castrate or cruelly scald, burn, or deprive any slave of any limb or member, or shall inflict any other cruel punishment, other than by whipping or beating with a horsewhip, cow-skin, switch or small stick, or by putting irons on, or confining or imprisoning such slave; every such person shall for every such offence, forfeit the sum of £100 current money.

XXXVIII. That in case any person in this Province, who shall be owner, or who shall have the care government or charge of any slave, or slaves, shall deny, neglect or refuse to allow such slave or slaves under his or her charge, sufficient cloathing, covering or food, it shall and may be lawfull for any person or persons, on behalf of such slave or slaves, to make complaint to the next neighbouring justice in the parish where such slave or slaves live, or are usually employed; and if there shall be no justice in the parish, then to the next justice in nearest parish: and the said justice shall summons the party against whom such complaint shall be made, and shall enquire of, hear and determine the same: and if the said justice shall find the said complaint to be true, or that such person will not exculpate or clear himself from the charge, by his or her own oath, which such person shall be at liberty to do in all cases where positive proof is not given of the offence, such justice shall and may make such orders upon the same for the relief of such slave or slaves, as he in his discretion shall think fit, and shall and may let and impose a fine or penalty on any person who shall offend in the premises, in any sum not exceeding £20 current money, for each offence.

◆ ◆ ◆

XLIV. And whereas many owners of slaves, and others who have the care, management and overseeing of slaves, do confine them so closely to hard labour; that they have not sufficient time for natural rest—Be it therefore enacted, That if any owner of slaves, or other person who shall have the care, management, or overseeing of any slaves, shall work or put any such slave or slaves to labour, more than 15 hours in 24 hours, from the 25th day of March to the 25th day of September, or more than 14 hours in 24 hours, from the 25th day of September to the 25th day of March; every such person shall forfeit any sum not exceeding or under £20, nor under £5 current money, for every time he, she or they shall offend herein, at the discretion of the justice before whom the complaint shall be made.

XLV. And whereas the having of slaves taught to write, or suffering them to be employed in writing, may be attended with great inconveniences; Be it enacted, that all and every person and persons whatsoever, who shall hereafter teach, or cause any slave or slaves to be taught to write, or shall use or employ any slave as a scribe in any manner of writing whatsoever, hereafter taught to write; every such person and persons shall, for every such offence, forfeit the sum of £100 current money.

The New York "Negro Plot"
1741

In 1741, a time of heightened tensions among English colonists because of the mother country's involvement in a war against Spain (the so-called War of Jenkins' Ear, 1739–1742), some white inhabitants of New York City were convulsed by a spasm of fear that enslaved blacks of the city, guided by Spanish agents (including the inevitable but fictitious Jesuit priest), were about to rise up in insurrection, torch the city, slaughter the whites, and rape white women—all this as a prelude to some eventual Spanish attack. Spurred on by the increasingly extravagant, not to say mad, revelations of a white servant girl, white New Yorkers resorted to law to try the supposed insurrectionists of both races. By the time the chief witness's disclosures crossed the line into lunacy, thirteen slaves had been burned at the stake, eighteen hanged (plus two white confederates), and seventy transported to various non-English colonies. Many level-headed contemporaries scoffed at the idea that there was any plot at all. So Daniel Horsmanden, a judge of the Supreme Court of Judicature who presided at the trials, compiled a record of the hearing to convince the skeptics. The following excerpts, the charge to the grand jury investigating events and the grand jury's return, reveal the public mind at the earliest and therefore least hysterical stage.

Mr. Justice Philipse gave the charge to the grand jury, as followeth:

Gentlemen of the grand jury,

It is not without some concern, that I am obliged at this time to be more particular in your charge than for many preceding terms there hath been occasion. The many frights and terrors which the good people of this city have of late been put into, by repeated and unusual fires, and burning of houses, give us too much room to suspect, that some of them at least, did not proceed from mere chance, or common accidents; but on the contrary, from the premeditated malice and wicked pursuits of evil and designing persons; and therefore, it greatly behoves us to use our utmost diligence, by all lawful ways and means, to discover the contrivers and perpetrators of such daring and flagitious undertakings: that, upon conviction, they may receive condign punishment; for although we have the happiness of living under a government which exceeds all others in the excellency of its constitution and laws, yet if those to whom the execution of them (which my lord Coke calls the life and soul of the law) is committed, do not exert themselves in a conscientious discharge of their respective duties, such laws which were intended for a terror to the evil-doer, and a protection to the good, will become a dead letter, and our most excellent constitution turned into anarchy and confusion; every one practising what he listeth, and doing what shall seem good in his own eyes: to prevent which, it is the duty of all grand juries to in-

quire into the conduct and behaviour of the people in their respective counties; and if, upon examination, they find any to have transgressed the laws of the land, to present them, that so they may by the court be put upon their trial, and then either to be discharged or punished according to their demerits.

I am told there are several prisoners now in jail, who have been committed by the city magistrates, upon suspicion of having been concerned in some of the late fires; and others, who under pretence of assisting the unhappy sufferers, by saving their goods from the flames, for stealing, or receiving them. This indeed, is adding affliction to the afflicted, and is a very great aggravation of such crime, and therefore deserves a narrow inquiry: that so the exemplary punishment of the guilty (if any such should be so found) may deter others from committing the like villainies; for this kind of stealing, I think, has not been often practised among us.

Gentlemen,

Arson, or the malicious and voluntary burning, not only a mansion house, but also any other house, and the out buildings, or barns, and stables adjoining thereto, by night or by day, is felony at common law; and if any part of the house be burned, the offender is guilty of felony, notwithstanding the fire afterwards be put out, or go out of itself.

This crime is of so shocking a nature, that if we have any in this city, who, having been guilty thereof, should escape, who can say he is safe, or tell where it will end?

Gentlemen,

Another Thing which I cannot omit recommending to your serious and diligent inquiry, is to find out and present all such persons who sell rum, and other strong liquor to negroes. It must be obvious to every one, that there are too many of them in this city who, under pretence of selling what they call a penny dram to a negro, will sell to him as many quarts or gallons of rum, as he can steal money or goods to pay for.

How this notion of its being lawful to sell a penny dram, or a pennyworth of rum to a slave, without the consent or direction of his master, has prevailed, I know not; but this I am sure of, that there is not only no such law, but that the doing of it is directly contrary to an act of the assembly now in force, for the better regulating of slaves. The many fatal consequences flowing from this prevailing and wicked practice, are so notorious, and so nearly concern us all, that one would be almost surprised, to think there should be a necessity for a court to recommend a suppressing of such pernicious houses: thus much in particular; now in general.

My charge, gentlemen, further is, to present all conspiracies, combinations, and other offences, from treasons down to trespasses; and in your inquiries, the oath you, and each of you have just now taken will, I am persuaded, be your guide, and I pray God to direct and assist you in the discharge of your duty.

◆ ◆ ◆

This evidence of a conspiracy, not only to bum the city, but also destroy and murder the people, was most astonishing to the grand jury, and that any white people should become so abandoned as to confederate with slaves in such an execrable and detestable purpose, could not but be very amazing to every one that heard it; what could scarce be credited; but that the several fires had been occasioned by some combination of villains, was, at the time of them naturally to be collected from the manner and circumstances attending them.

COLONIAL WELFARE SYSTEMS

The British colonies attempted to provide supplementary and residual systems for relief of the poor, disabled, and infirm. Primary responsibility for the disabled rested on their families; where there were no near relatives available to foot the bill, care of the poor and infirm rested with the towns.

An Act for the Relief of the Poor
1742

Colonial laws were modeled on the Poor Laws of the reign of Elizabeth I. First enacted in 1598 and then reenacted in definitive form in 1601, the English Poor Laws provided for appointment of overseers of the poor in every parish. These officers had comprehensive authority to bind out the children of the poor as apprentices, as well as those adults "married or unmarried as, having no means to maintain them, use no ordinary and daily trade of life to get their living by." They were empowered to raise taxes in money and in kind (flax, wool, iron, etc.), to build "convenient houses of dwelling for the said impotent poor," and in general to operate a parish-based welfare system vaguely resembling modern workfare experiments.[26] The colonies were content either to imitate the Elizabethan legislation or to elaborate on it, as in the following 1742 Delaware statute.

For the Prevention of straggling and indigent Persons from coming into and being chargeable to the Inhabitants, and for the better Relief of the Poor of this Government; Be It Enacted. . . .

That the Constables and Overseers of the Poor in each Hundred within the several Counties of this Government, shall and are hereby required to make diligent Inspection and Enquiry in their respective Districts after all vagrant, poor and impotent Persons coming into the same in order to settle or otherwise; and if any such shall be found as aforesaid, such Overseer or Constable shall and is hereby required to make Report thereof to the next Justice of the Peace of the said County; and the said Justice shall and is hereby required, by Warrant under his Hand and Seal, to cause such vagrant, poor or impotent Persons to be apprehended, and brought before him or some other Justice of the Peace of the same County; and if it appear to the Justice before whom such Person is or shall be brought, that such Person is likely to become chargeable as aforesaid, such Justice shall and is hereby required to order such vagrant, poor or impotent Person, if able to travel, immediately to depart the County, or to give sufficient Security to indemnify the County, as herein after mentioned; and upon Refusal or Neglect of such vagrant, poor or impotent Person to depart or give Security as aforesaid, it shall and may be lawful to and for any Two Justices of the Peace of the same County, to cause every such Person so refusing or neglecting, to be publickly whipp'd at the common Whipping-Post, with any Number of Lashes not exceeding Fifteen, and the same Punishment to be repeated every Day, or so often as he or she shall not be depart the same as aforesaid.

◆ ◆ ◆

[T]he Father and Grandfather, Mother and Grandmother, being of sufficient Ability, shall at their own Charges relieve and maintain their poor, blind, lame and impotent Children and Grand-children, as the Justices of the Peace at their General Court of Quarter-Sessions shall order and direct; and the Children and Grand-children, being of Ability, shall, by such Order of the Justices as aforesaid, at their own Charges relieve and maintain their Fathers and Mothers, Grand-fathers and Grand-mothers, not having any Estate, nor being of Ability to work; upon Pain of forfeiting Forty Shillings for every Month they or any of them shall fail therein, to be levied monthly, together with Costs, by Distress and Sale of the Goods and Chattels of such Father, Mother, Grandfather, Grandmother, Child or Children respectively, by Warrant under the Hands and Seals of any Two Justices of the Peace of the same County, and paid to the Treasurer for the Use of the Poor of the same County.

◆ ◆ ◆

Every poor Person, whose Name shall stand on the List of any of the Counties of this Government as one of the Poor of the said County, shall on the Right Sleeve, or on the Back of his or her upper Garment, in an open and visible Manner, wear such Badge or Mark as herein after is mentioned and expressed, That is to say, A large Roman or Capital P, together with the first Letter of the Name of the County whereof such poor Person is an Inhabitant, cut either in Red or Blue Cloath, as by the Overseers of the Poor of the Hundred wherein such poor Persons doth reside, shall be directed and appointed.

Note: Colonial Workfare

There was nothing gentle or humane about the colonial poor laws by the standards of the late twentieth century. Over all of them hung the odor of moral disapproval. At times these laws approached the criminalization of poverty. A Massachusetts statute of 1646 provided:

> Every township, or such as are deputed to order the prudentials thereof, shall have power to present to the Quarter Courte all idle & unprofitable persons, & all children, who are not diligently implied [employed] by their parents, which Courte shall have power to dispose of them, for their owne welfare & improvement of the common good.[27]

CLASS LEGISLATION AND SUMPTUARY LAWS

Note: Class and Status in Early America

The English settlers saw no reason to question the stratification of their society, even in the New World. God ordained that "in all times some must be rich, some poor, some high and eminent in power and dignity, others mean and in subjection," John Winthrop declared in his 1629 shipboard sermon.[28] The Cambridge Platform of 1648 required the elders of the churches "to see that none in the church live inordinately, out of rank and place."[29] To accomplish this end, the elites of all the colonies tried to regulate the wages, dress, and recreation of the lower classes as a means of disciplining their behavior and attitudes. Massachusetts Bay magistrates frowned on high wages, which only encouraged "vaine and idle waste of much precious tyme."[30] Responding to the crisis of King Philip's War in 1675, Massachusetts enacted the "Provoking Evils" laws, which prohibited excessive wages, with punishment for only the worker, not the master.[31] Even more annoying to the elites were the social pretensions of the lower orders, whereby persons of "meane condition, educations and callings" should presume to "take upon them the garbe of Gentlemen." Consequently, the Massachusetts General Court attempted to punish those who dressed "exceeding the quality and condition of their Persons and Estate."[32] Legislation over the years prohibited various sorts of finery and ostentation to the common people: lace, buttons, "silke or tiffany hoodes," long hair on men, silks, girdles, hatbands, silver and gold thread, slashed sleeves, short sleeves, needlework caps, ruffs, and beaver hats. All who violated the dress code "shalbe looked at as contemnors of authority, & regardless of the publike weale."[33] But Massachusetts Bay magistrates readily discharged ladies from prosecution for violation of the laws when it was proved that their husbands had a net worth of £200 and another lady "upon testimony of her being brought up above the ordinary rank."[34] Virginia hit on a clever enforcement device: it permitted tax assessments "according to his apparell, if he be married, according to his owne & his wives, or either of their apparel."[35] The Old Dominion reenacted an English benchmark of meanness when it prohibited seven occupational categories or groups of the lower classes—farmers, sailors, fishermen, craftsmen, laborers, apprentices, and servants—from playing at "Bear-baiting, Bull-baiting, Bowling, Cards, Cock-fighting, Colts, Dice, Foot-ball, Nine-pins, Tennis."[36]

Yet the sumptuary laws of New England largely went unenforced. They had to be reenacted recurrently because existing legislation was universally disregarded. It was one thing to denounce extravagant dress for the poor; it was something else altogether to make such prohibitions stick. The statutes therefore are gauges of ruling-class attitudes only and not of actual behavior (except in a negative way). Their proliferation attests only to universal disregard and nonenforcement. This problem was endemic to all other kinds of morals legislation.[37]

If unseemly ostentation in dress was offensive in the poorer classes, it was obnoxious in slaves. South Carolina legislators found it necessary to include a special sumptuary law in the 1740 slave code because "many of the slaves in the Province wear clothes much above the condition of slaves." With absurd specificity, the statute obliged masters to prohibit their slaves from wearing "any sort of apparel whatsoever, finer, other, or of greater value than negro cloth, duffils, kerseys, osnabrings, blue linen, check linen or coarse garlix, or callicoes, checked cottons, or Scotch plaids."[38] In reality, of course, masters dressed their slaves as they wished, and while a field worker might have the roughest clothing possible, a house servant or the mistress of a master might be dressed in the finest clothing available.

DEMOCRACY AND DEFERENCE

English society in the seventeenth and eighteenth centuries placed a high value on order, social ranking, and deference. Despite attempts to replicate this in the colonies, the elite in America never had the same power, authority, or status they did in England. Neither custom nor law would support the English system in the New World. The failure of sumptuary laws to make people dress according to their proper status dovetailed with the failure of the lower classes to give "proper" respect to the elite.

The Incident of the Roxbury Carters
1705

An incident reported by Massachusetts governor Joseph Dudley in 1705 suggests that democratic impulses may have been breaking through the crust of social constraint, changing the social matrix from which laws emerged. Dudley's version must be read with a great deal of skepticism: it is unlikely that the event occurred just as he described it. Yet this vignette of the stubborn, almost insolent, egalitarianism of the farmers confronting the social pretensions of an unpopular governor provides a glimpse of a social order churning from below.

Roxbury 23 Janu: 1705.

Revered and Dear Sir,—That you may not be imposed upon I have conveyed to you my memorial to the Judges referring to the ingures offered mee upon the road, which I desire you will communicate to the ministers of your circle whose good opinion I desire to mayntain, and have not in the matter by any means forfeited.

I am Sir Your humble servant
J. Dudley.

The Governour informs the Queen's Justices of her majestys Superior Court that on friday, the seventh of December last past, he took his Journey from Roxbury towards newhampshire and the Province of mayn for her majestys immediate service there: and for the ease of the Guards had directed them to attend him the next morning at Rumney house, and had not proceeded above a mile from home before he mett two Carts in the Road loaden with wood, of which the Carters were, as he is since informed, Winchester and Trobridge.

The Charet wherein the Governour was, had three sitters and three servants depending, with trunks and portmantles for the journey, drawn by four horses one very unruly, and was attended only at that instant by Mr. William Dudley, the Governours son.

When the Governour saw the carts approaching, he directed his son to bid them give him the way, having a Difficult drift, with four horses and a tender Charet so heavy loaden, not fit to break the way. Who accordingly did Ride up and told them the Governour was there, and they must give way: immediately upon it, the second Carter came up to the first, to his assistance, leaving his own cart, and one of them says aloud, he would not goe out of the way for the Governour: whereupon the Govr came out of the Charet and told Winchester he must give way to the Charet. Winchester answered boldly, without any other words, "I am as good flesh and blood as you; I will not give way; you may goe out of the way:" and came towards the Governour.

Whereupon the Governour drew his sword, to secure himself and command the Road, and went forward; yet without either saying or intending to hurt the carters, or once pointing or passing at them; but justly supposing they would obey and give him the way; and again commanded them to give way. Winchester answered that he was a Christian and would not give way: and as the Governour came towards him, he advanced and at len[g]th layd hold on the Gov.r and broke the sword in his hand. Very soon after came a justice of peace, and sent the Carters to prison. The Justices are further informed that during this talk with the carters, the Gov.r demanded their names, which they would not say, Trobridg particularly saying he was well known, nor did they once in the Govrs hearing or sight pull of their hatts or say they would go out of the way, or any word to excuse the matter, but absolutely stood upon it, as above is sayd; and once, being two of them, one on each side of the fore-horse, laboured and put forward to drive upon and over the Governour.

And this is averred upon the honour of the Governour.

J. Dudley

LAW AND THE COLONIAL ECONOMY

Throughout the seventeenth century, the mainland colonies attempted to control their economies extensively, regulating prices, wages, and the quality of output. Early in the seventeenth century, the colonies sought to re-create the British system of regulating wages and labor. These efforts at wage control drew on the models of the English Statute of Labourers (1351) and the Statute of Artificers (1563). But wage control was doomed to failure for two reasons: workers were scarce and they were mobile. In the end, the market persistently drove wages through the statutory ceilings, and the legislature could only respond, with a growing sense of futility, with yet another (and inevitably unsuccessful) attempt at capping them.

Wage regulation was not the only kind of economic regulation tried by the colonies. Early in the seventeenth century, Massachusetts attempted to reenact the English assize of bread. All colonies regulated weights and measures. In those colonies that exported a valuable staple, principally tobacco in the Chesapeake, colonial authorities vigilantly controlled the grades and quality of the export. Virginia planters reluctantly accepted the wisdom of this effort in the early eighteenth century. New England regulated the manufacture of barrels and the cooperage trade generally. All colonies offered bounties, either for the killing of pestiferous wildlife or for the manufacture of valuable products like potash. Some examples of such forms of economic regulation, quality control, and subsidization follow.

The Laws and Liberties of Massachusetts
1648

CASK & COOPER

It is ordered by this Court and authoritie thereof, that all cask used for any liquor, fish, or other commoditie to be put to sale shall be of London assize, and that fit persons shal be appointed from time to time in all places needfull, to gage all such vessels or cask & such as shal be found of due assize shal be marked with the Gagers marks, & no other who shal have for his paines four pence for every tun, & so proportionably. And every County court or any one Magistrate upon notice given them shall appoint such Gagers to view the said cask, & to see that they be right, & of sound & wel seasoned timber, & that everie Cooper have a distinct brand-mark on his own cask, upon payn of forfeiture of twenty shilling in either case, & so proportionably for lesser vessels.

The Laws of South Carolina
1734

For Encouragement to introduce into this Collony the Art of making Potash, Be it Enacted by the Authority aforesaid, That any Person now residing in this Province, or who shall hereafter come into the same, shall within Ten Years after the Ratification of this Act instruct the Inhabitants of this Collony in making Potash, (that is such as are willing to undertake the same) in such Manner that the said Commodity be made fit for the Market in Great-Britain, that such Persons shall receive Forty Shillings per Ton out of the publick Treasury of this Province for the first Five Hundred Tons that shall be entered or ship'd on board any Ship or Vessel sailing out of any Ports in this partof the Province, and the Receiver for the time being is hereby required to pay Forty Shillings aforesaid, for every Ton of Potash that is ship'd on board any Vessel sailing out of this Collony.

In this Province the Number of the Inhabitants being few for so great Extent of Land, the erecting of Mills of all kinds, and other Mechanick Engines, will greatly improve the Country itself and its Trade and Navigation: Be it therefore Enacted by the Authority aforsaid, That whatsoever Person or Persons shall after the Ratification of this Act erect a Mill, to saw with the Wind or Water, so as to bring the same to compleate Perfection, as in Holland or in any other Countries, he or they shall have the Privilege of erecting Wind or Water Sawmills in part of this Province exclusive of all others, for the Term of Eight Years, after the first Sawmill begins to Work, and if any other Person or Persons erect or cause to be erected in this Collony, any Wind or Water Sawmills within the Term of Eight years after the time aforesaid, without the Consent and Licence of those who erects the first, he shall forfeit the Sum of One Thousand Pounds, to be recovered for the Use of those to whom this Privilege exclusive of others doth belong.

EARLY CRIMINAL LAW

In early America, criminal law served several distinct objectives. Most fundamentally, it was one of the principal means of keeping the peace—the most basic purpose of criminal law in any society. Another was to regulate morality. Illustrations of these can be seen in the various statutes and some of the cases in early parts of this chapter.

The criminal law was also used to create social and political cohesion. This objective took on a special urgency in colonial America because the English settlers who framed and administered criminal law considered their societies to be beset by constant peril from three sources: the physical environment, external enemies, and internal foes (Indians, blacks, and others ethnically or religiously distinct). These pressures sometimes induced a state of mind close to mass paranoia, as in the case of the rumored slave insurrections known as the 1712 and 1741 "Negro Plots" in New York.

An important means of keeping the peace was identifying and protecting group identity by policing deviant behavior. Sociologists such as Emile Durkheim, Kai Erikson, and Harold Garfinkel have stressed the importance of societies determining what behavior is acceptable and what is threatening, constantly redefining boundaries between the two. In Erikson's vivid figure, "Morality and immorality meet at the public scaffold, and it is during this meeting that the line between them is drawn."[39]

But criminal law also served purposes other than the constabulary one. To a greater extent than today, criminal law was an adjunct to economic regulation, a convenient means of enforcing the pervasive regulatory apparatus of the seventeenth and eighteenth centuries. In this capacity, it promoted economic development in the specie-starved, investment-hungry economies of colonial America. Particularly in the New England colonies (except, as always, Rhode Island), criminal law was used to punish sin and other transgressions of the moral order, at least before independence. Criminal law was also a means of social control, imposing fines, whipping, banishment, and forms of public degradation (the stocks, for example, or branding), by which the ruling classes policed the behavior of those inferior to them on social and economic scales.

Many of the social and political purposes of the criminal law emerged in the last two legal incidents discussed in this chapter: the Salem witch trials and the seditious libel trial of John Peter Zenger.

The Salem Witch Trials
1692

The most notorious criminal trials of colonial America occurred during the summer of 1692, when over 150 women and men of Salem, Massachusetts, were accused of witchcraft. Nineteen were hanged as witches, and one man was pressed to death for refusing to plead. One of these victims was George Burroughs, a former minister. Some of the evidence and testimony against him follows.

The community hysteria that produced the prosecutions abated because of efforts by laymen like Thomas Brattle and clergy like Increase Mather, who condemned the trial court's reliance on what was called "spectral evidence"—that is, the testimony of the afflicted about supernatural apparitions. The second excerpt is from a tract published by Mather's son, the already-prominent divine Cotton Mather, that recommended a more cautious approach to evidentiary problems. Neither Mather père nor fils doubted the reality of witchcraft and the actual presence of evil spirits among humans; but both, especially the elder, were troubled by the loose evidentiary standards that characterized the witchcraft trials in the specially convened Court of Oyer and Terminer.

The witchcraft frenzy in Massachusetts ended as abruptly as it had begun. By the autumn of 1692, many persons outside Salem began to have doubts about the persecutions. The court was discharged, and the remaining accused were freed. The General Court (the legislative body of the colony) later enacted a resolution expressing its regret to the survivors of the condemned.

THE EXAMINATION OF GEO. BURROUGHS, 9 MAY, 1692

[Burroughs] denied that his house [at] Casco was haunted, yet he owned there were Toads. He denied that he made his wife swear, that she could not write to his father Ruck without his approbation of her letter to her Father. He owned that none of his children, but the eldest was Baptized The above was in private none of the Bewitched being present, At his entry into the Room many (if not all the Bewitched) were grievously tortured.

1. Sus. Sheldon testified that Burroughs' two wives appeared in their winding sheets, and said that man killed them.

He was bid to look upon Sus. Sheldon.

He looked back and knocked down all (or most), of the afflicted who stood behind him.

2. Mary Lewis' deposition going to be read and he looked upon her and she fell into a dreadful and tedious fit,

3. Mary Walcott

4. Eliz Hubbard	Testimony going
Susan Sheldon	to be read and they
	all fell into fits

Being asked what he thought of these things. He answered it was an amazing and humbling Providence, but he understood nothing of it and he said (some of you may observe, that) when they begin to name my name, they cannot name it.

Ann Putnam junior	Testified that his
Susan Sheldon	2 wives & 2
	children were de-
	stroyed by him.

The Bewitched were so tortured that Authority ordered them to be taken away some of them.

◆   ◆   ◆

VIEW OF BODY OF GEO. BURROUGHS

We whose names are under written received an order from the sheriff for to search the bodies of George Burroughs and George Jacobs we find nothing upon the body of the above said burroughs but what is natural, but upon the body of George Jacobs we find 3 teats which according to the best of our Judgments we think is not natural for we run a pin through 2 of them and he was not sensible of it, one of them being within his mouth upon the Inside of his right cheek and 2nd upon his right shoulder blade an[d] a 3rd upon his right hip.

◆   ◆   ◆

ANN PUTNAM V. GEO. BURROUGHS

The Deposition of Ann putnam who testifieth and saith that on 20th of April 1692 at evening she saw the Apparition of a minister at which she was grievously affrighted and cried out oh dreadful: dreadful here is a minister com[e], what are Ministers witches to: whence com[e] you and What is your name for I will complain of you though you be A minister: if you be a wizard: and immediately i was tortured by him being Racked and almost choked by him: and he tempted me to write in his book which I Refused with loud out cries and said I would not write in his book though he tore me all to pieces but told him that it was a dreadful thing: that he which was a Minister that should teach children to fear God should com[e] to persuade poor creatures to give their souls to the devil: Oh, dreadful, dreadful, tell me your name that I may know who you are: then again he tortured me and urged me to write in his book: which I Refused: and then presently he told me that his name was George Burroughs and that he had had three wives: and that he had bewitched the Two first of them to death; and that he killed Mistress Lawson because she was unwilling to go from the village and also killed Mr. Lawson's child because he went to the eastward with Sir Edmon[d Andros] and preached so to the soldiers and that he had bewitched a great many soldiers to death at the eastward when Sir Edmon was there, and that he had made Abigail Hobbs a witch and several witches more: and he has continued ever since; by times tempting me to write in his book and grievously torturing me by beating pinching and almost choking me several times a day and he also told me that he was above a witch he was a conjurer.

Jurat in Curia.

ANN PUTNAM V. GEO. BURROUGHS

The deposition of Ann putnam who testifieth and saith that on the 3th of may, 1692, at evening I saw the Apparition of Mr. George Burroughs who grievously tortured me and urged me to write in his book which I refused then he told me that his Two first wives would appear to me presently and tell me a great many lies but I should not believe them, then Immediately appeared to me the form of Two women in winding sheets and napkins about their heads, at which I was greatly affrighted, and they turned their faces towards Mr. Burroughs and looked very red and angry and told him that he had been a cruel man to them, and that their blood did cry vengeance against him: and also told him that they should be clothed with white Robes in heaven, when he should be cast into hell, and immediately he vanished away, and as soon as he was gone the Two women turned their faces towards me and looked as pale as a white wall: and told me that they were Mr. Burroughs Two first wives and that he had murdered them; and one told me that she was his first wife and he stabbed her under the left Arm and put a piece of ceiling wax on the wound and she pulled aside the winding sheet, and showed me the place and also told me that she was in the house Mr parris now lived where it was done, and the other told me that Mr. Burroughs and that wife which he hath now killed her in the vessel as she was coming to see her friends because they would have one another; and they both charged me that I should tell these things to the Magistrates before Mr Burroughs face and if he did now own them they did not know but they should appear there: this morning, also Mistress Lawson and her daughter Ann appeared to me whom I knew, and told me that Mr. Burroughs murdered them, this morning also appeared to me another woman in a winding sheet and told me that she was goodman Fuller's first wife and Mr. Burroughs killed her because there was some difference between her husband and him, also on the 9th may during the time of his examination he did most grievously torment and afflict mary Walcott mercy lewin Eliz. Hubbard and Abigail williams by pinching pricking and choking them.

INCREASE MATHER

"Cases of Conscience Concerning Evil Spirits Personating Men"
1692

Rev. Increase Mather, the father of Cotton Mather, was in England when the witchcraft outbreak began. When he returned to Massachusetts, the senior Mather was appalled to discover that people had been hanged as witches on the basis of "spectral evidence." Mather attacked the use of this evidence in an essay he read to the Boston ministers in October 1692. Mather's views on spectral evidence helped bring an end to the trials. It is worth noting that in this essay, Increase Mather admonishes the people of Massachusetts to protect the lives of innocent people, even if it means some of the guilty may escape.

The First Case that I am desired to express my judgment in, is this, whether it is not Possible for the Devil to impose on the imaginations of persons Bewitched, and to cause them to Believe that an Innocent, yea that pious person does torment them, when the Devil himself doth it; or whether satan may not appear in the Shape of an Innocent and Pious, as well as of a and Wicked Person, to Afflict such as suffer by Diabolical Molestations.

The Answer to the Question must be Affirmative; Let the following Arguments be duly weighed in the Balance of the Sanctuary.

Argu. I. There are several Scriptures from which we may infer the Possibility of what is Affirmed.

I. We find that the Devil by the Instigation of the Witch at Endor appeared in the Likeness of the Prophet Samuel. I am not ignorant that some have asserted that, which, if it were proved, would evert [i.e., overthrow] this Argument viz. that it was the true and not a delusive Samuel which the Witch brought to converse with Saul. . . . Moreover, had it been the true Samuel from Heaven reprehending Saul, is great Reason to believe, that he would not only have reproved him for his sin, in not executing Judgment on the Amalekites; as in Ver. 18. But for his Wickedness in consulting with familiar Spirits: For which Sin it was in special that he died. 2 Chron. 10. 13. But inasmuch as there is not one word to testify against that Abomination, we may conclude that. it was not real Samuel that appeared to Saul: and if it were the Devil in his likeness, the Argument seems very strong, that if the Devil may appear in the form of a Saint in Glory, much more is it possible for him to put on the likeness of the most Pious and Innocent Saint on Earth. There are, who acknowledge that a Demon may appear in the shape of a Godly Person, But not as doing Evil. Whereas the Devil in Samuel's likeness told a pernicious Lie, when he said, Thou hath disquieted me. It was not in the Power of Saul, nor of all the Devils in Hell, to disquiet a Soul in Heaven, where Samuel had been for Two years before this apparition. Nor did the Specter speak true, when he said, Thou and thy Sons shall be with me: Tho' Saul himself at his Death went to be with the Devil, his Son Jonathan did not so. Besides, (which suits with the matter on hand) the Devil in Samuels shape confirmed Necromancy and Cursed Witchery. He that can in the likeness of Saints encourage Witches to Familiarity with Hell, may possibly in the likeness of a Saint afflict a Bewitched person. But this we see from Scripture, Satan may be permitted to do.

It is evident from another Scripture, viz. that in 2 Cor. II. 14. For Satan himself is transformed into an Angel of Light. He seems to be what he is not, and makes others seem to be what they are not. He represents evil men as good, and good men as evil.

◆   ◆   ◆

It is not for men to determine how far the Holy God may permit the wicked one to proceed in his Accusations. The sacred story of Job giveth us to understand, that the Lord whose ways are past finding out, does for wise and Holy Ends suffer Satan by immediate Operation (and consequently by Witchcraft), greatly to afflict innocent Persons, as in their Bodies and Estates, so in their Reputations. I shall mention but one Scripture more to confirrn the Truth in hand: It is that in Eccles. 9. 2, 3. where it is said, All things come alike to all, there is one event to the Righteous and to the Wicked, as is the Good, so is the Sinner, this is an evil amongst all things under the Sun, that there is one Event happeneth to all. And in Eccles. 7. 15. 'tis said, There is a just man that perisheth in his Righteousness.

From hence we infer, that there is no outward Affliction whatsoever but may befall a good Man; now to be represented by Satan as a Tormentor of Bewitched or Possessed Persons, is a sore Affliction to a good man. To be tormented by Satan is a sore Affliction, yet nothing but what befell job, and a Daughter of Abraham, whom we read of in the Gospel: To be represented by Satan as tormenting others, is an Affliction like the former; the Lord may bring such extraordinary Temptations on his own Children, to afflict and humble them, for some Sin they have been guilty of before him. . . . Have we not known some that have bitterly censured all that have been complained of by bewitched Persons, saying it was impossible they should not be guilty; soon upon which themselves or some near Relations of theirs, have been to the lasting Infamy of their Families, accused after the same manner, and Personated by the Devil! Such tremendous Rebukes on a few, should the make all men to be careful how they join with Satan in Condemning the Innocent.

◆   ◆   ◆

I have heard of an Enchanted Pin, that has caused the Condemnation and Death of many scores of innocent Persons. There was notorious Witchfinder in Scotland, that undertook by a Pin, to make an infallible Discovery of suspected Persons, whether they were Witches or not, when the Pin was run an Inch or two into the Body of the accused Party Blood appeared, nor any sense of Pain, then he declared them to be witches; by means hereof my Author tells me no less then 300 persons were condemned for Witches in that Kingdom. This Bloody juggler . . . thrust great Brass Pin two Inches into the Body of one, that some would in that may try whether there was Witchcraft in the Case or no: the accused Party was not in the least sensible of what was done, and therefore in danger of receiving the Punishment justly due for Witchcraft only it so happened, that Colonel Fenwick (that worthy Gentleman, who many years since lived in New-England) was then the Military Governor in that Town; he sent for the Mayor and Magistrates advising them to be careful and cautious in their proceedings; for he told them, it might be an Enchanted Pin, which the Witchfinder made use of: Whereupon the Magistrates of the place ordered that he should make his Experiment with some other Pin as they should appoint: But that he would by no means be induced unto, which was a sufficient Discovery of the Knavery and Witchery of the Witchfinder.

♦ ♦ ♦

I have myself known several of whom I ought to think that they are now on Heaven, considering that they were of good Conversation, and reputed Pious by those that had the greatest Intimacy with them, of whom nevertheless, some complained that their Shapes appeared to them, and threatened them: Nor is this answered by saying, we do not know but those Persons might be Witches: We are bound by the Rule of Charity to think otherwise: And they that censure any, merely because such a sad Affliction as their being falsely represented by Satan has befallen them, do not do as they would be done by. I bless the Lord, it was never the portion allotted to me, nor to any Relation of mine to be thus abused: But no Man knoweth what may happen to him, since there be just Men unto whom it happeneth according to the Work of the Wicked, Eccles. 8. 14. But what needs more to be said, since there is one amongst ourselves whom no Man that knows him, can think him to be a Wizzard, whom yet some bewitched Persons complained of that they are in his Shape tormented: And the Devils have of late accused some eminent Persons.

It is an awful thing which the Lord has done to convince some amongst us of their Error: This then I declare and testify, that to take away the Life anyone, merely because a Specter or Devil, in a bewitched or possessed Person does accuse them, will bring the Guilt of innocent Blood on the Land, where such a thing shall be done: Mercy forbid that it should (and I trust that as it has not it never will be so), in New-England. What does such an Evidence amount unto more than this: Either such an one did afflict such an one, or the Devil in his likeness, or his Eyes were bewitched.

♦ ♦ ♦

Now no Credit ought to be given to what Demons in such as are by them obsessed shall say. Our Saviour by his own unerring Example has taught us not to receive the Devil's Testimony in anything. . . . The Father of Lies is never to be believed: He will utter twenty great truths to make way for one lie: He will accuse twenty Witches, if he can but thereby bring one innocent Person into trouble: He mixeth Truths with Lies, that so those truths giving credit unto lies, Men may believe both, and so be deceived.

♦ ♦ ♦

As for that which concerns the Bewitched Persons being recovered out of their Agonies by the Touch of the suspected Party, it is various and falible.

For sometimes the afflicted Person is made sick, (instead of being made whole) by the Touch of the Accused; sometimes the Power of Imagination is such, as that the Touch of a Person innocent and not accused shall have the same effect. It is related in the Account of the Trials of Witches at Bury in Suffolk 1664, during the time of the Trial, there were some Experiments made with the Persons afflicted, by bringing the accused to touch them, and it was observed that by the least Touch of one of the supposed Witches, they that were in their Fits, to all men's Apprehension wholly deprived of an Sense and Understandings, would suddenly shriek out and open their Hands.

♦ ♦ ♦

4. There are [those] that Question the Lawfulness of the Experiment. For if this healing power in the Witch is not a Divine but a Diabolical Gift, it may be dangerous to meddle too much with it. If the Witch may be ordered to touch afflicted Persons in order to their healing or recovery out of a sick Fit, why may not the Diseased Person be as well ordered to touch the Witch for the same cause? And if to touch him, why not to scratch him, and fetch Blood out of him, which is but an harder kind of touch? But as for this Mr. Perkins doubts not to call it a Practice of Witchcraft. It is not safe to meddle with any of the Devil's Sacraments or Institutions; For my own part, I should be loath to say to a Man, that I knew or thought was a Witch, do you look on such a Person, and see if you can Witch them into a Fit, and there is such an afflicted Person do you take them by the Hand, and see it You can Witch them well again. If it is by virtue of some Contract with the Devil that witches have Power to do such without [their judges'] being too much concerned in that Hellish Covenant. I take it to be . . . a solid Principle, . . . That they who force another to do that which he cannot possibly do, but by virtue of a Compact with the Devil, have themselves implicitly Communion with the Diabolical Covenant. The Devil is pleased and honored when any of his Institutions are made use of; this way of discovering Witches, is no better than that of putting the Urine of the afflicted Person into a Bottle that so the Witch may be tormented and discovered: The Vanity and Superstition of which practice I have formerly showed, and testified against. . . .

5. If the Testimony of a bewitched or possessed Person, is of validity as to what they see done to themselves., then it is so as to others, whom they see afflicted no less than themselves: But what they affirm concerning others, is not to be taken for Evidence. Whence had they this Supernatural Sight? It must needs be either from Heaven or from Hell: If from Heaven, (as Elisha's Servant, and Balaam's Ass could discern Angels) let their Testimony be received: But if they had this Knowledge from Hell, tho' there may possibly be truth in what they affirm, they are not legal Witnesses: For the Law of God allows of no Revelation from any other Spirit but himself, Isa. 8. 19. It is a Sin against God to make use of the Devil's help to know that which cannot be otherwise known: And I testify against it, as a great Transgresion, which may justly provoke the Holy One of Israel, to let loose Devils on the whole Land, Luke 4. 35. . . . The Persons, concerning whom the Question is, see things through Diabolical Mediums; on which account their Evidence is not mere human Testimony; and if it be in any part Diabolical, it is not to be owned as Authentic; for the Devil's Testimony ought not to be received neither in whole nor in part.

◆ ◆ ◆

To conclude; judicious Casuists have determined, that to make use of those Media to come to the Knowledge of any Matter, which have no such power in them by Nature, nor by Divine Institution is an Implicit going to the Devil to make a discovery: Now there is no natural Power in the Look or Touch of a Person to bewitch another; nor is this by Divine Institution the means whereby Witchcraft is discovered: Therefore it is an unwarrantable Practice.

◆ ◆ ◆

If a Crime cannot be found out but by Miracle, it is not for any judge on Earth to usurp that judgment which is reserved for the Divine Throne. These things being premised, I answer the Question affirmatively; Therefore proofs for the Conviction of Witches which Jurors may with a safe Consceience proceed upon, so as to bring them in guilty. The Scripture which saith, Thou shalt not suffer a Witch to live, clearly implies, that some in the World may be known and proved to be Witches: For until they be so, they may and must be suffered to live. . . .

Q. But then the Inquiry is, *What is sufficient Proof?*

◆ ◆ ◆

1. *That a free and voluntary Confession of the Crime made by the Person suspected and accused after Examination, is a sufficient Ground of Conviction.*

Indeed, if Persons are Distracted, or under the Power of Phrenetic Melancholy, that alters the Case; but the Jurors that examine them, and their neighbors that know them, may easily determine that Case; or if Confesion be extorted, the Evidence is not so clear and convictive; but if any Persons out of Remorse of Conscience, or from a Touch of God in their Spirits, confess and show their Deeds, as the Converted Magicians in Ephesus did, Acts 19 . . . nothing can be more clear. . . .

. . . But as for the Testimony of Confessing Witches against others, the case is not so clear as against themselves, they are not such credible Witnesses, as in a Case of Life and Death is to be desired: It is beyond dispute, that the Devil makes his Witches to dream strange things of themselves and others which are not so. . . . What Credit can be given to those that say they can turn Men into Horses? If so, they can as well turn Horses into Men; but all the Witches on Earth in Conjunction with all the Devils in Hell can never make or unmake a rational Soul. . . . In a word, there is no more Reality in what many Witches confess of strange things seen or done by them, whilst Satan had them in his full Power, than there is in Lucian's ridiculous Fable of his being Bewitched into an Ass, and what strange Feats he then played; so that what such persons relate concerning Persons and Things at Witch-meetings, ought not to be received with too much Credulity.

♦   ♦   ♦

2. *If two credible Persons shall affirm upon Oath that they have seen the party accused speaking such words, or doing things which none but such as have Familiarity with the Devil ever did or can do, that's a sufficient Ground for Conviction.*

The Devil never assists men to do supernatural things undesired. When therefore such like things shall be testified against the accused Party not by Specters which are Devils in the Shape of Persons either living or dead, but by real men or women who may be credited; it is proof enough that such an one has that Conversation and Correspondence with the Devil, as that he or she, whoever they be, ought to be exterminated from amongst Men. This notwithstanding I will add; It were better that ten suspected Witches should escape, than that one innocent Person should be Condemned. . . . that is an old saying, and true. . . . It is better that a Guilty Person should be Absolved, than that he should without sufficient ground of Conviction be condemned. I had rather judge a Witch to be an honest woman, than judge an honest woman as a Witch. The Word of God directs men not to proceed to the execution of the most capital offender; until such time as upon searching diligently, the matter is found to be Truth, and the thing certain, Deut. 13. 14, 15.

COTTON MATHER

The Wonders of the Invisible World
1693

Written in 1692 and published in London the following year, this book was Mather's attempt to justify his pivotal role in the trials.

Quaere, Whether if God would have us to proceed any further than bare Enquiry upon what Report there may come against any Man, from the World of Spirits, he will not by his Providence at the same time have brought into our hands, these more evident and sensible things, whereupon a man is to be esteemed a Criminal. But I will venture to say this further, that it will be safe to account the Names as well as

the Lives of our Neighbors; two considerable things to be brought under a Judicial Process, until it be found by Humane Observations that the Peace of Mankind is thereby disturbed. We are Humane Creatures, and we are safe while we say, they must be Humane Witnesses, who also have in the particular Act of Seeing, or Hearing, which enables them to be Witnesses, had no more than Humane Assistances that are to turn the Scale when Laws are to be executed.

I was going to make one Venture more; that is, to offer some safe Rules, for the finding out of the Witches, which are at this day our accursed Troublers: but this were a Venture too Presumptuous and Icarian for me to make; I leave that unto those Excellent and Judicious Persons, with whom I am not worthy to be numbered: All that I shall do, shall be to lay before my Readers, a brief Synopsis of what has been written on that Subject, by a Triumvirate of as Eminent Persons as have ever handled it. I will begin with,

An Abstract of Mr. Perkins's Way for the Discovery of Witches

I. There are Presumptions, which do at least probably and conjecturally note one to be a Witch.

These give occasion to Examine, yet they are no sufficient Causes of Conviction.

II. If any Man or Woman be notoriously defamed for a Witch, this yields a strong Suspicion. Yet the Judge ought carefully to look, that the Report be made by Men of Honesty and Credit.

III. If a Fellow-Witch, or Magician, give Testimony of any Person to be a Witch; this method is not sufficient for Condemnation; but it is a fit Presumption to cause a straight Examination.

IV. If after Cursing there follow Death, or at least some mischief: for Witches are wont to practice their mischievous Facts by Cursing and Banning: This also is a sufficient matter of Examination, tho' not of Conviction.

V. If after Enmity, Quarrelling, or Threatening, a present mischief does follow: that also is a great Presumption.

VI. If the Party suspected be the Son or Daughter, the man-servant or maid-servant, the Familiar Friend, near Neighbor, or old Companion, of a known and convicted Witch; this may be likewise a Presumption; for Witchcraft is an Art that may be learned, and conveyed from man to man.

VII. Some add this for a Presumption: If the Party suspected be found to have the Devil's mark; for it is commonly thought, when the Devil makes his covenant with them, he always leaves his mark behind them, whereby he knows them for his own: —a mark whereof no evident Reason in Nature can be given.

VIII. Lastly, If the party examined be Unconstant, or contrary to himself, in his deliberate Answers, it argueth a Guilty Conscience, which stops the freedom of Utterance. And yet there are causes of Astonishment, which may befal the Good, as well as the Bad.

IX. But then there is a Conviction, discovering the Witch, which must proceed from just and sufficient proofs, and not from bare presumptions.

X. Scratching of the suspected party, and Recovery thereupon, with several other such weak Proofs; as also, the fleeting [floating] of the suspected Party, thrown upon the Water; these Proofs are so far from being sufficient, that some of them are, after a sort, practices of Witchcraft.

XI. The Testimony of some Wizzard, tho' offering to shew the Witches Face in a Glass: This, I grant, may be a good Presumption, to cause a strait Examination; but a sufficient Proof of Conviction it cannot be. If the Devil tell the Grand Jury, that the person in question is a Witch, and offers withal to confirm the same by Oath, should the Inquest receive his Oath or Accusation to condemn the man? Assuredly no. And yet, that is as much as the Testimony of another Wizzard, who only by the Devil's help reveals the Witch.

XII. If any man, being dangerously sick, and like to dy, upon Suspicion, will take it on his Oath, that such an one hath bewitched him, it is an Allegation of the same nature, which may move the Judge to examine the Party, but it is of no moment for Conviction.

XIII. Among the sufficient means of Conviction, the first is, the free and voluntary Confession of the Crime, made by the party suspected and accused, after Examination. I say not, that a bare confession is sufficient, but a Confession after due Examination, taken upon pregnant presumptions. What needs now more witness or further Enquiry?

XIV. There is a second sufficient Conviction, by the Testimony of two Witnesses, of good and honest Report, avouching before the Magistrate, upon their own Knowledge, the two things: either that the party accused hath made a League with the Devil, or hath done some known practices of witchcraft. And, all Arguments that do necessarily prove either of these, being brought by two sufficient Witnesses, are of force fully to convince the party suspected.

XV. If it can be proved, that the party suspected hath called upon the Devil, or desired his Help, this is a pregnant proof of a League formerly made between them.

XVI. If it can be proved, that the party hath entertained a Familiar Spirit, and had Conference with it, in the likeness of some visible Creatures; here is Evidence of Witchcraft.

XVII. If the witnesses affirm upon Oath, that the suspected person hath done any action or work which necessarily infers a Covenant made, as, that he hath used Enchantments, divined things before they come to pass, and that peremptorily, raised Tempests, caused the Form of a dead man to appear; it proveth sufficiently, that he or she is a Witch.

POLITICS AND CRIMINAL LAW: TOWARD A NEW AMERICA

The Salem witch trials can be seen as the last gasp of a dying view of the world and how it worked. Spectral evidence, magic, and witches are the fears of another time, another place. Later generations would have their own fears of the unknown, of conspiracies, and would hunt their own "witches" in political and social contexts. But the Salem trials seem a distant reflection of a distant time. Nevertheless, they help us understand the relationship between law and society, and underscore the dangers of misusing the legal system in times of crisis. They are also a model of how *not* to conduct a trial. A century after these trials Americans would still remember them and recall what a legal system might look like without procedural protections for the accused, due process, attorneys to represent those on trials, and standards of evidence that have meaning.

The Zenger Trial
1735

The 1735 trial of John Peter Zenger for seditious libel in New York can be seen as an early step toward the American Revolution, the Constitution, and the Bill of Rights. Zenger was prosecuted for his unflattering comments in newspaper stories about the colony's governor, William Cosby. Cosby first tried to have Zenger indicted for the felony of seditious libel, but a grand jury of New Yorkers would not indict him. Thus, Cosby contrived to have him tried by information for the misdemeanor of seditious libel. Under existing libel law, the truth of an article was no defense. Indeed, "The greater the truth, the greater the libel" was the maxim of English law. This made sense in a monarchy, where the Crown depended on goodwill and the admiration of the people for its authority. A true but unflattering article about the government would have more impact than false and unbelievable complaints about the government. Under existing law, the jury in a libel case was only asked to determine if the person arrested published the allegedly libelous statements. The judge reserved for himself the decision whether the statements were actually libelous. The traditional defense was to deny publication.

In a radical departure, Philadelphia attorney Andrew Hamilton (no relation to Alexander Hamilton) argued that Zenger should be acquitted because what he said was true. Hamil-

*ton drew on several themes of continuing significance in American public law. His empha-
sis on the differing social and economic bases of law in America and the mother country
was pertinent for the reception of the common law. His concluding peroration, which at first
glance seems to be empty and exaggerated rhetoric, was in fact an extrapolation of legal arguments in their broader ideological significance. The jury, sympathetic to Zenger and hostile to Governor Cosby, acquitted Zenger, despite the charge of the judge that he be found
guilty. This was not a legal precedent—it was nothing more than an example of jury nullification in support of a popular defendant. But it served to be a strong and powerful political precedent for the idea that Americans should be free to criticize their rulers and their
leaders.*

Mr. Hamilton. May it please Your Honor; I agree with Mr. Attorney, that government is a sacred thing, but I differ very widely from him when he would insinuate that the just complaints of a number of men who suffer under a bad administration is libeling that administration.

♦   ♦   ♦

What strange doctrine is it to press everything for law here which is so in England? I believe we should not think it a favor, at present at least, to establish this practice. In England, so great a regard and reverence is had to the judges, that if any man strikes another in Westminster Hall while the judges are sitting, he shall lose his right hand and forfeit his land and goods for so doing. And though the judges here claim all the powers and authorities within this government that a Court of King's Bench has in England, yet I believe Mr. Attorney will scarcely say that such a punishment could be legally inflicted on a man for committing such an offense in the presence of the judges sitting any court within the Province of New York. The reason is obvious; a quarrel or riot in New York cannot possibly be attended with those dangerous consequences that it might in Westminster Hall; nor (I hope) will it be alleged that any misbehavior to a governor in the plantations will, or ought to be, judged of or punished as a like undutifulness would be to our Sovereign. From all which, I hope Mr. Attorney will not think it proper to apply his law cases (to support the cause of his Governor) which have only been judged where the King's safety or honor was concerned. It will not be denied but that a freeholder in the Province of New York has as

good a right to the sole and separate use of his lands as a freeholder in England, who has a right to bring an action of trespass against his neighbor for suffering his horse or cow to come and feed upon his land, or eat his corn, whether enclosed or not enclosed; and yet I believe it would be looked upon as a strange attempt for one man here to bring an action against another, whose cattle and horses feed upon his grounds not enclosed, or indeed for eating and treading down his corn, if that were not enclosed. Numberless are the instances of this kind that might be given, to show that what is good law at one time and in one place is not so at another time and in another place; so that I think the law seems to expect that in these parts of the world men should take care, by a good fence, to preserve their property from the injury of unruly beasts. And perhaps there may be as good reason why men should take the same care to make an honest and upright conduct a fence and security against the injury of unruly tongues.

♦   ♦   ♦

Mr. Chief Justice. You cannot be admitted, Mr. Hamilton, to give the truth of a libel in evidence. A libel is not to be justified; for it is nevertheless a libel that is true.

Mr. Hamilton. I am sorry the Court has so soon resolved upon that piece of law; I expected first to have been heard to that point. I have not in all my reading met with an authority that says we cannot be admitted to give the truth in evidence upon an information for a libel.

Mr. Chief Justice. The law is clear, that you cannot justify a libel.

♦   ♦   ♦

Mr. Chief Justice. Mr. Hamilton, the court is of opinion, you ought not to be permitted to prove the facts in the papers: These are the words of the book, "It is far from being a justification of a libel, that the contents thereof are true, or that the person upon whom it is made had a bad reputation, since the greater appearance there is of truth in any malicious invective, so much the more provoking it is."

Mr. Hamilton. These are Star Chamber cases, and I was in hopes that practice had been dead with the Court.

Mr. Chief Justice. Mr. Hamilton, the Court have delivered their opinion, and we expect you will use us with good manners; you are not to be permitted to argue against the opinion of the Court.

Mr. Hamilton. With submission, I have seen the practice in very great courts, and never heard it deemed unmannerly to

Mr. Chief Justice. After the Court have declared their opinion, it is not good manners to insist upon a point in which you are overruled.

Mr. Hamilton. I will say no more at this time; the Court I see is against us in this point; and that I hope I may be allowed to say.

♦ ♦ ♦

Mr. Chief Justice. No, Mr. Hamilton; the jury may find that Zenger printed and published those papers, and leave it to the Court to judge whether they are libelous; you know this is very common; it is in the nature of a special verdict, where the jury leave the matter of law to the Court.

Mr. Hamilton. I know, may it please Your Honor, the jury may do so; but I do likewise know they may do otherwise. I know they have the right beyond all dispute to determine both the law and the fact, and where they do not doubt of the law, they ought to do so. This leaving it to the judgment of the Court whether the words are libelous or not in effect renders juries useless (to say no worse) in many cases; but this I shall have occasion to speak to by and by; and I will with the Court's leave proceed to examine the inconveniences that must inevitably arise from the doctrines Mr. Attorney has laid down: and I observe in support of

this prosecution, he has frequently repeated the words taken from the case of Libel. Famosis in 5.Co. This is indeed the leading case, and to which almost all the other cases upon the subject of libels do refer; and I must insist that upon saying that according as this case seems to be understood by the Court and Mr. Attorney, it is not law at this day: For though I own it to be base and unworthy to scandalize any man, yet I think it is even villainous to scandalize a person of public character, and I will go so far into Mr. Attorney's doctrine as to agree that if the faults, mistakes, nay even the vices of such a person be private and personal, and don't affect the peace of the public, or the liberty or property of our neighbor, it is unmanly and unmannerly to expose them either by word or writing. But when a ruler of people brings his personal failings, but much more his vices, into his administration, and the people find themselves affected by them, either in their liberties or properties, that will alter the case mightily, and all the high things that are said in favor of rulers, and of dignities, and upon the side of power, will not be able to stop people's mouths when they feel themselves oppressed, I mean in a free government. It is true in times past it was a crime to speak truth, and in that terrible Court of Star Chamber, many worthy and brave men suffered for so doing; and yet even in that Court and in those bad times, a great and good man durst say, what I hope will not be taken amiss of me to say in the place, to wit, The practice of informations for libels is a sword in the hands of a wicked king and an arrant coward to cut down and destroy the innocent; the one cannot because of his high station, and the other dares not because of his want of courage, revenge himself in another manner.

♦ ♦ ♦

But to conclude; the question before the Court and you gentlemen of the jury is not of small nor private concern, it is not the cause of a poor printer, nor of New York alone, which you are now trying: No! It may in its consequence affect every freeman that lives under a British government on the main of America. It is the best cause.

→ 2 ←

Law in a Republican Revolution
1760–1815

The American Revolution profoundly affected the development of American law. In the years between 1760 and 1783 Americans created a self-conscious national identity, achieved political independence, and successfully waged a war of national liberation against the world's strongest military power. In these years, the British mainland colonies became republican states, while Americans implemented republican self-government as a working system in their newly created states. Throughout the period, ideology and law played decisive roles, driving and at the same time constraining the course of revolutionary political development.

After declaring independence, Americans combined republican ideology and practical experience to create a national government, first as a loose confederation that managed to see them through the war with Britain, and then as a national republic that was itself a state having sufficient powers of governance. By 1791 Americans had created a national state based on representative government, democratically elected. The new constitutional order balanced the right of the majority to self-government with the need to guarantee protections for minorities. One of the essential characteristics of that national government was a judiciary that could enforce its laws, protect national policy against state particularism, and at least in theory protect minority rights from what the French intellectual Alexis de Tocqueville would later call "the tyranny of the majority."

Without being conscious of it, Americans and Britons had been drifting apart in their understanding of their shared constitutional heritage. The basis for differences between them had existed from the time of the earliest seventeenth-century settlements, but those divisive potentials remained latent during the century-long struggle between Britain and France for dominance on the European continent, in North America, and in Asia. In 1763, that struggle concluded triumphantly for Great Britain, which then turned to two long-neglected problems in colonial affairs: tightening up colonial administration and increasing the revenue from the colonies.

From the beginning of settlement, Americans regarded themselves as English people, entitled to all the rights of their fellow subjects still resident within the realm, plus certain rights peculiar to their situation. Attempts by Britain to assert authority and control on the colonies after 1783 only served to reinforce the Americans' sense of their rights. When challenged on a particular belief, such as the autonomy of colonial government, they would re-think the implications of something they had long taken for granted, and this forced recon-sideration would then lead them to an extension of their original position.

Through their struggles with Parliament and the king, Americans discovered their most important revolutionary concept—popular sovereignty—the idea that the people should in effect rule themselves. At the outset of the American Revolution, no one in the colonies en-tertained any idea of disavowing loyalty to the Crown or of locating sovereign authority in the people themselves. Americans came to that belief slowly between 1760 and 1776. As late as 1774, in the Declaration and Resolves of the First Continental Congress, they sin-cerely insisted on their allegiance to the Crown. But Whig-minded Americans gradually came to see that Parliament's claim of full legislative power over the colonies was incompatible with their rights as colonists, especially self-government.

Americans also rejected the English claim that through "virtual representation" the colonies had a voice in Parliament. Proponents of "virtual representation" asserted that Par-liament legislated for the best interest of the entire British Empire and thus all the empire was virtually represented in Parliament. One Englishman asserted that a member of Parlia-ment sat "not as a representative of his own constituents, but as one of the august assembly by which the commons of Great Britain are represented." Under such a theory, the English claimed that Americans were "virtually" represented in Parliament. James Otis, a radical lawyer in Boston, scoffed, arguing that by this theory you could "as well prove that the British House of Commons in fact represents all the people of the globe as those in Amer-ica." Americans were used to elected local officials and colonial legislatures, and had no pa-tience for such sophistries. Arthur Lee of Virginia proclaimed in 1768 that "our privileges are all *virtual*, our sufferings are all *real*." Thus he argued that "a *virtual obedience* would have exactly corresponded with a *virtual representation*."

After independence, Americans evolved a coherent republican ideology that protected individual and collective rights, specified the sources of those rights, identified dangers to them, and provided a vision of America's destiny. This ideology emerged from two sources. First, Americans remembered and applied their heritage as English people and the history of England, especially the struggles against the Stuart kings. Second, they relied on their actual experience in the colonies during the preceding 150 years. During that period they had de-veloped elected legislatures and to a great extent practiced self-government. These two tra-ditions—the English and the colonial—produced a political philosophy based on the most revolutionary idea about government the world has yet known: the people are capable of governing themselves, without the superintendence of king, nobility, church, party, or tyrant.

Americans promptly put republicanism to practical use in structuring their state gov-ernments. Not surprisingly, they discovered that they were not of one mind about the mean-ing of republicanism. Their beliefs and hopes sorted themselves out along a spectrum, with conservative and radical poles. The radical-minded were inclined to a pure democracy, in which government would be as closely in the hands of the people as the circumstances of time, space, and technology would permit. This vision was realized in the Pennsylvania Con-stitution of 1776, with its array of democratic features tying the day-to-day operations of government immediately to the people. Conservatives condemned such experiments, fearing that popular majorities in direct control of government would threaten property rights and the stability of society. In their vision of popular sovereignty the structures of government would distance the people from the actual exercise of power.

Americans at first had less success in creating a national government than they had experienced in establishing state governments. They had accumulated over a century of experience in provincial governance, which easily transformed into governing the new states. But, their attempts at transcolonial integration (the New England Confederation of 1643, the Albany Plan of Union of 1754) had been failures. Furthermore, the Revolution against England was part of a battle against a distant, powerful central government. Thus, after independence many Americans opposed the creation of strong national government with a seat of power distant from where they lived. They were reluctant to exchange one powerful central government for another. Thus, the Articles of Confederation, approved by Congress in 1777, but not ratified until 1781, created a loose confederacy that had some characteristics of a true government, but eventually proved incapable of serving as a vehicle for long-term peacetime governance of the nation. The Framers' success in establishing a national government under the Constitution of 1787 has impressed later generations as almost superhuman, given the sectional divisions and particularist antagonisms that had to be overcome. In accomplishing this, the Framers produced an impressive body of political theory that enriched republican thought.

In the first decade of its operation, the new national government established precedents that became elements of American constitutionalism scarcely less significant than the Constitution itself. But the sectional and policy conflicts of the first decades of independence also spawned competing theories about the nature of the Union. Located in the doctrines of Alexander Hamilton, John Marshall, Joseph Story, and Daniel Webster, a nationalistic vision extolled the power of the national government as a unifying force overriding the local self-interest of state public policy. Eventually this ideology would be the driving force behind the Union cause in 1861–1865 and Abraham Lincoln's opposition to secession.

The other vision was propounded by Thomas Jefferson, James Madison in the Virginia Resolutions, and a claque of Virginia political theorists and jurists, most prominently Judge Spencer Roane, and later by the South Carolina southern nationalist John C. Calhoun. From the 1830s until 1861, various Democratic party leaders, such as James Buchanan, Stephen A. Douglas, and Roger B. Taney, would embrace much of this ideology. In the late antebellum period, southern extremists, such as Jefferson Davis, James Henry Hammond, and William Yancey, would use these theories in their most extreme incarnation to justify secession and civil war. Proponents of this localized vision, from Thomas Jefferson to Jefferson Davis, emphasized the primacy of the states as embodiments of popular sovereignty and squinted suspiciously at national power. The conflict between these competing visions, given practical relevance by the expansion of slavery, dominated political debate in the United States until the Civil War. Although the nationalist vision eventually triumphed, the state-power theory left a lingering suspicion of national power.

THE AMERICAN REVOLUTION

A 1750 election-day sermon delivered in Boston by the Reverend Jonathan Mayhew demonstrated just how provincial Americans had become in the development of their political life. James Otis, Jr., of Massachusetts attempted to identify American rights in the 1760s, but he could not escape the ambivalence of the early American position, defending colonial liberties while retaining loyalty to the British system. Perceiving the chasm that separated them from the Americans, the British articulated their own position, officially in the Declaratory Act of 1766 and unofficially in William Blackstone's *Commentaries*. The relentless erosion of relations between Great Britain and its colonies was signaled in 1774 by the Declaration and Resolves of the First Continental Congress, which set forth the essential American constitutional position. In 1776, Thomas Jefferson's Declaration of Independence cut the final emotional and ideological ties binding the former American colonies to the British Empire.

Jonathan Mayhew

"Unlimited Submission and Non-resistance to the Higher Powers"
1750

Starting from a shared fund of political theory in the early eighteenth century, British and American thinking about constitutional issues diverged, without either mother country or colonies being aware of how far apart from each other they were growing. A good example of this divergence was provided in an election sermon delivered by the Massachusetts Congregational minister Jonathan Mayhew in 1750, more than a decade before overt stirring of revolutionary sentiment. Taking as his text an admonition of St. Paul, "Let every soul be subject unto the higher powers . . . the powers that be are ordained of God" (Romans 13:1), Mayhew stood the apostle on his head.

Common tyrants and public oppressors are not entitled to obedience from their subjects by virtue of anything here laid down by the inspired apostle.

I now add, further, that the apostle's argument is so far from proving it to be the duty of people to obey and submit to such rulers as act in contradiction to the public good, and so to the design of their office, that it proves the direct contrary. For, please to observe, that if the end of all civil government be the good of society; if this be the thing that is aimed at in constituting civil rulers; and if the motive and argument for submission to government be taken from the apparent usefulness of civil authority,—it follows, that when no such good end can be answered by submission, there remains no argument or motive to enforce it; and if, instead of this good end's being brought about by submission, a contrary end is brought about, and the ruin and misery of society effected by it, here is a plain and positive reason against submission in all such cases, should they ever happen. And therefore, in such cases, a regard to the public welfare ought to make us withhold from our rulers that obedience and submission which it would otherwise be our duty to render to them.

Note: Litigation and the Coming of the Revolution

John Peter Zenger's case (see Chapter 1) was the earliest example of a process that promoted the Revolution. A case would come before local courts, growing out of a local political controversy, such as Zenger's criticism of the administration of royal governor William Cosby. The attorney representing one of the parties would appeal to the jury with arguments about political theory, rather than focusing on legal precedents. These arguments might appear to us, on their face, to be empty rhetoric. But the rhetorical appeal couched an articulation of a fundamental constitutional belief cherished by Americans (e.g., truth as a defense in a prosecution for seditious libel). This doctrinal advance thereupon became embedded in American belief as a constitutional principle.

This process was often repeated before and during the American Revolution. In the *Writs of Assistance Case* of 1761 in Massachusetts, a young attorney, James Otis, Jr., denounced the Crown's resort to general writs used in investigations of smuggling. After condemning such writs in uncompromising terms, Otis declaimed:

> But had this writ been in any book whatever, it would have been illegal. All prece-
> dents are under the control of the principles of law. . . . No Acts of Parliament can
> establish such a writ; though it should be made in the very words of the petition, it
> would be void. An act against the constitution is void.

John Adams, who was present at Otis's argument, later noted in his diary that "then and there the brat Independence was born."

In the "Parson's Cause" of 1763 (sometimes known as the *Two-Penny Act Case*), Patrick Henry made an even more dramatic leap from rhetorical appeal to constitutional principle. He argued that a Virginia statute regulating the pay of clergy of the established church, which had the effect of diminishing the curates' salaries, was a good law that contributed to the welfare of the people, and that its disallowance by King George III consequently violated the compact between king and people. By such action, the King degenerated into a tyrant and forfeited the right to his subjects' obedience. The attorney general, aghast, leapt up to object: "The gentleman speaks treason!" Nonetheless, the jury endorsed Henry's argument and returned only a nominal verdict for the plaintiff-clergyman.

JAMES OTIS

"The Rights of the British Colonies"
1764

This disjointed essay, frequently self-contradictory and at times approaching incoherence, reflects the confusion in the minds of Americans generally in 1764. Otis mirrored the am- bivalence of Americans in the early stages of the Revolution. On one hand, they considered themselves British subjects and appealed to the British constitution as a barrier to arbitrary power. On the other hand, they claimed rights inconsistent with the allegiance they pro- fessed, claims that their British fellow subjects found incomprehensible and revolutionary.

I affirm that government is founded on the necessity of our natures and that an original supreme, sovereign, absolute, and uncontrol- lable earthly power must exist in and preside over every society, from whose final decisions there can be no appeal but directly to Heaven. It is therefore originally and ultimately in the people. I say this supreme absolute power is originally and ultimately in the people; and they never did in fact freely, nor can they rightfully make an absolute, unlimited renunciation of this divine right. It is ever in the nature of the thing given in trust and on a condition the perfor- mance of which no mortal can dispense with,

namely, that the person or persons on whom the sovereignty is conferred by the people shall in- cessantly consult their good.

◆ ◆ ◆

I also lay it down as one of the first prin- ciples from whence I intend to deduce the civil rights of the British colonies, that all of them are subject to and dependent on Great Britain and that therefore as over subordinate govern- ments the Parliament of Great Britain has an undoubted power and lawful authority to make acts for the general good that by naming them shall and ought to be equally binding as upon the subjects of Great Britain within the realm. This principle, I presume, will be readily granted on the other side of the Atlantic. It has been practised upon for twenty years to my knowledge, in the province of Massachusetts Bay and I have ever received it that it has been so from the beginning in this and the sister provinces through the continent.

I am aware some will think it is time for me to retreat, after having expressed the power of the British Parliament in quite so strong terms. But 'tis from and under this very power and its acts, and from the common Law, that the political and civil rights of the colonists are derived; and upon those grand pillars of liberty shall my defense be rested. No act of Parliament can deprive them of the liberties of such, unless any will contend that an act of Parliament can make slaves not only of one but two millions of the commonwealth. And if so, why not of the whole? I freely own that I can find nothing in the laws of my country that would justify the Parliament in making one slave, nor did they ever professedly undertake to make one.

♦ ♦ ♦

Every British subject born on the continent of America or in any other of the British dominions is by the law of God and nature, by the common law, and by act of Parliament (exclusive of all charters from the crown) entitled to all the natural, essential, inherent, and inseparable rights of our fellow subjects in Great Britain. Among those rights are the following, which it is humbly conceived no man or body of men, not excepting the Parliament, justly, equitably, and consistently with their own rights and the constitution can take away.

♦ ♦ ♦

These are their bounds, which by God and nature are fixed; hitherto have they a right to come, and no further.

1. To govern by stated laws.
2. Those laws should have no other end ultimately but the good of the people.
3. Taxes are not to be laid on the people but by their consent in person or by deputation.

♦ ♦ ♦

That the colonists, black and white, born here are freeborn British subjects, and entitled to all the essential civil rights of such is a truth not only manifest from the provincial charters, from the principles of the common law, and acts of Parliament, but from the British constitution, which was re-established at the [Glorious] Revolution with a professed design to secure the liberties of all the subjects to all generations.

♦ ♦ ♦

The power of Parliament is uncontrollable but by themselves, and we must obey. They only can repeal their own acts. There would be an end of all government if one or a number of subjects or subordinate provinces should take upon them so far to judge of the justice of an act of Parliament as to refuse obedience to it. If there was nothing else to restrain such a step, prudence ought to do it, for forceably resisting the Parliament and the King's laws is high treason. Therefore let the Parliament lay what burdens they please on us, we must, it is our duty to submit and patiently bear them till they will be pleased to relieve us. And 'tis to be presumed the wisdom and justice of that august assembly always will afford us relief by repealing such acts as through mistake or other human infirmities have been suffered to pass, if they can be convinced that their proceedings are not constitutional or not for the common good.

♦ ♦ ♦

To say the Parliament is absolute and arbitrary is a contradiction. The Parliament cannot make 2 and 2, 5: omnipotency cannot do. The supreme power in a state is jus dicere only: jus dare strictly speaking, belongs alone to GOD. Parliaments are in all cases to declare what is for the good of the whole; but it is not the declaration of Parliament that makes it so. There must be in every instance a higher authority, viz., GOD. Should an act of Parliament be against any of his natural laws, which are immutably true, their declaration would be contrary to eternal truth, equity, and justice, and consequently void: and so it would be adjudged by the Parliament itself when convinced of their mistake.

William Blackstone on the Imperial Constitution
1765

Sir William Blackstone (1723–1780) was the first Vinerian Professor of Law at Oxford, where he introduced courses on English law. His lectures, published in 1765 as Commentaries on the Laws of England, *have stood for two centuries as the classic exposition of English law. The following passages on reception of the common law and parliamentary power represented the core of orthodoxy in the English view of the imperial constitution. In this outlook, there was obviously little room for accommodating the American position. Thus from the outset of the Revolutionary period, the leading theorists on both sides held irreconcilable positions.*

[O]ur more distant plantations in America, and elsewhere, are also in some respects subject to the English laws. Plantations or colonies, in distant countries, are either such where the lands are claimed by right of occupancy only by finding them desert and uncultivated, and peopling them from the mother-country; or where, when already cultivated, they have been either gained by conquest, or ceded to us by treaties. And both these rights are founded upon the law of nature, or at least upon that of nations. But there is a difference between these two species of colonies, with respect to the laws by which they are bound. For it hath been held that if an uninhabited country be discovered and planted by English subjects, all the English laws then in being, which are the birthright of every subject, are immediately there in force. But this must be understood with very many and very great restrictions. Such colonists carry with them only so much of the English law as is applicable to their own situation and the condition of an infant colony; such, for instance, as the general rules of inheritance, and of protection from personal injuries. The artificial refinements and distinctions incident to the property of a great and commercial people, the laws of police and revenue, (such especially as are enforced by penalties,) the mode of maintenance for the established clergy, the jurisdiction of spiritual courts, and a multitude of other provisions, are neither necessary nor convenient for them, and therefore are not in force. What shall be admitted and what rejected, at what times, and under what restrictions, must, in case of dispute, be decided in the first instance by their own

provincial judicature, subject to the revision and control of the king in council: the whole of their constitution being also liable to be new-modelled and reformed by the general superintending power of the legislature in the mother-country. But in conquered or ceded countries, that have already laws of their own, the king may indeed alter and change those laws; but till he does actually change them, the ancient laws of the country remain, unless such as are against the law of God, as in the case of an infidel country. Our American plantations are principally of this latter sort, being obtained in the last century either by right of conquest and driving out the natives (with what natural justice I shall not at present inquire), or by treaties. And therefore the common law of England, as such, has no allowance or authority there; they being no part of the mother-country, but distinct (though dependent) dominions. They are subject, however, to the control of the parliament; though (like Ireland, Man, and the rest) not bound by any acts of parliament, unless particularly named.

◆ ◆ ◆

III. We are next to examine the laws and customs relating to parliament, thus united together and considered as one aggregate body.

The power and jurisdiction of parliament, says sir Edward Coke, is so transcendent and absolute, that it cannot be confined, either for causes or persons, within any bounds. It has sovereign and uncontrollable authority in the making, confirming, enlarging, restraining, abrogating, repealing, reviving, and expounding of laws, concerning matters of all possible denominations, ecclesiastical, or temporal, civil, military, maritime, or criminal: this being the place where that absolute despotic power, which must in all governments reside somewhere, is intrusted by the constitution of these kingdoms.

◆　◆　◆

It must be owned that Mr. Locke and other theoretical writers, have held, that "there remains still inherent in the people a supreme power to remove or alter the legislative, when they find the legislative act contrary to the trust reposed in them; for when such trust is abused, it is thereby forfeited, and devolves to those who gave it." But, however just this conclusion may be in the theory, we cannot practically adopt it, nor take any legal steps for carrying it into execution under any dispensation of government at present actually existing. For this devolution of power, to the people at large, includes in it a dissolution of the whole form of government established by that people; reduces all the members to their original state of equality; and, by annihilating the sovereign power, repeals all positive laws whatsoever before enacted. No human laws will therefore suppose a case, which at once must destroy all law, and compel men to build afresh upon a new foundation; nor will they make provision for so desperate an event, as must render all legal provisions ineffectual. So long therefore as the English constitution lasts, we may venture to affirm, that the power of parliament is absolute and without control.

The Declaratory Act
1766

In 1765 Britain imposed the Stamp Act on the colonies, requiring the payment of tax (signified by the purchase of a stamp) for all paper goods sold in the colonies. Newspapers, legal documents, even personal stationery required a tax stamp before being sold. Americans responded vigorously, and violently, to the Stamp Act, burning stamps and intimidating the tax collectors. Emerging out of these protests were loosely formed organizations known as the Sons of Liberty. Within a decade they would become the backbone of the Revolutionary movement. Most important, in October 1765 thirty-seven delegates from nine colonies went to New York for the first inter-colony assembly, known as the Stamp Act Congress. The Congress denounced the Stamp Act. In March 1766 Parliament repealed the Stamp Act, but at the same time asserted its theoretical power to govern in the colonies in the Declaratory Act, which follows. The repeal of the Stamp Act might have defused the growing crisis in the empire, but the Declaratory Act prevented this and only served to anger Americans, who now denied that Parliament had the right or power to tax them.

AN ACT FOR THE BETTER SECURING THE DEPENDENCY OF HIS MAJESTY'S DOMINIONS IN AMERICA UPON THE CROWN AND PARLIAMENT OF GREAT BRITAIN

Whereas several of the houses of representatives in his Majesty's colonies and plantations in America, have of late, against law, claimed to themselves, or to the general assemblies of the same, the sole and exclusive right of imposing duties and taxes upon his Majesty's subjects in the said colonies and plantations; and have, in pursuance of such claim, passed certain votes, resolutions, and orders, derogatory to the legislative authority of parliament, and inconsistent with the dependency of the said colonies and plantations upon the crown of Great Britain: may it therefore please your most excellent Majesty, that it may be declared; and be it declared by the King's most excellent majesty, by and with the advice and consent of the lords spiritual and temporal, and commons, in this present parliament assembled, and by the authority of the same, that the said colonies and plantations in America have been, are, and of right ought to be, subordinate unto, and dependent upon the imperial crown and parliament of Great Britain; and that the King's majesty, by and with the advice and consent of the lords spiritual and temporal, and commons of Great Britain, in parliament assembled, had, hath, and of right ought to have, full power and authority to make laws and statutes of sufficient force and validity to bind the colonies and people of America, subjects of the crown of Great Britain, in all cases whatsoever.

The Declaration and Resolves of the Continental Congress
1774

Between 1765 and 1774, relations between the colonies and mother country continued to deteriorate. England tried various ways to control and tax the colonies, and each one met with resistance. In 1768 Americans began to boycott British goods and the Massachusetts House of Representatives issued a "Circular Letter" declaring that a series of British taxes known as the Townshend duties were "unconstitutional" because they violated the principle that tied taxation to representation. When the Massachusetts House refused to rescind the letter, Lord Hillsboro ordered the House dissolved. British troops were sent to Boston in 1769 and on March 5, 1770, British troops fired on unarmed Bostonians who were heckling them and pelting them with snowballs. The "Boston Massacre" left five people dead and led to new tensions. The Tea Act forced colonists to buy tea from one source, the East India Company, and made collection of the tax on imported tea easier. The result was boycotts across the continent. In December 1773 members of the Sons of Liberty in Boston boarded ships carrying tea and threw the cargo into the ocean. The Boston Tea Party led to new laws known as the Coercive Acts, or Intolerable Acts, which among other things closed the Port of Boston, reorganized the Massachusetts colonial government, allowed British troops to be quartered in homes in Massachusetts without the owner's consent, and made the commander-in-chief of the British army in America, General Thomas Gage, the governor of the colony. In September 1774 fifty-five delegates, representing every colony but Georgia, met in Philadelphia at the First Continental Congress. Not yet ready for revolution, the delegates issued the Declaration and Resolves on October 14, 1774. The declaration conceded Parliament's power to regulate the foreign affairs of the colonies, but nevertheless set forth the essential American constitutional position. By this time the conflict between Britain and America seemed inevitable. Britain ignored the declaration and refused to consider compromise or negotiation. What seemed obvious and equitable to Americans appeared irrational and treasonous to the British.

That the inhabitants of the English colonies in North-America, by the immutable laws of nature, the principles of the English constitution, and the several charters or compacts, have the following Rights:

Resolved, 1. That they are entitled to life, liberty and property: and they have never ceded to any foreign power whatever, a right to dispose of either without their consent.

Resolved, 2. That our ancestors, who first

settled these colonies, were at the time of their emigration from the mother country, entitled to all the rights, liberties, and immunities of free and natural-born subjects, within the realm of England.

Resolved, 3. That by such emigration they by no means forfeited, surrendered, or lost any of those rights, but that they were, and their descendants now are, entitled to the exercise and enjoyment of all such of them, as their local and other circumstances enable them to exercise and enjoy.

Resolved, 4. That the foundation of English liberty, and of all free government, is a right in the people to participate in their legislative council and as the English colonists are not represented, and from their local and other circumstances, cannot properly be represented in the British parliament, they are entitled to a free and exclusive power of legislation in their several provincial legislatures, where their right of representation can alone be preserved, in all cases of taxation and internal policy, subject only to the negative of their sovereign, in such manner as has been heretofore used and accustomed; But, from the necessity of the case, and a regard to the mutual interest of both countries, we cheerfully consent to the operation of such acts of the British parliament as are bona fide, restrained to the regulation of external commerce, for the purpose of securing the commercial advantages of the whole empire to the mother country, and the commercial benefits of its respective members; excluding every idea of taxation internal or external, for raising a revenue on the subjects, in America, without their consent.

Resolved, 5. That the respective colonies are entitled to the common law of England, and more especially to the great and inestimable privilege of being tried by their peers of the vicinage, according to the course of that law.

Resolved, 6. That they are entitled to the benefit of such of the English statutes, as existed at the time of their colonization; and which they have, by experience, respectively found to be applicable to their several local and other circumstances.

TOM PAINE

Common Sense
1776

The Declaration and Resolves led nowhere, and in April 1775, war broke out when British troops marched out of Boston toward Concord, Massachusetts, seeking to arrest patriot leaders. They faced off against the local militia at Lexington, and the war began. In May 1775 delegates from all the colonies gathered in Philadelphia for the Second Continental Congress. But even after the shooting war began in 1775, most Americans probably hoped for a reconciliation of some sort with the mother country. In July the Second Continental Congress sent the king an "Olive Branch Petition," seeking a reconciliation. The king ignored it. While British actions pushed the colonists toward independence, the brilliant propaganda of Tom Paine, in his book Common Sense, *helped sever the final remaining psychological and constitutional links with Britain, especially undermining the individual's sense of personal loyalty to the king, the "royal brute" and the "crowned ruffian," as Paine called him. Paine, a recent immigrant from England, held the monarchy in contempt. He argued that the origin of the monarchy would not stand careful scrutiny, noting that "the present race of kings in the world" lacked an "honorable origin." He declared that if we could "take off the dark covering of antiquity and trace them to their first rise, we should find the first of them nothing better than the principal ruffian of some restless gang; whose savage manners or preeminence in subtility obtained him the title of chief among plunderers: and who by in-*

creasing in power and extending his depredations, overawed the quiet and defenceless" to gain power. His history of the origin of the English monarchy was particularly devastating and helped convince Americans that they owed nothing to the king.

England since the conquest hath known some few good monarchs, but groaned beneath a much larger number of bad ones; yet no man in his senses can say that their claim under William the Conqueror is a very honorable one. A French bastard landing with an armed banditti and establishing himself king of England against the consent of the natives is in plain terms a very paltry rascally original. It certainly hath no divinity in it. However it is needless to spend much time in exposing the folly of hereditary rights: if there were any so weak as to believe it, let them promiscuously worship the ass and the lion, and welcome. I shall neither copy their humility, nor disturb their devotion. . . . The plain truth is, that the antiquity of English monarchy will not bear looking into.

◆　◆　◆

In England a king hath little more to do than to make war and give away places; which, in plain terms, is to empoverish the nation and set it together by the ears. A pretty business indeed for a man to be allowed eight hundred thousand sterling a year for, and worshipped into the bargain! Of more worth is one honest man to society, and in the sight of God, than all the crowned ruffians that ever lived.

◆　◆　◆

But where, say some, is the king of America? I'll tell you, he reigns above, and doth not make havoc of mankind like the royal brute of Great Britain. Yet that we may not appear to be defective even in earthly honors, let a day be solemnly set apart for proclaiming the charter; let it be brought forth placed on the divine law, the Word of God; let a crown be placed thereon, by which the world may know, that so far as we approve of monarchy, that in America the law is king. For as in absolute governments the king is law, so in free countries the law ought to be king; and there ought to be no other. But lest any ill use should afterwards arise, let the crown at the conclusion of the ceremony be demolished, and scattered among the people whose right it is.

The Declaration of Independence
1776

Thomas Jefferson's great masterpiece of political theory and propaganda divides into two sections. The first is a brilliantly succinct restatement of liberal political theory, as previously articulated by John Locke and others. The second section is an extended indictment of the misdeeds of King George III. It served the essential function of severing Americans' psychological loyalty and allegiance to the king. It also underscored the belief held by most Americans that Parliament did not represent them and therefore had no legitimate authority over them. The logic of the declaration is clear: if neither the king nor Parliament can rule America, then Americans must be independent and rule themselves. Many of the specific condemnations of the king are exaggerations, but on the whole, Jefferson spells out the general sense Americans had of the "oppression" of the king. The declaration begins with an assertion of universal equality and the fundamental right to liberty; but ironically, the man who wrote these words owned about 175 slaves at the time and would own over 200 at the time of his death. Clearly, there was a huge chasm between American ideals and Amer-

ican reality. In his original draft of the declaration, Jefferson has condemned the king for supporting the African slave trade—but not slavery itself. Many of the delegates in the Congress had purchased slaves from Africa and were ready to do so again; thus, they took this criticism out. The Congress did not even consider a condemnation of slavery itself, leading the English intellectual Samuel Johnson, who opposed the American cause, to ask the profound question: "How is it that we hear the loudest yelps *for liberty among the drivers of negroes?"*

THE UNANIMOUS DECLARATION OF THE THIRTEEN UNITED STATES OF AMERICA

When in the course of human events, it becomes necessary for one people to dissolve the political bands which have connected them with another, and to assume, among the Powers of the earth, the separate and equal station to which the Laws of Nature and of Nature's God entitle them, a decent respect to the opinions of mankind requires that they should declare the causes which impel them to the separation.

We hold these truths to be self-evident, that all men are created equal, that they are endowed by their Creator with certain unalienable Rights, that among these, are Life, Liberty, and the pursuit of Happiness. That, to secure these rights, Governments are instituted among Men, deriving their just Powers from the consent of the governed. That, whenever any form of Government becomes destructive of these ends, it is the Right of the People to alter or to abolish it, and to institute new Government, laying its foundation on such Principles, and organizing its Powers in such form, as to them shall seem most likely to effect their Safety and Happiness. Prudence, indeed, will dictate that Governments long established should not be changed for light and transient causes; and, accordingly, all experience hath shewn, that mankind are more disposed to suffer, while evils are sufferable, than to right themselves by abolishing the forms to which they are accustomed. But, when a long train of abuses and usurpations, pursuing invariably the same Object, evinces a design to reduce them under absolute Despotism, it is their right, it is their duty, to throw off such Government, and to provide new Guards for their future Security. Such has been the patient suf-

ferance of these Colonies; and such is now the necessity which constrains them to alter their former Systems of Government. The history of the present King of Great Britain is a history of repeated injuries and usurpations, all having in direct object the establishment of an absolute Tyranny over these States. To prove this, let Facts be submitted to a candid world.

He has refused his Assent to Laws, the most wholesome and necessary for the public good.

He has forbidden his Governors to pass Laws of immediate and pressing importance, unless suspended in their operation till his Assent should be obtained; and when so suspended, he has utterly neglected to attend to them.

He has refused to pass other Laws for the accommodation of large districts of people, unless those people would relinquish the right of Representation in the Legislature, a right inestimable to them and formidable to tyrants only.

He has called together legislative bodies at places unusual uncomfortable, and distant from the depository of their public records, for the sole purpose of fatiguing them into compliance with his measures.

He has dissolved representative houses repeatedly, for opposing, with manly firmness, his invasions on the rights of the people.

He has refused for a long time, after such dissolutions, to cause others to be elected; whereby the legislative powers, incapable of annihilation, have returned to the people at large for their exercise; the state remaining, in the mean time, exposed to all the dangers of invasions from without and convulsions within.

He has endeavored to prevent the population of these states; for that purpose obstructing the laws for naturalization of foreigners; refusing to pass others to encourage their migration hither, and raising the conditions of new appropriations of lands.

He has obstructed the administration of justice, by refusing his assent to laws for establishing judiciary powers.

He has made Judges dependent on his Will alone, for the tenure of their offices, and the amount and payment of their salaries.

He has erected a multitude of New Offices, and sent hither swarms of Officers to harass our People, and eat out their substance.

He has kept among us, in times of peace, Standing Armies without the Consent of our legislature.

He has affected to render the Military independent of and superior to the Civil Power.

He has combined with others to subject us to a jurisdiction foreign to our constitution, and unacknowledged by our laws; giving his Assent to their Acts of pretended Legislation:

For quartering large bodies of armed troops among us:

For protecting them, by a mock Trial, from Punishment for any Murders which they should commit on the Inhabitants of these States:

For cutting off our Trade with all parts of the world:

For imposing taxes on us without our Consent:

For depriving us in many cases, of the benefits of Trial by jury:

For transporting us beyond Seas to be tried for pretended offences:

For abolishing the free System of English Laws in a neighbouring Province, establishing therein an Arbitrary government, and enlarging its Boundaries so as to render it at once an example and fit instrument for introducing the same absolute rule into these Colonies:

For taking away our Charters, abolishing our most valuable Laws, and altering fundamentally the Forms of our Governments:

For suspending our own Legislatures, and declaring themselves invested with Power to legislate for us in all cases whatsoever.

He has abdicated Government here, by declaring us out of his Protection and waging War against us.

He has plundered our seas, ravaged our Coasts, burnt our towns, and destroyed the lives of our people.

He is at this time transporting large armies of foreign mercenaries to compleat the works of death, desolation, and tyranny, already begun with circumstances of Cruelty & perfidy scarcely paralleled in the most barbarous ages, and totally unworthy the Head of a civilized nation.

He has constrained our fellow Citizens taken Captive on the high seas to bear Arms against their Country, to become the executioners of their friends and Brethren, or to fall themselves by their Hands.

He has excited domestic insurrections amongst us, and has endeavoured to bring on the inhabitants of our frontiers, the merciless Indian savages, whose known rule of warfare, is an undistinguished destruction of all ages, sexes, and conditions. In every stage of these Oppressions We have Petitioned for Redress in the most humble terms: Our repeated Petitions have been answered only by repeated injury. A Prince, whose character is thus marked by every act which may define a Tyrant, is unfit to be the ruler of a free people.

Nor have We been wanting in attention to our British brethren. We have warned them from time to time of attempts by their legislature to extend an unwarrantable jurisdiction over us. We have reminded them of the circumstances of our emigration and settlement here. We have appealed to their native justice and magnanimity, and we have conjured them by the ties of our common kindred to disavow these usurpations, which, would inevitably interrupt our connections and correspondence. They too must have been deaf to the voice of justice and of consanguinity. We must, therefore, acquiesce in the necessity, which denounces our Separation, and hold them, as we hold the rest of mankind, Enemies in War, in Peace Friends.

We, therefore, the Representatives of the United States of America, in General Congress, Assembled, appealing to the Supreme Judge of the world for the rectitude of our intentions, do, in the Name, and by Authority of the good People of these Colonies, solemnly publish and declare, That these United Colonies are, and of Right ought to be free and independent states; that they are Absolved from all Allegiance to the British Crown, and that all political connection between them and the State of Great Britain, is and ought to be totally dissolved; and that as Free and Independent States, they have full Power to levy War, conclude Peace, contract Alliances, establish Commerce, and to do all other Acts and Things which Independent States may of right do. And for the support of this Declaration, with a firm reliance on the Protection of Divine Providence, we mutually pledge to each other our Lives, our Fortunes, and our sacred Honor.

REPUBLICAN STATE CONSTITUTIONALISM

The American Revolution was the hothouse in which republican ideology was nurtured. Independence provided Americans the opportunity of applying republican principles to create actual mechanisms of state governance. The first vehicles for incorporating these tenets into actual governments were the state constitutions, drafted by the state legislatures between 1776 and 1790. Reflecting a continuum of republican thought, these constitutions ranged themselves along a radical to conservative spectrum, with Pennsylvania's 1776 constitution embodying the democratic sentiments expressed in the anonymous radical pamphlet *The People the Best Governors.* By contrast, the constitution that the people of Massachusetts eventually ratified in 1780 reflected, in some ways, the more conservative republicanism of John Adams, who warned of the dangers of too immediate and powerful popular control over the actual workings of government. However, this constitution had its radical elements as well: ending slavery and providing universal adult male suffrage, without any property or racial qualifications.

The early state constitutions often contained some law-reform mandates. The state legislatures implemented other reforms. Some of these law-reform efforts encompassed private law, like the abolition of primogeniture and entail in Virginia. Most, however, dealt with public law as some of the new states reduced the number of capital offenses, provided for some public education, and expanded the right of suffrage.

Illustrative of the complexity of the reform in the Revolutionary era are the laws regarding religion and slavery. At the beginning of the Revolution, slavery was legal in every colony. Similarly, most of the colonies had, at least nominally, an established church, and all the colonies had religious tests for officeholding. During and immediately after the Revolution, Pennsylvania, Connecticut, and Rhode Island passed laws to gradually end slavery, while Massachusetts, New Hampshire, and the independent republic of Vermont (soon to be the fourteenth state) ended slavery through their constitutions. But deeply held notions of private property, economic self-interest, and racism prevented the adoption of gradual abolition laws in New York and New Jersey until 1799 and 1804. In the South abolition was never considered. The best reformers could hope for were laws like Virginia's of 1782, which allowed masters to voluntarily free their slaves, or the North Carolina Act of 1791, declaring that murder of a slave would be treated the same as murder of a freeman. Most southern whites agreed with Thomas Jefferson, who prevented a gradual abolition act from ever reaching the floor of the Virginia legislature. He considered free blacks to be "pests" and urged his fellow Virginians not to free them.

Religious disestablishment was equally complex. New England maintained official support for its churches into the 1830s and beyond. Disestablishment in Virginia happened relatively quickly, but only after a ferocious struggle led first by Jefferson and then taken to its successful conclusion by James Madison. In the Middle Atlantic states, religious heterogeneity ended what little remained of state support for religion. However, despite the general movement toward disestablishment, every state except New York maintained a religious test for officeholding during this period. The following constitutional provisions and state laws illustrate how the states changed—and did not change—their legal regimes in the wake of the Revolution.

The Virginia Declaration of Rights
1776

The Virginia Declaration of Rights, drafted by George Mason, served as a prototype for many subsequent bills of rights in state constitutions. It contains many of the essential ingredients of a free republican society. However, it also illustrates the contradiction inherent in creating a slaveholder's republic. The phrase of Section 1, "when they enter into a state of society," was inserted by the Virginia legislature to prevent the language of freedom and equality from being applied to slaves.

A declaration of rights made by the representatives of the good people of Virginia, assembled in full and free convention; which rights do pertain to them and their posterity, as the basis and foundation of government.

Section 1. That all men are by nature equally free and independent, and have certain inherent rights, of which, when they enter into a state of society, they cannot, by any compact, deprive or divest their posterity; namely, the enjoyment of life and liberty, with the means of acquiring and possessing property, and pursuing and obtaining happiness and safety.

Sec. 2. That all power is vested in, and consequently derived from, the people; that magistrates are their trustees and servants, and at all times amenable to them.

Sec. 3. That government is, or ought to be, instituted for the common benefit, protection, and security of the people, or community; of all the various modes and forms of government, that is best which is capable of producing the greatest degree of happiness and safety, and is most effectually secured against the danger of maladministration; and that, when any government shall be found inadequate or contrary to these purposes, a majority of the community hath an indubitable, inalienable, and indefeasible right to reform, alter, or abolish it, in such manner as shall be judged most conducive to the public weal.

Sec. 4. That no man, or set of men, are entitled to exclusive or separate emoluments or privileges from the community, but in consideration of public services; which, not being descendible, neither ought the offices of magistrate, legislator, or judge to be hereditary.

Sec. 5. That the legislative and executive powers of the State should be separate and distinct from the judiciary; and that the members of the two first may be restrained from oppression, by feeling and participating in the burdens of the people, they should, at fixed periods, be reduced to a private station, returning into that body from which they were originally taken, and the vacancies be supplied by frequent, certain and regular elections, in which all, or any part of the former members, to be again eligible, or ineligible, as the law shall direct.

Sec. 6. That elections of members to serve as representatives of the people, in assembly, ought to be free; and that all men, having sufficient evidence of permanent common interest with, and attachment to the community, have the right of suffrage, and cannot be taxed or deprived of their property for public uses, without their own consent, or that of their representatives so elected, nor bound by any law to which they have not, in like manner, assembled, for the public good.

Sec. 7. That all power of suspending laws, or the execution of laws, by any authority, without consent of the representatives of the people, is injurious to their rights, and ought not to be exercised.

Sec. 8. That in all capital or criminal prosecutions a man hath a right to demand the cause and nature of his accusation, to be confronted with the accusers and witnesses, to call for evidence in his favor, and to a speedy trial by an impartial jury of twelve men of his vicinage, without whose unanimous consent he cannot be found guilty; nor can he be compelled to give evidence against himself; that no man be deprived of his liberty, except by the law of the land or the judgment of his peers.

Sec. 9. That excessive bail ought not to be required, nor excessive fines imposed, nor cruel and unusual punishments inflicted.

Sec. 10. That general warrants, whereby an officer or messenger may be commanded to search suspected places without evidence of a fact committed, or to seize any person or persons not named, or whose offence is not particularly described and supported by evidence, are grievous and oppressive, and ought not to be granted.

Sec. 11. That in controversies respecting property, and in suits between man and man, the ancient trial by jury is preferable to any other, and ought to be held sacred.

Sec. 12. That the freedom of the press is one of the great bulwarks of liberty, and can never be restrained but by despotic governments.

Sec. 13. That a well-regulated militia, composed of the body of the people, trained to arms, is the proper, natural, and safe defence of a free State; that standing armies, in time of peace, should be avoided, as dangerous to liberty; and that in all cases the military should be under strict subordination to, and governed by, the civil power.

Sec. 14. That the people have a right to uniform government; and, therefore, that no government separate from, or independent of the government of Virginia, ought to be erected or established within the limits thereof.

Sec. 15. That no free government, or the blessings of liberty, can be preserved to any people, but by a firm adherence to justice, moderation, temperance, frugality, and virtue, and by frequent recurrence to fundamental principles.

Sec. 16. That religion, or the duty which we owe to our Creator, and the manner of discharging it, can be directed only by reason and conviction, not by force or violence; and therefore all men are equally entitled to the free exercise of religion, according to the dictates of conscience; and that it is the mutual duty of all to practise Christian forbearance, love, and charity towards each other.

The People the Best Governors
1776

The anonymous and well-read author of this pamphlet, probably a New Englander, advocated a number of radical ideas that aimed at a single objective: enhancing the role of the people in their own government. To this end, he would shorten as much as possible the leash of representation, removing all mechanisms of government that tended to transfer control of governmental power farther from the people.

God gave mankind freedom by nature, made every man equal to his neighbor, and has virtually enjoined them to govern themselves by their own laws. . . . The people best know their own wants and necessities, and therefore are best able to rule themselves. . . . That I might help in some measure to eradicate the notion of arbitrary power, heretofore drank in, and to establish the liberties of the people of this country upon a more generous footing, is the design of the following impartial work, now dedicated by the Author to the honest farmer and citizen.

The just power of a free people respects first the making and secondly the executing of laws. The liberties of people are chiefly, I may say entirely guarded by having the control of these two branches in their own hands.

♦ ♦ ♦

The question now that closes the whole arises, what it is that ought to be the qualification of a representative. In answer, we observe that fear is the principle of a despotic, honour of a kingly, and virtue is the principle of a republican government. Social virtue and knowledge, I say then is the best and only necessary qualification of the person before us. But it will be said that an estate of two hundred, four hundred pounds, or some other sum is essential. So sure as we make interest necessary in this case, as sure we root out virtue; and what will then become of the genuine principle of freedom? This notion of an estate has the directest tendency to set up the avaricious over the heads of the poor, though the latter are ever so virtuous. Let it not be said in future generations that money was made by the founders of the American States an essential qualification in the rulers of a free people.

♦ ♦ ♦

Lastly, let every government have an equal weight in the general congress, and let the representatives of the respective states be chosen by the people annually by ballot in their stated town meetings; the votes to be carried in and published at the appointed election as with respect to a governor, council, &c., in manner aforesaid; and the assemblies of the respective states may have power to instruct the said representatives from time to time as they shall think proper. It appears that the forms of government that have hitherto been proposed since the breach with Great Britain, by the friends of the American States, have been rather too arbitrary. The people are now contending for freedom; and would to God they might not only obtain, but likewise keep it in their own hands. I own myself a friend to a popular government; have freely submitted my reasons upon it. And although the plan here proposed might not ever [have] been adopted as yet, nevertheless those as free have alone secured the liberties of former ages, and a just notion of them has guarded the people against the sly insinuations and proposals of those of a more arbitrary turn, whose schemes have a tendency to deprive mankind of their natural rights.

Note: The Pennsylvania Constitution of 1776

Of all the thirteen new states (plus Vermont, for the time being an independent republic), none came closer to achieving the radical vision of *The People the Best Governors* than Pennsylvania. In its 1776 constitution, it incorporated a number of democratic innovations, including a unicameral legislature (an inheritance of the colonial period, when Pennsylvania had the only legislature of that sort on the mainland). The new constitution also added the following devices: male taxpayer suffrage, annual elections, requirements that the doors of the assembly always be open and that its deliberations and votes be printed weekly, septennial reapportionment, mandatory rotation in office, a collegial executive that could act only as a body (in place of a unitary governor), judges who were elected every seven years and were removable by the legislature for "misbehaviour," abolition of imprisonment for debt, mandated penal reform, compulsory public education, and a septennial Council of Censors that was to determine whether the constitution had been observed. However, even with all of these radical provisions, the 1776 constitution had provisions that were out-of-step with true revolutionary change. The constitution acknowledged slavery and did nothing about it, and limited officeholding to men who acknowledged God and the "scriptures of the Old and New Testament to be given by Divine inspiration." This provision, if enforced, would have prevented not only Jews but also deists, like Benjamin Franklin and Tom Paine, from holding office.

This constitution was short-lived because it was widely unpopular throughout its sixteen-year life, due in some measure to the fact that its supporters virtually disfranchised opponents of the constitution by means of an unacceptable oath. In what some historians consider a counterrevolution, Pennsylvanians opposed to the constitution managed to annul it in 1790, replacing it with a document that conformed more closely to those of other states.

SLAVERY AND THE NEW NATION

Slavery presented the greatest complication and the greatest contradiction for the new nation. Even before the Revolution, many reformers in England and America had started to challenge human bondage. The ideas of liberty found in the Declaration of Independence could not be easily reconciled with a nation of slaveholders. Furthermore, by the end of the Revolution, thousands of blacks had served the patriot cause; at Yorktown about one-fourth of Washington's army was made up of free blacks, mostly former slaves. At the same time, slaves were the most valuable form of private property in the nation, with the exception of real estate. Southerners were convinced they could not live without slaves and that they could never live among large numbers of free blacks. While some in the North saw the Revolution as a chance to end slavery, South Carolinians and Georgians looked forward to the end of the war so they might renew their imports of slaves. At the Constitutional Convention the Southerners would demand—and get—many protections for slavery. In other ways, however, the lawmaking of the Revolutionary era provided the greatest challenge to slavery until the Civil War.

Somerset v. *Stewart*
Lofft 1, 98 Eng. Rep. 499 (K.B. 1772)

Somerset v. Stewart was the foundation of all subsequent legal debate over slavery in the United States. It exercised a profound influence on the law of slavery in America, passing as it did into the common law of the states after independence. It is significant for opponents of slavery because of its condemnation of the nature of slavery and its assertion that the slave law of a foreign state does not control the law of the forum state. However, while never used to support slavery, the opinion of Lord Mansfield illustrates the power of the institution. Even as he freed Somerset, and gave all slaves in England a precedent that they could use to gain their freedom, he conceded that slaves would be legally held as property, subject to sale under the law of contracts, and that slavery could be established by positive law.

James Somerset, a slave in Virginia, accompanied his master to England. Once there, he ran off to freedom but was caught and consigned to a ship captain to be sold in Jamaica. The great British abolitionist Granville Sharp obtained a writ of habeas corpus from Lord Mansfield, Chief Justice of King's Bench, to inquire into the cause of Somerset's detention. Mansfield's opinion, although it did not abolish slavery in England (as Sharp hoped it would), did articulate principles that dominated all later controversies about slavery. As the first part of this opinion indicates, Lord Mansfield tried to avoid reaching a decision in this case, but when forced to do so, he accepted his duty, declaring that Justice would be done, "though the heavens may fall."

The question is, if the owner had a right to detain the slave, for the sending of him over to be sold in Jamaica. In five or six cases of this nature, I have known it to be accommodated by agreement between the parties: on its first coming before me, I strongly recommended it here. But if the parties will have it decided, we must give our opinion. Compassion will not, on the one hand, nor inconvenience on the other, be to decide; but the law: in which the difficulty will be principally from the inconvenience on both sides. Contract for sale of a slave is good here; the sale is a matter to which the law properly and readily attaches, and will maintain the price according to the agreement. But here the person of the slave himself is immediately the object of enquiry; which makes a very material difference. The now question is, whether any dominion, authority or coercion can be exercised in this country, on a slave according to the American laws? The difficulty of adopting the relation, without adopting it in all its consequences, is indeed extreme; and yet, many of those consequences are absolutely contrary to the municipal law of England. We have no authority to regulate the conditions in which law shall operate. On the other hand, should we think the coercive power cannot be exercised. . . . The setting 14,000 or 15,000 men at once free loose by a solemn opinion, is much disagreeable in the effects it threatens. . . . Mr. Stewart advances no claim on contract; he rests his whole demand on a right to the negro as slave, and mentions the purpose of detainure to be the sending of him over to be sold in Jamaica. If the parties will have judgment, fiat justitia, ruat coelum, let justice be done whatever the consequence. 50 a head may not be a high price; then a loss follows to the proprietors of above 700,000£ sterling. How would the law stand with respect to their settlement; their wages? How many actions for any slight coercion by the master? We cannot in any of these points direct the law; the law must rule us. In these particulars, it may be matter of weighty consideration, what provisions are made or set by law. Mr. Stewart may end the question, by discharging or giving freedom to the negro. I did think at first to put the matter to a more solemn way of argument: but . . . I do not imagine, after the point has been discussed on both sides so extremely well, any new light could be thrown on the subject. If the parties chuse to refer it to the Common Pleas, they can give them that satisfaction whenever they think fit. An application to Parliament, if the merchants think the question of great commercial concern, is the best, and perhaps the only method of settling the point for the future. The Court is greatly obliged to the gentlemen of the Bar who have spoke on the subject; and by whose care and abilities so much has been effected, that the rule of decision will be reduced to a very easy compass. . . . I think it right the matter should stand over.

♦   ♦   ♦

[T]he only question before us is, whether the cause on the return is sufficient? If it is, the negro must be remanded; if it is not, he must be discharged. Accordingly, the return states, that the slave departed and refused to serve; whereupon he was kept, to be sold abroad. So high an act of dominion must be recognized by the law of the country where it is used. The power of a master over his slave has been extremely different, in different countries. The state of slavery is of such a nature, that it is incapable of being introduced on any reasons, moral or political; but only positive law, which preserves its force long after the reasons, occasion, and time itself from whence it was created, is erased from memory: it's so odious, that nothing can be suffered to support it, but positive law. Whatever inconveniences, therefore, may follow from a decision, I cannot say this case is allowed or approved by the law of England; and therefore the black must be discharged.

The Pennsylvania Gradual Abolition Act
1780

This far-sighted statute reflected one of the first domestic social consequences of the American Revolution. Its rhetorical preamble was not cynically self-serving, as the detailed provisions that follow for protecting the freedom of former slaves attest. However, the provisions for apprenticeship of children born to slaves approximated the cost of raising the children. The statute in its criminal law provisions also began the long and tortured progression toward equality of all races before the law.

AN ACT FOR THE GRADUAL ABOLITION OF SLAVERY

Section 1. . . . We esteem it a peculiar blessing granted to us, that we are enabled this day to add one more step to universal civilization, by removing as much as possible the sorrows of those who have lived in undeserved bondage, and from which, by the assumed authority of the kings of Great Britain, no effectual, legal relief could be obtained. Weaned by a long course of experience from those narrow prejudices and partialities we had imbibed, we find our hearts enlarged with kindness and benevolence towards men of all conditions and nations; and we conceive ourselves at this particular period extraordinarily called upon, by the blessings which we have received, to manifest the sincerity of our profession, and to give a substantial proof of our gratitude.

Sect. 2. And whereas the condition of those persons, who have heretofore been denominated Negro and Mulatto slaves, has been attended with circumstances, which not only deprived them of the common blessings that they were by nature entitled to, but has cast them into the deepest afflictions, by an unnatural separation and sale of husband and wife from each other and from their children, an injury, the greatness of which can only be conceived by supposing that we were in the same unhappy case. In justice, therefore, to persons so unhappily circumstanced, and who, having no prospect before them whereon they may rest their sorrows and their hopes, have no reasonable inducement to render their service to society, which they otherwise might, and also in grateful commemoration of our own happy deliverance from that state of unconditional submission, to which we were doomed by the tyranny of Britain.

Sect. 3. Be it enacted, . . . That all persons, as well Negroes and Mulattoes as who shall be born within this state from and after the passing of this act, shall not be deemed and considered as servants for life, or slaves; and that all servitude for life, or slavery of children, in consequence of the slavery of their mothers, in the case of all children born within this state, from and after the passing of this act as aforesaid, shall be, and hereby is utterly taken away, extinguished and for ever abolished.

Sect. 4. Provided always, and be it further enacted by the authority aforesaid, That every Negro and Mulatto child born within this state after the passing of this act as aforesaid (who would, in case this act had not been made, have been born a servant for years, or life, or a slave) shall be deemed to be and shall be by virtue of this act the servant of such person or his or her assigns, who would in such case have been entitled to the service of such child, until such child shall attain unto the age of twenty eight years, in the manner and on the conditions whereon servants bound by indenture for four years are or may be retained and holden.

♦ ♦ ♦

Sect. 7. And be it further enacted by the authority aforesaid, That the offences and crimes of Negroes and Mulattoes, as well slaves and servants as freemen, shall be enquired of, adjudged, corrected and punished in like manner as the offences and crimes of the other inhabitants of this state are and shall be enquired of, adjudged, corrected and pun- ished, and not otherwise, except that a slave shall not be admitted to bear witness against a freeman.

Massachusetts Constitution of 1780

Massachusetts abolished slavery quickly, through a combination of a constitutional provision and a judicial interpretation of that provision. In 1790 the first census found no one enslaved in the Bay State.

DECLARATION OF RIGHTS.
ARTICLE I

All men are born free and equal, and have certain natural, essential and inalienable rights, among which may be reckoned the right of enjoying and defending their lives and liberties; that of acquiring, possessing and protecting property, and in fine of seeking and obtaining their safety and happiness.

Commonwealth v. Jennison
1783

In 1781 Nathaniel Jennison was indicted "for an assault on Quack Walker, and beat with a stick 1st May, 1781, and imprisoned two hours." At the end of the trial, Chief Justice William Cushing delivered the following charge to the jury.

The defense set up in this case afforded much scope for discussion and has been fully considered. It is founded on the assumed proposition that slavery had been by law established in this province: that rights to slaves, as property, acquired by law, ought not to be divested by any construction of the Constitution by implication; and that slavery in that instrument is not expressly abolished. It is true, without investigating the right of christians to hold Africans in perpetual servitude, that they had been considered by some of the Province laws as actually existing among us; but nowhere do we find it expressly established. It was a usage, —a usage which took its origins from the practice of some of the European nations and the regulations for the benefit of trade of the British government respecting its then colonies. But whatever usages formerly prevailed or slid in upon us by the example of others on the subject, they can no longer exist. Sentiments more favorable to the natural rights of mankind, and to that innate desire for liberty which heaven, without regard to complexion or shape, has planted in the human breast—have prevailed since the—glorious struggle for our rights began. And these sentiments led the framers of our constitution of government—by which the people of this commonwealth have solemnly bound themselves to each other to declare—*that all men are born free and equal;* and that *every subject is entitled to liberty,* and to have it guarded by the laws as well as his life and property. In short, without resorting to implication in constructing the constitution, slavery is in my judgement as effectively abolished as it can be by the granting of rights and privileges wholly incompatible and repugnant to its existence. The court are therefore fully of the opinion that perpetual servitude can no longer be tolerated in our government, and that liberty can only be forfeited by some criminal conduct or relinquished by personal consent or contract. . . . The Def[endan]t must be found guilty as the facts charged are not contraverted.

Virginia Manumission Act
Laws of Virginia, 1782

Virginia took no steps to end slavery, but during the Revolution it passed the following law, which allowed masters to voluntarily free their slaves. In 1806 the legislature backed away from this law and required that manumitted slaves leave the state. Virginia would go back and forth on this issue until 1852, when the state constitution explicitly prohibited manumitted slaves from remaining in the state.

AN ACT TO AUTHORIZE THE MANUMISSION OF SLAVES

I. Whereas application hath been made to this present general assembly, that those persons who are disposed to emancipate their slaves may be empowered so to do, . . . *Be it therefore enacted,* That it shall hereafter be lawful for any person, by his or her last will and testament, or by any other instrument in writing under his or her hand and seal attested and proved in the county court by two witnesses, or acknowledged by the part in the court of the county where he or she resides, to emancipate and set free, his or her slaves, or any of them, who shall thereupon be entirely and fully discharged from the performance of any contract entered into during servitude, and enjoy as full freedom as if they had been particularly named and freed by this act.

II. *Provided always, and be it further enacted,* That all slaves so set free, not being in the judgment of the court, of sound mind and body, or being above the age of forty-five years, or being males under the age of twenty-one, or females under the age of eighteen years, shall respectively be supported and maintained by the person so liberating them, or by his or her estate; and upon neglect or refusal so to do, the court of the county where

such neglect or refusal may be, is hereby empowered . . . to order the sheriff to distrain and sell so much of the person's estate as shall be sufficient for that purpose. *Provided also,* That every person by written instrument in his life time, or if by last will and testament, the executors of every person freeing any slave, shall cause to be delivered to him or her, a copy of the instrument of emancipation, attested by the clerk of the court of the county, who shall be paid therefore, by the person emancipating, five shillings, to be collected in the manner of other clerk's fees. Every person neglecting or refusing to, deliver to any slave by him or her set free, such copy, shall forfeit and pay ten pounds, . . . It shall be lawful for any justice of the peace to commit to the gaol of his county, any emancipated slave travelling out of the county of his or her residence without a copy of the instrument of his or her emancipation, there to remain till such copy is produced and the gaoler's fees paid.

III. *And be it further enacted,* That in case any slave so liberated shall neglect in any year to pay all taxes and levies imposed or to be imposed by law, the court of the county shall order the sheriff to hire out him or her for so long time as will raise the said taxes and levies. *Provided* sufficient distress cannot be made upon his or her estate.

North Carolina Statute on Slave Murder

North Carolina's statute regulating the killing of slaves, passed in 1791, illustrates the influence of the Revolution on criminal law and notions of slavery. While not ready to end slavery or even discuss its end, North Carolinians were no longer willing to allow the cold-blooded murder of slaves.

III. And whereas by another act of Assembly passed in the year 1774, the killing a slave, however wanton, cruel and deliberate, is only punishable in the first instance by imprisonment and paying the value thereof to the owner; which distinction of criminality between the murder of a white person and of one who is equally an human creature, but merely of a different complexion, is disgraceful to humanity and degrading in the highest degree to the laws and principles of a free, christian and enlightened country: *Be it enacted by the authority aforesaid,*

That if any person shall hereafter be guilty of wilfully and maliciously killing a slave, such offender shall upon the first conviction thereof be adjudged guilty of murder, and shall suffer the same punishment as if he had killed a free man; any law, usage or custom to the contrary notwithstanding. Provided always, That this act shall not extend to any person killing a slave outlawed by virtue of any act of Assembly of this state, or to any slave in the act of resistance to his lawful owner or master, or to any slave dying under moderate correction.

THOMAS JEFFERSON ON SLAVERY
Notes on the State of Virginia
1784

Thomas Jefferson in many ways embodied the Revolution and its contradictions. In 1784 he wrote Notes on the State of Virginia. *The book was written for a French audience, to explain to his French friends what life in Virginia was like. His musings on slavery reveal much about the issue in the Revolutionary period. Jefferson wrote a long chapter about the laws of Virginia. He mentioned the possibility of a law to free all the slaves in Virginia and remove them to another country. This led him to a long discussion about slavery and society, which illustrates why Jefferson, and other southern masters with similar ideas, could not support an end to slavery.*

It will probably be asked, Why not retain and incorporate the blacks into the state, and thus save the expence of supplying, by importation of white settlers, the vacancies they will leave? Deep rooted prejudices entertained by the whites; ten thousand recollections, by the blacks, of the injuries they have sustained; new provocations; the real distinctions which nature has made; and many other circumstances, will divide us into parties, and produce convulsions which will probably never end but in the extermination of the one or the other race. —To these objections, which are political, may be added others, which are physical and moral. The first difference which strikes us is that of colour. Whether the black of the negro resides in the reticular membrane between the skin and scarf-skin, or in the scarf-skin itself; whether it proceeds from the colour of the blood, the colour of the bile, or from that of some other secretion, the difference is fixed in nature, and

is as real as if its seat and cause were better known to us. And is this difference of no importance? Is it not the foundation of a greater or less share of beauty in the two races? Are not the fine mixtures of red and white, the expressions of every passion by greater or less suffusions of colour in the one, preferable to that eternal monotony, which reigns in the countenances, that immoveable veil of black which covers all the emotions of the other race? Add to these, flowing hair, a more elegant symmetry of form, their own judgment in favour of the whites, declared by their preference of them, as uniformly as is the preference of the Oranootan for the black women over those of his own species. The circumstance of superior beauty, is thought worthy attention in the propagation of our horses, dogs, and other domestic animals; why not in that of man? Besides those of colour, figure, and hair, there are other physical distinctions proving a difference of race. They have less hair on the face and body. They secrete less by the kidnies, and more by the glands of the skin, which gives them a very strong and disagreeable odour. This greater degree of transpiration renders them more tolerant of heat, and less so of cold, than the whites. Perhaps too a difference of structure in the pulmonary apparatus, which a late ingenious experimentalist has discovered to be the principal regulator of animal heat, may have disabled them from extricating, in the act of inspiration, so much of that fluid from the outer air, or obliged them in expiration, to part with more of it. They seem to require less sleep. A black, after hard labour through the day, will be induced by the slightest amusements to sit up till midnight, or later, though knowing he must be out with the first dawn of the morning. They are at least as brave, and more adventuresome. But this may perhaps proceed from a want of forethought, which prevents their seeing a danger till it be present. When present, they do not go through it with more coolness or steadiness than the whites. They are more ardent after their female: but love seems with them to be more an eager desire, than a tender delicate mixture of sentiment and sensation. Their griefs are transient. Those numberless afflictions, which render it doubtful whether heaven has given life to us in mercy or in wrath, are less felt, and sooner forgotten with them. In general, their existence appears to participate more of sensation than reflection. To this must be ascribed their disposition to sleep when abstracted from their diversions, and unemployed in labour. An animal whose body is at rest, and who does not reflect, must be disposed to sleep of course. Comparing them by their faculties of memory, reason, and imagination, it appears to me, that in memory they are equal to the whites; in reason much inferior, as I think one could scarcely be found capable of tracing and comprehending the investigations of Euclid; and that in imagination they are dull, tasteless, and anomalous. It would be unfair to follow them to Africa for this investigation. We will consider them here, on the same stage with the whites, and where the facts are not apocryphal on which a judgment is to be formed. It will be right to make great allowances for the difference of condition, of ed-

ucation, of conversation, of the sphere in which they move. Many millions of them have been brought to, and born in America. Most of them indeed have been confined to tillage, to their own homes, and their own society: yet many have been so situated, that they might have availed themselves of the conversation of their masters; many have been brought up to the handicraft arts, and from that circumstance have always been associated with the whites. Some have been liberally educated, and all have lived in countries where the arts and sciences are cultivated to a considerable degree, and have had before their eyes samples of the best works from abroad. The Indians, with no advantages of this kind, will often carve figures on their pipes not destitute of design and merit. They will crayon out an animal, a plant, or a country, so as to prove the existence of a germ in their minds which only wants cultivation. They astonish you with strokes of the most sublime oratory; such as prove their reason and sentiment strong, their imagination glowing and elevated. But never yet could I find that a black had uttered a thought above the level of plain narration; never see even an elementary trait of painting or sculpture. In music they are more generally gifted than the whites with accurate ears for tune and time, and they have been found capable of imagining a small catch. Whether they will be equal to the composition of a more extensive run of melody, or of complicated harmony, is yet to be proved. Misery is often the parent of the most affecting touches in poetry. —Among the blacks is misery enough, God knows, but no poetry. Love is the peculiar oestrum of the poet. Their love is ardent, but it kindles the senses only, not the imagination. Religion indeed has produced a Phyllis Whately; but it could not produce a poet. The compositions published under her name are below the dignity of criticism. . . . The improvement of the blacks in body and mind, in the first instance of their mixture with the whites, has been observed by every one, and proves that their inferiority is not the effect merely of their condition of life. We know that among the Romans, about the Augustan age especially, the condition of their slaves was much more deplorable than that of the blacks on the continent of America. The two sexes were confined in separate apartments, because to raise a child cost the master more than to buy one. Cato, for a very restricted indulgence to his slaves in this particular, took from them a certain price. But in this country the slaves multiply as fast as the free inhabitants. Their situation and manners place the commerce between the two sexes almost without restraint. . . . Whether further observation will or will not verify the conjecture, that nature has been less bountiful to them in the endowments of the head, I believe that in those of the heart she will be found to have done them justice. That disposition to theft with which they have been branded, must be ascribed to their situation, and not to any depravity of the moral sense. The man, in whose favour no laws of property exist, probably feels himself less bound to respect those made in favour of others. When arguing for ourselves, we lay it down as a fundamental, that laws, to be just, must give a reciprocation of right: that, without this, they are mere arbitrary rules of conduct, founded in force, and not in conscience: and it is a problem which I give to the master to solve, whether the religious precepts against the violation of property were not framed for him as well as his slave? And whether the slave may not as justifiably take a little from one, who has taken all from him, as he may slay one who would slay him? That a change in the relations in which a man is placed should change his ideas of moral right and wrong, is neither new, nor peculiar to the colour of the blacks. Homer tells us it was so 2600 years ago. . . . But the slaves of which Homer speaks were whites. Notwithstanding these considerations which must weaken their respect for the laws of property, we find among them numerous instances of the most rigid integrity, and as many as among their better instructed masters, of benevolence, gratitude, and unshaken fidelity. —The opinion, that they are inferior in the faculties of reason and imagination, must be hazarded with great diffidence. To justify a general conclusion, requires many ob-

servations, even where the subject may be submitted to the Anatomical knife, to Optical glasses, to analysis by fire, or by solvents. How much more then where it is a faculty, not a substance, we are examining; where it eludes the research of all the senses; where the conditions of its existence are various and variously combined; where the effects of those which are present or absent bid defiance to calculation; let me add too, as a circumstance of great tenderness, where our conclusion would degrade a whole race of men from the rank in the scale of beings which their Creator may perhaps have given them. To our reproach it must be said, that though for a century and a half we have had under our eyes the races of black and of red men, they have never yet been viewed by us as subjects of natural history. I advance it therefore as a suspicion only, that the blacks, whether originally a distinct race, or made distinct by time and circumstances, are inferior to the whites in the endowments both of body and mind. It is not against experience to suppose, that different species of the same genus, or varieties of the same species, may possess different qualifications. Will not a lover of natural history then, one who views the gradations in all the races of animals with the eye of philosophy, excuse an effort to keep those in the department of man as distinct as nature has formed them? This unfortunate difference of colour, and perhaps of faculty, is a powerful obstacle to the emancipation of these people. Many of their advocates, while they wish to vindicate the liberty of human nature, are anxious also to preserve its dignity and beauty. Some of these, embarrassed by the question "What further is to be done with them?" join themselves in opposition with those who are actuated by sordid avarice only. Among the Romans emancipation required but one effort. The slave, when made free, might mix with, without staining the blood of his master. But with us a second is necessary, unknown to history. When freed, he is to be removed beyond the reach of mixture.

RELIGION

Slavery was just one social issue that complicated law in the new Republic. Religion was another. All of the colonies had supported religion in some ways and most had established churches, although in many they were weak. In some colonies there was a strong movement to fully separate church and state. Virginia began this process by statute in 1786; New York accomplished this more fully in its first constitution. But as the excerpts from the New Hampshire Constitution illustrate, some Americans saw independence as an opportunity to enforce their religious views at the expense of others.

The Virginia Statute for Religious Freedom
1786

When Thomas Jefferson composed his own epitaph, he commemorated himself for three things: the Declaration of Independence, the creation of the University of Virginia, and the authorship of this statute. Its preamble is a long-winded compendium of the author's liberal opinions. In a nation as heterogeneous as America, a disestablishment policy was necessarily the wave of the future. But religious bigotry died hard. In the 1780s Baptist ministers were whipped in Virginia for preaching without a license. At the time Jews were barred from public office in every state but New York, and Catholics were barred in more than half the states. As late as the 1820s Maryland would still bar Jews from public office, and not until after the Civil War did New Hampshire finally end its support for some churches. The Virginia act, however, was one of the most important steps in establishing religious liberty in the new nation.

AN ACT FOR ESTABLISHING RELIGIOUS FREEDOM

I. Whereas Almighty God hath created the mind free; that all attempts to influence it by temporal punishments or burthens, or by civil incapacitations, tend only to beget habits of hypocrisy and meanness; and are a departure from the plan of the Holy author of our religion, who being Lord both of body and mind, yet chose not to propagate it by coercions on either, as was in his Almighty power to do; that the impious presumption of legislators and rulers, civil as well as ecclesiastical, who being themselves but fallible and uninspired men, have assumed dominion over the faith of others, setting up their own opinions and modes of thinking as the only true and infallible, and as such endeavouring to impose upon others, hath established and maintained false religions over the greatest part of the world, and through all time; that to compel a man to furnish contributions of money for the propagation of opinions which he disbelieves, is sinful and tyrannical;

that even the forcing him to support this or that teacher of his own religious persuasion, is depriving him of the comfortable liberty of giving his contributions to the particular pastor, whose morals he would make his pattern, and whose powers he feels most persuasive to righteousness, and is withdrawing from the ministry those temporary rewards, which proceeding from an approbation of their personal conduct are an additional incitement to earnest and unremitting labours for the instruction of mankind; that our civil rights have no dependence on our religious opinions, any more than our opinions in physics and geometry; and therefore the proscribing any citizen as unworthy the public confidence by laying upon him an incapacity of being called to offices of trust and emolument, unless he profess or renounce this or that religious opinion, is depriving him injuriously of those privileges and advantages to which in common with his fellow-citizens he has a natural right; that it tends only to corrupt the principles of that religion it is meant to encourage, by bribing with a monopoly of worldly honours and emoluments, those who will externally profess and conform to it; that though indeed these are criminal who do not withstand such temptation, yet neither are those innocent who lay the bait in their way; that to suffer the civil magistrate to intrude his powers into the field of opinion, and to restrain the profession or propagation of principles on supposition of their ill tendency, is a dangerous fallacy, which at once destroys all religious liberty, because he being of course judge of that tendency will make his opinions the rule of judgment, and approve or condemn the sentiments of others only as they shall square with or differ from his own; that it is time enough for the rightful purposes of civil government, for its officers to interfere when principles break out into overt acts against peace and good order; and finally, that truth is great and will prevail if left to herself, that she is the proper and sufficient antagonist to error, and has nothing to fear from the conflict, unless by human interposition disarmed of her natural weapons, free argument and debate, errors ceasing to be dangerous when it is permitted freely to contradict them.

II. Be it enacted by the General Assembly, That no man shall be compelled to frequent or support any religious worship, place, or ministry whatsoever, nor shall be enforced, restrained, molested, or burthened in his body or goods, nor shall otherwise suffer on account of his religious opinions or belief; but that all men shall be free to profess, and by argument to maintain, their opinion in matters of religion, and that the same shall in no wise diminish, enlarge, or affect their civil capacities.

III. And though we well know that this assembly elected by the people for the ordinary purposes of legislation only, have no power to restrain the acts of succeeding assemblies, constituted with the powers equal to our own, and that therefore to declare this act to be irrevocable would be of no effect in law; yet we are free to declare, and do declare, that the rights hereby asserted are of the natural rights of mankind, and that if any act shall be hereafter passed to repeal the present, or to narrow its operation, such act will be an infringement of natural right.

New Hampshire Constitution
1784

The New Hampshire Constitution of 1784 reflected the Protestant majority's fear and perhaps even hatred of Catholics (as well as Jews and other non-Christians). The religious tests for officeholding remained in force until 1877, while the provisions for support of religion in Article VI of the Bill of Rights were incorporated in subsequent state constitutions and not amended until 1962.

PART I: THE BILL OF RIGHTS

♦ ♦ ♦

VI. As morality and piety, rightly grounded on evangelical principles, will give the best and greatest security to government, and will lay in the hearts of men the strongest obligations to due subjection; and as the knowledge of these, is most likely to be propagated through a society by the institution of the public worship of the DEITY, and of

public instruction in morality and religion; therefore, to promote those important purposes, the people of this state have a right to impower, and do hereby fully impower the legislature to authorize from time to time, the several towns, parishes, bodies-corporate, or religious societies within this state, to make adequate provision at their own expence, for the support and maintenance of public protestant teachers of piety, religion and morality:

Provided notwithstanding, That the several towns, parishes, bodies-corporate, or religious societies, shall at all times have the exclusive right of electing their own public teachers, and of contracting with them for their support and maintenance. And no person of any one particular religious sect or denomination, shall ever be compelled to pay towards the support of the teacher or teachers of another persuasion, sect or denomination.

And every denomination of christians demeaning themselves quietly, and as good subjects of the state, shall be equally under the protection of the law: and no subordination of any one sect or denomination to another, shall ever be established by law.

And nothing herein shall be understood to affect any former contracts made for the support of the ministry; but all such contracts shall remain, and be in the same state as if this constitution had not been made.

♦ ♦ ♦

XIII. No person who is conscientiously scrupulous about the lawfulness of bearing arms, shall be compelled thereto, provided he will pay an equivalent.

♦ ♦ ♦

PART II: SENATE

♦ ♦ ♦

Provided nevertheless, That no person shall be capable being elected a senator, who is not of the protestant religion.

♦ ♦ ♦

House of Representatives

. . . Every member of the house of representatives . . . shall be of the protestant religion.

♦ ♦ ♦

Executive Power: President

. . . [H]e shall be of the Protestant religion.

♦ ♦ ♦

Council

. . . The qualifications for counselors, shall be the same as those required for senators.

♦ ♦ ♦

Delegates to Congress

The delegates of this state to the Congress of the United States, shall . . . have the same qualifications, in all respects, as by this constitution are required for the president.

RELIGION AND LAW REFORM

THOMAS JEFFERSON

Notes on the State of Virginia
1784

One of the most important effects of the Revolution was its stimulation of long-standing movements for the reform of both public and private law. Thomas Jefferson was more prominent in such efforts than others, having drafted several proposed constitutions for his state and having actively participated in the enactment of statutes embodying law-reform goals, such as the 1786 Statute for Religious Freedom. In 1784, he published a conspectus of the physical and social characteristics of Virginia, Notes on the State of Virginia, *in which he summarized post-independence efforts at law reform.*

This constitution [of Virginia] was formed when we were new and unexperienced in the science of government. It was the first, too, which was formed in the whole United States.

No wonder then that time and trial have discovered very capital defects in it.

1. The majority of the men in the State,
who pay and fight for its support, are unrepre-
sented in the legislature, the roll of freeholders
entitled to vote not including generally the half
of those on the roll of the militia, or of the
tax-gatherers.

2. Among those who share the representation, the shares are very unequal. Thus the
county of Warwick, with only one hundred
fighting men, has an equal representation with
the county of Loudon, which has one thousand
seven hundred and forty-six. So that every man
in Warwick has as much influence in the government as seventeen men in Loudon.

◆ ◆ ◆

3. The senate is, by its constitution, too
homogeneous with the house of delegates. Being chosen by the same electors, at the same
time, and out of the same subjects, the choice
falls of course on men of the same description.
The purpose of establishing different houses of
legislation is to introduce the influence of different interests or different principles.

◆ ◆ ◆

4. All the powers of government, legislative, executive, and judiciary, result to the
legislative body. The concentrating [of] these
in the same hands is precisely the definition
of despotic government. It will be no allevia-
tion that these powers will be exercised by a
plurality of hands, and not by a single one.
One hundred and seventy-three despots would
surely be as oppressive as one. Let those who
doubt it turn their eyes on the republic of
Venice. As little will it avail us that they are
chosen by ourselves. An elective despotism
was not the government we fought for, but one
which should not only be founded on free
principles, but in which the powers of government should be so divided and balanced
among several bodies of magistracy, as that
no one could transcend their legal limits,
without being effectually checked and restrained by the others.

◆ ◆ ◆

5. That the ordinary legislature may alter
the constitution itself.

◆ ◆ ◆

Many of the laws which were in force during the monarchy being relative merely to that
form of government, or inculcating principles
inconsistent with republicanism, the first assembly which met after the establishment of the
common-wealth appointed a committee to revise the whole code, to reduce it into proper
form and volume, and report it to the assembly.
This work has been executed by three gentlemen, and reported; but probably will not be
taken up till a restoration of peace shall leave
to the legislature leisure to go through such a
work.

The plan of the revisal was this. The common law of England, by which is meant, that
part of the English law which was anterior to
the date of the oldest statutes extant, is made
the basis of the work. It was thought dangerous
to attempt to reduce it to a text; it was therefore left to be collected from the usual monuments of it. Necessary alterations in that, and
so much of the whole body of the British
statutes, and of acts of assembly, as were
thought proper to be retained, were digested
into one hundred and twenty-six new acts, in
which simplicity of style was aimed at, as far
as was safe. The following are the most remarkable alterations proposed:

To change the rules of descent, so as that
the lands of any person dying intestate shall be
divisible equally among all his children, or
other representatives, in equal degree.

To make slaves distributable among the
next of kin, as other movables.

To have all public expenses, whether of the
general treasury, or of a parish or county, (as
for the maintenance of the poor, building
bridges, court-houses, etc.,) supplied by assessment on the citizens, in proportion to their
property.

To hire undertakers for keeping the public
roads in repair, and indemnify individuals
through whose lands new roads shall be opened.

To define with precision the rules whereby
aliens should become citizens, and citizens
make themselves aliens.

To establish religious freedom on the broadest bottom.

To emancipate all slaves born after the passing [of] the act. [This act was never proposed or passed, indeed, as chairman of the committee to revise Virginia's laws, Jefferson had prevented this act from reaching the floor of the Virginia legislature.]

[Here follow Jefferson's extensive, ambivalent, and tortured musings on slavery and race, wherein he called for the gradual abolition of slavery in the Old Dominion, followed by the immediate expulsion of free blacks. His meditations on the inferiority of blacks, as he saw it, were anthropological yet reflected the racism universal among whites of his time.]

◆ ◆ ◆

The revised code further proposes to proportion crimes and punishments.

Pardon and privilege of clergy are proposed to be abolished; but if the verdict be against the defendant, the court in their discretion may allow a new trial. No attainder to cause a corruption of blood, or forfeiture of dower. Slaves guilty of offences punishable in others by labor, to be transported to Africa, or elsewhere, as the circumstances of the time admit, there to be continued in slavery. A rigorous regimen proposed for those condemned to labor.

Another object of the revisal is, to diffuse knowledge more generally through the mass of the people. This bill proposes to lay off every county into small districts of five or six miles square, called hundreds, and in each of them to establish a school, for teaching, reading, writing, and arithmetic. The tutor to be supported by the hundred, and every person in it entitled to send their children three years gratis, and as much longer as they please, paying for it. These schools to be under a visitor who is annually to choose the boy of best genius in the school, of those whose parents are too poor to give them further education, and to send him forward to one of the grammar schools, of which twenty are proposed to be erected in different parts of the country, for teaching, Greek, Latin, Geography, and the higher branches of numerical arithmetic. Of the boys thus sent in one year, trial is to be made at the grammar schools one or two years, and the best genius of the whole selected, and continued six years, and the residue dismissed. By this means twenty of the best geniuses will be raked from the rubbish annually, and be instructed, at the public expense, so far as the grammar schools go. At the end of six years instruction, one half are to be discontinued (from among whom the grammar schools will probably be supplied with future masters); and the other half, who are to be chosen for the superiority of their parts and disposition, are to be sent and continued three years in the study of such sciences as they shall choose, at William and Mary college, the plan of which is proposed to be enlarged, as will be hereafter explained, and extended to all the useful sciences. The ultimate result of the whole scheme of education would be the teaching all the children of the State reading, writing, and common arithmetic; turning out ten annually, of superior genius, well taught in Greek, Latin, Geography, and the higher branches of arithmetic; turning out ten others annually, of still superior parts, who, to those branches of learning, shall have added such of the sciences as their genius shall have led them to; the furnishing to the wealthier part of the people convenient schools at which their children may be educated at their own expense. The general objects of this law are to provide an education adapted to the years, to the capacity, and the condition of every one, and directed to their freedom and happiness.

REPUBLICAN NATIONAL CONSTITUTIONALISM

The first revolution in government occurred at the state level, but it was just as necessary to adapt republican principles to structuring a national government. The Articles of Confederation, ratified in 1781, provided the beginning of such a government, in the form of a federation having some attributes of national authority. Under its authority, the Confederation Congress successfully waged war, conducted diplomacy, and carried on essential govern-

mental functions, including providing government for some of the western territories under
the Northwest Ordinance. But such success did not satisfy nationalist leaders like James
Madison, Alexander Hamilton, and eventually George Washington. They ultimately sought
to replace the Confederation with a more vigorous national authority.

The Philadelphia Convention of 1787 successfully resolved many of the conflicts among
the states and sections; those that the delegates could not resolve were ignored or sidestepped.
Throughout the convention Madison kept notes, which despite it being an incomplete record
of the convention, managed to capture much of the debate there. Controversy continues,
though, on what precisely the convention did accomplish and what it left undone or fatally
compromised.

Modern historians are not the only ones skeptical of the achievements of the convention; opponents of ratification, called Antifederalists, raised an array of both serious and minor criticisms of the Constitution of 1787. Some of the critics were genuinely fearful of what
the Constitution contained, or in the case of a Bill of Rights, did not contain. Others—often
local and state politicians—simply opposed a stronger national government because they did
not like centralized power or they understood (correctly) that the Constitution might undermine their power and influence. Madison, Hamilton, and John Jay (who was not at the convention) rebutted many of these arguments brilliantly in *The Federalist Papers* of 1787 to
1788. In Number 10 Madison developed his synthesis of republican theory and federations,
while Hamilton anticipated judicial review as a consequence of the same republican theory
in Number 78.

The Articles of Confederation
1781

*America's first national Constitution was a hybrid document. It clearly established a federation
rather than a nation, and numerous provisions prevented the emergence of full nationhood, especially the "expressly delegated" clause of Article II. The Articles gave each state a single vote
in the Congress, thus leading to perpetual frustration from the larger states, which provided the
most money to the national treasury and the most men to the national army during the Revolution. The Articles could not be amended without the unanimous vote of the state legislatures—
something that almost never happened. Under the Articles the nation did defeat England and
successfully signed a peace treaty, but the nation was weak and not fully united; it was clearly
more of a league organized for defense than a true nation-state. Historians have long disputed
the Articles' prospects for evolving into a permanent national charter.*

Articles of Confederation and perpetual Union
between the states of Newhampshire, Massa-
chusetts-bay, Rhodeisland and Providence Plantations, Connecticut, New-York, New-Jersey,
Pennsylvania, Delaware, Maryland, Virginia,
North-Carolina, South-Carolina and Georgia.

◆ ◆ ◆

Article II. Each state retains its sovereignty, freedom, and independence, and every
Power, Jurisdiction and right, which is not by
the confederation expressly delegated to the
United States, in Congress assembled.

Article III. The said states hereby severally enter into a firm league of friendship with
each other, for their common defence, the se-

curity of their Liberties, and their mutual and general welfare, binding themselves to assist each other, against all force offered to, or attacks made upon them, or any of them, on account of religion, sovereignty, trade, or any other pretence whatever.

◆ ◆ ◆

Article V. For the more convenient management of the general interests of the united states, delegates shall be annually appointed in such manner as the legislature of each state shall direct, to meet in Congress on the first Monday in November, in every year, with a power reserved in each state, to recall its delegates, or any of them, at any time within the year, and to send others in their stead, for the remainder of the Year.

In determining questions in the united states in Congress assembled, each state shall have one vote.

◆ ◆ ◆

Article VIII. All charges of war, and all other expences that shall be incurred for the common defence or general welfare, and allowed by the united states in congress assembled, shall be defrayed out of a common treasury, which shall be supplied by the several states in proportion to the value of all land within each state, granted to or surveyed for any Person, as such land and the buildings and improvements thereon shall be estimated according to such mode as the united states in congress assembled, shall from time to time direct and appoint.

The Philadelphia Convention
1787

James Madison took detailed notes of the debates at the Philadelphia Convention while participating in those debates more actively than all but a handful of his colleagues. The following excerpts present the highly nationalistic Randolph Plan (actually drafted by Madison) and the ensuing debate that focused on the problem of the representation of states in the new Congress. In the course of that debate, Madison, James Wilson, and George Mason made penetrating observations on democracy, interest-group politics, and federalism.

THE RANDOLPH OR VIRGINIA PLAN
MAY 29, 1787

[Virginia Governor Edmund Randolph] then commented on the difficulty of the crisis, and the necessity of preventing the fulfillment of the prophecies of the American downfall.

He observed that in revising the federal system we ought to inquire 1. into the properties, which such a government ought to possess, 2. the defects of the confederation, 3. the danger of our situation & 4. the remedy.

I. The Character of such a government ought to secure 1. against foreign invasion: 2. against dissensions between members of the Union, or seditions in particular states: 3. to procure to the several States various blessings, of

which an isolated situation was incapable: 4. to be able to defend itself against incroachment: & 5. to be paramount to the state constitutions.

◆ ◆ ◆

II. . . . He then proceeded to enumerate the defects:

1. that the confederation produced no security against foreign invasion; congress not being permitted to prevent a war nor to support it by their own authority—Of this he cited many examples; most of which tended to shew, that they could not cause infractions of treaties or of the law of nations, to be punished: that particular states might by their conduct provoke war without control; and

that neither militia nor draughts being fit for defence on such occasions, inlistments only could be successful, and these could not be executed without money.

2. that the federal government could not check the quarrels between states, nor a rebellion in any, not having constitutional power nor means to interpose according to the exigency:

3. that there were many advantages, which the U.S. might acquire, which were not attainable under the confederation—such as a productive impost—counteraction of the commercial regulations of other nations—pushing of commerce ad libitum—etc.etc.

4. that the federal government could not defend itself against the incroachments from the states.

5. that it was not even paramount to the state constitutions, ratified, as it was in ma[n]y of the states.

III. He next reviewed the danger of our situation, appealed to the sense of the best friends of the U.S.—the prospect of anarchy from the laxity of government every where; and to other considerations.

IV. He then proceeded to the remedy; the basis of which he said must be the republican principle.

He proposed as conformable to his ideas the following resolutions, which he explained one by one. . . .

1. Resolved that the Articles of Confederation ought to be so corrected & enlarged as to accomplish the objects proposed by their institution; namely, "common defence, security of liberty, and general welfare."

2. Resolved therefore that the rights of suffrage in the National Legislature ought to be proportioned to the Quotas of contribution, or to the number of free inhabitants, as the one or the other rule may seem best in different cases.

3. Resolved that the National Legislature ought to consist of two branches.

4. Resolved that the members of the first branch of the National Legislature ought to be elected by the people of the several States every ____ for the term of ____.

◆ ◆ ◆

5. Resolved that the members of the second branch of the National Legislature ought to be elected by those of the first, out of a proper number of persons nominated by the individual Legislatures.

◆ ◆ ◆

6. Resolved that each branch ought to possess the right of originating Acts; that the National Legislature ought to be empowered to enjoy the Legislative Rights vested in Congress by the Confederation & moreover to legislate in all cases to which the separate States are incompetent, or in which the harmony of the United States may be interrupted by the exercise of individual Legislation; to negative all laws passed by the several States, contravening in the opinion of the National Legislature the articles of Union; and to call forth the force of the Union against any member of the Union failing to fulfill its duty under the articles thereof.

7. Resolved that a National Executive be instituted; to be chosen by the National Legislature for the term of ____ years, to receive punctually at stated times, a fixed compensation for the services rendered, in which no increase or diminution shall be made so as to affect the Magistracy, existing at the time of increase or diminution, and to be ineligible a second time; and that besides a general authority to execute the National laws, it ought to enjoy the Executive rights vested in Congress by the Confederation.

8. Resolved that the Executive and a convenient number of the National Judiciary, ought to compose a Council of revision with authority to examine every act of the National Legislature before it shall operate, & every act of a particular Legislature before a Negative thereon shall be final; and that the dissent of the said Council shall amount to a rejection, unless the Act of the National Legislature be again passed, or that of a particular Legislature be again negatived by ____ of the members of each branch.

9. Resolved that a National Judiciary be established to consist of one or more supreme tribunals, and of inferior tribunals to be chosen by the National Legislature, to hold their offices during good behaviour; and to receive punctu-

ally at stated times fixed compensation for their services, in which no increase or diminution shall be made so as to affect the persons actually in office at the time of such increase or diminution; that the jurisdiction of the inferior tribunals shall be to hear & determine in the first instance, and of the supreme tribunal to hear and determine in the dernier resort, all piracies & felonies on the high seas, captures from an enemy, cases in which foreigners or citizens of other States applying to such jurisdictions may be interested, or which respect the collection of the National revenue; impeachments of any National officers, and questions which may involve the national peace and harmony.

◆ ◆ ◆

Mr. Wilson. He wished for vigor in the Government, but he wished that vigorous authority to flow immediately from the legitimate source of all authority. The Government ought to possess not only first the force, but secondly the mind or sense of the people at large. The Legislature ought to be the most exact transcript of the whole Society. Representation is made necessary only because it is impossible for the people to act collectively. The opposition was to be expected he said from the Governments, not from the Citizens of the States. The latter had parted as was observed (by Mr. King) with all the necessary powers; and it was immaterial to them, by whom they were exercised, if well exercised. The State officers were to be the losers of power. The people he supposed would be rather more attached to the national Government than to the State Governments as being more important in itself, and more flattering to their pride. There is no danger of improper elections if made by large districts. Bad elections proceed from the smallness of the districts which give an opportunity to bad men to intrigue themselves into office.

◆ ◆ ◆

Colonel Mason. Under the existing Confederacy, Congress represent the States not the people of the States; their acts operate on the States, not on the individuals. The case will be changed in the new plan of Government. The people will be represented; they ought therefore to choose the Representatives. The requisites in actual representation are that the Representatives should sympathize with their constituents; should think as they think, & feel as they feel; and that for these purposes should even be residents among them. Much he said had been alleged against democratic elections. He admitted that much might be said; but it was to be considered that no Government was free from imperfections & evils; and that improper elections in many instances, were inseparable from Republican Governments. But compare these with the advantage of this Form in favor of the rights of the people, in favor of human nature. He was persuaded there was a better chance for proper elections by the people, if divided into large districts, than by the State Legislatures.

THE PATERSON OR SMALL STATES PLAN
JUNE 15, 1787

Mr. Paterson, said as he had on a former occasion given his sentiments on the plan proposed by Mr. Randolph he would now avoiding repetition as much as possible give his reasons in favor of that proposed by himself. He preferred it because it accorded 1. with the powers of the Convention, 2. with the sentiments of the people. If the confederacy was radically wrong, let us return to our States, and obtain larger powers, not assume them of ourselves.

◆ ◆ ◆

If the sovereignty of the States is to be maintained, the Representatives must be drawn immediately from the States, not from the people: and we have no power to vary the idea of equal sovereignty. The only expedient that will cure the difficulty, is that of throwing the States into Hotchpot.

◆ ◆ ◆

Mr. Wilson entered into a contrast of the principal points of the two plans so far he said as there had been time to examine the one last proposed. These points were 1. in the Virginia plan there are two & in some degree three branches in the Legislature: in the plan from N.J. there is to be a single legislature only—2.

Representation of the people at large is the basis of the one:—the State Legislatures, the pillars of the other—3. proportional representation prevails in one:—equality of suffrage in the other—4. A single Executive Magistrate is at the head of the one:—a plurality is held out in the other.—5. in the one the majority of the people of the U.S. must prevail:—in the other a minority may prevail. 6. the National Legislature is to make laws in all cases to which the separate States are incompetent &—:—in place of this Congress are to have additional power in a few cases only—7. A negative on the laws of the States:—in place of this coertion to be substituted—8. The Executive to be removable on impeachment & conviction;—in one plan: in the other to be removeable at the instance of majority of the Executives of the States—9. Revision of the laws provided for in one:—no such check in the other—10. inferior national tribunals in one:—none such in the other. 11. In the one jurisdiction of National tribunals to extend etc.—; an appellate jurisdiction only allowed in the other. 12. Here the jurisdiction is to extend to all cases affecting the National peace & harmony: there, a few cases only are marked out. 13. finally the ratification is in this way to be by the people themselves:—in that by the legislative authorities according to the thirteenth article of Confederation.

THE SLAVE TRADE DEBATE

[The delegates ultimately reconciled the issue of representation in Congress by giving the states equality in the Senate and basing representation in the House on population. This resolution was known as the Connecticut Compromise or Great Compromise. This displeased Madison, who believed that state equality in the Senate violated the basic principles of republican government. Population-based representation also raised the question of who would be counted to determine the state's population. Most Northerners argued that only free people should be counted; most Southerners wanted to count slaves as well. In the end a second compromise—the three-fifths compromise—settled this issue. The population of the states, for pur-

poses of representation, would be based on the whole number of free people plus 60 percent (three-fifths) of all slaves. Most Southerners considered this a big victory, while a number of Northerners felt it a betrayal of American principles of liberty. During one debate over the three-fifths clause, William Paterson of New Jersey sarcastically asked, "Has a man in Virga. a number of votes in proportion to the number of his slaves?" Later in the convention Gouverneur Morris, who represented Pennsylvania, bitterly complained, "When fairly explained [it] comes to this: that the inhabitant of Georgia and South Carolina who goes to the Coast of Africa, and in defiance of the most sacred laws of humanity tears away his fellow creatures from their dearest connections and damns them to the most cruel bondages, shall have more votes in a Government instituted for protection of the rights of mankind, than the Citizen of Pennsylvania or New Jersey who views with a laudable horror, so nefarious a practice." Even more than counting slaves for representation, many northern delegates objected to the clause that prohibited Congress from ending the slave trade before 1808. The following excerpt from that debate reveals the intensity on both sides of this issue. Ultimately Congress would ban the African trade, but not before South Carolina and Georgia imported about 100,000 new slaves to the United States. It is worth noting that this debate, unlike the debate over counting slaves, was not entirely sectional. Virginian opposed the slave trade, while the Connecticut delegation supported the South Carolinians.]

August 21, 1787

Mr. L—Martin [Md.], proposed . . . a prohibition or tax on the importation of slaves.

1. As five slaves are to be counted as 3 free men in the apportionment of Representatives; such a clause wd. leave an encouragement to this trafic. 2 slaves weakened one part of the Union which the other parts were bound to protect: the privilege of importing them was therefore unreasonable. . . .

3. it was inconsistent with the principles of the revolution and dishonorable to the American character to have such a feature in the Constitution.

Mr. Rutlidge [S.C.] did not see how the importation of slaves could be encouraged by this section. He was not apprehensive of insurrections and would readily exempt the other States from (the obligation to protect the Southern against them). . . . Religion & humanity had nothing to do with this question. . . . Interest alone is the governing principle with Nations. . . . The true question at present is whether the Southn. States shall or shall not be parties to the Union. If the Northern States consult their interest, they will not oppose the increase of Slaves which will increase the commodities of which they will become the carriers.

Mr. Elseworth [Conn.] was for leaving the clause as it stands. Let every State import what it pleases. The morality or wisdom of slavery are considerations belonging to the States themselves. . . . What enriches a part enriches the whole, and the States are the best judges of their particular interest. The old confederation had not meddled with this point, and he did not see any greater necessity for bringing it within the policy of the new one:

Mr. Pinkney [S.C.]. South Carolina can never receive the plan if it prohibits the slave trade. In every proposed extension of the powers of Congress, that State has expressly & watchfully excepted that of meddling with the importation of negroes. If the States be all left at liberty on this subject, S. Carolina may perhaps by degrees do of herself what is wished, as Virginia & Maryland have already done.

◆ ◆ ◆

Wednesday August 22

. . . Mr. Sherman [Conn.] was for leaving the clause as it stands. He disapproved of the slave trade: yet as the States were now possessed of the right to import slaves, as the public good did not require it to be taken from them, & as it was expedient to have as few objections as possible to the proposed scheme of Government, he thought it best to leave the matter as we find it. He observed that he abolition of slavery seemed to be going on in the U.S. & that the good sense of the several States would probably by degrees compleat it. He urged on the

Convention the necessity of despatch(ing its business.)

Col. Mason [Va.]. This infernal trafic originated in the avarice of British Merchants. The British Govt. constantly checked the attempts of Virginia to put a stop to it. The psent question concerns not the importing States alone but the whole Union. The evil of having slaves was experienced during the late war. Had slaves been treated as they might have been by the Enemy, they would have proved dangerous instruments in their hands. But their folly dealt by the slaves, as it did by the Tories. He mentioned the dangerous insurrections of the slaves in Greece and Sicily; and the instructions given by Cromwell to the Commissioners sent to Virginia, to arm the servants & slaves, in case other means of obtaining its submission should fail. Maryland & Virginia he said had already prohibited the importation of slaves expressly. N. Carolina had done the same in substance. All this would be in vain if S. Carolina & Georgia be at liberty to import. The Western people are already calling out for slaves for their new lands; and will fill that Country with slaves if they can be got thro' S. Carolina & Georgia. Slavery discourages arts & manufactures. The poor despise labor when performed by slaves. They prevent the immigration of Whites, who really enrich & strengthen a Country. They produce the most pernicious effect on manners. Every master of slaves is born a petty tyrant. They bring the judgment of heaven on a Country. As nations can not be rewarded or punished in the next world they must be in this. By an inevitable chain of causes & effects providence punishes national sins, by national calamities. He lamented that some of our Eastern brethren had from a lust of gain embarked in this nefarious traffic. As to the States being in possession of the Right to import, this was the case with many other rights, now to be properly given up. He held it essential in every point of view, that the Genl. Govt. should have power to prevent the increase of slavery.

Mr. Elsworth [Conn.]. As he had never owned a slave could not judge of the effects of slavery on character. He said however that if it was to be considered in a moral light we ought to go farther and free those already in the Country. . . . As slaves also multiply so fast in Virginia & Maryland that it is cheaper to raise than import them, whilst in the sickly rice swamps foreign supplies are necessary, if we go no farther than is urged, we shall be unjust towards S. Carolina & Georgia. . . . Let us not intermeddle. As population increases; poor laborers will be so plenty as to render slaves useless. Slavery in time will not be a speck in our Country. Provision is already made in Connecticut for abolishing it. And the abolition has already taken place in Massachusetts. As to the danger of insurrections from foreign influence, that will become a motive to kind treatment of the slaves.

Mr. [Charles] Pinkney [S.C.] . . . If slavery be wrong, it is justified by the example of all the world. He cited the case of Greece Rome & other antient States; the sanction given by France England, Holland & other modern States. In all ages one half of mankind have been slaves. If the S. States were let alone they will probably of themselves stop importations. He wd. himself as a Citizen of S. Carolina vote for it. An attempt to take away the right as proposed will produce serious objections to the Constitution which he wished to see adopted.

General [Charles Cotesworth] Pinkney declared it to be his firm opinion that if himself & all his colleagues were to sign the Constitution & use their personal influence, it would be of no avail towards obtaining the assent of their Constituents. S. Carolina & Georgia cannot do without slaves. As to Virginia she will gain by stopping the importations. Her slaves will rise in value, & she has more than she wants. It would be unequal to require S.C. & Georgia to confederate on such unequal terms. He said the Royal assent before the Revolution had never been refused to S. Carolina as to Virginia. He contended that the importation of slaves would be for the interest of the whole Union. The more slaves, the more produce to employ the carrying trade; The more consumption also, and the more of this, the more of revenue for the common treasury. He admitted it to be reasonable that slaves should be dutied like other imports, but should consider a rejection of the clause as an exclusion of S. Carola from the Union.

Mr. Baldwin [Ga.] had conceived national objects alone to be before the Convention, not such as like the present were of a local nature. Georgia was decided on this point. That State has always hitherto supposed a Genl Governmt to be the pursuit of the central States who wished to have a vortex for every thing . . . that her distance would preclude her from equal advantage . . . & that she could not prudently purchase it by yielding national powers. From this it might be understood in what light she would view an attempt to abridge one of her favorite prerogatives. If left to herself, she may probably put a stop to the evil. As one ground for this conjecture, he took notice of the sect of which he said was a respectable class of people, who carryed their ethics beyond the mere equality of men, extending their humanity to the claims of the whole animal creation.

Mr. Wilson [Pa.] observed that if S.C. & Georgia were themselves disposed to get rid of the importation of slaves in a short time as had been suggested, they would never refuse to Unite because the importation might be prohibited. As the Section now stands all articles imported are to be taxed. Slaves alone are exempt. This is in fact a bounty on that article.

Mr. Gerry [Mass.] thought we had nothing to do with the conduct of the States as to Slaves, but ought to be careful not to give any sanction to it.

Mr. Dickenson [Del.] considered it as inadmissible on every principle of honor & safety that the importation of slaves should be authorized to the States by the Constitution. The true question was whether the national happiness would be promoted or impeded by the importation, and this question ought to be left to the National Govt. not to the States particularly interested. If Engd. & France permit slavery, slaves are at the same time excluded from both those Kingdoms. Greece and Rome were made unhappy by their slaves. He could not believe that the Southn. States would refuse to confederate on the account apprehended; especially as the power was not likely to be immediately exercised by the Genl. Government.

Mr. Williamson [N.C.] stated the law of N. Carolina on the subject to wit that it did not directly prohibit the importation of slaves. It imposed a duty of lb 5. on each slave imported from Africa. lb 10. on each from elsewhere, & lb 50 on each from a State licensing manumission. He thought the S. States could not be members of the Union if the clause should be rejected, and that it was wrong to force any thing down, not absolutely necessary, and which any State must disagree to.

Mr. King [Mass.] thought the subject should be considered in a political light only. If two States will not agree to the Constitution as stated on one side, he could affirm with equal belief on the other, that great & equal opposition would be experienced from the other States. He remarked on the exemption of slaves from duty whilst every other import was subjected to it, as an inequality that could not fail to strike the commercial sagacity of the Northn. & middle States.

Mr. Langdon [N.H.] was strenuous for giving the power to the Genl. Govt. He cd. not with a good conscience leave it with the States who could then go on with the traffic, without being restrained by the opinions here given that they will themselves cease to import slaves.

Genl. Pinkney [S.C.] thought himself bound to declare candidly that he did not think S. Carolina would stop her importations of slaves in any short time, but only stop them occasionally as she now does. He moved to commit the clause that slaves might be made liable to an equal tax with other imports which he he thought right & wch. wd. remove one difficulty that had been started.

Mr. Rutledge [S.C.]. If the Convention thinks that N.C; S.C. & Georgia will ever agree to the plan, unless their right to import slaves

be untouched, the expectation is vain. The people of those States will never be such fools as to give up so important an interest. . . .

Mr. Govr. Morris [Pa.] wished the whole subject to be committed including the clauses relating to taxes on exports & to a navigation act. These things may form a bargain among the Northern & Southern States.

Mr. Butler [S.C.] declared that he never would agree to the power of taxing exports.

Mr. Sherman [Conn.] said it was better to let the S. States import slaves than to part with them, if they made that a sine qua non. He was opposed to a tax on slaves imported as making the matter worse, because it implied they were property. He acknowledged that if the power of prohibiting the importation should be given to the Genl. Government that it would be exercised. He thought it would be its duty to exercise the power.

Mr. Read [Del.] was for the commitment provided the clause concerning taxes on exports should also be committed.

Mr. Sherman [Conn.] observed that that clause had been agreed to & therefore could not committed.

Mr. Randolph [Va.] was for committing in order that some middle ground might, if possible, be found. He could never agree to the clause as it stands. He wd. sooner risk the constitution—He dwelt on the dilemma to which the Convention was exposed. By agreeing to the clause, it would revolt the Quakers, the Methodists, and many others in the States having no slaves. On the other hand, two States might be lost to the Union. Let us then, he said, try the chance of a commitment.

Debating the Constitution

After it was written, the Constitution was sent to the states for their approval. Supporters of the Constitution were known as "Federalists" and the opponents were known as "Antifederalists." Had the Constitution been voted up or down immediately after the convention, it would probably have failed. But in the nine months following the convention, the Federalists outmaneuvered and outargued their opponents. The debates on both sides were rich and varied. What follows is just a brief sample of the arguments for and against the Constitution.

Antifederalist Critiques of the Constitution:
Elbridge Gerry's Report on the Constitution
as Printed in *Massachusetts Centinel*
November 3, 1787

Although a Massachusetts delegate to the Philadelphia Convention and an advocate of a strong national government there, Elbridge Gerry, a republican Patriot and statesman of the Confederation Congress, eventually opposed ratification on the grounds that the document subordinated the states. Such inconsistency was characteristic of Gerry's later career, but the views expressed in the following report faithfully express and recapitulate one strand of Antifederalist thought.

New-York, 18th October, 1787.

Gentlemen,

I have the honour to inclose, pursuant to my commission, the constitution proposed by the federal Convention.

To this system I gave my dissent, and shall submit my objections to the honourable Legislature.

It was painful for me, on a subject of such national importance, to differ from the respectable members who signed the constitution: But conceiving as I did, that the liberties of America were not secured by the system, it was my duty to oppose it.—

My principal objections to the plan, are, that there is no adequate provision for a representation of the people—that they have no security for the right of election—that some of the powers of the Legislature are ambiguous, and others indefinite and dangerous—that the Executive is blended with and will have undue influence over the Legislature—that the judicial department will be oppressive—that treaties of the highest importance may be formed by the President with the advice of two thirds of a quorum of the Senate—and that the system is without security of a bill of rights. These are objections which are not local, but apply equally to all the States.

As the Convention was called for "the sole and express purpose of revising the Articles of Confederation, and reporting to Congress and the several Legislatures such alterations and provisions as shall render the Federal Constitu-

tion adequate to the exigencies of government and the preservation of the union," I did not conceive that these powers extended to the formation of the plan proposed, but the Convention being of a different opinion, I acquiesced in it, being fully convinced that to preserve the union, an efficient government was indispensibly necessary: and that it would be difficult to make proper amendments to the articles of Confederation.

The Constitution proposed has few, if any federal features, but is rather a system of national government: Nevertheless, in many respects I think it has great merit, and by proper amendments, may be adapted to the "exigencies of government," and preservation of liberty.

The question on this plan involves others of the highest importance—1st. Whether there shall be a dissolution of the federal government? 2dly. Whether the several State Governments shall be so altered, as in effect to be dissolved? and 3dly, Whether in lieu of the federal and State Governments, the national Constitution now proposed shall be substituted without amendment? Never perhaps were a people called on to decide a question of greater magnitude—Should the citizens of America adopt the plan as it now stands, their liberties may be lost: Or should they reject it altogether Anarchy may ensue. It is evident therefore, that they should not be precipitate in their decisions; that the subject should be well understood, lest they should refuse to support the government, after having hastily accepted it.

If those who are in favor of the Constitution, as well as those who are against it, should preserve moderation, their discussions may afford much information and finally direct to an happy issue.

It may be urged by some, that an implicit confidence should be placed in the Convention: But, however respectable the members may be who signed the Constitution, it must be admitted, that a free people are the proper guardians of their rights and liberties—that the greatest men may err—and that their errours are sometimes, of the greatest magnitude.

Others may suppose, that the Constitution may be safely adopted, because therein provision is made to amend it: But cannot this object be better attained before a ratification, than after it? And should a free people adopt a form of Government, under conviction that it wants amendment?

And some may conceive, that if the plan is not accepted by the people, they will not unite in another: But surely whilst they have the power to amend, they are not under the necessity of rejecting it.

♦ ♦ ♦

I shall only add, that as the welfare of the union requires a better Constitution than the Confederation, I shall think it my duty as a citizen of Massachusetts, to support that which shall be finally adopted, sincerely hoping it will secure the liberty and happiness of America. . . .

E. Gerry

Federalist, Number 10
1787

James Madison's first contribution as "Publius" is the most frequently quoted of the Federalist essays. It is a masterly summation of the premises of what has come to be called, in the twentieth century, interest-group pluralism. It also presented the heart of modern "liberal" (as contrasted with "republican") thought. Madison used the contrast between republics and democracies to great effect.

Among the numerous advantages promised by a well constructed Union, none deserve to be more accurately developed than its tendency to break and control the violence of faction. The friend of popular governments, never finds himself so much alarmed for their character and fate, as when he contemplates their propensity to this dangerous vice. He will not fail therefore to set a due value on any plan which, without violating the principles to which he is attached, provides a proper cure to it. The instability, injustice and confusion introduced into the public councils, have in truth been the mortal diseases under which popular governments have every where perished; as they continue to be the favorite and fruitful topics from which the adversaries to liberty derive their most specious declamations. The valuable improvements made by the American Constitu-

tions on the popular models, both ancient and modern, cannot certainly be too much admired; but it would be an unwarrantable partiality, to contend that they have as effectually obviated the danger on this side as was wished and expected. Complaints are every where heard from our most considerate and virtuous citizens, equally the friends of public and private faith, and of public and personal liberty; that our governments are too unstable; that the public good is disregarded in the conflicts of rival parties; and that measures are too often decided, not according to the rules of justice, and the rights of the minor party; but by the superior force of an interested and over-bearing majority. However anxiously we may wish that these complaints had no foundation, the evidence of known facts will not permit us to deny that they are in some degree true. It will be found indeed, on a candid review of our situation, that some of the distresses under which we labor, have been erroneously charged on the operation of our governments; but it will be found, at the same time, that other causes will not alone account for many of our heaviest misfortunes; and particularly, for the prevailing and increasing distrust of public engagements, and alarm for private rights, which are echoed from one end of the continent to the other. These must be chiefly, if not wholly, effects of the unsteadiness and injustice, with which a factious spirit has tainted our public administrations.

By a faction I understand a number of citizens, whether amounting to a majority or minority of the whole, who are united and actuated by some common impulse of passion, or of interest, adverse to the rights of other citizens, or to the permanent and aggregate interest of the community.

◆ ◆ ◆

As long as the reason of man continues fallible, and he is at liberty to exercise it, different opinions will be formed. As long as the connection subsists between his reason and his self-love, his opinions and passions will have a reciprocal influence on each other; and the former will be objects to which the latter will attach themselves. The diversity in the faculties of men from which the rights of property originate, is not less an insuperable obstacle to a uniformity of interests. The protection of these faculties is the first object of Government. From the protection of different and unequal faculties of acquiring property, the possession of different degrees and kinds of property immediately results; and from the influence of these on the sentiments and views of the respective proprietors, ensues a division of the society into different interests and parties.

The latent causes of faction are thus sown in the nature of man; and we see them every where brought into different degrees of activity, according to the different circumstances of civil society. A zeal for different opinions concerning religion, concerning Government and many other points, as well of speculation as of practice; and attachment to different leaders ambitiously contending for pre-eminence and power; or to persons of other descriptions whose fortunes have been interesting to the human passions, have in turn divided mankind into parties, inflamed them with mutual animosity, and rendered them much more disposed to vex and oppress each other, than to co-operate for their common good. So strong is this propensity of mankind to fall into mutual animosities, that where no substantial occasion presents itself, the most frivolous and fanciful distinctions have been sufficient to kindle their unfriendly passions, and excite their most violent conflicts. But the most common and durable source of factions, has been the various and unequal distribution of property. Those who hold, and those who are without property, have ever formed distinct interests in society. Those who are creditors, and those who are debtors, fall under a like discrimination. A landed interest, a manufacturing interest, a mercantile interest, a monied interest, with many lesser interests, grow up of necessity in civilized nations, and divide them into different classes, actuated by different sentiments and views. The regulation of these various and interfering interests forms the principal task of modern Legislation, and involves the spirit of party and faction in the necessary and ordinary operations of Government.

◆ ◆ ◆

The inference to which we are brought, is, that the causes of faction cannot be removed; and that relief is only to be sought in the means of controlling its effects.

If a faction consists of less than a majority, relief is supplied by the republican principle, which enables the majority to defeat its sinister views by regular vote: It may clog the administration, it may convulse the society; but it will be unable to execute and mask its violence under the forms of the Constitution. When a majority is included in a faction, the form of popular government on the other hand enables it to sacrifice to its ruling passion or interest, both the public good and the rights of other citizens. To secure the public good, and private rights, against the danger of such a faction, and at the same time to preserve the spirit and the form of popular government, is then the great object to which our enquiries are directed: Let me add that it is the great desideratum, by which alone this form of government can be rescued from the opprobrium under which it has so long labored, and be recommended to the esteem and adoption of mankind.

By what means is this object attainable? Evidently by one of two only. Either the existence of the same passion or interest in a majority at the same time, must be prevented; or the majority, having such co-existent passion or interest, must be rendered, by their number and local situation, unable to concert and carry into effect schemes of oppression. If the impulse and the opportunity be suffered to coincide, we well know that neither moral nor religious motives can be relied on as an adequate control. They are not found to be such on the injustice and violence of individuals, and lose their efficacy in proportion to the number combined together; that is, in proportion as their efficacy becomes needful.

From this view of the subject, it may be concluded, that a pure Democracy, by which I mean, a Society, consisting of a small number of citizens, who assemble and administer the Government in person, can admit of no cure for the mischiefs of faction. A common passion or interest will, in almost every case, be felt by a majority of the whole; a communication and concert results from the form of Government itself; and there is nothing to check the inducements to sacrifice the weaker party, or an obnoxious individual. Hence it is, that such Democracies have ever been spectacles of turbulence and contention; have ever been found incompatible with personal security, or the rights of property; and have in general been as short in their lives, as they have been violent in their deaths. Theoretic politicians, who have patronized this species of Government, have erroneously supposed, that by reducing mankind to a perfect equality in their political rights, they would, at the same time, be perfectly equalized and assimilated in their possessions, their opinions, and their passions.

A Republic, by which I mean a Government in which the scheme of representation takes place, opens a different prospect, and promises the cure for which we are seeking. Let us examine the points in which it varies from pure Democracy, and we shall comprehend both the nature of the cure, and the efficacy which it must derive from the Union.

The two great points of difference between a Democracy and a Republic are, first, the delegation of the Government, in the latter, to a small number of citizens elected by the rest: secondly, the greater number of citizens, and greater sphere of country, over which the latter may be extended.

The effect of the first difference is, on the one hand to refine and enlarge the public views, by passing them through the medium of a chosen body of citizens, whose wisdom may best discern the true interest of their country, and whose patriotism and love of justice, will be least likely to sacrifice it to temporary or partial considerations. Under such a regulation, it may well happen that the public voice pronounced by the representatives of the people, will be more consonant to the public good, than if pronounced by the people themselves convened for the purpose. On the other hand, the effect may be inverted. Men of factious tempers, of local prejudices, or of sinister designs, may by intrigue, by corruption or by other means, first obtain the suffrages, and then betray the interests of the people. The question resulting is, whether small or extensive Republics are most favorable to the election of proper guardians of the public weal: and it is clearly decided in favor of the latter by two obvious considerations.

In the first place it is to be remarked that however small the Republic may be, the Representatives must be raised to a certain number, in order to guard against the cabals of a few; and that however large it may be, they must be limited to a certain number, in order to guard against the confusion of a multitude. Hence the number of Representatives in the two cases, not being in proportion to that of the Constituents, and being proportionally greatest in the small Republic, it follows, that if the proportion of fit characters, be not less, in the large than in the small Republic, the former will present a greater option, and consequently a greater possibility of a fit choice.

In the next place, as each Representative

will be chosen by a greater number of citizens in the large than in the small Republic, it will be more difficult for unworthy candidates to practise with success the vicious arts, by which elections are too often carried; and the suffrages of the people being more free, will be more likely to centre on men who possess the most attractive merit, and the most diffusive and established characters.

◆ ◆ ◆

The other point of difference is, the greater number of citizens and extent of territory which may be brought within the compass of Republican, than of Democratic Government; and it is this circumstance principally which renders factious combinations less to be dreaded in the former, than in the latter. The smaller the society, the fewer probably will be the distinct parties and interests composing it; the fewer the distinct parties and interests, the more frequently will a majority be found of the same party; and the smaller the number of individuals composing a majority, and the smaller the compass within which they are placed, the more easily will they concert and execute their plans of oppression. Extend the sphere, and you take in a greater variety of parties and interests; you make it less probable that a majority of the whole will have a common motive to invade the rights of other citizens; or if such a common motive exists, it will be more difficult for all who feel it to discover their own strength, and to act in unison with each other.

Federalist, **Number 78**
1788

Number 78 is the first of Alexander Hamilton's great essays on the judiciary. Here he candidly laid out a defense of judicial review, an extraordinarily bold move at the time. Judicial review had been broached in a few states by 1788, but it was nowhere widely accepted as legitimate or desirable. Hamilton, unlike Madison, had the gift of writing aphoristically, and this essay contains some of his most memorable phrases.

According to the plan of the convention, all the judges who may be appointed by the United States are to hold their offices during good behaviour, which is conformable to the most approved of the state constitutions; and among the rest, to that of this state. Its propriety having been drawn into question by the adversaries of that plan, is no light symptom of the rage for objection which disorders their imaginations and judgments. The standard of good behaviour for the continuance in office of the judicial magistracy is certainly one of the most valuable of the modem improvements in the practice of government. In a monarchy it is an excellent barrier to the depotism of the prince: In a republic it is a no less excellent barrier to the encroachments and oppressions of the representative body. And it is the best expedient which can be devised in any government, to secure a steady, upright and impartial administration of the laws.

Whoever attentively considers the different departments of power must perceive, that in a government in which they are separated from each other, the judiciary, from the nature of its functions, will always be the least dangerous to the political rights of the constitution; because it will be least in a capacity to annoy or injure them. The executive not only dispenses the honors, but holds the sword of the community. The legislature not only commands the purse, but prescribes the rules by which the duties and rights of every citizen are to be regulated. The judiciary on the contrary has no influence over either the sword or the purse, no direction either of the strength or of the wealth of the society, and can take no active resolution whatever. It may truly be said to have neither Force nor Will, but merely judgment; and must ultimately depend upon the aid of the executive arm even for the efficacy of its judgments.

This simple view of the matter suggests several important consequences. It proves incontestibly that the judiciary is beyond comparison the weakest of the three departments of power; that it can never attack with success either of the other two; and that all possible care is requisite to enable it to defend itself against their attacks. It equally proves, that though individual oppression may now and then proceed from the courts of justice, the general liberty of the people can never be endangered from that quarter: I mean, so long as the judiciary remains truly distinct from both the legislative and executive. For I agree that "there is no liberty, if the power of judging be not separated from the legislative and executive powers." And it proves, in the last place, that as liberty can have nothing to fear from the judiciary alone, but would have everything to fear from its union with either of the other departments; that as all the effects of such an union must ensue from a dependence of the former on the latter, notwithstanding a nominal and apparent separation; that as from the natural feebleness of the judiciary, it is in continual jeopardy of being overpowered, awed or influenced by its coordinate branches; and that as nothing can contribute so much to its firmness and independence, as permanency in office, this quality may therefore be justly regarded as an indispensable ingredient in its constitution; and in a great measure as the citadel of the public justice and the public security.

The complete independence of the courts of justice is peculiarly essential in a limited constitution. By a limited constitution I understand one which contains certain specified exceptions to the legislative authority; such for instance as that it shall pass no bills of attainder, no ex post facto laws, and the like. Limitations of this kind can be preserved in practice no other way than through the medium of the courts of justice; whose duty it must be to declare all acts contrary to the manifest tenor of the constitution void. Without this, all the reservations of particular rights or privileges would amount to nothing.

Some perplexity respecting the right of the courts to pronounce legislative acts void, because contrary to the constitution, has arisen from an imagination that the doctrine would imply a superiority of the judiciary to the legislative power. It is urged that the authority which can declare the acts of another void, must necessarily be superior to the one whose acts may be declared void. As this doctrine is of great importance in all the American constitutions, a brief discussion of the grounds on which it rests cannot be unacceptable.

There is no position which depends on clearer principles, than that every act of a delegated authority, contrary to the tenor of the commission under which it is exercised, is void. No legislative act therefore contrary to the constitution can be valid. To deny this would be to affirm that the deputy is greater than his principal; that the servant is above his master; that the representatives of the people are superior to the people themselves; that men acting by virtue of powers may do not only what their powers do not authorise, but what they forbid.

If it be said that the legislative body are themselves the constitutional judges of their own powers, and that the construction they put upon them is conclusive upon the other departments, it may be answered, that this cannot be the natural presumption, where it is not to be collected from any particular provisions in the constitution. It is not otherwise to be supposed that the constitution could intend to enable the representatives of the people to substitute their will to that of their constituents. It is far more rational to suppose that the courts were designed to be an intermediate body between the people and the legislature, in order, among other things, to keep the latter within the limits assigned to their authority. The interpretation of the laws is the proper and peculiar province of the courts. A constitution is in fact, and must be, regarded by the judges as a fundamental law. It therefore belongs to them to ascertain its meaning as well as the meaning of any particular act proceeding from the legislative body. If there should happen to be an irreconcileable variance between the two, that which has the superior obligation and validity ought of course to be preferred; or in other words, the constitution ought to be preferred to the statute, the intention of the people to the intention of their agents.

Nor does this conclusion by any means suppose a superiority of the judicial to the legislative power. It only supposes that the power of the people is superior to both; and that where the will of the legislature declared in its statutes, stands in opposition to that of the people declared in the constitution, the judges ought to be governed by the latter, rather than the former. They ought to regulate their decisions by the fundamental laws, rather than by those which are not fundamental.

This exercise of judicial discretion in determining between two contradictory laws, is exemplified in a familiar instance. It not uncommonly happens, that there are two statutes existing at one time, clashing in whole or in part with each other, and neither of them containing any repealing clause or expression. In such a case, it is the province of the courts to liquidate and fix their meaning and operation; so far as they can by any fair construction be reconciled to each other; reason and law conspire to dictate that this should be done. Where this is impracticable, it becomes a matter of necessity to give effect to one, in exclusion of the other. The rule which has obtained in the courts for determining their relative validity is that the last in order of time shall be preferred to the first. But this is mere rule of construction, not derived from any positive law, but from the nature and reason of the thing. It is a rule not enjoined upon the courts by legislative provision, but adopted by themselves, as consonant to truth and propriety, for the direction of their conduct as interpreters of the law. They thought it reasonable, that between the interfering acts of an equal authority, that which was the last indication of its will, should have the preference.

But in regard to the interfering acts of a superior and subordinate authority, of an original and derivative power, the nature and reason of the thing indicate the converse of that rule as proper to be followed. They teach us that the prior act of a superior ought to be preferred to the subsequent act of an inferior and subordinate authority; and that, accordingly, whenever a particular statute contravenes the constitution,

it will be the duty of the judicial tribunals to adhere to the latter, and disregard the former.

It can be of no weight to say, that the courts on the pretense of a repugnancy, may substitute their own pleasure to the constitutional intentions of the legislature. This might as well happen in the case of two contradictory statutes; or it might as well happen in every adjudication upon any single statute. The courts must declare the sense of the law; and if they should be disposed to exercise will instead of judgment, the consequence would equally be the substitution of their pleasure to that of the legislative body. The observation, if it proved anything, would prove that there ought to be no judges distinct from that body.

If then the courts of justice are to be considered as the bulwarks of a limited constitution against legislative encroachments, this consideration will afford a strong argument for the permanent tenure of judicial offices, since nothing will contribute so much as this to that independent spirit in the judges, which must be essential to the faithful performance of so arduous a duty.

This independence of the judges is equally requisite to guard the constitution and the rights of individuals from the effects of those ill humours which the arts of designing men, or the influence of particular conjunctures, sometimes disseminate among the people themselves, and which, though they speedily give place to better information and more deliberate reflection, have a tendency in the mean time to occasion dangerous innovations in the government, and serious oppressions of the minor party in the community. Though I trust the friends of the proposed constitution will never concur with its enemies in questioning that fundamental principle of republican government, which admits the right of people to alter or abolish the established constitution whenever they find it inconsistent with their happiness; yet it is not to be inferred from this principle, that the representatives of the people, whenever a momentary inclination happens to lay hold of a majority of their constituents incompatible with the provisions in the existing constitution, would on that account be justifiable in a violation of those provisions; or that the courts would be under a greater obligation to connive at infractions in this shape, than when they had proceeded wholly from the cabals of the representative body. Until the people have by some solemn and authoritative act annulled or changed the established form, it is binding upon themselves collectively, as well as individually; and no presumption, or even knowledge of their sentiments, can warrant their representatives in a departure from it, prior to such an act.

The Northwest Ordinance
1787

While the delegates met in Philadelphia, the Confederation Congress passed its most significant piece of legislation: the Northwest Ordinance. The ordinance led to the settlement of the Northwest and eventually the creation of the present-day states of Ohio, Indiana, Illinois, Michigan, Wisconsin, and part of Minnesota. The ordinance set the stage for the national government selling large tracts of land, which helped stabilize the nation's finances and led to a smoother transition from the Confederation government to the government under the Constitution. The ordinance rejected the policy of colonial status for American territories, laying the basis for equality of status among all the American states. It also projected principles of liberal government into the new territories and excluded slavery north of the Ohio River. After the Constitution went into effect, the new Congress reaffirmed the validity of the ordinance.

Sec. 5. The governor and judges, or a majority of them, shall adopt and publish in the district such laws of the original States, criminal and civil, as may be necessary, and best suited to the circumstances of the district, and report them to Congress from time to time, which laws shall be in force in the district until the organization of the general assembly therein, unless disapproved of by Congress; but afterwards the legislature shall have authority to alter them as they shall think fit.

♦ ♦ ♦

Sec. 9. So soon as there shall be five thousand free male inhabitants, of full age, in the district, upon giving proof thereof to the governor, they shall receive authority, with time and place, to elect representatives from their counties and townships, to represent them in the general assembly: Provided, That for every five hundred free male inhabitants there shall be one representative, and so on, progressively, with the number of free male inhabitants, shall the right of representation increase, until the number of representatives shall amount to twenty-five; after which the number and proportion of representatives shall be regulated by the legislature.

♦ ♦ ♦

Sec. 13. And for extending the fundamental principles of civil and religious liberty, which form the basis whereon these republics, their laws and constitutions, are erected; to fix and establish those principles as the basis of all laws, constitutions, and governments, which forever hereafter shall be formed in the said territory; to provide, also, for the establishment of States, and permanent government therein, and for their admission to a share in the Federal councils on an equal footing with the original States, at as early periods as may be consistent with the general interest:

Sec. 14. It is hereby ordained and declared, by the authority aforesaid, that the following articles shall be considered as articles of compact, between the original States and the people and States in the said territory, and forever remain unalterable, unless by common consent, to wit:

ARTICLE I

No person, demeaning himself in a peaceable and orderly manner, shall ever be molested on account of his mode of worship, or religious sentiments, in the said territory.

ARTICLE II

The inhabitants of the said territory shall always be entitled to the benefits of the writs of habeas corpus, and of the trial by jury; of a proportionate representation of the people in the legislature, and of judicial proceedings according to the course of the common law. All persons shall be bailable, unless for capital offences, where the proof shall be evident, or the presumption great. All fines shall be moderate; and no cruel or unusual punishment shall be inflicted. No man shall be deprived of his liberty or property, but by the judgment of his peers, or the law of the land, and should the public exigencies make it necessary, for the common preservation, to take any person's property, or to demand his particular services, full compensation shall be made for the same. And, in the just preservation of rights and property, it is understood and declared, that no law ought ever to be made or have force in the said territory, that shall, in any manner whatever, interfere with or affect private contracts, or engage-

ments, bona fide, and without fraud previously formed.

ARTICLE III

Religion, morality, and knowledge being necessary to good government and the happiness of mankind, schools and the means of education shall forever be encouraged. The utmost good faith shall always be observed towards the Indians; their lands and property shall never be taken away from them without their consent; and in their property, rights, and liberty they never shall be invaded or disturbed unless in just and lawful wars authorized by Congress; but laws founded in justice and humanity shall, from time to time, be made, for preventing wrongs being done to them, and for preserving peace and friendship with them.

♦ ♦ ♦

ARTICLE VI

There shall be neither slavery nor involuntary servitude in the said territory, otherwise than in the punishment of crimes, whereof the party shall have been duly convicted: Provided always, That any person escaping into the same, from whom labor or service is lawfully claimed in any one of the original States, such fugitive may be lawfully reclaimed, and conveyed to the person claiming his or her labor or service as aforesaid.

THE NEW REPUBLIC

Ratification of the Constitution marked the beginning, not the end, of controversy over the new government's powers, particularly those that involved conflict with state authority. Continuing sectional controversy, plus the outbreak of the French Revolution and the resumption of world war between England and France, led to the emergence of parties espousing differing constitutional programs. These divisions cut across all issues coming before the new national government. Hamilton and Madison debated presidential power in the Helvidius–Pacificus essays of 1793. Political unrest throughout the 1790s raised recurrent questions of national authority. The Whiskey Rebellion provided the first major test of the nation's ability to suppress resistance to its laws. In his Farewell Address of 1796, President George

Washington laid down principles governing the conduct of both domestic and foreign policy that reflected the conservative republicanism of his principal adviser, Alexander Hamilton. The outbreak of the undeclared naval war between France and America in 1798 led to Federalist enactment of the Alien and Sedition Acts, which in turn produced a series of prosecutions for seditious libel. Madison and Jefferson articulated an alternative theory of national power under the Constitution in the Virginia and Kentucky Resolutions of 1798 and 1799, arguing for the unconstitutionality of the Alien and Sedition Acts, and of prosecutions under them.

THE BILL OF RIGHTS

Antifederalists, such as Elbridge Gerry, objected to the Constitution as it came from the Philadelphia Convention, in part because they believed it threatened fundamental liberty. At the convention George Mason had asked that a bill of rights be appended to the proposed plan of government, but the other delegates voted it down. They believed they had created a government of enumerated and limited powers, and therefore a bill of rights was unnecessary. They also argued that a bill of rights was something that the subjects of a monarchy demanded from a king, but in the American Republic, where the people were sovereign, a bill of rights was unnecessary. In addition, some delegates, including Madison, believed that a bill of rights was useless in restraining a majority determined to ride roughshod over the liberties of the minority. Madison thought the Virginia Declaration of Rights was a "parchment barrier" that had proved useless in protecting fundamental rights. During the struggle for ratification, Antifederalists continued to demand a bill of rights. Initially, Federalists saw these demands as insincere—the work of selfish, narrow-minded politicians. Such views reflected the contempt that many Federalists had for the opponents of the Constitution. A North Carolina Federalist called his opponents "a blind stupid set, that wish Damnation to their Country," who were "fools and knaves" opposed to "any man of abilities and virtue." A New Hampshire Federalist predicted "that none but *fools, blockheads,* and *mad men*" opposed the Constitution. In New York the anonymous "Caesar" thought that the demands for a bill of rights were made by "designing croakers" in order "to frighten the people with ideal bugbears."

However, as the struggle for ratification progressed, some Federalists, including Madison, concluded that many who demanded a bill of rights were not extreme antinationalists, but were in fact sincerely worried about a national government that was not constrained by a bill of rights. To achieve harmony in his state and to secure his election to the first Congress, Madison promised his constituents that he would support of bill of rights if elected to the House of Representatives. In 1789 Madison promptly redeemed this promise, and under his leadership the Congress sent twelve amendments to the states; ten were ratified by 1791, and those ten are known today as the Bill of Rights. They are a somewhat more concise catalogue of individual liberties than comparable declarations of rights in most state constitutions of the period. Most were framed as negative rights—what the Congress could *not* do, for example—but some, such as the right to counsel in the Sixth Amendment, were framed as positive rights.

The Bill of Rights appears in the appendix of this book and accordingly is not reprinted here.

James Madison

"Property"
National Gazette,
March 29, 1792

While he had never believed a bill of rights was necessary, Madison was devoted to the idea of rights and to their protection. This essay, published in the National Gazette *in 1792, illustrates Madison's views that liberty and property are interconnected. In many ways, this is an incredibly modern notion of property, reflective of the theories of courts and lawyers in the twentieth and twenty-first centuries.*

March 27, 1792

This term in its particular application means "that dominion which one man claims and exercises over the external things of the world, in exclusion of every other individual."

In its larger and juster meaning, it embraces every thing to which a man may attach a value and have a right; and *which leaves to every one else the like advantage.*

In the former sense, a man's land, or merchandize, or money is called his property.

In the latter sense, a man has a property in his opinions and the free communication of them.

He has a property of peculiar value in his religious opinions, and in the profession and practice dictated by them.

He has a property very dear to him in the safety and liberty of his person.

He has an equal property in the free use of his faculties and free choice of the objects on which to employ them.

In a word, as a man is said to have a right to his property, he may be equally said to have a property in his rights.

Where an excess of power prevails, property of no sort is duly respected. No man is safe in his opinions, his person, his faculties, or his possessions.

Where there is an excess of liberty, the effect is the same, tho' from an opposite cause.

Government is instituted to protect property of every sort; as well that which lies in the various rights of individuals, as that which the term particularly expresses. This being the end of government, that alone is a just government, which impartially secures to every man, whatever is his own.

According to this standard of merit, the praise of affording a just securing to property, should be sparingly bestowed on a government which, however scrupulously guarding the possessions of individuals, does not protect them in the enjoyment and communication of their opinions, in which they have an equal, and in the estimation of some, a more valuable property.

More sparingly should this praise be allowed to a government, where a man's religious rights are violated by penalties, or fettered by tests, or taxed by a hierarchy. Conscience is the most sacred of all property; other property depending in part on positive law, the exercise of that, being a natural and unalienable right. To guard a man's house as his castle, to pay public and enforce private debts with the most exact faith, can give no title to invade a man's conscience which is more sacred than his castle, or to withhold from it that debt of protection, for which the public faith is pledged, by the very nature and original conditions of the social pact.

That is not a just government, nor is property secure under it, where the property which a man has in his personal safety and personal liberty, is violated by arbitrary seizures of one class of citizens for the service of the rest. A magistrate issuing his warrants to a press gang, would be in his proper functions in Turkey or Indostan, under appellation proverbial of the most compleat despotism.

That is not a just government, nor is property secure under it, where arbitrary restrictions, exemptions, and monopolies deny to part of its citizens that free use of their faculties, and free choice of their occupations, which not only constitute their property in the general sense of the word; but are the means of acquiring property strictly so called. What must be the spirit of legislation where a manufacturer of linen cloth is forbidden to bury his own child in a linen shroud, in order to favour his neighbour who manufactures woolen cloth; where the manufacturer and wearer of woolen cloth are again forbidden the economical use of buttons of that material, in favor of the manufacturer of buttons of other materials!

A just security to property is not afforded by that government, under which unequal taxes oppress one species of property and reward another species: where arbitrary taxes invade the domestic sanctuaries of the rich, and excessive taxes grind the faces of the poor; where the keenness and competitions of want are deemed an insufficient spur to labor, and taxes are again applied, by an unfeeling policy, as another spur; in violation of that sacred property, which Heaven, in decreeing man to earn his bread by the sweat of his brow, kindly reserved to him,

in the small repose that could be spared from the supply of his necessities.

If there be a government then which prides itself in maintaining the inviolability of property; which provides that none shall be taken directly even for public use without indemnification to the owner, and yet directly violates the property which individuals have in their opinions, their religion, their persons, and their faculties; nay more, which indirectly violates their property, in their actual possessions, in the labor that acquires their daily subsistence, and in the hallowed remnant of time which ought to relieve their Fatigues and soothe their cares, the influence will have been anticipated, that such a government is not a pattern for the United States.

If the United States mean to obtain or deserve the full praise due to wise and just governments, they will equally respect the rights of property, and the property in rights: they will rival the government that most sacredly guards the former; and by repelling its example in violating the latter, will make themselves a pattern to that and all other governments.

Hamilton Versus Madison on Presidential Power
1793

This classic confrontation between Alexander Hamilton, writing under the pen name "Pacificus," and James Madison, writing as "Helvidius," was an important early exploration of presidential power in the conduct of foreign and military affairs. Hamilton contended for a general, interstitial, and residual executive power: the president can do anything he is not explicitly forbidden to do. Madison, relying on a separation-of-powers theory, rejected his antagonist's ample concept of presidential power in favor of one by which the president is narrowly bounded by the Constitution, particularly by grants of power to Congress. The dichotomy these two men exposed is more pertinent than ever today.

[Hamilton:]

The second Article of the Constitution of the UStates, section 1st, established this general Proposition, That "The Executive Power shall be vested in a President of the United States of America."

The same article in a succeeding Section proceeds to designate particular cases of Ex-

ecutive Power. It declares among other things that the President shall be Commander in Chief of the army and navy of the UStates and of the Militia of the several states when called into the actual service of the UStates, that he shall have power by and with the advice of the senate to make treaties; that it shall be his duty to receive ambassadors and other public Ministers and to take care that the laws be faithfully executed.

It would not consist with the rules of sound construction to consider this enumeration of particular authorities as derogating from the more comprehensive grant contained in the general clause, further than as it may be coupled with express restrictions or qualifications; as in regard to the cooperation of the Senate in the appointment of Officers and the making of treaties; which are qualifications of the general executive powers of appointing officers and making treaties: Because the difficulty of a complete and perfect specification of all the cases of Executive authority would naturally dictate the use of general terms—and would render it improbable that a specification of certain particulars was designed as a substitute for those terms, when antecedently used. The different mode of expression employed in the constitution in regard to the two powers the Legislative and the Executive serves to confirm this inference. In the article which grants the legislative powers of the Government the expressions are—"All Legislative powers herein granted shall be vested in a Congress of the UStates;" in that which grants the Executive Power the expressions are, as already quoted "The Executive Power shall be vested in a President of the UStates of America."

The enumeration ought rather therefore to be considered as intended by way of greater caution, to specify and regulate the principal articles implied in the definition of Executive Power; leaving the rest to flow from the general grant of that power, interpreted in conformity to other parts [of] the constitution and to the principles of free government.

The general doctrine then of our constitution is, that the Executive Power of the Nation is vested in the President; subject only to the exceptions and qualifications which are expressed in the instrument.

[Madison:]

The basis of [Hamilton's] reasoning is, we perceive, the extraordinary doctrine, that the powers of making war and treaties, are in their nature executive; and therefore comprehended in the general grant of executive power, where not specially and strictly excepted out of the grant.

◆   ◆   ◆

If we consult for a moment, the nature and operation of the two powers to declare war and make treaties, it will be impossible not to see that they can never fall within a proper definition of executive powers. The natural province of the executive magistrate is to execute laws, as that of the legislature is to make laws. All his acts therefore, properly executive, must presuppose the existence of the laws to be executed. A treaty is not an execution of laws; it does not pre-suppose the existence of laws. It is, on the contrary, to have itself the force of a law, and to be carried into execution, like all other laws, by the executive magistrate. To say then that the power of making treaties which are confessedly laws, belongs naturally to the department which is to execute the laws, is to say, that the executive department naturally includes a legislative power. In theory, this is an absurdity—in practice a tyranny.

The power to declare war is subject to similar reasoning. A declaration that there shall be war, is not an execution of laws: it does not suppose pre-existing laws to be executed: it is not in any respect, an act merely executive. It is, on the contrary, one of the most deliberative acts that can be performed; and when performed, has the effect of repealing all the laws operating in a state of peace, so far as they are inconsistent with a state of war: and of enacting as a rule for the executive, a new code adapted to the relation between the society and its foreign enemy. In like manner a conclusion of peace annuls all the laws peculiar to a state of war, and revives the general laws incident to a state of peace.

These remarks will be strengthened by adding that treaties, particularly treaties of peace, have sometimes the effect of changing not only the external laws of the society, but operate also on the internal code, which is purely municipal, and to which the legislative authority of the country is of itself competent and compleat.

From this view of the subject it must be evident, that although the executive may be a convenient organ of preliminary communications with foreign governments, on the subjects of treaty or war; and the proper agent for carrying into execution the final determinations of the competent authority; yet it can have no pretensions from the nature of the powers in question compared with the nature of the executive trust, to that essential agency which gives validity to such determinations. It must be further evident that, if these powers be not in their nature purely legislative, they partake so much more of that, than of any other quality, that under a constitution leaving them to result to their most natural department, the legislature would be without a rival in its claim.

Another important inference to be noted is, that the powers of making war and treaty being substantially of a legislative, not an executive nature, the rule of interpreting exceptions strictly, must narrow instead of enlarging executive pretensions on those subjects.

GEORGE WASHINGTON

Farewell Address
1796

George Washington's Farewell Address is usually recalled for the foreign policy advice (no entangling alliances) contained in its latter section. But its ghost author, Alexander Hamilton, considered the conservative homily on domestic affairs that preceded the foreign policy section to be at least equally important. In several eloquent passages, Hamilton restated the precepts of conservative republicanism first voiced by John Adams twenty years earlier, enlightened by the experience of two decades of self-government.

This government, the offspring of your own choice, uninfluenced and unawed; adopted upon full investigation and mature deliberation; completely free in its principles; in the distribution of its powers uniting security with energy, and containing within itself provision for its own amendment, has a just claim to your confidence and your support. Respect for its authority, compliance with its laws, acquiescence in its measures, are duties enjoined by the fundamental maxims of true liberty. The basis of our political system is the right of the people to make and to alter their constitutions of government. But the constitution which at any time exists, until changed by an explicit and authentic act of the whole people, is sacredly obligatory upon all. The very idea of the power and the right of the people to establish government, presupposes the duty of every individual to obey the established government.

All obstructions to the execution of the laws, all combinations and associations, under whatever plausible character, with the real design to direct, control, counteract, or awe the regular deliberations and action of the constituted authorities, are destructive of this fundamental principle, and of fatal tendency. They serve to organize faction; to give it an artificial and extraordinary force; to put in the place of the delegated will of the nation, the will of party, often a small, but artful and enterprising minority of the community; and according to the alternate triumphs of different parties, to make the public administration the mirror of the ill concerted and incongruous projects of faction, rather than the organ of consistent and wholesome plans, digested by common councils, and modified by mutual interests.

Towards the preservation of your government, and the permanency of your present happy state, it is requisite not only that you steadily discountenance irregular opposition to its acknowledged authority, but also that you resist with care the spirit of innovation upon its principles, however specious the pretext. One method of assault may be to affect in the forms of the constitution alterations which will impair the energy of the system, and thus to undermine what cannot be directly overthrown. In all the changes to which you may be invited, remember that time and habit are at least as necessary to fix the true character of governments, as of other human institutions; that experience is the surest standard by which to test the real tendency of the existing constitutions of a country; that facility in changes upon the credit of mere hypothesis and opinion, exposes to perpetual change, from the endless variety of hypothesis and opinion; and remember especially, that from the efficient management of your common interests, in a country so extensive as ours a government of as much vigor as is consistent with the perfect security of liberty, is indispensable. Liberty itself will find in such a government, with powers properly distributed and adjusted, its surest guardian. It is, indeed, little else than a name, where the government is too feeble to withstand the enterprises of faction, to confine each member of society within the limits prescribed by the laws, and to maintain all in the secure and tranquil enjoyment of the rights of person and property.

The Sedition Act
1798

Taken with the Alien Acts enacted in the same year, this statute was part of a package of measures by which the Federalists harassed the Jeffersonian Republicans after the outbreak of the naval quasi-war with France. The statute enacted the common law of seditious libel. Although modern scholars considers it flagrantly unconstitutional, the Sedition Act was in its time actually a progressive measure in many respects. Unlike the existing law of libel, the law allowed juries to decide if the publication was in fact libelous, rather than leaving that decision to the judge. Furthermore, the law rejected the existing English rule that truth was not a defense to a libel. This law specifically allowed the defendant to argue truth as a defense. These were the protections demanded by John Peter Zenger's attorney two generations earlier. However, as defendants would find in the late 1790s, these provisions were hollow protection. The first man charged under the law, the Jeffersonian congressman Matthew Lyon, was tried far from his home, before a jury handpicked by a Federalist U.S. district attorney. Lyon was charged with calling President John Adams "pompous," an assertion that was hardly subject to a defense of "truth," since the president's pomposity was clearly in the eyes of the beholder.

The law expired of its own force but not before numerous prosecutions under it vexed the Federalists' opponents. The statute went a long way toward making legitimate political opposition a criminal offense. Disgust over the law discouraged any further attempts of Congress to punish people for their ideas. Ironically, when he became president, Thomas Jefferson approved the common-law prosecution of Federalist newspaper editors in Connecticut. He also urged his allies in the states to use state law to prosecute and jail his opponents. Both tactics failed, and in United States v. Hudson and Goodwin *(1812), the U.S. Supreme Court held that there was no federal common law of crimes.*

Sec. 2. And be it further enacted, That if any person shall write, print, utter or publish, or shall cause or procure to be written, printed, uttered, or published, or shall knowingly and willingly assist or aid in writing, printing, uttering or publishing any false, scandalous and malicious writing or writings against the government of the United States, or either house of the Congress of the United States, or the President of the United States, with intent to defame the said government, or either house of the said Congress, or the said President, or to bring them, into contempt or disrepute; or to excite against them, or either or any of them, the hatred of the good people of the United States, or to stir up sedition within the United States, or to excite any unlawful combinations therein, for opposing or resisting any law of the United States, or any act of the President of the United States, done in pursuance of any such law, or of the powers in him vested by the constitution of the United States, or to resist, oppose, or defeat, any such law or act, or to aid, encourage or abet any hostile designs or any foreign nation against the United States, their people or government, then such person, being thereof convicted before any court of the United States

having jurisdiction thereof, shall be punished by a fine not exceeding two thousand dollars, and by imprisonment not exceeding two years.

Sec. 3. And be it further enacted and declared, That if any person shall be prosecuted under this act, for the writing or publishing any libel aforesaid, it shall be lawful for the defendant, upon the trial of the cause, to give in evidence in his defence, the truth of the matter contained in the publication charged as libel. And the jury who shall try the cause, shall have a right to determine the law and the fact, under the direction of the court, as in other cases.

Sec. 4. And be it further enacted, That this act shall continue and be in force until the third day of March, one thousand eight hundred and one, and no longer.

The Virginia and Kentucky Resolutions
1798–1799

If the Constitution of 1787 implicitly embodied a nationalist outlook on government, the Virginia and Kentucky Resolutions expressed what might be considered a state-sovereignty counter-Constitution. James Madison contributed to both traditions, being a key figure at the Constitution, the "father" of the Bill of Rights, and the author of the Virginia Resolutions, a leading document of the counter-Constitution tradition. These resolutions ultimately took on a life of their own, providing the constitutional foundation of all later anticonsolidationist thought, and were the ancestors of nullification and secession. The resolutions and the vision of the Union they embody contrast dramatically with the vision of the Union articulated by Chief Justice John Marshall from 1810 through 1824. In the two visions we see the polarity that dominated constitutional controversy until it was resolved by the Civil War.

Besides the two visions of the Union, these resolutions illustrate some of the ironies of American politics and law. President Jefferson, the author of the Kentucky Resolutions, urged libel prosecutions at the state level and approved them at the federal level. Furthermore, although both Madison and Jefferson articulated a theory of limited national power, during their presidencies they aggressively expanded the power of the national government through the Louisiana Purchase, the beginning of Indian removal, various embargoes, the War of 1812, and at the end of his term, Madison's support, with Jefferson's endorsement, of a new Bank of the United States.

KENTUCKY RESOLUTIONS
NOVEMBER 10, 1798

1. Resolved, That the several states composing the United States of America are not united on the principle of unlimited submission to their

general government; but that, by compact, under the style and title of a Constitution for the United States, and of amendments thereto, they constituted a general government for special purposes, delegated to that government certain definite powers, reserving, each state to itself, the residuary mass of right to their own self-government; and that whensover the general government assumes undelegated powers, its acts are unauthoritative, void, and no force; that to this compact each state acceded as a state, and is an integral party; that this government, created by this compact, was not made the exclusive or final judge of the extent of the powers delegated to itself, since that would have made its discretion, and not the Constitution, the measure of its powers; but that, as in all other cases of compact among parties having no common judge, each party has an equal right to judge for itself, as well of infractions as the mode and measure of redress.

2. Resolved, That the Constitution of the United States having delegated to Congress a power to punish treason, counterfeiting the securities and current coin of the United States, piracies and felonies committed on the high seas, and offences against the laws of nations, and no other crimes whatever; and it being true, as a general principle, and one of the amendments to the Constitution having also declared "that the powers not delegated to the United States by the Constitution, nor prohibited by it to the states, are reserved to the states respectively, or to the people,"—therefore, also, the [Sedition Act] (and all other their acts which assume to create, define, or punish crimes other than those enumerated in the Constitution,) are altogether void, and of no force; and that the power to create, define, and punish, such other crimes is reserved, and of right appertains, solely and exclusively, to the respective states, each within its own territory.

3. Resolved, That it is true, as a general principle, and is also expressly declared by one of the amendments to the Constitution, that "the powers not delegated to the United States by the Constitution, nor prohibited by it to the states, are reserved to the states respectively, or to the people;" and that, no power over the freedom of religion, freedom of speech, or freedom of the press, being delegated to the United States by the Constitution, nor prohibited by it to the states, all lawful powers respecting the same did of right remain, and were reserved to the states, or to the people; . . . That therefore the act of the Congress of the United States,

passed on the 14th of July, 1798, entitled "An Act in Addition to the Act entitled 'An Act for the Punishment of certain Crimes against the United States,'" which does abridge the freedom of the press, is not law, but is altogether void, and of no force.

◆ ◆ ◆

7. Resolved, That the construction applied by the general government [of the necessary-and-proper clause] goes to the destruction of all the limits prescribed to their power by the Constitution; that words meant by that instrument to be subsidiary only to the execution of the limited powers, ought not to be so construed as themselves to give unlimited powers, nor a part so to be taken as to destroy the whole residue of the instrument.

◆ ◆ ◆

In questions of power, then, let no more be said of confidence in man, but bind him down from mischief by the chains of the Constitution. That this commonwealth does therefore call on its co-states for an expression of their sentiments on the acts concerning aliens, and for the punishment of certain crimes herein before specified, plainly declaring whether these acts are or are not authorized by the federal compact. And it doubts not that their sense will be so announced as to prove their attachment to limited government, whether general or particular, and that the rights and liberties of their co-states will be exposed to no dangers by remaining embarked on a common bottom with their own; but they will concur with this commonwealth in considering the said acts as so palpably against the Constitution as to amount to an undisguised declaration, that the compact is not meant to be the measure of the powers of the general government, but that it will proceed in the exercise over these states of all powers whatsoever. That they will view this as seizing the rights of the states, and consolidating them in the hands of the general government, with a power assumed to bind the states, not merely in cases made federal, but in all cases whatsoever, by laws made not with their consent, but by others against their consent; that this would be to surrender the form of government we have chosen, and live under one deriving its powers from its own will, and not from our authority; and that the co-states, recurring to their natural rights not made federal, will concur in declaring these void and of no force, and will each unite with this commonwealth in requesting their repeal at the next session of Congress.

VIRGINIA RESOLUTIONS
DECEMBER 21, 1798

That this Assembly doth explicitly and peremptorily declare, that it views the powers of the federal government as resulting from the compact to which the states are parties, as limited by the plain sense and intention of the instrument constituting that compact, as no further valid than they are authorized by the grants enumerated in that compact; and that, in case of a deliberate, palpable, and dangerous exercise of other powers, not granted by the said compact, the states, who are parties thereto, have the right, and are in duty bound, to interpose, for arresting the progress of the evil, and for maintaining, within their respective limits, the authorities, rights and liberties, appertaining to them.

That the General Assembly doth also express its deep regret, that a spirit has, in sundry instances, been manifested by the federal government to enlarge it powers by forced constructions of the constitutional charter which defines them; and that indications have appeared of a design to expound certain general phrases (which, having been copied from the very limited grant of powers in the former Articles of Confederation, were the less liable to be misconstrued) so as to destroy the meaning and effect of the particular enumeration which necessarily explains and limits the general phrases, and so as to consolidate the states, by degrees, into one sovereignty, the obvious tendency and inevitable result of which would be, to transform the present republican system of the United States into an absolute, or, at best, a mixed monarchy.

KENTUCKY RESOLUTIONS
NOVEMBER 14, 1799

Resolved, That this commonwealth considers the federal Union, upon the terms and for the purposes specified in the late compact, conducive to the liberty and happiness of the several states: That it does now unequivocally declare its attachment to the Union, and to that compact, agreeably to its obvious and real intention, and will be among the last to seek its dissolution: That, if those who administer the general government be permitted to transgress the limits fixed by that compact, by a total disregard to the special delegations of power therein contained, an annihilation of the state governments, and the creation, upon their ruins, of a general consolidated government, will be the inevitable consequence: That the principle and construction, contended for by sundry of the state legislatures, that the general government is the exclusive judge of the extent of the powers delegated to it, stop not short of despotism—since the discretion of those who administer the government, and not the Constitution, would be the measure of their powers: That the several states who formed that instrument, being sovereign and independent, have the unquestionable right to judge of the infraction; and, That a nullification, by those sovereignties, of all unauthorized acts done under color of that instrument, is the rightful remedy: That this commonwealth does, under the most deliberate reconsideration declare, that the said Alien and Sedition Laws, are in their opinion, palpable violations of the said Constitution; and however cheerfully it may be disposed to surrender its opinion to a majority of its sister states, in matters of ordinary or doubtful policy, yet, in momentous regulations like the present, which so vitally wound the best rights of the citizen, it would consider a silent acquiescence as highly criminal: That, although this commonwealth, as a party to the federal compact, will bow to the laws of the Union, yet it does, at the same time, declare, that it will not now, or ever hereafter, cease to oppose, in a constitutional manner, every attempt, at what quarter soever offered, to violate that compact: And finally, in order that no pretext or arguments may be drawn from a supposed acquiescence, on the part of this commonwealth, in the constitutionality of those laws, and be thereby used as precedents for similar future violations of the federal compact, this commonwealth now enter against them in solemn Protest.

THOMAS JEFFERSON

First Inaugural Address
1801

Jefferson called his election the "Revolution of 1800." More correctly, it can be seen as part of the final act of the American Revolution. After a bitter and nasty election campaign, Jefferson narrowly defeated the incumbent president, John Adams. On inauguration day Adams peacefully left the new national capital, Washington, D.C., and Jefferson peacefully took office. For the first time in modern history—perhaps the first time in human history—an entrenched leader of a nation peacefully left office so that his chief rival could take over.

Given the personally vicious campaign on both sides, Jefferson's inaugural is remarkable for its conciliatory approach to Jefferson's inveterate and embittered political enemies. His claim that Americans were now "all Republicans" and "all Federalists" illustrated the triumph of republican and democratic theory. In this address, Jefferson succinctly stated the ideals of his administration in phrases that could have served throughout the nineteenth century as a program for a republic blessed by abundance and untroubled by external enemies. More important, Jefferson's address offered a brilliant analysis of politics in the new Republic and an eloquent statement about the nature of a free society, in which dissent and disagreement are not a sign of weakness but a sign of strength. His characterization of the election as a "contest of opinion" spoke to the highest ideals and loftiest principles of republican thought and democratic theory. The peaceful transition from one administration to another proved that the Revolution had succeeded.

During the contest of opinion through which we have passed the animation of discussions and of exertions has sometimes worn an aspect which might impose on strangers unused to think freely and to speak and to write what they think; but this being now decided by the voice of the nation, announced according to the rules of the Constitution, all will, of course, arrange themselves under the will of the law, and unite in common efforts for the common good. All, too, will bear in mind this sacred principle, that though the will of the majority is in all cases to prevail, that will to be rightful must be reasonable; that the minority possesses their equal rights, which equal law must protect, and to violate would be oppression. Let us, then, fellow-citizens, unite with one heart and one mind. Let us restore to social intercourse that harmony and affection without which liberty and even

life itself are but dreary things. And let us reflect that, having banished from our land that religious intolerance under which mankind so long bled and suffered, we have yet gained little if we countenance a political intolerance as despotic, as wicked, and capable of as bitter and bloody persecutions. During the throes and convulsions of the ancient world, during the agonizing spasms of infuriated man, seeking through blood and slaughter his long-lost liberty, it was not wonderful that the agitation of the billows should reach even this distant and peaceful shore; that this should be more felt and feared by some and less by others, and should divide opinions as to measures of safety. But every difference of opinion is not a difference of principle. We have called by different names brethren of the same principle. We are all Republicans, we are all Federalists. If there be any among us who would wish to dissolve this Union or to change its republican form, let them stand undisturbed as monuments of the safety which error of opinion may be tolerated where reason is left free to combat it. I know, indeed, that some honest men fear that a republican government can not be strong, that this Government is not strong enough; but would the honest patriot, in the full tide of successful experiment, abandon a government which has so far kept us free and firm on the theoretic and visionary fear that this Government, the world's best hope, may by possibility want energy to preserve itself? I trust not. I believe this, on the contrary, the strongest Government on earth. I believe it the only one where every man, at the call of the law, would fly to the standard of the law, and would meet invasions of the public order as his own personal concern. Sometimes it is said that man can not be trusted with the government of himself. Can he, then, be trusted with the government of others? Or have we found angels in the forms of kings to govern him? Let history answer this question.

♦ ♦ ♦

About to enter, fellow-citizens, on the exercise of duties which comprehend everything dear and valuable to you, it is proper you should understand what I deem the essential principles of our Government and consequently those which ought to shape its Administration. I will compress them within the narrowest compass they will bear, stating the general principle, but not all its limitations. Equal and exact justice to all men, of whatever state or persuasion, religious or political; peace, commerce, and honest friendship with all nations, entangling alliances with none; the support of the State governments in all their rights, as the most competent administrations for our domestic concerns and the surest bulwarks against antirepublican tendencies; the preservation of the General Government in its whole constitutional vigor, as the sheet anchor of our peace at home and safety abroad; a jealous care of the right of election by the people—a mild and safe corrective of abuses which are lopped by the sword of revolution where peaceable remedies are unprovided; absolute acquiescence to the decisions of the majority, the vital principle of republics, from which is no appeal but to force, the vital principle and immediate parent of despotism; a well-disciplined militia, our best reliance in peace and for the first moments of war, till regulars may relieve them; the supremacy of the civil over the military authority; economy in the public expense, that labor may be lightly burthened; the honest payment of our debts and sacred preservation of the public faith; encouragement of agriculture, and of commerce as its handmaid; the diffusion of information and arraignment of all abuses at the bar of the public reason; freedom of religion; freedom of the press, and freedom of person under the protection of the habeas corpus, and trial by juries impartially selected. These principles form the brightest constellation which has gone before us and guided our steps through an age of revolution and reformation. The wisdom of our sages and blood of our heroes have been devoted to their attainment. They should be the creed of our political faith, the text of civic instruction, the touchstone by which to try the services of those we trust; and should we wander from them in moments of error or of alarm, let us hasten to retrace our steps and to regain the road which alone leads to peace, liberty, and safety.

COURTS AND JUDGES IN THE NEW NATION

From the outset, courts played a prominent role in both state and national governments. The scope of that role remained unclear, however, at both the federal and state levels. The inability of the Philadelphia Convention to establish a clear place for lower federal courts was emblematic of controversies surrounding the national judiciary. The so-called Madisonian Compromise, by which Congress was given power to create lower federal courts but was not required to do so, merely passed the political controversy from the convention to the new government. Congress partially resolved the problem by creating lower federal courts in the

Judiciary Act of 1789, but it, too, compromised on their role. Congress gave the new national judiciary less than all the jurisdiction authorized by the Constitution's Article III, and it provided that state substantive law would furnish the rules of decision for cases that came to federal courts because the parties were citizens of different states.

In its first decade, the United States Supreme Court handed down a number of important decisions. None had a more lasting influence than *Calder* v. *Bull* (1798), which embedded the doctrine of higher law into American law. The proponent of that idea, Justice Samuel Chase, proved to be an intemperate and partisan Federalist off and on the bench. When they came to power, Jeffersonian Republicans, who regarded Chase as an epitome of Federalist reaction entrenched on the bench after its rejection at the polls, attempted to impeach him. The failure of that impeachment effort signaled the permanence, if not the invulnerability, of federal judicial power.

Federalist jurists like Chief Justices John Jay and John Marshall succeeded in ensconcing their vision of the rule of law in the Constitution. In order for Chief Justice Marshall to establish courts as ultimate guardians of the rule of law, he had to elevate Alexander Hamilton's views in *The Federalist,* Number 78, to the status of constitutional dogma. The 1803 case of *Marbury* v. *Madison* provided Marshall with an opportunity to do just that, asserting the doctrine of judicial review: the power of courts to hold a statute or an action of the executive branch unconstitutional and accordingly to refuse to give it effect.

The Judiciary Act
1789

In 1911, Justice Henry B. Brown hailed this statute as "the most important and the most satisfactory Act ever passed by Congress." For once, the hyperbole is justified. Over time, the statute proved to be the keystone in the arch of the federal union. Yet in its time it was a compromise measure, and its Section 34 made a considerable concession to the supporters of state judicial power, who feared that the federal courts would overshadow the state courts. Both Sections 25 and 34 remain central to the evolution of federal judicial power.

Sec. 25. And be it further enacted, That a final judgment or decree in any suit, in the highest court of law or equity of a State in which a decision in the suit could be had, where is drawn in question the validity of a treaty or statute of, or an authority exercised under the United States, and the decision is against their validity; or where is drawn in question the validity of a statute of, or an authority exercised under any State, on the ground of their being repugnant to the constitution, treaties or laws of the United States, and the decision is in favour of such their validity, or where is drawn in question the construction of any clause of the constitution, or of a treaty, or statute of, or commission held under the United States, and the decision is against the title, right, privilege or exemption specially set up or claimed by either party, under such clause of the said constitution, treaty, statute, or commission, may be re-examined and reversed or affirmed in the Supreme Court of the United States upon a writ of error, . . . and the proceeding upon the reversal shall also be the same, except that the Supreme Court, instead of remanding the cause for a final decision as before provided, may at their discretion, if the cause shall have been once remanded before, proceed to a final decision of the same, and award execution. But no other error shall be assigned or regarded as a ground of reversal in any case as aforesaid, than such as appears on the face of the record, and immediately respects the before mentioned questions of validity or construction of the said constitution, treaties, statutes, commissions, or authorities in dispute.

♦   ♦   ♦

Sec. 34. And be it further enacted, That the laws of the several states, except where the constitution, treaties or statutes of the United States shall otherwise require or provide, shall be regarded as rules of decision in trials at common law in the courts of the United States in cases where they apply.

Jefferson Versus Hamilton on the Bank of the United States
1791

In 1791, Secretary of the Treasury Alexander Hamilton proposed that Congress grant a corporate charter to the Bank of the United States. The bank would be a depository for public revenues and act as the government's central financial institution, regulating currency and lending money to the national treasury. But it would also be a private corporation, with profits going to its stockholders.

President Washington had doubts about the constitutionality of the bank bill because nothing in the Constitution explicitly authorized Congress to charter corporations. So he requested the members of his cabinet to render advisory opinions on the constitutional question. The opinions submitted by Secretary of State Jefferson and Secretary of the Treasury Hamilton set forth two opposing ways of interpreting the Constitution, loosely called in our day strict versus loose construction. John Marshall virtually plagiarized Hamilton's argument for his opinion in McCulloch v. Maryland *(1819), upholding the constitutionality of the Second Bank of the United States and rejecting Jefferson's narrow interpretive approach.*

[Jefferson:]

I consider the foundation of the Constitution is laid on this ground: That "all powers not delegated to the United States, by the Constitution, nor prohibited by it to the States, are reserved to the States or to the people." . . . To take a single step beyond the boundaries thus specially drawn around the powers of Congress, is to take possession of a boundless field of power, no longer susceptible of any definition.

The incorporation of a bank, and the powers assumed by this bill, have not, in my opinion, been delegated to the United States, by the Constitution.

I. They are not among the powers specially enumerated. . . .

II. Nor are they within either of the general phrases, which are the two following:—

1. To lay taxes to provide for the general welfare of the United States, that is to say, "to lay taxes for the purpose of providing for the general welfare." For the laying of taxes is the power, and the general welfare the purpose for which the power is to be exercised. They are not to lay taxes ad libitum for any purpose they please; but only to pay the debts or provide for the welfare of the Union. In like manner, they are not to do anything they please to provide for the general welfare, but only to lay taxes for that purpose. To consider the latter phrase, not as describing the purpose of the first, but as giving a distinct and independent power to do any act they please, which might be for the good of the Union, would render all the preceding and subsequent enumerations of power completely useless.

It would reduce the whole instrument to a single phrase, that of instituting a Congress with power to do whatever would be for the good of the United States; and, as they would be the sole judges of the good or evil, it would be also a power to do whatever evil they please.

♦ ♦ ♦

2. The second general phrase is, "to make all laws necessary and proper for carrying into execution the enumerated powers." But they can all be carried into execution without a bank. A bank therefore is not necessary, and consequently not authorized by this phrase.

It has been urged that a bank will give great facility or convenience in the collection of taxes. Suppose this were true: yet the Constitution allows only the means which are "necessary" not those which are merely "convenient" for effecting the enumerated powers. If such a latitude of construction be allowed to this phrase as to give any non-enumerated power, it will go to every one, for there is not one which ingenuity may not torture into convenience in some instance or other, to some one of so long a list of enumerated powers. It would swallow up all the delegated powers, and reduce the whole to one power, as before observed. Therefore it was that the Constitution restrained them to the necessary means, that is to say, to those means without which the grant or power would be nugatory.

[Hamilton:]
It is not denied that there are implied, as well as express powers, and that the former are as effectually delegated as the latter. And for the sake of accuracy it shall be mentioned, that there is another class of powers, which may be properly denominated resulting powers.

♦ ♦ ♦

It is conceded, that implied powers are to be considered as delegated equally with express ones.

Then it follows, that as a power of erecting a corporation may as well be implied as any other thing; it may as well be employed as an instrument or means of carrying into execution any of the specified powers, as any other instrument or means whatever. The only question must be, in this as in every other case, whether the means to be employed, or in this instance the corporation to be erected, has a natural re-

lation to any of the acknowledged objects or lawful ends of the government.

♦ ♦ ♦

To this mode of reasoning respecting the right of employing all the means requisite to the execution of the specified powers of the Government, it is objected that none but necessary & proper means are to be employed, & the Secretary of State [Jefferson] maintains, that no means are to be considered as necessary, but those without which the grant of the power would be nugatory.

♦ ♦ ♦

All the arguments therefore against the constitutionality of the bill derived from the accidental existence of certain State-banks: institutions which happen to exist to day, & for aught that concerns the government of the United States, may disappear tomorrow, must not only be rejected as fallacious, but must be viewed as demonstrative, that there is a radical source of error in the reasoning.

It is essential to the being of the National government, that so erroneous a conception of the meaning of the word necessary, should be exploded.

It is certain, that neither the grammatical, nor popular sense of the term requires that construction. According to both, necessary often means no more than needful, requisite, incidental, useful, or conducive to. It is a common mode of expression to say, that it is necessary for a government or a person to do this or that thing, when nothing more is intended or understood, than that the interests of the government or person require, or will be promoted, by the doing of this or that thing. The imagination can be at no loss for exemplifications of the use of the word in this sense.

And it is the true one in which it is to be understood as used in [the] constitution. The whole turn of the clause containing it, indicates, that it was the intent of the convention, by that clause to give a liberal latitude to the exercise of the specified powers.

♦ ♦ ♦

The truth is that difficulties on this point are inherent in the nature of the federal constitution. They result inevitably from a division of the legislative power. The consequence of this division is, that there will be cases clearly within the power of the National Government; others clearly without its power; and a third class, which will leave room for controversy & difference of opinion, & concerning which a reasonable latitude of judgment must be allowed.

But the doctrine which is contended for is not chargeable with the consequence imputed to it. It does not affirm that the National government is sovereign in all respects, but that it is sovereign to a certain extent: that is, to the extent of the objects of its specified powers.

It leaves therefore a criterion of what is constitutional, and of what is not so. This criterion is the end to which the measure relates as a mean. If the end be clearly comprehended within any of the specified powers, & if the measure have an obvious relation to that end, and is not forbidden by any particular provision of the constitution—it may safely be deemed to come within the compass of the national authority.

Calder v. Bull
3 Dall. (3 U.S.) 386 (1798)

Calder v. Bull *was a complicated inheritance case in which the Connecticut legislature, acting as a court of last resort, had overturned the decision of a lower court that refused to enforce a will awarding Bull his inheritance. The legislature ordered a new trial, which upheld the will and gave the property to Bull. Calder then sued, arguing that the action of the legislature constituted an ex post facto law. In upholding the act of the legislature, justices Samuel Chase and James Iredell presented two distinctly different views of the role of natural law under the new Constitution. Chase's opinion in this case is the clearest and most definitive expression of higher-law doctrine to emanate from the United States Supreme Court. But opinions in the pre-Marshall era were delivered seriatim, so it was not necessarily of more binding precedential authority than Justice James Iredell's, which expressed diametrically contrasting views. Nevertheless, the eminent twentieth-century constitutional authority Edward S. Corwin thought that Chase's opinion expounded what he called "the basic doctrine of American constitutional law."*

[Chase:]

I cannot subscribe to the omnipotence of a state legislature, or that it is absolute and without control; although its authority should not be expressly restrained by the constitution, or fundamental law of the state. The people of the United States erected their constitutions or forms of government, to establish justice, to promote the general welfare, to secure the blessings of liberty, and to protect their persons and property from violence. The purposes for which men enter into society will determine the nature and terms of the social compact; and as they are the foundation of the legislative power, they will decide what are the proper objects of it. The nature, and ends of legislative power will limit the exercise of it. This fundamental principle flows from the very nature of our free republican governments, that no man should be compelled to do what the laws do not require; nor to refrain from acts which the laws permit. There are acts which the federal, or state legislature cannot do, without exceeding their authority. There are certain vital principles in our free republican governments, which will determine and overrule an apparent and flagrant abuse of legislative power; as to authorize manifest injustice by positive law; or to take away that security for personal liberty, or private property, for the protection whereof the government was established. An act of the legislature (for I cannot call it a law), contrary to the great first principles of the social compact, cannot be considered a rightful exercise of legislative authority. The obligation of a law, in governments established on express compact, and on republican principles, must be determined by the nature of the power on which it is founded.

A few instances will suffice to explain what I mean. A law that punished a citizen for an innocent action, or, in other words, for an act, which, when done, was in violation of no existing law; a law that destroys or impairs the lawful private contracts of citizens; a law that makes a man a judge in his own cause; or a law that takes property from A. and gives it to B.; it is against all reason and justice, for a people to intrust a legislature with such powers; and therefore, it cannot be presumed that they have done it. The genius, the nature and the spirit of our state governments, amount to a prohibition of such acts of legislation; and the general principles of law and reason forbid them. The legislature may enjoin, permit, forbid and punish; they may declare new crimes; and establish rules of conduct for all its citizens in future cases; they may command what is right, and prohibit what is wrong; but they cannot change innocence into guilt; or punish innocence as a crime; or violate the right of an antecedent lawful private contract; or the right of private property. To maintain that our federal, or state legislature possesses such powers, if they had not been expressly restrained, would, in my opinion, be a political heresy, altogether inadmissible in our free republican governments.

[Iredell:]

If, then, a government, composed of legislative, executive and judicial departments, were established, by a constitution which im-

posed no limits on the legislative power, the consequence would inevitably be, that whatever the legislative power chose to enact, would be lawfully enacted, and the judicial power could never interpose to pronounce it void. It is true, that some speculative jurists have held, that a legislative act against natural justice must, in itself, be void; but I cannot think that, under such a government any court of justice would possess a power to declare it so.

♦ ♦ ♦

In order, therefore, to guard against so great an evil, it has been the policy of all the American states, which have, individually, framed their state constitutions, since the revolution, and the people of the United States, when they framed the federal constitution, to define with precision the objects of the legislative power; and to restrain its exercise within marked and settled boundaries. If any act of Congress, or of the legislature of a state, violates those constitutional provisions, it is unquestionably void; though, I admit, that as the authority to declare it void is of a delicate and awful nature, the court will never resort to that authority, but in a clear and urgent case. If, on the other hand, the legislature of the Union, or the legislature of any member of the Union, shall pass a law, within the general scope of their constitutional power, the court cannot pronounce it to be void, merely because it is, in their judgment, contrary to the principles of natural justice. The ideas of natural justice are regulated by no fixed standard: the ablest and the purest men have differed upon the subject; and all that the court could properly say, in such an event, would be, that the legislature (possessed of an equal right of opinion) had passed an act which, in the opinion of the judges, was inconsistent with the abstract principles of natural justice.

Marbury v. Madison
1 Cranch (5 U.S.) 137 (1803)

The principle of judicial review had been asserted and in some states established before 1803. The North Carolina case of Bayard v. Singleton *(1787) was the first to do so explicitly, but numerous cases before and after 1787 asserted the power implicitly. Thus it is in-*

correct to think of Marbury *as being the first case to establish the power. But if not first in time, it is certainly the most important of any.*

In his discursive and prolix opinion, Marshall broached the doctrine of political questions, to be developed by his successor Roger Taney in Luther v. Borden *(1849). He implicitly chastised President Jefferson and Secretary of State Madison for having committed an illegal act, yet by declining jurisdiction left himself invulnerable to executive retaliation (and it is uncertain which Jefferson felt more keenly: Marshall's rebuke or the frustration of not being able to disregard it).*

But far greater than any of this are the last few pages of the opinion, where Marshall asserted the power of judicial review and attempted to show its inevitability on the basis of fundamental principles. Yet his reasoning was both vulnerable and ambiguous on its central point. Is the power of judicial review merely an incident of the Court's ordinary function of deciding cases—and in doing so, choosing between conflicting laws? Or did Marshall assert here some special and extraordinary power for the Court, a unique function entrusted to it of superintending the separation of powers and the proper operation of the Constitution? Finally, the pivotal point of Marshall's reasoning is his assertion that the Constitution is law; all else follows from this one basic proposition.

In the order in which the court has viewed this subject, the following questions have been considered and decided.

1st. Has the applicant a right to the commission he demands?

2dly. If he has a right, and that right has been violated, do the laws of his country afford him a remedy?

3dly. If they do afford him a remedy, is it a mandamus issuing from this court?

♦ ♦ ♦

Mr. Marbury, then, since his commission was signed by the president, and sealed by the secretary of state, was appointed. . . .

To withhold his commission, therefore, is an act deemed by the court not warranted by law, but violative of a vested legal right.

This brings us to the second inquiry; which is,

2dly. If he has a right, and that right has been violated, do the laws of his country afford him a remedy?

The very essence of civil liberty certainly consists in the right of every individual to claim the protection of the laws, whenever he receives an injury. One of the first duties of government is to afford that protection.

♦ ♦ ♦

Is the act of delivering or withholding a commission to be considered as a mere political act, belonging to the executive department alone, for the performance of which entire confidence is placed by our constitution in the supreme executive; and for any misconduct respecting which, the injured individual has no remedy?

♦ ♦ ♦

It is not believed that any person whatever would attempt to maintain such a proposition.

It follows, then, that the question, whether the legality of an act of the head of a department be examinable in a court of justice or not, must always depend on the nature of that act.

♦ ♦ ♦

By the constitution of the United States, the president is invested with certain important political powers, in the exercise of which he is to use his own discretion, and is accountable only to his country in his political character and to his own conscience. To aid him in the performance of these duties, he is authorized to appoint certain officers, who act by his authority, and in conformity with his orders.

In such cases, their acts are his acts; and whatever opinion may be entertained of the manner in which executive discretion may be used, still there exists, and can exist, no power to control that discretion. The subjects are political. They respect the nation, not individual rights, and being intrusted to the executive, the decision of the executive is conclusive.

♦ ♦ ♦

The conclusion from this reasoning is, that where the heads of departments are the political or confidential agents of the executive, merely to execute the will of the president, or rather to act in cases in which the executive possesses a constitutional or legal discretion, nothing can be more perfectly clear than their acts are only politically examinable. But where a specific duty is assigned by law, and individual rights depend upon the performance of that duty, it seems equally clear that the individual who considers himself injured, has a right to resort to the laws of his country for a remedy.

♦ ♦ ♦

It is, then, the opinion of the court,

1st. That by signing the commission of Mr. Marbury, the President of the United States appointed him a justice of peace for the county of Washington, in the district of Columbia; and that the seal of the United States, affixed thereto by the secretary of state, is conclusive testimony of the verity of the signature, and of the completion of the appointment; and that the appointment conferred on him a legal right to the office for the space of five years.

2dly. That, having this legal title to the office, he has a consequent right to the commission; a refusal to deliver which is a plain violation of that right, for which the laws of his country afford him a remedy.

It remains to be inquired whether,

3dly. He is entitled to the remedy for which he applies.

♦ ♦ ♦

This, then, is a plain case for a mandamus, either to deliver the commission, or a copy of it from the record; and it only remains to be inquired,

Whether it can issue from this court.

♦ ♦ ♦

When an instrument organizing fundamentally a judicial system, divides it into one supreme, and so many inferior courts as the legislature may ordain and establish; then enumerates its powers, and proceeds so far to distribute them, as to define the jurisdiction of the supreme court by declaring the cases in which it shall take original jurisdiction, and that in others it shall take appellate jurisdiction; the plain import of the words seems to be, that in one class of cases its jurisdiction is original, and not appellate; in the other it is appellate, and not original. If any other construction would render the clause inoperative, that is an additional reason for rejecting such other construction, and for adhering to their obvious meanings.

To enable this court, then, to issue a mandamus, it must be shown to be an exercise of appellate jurisdiction, or to be necessary to enable them to exercise appellate jurisdiction. It is the essential criterion of appellate jurisdiction, that it revises and corrects the proceedings in a cause already instituted, and does not create that cause. Although, therefore, a mandamus may be directed to courts, yet to issue such a writ to an officer for the delivery of a paper, is in effect the same as to sustain an original action for that paper, and, therefore, seems not to belong to appellate, but to original jurisdiction. Neither is it necessary in such case as this, to enable the court to exercise its appellate jurisdiction.

The authority, therefore, given to the supreme court, by the act establishing the judicial courts of the United States, to issue writs of mandamus to public officers, appears not to be warranted by the constitution; and it becomes necessary to inquire whether a jurisdiction so conferred can be exercised.

The question, whether an act, repugnant to the constitution, can become the law of the land, is a question deeply interesting to the United States; but, happily, not of an intricacy proportioned to its interest. It seems only necessary to recognise certain principles, supposed to have been long and well established, to decide it.

That the people have an original right to establish, for their future government, such principles as, in their opinion, shall most conduce to their own happiness is the basis on which their whole American fabric has been erected. The exercise of this original right is a very great exertion; nor can it, nor ought it, to be frequently repeated. The principles, therefore, so established are deemed fundamental. And as the authority from which they proceed is supreme, and can seldom act, they are designed to be permanent.

This original and supreme will organizes the government, and assigns to different departments their respective powers. It may either stop here, or establish certain limits not to be transcended by those departments.

The government of the United States is of the latter description. The powers of the legislature are defined and limited; and that those limits may not be mistaken, or forgotten, the constitution is written. To what purpose are powers limited, and to what purpose is that limitation committed to writing, if these limits may, at any time, be passed by those intended to be restrained? The distinction between a government with limited powers is abolished, if those limits do not confine the persons on whom they are imposed, and if acts prohibited and acts allowed, are of equal obligation. It is a proposition too plain to be contested, that the constitution controls any legislative act repugnant to it; or, that the legislature may alter the constitution by an ordinary act.

Between these alternatives there is no middle ground. The constitution is either a superior paramount law, unchangeable by ordinary means, or it is on a level with ordinary legislative acts, and, like other acts, is alterable when the legislature shall please to alter it.

If the former part of the alternative be true, then a legislative act contrary to the constitution is not law; if the latter part be true, then written constitutions are absurd attempts, on the part of the people, to limit a power in its own nature illimitable.

Certainly all those who have framed constitutions contemplate them as forming the fundamental and paramount law of the nation, and, consequently, the theory of every such government must be, that an act of the legislature, repugnant to the constitution, is void.

This theory is essentially attached to a written constitution, and, is consequently, to be considered, by this court, as one of the fundamental principles of our society. It is not therefore to be lost sight of in the further consideration of this subject.

If an act of the legislature, repugnant to the constitution is void, does it, notwithstanding its validity, bind the courts, and oblige them to give it effect? Or, in other words, though it be not law, does it constitute a rule as operative as if it was a law? This would be to overthrow in fact what was established in theory; and would seem at first view, an absurdity too gross to be insisted on. It shall, however, receive a more attentive consideration.

It is emphatically the province and duty of the judicial department to say what the law is. Those who apply the rule to particular cases, must of necessity expound and interpret that rule. If two laws conflict with each other, the courts must decide on the operation of each.

So if a law be in opposition to the constitution; if both the law and the constitution apply to a particular case, so that the court must either decide that case conformably to the law, disregarding the constitution; or conformably to the constitution, disregarding the law; the court must determine which of these conflicting rules governs the case. This is of the very essence of judicial duty.

If, then, the courts are to regard the constitution, and the constitution is superior to any ordinary act of the legislature, the constitution, and not such ordinary act, must govern the case to which they both apply.

Those, then, who controvert the principle that the constitution is to be considered, in court, as a paramount law, are reduced to the necessity of maintaining that courts must close their eyes on the constitution, and see only the law. This doctrine would subvert the very foundation of all written constitutions. It would declare that an act which, according to the principles and theory of our government, is entirely void, is yet, in practice, completely obligatory. It would declare that if the legislature shall do what is expressly forbidden, such act, notwithstanding the express prohibition, is in reality effectual. It would be giving to the legislature a practical and real omnipotence, with the same breath which professes to restrict their powers within narrow limits. It is prescribing limits, and declaring that those limits may be passed at pleasure.

♦   ♦   ♦

It is also not entirely unworthy of observation, that in declaring what shall be the supreme law of the land, the constitution itself is first mentioned; and not the laws of the United States generally, but those only which shall be made in pursuance of the constitution, have that rank.

Thus, the particular phraseology of the constitution of the United States confirms and strengthens the principle, supposed to be essential to all written constitutions, that a law repugnant to the constitution is void; and that courts, as well as other departments, are bound by that instrument.

3

The Active State and the Mixed Economy
1812–1860

THE GOLDEN AGE OF AMERICAN LAW

The period from 1787 to 1861 has been called the "golden age" of American law. Scholarship on the era describes it as "the creative period," "the transformation" of law, and "the Americanization" of the law. Well before the current resurgence in American legal history, Roscoe Pound called this the "formative era of American law." Historian Daniel J. Boorstin argues that it was an era of "creative outbursts" in "legal history."[1]

In this period, the United States Supreme Court was the most prominent judicial body in the nation, and many of its decisions shaped both public and private law. However, collectively the state courts had far greater influence on the development of law. The federal courts had limited jurisdiction, while the state courts determined most issues of private law and many important issues of public law as well. Chief Justice Lemuel Shaw of Massachusetts, Chancellor James Kent of New York, and Chief Justice Thomas Ruffin of North Carolina were particularly influential, but a host of other state judges also contributed to legal developments.

Treatise writers were also important to legal developments. Before the Civil War, access to law was limited; there was no national reporter system. Reports from other states were also difficult to acquire. Rhode Island and Georgia did not even report their supreme court decisions until 1828 and 1845. South Carolina had no unified courts of equity and law; thus reports for that state were divided. For a time, New York and North Carolina also published separate equity reports. Statutes were even more difficult to find. Most lawyers and judges relied on treatise writers, who ascertained the state of the law and provided voluminous citations to state, federal, and English cases. William Wetmore Story's *Treatise on the Law of Contracts* (1844), for example, cited over 3,500 cases. Story was the son of the greatest treatise writer of the age, Justice Joseph Story, whose various *Commentaries* on Agency, Bailments, Conflicts, Equity, Promissory Notes, and the Constitution made him "a one-man West Publication Company."[2] James Kent's four-volume *Commentaries on American Law* went through twelve editions between 1830 and 1873. These and more specialized treatises, such as Joseph Angell's *A Treatise on the Law of Watercourses* (five editions before 1854) and Francis Hilliard's *The Law of Torts and Private Wrongs* (1859), helped create a national legal system by giving Americans access to the growing number of reported cases, the various printed codes, and statutes. Treatises and commentaries enabled state judges from throughout the country to cite one another.

The growth of American law also mirrored changes in technology, commerce, and settlement. Steamboats, water-powered mills, and railroads revolutionized the economy as the new technology changed everything it touched. Workplaces became increasingly dangerous and impersonal, while machines gradually replaced skilled artisans. These changes led to litigation involving injured workers and labor unions. Technology also affected the property, safety, and lives of third parties. Cinders from trains could cause catastrophic fires, while crashes of steamboats or trains could harm freight, passengers, and even bystanders.

Business organizations became increasingly complex. Large factories, steamboats, and railroads required unprecedented capital formation. Initially, economic development depended on government intervention through public works projects (such as the Erie Canal), through monopolies (such as the New York steamboat franchise), or through special charters (such as that given to the First and Second Banks of the United States). Economic development depended on government intervention to protect or support particular industries and entrepreneurs. Supporters of these distributive governmental activities argued that the people of the state and the nation benefited from technological and economic developments. Chief Justice James Kent of New York applauded the steamboat monopoly because "under its auspices the experiment of navigating boats by steam has been made and crowned with triumphant success." Through such successes, the stockholders of the Bank of the United States and the owners of the steamboat monopoly—men of prominence, wealth, and political connection—benefited from the actions of the government.

Opponents of monopolies saw little justice in such governmental support, which they argued was a gift to special interests at the expense of the taxpayers. President Andrew Jackson thought government should "shower its favors alike on the high and the low, the rich and poor" and not give special benefits to powerful individuals. Competitors of state-supported monopolies argued that special charters and grants hurt consumers. Advocates of laissez-faire, they insisted that the law of the marketplace rather than government subsidies would bring about lower prices and better service.

By the mid-1830s, governments were moving away from direct support for economic development. Their place was taken by thousands of newly organized corporations. In the nineteenth century, Americans remade the corporation into a dynamic legal tool that enabled investors to pool their resources for rapid capital formation. This economic development led to an explosion in contract law. In 1765 William Blackstone's influential *Commentaries on the Laws of England* devoted only about forty pages, out of nearly two thousand, to contracts. But as changing national and international markets affected the price of goods and labor, agreements among corporations and individuals grew increasingly complex. By 1850 contracts had become the dominant field of American private law. This expanded contract law jettisoned old ideas of equity, fairness, and reasonableness. New measures of damages, based on expectations and changing values of goods, emerged. A meeting of the minds of two contractors replaced the older, and some would say paternalistic, concept that a contract was a fair exchange of goods or labor for money. The doctrine of caveat emptor replaced the idea that "a sound price warrants a sound commodity."

Similar changes swept tort law. In 1776 torts was almost unknown as a field. As late as 1835, Francis Hilliard's *The Elements of Law; Being a Comprehensive Summary of American*

Jurisprudence barely recognized the existence of tort law. However, tort law developed so rapidly that by 1859 Hilliard published a two-volume treatise on the subject, *The Law of Torts and Private Wrongs,* with citations to more than five thousand cases. Railroads, steamboats, mills, and urbanization were the great engines driving this revolution in tort law. By the end of the Civil War, some courts were beginning to conclude that an insurance policy rather than a lawsuit was the proper way for a society to allocate the costs of accidents due to technological change. Others, however, argued that industries that sought to profit from technology also had to bear the costs of damages to property and persons caused by the new technology.

Not every state court and state legislature embraced all these changes and developments. Southern states frequently rejected the application of certain rules, at least as they applied to slaves. Louisiana, continuing its civil law heritage, likewise rejected the concept of caveat emptor. In the West, a distinctly American law of water arose, to take into account differences of climate and topology.

Changing attitudes toward government intervention in the economy also affected economic growth and legal development. Before 1830, the federal government chartered a national bank, established protective tariffs, and built roads. But after 1835, the national government retreated from active participation in the economy and, with a few exceptions, left stimulation, promotion, and regulation to the states.

The states took various positions on economic development. New York led the way with the nation's most dramatic, ambitious, expensive, and ultimately successful internal improvement program—the Erie Canal and its system of feeder canals. Some states subsidized corporations, while others specifically prohibited subsidies. All the states gave railroads the right to take land through eminent domain proceedings, and most extended this right to mills and factories as well. Some states prohibited liquor sales on moral grounds, while others were the home of a growing alcoholic beverage industry. Mississippi prohibited the importation of slaves for sale, not on moral grounds, but in a futile attempt to limit the outflow of money from the state. The northern states ended slavery outright, and in the process not only destroyed the value of vast amounts of property in their own states, but challenged the rights of Southerners to bring their slave property into the free states.

The history of the nineteenth century demonstrates that the legal system facilitated the development of the economy. Legal historians disagree about the merits of this development. James Willard Hurst argues that "the central purpose of our legal order, [is] that law exists for the benefit of people and not people for the benefit of law." Hurst places particular emphasis on legislators who passed new laws that facilitated "the release of creative energies." Morton J. Horwitz, on the contrary, emphasizes "common law judges . . . play[ing] a central role in directing the course of social change." Numerous scholars have challenged this view. Peter Karsten, for example, argues that courts in fact were often sympathetic to those who sued corporations or in other ways challenged them. William J. Novak has argued that the thrust of antebellum law was not to support corporations or individuals, but rather to enhance the public welfare and that "public regulation—the power of the state to restrict individual liberty and property for the common welfare—colored all facets of early American development."[3] Hurst and Karsten see the law helping the common people of America; Horwitz finds a more narrowly directed "instrumentalism" that aided entrepreneurs and stockholders at the expense of poorer people; while Novak sees a regulated society in which lawmakers sought to serve the general public and thus might help entrepreneurs at one moment and then regulate them at the next.

The differences between these scholars illustrate some of the questions raised by the development of law in mid-nineteenth-century America. The debates among today's scholars reflect similar discussions among antebellum legislators, jurists, lawyers, and theorists. These debates over economic and legal policy were also affected by political questions that embraced not only the economy of the nation, but also the emerging sectional conflicts over slavery and the nature of the national Union itself. The important issues of slavery and the Union are dealt with in Chapter 4 of this book. Nevertheless, these public law questions should be kept in mind as we consider how the state and national governments affected the development of the economy and of private law in the nineteenth century. For example, behind almost every decision concerning interstate commerce U.S. Supreme Court justices weighed how the case might affect slavery and the interstate movement of slaves.

COMMERCE, LEGISLATIVE PROMOTION, AND LAW IN THE NEW REPUBLIC

From the end of the War of 1812 until the Civil War, private investors and the government were partners in the development of the economy. State courts and legislatures were often more important than individual entrepreneurs in stimulating commercial expansion and economic growth. The states encouraged new industries in a variety of ways, including subsidies, monopolies, enabling acts, and charters. States were particularly interested in expanding their transportation networks. Even before steam technology was perfected, New York granted monopolies to stimulate regular steamboat service in the state.

THE NEW YORK STEAMBOAT MONOPOLY AND THE FEDERAL COMMERCE POWER

New York's steamboat monopoly is a classic example of state economic intervention. In 1798 New York gave Robert R. Livingston an exclusive fourteen-year franchise to operate a steamboat "within" the state. In 1803 Livingston and Robert Fulton launched the nation's first steamboat. New York then granted Livingston and Fulton a new twenty-year franchise. In April 1808, when Livingston and Fulton finally began operating regular steamboat service between Albany and New York City, the legislature rewarded them by extending the monopoly until 1838 if they were able to put three more boats into operation. Anyone competing with the monopoly, in violation of this charter, "would forfeit" their "boats and vessels" and "engines."

Sometime after April 1808, James Van Ingen began to operate a steamboat between New York City and Albany, "in contravention of" Livingston's grant. In September 1811, Livingston and Fulton filed a bill in Chancery, asking that Van Ingen be enjoined from operating his steamboat in New York waters without their permission. On November 18, Chancellor John Lansing refused to grant Livingston and Fulton the injunction. In his opinion, Lansing wrote:

> Suppose this grant valid; if the legislature of this state could make an exclusive
> grant of that nature, could they not have extended it to vessels impelled *by the*

winds or *by oars,* and to vessels of every other description, capable of floating? If they cannot, where is the line of distinction to be drawn between what has been granted, and what is unsusceptible of grant? If carried to this extent, would it not be an abridgement of common rights? Could it comport with the constitutional provision, that the citizens of all the states are to have like privileges and immunities with the citizens of the several states? With whom are they to be ranked? With the class who hold exclusive rights in the state, or with the excluded class of citizens? If the most favored citizens are not to give the test, what proportion of the collective number of the citizens of this state are to constitute it? If a numerical calculation is to be admitted, are a tenth, a hundredth or a thousandth part to afford such test? Would it consist with the intent of the constitution of the *United States,* that any portion of the citizens of an individual state, described by their age, their occupations, or estates, should have the exclusive right of using the navigable waters of such state? Can the constitution be so constructed as to give rights to the citizens of all the states, superior to the rights of that state in which they are to be exercised? Or was the second section of the fourth article intended to secure equal rights to all? And should the grant in this case partake of the nature of a contract, could Its consideration be legally carved out of the *jus publicum* of the citizens of the *United States?*

Livingston v. Van Ingen
9 Johns. (N.Y.) 507 (1812)

After losing in Chancery Court, Livingston and Fulton appealed to the New York Court for the Trial of Impeachments and the Correction of Errors, which unanimously reversed Chancellor Lansing's decision and issued the injunction against Van Ingen. The decision was written by James Kent, one of the leading jurists and legal commentators of the first half of the nineteenth century.

Kent, Ch.J. The great point in this cause is, whether the several acts of the legislature which have been passed in favor of the appellants, are to be regarded as constitutional and binding.

In the first place, the presumption must be admitted to be extremely strong in favor of their validity. The act in the year 1798 was peculiarly calculated to awaken attention, as it was the first act that was passed upon the subject, after the adoption of the federal constitution, and it would naturally lead to a consideration of the power of the state to make such a grant. That act was, therefore, a legislative exposition given to the powers of the state governments, and there were circumstances existing at the time, which gave that exposition singular weight and importance. It was a new and original grant to one of the appellants, encouraging him, by the pledge of an exclusive privilege for twenty years, to engage, according to the language of the preamble to the statute, in the "uncertainty and hazard of a very expensive experiment." The legislature must have been clearly satisfied of their competency to make this pledge, or they acted with deception and injustice towards the individual on whose account it was made. There were members in that legislature, as well as in all the other departments of the government, who had been deeply concerned in the study of the constitution of the United States, and who were masters of all the critical discussions which had attended the interesting progress of its adoption. Several of them had been members of the state convention, and this was particularly the case with the exalted character, who at that time was chief magistrate of this state, (Mr. [John] Jay,) and who was distinguished, as well in the council of revision, as elsewhere, for the scrupulous care and profound attention with which he examined every question of a constitutional nature.

If they are void, it must be because the people of this state have alienated to the government of the United States their whole original power over the subject matter of the grant. No one can entertain a doubt of a competent power existing in the legislature, prior to the adoption of the federal constitution. The capacity to grant separate and exclusive privileges appertains to every sovereign authority. It is a necessary attribute of every independent government. All our bank charters, turnpike, canal and bridge companies, ferries, markets, &c. are grants of exclusive privileges for beneficial public purposes. These grants may possibly be inexpedient or unwise, but that has nothing to do with the question of constitutional right. In the present case, the grant to the appellants took away no vested right. It interfered with no man's property. It left every citizen to enjoy all the rights of navigation, and all the use of the waters of this state which he before enjoyed. There was, then, no injustice, no violation of first principles, in a grant to the appellants, for a limited time, of the exclusive benefit of their own hazardous and expensive experiments. The first impression upon every unprejudiced mind would be, that there was justice and policy in the grant. Clearly, then, it is valid, unless the power to make it be taken away by the constitution of the United States.

1. As to the power to regulate commerce. This power is not, in express terms, exclusive, and the only prohibition upon the states is, that they shall not enter into any treaty or compact with each other, or with a foreign power, nor lay any duty on tonnage, or on imports or exports, except what may be necessary for executing their inspection laws. Upon the principles above laid down, the states are under no other constitutional restriction, and are, consequently, left in possession of a vast field of commercial regulation; all the internal commerce of the state by land and water remains entirely, and

I may say exclusively, within the scope of its original sovereignty. The congressional power relates to external not to internal commerce, and it is confined to the regulation of that commerce. . . .

The states are under no other restrictions than those expressly specified in the constitution, and such regulations as the national government may, by treaty, and by laws, from time to time, prescribe. Subject to these restrictions, I contend, that the states are at liberty to make their own commercial regulations. There can be no other safe or practicable rule of conduct, and this, as I have already shown, is the true constitutional rule arising from the nature of our federal system. This does away all color: for the suggestion that the steam-boat grant is illegal and void under this clause in the constitution. It comes not within any prohibition upon the states, and it interferes with no existing regulation. Whenever the case shall arise of an exercise of power by congress which shall be directly repugnant and destructive to the use and enjoyment of the appellants' grant, it would fall under the cognizance of the federal courts, and they would, of course, take care that the laws of the union are duly supported. I must confess, however, that I can hardly conceive of such a case, because I do not, at present, perceive any power which congress can lawfully carry to that extent. But when there is no existing regulation which interferes with the grant, nor any pretence of a constitutional interdict, it would be extraordinary for us to adjudge it void, on the mere contingency of a collision with some future exercise of congressional power. Such a doctrine is a monstrous heresy. It would go, in a great degree, to annihilate the legislative power of the states. . . .

The grant to the appellants may, then, be considered as taken subject to such future commercial regulations as congress may lawfully prescribe. Congress, indeed, has not any direct jurisdiction over our interior commerce or waters. Hudson river is the property of the people of this state, and the legislature have the same jurisdiction over it that they have over the land, or over any of our rivers or lakes. They may, in their sound discretion, regulate and control, enlarge or abridge the use of its waters, and they are in the habitual exercise of that sovereign right. . . .

What has been the uniform, practical construction of this power? Let us examine the code of our statute laws. Our turnpike roads, our toll-bridges, the exclusive grant to run stage-wagons, our laws relating to paupers from other states, our Sunday laws, our rights of ferriage over navigable rivers and lakes, our auction licenses, our licenses to retail spirituous liquors, the laws to restrain hawkers and peddlers; what are all these provisions but regulations of internal commerce, affecting as well the intercourse between the citizens of this and other states, as between our own citizens? So we also exercise, to a considerable degree, a concurrent power with congress in the regulation of external commerce. What are our inspection laws relative to the staple commodities of this state, which prohibit the exportation, except upon certain conditions, of flour, of salt provisions, of certain articles of lumber, and of pot and pearl ashes, but regulations of external commerce? Our health and quarantine laws, and the laws prohibiting the importation of slaves, are striking examples of the same kind.

Are we prepared to say, in the face of all these regulations, which form such a mass of evidence of the uniform construction of our powers, that a special privilege for the exclusive navigation by a steam-boat upon our waters, is void, because it may, by possibility, and in the course of events, interfere with the power granted to congress to regulate commerce? Nothing, in my opinion, would be more preposterous and extravagant. Which of our existing regulations may not equally interfere with the power of congress? It is said that a steamboat may become the vehicle of foreign commerce; and, it is asked, can then the entry of them into this state, or the use of them within it, be prohibited? I answer yes, equally as we may prohibit the entry or use of slaves, or of pernicious animals, or an obscene book, or infectious goods, or any thing else that the legislature shall deem noxious or inconvenient. Our quarantine laws amount to an occlusion of the port of New-York from a portion of foreign commerce, for several months in the year; and the mayor is even authorized under those laws

to stop all commercial intercourse with the ports of any neighboring state.

The grant of 1798, was made to Chancellor Livingston, as "the possessor of a mode of applying the steam engine to propel a boat on new and advantageous principles." This power to encourage the importation of improvements, by the grant of an exclusive enjoyment, for a limited period, is extremely useful, and the English nation have long perceived and felt its beneficial effects. This will appear by a cursory view of the law of that country. The creation of monopolies was anciently claimed and exercised as a branch of the royal prerogative.

. . . [T]he uniform opinion, in England . . . has been that imported improvements, no less than original inventions ought to be encouraged by patent. And can we for a moment suppose that such a power does not exist in the several states? We have seen that it does not belong to congress, and if it does not reside in the states, it resides nowhere, and is wholly extinguished. This would be leaving the states in a condition of singular and contemptible imbecility. The power is important in itself, and may be most beneficially exercised for the, encouragement of the arts; and if well and judiciously exerted, it may ameliorate the condition of society, by enriching and adorning the country with useful and elegant improvements. This ground is clear of any constitutional difficulty, and renders the argument in favor of the validity of the statutes perfectly conclusive. And permit me here to add, that I think the power has been wisely applied, in the instance before us, to the creation of the privilege now in controversy. Under its auspices the experiment of navigating boats by steam has been made, and crowned with triumphant success. Every lover of the arts, every patron of useful improvement, every friend to his country's honor, has beheld this success with pleasure and admiration. From this single source the improvement is progressively extending to all the navigable waters of the United States, and it promises to become a great public blessing, by giving astonishing facility, despatch and safety, not only to travelling, but to the internal commerce of this country. It is difficult to consider even the known results of the undertaking, without feeling a sentiment of good will and gratitude towards the individuals by whom they have been procured, and who have carried on their experiment with patient industry, at great expense, under repeated disappointments, and while constantly exposed to be held up, as dreaming projectors, to the whips and scorns of time. So far from charging the authors of the grant with being rash and inconsiderate, or from wishing to curtail the appellants of their liberal recompense, I think the prize has been dearly earned and fairly won, and that the statutes bear the stamp of an enlightened and munificent spirit.

I am accordingly of opinion . . . that an injunction be awarded.

Note: The Mix of Economics, Politics, and Law

Besides the constitutional issues, *Livingston* v. *Van Ingen* raised questions about how the economy ought to be organized. Supporters of exclusive franchises argued that technological change was expensive and risky, and that grants such as the steamboat monopoly encouraged entrepreneurs to take risks and make investments that would benefit the entire society. Opponents argued that the franchise was a special privilege, granted to those with money and power.

This case also had political overtones. Lansing had been a leading Antifederalist in 1787, while Livingston had been one of New York's most vocal Federalists. Both Livingston and Lansing later allied themselves with Jefferson, but relations between the two were strained. James Kent, however, was an unabashed Federalist who disagreed with Lansing on almost all political and economic issues.

Article I, Section 8, of the Constitution gave Congress power to regulate commerce among the states, with foreign nations, and with Indians. In *The Federalist,* Number 42, James Madison argued that this clause would prevent "unceasing animosities" over commerce that would "terminate in serious interruptions of the public tranquility." *Gibbons* v. *Ogden* illustrates the interstate rivalries and hostility that Madison feared.

Gibbons v. *Ogden*
9 Wheat. (22 U.S.) 1 (1824)

In 1815 Aaron Ogden, a former governor of New Jersey, purchased from the owners of the Livingston-Fulton franchise the right to operate a steamboat from New York City to Elizabethtown, New Jersey. In 1819 Ogden sued his former partner, Thomas Gibbons, for infringing on his franchise rights by independently operating a steamboat service between New York and New Jersey. This case raised a critical federal issue. Gibbons argued that his federal coasting license entitled him to operate his boats anywhere in the United States. In upholding the right of New York to grant a steamboat monopoly, Chancellor Kent rejected this argument. In Gibbons v. Ogden, *17 Johns. (N.Y.) 488 (1820), New York's highest court affirmed Kent's ruling. Gibbons appealed to the United States Supreme Court. By this time, New Jersey and Connecticut had adopted laws retaliating against New York ships. Although docketed in 1820, the case was not finally decided until 1824, when Chief Justice Marshall rejected the New York monopoly with his crucial interpretation of the commerce clause.*

Mr. Chief Justice Marshall. . . .

The appellant contends that this decree [the injunction against Gibbons] is erroneous, because the laws which purport to give the exclusive privilege it sustains, are repugnant to the constitution and laws of the United States.

They are said to be repugnant—

1st. To that clause in the constitution which authorizes Congress to regulate commerce.

The words are, "Congress shall have power to regulate commerce with foreign nations, and among the several States, and with the Indian tribes."

The subject to be regulated is commerce. . . . The counsel for the appellee would limit it to traffic, to buying and selling, or the interchange of commodities, and do not admit that it comprehends navigation. This would restrict a general term, applicable to many objects, to one of its significations. Commerce, undoubtedly, is traffic, but it is something more: it is intercourse. It describes the commercial intercourse between nations, and parts of nations, in all its branches, and is regulated by prescribing rules for carrying on that intercourse. The mind can scarcely conceive a system for regulating commerce between nations, which shall be silent on the admission of the vessels of the one nation into the ports of the other, and be confined to prescribing rules for the conduct of individuals, in the actual employment of buying and selling, or of barter.

If commerce does not include navigation, the government of the Union has no direct power over that subject, and can make no law prescribing what shall constitute American vessels, or requiring that they shall be navigated by American seamen. Yet this power has been exercised from the commencement of the government, has been exercised with the consent of all, and has been understood by all to be a commercial regulation. All America understands, and has uniformly understood, the word "commerce," to comprehend navigation. It was so understood, and must have been so understood, when the constitution was framed. The power over commerce, including navigation, was one of the primary objects for which the people of America adopted their government, and must have been contemplated in forming it. The convention must have used the word in that sense, because all have understood it in that sense; and the attempt to restrict it comes too late.

The word used in the constitution, then, comprehends, and has been always understood to comprehend, navigation within its meaning; and a power to regulate navigation, is as expressly granted, as if that term had been added to the word "commerce."

The subject to which the power is next applied, is to commerce "among the several States." The word "among" means intermingled with. . . . Commerce among the States, cannot stop at the external boundary line of each State, but may be introduced into the interior.

It is not intended to say that these words comprehend that commerce, which is completely internal, which is carried on between man and man in a State, or between different parts of the same State, and which does not extend to or affect other States. Such a power would be inconvenient, and is certainly unnecessary.

Comprehensive as the word "among" is, it may very properly be restricted to that commerce which concerns more States than one. The phrase is not one which would probably have been selected to indicate the completely interior traffic of a State, because it is not an apt phrase for that purpose. . . . The completely internal commerce of a State, then, may be considered as reserved for the State itself.

But, in regulating commerce with foreign nations, the power of Congress does not stop at jurisdictional lines of the several States. It would be a very useless power, if it could not pass those lines. The commerce of the United States with foreign nations, is that of the whole United States. Every district has a right to participate in it. The deep streams which penetrate our country in every direction, pass through the interior of almost every State in the Union, and furnish the means of exercising this right. If Congress has the power to regulate it, that power must be exercised whenever the subject exists. If it exists within the States, if a foreign voyage may commence or terminate at a port within a State, then the power of Congress may be exercised within a State.

This principle is, if possible, still more clear, when applied to commerce "among the several States." They either join each other, in which case they are separated by a mathematical line, or they are remote from each other, in which case other States lie between them. What is commerce "among" them; and how is it to be conducted? Can a trading expedition between two adjoining States, commence and terminate outside of each? And if the trading intercourse be between two States remote from each other, must it not commence in one, terminate in the other, and probably pass through a third? Commerce among the States must, of necessity, be commerce with the States. . . . We are now arrived at the inquiry—What is this power?

It is the power to regulate; that is, to prescribe the rule by which commerce is to be governed. This power, like all others vested in Congress, is complete in itself, may be exercised to its utmost extent, and acknowledges no limitations, other than are prescribed in the constitution. These are expressed in plain terms, and do not affect the questions which arise in this case. . . . [T]he sovereignty of Congress, though limited to specified objects, is plenary as to those objects, the power over commerce with foreign nations, and among the several States, is vested in Congress as absolutely as it would be in a single government, having in its constitution the same restrictions on the exercise of the power as are found in the constitution of the United States. The wisdom and the discretion of Congress, their identity with the people, and the influence which their constituents possess at elections, are, in this, as in many other instances, as that, for example, of declaring war, the sole restraints on which they have relied, to secure them from its abuse. They are the restraints on which the people must often rely solely, in all representative governments.

The power of Congress, then, comprehends navigation, within the limits of every State in the Union; so far as that navigation may be, in any manner, connected with "commerce with foreign nations, or among the several States, or with the Indian tribes." It may, of consequence, pass the jurisdictional line of New York, and act upon the very waters to which the prohibition now under consideration applies.

But it has been urged that, although the power of Congress to regulate commerce . . . have no other limits than are prescribed in the constitution, yet the States may severally exercise the same power, within their respective jurisdictions. In support of this argument, it is said, that they possessed it as an inseparable attribute of sovereignty, before the formation of the constitution, and still retain it, except so far as they have surrendered it by that instrument; that this principle results from the nature of the government, and is secured by the tenth amendment; that an affirmative grant of power is not exclusive, unless in its own nature it be such that the continued exercise of it by the former possessor is inconsistent with the grant, and that this is not of that description.

The grant of the power to lay and collect taxes is like the power to regulate commerce, made in general terms, and has never been understood to interfere with the exercise of the same power by the States; and hence . . . has been applied to the question under consideration. But the two grants are not . . . similar in their terms or their nature. Although many of the powers formerly exercised by the States, are transferred to the government of the Union, yet the State governments remain, and constitute a most important part of our system. The power of taxation is indispensable to their existence, and is a power which . . . is capable of residing in, and being exercised by, different authorities at the same time. We are accustomed to see it placed, for different purposes, in different heads. Taxation . . . is not incompatible with a power in another to take what is necessary for other purposes. Congress is authorized to lay and collect taxes, &c. to pay the debts, and provide for the common defence and general welfare of the United States. This does not interfere with the power of the States to tax for the support of their own governments; nor is the exercise of that power by the States an exercise of any portion of the power that is granted to the United States. . . . But, when a State proceeds to regulate commerce with foreign nations, or among the several States, it is exercising the very power that is granted to Congress, and is doing the very thing which Congress is authorized to do. There is no analogy, then, between the power of taxation and the power of regulating commerce.

. . . The sole question is, can a State regulate commerce with foreign nations and among the States, while Congress is regulating it?

◆ ◆ ◆

In argument . . . it has been contended that if a law, passed by a state in the exercise of its acknowledged sovereignty, comes into conflict with a law passed by Congress in pursuance of the constitution, they affect the subject, and each other, like equal opposing powers.

But the framers of our constitution foresaw this state of things, and provided for it, by declaring the supremacy not only of itself, but of the laws made in pursuance of it. The nullity of any act, inconsistent with the constitution, is produced by the declaration that the constitution is the supreme law. . . . In every case the act of Congress or the treaty, is supreme; and the law of the state, though not enacted, in the exercise of powers not controverted, must yield to it.

In pursuing this inquiry at the bar, it has been said that the constitution does not confer the right of intercourse between state and state. That right derives its source from those laws whose authority is acknowledged by civilized man throughout the world. This is true. The constitution found it an existing right, and gave to Congress the power to regulate it. In the exercise of this power, Congress has passed "an act for enrolling or licensing ships or vessels to be employed in the coasting trade and fisheries, and for regulating the same." The counsel for the respondent contend, that this act does not give the right to sail from port to port, but confines itself to regulating a pre-existing right, so far only as to confer certain privileges on enrolled and licensed vessels in its exercise.

♦   ♦   ♦

This act demonstrates the opinion of Congress, that steam boats may be enrolled and licensed, in common with vessels using sails. They are, of course, entitled to the same privileges, and can no more be restrained from navigating waters, and entering ports which are free to such vessels, than if they were wafted on their voyage by the winds, instead of being propelled by the agency of fire. The one element may be as legitimately used as the other, for every commercial purpose authorized by the laws of the Union; and the act of a State inhibiting the use of either to any vessel having a license under the act of Congress comes, we think, in direct collision with that act.

Note: The Effect of *Gibbons*

Marshall's opinion was generally greeted with praise. Most Americans believed that the transportation monopolies hindered economic growth and led to unnecessary interstate conflicts. Within two weeks after the decision, a ship from Connecticut arrived in New York harbor. This was the end of interstate rivalries and retaliation over shipping monopolies. Within a year, the New York court struck down the Livingston monopoly for shipping solely within the state. *Gibbons* is the most important commerce clause case in Supreme Court history. All subsequent nineteenth-century commerce clause cases (and many twentieth-century ones) were, to a great extent, merely commentary on *Gibbons.*

THE SECOND BANK OF THE UNITED STATES

In 1791, Secretary of the Treasury Alexander Hamilton proposed that Congress charter the Bank of the United States, which would be a depository for public funds and serve as the government's central financial institution, regulating currency and lending money to the national treasury. The bank would also be a private corporation whose stockholders would share the profits. The bank raised fundamental questions of distributive justice. Should the government give public support to a private enterprise in such a way that some would benefit and others might be harmed? Or should the government avoid such economic activity, even if the commerce of the entire nation suffered? These continued as political and legal issues for the next forty years.

Hamilton believed that the bank was vital for economic development and that it would make the young nation prosperous, vigorous, and glorious. He argued that the bank was constitutionally permissible, under the necessary and proper clause of Article I. Congressman James Madison and Secretary of State Thomas Jefferson opposed the bank because it would aid business interests and argued that Congress lacked the power to grant corporate charters. After considering these arguments, President Washington signed the bill granting the bank a twenty-year charter. In 1811, Congress refused to recharter the bank, in part on constitutional grounds similar to those used by Jefferson and Madison in 1791.

In 1816, in the aftermath of the War of 1812, Congress rechartered the bank as the Second Bank of the United States. President Madison now supported the bank, believing that the constitutional question was "precluded . . . by repeated circumstances of the validity of such an institution in acts of the legislative, executive, and judicial branches, of the Government . . . [and] a concurrence of the general will of the nation."

Private investors held 80 percent of the Second Bank's stock and elected twenty directors. The federal government owned the remaining stock, and the president appointed five directors. The bank's notes were legal tender for payment of debts and federal taxes and functioned as the only national currency. Congress guaranteed it would not charter any competing banks. The charter regulated the types of loans the bank could make, required that the bank make reports to the Secretary of the Treasury, made the bank's records available to congressional committees, and stipulated that the bank maintain branch offices throughout the nation. The charter also required the bank to pay the United States government $1.5 million.

By 1818, much of the bank's support had evaporated, especially in the South and the West. The bank's monopoly seemed undemocratic, and some of its speculative investments and a few fraudulent activities by some bank officials led to local opposition. The bank's tight credit policies were constricting the economy, gradually pushing the nation toward the Panic of 1819. In this atmosphere, two states prohibited the bank outright, while six others taxed the bank's operations.

McCulloch v. Maryland
4 Wheat. (17 U.S.) 316 (1819)

Maryland imposed a tax of $15,000 on all banks operating in the state that were not chartered by the state. Only the Bank of the United States fit this description. The bank's cashier at the Baltimore branch, James McCulloch, refused to pay the tax. The Maryland Supreme Court upheld the tax, and McCulloch appealed to the United States Supreme Court.

Mr. Chief Justice Marshall delivered the opinion of the Court.

In the case now to be determined, the defendant, a sovereign State, denies the obligation of a law enacted by the legislature of the Union, and the plaintiff, on his part, contests the validity of an act which has been passed by the legislature of that State. The constitution of our country, in its most interesting and vital parts, is to be considered; the conflicting powers of the government of the Union and of its members, as marked in that constitution, are to be discussed; and an opinion given, which may essentially influence the great operations of the government.

The first question made in the cause is, has Congress power to incorporate a bank?

It has been truly said, that this can scarcely be considered as an open question. . . . The principle now contested was introduced at a very early period of our history, has been recognized by many successive legislatures, and has been acted upon by the judicial department, in cases of peculiar delicacy, as a law of undoubted obligation.

♦ ♦ ♦

In discussing this question, the counsel for the State of Maryland have deemed it of some importance, in the construction of the constitution, to consider that instrument not as emanating from the people, but as the act of sovereign and independent States. The powers of the general government, it has been said, are delegated by the States, who alone are truly sovereign; and must be exercised in subordination to the States, who alone possess supreme dominion.

It would be difficult to sustain this proposition. The Convention which framed the constitution was indeed elected by the State legislatures. But the instrument, when it came from their hands, was a mere proposal, without obligation. . . . It was reported to the then existing Congress of the United States, with a request that it might "be submitted to a Convention of Delegates, chosen in each State by the people thereof, under the recommendation of its Legislature, for their assent and ratification." This mode of proceeding was adopted; and by the Convention, by Congress, and by the State Legislatures, the instrument was submitted to the people. They acted upon it in the only manner in which they can act safely, effectively, and wisely, on such a subject, by assembling in Convention.

From these Conventions the constitution derives its whole authority. The government proceeds directly from the people; is "ordained and established" in the name of the people; and is declared to be ordained, "in order to form a more perfect union, establish justice, ensure domestic tranquility, and the blessings of liberty to themselves and to their posterity." The assent of the States, in their sovereign capacity, is implied in calling a Convention, and thus submitting that instrument to the people. But the people were at perfect liberty to accept or reject it; and their act was final. It required not the affirmance, and could not be negatived, by the State governments. The constitution, when thus adopted, was of complete obligation, and bound the State sovereignties.

The government of the Union, then . . . is, emphatically, and truly, a government of the people. In form and in substance it emanates from them. Its powers are granted by them, and are to be exercised directly on them, and for their benefit.

This government is acknowledged by all to be one of enumerated powers. The principle, that it can exercise only the powers granted to it . . . is now universally admitted. But the question respecting the extent of the powers actually granted, is perpetually arising, and will probably continue to arise, as long as our system shall exist.

♦ ♦ ♦

If any one proposition could command the universal assent of mankind, we might expect it would be this—that the government of the Union, though limited in its powers, is supreme within its sphere of action. This would seem to result necessarily from its nature. It is the government of all; its powers are delegated by all; it represents all, and acts for all. The nation, on those subjects on which it can act, must necessarily bind its component parts. But this question is not left to mere reason: the people have, in express terms, decided it, by saying, "this constitution, and the laws of the United States, which shall be made in pursuance thereof," "shall be the supreme law of the land," and by requiring that the members of the State legislatures, and the officers of the executive and judicial departments of the States, shall take the oath of fidelity to it.

The government of the United States, then, though limited in its powers, is supreme; and its laws, when made in pursuance of the constitution, form the supreme law of the land, "any thing in the constitution or laws of any State to the contrary notwithstanding."

Among the enumerated powers, we do not find that of establishing a bank or creating a corporation. But there is no phrase in the instrument which, like the articles of confederation, excludes incidental or implied powers; and which requires that every thing granted shall be expressly and minutely described. Even the 10th amendment, which was framed for the purpose of quieting the excessive jealousies which had been excited, omits the word "expressly," and declares only that the powers "not delegated to the United States, nor prohibited to the States, are reserved to the States or to the people;" thus leaving the question, whether the particular power which may become the subject of contest has been delegated to the one government, or prohibited to the other, to depend on a fair construction of the whole instrument. The men who drew and adopted this amendment had experienced the embarrassments resulting from the insertion of this word in the articles of confederation, and probably omitted it to avoid those embarrassments. A constitution, to contain an accurate detail of all the subdivisions of which its great powers will admit, and of all the means by which they may be carried into execution, would partake of the prolixity of a legal code, and could scarcely be embraced by the human mind. It would probably never be understood by the public. Its nature, therefore, requires, that only its great outlines should be marked, its important objects designated, and the minor ingredients which compose those objects be deduced from the nature of the objects themselves. That this idea was entertained by the framers of the American constitution, is not only to be inferred from the nature of the instrument, but from the language. Why else were some of the limitations, found in the ninth section of the 1st article, introduced? It is also, in some degree, warranted by their having omitted to use any restrictive term which might prevent its receiving a fair and just interpretation. In considering this question, then we must never forget, that it is a *constitution* we are expounding.

Although, among the enumerated powers of government, we do not find the word "bank" or "incorporation," we find the great powers to lay and collect taxes; to borrow money; to regulate commerce; to declare and conduct a war; and to raise and support armies and navies. The sword and the purse, all the external relations,

and no inconsiderable portion of the industry of the nation, are intrusted to its government. It can never be pretended that these vast powers draw after them others of inferior importance, merely because they are inferior. Such an idea can never be advanced. But it may with great reason be contended, that a government, entrusted with such ample powers, on the due execution of which the happiness and prosperity of the nation so vitally depends, must also be entrusted with ample means for their execution. The power being given, it is the interest of the nation to facilitate its execution. . . . Throughout this vast republic, revenue is to be collected and expended, armies are to be marched and supported. The exigencies of the nation may require that the treasure raised in the north should be transported to the south, that raised in the east conveyed to the west, or that this order should be reversed. Is that construction of the constitution to be preferred which would render these operations difficult, hazardous, and expensive? Can we adopt that construction, (unless the words imperiously require it,) which would impute to the framers of that instrument, when granting these powers for the public good, the intention of impeding their exercise by withholding a choice of means? If, indeed, such be the mandate of the constitution, we have only to obey; but that instrument does not profess to enumerate the means by which the powers it confers may be executed; nor does it prohibit the creation of a corporation, if the existence of such a being be essential to the beneficial exercise of those powers. It is, then, the subject of fair inquiry, how far such means may be employed.

◆   ◆   ◆

The creation of a corporation, it is said, appertains to sovereignty. This is admitted. . . . In America, the powers of sovereignty are divided between the government of the Union, and those of the States. They are each sovereign with respect to the objects committed to the other. . . . The power of creating a corporation, though appertaining to sovereignty, is not, like the power of making a war, or levying taxes, or of regulating commerce, a great substantive and independent power. . . . It is never the end for which other powers are exercised, but a means by which other objects are accomplished. . . . No sufficient reason is, therefore, perceived, why it may not pass as incidental to those powers which are expressly given, if it be a direct mode of executing them.

But the constitution of the United States has not left the right of Congress to employ the necessary means, for the execution of the powers conferred on the government, to general reasoning. To its enumeration of powers is added that of making "all laws which shall be necessary and proper, for carrying into execution the foregoing powers, and all other powers vested by this constitution, in the government of the United States, or in any department thereof."

♦ ♦ ♦

The subject is the execution of those great powers on which the welfare of a nation essentially depends. It must have been the intention of those who gave these powers, to insure, as far as human prudence could insure, their beneficial execution. This could not be done by confiding the choice of means to such narrow limits as not to leave it in the power of Congress to adopt any which might be appropriate, and which were conducive to the end. This provision is made in a constitution intended to endure for the ages to come, and consequently, to be adapted to the various *crises* of human affairs. To have prescribed the means by which government should, in all future time, execute its powers, would have been to change, entirely, the character of the instrument, and give it the properties of a legal code. It would have been an unwise attempt to provide, by immutable rules, for exigencies which, if foreseen at all, must have been seen dimly, and which can be best provided for as they occur. To have declared that the best means shall not be used, but that those alone without which the power given would be nugatory, would have been to deprive the legislature of the capacity to avail itself of experience, to exercise its reason, and to accommodate its legislation to circumstances. If we apply this principle of construction to any of the powers of the government, we shall find it so pernicious in its

operation that we shall be compelled to discard it.

♦ ♦ ♦

In ascertaining the sense in which the word "necessary" is used in this clause of the constitution, we may derive some aid from that with which it is associated. Congress shall have power "to make all laws which shall be necessary and proper to carry into execution" the powers of the government. If the word "necessary" was used in that strict and rigorous sense for which the counsel for the State of Maryland contend, it would be an extraordinary departure from the usual course of the human mind, as exhibited in composition, to add a word, the only possible effect of which is to qualify that strict and rigorous meaning; to present to the mind the idea of some choice of means of legislation not straitened and compressed within the narrow limits for which gentlemen contend.

But the argument which most conclusively demonstrates the error of the construction contended for by the counsel for the State of Maryland, is founded on the intention of the Convention, as manifested in the whole clause. . . . That it might employ those which, in its judgement, would most advantageously effect the object to be accomplished. That any means adapted to the end, any means which tended directly to the execution of the constitutional powers of the government, were in themselves constitutional. This clause, as constructed by the State of Maryland, would abridge, and almost annihilate this useful and necessary right of the legislature to select its means. That this could not be intended, is . . . too apparent for controversy. We think so for the following reasons:

1st. The clause is placed among the powers of Congress, not among the limitations on those powers.

2nd. Its terms purport to enlarge, not to diminish the powers vested in the government. It purports to be an additional power, not a restriction on those already granted. No reason has been, or can be assigned for this concealing an intention to narrow the discretion of the national legislature under words which purport to enlarge it. The framers of the constitution wished its adoption, and well knew that it would be endangered by its strength, not by its weakness.

. . . If no other motive for its insertion can be suggested, a sufficient one is found in the desire to remove all doubts respecting the right to legislate on that vast mass of incidental powers which must be involved in the constitution, if that instrument be not a splendid bauble.

We admit, as all must admit, that the powers of the government are limited, and that its limits are not to be transcended. But we think the sound construction of the constitution must allow to the national legislature that discretion, with respect to the means by which the powers it confers are to be carried into execution, which will enable that body to perform the high duties assigned to it, in the manner most beneficial to the people. Let the end be legitimate, let it be within the scope of the constitution, and all means which are appropriate, which are plainly adapted to that end, which are not prohibited, but consist with the letter and spirit of the constitution, are constitutional.

♦ ♦ ♦

It being the opinion of the Court, that the act incorporating the bank is constitutional; and that the power of establishing a branch in the State of Maryland might be properly exercised by the bank itself, we proceed to inquire—

2. Whether the State of Maryland may, without violating the constitution, tax that branch?

That the power to tax involves the power to destroy; that the power to destroy may defeat and render useless the power to create; that there is a plain repugnance, in conferring on one government a power to control the constitutional measures of another, which other, with respect to those very measures, is declared to be supreme over that which exerts the control, are propositions not to be denied. But all inconsistencies are to be reconciled by the magic of the word *confidence*. Taxation, it is said, does not necessarily and unavoidably destroy. To

carry it to the excess of destruction would be an abuse, to presume which, would banish that confidence which is essential to all government.

But is this a case of confidence? Would the people of any one State trust those of another with a power to control the most insignificant operations of their State government? We know they would not. Why, then, should we suppose that the people of any one State should be willing to trust those of another with a power to control the operations of a government to which they have confided their most important and most valuable interests? In the legislature of the Union alone, are all represented. The legislature of the Union alone, therefore, can be trusted by the people with the power of controlling measures which concern all, in the confidence that it will not be abused. This, then, is not a case of confidence, and we must consider it as it really is.

If the States may tax one instrument, employed by the government in the execution of its powers, they may tax any and every other instrument. They may tax the mail; they may tax the mint; they may tax patent rights; they may tax the papers of the custom-house; they may tax judicial process; they may tax all the means employed by the government, to an excess which would defeat all the ends of government. This was not intended by the American people. They did not design to make their government dependent on the States.

The Court has bestowed on this subject its most deliberate consideration. The result is a conviction that the States have no power, by taxation or other-wise, to retard, impede, burden, or in any manner control, the operations of the constitutional laws enacted by Congress to carry into execution the powers vested in the general government. This is, we think, the unavoidable consequence of that supremacy which the constitution has declared.

We are unanimously of opinion, that the law passed by the legislature of Maryland, imposing a tax on the Bank of the United States, is unconstitutional and void.

Note: A Court Opinion as Political Theory

Next to *Marbury* v. *Madison, McCulloch* was Chief Justice John Marshall's most important decision. The power of the reasoning, the strength of the argument, and the overall vision of the national government make this Marshall's "greatest" opinion. But was this thirty-seven-page opinion (remarkably long for the era) a work of law or of political theory? Marshall cited no cases at all. *The Federalist,* congressional debates, the Articles of Confederation, and the Constitution are the only external sources he noted. Marshall argued that the Framers intended to write a Constitution that would "endure for ages to come." He interpreted the intentions from the text, and argued that the text was open-ended so that the Constitution could grow and develop over time. The opinion has shaped most subsequent American constitutional and political history because of Marshall's expansive interpretation of the necessary and proper clause.

ANDREW JACKSON

Veto Message
July 10, 1832

In June 1832, Congress extended the charter of the bank. Friends of the bank believed President Andrew Jackson would sign the bill because it had passed by large margins in both houses. But the bank's supporters miscalculated. Jackson despised the Second Bank of the United States, which he blamed for causing the Panic of 1819, in which Jackson personally lost money. Jackson, the nation's first western president, also saw the bank as the symbol of eastern power and privilege. He also objected to the fact that the bank was controlled by only a few hundred American stockholders and that nearly one-quarter of the stock was owned by foreigners. Furthermore, he thought the bill would enrich these already wealthy people at the expense of the nation. Finally, Jackson disliked monopolies and thought they should rarely be granted because their profits ultimately came "directly or indirectly out of the earnings of the American people." Having established the impolicy of the bank in the first part of his veto message, Jackson turned to its constitutionality.

It is maintained by the advocates of the bank that its constitutionality in all its features ought to be considered as settled by precedent and by the decision of the Supreme Court. To this conclusion I can not assent. Mere precedent is a dangerous source of authority, and should not be regarded as deciding questions of constitutional power except where the acquiescence of the people and the States can be considered as well settled. So far from this being the case on this subject, an argument against the bank might be based on precedent. One Congress, in 1791, decided in favor of a bank; another, in 1811, decided against it. One Congress, in 1815, decided against a bank; another, in 1816, decided in its favor. Prior to the present Congress, therefore, the precedents drawn from that source were equal. If we resort to the States, the expressions of legislative, judicial, and executive opinions against the bank have been probably to those in its favor as 4 to 1. There is nothing in precedent, therefore, which, if its authority were admitted, ought to weigh in favor of the act before me.

If the opinion of the Supreme Court covered the whole ground of this act, it ought not to control the coordinate authorities of this Government. The Congress, the Executive, and the Court must each for itself be guided by its own opinion of the Constitution. Each public officer who takes an oath to support the Constitution swears that he will support it as he understands it, and not as it is understood by others. It is as much the duty of the House of Representatives, of the Senate, and of the President to decide upon the constitutionality of any bill or resolution . . . as it is of the supreme judges. . . . The opinion of the judges has no more authority over Congress than the opinion of Congress has over the judges, and on that point the President is independent of both. The authority of the Supreme Court must not, therefore, be permitted to control the Congress or the Executive when acting in their legislative capacities, but to have only such influence as the force of their reasoning may deserve.

It is to be regretted that the rich and powerful too often bend the acts of government to their selfish purposes. Distinctions in society will always exist under every just government. Equality of talents, of education, or of wealth can not be produced by human institutions. In the full enjoyment of the gifts of Heaven and the fruits of superior industry, economy, and virtue, every man is equally entitled to protection by law; but when the laws undertake to add to these natural and just advantages artificial distinctions, to grant titles, gratuities, and exclusive privileges, to make the rich richer and the potent more powerful, the humble members of society—the farmers, mechanics, and laborers—who have neither the time nor the means of securing like favors to themselves, have a right to complain of the injustice of their Government. There are no necessary evils in government. Its evils exist only in its abuses. If it would confine itself to equal protection, and, as Heaven does its rains, shower its favors alike on the high and the low, the rich and the poor, it would be an unqualified blessing. In the act before me there seems to be a wide and unnecessary departure from these just principles.

Nor is our Government to be maintained or our Union preserved by invasions of the rights and powers of the several States. In thus attempting to make our General Government strong we make it weak. Its true strength consists in leaving individuals and States as much as possible to themselves—in making itself felt, not in its power, but in its beneficence; not in its control, but in its protection; not in binding the States more closely to the center, but leaving each to move unobstructed in its proper orbit.

Experience should teach us wisdom. Most of the difficulties our Government now encounters and most of the dangers which impend over our Union have sprung from an abandonment of the legitimate objects of Government by our national legislation, and the adoption of such principles as are embodied in this act. Many of our rich men have not been content with equal protection and equal benefits, but have besought us to make them richer by act of Congress. By attempting to gratify their desires we have in the results of our legislation arrayed section against section, interest against interest, and man against man, in a fearful commotion which threatens to shake the foundations of our Union. It is time to pause in our career to review our principles, and if possible revive that devoted patriotism and spirit of compromise which distinguished the sages of the Revolution and the fathers of our Union. We can at least take a stand against all new grants of monopolies and exclusive privileges, against any prostitution of our Government to the advancement of the few at the expense of the many.

Note: Jacksonian Economics

This veto illustrates the hostility of Jackson and his followers to government intervention in the economy and to the privileged rich. After the veto, he ordered the removal of all government deposits in the bank. Two Secretaries of the Treasury refused to remove the deposits because they feared that such an act would destroy the economy. Jackson finally appointed Roger B. Taney to the post, and he removed the deposits. In 1832, Jackson was reelected, campaigning against the "monster bank." Jackson rewarded Taney by appointing him Chief Justice of the United States. Shortly after Jackson left office, the Panic of 1837 broke out, dooming his successor, Martin Van Buren. With a few exceptions, Jackson's veto also ended any active role for the antebellum federal government in the nation's economy.

After the War of 1812, there was widespread support for federal aid to economic development. John C. Calhoun's "Bonus Bill" (1817) provided funds for internal improvements from money paid to the government by the Second Bank of the United States. President

Madison vetoed this bill on constitutional grounds. President Monroe supported "the systematic and fostering care of the government for our manufacturers," but agreed with Madison that the Constitution prohibited federal funding of internal improvements. Monroe asked for a constitutional amendment to change this situation. No amendment was adopted, and in 1830 Andrew Jackson vetoed the Maysville Road Bill, asserting that because the road would be built entirely within one state (Kentucky), Congress had no power to fund it. This veto was also a slap at Jackson's Whig rival, Kentuckian Henry Clay. Jackson signed the Cumberland Road Bill in 1830, but that ended his support for internal improvements. In 1832, Jackson vetoed the rechartering of the Second Bank of the United States.

Note: A Federal Common Law

In *United States* v. *Hudson and Goodwin* (1812) and *United States* v. *Coolidge* (1816), the Supreme Court held that there was no federal common law of crimes and that prosecutions in federal court had to be based on a federal statute. However, in *Swift* v. *Tyson* (1842), a unanimous Supreme Court held that for civil litigation there was a federal common law, and federal district judges could develop their own rules, independent of state decisions and laws, consistent with final review by the Supreme Court. This resulted in a nationalization of commercial common-law jurisprudence at a time when access to state decisions was often difficult. For this reason, *Swift* is usually regarded as a "lawyer's" case.

Swift illustrates the connection between legal rules and nineteenth-century economic growth. In his opinion, Justice Joseph Story pointed out that without this rule, almost all interstate transactions would be uncertain. In an age when private bank notes and bills of exchange functioned in the absence of a national currency, predictability and uniformity of commercial and legal rules were vital to the nation's economy. Even some Jacksonian states'-rights jurists, such as Roger B. Taney and Peter V. Daniel, joined Story because they understood that economic development and growth required consistent rules for commercial transactions. Nevertheless, Story's decision must also be seen as part of the ongoing tension between supporters of a strong federal judiciary and supporters of states' rights. The outcome was consistent with Story's lifelong goal of strengthening the federal courts and nationalizing law. *Swift* dovetails with Story's opinion in the same Court term in *Prigg* v. *Pennsylvania* (1842), which created a common-law right of recaption in fugitive slave cases (see Chapter 4).

Note: Canals, Internal Improvements, and the States

In the first half of the nineteenth century, the states led the development of the nation's transportation network. State activism included direct state construction of, investment in, and subsidies to canals, turnpikes, and railroads. State commissions established to promote economic development also simplified incorporation proceedings, expedited eminent domain condemnations, and aided the growth of transportation networks as well as water-powered manufacturing. New York's Erie Canal was the most dramatic, and most profitable, example of direct state involvement in internal development. Canal revenue more than made up for the cost of construction while helping to make New York the richest state in the nation. In 1825, after the canal opened but before its final completion, Governor DeWitt Clinton bragged to his legislature:

For almost all useful purposes, the city of Detroit, will . . . be brought within a hundred miles of the city of Albany. Already have we witnessed the creative power of these communications, in the flourishing villages which have sprung up or been extended; in the increase of our towns; and, above all, in the prosperity of the city of New York . . . it is highly probable that in fifteen years its population will be doubled, and that in less than thirty years it will be the third city in point of numbers, in the civilized world, and the second, if not the first, in commerce.

Clinton's predictions proved basically correct. Other states, like Pennsylvania and Ohio, also built elaborate, although less successful, canal systems.

The background of the Erie Canal illustrates the necessity of government intervention in the construction of canals. As early as 1792, New York chartered (and invested in) two private canal companies. One quickly collapsed. The other barely survived. This experience showed that private enterprise could not raise sufficient capital to build and operate a large canal system. In 1808, the Secretary of the Treasury advocated federal support for canals. In anticipation of federal funds, New York surveyed a canal route from the Hudson River to Lake Erie. In 1810, the state appointed a Canal Commission, which concluded that private investment was insufficient to build a canal across New York. The next year, the legislature appointed DeWitt Clinton and Gouverneur Morris to lobby Congress for canal funding. A bill on this subject died in a House committee. After the War of 1812, Congress supported internal improvements, but Madison's 1817 veto of Calhoun's "Bonus Bill" made it clear that any canal in New York would have to be funded by the state.

Opponents of New York's canal program feared higher taxes. Party politics, not laissez-faire ideology, also led to opposition. Martin Van Buren and other Democrats opposed the canal because they did not want DeWitt Clinton to get credit for the project. Nevertheless, in 1816 the legislature appointed Clinton as head of a new Canal Commission. In 1817, construction of the canal began. That same year, Clinton became governor. He was also governor in 1825, when the canal was completed.

STATE CONSTITUTIONS AND THE ACTIVE STATE

Most of the state constitutions written between 1776 and 1803 said little about economic development. This left the question entirely in the hands of the state legislatures. Post-Revolutionary state governments regulated industries, granted charters to companies, and created monopolies. Some states gave direct cash subsidies to some industries or invested directly in private corporations. Even when such investments were honestly made and carefully managed, much of the public objected to this use of tax dollars, which enriched individual stockholders through the infusion of public money into private business.

Grants of monopolies to steamboat companies, bridges, and other enterprises also led to public opposition. Finally, the whole process of creating corporations came under public scrutiny. Without general incorporation laws, entrepreneurs were forced to seek legislative charters for their new companies. This process was time-consuming, expensive, and subject to political abuse. Equally important, some Americans disliked the whole idea of corporations, which limited the liabilities of investors and allowed irresponsible corporate owners and managers to avoid the costs of their negligence or mismanagement.

During the nation's second wave of state constitution making, from about 1820 to 1860, many constitutions severely restricted state involvement in the economy through provisions limiting state investment, state debt, and corporations.

Ohio Constitution
1851

Ohio's 1803 Constitution had no limitations on state expenditures or state intervention in the economy. However, the 1851 Constitution, like many of the state constitutions of the late antebellum period, severely limited state economic activity.

ARTICLE VIII: PUBLIC DEBT AND PUBLIC WORKS

Section 1. The State may contract debts to supply casual deficits or failures in revenues, or to meet expenses not otherwise provided for; but the aggregate amount of such debts, direct or contingent . . . shall never exceed seven hundred and fifty thousand dollars; and the money, arising from the creation of such debts, shall be applied to the purpose for which it was obtained, or to repay the debts so contracted, and to no other purpose whatever.

Section 2. In addition to the above limited power, the State may contract debts to repel invasion, suppress insurrection, defend the State in war, or to redeem the present outstanding indebtedness of the State; but the money, arising from the contracting of such debts, shall be applied to the purpose for which it was raised, or to repay such debts, and to no other purpose whatever; and all debts, incurred to redeem the present outstanding indebtedness of the State shall be so contracted as to be payable by the sinking fund, hereinafter provided for, as the same shall accumulate.

Section 3. Except the debts above specified . . . [in] this article, no debt whatever shall hereafter be created by or on behalf of the State.

Section 4. The credit of the State shall not, in any manner be given or loaned to, or in aid of, any individual association or corporation whatever; nor shall the State ever hereafter become a joint owner, or stockholder, in any company or association in this State, or elsewhere, formed for any purpose whatever.

Section 5. The State shall never assume the debts of any county, city, town, or township, or of any corporation whatever, unless such debt shall have been created to repel invasion, suppress insurrection, or defend the State in war.

Section 6. The General Assembly shall never authorize any county, city, town, or township, by vote of its citizens, or otherwise, to become a stockholder in any joint stock company, corporation, or association whatever; or to raise money for, or loan its credit to, or in aid of, any such company, corporation, or association.

♦ ♦ ♦

ARTICLE XII: FINANCE AND TAXATION

♦ ♦ ♦

Section 3. The general assembly shall provide, by law, for taxing the notes and bills discounted or purchased, moneys loaned, and all other property, effects, or dues . . . of all banks, now existing or hereafter created, and of all bankers, so that all property employed in banking shall always bear a burden of taxation equal to that imposed on the property of individuals.

♦ ♦ ♦

Section 6. The State shall never contract any debt for purposes of internal improvement.

ARTICLE XIII: CORPORATIONS

Section 1. The general assembly shall pass no special act conferring corporate powers.

Section 2. Corporations may be formed under general laws; but all such laws may, from time to time, be altered or repealed.

Section 3. Dues from corporations shall be secured by such individual liability of the stockholders, and other means, as may be prescribed by law; but, in all cases, each stockholder shall be liable, over and above the stock by him or her owned, and any amount unpaid thereon, to a further sum at least equal in amount to such stock.

Section 4. The property of corporations, now existing or hereafter created, shall forever be subject to taxation, the same as the property of individuals.

Section 5. No right of way shall be appropriated to the use of any corporation, until full compensation therefor shall be first made in money, or first secured by a deposit of money, to the owner, irrespective of any benefit from any improvement proposed by such corporation; which compensation shall be ascertained by a jury of twelve men, in a court of record, as shall be prescribed by law.

♦ ♦ ♦

Section 7. No act of the general assembly, authorizing associations with banking powers, shall take effect, until it shall be submitted to the people, at the general election next succeeding the passage thereof, and be approved by a majority of all the electors voting at such election.

Mississippi Constitution
1817

Like Ohio, Mississippi was a new western state on a developing frontier. Mississippi entered the Union thirteen years after Ohio, and some provisions of its first constitution reflect the political issues of America after the War of 1812. The 1832 constitution also reflects the changing nature of the economy, as well as other important socioeconomic influences on the state.

ARTICLE VI: GENERAL PROVISIONS

Section 9. No bank shall be incorporated by the legislature without the reservation of a right to subscribe for, in behalf of the State, at least one-fourth part of the capital stock thereof, and the appointment of a proportion of the directors equal to the stock subscribed for.

♦ ♦ ♦

Section 17. Divorces from the bonds of matrimony shall not be granted, but in cases provided for by law, by suit in chancery; Provided, That no decree for such divorce shall have effect until the same shall be sanctioned by two-thirds of both branches of the general assembly.

Mississippi Constitution
1832

ARTICLE VII: GENERAL PROVISIONS

Section 8. No money from the treasury shall be appropriated to objects of internal improvement, unless the bill for that purpose be passed by two-thirds of both branches of the legislature. . . .

Section 9. No law shall ever be passed to raise a loan of money upon the credit of the State, or to pledge the faith of the State, for the redemption of any loan or debt, unless such law be proposed in the senate or house of representatives, and be agreed to by a majority of the members of each house, and entered on the journals with the yeas and nays taken thereon, and be referred to the next succeeding legislature, and published for three months previous to the next regular election, in three newspapers of this State; and unless a majority of each branch of the legislature, so elected, after such publication, shall agree to and pass such a law; and in such case the yeas and nays shall be taken and entered on the journals of each house.

♦ ♦ ♦

SLAVES

Section 1. The legislature shall have no power to pass laws for the emancipation of slaves without the consent of the owners, unless where the slave shall have rendered to the State some distinguished service; in which case the owner shall be paid a full equivalent for the slave so emancipated. They shall have no power to prevent emigrants to this State from bringing with them such persons as are deemed slaves by the laws of any one of the United States, so long as any person of the same age or description shall be continued in slavery by the laws of this State: Provided, That such person or slave be the bona-fide property of such immigrants: And

provided also, That laws may be passed to prohibit the introduction into this State of slaves who may have committed high crimes in other States. They shall have power to pass laws to permit the owners of slaves to emancipate them, saving the rights of creditors, and preventing them from becoming a public charge. They shall have full power to oblige the owners of slaves to treat them with humanity; to provide for them necessary clothing and provisions; to abstain from all injuries to them, extending to life or limb; and, in case of their neglect or refusal to comply with the directions of such laws, to have such slave or slaves sold for the benefit of the owner or owners.

Section 2. The introduction of slaves into this State as merchandise, or for sale, shall be prohibited from and after the first day of May, eighteen hundred and thirty-three: Provided, That the actual settler or settlers shall not be prohibited from purchasing slaves in any State in this Union, and bringing them into this State for their own individual use, until the year eighteen hundred and forty-five.

SUBSTANTIVE LAW AND ECONOMIC GROWTH

The developing economy of the nineteenth century led to dramatic changes in the substantive law of the United States. Some decisions of the United States Supreme Court interpreting the commerce clause and the contracts clause of the Constitution were particularly important to economic development. As noted earlier, in *Gibbons* v. *Ogden* (1824) the Supreme Court used the commerce clause to strike down the steamboat monopoly that the New York courts had upheld in *Livingston* v. *Van Ingen* (1812).

Despite the importance of major federal cases, most of the substantive legal changes of the period came from the state courts. Property law and water law changed dramatically as English common-law rules dating from the Middle Ages seemed increasingly irrelevant to American conditions. Corporations increased in number, and a new field of law emerged. Tort law, virtually an unknown field before the Revolution, became a mainstay of litigation by 1860.

Nineteenth-century courts fashioned law to fit changing circumstances resulting from new technologies, industries, and business methods. Contract law, which evolved to fit the exigencies of world markets, placed new burdens on both consumers and businessmen through the rise of caveat emptor. Cases involving property and corporations often pitted older industries and technologies against newer ones, usually aiding the growth of new industries and the replacement of old ones. Even when the newer corporations lost a case, the precedents set were often helpful to the general growth of corporations. Thus in *Dartmouth College* v. *Woodward* (1819), the court sided with an older corporation but created a precedent that affected the vested rights of all new corporations.

More dramatic than suits between corporations were cases involving individuals who asked the courts to protect them from the more powerful economic entities they encountered. Initially, no American court recognized the right of workers to strike or bargain collectively. In *Commonwealth* v. *Hunt* (1842), Chief Justice Lemuel Shaw of the Massachusetts Supreme Judicial Court ruled that labor unions were not illegal conspiracies per se. This limited victory was not labor's "emancipation proclamation," as some historians have hailed it, but under it a few antebellum laborers, mostly skilled workers, were able to unionize and improve their working conditions and wages.

Workers were even less successful in protecting themselves from unsafe working conditions. In *Farwell* v. *Boston and Worcester Railroad* (1842), Chief Justice Shaw drastically limited the opportunity for injured workers to recover for job-related injuries. Thus the workers, not the investors, would bear the often tragic human costs of industrialization.

Courts were only slightly more sympathetic to shippers, passengers, and innocent bystanders harmed by the dangerous machines of nineteenth-century industrialization. Antebellum courts generally limited the liabilities of industries and placed the costs of industrial accidents on individuals. Courts denied bereaved plaintiffs the right to sue for the "wrongful death" of their relatives. Courts limited or barred recovery by victims of accidents through the adoption of the doctrine of contributory negligence. Courts also limited the liabilities of common carriers for lost goods, holding that property owners could not always sue industrial actors who negligently damaged their property. Insurance, not lawsuits, was the appropriate defense for property in the dangerous world of industrializing America.

THE ADVENT OF THE CORPORATION

William Blackstone defined corporations as "artificial persons, who may maintain a perpetual succession, and enjoy a kind of legal immortality."[4] Before 1800, corporations usually created such institutions as colleges, hospitals, and, most common of all, governmental entities. New York City, for example, is a corporation. A few government-sponsored economic initiatives were also incorporated, such as the Virginia Company, which settled Jamestown in 1607, and the Royal Africa Company, which had a monopoly over English participation in the African slave trade. Private business, such as banks and insurance companies, were the least common corporations. In 1780, the United States had fewer than 20 business corporations. Forty years later, the nation boasted more than 1,800 corporations, engaged in transportation, commerce, finance, and manufacturing.

Incorporation offered three important advantages. First, corporations do not end with the death of their owners, but can exist beyond the life of any single individual or group of individuals. This advantage made them useful for creating government entities, like cities, and charitable operations, like hospitals or schools. The effects of this are obvious for businesses. Unlike a sole proprietorship or a partnership, a business corporation can continue long after its founders have died or retired. The second key aspect of a corporation is the limited liability it usually places on the stockholders. Each member of a partnership can be held personally liable for all debts that the partnership might incur. But in a corporation, a stockholder's liability is usually limited to his or her actual investment. Finally, a corporation facilitated the pooling of capital to raise the enormous sums necessary to build new forms of manufacturing, commerce, and transportation. Investors could place their funds with corporate directors, without having to worry about the day-to-day operations of the business. This allowed for rapid economic development in the nineteenth century.

During the early national period, corporations were viewed as monopolistic and partial to the rich. They were fundamentally antirepublican. Nevertheless, many Republicans recognized their value. Thus in *Currie's Administrator* v. *The Mutual Assurance Society* (Va., 1809), Judge Spencer Roane, a staunch Jeffersonian and a vigilant opponent of privilege, conceded that "those artificial persons are rendered necessary in the law from the inconvenience, if not impracticability of keeping alive the rights of associated bodies, by devolving them on one series of individuals after another."

The realization that corporations were a useful necessity led to their expanded use, even though they had antirepublican tendencies. State legislatures gradually democratized the incorporation process through "general incorporation laws," which allowed the creation of new corporations without special legislative acts. This is an example of what legal historian James Willard Hurst has called the use of law to facilitate "the release of creative energies."[5] This solution, while answering the republican critique of corporations as monopolies, led to a new problem: the proliferation of corporations and the subsequent concentration of wealth and power in the hands of these fictitious persons. Moreover, critics considered such bodies to be "soulless." Corporations were, after all, not human beings, but legal fictions whose sole reason for existence was the profit of stockholders who were themselves often removed from the operation of the business.

Dartmouth College v. Woodward
4 Wheat. (17 U.S.) 518 (1819)

In 1769, Dr. Eleazar Wheelock received a royal charter creating Dartmouth College, with a self-perpetuating board of trustees. This charter allowed Wheelock to appoint his own successor, unless the choice was "disapproved by the trustees." Ten years later, Wheelock's son John became the college's second president. In 1816, the trustees removed the autocratic John Wheelock. The state legislature then amended the 1769 charter by creating "Dartmouth University," with a board of trustees and overseers favorable to Wheelock. In 1817, the old trustees operated Dartmouth College, with ninety-five students, while the new trustees operated Dartmouth University, with only fourteen students. Meanwhile, the old college trustees hired Daniel Webster (an alumnus) to sue William Woodward (the treasurer of the new Dartmouth University) for possession of the records, seal, and charter, as well as for $50,000 in damages. The case would determine the validity of the 1816 law, modifying the original corporate charter. The college trustees lost before the New Hampshire Supreme Court, but appealed to the United States Supreme Court. There Webster argued that the amendment of the corporate charter was actually a "law impairing the obligation of contracts," which violated Article I, Section 10, of the United States Constitution.

The opinion of the Court was delivered by Mr. Chief Justice Marshall.

♦ ♦ ♦

The single question now to be considered is, do the acts [creating Dartmouth University] to which the verdict refers violate the constitution of the United States?

This Court can be insensible neither to the magnitude nor delicacy of this question. The validity of a legislative act is to be examined; and the opinion of the highest law tribunal of a

State is to be revised: . . . On more than one occasion, this Court has expressed the cautious
circumspection with which it approaches the
consideration of such questions; and has declared, that, in no doubtful case, would it pronounce a legislative act to be contrary to the
constitution. But the American people have
said, in the constitution of the United States,
that "no State shall pass any . . . law impairing
the obligation of contracts." In the same instrument they also said, "that the judicial power
shall extend to all cases in law and equity arising under the constitution." On the judges of
this Court, then, is imposed the high and solemn
duty of protecting, from even legislative violation, those contracts which the constitution of
our country has placed beyond legislative control; and, however irksome the task may be, this
is a duty from which we dare not shrink.

The title of the plaintiffs originates in a
charter dated . . . 1769, incorporating twelve
persons [as] . . . "The Trustees of Dartmouth
College," granting to them and their successors
the usual corporate privileges and powers, and
authorizing the trustees, who are to govern the
college, to fill up all vacancies which may be
created in their own body.

The defendant claims under three acts of
the legislature of New-Hampshire, the most material of which was passed on the 27th of June,
1816, and is entitled, "an act to amend the charter, and enlarge and improve the corporation of
Dartmouth College."

◆　◆　◆

It can require no argument to prove, that
the circumstances of this case constitute a contract. An application is made to the crown for
a charter to incorporate a religious and literary
institution. In the application, it is stated that
large contributions have been made for the object, which will be conferred on the corporation, as soon as it shall be created. The charter
is granted, and on its faith the property is conveyed. Surely in this transaction every ingredient of a complete and legitimate contract is to
be found.

The points for consideration are,

1. Is this contract protected by the constitution of the United States?

2. Is it impaired by the acts under which
the defendant holds?

. . . This is the point on which the cause
essentially depends. If the act of incorporation
be a grant of political power, if it create a civil
institution to be employed in the administration
of the government, or if the funds of the college be public property, or if the State of New
Hampshire, as a government, be alone interested in its transactions, the subject is one in
which the legislature of the State may act according to its own judgement, unrestrained by
any limitation of its power imposed by the constitution of the United States.

But if this be a private eleemosynary institution, endowed with a capacity to take
property for objects unconnected with government, whose funds are bestowed by individuals on the faith of the charter . . . there
may be more difficulty in the case, although
neither the persons who have made these stipulations, nor those for whose benefit they were
made, should be parties to the cause. Those
who are no longer interested in the property,
may yet retain such an interest in the preservation of their own arrangements, as to have
a right to insist that those arrangements shall
be held sacred . . . the trustees [may be] . . .
so completely their representatives in the eye
of the law, as to stand in their place, not only
as respects the government of the college, but
also as respects the maintenance of the college
charter.

◆　◆　◆

[Here Marshall discussed Dartmouth's history, demonstrating that its funds "consisted entirely of private donations" solicited by Dr.
Eleazar Wheelock and that the "charter of incorporation was granted at his instance." Marshall concluded, "It is then an eleemosynary,
and, as far as respects its funds, a private corporation." Marshall noted that "education is an
object of national concern and a proper subject
of legislation" and that governments could create colleges. But, he asked, was Dartmouth a
government-created "institution"?]

Whence, then, can be derived the idea, that
Dartmouth College has become a public institution, and its trustees public officers, exercising

powers conferred by the public for public objects? Not from the source whence its funds were drawn; for its foundation is purely private and eleemosynary—Not from the application of those funds; for money may be given for education, and the persons receiving it do not, by being employed in the education of youth, become members of the civil government. Is it from the act of incorporation? Let this . . . be considered.

A corporation is an artificial being, invisible, intangible, and existing only in contemplation of law. Being the mere creature of law, it possesses only those properties which the charter of its creation confers upon it, either expressly, or as incidental to its very existence. These are such as are supposed best calculated to effect the object for which it was created. Among the most important are immortality; and if the expression be allowed, individuality; properties, by which a perpetual succession of many persons are considered as the same, and may act as a single individual. They enable a corporation to manage its own affairs, and to hold property without the perplexing intricacies, the hazardous and endless necessity, of perpetual conveyances for the purpose of transmitting it from hand to hand. It is chiefly for the purpose of clothing bodies of men, in succession, with these qualities and capacities, that corporations were invented, and are in use. By these means, a perpetual succession of individuals are capable of acting for the promotion of the particular object, like one immortal being. But this being does not share in the civil government of the country, unless that be the purpose for which it was created. Its immortality no more confers on it political power, or a political character, than immortality would confer such power or character on a natural person. It is no more a State instrument, than a natural person exercising the same powers would be. . . . Because the government has given it the power to take and to hold property in a particular form, and for particular purposes, has the government a consequent right substantially to change that form, or to vary the purposes to which the property is to be applied? This principle has never been asserted or recognized, and is supported by no authority. Can it derive aid from reason?

The objects for which a corporation is created are universally such as the government wishes to promote. They are deemed beneficial to the country; and this benefit constituted the consideration, and, in most cases, the sole consideration of the grant. In most eleemosynary institutions, the object would be difficult, perhaps unattainable, without the aid of a charter of incorporation. Charitable, or public spirited individuals, desirous of making permanent appropriations for charitable or other useful purposes . . . apply to the government, state their beneficial object, and offer to advance the money necessary for its accomplishment, provided the government will confer on the instrument which is to execute their designs the capacity to execute them. . . . The benefit to the public is considered as an ample compensation for the faculty it confers, and the corporation is created. If the advantages to the public constitute a full compensation for the faculty it gives, there can be no reason for exacting a further compensation, by claiming a right to exercise over this artificial being a power which changes its nature, and touches the fund, for the security and application of which it was created. There can be no reason for implying in a charter, given for a valuable consideration, a power which is not only not expressed, but is in direct contradiction to its express stipulations.

◆　◆　◆

From this review of the charter, it appears, that Dartmouth College is an eleemosynary institution, incorporated for the purpose of perpetuating the application of the bounty of the donors, to the specified objects of that bounty; that its trustees or governors were originally named by the founder, and invested with the power of perpetuating themselves; that they are not public officers, nor is it a civil institution, participating in the administration of government; but a charity school, or a seminary of education, incorporated for the preservation of its property, and the perpetual application of that property to the objects of its creation.

◆　◆　◆

This is plainly a contract to which the donors, the trustees, and the crown, (to whose

rights and obligations New Hampshire succeeds,) were the original parties. It is a contract
made on a valuable consideration. It is a contract for the security and disposition of property. It is a contract, on the faith of which, real
and personal estate has been conveyed to the
corporation. It is then a contract within the letter of the constitution, and within its spirit also.

♦ ♦ ♦

The opinion of the Court, after mature deliberation, is, that this is a contract, the obligation of which cannot be impaired, without violating the constitution of the United States. This
opinion appears to us to be equally supported
by reason, and by the former decisions of this
Court.

. . . We next proceed to the inquiry, whether
its obligation has been impaired by those acts of
the legislature of New Hampshire. . . .

From the review of this charter, which has
been taken, it appears, that the whole power of
governing the college, of appointing and removing tutors, of fixing their salaries, of directing the course of study to be pursued by the
students, and of filling up vacancies created in
their own body, was vested in the [twelve]
trustees.

♦ ♦ ♦

It has been already stated, that the act "to
amend the charter . . . " increases the number of
trustees to twenty-one, gives the appointment of
the additional members to the executive of the
State, and creates a board of overseers, to consist of twenty-five persons, of whom twenty-one

are also appointed by the executive of New-
Hampshire, who have power to inspect and control the most important acts of the trustees.

. . . The whole power of governing the college is transferred from trustees appointed according to the will of the founder, expressed in
the charter, to the executive of New Hampshire.
The management and application of the funds
of this eleemosynary institution, which are
placed by the donors in the hands of trustees
named in the charter, and empowered to perpetuate themselves, are placed by this act under the control of the government of the State.
The will of the State is substituted for the will
of the donors, in every essential operation of
the college. This is not an immaterial change.
The founders of the college contracted, not
merely for the perpetual application of the funds
which they gave, to the objects for which those
funds were given; they contracted also, to secure that application by the constitution of the
corporation. They contracted for a system,
which should, as far as human foresight can
provide, retain forever the government of the
literary institution they had formed, in the hands
of persons approved by themselves. This system is totally changed.

♦ ♦ ♦

It results from this opinion, that the acts of
the legislature of New Hampshire, which are
stated in the special verdict found in this cause,
are repugnant to the constitution of the United
States; and that the judgement . . . ought to have
been for the plaintiffs. The judgement of the
State Court must, therefore, be reversed.

Note: The Politics of the *Dartmouth College* Case

The Republican governor and state legislature viewed the old college as a bastion of Federalism tainted by a "royal" charter and wanted to democratize Dartmouth by making it a state
institution. Thus, in part, this case must be placed in the context of the decline of New England Federalism and the rise of Jeffersonian Republicanism.

By interpreting a corporate charter to be a contract between the corporation owners or
trustees and the state, Chief Justice Marshall laid out the constitutional protections and limitations that corporations would come to rely on for the rest of the nineteenth century and
well into the twentieth.

Charles River Bridge Company v. Warren Bridge Company
11 Pet. (36 U.S.) 420 (1837)

By acts of 1785 and 1792, the Massachusetts legislature gave the Charles River Bridge Company a seventy-year charter to operate a toll bridge between Charlestown and Boston. In 1828, the legislature chartered the Warren Bridge Company to construct a second bridge, which would revert to the state as a toll-free bridge in six years or less. The proprietors of the Charles River Bridge sought an injunction against the new bridge, arguing that their charter constituted an exclusive contract with the state, that the new bridge charter violated that contract, and that a free bridge would destroy the value of their charter, which had almost thirty more years to run. Although brought to the United States Supreme Court under the contracts clause of the Constitution, this case illustrates how new technologies and new corporations affected nineteenth-century economic and legal development. Put simply, the case asked if a state could create new corporations that might compete with or destroy the vested interests of existing corporations.

Mr. Chief Justice Taney delivered the opinion of the court.

The questions involved in this case are of the gravest character, and the Court have given to them the most anxious and deliberate consideration. The value of the right claimed by the plaintiffs is large in amount; and many persons may no doubt be seriously affected in their pecuniary interests by any decision which the court may pronounce; and the questions which have been raised as to the power of the several states, in relation to the corporations they chartered, are pregnant with important consequences; not only to the individuals who are concerned in the corporate franchises, but to the communities in which they exist.

♦ ♦ ♦

The plaintiffs in error insist, mainly, upon two grounds: 1st. That by virtue of the grant of 1650, Harvard College was entitled, in perpetuity, to the right of keeping a ferry between Charlestown and Boston; that this right was exclusive; and that the legislature had not the power to establish another ferry on the same line of travel, because it would infringe the rights of the college; and that these rights, upon the erection of the bridge in the place of the ferry, under the charter of 1785, were transferred to, and became vested in "the proprietors

of the Charles river bridge;" and . . . by virtue of this transfer of the ferry right, the rights of the bridge company were as exclusive in that line of travel, as the rights of the ferry. 2nd. That independently of the ferry right, the acts of the legislature of Massachusetts of 1785, and 1792 . . . necessarily implied that the legislature would not authorize another bridge, and especially a free one, by the side of this, and placed in the same line of travel, whereby the franchise granted to the "proprietors of the Charles River Bridge" should be rendered of no value; and the plaintiffs in error contend, that the grant of the ferry to the college, and of the charter to the proprietors of the bridge, are both contracts on the part of the state; and that the law authorizing the erection of the Warren bridge in 1828, impairs the obligation of one or both of these contracts.

♦ ♦ ♦

But upon what ground can the plaintiffs in error contend that the ferry rights of the college have been transferred to the proprietors of the bridge? . . . It is not suggested that there ever was, in point of fact, a deed of conveyance executed by the college to the bridge company. . . . The petition to the legislature, in 1785, on which the charter was granted, does not suggest an assignment, nor any agreement or consent on the part of the college; and the petitioners do not appear to have regarded the wishes of that institution, as by any means necessary to ensure their success. . . . The legislature, in granting the charter . . . acted on the principles assumed by the petitioners. The preamble recites that the bridge "will be of great public utility;" and that is the only reason they assign, for passing the law which incorporated this company. . . . The ferry, with all its privileges was intended to be for ever at an end, and a compensation in money was given in lieu of it. The college acquiesced in this arrangement, and there is proof, in the record, that it was all done with their consent. Can a deed of assignment to the bridge company which would keep alive the ferry rights in their hands, be presumed under such circumstances?

◆ ◆ ◆

Neither can the extent of the pre-existing ferry right, whatever it may have been, have any influence upon the construction of the written charter for the bridge. It does not, by any means, follow, that because the legislative power in Massachusetts, in 1650, may have granted to a justly favored seminary of learning, the exclusive right of ferry between Boston and Charlestown, they would, in 1785, give the same extensive privilege to another corporation, who were about to erect a bridge in the same place. The fact that such a right was granted to the college, cannot . . . be used to extend the privileges of the bridge company beyond what the words of the charter naturally and legally import . . . and as the franchise of the ferry, and that of the bridge, are different in their nature, and were each established by separate grants, which have no words to connect the privileges of the one with the privileges of the other; there is no rule of legal interpretation, which would authorize the court to associate these grants together, and to infer that any privilege was intended to be given to the bridge company, merely because it had been conferred on the ferry. The charter to the bridge is a written instrument which must speak for itself, and be interpreted by its own terms.

◆ ◆ ◆

[T]he case most analogous to this, and in which the question came more directly before the court, is . . . *Providence Bank* v. *Billings* [1830]. . . . In that case, it appeared that the legislature of Rhode Island had chartered the bank, in the usual form of such acts of incorporation. The charter contained no stipulation on the part of the state, that it would not impose a tax on the bank, nor any reservation of the right to do so. It was silent on this point. Afterwards, a law was passed, imposing a tax on all banks in the state; and the right to impose this tax was resisted by the Providence Bank, upon the ground, that if the state could impose a tax, it might tax so heavily as to render the franchise of no value, and destroy the institution; that the charter was a contract, and that a power which may in effect destroy the charter is inconsistent with it, and is impliedly renounced by granting it. But the court said that the taxing power was of vital importance, and essential to the existence of government; and that the relinquishment of such a power is never to be assumed. . . . The case now before the court is, in principle, precisely the same. It is a charter from a state. The act of incorporation is silent in relation to the contested power. The argument in favor of the proprietors of the Charles river bridge, is the same, almost in words, with that used by the Providence Bank; that is, that the power claimed by the state, if it exists, may be so used as to destroy the value of the franchise they have granted to the corporation. The argument must receive the same answer. . . .

It may, perhaps, be said, that in the case of The Providence Bank, this court were speaking of the taxing power; which is of vital importance to the very existence of every government. But the object and end of all government is to promote the happiness and prosperity of the community by which it is established; and it can never be assumed, that the government intended to diminish its power of accomplishing the end for which it was created. And in a country like ours, free, active, and enterprising, continually advancing in numbers and wealth; new channels of communication are daily found necessary, both for travel and trade; and are essential to the comfort, convenience, and prosperity of the people. A state ought never to be presumed to surrender this power, because, like the taxing power, the whole community have an interest in preserving it undiminished. And when a corporation alleges, that a state has surrendered for seventy years, its power of improvement and public accommodation, in a great and important line of travel, along which a vast number of citizens must daily pass; the community have a right to insist, in the language of this court above quoted, "that its abandonment ought not to be presumed, in a case, in which the deliberate purpose of the state to abandon it does not appear." The continued existence of a government would be of no great value, if by implications and presumptions, it was disarmed of the powers necessary to accomplish the ends of its creation; and the functions it was designed to perform, transferred to the hands of privileged corporations. . . . No one will question that the interests of the great body of the people of the state, would, in this instance, be affected by the surrender of this great line of travel to a single corporation, with the right to exact toll, and exclude competition for seventy years. While the rights of private property are sacredly guarded, we must not forget that the community also have rights, and that the happiness and well being of every citizen depends on their faithful preservation.

◆ ◆ ◆

The . . . Warren bridge . . . does not interrupt the passage over the Charles river bridge, nor make the way to it or from it less convenient. None of the faculties or franchises granted to that corporation, have been revoked by the legislature; and its right to take the tolls granted by the charter remains unaltered. In short, all the franchises and rights of property enumerated in the charter, and there mentioned to have been granted to it, remain unimpaired. But its income is destroyed by the Warren bridge; which, being free, draws off the passengers and property which would have gone over it, and renders their franchise of no value. This is the gist of the complaint. For it is not pretended, that the erection of the Warren bridge would have done them any injury, or in any degree affected their right of property; if it had not diminished the amount of their tolls. In order then

to entitle themselves to relief, it is necessary to show, that the legislature contracted not to do the act of which they complain; and that they impaired, or in other words, violated that contract by the erection of the Warren bridge.

The inquiry then is, does the charter contain such a contract on the part of the state? Is there any such stipulation to be found in that instrument? It must be admitted on all hands, that there is none—no words that even relate to another bridge, or to the diminution of their tolls, or to the line of travel. If a contract on that subject can be gathered from the charter, it must be by implication. . . . Can such an agreement be implied? The rule of construction before stated is an answer to the question. In charters of this description, no rights are taken from the public, or given to the corporation, beyond those which the words of the charter, by their natural and proper construction, purport to convey. There are no words which import such a contract as the plaintiffs in error contend for, and none can be implied; and the same answer must be given to them that was given by this court to the Providence Bank. The whole community are interested in this inquiry, and they have a right to require that the power of promoting their comfort and convenience, and of advancing the public propriety, by providing safe, convenient, and cheap ways for the transportation of produce, and the purposes of travel, shall not be construed to have been surrendered or diminished by the state; unless it shall appear by plain words, that it was intended to be done.

◆ ◆ ◆

Indeed, the practice and usage of almost every state in the Union, old enough to have commenced the work of internal improvement, is opposed to the doctrine contended for on the part of the plaintiffs in error. Turnpike roads have been made in succession, on the same line of travel; the later ones interfering materially with the profits of the first. These corporations have, in some instances, been utterly ruined by the introduction of newer and better modes of transportation. . . . In some cases, rail roads have rendered the turnpike roads on the same line of travel so entirely useless, that the franchise of the turnpike corporation is not worth preserving. Yet in none of these cases have the corporation supposed that their privileges were invaded, or any contract violated on the part of the state. . . .

And what would be the fruits of this doctrine of implied contracts on the part of the states, and of property in a line of travel by a corporation, if it should now be sanctioned by this court? To what results would it lead us? If it is to be found in the charter to this bridge, the same process of reasoning must discover it, in the various acts which have been passed, within the last forty years, for turn-pike companies. And what is to be the extent of the privileges of exclusion on the different sides of the road? The counsel who have so ably argued this case, have not attempted to define it by any certain boundaries. How far must the new improvement be distant from the old one? How near may you approach without invading its rights in the privileged line? If this court should establish the principles now contended for, what is to become of the numerous rail roads established on the same line of travel with turnpike companies; and which have rendered the franchises of the turnpike corporations of no value? Let it once be understood that such charters carry with them these implied contracts, and give this unknown and undefined property in a line of traveling; and you

will soon find the old turnpike corporations awakening from their sleep, and calling upon this court to put down the improvements which have taken their place. The millions of property which have been invested in rail roads and canals, upon lines of travel which had been before occupied by turnpike corporations, will be put in jeopardy. We shall be thrown back to the improvements of the last century, and obliged to stand still, until the claims of the old turnpike corporations shall be satisfied; and they shall consent to permit these states to avail themselves of the lights of modem science, and to partake of the benefit of those improvements which are now adding to the wealth and prosperity, and the convenience and comfort, of every other part of the civilized world. Nor is this all. This court will find itself compelled to fix, by some arbitrary rule, the width of this new kind of property in a line of travel; for if such a right of property exists, we have no lights to guide us in marking out its extent, unless, indeed, we resort to the old feudal grants, and to the exclusive rights of ferries, by prescription, between towns; and are prepared to decide that when a turnpike road from one town to another, had been made, no rail road or canal, between these two points, could afterwards be established. This court are not prepared to sanction principles which must lead to such results.

Note: The Limited Liability of Stockholders

Vose v. *Grant* (Mass., 1819) and *Spear* v. *Grant* (Mass., 1819) endorsed the principle that stockholders are not personally liable for the actions of a company. Grant owned stock in a bank incorporated by the Massachusetts legislature in 1804. Vose and Spear held notes issued by the bank. An act of 1812 terminated the charters of all banks in the state, but required that the banks remain in operation until 1816, in order to pay off their notes, settle their accounts, and disburse remaining funds among the stockholders.

In 1813, the shareholders divided 75 percent of the capital among themselves, believing that the remaining capital was sufficient to pay off all outstanding notes. This was a miscalculation, and subsequently the bank failed to meet its obligations. Vose and Spear sued Grant, alleging that as a shareholder he was not entitled to his disbursement until all other obligations had been redeemed.

In *Vose,* the court asserted that "the stockholders are not liable to an action on account of a mistaken opinion, or vote, expressed or given at a legal meeting." The court concluded that "every holder of a bank note ought to understand that he holds only the promise of an individual to pay him the sum expressed in it. That individual is a corporation; a creature of the legislature. It may die, or become insolvent, like any other person." In *Spear,* Chief Justice Parker asserted that a bank note "cannot be the basis of an implied promise by the stockholders individually." Otherwise, "a stockholder, wholly innocent and ignorant of the mismanagement, which has brought the bank into discredit, might be ruined by reason of owning a single share in the stock of the corporation." In both cases, the court implied that equity proceedings might force the stockholders to disgorge their disbursements, to be divided among the noteholders. But without evidence of fraud, there was no common-law action "by which any one creditor can compel any one stockholder to pay him the amount of his stock."

LABOR IN AN INDUSTRIALIZING SOCIETY

Antebellum labor law focused on two major issues: the right of workers to organize unions and take collective action, and the liability of employers for accidents to workers.

Traditionally, strikes, boycotts, and other collective action by labor organizations were considered illegal conspiracies. Between 1787 and 1842, there were seventeen labor conspiracy trials. Nine involved shoemakers or bootmakers, known as cordwainers. The *Philadelphia Cordwainers Case* (1806) was the first major American labor conspiracy trial. The Philadelphia cordwainers struck to protest the rise of retail shoe stores and mass-produced footwear. In 1809, there was a similar strike and conspiracy trial in New York. Both strikes were broken, the unions destroyed, and the labor organizers convicted and fined.

Safety was also important to workers. Industrialization, with its steamboats, railroads, and factories, was extremely hazardous. Before the industrial revolution, accidents were fewer and the common law assumed that an employer would provide a safe workplace and, "at his peril, employ servants who are skillful and careful."[6] These old common-law ideas made both greater sense and no sense at all in the emerging industrial society. They made greater sense because the workplace was more dangerous. In large factories or on railroads and steamboats, workers no longer knew many of their fellow employees and could not judge if they were careful. Many workers did not even know their ultimate employer, and they increasingly had less input into the safety of their workplace. Thus holding the employer liable for all injuries made sense from the workers' perspective.

Employers had a different view. They could no longer supervise all their workers or the company property at any given time. No one from management could ride on every train, making sure the crew followed all safety rules. Thus owners preferred rules limiting their liability for industrial accidents. In what was perhaps the most instrumental decision in his career, Chief Justice Shaw furthered the interests of industrialists in the Bay State, in holding that a railroad was not liable for the injuries to an engineer caused by a negligent "fellow servant" of the corporation. The result was that workers would be unable to recover for on-the-job injuries. Thus the cost of industrial injuries would be born by those least able to afford it—the workers and their families. Not until the adoption of workers' compensation schemes in the twentieth century would this change.

Note: The Traditional Theory of Labor Conspiracy

In *People* v. *Fisher* (1835), the New York Supreme Court upheld the indictment of journeyman bootmakers for conspiracy to prevent others from working and for "unlawfully and unjustly" intending to extort "large and exorbitant sums" from employers. The indictment noted that a shoemaker named Pennock, who had worked for a lower wage, was fired when other journeymen refused to work for anyone who employed Pennock. The court found that a "conspiracy" to raise wages would undermine the social and economic fabric of the country:

> It is important to the best interests of society that the price of labor be left to regu-
> late itself, or rather be limited by the demand for it. Combinations and confederacies
> to enhance or reduce the prices of labor, or of any articles of trade or commerce, are
> injurious. They may be oppressive, by compelling the public to give more for an ar-
> ticle of necessity or of convenience than it is worth; or on the other hand, of com-
> pelling the labor of the mechanic for less than its value. Without . . . improper in-
> terference . . . the price of labor or the wages of mechanics will be regulated by the
> demand for the manufactured article, and the value of that which is paid for it; but
> the right does not exist either to enhance the price of the article, or the wages of the
> mechanic, by any forced and artificial means. The man who owns an article of trade
> or commerce is not obliged to sell it for any particular price, nor is the mechanic,
> obliged by law to labor for any particular price. He may say that he will not make
> coarse boots for less than one dollar per pair, *but he has no right to say that no other
> mechanic shall make them for less.* The cloth merchant may say that he will not sell
> his goods for less than so much per yard, but has no right to say that any other mer-
> chant shall not sell for a less price. . . . All combinations therefore to effect such an
> object are injurious, not only to the individual particularly oppressed, but to the pub-
> lic at large.

In this case, the court found that "an industrious man was driven out of employment by the unlawful measures pursued by the defendants," which injured the community "by diminishing the quantity of productive labor, and of internal trade." The court continued:

> Competition is the life of trade. If the defendants cannot make coarse boots for less
> than one dollar per pair, let them refuse to do so; but let them not directly or indi-
> rectly undertake to say that others shall not do the work for a less price. It may be
> that Pennock, from greater industry or greater skill, made more profit by making
> boots at seventy-five cents per pair than the defendants at a dollar. He had a right to
> work for what he pleased. His employer had a right to employ him for such price as
> they could agree upon. The interference of the defendants was unlawful; its tendency
> is not only to individual oppression, but to public inconvenience and embarrassment.

Commonwealth v. Hunt
4 Met. (45 Mass.) 111 (1842)

The defendants, members of the Boston Journeymen Bootmakers' Society, refused to work for any employer who hired nonunion journeymen. When their employer, Isaac Wait, hired Jeremiah Horne, a nonunion journeyman, the defendants threatened to quit. Unwilling to lose all his employees, Wait fired Horne. District Attorney Samuel D. Parker, a Whig known for his opposition to labor organizers, abolitionists, and other reformers, prosecuted the union members for conspiracy. Robert Rantoul, a leading Jacksonian Democrat, defended

Hunt, the president of the union. A jury of "gentlemen" took only twenty minutes to convict the workers, but the Massachusetts Supreme Judicial Court reversed the conviction.

[Chief Justice Shaw] . . . [W]e are of the opinion, that as a general description, though perhaps not a precise and accurate definition, a conspiracy must be a combination of two or more persons, by some concerted action, to accomplish some criminal or unlawful purpose, or to accomplish some purpose, not in itself criminal or unlawful, by criminal or unlawful means.

◆ ◆ ◆

The first count set forth, that the defendants, with diverse others unknown, on the day and at the place named, being workmen, and journeymen, in the art and occupation of bootmakers, unlawfully, perniciously and deceitfully designing and intending to continue, keep up, form, and unite themselves, into an unlawful club, society and combination, and make unlawful by-laws, rules and orders among themselves, and thereby govern themselves and other workmen, in the said art, and unlawfully and unjustly to extort great sums of money by means thereof, did unlawfully assemble and meet together, and being so assembled, did unjustly and corruptly conspire, combine, confederate and agree together, that none of them should thereafter, and that none of them would, work for any master or person whatsoever, in the said art, mystery and occupation, who should employ any workman or journeyman, or other person, in the said art, who was not a member of said club, society or combination, after notice given him to discharge such workman, from the employ of such master; to the great damage and oppression, &c.

◆ ◆ ◆

Stripped then of these introductory recitals and alleged injurious consequences, and of the qualifying epithets attached to the facts, the averment is this: that the defendants and others formed themselves into a society, and agreed not to work for any person, who should employ any journeyman or other person, not a member of such society. . . .

The manifest intent of the association is, to induce all those engaged in the same occupation to become members of it. Such a purpose is not unlawful. It would give them a power which might be exerted for useful and honorable purposes, or for dangerous and pernicious ones. If the latter were the real and actual object, and susceptible of proof, it should have been specially charged. Such an association might be used to afford each other assistance in times of poverty, sickness and distress; or to raise their intellectual, moral and social condition; or to make improvement in their art; or for other proper purposes. Or the association might be designed for purposes of oppression and injustice. But in order to charge all those, who become members of an association, with the guilt of a criminal conspiracy, it must be averred and proved that the actual, if not the avowed object of the association, was criminal. . . .

Nor can we perceive that the objects of this association, whatever they may have been were to be attained by criminal means. The means which they proposed to employ, as averred in this count, and which, as we are now to presume, were established by the proof, were, that they would not work for a person, who, after due notice, should employ a journeyman not a member of their society. Supposing the object of the association to be laudable and lawful, or at least not unlawful, are these means criminal? The case supposes that these persons are not bound by contract, but free to work for whom they please, or not to work, if they so prefer. In this state of things, we cannot perceive, that it is criminal for men to agree together to exercise their own acknowledged rights. . . . One way to test this is, to consider the effect of such an agreement, where the object of the association is acknowledged on all hands to be a laudable one. Suppose a class of workmen, impressed with the manifold evils of intemperance, should agree with each other not to work in a shop with any one who used it, or not to work for an employer, who should, after notice, employ a journeyman who habitually used it. The consequences might be the same. A workman, who should still persist in the use of ardent spirit, would find it more difficult to get employment; a master employing such an one might, at times, experience inconvenience in his work, in losing the services of a skilful but intemperate workman. Still . . . that as the object would be lawful, and the means not unlawful, such an agreement could not be pronounced a criminal conspiracy.

From this count in the indictment, we do not understand that the agreement was, that the defendants would refuse to work for an employer, to whom they were bound by contract for a certain time, in violation of that contract; nor that they would insist that an employer should discharge a workman engaged by contract for a certain time, in violation of such contract. It is perfectly consistent with every thing stated in this count, that the effect of the agreement was, that when they were free to act, they would not engage with an employer, or continue in his employment, if such employer, when free to act, should engage with a workman, or continue a workman in his employment, not a member of the association. If a large number of men . . . should combine together to violate their contract, and quit their employment together, it would present a very different question. Suppose a farmer, employing a large number of men, engaged for the year, at fair monthly wages, and suppose that just at the moment that his crops were ready to harvest, they should all combine to quit his service, unless he would advance their wages, at a time when other laborers could not be obtained. It would surely be a conspiracy to do an unlawful act, though of such a character, that if done by an individual, it would lay the foundation of a civil action only, and not of a criminal prosecution. It would be a case very different from that stated in this court.

The second count . . . alleges that the defendants . . . did assemble, conspire, confederate and agree together, not to work for any master of person who should employ any workman not being a member of . . . the Boston Journeymen Bootmaker's Society . . . and that by means of said conspiracy they did compel one

Isaac B. Wait, a master cordwainer, to turn out of his employ one Jeremiah Horne, a journeyman boot-maker, &c. in evil example, &c. So far as the averment of a conspiracy is concerned, all the remarks made in reference to the first count are equally applicable to this. It is simply an averment of an agreement amongst themselves not to work for a person, who should employ any person not a member of a certain association. It sets forth no illegal or criminal purpose to be accomplished, nor any illegal or criminal means to be adopted for the accomplishment of any purpose. It was an agreement, as to the manner in which they would exercise an acknowledged right to contract with others for their labor. It does not aver a conspiracy or even an intention to raise their wages; and it appears by the bill of exceptions, that the case was not put upon the footing of a conspiracy to raise their wages. Such an agreement, as set forth in this count, would be perfectly justifiable.

♦ ♦ ♦

The third count, reciting a wicked and unlawful intent to impoverish one Jeremiah Horne . . . charges the defendants . . . with an unlawful conspiracy, by wrongful and indirect means, to impoverish said Home and to deprive and hinder him, from his said art and trade and getting his support thereby, and that, in pursuance of said unlawful combination, they did . . . impoverish him.

If the fact of depriving Jeremiah Horne of the profits of his business, by whatever means it might be done, would be unlawful and criminal, a combination to compass that object would be an unlawful conspiracy, and it would be unnecessary to state the means. . . .

Suppose a baker in a small village had the exclusive custom of his neighborhood, and was making large profits by the sale of his bread. Supposing a number of those neighbors, believing the price of his bread too high, should propose to him to reduce his prices, or if he did not, that they would introduce another baker; and on his refusal, such other baker should, under their encouragement, set up a rival establishment, and sell his bread at lower prices; the effect would be to diminish the profit of the former baker, and to the same extent to impover-ish him. And it might be said and proved, that the purpose of the associates was to diminish his profits, and thus impoverish him, though the ultimate and laudable object of the combination was to reduce the cost of bread to themselves and their neighbors. The same thing may be said of all competition in every branch of trade and industry; and yet it is through that competition, that the best interests of trade and industry are promoted. It is scarcely necessary to allude to the familiar instances of opposition lines of con-veyance, rival hotels, and the thousand other in-stances, where each strives to gain custom to himself, by ingenious improvements, by in-creased industry, and by all the means by which he may lessen the price of commodities, and thereby diminish the profits of others.

We think, therefore, that associations may be entered into, the object of which is to adopt measures that may have a tendency to impov-erish another, that is, to diminish his gains and profits, and yet so far from being criminal or unlawful, the object may be highly meritorious and public spirited. The legality of such an as-sociation will therefore depend upon the means

to be used for its accomplishment. If it is to be carried into effect by fair or honorable and law-ful means, it is, to say the least, innocent; if by falsehood or force, it may be stamped with the character of conspiracy.

♦ ♦ ♦

One case was cited, which was supposed to be much in point, and which is certainly de-serving of great respect. The People v. Fisher. . . . was a conspiracy by journeymen to raise their wages, and it was decided to be a viola-tion of the statutes, making it criminal to com-mit any act injurious to trade or commerce. It has, therefore, an indirect application only to the present case.

♦ ♦ ♦

[L]ooking solely at the indictment, disre-garding the qualifying epithets, recitals and im-material allegations, and confining ourselves to facts so averred as to be capable of being tra-versed and put in issue, we cannot perceive that it charges a criminal conspiracy punishable by law. The exceptions must, therefore, be sus-tained, and the judgment arrested.

Note: The Fellow Servant Rule

The fellow servant rule precluded a worker from suing an employer for job-related injuries caused by the negligence of another worker, or "fellow servant." Instead, the injured worker was forced to sue the negligent fellow servant, who in all probability was judgment proof. The rule was first announced in England, in *Priestly* v. *Fowler* (1837). Four years later, a divided South Carolina Supreme Court adopted the rule in *Murray* v. *South Carolina Rail Road* (1841), with the most distinguished member of the court, John Belton O'Neall, dis-senting. Chief Justice Lemuel Shaw's enthusiastic embrace of the rule three years later paved the way for its spread to most states.

Farwell v. *The Boston and Worcester Railroad Co.*
4 Met. (45 Mass.) 49 (1842)

Farwell was an engineer for the Boston and Worcester Railroad. In 1837, his train derailed because a switchman—another employee, or fellow servant—failed to correctly move a track. In the accident, "the wheels of one of said cars passed over the right hand of the plaintiff, crushing and destroying the same."

Shaw, C.J. This is an action of new impression in our courts, and involves a principle of great importance. It presents a case, where two persons are in the service and employment of one company, whose business it is to construct and maintain a rail road, and to employ their trains of cars to carry persons and merchandise for hire. They are appointed and employed by the same company to perform separate duties and services, all tending to the accomplishment of one and the same purpose—that of the safe and rapid transmission of the trains; . . . The question is, whether, for damages sustained by one of the persons so employed, by means of the carelessness and negligence of another, the party injured has a remedy against the common employer. It is an argument against such an action, though certainly not a decisive one, that no such action has before been maintained.

It is laid down by Blackstone, that if a servant, by his negligence, does any damage to a stranger, the master shall be answerable for his neglect. But the damage must be done while he is actually employed in the master's service; otherwise, the servant shall answer for his own misbehavior. . . . This rule is obviously founded on the great principle of social duty, that every man, in the management of his own affairs, whether by himself or by his agents or servants, shall so conduct them as not to injure another; and if he does not, and another thereby sustains damage, he shall answer for it. If done by a servant, in the course of his employment, and acting within the scope of his authority, it is considered, in contemplation of law, so far the act of the master, that the latter shall be answerable *civiliter*. . . . The maxim *respondeat superior* is adopted in that case, from general considerations of policy and security.

But this does not apply to the case of a servant bringing his action against his own employer to recover damages for an injury arising in the course of that employment, where all such risks and perils as the employer and the servant respectively intend to assume and bear may be regulated by the express or implied contract between them, and which, in contemplation of law, must be presumed to be thus regulated.

The same view seems to have been taken by the learned counsel for the plaintiff in the argument; and it was conceded, that the claim could not be placed on the principle indicated by the maxim *respondeat superior*, which binds the master to indemnify a stranger for the damage caused by the careless, negligent or unskilful act of his servant in the conduct of his affairs. The claim, therefore, is placed, and must be maintained . . . on the ground of contract. . . . It would be an implied promise, arising from the duty of the master to be responsible to each person employed by him, in the conduct of every branch of business, where two or more persons are employed, to pay for all damage occasioned by the negligence of every other person employed in the same service. If such a duty were established by law— like that of a common carrier, to stand to all losses of goods not caused by the act of God or of a public enemy . . . it would be a rule of frequent and familiar occurrence, and its existence and application with all its qualifications and restrictions, would be settled by judicial precedents. But we are of opinion that no such rule has been established, and the authorities, as far as they go, are opposed to the principle. *Priestly* v. *Fowler, Murray* v. *South Carolina Rail Road Company*. The general rule, resulting from considerations as well of justice as of policy, is that he who engages in the employment of another for the performance of specified duties and services, for compensation, takes upon himself the natural and ordinary risks and perils incident to the performance of such services, and in legal presumption, the compensation is adjusted accordingly. And we are not aware of any principle which should except the perils arising from the carelessness and negligence of those who are in the same employment. These are perils which the servant is as likely to know, and against which he can as effectually guard, as the master. They are perils incident to the service, and which can be as distinctly foreseen and provided for in the rate of compensation as any others. To say that the master shall be responsible because the damage is caused by his agents, is assuming the very point which remains to be proved. They are his agents to some extent, and for some purposes; but whether he is responsible, in a particular case, for their negligence, is not decided by the single fact that they are, for some purposes, his agents.

◆   ◆   ◆

[Here Shaw examined the legal obligations of common carriers and innkeepers to protect freight, passengers, and guests, concluding they are held] . . . to the strictest responsibility for care, vigilance, and skill, on the part of themselves and all persons employed by them, and they are paid accordingly. The rule is founded on the expediency of throwing the risk upon those who can best guard against it.

We are of opinion that these considerations apply strongly to the case in question. Where several persons are employed in the conduct of one common enterprise or undertaking, and the safety of each depends much on the care and skill with which each other shall perform his appropriate duty, each is an observer of the conduct of the others, can give notice of any misconduct, incapacity or neglect of duty, and leave the service, if the common employer will not take such precautions, and employ such agents as the safety of the whole party may require. By these means, the safety of each will be much more effectually secured, than could be done by a resort to the common employer for indemnity in case of loss by the negligence of each other. Regarding it in this light, it is the ordinary case of one sustaining an injury in the course of his own employment, in which he must bear the loss himself, or seek his remedy, if he have any, against the actual wrong-doer.

In applying these principles to the present case, it appears that the plaintiff was employed by the defendants as an engineer, at the rate of wages usually paid in that employment, being a higher rate than the plaintiff had before received as a machinist. It was a voluntary undertaking on his part, with a full knowledge of the risks incident to the employment; and the loss was sustained by means of an ordinary casualty, caused by the negligence of another servant of the company. Under these circumstances, the loss must be deemed to be the result of a pure accident, like those to which all men, in all employments, and at all times, are more or less exposed; and like similar losses

from accidental causes, it must rest where it first fell, unless the plaintiff has a remedy against the person actually in default; of which we give no opinion.

It was strongly pressed in the argument, that although this might be so, where two or more servants are employed in the same department of duty, where each can exert some influence over the conduct of the other, and thus to some extent provide for his own security; yet that it could not apply where two or more are employed in different departments of duty, at a distance from each other, and where one in no degree control or influence the conduct of another. But we think this is founded upon a supposed distinction, on which it would be extremely difficult to establish a practical rule. When the object to be accomplished is one and the same, when the employers are the same, and the several persons employed derive their authority and their compensation from the same source, it would be extremely difficult to distinguish, what constitutes one department and what a distinct department of duty. . . . If it were made to depend upon the nearness or distance of the persons from each other, the question would immediately arise, how near or how distant must they be, to be in the same or different departments. In a blacksmith's shop, persons working in the same building, at different fires, may be quite independent of each other, though only a few feet distant. In a ropewalk, several may be at work on the same piece of cordage, at the same time, at many hundred feet distant from each other, and beyond the reach of sight and voice, and yet acting together.

Besides, it appears to us, that the argument rests upon an assumed principle of responsibility which does not exist. The master . . . is not exempt from liability, because the servant has better means of providing for his safety, when he is employed in immediate connexion with those from whose negligence he might suffer; but because the implied contract of the master does not extend to indemnify the servant against the negligence of any one but himself; and he is not liable in tort, as for the negligence of his servant, because the person suffering does not stand towards him in the relation of a stranger, but is one whose rights are regulated by contract express or implied. The exemption of the master, therefore, from liability for the negligence of a fellow servant, does not depend exclusively upon the consideration, that the servant has better means to provide for his own safety, but upon other grounds. Hence the separation of the employment into different departments cannot create that liability, when it does not arise from express or implied contract, or from a responsibility created by law to third persons, and strangers, for the negligence of a servant.

Note: Chief Justice Shaw and Labor

Since the fellow servant rule involved personal injury, it might easily be categorized as a subspecies of tort law. Or, since the rule, as laid out by Chief Justice Shaw, also involved labor contracts, it might be considered a development in contract law. However, its most dramatic effect was on American workers injured on the job, and hence was a development in labor law. Embedded in Shaw's opinion is also the concept of "assumption of risk" applied to workers who take dangerous jobs.

Shaw's biographer, historian Leonard W. Levy, described *Commonwealth* v. *Hunt* as "the Magna Charta of American trade-unionism, for it removed the stigma of criminality from labor organizations."[7] Like the Magna Charta, however, the decision had little actual effect on the lot of working people in America. Shortly after the Civil War, lawyers, judges, and employers found other methods, most notably the labor injunction, to stifle labor organizations. Scholars have often wondered why in the same term of the Supreme Judicial Court, Shaw wrote the apparently prolabor decision in *Commonwealth* v. *Hunt,* and the apparently antilabor decision in *Farwell* v. *Boston and Worcester Railroad Co.* Can the two decisions be reconciled? Consider the kind of positive collective action that Shaw postulates in *Hunt.* Is such action similar to what he expects from workers in *Farwell?*

Note: Fellow Servants and Slaves

Most southern states refused to apply the fellow servant rule to slaves. In *Louisville* and *Nashville Railroad Co.* v. *Yandell* (1856), the Kentucky court wrote: "Whatever may be the wisdom and policy of this rule of law, when applied to free persons . . . we do not hesitate to reject its application to the present case, in which a slave was an employee." The court found that a slave could not be a fellow servant because:

> [A] slave may not, with impunity, remind and urge a free white person, who is a co-employee, to a discharge of his duties, or reprimand him for his carelessness and neglect; nor may he, with impunity, desert his post at discretion when danger is impending, nor quit his employment on account of the unskillfulness, bad management, inattention, or neglect of others of the crew. Whatever may be the danger by reason of any of these causes, he must stand to his post, though destruction of life or limb may never be so imminent. He is fettered by the stern bonds of slavery—necessity is upon him, and he must hold on to his employment. Slaves, to be sure, are rational beings but without the power of obeying, at pleasure, the dictates of their reason and judgment.

PROPERTY

In describing traditional English property law, Blackstone asserted that "occupancy," which was "the taking possession of those things, which before belonged to nobody," was "the true ground and foundation of all property." This primitive concept of property, Blackstone noted, was modified by such legal actions as contract, forfeiture, bankruptcy, succession, marriage, and, most important of all, the royal prerogative, which gave the monarch title to all land "found without any owner."[8]

By the time of the American Revolution, "real property law had become the victim of too many able minds refining too many distinctions for too long. It was of almost incredible complexity; cynics like Oliver Cromwell called it an ungodly jumble. It had become a mystery, unintelligible except to experts."[9] This nearly incomprehensible system of land tenure and ownership—based on feudal tenancies, conveyances, deeds, the doctrine of estates, and common-law precedents—supported the social reality that most land in England was in the hands of a very small number of people and that often this land was not actually owned by any single individual, but was part of an "estate." The concept of an estate was described in the sixteenth century in *Walsingham's Case:*

> The land itself is one thing and the estate in land is another thing: for an estate in the land is a time in the land, or land for a time: and there are diversities of estates, which are no more than diversities of time; for he who hath a fee simple in the land has a time in the land without end, or land for a time without end; and he who has land in tail has a time in land, or the land for a time, as he has issue of his body; and he who has an estate in land for life has no time in it longer than his own life; and so of one who has an estate in land for the life of another, or for years.[10]

Unlike England, America lacked a feudal history and had an abundance of "land found without owner," since white Americans rarely recognized that Native Americans occupied and owned land. Furthermore, after 1776 Americans had no king to claim a prerogative right. Thus in the United States, important aspects of English property law was irrelevant. What America needed was a dynamic and flexible property law. To accommodate the American experience, some changes in property law developed in the colonial period. The most dramatic change was the enslavement of human beings and their conversion to chattel or real estate. In the wake of the Revolution, most of the states dispensed with entail for land ownership and primogeniture for intestate succession. One of the few restrictions on the land to survive the Revolution was dower rights for widows. Nineteenth-century courts and legislatures facilitated the growth of the economy by the abandonment of useless and counterproductive common-law rules. The rejection of implied monopolies, as described in the *Charles River Bridge Company* case, shows how antebellum judges favored dynamic economic growth over vested property rights. The proliferation of eminent domain laws, and their support by courts, facilitated the taking of private property for the construction of mill dams, roads, canals, and railroads. By mid-century, a "man's home" was no longer "his castle" if it stood along the route of a proposed railroad. The circumstances of the West especially affected water and mineral law, as well as the law of real property. Yet, despite these changes, migrating Americans usually carried with them eastern notions of property and private ownership.

Van Ness v. Pacard
2 Pet. (27 U.S.) 137 (1829)

Pacard erected a building on land rented from Van Ness. Before the lease expired, Pacard removed the building. Van Ness sued for trespass, under the common-law rule that struc-

tures built on leased land became part of that land, and could not be removed by the renter
when the lease expired. In upholding a lower court decision in favor of Pacard, Justice
Joseph Story explained that much of English property law was often irrelevant in America.

The general rule of the common law certainly is, that whatever is once annexed to the freehold becomes part of it, and cannot afterwards be removed, except by him who is entitled to the inheritance. . . .

The common law of England is not to be taken in all respects to be that of America. Our ancestors brought with them its general principles, and claimed it as their birthright; but they brought with them and adopted only that portion which was applicable to their situation. There could be little or no reason for doubting, that the general doctrine as to things annexed to the freehold, so far as it respects heirs and executors, was adopted by them. . . . But, between landlord and tenant, it is not so clear that the rigid rule of the common law, . . . was so applicable to their situation, as to give rise to necessary presumption in its favour. The coun-

try was a wilderness, and the universal policy was to procure its cultivation and improvement. The owner of the soil, as well as the public, had every motive to encourage the tenant to devote himself to agriculture, and to favour any erections which should aid this result; yet, in the comparative poverty of the country, what tenant could afford to erect fixtures of much expense or value, if he was to lose his whole interest therein by the very act of erection? His cabin or log-hut, however necessary for any improvement of the soil would cease to be his the moment it was finished. It might, therefore deserve consideration, whether, in case the doctrine were not previously adopted in a state by some authoritative practice of adjudication, it ought to be assumed by this Court as part of the jurisprudence of such state, upon the mere footing of its existence to the common law.

Note: Eminent Domain

Eminent domain allows the taking of land, without the consent of the owner, by the government or by a private party, under certain circumstances. This process requires a formal condemnation of property, followed by a payment for the value of the property. Eminent domain was vital to the development of roads, railroads, and factories in the nineteenth century.

Parham v. The Justices of Decatur County
9 Ga. 341 (1851)

Parham objected to the taking of his land for the construction of a road. This case allowed
Judge Eugenius Nisbet of the Georgia Supreme Court to explain the theory behind eminent
domain.

It is very clear, that the Legislature may take the property of a citizen for purposes of public necessity or public utility. All grants of land are in subordination to the eminent domain which remains in the State; and from the necessities of the social compact, they are sub-

ject to this condition. The sovereign authority of the States, acting through the Legislature, is bound to protect and defend the States, and to promote the public happiness and prosperity of the people; and the Legislature is to judge when the public necessity or public utility requires the appropriation of the property of the citizen. I need not enlarge on these propositions—they are the law of this Court, more than once promulgated. Nor do we deny, that a highway is a work of public utility. It is necessary to commerce and intercourse. Nothing can be more conducive to the social well-being and commercial prosperity of a State, than roads. It were pagan and aboriginal not to have them. Our doctrine farther is, however, that the property of the citizen cannot be taken for any purpose of public utility or convenience, unless the law which appropriates it, makes provision for a just compensation to the proprietor. This is true at Common Law . . . recognized and affirmed by *Magna Charta,* and it is true by the special ordainment of the Constitution of the United States.

♦   ♦   ♦

The general doctrine, that private property cannot be taken for public use, without compensation, has been more than once held here. The question, it is true, has come before us, except in one instance, in the construction of rail road charters, or bridge or ferry grants. The principle is the same in this case. Whether the property of a citizen can be taken at all or not, depends upon the use or necessity which requires it. The principle upon which the right of way for a rail road has been sustained is, that the rail road is of public utility, and, therefore, when property is taken for that object, it is taken for public use. So, in the case of a public road, the ground of the rightful assumption is public use. If, in the former case, compensation must be made, as we have held, so in the latter case. I see no difference, so far as the principle is concerned, between a common highway and a rail road.

Barron v. Baltimore
7 Pet. 243 (1833)

Not all property destroyed by industrial development was taken through eminent domain. When public works improvements lowered the water level of the Baltimore harbor, ships could no longer reach Barron's wharf, leaving it "of little or no value." Barron sued the city for this "taking" of his property, and a county court awarded him $4,500. The Maryland Court of Appeals reversed this judgment because the state constitution had no just compensation provision. On appeal to the United States Supreme Court, Barron argued that he was entitled to compensation under the Fifth Amendment to the Constitution.

In dismissing the case for want of jurisdiction, Chief Justice Marshall concluded that "the fifth amendment must be understood as restraining the power of the general government, not as applicable to the States." Marshall asserted that the state constitutions were designed to protect the rights and liberties of the people from state action.

Barron illustrates the willingness of states to ignore vested interests in promoting economic development and the reluctance of the Supreme Court to interfere with the states on this issue. Barron is most important, however, for ensuring that the Bill of Rights would not be applicable to the states before the Civil War. Some abolitionists and Republicans argued that Barron was incorrectly decided and that the Bill of Rights did limit state action. This minority position came into its own after the Civil War began, and the Fourteenth Amendment was written in part to apply the Bill of Rights to the states. Not until Gitlow v. New York (1925), however, would the Supreme Court begin to accept this result of the Civil War.

Chief Justice Marshall, delivered the opinion of the Court.

The plaintiff in error contends [the Court has jurisdiction under] . . . that clause in the fifth amendment to the constitution, which inhibits the raking of private property for public use, without just compensation. He insists that this amendment, being in favour of the liberty of the citizen, ought to be so construed as to restrain the legislative power of a state, as well as that of the United States.

♦   ♦   ♦

The constitution was ordained and established by the people of the United States for themselves, for their own government, and not for the government of the individual states. Each state established a constitution for itself, and, in that constitution, provided such limitations and restrictions on the powers of its particular government as its judgment dictated. The people of the United States framed such a government for the United States as they supposed best adapted to their situation and best calculated to promote their interests. The powers they conferred on this government were to be exercised by itself; and the limitations on power, if expressed in general terms, are naturally, and, we think, necessarily applicable to the government created by the instrument. They are limitations of power granted in the instrument itself; not of distinct governments, framed by different persons and for different purposes.

If these propositions be correct, the fifth amendment must be understood as restraining the power of the general government, not as applicable to the states. In their several constitutions they have imposed such restrictions on their respective governments as their own wisdom suggested; such as they deemed most proper for themselves. It is a subject on which they judge exclusively, and with which others interfere no farther than they are supposed to have a common interest.

The counsel for the plaintiff in error insists that the constitution was intended to secure the people of the several states against the undue exercise of power by their respective state governments; as well as against that which might be attempted by their general government. In support of this argument he relies on the inhibitions contained in the tenth section of the first article.

We think that section affords a strong if not a conclusive argument in support of the opinion already indicated by the court.

The preceding section contains restrictions which are obviously intended for the exclusive purpose of restraining the exercise of power by the departments of the general government. Some of them use language applicable only to congress: others are expressed in general terms. The third clause, for example, declares that "no bill of attainder or ex post facto law shall be passed." No language can be more general; yet the demonstration is complete that it applies solely to the government of the United States. In addition to the general arguments furnished by the instrument itself, some of which have been already suggested, the succeeding section, the avowed purpose of which is to restrain state legislation, contains in terms the very prohibition. It declares that "no state shall pass any bill of attainder or ex post facto law." This provision, then, of the ninth section, however comprehensive its language, contains no restriction on state legislation.

The ninth section having enumerated, in the nature of a bill of rights, the limitations intended to be imposed on the powers of the general government, the tenth proceeds to enumerate those which were to operate on the state legislatures. These restrictions are brought together in the same section, and are by express words applied to the states. . . .

If the original constitution, in the ninth and tenth sections of the first article, draws this plain and marked line of discrimination between the limitations it imposes on the powers of the general government, and on those of the state; if in every inhibition intended to act on state power, words are employed which directly express that intent; some strong reason must be assigned for departing from this safe and judicious course in framing the amendments, before that departure can be assumed.

We search in vain for that reason.

Had the people of the several states, or any of them, required changes in their constitutions; had they required additional safeguards to liberty from the apprehended encroachments of their particular governments: the remedy was in their own hands, and would have been applied by themselves. A convention would have been assembled by the discontented state, and the required improvements would have been made by itself. The unwieldy and cumbrous machinery of procuring a recommendation from two-thirds of congress, and the assent of three-fourths of their sister states, could never have occurred to any human being as a mode of doing that which might be effected by the state itself. Had the framers of these amendments intended them to be limitations on the powers of the state governments, they would have imitated the framers of the original constitution, and have expressed that intention. Had congress engaged in the extraordinary occupation of improving the constitutions of the several states by affording the people additional protection from the exercise of power by their own governments in matters which concerned themselves alone, they would have declared this purpose in plain and intelligible language.

But it is universally understood, it is a part of the history of the day, that the great revolution which established the constitution of the United States, was not effected without immense opposition. Serious fears were extensively entertained that those powers which the patriot statesmen, who then watched over the interests of our country, deemed essential to union, and to the attainment of those invaluable objects for which union was sought, might be exercised in a manner dangerous to liberty. In almost every convention by which the constitution was adopted, amendments to guard against the abuse of power were recommended. These amendments demanded security against the apprehended encroachments of the general government—not against those of the local governments.

In compliance with a sentiment thus generally expressed, to quiet fears thus extensively entertained, amendments were proposed by the required majority in congress, and adopted by the states. These amendments contain no expression indicating an intention to apply them to the state governments. This court cannot so apply them.

We are of opinion that the provision in the fifth amendment to the constitution, declaring that private property shall not be taken for public use without just compensation, is intended solely as a limitation on the exercise of power by the government of the United States, and is not applicable to the legislation of the states. We are therefore of opinion that there is no repugnancy between the several acts of the general assembly of Maryland, given in evidence by the defendants at the trial of this cause, in the court of that state, and the constitution of the United States. This court, therefore, has no jurisdiction of the cause; and it is dismissed.

JOSEPH ANGELL

A Treatise on the Law of Watercourses
1854

While the steam engine revolutionized transportation, an expanded use of dams and water power changed the nature of manufacturing. The following selection from Joseph Angell's treatise illustrates the important connection between eminent domain law and water law in the nineteenth century.

Sec. 466. As a general rule, it must undoubtedly rest in the discretion and wisdom of the legislature to determine when public uses require the assumption and appropriation of private property; although the question is one not without embarrassment, as the line of demarcation between a use that is public, and one that is strictly private, is not to be drawn without much consideration. It has been said by a learned Judge [Chief Justice Shaw], that "it is difficult, perhaps impossible, to lay down any general rule, that would precisely define the power of the government, in the exercise of the acknowledged right of eminent domain; it must be large and liberal, so as to meet the public exigencies, and it must be so limited and restrained, as to secure effectually the rights of the citizen; and it must depend, in some instances, upon the nature of the exigencies as they arise, and the circumstances of particular cases." One thing is incontrovertible, and that is, that the necessities of the public for the use to which the property is to be appropriated must exist as *the basis* upon which the right is founded. Where private property, therefore, is wanted merely for *ornamental* purposes, this right cannot be exercised, as the purpose must be *useful.*

Sec. 467. Although it rests with the wisdom of the legislature to determine what is a "public use," and also the necessity for taking the property of an individual for that purpose; yet the right of eminent domain does not authorize the government, even for a full compensation, *to take the property of one citizen and transfer it to another,* when the public is not interested in the transfer. The possession and exertion of such a power would be incompatible with the nature and very object of all government; for, it being admitted, that a chief end for which government is instituted, is, that every man may enjoy his own; it follows, necessarily, that the rightful exercise of a power by the government of taking arbitrarily from any man what is his own, for the purpose of giving it to another, would subvert the very foundation principle upon which the government was organized. . . . [New York's] Chief Justice Savage . . . says, that, "the constitution, by authorizing appropriation of private property to public use, impliedly declares, that for any other use, private property shall not be taken from one and applied to the private use of another." It is in violation, he says, of natural right; and if it is not in violation of the *letter* of the constitution, it is of its spirit. . . . As has been declared by a learned Judge in Virginia, "Liberty itself consists essentially, as well as in the security of private property, as of the persons of individuals; and this security of private property is one of the primary objects of civil government, which our ancestors, in framing our Constitution, intended to secure to themselves and their posterity, effectually, and forever."

♦ ♦ ♦

Sec. 476. The constitutionality of the legislative power of taking private property depends upon the provision for a just indemnity; so that a statute incorporating a company to take private property without the consent of the owner, to promote any work for the public benefit, and making *no* provision for his indemnity, is unconstitutional and void. Thus the erection of a dam across a navigable water by an individual, under the authority of a statute of New Jersey, providing no remedy to the owner of a meadow overflowed by means of the dam, was held to be an injury for which the owner had his action for damages.

♦ ♦ ♦

Sec. 479. The Supreme Court of the State of New York, . . . say: "The Legislature of this State, it is believed, has never exercised the right of eminent domain in favor of mills of any kind. . . . " But nothing can be more clear, than that legislative acts of this character and for such object essentially promote the good of a community in its progress from a wilderness to cultivation, as was the case with the North American Colonies . . . when . . . the support of grist-mills and saw-mills was a measure of even vital necessity; and they were consequently encouraged in every possible manner. Mill-sites were, in some instances, appropriated from common lands, by the votes of their proprietors; and mills were often exempted from taxation. . . . In many instances they were erected in parts of the country still covered by the primitive forests, and where the extent of the flowing, and even the owners of the lands, were unknown. Even at the present day in . . . Georgia, the legislature have provided, that whoever will build a grist-mill on land so circumstanced, shall be entitled to the grant of an extensive tract of land, and whoever will build a saw-mill, to a grant of a much more extensive tract.

♦ ♦ ♦

Sec. 484. The effect of the statutes authorizing the flowing of land not belonging to the mill-owner, and providing a mode for estimating and recovering compensation therefor, take away . . . the right which the land-owner *prima facie* possesses of removing from his land a nuisance. For the same reason the only judicial remedy of the land-owner is the one prescribed by the statute, which is substituted for the action on the case. This was so expressly held in Massachusetts, . . . [that] the acts authorizing flowing, made expressly to relieve mill-owners from the difficulties and disputes to which they were before subject . . . [took] away the action at Common Law; an action which might be renewed for every new injury, and so harass the owner of a mill with continual lawsuits.

Note: Water Rights in the East

Like England, the eastern United States was blessed with abundant water resources, which allowed for industrialization through the building of mills and dams. The problem of mill dams flooding adjacent lands was dealt with through mill dam acts, eminent domain law, and judicially determined compensation to landowners. Mills competing for the same water raised a more complex problem. The placement of water wheels by an upstream mill might flood out a mill downstream. Similarly, if a mill downstream raised the height of its dam, it might force water to back up into a mill farther upstream and disrupt the water's flow.

Cary v. *Daniels*
8 Met. (Mass.) 466 (1844)

In 1837, James Wilson owned two mills, known as the upper mill and lower mill, and a dam, known as the middle dam. The middle dam was conveniently located so that when water behind it backed up into the water wheels of the upper mill, the operators of that mill could easily walk to the middle dam and open the waste gate, to lower the water level between the two mills and prevent the interference with the upper mill. In 1837, Wilson sold the upper mill to Cary. Later that year, a flood destroyed the middle dam. Daniels bought the lower mill in 1838 and built a new, larger dam farther downstream. This dam was too far from Cary's mill to allow him to easily open the waste gates when the water began to back up. Furthermore, the new dam was higher and thus more frequently caused the river to back up into Cary's mill, disrupting its operation. Cary sued Daniels, arguing that he had a right to the unobstructed use of his mill, and that Daniels was obligated to allow him to open the new dam when necessary for the operation of his own mill. Chief Justice Shaw delivered the opinion of the court.

The complaint is, that the lower dam is so raised as to set back the water and obstruct the free use of the plaintiff's water wheels.

Two questions were made at the trial. 1. Whether, as contended for by the plaintiff, he is not entitled, as against the defendant, to a free and unobstructed use of the stream below his mill, including a right to have the water run off as low as it would run in its natural bed. . . .

On the first point, we are of opinion that the claim cannot be maintained.

It is agreed on all hands, that the owner of a parcel of land, through which a stream of water flows, has a right to the use and enjoyment of the benefits to be derived therefrom, as it passes through his own land; but as this right is common to all through whose lands it flows, it follows that no one can wholly destroy or divert it; so as to prevent the water from coming to the proprietor below; nor can a lower proprietor wholly obstruct it, so as to throw it back upon the mills or lands of the proprietor above. We, of course, now speak of rights at common law, independent of any modification thereof by statute. But one of the beneficial uses of a water-course, and in this country one of the most important, is its application to the working of mills and machinery; a use profitable to the owner, and beneficial to the public. It is therefore held, that each proprietor is entitled to such use of the stream, so far as it is reasonable, conformable to the usages and wants of the community, and having regard to the progress of improvement in hydraulic works, and not inconsistent with a like reasonable use by the other proprietors of land, on the same stream, above and below. This last limitation of the right must be taken with one qualification, growing out of the nature of the case. The usefulness of water for mill purposes depends as well on its fall as its volume. But the fall depends upon the grade of the land over which it runs. The descent may be rapid, in which case there may be fall enough for mill sites at short distances; or the descent may be so gradual as only to admit of mills at considerable distances. In the latter case, the erection of a mill on one proprietor's land may raise and set the water back to such a distance as to prevent the proprietor above from having sufficient fall to erect a mill on his land. It seems to follow, as a necessary consequence from these principles, that in such case, the proprietor who first erects his dam for such a purpose has a right to maintain it, as against the proprietors above and below; and to this extent, prior occupancy gives a prior title to such use. It is a profitable, beneficial, and reasonable use, and therefore one which he has a right to make. If it necessarily occupy so much of the fall as to prevent the proprietor above from placing a dam and mill on his land, it is *damnum absque injuria* [loss without injury]. For the same reason, the proprietor below cannot erect a dam in such a manner as to

raise the water and obstruct the wheels of the first occupant. He had an equal right with the proprietor below to a reasonable use of the stream; he had made only a reasonable use of it; his appropriation to that extent, being justifiable and prior in time, necessarily prevents the proprietor below from raising the water, without interfering with a rightful use already made; and it is therefore not an injury to him. Such appears to be the nature and extent of the prior and exclusive right, which one proprietor acquires by a prior reasonable appropriation of the use of the water and its fall; and it results, not from any originally superior legal right, but from a legitimate exercise of his own common right, the effect of which is, de facto, to supersede and prevent a like use by other proprietors originally having the same common right. It is, in this respect, like the right in common, which any individual has, to use a highway; whilst one is reasonably exercising his own right, by a temporary occupation of a particular part of the street with his carriage or team, another cannot occupy the same place at the same time.

♦ ♦ ♦

So the proprietor above may, in like manner, make any reasonable uses of the stream and fall of water which he can do consistently with the previous appropriation of the proprietor below. If, with a view of gaining an advantage to his mill, in low stages of water, which may occur perhaps during the greatest part of the year, he places his mill so low that, in high stages of water, the dam below will throw back water on his wheels, he may do so if he choose, because he thereby does no injury to any other proprietor. But if he sustains a damage from such back water, it is a damage resulting from no wrong done by the lower proprietor who had previously established his dam, and it is an inconvenience to which he subjects his mill for the sake of greater advantages; and he has no cause to complain.

♦ ♦ ♦

The next claim of the plaintiff's is this; that he had a right, founded upon the usage and practice of his grantors, to open the waste gates of the middle dam, and thereby relieve his own mill from back water; and that the defendant, by taking down the middle dam, and erecting a new dam further down the stream, had either prevented him from the exercise of this right, or rendered the exercise of it more onerous and expensive. The court are of opinion, that this claim cannot be sustained. At the time of the practice relied on, the grantors were owners of both mills, and might favor one at the expense of the other, as the exigencies of their business might require, or at their own mere pleasure. But no right could be founded on such practice; because it was not adverse. When the estates were severed, and the rights of the respective proprietors became adverse, they stood upon the same footing as if no such usage had existed. The damages, therefore, which were given by the jury, for the violation of this supposed right, must be deducted from the verdict. . . .

But, for the reasons already given, the court are of opinion, that the defendant had no right to erect his new dam higher than his old one, so as to appropriate an increased portion of the stream to his own use, and thereby set back water upon the mill wheels of the plaintiff. The jury having found that he had so raised his dam, to the injury of the plaintiff, and assessed damages therefor separately, we think the verdict must be amended, so as to stand as a verdict for the latter sum only, and that judgment be rendered thereon for the plaintiff.

Note: Water Rights in the West

Cary v. *Daniels* illustrates the limitations on water use where water was abundant, population relatively dense, and settlement long-standing. In England and the East, the common law of water developed over many years to protect all users of a particular stream or river. Simply stated, under the common law people were free to use the water flowing by their property, as long as they did not diminish the water available to persons farther downstream or unreasonably disrupt the flow downstream and adversely affect users and landowners upstream. This rule, modified by eminent domain law and statutes protecting mill dams, was workable and sensible where streams, ponds, lakes, and rivers were common and rainfall was adequate for most crops. However, much of the common law of water and property was useless in the West, where the average annual rainfall of sixteen inches was less than half that in the East. For example, abundant water resources meant that irrigation was virtually unknown in the East and in England. Thus Westerners had to develop statutes and a new common law to facilitate irrigation and other uses of water unknown in the East. The common law of water rights in the West was based on the concept of "reasonable use."

WALTER PRESCOTT WEBB

The Great Plains
1931

Drawing on Charles S. Kinney, Law of Irrigation and Water Rights and the Arid Region Doctrine of Appropriation of Waters *(1912), historian Webb described how a western law of water emerged.*

The custom or practice that came in to supplement or entirely displace the common law of riparian rights was that of prior appropriation for beneficial use, which practice Kinney has named the "Arid Region Doctrine of appropriation."

The Arid Region Doctrine of appropriation may be defined as that doctrine or rule of law which has grown up in this Western portion of our country, governing the use of water of the natural streams and other bodies, by its appropriation for any useful or beneficial purpose, based upon the physical necessities of the case; and, whereby for the purpose of applying the water to some beneficial use, the water must be diverted from its natural channels, and, in contradistinction to the strict construction of the common law of riparian rights, the place of use may be on either riparian or nonriparian lands, and the right based on priority. In fact, this doctrine is in derogation of the common law, and as said in an early California case, it is "without judicial or legislative precedent, either in our own country or in that from which we have borrowed our jurisprudence."

This doctrine is distinguished by the following characteristics:

1. It had its origin west of the hundredth meridian, and was and is unknown to the humid portion of the country.

2. It permits the use of water for beneficial or useful purposes as distinguished from the reasonable use of the modified common law.

3. It permits the diversion of water from the stream regardless of the diminution of the stream.

4. The water may be used either on riparian or on nonriparian lands. According to the common law all the land not immediately adjacent to the stream would have been left high and dry, but under the arid-region doctrine the reclamation of this land became possible.

5. The arid-region doctrine denies the equality among users so steadfastly maintained by the common law of riparian rights. It grants to the first appropriator an exclusive right and to later appropriators rights conditioned upon the prior rights of those who have gone before.

6. Under the common law a riparian owner's rights, though not inalienable, remain his without any specific act of commission or omission on his part—his by virtue of ownership of the land. He does not forfeit the right if he does not use it. Under the arid-region doctrine, on the contrary, the continuation of the privilege or right depends upon beneficial use combined with prior appropriation. Not to use the water, for example, is to forfeit it.

Irwin v. Phillips, et al.
5 Cal. 140 (1855)

Irwin v. Phillips *illustrates the rules of western water rights. Matthew Irwin, a California miner, diverted a stream from its natural course to his mining operation. Robert Phillips and others later began mining farther downstream and found that they lacked sufficient water for their operation. Thus they began to "trench on" Irwin's dam, in an attempt to divert the water back into the original streambed. Irwin won a suit for trespass at the trial level, and Phillips appealed to the California Supreme Court, raising the question: Did the common law of England and the eastern United States apply to California? If it did, then Irwin had no right to divert water from its natural course. Phillips supported this position by citations to numerous cases from Massachusetts, New York, and Britain, and to American and English treatises, including Angell's Watercourses. Irwin argued that a substantially new law had developed in California, which allowed a first user to take as much water as he needed. This case illustrates the difficulties of allocating a scarce resource—water—according to common-law rules developed where the resource was plentiful. The case also illustrates nicely Oliver Wendell Holmes's assertion that the life of the law has not been logic, but has been "experience."*

Heydenfeldt, J. . . .

. . . The proposition to be settled is whether the owner of a canal in the mineral region of this State, constructed for the purpose of supplying water to miners, has the right to divert the water of a stream from its natural channel, as against the claims of those who, subsequent to the diversion, take up lands along the banks of the stream, for the purpose of mining. It must be premised that it is admitted on all sides that the mining claims in controversy, and the lands through which the stream runs and through which the canal passes, are a part of the public domain, to which there is no claim of private proprietorship; and that the miners have the right to dig for gold on the public lands. . . .

It is insisted by the appellants [Phillips] that in this case the common law doctrine must be invoked, which prescribes that a water course must be allowed to flow in its natural channel. But upon an examination of the authorities which support that doctrine, it will be found to rest upon the fact of the individual rights of landed proprietors upon the stream, the principle being both at the civil and common law that the owner of lands on the banks of a water course owns to the middle of the stream, and has the right in virtue of his proprietorship to the use of the water in its pure and natural condition. In this case the lands are the property either of the State or the United States. . . . It is certain that at the common law the diversion of water courses could only be complained of by riparian owners, who were deprived of the use, or those claiming directly under them. Can the appellants assert their present claim as tenants at will? To solve this question it must be kept in mind that their tenancy is of their own creation, their tenements of their own selection, and subsequent, in point of time, to the diversion of the stream. They had the right to mine where they pleased throughout an extensive region, and they selected the bank of a stream from which the water had been already turned, for the purpose of supplying the mines at another point.

Courts are bound to take notice of the political and social condition of the country which they judicially rule. In this State the larger part of the territory consists of mineral lands, nearly the whole of which are the property of the public. No right or intent of disposition of these lands has been shown either by the United States or the State governments, and . . . a system has been permitted to grow up by the voluntary action and assent of the population, whose free and unrestrained occupation of the mineral region has been tacitly assented to by the one government, and heartily encouraged by the expressed legislative policy of the other. If there are, as must be admitted, many things connected with this system, which are crude and undigested, and subject to fluctuation and dispute, there are still some which a universal sense of necessity and propriety have so firmly fixed as that they have come to be looked upon as having the force and effect of res judicata. Among these the most important are the rights of miners to be protected in the possession of their selected localities, and the rights of those who, by prior appropriation, have taken the waters from their natural beds, and by costly artificial works have conducted them for miles over mountains and ravines, to supply the necessities of gold diggers, and without which the most important interests of the mineral region would remain without development. So fully recognized have become these rights, that without any specific legislation conferring or confirming them, they are alluded to and spoken of in various acts of the Legislature in the same manner as if they were rights which had been vested by the most distinct expression of the will of the law makers; as for instance, in the Revenue Act "canals and water races" are declared to be property subject to taxation, and this when there was none other in the State than such as were devoted to the use of mining. . . . This simply goes to prove . . . that however much the policy of the State, as indicated by her legislation, has conferred the privilege to work the mines, it has equally conferred the right to divert the streams from their natural channels, and as these two rights stand upon an equal footing, when they conflict, they must be decided by the fact of priority, upon the maxim of equity, *qui prior est in tempore, potior est injure* [he who is prior in time is better in right]. The miner who selects a piece of ground to work, must take it as he finds it, subject to prior rights, which have an equal equity, on account of an equal recognition from the sovereign power. If it is upon a stream, the waters of which have not been taken from their bed, they cannot be taken to his prejudice; but if they have been already diverted, and for as high and legitimate a purpose as the one he seeks to accomplish,

he has no right to complain, no right to interfere with the prior occupation of his neighbor, and must abide the disadvantages of his own selection.

It follows from this opinion that the judgment of the Court below was substantially correct . . . and it is therefore affirmed.

Note: Law and Westward Migration

Most Americans have an image of "the West" as lawless and violent. While there is some basis for this view, there is another side to western migration. In his innovative study *Law for the Elephant: Property and Social Behavior on the Overland Trail* (1980), John Phillip Reid argues that Americans moving west brought with them both a respect for the law and a rudimentary knowledge of the law. He demonstrates that without lawyers, judges, or courts, the western settlers implemented such legal concepts as property, contract, and partnership. Reid finds that "except for definitions of possession and rules governing exclusive control of minerals, water, and open range, the law of the east was the law of the west. The concept of private property remained largely inviolable, even when conditions were trying and people desperate." Reid notes that

> few emigrants traveling the overland trail to the Pacific coast could have explained the meaning of "words of purchase" or fee simple absolute, yet all understood and a vast majority respected the legal principles vesting in their individual exclusive enjoyment of property lawfully possessed. . . . [T]hey respected the rights of property owners much as if still back east in the midst of plenty. By respect of their neighbor and their neighbor's property they were, more often than not, adhering to a morality of law.

THE GROWTH OF CONTRACT LAW IN THE NINETEENTH CENTURY

The nineteenth century "was the golden age of contract law."[11] An almost unknown field in 1800, by 1860 it dominated American law. Examination of the legal treatises reveals this sudden development of contract law. In 1765, Blackstone devoted an entire volume of *Commentaries on the Laws of England* to property, but only a few pages to contracts. William Wetmore Story's 1844 contract treatise was over 400 pages long and cited more than 3,500 English and American cases. Three years later, he published a revised and expanded edition. In the 1850s, Theophilus Parsons published three editions of his two-volume *The Law of Contracts*.

Nineteenth-century law retained common-law notions that contracts with children, drunkards, and married women might be void because of the legal incompetence of the parties. Generally, slaves and southern free blacks were not allowed to make contracts. However, industrialization and the rise of national and international markets led to dramatic changes in other aspects of contract law.

Before the nineteenth century, a legally enforceable contract had to be fair; the exchange of money for goods or services had to be reasonable, under the theory that a "sound price warrants a sound commodity." By the 1840s, this was no longer true. Story's treatise noted that a contract required only "mutual assent of the parties" and a "valuable consideration," which he defined as "a legal consideration emanating from some injury or inconvenience to the one party, or some benefit to the other party." Courts no longer cared if the exchange of consideration was fair. "It is not necessary," Story noted, "that the consideration and promise should be equivalents in actual value, for it would be impossible, ever precisely to determine, whether in a given case the consideration was adequate, without a psychological investigation into the motives of the parties." Antebellum courts demanded only that

> each party to a contract may exercise his own discretion, as to the adequacy of consideration; and if the agreement be made bona fide, it matters not how insignificant the benefit may apparently be to the promisor, or how slight the inconvenience or damage appear to be to the promisee.

Story's explanation reveals much about the attitudes that mid-nineteenth-century capitalism fostered. Story declared that "if no contracts were good, but those, which were apparently of equal benefit to both parties, probably very few contracts, which are made, would be legally valid."[12] In other words, the law of the nineteenth century recognized and supported the belief that unfair bargains were necessary for the commercial and industrial development of the day. The maker of sharp bargains, the shrewd businessman, was legally protected unless there was "evidence of fraud or imposition."[13]

Morton Horwitz has noted that in the nineteenth century,

> judges and jurists finally reject[ed] the longstanding belief that the justification of contractual obligation is derived from the inherent justice or fairness of an exchange. In its place, they asserted for the first time that the source of the obligation of contract is the convergence of the wills of the contracting parties.[14]

In such a world, those with the most knowledge and greatest economic power tended to dictate the terms of contracts. Thus contract law generally favored sellers over buyers and employers over laborers and served as an instrument that aided the industrial and commercial entrepreneurs of the nineteenth century. This led to the "triumph of contract" over property, tort, and equity, as the law came "to ratify those forms of inequality that the market system produced."[15]

Seixas and Seixas v. *Woods*
2 Cai. R. (N.Y.) 48 (1804)

The Seixases purchased from Woods what he alleged was valuable brazilletto wood but was actually almost worthless peachum wood. Woods had purchased this shipment from a third party, without inspecting it, and, similarly, the Seixases bought the shipment without examining it. When the Seixases discovered the error, they sought to return the shipment to Woods, who refused to accept it or give a refund. The Seixases did not allege fraud by Woods, merely that he had improperly labeled his goods and had sold them as something they were not. Judges Smith Thompson and James Kent spoke for the New York Supreme Court, in finding for Woods on the grounds that there was no implied warranty and thus the buyers should have relied on caveat emptor.

Thompson, J. . . .

From the facts . . . it appears there was no *express warranty* by the defendant, or any *fraud* in the sale. The wood was sold and purchased as *brazilletto* wood, and a fair price for such wood paid, when in fact the wood was of a different quality, and of little or no value. The plaintiff's agent, who made the purchase, saw the wood when unloaded and delivered, and did not discover or know that it was of a different quality from that described in the bills of parcels; neither did the defendant, who was only consignee of this cargo, know that the wood was not *brazilletto*. The question then arises, whether there was an implied warranty, so as to afford redress to the plaintiffs, or whether the maxim caveat emptor must be applied to them. From an examination of the decisions in courts of common law, I can find no case where an action has been sustained under similar circumstances: an express warranty, or some fraud in the sale, are deemed indispensably necessary to be shown. . . . I see no injustice or inconvenience resulting from this doctrine, but, on the contrary, think it is best calculated to excite that caution and attention which all prudent men ought to observe in making their contracts. I [find for] . . . the defendant. . . .

Kent, J. . . . That without a warranty by the seller, or fraud on his part, the buyer must stand to all losses arising from latent defects, and that there is no instance in the *English* law of a contrary rule being laid down. The civil law, and the law of those countries which have adopted the civil as their common law, is more rigorous towards the seller, and make him responsible in every case for a latent defect . . . and, if the question was *res integra* in our law, I confess I should be overcome by the reasoning of the *Civilians*. And yet the rule of the common law has been well and elegantly vindicated . . . as most happily reconciling the claims of convenience with the duties of good faith. It requires the *purchaser* to apply his attention to those particulars which may be supposed within the reach of his observation and judgment, and the vendor to communicate those particulars and defects which cannot be supposed to be immediately within the reach of such attention. And even against his want of vigilance, the purchaser may provide, by requiring the vendor expressly to warrant the article. The mentioning the wood as *brazilletto* wood, in the bill of parcels, and in the advertisement some days previous to the sale, did not amount to a warranty to the plaintiffs. To make an affirmation at the time of the sale, a warranty, it must appear by evidence to be so intended, and not to have been a mere matter of judgment and opinion, and of which the defendant had no particular knowledge. Here it is admitted the defendant was equally ignorant with the plaintiffs, and could have had no such intention.

McFarland v. Newman
Watts (Pa.) 55 (1839)

McFarland *v.* Newman *shows the further advance of caveat emptor. Newman purchased McFarland's colt, which turned out to have "an incurable disease called glanders." At trial, Newman proved that the horse had "exhibited . . . symptoms all the time McFarland had him (a period of ten or eleven months)" but that at the sale McFarland declared the horse had been ill for only a few days and was suffering from "the ordinary distemper to which colts are subject." The jury awarded Newman $75 based on McFarland's "alleged warranty," and McFarland appealed.*

Gibson, C.J. . . . The civil law maxim is, doubtless, that a sound article is warranted by a sound price; but the common-law courts started with the doctrine that though the sale of a chattel is followed by an implied warranty of title, and a right of action *ex delicto* [out of the fault] for wilful misrepresentation of the quality; yet that maxim caveat emptor, disposes of all beside. Thus was the common law originally settled; and the current of decision ran smooth and clear in the channel thus marked out for it, from the days of the year books, till within a few years past, when it suddenly became turgid and agitated; and . . . it finally ran wild. The judges, in pursuit of a phantom in the guise of a principle of impracticable policy and questionable morality, broke away from the common law, not, however, by adopting the civil law principle of implied warranty as to soundness, but by laying hold on the vendor's commendation of his commodity, and not at first as absolutely constituting an express warranty, but as evidence of it. I say the policy of this principle is impracticable, because the operations of commerce are such as to require that the rules for its regulation admit of as few occasions for reclamation as possible; and I say its morality is questionable, because I am unable to discern anything immoral in the bona fide sale of an article represented to be exactly that as which the vendor had purchased it. It is to be remembered that I am speaking of the sale of a thing accepted by the vendee after opportunity had to inspect and test it, and not of a sale of which he was necessarily compelled by the circumstances to deal on the faith of the vendor's description; nor yet a sale on the concoction of which he was overreached by misrepresentation or trick.

◆ ◆ ◆

As the case goes back to another jury, it is proper to intimate the principle on which a correct decision of it must depend. Though to constitute a warranty requires no particular form of words, the naked averment of a fact is neither a warranty itself, nor evidence of it. In connection with other circumstances, it certainly may be taken into consideration; but the jury must be satisfied from the whole that the vendor actually, and not constructively, consented to be bound for the truth of his representation. Should he have used expressions fairly importing a willingness to be thus bound, it would furnish a reason to infer that he had intentionally induced the vendee to treat on that basis; but a naked affirmation is not to be dealt with as a warranty, merely because the vendee had gratuitously relied on it; for not to have exacted a direct engagement, had he desired to buy on the vendor's judgment, must be accounted an instance of folly. Testing the vendor's responsibility by these principles, justice will be done without driving him into the toils of an imaginary contract.

Judgment reversed, and a *venire de novo* awarded.

Icar v. Suares
7 La. 517 (1835)

Because of its civil-law heritage, Louisiana completely rejected the concept of caveat emptor. *Instead, the state required the vendor to disclose all known defects. A dissatisfied purchaser could file an action of redhibition, to rescind a sale if defects were not disclosed. The redhibition laws stemmed from Roman law concerning the sale of slaves, and in Louisiana this applied to the sale of slaves and other property. Icar initiated this redhibitory action to annul the sale of Kate, a slave, and recover his purchase price and other costs, on the ground that Kate had "the redhibitory vices of craziness and running away."*

Bullard, J., delivered the opinion of the court.

The plaintiff seeks to be relieved from a contract, by which he purchased from the defendant a recently imported slave, on account of two redhibitory vices, to wit: the habit of running away and madness. Judgment was rendered in his favor, and the defendant appealed.

The case turns altogether on matters of fact. We doubt whether the evidence establishes the habit of running away previous to the sale, but the opinion we have formed on the second ground, renders it unnecessary to give any positive opinion on the first.

It is contended that Kate was not crazy, but only stupid, and that stupidity is not madness, but on the contrary an apparent defect, against which the defendant did not warrant. . . . The code enumerates madness (folie) among the absolute vices of slaves, which give rise to the action of redhibition. Whether the subject of this action is idiotick . . . we [do not] consider it material, inasmuch as the code has declared, that a sale may be avoided on account of any vice or defect, which renders the thing absolutely useless, or its use so inconvenient and imperfect, that it must be supposed the buyer would not have purchased with a knowledge of the vice. La. Code. art. 2496.

We are satisfied from the evidence in the record . . . the slave in question was wholly, and perhaps worse than useless.

It is, therefore, ordered, adjudged and decreed, that the judgment of the District Court be affirmed, with costs.

Seymour v. *Delancey, et al.*
3 Cow. (N.Y.) 445 (1824)

Thomas Ellison contracted to give Seymour two farms for a one-third interest in a group of lots in the village of Newburgh, New York. The exchange of land was never carried out, and Seymour sued Ellison's heirs, the Delanceys, to require specific performance of the contract. In Seymour v. Delancey, et al., *6 Johns. Ch. (N.Y.) 222 (1822), Chancellor James Kent refused to order specific performance of the contract. Kent found that "at the date of the agreement, the village lots were not worth half the value of the country farms." Kent then asserted that*

> *there is a very great weight of authority against enforcing a contract, where the consideration is so inadequate as to render it a hard bargain, and an unequal and an unreasonable bargain; the argument is exceedingly strong against it in such cases, when it is considered that if equity acts at all, it must act ex* vigore, *and carry the contract into execution, with unmitigated severity.*

Kent concluded

> *that inadequacy of price may, of itself, and without fraud or other ingredient, be sufficient to stay the application of the power of this Court to enforce a specific performance of a private contract to sell land. . . . In the present case, the inadequacy is so great as to give the character of hardship, unreasonableness and inequality to the contract, and to render it discreet and proper, under the established principles of the Court, to refuse to decree a specific performance.*

Seymour appealed to the New York Court for the Trial of Impeachments and the Correction of Errors. This unique body consisted of the entire New York State Senate, the justices of the New York Supreme Court, the chancellor, and the lieutenant governor. Chief Justice John Savage and nine senators voted to uphold Kent's decree. But Senator John Sudam wrote for the majority, which voted to reverse Kent.

[I]t cannot be sustained, in my opinion, that *mere inequality* in value, which is not so gross as to strike the moral feeling of an indifferent man, would be sufficient to warrant the Chancellor in witholding a decree for specific performance. I admit that the exercise of the power, in a Court of Chancery, to enforce the specific performance of contracts for the sale or the exchange of land, rests in the sound discretion of the Court: but this is a sound legal discretion; and not the exercise of an arbitrary power, interfering with the contracts of individuals, and sporting with their vested rights. I also admit, that the party claiming the specific performance must present a case *fair, just* and *reasonable; that the contract must be founded on adequate consideration;* and that it must be free from *fraud, misrepresentation, deceit,* or *surprise.*

To determine whether, in fact, the agreement for exchange was hard, unequal, and disproportionate, and whether it was free from *fraud, surprise, &c.,* it will be necessary to examine, with as much brevity as possible, the history of this transaction.

◆ ◆ ◆

[Here Senator Sudam pointed out that before agreeing to trade the farms for the one-third interest in the village lots, Ellison had purchased the other two-thirds interest in the lots from Seymour's relatives. Sudam continued:] . . . It is also in evidence that Ellison, during the summer, resided in New Windsor, in the county of Orange, adjoining the village of Newburgh, and that he was well acquainted with the property of the appellant, proposed to be exchanged for his two farms. It also appears that Ellison had a favorable opinion of Newburgh as a business place; and he may have been influenced by the consideration, that property there would rise in value, in consequence of the expected establishment of a navy yard.

◆ ◆ ◆

The whole presents a very strong case, and one in which the contract should be carried into effect, unless some controlling rule of decision in our Equity Courts shall require the contrary.

There can be no doubt, from a review of the evidence, that Ellison made his bargain, well knowing all the facts in relation to the Newburgh lots, as well as his farms proposed to be exchanged for them. . . . It could not be pretended, that after a purchase of two-thirds of the whole property, he had never examined the premises, or that he had not ascertained the situation and comparative value of the Newburgh lots; for it is admitted by all parties, that at the time of the purchase from Drake Seymour, and his agreeing to purchase of S. S. Seymour, he was not incompetent to transact business of any kind. Immediately after this, the negotiation for the one-third of the appellant's lots commenced. . . . There is, therefore, no pretence, in my opinion, that Ellison was not fully acquainted with the premises, proposed to be exchanged with him, by the appellant. . . . He was in a situation deliberately to form his opinion, and unquestionably he did do so, as to the value of the Newburgh lots; and from his previous purchases, he must have ascertained their value, to his own satisfaction. Under the advice of his agent, he knew the value of the property to be conveyed by him to the appellant. We must take it, then, that Ellison deliberately, and with his eyes open, entered into the contract which the appellant now seeks to enforce by a decree of a Court of Equity.

I am, therefore, of opinion, from a review of the whole evidence, that this contract was, at the time the negotiation was first entered into, and at the time the articles were executed by Seymour and Ellison, certain fair and just, in all its parts.

The next question which presents itself to the consideration of the Court is, whether the contract between the appellant and Ellison is so *hard, unreasonable, or unequal,* that this Court will not aid to enforce it.

In reviewing this part of the case, it will be the duty of the Court to investigate the evidence as to the value of the Newburgh lots, and the farms to be exchanged for them. Should they arrive at the conclusion that *mere inadequacy in value, where there is no fraud, misrepresentation, imposition, or concealment of facts, is of itself sufficient to avoid the contract,* it will save a great deal of the labor and investigation which might otherwise be required. I admit, however, that where the inadequacy of price in a contract is so flagrant and palpable as to convince a man at the first blush, that one of the contracting parties had been imposed on by some false pretence, such a contract ought not to be enforced by this, or any other Court of Equity. It is not to be denied, that it is the settled doctrine of the Court of Chancery, that it will not carry into effect, specifically, a contract where the inadequacy of price amounts to conclusive evidence of fraud.

◆ ◆ ◆

I cannot assent to the doctrine, that inadequacy of price may, of itself and without fraud or other ingredient, be sufficient to stay the application of the power of a Court of Chancery, to enforce a specific performance of a private contract to sell land.

To establish this doctrine in the state of New York, would, to my mind, be sanctioning a principle, which would lead to very injurious results. Every member of this Court must be well aware how much property is held by contract; that purchases are constantly made upon speculation; that the value of real estate is fluctuating; and that there, most generally, exists an honest difference of opinion in regard to any bargain, as to its being a beneficial one, or not. To say, when all is fair, and the parties deal on equal terms, that a Court of Equity will not interfere, does not appear to me to be supported by authority . . . and unless I am bound down by some rigid rule of law, I, for one cannot consent to its introduction into our equity code.

◆ ◆ ◆

There may be such inadequacy of price as, of itself, to be an evidence of fraud. But wherever this does not exist, and resort is had to the testimony of witnesses, and they differ in their valuation, as in the present case, the contract should be executed. . . .

The cause must therefore be remitted to the Court of Chancery, that the Chancellor may direct a Master to inquire whether the appellant can give to the respondents a clear and unincumbered title to the Newburgh lots; and if he can, a decree for a specific performance, according to the contract, must be entered against the respondents.

Note: Contracts and the Emerging Speculative Economy

Senator Sudam's opinion notes that "purchases are constantly made upon speculation." This statement anticipates a modern marketplace, based on securities, speculative contracts, and other kinds of risky investments. Sudam's opinion supports such an economic environment, but at the expense of those who might enter into blatantly unfair bargains out of ignorance.

Note: Contracts and the Federal Constitution

In antebellum America, contracts was the only area of substantive civil law with a major federal component. Article I, Section 10, of the Constitution prohibited states from "impairing the obligations of contracts." Both the *Dartmouth College* and *Charles River Bridge* cases reached the Court under the contracts clause. The first major contracts clause case was *Fletcher* v. *Peck,* 6 Cranch (U.S.) 87 (1810), which stemmed from one of America's greatest political scandals, the Yazoo Land Fraud.

In January 1795, the Georgia legislature sold 35 million acres near the Yazoo River to four land companies for a paltry $500,000, less than $1\frac{1}{2}$ cents an acre. Many members of the 1795 legislature held stock in the land companies, as did various state and federal officeholders. In 1796, a new legislature rescinded this sale, burned all records of the purchase, but did not return the $500,000 purchase price.

Fletcher v. *Peck* was a collusive suit brought to test the 1796 repeal. Peck, of Massachusetts, a holder of land under the 1795 law, sold 15,000 acres to Fletcher, of New Hampshire. Fletcher then sued Peck, arguing that the 1796 law rescinding the original grant prevented Peck from giving him good title to the land. Chief Justice Marshall, speaking for the Supreme Court, declared that the 1796 law was unconstitutional because the 1795 law was "in its nature a contract," and "absolute rights" had "been vested under that contract" and a repeal of the law could not "devest those rights." The Chief Justice admitted that "corruption" might "contaminate the very source of legislation or that impure motive" might "contribute to the passage of a law." But he rejected the idea that "the validity of a law depends upon the motives of its framers." Ignoring the notoriety of the land fraud, Marshall said of the Yazoo purchaser:

> He has paid his money for a title good at law; he is innocent, whatever may be the guilt of others, and equity will not subject him to the penalties attached to that guilt. All titles would be insecure, and the intercourse between man and man would be very seriously obstructed, if this principle be overturned.

This case provided constitutional precedent for protecting vested rights, but did not solve the questions surrounding the Yazoo land titles. In 1814, Congress indemnified all Yazoo landholders with a $5 million buyout. This was a political solution to what was from the beginning a political problem.

The Evolution of Modern Tort Law

The lack of a recognizable system of tort is one of the major differences between liability law before 1800 and after about 1850. The term "tort" appears only once in the index of Blackstone's *Commentaries on the Laws of England.* Book 3 of Blackstone, *Of Private Wrongs,* is "primarily devoted to English civil procedure: the jurisdictional allocations among the courts and the procedures for litigating them."[16] Blackstone did not discuss torts because the substance of the common law of wrongs was almost nonexistent before the mid–nineteenth century.

Before the nineteenth century, a variety of private wrongs—such as assault, libel, and trespass—were dealt with as separate legal actions. Under the writ system, courts "identified a residual category of noncriminal wrongs not arising out of contract,"[17] which were litigated under the old common-law writ system as "trespass" or "trespass on the case" (often called "case"). At this time " 'torts' was not an autonomous branch of law," but was, as Oliver Wendell Holmes, Jr., noted in 1871, "a collection of unrelated writs."[18] Suits for harms that we would now call torts were not categorized as such, nor did lawyers use such modern legal concepts as "negligence," "duty," and "fault." At that time, "negligence" and "breach of duty" usually referred to the failure to perform the requirements of a contract or the failure of a government official to perform his function as established by common law or statute. Indeed, "perhaps the most important eighteenth century of line of cases in which negligence was a factor involved both common law and statutory actions against sheriffs for taking insufficient bond or for allowing imprisoned debtors to escape."[19]

In the mid–nineteenth century, the law of torts rapidly changed. Francis Hilliard's treatise *The Elements of Law* (1835) had only seven minor references to tort law; however, in 1859 his two-volume, 1,200 page *The Law of Torts* contained citations to over 5,000 cases. This phenomenal growth in tort law resulted from two quite different—although ultimately interrelated—changes in Anglo-American society.

By mid-century, the old common-law system of writs and pleadings began to collapse because it could no longer efficiently serve the needs of the expanding legal system and a dynamic economy. The writ system was too slow and cumbersome. Technical pleadings, rather than the substance of a case, too often determined outcomes. The demise of the writ system ended the archaic distinctions between "trespass" and "trespass on the case," allowed for the substitution of more meaningful terminology, and forced lawyers and judges to think more systematically and categorically.

The end of the writ system did not, by itself, lead to either an explosion in tort law or doctrinal change. Both evolved with a changing economy. Industrialization led to more accidents and harms—more torts. The new machines of the nineteenth century—especially railroads and steamboats—all too frequently injured or killed bystanders, passengers, and operators. The old writ system was simply incapable of handling the exploding number and variety of suits caused by industrial mishaps. Moreover, these torts increasingly took place between strangers. In an earlier age, community relationships might have allowed for the compensation for losses without resort to law. But in the bustling and impersonal world of the railroad, the factory, and the city, courts provided the only forum for compensating accident victims. Out of these increasingly frequent accidents the modern law of torts emerged with its elements of fault, negligence, duty, and proximate causation.

The emerging tort law made tortfeasors generally liable for the harms they caused others. However, four rules evolved that undermined the likelihood of injured parties recovering damages. "Contributory negligence" prevented an injured person from winning damages if the defendant could prove that even a small part of the accident was caused by the injured party. The rule against "wrongful death" suits prevented the families of persons killed in accidents from recovering damages. The fellow servant rule (presented as part of the labor law section of this chapter) prevented most workers from recovering damages for job-related injuries. Finally, courts refused to hold tortfeasors responsible for damages resulting from "remote causation." These rules tended to aid the new nineteenth-century industries, especially the emerging railroads and steamboat companies.

Spencer v. *Campbell*
9 Watts & Serg. (Pa.) 32 (1845)

Campbell took his grain to the Spencers' mill, where a defective steam boiler exploded, killing Campbell's horse. Campbell sued in "trespass on the case," asserting that the Spencers had a duty to "use safe and convenient machinery" in their business and that "in disregard to this duty they procured a defective steamboiler, and well knowing it to be defective used it." Campbell also argued that the Spencers "negligently managed their engine." The Spencers argued that they had purchased the boiler from one Meixsell, a reputable machinist, that they were not experts in this technology, and that they could not be held responsible for a manufacturer's defects. The presiding judge charged the jury in the following manner.

Woodward (President).—There is little ground to doubt the legal duty that was upon the defendants to provide reasonably sufficient and safe machinery for carrying on their business.

This duty is on men in every branch of business, when they ask people to risk life and property in their hands and for their profit. The transporter of passengers or property . . . is required to have all the means and appliances necessary for a safe accomplishment of the work in hand; the innkeeper is bound to provide safe and convenient house-room for his guests and stabling for horses; and the rule applies with peculiar force to manufacturers and mechanics whose occupation brings customers . . . into the immediate vicinity of their machinery.

But whilst the defendants do not deny the alleged defectiveness of their steam-boiler, nor controvert the general principle of law applicable to all machinery, they seek to excuse themselves from liability in this case on the ground that being themselves unacquainted with steam engines, they applied to an experienced machinist for a competent and good engine for their grist mill, paid him a sound price, and received a machine which he represented to be safe and sufficient for their purposes; that he put it up for them, and instructed them in the use of it, and that they never applied all the power to the boiler which he assured them they might with safety put on; and that, until the explosion occurred, they did not know that the boiler was defective. The plaintiff charges them with "well knowing" the defective character of the boiler; and the negligence which constitutes the tort in this case depends on this question of knowledge. It is well known now and admitted that the boiler was defective; but did the defendants know this whilst they were using it? If they did, it was the grossest negligence in them to continue to use the boiler; if they did not, the plaintiff cannot recover on the first count of his declaration.

♦ ♦ ♦

If the jury should find it necessary thus to impute knowledge of the defectiveness of the engine to the defendants, they are not to be excused on account of any false security into which the representations of Meixsell, the machinist, may have betrayed them. They employed him at their own risk; they took his advice at their peril. Their customers never trusted in Meixsell; their confidence was in the

Spencers. As between one of those customers and the Spencers, the opinions and assurances of Meixsell become unimportant. If the defendants chose to make his opinions the rule of their conduct in opposition to the testimony of their own senses, they have no right to visit the consequences of their folly on their innocent customers. The public repaired to their mill on the presumption that they employed all the precautions and care in conducting their business that men of ordinary prudence do commonly employ, and they were bound to know that the faith and confidence of their customers were in them, rather than in some irresponsible and unknown individual whose advice they had sought and obtained. Meixsell was undoubtedly false to the defendants, but this is their misfortune. They cannot transfer it to another innocent party who was a stranger to all that occurred between Meixsell and the defendants. They brought on the misfortune, and must therefore bear it.

♦ ♦ ♦

[Under this charge the jury found for Campbell, and the Spencers appealed to the Pennsylvania Supreme Court. Chief Justice John Bannister Gibson upheld the jury verdict.]

♦ ♦ ♦

The only material inquiry, in the case before us, regards the nature and extent of the defendant's responsibility to their customers. It is true that the judge put the responsibility of a carrier or an innkeeper as illustration, not of the degree of diligence required but of the duty which the law imposed on him to provide all the means and appliances necessary for a safe accomplishment of his business; but he put the question on the true ground as a conclusion from the whole, that of ordinary care and skill. As the defendants were bound to use reasonable diligence to ascertain the quality of their machinery in regard to safety, they were answerable certainly for gross negligence of which there was evidence. They were warned of the danger not only to others, but by their own eyes; yet they preferred to rely on the assurances of the manufacturer; and the judge was right in charging that "if they chose to make his opinion the rule of their conduct in opposition to the evidence of their own senses, they had no right to visit the consequences of their folly on their customers." To work the engine under an extraordinary head of steam, though the boiler-head had been perceptibly sprung at the lowest pressure, was an act of rashness; and it is to be remembered that they were bound, not only to use due care, but to possess a competent share of skill on the principle by which the law implies an agreement to that effect on the part of every one who undertakes to perform a business, an office, or a duty. . . . [Here Chief Justice Gibson discussed the negligent operation of the boiler, implying that because it was defective, the Spencers used it negligently.] It is not to be doubted, then, that the disaster which ensued is one which he was bound to prevent, and for which all are answerable.

Judgment affirmed.

Brown v. Kendall
6 Cush. (60 Mass.) 292 (1850)

In attempting to separate their fighting dogs with a stick, Kendall accidentally hit Brown, injuring his eye.

Shaw, C.J. This is an action of trespass, *vi et armis,* brought by George Brown against George K. Kendall, assault and battery; . . .

The facts set forth in the bill of exceptions preclude the supposition, that the blow . . . was intentional. The whole case proceeds on the assumption, that the damage sustained by the plaintiff . . . was inadvertent and unintentional; and the case involves the question how far, and under what qualifications, the party by whose unconscious act the damage was done is responsible for it. We use the term "unintentional" rather than involuntary, because in some of the cases, it is stated, that the act of holding and using weapon or instrument, the movement of which is the immediate cause of hurt to another, is a voluntary act, although its particular effect in hitting and hurting another is not within the purpose or intention of the party doing the act.

◆ ◆ ◆

We think . . . that the plaintiff must come prepared with evidence to show either that the *intention* was unlawful, or that the defendant was *in fault;* for if the injury was unavoidable, and the conduct of the defendant was free from blame, he will not be liable. . . . If, in the prosecution of a lawful act, a casualty purely accidental arises, no action can be supported for an injury arising therefrom. . . . In applying these rules to the present case, we can perceive no reason why the instructions asked for by the defendant ought not to have been given; to this effect, that if both plaintiff and defendant at the time of the blow were using ordinary care, and the plaintiff was not, or if at that time, both the plaintiff and defendant were not using ordinary care, then the plaintiff could not recover.

In using this term, ordinary care, it may be proper to state, that what constitutes ordinary care will vary with the circumstances of cases. In general, it means that kind and degree of care, which prudent and cautious men would use, such as is required by the exigency of the case, and such as is necessary to guard against probable danger. A man, who should have occasion to discharge a gun, on an open and extensive marsh, or in a forest, would be required to use less circumspection and care, than if he were to do the same thing in an inhabited town, village, or city. To make an accident, or casualty, or as the law sometimes states it, inevitable accident, it must be such an accident as the defendant could not have avoided by the use of the kind and degree of care necessary to the exigency, and in the circumstances in which he was placed.

We are not aware of any circumstances in this case, requiring a distinction between acts which it was lawful and proper to do, and acts of legal duty. There are cases, undoubtedly, in which officers are bound to act under process, for the legality of which they are not responsible, and perhaps some others in which this distinction would be important. We can have no doubt that the act of the defendant in attempting to part the fighting dogs, one of which was his own, and for the injurious acts of which he might be responsible, was a lawful and proper act, which he might do by proper and safe means. If then, in doing this act, using due care and all proper precautions necessary to the exigency of the case, to avoid hurt to others, in raising his stick for that purpose, he accidentally hit the plaintiff in his eye, and wounded him, this was the result of pure accident, or was involuntary and unavoidable, and therefore the action would not lie. Or if the defendant was chargeable with some negligence, we think the plaintiff cannot recover without showing that the damage was caused wholly by the act of the defendant, and that the plaintiff's own negligence did not contribute as an efficient cause to produce it.

The court instructed the jury, that if it was not a necessary act, and the defendant was not in duty bound to part the dogs, but might with propriety interfere or not as he chose, the defendant was responsible for the consequences of the blow, unless it appeared that he was in the exercise of extraordinary care, so that the accident was inevitable, using the word not in a strict but a popular sense. This is to be taken in connection with the charge afterwards given, that if the jury believed, that the act of inter-

ference in the fight was unnecessary, (that is, as before explained, not a duty incumbent on the defendant,) then the burden of proving extraordinary care on the part of the defendant, or want of ordinary care on the part of the plaintiff, was on the defendant.

The court are of opinion that these directions were not conformable to law. If the act of hitting the plaintiff was unintentional, on the part of the defendant, and done in the doing of a lawful act, then the defendant was not liable, unless it was done in the want of exercise of due care, adapted to the exigency of the case, and therefore such want of due care became part of the plaintiff's case, and the burden of proof was on the plaintiff to establish it. . . .

. . . [W]e are of opinion, that the other part of the charge, that the burden of proof was on the defendant, was incorrect. Those facts which are essential to enable the plaintiff to recover, he takes the burden of proving. The evidence may be offered by the plaintiff or by the defendant; the question of due care, or want of care, may be essentially connected with the main facts, and arise from the same proof; but the effect of the rule, as to the burden of proof, is this, that when the proof is all in, and before the jury . . . if it appears that the defendant was doing a lawful act, and unintentionally hit and hurt the plaintiff, then unless it also appears to the satisfaction of the jury, that the defendant is chargeable with some fault, negligence, carelessness, or want of prudence, the plaintiff . . . is not entitled to recover.

New trial ordered.

Note: The Emergence of Negligence

Brown v. *Kendall* is central to the development of tort law. Charles Gregory, echoing an earlier assessment by Oliver Wendell Holmes, asserts that Chief Justice Shaw's opinion was a "marked departure from the past," which led to "the establishment of a consistent theory of liability for unintentionally caused harm." Morton Horwitz argues that scholars have given "an exaggerated significance" to the case, but he does accept the argument that before the 1850s "negligence" did not apply in tort actions and that all actions for trespass were based on strict liability.[20] Whoever is right in this debate, *Brown* v. *Kendall* is an important case, as either a major new precedent or the best summary of the law as it already had developed.

In addition to articulating the need to establish negligence to win a tort suit, Shaw clearly stated the doctrine of "contributory negligence." Under this theory, an injured party cannot recover from a negligent tortfeasor if the injured party was even slightly responsible for the accident. In articulating a theory of contributory negligence, Shaw gave a great boon to America's industries. For the rest of the nineteenth century, and well into the twentieth, railroads and other industries often avoided paying tort damages because of the doctrine of contributory negligence.

Note: Toward the Future

The proliferation of accidents in an increasingly impersonal world of large cities, new technologies, and dangerous industries led to changes in behavior that went beyond using courts to recompense the injured for their losses. By 1866, the courts in New York believed that insurance against accidental damages was no longer a luxury; it was a standard and accepted practice in an age when remote causation led to damages where there was no clear tortfeasor who might be sued. While this seemed logical to the New York courts, a court in Illinois could not accept it, nor could the Missouri legislature. In the two cases and statute that follow, we see the heart of the debate of industrialization and its costs.

Ryan v. *New York Central Railroad Co.*
35 N.Y. 210 (1866)

This case illustrates how the courts began to deal with the kinds of catastrophic accidents that could develop because of industrialization. Ryan's house was destroyed by a fire, which was initially caused by a New York Central Railroad train. The fire spread to Ryan's house from other buildings. Ryan sued the railroad, on the grounds that it had caused the original fire. The court ruled that Ryan could not recover from the railroad and, in the process, suggested that the future road to protection from liability lay in insurance, not lawsuits. The court, of course, was both right and wrong about how the future would play out in this area of law in industrial America.

Hunt, J. On the 15th day of July, 1854, in the city of Syracuse, the defendant, by the careless management . . . of one of its engines, set fire to its woodshed, and a large quantity of wood therein. The plaintiff's house, situated at a distance of one hundred and thirty feet from the shed, soon took fire from the heat and sparks, and was entirely consumed, notwithstanding diligent efforts were made to save it. . . .

The question may be thus stated: A house in a populous city takes fire, through the negligence of the owner or his servant; the flames extend to and destroy an adjacent building: Is the owner of the first building liable to the second owner for the damage sustained by such burning?

It is a general principle that every person is liable for the consequences for his own acts. He is thus liable in damages for the proximate results of his own acts, but not for remote damages. It is not easy at all times to determine what are proximate and what are remote damages. In *Thomas* v. *Winchester* . . . Judge Ruggles defines the damages for which a party is liable, as those which are the natural or necessary consequences of his acts. Thus, the owner of a loaded gun, who puts it in the hands of a child, by whose indiscretion it is discharged, is liable for the injury sustained by a third person from such discharge. . . . The injury is a natural and ordinary result of the folly of placing a loaded gun in the hands of one ignorant of the manner of using it, and incapable of appreciating its effects. The owner of a horse and cart, who leaves them unattended in the street, is liable for an injury done to a person or his property, by the running away of the horse . . . for the same reason. The injury is the natural result of the negligence. If the party thus injured had, however, by the delay or confinement from his injury, been prevented from completing a valuable contract, from which he expected to make large profits, he could not recover such expected profits from the negligent party, in the cases supposed. Such damages would not be the necessary or natural consequences, nor the results ordinarily to be anticipated, from the negligence committed.

. . . So if an engineer upon a steamboat or locomotive, in passing the house of A., so carelessly manages its machinery that the coals and sparks from its fires fall upon and consume the house of A., the railroad company or the steamboat proprietors are liable to pay the value of the property thus destroyed.

. . . Thus far the law is settled and the principle is apparent. If, however, the fire communicates from the house of A. to that of B., and that is destroyed, is the negligent party liable for his loss? And if it spreads thence to the house of C., and thence to the house of D., and thence consecutively through the other houses, until it reaches and consumes the house of Z., is the party liable to pay the damages sustained by these twenty-four sufferers? The counsel for the plaintiff does not distinctly claim this, and I think it would not be seriously insisted that the sufferers could recover in such case. Where, then, is the principle upon which A. recovers and Z. fails?

◆　◆　◆

[I] place my opinion upon the ground that, in the one case, to wit, the destruction of the building upon which the sparks were thrown by the negligent act of the party sought to be charged, the result was to have been anticipated the moment the fire was communicated to the building; that its destruction was the ordinary and natural result of its being fired. In the second, third or twenty-fourth case, as supposed,

the destruction of the building was not a natural and expected result of the first firing. That a building upon which sparks and cinders fall should be destroyed or seriously injured must be expected, but that the fire should spread and other buildings be consumed, is not a necessary or an usual result. That it is possible, and that it is not unfrequent, cannot be denied. The result, however, depends, not upon any necessity of a further communication of the fire, but upon a concurrence of accidental circumstances, such as the degree of the heat, the state of the atmosphere, the condition and materials of the adjoining structures and the direction of the wind. These are accidental and varying circumstances. The party has no control over them, and is not responsible for their effects.

My opinion, therefore, is, that this action cannot be sustained, for the reason that the damages incurred are not the immediate but the remote result of the negligence of the defendants. The immediate result was the destruction of their own wood and sheds; beyond that, it was remote.

◆　◆　◆

To sustain such a claim as the present . . . would subject to a liability against which no prudence could guard, and to meet which no private fortune would be adequate. Nearly all fires are caused by negligence, in its extended sense. In a country where wood, coal, gas and oils are universally used, where men are crowded into cities and villages, where servants are employed, and where children find their home in all houses, it is impossible that the most vigilant prudence should guard against the occurrence of accidental or negligent fires. A man may insure his own house or his own furniture, but he cannot insure his neighbor's building or furniture, for the reason that he has no interest in them. To hold that the owner must not only meet his own loss by fire, but that he must guarantee the security of his neighbors on both sides . . . would be to create a liability which would be the destruction of all civilized society. No community could long exist, under the operation of such a principle. In a commercial country, each man, to some extent, runs the hazard of his neighbor's conduct, and each, by insurance against such hazards, is enabled to obtain a reasonable security against loss. To neglect such precaution, and to call upon his neighbor, on whose premises a fire originated, to indemnify him instead, would be to award a punishment quite beyond the offense committed. It is to be considered, also, that if the negligent party is liable to the owner of a remote building thus consumed, he would also be liable to the insurance companies who should pay losses to such remote owners. The principle of subrogation would entitle the companies to the benefit of every claim held by the party to whom a loss should be paid.

In deciding this case, I have examined the authorities cited from the Year Books, and have not overlooked the English statutes on the subject, or the English decisions extending back for many years. It will not be useful further to refer to these authorities, and it will be impossible to reconcile some of them with the view I have taken.

The remoteness of the damage, in my judgment, forms the true rule on which the question should be decided, and which prohibits a recovery by the plaintiff in this case.

Fent et al. v. Toledo, Peoria & Warsaw Railway Co.
59 Ill. 349 (1871)

A decade after the decision in Ryan *the Illinois court emphatically rejected the reasoning and logic of the New York decision.*

Mr. Chief Justice Lawrence delivered the opinion of the Court:

On the 1st of October, 1867, a locomotive, with a train of freight cars, belonging to the appellee, in passing eastwardly through the village of Fairbury, threw out great quantities of unusually large cinders, and set on fire two buildings and a lumber yard. The weather at the time was very dry, and the wind blowing freely from the south. One of the buildings ignited by the sparks was a warehouse near the track. The heat and flames from this structure speedily set on fire the building of plaintiffs [Fent et al.], situated about two hundred feet from the warehouse, and destroyed it and most of its contents. To recover damages for this loss, the plaintiffs have brought this suit.

The defendant in the circuit court demurred to the plaintiffs' evidence, and the court sustained the demurrer. To reverse this judgment, the plaintiffs bring up the record.

The evidence shows great negligence on the part of defendant, but it is unnecessary to discuss this question. Where a demurrer is interposed to the evidence, the rule is, that the demurrer admits not only all that the plaintiffs' testimony has proved, but all that it tends to prove. In this case, therefore, the defendant's negligence must be regarded as admitted. It is not, indeed, controverted, but the counsel rely for defense solely upon the ground that the plaintiffs' building was not set on fire directly by sparks from the defendant's locomotive, but by the burning of the intermediate warehouse, and that therefore the defendant is to be held harmless, under the maxim "*causa proxima, non remota, spectatur.*"

There are not many of the maxims of the law which touch so closely upon metaphysical speculation. The rule itself is one of universal application, but the difficulty lies in establishing a criterion by which to determine when the cause of an injury is to be considered proximate, and when merely remote. Greenleaf [on Evidence] . . . lays down the rule that "the damage, to be recovered, must always be the *natural and proximate consequence* of the act complained of." But this seems little more than the substitution of one form of general expression for another.

Parsons [on Contracts] . . . after alluding to the confusion in which the adjudged cases leave this question, says: "We have been disposed to think that there is a principle derivable on the one hand from the general reason and justice of the question, and on the other applicable as a test in many cases, and perhaps useful, if not decisive, in all. It is, that every defendant shall be held liable for all of those consequences which might have been foreseen and expected as the results of his conduct, but not for those which he could not have foreseen, and was therefore under no moral obligation to take into consideration." We are disposed to regard this explanation of the rule as clearer, and capable of more precise application, than any other we have met with in our examination of this subject.

◆ ◆ ◆

With the exception of two recent cases decided in this country upon the precise question before us, it can not be denied that the great current of English and American authorities would bring the defendant in this case within the category of proximate causes. The great effort of the counsel for defendant has been to explain away, as far as possible, the effect of these authorities, and to draw a distinction between them and the case at bar. However successful they may have been in showing a difference between some of the cases cited by appellants' counsel and that under consideration, on the other hand, they cite no English case, and but two American cases, in which a wrong doer has been excused from liability under circumstances analogous to those disclosed by this record, on the ground that he was a remote, and not a proximate, cause of the injury done.

. . . [T]he English reports abound with instances in which causes more remote than the cause in this case have been held sufficiently direct and proximate to be made a ground of damages. . . . [In *Montoyer* v. *London Insurance Co.*, 6 Exch. 451] the defendant had insured the plaintiff's tobacco against perils of the sea. Hides were shipped in the same vessel. The vessel shipped sea water, which, coming in contact with the hides, caused them to ferment. The fermentation created a noxious vapor which acted on the tobacco and spoiled its flavor. Suit was brought against the company, and the defense was the same relied upon in this case. The court held the defendant responsible, and said

in its opinion: "The sea water having caused the hides to ferment, and thereby the tobacco to be spoiled, it is merely playing with terms to say the injury is not occasioned by the sea water. The action of the sea water, which had been shipped in consequence of bad weather, occasioned the fermentation, and is the proximate cause."

If we turn to the American courts, we shall find the general current of authorities to be in harmony with the English precedents.

◆ ◆ ◆

The case of *Hart* v. *Western Railroad Co.* [Mass. 1847] . . . presented precisely the same question with that before us. The locomotive set fire to a shop, and the fire crossed the street and destroyed a dwelling house. The court held the company liable.

◆ ◆ ◆

Counsel for appellee seek to weaken the authority of these cases by adverting to the fact that they were decided under a statute of Massachusetts making railway companies liable for all losses by fire communicated from their locomotives, and authorizing them to insure against such risks. But the statute does not in the least degree affect the common law principle under consideration, and was not so regarded by the court in these decisions. It simply makes the companies liable for fires caused by them, irrespective of the question of negligence. But if the locomotive was the remote, instead of the proximate cause, in the sense of the maxim we are now discussing, there would have been no liability under the statute any more than at common law. Upon this question of cause, the cases are as much in point as if there had been no statute

◆ ◆ ◆

We now come to the two cases chiefly relied upon by appellee's [railroad's] counsel. They are quite in point, but we are wholly unable to agree with their conclusions. One is *Ryan* v. *The New York Central Railroad* [N.Y. 1860] and the other is *Kerr* v. *The Pennsylvania Railroad Co.* [Pa., 1870]. . . . These two cases stand alone, and we believe they are directly in conflict with every English or American case, as yet reported, involving this question.

As we understand these cases, they hold that, where the fire is communicated by the locomotive to the house of A, and thence to the house of B, there can be no recovery by the latter. It is immaterial, according to the doctrine of these cases, how narrow may be the space between the two houses, or whether the destruction of the second would be the natural consequence of the burning of the first. The principle laid down by these authorities and urged by counsel in this case is, that, in order to a recovery, the fire which destroys the plaintiff's property must be communicated directly from the railway, and not through the burning of intermediate property. With all our respect for these courts, we can not adopt this principle, and it is admitted by the judges who delivered the opinions to have no precedent for its support, and to be absolutely in conflict with former adjudications.

♦ ♦ ♦

The Court of Appeals in New York, and the Supreme Court of Pennsylvania, seem, from their opinions, to have attached great weight to an argument urged upon us by the counsel for appellee [the railroad], and indeed that argument seems to have been the chief reason for announcing a rule which both courts struggle in vain to show is not in conflict with all prior adjudications. That argument is, in brief, that an entire village or town is liable to be burned down by the passing of the fire from house to house, and if the railway company, whose locomotive has emitted the cinders that caused the fire, is to be charged with all the damages, these companies would be in constant danger of bankruptcy, and of being obliged to suspend their operation. We confess ourselves wholly unable to see the overpowering force of this argument. It proceeds upon the assumption that, if a great loss is to be suffered, it had better be distributed among a hundred innocent victims than wholly visited upon the wrong doer.

As a question of law or ethics, the proposition does not commend itself to our reason. We must still cling to the ancient doctrine, that the wanton wrong doer must take the consequences of his own acts, whether measured by a thousand dollars or a hundred thousand.

As to the railroads, however useful they may be to the regions they traverse, they are not operated by their owners for benevolent purposes, or to promote the public welfare. Their object is pecuniary profit. It is a perfectly legitimate object, but we do not see why they should be exempted from the moral duty of indemnification for injuries committed by the careless or wanton spread of fire along their track, because such indemnity may sometimes amount to so large a sum as to sweep away all their profits. The simple question is, whether a loss, that must be borne somewhere, is to be visited on the head of the innocent or the guilty. If, in placing it where it belongs, the consequence will be the bankruptcy of a railway company, we may regret it, but we should not, for that reason, hesitate in the application of a rule of such palpable justice.

But is it true that railroads can not thrive under such a rule? They have now been in operation many years, and extend over very many thousand miles, and we have never yet heard of town or village that has been destroyed by a fire ignited by their locomotives. Improved methods of construction, and a vigilant care in the management of locomotives, have made the probability of loss from this cause so slight that we can not but regard the fears of the disastrous consequences to the railway companies which may follow from an adherence to the ancient rule, as in a large degree chimerical. A case may occur at long intervals in which they will be required to respond in heavy damages; but better this, than that they should be permitted to evade the just responsibilities of their own negligence, under the pretence that the existence of the road may be endangered. It were better that a railway company should be reduced to bankruptcy, and even suspend its operations, than that the courts should establish for its benefit a rule intrinsically unjust, and repugnant not merely to ancient precedent, but to the universal sense of right and wrong.

Our position on this subject is briefly this: We do not desire to impose upon the railway companies unreasonable obligations, or to subject them to unreasonable danger of great pecuniary loss. We do not wish to make them insurers against all damages by fire that may result from the passage of their trains, without reference to the question of remote and proximate cause. But, on the other hand, we do insist on applying to them the same rule that has been held through all the administration of the common law, with the exception of the two cases upon which we have been commenting. As already stated, we understand the doctrine of those two cases, and the position of counsel for appellee to be, that, if fire is communicated from a locomotive to the house of A, and thence to the house of B, it is a conclusion of law that the fire sent forth by the locomotive is to be regarded as the remote, and not the proximate, cause, of the injury to B; and the railway company is, for this reason alone, to be held not responsible. This rule we repudiate as in the teeth of almost numberless decisions, and as unsupported by that reason which is the life of the law.

We hold, on the contrary . . . it is in each case a question of fact, to be determined by the jury under the instructions of the court. Those instructions should be, in substance, what we have already stated. If the fire is the consequence of the carelessness of the railway company, and the question of remote or proximate cause is raised, the jury should be instructed that, so far as the case turns upon that issue, the company is to be held responsible, if the loss is a natural consequence of its alleged carelessness which might have been foreseen by any reasonable person, but is not to be held responsible for injuries which could not have been foreseen or expected as the results of its negligence or misconduct.

In the case before us, owing to the distance of the plaintiff's building from the one first set on fire, this question might not have been one of easy determination. The defendant, however, thought it better not to take the risks of this issue, but, by a demurrer to the evidence, to rest his defense upon the theory that, even admitting all that the evidence tends to prove, there is still no liability.

In this court, the counsel for the company have not discussed the evidence. They place the case on the single ground, that the company is free from liability, because the plaintiff's house was set on fire, not immediately by cinders thrown from the locomotive, but by the burning of another house. Their position is, that this alone exonerates the company, without any reference whatever to the question whether the second house was so near the first that in the then state of the wind and weather, its destruction was a natural consequence of the burning of the first, which any reasonable person could have foreseen and would have expected. This question they have not discussed.

On the legal question upon which appellee's counsel thus rest the case, we can not adopt their views.

On the demurrer to the evidence, we must hold it tended to prove that the fire escaped through the carelessness of the defendant, and that the destruction of the plaintiffs' house was its natural consequence, which any reasonable person could have foreseen. The demurrer should, therefore, have been overruled.

The judgment is reversed, and the case remanded for trial.

An Act to Establish the Responsibility of Railroad Corporations, Companies and Persons Owning or Operating Railroads, for Damages by Fires Communicated by Locomotive Engines
Missouri Laws, Act of March 31, 1887

Ryan v. New York Central *recognized the importance of insurance for the industrial economy, but placed the burden on countless individuals who might be harmed by a railroad, but in effect had no defense against the railroad. The Missouri legislature adopted a different approach that gave the railroads a huge incentive to improve the safety of their operations.*

Be it enacted by the General Assembly of . . . Missouri, as follows:

Section 1. Each railroad corporation owning or operating a railroad in this state shall be responsible in damages to every person an corporation who property may be injured or destroyed by fire communicated directly or indirectly by locomotive engines in use upon the railroad owned or operated by such railroad corporation, and each such railroad corporation shall have an insurable interest in the property upon the route of the railroad owned operated by it, and may procure insurance thereon on its own behalf for its protection against such damages.

Note: Wrongful Death and Tort Law

The most bizarre development in nineteenth-century American tort law was the conclusion that there could be no tort action if the injured person died. Peter Karsten notes that in the colonial period and in the early nineteenth century, American courts awarded damages to the survivors of those wrongfully killed by others. Thus, as late as 1838 a New York court upheld "an award of two hundred dollars to the parents of a boy killed by a carriage," but in 1859 "the same court cited [the English case of] *Baker* v. *Bolton* and observed, apologetically, that 'the law will not bend to accommodate our private views, or gratify our personal desires.'"[21] The New York court was simply following the route set out by the Massachusetts Supreme Judicial Court in *Carey* v. *Berkshire Railroad* and *Skinner* v. *Housatonic Railroad,* 1 Cush. (Mass.) 475 (1848). In that case the Massachusetts court ruled against an action for wrongful death. As Chief Justice Shaw's biographer concluded, "The common law as construed by the Shaw Court made it costly for carriers to scratch but cheap to kill, particularly if the killing were instantaneous." This ruling survived the Civil War. In the 1870s, a "dead victim's survivors could only seek retribution through a criminal indictment, because the common law provided no civil remedy for wrongful death."[22] In 1883, the Massachusetts legislature allowed survivors to sue for wrongful death of their relatives killed in accidents. Other states made similar changes, through legislation and through decisions in state and some federal courts. These were usually, but not always, limited to economic losses. As early as 1865 a Connecticut court allowed some recovery beyond economic loss that would include the "pain and suffering" of a widow. Nevertheless, such changes in the law were slow. Most important, perhaps, the families of those killed on the job—the most likely place for fatal accidents at this time—could not recover from the employer. Under the Massachusetts law of 1883, and most common-law decisions, employers remained immune from suit under the fellow servant rule until an 1887 statute allowed such suits. Only gradually did other states overrule, through statutes, the common-law development that prevented tort suits for wrongful death. The Federal Employers' Liability Act, first passed in 1906 and rewritten in 1908 to meet constitutional objections, gave the families of railroad workers a right to sue for wrongful death. This law "abolished the fellow servant rule completely for railroad workers" and "made the railroad liable for any death or injury resulting from 'the negligence of any . . . employees . . . or by reason of any defect or insufficiency, due to . . . negligence in its cars, engines, appliances, machinery, track, roadbed, works, boats, wharves, or other equipment.'"[23] This change in the law, and others, were a product of the Progressive Era and a changing economy and changing social realities. In the mid–nineteenth century the families of those killed in accidents had little hope of recovering for their loved ones' wrongful deaths.

→ 4 ←

Slavery, the Civil War, Reconstruction, and Segregation

From 1787 until the end of the Civil War, slavery was central to most national political debates. Slavery and race relations also affected interstate relations and led to conflicts both among the states and between the states and the national government. Americans debated—and disputed—the role of the federal government or the states in the return of fugitive slaves; the power of the national government to regulate or limit slavery in the federal territories; and what limits the free states could place on the movement of slaves within their jurisdiction.

Even when not immediately on the agenda, slavery lurked in the background of most legal and constitutional wrangling. States'-rights Virginians, for example, worried that Chief Justice Marshall's opinion in *McCulloch* v. *Maryland* (1819) upholding the constitutionality of the Bank of the United States set a precedent that could harm slavery. Similarly, while the Nullification Crisis of 1832 was ostensibly over a tariff, much of South Carolina's general discomfort stemmed from the fear of slave revolts, a decline in the price of cotton, and the rejuvenated abolitionist movement.

From 1787 until the Civil War, the constitutional status of the states within the Union remained contested. The Constitution created a federal Union with powers shared by the states and the national government, and with uncertain jurisdictional boundaries between these entities. The Constitution placed certain obligations on the states, but did not clearly indicate how those obligations were to be met or the role of the federal government in enforcing them. Although the Framers of the Constitution presumed that interstate comity would be voluntarily observed, the antebellum Constitution offered few mechanisms for settling interstate disputes when such cooperation was not forthcoming. Debates over slavery, more than any other issue, forced these controversies into the open.

The Constitution explicitly recognized slavery in five places, referring to slaves as "other Persons" and "Person[s] held to Service or Labour." Slavery influenced at least ten other clauses. One of the most important was the "domestic insurrections clause," which obligated the national government to suppress slave rebellions.

Under the Constitution, Congress lacked power to interfere with slavery in the states. By 1804, all of the states in the North had either ended slavery outright or passed gradual abolition acts. Southern free blacks were pariahs, living perilously between slavery and freedom. Ninety-five percent of the nation's blacks were slaves, subject to the whims of their masters and the rules set out by southern courts and legislatures. They were property, to be bought, sold, inherited, and seized for debts. Short of murder and mutilation, their masters could generally treat them as they wished.

While the Constitution left the states free to regulate the status of slaves within their borders, the federal government had some jurisdiction over slavery. Congress prohibited the African slave trade in 1808, although enforcement was lax until 1861. The question of slavery in the territories led to federal laws, political debates, and the case of the era—*Dred Scott* v. *Sandford.* The problem of fugitive slaves led to debates, legal cases, and riots. Southerners argued that the Constitution protected their rights to reclaim fugitive slaves; some Northerners responded that "a higher law" compelled them to protect the freedom of those who sought to escape bondage. Among the reasons for leaving the Union that Southerners offered in 1861 was the failure of Northerners to cooperate in the rendition of fugitive slaves.

Although the Constitution was the "supreme law of the land," antebellum state officials jealously resisted assertions of power by the federal government. By 1861, almost every state had, at some point, asserted its "sovereignty" and claimed the right to resist or nullify federal law, or even to secede from the Union. Antebellum federal officials were cautious about treading too heavily on the prerogatives of the states.

Despite general deference to the states, early on the United States Supreme Court asserted its power to declare state laws unconstitutional. States complained, sometimes resisted, and occasionally ignored mandates from the federal courts. State officials disregarded the ruling in *Worcester* v. *Georgia* (1832) that Georgia had no authority over the Cherokee Indians. In *Ableman* v. *Booth* (1859), the United States Supreme Court rejected the attempts of the Wisconsin Supreme Court to strike down as unconstitutional the federal Fugitive Slave Law of 1850. In its attempt to resist federal law, the Wisconsin court refused to comply with the United States Supreme Court's request for a copy of the record of the state proceedings. South Carolina officials ignored Justice William Johnson's opinion in *Elkison* v. *Deliesseline* (1823) that the state's Negro Seamen's Act was unconstitutional. Despite Johnson's opinion, most other southern states adopted similar legislation. Court decisions were not the only federal actions that states opposed. South Carolina declared a tariff to be null and void within its jurisdiction. Although the state backed down in the face of overwhelming federal power, nullification remained part of the nation's political and legal lexicon until the Civil War.

More dangerous than nullification was the claim that a state could leave the Union at will. If such a right existed, the Union was little more than a voluntary association. The dispute over the right to secede turned on differing theories of the Union. In the 1820s and 1830s, John Quincy Adams and Daniel Webster laid out the theory of a "perpetual Union," while Andrew Jackson threatened to march an army into South Carolina if the state did not back down from its attempts to nullify the federal tariff. In 1861 Lincoln drew from the positions set out by Adams, Webster, and Jackson in 1861 as part of his constitutional arguments against secession. Lincoln believed that the Constitution and the nation were created by the people, and the Union formed a perpetual contract that no state could break without the consent of the American people.

The alternative view argued that the Union was a compact of sovereign states. During the Sedition Act Crisis of 1798, Thomas Jefferson and James Madison endorsed this theory but did not advocate secession. Between the late 1820s and his death in 1850, South Carolina's John C. Calhoun refined the compact theory into an argument for state sovereignty, nullification, and secession. Calhoun argued that the states had created a national government with limited powers, and that if the national government exceeded its powers by threatening the rights and privileges of the states, the states were free to leave the Union.

The Civil War was partially a war over competing theories of constitutional interpretation and the meaning of the Constitution itself. During the war, theory and practice merged. The legal and intellectual arguments for a strong central government, a perpetual Union, and national supremacy that were used to oppose secession also helped create the ideological support for strengthening the national government, as well as consolidating enormous power in the hands of the president. Such centralization of power helped win the war. These theories also carried over to three new constitutional amendments, which fundamentally changed the nature of the Union.

Support for states' rights did not totally disappear with the end of the war. Andrew Johnson combined a states'-rights ideology with racism to frustrate congressional attempts to protect and enhance black freedom. The Supreme Court remained uncomfortable with the nationalization of power brought about by the war. For the rest of the century, the Court rejected many of the changes mandated by the Civil War Amendments and the statutes enacted to implement them. Tragically, the postwar justices were unable to escape their own past and to see that the Civil War and the new amendments had thoroughly altered the relationship of the states to the national government.

Black Americans suffered most from the Court's failure to appreciate the revolution in constitutional law brought about by the Civil War. Decisions in the *Slaughterhouse Cases* (1873), the *Civil Rights Cases* (1883), *Plessy* v. *Ferguson* (1896), and numerous other cases undermined Congress's attempts to protect the rights that blacks had won during and immediately after the war. The Court failed to see how the war, the new federalism it produced, and the three new constitutional amendments had permanently altered race relations. The Court's failure to acknowledge and support the new federal structure in order to protect former slaves is ironic because as Lincoln recognized in his second inaugural, "All knew" that slavery "was somehow the cause of the war" and that only its eradication justified the horrors of the war itself. Tragically, the postwar Court made decisions affecting black rights as though nothing significant had occurred between 1861 and 1870, ignoring that the whole nature of the Constitution and the political system had changed because of the war against slavery.

The Civil War destroyed forever the once commonly accepted theory of state sovereignty. Federal supremacy was secured, not by legal theory and doctrine, but by the unanswerable arguments set forth by Generals Grant and Sherman. Appomattox signaled the end of state sovereignty and the viability of secession. The war also ended the debate over slavery by destroying the institution. Legally and rhetorically, Lincoln was the great emancipator. Practically, the title must be shared with the Union Army, which brought freedom to 3 million slaves through the force of arms. Among those under arms were nearly 200,000 blacks, many of whom had only recently been slaves.

While the Civil War ended arguments over state sovereignty, a rejuvenated states'-rights doctrine emerged from the ashes of the Confederacy. Southerners no longer claimed that their state laws were supreme; instead, they persuaded Congress and the Supreme Court that race relations was a local problem that the federal government should ignore. Blacks found that slavery had been replaced with a new kind of oppression, which took the form of segregation, separate and *unequal* access to public schools and other facilities, and a kind of economic bondage in the form of debt peonage. In the nineteenth century, blacks gained their freedom, but the promise of the Civil War Amendments remained unredeemed.

SLAVERY AND STATE LAW

At its height, the South's "peculiar institution" directly involved about 385,000 masters and some 4 million slaves worth over $1 billion. Indirectly, most white Southerners and more than 250,000 free blacks in the South were also affected by this system of bondage.

As property, slaves were bought and sold and were the objects of suits in tort, contract, property, and insurance law. As human beings, slaves could be prosecuted for crimes or be victims of crimes. For white lawmakers, slaves were an alien race to be controlled by the state and exploited by their masters, and a form of property to be protected from white strangers who might harm them. Jurists and legislators struggled with slaves' dual status as both property and persons.

RACE AND THE LAW OF NEGRO SLAVERY

Slavery violated the tenets of American liberty and democracy. Nevertheless, it was an integral part of the economy of half the nation. Southerners justified slavery as an economic necessity and argued that American slavery was consistent with natural law because the system, unlike its counterpart in ancient or medieval Europe, was racially based. Southerners contended that blacks were racially inferior, and, therefore, enslaving them was not only legitimate, but a positive good for blacks as well as whites.

THOMAS R. R. COBB

An Inquiry into the Law of Negro Slavery
1858

Cobb was the reporter for the Georgia Supreme Court (1849–1857), a professor at the Lumpkin School of Law in Athens, and the man most responsible for drafting the Confederate Constitution. As a brigadier general in the Confederate Army, he was killed in action at Fredericksburg in 1862. Cobb was the only Southerner to write a treatise on slave law. Here he mixes racist theories with legal argument as he summarizes the rationales used by lawyers and judges to defend slavery.

18.   . . . [W]e recognize in the negro a man, endowed with reason, will, and accountability, and in order to justify his subjection we must inquire of his intellectual and moral nature, and must be satisfied that its development is thereby promoted. If this be true, if the physical, intellectual, and moral development of the African race are promoted by a state of slavery, and their happiness secured to a greater extent than if left at liberty then their enslavement is consistent with the law of nature, and violative of none of its provisions. Is the negro's own happiness thereby best promoted? Is he therein most useful to his fellowman? Is he thereby more surely led to the discharge of his duty to God?

◆   ◆   ◆

20. *First* then is the inquiry as to the physical adaptation of the negro to a state of servitude. His black color peculiarly fits him for the endurance of the heat of long-continued summers. The arched leg and receding heel seem to indicate a natural preparation for strength and endurance. The absence of nervous irritability gives to him a complete exemption from those inflammatory diseases so destructive in hot and damp atmospheres, and hence the remarkable fact, that the ravages of that scourge of the tropics, the yellow fever, never reach the negro race.

♦   ♦   ♦

22. *Second.* The mental inferiority of the negro has been often asserted and never successfully denied. An inviting field for digression is offered here, in the much-mooted question of the unity of the human race. It is unnecessary for our purposes to enter these lists. The law deals with men and things as they are, and whether the negro was originally a different species, or is a degeneration of the same, is a matter indifferent in the inquiry as to his proper status in his present condition. We deal with him as we find him, and according to the measure of his capacity, it is our duty to cultivate and improve him.

♦   ♦   ♦

31. The prominent defect in the mental organization of the negro, is a want of judgment. He forms no definite idea of effects from causes. He cannot comprehend, so as to execute the simplest orders, unless they refresh his memory as to some previous knowledge. He is imitative, sometimes eminently so, but his mind is never inventive or suggestive. Improvement never enters into his imagination. . . . This mental defect, connected with the indolence and want of foresight of the negro, is the secret of his degradation. The imitative faculty makes the negro a good musician, yet he never originates a single air, nor invents a musical instrument.

32. Our next inquiry is as to the moral character of the Negro. . . . The degraded situation of the barbarous tribes of Africa is well attested by every observer. So debased is their condition generally, that their humanity has been even doubted.

♦   ♦   ♦

69. As all the negroes introduced into America were brought as slaves, the black color of the race raises the presumption of slavery, contrary to the principles of the common law, which would presume freedom. . . . This presumption is extended, in most of the States, to mulattoes or persons of mixed blood, casting upon them the onus of proving a free maternal ancestor.

70. The issue and descendants of slaves, in the maternal line, are slaves. The rule, *partus sequitur ventrem,* has been adopted in all the States. The reason of this rule, as given by the civilians, was . . . "From principles of justice, the offspring, the increase of the womb, belongs to the master of the womb." This rule has been almost universal among those nations recognizing slavery.

♦   ♦   ♦

86. Of the three great absolute rights guaranteed to every citizen by the common law, viz., the right of personal security, the right of personal liberty, and the right of private property, the slave, in a state of pure or absolute slavery, is totally deprived, being, as to life, liberty, and property, under the absolute and uncontrolled dominion of his master . . . however, no such state of slavery exists in these States. . . . [Because] modified is the slavery here, partly by natural law, partly by express enactment, and more effectually by the influence of civilization and Christian enlightenment . . . [producing] many of those protecting barriers, the denial of whose existence would shock an enlightened public sense.

87. Statute law has done much to relieve the slave from this absolute dominion [of the master]. . . . In all of the slaveholding States, the homicide of a slave is held to be murder. . . . Nor has the legislation of the States stopped at the protection of their lives, but the security of limbs and the general comfort of the body are, in most of the States, amply provided for, various penalties being inflicted on masters for their cruel treatment.

THE POWER OF THE MASTER OVER THE SLAVE

By the late antebellum period, the South universally accepted the idea that the law should punish strangers who harmed or killed slaves. Less certain was how a master's conduct might be limited by the law. The cases in this section confront three key issues involving a master's rights over the slave: whether a master had the right to punish a slave, whether a master could kill a slave, and whether a master had the right to free a slave.

State v. *Mann*
2 Dev. (N.C.) 263 (1829)

Elizabeth Jones rented her slave, Lydia, to John Mann. When Mann attempted to chastise Lydia for some "minor offence," she "ran off" and Mann shot her in the back. There was no allegation that Lydia was attempting to escape from bondage, only that she was attempting to avoid a beating. Jones procured Mann's indictment and conviction for battery, which Mann appealed. In his opinion of the court, Judge Thomas Ruffin conceded that a stranger could be indicted for battery on a slave. Ruffin also found that Jones had a right to sue Mann for any damages to Lydia "upon the general doctrine of bailment." But in the context of the criminal law, Ruffin equated the renter (Mann) with an owner and thus outlined the right of a master to punish a slave, and the right of the state to interfere with the master-slave relationship. Ruffin explored whether the state could interfere with an owner's treatment of his or her own slaves.

Ruffin, Judge—A Judge cannot but lament when such cases as the present are brought into judgment. It is impossible that the reasons on which they go can be appreciated, but where institutions similar to our own, exist and are thoroughly understood. The struggle, too, in the Judge's own breast between the feeling of the man, and the duty of the magistrate is a severe one, presenting strong temptation to put aside such questions, if it be possible. It is useless however, to complain of things inherent in our political state. And it is criminal in a Court to avoid any responsibility which the laws impose. With whatever reluctance therefore it is done the Court is compelled to express an opinion upon the extent of the dominion of the master over the slave in North-Carolina.

The indictment charges a battery on *Lydia,* a slave of *Elizabeth Jones.* . . . The enquiry here is whether a cruel and unreasonable battery on a slave, by the hirer, is indictable. . . . [Here Ruffin asserted that in a criminal case the hirer should be treated as though he were the owner of the slave.] [U]pon the general question, whether the owner is answerable *criminaliter* for a battery upon his own slave, or other exercise of authority or force not forbidden by statute, the Court entertains but little doubt.— That he is so liable, has never yet been decided; nor, as far as is known, been hitherto contended. There have been no prosecutions of the sort. The established habits and uniform practice of the country in this respect, is the best evidence of the portion of power, deemed by the whole community, requisite to the preservation of the master's dominion. . . . [A]rguments drawn from the well established principles which confer and restrain the authority of the parent over the child, the tutor over the pupil, the master over the apprentice, have been pressed on us. The Court does not recognize their application. There is no likeness between the cases. They are in opposition to each other, and there is an impassable gulf between them. The difference is that which exists between freedom and slavery—and a greater cannot be imagined. In the one, the end in view is the happiness of the youth, born to equal rights with that governor, on whom the duty devolves of training the young to usefulness, in a station which he is afterwards to assume among freemen. To such an end, and with such a subject, moral and intellectual instruction seem the natural means; and for the most part, they are found to suffice. Moderate force is superadded, only to make the others effectual. If that fail, it is better to leave the party to his own headstrong passions, and the ultimate correction of the law, than to allow it to be immoderately inflicted by a private person. With slavery it is far otherwise. The end is the profit of the master, his security and the public safety; the subject, one doomed in his own person, and his posterity, to live without knowledge, and without the capacity to make any thing his own, and to toil that another may reap the fruits. What moral considerations shall be addressed to such a being to convince him what it is impossible but that the most stupid must feel and know can never be true—that he is thus to labor upon a principle of natural duty, or for the sake of his own personal happiness, such services can only be expected from one who has no will of his own, who surrenders his will in implicit obedience to that of another. Such obedience is the consequence only of uncontrolled authority over the body. There is nothing else which can operate to produce the effect. The power of the master must be absolute, to render the submission of the slave perfect. I most freely confess my sense of the harshness of this proposition. I feel it as deeply as any man can. And as a principle of moral right, every person in his retirement must repudiate it. But in the actual condition of things, it must be so.—There is no remedy. This discipline belongs to the state of slavery. They cannot be disunited, without abrogating at once the rights of the master, and absolving the slave from his subjection. It constitutes the curse of slavery to both the bond and free portions of our population. But it is inherent in the relation of master and slave.

That there may be particular instances of cruelty and deliberate barbarity, where, in conscience the law might properly interfere, is most probable. The difficulty is to determine, where a Court may properly begin. Merely in the abstract it may well be asked, which power of the master accords with right. The answer will probably sweep away all of them. But we cannot look at the matter in that light. The truth is, that we are forbidden to enter upon a train of general reasoning on the subject. We cannot allow the right of the master to be brought into discussion in the Courts of Justice. The slave, to remain a slave, must be made sensible, that there is no appeal from his master; that his power is in no instance, usurped; but is conferred by the laws of man at least, if not by the law of God. The danger would be great indeed, if the tribunals of justice should be called on to graduate the punishment appropriate to every temper, and every dereliction of menial duty. No man can anticipate the many and aggravated provocations of the master, which the slave would be constantly stimulated by his own passions, or the instigation of others to give; or the consequent wrath of the master prompting him to bloody vengeance, upon the turbulent traitor—a vengeance generally practised with impunity by reason of its privacy. The Court therefore disclaims the power of changing the relation, in which these parts of our people stand to each other.

We are happy to see, that there is daily less and less occasion for the interposition of the Courts. The protection already afforded by several statutes, that all-powerful motive, the private interest of the owner, the benevolence towards each other, seated in the hearts of those who have been born and bred together, the frowns and deep execrations of the community upon the barbarian, who is guilty of excessive and brutal cruelty to his unprotected slave, all combined, have produced a mildness of treatment, and attention to the comforts of the unfortunate class of slaves, greatly mitigating the rigors of servitude, and ameliorating the condition of the slaves. The same causes are operating, and will continue to operate with increased action, until the disparity in numbers between the whites and blacks, shall have rendered the latter in no degree dangerous to the former, when the police now existing may be further relaxed. This result, greatly to be desired, may be much more rationally expected from the events above alluded to, and now in progress, than from any rash expositions of abstract truths, by a Judiciary tainted with a false and fanatical philanthropy, seeking to redress an acknowledged evil, by means still more wicked and appalling than even that evil.

I repeat, that I would gladly have avoided this ungrateful question. But being brought to it, the Court is compelled to declare, that while slavery exists amongst us in its present state, or until it shall seem fit to the Legislature to interpose express enactments to the contrary, it will be imperative duty of the Judges to rec-

ognize the full dominion of the owner over the slave, except where the exercise of it is forbidden by statute. And this we do upon the ground, that this dominion is essential to the value of slaves as property, to the security of the master, and the public tranquility, greatly dependent upon their subordination; and in fine, as most effectually securing the general protection and comfort of the slaves themselves.

Per Curiam—Let the judgment below be reversed, and judgment entered for the Defendant.

Note: Harriet Beecher Stowe on Southern Judges

The author of this opinion, Judge Thomas Ruffin, is generally considered to be one of the finest antebellum southern jurists. In her *Key to Uncle Tom's Cabin,* Harriet Beecher Stowe concluded: "No one can read this decision, so fine and clear in its expression, so dignified and solemn in its earnestness, and so dreadful in its results, without feeling at once a deep respect of the man [Ruffin] and the horror of the system."

Stowe referred to the next case as the "Ne Plus Ultra of Legal Humanity." "Nobody," she wrote, "could willingly read" this indictment "twice." She noted that Souther was sentenced to only five years in jail and, afterward, could buy "as many more negroes as he chooses."

Souther v. *Commonwealth*
7 Gratt. (Va.) 672 (1851)

Simeon Souther was indicted for murdering his own slave.

The count charged that on the first day of September 1849, the prisoner tied his negro slave Sam, with ropes about his wrists, neck, body, legs, and ankles, to a tree. That whilst so tied, the prisoner first whipped the slave with switches. That he next beat and cobbed the slave with a shingle, and compelled two of his slaves, a man and a woman, also to cob the deceased with the shingle. That whilst the deceased was so tied to the tree, the prisoner did strike, knock, kick, stamp, and beat him, upon various parts of his head, face and body; that he applied fire to his body, back, sides belly, groins and privy parts; that he then washed his body, & c., with warm water, in which pods of

red pepper had been put and steeped, and he compelled his two slaves aforesaid, also to wash him with this same preparation of warm water and red pepper. . . . [Then] the prisoner untied the deceased from the tree, in such way as to throw him with violence to the ground, and he then and there did knock, kick, stamp, and beat the deceased upon his head, temples, and various parts of his body. That the prisoner then had the deceased carried into a shed room of his house, and there he compelled one of his slaves in his presence, to confine the deceased's feet in stocks . . . and to tie a rope about the neck of the deceased, and fasten it to a bed post in the room, there by strangling, choking and suffocating the deceased. And that whilst the deceased was thus made fast in stocks as aforesaid, the prisoner did kick, knock, stamp, and beat him, upon his head, face, breast, belly, sides, back, and body. And he again compelled his two slaves to apply fire to the body of the deceased whilst he was so made fast as aforesaid. And . . . from these various modes of punishment and torture, the slave Sam then and there died. It appeared that the prisoner commenced the punishment of the deceased in the morning, and that it was continued throughout the day; and that the deceased died in the presence of the prisoner and one of his slaves and one of the witnesses, whilst the punishment was still progressing.

Field, J. . . . The prisoner was indicted and convicted of murder in the second degree, in the Circuit court of Hanover at its April term last past, and was sentenced to the penitentiary for five years, the period of time ascertained by the jury.

♦ ♦ ♦

It is believed that the records of criminal jurisprudence do not contain a case of more atrocious and wicked cruelty than was presented upon the trial of Souther; and yet it has been gravely and earnestly contended here by his counsel, that his offence amounts to manslaughter only.

It has been contended by the counsel of the prisoner, that a man cannot be indicted and prosecuted for the cruel and excessive whipping

of his own slave. That it is lawful for the master to chastise his slave; and that if death ensues from such chastisement, unless it was intended to produce death, it is like the case of homicide, which is committed by a man in the performance of a lawful act, which is manslaughter only. It has been decided by this Court . . . that the owner of a slave, for the malicious, cruel and excessive beating of his own slave, cannot be indicted; yet it by no means follows when such malicious, cruel and excessive beating results in death though not intended and premeditated, that the beating is to be regarded as lawful, for the purpose of reducing the crime to manslaughter, when the whipping is inflicted for the sole purpose of chastisement. It is the policy of the law in respect to the relation of master and slave, and for the sake of securing proper subordination and obedience on the part of the slave, to protect the master from prosecution in all such cases, even if the whipping and punishment be malicious, cruel and excessive. But in so inflicting punishment for the sake of punishment, the owner of the slave acts at his peril; and if death ensues in consequence of such punishment, the relation of master and slave affords no ground of excuse or palliation. The principles of the common law in relation to homicide, apply to his case, without qualification or exception; and according to those principles, the act of the prisoner, in the case under consideration, amounted to murder. Upon this point we are unanimous. [The court affirmed Souther's five-year sentence.]

State v. Hoover
4 Dev. and Bat. (N.C.) 365 (1839)

This case illustrates that in the most extreme cases southern courts were willing to execute whites—even slave owners—for the murder of their slaves. The defendant in this case was hanged shortly after the North Carolina Supreme Court rejected his appeal.

The prisoner was put upon his trial . . . for the murder of his own female slave, a woman named Mira. The witnesses, . . . testified to a series of the most brutal and barbarous whippings, scourgings and privations, inflicted by

the prisoner upon the deceased, from about the first of December, to the time of her death in the ensuing March, while she was in the latter stages of pregnancy, and afterwards, during the period of her confinement and recovery from a recent delivery. A physician, who was one of the coroner's inquest, called to view the body of the deceased, stated that there were five wounds on the head of the deceased, four of which appeared to have been inflicted a week or more before her death; that the fifth was a fresh wound, about one and a half inches long, and to the bone, and was, in his opinion, sufficient to have produced her death; that there were many other wounds on different parts of her body, which were sufficient, independent of those on the head, to have caused death. The reasons assigned by the prisoner to those who witnessed his inhuman treatment of the deceased, were, at one time, that she stole his turnips and sold them to the worthless people in the neighborhood, and that she had attempted to burn his barn, and was disobedient and impudent to her mistress; at another, that she had attempted to burn his still house, and had put something in a pot to poison his family. There was no evidence except her own confessions, extorted by severe whippings, that the deceased was guilty of any of the crimes imputed to her; nor did it appear that she was disobedient or impertinent to her master or mistress; on the contrary, she seemed, as some of the witnesses testified, to do her best to obey the commands of her master, and that when she failed to do so, it was from absolute inability to comply with orders to which her condition and strength were unequal. The prisoner offered no testimony.

◆　◆　◆

Ruffin, Chief Justice.

With deep sorrow we have perused the statement of the case as it appeared upon the evidence; and we cannot surmise a ground on which the prisoner could expect a *venire de novo*. Indeed, it seems to us, that the case was left hypothetically to the jury, much more favourably for the prisoner than the circumstances authorized.

A master may lawfully punish his slave; and the degree must, in general, be left to his own judgment and humanity, and cannot be judicially questioned. *State* v. *Mann.* . . . But the master's authority is not altogether unlimited. He must not kill. There is, at the least, this restriction upon his power: he must stop short of

taking life. It has been repeatedly held, that independent of the act of 1791, the killing of a slave may amount to murder; and this rule includes a killing by the master as well as that by a stranger. . . . It must indeed be true, in the nature of things, that a killing by the owner may be extenuated by many circumstances, from which no palliation could be derived in favour of a stranger. But it is almost self-evident that this prisoner can claim no extenuation of his guilt below the highest grade. It is, perhaps, sufficient merely to declare that to be the opinion of the Court, without undertaking the revolting task of collating and minutely commenting on the horrid enormities detailed by the witnesses. But some of the terms used in laying the case before the jury, render it our duty, as we think, to notice the circumstances somewhat more particularly.

If death unhappily ensue from the master's chastisement of his slave, inflicted apparently with a good intent, for reformation or example, and with no purpose to take life, or to put it in jeopardy, the law would doubtless tenderly regard every circumstance which, judging from the conduct generally of masters towards slaves, might reasonably be supposed to have hurried the party into excess. But the acts imputed to this unhappy man do not belong to a state of civilization. They are barbarities which could only be prompted by a heart in which every humane feeling had long been stifled; and indeed there can scarcely be a savage of the wilderness so ferocious as not to shudder at the recital of them. Such acts cannot be fairly attributed to an intention to correct or to chastise. They cannot, therefore, have allowance, as being the exercise of an authority conferred by the law for the purposes of the correction of the slave, or of keeping the slave in due subjection. The Court is at a loss to comprehend how it could have been submitted to the jury that they might find an extenuation from provocation. There is no opening for such an hypothesis. There was no evidence of the supposed acts, which, it was thought, might be provocations. But if they had been proved, this Court could not have concurred in the instructions—given, doubtless, from abundant caution and laudable tenderness of life. We could not have concurred, because however flagrant the provocation, the acts of the prisoner were not perpetrated in sudden heat of blood, but must have flowed from a settled and malignant pleasure in inflicting pain, or a settled and malignant insensibility to human suffering. There was none of that *brief fury* to which the law has regard, as an infirmity of our nature. On the contrary, without any consideration for the sex, health, or strength of the deceased, through a period of four months, including the latter stages of pregnancy, delivery, and recent recovery there from, by a series of cruelties and privations in their nature unusual, and in degree excessive beyond the capacity of a stout frame to Sustain, the prisoner employed himself from day to day in practising grievous tortures upon an enfeebled female, which finally wore out the energies of nature and destroyed life. He beat her with clubs, iron chains, and other deadly weapons, time after time; burnt her; inflicted stripes over and often, with scourges, which literally excoriated her whole body; forced her out to work in inclement seasons, without being duly clad; provided for her insufficient food; exacted labour beyond her strength, and wantonly beat her because she could not comply with his requisitions. These enormities, besides others too disgusting to be particularly designated, the prisoner, without his heart once relenting or softening, practiced from the first of December until the latter end of the ensuing March; and he did not relax even up to the last hour of his victim's existence. In such a case, surely, we do not speak of provocation; for nothing could palliate such a course of conduct. Punishment thus immoderate and unreasonable in the measure, the continuance, and the instruments, accompanied by other hard usage and painful privations of food, clothing, and rest, loses all character of correction *in foro domestico*, and denotes plainly that the prisoner must have contemplated the fatal termination, which was the natural consequence of such barbarous cruelties.

In such a case, too, we think it incorrect to say that the jury must be satisfied the prisoner intended to kill the deceased, before he, could be properly convicted. It is ordinarily true, that an actual intent to kill is involved in the idea of murder. But it is not always so. If great bodily harm, be intended, and that can be gathered from the nature of the means used or other circumstances, and death ensue, the party will be guilty of murder, although he may not have intended death. The intent, by severe and protracted cruelties and torments, to inflict grievous and dangerous suffering, or, in other words, to do great bodily harm, imports, from the means and manner thereof, a disregard of consequences; and consequently, the party is justly answerable for all the harm he did, although he did not specially design the whole. . . .

In conclusion, the Court is obliged to say, that whatever error crept into the trial, was in favour of the prisoner; and that nothing occurred of which he can complain. It is the opinion of this Court that the judgment ought not to be reversed; . . . Judgment affirmed.

Mitchell v. *Wells*
35 Miss. 235 (1859)

In 1846, Edward Wells emancipated his slave (and also his daughter by a slave mistress) Nancy Wells in Ohio. Wells then returned to Mississippi, where he subsequently died, bequeathing $3,000 and other property to Nancy. Wells's executor, William Mitchell, refused to give Nancy her legacy, arguing that she was a slave. A chancery court awarded Nancy her estate, and Mitchell appealed to Mississippi's highest court, which examined whether Nancy's emancipation in Ohio affected her status in Mississippi. The two opinions illustrate the connections between slavery and politics in the late antebellum period. They also illustrate the dilemma faced by slave societies between interfering with the actions of masters, *as Justice William Harris's majority opinion urges, and conceding that the right of masters to control their property was the essence of slavery, as Justice Alexander Handy's dissent argues. This case reached the Mississippi court two years after the United States Supreme Court ruled in* Dred Scott v. Sandford *that blacks were not citizens of the United States.*

[Handy, J.] [It is] . . . the obvious policy of the State on the subject of emancipation, as declared by her latest legislation, as well as by her settled conviction, that the interests of both races are best promoted by the institution of slavery as it exists amongst us, and most seriously prejudiced by either manumission in the Union, or colonization elsewhere.

I think it demonstrable, both upon principle and the weight of authority, that a slave, once domiciliated as such, in this State, can acquire no right, civil or political, within her limits, by manumission elsewhere. That manumission and citizenship, elsewhere conferred, cannot, even upon principles of comity, under our laws and policy, vest any right here.

♦ ♦ ♦

Mississippi came into the Union under this Federal Constitution as a member of this political family, to be associated on terms of political equality, comity, or courtesy with the white race, who alone by that compact had a right to be thus associated. She came into the Union, not only recognizing the institution of slavery as her best policy, but forbidding the legislature from passing laws for the emancipation of slaves except by the consent of the owner. She came into the Union with this institution, not only sanctioned, provided for, and protected by her own Constitution, by the direct act and recognition of the other States of the Union, and by the express provisions of that same Constitution which had originally excluded the African race from the privileges of citizenship, but with a right to full protection, under that instrument, both for the enjoyment of her property in slaves, and against the degradation of political companionship, association, and equality with them in the future. Her climate, soil, and productions, and the pursuits of her people, their habits, manners, and opinions, all combine not only to sanction the wisdom, humanity, and policy of the system thus estab-

lished by her organic law and fostered by her early legislation, but they require slave labor.

It was declared in the convention that framed the Federal Constitution, by some of their delegates, that Georgia and South Carolina would become barren wastes without slave labor, and so important did they deem it to their prosperity, that they openly announced that these States would not become parties to the Union if the slave trade should be prohibited.

. . . [In Mississippi] as early as 1822, emancipation, except for some distinguished service, and even then proven to and sanctioned by the legislature, was prohibited.

♦ ♦ ♦

[A]s late as February, 1857, the legislature of this State declared that "It shall not be lawful for any person, either by deed, will, or other conveyance, directly or in trust, . . . to make any disposition of any slave or slaves, for the purpose or with the intent to emancipate such slave or slaves in this State, or to provide that such slaves be removed to be emancipated elsewhere."

♦ ♦ ♦

I cannot therefore doubt, in view of the whole subject, that it *now* is and *ever has been,* the policy of Mississippi to protect, preserve, and perpetuate the institution of slavery as it exists amongst us, and to prevent emancipation generally of Mississippi slaves.

♦ ♦ ♦

A slave once domiciliated here, *during the continuance of that domicile* has no such rights [to inherit property]. If the appellee possess them at all, then she must have derived them from the law of her new domicile. That law, *proprio vigore,* has no extra-territorial operation, and could vest no right in the appellee *here,* except by the comity or consent of the State of Mississippi. She stands before the authorities of this State with no vested right, [and] . . . is entitled, therefore, to such *rights only,* as are not inconsistent with our laws or policy. . . . By our law she had neither capacity to sue, nor take, nor hold property, originally, before she left this State. The law of her new domicile confirming such rights in Ohio, are limited to that domicile, and cannot be made to extend over us without our consent, as she can have no *vested right* to claim or demand a mere favor, *a gratuity dependent at all times on the will of the donor;* when that favor or courtesy is withheld by the State, her right must cease with it, in obedience to the *will of the sovereign* . . . irrespective of rights acquired in another State.

[Here Harris quoted from Chief Justice Taney's opinion in *Dred Scott* v. *Sandford* that blacks were not citizens of the United States under the Constitution, but were, at the Founding, "considered a subordinate and inferior class of beings, . . . and whether emancipated or not, yet remained subject to their authority, and had no rights or privileges but such as those who held the power and the Government might choose to grant them."]

♦ ♦ ♦

I wholly dissent from the application of the doctrine of "comity" to cases like this. "Comity" forbids that a sister State of this confederacy should seek to introduce into the family of States, as equals or associates, a caste of different color, and of acknowledged inferiority, who, though existing among us at the time of our compact of Union, were excluded from the sisterhood by common consent.

♦ ♦ ♦

No people are bound, or ought to enforce or hold valid, *in their courts of justice,* any contract which is injurious to their public rights, or offends their morals, or contravenes their policy, or violates a public law. [Citing James Kent]

♦ ♦ ♦

The State of Ohio, forgetful of her Constitutional obligations to the whole race, and afflicted with a *negro-mania,* which inclines her to *descend,* rather than elevate herself in the scale of humanity, chooses to take to her embrace, as citizens, the neglected race, who by common consent of the States united, were regarded, at the formation of our government, as an inferior caste, incapable of the blessings of free government, and occupying, in the order of nature, an intermediate state between the irrational animal and the white man.

In violation of good faith, as well as of the guarantees of the Constitution, efforts are made to destroy the rights of property in this race, which, at the time of the adoption of that instrument, was in servitude, in all or nearly all the States originally parties to the compact of Union. Mississippi and other States, under the firm conviction that the relation of master and slave . . . is mutually productive of the happiness and best interests of both, continues the institution, and desires to perpetuate it. She is unwilling to extend to the slave race freedom and equality of rights, or to elevate them into political association with the family of States.

Ohio persists; and not only so introduces slaves into her own political organization, but her citizens extend encouragement and inducement to the removal of slaves from Mississippi into the limits of Ohio; and then, in violation of the laws and policy of Mississippi, and in violation of the laws of the United States in relation to the rendition of fugitive slaves, introduces them into her limits as citizens.

Looking at the transaction in the light of comity, courtesy, founded on mutual respect and mutual good-will, regarding it as a question of neighborly politeness and good breeding, or in the more intimate relation of constitutional brotherhood, in which the advocates of this doctrine of comity choose to place it, and it seems to me that comity is terminated by Ohio, in the very act of degrading herself and her sister States, by the offensive association, and that the rights of Mississippi are outraged, when Ohio ministers to emancipation and the abolition of our institution of slavery, by such unkind, disrespectful, lawless interference with our local rights.

But when I am told that Ohio has not only the right thus to degrade and disgrace herself, and wrong us, but also, that she has the right to force her new associates into the Mississippi branch of the American family, to claim and exercise rights *here,* which our laws have always denied to this inferior race, and that Mississippi is bound to yield obedience to such demand, I am at a loss to understand upon what *principle* of law or reason, of courtesy or justice, such claim can be founded.

Suppose that Ohio, still further afflicted with her peculiar philanthropy, should determine to descend another grade in the scale of *her peculiar* humanity, and claim to confer citizenship on the chimpanzee or the ourang-outang (the most respectable of the monkey tribe), are we to be told that "comity" will require of the States not thus demented, to forget their own policy and self-respect, and lower their own citizens and institutions in the scale of being, to meet the necessities of the mongrel race thus attempted to be introduced into the family of sisters in this confederacy?

Ohio, by allowing the manumission of defendant in error in her jurisdiction, and conferring rights of citizenship *there,* contrary to the known policy of Mississippi, can neither confer freedom on a Mississippi slave, nor the right to acquire, hold, sue for, nor enjoy property in Mississippi.

Let the decree be reversed.

◆ ◆ ◆

[Justice Alexander Handy dissented.]

It is said that the violation by the non-slaveholding States, of the constitutional rights of the Southern States, in harboring our fugitive slaves . . . deprives them of all claim to international comity in reference to the rights of their free negroes who may seek to assert rights in our courts.

But this sacred duty,—to respect and enforce the rights of residents of other States, secured to them by the laws of those States,—can never be destroyed, whilst the confederacy continues, by the fact that the State under which the right is claimed, has been recreant to her obligations to the compact which binds the States together. If their courts of justice have been prostituted to the purposes of fanaticism and lawlessness, that is no reason why we should descend from our elevated position, which should be superior to such influences,

follow their unworthy example, and make this court the medium of propagating our political theories upon the same subject. Whilst the confederacy continues, we cannot justify ourselves as a State in violating its spirit and principles, because other States have . . . been false to their duties and obligations. It may justify us in dissolving the compact, but not in violating our obligations under it whilst it continues.

◆ ◆ ◆

The fundamental and controlling idea upon which property in slaves rests is, the *right of absolute disposition;* and this is paramount to any question as to how, or in whose behalf, the right shall be exercised. That right, so far as it refers to the disposition of the person of the slave, is unlimited, except as it is restricted by regulations of positive law. The restrictive policy, as declared by this State, is limited to emancipation of slaves in this State, to take effect here or elsewhere. But it does not extend to removal out of this State and emancipation there, and could not, for want of power to carry out any such policy. It would be contrary to all reason and principle for us to attempt to establish any law or policy prohibiting the owner in this State from removing his slave to England or India, and manumitting him there to reside there; and for the same reason, we have none interdicting the removal to Ohio for manumission and residence there. Our abstract opinions are, that such a course is impolitic; but such opinions have not been established *as a policy.* Our policy, *as a State,* has no reference whatever to free negroes out of the State, except to prevent them from coming to this State and residing here. It is based upon the same principle as all our domestic policy; having reference to our own internal welfare and protection, and to the promotion of the morality and happiness of society. . . . So our domestic policy has been strongly against banking in this State; yet no one would contend that a foreign bank might not sue in this State upon any legal right acquired in another State. These things, though contrary to a policy of a domestic character, contemplated by our laws, are not within their prohibition, because our laws have reference solely to the prevention of the mischiefs within this State.

Note: The *Somerset* Precedent in America

Before the 1830s, most southern states had recognized the right of masters to emancipate their slaves in the free states, as well as the power of the free states to emancipate any slaves voluntarily brought within their jurisdiction. *Mitchell* v. *Wells* was the last of a number of southern decisions rejecting the notion, dating from *Somerset* v. *Stewart* (1772), that slaves could gain freedom by being brought to a free state.

SLAVERY AND THE CONSTITUTION

Slavery was the most divisive constitutional issue in pre–Civil War America. A federal republic that was, in Lincoln's words, "half slave and half free" required accommodations and compromises over slavery. Indeed, much of the debate at the Constitutional Convention centered on slavery in the new nation.

In 1788, during the ratification struggle, General Charles Cotesworth Pinckney told the South Carolina legislature that

> we have a security that the general government can never emancipate them, for no such authority is granted, and it is admitted on all hands, that the general government has no powers but what are expressly granted by the constitution; and that all rights not expressed were reserved by the several states.

Mainstream nineteenth-century constitutional interpretation accepted this understanding that the national government had no power over slavery in the states where it existed. However, federal jurisdiction arose over (1) the African slave trade and the regulation of the interstate commerce in slaves, (2) the return of fugitive slaves, (3) slavery in the federal territories and District of Columbia, (4) the admission of new slave states into the Union, and (5) the interstate transit or sojourn of slaves through or in free states.

The Constitution prohibited any federal interference with the African slave trade until 1808, when Congress prohibited the importation of slaves and declared the African trade to be piracy. Enforcement of the laws prohibiting the trade was lax, and not until Lincoln's administration did the government seek the death penalty for a slave trader. While important for the development of admiralty law and international law, the cases on the slave trade had relatively little impact on domestic slavery or domestic legal developments. Their indifferent enforcement, however, illustrates the extent to which slave owners and their northern "doughface" sympathizers controlled Congress, the judiciary, and the executive branch before the Civil War. In the 1850s, some proslavery extremists wanted to reopen the slave trade, but most Southerners rejected this idea. In 1861, the Confederate Constitution banned the African slave trade.

Although most antebellum lawyers and lawmakers would have conceded that Congress had the *power* to regulate the interstate slave trade, legislation on the subject was politically unthinkable because it would have threatened the Union. Commerce clause cases, such as *Gibbons* v. *Ogden,* recognized the special status of slaves in the general regulation of commerce. It is possible to see the influence of slavery, directly or indirectly, in almost every commerce clause case from 1820 to 1861.

The issues of fugitive slaves, slavery in the federal territories, and slave transit led to divisive debates in state legislatures and Congress, and before state and federal courts. Ultimately, these issues were decided not by constitutional arguments and ballots, but by battlefield tactics and bullets.

THE PROBLEM OF FUGITIVE SLAVES

The fugitive slave clause's wording and its placement in Article IV, Section 2, of the Constitution suggest that the Framers did not anticipate a federal law to enforce it. However, in 1793 Congress spelled out procedures for the return of fugitive slaves. The 1793 act allowed masters or their agents who captured runaways to bring them to any magistrate, state or federal, to obtain a "certificate of removal," authorizing the claimants to take the runaway slaves out of the states where they were found, and back to the state where the slaves owed service. By this time, all the New England states and Pennsylvania either had abolished slavery outright or were in the process of gradually eliminating it. By 1804, New York and New Jersey had joined this "first emancipation." These changes in northern law meant that in more than half the nation a presumption of servitude, based on race, no longer existed. The Fugitive Slave Law of 1793, with its lax evidentiary standards, gravely threatened the growing northern free black population. To prevent kidnapping, many free states passed "personal liberty laws," which supplemented the requirements of the federal law. In 1842, Pennsylvania's law led to the first United States Supreme Court decision on fugitive slaves.

Prigg v. *Pennsylvania*
16 Pet. (41 U.S.) 539 (1842)

In 1837 Edward Prigg and three other Maryland men seized Margaret Morgan and her children in Pennsylvania, claiming them as a fugitive slaves. Margaret's parents (whose names are unknown) had been slaves owned by a man named John Ashmore, but sometime around the War of 1812, he allowed them to live as free people. Margaret grew up assuming she was free, married a free black from Pennsylvania named Jerry Morgan, and lived in Harford County, Maryland. In 1830 the U.S. census recorded her as being a "free person of color." In 1832 the Morgans moved to York, Pennsylvania. Margaret subsequently had at least one, and maybe two, children while living in Pennsylvania. In 1837 John Ashmore's widow sent her son-in-law and three other men, including Prigg, to Pennsylvania to recover Margaret. The Marylanders applied to a justice of the peace for certificates of removal under the federal law of 1793 and Pennsylvania's personal liberty law of 1826, which had higher evidentiary requirements than the federal law. The justice refused Prigg's request, probably because some of Margaret's children had been born in Pennsylvania and were free under that state's laws, as well as because her status was murky at best. Without any legal authority, Prigg removed Morgan and her children, including at least one conceived and born in Pennsylvania. Convicted of kidnapping under the 1826 law, Prigg appealed to the United States Supreme Court. At issue was the constitutionality of both the federal law of 1793 and the Pennsylvania law of 1826.

Mr. Justice Story delivered the opinion of the Court.

♦ ♦ ♦

Historically, it is well known, that the object of [the fugitive slave] clause was to secure to the citizens of the slaveholding states the complete right and title of ownership in their slaves, as property, in every state in the Union into which they might escape from the state where they were held in servitude. The full recognition of this right and title was indispensable to the security of this species of property in all the slaveholding states; and indeed, was so vital to the preservation of their domestic interests and institutions, that it cannot be doubted that it constituted a fundamental article, without the adoption of which the Union could not have been formed. Its true design was to guard against the doctrines and principles prevalent in the non-slaveholding states, by preventing them from intermeddling with, or obstructing, or abolishing the rights of the owners of slaves.

. . . [I]f the Constitution had not contained this clause, every non-slaveholding state in the Union would have been at liberty to . . . free all runaway slaves coming within its limits, and to have given them entire immunity and protection against the claims of their masters; a course which would have created the most bitter animosities, and engendered perpetual strife between the different states. The clause was, therefore, of the last importance to the safety and security of the southern states; and could not have been surrendered by them without endangering their whole property in slaves. The clause was accordingly adopted into the Constitution by the unanimous consent of the framers of it; a proof at once of its intrinsic and practical necessity.

The clause manifestly contemplates the existence of a positive, unqualified right on the part of the owner of the slave, which no state law or regulation can in any way qualify, regulate, control, or restrain. The slave is not to be discharged from service or labour, in consequence of any state law or regulation. Now, certainly . . . any state law or state regulation, which interrupts, limits, delays, or postpones the right of the owner to the immediate possession of the slave, and the immediate command of his service and labour, operates, pro tanto, a discharge of the slave therefrom. . . .

We have said that the clause contains a positive and unqualified recognition of the right of the owner in the slave, unaffected by any state law or regulation whatsoever. . . . If this be so, then all the incidents to that right attach also; the owner must, therefore, have the right to seize and repossess the slave, which the local laws of his own state confer upon him as property. . . . Upon this ground we have not the slightest hesitation in holding that, under and in

virtue of the Constitution, the owner of a slave is clothed with entire authority, in every state in the Union, to seize and recapture his slave, whenever he can do it without any breach of the peace, or any illegal violence. In this sense, and to this extent this clause of the Constitution may properly be said to execute itself; and to require no aid from legislation, state or national.

◆ ◆ ◆

If, therefore, the clause of the Constitution had stopped at the mere recognition of the right, without providing or contemplating any means by which it might be established and enforced in cases where it did not execute itself, it is plain that it would have, in a great variety of cases, a delusive and empty annunciation.

. . . [The slaveowners] require the aid of legislation to protect the right, to enforce the delivery, and to secure the subsequent possession of the slave. If, indeed, the Constitution guarantees the right, and if it requires the delivery upon the claim of the owner, (as cannot well be doubted,) the natural inference certainly is, that the national government is clothed with the appropriate authority and functions to enforce it. The fundamental principle applicable to all cases of this sort, would seem to be, that where the end is required, the means are given; and where the duty is enjoined, the ability to perform it is contemplated to exist on the part of the functionaries to whom it is entrusted. The clause is found in the national Constitution, and not in that of any state. It does not point out any state functionaries, or any state action to carry its provisions into effect. The states cannot, therefore, be compelled to enforce them; and it might well be deemed an unconstitutional exercise of the power of interpretation, to insist that the states are bound to provide means to carry into effect the duties of the national government, nowhere delegated or intrusted to them by the Constitution. On the contrary, the natural, if not the necessary conclusion is, that the national government, in the absence of all positive provisions to the contrary, is bound, through its own proper departments, legislative, judicial, or executive, as the case may require, to carry into effect all the rights and duties imposed upon it by the Constitution. . . .

Congress has taken this very view of the power and duty of the national government. . . . The result of their deliberations, was the passage of the act of the 12th of February, 1793.

◆ ◆ ◆

We hold the [Fugitive Slave] act to be clearly constitutional in all its leading provisions, and, indeed, with the exception of that part which confers authority upon state magistrates, to be free from reasonable doubt and difficulty upon the grounds already stated. As to the authority so conferred upon state magistrates, while a difference of opinion . . . may exist still on the point, in different states, whether state magistrates are bound to act under it; none is entertained by this Court that state magistrates may, if they choose, exercise that authority, unless prohibited by state legislation.

The remaining question is, whether the power of legislation upon this subject is exclusive in the national government. . . . In our opinion it is exclusive. . . .

It is scarcely conceivable that the slave-holding states would have been satisfied with leaving to the legislation of the non-slaveholding states, a power of regulation, in the absence of that of Congress, which would or might practically amount to a power to destroy the rights of the owner. If the argument, therefore, of a concurrent power in the states to act upon the subject-matter in the absence of legislation by Congress, be well founded; then, if Congress had never acted at all . . . there would be a resulting authority in each of the states to regulate the whole subject as its pleasure; and to dole out its own remedial justice, or withhold it at its pleasure and according to its own views of policy and expediency. Surely such a state of things never could have been intended, under such a solemn guarantee of right and duty. On the other hand, construe the right of legislation as exclusive in Congress, and every evil, and every danger vanishes. The right and the duty are then coextensive and uniform in remedy and operation throughout the whole Union. The owner has the same security, and the same remedial justice, and the same exemption from state regulation and control, through however many states he may pass with

his fugitive slave in his possession, in transitu, to his own domicile. . . .

These are some of the reasons . . . upon which we hold the power of legislation on this subject to be exclusive in Congress. To guard, however, against any possible misconstruction of our views, it is proper to state, that we are by no means to be understood in any manner whatsoever to doubt or to interfere with the police power belonging to the states in virtue of their general sovereignty. That police power extends over all subjects within the territorial limits of the states; and has never been conceded to the United States. It is wholly distinguishable from the right and duty secured by the provision now under consideration. . . . We entertain no doubt whatsoever, that the states, in virtue of their general police power, possess full jurisdiction to arrest and restrain in runaway slaves, and remove them from their borders, and otherwise to secure themselves against their depredations and evil example, as they certainly may do in cases of idlers, vagabonds, and paupers. The rights of the owners of fugitive slaves are in no just sense interfered with, or regulated by such a course; and in many cases, the operations of this police power, although designed essentially for . . . the protection, safety, and peace of the state, may essentially promote and aid the interests of the owners. But such regulations can never be permitted to interfere with or to obstruct the just rights of the owner to reclaim his slave, derived from the Constitution of the United States; or with the remedies prescribed by Congress to aid and enforce the same.

Upon these grounds, we are of opinion that the act of Pennsylvania . . . is unconstitutional.

◆ ◆ ◆

[Chief Justice Taney concurred with the result in *Prigg,* but objected to Story's assertions that state officials could not be required to enforce the federal law. Taney also misconstrued Story's opinion to mean that the states were prohibited from adopting legislation to aid in the return of fugitive slaves.]

The opinion of the Court maintains that the power over this subject is so exclusively vested in Congress, that since the adoption of the Constitution, no state can pass any law in relation to it. In other words the state authorities are prohibited from interfering for the purpose of protecting the right of the master and aiding him in the recovery of his property. I think the states are not prohibited; and that, on the contrary, it is enjoined upon them as a duty to protect and support the owner when he is endeavouring to obtain possession of his property found within their respective territories.

◆ ◆ ◆

Indeed, if the state authorities are absolved from all obligation to protect this right, and may stand by and see it violated without an effort to defend it, the act of Congress of 1793 scarcely deserves the name of a remedy . . . [because the law would] depend altogether for its execution upon the officers of the United States named in it. And the master must take the fugitive, after he has seized him, before a judge of the District or Circuit Court, residing in the state, and

exhibit his proofs, and procure from the judge his certificate of ownership, in order to obtain the protection in removing his property which this act of Congress professes to give.

Now, in many of the states there is but one district judge, and there are only nine states which have judges of the Supreme Court residing within them. The fugitive will frequently be found by his owner in a place very distant from the residence of either of these judges; and would certainly be removed beyond his reach, before a warrant could be procured from the judge to arrest him, even if the act of Congress authorized such a warrant. But it does not authorize the judge to issue a warrant to arrest the fugitive; but evidently relied on the state authorities to protect the owner in making the seizure. . . . It is only necessary to state the provisions of this law in order to show how ineffectual and delusive is the remedy provided by Congress, if state authority is forbidden to come to its aid.

Note: *Prigg* and the Use of History

In *Prigg,* Justice Story characterized the fugitive slave clause as "a fundamental article, without the adoption of which the Union could not have been formed." The history of the clause undermined this argument. Late in the Constitutional Convention, South Carolina's Pierce Butler proposed a clause to "require fugitive slaves and servants to be delivered up like criminals." James Wilson objected that this "obliged the Executive of the State to do it, at the public expense." Roger Sherman sarcastically added that there was "no more propriety in the public seizing and surrendering a slave or servant, than a horse." In the face of this opposition, Butler withdrew his proposal. The next day, without any further debate or even a recorded vote, the delegates adopted what became the fugitive slave clause.

Note: *Prigg* and Its Aftermath

Justice Story's opinion did not in fact prohibit state enforcement of the 1793 law. Nevertheless, in the 1840s some northern jurists refused to hear fugitive slave cases, claiming that the Supreme Court's decision precluded them from taking jurisdiction. Various states adopted new personal liberty laws that removed state support for enforcement of the 1793 law. A Massachusetts act of 1843, for example, prohibited any state official, including sheriffs and judges, from participating in the return of a fugitive slave under the law of 1793, and denied slave catchers access to public jails and other facilities.

The new personal liberty laws led to southern demands for a more stringent federal law. The Fugitive Slave Law of 1850 authorized the appointment of a federal commissioner in every county of the United States who could issue certificates of removal for fugitive slaves and call for aid from federal marshals, the military, and "bystanders, or *posse comitatus.*" People interfering in the enforcement of the law could be jailed for up to six months and fined up to $1,000. An alleged fugitive could be seized on minimal evidence and brought before the commissioner, who issued the arrest warrant for a summary and juryless proceeding. At this hearing, the alleged fugitive was prohibited from testifying on his own behalf. A successful claimant was required to pay the federal commissioner a fee of $10, but if the commissioner decided against the claimant the fee was only $5. Congress justified this differential because the commissioner had more paperwork if he found in favor of the claimant; but to many Northerners, this seemed like a blatant attempt at bribery.

Reaction to the 1850 law took many forms. Some blacks, free and fugitive, living in the North fled to Canada. In a number of northern cities, blacks and their white allies formed self-defense groups. While most fugitive slave seizures ended in successful renditions, riots and rescues in Massachusetts, Pennsylvania, New York, Ohio, Illinois, and Wisconsin gave Americans—especially Southerners—the impression that the law was not being enforced. These incidents made national headlines as alleged fugitive slaves avoided the clutches of federal officers, and on one occasion a slave owner lost his life as a group of fugitive slaves in Christiana, Pennsylvania, successfully resisted being returned to bondage.

Note: Northern States'-Rights Arguments

In January 1855, a federal court convicted Sherman Booth for having rescued a fugitive slave, but less than two weeks later the Wisconsin Supreme Court declared the 1850 Fugitive Slave Law unconstitutional and released Booth from federal custody. Federal Marshal Stephen Ableman's appeal of the state court decision was delayed for three years because the Wisconsin court refused to send a record of the case to the United States Supreme Court. Chief Justice Taney's opinion for a unanimous court in *Ableman* v. *Booth,* 21 How. (U.S.) 506 (1859), upheld the 1850 law and asserted that no state could interfere with the rendition process or question the power of federal officers to arrest people under the law.

SLAVERY, THE TERRITORIES, AND INTERSTATE COMITY

The issue of slavery in the territories first emerged when Missouri sought to enter the Union as a slave state. Northerners argued that Missouri was north and west of the Ohio River and thus should be free under the Northwest Ordinance. The ensuing debate led to the Compromise of 1820, also called the Missouri Compromise, which brought Missouri into the Union as a slave state, but barred slavery from those territories north and west of the southern boundary of Missouri.

The acquisition of land during the Mexican War reopened the question of slavery in the territories. In 1846, northern congressmen tried to keep slavery out of all the territories acquired from Mexico through the Wilmot Proviso, but the proposal died in the Senate. Southerners, meanwhile, demanded the right to take their slaves into all the federal territories, even those free under the Compromise of 1820.

Political deadlock ended with the Compromise of 1850, which brought California into the Union as a free state, prohibited the public sale of slaves in the District of Columbia, led to the passage of the new Fugitive Slave Law, and opened some of the new territories to slavery. In 1854, the Kansas-Nebraska Act allowed slavery into some territories previously closed to slavery under the Missouri Compromise of 1820. The Kansas-Nebraska Act led to the formation of the Republican party, which was dedicated to stopping the spread of slavery in the territories.

Dred Scott v. *Sandford*
19 How. (60 U.S.) 393 (1857)

As the slave of John Emerson, an Army surgeon, Dred Scott lived on military bases in Illinois and at Fort Snelling (present-day Minnesota), an area that was free under the Missouri Compromise. In 1850, after Emerson's death, a St. Louis court, following Missouri precedents dating from 1824, held that Dred Scott had become free while living in nonslave jurisdictions and remained free, despite his return to Missouri. The Missouri Supreme Court reversed this result. Reflecting the proslavery ideology of the South, the Missouri court, in Scott v. Emerson, *15 Mo. 576 (1852), disavowed the old precedents:*

> *Times are not as they were when the former decisions on this subject were made. Since then not only individuals but States have been possessed of a dark and fell spirit in relation to slavery, whose gratification is sought in the pursuit of measures, whose inevitable consequence must be the overthrow and destruction of our government. Under such circumstances it does not behoove the State of Missouri to show the least countenance to any measure which might gratify this spirit.*

By this time, Emerson's widow had remarried and no longer claimed ownership of Dred Scott and his family. Scott's new owner was Mrs. Emerson's brother, John F. A. Sanford, a native-born Southerner who by this time lived in New York. Sanford's residence allowed Scott to sue Sanford under diversity jurisdiction.[1] Sanford argued in a plea in abatement that as a black, Scott could not be a citizen of the United States. United States District Judge Robert W. Wells denied this plea, ruling that if Scott was free, then he was a citizen, for purposes of diversity jurisdiction. If he was not free, then his standing to sue was moot. On the merits of the case, Wells ruled that Scott's status was legitimately determined by the Missouri Supreme Court, and upheld his enslavement. Scott appealed to the United States Supreme Court. In his opinion, Chief Justice Roger B. Taney resolved two issues: the status of blacks, slave or free, under the Constitution, and the power of Congress to regulate slavery in the territories.

Mr. Chief Justice Taney delivered the opinion of the court.

♦ ♦ ♦

The question is simply this: Can a negro, whose ancestors were imported into this country, and sold as slaves, become a member of the political community formed and brought into existence by the Constitution of the United States, and as such become entitled to all the rights, and privileges, and immunities, guaranteed by that instrument to the citizen? One of which rights is the privilege of suing in a court of the United States in the cases specified in the Constitution.

♦ ♦ ♦

The words "people of the United States" and "citizens" are synonymous terms, and mean the same thing. They both describe the political body who, according to our republican institutions, form the sovereignty, and who hold the power and conduct the Government through their representatives. . . . The question before us is, whether the class of persons described in the plea in abatement compose a portion of this people, and are constituent members of the sovereignty? We think they are not, and that they are not included, and were not intended to be included, under the word "citizen" in the Constitution, and can therefore claim none of the rights and privileges which that instrument provides for and secure to citizens of the United States. On the contrary, they were at that time [1787] considered as a subordinate and inferior class of beings, who had been subjugated by the dominant race, and, whether emancipated or not, yet remained subject to their authority, and had no rights or privileges but such as those who held the power and the Government might choose to grant them.

It is not the province of the court to decide upon the justice or injustice, the policy or impolicy, of these laws. The decision of that question belonged to the political or law-making power; to those who formed the sovereignty and framed the Constitution. . . .

In discussing this question, we must not confound the rights of citizenship which a State may confer within its own limits, and the rights of citizenship as a member of the Union. It does not by any means follow, because he has all the rights and privileges of a citizen of a State, that he must be a citizen of the United States. . . . The Constitution has conferred on Congress the right to establish an uniform rule of naturalization, and this right is evidently exclusive, and has always been held by this court to be so. Consequently, no State, since the adoption of the Constitution, can by naturalizing an alien invest him with the rights and privileges secured to a citizen of a State under the Federal Government.

◆ ◆ ◆

The question then arises, whether the provisions of the Constitution, in relation to the personal rights and privileges to which the citizen of a State should be entitled, embraced the Negro African race, at that time in this country, or who might afterwards be imported, who had then or should afterwards be made free in any State; and to put it in the power of a single State to make him a citizen of the United States, and endue him with the full rights of citizenship in every other State without their consent? Does the Constitution of the United States act upon him whenever he shall be made free under the laws of a State, and raised there to the rank of a citizen, and immediately clothe him with all the privileges of a citizen in every other State, and in its own courts?

The court think the affirmative of these propositions cannot be maintained. And if it cannot, the plaintiff in error could not be a citizen of the State of Missouri, within the meaning of the Constitution of the United States, and, consequently, was not entitled to sue in its courts.

◆ ◆ ◆

In the opinion of the court, the legislation and histories of the times, and the language used in the Declaration of Independence, show, that neither the class of persons who had been imported as slaves, nor their descendants, whether they had become free or not, were then acknowledged as a part of the people, nor intended to be included in the general words used in that memorable instrument.

◆ ◆ ◆

They had for more than a century before been regarded as beings of an inferior order, and altogether unfit to associate with the white race, either in social or political relations; and so far inferior, that they had no rights which the white man was bound to respect; and that the negro might justly and lawfully be reduced to slavery for his benefit. He was bought and sold, and treated as an ordinary article of merchandise and traffic, whenever a profit could be made by it. This opinion was at that time fixed and universal in the civilized portion of the white race. It was regarded as an axiom in morals as well as in politics, which no one thought of disputing, or supposed to be open to dispute; and men in every grade and position in society daily and habitually acted upon it in their private pursuits, as well as in matters of public concern, without doubting for a moment the correctness of this opinion.

♦ ♦ ♦

And, accordingly, a negro of the African race was regarded by them as an article of property, and held, and bought and sold as such, in every one of the thirteen colonies which united in the Declaration of Independence, and afterwards formed the Constitution of the United States.

♦ ♦ ♦

This state of public opinion had undergone no change when the Constitution was adopted, as is equally evident from its provisions and language.

♦ ♦ ♦

It is obvious that they [blacks] were not even in the minds of the framers of the Constitution when they were conferring special rights and privileges upon the citizens of the States. . . .

[Taney then discussed statutes and cases from various states, North and South, arguing that these precedents illustrated "the entire repudiation of the African Race."]

♦ ♦ ♦

The legislation of the States therefore shows, in a manner not to be mistaken, the inferior and subject condition of that race at the time the Constitution was adopted, and long afterwards, throughout the thirteen States . . . and it is hardly consistent with the respect due to these States, to suppose that they regarded at that time, as fellow-citizens and members of the sovereignty, a class of beings whom they had thus stigmatized. . . . It cannot be supposed that they intended to secure to them rights, and privileges, and rank, in the new political body throughout the Union, which every one of them denied within the limits of its own dominion. More especially, it cannot be believed that the large slaveholding States regarded them as included in the word citizens, or would have consented to a Constitution which might compel them to receive them in that character from an-

other State. For if they were so received, and entitled to the privileges and immunities of citizens, it would exempt them from the operation of the special laws and from the police regulations which they considered to be necessary for their own safety. It would give to persons of the negro race, who were recognized as citizens in any one State of the Union, the right to enter every other State whenever they pleased, singly or in companies, without pass or passport, and without obstruction, to sojourn there as long as they pleased, to go where they pleased at every hour of the day or night without molestation, unless they committed some violation of law for which a white man would be punished; and it would give them the full liberty of speech public and in private upon all subjects upon which its own citizens might speak; to hold public meetings upon political affairs, and to keep and carry arms wherever they went. And all of this would be done in the face of the subject race of the same color, both free and slaves, and inevitably producing discontent and insubordination among them, and endangering the peace and safety of the State.

It is impossible, it would seem, to believe that the great men of the slaveholding States, who took so large a share in framing the Constitution of the United States, and exercised so much influence in procuring its adoption, could have been so forgetful or regardless of their own safety and the safety of those who trusted and confided in them.

♦ ♦ ♦

No one, we presume, supposes that any change in public opinion or feeling, in relation to this unfortunate race, in the civilized nations of Europe or in this country, should induce the Court to give to the words of the Constitution a more liberal construction in their favor than they were intended to bear when the instrument was framed and adopted. Such an argument would be altogether inadmissible in any tribunal called on to interpret it. If any of its provisions are deemed unjust, [the Constitution] . . . may be amended; but while it remains unaltered, it must be construed now as it was understood at the time of its adoption. It is not only the same in words, but the same in meaning, and delegates the same powers to the Government, and reserves and secures the same rights and privileges to the citizen; and as long as it continues to exist in its present form, it speaks not only in the same words, but with the same meaning and intent with which it spoke when it came from the hands of its framers, and was voted on and adopted by the people of the United States. Any other rule of construction would abrogate the judicial character of this court, and make it the mere reflex of the popular opinion or passion of the day. This court was not created by the Constitution for such purposes. Higher and graver trusts have been confided to it, and it must not falter in the path of duty.

♦ ♦ ♦

[Thus] the court is of opinion that, upon the facts stated in the plea in abatement, Dred Scott was not a citizen of Missouri within the meaning of the Constitution of the United States, and not entitled as such to sue in its courts.

♦ ♦ ♦

The act of Congress, upon which the plaintiff relies [to claim his freedom], declares that slavery and involuntary servitude, except as a punishment for crime, shall be forever prohibited in all that part of the territory ceded by France, under the name of Louisiana, which lies north of thirty-six degrees thirty minutes north latitude, and not included within the limits of Missouri. And the difficulty which meets us at the threshold of this part of the inquiry is, whether Congress was authorized to pass this law under any of the powers granted to it by the Constitution; for if the authority is not given by that instrument, it is the duty of this court to declare it void and inoperative, and incapable of conferring freedom upon any one who is held as a slave under the laws of any one of the States.

The counsel for the plaintiff has laid much stress upon that article in the Constitution which confers on Congress the power "to dispose of and make all needful rules and regulations respecting the territory or other property belonging to the United States;" but, in the judgment

of the court, that provision has no bearing on the present controversy, and the power there given . . . was intended to be confined, to the territory which at that time belonged to, or was claimed by, the United States, and was within their boundaries as settled by the treaty with Great Britain, and can have no influence upon a territory afterwards acquired from a foreign Government. It was a special provision for a known and particular territory, and to meet a present emergency, and nothing more.

♦ ♦ ♦

[Taney then discussed the power of Congress to acquire new territories for the United States.]

There is certainly no power given by the Constitution to the Federal Government to establish or maintain colonies bordering on the United States or at a distance, to be ruled and governed at its own pleasure; nor to enlarge its territorial limits in any way, except by the admission of new States. That power is plainly given. . . . But no power is given to acquire a Territory to be held and governed permanently in that character.

♦ ♦ ♦

[I]t may be safely assumed that citizens of the United States who migrate to a Territory belonging to the people of the United States, cannot be ruled as mere colonists, dependent upon the will of the General Government, and to be governed by any laws it may think proper to impose. The principle upon which our Governments rest, and upon which alone they continue to exist, is the union of States, sovereign and independent within their own limits in their internal and domestic concerns, and bound together as one people by a General Government, possessing certain enumerated and restricted powers, delegated to it by the people of the several States, and exercising supreme authority within the scope of the powers granted to it. . . . A power, therefore, in the General Government to obtain and hold colonies and dependent territories, over which they might legislate without restriction, would be inconsistent with its own existence in its present form. Whatever it acquires, it acquires for the benefit of the people of the several States who created it. It is their trustee acting for them, and charged with the duty of promoting the interests of the whole people of the Union in the exercise of the powers specifically granted.

◆ ◆ ◆

But the power of Congress over the person or property of a citizen can never be a mere discretionary power under our Constitution and form of Government. The powers of the Government and the rights and privileges of the citizens are regulated and plainly defined by the Constitution itself. . . . The Territory being a part of the United States, the Government and the citizen both enter it under the authority of the Constitution, with their respective rights defined and marked out; and the Federal Government can exercise no power over his person or property, beyond what that instrument confers, nor lawfully deny any right which it has reserved.

A reference to a few of the provisions of the Constitution will illustrate this proposition.

For example, no one, we presume, will contend that Congress can make any law in a Territory respecting the establishment of religion, or the free exercise thereof, or abridging the freedom of speech or of the press, or the right of the people of the Territory peaceably to assemble, and to petition the Government for the redress of grievances.

◆ ◆ ◆

These powers, and others, in relation to rights of person, . . . are, in express and positive terms, denied to the General Government; and the rights of private property have been guarded with equal care. Thus the rights of property are united with the rights of person, and placed on the same ground by the fifth amendment to the Constitution, which provides that no person shall be deprived of life, liberty, and property, without due process of law. And an act of Congress which deprives a citizen of the United States of his liberty or property, merely because he came himself or brought his property into a particular Territory of the United States, and who had committed no offense against the laws, could hardly be dignified with the name of due process of law.

◆ ◆ ◆

Now, as we have already said . . . the right of property in a slave is distinctly and expressly affirmed in the Constitution. The right to traffic in it, like an ordinary article of merchandise and property, was guaranteed to the citizens of the United States, in every State that might desire it, for twenty years. And the Government in express terms is pledged to protect it in all future time, if the slave escapes from his owner. This is done in plain words—too plain to be misunderstood. And no word can be found in the Constitution which gives Congress a greater power over slave property, or which entitles property of that kind to less protection than property of any other description. The only power conferred is the power coupled with the duty of guarding and protecting the owner in his rights.

Upon these considerations, it is the opinion of the court that the act of Congress which prohibited a citizen from holding and owning property of this kind in the territory of the United States . . . is not warranted by the Constitution, and is therefore void; and that neither Dred Scott himself, nor any of his family, were made free by being carried into this territory; even if they had been carried there by the owner, with the intention of becoming a permanent resident.

Note: The Reaction to *Dred Scott*

The unabashedly proslavery Chief Justice Taney hoped that his magisterial, fifty-four-page opinion would finally settle, in the South's favor, the controversy over slavery in the territories, determine forever the status of blacks in America, and help destroy the new Republican party. His opinion had the opposite effect, in part because, as historian Don Fehrenbacher has written, "Taney's opinion, carefully read, proved to be a work of unmitigated partisanship, polemical in spirit though judicial in its language, and more like an ultimatum than a formula for sectional accommodation. Peace on Taney's terms resembled the peace implicit in a demand for unconditional surrender."[2]

In a sixty-nine-page dissent opinion, Justice Benjamin R. Curtis of Massachusetts took Taney to task at almost every point. Curtis argued that United States citizenship preceded the Constitution, that free blacks had been citizens of at least five states before 1787, and thus they had also been citizens of the United States at the time the Constitution was adopted. Curtis also argued that under a "reasonable interpretation of the language of the Constitution," Congress had the power to regulate slavery in the federal territories. This dissent, along with a powerful attack on Taney's opinion in Justice John McLean's dissent, heartened Northerners like Horace Greeley, who wrote that Taney's decision was "atrocious," "wicked," "abominable," "false," and built on "shallow sophistries" and "detestable hypocrisy." The *Chicago Tribune,* reflecting the shock and horror of many Northerners, wrote, "We scarcely know how to express our detestation of its inhuman dicta, or to fathom the wicked consequences which may flow from it."

One of the potential "wicked consequences" of the case was broadly hinted at by Justice Samuel Nelson, a New York Democrat, who noted in his concurrence that "except as restrained by the Federal Constitution," the states had "complete and absolute power over the subject" of slavery. This may have referred to only the fugitive slave clause. But Republicans saw a darker side to Nelson's opinion, especially because the justice also noted there was some question about the

> right of the master with his slave, of transit into or through a free State, on business or commercial pursuits, or in the exercise of a federal right, or the discharge of a federal duty, being a citizen of the United States. . . . This question depends upon different considerations and principles from the one in hand, and turns upon the rights and privileges secured to a common citizen of the republic, under the Constitution of the United States. When that question arises, we shall be prepared to decide it.

ABRAHAM LINCOLN

"House Divided" Speech
June 16, 1858

After being nominated for the United States Senate, Abraham Lincoln gave his famous "House Divided" speech to the Illinois Republican Convention. Lincoln accused his opponent, Stephen A. Douglas, of being part of a conspiracy to open up all the territories to slavery and ultimately to force slavery on the North. The key elements of this conspiracy were the Kansas-Nebraska Act of 1854 and the Dred Scott *decision. The Kansas-Nebraska Act allowed slavery in some territory from which it had been prohibited under the Missouri Compromise. Douglas accomplished this through "popular sovereignty," which allowed the people of a territory to decide for themselves if they wanted slavery. Lincoln believed that the 1854 act and popular sovereignty were preludes to the* Dred Scott *decision, which opened up all the territories to slavery. Lincoln feared that another* Dred Scott *decision would legalize slavery in the North.*

"A house divided against itself cannot stand."

I believe this government cannot endure, permanently half *slave* and half *free.*

I do not expect the Union to be *dissolved*— I do not expect the house to *fall*—but I *do* expect it will cease to be divided.

It will become *all* one thing, or *all* the other.

Either the *opponents* of slavery, will arrest the further spread of it, and place it where the public mind shall rest in the belief that it is in course of ultimate extinction; or its *advocates* will push it forward, till it shall become alike lawful in *all* the states, *old* as well as *new*— *North* as well as *South.*

Have we no *tendency* to the latter condition?

Let any one who doubts, carefully contemplate that now almost complete legal combination—piece of *machinery* so to speak— compounded of the Nebraska doctrine, and the Dred Scott decision.

♦ ♦ ♦

[The Kansas-Nebraska Act] opened all the national territory to slavery. . . . This . . . had been provided for . . . in the notable argument of *"squatter sovereignty,"* otherwise called *"sacred right of self government,"* which latter phrase, though expressive of the only rightful basis of any government, was so perverted in this attempted use of it as to amount to just this: That if any *one* man, choose to enslave *another,* no *third* man shall be allowed to object.

♦ ♦ ♦

While the Nebraska Bill was passing through Congress, a law case, involving the question of a negro's freedom . . . was passing through the U.S. Circuit Court for the District of Missouri; and both Nebraska Bill and law suit were brought to a decision in the same month of May, 1854. The Negro's name was "Dred Scott."

♦ ♦ ♦

[The points decided by the *Dred Scott* decision include] that whether the holding a negro in actual slavery in a free state, makes him free, as against the holder, the United States courts will not decide, but will leave to be decided by the courts of any slave state the negro may be forced into by the master.

This point is made, not to be pressed immediately . . . [that] the logical conclusion that what Dred Scott's master might lawfully do with Dred Scott, in the free state Illinois, every other master may lawfully do with any other *one,* or one *thousand* slaves, in Illinois, or in any other free state.

♦ ♦ ♦

While the opinion of . . . Chief Justice Taney, in the Dred Scott case . . . expressly declare[s] that the Constitution of the United States neither permits congress nor a territorial legislature to exclude slavery from any United States territory, . . . [Taney] *omit* to declare whether or not the same constitution permits a *state,* or the people of a state, to exclude it.

Possibly, this was a mere omission; but who can be quite sure. . . . The nearest approach to the point of declaring the power of a state over slavery, is made by Judge Nelson. He approaches it more than once, using the precise idea, and *almost* the language too, of the Nebraska Act. On one occasion his exact language is, "except in cases where the power is restrained by the Constitution of the United States, the law of the State is supreme over the subject of slavery within its jurisdiction."

In what *cases* the power of the *states* is so restrained by the U.S. Constitution, is left an *open* question, precisely as the same question, as to the restraint on the power of the *territories* was left open in the Nebraska Act. Put *that* and *that* together, and we have another nice little niche, which we may, ere long, see filled with another Supreme Court decision, declaring that the Constitution of the United States does not permit a *state* to exclude slavery from its limits.

♦ ♦ ♦

Such a decision is all that slavery now lacks of being alike lawful in all the states.

Welcome or unwelcome, such decision *is* probably coming, and will soon be upon us, unless the power of the present political dynasty shall be met and overthrown.

We shall *lie down* pleasantly dreaming that the people of Missouri are on the verge of mak-ing their state *free;* and we shall *awake* to the *reality,* instead, that the Supreme Court has made *Illinois* a *slave* state.

Note: The Next *Dred Scott* Decision

The next *Dred Scott* case that Lincoln feared was already making its way through the courts. *Lemmon* v. *The People* (N.Y., 1860) was the last of a line of cases that began with the English case *Somerset* v. *Stewart* (1772) (discussed in Chapter 2 of this book). In *Somerset,* Lord Chief Justice Mansfield of the Court of King's Bench held that a slave could not forcibly be removed from England. Somerset's counsel, William Davy, provided a metaphor for England and other free jurisdictions, declaring that "the air of England . . . is too pure for a slave to breathe in." In *Commonwealth* v. *Aves* (1836), Chief Justice Lemuel Shaw applied the principles of *Somerset,* holding that slavery was a creature of municipal law and no laws of Massachusetts would jus-tify the enslavement of anyone except fugitive slaves. Thus Med, a six-year-old slave girl, was free because her owner voluntarily took her into Massachusetts.

In 1852, the Lemmons, who were from Virginia, traveled to New York City to change ships for direct steamboat passage to New Orleans. Although they planned to be in New York for only a day or two, a judge freed their eight slaves. New York businessmen raised money to recompense the Lemmons for the value of their slaves, but the state of Virginia appealed the case. In *Lemmon* v. *The People,* the New York Court of Appeals held that all slaves (except fugitives) became free the moment they entered the state. Citing *Somerset* and *Aves,* the court asserted that

> every sovereign State has a right to determine by its laws the condition of all per-
> sons who may at any time be within its jurisdiction; to exclude therefrom those whose
> introduction would contravene its policy, or to declare the conditions upon which
> they may be received, and. . . . Each State, has, moreover, the right to enact such
> rules as it may see fit respecting the title to property.

The court emphatically denied that "a citizen carries with him, into every State into which he may go, the legal institutions of the one in which he was born."

In dissent, Judge Thomas W. Clerke rhetorically asked: "Is it consistent with this pur-pose of perfect union, and of perfect and unrestricted intercourse, that property which the citizen of one State brings into another State, for the purpose of passing through it to a State where he intends to take up his residence, shall be confiscated in the State through which he is passing, or shall be declared no property . . . ?" Clerke believed that the decision was "wanton aggression" for "mere propagandism." Clerke warned that under international law, the act of New York "would be a valid cause" of war.

Later that year, South Carolina referred to *Lemmon* as one of its reasons for seceding. It is likely that the Taney Court would have overturned this decision, but before that could happen, the national compact fell apart.

SECESSION AND CONSTITUTIONAL THEORY

The nation had hardly begun when some of the politicians had asserted the right of the states to withdraw from the Union. In 1776 Thomas Lynch of South Carolina declared in the Continental Congress that if there was to be a debate over whether slaves were property, the Union would come to an end. At the Constitutional Convention South Carolinians made similar threats. During the War of 1812 New England Federalists at the Hartford Convention suggested they should leave the Union, but such proposals had little support in that region. The most important challenge to the Union before the Civil War came from South Carolina, during the nullification crisis of 1832–1833.

South Carolina Ordinance of Nullification
1 S.C. Statutes at Large 329 (1832)

The nullification crisis began when South Carolina protested the high import duties under the tariff of 1828, also known as the Tariff of Abominations. The protests led to major reductions in the taxes in the tariff of 1832. But by then South Carolinians had become obsessed with issues of state sovereignty and the theory that the states could nullify federal law. Supporters of nullification carried every county in the 1832 election, and Governor James Hamilton called for a special legislative session, which led to a state nullification convention and then to the ordinance of nullification.

Whereas the Congress of the United States, by various acts, purporting to be acts laying duties and imposes on foreign imports, but in reality intended for the protection of domestic manufactures, and the giving of bounties to classes and individuals engaged in particular employments, at the expense and to the injury and oppression of other classes and individuals, and by wholly exempting from taxation certain foreign commodities, such as are not produced or manufactured in the United States, to afford a pretext for imposing higher and excessive duties on articles similar to those intended to be protected, hath exceeded its just powers under the Constitution, which confers on it no authority to afford such protection, and hath violated the true meaning and intent of the Constitution, which provides for equality in imposing the burthens of taxation upon the several States and portions of the Confederacy:—

And whereas the said Congress, exceeding its just power to impose taxes and collect revenue for the purpose of effecting and accomplishing the specific objects and purposes which the Constitution of the United States authorizes it to effect and accomplish, hath raised and collected unnecessary revenue for objects unauthorized by the Constitution:—

We, therefore, the people of the State of South Carolina in Convention assembled, do *declare and ordain,* . . . That the several acts and parts of acts of the Congress of the United Seates, purporting to be laws for the imposing of duties and imposts on the importation of foreign commodities, . . . are unauthorized by the Constitution of the United States, and violate the true meaning and intent thereof, and are null, void, and no law, nor binding upon this State, its officers or citizens; and all promises, contracts, and obligations, made or entered into, or to be made or entered into, with purpose to secure the duties imposed by the said acts, and all judicial proceedings which shall be hereafter had in affirmance thereof, are and shall be held utterly null and void.

And it is further Ordained, That it shall not be lawful for any of the constituted authorities, whether of this State or of the United States, to enforce the payment of duties imposed by the said acts within the limits of this State; but it shall be the duty of the Legislature to adopt such measures and pass such acts as may be necessary to give full effect to this Ordinance, and to prevent the enforcement and arrest the operation of the said acts and parts of acts of the Congress of the United States within the limits of this State, from and after the 1st day of February next, . . .

And it is further Ordained, That in no case of law or equity, decided in the courts of this State, wherein shall be drawn in question the authority of this ordinance, or the validity of such act or acts of the Legislature as may be passed for the purpose of giving effect thereto, or the validity of the aforesaid acts of Congress, imposing duties, shall any appeal be taken or allowed to the Supreme Court of the United States, nor shall any copy of the record be printed or allowed for that purpose; and if any such appeal shall be attempted to be taken, the courts of this State shall proceed to execute and enforce their judgments, according to the laws and usages of the State, without reference to such attempted appeal, and the person or persons attempting to take such appeal may be dealt with as for a contempt of the court.

And it is further Ordained, That all persons now holding any office of honor, profit, or trust, civil or military, under this State, (members of the Legislature excepted), shall, within such time, and in such manner as the Legislature shall prescribe, take an oath well and truly to obey, execute, and enforce, this Ordinance, and such act or acts of the Legislature as may be passed in pursuance thereof, according to the true intent and meaning of the same; and on the neglect or omission of any such person or persons so to do, his or their office or offices shall be forthwith vacated, . . . and no person hereafter elected to any office of honor, profit, or trust, civil or military, (members of the Legislature excepted), shall, until the Legislature shall otherwise provide and direct, enter on the execution of his office, . . . until he shall, in like manner, have taken a similar oath; and no juror shall be empannelled in any of the courts of this State, in any cause in which shall be in question this Ordinance, or any act of the Legislature passed in pursuance thereof, unless he shall first, in addition to the usual oath, have taken an oath that he will well and truly obey, execute, and enforce this Ordinance, and such act or acts of the Legislature as may be passed to carry the same into operation and effect, according to the true intent and meaning thereof.

And we, the People of South Carolina, to the end that it may be fully understood by the Government of the United States, and the people of the co-States, that we are determined to maintain this, our Ordinance and Declaration, at every hazard, Do further Declare that we will not submit to the application of force, on the part of the Federal Government, to reduce this State to obedience; but that we will consider the passage, by Congress, of any act . . . to coerce the State, shut up her ports, destroy or harass her commerce, or to enforce the acts hereby declared to be null and void, otherwise than through the civil tribunals of the country, as inconsistent with the longer continuance of South Carolina in the Union: and that the people of this State will thenceforth hold themselves absolved from all further obligation to maintain or preserve their political connexion with the people of the other States, and will forthwith proceed to organize a separate Government, and do all other acts and things which sovereign and independent States may of right to do.

President Jackson's Proclamation Regarding Nullification
December 10, 1832

President Jackson responded to South Carolina's nullification with barely restrained fury. A native of South Carolina, Jackson had spent almost his entire life in government service. His proclamation was nearly nine thousand words long, running almost forty double-spaced pages. He berated, threatened, and cajoled the people of South Carolina, reminding them of their patriot heritage and warning them of the military force they would face if they persisted in challenging the United States government. At the same time, he offered a powerful constitutional argument against nullification and secession. Less than two decades before this event, Jackson, as a general, had invaded Spanish Florida where he captured and hanged British citizens he believed were conspiring with Indians to harm the United States. Although no longer a young general, the president revealed in this proclamation seemed fully pre-pared to lead an army into South Carolina to hang the leaders of what he considered to be a treasonous rebellion.

Whereas a convention, assembled in the State of South Carolina, have passed an ordinance by which they declare "that the several acts and parts of acts of the Congress of the United States . . . are unauthorized by the Constitution of the United States, and violate the true meaning and intent thereof, and are null and void, and no law," nor binding on the citizens of that State or its officers . . . and

♦   ♦   ♦

Whereas the said ordinance prescribes to the people of South Carolina a course of conduct in direct violation of their duty as citizens of the United States, contrary to the laws of their country, subversive of its Constitution, and having for its object the destruction of the Union . . . that sacred Union, hitherto inviolate, which, perfected by our happy Constitution, has brought us, by the favor of Heaven, to a state of prosperity at home, and high consideration abroad, rarely, if ever, equaled in the history of nations:

To preserve this bond of our political existence from destruction, to maintain inviolate this state of national honor and prosperity, and to justify the confidence my fellow-citizens have reposed in me, I, Andrew Jackson, President of the United States, have thought proper to issue this my proclamation, stating my views of the Constitution and laws applicable to the measures adopted by the Convention of South Carolina . . . declaring the course which duty will require me to pursue, and, appealing to the understanding and patriotism of the people, warn them of the consequences that must inevitably result from an observance of the dictates of the convention.

♦   ♦   ♦

The ordinance is founded, not on the indefeasible right of resisting acts which are plainly unconstitutional, and too oppressive to be endured, but on the strange position that any one State may not only declare an act of Congress void, but prohibit its execution—that they may do this consistently with the Constitution—that the true construction of that instrument permits a State to retain its place in the Union, and yet be bound by no other of its laws than those it may choose to consider as constitutional. . . . [O]ur social compact in express terms declares, that the laws of the United States, its Constitution, and treaties made under it, are the supreme law of the land; and for greater caution adds, "that the judges in every State shall be bound thereby, anything in the Constitution or laws of any State to the contrary notwithstanding." And it may be asserted, without fear of refutation, that no federative government could exist without a similar provision. Look, for a moment, to the consequence. If South Carolina considers the revenue laws unconstitutional, and has a right to prevent their execution in the port of Charleston, there would be a clear constitutional objection to their collection in every other port, and no revenue could be collected anywhere; for all imposts must be equal. . . .

If this doctrine had been established at an earlier day, the Union would have been dissolved in its infancy. The excise law in Pennsylvania, the embargo and non-intercourse law in the Eastern States, the carriage tax in Virginia, were all deemed unconstitutional, and were more unequal in their operation than any of the laws now complained of; but, fortunately, none of those States discovered that they had the right now claimed by South Carolina. The war into which we were forced, to support the dignity of the nation and the rights of our citizens, might have ended in defeat and disgrace instead of victory and honor, if the States, who supposed it a ruinous and unconstitutional measure, had thought they possessed the right of nullifying the act by which it was declared, and denying supplies for its prosecution. Hardly and unequally as those measures bore upon several members of the Union, to the legislatures of none did this efficient and peaceable remedy, as it is called, suggest itself. The discovery of this important feature in our Constitution was reserved to the present day. To the statesmen of South Carolina belongs the invention, and upon the citizens of that State will, unfortunately, fall the evils of reducing it to practice.

◆　◆　◆

[O]ur present happy Constitution was formed, but formed in vain, if this fatal doctrine prevails. It was formed for important objects that are announced in the preamble made in the name and by the authority of the people of the United States, whose delegates framed, and whose conventions approved it. The most important among these objects, that which is placed first in rank, on which all the others rest, is *"to form a more perfect Union."* Now, is it possible that, even if there were no express provision giving supremacy to the Constitution and laws of the United States over those of the States, it can be conceived that an Instrument made for the purpose of *"forming a more perfect Union"* than that of the confederation, could be so constructed by the assembled wisdom of our country as to substitute for that confederation a form of government, dependent for its existence on the local interest, the party spirit of a State, or of a prevailing faction in a State? Every man, of plain, unsophisticated understanding, who hears the question, will give such an answer as will preserve the Union. Metaphysical subtlety, in pursuit of an impracticable theory, could alone have devised one that is calculated to destroy it.

I consider, then, the power to annul a law of the United States, assumed by one State, *incompatible with the existence of the Union, contradicted expressly by the letter of the Constitution, unauthorized by its spirit, inconsistent with every principle on which It was founded, and destructive of the great object for which it was formed.*

◆　◆　◆

We have hitherto relied on it [the Constitution] as the perpetual bond of our Union. We have received it as the work of the assembled wisdom of the nation; we have trusted to it as to the sheet-anchor of our safety, in the stormy times of conflict with a foreign or domestic foe; we have looked to it with sacred awe as the palladium of our liberties, and with all the solemnities of religion have pledged to each other our lives and fortunes here, and our hopes of happiness hereafter, in its defense and support. Were we mistaken, my countrymen, in attaching this importance to the Constitution of our country? Was our devotion paid to the wretched, inefficient, clumsy contrivance, which this new doctrine would make it? Did we pledge ourselves to the support of an airy nothing—a bubble that must be blown away by the first breath of disaffection? Was this self-destroying, visionary theory the work of the profound statesmen, the exalted patriots, to whom the task of constitutional reform was intrusted? Did the name of Washington sanction, did the States deliberately ratify, such an anomaly in the history of fundamental legislation? No; we were not mistaken. The letter of this great instrument is free from this radical fault. Its language directly contradicts the imputation, its spirit, its evident intent, contradicts it. No; we did not err. Our Constitution does not contain the absurdity of giving power to make laws, and another power to resist them. The sages, whose memory will always be reverenced, have given us a practical, and, as they hoped, a permanent constitutional compact. The Father of his Country did not affix his revered name to so palpable an absurdity. Nor did the States, when they severally ratified it, do so under the impression that a veto on the laws of the United States was reserved to them, or that they could exercise it by application. Search the debates in all their conventions—examine the speeches of the most zealous opposers of federal authority—look at the amendments that were proposed. They are all silent—not a syllable uttered, not a vote given, not a motion made, to correct the explicit supremacy given to the laws of the Union over those of the States, or to show that implication, as is now contended, could defeat it. No, we have not erred! The Constitution is still the object of our reverence, the bond of our Union, our defense in danger, the source of our prosperity in peace.

◆   ◆   ◆

The Constitution declares that the judicial powers of the United States extend to cases arising under the laws of the United States, and that such laws, the Constitution and treaties, shall be paramount to the State constitutions and laws. The judiciary act prescribes the mode by which the case may be brought before a court of the United States, by appeal, when a State tribunal shall decide against this provision of the Constitution. The ordinance declares there shall be no appeal—makes the State law paramount to the Constitution and laws of the United States; forces judges and jurors to swear that they will disregard their provisions; and even makes it penal in a suitor to attempt relief by appeal. . . .

Here is a law of the United States, not even pretended to be unconstitutional, repealed by the authority of a small majority of the voters of a single State. Here is a provision of the Constitution which is solemnly abrogated by the same authority.

On such expositions and reasonings, the ordinance grounds not only an assertion of the right to annul the laws of which it complains, but to enforce it by a threat of seceding from the Union if any attempt is made to execute them.

This right to secede is deduced from the nature of the Constitution, which they say is a compact between sovereign States who have preserved their whole sovereignty, and therefore are subject to no superior; that because they made the compact, they can break it when in their opinion it has been departed from by the other States. Fallacious as this course of reasoning is, it enlists State pride, and finds advocates in the honest prejudices of those who have not studied the nature of our government sufficiently to see the radical error on which it rests.

The people of the United States formed the Constitution, acting through the State legislatures, in making the compact, to meet and discuss its provisions, and acting in separate conventions when they ratified those provisions;

but the terms used in its construction show it to be a government in which the people of all the States collectively are represented. We are *one people* in the choice of the President and Vice-President.

◆   ◆   ◆

The States severally have not retained their entire sovereignty. It has been shown that in becoming parts of a nation, not members of a league, they surrendered many of their essential parts of sovereignty. The right to make treaties, declare war, levy taxes, exercise exclusive judicial and legislative powers, were all functions of sovereign power. The States, then, for all these important purposes, were no longer sovereign. The allegiance of their citizens was transferred in the first instance to the government of the United States; they became American citizens, and owed obedience to the Constitution of the United States, and to laws made in conformity with the powers vested in Congress. . . . What shows conclusively that the States cannot be said to have reserved an undivided sovereignty, is that they expressly ceded the right to punish treason—not treason against their separate power, but treason against the United States. Treason is an offense against sovereignty, and sovereignty must reside with the power to punish it. . . . We were the *United States* under the Confederation, and the name as perpetuated and the Union rendered more perfect by the federal Constitution. In none of these stages did we consider ourselves in any other light than as forming one nation. Treaties and alliances were made in the name of all. Troops were raised for the joint defense. How, then, with all these proofs, that under all changes of our position we had, for designated purposes and with defined powers, created national governments—how is it that the most perfect of these several modes of union should now be considered as a mere league that may be dissolved at pleasure? . . .

So obvious are the reasons which forbid this secession, that it is necessary only to allude to them. The Union was formed for the benefit of all. It was produced by mutual sacrifice of interest and opinions. Can those sacrifices be recalled? Can the States, who magnanimously surrendered their title to the territories of the West, recall the grant? Will the inhabitants of the inland States agree to pay the duties that may be imposed without their assent by those on the Atlantic or the Gulf, for their own benefit? Shall there be a free port in one State, and enormous duties in another? No one believes that any right exists in a single State to involve all the others in these and countless other evils, contrary to engagements solemnly made. Everyone must see that the other States, in self-defense, must oppose it at all hazards.

These are the alternatives that are presented by the convention: A repeal of all the acts for raising revenue, leaving the government without the means of support; or an acquiescence in the dissolution of our Union by the secession of one of its members. . . .

This, then, is the position in which we stand. A small majority of the citizens of one State in the Union have elected delegates to a State convention; that convention has ordained that all the revenue laws of the United States must be repealed, or that they are no longer a member of the Union. The governor of that State has recommended to the legislature the raising of an army to carry the secession into effect, and that he may be empowered to give clearances to vessels in the name of the State. No act of violent opposition to the laws has yet been committed, but such a state of things is hourly apprehended, and it is the intent of this instrument to *proclaim*, not only that the duty imposed on me by the Constitution, "to take care that the laws be faithfully executed," shall be performed to the extent of the powers already vested in me by law or of such others as the wisdom of Congress shall devise and Entrust to me for that purpose; but to warn the citizens of South Carolina, who have been deluded into an opposition to the laws, of the danger they will incur by obedience to the illegal and disorganizing ordinance of the convention; to exhort those who have refused to support it to persevere in their determination to uphold the Constitution and laws of their country, and to point out to all the perilous situation into which the good people of that State have been led, and that the course they are urged to pursue is one of ruin and disgrace to the very State whose rights they affect to support.

Fellow-citizens of my native State, let me not only admonish you, as the First Magistrate of our common country, not to incur the penalty of its laws, but use the influence that a father would over his children whom he saw rushing to a certain ruin. In that paternal language, with that paternal feeling, let me tell you, my countrymen, that you are deluded by men who are either deceived themselves or wish to deceive you. . . . Eloquent appeals to your passions, to your State pride, to your native courage, to your sense of real injury, were used to prepare you for the period when the mask which concealed the hideous features of *disunion* should be taken off. It fell, and you were made to look with complacency on objects which not long since you would have regarded with horror. Look back to the arts which have brought you to this state; look forward to the consequences to which it must inevitably lead! . . . Ponder well on this circumstance, and you will know how to appreciate the exaggerated language they [the leaders of the Nullification movement] address to you. They are not champions of liberty emulating the fame of our Revolutionary fathers, nor are you an oppressed people, contending, as they repeat to you, against worse than colonial vassalage. You are free members of a flourishing and happy Union. There is no settled design to oppress you. . . .

. . . Contemplate the condition of that country of which you still form an important part; consider its government uniting in one bond of common interest and general protection so many different States—giving to all their inhabitants the proud title of *American citizen*, protecting their commerce—securing their literature and arts—facilitating their intercommunication, defending their frontiers, and making their name respected in the remotest parts of the earth. Consider the extent of its territory, its increasing and happy population, its advance in arts, which render life agreeable, and the sciences which elevate the mind! See education spreading the lights of religion, morality, and general information into every cottage in this wide extent of our Territories and States. Behold it as the asylum where the wretched and the oppressed find a refuge and support! Look on this picture of happiness and honor. . . . For what do you throw away these inestimable blessings? For what would you exchange your share in the advantages and honor of the Union? For the dream of a separate independence—a dream interrupted by bloody conflicts with your neighbors, and a vile dependence on a foreign power. If your leaders could succeed in establishing a separation, what would be your situation? Are you united at home? Are you free from the apprehension of civil discord, with all its fearful consequences? Do our neighboring republics, every day suffering some new revolution or contending with some new insurrection, do they excite your envy? But the dictates of a high duty oblige me solemnly to announce that you cannot succeed. The laws of the United States must be executed. I have no discretionary power on the subject—my duty is emphatically pronounced in the Constitution. Those who told you that you might peaceably prevent their execution, deceived you—they could not have been deceived themselves. They know that a forcible opposition could alone prevent the execution of the laws, and they know that such opposition must be repelled. Their object is disunion, but be not deceived by names; disunion, by armed force, is *treason*. Are you really ready to incur its guilt? . . . On your unhappy State will inevitably fall all the evils of the conflict you force upon the government of your country. It cannot accede to the mad project of disunion, of which you would be the first victims. Its First Magistrate can not, if he would, avoid the performance of his duty. The consequence

must be fearful for you, distressing to your fellow-citizens here, and to the friends of good government throughout the world. Its enemies have beheld our prosperity with a vexation they could not conceal; it was a standing refutation of their slavish doctrines, and they will point to our discord with the triumph of malignant joy. It is yet in your power to disappoint them. There is yet time to show that the descendants of the Pinckneys, the Sumpters, the Rutledges, and of the thousand other names which adorn the pages of your Revolutionary history, will not abandon that Union to support which so many of them fought and bled and died. I adjure you, as you honor their memory, as you love the cause of freedom, to which they dedicated their lives, as you prize the peace of your country, the lives of its best citizens, and your own fair fame, to retrace your steps.

◆ ◆ ◆

Fellow-citizens, the momentous case is before you. On your undivided support of your government depends the decision of the great question it involves, whether your sacred Union will be preserved, and the blessing it secures to us as one people shall be perpetuated. No one can doubt that the unanimity with which that decision will be expressed, will he such as to inspire new confidence in republican institutions, and that the prudence, the wisdom, and the courage which it will bring to their defense, will transmit them unimpaired and invigorated to our children.

NULLIFICATION AND SECESSION

In response to Jackson's proclamation and his threat to use military force to suppress South Carolina's incipient rebellion, the state repealed its ordinance of nullification. However, defiant to the end, the state adopted a new series of resolutions, including one that asserted

> that each state of the Union has the right, whenever it may deem such a course necessary for the preservation of its liberties or vital interests, to secede peaceably from the Union, and that there is no constitutional power in the general government, much less in the executive department, of that government, to retain by force such state in the Union.

Such claims remained entirely theoretical from 1833 until 1860. However, during Lincoln's campaign for the presidency, South Carolinians and other southern nationalists began to revive the arguments of the nullification crisis and the theories of John C. Calhoun that the states were sovereign members of a compact and could withdraw from the compact at will.

Throughout his presidential campaign, Lincoln reiterated that the federal government could not interfere with slavery in the states where it already existed. Lincoln also indicated that although he thought the fugitive slave law might be unjust, he was prepared to enforce it as he would any other federal law.

Proslavery ideologues ignored such statements and focused on Lincoln's opposition both to slavery in the territories and to the admission to the Union of any new slave states. Shortly after Lincoln's election, South Carolina elected a convention that unanimously endorsed secession. South Carolina justified secession by arguing that Lincoln's "opinions and purposes" were "hostile to slavery."

President James Buchanan rejected this theory and agreed with Republicans that secession was illegal. But as a states'-rights Democrat (with strong southern sympathies), Buchanan also took no steps to stop secession. He believed that the federal government lacked the power to interfere with the states, even if they left the Union.

The Supreme Court supported this position in *Kentucky* v. *Dennison* (1861) by refusing to order Ohio to return a fugitive from justice who was wanted for having helped a slave escape from Kentucky. Taney had no sympathy for the free black—Willis Lago—who had helped a slave escape from Kentucky. Nor did he support the Ohio governor's antislavery position. Taney agreed with Kentucky that Lago was a slave stealer who should be properly tried in Kentucky. But Chief Justice Taney nevertheless concluded that the criminal extradition clause of the Constitution "is left to depend on the fidelity of the State Executive to the compact entered into with the other States when it adopted the Constitution" and that there was "no power delegated to the General Government . . . to use any coercive means to compel" a state governor to act. Delivered just before the Civil War began, Taney's opinion was obviously meant to deny Lincoln the power to coerce states back into the Union.

Upon taking office, Lincoln declared that the Union was "perpetual" and took actions to resupply Union troops stationed along the south Atlantic coast. Rather than allow Fort Sumter in Charleston Harbor to be resupplied, South Carolina authorities fired on it. For the next four years, the theory of secession was tested in a trial by battle. When the Civil War ended, all but one of the defeated Confederate states renounced secession; South Carolina, defiant to the end, merely repealed its ordinance of secession.

Declaration of the Immediate Causes Which Induce and Justify the Secession of South Carolina
December 24, 1860

Between the election of Lincoln in November 1860 and his inauguration in March 1861, seven states adopted ordinances of secession and declared they were no longer members of the Union. After the Civil War began, four more states left the Union. Immediately after Lincoln's election, South Carolina resurrected the popularly elected convention, previously used in the nullification crisis of 1832–1833, to consider secession. On December 24, this convention voted to leave the Union.

We hold that the Government . . . established [by the Constitution] is subject to the . . . fundamental principle, namely: the law of compact. We maintain that in every compact between two or more parties, the obligation is mutual; that the failure of one of the contracting parties to perform a material part of the agreement, entirely releases the obligation of the other; and that where no arbiter is provided, each party is remitted to his own judgment to determine the fact of failure, with all its consequences.

In the present case, that fact is established with certainty. We assert that fourteen of the States have deliberately refused, for years past, to fulfill their constitutional obligations, and we refer to their own Statutes for the proof.

The Constitution of the United States, in its fourth Article, provides as follows:

"No person held to service or labor in one State, under the laws thereof, escaping into another, shall, in consequence of any law or regulation therein, be discharged from such service or labor, but shall be delivered up, on claim of the party to whom such service or labor may be due."

This stipulation was so material to the compact, that without it that compact would not have been made. The greater number of the contracting parties held slaves, and they had previously evinced their estimate of the value of such a stipulation by making it a condition in the Ordinance for the government of the territory ceded by Virginia, which now composes the States north of the Ohio River.

♦ ♦ ♦

The General Government, as the common agent, passed laws to carry into effect these stipulations of the States. For many years these laws were executed. But an increasing hostility on the part of the non-slaveholding States to the institution of slavery, has led to a disregard of their obligations, and the laws of the General Government have ceased to effect the objects of the Constitution. The States of Maine, New Hampshire, Vermont, Massachusetts, Connecticut, Rhode Island, New York, Pennsylvania, Illinois, Indiana, Michigan, Wisconsin and Iowa, have enacted laws which either nullify the Acts of Congress or render useless any attempt to execute them. In many of these States the fugitive is discharged from the service or labor claimed, and in none of them has the State Government complied with the stipulation made in the Constitution. . . . In the State of New York even the right of transit for a slave has been denied by her tribunals; and the States of Ohio and Iowa have refused to surrender to justice fugitives charged with murder, and with inciting servile insurrection in the State of Virginia. Thus the constituted compact has been deliberately broken and disregarded by the non-slaveholding States, and the consequence follows that South Carolina is released from her obligation.

♦ ♦ ♦

[In the Constitution, the] right of property in slaves was recognized by giving to free persons distinct political rights, by giving them the right to represent, and burthening them with direct taxes for three-fifths of their slaves; by authorizing the importation of slaves for twenty years; and by stipulating for the rendition of fugitives from labor.

We affirm that these ends for which this Government was instituted have been defeated, and the Government itself has been made destructive of them by the action of the non-slaveholding States. Those States have assumed the right of deciding upon the propriety of our domestic institutions; and have denied the rights of property established in fifteen of the States and recognized by the Constitution; they have denounced as sinful the institution of slavery; they have permitted the open establishment among them of societies, whose avowed object is to disturb the peace and to eloign the property of the citizens of other States. They have encouraged and assisted thousands of our slaves to leave their homes; and those who remain, have been incited by emissaries, books and pictures to servile insurrection.

For twenty-five years this agitation has been steadily increasing, until it has now secured to its aid the power of the common Government. Observing the forms of the Constitution, a sectional party has found within that Article establishing the Executive Department, the means of subverting the Constitution itself. A geographical line has been drawn across the Union, and all the States north of that line have united in the election of a man to the high office of President of the United States, whose opinions and purposes are hostile to slavery. He is to be entrusted with the administration of the common Government, because he has declared that that "Government cannot endure permanently half slave, half free," and that the public mind must rest in the belief that slavery is in the course of ultimate extinction.

This sectional combination for the submersion of the Constitution has been aided in some of the States by elevating to citizenship, persons who, by the supreme law of the land, are incapable of becoming citizens; and their votes have been used to inaugurate a new policy, hostile to the South, and destructive of its beliefs and safety.

On the 4th of March next, this party will take possession of the Government. It has announced that the South shall be excluded from the common territory, that the judicial tribunals shall be made sectional and that a war must be waged against slavery until it shall cease throughout the United States.

The guaranties of the Constitution will then no longer exist; the equal rights of the States will be lost. The slaveholding States will no longer have the power of self-government, or self-protection, and the Federal Government will have become their enemy.

◆ ◆ ◆

We, therefore, the People of South Carolina, by our delegates Convention assembled, appealing to the Supreme Judge of the world for the rectitude of our intentions, have solemnly declared that the Union heretofore existing between this State and the other States of North America, is dissolved, and that the State of South Carolina has resumed her position among the nations of the world, as a separate and independent State; with full power to levy war, conclude peace, contract alliances, establish commerce, and to do all other acts and things which independent States may of right do.

ABRAHAM LINCOLN

First Inaugural Address
March 4, 1861

Upon taking office, Lincoln faced the greatest crisis in the nation's history. Seven states had seceded, and civil war seemed likely. Although personally opposed to slavery, Lincoln had made it clear throughout his campaign that he posed no threat to slavery where it already existed. While seeking peace, Lincoln was determined to preserve the Union and not to back down from his commitment to prevent the spread of slavery to the western territories.

Fellow citizens of the United States:

◆ ◆ ◆

Apprehension seems to exist among the people of the Southern States, that by the accession of a Republican Administration, their property, and their peace, and personal security, are to be endangered. There has never been any reasonable cause for such apprehension. Indeed, the most ample evidence to the contrary has all the while existed, and been open to their inspection. It is found in nearly all [my] published speeches. . . . I do but quote from one of those speeches when I declare that "I have no purpose, directly or indirectly, to interfere with the institution of slavery in the States where it exists. I believe I have no lawful right to do so, and I have no inclination to do so." Those who nominated and elected me did so with full knowledge that I had made this, and many similar declarations, and had never recanted them. And more than this, they placed in the platform . . . [this] clear and emphatic resolution. . . .

"*Resolved,* That the maintenance inviolate

of the rights of the States, and especially the right of each State to order and control its own domestic institutions according to its own judgment exclusively, is essential to that balance of power on which the perfection and endurance of our political fabric depend; and we denounce the lawless invasions by armed force of the soil of any State or Territory, no matter under what pretext, as among the gravest of crimes."

I now reiterate these sentiments: and in doing so, I only press upon the public attention the most conclusive evidence of which the case is susceptible, that the property, peace and security of no section are to be in anywise endangered by the now incoming Administration. I add too, that all the protection which, consistently with the Constitution and the laws, can be given, will be cheerfully given to all the States when lawfully demanded, for whatever cause—as cheerfully to one section, as to another.

♦ ♦ ♦

I hold that in contemplation of universal law, and of the Constitution, the Union of these States is perpetual. Perpetuity is implied, if not expressed, in the fundamental law of all national governments. It is safe to assert that no government power, ever had a provision in its organic law for its own termination. Continue to execute all the express provisions of our national Constitution, and the Union will endure forever—it being impossible to destroy it, except by some action not provided for in the instrument itself.

♦ ♦ ♦

Descending from these general principles, we find the proposition that, in legal contemplation, the Union is perpetual, confirmed by the history of the Union itself. The Union is much older than the Constitution. It was formed in fact, by the Articles of Association in 1774. It was matured and continued by the Declaration of Independence in 1776. It was further matured and the faith of all the then thirteen States expressly plighted and engaged that it should be perpetual, by the Articles of Confederation in 1778. And finally, in 1787, one of the declared objects for ordaining and establishing the Constitution, was *"to form a more perfect union."*

But if destruction of the Union, by one, or by a part only, of the States, be lawfully possible, the Union is *less* perfect than before the Constitution, having lost the vital element of perpetuity.

It follows from these views that no State, upon its own mere motion, can lawfully get out of the Union,—that *resolves* and *ordinances* to that effect are legally void; and that acts of violence, within any State or States, against the authority of the United States, are insurrectionary or revolutionary. . . .

I therefore consider that, in view of the Constitution and the laws, the Union is unbroken; and, to the extent of my ability, I shall take care, as the Constitution itself expressly enjoins upon me, that the laws of the Union be faithfully executed in all the States. Doing this I deem to be only a simple duty on my part; and I shall perform it, so far as practicable, unless my rightful masters, the American people, shall withhold the requisite means, or, in some authoritative manner, direct the contrary. I trust this will not be regarded as a menace, but only as the declared purpose of the Union that it *will* constitutionally defend, and maintain itself.

In doing this there needs to be no bloodshed or violence; and there shall be none, unless it be forced upon the national authority. The power confided to me, will be used to hold, occupy, and possess the property, and places belonging to the government, and to collect the duties and imposts; but beyond what may be necessary for these objects, there will be no invasion—no using of force against, or among the people anywhere. Where hostility to the United States, in any interior locality, shall be so great and so universal, as to prevent competent resident citizens from holding the Federal offices, there will be no attempt to force obnoxious strangers among the people for that object. While the strict legal right may exist in the government to enforce the exercise of these offices, the attempt to do so would be so irritating, and so nearly impracticable with all, that I deem it better to forgo, for the time, the uses of such offices.

That there are persons in one section, or another who seek to destroy the Union at all events, and are glad of any pretext to do it . . . I need address no word to them. To those, however, who really love the Union, may I not speak?

Before entering upon so grave a matter as the destruction of our national fabric, with all its benefits, its memories, and its hopes, would it not be wise to ascertain precisely why we do it? Will you hazard so desperate a step, while there is any possibility that any portion of the ills you fly from, have no real existence? Will you, while the certain ills you fly to, are greater than all the real ones you fly from? Will you risk the commission of so fearful a mistake?

All profess to be content in the Union, if all constitutional rights can be maintained. Is it true, then, that any right, plainly written in the Constitution, has been denied? I think not. . . . Think, if you can, of a single instance in which a plainly written provision of the Constitution has ever been denied. . . . Shall fugitives from labor be surrendered by national or by State authority? The Constitution does not expressly say. *May* Congress prohibit slavery in the territories? The Constitution does not expressly say. *Must* congress protect slavery in the territories? The Constitution does not expressly say.

♦ ♦ ♦

Plainly, the central idea of secession, is the essence of anarchy. A majority, held in restraint by constitutional checks, and limitations, and always changing easily, with deliberate changes of popular opinions and sentiments, is the only true sovereign of a free people. Whoever rejects it, does, of necessity, fly to anarchy or to despotism. Unanimity is impossible; the rule of a minority, as a permanent arrangement, is wholly inadmissible; so that, rejecting the majority principle, anarchy, or despotism . . . is all that is left.

I do not forget the position assumed by some, that constitutional questions are to be decided by the Supreme Court; nor do I deny that such decisions must be binding in any case, upon the parties to a suit, as to the object of that suit, while they are also entitled to very high respect and consideration, in all parallel cases, by all other departments of the government. And while it is obviously possible that such de-

cision may be erroneous in any given case, still the evil effect following it, being limited to that particular case, with the chance that it may be over-ruled, and never become a precedent for other cases, can better be borne than could the evils of a different practice. At the same time the candid citizen must confess that if the policy of the government, upon vital questions, affecting the whole people, is to be irrevocably fixed by decisions of the Supreme Court, the instant they are made, in ordinary litigation between parties, in personal actions, the people will have ceased, to be their own rulers, having, to that extent, practically resigned their government, into the hands of that eminent tribunal. Nor is there, in this view, any assault upon the court, or the judges. It is a duty, from which they may not shrink, to decide cases properly brought before them; and it is no fault of theirs, if others seek to turn their decisions to political purposes.

One section of our country believes slavery is right, and ought to be extended, while the other believes it is wrong, and ought not to be extended. This is the only substantial dispute. The fugitive slave clause of the Constitution, and the law for the suppression of the foreign slave trade, are each as well enforced, perhaps, as any law can ever be in a community where the moral sense of the people imperfectly supports the law itself. The great body of the people abide by the dry legal obligation in both cases, and a few break over in each. This, I think, cannot be perfectly cured; and it would be worse in both cases after the separation of the sections, than before. The foreign slave trade, now imperfectly suppressed, would be ultimately revived without restriction, in one section; while fugitive slaves, now only partially surrendered, would not be surrendered at all, by the other.

Physically speaking, we cannot separate. We cannot remove our respective sections from each other, nor build an impassable wall between them. A husband and wife may be divorced, and go out of the presence, and beyond the reach of each other; but the different parts of our country cannot do this. They cannot but remain face to face; and intercourse, either amicable or hostile, must continue between them.

Is it possible then to make that intercourse more advantageous, or more satisfactory, after separation than before? Can aliens make treaties easier than friends can make laws? Can treaties be more faithfully enforced between aliens, than laws can among friends? Suppose you go to war, you cannot fight always; and when, after much loss on both sides, and no gain on either, you cease fighting, the identical old questions, as to terms of intercourse, are again upon you.

♦ ♦ ♦

While the people retain their virtue, and vigilance, no administration, by any extreme of wickedness or folly, can very seriously injure the government, in the short space of four years.

My countrymen, one and all, think calmly and well, upon this whole subject. Nothing valuable can be lost by taking time. If there be an object to hurry any of you, in hot haste, to a step which you would never take deliberately, that object will be frustrated by taking time; but no good object can be frustrated by it. Such of you as are now dissatisfied, still have the old Constitution unimpaired, and, on the sensitive point, the laws of your own framing under it;

while the new administration will have no immediate power, if it would, to change either. If it were admitted that you who are dissatisfied, hold the right side in the dispute, there still is no single good reason for precipitate action. Intelligence, patriotism, Christianity, and a firm reliance on Him, who has never yet forsaken this favored land, are still competent to adjust, in the best way, all our present difficulty.

In your hands, my dissatisfied fellow countrymen, and not in mine, is the momentous issue of civil war. The government will not assail you. You can have no conflict, without being yourselves the aggressors. You have no oath registered in Heaven to destroy the government, while I shall have the most solemn one to "preserve, protect and defend" it.

I am loth to close. We are not enemies, but friends. We must not be enemies. Though passion may have strained, it must not break our bonds of affection. The mystic chords of memory, stretching from every battlefield, and patriot grave, to every living heart and hearthstone, all over this broad land, will yet swell the chorus of the Union, when again touched, as surely they will be, by the better angels of our nature.

THE CIVIL WAR AND EMANCIPATION

During the Civil War, the president and Congress discovered new solutions to the problems that caused the war and to those that were created by the war. What could not be accomplished legally in peacetime became possible during the war. The president, Congress, and the army were the chief actors in shaping constitutional developments.

At the beginning of the war, Lincoln unilaterally suspended habeas corpus while Congress was not in session. Acting in his capacity as a circuit judge, Chief Justice Taney, in *Ex parte Merryman* (1861), declared Lincoln's suspension of habeas corpus unconstitutional. Lincoln ignored Taney's order to release the Confederate activist Merryman. Congress subsequently ratified Lincoln's actions with the Habeas Corpus Act of 1863. After the *Merryman* case, all the federal courts showed enormous deference to the administration. In the *Prize Cases* (1863), the Supreme Court affirmed Lincoln's unilateral use of a blockade against southern ports. In *Ex parte Vallandingham* (1864), the Court refused to intervene on behalf of a civilian arrested, tried, and sentenced by a military tribunal.

The greatest legal change of the Civil War era was the conversion of billions of dollars worth of slave property into millions of free citizens of the nation. In April 1862, Congress ended slavery in the District of Columbia through compensated emancipation. In June, Congress rejected the *Dred Scott* precedent by abolishing slavery in the territories. In July, Congress took the first step toward black citizenship by granting blacks the right to testify in all court cases in the nation's capital. No one challenged these laws in the courts. It is likely that the Supreme Court, with Taney still the chief justice, would have sided with the slaveholders in such a case, but no one doubted that Lincoln and Congress would have ignored the Court on this issue. In 1862, Congress also passed the Second Confiscation Act, which declared forever free the slaves of certain rebellious masters and authorized the use of black troops. The Supreme Court would uphold this law in *Miller* v. *United States* (1870).

Many of the constitutional developments of the Civil War are extraordinarily ironic. Before the war, the South accused Lincoln of wanting to destroy slavery, while Lincoln claimed he had no plans and no power to take such an action. But during the war, both the president and Congress found powers to do what could not have been done in peacetime. Secession and war became self-fulfilling prophecies for the South. By leaving the Union, Southerners gave the Republicans a majority in Congress they would never have had otherwise. By fighting the war, the South gave Lincoln powers he never dreamed of before 1861. The war began as a revolution by the South, and ended as a revolution in constitutional law, race relations, and national power.

ABRAHAM LINCOLN

The Emancipation Proclamation
January 1, 1863

Although few slaves actually gained their freedom under the law, the Second Confiscation Act and congressional abolition in federal jurisdictions set the stage for the Emancipation Proclamation, which Lincoln secretly drafted in July 1862. In August, Lincoln publicly denied any plans for emancipation, but on September 22, 1862, acting as commander-in-chief, Lincoln issued the Preliminary Emancipation Proclamation, declaring that it would go into effect in one hundred days.

Now, therefore I, Abraham Lincoln, President of the United States, by virtue of the power in me vested as Commander-in-Chief, of the Army and Navy of the United States in time of actual armed rebellion against authority and government of the United States, and as a fit and necessary war measure for suppressing said rebellion, do, on this first day of January, in the year of our Lord one thousand eight hundred and sixty three, and in accordance with my purpose so to do publicly proclaimed for the full period of one hundred days, from the day first above mentioned, order and designate as the States and parts of States wherein the people thereof respectively, are this day in rebellion against the United States, the following, to wit:

Arkansas, Texas, Louisiana, (except [thirteen listed Parishes] . . . including the City of New-Orleans) Mississippi, Alabama, Florida, Georgia, South-Carolina, North-Carolina, and Virginia, (except the forty-eight counties designated as West Virginia, and also [seven listed counties] . . . [)]; and which excepted parts are, for the present, left precisely as if this proclamation were not issued.

And by virtue of the power, and for the purpose aforesaid, I do order and declare that all persons held as slaves within said designated States, and parts of States, are, and henceforward shall be free; and that the Executive government of the United States, including the military and naval authorities thereof, will recognize and maintain the freedom of said persons. And I hereby enjoin upon the people so declared to be free to abstain from all violence, unless in necessary self-defence; and I recommend to them that, in all cases when allowed, they labor faithfully for reasonable wages.

And I further declare and make known, that such persons of suitable condition, will be received into the armed service of the United States to garrison forts, positions, stations, and other places, and to man vessels of all sorts in said service.

And upon this act, sincerely believed to be an act of justice, warranted by the Constitution, upon military necessity, I invoke the considerate judgment of mankind, and the gracious favor of Almighty God.

Note: The Effect of the Emancipation Proclamation

The Emancipation Proclamation applied only to areas of the nation that were under Confederate control. Thus it emancipated no slaves when issued. However, each movement of Union troops farther south resulted in the emancipation of more slaves. From 1863 to 1865, the Union Army became the actual emancipator of millions of slaves. In 1864, Congress sent to the states the Thirteenth Amendment, declaring that "neither slavery nor involuntary servitude . . . shall exist within the United States." When ratified in 1865, this amendment ended slavery everywhere in the nation. Meanwhile, between 1863 and 1865 many slave owners in the border states allowed their male slaves to enlist in the army. The owner usually claimed the enlistment bounty, while the slave gained his freedom and the opportunity to fight for the freedom of all American slaves.

ABRAHAM LINCOLN

Second Inaugural Address
March 4, 1865

Lincoln's Second Inaugural Address is a masterpiece of political writing. Lincoln sketched out an agenda for Reconstruction by attributing the underlying cause of the war to slavery and by stressing the shared heritage of Northerners and Southerners. Thus the inaugural set the stage for ending all vestiges of slavery and for bringing the nation back together with "malice toward none" and with "charity for all."

On the occasion corresponding to this four years ago all thoughts were anxiously directed to an impending civil war. All dreaded it, all sought to avert it. While the inaugural address was being delivered from this place, devoted altogether to saving the Union without war, insurgent agents were in the city seeking to destroy it without war—seeking to dissolve the Union and divide effects by negotiation. Both parties deprecated war, but one of them would make war rather than let the nation survive, and the other would accept war rather than let it perish, and the war came.

One-eighth of the whole population were colored slaves, not distributed generally over the Union, but localized in the southern part of it. These slaves constituted a peculiar and powerful interest. All knew that this interest was somehow the cause of the war. To strengthen, perpetuate, and extend this interest was the object for which the insurgents would rend the Union even by war, while the Government claimed no right to do more than to restrict the territorial enlargement of it. Neither party expected for the war the magnitude or the duration which it has already attained. Neither anticipated that the cause of the conflict might cease with or even before the conflict itself should cease. Each looked for an easier triumph, and a result less fundamental and astounding. Both read the same Bible and pray to the same God, and each invokes His aid against the other. It may seem strange that any men should dare to ask a just God's assistance in wringing their bread from the sweat of other men's faces, but let us judge not, that we be not judged. The prayers of both could not be answered. That of neither has been answered fully. The Almighty has His own purposes. "Woe unto the world because of offenses; for it must needs be that offenses come, but woe to that man by whom the offense cometh." If we shall suppose that American slavery is one of those offenses which, in the providence of God, must needs come, but which, having continued through His appointed time, He now wills to remove, and that He gives to both North and South this terrible war as the woe due to those by whom the offense came, shall we discern therein any departure from those divine attrib-

utes which the believers in a living God always ascribe to Him? Fondly do we hope, fervently do we pray, that this mighty scourge of war may speedily pass away. Yet, if God wills that it continue until all the wealth piled by the bondsman's two hundred and fifty years of unrequited toil shall be sunk, and until every drop of blood drawn with the lash shall be paid by another drawn with the sword, as was said three thousand years ago, so still it must be said "the judgments of the Lord are true and righteous altogether."

With malice toward none, with charity for all, with firmness in the right as God gives us to see the right, let us strive on to finish the work we are in, to bind up the nation's wounds, to care for him who shall have borne the battle and for his widow and his orphan, to do all which may achieve and cherish a just and lasting peace among ourselves and with all nations.

RECONSTRUCTION AND ITS AFTERMATH: POLITICAL CHANGE, BLACK FREEDOM, AND THE NADIR OF BLACK RIGHTS

Peace brought as many complex constitutional and legal problems as had the war. The nation could not re-create itself into the antebellum federal system, with the states retaining great power. A new federalism had emerged that made the states unambiguously subordinate to the national government. State sovereignty was forever dead; the concept of states' rights remained, but it had been weakened and altered by the war. One price of peace was the repudiation of secession.

A second price was the recognition of the end of slavery. Emancipation had been accomplished by congressional action, presidential proclamation, and Union military success. The federal government demanded that the former Confederate states accept and endorse this change in their new state constitutions and with their ratification of the Thirteenth Amendment.

But what was to happen to the ex-slaves? Were they to be left to the mercies of their defeated masters? Were they to be enfranchised and made full citizens? Who would protect them from exploitation and violence? How would they feed themselves, gain an economic foothold, acquire an education? Such questions puzzled the victorious Republicans as they began to reconstruct the Union.

Complicating this task was the assassination of Lincoln and the ascension of Andrew Johnson, a native Southerner who disliked slavery and had been a political opponent of the planter elite in Tennessee, but who also despised blacks. Johnson's views of black freedom were not in tune with those of most Republicans or most Northerners. Even by the standards of the 1860s, Johnson was a thoroughgoing racist. Poorly educated, unsophisticated, intemperate, and stubborn, Johnson's behavior would lead to his impeachment. More important, his policies undermined the "new birth of freedom" that Lincoln had spoken of shortly before his death.

Central to Reconstruction were the Thirteenth, Fourteenth, and Fifteenth Amendments. Debate still rages over the purpose or "intent" of these amendments. Historians Harold Hyman and William M. Wiecek have persuasively argued that the Thirteenth Amendment was designed to do more than end slavery: it was a statement of "protection" guaranteed by the federal government "from involuntary servitude and violence" and a promise "of all the full and equal rights of freedom, some of which history had identified and a multitude of which remained for the inscrutable future to reveal."[3] The enforcement provision of the amendment—the first in the Constitution—particularly troubled Southerners because it implied open-ended federal power to protect the freedmen and to regulate race relations. Congress quickly exercised power under the enforcement clause to protect the basic rights of the freedmen, through the Civil Rights Act of 1866, enacting it over President Johnson's veto.

The Thirteenth Amendment was the beginning of the process of constitutionalizing the revolution in federalism and race relations. The Fourteenth Amendment contained an enforcement provision as well, along with open-ended language guaranteeing the freedmen "privileges and immunities," "due process," and "equal protection of the law." We can never know exactly what the authors of this amendment had in mind. They probably did not completely know themselves. But, at a minimum, the framers of the two amendments believed they were expanding the Bill of Rights to the states and giving Congress broad plenary power to protect both civil rights and civil liberties throughout the nation. The Fifteenth Amendment, ratified in 1870, was designed to prohibit voting discrimination based on race.

Congress passed civil rights acts in 1866 and 1875 and various other laws to protect black freedom. The Supreme Court, however, failed to appreciate the revolution in law that the Civil War and Reconstruction produced. Too often, the justices looked at congressional actions through the lens of antebellum legal theory, rather than through the expansive language of the new amendments. Uncomfortable with the revolution in federalism and race relations, the Court interpreted the new amendments in constricted and narrow ways.

By the end of the century, the Court had abandoned the freedmen to the tender mercies of southern white politicians. The results were political disfranchisement, legal isolation, economic peonage, and segregation everywhere. This was "the Nadir" of American black life, the "Betrayal of the Negro" by Congress and the courts, and the betrayal of the principles of the Reconstruction amendments.[4]

POLITICAL CHANGE

With the Union preserved, the overwhelming political question facing the nation was how the Union should be reconstructed. Was Congress or the president to set policy? Should the southern states be readmitted quickly to encourage reconciliation, or should the former Confederate states be denied full political self-determination until they had fully accepted the consequences of the war, including black freedom, citizenship, and equality?

Starting in Louisiana in late 1863, Lincoln sought to impose a Reconstruction program through provisional governments under his control. Lincoln wanted a speedy Reconstruction, but Republican congressional leaders opposed it and refused to seat senators and congressmen elected by the reconstructed states in 1864 and 1865.

The conflict between Congress and the president turned to open warfare under Andrew Johnson. Johnson consistently attempted to thwart Congress, often by failing to implement Reconstruction acts passed over his intemperate and unnecessarily antagonistic vetoes. He arbitrarily fired a large number of local federal officeholders in a clumsy attempt to control northern state politics. Johnson angered Congress by pardoning many former Confederates and pressing for a quick Reconstruction of the South. Johnson's racism and hostility to black rights endangered the lives of blacks and white Unionists in the South. His policies had

> a staggering effect on the South. He converted a conquered people, bitter but ready to accept the consequences of defeat, into a hostile, aggressive, uncooperative unit. He restored them to political and economic power . . . [allowing them to dominate] the men and women they had recently held as slaves. He had set back the work of Reconstruction, as it turned out, two full years.[5]

Johnson undermined the Freedmen's Bureau, the 1866 Civil Rights Act, and other congressionally mandated policies and programs. He placated southern whites while ignoring the plight of southern blacks. In July 1866, Johnson overruled Philip Sheridan when the general removed from office local officials who were responsible for "the absolute massacre" in New Orleans of black army veterans and Republican delegates to the Louisiana Constitutional Convention. Another general complained that Johnson's policy of overruling military commanders led to "barbarism" in Louisiana and throughout the South. To curb Johnson's obstruction of its will, Congress passed the Tenure of Office Act in 1867, barring Johnson from removing various federal officials until the Senate confirmed their replacements. This law was aimed at preventing the removal of Secretary of War Edwin Stanton, an ally of Congress and a supporter of black rights. In February 1868, Johnson nevertheless removed Stanton from office, which was the final event before his impeachment.

Articles of Impeachment of Andrew Johnson
March 2 and 3, 1868

Articles exhibited by the House of Representatives of the United States, in the name of themselves and all the people of the United States, against Andrew Johnson, President of the United States, in maintenance and support of their impeachment against him for high crimes and misdemeanors in office.

Article I. That said Andrew Johnson, President of the United States, on the 21st day of February, A.D. 1868 . . . unmindful of the high duties of his office, of his oath of office, and of the requirement of the Constitution that he should take care that the laws be faithfully executed, did unlawfully and in violation of the Constitution and laws of the United States issue an order in writing for the removal of Edwin M. Stanton from the office of Secretary for the Department of War, . . . and . . . on the 12th day of December, in the year last aforesaid—

having reported to said Senate such suspension, with the evidence and reasons for his action in the case . . . and said Senate thereafterwards, on the 13th day of January, A.D. 1868, having duly considered the evidence and reasons reported by said Andrew Johnson for said suspension, and having refused to concur in said suspension, whereby and by force of the provisions of an act entitled "An act regulating the tenure of certain civil offices," passed March 2, 1867, said Edwin M. Stanton did forthwith resume the functions of his office, whereof the said Andrew Johnson . . . unlawfully issued with intent then and there to violate . . . [the Tenure of Office Act], and with the further intent, contrary to the provisions of said act, in violation thereof, and contrary to the provisions of the Constitution of the United States, and without the advice and consent of the Senate of the United States . . . to remove said Edwin M.

Stanton from the office of the Secretary for the Department of War, the said Edwin M. Stanton being then and there Secretary for the Department of War, . . . whereby said Andrew Johnson, President of the United States, did then and there commit and was guilty of a high misdemeanor in office.

♦ ♦ ♦

Art. X. That said Andrew Johnson, President of the United States, unmindful of the high duties of his office and the dignity and proprieties thereof, and of the harmony and courtesies which ought to exist and be maintained between the executive and legislative branches of the Government of the United States, designing and intending to set aside the rightful authority and powers of Congress, did attempt to bring into disgrace, ridicule, hatred, contempt, and reproach the Congress of the United States and the several branches thereof, to impair and destroy the regard and respect of all the good people of the United States for the Congress and legislative power thereof (which all officers of the Government ought inviolably to preserve and maintain), and to excite the odium and resentment of all the good people of the United States against Congress and the laws by it duly and constitutionally enacted; and, in pursuance of his said design and intent, openly and publicly, and before divers assemblages of the citizens of the United States, convened in divers parts thereof to meet and receive said Andrew Johnson as the Chief Magistrate of the United States, did, on the 18th day of August, A.D. 1866, and on divers other days and times, as well before as afterwards, make and deliver with a loud voice certain intemperate, inflammatory, and scandalous harangues, and did therein utter loud threats and bitter menaces, as well against Congress as the laws of the United States, duly enacted thereby, amid the cries, jeers, and laughter of the multitudes then assembled and in hearing . . . [Here the charges included specific examples of his speeches, with long quotations from them] which said utterances, declarations, threats, and harangues, highly censurable in any, are peculiarly indecent and unbecoming in the Chief Magistrate of the United States, by means whereof said An-

drew Johnson has brought the high office of the President of the United States into contempt, ridicule, and disgrace, to the great scandal of all good citizens; whereby said Andrew Johnson, President of the United States, did commit and was then and there guilty of a high misdemeanor in office.

Art. XI. That said Andrew Johnson, President of the United States, unmindful of the high duties of his office and of his oath of office, and in disregard of the Constitution and laws of the United States, did heretofore, to wit, on the 18th day of August, A.D. 1866, at the city of Washington, in the District of Columbia, by public speech, declare and affirm in substance that the Thirty-ninth Congress of the United States was not a Congress of the United States authorized by the Constitution to exercise legislative power under the same, but, on the contrary, was a Congress of only part of the States; thereby denying and intending to deny that the legislation of said Congress was valid or obligatory upon him, the said Andrew Johnson, except in so far as he saw fit to approve the same, and also thereby denying and intending to deny the power of the said Thirty-ninth Congress to propose amendments to the Constitution of the United States; and in pursuance of said declaration the said Andrew Johnson, President of the United States, afterwards, to wit, on the 21st day of February, A.D. 1868, . . . did unlawfully, and in disregard of the requirement of the Constitution that he should take care that the laws be faithfully executed, attempt to prevent the execution of an act entitled "An act regulating the tenure of certain civil offices," passed March 2, 1867, by unlawfully devising and contriving, and attempting to devise and contrive, means by which he should prevent Edwin M. Stanton from forthwith resuming the functions of the office of Secretary for the Department of War, notwithstanding the refusal of the Senate to concur in the suspension theretofore made by said Andrew Johnson of said Edwin M. Stanton from said office of Secretary for the Department of War, and also by further unlawfully devising and contriving, and attempting to devise and contrive, means then and there to prevent the execution of an act entitled "An act making appropriations for the support of the

Army for the fiscal year ending June 30, 1868 and for other purposes," approved March 2, 1867, and also to prevent the execution of an act entitled "An act to provide for the more efficient government of the rebel States," passed March 2, 1867, whereby the said Andrew Johnson, President of the United States, did then, to wit, on the 21st day of February, A.D. 1868, at the city of Washington, commit and was guilty of a high misdemeanor in office.

[On May 16, thirty-five senators voted for conviction, one short of the two-thirds majority needed for removal from office.]

Note: The Courts and the Politics of Reconstruction

For the most part, the courts rarely interfered with Reconstruction policy. In *Ex parte Milligan* (1866), the Supreme Court reversed Milligan's conviction because he was a civilian who had been tried by a military court in Indiana at a time when the civilian courts were open and functioning. Although a great victory for civil liberties, the case had little effect on Reconstruction policy. Somewhat more significant to Reconstruction policies were *Cummings* v. *Missouri* (1867) and *Ex parte Garland* (1867), striking down, as ex post facto laws, state and federal requirements of oaths that made voters, attorneys, and others swear that they had never aided the rebellion or even expressed sympathy for the Confederate cause.

The Supreme Court was exceedingly restrained on the key issue of congressional power over Reconstruction. The Court accepted the reality that Congress would decide the political issue of the status of the former Confederate states. In *Mississippi* v. *Johnson* (1867), *Georgia* v. *Stanton* (1868), and *Ex parte McCardle* (1869), the Court refused to interfere with the implementation of the military reconstruction acts. In *Texas* v. *White* (1869), the Court accepted Congress's theory of Reconstruction—that "the rights of the State as a member" of the Union "were suspended" by secession and that only Congress could end that suspension.

BLACK FREEDOM

The Thirteenth Amendment, ratified in late 1865, proclaimed the end of slavery and empowered Congress to enforce the amendment "by appropriate legislation." The Fourteenth and Fifteenth Amendments, adopted in 1868 and 1870, contained similar enforcement clauses.

After the war, most southern whites acquiesced in the demise of chattel slavery but did not accept the freedmen as equals or as citizens. In 1865 and 1866, President Johnson allowed former Confederates to participate in the reorganization of state and local governments. These new governments quickly moved to force blacks into a state of subservience and subjugation with laws collectively known as the black codes. These laws required that blacks, but not whites, obtain licenses to do such things as live in a city or town, own guns or other weapons, or "exercise the function of a minister of the Gospel." Black children could be apprenticed against the wishes of their parents, while strict vagrancy laws allowed the virtual enslavement of any free black who was unwilling to work for his or her former master. The laws "created a quasi-slavery or serfdom which was offensive to liberal, humanitarian sentiment" and "represented an attempt to make the freedmen in effect slaves of the community by treating them as a distinct class and by severely restricting their access to the ordinary civil rights and liberties that white persons enjoyed."[6]

Congress countered the black codes with the Civil Rights Act of 1866. In *In re Turner* (1867), Chief Justice Salmon P. Chase held, while riding circuit, that a Maryland apprentice law leading to the virtual enslavement of the minor children of former slaves violated the 1866 act. Increased violence against blacks and white Unionists by the Ku Klux Klan led to the "Force Acts," adopted by Congress in 1870 and 1871. Congressional protection of blacks culminated with the Civil Rights Act of 1875.

Congressional support for black freedom had mixed results. President Johnson resisted Congress's attempts to protect the freedmen. Congress enacted both the Second Freedmen's Bureau Act and the Civil Rights Act of 1866 over Johnson's vetoes. Johnson refused to use his powers to protect blacks and, instead, removed numerous civilian officials and military officers in the South who attempted to help blacks and treat them justly. More important, Johnson's policies encouraged white resistance to civil rights, which continued during the Grant administration. Ultimately, southern white resistance, a series of adverse Supreme Court decisions, and northern disinterest in the fate of southern blacks doomed the former slaves to poverty, political disfranchisement, segregation, and legally sanctioned second-class status.

Mississippi Black Codes
1865

By late 1865, President Johnson had established new governments in the South that were dominated by whites, including many former Confederates. Johnson required only that the governments ratify the Thirteenth Amendment, repudiate the Confederate debt, and repeal their ordinances of secession. These new governments sought to control the freedmen through black codes.

AN ACT TO CONFER CIVIL RIGHTS ON FREEDMEN, AND FOR OTHER PURPOSES

Section 1. Be it enacted by the Legislature of the State of Mississippi, That all freedmen, free negroes and mulattoes may sue and be sued, implead and be impleaded in all the courts of law and equity of this State, and may acquire personal property and choses in action, by descent or purchase, and may dispose of the same, in the same manner, and to the same extent that white persons may: Provided that the provisions of this section shall not be so construed as to allow any freedmen, free negro or mulatto, to rent or lease any lands or tenements, except in incorporated towns or cities in which places the corporate authorities shall control the same.

Section 2. Be it further enacted, That all freedmen, free negroes, and mulattoes may intermarry with each other, in the same manner and under the same regulations that are provided by law for white persons: Provided, that the clerk of probate shall keep separate records of the same.

Section 3. Be it further enacted, That all freedmen, free negroes and mulattoes, who do now and have heretofore lived and cohabitated together as husband and wife shall be taken and held in law as legally married, and the issue shall be taken and held as legitimate for all purposes. That it shall not be lawful for any freedmen [etc.] . . . to intermarry with any white person; nor for any white person to intermarry with any freedmen [etc.] . . . ; and any person who shall so intermarry shall be deemed guilty of felony, and on conviction thereof, shall be confined in the State Penitentiary for life; and those shall be deemed freedmen, free negroes and mulattoes who are of pure negro blood, and those descended from a negro to the third generation inclusive, though one ancestor of each generation may have been a white person.

◆ ◆ ◆

Section 6. Be it further enacted, That all contracts for labor made with freedmen, free negroes and mulattoes, for a longer period than one month shall be in writing and in duplicate, attested and read to said freedmen [etc.] . . . and if the laborer shall quit the service of the employer, before expiration of his term of service, without good cause, he shall forfeit his wages for that year, up to the time of quitting.

Section 7. Be it further enacted, That every civil officer shall, and every person may arrest and carry back to his or her legal employer any freedman, free negro or mulatto, who shall have quit the service of his or her employer before the expiration of his or her term of service without good cause, and said officer and person shall be entitled to receive for arresting and carrying back every deserting employee aforesaid, the sum of five dollars, and ten cents per mile from the place of arrest to the place of delivery, and the same shall be paid by the employer, and held as a set-off for so much against the wages of said deserting employee: Provided that said arrested party after being so returned may appeal to a justice of the peace or member of the board of police of the county, who on notice to the alleged employer, shall try summarily whether said appellant is legally employed by the alleged employer and has good cause to quit said employer; either party shall have the right of appeal to the county court, pending which the alleged deserter shall be remanded to the alleged employer, or otherwise disposed of as shall be right and just, and the decision of the county court shall be final.

◆ ◆ ◆

Section 9. Be it further enacted, That if any person shall persuade or attempt to persuade, entice or cause any freedman [etc.] . . . to desert from the legal employment of any person, before the expiration of his or her term of service, or shall knowingly employ any such deserting freedman [etc.] . . . or shall knowingly give or sell to any such deserting freedman [etc.] . . . any food, payment or other thing, he or she shall be guilty of a misdemeanor, and upon conviction, shall be fined not less than twenty-five dollars and not more than two hundred dollars and the costs, and if said fine and

costs shall not be immediately paid, the court shall sentence said convict to not exceeding two months imprisonment in the county jail, and he or she shall moreover be liable to the party injured in damages: Provided, if any person shall, or shall attempt to persuade, entice, or cause any freedman [etc.] . . . to desert from any legal employment of any person, with the view to employ said freedman [etc.] . . . without the limits of this State, such person, on conviction, shall be fined not less than fifty dollars and not more than five hundred dollars and costs, and if said fine and costs shall not be immediately paid, the court shall sentence said convict to not exceeding six months imprisonment in the county jail.

AN ACT TO AMEND THE VAGRANT LAWS OF THE STATE

◆ ◆ ◆

Sec. 2. Be it further enacted, That all freedmen, free negroes and mulattoes in this state, over the age of eighteen years, found on the second Monday in January, 1866, or thereafter, with no lawful employment or business, or found unlawfully assembling themselves together either in the day or night time, and all white persons so assembling with freedmen [etc.] . . . or usually associating with freedmen [etc.] . . . on terms of equality, or living in adultery or fornication with a freedwoman, free negro, or mulatto, shall be deemed vagrants, and on conviction thereof, shall be fined in the sum of not exceeding, in the case of a freedman, free negro or mulatto, fifty dollars and a white man twelve hundred dollars, and imprisoned at the discretion of the court, the free negro not exceeding ten days, and the white man not exceeding six months.

◆ ◆ ◆

Sec. 7. Be it further enacted, That if any freedman, free negro or mulatto shall fail, or refuse to pay any tax levied according to the provisions of the sixth section of this act, it shall be prima facie evidence of vagrancy, and it shall be the duty of the sheriff to arrest such freedman, free negro or mulatto or such person refusing or neglecting to pay such tax and proceed at once to hire, for the shortest time, such delinquent tax payer to any one who will pay the said tax, with accruing costs, giving preference to the employer, if there be one.

An Act to Protect All Persons in the United States in Their Civil Rights, and Furnish Means of Their Vindication
1866

Congress responded to the proliferation of southern black codes with the Civil Rights Act of 1866. This was the first congressional protection of individual liberty in American history. The bill became law over President Johnson's veto.

Be it enacted . . . That all persons born in the United States and not subject to any foreign power, excluding Indians not taxed, are hereby declared to be citizens of the United States; and such citizens, of every race and color, without regard to any previous condition of slavery or involuntary servitude . . . shall have the same right, in every state and Territory . . . to make and enforce contracts, to sue, be parties, and give evidence, to inherit, purchase, lease, sell, hold, and convey real and personal property, and to full and equal benefit of all laws and proceedings for the security of person and property, as is enjoyed by white citizens, and shall be subject to like punishment, pains, and penalties, and to none other. . . .

Sec. 2. . . . That any person who, under color of any law, statute, ordinance, regulation, or custom, shall subject, or cause to be subjected, any inhabitant of any State or Territory to the deprivation of any right secured or protected by this act, or to different punishment, pains, or penalties on account of such person having at any time been held in a condition of slavery or involuntary servitude, . . . or by reason of his color or race, than is prescribed for the punishment of white persons, shall be deemed guilty of a misdemeanor, and, on conviction, shall be punished by fine not exceeding one thousand dollars, or imprisonment not exceeding one year, or both. . . .

Sec. 3. . . . That the district courts of the United States, within their respective districts, shall have, exclusively of the courts of the several States, cognizance of all crimes and offenses committed against the provisions of this act, and also, concurrently with the circuit courts of the United States, of all causes, civil and criminal, affecting persons who are denied or cannot enforce in the courts of judicial tribunals of the State or locality where they may be any of the rights secured to them by the first section of this act. . . .

Sec. 4. . . . That the district attorneys, marshals, and deputy marshals of the United States, the commissioners appointed by the circuit and territorial courts of the United States . . . the officers and agents of the Freedmen's Bureau, and every other officer who may be specially empowered by the President of the United States . . . are hereby, specially authorized and required, at the expense of the United States, to institute proceedings against all and every person who shall violate the provisions of this act, and cause him or them to be arrested . . . for trial before such court of the United States or territorial court. . . . And with a view to affording reasonable protection to all persons in their constitutional rights of equality before the law, without distinction of race or color, or previous condition of slavery . . . and to the prompt discharge of the duties of this act, it shall be the duty of the circuit courts [and territorial courts] of the United States . . . from time to time, to increase the number of commissioners, so as to afford a speedy and convenient means for the

arrest and examination of persons charged with
a violation of this act.

 [The remaining sections of the law contained various enforcement provisions and penalties. These provisions included the use of
federal troops and local militia for enforcement.]

Note: The Civil Rights Act and the Fourteenth Amendment

Some members of Congress doubted the constitutionality of the 1866 Civil Rights Act, but
most were convinced that the enforcement provision of the Thirteenth Amendment gave Congress sufficient power to protect the freedmen against both private action and state action.
Following the override of President Johnson's veto of the Civil Rights Act, Congress passed
the Fourteenth Amendment and sent it to the states. In 1870, Congress "reenacted" the 1866
act, on the assumption that the newly adopted Fourteenth and Fifteenth Amendments gave
additional constitutional authority to the law.

Note: Andrew Johnson's Veto of the 1866 Civil Rights Act

The Civil Rights Act of 1866 became law over Johnson's veto. In his veto message, Johnson complained that the bill gave citizenship to all persons born in the United States, including "the Chinese of the Pacific States, Indians subject to taxation, the people called gypsies, as well as the entire race designated as blacks, people of color, negroes, mulattos, and
persons of African blood." He condemned the law for creating "a perfect equality of white
and colored races . . . fixed by Federal law in every state of the Union," arguing that "in
fact, the distinction of race and color is by the bill made to operate in favor of the colored
and against the white race."

Note: The Freedmen's Bureau

In 1865, Congress established the Bureau of Refugees, Freedmen, and Abandoned Lands
as an arm of the Department of War, staffed by a combination of military and civilian
agents and headed by a Civil War hero, General Oliver O. Howard. The bureau, which
was the country's first federally funded public-welfare program, coordinated private relief efforts with government initiatives to provide food, shelter, education, and legal protection to the recently emancipated slaves. Its ties to private charity suggest the discomfort of most members of Congress with federal aid to individuals; its failure to redistribute
land to former slaves underscores the conservative nature of Reconstruction. The Freedmen's Bureau was to be in existence for one year after the war ended, but in July 1866
Congress re-created the bureau, passing the law over Johnson's veto. The 1866 act created Freedmen's Bureau courts to hear cases where "the ordinary course of judicial proceedings" had been "interrupted" or until a state was "duly represented in Congress."
These courts adjudicated a full range of cases, using the military to protect the privileges
and immunities of black citizens, and provided some legal protection and due process to
former slaves, who faced discrimination and legal harassment at the hands of their former masters. Ultimately, the bureau's greatest success was in establishing schools for the
freedmen.

Note: The Civil Rights Act of 1875

Officially titled "An Act to Protect all Citizens in their Civil and Legal Rights," the Civil Rights Act of 1875 was the last gasp of Reconstruction legislation. The law's preamble asserted that it was "essential to a just government" to "recognize the equality of all men before the law" and that it was "the duty of government in all its dealing with the people to mete out equal and exact justice to all; of whatever nativity, race, color, or persuasion, religious or political." It prohibited racial discrimination in jury selection at the state and federal levels, and allowed both civil damages and criminal penalties for any individuals who discriminated in "public accommodations . . . inns, public conveyances on land or water, theaters, and other places of public assessment." The act had almost no effect on American blacks, and most of it was declared unconstitutional in the *Civil Rights Cases* (1883).

THE END OF CIVIL RIGHTS

The revolution in civil rights law began in 1862 with the confiscation acts and the first steps at congressional emancipation. The legislative initiatives continued until the passage of the Civil Rights Act of 1875. However, by this time, the United States Supreme Court had already begun to undermine the statutes and the amendments of the Civil War era.

Initially, the federal courts supported civil rights. Two cases decided by Supreme Court justices while on circuit court duty illustrate this. In *U.S. v. Rhodes* (1866), Justice Noah Swayne upheld the constitutionality of the 1866 Civil Rights Act under the enforcement clause of the Thirteenth Amendment. In *In re Turner* (1866), Chief Justice Salmon P. Chase used the new amendment and the 1866 act to prohibit virtual reenslavement of black children under apprentice laws. In 1870 and 1871, trials under the enforcement acts (or Ku Klux Klan acts, as they were known) helped destroy the Klan.

However, after 1873, support for civil rights diminished. Reconciliation captured the imagination of the North, while Democrats, including former Confederates, began to take control of southern state governments. In *U.S. v. Cruikshank* (1874) and *U.S. v. Harris* (1883), the Court undermined the use of the Ku Klux Klan acts, while in the *Civil Rights Cases* (1883), the Court found most of the 1875 Civil Rights Act to be unconstitutional. In the following decades, the Court and the national legislature did little to protect black rights and liberties. The beginning of the nadir for black civil rights was Justice Samuel F. Miller's majority opinion in the *Slaughterhouse Cases*.

The *Slaughterhouse Cases*
16 Wall. (83 U.S.) 36 (1873)

In 1869, Louisiana confined all slaughtering in New Orleans to the Crescent City Live-Stock Landing & Slaughterhouse Company. This monopoly required individual butchers to rent space from the Crescent City Company in order to carry out their business. The state and city claimed this was a legitimate health regulation under the state's police powers. The butchers argued that the monopoly violated the Thirteenth and Fourteenth Amendments to the Constitution. Slaughterhouse *was the first case the Supreme Court heard under the Four-*

teenth Amendment. In rejecting the claims of the butchers, the Court severely limited the application of the Fourteenth Amendment and virtually destroyed the value of the privileges and immunities clause of that amendment.

Mr. Justice Miller

♦ ♦ ♦

The most cursory glance at these articles [the Civil War Amendments] discloses a unity of purpose, when taken in connection with the history of the times, which cannot fail to have an important bearing on any question of doubt concerning their true meaning. Nor can such doubts, when any reasonably exist, be safely and rationally solved without a reference to that history; for in it is found the occasion and the necessity for recurring again to the great source of power in this country, the people of the States, for additional guarantees of human rights; additional powers to the Federal government; additional restraints upon those of the States. Fortunately that history is fresh within the memory of us all, and its leading features, as they bear upon the matter before us, free from doubt.

The institution of African slavery, as it existed in about half the states of the Union, and the contests pervading the public mind for many years, between those who desired its curtailment and ultimate extinction and those who desired additional safeguards for its security and perpetuation, culminated in the effort, on the part of most of the States in which slavery existed, to separate from the Federal government, and to resist its authority. This constituted the war of the rebellion, and whatever auxiliary causes may have contributed to bring about this war, undoubtedly the over-shadowing and efficient cause was African slavery.

In that struggle slavery, as a legalized social relation, perished. . . . Hence the thirteenth article of amendment. . . .

To withdraw the mind from the contemplation of this grand yet simple declaration of the personal freedom of all the human race within the jurisdiction of this government—a declaration designed to establish the freedom of four millions of slaves—and with a microscopic search endeavor to find in it a reference to servitudes, which may have been attached to property in certain localities, requires an effort, to say the least of it.

That a personal servitude was meant is proved by the use of the word "involuntary," which can only apply to human beings. The exception of servitude as a punishment for crime gives an idea of the class of servitude that is meant. The word servitude is of larger meaning than slavery, as the latter is popularly understood in this country, and the obvious purpose was to forbid all shades and conditions of African slavery. It was very well understood that in the form of apprenticeship for long terms, as it had been practiced in the West India Islands, on the abolition of slavery by the English government, or by reducing the slaves to the condition of serfs attached in the plantation, the purpose of the article might have been evaded, if only the word slavery had been used. The case of the apprentice slave, held under a law of Maryland, liberated by Chief Justice Chase [*In re Turner* (1866)], on a writ of habeas corpus under this article, illustrates this course of observation. And it is all that we deem necessary to say on the application of that article to the statute of Louisiana, now under consideration.

♦ ♦ ♦

We repeat, then in the light of this recapitulation of events, almost too recent to be called history, but which are familiar to us all; and on the most casual examination of the language of these amendments, no one can fail to be impressed with the one pervading purpose found in them all, lying at the foundation of each, and without which none of them would have been even suggested; we mean the freedom of the slave race, the security and firm establishment of that freedom, and the protection of the newly-made freeman and citizen from the oppression of those who had formerly exercised unlimited dominion over him. It is true that only the fifteenth amendment, in terms, mentions the negro by speaking of his color and his slavery. But it is just as true that each of the other articles was addressed to the grievances of that race.

♦   ♦   ♦

The first section of the fourteenth article, to which our attention is more specially invited, opens with a definition of citizenship—not only citizenship of the United States, but citizenship of the States.

♦   ♦   ♦

It is quite clear, then, that there is a citizenship of the United States, and a citizenship of a State, which are distinct from each other, and which depend upon different characteristics or circumstances in the individual.

We think this distinction and its explicit recognition in this amendment of great weight in this argument, because the next paragraph of this same section, which is the one mainly relied on by the plaintiffs in error, speaks only of privileges and immunities of citizens of the United States, and does not speak of those of citizens of the several States. The argument, however, in favor of the plaintiffs rests wholly on the assumption that the citizenship is the same, and the privileges and immunities guaranteed by the clause are the same.

The language is "No state shall make or enforce any law which shall abridge the privileges or immunities of citizens of *the United States*." It is a little remarkable, if this clause was intended as a protection to the citizen of a State against the legislative power of his own State, that the word citizen of the State should be left out when it is so carefully used, and used in contradiction to citizens of the United States, in the very sentence which precedes it. It is too clear for argument that the change in phraseology was adopted . . . with a purpose.

Of the privileges and immunities of the citizen of the United States, and of the privileges and immunities of the citizen of the State, and what they respectively are, we will presently consider; but we wish to state here that it is only the former which are placed by this clause under the protection of the Federal Constitution, and that the latter, whatever they may be, are not intended to have any additional protection by this paragraph of the amendment.

♦   ♦   ♦

Was it the purpose of the fourteenth amendment, by the simple declaration that no State should make or enforce any law which shall abridge the privileges and immunities of citizens of the United States, to transfer the security and protection of all the civil rights which we have mentioned, from the States to the Federal government? And where it is declared that Congress shall have the power to enforce that article, was it intended to bring within the power of Congress the entire domain of civil rights heretofore belonging exclusively to the States?

All this and more must follow, if the proposition of the plaintiffs in error be sound. For not only are these rights subject to the control of Congress whenever in its discretion any of them are supposed to be abridged by State Legislation, but that body may pass laws in advance, limiting and restricting the exercise of legislative power by the States, in their most ordinary and usual functions, as in its judgment it may think proper on all such subjects. And still further, such a construction followed by the reversal of the judgments of the Supreme Court of Louisiana in these cases, would constitute this court a perpetual censor upon all legislation of the States, on the civil rights of their own citizens, with authority to nullify such as it did not approve as consistent with those rights, as they existed at the time of the adoption of this amendment. The argument we admit is not always the most conclusive which is drawn from the consequences urged against the adoption of a particular construction of an instrument. But when, as in the case before us, these consequences are so serious, so far reaching and pervading, so great a departure from the structure and spirit of our institutions; when the effect is to fetter and degrade the State governments by subjecting them to the control of Congress, in the exercise of powers heretofore universally conceded to them of the most ordinary and fundamental character; when in fact it radically changes the whole theory of the relations of the State and Federal governments to each other and of both these governments to the people; the argument has been a force that is irresistible, in the absence of language which expresses such a purpose too clearly to admit of doubt.

We are convinced that no such results were intended by the Congress which proposed these amendments, nor by the legislature of the States which ratified them.

♦ ♦ ♦

But lest it should be said that no such privileges and immunities are to be found.

♦ ♦ ♦

[The Court offered some examples of "privileges and immunities" protected by the Fourteenth Amendment. These included the right to travel and a right to claim protection of the government on the high seas.] The right to peaceably assemble and petition for redress of grievances, the privilege of the writ of habeas corpus, are rights of the citizen guaranteed by the Federal Constitution. The right to use the navigable waters of the United States, however they may penetrate the territory of the several States, all rights secured to our citizens by treaties with foreign nations, are dependent upon citizenship of the United States, and not citizenship of a State. One of these privileges is conferred by the very article under consideration. It is that a citizen of the United States can, of his own volition, become a citizen of any State of the Union by a bona fide residence therein, with the same rights as other citizens of that State. To these may be added the rights secured by the thirteenth and fifteenth articles of amendment, and by the other clause of the fourteenth, next to be considered.

♦ ♦ ♦

The argument has not been much pressed in these cases that the defendant's charter deprives the plaintiffs of their property without due process of law, or that it denies them the equal protection of the law. . . . [Here the court noted that such clauses existed in most state constitutions as well as in the Fifth Amendment to the United States Constitution.]

We are not without judicial interpretation, therefore, both state and nation, of the meaning to this clause. And it is sufficient to say that under no construction of that provision that we have ever seen, or any that we deem admissible, can the restraint imposed by the state of Louisiana . . . be held to be a deprivation of property within the meaning of that provision.

♦ ♦ ♦

"Nor shall any State deny to any person within its jurisdiction the equal protection of the laws."

In the light of the history of these amendments, and the pervading purpose of them, which we have already discussed, it is not difficult to give a meaning to this clause. The existence of laws in the States where the newly emancipated negroes resided, which discriminated with gross injustice and hardship against them as a class, was the evil to be remedied by this clause, and by it such laws are forbidden.

If, however, the States did not conform their laws to its requirements, then by the fifth section of the article of amendment Congress was authorized to enforce it by suitable legislation. We doubt very much whether any action of a State not directed by way of discrimination against the negroes as a class, or an account of their race, will ever be held to come within the purview of this provision. It is so clearly a provision for that race and that emergency, that a strong case would be necessary for its application to any other.

♦ ♦ ♦

It was then discovered [when the Civil War occurred] that the true danger to the perpetuity of the Union was in the capacity of the State organization to combine and concentrate all the powers of the State, and of contiguous States, for a determined resistance to the General Government.

Unquestionably this has given great force to the argument, and added largely to the number of those who believe in the necessity of a strong National government.

But, however pervading this sentiment, and however it may have contributed to the adoption of the amendments we have been considering, we do not see in those amendments any purpose to destroy the main features of the general system. Under the pressure of all the excited feeling growing out of the war, our statesmen have still believed that the existence of the States with powers for domestic and local government, including the regulation of civil rights—the rights of person and of property—was essential to the perfect working of our complex form of government, though they have thought proper to impose additional limitations on the States, and to confer additional power on that of the Nation.

Note: The *Slaughterhouse* Legacy

Chief Justice Chase and Justices Swayne, Bradley, and Field dissented, arguing for a more expansive interpretation of the Fourteenth Amendment. These dissents stressed the nationalization of liberty under the amendment. The Bradley dissent in particular set the stage for the late-nineteenth-century developments in substantive due process, as is presented in Chapter 6 of this book.

The more pernicious result of *Slaughterhouse* is outlined in the following paragraph from a recent book on the constitutional history of this period.

> Herein lay a terrible irony for blacks. After having construed the "pervading purpose" of the Civil War amendments to be the freedom of black people, Miller relegated freedmen, for the effective protection of their new freedom, to precisely those governments—the southern states—least likely to respect either their rights or their freedom should the Republican regimes fall from power. The federal government could protect only the privileges and immunities of federal citizenship. As enumerated by Miller, these included the right of access to Washington, D.C., and the coastal seaports; the right to protection on the high seas and abroad; the right to use navigable waters of the United States; the right of assembly and petition; the privilege of habeas corpus. Of these, only the last two would be significant for most blacks.[7]

Note: *Civil Rights Cases*, 109 U.S. 3 (1883)

The *Civil Rights Cases* were five prosecutions and civil suits from California, Kansas, Missouri, New York, and Tennessee, for denying blacks access to public accommodations and facilities under the Civil Rights Act of 1875. The defendants had denied blacks access to hotels, theaters, and railroad cars. Speaking for the Court, Justice Joseph Bradley found the 1875 Civil Rights Act unconstitutional because he believed that the Fourteenth Amendment prohibited only state action and did not protect blacks against private discrimination. He admitted that the Thirteenth Amendment allowed for the elimination of "badges of slavery," but would not apply this to prohibitions of racial discrimination in "an inn, a public conveyance, or a theatre." He believed that antidiscrimination laws belonged to the jurisdiction of the states, not the national government. He concluded:

> When a man has emerged from slavery, and by the aid of beneficent legislation has shaken off the inseparable concomitants of that state, there must be some stage in the progress of his elevation when he takes the rank of a mere citizen, and ceases to be the special favorite of the laws, and when his rights as a citizen, or a man, are to be protected in the ordinary modes by which other men's rights are protected. There were thousands of free colored people in this country before the abolition of slavery,

enjoying all the essential rights of life, liberty and property the same as white citizens; yet no one, at that time, thought that it was any invasion of his personal status as a freeman because he was not admitted to all the privileges enjoyed by white citizens, or because he was subjected to discriminations in the enjoyment of accommodations in inns, public conveyances and places of amusement. Mere discriminations on account of race or color were not regarded as badges of slavery. If, since that time, the enjoyment of equal rights in all these respects has become established by constitutional enactment, it is not by force of the Thirteenth Amendment (which merely abolishes slavery), but by force of the Fourteenth and Fifteenth Amendments.

Justice John Marshall Harlan, a former slave owner from Kentucky, dissented, arguing that the Court's opinion rested "upon grounds entirely too narrow and artificial." He urged a broad reading of both the Thirteenth and Fourteenth Amendments. Of the former he noted:

The Thirteenth Amendment, it is conceded, did something more than to prohibit slavery as an *institution,* resting upon distinctions of race, and upheld by positive law. My brethren admit that it established and decreed universal *civil freedom* throughout the United States. But did the freedom thus established involve nothing more than exemption from actual slavery? Was nothing more intended than to forbid one man from owning another as property? Was it the purpose of the nation simply to destroy the institution, and then remit the race, theretofore held in bondage, to the several States for such protection, in their civil rights, necessarily growing out of freedom, as those States, in their discretion, might choose to provide? Were the States against whose protest the institution was destroyed, to be left free, so far as national interference was concerned, to make or allow discriminations against that race, as such, in the enjoyment of those fundamental rights which by universal concession, inhere in a state of freedom?

Harlan also argued that the discrimination in public carriers and public facilities amounted to state action because the roads and highways were "established by authority of these States." Public inns were historically obligated to serve "all travelers or Wayfarers who might choose to" enter them. Theaters were licensed by the state, and that was sufficient state action to justify federal protection under the Civil War Amendments. Most important, Harlan challenged the cynical conclusions of Bradley that the former slaves had been the "special favorite of the laws."

My brethren say, that when a man has emerged from slavery, and by the aid of beneficent legislation has shaken off the inseparable concomitants of that state, there must be some stage in the progress of his elevation when he takes the rank of a mere citizen, and ceases to be the special favorite of the laws, and when his rights as a citizen, or a man, are to be protected in the ordinary modes by which other men's rights are protected. It is, I submit, scarcely just to say that the colored race has been the special favorite of the laws. The statute of 1875, now adjudged to be unconstitutional, is for the benefit of citizens of every race and color. What the nation, through Congress, has sought to accomplish in reference to that race, is—what had already been done in every State of the Union for the white race—to secure and protect rights belonging to them as freemen and citizens; nothing more. It was not deemed enough "to help the feeble up, but to support him after." The one underlying purpose of congressional legislation has been to enable the black race to take the rank of mere citizens. The difficulty has been to compel a recognition of the legal right of the black race to take the rank of citizens, and to secure the enjoyment of privileges belonging, under the law, to them as a component part of the people for whose welfare and happiness government is ordained. At every step, in this direction, the nation has been confronted with class tyranny, which a contemporary English historian says is, of all tyrannies, the most intolerable, "for it is ubiquitous in its operation, and weighs, perhaps, most heavily on those whose obscurity or distance would withdraw them from the notice of a single despot." To-day, it is the colored race which is denied, by corporations and individuals wielding public authority, rights fundamental in their freedom and citizenship. At some future time, it may be that some other race will fall under the ban of race discrimination. If the constitutional amendments be enforced, according to the intent with which, as I conceive, they were adopted, there cannot be, in this republic, any class of human beings in practical subjection to another class, with power in the latter to dole out to the former just such privileges as they may choose to grant. The supreme law of the land has decreed that no authority shall be exercised in this country upon the basis of discrimination, in respect of civil rights, against freemen and citizens because of their race, color, or previous condition of servitude.

RACE AND SEGREGATION IN NINETEENTH-CENTURY LAW AND SOCIETY

Throughout the nineteenth century, lawmakers in both the North and the South invoked race to define personal status. Slavery, of course, attached exclusively to black people. In the antebellum period approximately 95 percent of all African Americans were slaves. The small free black population—about 500,000 in 1860—was about equally divided between the North and the South. The status of free blacks varied from state to state.

On the eve of the Civil War, blacks had fundamental legal equality in all of the New England states except Connecticut. In those states blacks could vote, hold public office, and enter any profession they wanted. In *Roberts* v. *City of Boston* (1850), the Massachusetts Supreme Judicial Court upheld segregated schools in the state, but five years later the legislature banned the practice. In the rest of the North, black rights and opportunities varied by state and even within states. In New York, for example, there were integrated public schools in Syracuse and Rochester, but not in Albany or New York City. Similarly, blacks attended school with whites in much of northern Ohio, including Cleveland, Oberlin, and Toledo, while Cincinnati resisted spending any funds on black education, even when required by the state legislature to do so.

On the eve of the Civil War, most northern blacks could not vote, hold office, or attend schools with whites. But they were able to buy and sell property, enter almost any profession (a few states did not allow them to practice law), and move about from place to place. With the exception of Indiana, Illinois, and Oregon, they were free to take up residence in every northern state. Despite some legal restrictions and much social racism, blacks in the North attended schools and bought houses, and most important, exercised basic civil liberties to struggle for full equality.

In the South the rights of free blacks were more severely restricted. In no southern state could they vote, hold office, testify against a white person, or practice law or medicine. No free blacks in the South had access to publicly funded schooling, and a number of southern states prohibited free blacks from learning to read. All southern states restricted the intrastate movement of free blacks, as well as prohibited black immigration.

The end of slavery did not end racism. Most of the North adopted some discriminatory legislation, and as Reconstruction came to an end, southern whites began to develop a sophisticated system of race control that ultimately led to an entirely segregated society. This shift from slavery to segregation underscores the dynamic and pliable character of the relationship between race and law. This same ideology would also affect the treatment of Native Americans and Chinese. In each instance, the social and cultural assumptions of inferiority that whites attached to these groups found expression in the legal culture. Throughout the nineteenth century, a minority of white Americans embraced the arguments made by some anthropologists, physicians, and other scientists that nonwhites were actually a species of beings who had been placed on earth by God at a "separate creation." Most Americans rejected this extreme position, in large measure because it violated the biblical creation story set out in the book of Genesis. More common, at least in the South, was the view expressed by Senator James Henry Hammond of South Carolina in a famous 1858 speech on the floor of the Senate that blacks were simply a "race inferior" to whites who had a "low order of intellect" and "little skill," and were marked by "vigor, docility, [and] fidelity." Comparable statements about the Chinese and Native Americans were made by other nineteenth-century Americans. Not surprisingly, white Americans sought through the law to provide for the social control of each of these groups. But in each instance, the law also recognized important differences among these racial groups, and, as significant, there were important regional differences in ideas and practices. For example, after the Civil War, the Chinese, Native Americans, and Mexican Americans were a far greater source of concern than were blacks in the West; the opposite was true in the East and South.

The Civil War had ironic consequences for the adjustment of race relations in the United States. The war simultaneously exacerbated racial disharmony by emancipating some 4 million slaves while it fostered political changes necessary to establish a seemingly color-blind legal order through the Thirteenth, Fourteenth, and Fifteenth Amendments to the federal Constitution. As we have seen, these amendments and statutes passed by the Republican majority in Congress provided the legal scaffolding that made blacks citizens, promised them equal protection of the laws, and prohibited discrimination in federal elections. The amendments were only partially successful in creating substantive equality for black people. For example, in the late nineteenth century and twentieth century, southern state legislatures, with the acquiescence of the United States Supreme Court, enacted statutes that stripped blacks of their political rights and cast them into racial segregation. Conditions were better in the North, where blacks could testify against whites, freely migrate from state to state, enjoy public education, and vote. Yet even under the best circumstances, legal equality for nineteenth-century American blacks did not translate into equal social status with whites. In matters of public schooling, voting, and marrying, the legal order reflected an underlying social assumption that, for the most part, blacks were not to mix with whites.

Roberts v. The City of Boston
5 Cush. (59 Mass.) 198 (1850)

Roberts *v.* The City of Boston *(1850) was the first school desegregation case in the United States. Charles Sumner, a future United States senator, and Robert Morris, Jr., one of the first black attorneys in the nation, argued the case for Benjamin Roberts. He had sought to enroll his daughter, Sarah, in the school nearest to his house, rather than in a more distant school designated for black children. In order for Sarah to reach her assigned school, she had to pass five "whites only" schools. At the time, Boston was one of only a few places in Massachusetts that segregated black and white schoolchildren. Segregation in the schools was not required by any state statute or Boston ordinance. Rather, the Boston school committee used its powers to segregate the city's schools. Chief Justice Lemuel Shaw, one of the giant figures of nineteenth-century legal history, delivered the opinion of the court.*

[Sarah Roberts] The plaintiff, a colored child of five years of age, has commenced this action, by her father and next friend . . . upon the statute of 1845, c. 214, which provides, that any child unlawfully excluded from public school instruction, in this commonwealth, shall recover damages therefor, in an action against the city or town, by which such public school instruction is supported. The question therefore is, whether, upon the facts agreed, the plaintiff has been unlawfully excluded from such instruction.

By the agreed statement of facts, it appears that the defendants support a class of schools called primary schools, to the number of about one hundred and sixty, designed for the instruction of children of both sexes, who are between the ages of four and seven years. Two of these schools are appropriated by the primary school committee, having charge of that class of schools, to the exclusive instruction of colored children, and the residue to the exclusive instruction of white children.

The plaintiff, by her father, took proper measures to obtain admission into one of these schools appropriated to white children, but pursuant to the regulations of the committee . . . she was not admitted. Either of the schools appropriated to colored children was open to her; the nearest of which was about a fifth of a mile or seventy rods more distant from her father's house than the nearest primary school. It further appears, by the facts agreed, that the committee having charge of that class of schools, had, a short time previously to the plaintiff's application, adopted a resolution upon a report of a committee, that in the opinion of that board, the continuance of the separate schools for colored children and the regular attendance of all such children upon the schools, is not only legal and just, but is best adapted to promote the instruction of that class of the population.

♦   ♦   ♦

The plaintiff had access to a school, set apart for colored children, as well conducted in all respects, and as well fitted, in point of capacity and qualification of the instructors, to advance the education of children under seven years old, as the other primary schools; the objection is, that the schools thus open to the plaintiff are exclusively appropriated to colored children, and are at a greater distance from her home. Under these circumstances, has the plaintiff been unlawfully excluded from public school instruction? Upon the best consideration we have been able to give the subject, the court are all of opinion that she has not.

It will be considered, that this is a question of power, or of the legal authority of the committee intrusted by the city with this department of public instruction; because, if they have the legal authority, the expediency of exercising it in any particular way is exclusively with them.

The great principle, advanced by the learned and eloquent advocate of the plaintiff, is, that by the constitution and laws of Massachusetts, all persons without distinction of age or sex, birth or color, origin or condition, are equal before the law. This, as a broad general principle, such as ought to appear in a declaration of rights, is perfectly sound; it is not only expressed in terms, but pervades and animates the whole spirit of our constitution of free government. But, when this great principle comes to be applied to the actual and various conditions of persons in society, it will not warrant the assertion, that men and women are legally clothed with the same civil and political powers, and that children and adults are legally to have the same functions and be subject to the same treatment; but only that the rights of all, as they are settled arid regulated by law, are equally entitled to the paternal consideration and protection of the law, for their maintenance and security. What those rights are, to which individuals, in the infinite variety of circumstances by which they are surrounded in society, are entitled, must depend on laws adapted to their respective relations and conditions.

Conceding, therefore, in the fullest manner, that colored persons, the descendants of Africans, are entitled by law, in this commonwealth, to equal rights, constitutional and political, civil and social, the question then arises, whether the regulation in question, which provides separate schools for colored children, is a violation of any of these rights.

Legal rights must, after all, depend upon the provisions of law; certainly all those rights of individuals which can be asserted and maintained in any judicial tribunal. The proper province of a declaration of rights and constitution of government, after directing its form, regulating its organization and the distribution of its powers, is to declare great principles and fundamental truths, to influence and direct the judgment and conscience of legislators in making laws, rather than to limit and control them, by directing what precise laws they shall make. The provision, that it shall be the duty of legislatures and magistrates to cherish the interests of literature and the sciences, especially the university at Cambridge, public schools, and grammar schools, in the towns, is precisely of this character. Had the legislature failed to comply with this injunction, and neglected to provide public schools in the towns, or should they so far fail in their duty as to repeal all laws on the subject, and leave all education to depend on private means, strong and explicitly as the direction of the constitution is, it would afford no remedy or redress to the thousands of the rising generation, who now depend on these schools to afford them a most valuable education and an introduction to useful life.

♦ ♦ ♦

The power of general superintendence vests a plenary authority in the committee to arrange, classify, and distribute pupils, in such a manner as they think best adapted to their general proficiency and welfare. If it is thought expedient to provide for very young children, it may be, that such schools may be kept exclusively by female teachers, quite adequate to their instruction, and yet whose services may be obtained at a cost much lower than that of more highly-qualified male instructors. So if they should judge it expedient to have a grade of schools for children from seven to ten, and another for those from ten to fourteen, it would seem to be within their authority to establish such schools. So to separate male and female pupils into different schools. It has been found necessary, that is to say, highly expedient, at times, to establish special schools for poor and neglected children, who have passed the age of seven, and have become too old to attend the primary school, and yet have not acquired the rudiments of learning, to enable them to enter the ordinary schools. If a class of youth, of one or both sexes, is found in that condition, and it is expedient to organize them into a separate school, to receive the special training, adapted to their condition, it seems to be within the power of the superintending committee, to provide for the organization of such special school.

♦ ♦ ♦

In the absence of special legislation of this subject, the law has vested the power in the committee to regulate the system of distribution and classification; and when this power is reasonably exercised, without being abused or perverted by colorable pretences, the decision of the committee must be deemed conclusive. The committee, apparently upon great deliberation, have come to the conclusion, that the good of both classes of schools will be best promoted, by maintaining the separate primary schools for colored and for white children, and we can perceive no ground to doubt, that this is the honest result of their experience and judgment.

It is urged that this maintenance of separate schools tends to deepen and perpetuate the odious distinction of caste, founded in a deep-rooted prejudice in public opinion. This prejudice, if it exists, is not created by law, and probably cannot be changed by law. Whether this distinction and prejudice, existing in the opinion and feelings of the community, would not be as effectually fostered by compelling colored and white children to associate together in the same schools, may well be doubted; at all events, it is a fair and proper question for the committee to consider and decide upon, having in view the best interests of both classes of children placed under their superintendence, and

we cannot say, that their decision upon it is not founded on just grounds of reason and experience, and in the results of a discriminating and honest judgment.

The increased distance, to which the plaintiff was obliged to go to school from her father's house, is not such, in our opinion, as to render the regulation in question unreasonable, still less illegal.

On the whole the court are of opinion, that upon the facts stated, the action cannot be maintained.

Note: Free Blacks and the Law

At the beginning of the Civil War, there were approximately 500,000 free blacks in the United States. More than half of them lived in the South, where they enjoyed a precarious existence at best. There was great variety in the laws limiting their actions, but several broad trends were evident. They could not travel without passes, move to other slave states, practice certain professions, gather in groups, own weapons, and learn to read or write. The highpoint of southern antebellum hostility to free blacks appeared in *Mitchell* v. *Wells,* 37 Miss. 235 (1859). Nancy Wells was the daughter of a Mississippi slave owner, Edward Wells, and his slave mistress. Before his death, Edward Wells took his daughter to Ohio and emancipated her there. In his will, Wells bequeathed $3,000, a bed, and some property to his daughter. The executor of the will, William Mitchell, refused to give Nancy her legacy, even after a lower court ordered him to do so. Judge William Harris of the Mississippi High Court of Errors and Appeals reversed that decision and held that Nancy Wells, whatever her status in Ohio, would always be a slave in Mississippi.

The issue of the rights of free blacks also turned on the important question of the legal definition of race. The 1802 and 1851 constitutions of Ohio, for example, enfranchised only white males. But in *Anderson* v. *Millikin et al.,* 9 Ohio St. 586 (1859), the Ohio Supreme Court declared that the constitutional prohibition on black suffrage was limited to persons who were more than half black. The decision declared mulattos white, and it made Ohio one of two states (the other was Louisiana) to reject what might be called "the American rule of race"—that any visible black ancestry made a person black, rather than white.

The *Roberts* and *Anderson* cases illustrate the complexity of northern race relations. While the legislature in Massachusetts took a more liberal view of race relations than did the state's highest court, in Ohio the reverse happened. Moreover, while Massachusetts, Ohio, Iowa, California, and most other free states liberalized their laws on race in the late antebellum period and during the Civil War, Indiana and Illinois moved in the opposite direction. For example, in *Nelson (a mulatto)* v. *The People,* 33 Ill. 390 (1864), the Illinois Supreme Court was openly hostile to the rights of free blacks. The judges upheld the constitutionality of a law that prohibited free blacks from immigrating into the state. The same year, however, the Iowa legislature repealed a statute that had prohibited the immigration of blacks into the state (see 10 Iowa Laws 6 [1864]).

Plessy v. *Ferguson*
163 U.S. 537 (1896)

Plessy, a man of mixed racial ancestry, was prosecuted for sitting in a railroad car in the "whites only" section. He sought relief from the United States Supreme Court, asking for a writ of prohibition against Ferguson, the judge of the Orleans Parish criminal court, to end the prosecution. This litigation was organized by citizens in Louisiana, as a test case, to help stem the growing tide of southern segregation.

Mr. Justice Brown . . .

This case turns upon the constitutionality of an act of the General Assembly of the State of Louisiana, passed in 1890, providing for separate railway carriages for the white and colored races.

The first section of the statute enacts "that all railway companies carrying passengers in their coaches in this State, shall provide equal but separate accommodations for the white, and colored races, by providing two or more passenger coaches for each passenger train, or by dividing the passenger coaches by a partition so as to secure separate accommodations."

♦ ♦ ♦

1. That it does not conflict with the Thirteenth Amendment, which abolished slavery and involuntary servitude, except as a punishment for crime, is too clear for argument. Slavery implies involuntary servitude—a state of bondage; the ownership of mankind as a chattel, or at least the control of the labor and services of one man for the benefit of another, and the absence of a legal right to the disposal of his own person, property and services.

♦ ♦ ♦

[Here the Court cited the *Slaughterhouse Cases* (1873) and the *Civil Rights Cases* (1883).] A statute which implies merely a legal distinction between the white and colored races—a distinction which is founded in the color of the two races, and which must always exist so long as white men are distinguished from the other race by color—has no tendency to destroy the legal equality of the two races,

or reestablish a state of involuntary servitude. Indeed, we do not understand that the Thirteenth Amendment is strenuously relied upon by the plaintiff in error in this connection.

♦ ♦ ♦

The object of the [Fourteenth] amendment was undoubtedly to enforce the absolute equality of the two races before the law, but in the nature of things it could not have been intended to abolish distinctions based upon color, or to enforce social, as distinguished from political equality, or a commingling of the two races upon terms unsatisfactory to either. Laws permitting, and even requiring, their separation in places where they are liable to be brought into contact do not necessarily imply the inferiority of either race to the other, and have been generally, if not universally, recognized as within the competency of the state legislatures in the exercise of their police power. The most common instance of this is connected with the establishment of separate schools for white and colored children, which has been held to be a valid exercise of the legislative power even by courts of States where the political rights of the colored race have been longest and most earnestly enforced.

One of the earliest of these cases is that of *Roberts* v. *City of Boston* (1850), in which the Supreme Judicial Court of Massachusetts held that the general school committee of Boston had power to make provision for the instruction of colored children in separate schools established exclusively for them, and to prohibit their attendance upon the other schools.

♦ ♦ ♦

So far, then as a conflict with the Fourteenth Amendment is concerned, the case reduces itself to the question whether the statute of Louisiana is a reasonable regulation, and with respect to this there must necessarily be a large discretion on the part of the legislature. In determining the question of reasonableness it is at liberty to act with reference to the established usages, customs and traditions of the people, and with a view to the promotion of their comfort, and the preservation of the public peace and good order. Gauged by this standard, we cannot say that a law which authorizes or even requires the separation of the two races in public conveyances is unreasonable, or more obnoxious to the Fourteenth Amendment than the acts of Congress requiring separate schools for colored children in the District of Columbia, the constitutionality of which does not seem to have been questioned, or the corresponding acts of state legislatures.

We consider the underlying fallacy of the plaintiff's argument to consist in the assumption that the enforced separation of the two races stamps the colored race with a badge of inferiority. If this be so, it is not by reason of anything found in the act, but solely because the colored race chooses to put that construction upon it. The argument necessarily assumes that if, as has been more than once the case, and is not unlikely to be so again, the colored race should become the dominant power in the state legislature, and should enact a law in precisely similar terms, it would thereby relegate the white race to an inferior position. We imagine that the white race, at least, would not acquiesce in this assumption. The argument also assumes that social prejudices may be overcome by legislation, and that equal rights cannot be secured to the negro except by an enforced commingling of the two races. We cannot accept this proposition. If the two races are to meet upon terms of social equality, it must be the result of natural affinities, a mutual appreciation of each other's merits and a voluntary consent of individuals. . . . Legislation is powerless to eradicate racial instincts or to abolish distinctions based upon physical differences, and the attempt to do so can only result in accentuating the difficulties of the present situation. If the

civil and political rights of both races be equal one cannot be inferior to the other civilly or politically. If one race be inferior to the other socially, the Constitution of the United States cannot put them upon the same plane.

♦ ♦ ♦

Mr. Justice Harlan dissenting.

♦ ♦ ♦

In respect of civil rights, common to all citizens, the Constitution of the United States does not, I think, permit any public authority to know the race of those entitled to be protected in the enjoyment of such rights. Every true man has pride of race, and under appropriate circumstances when the rights of others, his equals before the law, are not to be affected, it is his privilege to express such pride and to take such action based upon it as to him seems proper. But I deny that any legislative body or judicial tribunal may have regard to the race of citizens when the civil rights of those citizens are involved. Indeed, such legislation, as that here in question, is inconsistent not only with that equality of rights which pertains to citizenship, National and State, but with the personal liberty enjoyed by everyone within the United States.

The Thirteenth Amendment does not permit the withholding or the deprivation of any right necessarily inhering in freedom. It not only struck down the institution of slavery as previously existing in the United States, but it prevents the imposition of any burdens or disabilities that constitute badges of slavery or servitude. It decreed universal civil freedom in this country. This court has so adjudged. But that amendment having been found inadequate to the protection of the rights of those who had been in slavery, it was followed by the Fourteenth Amendment, which added greatly to the dignity and glory of American citizenship, and to the security of personal liberty, by declaring that "all persons born or naturalized in the United States, and subject to the jurisdiction thereof, are citizens of the United States and of the State wherein they reside," and that "no State shall make or enforce any law which shall abridge the privileges or immunities of citizens of the United States; nor shall any State deprive any person of life, liberty or property without due process of law, nor deny to any person within its jurisdiction the equal protection of the laws." These two amendments, if enforced according to their true intent and meaning, will protect all the civil rights that pertain to freedom and citizenship.

♦ ♦ ♦

It was said in argument that the statute of Louisiana does not discriminate against either race, but prescribes a rule applicable alike to white and colored citizens. But this argument does not meet the difficulty. Every one knows that the statute in question had its origin in the purpose, not so much to exclude white persons from railroad cars occupied by blacks, as to exclude colored people from coaches occupied by or assigned to white persons. Railroad corporations of Louisiana did not make discrimination among whites in the matter of accommodation for travellers. The thing to accomplish was, under the guise of giving equal accommodation for whites and blacks, to compel the latter to keep to themselves while travelling in railroad passenger coaches. No one would be so wanting in candor as to assert the contrary. The fundamental objection, therefore, to the statute is that it interferes with the personal freedom of citizens.

♦ ♦ ♦

The white race deems itself to be the dominant race in this country. And so it is, in prestige, in achievements, in education, in wealth and in power. So, I doubt not, it will continue to be for all time, if it remains true to its great heritage and holds fast to the principles of constitutional liberty. But in view of the Constitution, in the eye of the law, there is in this country no superior, dominant, ruling class of citizens. There is no caste here. Our Constitution is color-blind, and neither knows nor tolerates classes among citizens. In respect of civil rights, all citizens are equal before the law. The humblest is the peer of the most powerful. The law regards man as man, and takes no account of his surroundings or of his color when his civil

rights as guaranteed by the supreme law of the land are involved. It is, therefore, to be regretted that this high tribunal, the final expositor of the fundamental law of the land, has reached the conclusion that it is competent for a State to regulate the enjoyment by citizens of their civil rights solely upon the basis of race.

In my opinion, the judgment this day rendered will, in time, prove to be quite as pernicious as the decision made by this tribunal in the *Dred Scott* case (1857). It was adjudged in that case that the descendants of Africans who were imported into this country and sold as slaves were not included nor intended to be included under the word "citizens" in the Constitution, and could not claim any of the rights and privileges which that instrument provided for and secured to citizens of the United States; that at the time of the adoption of the Constitution they were "considered as a subordinate and inferior class of beings, who . . . had no rights or privileges but such as those who held the power and the government might choose to grant them." The recent amendments of the Constitution, it was supposed, had eradicated these principles from our institutions. But it seems that we have yet, in some of the States, a dominant race—a superior class of citizens, which assumes to regulate the enjoyment of civil rights, common to all citizens, upon the basis of race. The present decision, it may well be apprehended, will not only stimulate aggressions, more or less brutal and irritating, upon the admitted rights of colored citizens, but will encourage the belief that it is possible, by means of state enactments, to defeat the beneficent purposes which the people of the United States had in view when they adopted the recent amendments of the Constitution, by one of which the blacks of this country were made citizens of the United States and of the States in which they respectively reside, and whose privileges and immunities, as citizens, the States are forbidden to abridge. Sixty millions of whites are in no danger from the presence here of eight millions of blacks. The destinies of the two races, in this country, are indissolubly linked together, and the interests of both require that the common government of all shall not permit the seeds of race hate to be planted under the sanction of law. What can more certainly arouse race hate, what more certainly create and perpetuate a feeling of distrust between these races, than state enactments, which, in fact, proceed on the ground that colored citizens are so inferior and degraded that they cannot be allowed to sit in public coaches occupied by white citizens? That, as all will admit, is the real meaning of such legislation as was enacted in Louisiana. . . .

State enactments, regulating the enjoyment of civil rights, upon the basis of race, and cunningly devised to defeat legitimate results of the war, under the pretence of recognizing equality of rights, can have no other result than to render permanent peace impossible, and to keep alive a conflict of races, the continuance of which must do harm to all concerned. This question is not met by the suggestion that social equality cannot exist between the white and black races in this country. That argument, if it can be properly regarded as one, is scarcely worthy of consideration; for social equality no more exists between two races when travelling in a passenger coach or a public highway than when members of the same races sit by each other in a street car or in the jury box, or stand or sit with each other in a political assembly, or when they use in common the streets of a city or town, or when they are in the same room for the purpose of having their names placed on the registry of voters, or when they approach the ballot-box in order to exercise the high privilege of voting.

There is a race so different from our own that we do not permit those belonging to it to become citizens of the United States. Persons belonging to it are, with few exceptions, absolutely excluded from our country. I allude to the Chinese race. But by the statute in question, a Chinaman can ride in the same passenger coach with white citizens of the United States,

while citizens of the black race in Louisiana, any of whom, perhaps, risked their lives for the preservation of the Union, who are entitled, by law, to participate in the political control of the State and nation, who are not excluded, by law or by reason of their race, from public stations of any kind, and who have all the legal rights that belong to white citizens, are yet declared to be criminals, liable to imprisonment, if they ride in a public coach occupied by citizens of the white race. It is scarcely just to say that a colored citizen should not object of occupying a public coach assigned to his own race. He does not object, nor, perhaps, would he object to separate coaches for his race, if his rights under the law were recognized. But he objects, and ought never to cease objecting to the proposition, that citizens of the white and black races can be adjudged criminals because they sit, or claim the right to sit, in the same public coach on a public highway.

The arbitrary separation of citizens, on the basis of race, while they are on a public highway, is a badge of servitude wholly inconsistent with the civil freedom and the quality before the law established by the Constitution. It cannot be justified upon any legal grounds.

If evils will result from the commingling of the two races upon public highways established for the benefit of all, they will be infinitely less than those that will surely come from state legislation regulating the enjoyment of civil rights upon the basis of race. We boast of the freedom enjoyed by our people above all other peoples. But it is difficult to reconcile that boast with a state of the law which, practically, puts the brand of servitude and degradation upon a large class of our fellow-citizens, our equals before the law. The thin disguise of "equal" accommodations for passengers in railroad coaches will not mislead any one, nor atone for the wrong this day done.

Note: Separate But Equal in the North

In *Board of Education of Ottawa* v. *Tinnon* (1881), the Kansas Supreme Court ordered Ottawa to integrate its schools. The court held that Kansas law did not allow Ottawa to impose segregation. Because the case turned on state law, the court did not decide the constitutionality of segregation. *Tinnon* illustrates the divergence between the North and the South on race at this time. Ironically, the case that ended school segregation, *Brown* v. *Board of Education of Topeka* (1954), would come out of Kansas.

In *Plessy,* Justice Brown cited the nation's first school desegregation case, *Roberts* v. *City of Boston,* 5 Cush. (59 Mass.) 198 (1850), to support segregation in Louisiana. In *Roberts,* Chief Justice Lemuel Shaw upheld Boston's segregated school system with a theory that resembled "separate but equal." The validity of the *Roberts* precedent in *Plessy* is undermined by three points. First, *Roberts* took place before the Civil War and Reconstruction worked a revolution in race relations. Did it make sense to use an antebellum case to justify segregation almost fifty years, a war, and three constitutional amendments later? Second, *Roberts* was decided under the Massachusetts Constitution, which did not have an equal protection clause similar to that in the Fourteenth Amendment. Finally, in 1855 the Massachusetts legislature banned all segregation in the state's public schools.

Segregation on the Eve of a New Century
1898

In 1898, an editor of the Charleston, South Carolina, News and Courier *attacked the growing segregation in his state with an argument of* reductio ad absurdum, *but, as C. Vann Woodward has observed, "apart from the Jim Crow counties and Jim Crow witness stands, all the improbable applications of the principle suggested by the editor in derision had been put into practice—down to and including the Jim Crow Bible."*[8]

If there must be Jim Crow cars on the railroads, there should be Jim Crow cars on the street railways. Also on all passenger boats. . . . If there are to be Jim Crow cars, moreover, there should be Jim Crow waiting saloons at all stations, and Jim Crow eating houses. . . . There should be Jim Crow sections of the jury box, and a separate Jim Crow dock and witness stand in every court—and a Jim Crow Bible for colored witnesses to kiss. It would be advisable to also have a Jim Crow section in county auditors' and treasurers' offices for the accommodation of colored taxpayers. . . . Perhaps, the best plan would be, after all, to take the short cut to the general end . . . establishing two or three Jim Crow counties at once.

→ 5 ←

Nineteenth-Century Law and Society
1800–1900

Industrialization, urbanization, territorial growth, and immigration transformed nineteenth-century American society. When the Civil War began in 1861, agriculture propelled the country's economic growth; forty years later, manufacturing had taken its place. The benefits of economic growth showered unevenly across the social order; wealth became increasingly concentrated in the rising urban middle and upper classes, even as the absolute numbers of persons in the ranks of both groups continued to swell.

Economic growth and accompanying demographic changes had powerful social ramifications. The rising urban middle class, for example, fostered new expectations about the role of women, children, and family life in general. In the seventeenth and eighteenth centuries, most American families functioned as independent economic units. But as men became enmeshed in the nineteenth century's money economy (whether through trade and commerce or market farming), the direct contributions of women and children to the family economy changed. The new order that began to emerge by the 1820s had women and men occupying separate spheres, with the former dominating the private realm of the home by serving as homemakers and guardians of their families' moral and cultural well-being.

The roles of women and children changed in other ways. Until the late eighteenth century, economic pressures guided many marriages, but in the new century the ideals of mutual emotional support and love increasingly shaped wedlock. In this configuration, the children of middle- and upper-class combinations emerged as objects of emotional attachment rather than economic assets. These changes in the underlying social basis of the middle-class family prompted new demands on the legal culture, and lawmakers and judges responded by revising the rules governing domestic relations, an area that government had previously regulated lightly. The law of marriage, birth control, abortion, divorce, and child custody all experienced significant changes.

The lines separating male and female spheres also became entangled during this century. Women social reformers, such as Elizabeth Cady Stanton, sought to broaden the legal status of women, but to do so, in most instances, meant removing them from the pedestal on which men had placed them and eliminating the laws that male legislators had ostensibly crafted to protect women and the family. A small but vocal band of women also asserted their claims to a role in public life through activism on behalf of several social reform causes, including the abolition of slavery, penal reform, temperance, and, most significantly, women's suffrage.

Economic growth and social change converged through the law in other ways. Throughout the century, labor remained dear. Black slaves, as we have seen in Chapter 4, supplied much of the needs of southern planters before the Civil War. Subsequently, newly emancipated slaves sought to find a place in the new American market economy in a legal and constitutional system that was almost always hostile to them. The experience of African Americans was only one example of the tensions inherent in a legal culture that struggled to reconcile an ostensible commitment to an impartial rule of law with persistent racism and xenophobia. Native American, Asians, and Latinos each strove to find their respective identities before the law and in the new post–Civil War economy.

Growing racial and ethnic diversity, however, exacerbated social tensions. A strong white nativist movement, for example, protested first the massive wave of Irish and European immigrants that beat on American shores, beginning in mid-century, and provided an enormous pool of labor. They then turned their attention to other ethnic groups, including Chinese and Japanese on the West Coast and the existing Latino population there as well.

The nation's population soared because of this flood of immigrants. In the decade 1820 to 1829, only about 4 percent of the population increase came from the foreign born; between 1880 and 1889 more than 40 percent of the population increase came from immigration. Most of these new immigrants swelled the population of American cities and stoked industrialization, but they also frightened the native-born Protestant population with their customs and Catholic religious beliefs.

Americanization, ethnic assimilation, and racism also became entwined with themes of law and order. Urban rioting, crime, and poverty were features of growing American cities, and public authorities, who were often native-born Protestants, linked these disorders to immigrants. Throughout the century, concerns about crime often merely disguised nativist wishes to control the "dangerous classes." Yet social control through the criminal justice system had another side: a genuinely free people required a stable social order in which their persons and property were secure.

Nativism and racism were invariably supportive of each other, and both lurked just below the surface of American society. The legal fate of Asians, Native Americans, and Latinos illustrates this point. The Chinese and Japanese were the most exotic component of the nineteenth-century migration. The Chinese first arrived in America in the 1840s with the opening of the California gold fields, and they shortly became the objects of racial contempt and of public policies as bizarre as, if not more bizarre than, those adopted to deal with free blacks. The Chinese labored with white settlers to open the American West, but they were as visibly different as blacks from the dominant Anglo-Saxon population, and their religious practices made then troublesome for a criminal justice system rooted in Christian oath taking.

Native Americans also drew the white population's contempt. As American settlers poured westward, they invariably competed with the Indians for lands. These successive collisions began in the Southeast early in the century, spread beyond the Mississippi in mid-century, and continued after the Civil War on the Great Plains. Ironically, while most of the white population viewed Native Americans with a degree of equanimity that they refused to extend to blacks and Chinese, no other racial group suffered greater cultural or physical destruction. At each turn in the history of white–Native American relations, the law figured prominently in defining the rights and duties of each group. The issue of Indian rights, however, was part of a greater debate about the relative power of the federal and state governments. If the tribes were treated as separate nations, then the states had limited authority to take tribal lands and impose state law. The white quest for Indian lands also raised questions about whether a policy of preserving tribal culture on reservations or granting Native Americans full citizenship made sense. American Indian policy mixed political expediency, philanthropy, and greed in often equal measures.

Latinos and Hispanics, like Native Americans, stood in the path of white expansion. Yet they also offered crucial skills to new immigrants in mining gold, channeling water, and herding cattle in the arid West.

For all of these groups, the underlying question became their constitutional status as citizens generally and specifically the force with which the new Civil War Amendments, notably the Fourteenth, applied to them. What is clear is that these groups faced legal and social struggles for civil rights as challenging as black Americans, although none of them had to undo the single most salient characteristic separating blacks—their color combined with a history of slavery.

By 1900, the rural Republic of a hundred years before had been swamped by a significantly more diverse and contentious social order. Whether involving matters of racial adjustment, domestic relations, women's rights, or crime and criminal justice, the relationship between law and society in the nineteenth century was typically one of demand and response. The documents that follow address the ways in which nineteenth-century Americans invoked legal authority to deal with the tensions created by a contradictory commitment to human equality on the one hand, and sexism, nativism, and racism on the other.

RACE

Paradigms of race shape our understanding and definition of racial problems. The most pervasive and powerful paradigm of race in the nineteenth-century United States was that of black/white. Such a paradigm, however, fails to address the broad complex of racial issues before the nation, not just in the nineteenth century but in the twenty-first century as well. Indeed, while the struggle for black civil rights forms one of the most important stories in American legal history, it is best interpreted as part of the fate of other people of color, notably Asians, Native Americans, and Latinos. Today, of course, scholars such as Harvard sociologist Orlando Patterson argue that race is increasingly disappearing as a meaningful category by which to sort the human population. Indeed, Patterson argues that by the middle of the twenty-first century, such distinctions are likely to be moot. Such, however, was not the case in the nineteenth century.

Nineteenth-century lawmakers invoked race to define personal status. Slavery, as you have seen in Chapter 4, attached exclusively to black people, and the southern system of Jim Crow segregation that rose to replace it after Reconstruction was also directed toward nonwhites only. This shift from slavery to segregation underscores the dynamic and pliable character of the relationship between race and law, and this same quality figures in the treatment accorded Native Americans, Chinese, and Latinos. In each instance, the social and cultural assumptions of inferiority that whites attached to these groups found expression in the legal culture. Throughout the nineteenth century, a minority of white Americans embraced the arguments made by some anthropologists, physicians, and other scientists that nonwhites were actually a species of beings who had been placed on earth by God at a "separate creation." Most Americans rejected this extreme position, in large measure because it violated the biblical creation story set out in the book of Genesis. More common, at least in the South, was the view expressed by Senator James Henry Hammond of South Carolina in a famous 1858 speech on the floor of the Senate. He argued that blacks were simply a "race inferior" to whites who had a "low order of intellect" and "little skill," and were marked by "vigor, docility, [and] fidelity." Comparable statements about the Chinese, Native Americans, and Latinos were made by other prominent white nineteenth-century Americans. Not surprisingly, white Americans sought through the law to provide for the social control of each of these groups. But in each instance, the law also recognized important differences among these racial groups, and, as significant, there were important regional differences in ideas and practices. For example, after the Civil War, the Chinese, Native Americans, and Latinos were a far greater source of concern than were blacks in the West; the opposite was true in the East and South.

NATIVE AMERICANS

As white settlers flooded into the interior of the new American nation, they found a land already occupied by Native Americans. By 1800, white settlement, disease, and warfare had decimated the native population along the Atlantic coast, leaving only a few tribal remnants scattered from Maine to Georgia. In the trans-Appalachian interior, powerful tribes still dominated, although by 1820 they too had succumbed to the tide of white migration.

During these years, the federal government established formative policies that framed the course of white–Native American relations for the rest of the century. Lawmakers attempted to balance competing goals. They at once pursued a paternalistic policy intended to protect Native Americans from unscrupulous traders and settlers while Christianizing them in preparation for admission into white society. The same federal government also championed a policy of territorial expansion that with each successive wave of white settlement pushed Native Americans ever farther west.

The acquisition of Native American lands emerged as the dominant objective of federal Indian policy, but the means to that end varied during the century. Initially, the federal government had set on a course of conquest, but during the 1790s that program changed to one that recognized the inherent rights of Native Americans to their lands. Land transfers were accomplished through treaty agreements, a policy that rested on the assumption that the several tribes composed a distinct nation capable of entering into treaty negotiations. The nature and scope of Native American sovereignty, therefore, emerged as the most important issue of federal Indian policy in the nineteenth century.

The Framers of the federal Constitution left the status of Native Americans indefinite, although, by implication, they were outside the constitutional system. They were denied citizenship, exempted from taxation, and not counted in the apportionment of representation and direct taxes. Congress had authority to regulate commerce with the Indian tribes, and a succession of presidents acted under the treaty-making and war powers to negotiate with the tribes. Throughout the nineteenth century, the federal government pursued a policy that inexorably eroded the independence of the tribes, reaching a point late in the century when, under the Dawes Act of 1887, it called for the wholesale assimilation of the tribes.

Cherokee Nation v. *Georgia*
5 Pet. (30 U.S.) 1 (1831)

The disposition of Native American lands was a point of controversy between federal and state governments, with each claiming that it had exclusive authority to deal with the tribes. During the 1820s, Georgia became dissatisfied with the slowness of the United States government in removing the Creek and Cherokee populations. Georgia lawmakers aggressively pushed for the removal of the tribes, so much so that they dispatched surveyors to prepare the land for sale. The Cherokees reacted by adopting a written constitution and proclaiming themselves an independent nation. When Andrew Jackson became president in 1829, he refused to take any action in defense of Indian treaty rights as previous chief executives, especially John Quincy Adams, had done. Friends of the Cherokees, however, sought an injunction from the Supreme Court to restrain Georgia from enforcing its laws over the Cherokees and from seizing their lands. Against this backdrop of events, Chief Justice John Marshall wrote the opinion of the Court.

Mr. Chief Justice Marshall delivered the opinion of the Court.

This bill is brought by the Cherokee nation, praying an injunction to restrain the state of Georgia from the execution of certain laws of that state, which, as is alleged, go directly to annihilate the Cherokees as a political society, and to seize, for the use of Georgia, the lands of the nation which have been assured to them by the United States in solemn treaties repeatedly made and still in force.

If courts were permitted to indulge their sympathies, a case better calculated to excite them can scarcely be imagined. A people once numerous, powerful, and truly independent, found by our ancestors in the quiet and uncontrolled possession of an ample domain, gradually sinking beneath our superior policy, our arts and our arms, have yielded their lands by successive treaties, each of which contains a solemn guarantee of the residue, until they retain no more of their formerly extensive territory than is deemed necessary to their comfortable subsistence. To preserve this remnant, the present application is made.

Before we can look into the merits of the case, a preliminary inquiry presents itself. Has this court jurisdiction of the cause?

The third article of the constitution describes the extent of the judicial power. The second section closes an enumeration of the cases to which it is extended, with "controversies" "between a state or the citizens thereof, and foreign states, citizens, or subjects." A subsequent clause of the same section gives the supreme court original jurisdiction in all cases in which a state shall be a party. The party defendant may then unquestionably be sued in this court. May the plaintiff sue in it? Is the Cherokee nation a foreign state in the sense in which that term is used in the constitution?

The counsel for the plaintiffs have maintained the affirmative of this proposition with great earnestness and ability. So much of the argument as was intended to prove the character of the Cherokees as a state, as a distinct political society, separated from others, capable of managing its own affairs and governing itself, has, in the opinion of a majority of the judges, been completely successful. They have been uniformly treated as a state from the settlement of our country. The numerous treaties made with them by the United States recognize them as a people capable of maintaining the relations of peace and war, of being responsible in their political character for any violation of their engagements, or for any aggression committed on the citizens of the United States by any individual of their community. Laws have been enacted in the spirit of these treaties. The acts of our government plainly recognize the Cherokee nation as a state, and the courts are bound by those acts.

A question of much more difficulty remains. Do the Cherokees constitute a foreign state in the sense of the constitution?

The counsel have shown conclusively that they are not a state of the union, and have insisted that individually they are aliens, not owing allegiance to the United States. An aggregate of aliens composing a state must, they say, be a foreign state. Each individual being foreign, the whole must be foreign.

This argument is imposing, but we must examine it more closely before we yield to it. The condition of the Indians in relation to the United States is perhaps unlike that of any other two people in existence. In the general, nations not owing a common allegiance are foreign to each other. The term *foreign nation* is, with strict propriety, applicable by either to the other. But the relation of the Indians to the United States is marked by peculiar and cardinal distinctions which exist no where else.

The Indian territory is admitted to compose a part of the United States. In all our maps, geographical treatises, histories, and laws, it is so considered. In all our intercourse with foreign nations, in our commercial regulations, in any attempt at intercourse between Indians and foreign nations, they are considered as within the jurisdictional limits of the United States, subject to many of those restraints which are imposed upon our own citizens. They acknowledge themselves in their treaties to be under the protection of the United States; they admit that the United States shall have the sole and exclusive right of regulating the trade with them, and managing all their affairs as they think proper; and the Cherokees in particular were allowed by the treaty of Hopewell, which preceded the constitution, "to send a deputy of their choice, whenever they think fit, to congress." Treaties were made with some tribes by the state of New York, under a then unsettled construction of the confederation, by which they ceded all their lands to that state, taking back a limited grant to themselves, in which they admit their dependence.

Though the Indians are acknowledged to have an unquestionable, and, heretofore, unquestioned right to the lands they occupy, until that right shall be extinguished by a voluntary cession to our government; yet it may well be doubted whether those tribes which reside within the acknowledged boundaries of the United States can, with strict accuracy, be denominated foreign nations. They may, more correctly, perhaps, be denominated domestic dependent nations. They occupy a territory to which we assert a title independent of their will, which must take effect in point of possession when their right of possession ceases. Meanwhile they are in a state of pupilage. Their relation to the United States resembles that of a ward to his guardian.

They look to our government for protection; rely upon its kindness and its power; appeal to it for relief to their wants; and address the president as their great father. They and their country are considered by foreign nations, as well as by ourselves, as being so completely under the sovereignty and dominion of the United States, that any attempt to acquire their lands, or to form a political connexion with them, would be considered by all as an invasion of our territory, and an act of hostility.

These considerations go far to support the opinion, that the framers of our constitution had not the Indian tribes in view, when they opened the courts of the union to controversies between a state or the citizens thereof, and foreign states.

In considering this subject, the habits and usages of the Indians, in their intercourse with their white neighbours, ought not to be entirely disregarded. At the time the constitution was framed, the idea of appealing to an American court of justice for an assertion of right or a redress of wrong, had perhaps never entered the mind of an Indian or of his tribe. Their appeal was to the tomahawk, or to the government. This was well understood by the statesmen who framed the constitution of the United States, and might furnish some reason for omitting to enumerate them among the parties who might sue in the courts of the union. Be this as it may, the peculiar relations between the United States and the Indians occupying our territory are such, that we should feel much difficulty in considering them as designated by the term *foreign state,* were there no other part of the constitution which might shed light on the meaning of these words. But we think that in construing them, considerable aid is furnished by that clause in the eighth section of the third article; which empowers congress to "regulate commerce with foreign nations, and among the several states, and with the Indian tribes."

In this clause they are as clearly contradistinguished by a name appropriate to themselves, from foreign nations, as from the several states composing the union. They are designated by a distinct appellation; and as this appellation can be applied to neither of the others, neither can the appellation distinguishing either of the others be in fair construction applied to them. The objects, to which the power of regulating commerce might be directed, are divided into three distinct classes—foreign nations, the several states, and Indian tribes. When forming this article, the convention considered them as entirely distinct. We cannot assume that the distinction was lost in framing a subsequent article, unless there be something in its language to authorize the assumption.

The counsel for the plaintiffs contend that the words "Indian tribes" were introduced into the article, empowering congress to regulate commerce, for the purpose of removing those doubts in which the management of Indian affairs was involved by the language of the ninth article of the confederation. Intending to give the whole power of managing those affairs to the government about to be instituted, the convention conferred it explicitly; and omitted those qualifications which embarrassed the exercise of it as granted in the confederation.

This may be admitted without weakening the construction which has been intimated. Had the Indian tribes been foreign nations, in the view of the convention; this exclusive power of regulating intercourse with them might have been, and most probably would have been, specifically given, in language indicating that idea, not in language contradistinguishing them from foreign nations. Congress might have been empowered "to regulate commerce with foreign nations, including the Indian tribes, and among the several states." This language would have suggested itself to statesmen who considered the Indian tribes as foreign nations, and were yet desirous of mentioning them particularly.

♦ ♦ ♦

The court has bestowed its best attention on this question, and, after mature deliberation, the majority is of opinion that an Indian tribe or nation within the United States is not a foreign state in the sense of the constitution and cannot maintain an action in the courts of the United States.

♦ ♦ ♦

If it be true that the Cherokee nation have rights, this is not the tribunal in which those rights are to be asserted. If it be true that wrongs have been inflicted, and that still greater are to be apprehended, this is not the tribunal which can redress the past or prevent the future.

The motion for an injunction is denied.

Note: The Federal Government and Native Americans

The year following *Cherokee Nation,* the Court decided *Worcester* v. *Georgia,* 6 Pet. 515 (1832). Samuel Worcester had been convicted in a state court of living on Indian lands without a state license. In this instance, Chief Justice Marshall, speaking for the Court, recognized the Cherokees as a distinct political community having territorial boundaries within which Georgia had no right of action. Georgia declined to appear in the Supreme Court to argue its position, and state officials refused to release Worcester from custody. President Andrew Jackson also dismissed the chief justice's opinion, supposedly proclaiming that "John Marshall had made his decision, now let him enforce it." Jackson decided that the best course of action was to apply further pressure on the Cherokees to give up their lands, and his administration oversaw the wholesale removal of the native tribes of the Southeast to lands beyond the Mississippi River. The federal Constitution failed to provide meaningful protection to the nation's largest free minority, the American Indians. The *Cherokee Nation* and *Worcester* cases also coincided with the nullification crisis. The defiance of Georgia officials seems to have further emboldened radical states'-rights elements in South Carolina. President Jackson acted with far greater energy in stemming that threat to federal authority than he did in dealing with recalcitrant Georgia officials.

The concept of tribal sovereignty came under attack after the Civil War. The federal government, for example, permitted gold prospectors to stream into the Black Hills, an area considered sacred by the Sioux. Despite a stunning victory in 1876 over General George Armstrong Custer at Little Big Horn, the native tribes proved no match for the U.S. Army. Furthermore, the slaughter of the buffalo by white hunters (some 13 million animals by 1883) decimated the natural supply of food and clothing of the tribes, to which the federal government turned a blind eye.

The concept of tribal sovereignty also came under congressional attack in the post–Civil War era. The Dawes Severalty Act of 1887 was the most important piece of congressional legislation involving Indians in the nineteenth century. The purpose of the act was simple: to end the traditional policy of treating individual Indians as members of their tribes. The Dawes Act sought to lure Indians away from their tribal commitments by offering them a homestead grant that promised both to destroy their culture and to turn them into white farmers. The great bulk of Native Americans opposed the Dawes Act, and Indian agents representing them in Washington made these sentiments known to Congress. The idea of making Indians American citizens, however, had great allure for lawmakers, since it held forth the promise of permanently settling the Indian question. More important, however, the Dawes Act, even with its allotment of 160 acres per Indian, created millions of "surplus" acres that could be sold to white settlers. By the end of the century, Native Americans had lost 60 percent of their lands, the sale of which went into a trust fund for use in further "civilizing" the tribes.

Lone Wolf v. *Hitchcock*
187 U.S. 553 (1903)

In Lone Wolf *the Supreme Court recognized a near absolute plenary congressional power over the affairs of Native Americans—in this instance the disposal of lands held by the Kiowas, Comanche, and Apache peoples. The Court's decision represented a decisive shift away from the doctrines of the* Cherokee Cases *(1831–1832) and their emphasis on the inherent rights of native peoples and toward a policy that emphasized the power of the federal government to appropriate and hold tribal lands in trust. In 1979 a federal judge described* Lone Wolf *as the "Indian's* Dred Scott*." In more recent times, the Supreme Court has accepted some limitations on federal control of native peoples, most notably in* Seminole Tribe of Florida v. Florida *(1996), in which the Court struck down a complex scheme by which the federal government had regulated gambling on reservation land. In* Lone Wolf, *Justice Edward D. White rejected the claim by Lone Wolf, the principal chief of the Kiowa tribe, that the federal policy of allotting the lands of native peoples violated the 1867 Treaty of Medicine Lodge. He found, instead, in favor of Ethan Hitchcock, Secretary of the Interior.*

Mr. Justice White . . . delivered the opinion of the court:

By the sixth article of the first of the two treaties . . . proclaimed on August 25, 1868 (15 Stat. at L. 581), it was provided that heads of families of the tribes affected by the treaty might select, within the reservation, a tract of land of not exceeding 320 acres in extent, which should thereafter cease to be held in common, and should be for the exclusive possession of the Indian making the selection so long as he or his family might continue to cultivate the land. The twelfth article reads as follows:

Article 12. No treaty for the cession of any portion or part of the reservation herein in described, which may be held in common, shall be of any validity or force, as against the said Indians, unless executed and signed by at least three fourths of all the adult male Indians occupying the same, and no cession by the tribe shall be understood or construed in such manner as to deprive, without his consent, any individual member of the tribe of his rights to any tract of land selected by him as provided in article 3 [6] of this treaty.

The appellants base their right to relief on the proposition that by the effect of the article just quoted the confederated tribes of Kiowas, Comanches, and Apaches were vested with an interest in the lands held in common within the reservation, which interest could not be divested by Congress in any other mode than that specified in the said twelfth article, and that as a result of the said stipulation the interest of the Indians in the common lands fell within the protection of the 5th Amendment to the Constitution of the United States, and such interest— indirectly at least—came under the control of the judicial branch of the government. We are unable to yield our assent to this view.

The contention in effect ignores the status of the contracting Indians and the relation of dependency they bore and continue to bear towards the government of the United States. To uphold the claim would be to adjudge that the indirect operation of the treaty was to materially limit and qualify the controlling authority of Congress in respect to the care and protection of the Indians, and to deprive Congress, in a possible emergency, when the necessity might be urgent for a partition and disposal of the tribal lands, of all power to act, if the assent of the Indians could not be obtained.

Now, it is true that in decisions of this court, the Indian right of occupancy of tribal lands, whether declared in a treaty or otherwise created, has been stated to be sacred, or, as sometimes expressed, as sacred as the fee of the United States in the same lands. *Johnson* v. *M'Intosh* (1823); *Cherokee Nation* v. *Georgia* (1831); *Worcester* v. *Georgia* (1832); *United States* v. *Cook* (1873); *Leavenworth, L. & G. R. Co.* v. *United States* (1875); *Beecher* v. *Wetherby* (1877). But in none of these cases was there involved a controversy between Indians and the government respecting the power of Congress to administer the property of the Indians. The questions considered in the cases referred to, which either directly or indirectly had relation to the nature of the property rights of the Indians, concerned the character and extent of such rights as respected states or individuals. In one of the cited cases it was clearly pointed out that Congress possessed a paramount power over the property of the Indians, by reason of its exercise of guardianship over their interests, and that such authority might be implied, even though opposed to the strict letter of a treaty with the Indians. Thus, in *Beecher* v. *Wetherby*, discussing the claim that there had been a prior reservation of land by treaty to the use of a certain tribe of Indians, the court said:

But the right which the Indians held was only that of occupancy. The fee was in the United States, subject to that right, and could be transferred by them whenever they chose. The grantee, it is true, would take only the naked fee, and could not disturb the occupancy of the Indians; that occupancy could only be interfered with or determined by the United States. It is to be presumed that in this matter the United States would be governed by such considerations of justice as would control a Christian people in their treatment of an ignorant and dependent race. Be that is it may, the propriety or justice of their action towards the Indians with respect to their lands is a question of governmental policy, and is not a matter open to discussion in a controversy between third parties, neither of whom derives title from the Indians.

Plenary authority over the tribal relations of the Indians has been exercised by Congress from the beginning, and the power has always been deemed a political one, not subject to be controlled by the judicial department of the government. Until the year 1871 the policy was pursued of dealing with the Indian tribes by means of treaties, and, of course, a moral obligation rested upon Congress to act in good faith in performing the stipulations entered into on its behalf. But, as with treaties made with foreign nations (*Chinese Exclusion Case* [1889]), the legislative power might pass laws in conflict with treaties made with the Indians.

The power exists to abrogate the provisions of an Indian treaty, though presumably such power will be exercised only when circumstances arise which will not only justify the government in disregarding the stipulations of the treaty, but may demand, in the interest of the country and the Indians themselves, that it should do so. When, therefore, treaties were entered into between the United States and a tribe of Indians it was never doubted that the power to abrogate existed in Congress, and that in a contingency such power might be availed of from considerations of governmental policy, particularly if consistent with perfect good faith towards the Indians. In *United States* v. *Kagama* (1885), speaking of the Indians, the court said:

After an experience of a hundred years of the treaty-making system of government Congress has determined upon a new departure,—to govern them by acts of Congress. This is seen in the act of March 3, 1871, embodied in § 2079 of the Revised Statutes: "No Indian nation or tribe, within the territory of the United States, shall be acknowledged or recognized as an independent nation, tribe, or power with whom the United States may contract by treaty; but no obligation of any treaty lawfully made

and ratified with any such Indian nation or tribe prior to March 3d, 1871, shall be hereby invalidated or impaired."

In upholding the validity of an act of Congress which conferred jurisdiction upon the courts of the United States for certain crimes committed on an Indian reservation within a state, the court said:

It seems to us that this is within the competency of Congress. These Indian tribes are the wards of the nation. They are communities dependent on the United States. Dependent largely for their daily food. Dependent for their political rights. They own no allegiance to the states, and receive from them no protection. Because of the local ill feeling, the people of the states where they are found are often their deadliest enemies. From their very weakness and helplessness, so largely due to the course of dealing of the Federal government with them and the treaties in which it has been promised, there arises the duty of protection, and with it the power. This has always been recognized by the executive and by Congress, and by this court, whenever the question has arisen.

♦ ♦ ♦

The power of the general government over these remnants of a race once powerful, now weak and diminished in numbers, is necessary to their protection, as well as to the safety of those among whom they dwell. It must exist in that government, because it never has existed anywhere else, because the theater of its exercise is within the geographical limits of the United States, because it has never been denied, and because it alone can enforce its laws on all the tribes.

That Indians who had not been fully emancipated from the control and protection of the United States are subject, at least so far as the tribal lands were concerned, to be controlled by direct legislation of Congress. . . .

In view of the legislative power possessed by Congress over treaties with the Indians and Indian tribal property, we may not specially consider the contentions pressed upon our notice that the signing by the Indians of the agreement of October 6, 1892, was obtained by fraudulent misrepresentations, and concealment, that the requisite three fourths of adult male Indians had not signed, as required by the twelfth article of the treaty of 1867, and that the treaty as signed had been amended by Congress without submitting such amendments to the action of the Indians since all these matters, in any event, were solely within the domain of the legislative authority, and its action is conclusive upon the courts.

The act of June 6, 1900, which is complained of in the bill, was enacted at a time when the tribal relations between the confederated tribes of Kiowas, Comanches, and Apaches still existed, and that statute and the statutes supplementary thereto dealt with the disposition of tribal property, and purported to give an adequate consideration for the surplus lands not allotted among the Indians or reserved for their benefit. Indeed, the controversy which this case presents is concluded by the decision . . . that full administrative power was possessed by Congress over Indian tribal property. In effect, the action of Congress now complained of was but an exercise of such power, a mere change in the form of investment of Indian tribal property, the property of those who, as we have held, were in substantial effect the wards of the government. We must presume that Congress acted in perfect good faith in the dealings with the Indians of which complaint is made, and that the legislative branch of the government exercised its best judgment in the premises. In any event, as Congress possessed full power in the matter, the judiciary cannot question or inquire into the motives which prompted the enactment of this legislation. If injury was occasioned, which we do not wish to be understood as implying, by the use made by Congress of its power, relief must be sought by an appeal to that body for redress, and not to the courts. The legislation in question was constitutional, and the demurrer to the bill was therefore rightly sustained.

The motion to dismiss does not challenge jurisdiction over the subject-matter. Without expressly referring to the propositions of fact upon which it proceeds, suffice it to say that we think it need not be further adverted to, since, for the reasons previously given and the nature of the controversy, we think the decree below should be affirmed.

And it is so ordered.

ASIANS

Although only 264,000 Chinese and about 10,000 Japanese came to the United States and Hawaii between 1860 and 1900, they constituted a significant minority on the West Coast. The Chinese initially labored in the gold fields, where they were particularly adept at finding what other miners overlooked. White American miners resented the Chinese presence, and they gradually applied physical violence and political pressure to force them out. The California General Assembly, for example, made an abortive attempt to declare illegal all mining by foreign persons, settling instead for a stiff tax on foreign miners (which the California Supreme Court ultimately declared unconstitutional). Under continuing pressure from the American population, the Chinese gravitated into San Francisco, Sacramento, and other urban areas. They did, however, continue throughout the West to perform some of the dirtiest and hardest work, ranging from railroad and levee construction to factory labor. They also engaged in a variety of trades, most notably the laundry business. American settlers in the West viewed the Chinese with double suspicion. They were considered heathens, exotic, backward, and immoral; they were also deeply resented by a white workforce fearful of its jobs and wages.

Yick Wo v. *Hopkins*
118 U.S. 356 (1886)

The hatred of white Americans for the Chinese surfaced in several ways, some of which appeared in what today would seem bizarre statutes and ordinances. Just as Southerners were erecting Jim Crow laws to segregate blacks and other nonwhites, Westerners sought to control the Chinese. A California statute of 1872, for example, authorized school districts to establish separate schools for the Chinese and Japanese. But it was their pocketbooks that Westerners were most interested in protecting, as the following case involving a San Francisco ordinance of 1880 makes clear. The ordinance made it unlawful to carry on a laundry in the city without the consent of the board of supervisors, unless the laundry was located in a building constructed of either brick or stone. Almost every San Francisco laundry was in a wooden building. The board turned down all applications of Chinese and granted all those of Caucasians. Its actions raised important questions about the meaning of the equal protection clause of the Fourteenth Amendment.

Mr. Justice Matthews delivered the opinion of the court.

In the case of the petitioner, brought here by writ of error to the Supreme Court of California, our jurisdiction is limited to the question, whether the plaintiff in error has been denied a right in violation of the Constitution, laws, or treaties of the United States.

We are consequently constrained at the outset to differ from the Supreme Court of California upon the real meaning of the ordinances in question. That court considered these ordinances as vesting in the board of supervisors a not unusual discretion in granting or withholding their assent to the use of wooden buildings as laundries, to be exercised in reference to the circumstances of each case, with a view to the protection of the public against the dangers of fire. We are not able to concur in that interpretation of the power conferred upon the supervisors. There is nothing in the ordinances which points to such a regulation of the business of keeping and conducting laundries. They seem intended to confer, and actually do confer, not a discretion to be exercised upon a consideration of the circumstances of each case, but a naked and arbitrary power to give or withhold consent, not only as to places, but as to persons.

The ordinance drawn in question . . . does not prescribe a rule and conditions for the regulation of the use of property for laundry purposes, to which all similarly situated may conform. It allows without restriction the use for such purposes of buildings of brick or stone; but, as to wooden buildings, constituting nearly all those in previous use, it divides the owners or occupiers into two classes, not having respect to their personal character and qualifications for the business, nor the situation and nature and adaptation of the buildings themselves, but merely by an arbitrary line, on one side of which are those who are permitted to pursue their industry by the mere will and consent of the supervisors, and on the other those from whom that consent is withheld at their mere will and pleasure. And both classes are alike only in this, that they are tenants at will, under the supervisors, of their means of living. The ordinance, therefore, also differs from the not unusual case, where discretion is lodged by law in public officers or bodies to grant or withhold licenses to keep taverns, or places for the sale of spirituous liquors, and the like, when one of the conditions is that the applicant shall be a fit person for the exercise of the privilege, because in such cases the fact of fitness is submitted to the judgment of the officer, and calls for the exercise of a discretion of a judicial nature.

♦ ♦ ♦   ♦ ♦ ♦

The rights of the petitioners, as affected by the proceedings of which they complain, are not less, because they are aliens and subjects of the Emperor of China.

◆　◆　◆

The Fourteenth Amendment to the Constitution is not confined to the protection of citizens. It says: "Nor shall any State deprive any person of life, liberty, or property without due process of law; nor deny to any person within its jurisdiction the equal protection of the laws." These provisions are universal in their application, to all persons within the territorial jurisdiction, without regard to any differences of race, of color, or of nationality; and the equal protection of the laws is a pledge of the protection of equal laws. . . . The questions we have to consider and decide in these cases, therefore, are to be treated as involving the rights of every citizen of the United States equally with those of the strangers and aliens who now invoke the jurisdiction of the court.

◆　◆　◆

When we consider the nature and the theory of our institutions of government, the principles upon which they are supposed to rest, and review the history of their development, we are constrained to conclude that they do not mean to leave room for the play and action of purely personal and arbitrary power. Sovereignty itself is, of course, not subject to law, for it is the author and source of law; but in our system, while sovereign powers are delegated to the agencies of government, sovereignty itself remains with the people, by whom and for whom all government exists and acts. And the law is the definition and limitation of power. It is, indeed, quite true, that there must always be lodged somewhere, and in some person or body, the authority of final decision; and in many cases of mere administration the responsibility is purely political, no appeal lying except to the ultimate tribunal of the public judgment, exercised either in the pressure of opinion or by means of the suffrage. But the fundamental rights to life, liberty, and the pursuit of happiness, considered as individual possessions, are secured by those maxims of constitutional law which are the monuments showing the victorious progress of the race in securing to men the blessings of civilization under the reign of just and equal laws, so that, in the famous language of the Massachusetts Bill of Rights, the government of the commonwealth "may be a government of laws and not of men." For, the very idea that one man may be compelled to hold his life, or the means of living, or any material right essential to the enjoyment of life, at the mere will of another, seems to be intolerable in any country where freedom prevails, as being the essence of slavery itself.

There are many illustrations that might be given of this truth, which would make manifest that it was self-evident in the light of our system of jurisprudence. The case of the political franchise of voting is one. Though not regarded strictly as a natural right, but as a privilege merely conceded by society according to its will, under certain conditions, nevertheless it is regarded as a fundamental political right, because preservative of all rights.

◆　◆　◆

[T]he cases present the ordinances in actual operation, and the facts shown establish an administration directed so exclusively against a particular class of persons as to warrant and require the conclusion, that, whatever may have been the intent of the ordinances as adopted, they are applied by the public authorities charged with their administration, and thus representing the State itself, with a mind so unequal and oppressive as to amount to a practical denial by the State of that equal protection of the laws which is secured to the petitioners, as to all other persons, by the broad and benign provisions of the Fourteenth Amendment to the Constitution of the United States. Though the law itself be fair on its face and impartial in appearance, yet, if it is applied and administered by public authority with an evil eye and an unequal hand, so as practically to make unjust and illegal discriminations between persons in similar circumstances, material to their rights, the denial of equal justice is still within the prohibition of the Constitution.

◆　◆　◆

The present case, as shown by the facts disclosed in the record, are within this class. It appears that both petitioners have complied with every requisite, deemed by the law or by the public officers charged with its administration, necessary for the protection of neighboring property from fire, or as a precaution against injury to the public health. No reason whatever, except the will of the supervisors, is assigned why they should not be permitted to carry on, in the accustomed manner, their harmless and useful occupation, on which they depend for a livelihood. And while this consent of the supervisors was withheld from them and from two hundred others who have also petitioned, all of whom happen to be Chinese subjects, eighty others, not Chinese subjects, are permitted to carry on the same business under similar conditions. The fact of this discrimination is admitted. No reason for it is shown, and the conclusion cannot be resisted, that no reason for it exists except hostility to the race and nationality to which the petitioners belong, and which in the eye of the law is not justified. The discrimination is, therefore, illegal, and the public administration which enforces it is a denial of the equal protection of the laws and a violation of the Fourteenth Amendment of the Constitution. The imprisonment of the petitioners is, therefore, illegal, and they must be discharged.

Note: The Chinese and Jim Crow

On first impression, the Court's treatment of the Chinese under the Fourteenth Amendment seems to contrast sharply with its approval of southern Jim Crow legislation. Yet there was an important difference, one that helps to place not just the Court but the role of race in late-nineteenth-century legal culture in perspective. What the justices worried about in *Yick Wo* was the threat posed by the city ordinance to property rights. The justices were certainly willing to recognize broad authority for local and state governments to regulate human activity in the name of health, safety, morals, and welfare. But in this instance, such regulation seemed capricious, arbitrary, and a species of class legislation. That is, the law, while not blatantly discriminatory on racial grounds, did threaten private property rights, which the justices held particularly dear. Most Jim Crow legislation did not labor under that particular handicap.

Note: Chinese Exclusion

Restricting the influx of Chinese into the United States through federal legislation was one of the goals of organized labor in the West. Congress bowed to this pressure in 1882 when it passed the first of the Chinese exclusion acts. These laws prohibited Chinese laborers and miners from entering the United States, and subsequent amendments to this basic law prevented Chinese laborers who left the United States from returning. Subsequent measures limited the access of the Chinese to bail bonds, required that they carry identification certificates or face deportation, and broadened the categories of persons covered to include merchants, laundry owners, and fishers. In 1902 Congress closed the door entirely to Chinese migration.

United States v. *Wong Kim Ark*
169 U.S. 649 (1898)

The Supreme Court initially fashioned narrow holdings designed to protect Chinese reentry into the United States and to accord some protection to Chinese who were American citi-

zens. In United States *v.* Wong Kim Ark, *169 U.S. 649 (1898), the justices voted 6 to 2 in favor of Wong Kim Ark, born to Chinese parents in San Francisco, who had been denied admission to the United States after traveling to China for a visit. The majority ruled that the Fourteenth Amendment guaranteed citizenship to all persons born in the United States, regardless of ethnic heritage, although the two dissenters (Chief Justice Fuller, who was joined by Justice Harlan) raised a competing theory of the power of Congress to control citizenship under the Fourteenth Amendment.*

Mr. Justice Gray delivered the opinion of the court.

The facts of this case, as agreed by the parties, are as follows: Wong Kim Ark was born in 1873 in the city of San Francisco, in the State of California and United States of America, and was and is a laborer. His father and mother were persons of Chinese descent, and subjects of the Emperor of China; they were at the time of his birth domiciled residents of the United States, having previously established and still enjoying a permanent domicil and residence therein at San Francisco; they continued to reside and remain in the United States until 1890, when they departed for China; and during all the time of their residence in the United States they were engaged in business, and were never employed in any diplomatic or official capacity under the Emperor of China. Wong Kim Ark, ever since his birth, has had but one residence, to wit, in California, within the United States, and has there resided, claiming to be a citizen of the United States, and has never lost or changed that residence, or gained or acquired another residence; and neither he, nor his parents acting for him, ever renounced his allegiance to the United States, or did or committed any act or thing to exclude him therefrom. In 1890 (when he must have been about seventeen years of age) he departed for China on a temporary visit and with the intention of returning to the United States, and did return thereto by sea in the same year, and was permitted by the collector of customs to enter the United States, upon the sole ground that he was a native-born citizen of the United States. After such return, he remained in the United States, claiming to be a citizen thereof, until 1894, when he (being about twenty-one years of age, but whether a little above or a little under that age does not appear) again departed for China on a tempo-

rary visit and with the intention of returning to the United States; and he did return thereto by sea in August, 1895, and applied to the collector of customs for permission to land; and was denied such permission, upon the sole ground that he was not a citizen of the United States.

It is conceded that, if he is a citizen of the United States, the acts of Congress, known as the Chinese Exclusion Acts, prohibiting persons of the Chinese race, and especially Chinese laborers, from coming into the United States, do not and cannot apply to him.

The question presented by the record is whether a child born in the United States, of parents of Chinese descent, who, at the time of his birth, are subjects of the Emperor of China, but have a permanent domicil and residence in the United States, and are there carrying on business, and are not employed in any diplomatic or official capacity under the Emperor of China, becomes at the time of his birth a citizen of the United States, by virtue of the first clause of the Fourteenth Amendment of the Constitution, "All persons born or naturalized in the United States, and subject to the jurisdiction thereof, are citizens of the United States and of the State wherein they reside."

To hold that the Fourteenth Amendment of the Constitution excludes from citizenship the children, born in the United States, of citizens or subjects of other countries, would be to deny citizenship to thousands of persons of English, Scotch, Irish, German or other European parentage, who have always been considered and treated as citizens of the United States.

♦ ♦ ♦

VI. Whatever considerations, in the absence of a controlling provision of the Constitution, might influence the legislative or the executive branch of the Government to decline to admit persons of the Chinese race to the status of citizens of the United States, there are none that can constrain or permit the judiciary to refuse to give full effect to the peremptory and explicit language of the fourteenth Amendment, which declares and ordains that "All persons born or naturalized in the United States, and subject to the jurisdiction thereof, are citizens of the United States."

Chinese persons, born out of the United States, remaining subjects of the Emperor of China, and not having become citizens of the United States, are entitled to the protection of and owe allegiance to the United States, so long as they are permitted by the United States to reside here; and are "subject to the jurisdiction thereof," in the same sense as all other aliens residing in the United States.

In *Yick Wo* v. *Hopkins* [1886] the decision was that an ordinance of the city of San Francisco, regulating a certain business, and which, as executed by the board of supervisors, made an arbitrary discrimination between natives of China, still subjects of the Emperor of China, but domiciled in the United States, and all other persons, was contrary to the Fourteenth Amendment of the Constitution. Mr. Justice Matthews, in delivering the opinion of the court, said: "The rights of the petitioners, as affected by the proceedings of which they complain, are not less, because they are aliens and subjects of the Emperor of China. . . . The Fourteenth Amendment to the Constitution is not confined to the protection of citizens. It says, 'Nor shall any State deprive any person of life, liberty or property, without due process of law; nor deny to any person within its jurisdiction the equal protection of the laws.' These provisions are universal in their application, to all persons within the territorial jurisdiction, without regard to any differences of race, of color, or of nationality; and the equal protection of the laws is a pledge of the protection of equal laws. It is accordingly enacted, by § 1977 of the Revised Statutes, that 'all persons within the jurisdiction of the United States shall have the same right in every State and Territory to make and enforce contracts, to sue, be parties, give evidence, and to the full and equal benefit of all laws and proceedings for the security of persons and property, as is

enjoyed by white citizens, and shall be subject to like punishment, pains, penalties, taxes, licenses and exactions of every kind, and to no other.' The questions we have to consider and decide in these cases, therefore, are to be treated as involving the rights of every citizen of the United States, equally with those of the strangers and aliens who now invoke the jurisdiction of this court."

The manner in which reference was made, in the passage above quoted, to § 1977 of the Revised Statutes, shows that the change of phrase in that section, reenacting § 16 of the statute of May 31, 1870, c. 114, 16 Stat. 144, as compared with § 1 of the Civil Rights Act of 1866—by substituting, for the words in that act, "of every race and color," the words, "within the jurisdiction of the United States"— was not considered as making the section, as it now stands, less applicable to persons of every race and color and nationality, than it was in its original form; and is hardly consistent with attributing any narrower meaning to the words "subject to the jurisdiction thereof" in the first sentence of the Fourteenth Amendment of the Constitution, which may itself have been the cause of the change in the phraseology of that provision of the Civil Rights Act.

The decision in *Yick Wo* v. *Hopkins*, indeed, did not directly pass upon the effect of these words in the Fourteenth Amendment, but turned upon subsequent provisions of the same section. But, as already observed, it is impossible to attribute to the words, "subject to the jurisdiction thereof," that is to say, of the United States, at the beginning, a less comprehensive meaning than to the words "within its jurisdiction," that is of the State, at the end of the same section; or to hold that persons, who are indisputably "within the jurisdiction" of the State, are not "subject to the jurisdiction" of the Nation.

It necessarily follows that persons born in China, subjects of the Emperor of China, but domiciled in the United States, having been adjudged, in *Yick Wo* v. *Hopkins*, to be within the jurisdiction of the State, within the meaning of the concluding sentence, must be held to be subject to the jurisdiction of the United States, within the meaning of the first sentence of this section of the Constitution; and their children, "born in the United States," cannot be less "subject to the jurisdiction thereof." . . . And we are not aware of any judicial decision to the contrary.

During the debates in the Senate in January and February, 1866, upon the Civil Rights Bill, Mr. Trumbull, the chairman of the committee which reported the bill, moved to amend the first sentence thereof so as to read, "All persons born in the United States, and not subject to any foreign power, are hereby declared to be citizens of the United States, without distinction of color." Mr. Cowan, of Pennsylvania, asked, "Whether it will not have the effect of naturalizing the children of Chinese and Gypsies, born in this country?" Mr. Trumbull answered, "Undoubtedly;" and asked, "Is not the child born in this country of German parents a citizen?" Mr. Cowan replied, "The children of German parents are citizens; but Germans are not Chinese." Mr. Trumbull rejoined: "The law makes no such distinction; and the child of an Asiatic is just as much a citizen as the child of a European." Mr. Reverdy Johnson suggested that the words, "without distinction of color," should be omitted as unnecessary; and said: "The amendment, as it stands, is that all persons born in the United States, and not subject to a foreign power, shall, by virtue of birth, be citizens. To that I am willing to consent; and that comprehends all persons, without any reference to race or color, who may be so born." And Mr. Trumbull agreed that striking out those words would make no difference in the meaning, but thought it better that they should be retained, to remove all possible doubt.

The Fourteenth Amendment of the Constitution, as originally framed by the House of Representatives, lacked the opening sentence. When it came before the Senate in May, 1866, Mr. Howard, of Michigan, moved to amend by prefixing the sentence in its present form, (less the words "or naturalized,") and reading, "All persons born in the United States, and subject to the jurisdiction thereof, are citizens of the United States and of the State wherein they reside." Mr. Cowan objected, upon the ground that the Mongolian race ought to be excluded; and said: "Is the child of the Chinese immigrant in California a citizen? . . . I do not know how my honorable friend from California looks upon Chinese, but I do know how some of his fellow-citizens regard them. I have no doubt that now they are useful, and I have no doubt that within proper restraints, allowing that State and the other Pacific States to manage them as they may see fit, they may be useful; but I would not tie their hands by the Constitution of the United States so as to prevent them hereafter from dealing with them as in their wisdom they see fit." Mr. Conness, of California, replied: "The proposition before us relates simply, in that respect, to the children begotten of Chinese parents in California, and it is proposed to declare that they shall be citizens. We have declared that by law; now it is proposed to incorporate the same provision in the fundamental instrument of the Nation. I am in favor of doing so. I voted for the proposition to declare that the children of all parentage whatever, born in California, should be regarded and treated as citizens of the United States, entitled to equal civil rights with other citizens of the United States. . . . We are entirely ready to accept the provision proposed in this Constitutional Amendment, that the children born here of Mongolian parents shall be declared by the Constitution of the United States to be entitled to civil rights and to equal protection before the law with others." It does not appear to have been suggested, in either House of Congress, that children born in the United States of Chinese parents would not come within the terms and effect of the leading sentence of the Fourteenth Amendment.

Doubtless, the intention of the Congress which framed and of the States which adopted this Amendment of the Constitution must be sought in the words of the Amendment; and the debates in Congress are not admissible as evidence to control the meaning of those words. But the statements above quoted are valuable as contemporary opinions of jurists and statesmen upon the legal meaning of the words themselves; and are, at the least, interesting as showing that the application of the Amendment to the Chinese race was considered and not overlooked.

The acts of Congress, known as the Chinese Exclusion Acts, the earliest of which was passed some fourteen years after the adoption of the Constitutional Amendment, cannot control its meaning, or impair its effect, but must be construed and executed in subordination to its provisions. And the right of the United States, as exercised by and under those acts, to exclude or to expel from the country persons of the Chinese race, born in China, and continuing to be subjects of the Emperor of China, though having acquired a commercial domicil in the United States, has been upheld by this court, for reasons applicable to all aliens alike, and inapplicable to citizens, of whatever race or color. . . .

It is true that Chinese persons born in China cannot be naturalized, like other aliens, by proceedings under the naturalization laws. But this is for want of any statute or treaty authorizing or permitting such naturalization, as will appear by tracing the history of the statutes, treaties and decisions upon that subject— always bearing in mind that statutes enacted by Congress, as well as treaties made by the President and Senate, must yield to the paramount and supreme law of the Constitution.

The power, granted to Congress by the Constitution, "to establish an uniform rule of naturalization," was long ago adjudged by this court to be vested exclusively in Congress. *Chirac* v. *Chirac*, (1817). For many years after the establishment of the original Constitution, and until two years after the adoption of the Fourteenth Amendment, Congress never authorized the naturalization of any but "free white persons." By the treaty between the United States and China, made July 28, 1868, and promulgated February 5, 1870, it was provided that "nothing herein contained shall be held to confer naturalization upon citizens of the United States in China, nor upon the subjects of China in the United States."

◆ ◆ ◆

The Convention between the United States and China of 1894 provided that "Chinese laborers or Chinese of any other class, either permanently or temporarily residing in the United States, shall have for the protection of their persons and property all rights that are given by the laws of the United States to citizens of the

most favored nation, excepting the right to become naturalized citizens."

◆ ◆ ◆

The Fourteenth Amendment of the Constitution, in the declaration that "all persons born or naturalized in the United States, and subject to the jurisdiction thereof, are citizens of the United States and of the State wherein they reside," contemplates two sources of citizenship, and two only: birth and naturalization. Citizenship by naturalization can only be acquired by naturalization under the authority and in the forms of law. But citizenship by birth is established by the mere fact of birth under the circumstances defined in the Constitution. Every person born in the United States, and subject to the jurisdiction thereof, becomes at once a citizen of the United States, and needs no naturalization. A person born out of the jurisdiction of the United States can only become a citizen by being naturalized, either by treaty, as in the case of the annexation of foreign territory; or by authority of Congress, exercised either by declaring certain classes of persons to be citizens, as in the enactments conferring citizenship upon foreign-born children of citizens, or by enabling foreigners individually to become citizens by proceedings in the judicial tribunals, as in the ordinary provisions of the naturalization acts.

The power of naturalization, vested in Congress by the Constitution, is a power to confer citizenship, not a power to take it away. "A naturalized citizen," said Chief Justice Marshall, "becomes a member of the society, possessing all the rights of a native citizen, and standing, in the view of the Constitution, on the footing of a native. The Constitution does not authorize Congress to enlarge or abridge those rights. The simple power of the National Legislature is to prescribe a uniform rule of naturalization, and the exercise of this power exhausts it, so far as respects the individual. The Constitution then takes him up, and, among other rights, extends to him the capacity of suing in the courts of the United States, precisely under the same circumstances under which a native might sue." *Osborn* v. *United States Bank* (1824). Congress having no power to abridge the rights conferred by the Constitution upon those who have become naturalized citizens by virtue of acts of Congress, a fortiori no act or omission of Congress, as to providing for the naturalization of parents or children of a particular race, can affect citizenship acquired as a birthright, by virtue of the Constitution itself, without any aid of legislation. The Fourteenth Amendment, while it leaves the power, where it was before, in Congress, to regulate naturalization, has conferred no authority upon Congress to restrict the effect of birth, declared by the Constitution to constitute a sufficient and complete right to citizenship.

No one doubts that the Amendment, as soon as it was promulgated, applied to persons of African descent born in the United States, wherever the birthplace of their parents might have been; and yet, for two years afterwards, there was no statute authorizing persons of that race to be naturalized. If the omission or the refusal of Congress to permit certain classes of persons to be made citizens by naturalization could be allowed the effect of correspondingly restricting the classes of persons who should become citizens by birth, it would be in the power of Congress, at any time, by striking negroes out of the naturalization laws, and limiting those laws, as they were formerly limited, to white persons only, to defeat the main purpose of the Constitutional Amendment.

The fact, therefore, that acts of Congress or treaties have not permitted Chinese persons born out of this country to become citizens by naturalization, cannot exclude Chinese persons born in this country from the operation of the broad and clear words of the Constitution, "All persons born in the United States, and subject to the jurisdiction thereof, are citizens of the United States."

VII. Upon the facts agreed in this case, the American citizenship which Wong Kim Ark acquired by birth within the United States has not been lost or taken away by anything happening since his birth. No doubt he might himself, after coming of age, renounce this citizenship, and become a citizen of the country of his parents, or of any other country; for by our law, as solemnly declared by Congress, "the right of expatriation is a natural and inherent

right of all people," and "any declaration, instruction, opinion, order or direction of any officer of the United States, which denies, restricts, impairs or questions the right of expatriation, is declared inconsistent with the fundamental principles of the Republic." Whether any act of himself, or of his parents, during his minority, could have the same effect, is at least doubtful. But it would be out of place to pursue that inquiry; inasmuch as it is expressly agreed that his residence has always been in the United States, and not elsewhere; that each of his temporary visits to China, the one for some months when he was about seventeen years old, and the other for something like a year about the time of his coming of age, was made with the intention of returning, and was followed by his actual return, to the United States; and "that said Wong Kim Ark has not, either by himself or his parents acting for him, ever renounced his allegiance to the United States, and that he has never done or committed any act or thing to exclude him therefrom."

The evident intention, and the necessary effect, of the submission of this case to the decision of the court upon the facts agreed by the parties, were to present for determination the single question, stated at the beginning of this opinion, namely, whether a child born in the United States, of parents of Chinese descent, who, at the time of his birth, are subjects of the Emperor of China, but have a permanent domicil and residence in the United States, and are there carrying on business, and are not employed in any diplomatic or official capacity under the Emperor of China, becomes at the time of his birth a citizen of the United States. For the reasons above stated, this court is of opinion that the question must be answered in the affirmative.

Order affirmed.

Dissent: Mr. Chief Justice Fuller dissenting.

I cannot concur in the opinion and judgment of the court in this case.

The proposition is that a child born in this country of parents who were not citizens of the United States, and under the laws of their own country and of the United States could not become such—as was the fact from the beginning of the Government in respect of the class of aliens to which the parents in this instance belonged—is, from the moment of his birth a citizen of the United States, by virtue of the first clause of the Fourteenth Amendment, any act of Congress to the contrary notwithstanding.

The argument is, that although the Constitution prior to that amendment nowhere attempted to define the words "citizens of the United States" and "natural-born citizen" as used therein, yet that it must be interpreted in the light of the English common law rule which made the place of birth the criterion of nationality; that that rule "was in force in all the English colonies upon this continent down to the time of the Declaration of Independence, and in the United States afterwards, and continued to prevail under the Constitution as originally established;" and "that before the enactment of the Civil Rights Act of 1866 and the adoption of the Constitutional Amendment, all white persons, at least, born within the sovereignty of the United States, whether children of citizens or

of foreigners, excepting only children of ambassadors or public ministers of a foreign Government, were native-born citizens of the United States."

Thus the Fourteenth Amendment is held to be merely declaratory except that it brings all persons, irrespective of color, within the scope of the alleged rule, and puts that rule beyond the control of the legislative power. If the conclusion of the majority opinion is correct, then the children of citizens of the United States, who have been born abroad since July 28, 1868, when the amendment was declared ratified, were, and are, aliens, unless they have, or shall on attaining majority, become citizens by naturalization in the United States; and no statutory provision to the contrary is of any force of effect. And children who are aliens by descent, but born on our soil, are exempted from the exercise of the power to exclude or to expel aliens, or any class of aliens, so often maintained by this court, an exemption apparently disregarded by the acts in respect of the exclusion of persons of Chinese descent.

Note: Gentleman's Agreement (1907)

President Theodore Roosevelt negotiated the so-called Gentleman's Agreement between the Japanese and U.S. governments to halt immigration from Japan to America. Japan had grown concerned in preceding years that many of its best citizens, particularly the young men it needed to support its growing military, had left for America. In the United States, the same virulent racism directed against the Chinese also figured in including the Japanese as part of the "the yellow peril." Thus both countries had an interest in slowing or halting immigration. The agreement was initially approved by representatives from both countries on January 24, 1907, although it was not formalized until February 18, 1908. It remained in effect until the United States superseded the agreement with the Immigration Act of 1924, which continued the restrictive immigration policies.

The agreement contemplated that the Japanese government would issue passports to the continental United States only to nonlaborers or to laborers who, in coming to the continent, sought to resume a formerly acquired domicile, to join a parent, wife, or children residing there, or to assume active control of an already possessed interest in a farming enterprise in this country. With respect to Hawaii, the Japanese government issued passports only to members of the laboring classes limited to former residents and parents, wives, or children of residents.

Oregon v. *Charley Lee Quong, Ah Lee, and Lee Jong*
7 Ore. 237 (1879)

The picture for the Chinese was also mixed on the state level. Until about 1882 the Chinese often received support from state appellate court judges in the West. For example, in Oregon v. Charley Lee Quong, Ah Lee, and Lee Jong *(1879), the Oregon Supreme Court overturned the conviction of three Chinese defendants found guilty of murder, because the trial judge failed to inform the jury that the Chinese, who did not believe in the sanctity of Christian oaths, might be lying. By the 1890s, however, the legal position of the Chinese had eroded and they increasingly fell prey to the anti-Chinese sentiment represented in the exclusion acts.*

By the Court, Boise, J.

These appellants were indicted at the October term of the Circuit Court of Multnomah County for the crime of murder in the first degree, jointly with Lee Jong, who escaped and fled the country, and were tried at the same term of the court, and convicted of the crime charged, and sentenced to be hanged by judgment of said court. . . .

The facts are, briefly, that the deceased, Chin Sue Ying, was mortally wounded by two blows in the head with a hatchet and two shots in the abdomen from a pistol or pistols, in the Chinese joss-house, at or about two o'clock of the afternoon of the third day of October, A.D. 1878, from the effect of which wounds he died at or about two o'clock of the morning of October 5, 1878; that deceased had been in said joss-house on the evening of the 2d of October, about nine or ten o'clock. Charley Lee Quong applied to a special policeman, who was on duty below stairs, to go up into the second story of the building, into the joss-room, and take deceased out, complaining that deceased had burst a Chinese stink-pot on the floor; that the policeman went up-stairs accordingly, and found that some dark-looking fluid had been poured on the floor, which had a very offensive odor, and the deceased, being accused by Lee Quong of having poured it there, he was accordingly put out of the house by said officer; that as he left the room Lee Quong followed as far as the door, exclaiming in an angry tone, "Ki Gi," which was interpreted to mean "a man who acts like a prostitute," and as being a term of re-

proach; that said officer inquired of Lee Quong why he did not have the deceased arrested, to which Lee Quong replied: "I will arrest him to-morrow," or "I will have him arrested tomorrow"; that about half-past one o'clock P.M. of October 3d, the two and only witnesses for the state who claimed to have witnessed the tragedy left their respective places of employment in the suburbs of the city and came to the store of Wing Hing & Co., about two blocks distant from the joss-house; that one of said witnesses met deceased at said store and they went directly to the joss-house; that the other of said witnesses, when he reached the store, followed on immediately to the joss-house, and the three had been in the joss-room but a few minutes when the affray occurred; that said witnesses had been in the habit of leaving their places of employment about one o'clock of each day previous to October 3d.

In giving an account of the killing, Wo Jung, a witness, testified: "That he is acquainted with defendants now on trial, and with Lee Jong, named in the indictment and not on trial, and was acquainted with the deceased in his lifetime; that deceased was wounded in the Chinese joss-house in the city of Portland; that witness was present in the joss-house at the time deceased was wounded, and was standing within seven or eight feet of deceased when he was attacked by the three defendants named in the indictment; that the first thing witness saw that indicated any difficulty between the defendants and deceased was that witness saw the defendant Lee Jong raise a hatchet and strike the deceased from behind; that the deceased turned his face in the direction of Lee Jaw, who then struck him a second blow with the hatchet; that deceased received both blows of the hatchet upon his head; that deceased was struck the first blow with the hatchet, and as he was in the act of turning his face towards Lee Jaw, the defendants, Charley Lee Quong and Lee Jong, each shot at deceased with pistols; that the pistols were fired from the side of the deceased,— the witness could not tell from which side; Charley Lee Quong fired one of the pistols and Lee Jong fired the other at deceased; that the shots were fired in quick succession, the one immediately after the other; that after the second shot the deceased fell to the floor, and the witness was badly frightened and ran away; that witness is positive that deceased was first struck by Lee Jaw; that Lee Jaw was standing behind deceased when he struck him the first blow with the hatchet, and that upon being so struck deceased turned his head to one side, about which time Charley Lee Quong and Lee Jong fired pistols at him from his side, and the defendant, Lee Jaw, about the same time struck the deceased a second blow on his head with the hatchet, whereupon deceased fell to the floor and witness ran away; that there were a large number of persons present in the joss-house at the time, but that there were no persons between witness and deceased at the time he was attacked and wounded by the three defendants named in the indictment; that a band of China musicians were performing upon their instruments in the joss-room at the time, and there was much noise in the room; that witness did not see deceased do anything nor hear him say anything to either of defendants before he was assaulted by them." The witness also testified to the situation of the tables in the room, and some other things not necessary to mention here.

Another witness, Lun Sing, was introduced by the prosecution, who testified that he was present in the joss-house at the time of the wounding, and was standing near the north wall of the room, which is opposite the side at which the difficulty occurred, which was near the south wall at the south end of the tables. This witness, in describing the same, says the first thing he saw to indicate trouble was that he saw

Lee Jaw raise a hatchet and strike deceased on the head; that Lee Jaw was standing behind deceased at the time, the back of deceased being toward Lee Jaw, who struck him from behind, and struck him on the head with the hatchet; that this blow was on the back of the head of deceased; that deceased when struck turned his head with his face towards Lee Jaw, who then struck him a second blow with the hatchet; that deceased received this second blow on his forehead; that Charley Lee Quong and Lee Jong were standing close to deceased at the time, and witness saw both of them put their hands in their pockets and draw them out again; they each, Charley Lee Quong and Lee Jong, raised their arms, having their hands under their sleeves, and two pistols were fired in rapid succession, but witness did not recognize by whom they were fired; they seemed to be fired from about where the defendants Charley Lee Quong and Lee Jong were standing, but witness could not recognize who fired either pistol; says he was at the north side of the room and at the north end of the same table that deceased was standing at the south end of; and that he could see him and what took place.

These witnesses, Wo Jung and Lun Sing, were the only witnesses introduced on the part of the prosecution who claimed to have been present up-stairs in the joss-room when deceased was wounded, and were the only witnesses on behalf of the state who testified to having seen the difficulty. Both of said witnesses testified that they were at and before the difficulty scholars in the Chinese mission school in the city of Portland, and that deceased was also a scholar in said school. Lun Sing testified that he went to the joss-house with the deceased, and the other witness went there about the same time; and they had been there but a short time when the difficulty occurred.

◆ ◆ ◆

Dr. Saylor, a witness for the state, testified that he made a post-mortem examination of the body of the deceased; that deceased had received two blows on the head, inflicted by some sharp instrument which witness supposed to be a hatchet; that the wounds were on the left side of the head, and both cuts penetrated through the skull into the brain. This witness also found on the deceased two gun-shot wounds,—one in the bowels near the navel, and the other in the pelvis; that the first gun-shot wound perforated the bowels, and was the immediate cause of his death; that the wounds in the head extended from about two and one half or three inches above the eye, backward to or beyond the curve of the skull behind; that these wounds were something over half an inch apart in front, and came together behind, thus forming a V-shape; that in the opinion of witness either of said wounds would most probably have proved fatal, but the immediate cause of the death was inflammation from the gun-shot wound in the bowels; that the gun-shot wounds were received from the front; that either of said cuts on the head would have knocked down any ordinary man; that in the opinion of the witness both blows on the head were inflicted by a party standing in front of deceased when the blows were struck; that deceased was probably not so tall as Lee Jaw or Charley Lee Quong by two or three inches; that wounds in the head might have been given by one standing behind deceased if deceased had been sitting down at the time or had been seized and drawn backwards; but that witness is of the opinion that both blows were struck by a person standing in front of deceased at the time; witness thinks all the wounds were given by a person standing in front of deceased, and that the wounds on the head were made with a hatchet having a blade from three and one half to four inches wide.

The dying declarations of deceased were also admitted, in which deceased said that Lee Jaw cut him and that Charley Lee Quong shot him. In these dying declarations the deceased did not explain how he knew that defendants were the parties; and if the statements of the witnesses Wo Jung and Lun Sing are true, it would seem that the deceased could not have seen Lee Jaw when he struck him with the hatchet, and he would not have been likely to have seen Charley Lee Quong shoot him when stunned by a blow that penetrated his brain. So the probabilities are, that if he knew these men to have been the parties, he must have learned it from those who witnessed the attack.

The defendants offered evidence tending to prove that neither of these prisoners, Lee Jaw or Charley Lee Quong, were present in the joss-room at the time the wounds were inflicted. The defendants then introduced three or four witnesses, who testified that they were present when deceased was wounded, and saw the whole difficulty; that deceased came to about the same place in the joss-room as stated by witnesses for the prosecution, and then raised his right hand, having a piece of meat in it, which he attempted to throw at the Joss; that the defendant, named Lee Jong in the indictment, was standing at the time immediately in front of deceased, between him and the Joss, and about three feet distant from deceased; that when deceased raised his hand to throw the meat, Lee Jong seized him with both hands by his arms, and exclaimed: "Don't do that!" That thereupon the scuffle ensued between Lee Jong and the deceased, during which Lee Jong drew a hatchet from under his coat or garment behind, and struck at the head of deceased with the hatchet.

The witnesses are not certain whether the hatchet came in contact with the head of deceased at that time, but think not; that thereupon deceased, having dropped the meat, seized the hatchet with both hands and Lee Jong did likewise, and a scuffle ensued between them for the possession of the hatchet; that Lee Jong, unable to wrest the hatchet from deceased, let go of it with his right hand, but still held on with his left and drew a pistol with his right hand from under his clothes and shot deceased; that deceased staggered, and Lee Jong again cocked said pistol and shot him a second time; that at the second shot deceased loosed his hold on the hatchet and fell to the floor, whereupon Lee Jong put the pistol back under his clothing, and taking the hatchet in his right hand, struck deceased twice in the head with the blade of the hatchet as he lay on his back on the floor. Each of these witnesses for defendant who so testified to having seen the difficulty also testified that they did not see either Lee Jaw or Charley Lee Quong present at the scene of the difficulty, and that neither of them participated in it.

From the testimony of these witnesses, who claimed they each saw the whole transaction, it is evident that there are different accounts as to the manner in which the wounds were given and who participated in the attack. The judge of the Circuit Court said to the jury in instructing them that this testimony could not be reconciled, and that perjury had been committed by the witnesses on the one side or the other, and we think he was warranted in making that statement, for the testimony of all the witnesses cannot be true. There is no reason to suppose that they were honestly mistaken; but to determine who among the witnesses had sworn falsely, or how much of the testimony of each or any of them was true or false, was a question for the jury.

The testimony of the witnesses for the prosecution, who state that the deceased was struck with a hatchet from behind, does not accord with the opinion of Dr. Saylor, who gives it as his opinion that the blows came from a person standing in front of deceased, and in addition to the reasons given by Dr. Saylor, the wounds were both on the left side of the head, where they would be likely to be made by a person standing in front and using the hatchet in his right hand. If they were made by a person standing behind they would be likely to be on the right side of the head, if the person assaulting used his right hand.

The witnesses for the defense describe the transaction with unusual minuteness and precision. They say that thereupon deceased, having dropped the meat he was going to throw at the Joss, seized the hatchet with both hands and Lee Jong did likewise, and a scuffle ensued between them for its possession; that Lee Jong being unable to wrest the hatchet from deceased, let go of it with his right hand, but still holding it with his left, drew a pistol with his right hand from under his clothes and shot deceased with said pistol from in front; that deceased staggered, and Lee Jong again cocked said pistol and shot him the second time; that at the second shot deceased loosed his hold on the hatchet and fell to the floor, whereupon Lee Jong put the pistol back under his clothing, and taking the hatchet in his right hand, struck deceased twice in the head with the blade of the hatchet as he lay upon his back upon the floor. If all these witnesses saw this transaction and describe it alike in all these minute details, their testimony is liable to

criticism, for witnesses to such a transaction rarely agree in details, and there was a large number present, and much noise and excitement in the room. The intrinsic value of this testimony is greatly weakened by the exact agreement of each witness in these minute details, and we think the criticism thereon by the court was just and proper.

It may be that each party (for it seems there were two parties in the room at the time) has given a highly colored and partially false statement of the real facts. At any rate, it was the province and the duty of the jury to pass on the value of all this evidence on both sides, and try to ascertain the real facts of the transaction from all the evidence.

After the evidence was closed, the court, among other things, charged the jury: "In this case there is no testimony tending to reduce the grade of the crime from murder in the first degree, except the testimony of those witnesses for the defense who give an account of the killing as they claim to have seen it. But if the testimony of these witnesses is true, then these defendants were not present at all. If therefore you believe these witnesses, these defendants are entitled to a verdict of acquittal. If you have a reasonable doubt as to whether or not they have told the truth, the defendant should be acquitted. If you think beyond a reasonable doubt that they have not told the truth, then there is no testimony, as stated, tending to reduce the grade of the crime below that of murder in the first degree. In other words, in the testimony tending to convict these defendants there is nothing that will justify you in finding the defendants guilty in any less degree than that charged." As before indicated, the evidence on both sides was liable to criticism. The witnesses for the prosecution did not agree as to the position of the parties, when the wounds were given, and the counsel for the defense had a right to submit to the jury the question as to the entire truth of their theory, and also the theory that some truth and some falsehold had been spoken by the witnesses on each side; that is, that if the jury should reject the theory of the alibi, still that the evidence tended to show that deceased was committing an act of sacrilege on the Chinese religion, which its votaries had avenged in the sudden heat of passion. This instruction puts the case to the jury by presenting each side separately, telling the jury to look at the evidence, and if they believe the witnesses for the prosecution, then it is murder in the first degree. If they believe the witnesses for the defense, then the defendants should be acquitted.

But suppose the jury believed from the appearance and conduct of the witnesses on each side that they had come into court to swear through their case, and that some truth and some falsehood had been testified to on each side, and though they believed there had been a crime committed, yet they doubted as to whether it had been premeditated or had arisen in a sudden quarrel, then the defendants had a right to the benefit of such doubt. And we think the last part of this instruction, which says: "In other words, in the testimony tending to convict these defendants there is nothing that will justify you in finding the defendants guilty in any degree less than that charged," is erroneous, for the jury probably understood by this the testimony for the prosecution. In that testimony the two Chinese witnesses swear that deceased was struck with a hatchet by Lee Jaw, standing behind him, while Dr. Saylor, a witness for the prosecution, gives it as his opinion from the position of the wounds that the blows were inflicted by a person standing in front of deceased, and also that either of these blows would have caused sudden paralysis and caused the deceased to fall, while the two Chinese witnesses say he stood up and looked around after he was struck. These facts had a tendency to contradict the theory that deceased was struck by a person standing behind him, which fact was the strongest one in the case to prove premeditation, which was one of the facts to be found by the jury in order to justify them in finding the prisoners guilty of murder in the first degree.

We think this instruction might have prejudiced the rights of the defendants. It is true that the court afterwards, in his instructions, told the jury that they must find the defendants guilty beyond a reasonable doubt, and also that

if they believed from the evidence that either of the defendants killed or assisted in killing Chin Sue Ying, and entertained a reasonable doubt as to the grade of the crime, the defendant was entitled to the benefit of that doubt, and the jury should find such defendant guilty of the lower grade.

But the court, having in the instruction referred to first told the jury that there was no evidence tending to reduce the degree of the crime from that charged unless they believed the defendants' witnesses, we think the instruction was likely to have influenced the jury against the defendants. There is exception taken also to the ruling of the court in admitting the dying declarations of the deceased. As to this we think, as that is a matter to a certain degree in the discretion of the Circuit Court who hears the witnesses, that this court should not hold such a ruling erroneous unless it is evidently so, and we hold from the evidence here presented that such ruling was correct. The defendants' counsel also asked the court to charge the jury that "if the jury find that none but Chinese witnesses testify to the circumstances of the killing and as to the parties concerned in it, and the jury are in such doubt as to the credibility or truthfulness of such witnesses as to feel uncertain whether they should be believed, the jury should acquit the defendants."

This instruction was refused, and we think properly, because the word "uncertain" may include any doubt, whether reasonable or not. There is more or less uncertainty as to all facts attempted to be established by parol evidence. Nothing is absolutely certain that rests on the testimony of men, and where evidence is given to establish any proposition tending to prove guilt, it is sufficient if it remove all reasonable doubt.

There are many other instructions and rulings of the court which were controverted in the argument, but we think they were substantially correct. The judgment of the Circuit Court will be reversed and a new trial ordered.

LATINOS AND HISPANICS

During the nineteenth century, Spanish was the predominate language spoken in the American Southwest. Hispanic explorers had covered more than one-half of the territory of the present-day United States, and Hispanics participated in the colonization of over half of the nation and served in the Continental Army during the American Revolution. The governor of the Louisiana Territory, General Bernardo de Gálvez, sent money, rifles, and other supplies to General George Washington for independence. Captain Jorge Farragut came to the United States from the Spanish island of Minorca to fight against the British—first in the Revolution and then in the War of 1812 as part of the U.S. Navy. In the Civil War, his son, David Glasgow Farragut, won fame as a Union hero by blocking southern ports. Moreover, during the nineteenth century, Latinos also participated directly in American political life, far more than blacks, Native Americans, and Asian immigrants. The first Latino to serve in Congress, Joseph Marion Hernández, was elected in 1822 as a delegate from Florida to the U.S. Congress.

As the new nation expanded across the continent, white pioneers sought both homes and wealth, although these same settlers often relied on the local Hispanic population to help unlock the riches of the region. When gold and other valuable metals were discovered in the Southwest, many prospectors knew only what they had. They had no idea how to get it out of the ground. To do so, they borrowed mining techniques from Mexico, Peru, and Chile. In a popular California mining legend, James Marshall, upon discovering gold, supposedly proclaimed the news, yelling, "Gold! Gold!" What he actually said was *"Chispa"*—Spanish for "bright speck."

Latinos played a similar role in helping immigrants from the humid East come to terms with the arid West. Managing the water supply was an art the settlers learned from the Mexicans, who learned it from the Pueblo Indians. Hispanics also taught eastern farmers the critical techniques associated with cattle and sheep ranching. Early songs and legends of the Old West featured an Americanized version of the *vaqueros* (cowboys) from México. Thus, the enduring legend of the cowboy of the Old West came almost entirely from Hispanic culture.

By the time the Treaty of Guadalupe Hidalgo ceded half of the Mexican territory to the United States in 1848, Mexican heritage had become inextricably woven into the historical fabric of the American Southwest. As they assessed their situation in the space that marked the intersection of the cultures of Mexico and the United States, Mexican Americans struggled with issues of identity in the decades following 1848.

Like Native Americans, blacks, and Asians, persons of Latino and Hispanic background also faced cultural and economic discrimination from the dominant white culture, especially with the de facto segregation of public schools in the late nineteenth and early twentieth centuries. As was true with these other groups, establishing citizenship became one of the key issues for the Latino population. Historically, Latinos' classification as white rather than as African American justified the admission of Mexicans as United States citizens after the Mexican-American War. The Treaty of Guadalupe Hidalgo stipulated that former Mexican citizens were to be given "all the rights of citizens of the United States." Despite the straightforward language of the treaty, Latinos struggled to claim their full rights as American citizen. When California gained statehood in 1850, its constitution allowed Latinos to become citizens by virtue of their whiteness. California courts followed their state constitution's lead, granting some Latinos the benefits of American citizenship—and then only because of their status as white males. Courts assigned Latinos a white racial identity for purposes of determining citizenship, but they did not agree that Latinos necessarily had the same social privileges as whites. Latino children often attended segregated schools; Latino neighborhoods were segregated from white neighborhoods; and Latinos suffered from employment discrimination. This characterization of Latinos as white was an outgrowth of the legacy of slavery. African Americans were not guaranteed United States citizenship until the passage of the Fourteenth Amendment in 1868, yet to have classified Latinos as African American would have been difficult for nineteenth-century courts, given the clarity of the two groups' different geographical and ethnic origins.

California ex rel. M. M. Kimberly v. Pablo de la Guerra
40 Cal. 311 (1870)

Pablo de la Guerra was a judge in Santa Barbara County, California, and formerly a Mexican citizen who became a citizen of the United States under the Treaty of Guadalupe Hidalgo. Matthew Kimberly contested his election, arguing that the judge was not a citizen and therefore could not hold office. The case raised the question of whether ethnicity served as a bar to citizenship for persons of Mexican heritage. The California Supreme Court held that the natural consequence of the cession of the territory by Mexico, and its acquisition by the United States, was that the allegiance of the inhabitants who remained in it were transferred to the new sovereign. The court also held that by the terms of the treaty, those who did not elect to remain citizens of Mexico lost their rights as Mexican citizens, and the conclusion was inevitable that they acquired the rights of citizens of the United States. Otherwise, the court held, they remained a people without a country. The court held that having admitted into the Union a state, of which the judge was a constituent member, the United States conferred upon him all the rights of citizenship.

Opinion by Temple:

The respondent was born at Santa Barbara, in 1819, and has ever since resided at that place, and is admitted to have been a white male citizen of Mexico at the date of the treaty of Guadalupe Hidalgo. After the ratification of that treaty he elected to become a citizen of the United States in the mode provided in the treaty. He was a member of the Constitutional Convention which framed the Constitution of California, and has almost continuously, since the adoption of that instrument, held office under its provisions. At the judicial election, held in 1869, he was elected Judge of the First Judicial District, and the relator [Kimberly] in this proceeding contests his right to the office, on the ground that he is not a citizen of the United States, as by an Act passed April 20, 1863, it is provided that "no person shall be eligible to the office of District Judge, who shall not have been a citizen of the United States and a resident of this State for two years."

Article IX of the treaty of Guadalupe Hidalgo is as follows: "The Mexicans who, in the Territories aforesaid, shall not preserve the character of citizens of the Mexican Republic, conformably with what is stipulated in the preceding Article, shall be incorporated into the Union of the United States and be admitted at the proper time (to be judged of by the Congress of the United States), to the enjoyment of all the rights of citizens of the United States, according to the principles of the Constitution; and in the meantime shall be maintained and protected in the free enjoyment of their liberty and property, and secured in the free exercise of their religion without restriction."

It is contended on the part of the relator that Mexicans who were resident in California at the date of the treaty, and who elected in the mode provided to become citizens of the United States, did not acquire the right of citizenship by the terms of the treaty, but an Act of Congress admitting them to such rights is necessary, and that no such Act having been passed, the respondent is not a citizen.

The question raised would be of very grave import to the people of this State, were it not for the fact that its solution is quite obvious. By the eighth article of the treaty it is provided that the Mexicans who were resident in the ceded territory might either remain or remove to the Mexican Republic, and should be protected in their property. It is then stipulated:

"Those who shall prefer to remain in said Territory may either retain the title and rights of Mexican citizens, or acquire those of citizens of the United States. But they shall be under the obligation to make their election within one year from the date of ratification of this treaty; and those who shall remain in the said Territories after the expiration of that year, without having declared their intention to retain their character of Mexicans, shall be considered to have elected to become citizens of the United States."

The natural consequence of the cession of the Territory by Mexico, and its acquisition by the United States, would be that the allegiance of the inhabitants who remained in it would be transferred to the new sovereign. By the stipulation of the treaty, however, three courses were left open to the inhabitants. One was to remove to the Republic of Mexico; in which event they would, of course, continue to be citizens of Mexico; the second was to remain in the ceded Territory and retain the title and rights of Mexican citizens; the third, to become citizens of the United States.

That the treaty was intended to operate directly, and of itself to fix the status of those inhabitants, does not admit of a doubt. That it had that effect, so far as those who elected to remain citizens of Mexico are concerned, is obvious, and there is no reason for a different construction as to those who elected to become citizens of the United States. In fact, this would have been the natural consequence of the treaty (so far as was possible under our form of Government), and it required this special treaty stipulation to enable the inhabitants to remain in the ceded territory and owe no allegiance to the new Government. But for this provision the Mexicans who remained would not have been considered aliens, but would have been vested with such rights of citizenship as can be conferred upon the inhabitants of a Territory who are not citizens of any of the States of the Union. But, by the terms of the treaty, those who did not elect to remain citizens of Mexico, lost their rights as Mexican citizens, at least as soon as the election was made, and the conclusion is irresistible that they acquired (so far as was possible) the rights of citizens of the United States at the time they lost those of Mexican citizens; otherwise they remained a people without a country.

This article of the treaty would probably never have received a different construction from that here given, were it not for the following article, which has been strangely misconstrued. It provides that these Mexicans in the ceded Territories, who do not retain the character of Mexican citizens, shall be incorporated into the Union of the United States, and be admitted at the proper time (to be judged of by the Congress of the United States), to the enjoyment of all the rights of citizens of the United States, according to the principles of the Constitution. The Union with which they are to be incorporated is, of course, the Union of the States composing the United States, and by which Union that Government is created. They can be incorporated into this Union only as a State, and the admission of the people to the full rights as citizens of the United States follows as the consequence of that act; and this is the only way in which it was possible for Congress to confer upon them all the rights of citizens of the United States. For this purpose it is not necessary to inquire whether, under our form of Government, there can be a citizen of one of the United States who is not a citizen of the States. I have no doubt that those born in the Territories, or in the District of Columbia, are so far citizens as to entitle them to the protection guaranteed to citizens of the United States in the Constitution, and to the shield of nationality abroad; but it is evident that they have not the political rights which are vested in citizens of the States. They are not constituents of any community in which is vested any sovereign power of government. Their position partakes more of the character of subjects than of citizens. They are subject to the laws of the United States, but have no voice in its management. If they are allowed to make laws, the validity of these laws is derived from the sanction of a Government in which they are not represented. Mere citizenship they may have, but the political rights of citizens they cannot enjoy until they are organized into a State, and admitted into the Union.

But the United States cannot acquire territory to hold and rule permanently in full government. Such acquisitions are in pursuance of its power to admit new States, and every Territory thus acquired must be held to have been acquired for the purpose of being erected into a State. Indeed that may be considered as the last act in the acquisition of the Territory, for it is then for the first time incorporated into the Union. Once admitted into the Union it requires no Act of Congress to define the rights of the inhabitants who were recognized as members of the community organized into a State, "because the Constitution itself defines the relative rights, powers and duties of the State, and the citizens of the State, and the General Government." (*Scott* v. *Sandford* [1857])

Having admitted into the Union a State, of which these inhabitants were constituent members, Congress could do no more. It has conferred upon them all the rights of citizens, or rather it has recognized these rights in the only mode provided by the Constitution which was applicable to them.

The question involved in this case seems to have been decided in the case of the *American Insurance Company* v. *Canter* (1828). This case involved the validity of a territorial law of Florida, establishing a certain Court. Chief Justice Marshall, in pronouncing the opinion of the Court, says: "On the 2d of February, 1819, Spain ceded Florida to the United States. The sixth article of the treaty of cession contains the following provision: 'The inhabitants of the Territories which His Catholic Majesty cedes to the United States by this treaty shall be incorporated in the Union of the United States as soon as may be consistent with the principles of the Federal Constitution; and admitted to the

enjoyment of the privileges, rights and immunities of the citizens of the United States.' "

"This treaty is the law of the land, and admits the inhabitants of Florida to the enjoyment of the privileges, rights and immunities of the citizens of the United States. It is unnecessary to inquire whether this is not their condition independent of stipulation. They do not, however, participate in political power; they do not share in the Government till Florida shall become a State. In the meantime, Florida continues to be a Territory of the United States, governed by virtue of that clause in the Constitution which empowers Congress 'to make all needful rules and regulations respecting the territory or other property belonging to the United States.' "

But it is suggested by counsel for relator, that if this construction be correct, then the Constitution of California is in conflict with the ninth article of the treaty, for that article provides that all Mexican citizens who elect to become citizens of the United States, shall be admitted to all the rights of citizens, while the Constitution discriminates. It declares that white male citizens of Mexico, who have elected to become citizens of the United States, shall be electors, while all, without distinction of color, including Indians, were Mexican citizens, and entitled to vote by the laws of Mexico.If this be so, it does not follow that the respondent is not a citizen of the United States, but that the elective franchise is denied to certain persons who had been entitled to its exercise under the laws of Mexico. The possession of all political rights is not essential to citizenship. When Congress admitted California as a State, the constituent members of the State, in their aggregate capacity, became vested with the sovereign powers of government, "according to the principles of the Constitution." They then had the right to prescribe the qualifications of electors, and it is no violation of the treaty that these qualifications were such as to exclude some of the inhabitants from certain political rights. They were excluded in accordance with the principles of the Constitution.

The respondent is clearly a citizen of the United States, and the judgment should be affirmed.

So ordered.

GENDER AND DOMESTIC RELATIONS

The American Revolution unleashed forces that had long-term effects on the status of women and the family. Republican ideology fostered a family order in which authority was accountable, property rights were equated with independence, and human relations were set in contractual terms. The family in the nineteenth century became a private, inward-looking institution, one sharply in contrast with the community-oriented little commonwealths of the colonial era. Market capitalism also molded the status of women, the family, and the role of children. The gradual separation of the workplace from the home granted wives new autonomy over the domestic sphere, opened men even more directly to the competitive forces of a market economy, and gave rise to the "economically worthless child." Thus new economic and social demands precipitated changes in the law affecting women and domestic relations (marriage, divorce, child custody, and birth control).

THE RIGHTS OF WOMEN

Gender, like race, was a defining category of nineteenth-century American law, and it is conspicuous in matters as diverse as protective legislation, domestic relations, suffrage, property rights, birth control, and abortion. Being female—and being female and married in particular—made a difference in the eyes of the law. Male lawmakers clung to paternalistic ideas that at once placed women on a pedestal and condemned them to second-class status. As the century progressed, however, a small group of feminist reformers sought to chart an independent course for women. They did so at a time when the growing pressures of a burgeoning market economy placed new pressures not only on women but also on men and the family unit as a whole.

"The Seneca Falls Declaration of Sentiments"
1848

In 1848, Elizabeth Cady Stanton and Lucretia Mott organized the Seneca Falls Convention, one of the most significant protest meetings of the antebellum era. They and other women had participated actively in a host of other social reforms, especially the antislavery movement. Males, however, dominated the leadership of these groups, often relegating women to second-class roles. At the World Anti-Slavery Conference in 1840, for example, male delegates refused to allow women to participate; they ordered both Stanton and Mott to sit behind curtains where they could not be seen. Modeling the language of their "Declaration of Sentiments" on that of the Declaration of Independence, the women at Seneca Falls charged that men had usurped women's freedom and dignity. The resolutions they appended to the declaration underscored their concern with gender bias in the law and the legal system.

When, in the course of human events, it becomes necessary for one portion of the family of man to assume among the people of the earth a position different from that which they have hitherto occupied, but one to which the laws of nature and of nature's God entitle them, a decent respect to the opinions of mankind requires that they should declare the causes that impel them to such a course.

We hold these truths to be self-evident: that all men and women are created equal; that they are endowed by their Creator with certain inalienable rights; that among these are life, liberty, and the pursuit of happiness; that to secure these rights governments are instituted, deriving their just powers from the consent of the governed. Whenever any form of government becomes destructive of these ends, it is the right of those who suffer from it to refuse allegiance to it, and to insist upon the institution of a new government, laying its foundation on such principles, and organizing its powers in such form, as to them shall seem most likely to effect their safety and happiness. Prudence, indeed, will dictate that governments long established should not be changed for light and transient causes; and accordingly all experience hath shown that mankind are more disposed to suffer, while evils are sufferable, than to right themselves by abolishing the forms to which they were accustomed. But when a long train of abuses and usurpations, pursuing invariably the same object evinces a design to reduce them under absolute despotism, it is their duty to throw off such government, and to provide new guards for their future security. Such has been the patient sufferance of the women under this government, and such is now the necessity which constrains them to demand the equal station to which they are entitled.

The history of mankind is a history of repeated injuries and usurpations on the part of man toward woman, having in direct object the establishment of an absolute tyranny over her. To prove this, let facts be submitted to a candid world.

He has never permitted her to exercise her inalienable right to the elective franchise.

He has compelled her to submit to laws, in the formation of which she had no voice.

He has withheld from her rights which are given to the most ignorant and degraded men— both natives and foreigners.

Having deprived her of this first right of a citizen, the elective franchise, thereby leaving her without representation in the halls of legislation, he has oppressed her on all sides.

He has made her, if married, in the eye of the law, civilly dead.

He has taken from her all right in property, even to the wages she earns.

He has made her, morally, an irresponsible being, as she can commit many crimes with impunity, provided they be done in the presence of her husband. In the covenant of marriage, she is compelled to promise obedience to her husband, he becoming, to all intents and purposes, her master—the law giving him power to deprive her of her liberty, and to administer chastisement.

He has so framed the laws of divorce, as to what shall be the proper causes, and in case of separation, to whom the guardianship of the children shall be given, as to be wholly regardless of the happiness of women—the law, in all cases, going upon a false supposition of the supremacy of man, and giving all power into his hands.

After depriving her of all rights as a married woman, if single, and the owner of property, he has taxed her to support a government which recognizes her only when her property can be made profitable to it.

He has monopolized nearly all the profitable employments, and from those she is permitted to follow, she receives but a scanty remuneration. He closes against her all the avenues to wealth and distinction which he considers most honorable to himself. As a teacher of theology, medicine, or law, she is not known.

He has denied her the facilities for obtaining a thorough education, all colleges being closed against her.

He allows her in Church, as well as State, but a subordinate position, claiming Apostolic authority for her exclusion from the ministry, and, with some exceptions, from any public participation in the affairs of the Church.

He has created a false public sentiment by giving to the world a different code of morals for men and women, by which moral delinquencies which exclude women from society, are not only tolerated, but deemed of little account in man.

He has usurped the prerogative of Jehovah

himself, claiming it as his right to assign for her a sphere of action, when that belongs to her conscience and to her God.

He has endeavored, in every way that he could, to destroy her confidence in her own powers, to lessen her self-respect, and to make her willing to lead a dependent and abject life.

Now, in view of this entire disfranchisement of one-half the people of this country, their social and religious degradation—in view of the unjust laws above mentioned, and because women do feel themselves aggrieved, oppressed, and fraudulently deprived of their most sacred rights, we insist that they have immedi-

ate admission to all the rights and privileges which belong to them as citizens of the United States.

In entering upon the great work before us, we anticipate no small amount of misconception, misrepresentation, and ridicule; but we shall use every instrumentality within our power to effect our object. We shall employ agents, circulate tracts, petition the State and National legislatures, and endeavor to enlist the pulpit and the press in our behalf. We hope this Convention will be followed by a series of Conventions embracing every part of the country.

The New York Married Women's Property Acts
1848

Unmarried women enjoyed the same legal position as men, save for the fact that they could not vote. Such was not the case for wives, whose condition some antebellum legal commentators equated with that of slaves. Such dependence, while suited to low-level economic activity, became increasingly costly as the mid-century American economy reached the stage of takeoff into sustained growth. Economic growth carried with it certain costs of credit associated with risk taking and with pauperization of the family should a husband slide into insolvency. State legislatures adopted married women's property acts as a means of dealing with the twin problems of providing greater stability to the economy and ensuring the equitable treatment of women (and minor children under their care) from spendthrift husbands. The first statutes appeared in Arkansas and Florida territories in the mid-1830s, but the first major state act was that of Mississippi, which came hard on the heels of the devastating Panic of 1837. The New York State act, passed in 1848 (the same year as the Seneca Falls Convention), emerged as the national model. During the next half-century, New York legislators refashioned and expanded this initial legislation, attempting to keep pace with changing economic demands and with growing pressure from increasingly well-organized women's groups.

AN ACT FOR THE MORE EFFECTUAL PROTECTION OF THE PROPERTY OF MARRIED WOMEN.
PASSED APRIL 7, 1848

The People of the State of New York, represented in Senate and Assembly, do enact as follows:

1. The real and personal property of any female who may hereafter marry, and which she

shall own at the time of marriage, and the rents, issues and profits thereof shall not be subject to the disposal of her husband, nor be liable for his debts, and shall continue her sole and separate property, as if she were a single female.

2. The real and personal property, and the rents, issues and profits thereof of any female now married shall not be subject to the disposal of her husband; but shall be her sole and separate property as if she were a single female ex-

cept so far as the same may be liable for the debts of her husband heretofore contracted.

3. It shall be lawful for any married female to receive, by gift, grant, devise or bequest, from any person other than her husband and hold to her sole and separate use, as if she were a single female, real and personal property, and the rents, issues, and profits thereof, and the same shall not be subject to the disposal of her husband, nor be liable for his debts.

4. All contracts made between persons in contemplation of marriage shall remain in full force after such marriage takes place.

♦ ♦ ♦

AN ACT TO AMEND AN ACT ENTITLED "AN ACT FOR THE MORE EFFECTUAL PROTECTION OF THE PROPERTY OF MARRIED WOMEN," PASSED APRIL 7, 1848. PASSED APRIL 11, 1849.

The People of the State of New York, represented in Senate and Assembly, do enact as follows:

1. The third section of the act entitled "An act for the more effectual protection of the property of married women," is hereby amended so as to read as follows:

2. Any married female may take by inheritance or by gift, grant, devise or bequest, from any person other than her husband and hold to her sole and separate use and convey and devise real and personal property, and any interest of estate therein, and the rents, issues and profits thereof in the same manner and with like effect as if she were unmarried, and the same shall not be subject to the disposal of her husband nor be liable for his debts.

3. Any person who may hold or who may hereafter hold as trustee for any married woman, any real or personal estate or other property under any deed of conveyance or otherwise, on the written request of such married woman accompanied by a certificate of a justice of the supreme court that he has examined the condition and situation of the property, and made due enquiry into the capacity of such married woman to manage and control the same, may convey such married woman by deed or otherwise, all or any portion of such property, or the rents issues or profits thereof, for her sole and separate use and benefit.

4. All contracts made between persons in contemplation of marriage shall remain in full force after such marriage takes place.

Note: Married Women and the Law

Under the doctrine of coverture, which had historical roots tracing back to the Middle Ages, the property of the wife came under the control of her husband. This practice left many wives economically dependent on their husbands. There were exceptions, however. For example, the practice of dower gave to widows a one-third life estate in the property of their husbands. Married women also could receive protection through separate equitable estates. This trust arrangement could be fashioned before marriage (in which case it became a prenuptial agreement) or later. The document, which was created in equity rather than law, designated a trustee who was charged with holding the property for the separate use of a particular married woman. The device protected the property of women from being ravaged by their husbands' creditors. Nevertheless, the impetus behind these measures was not to place women on an equal footing with men, but to secure them against financial ruin. Most married women did not have prenuptial agreements or separate equitable estates. The first wave of married women's property acts freed wives' estates from the debts of their husbands, leaving the traditional marital estate and coverture rules intact. Subsequent legislation extended the sweep of these laws by taking into account the changing workplace where women entered in small but growing numbers in the late nineteenth century. Married women's property acts were modest incursions on traditional patriarchy that provided for equity in wives' treatment rather than equality with husbands.

Bradwell v. *Illinois*
83 U.S. 130 (1873)

Discrimination based on sex figured in the debates over the Fourteenth Amendment, but ultimately its framers could not agree on adding a specific provision dealing with it. Instead, the term "person" was used, and the Court quickly proceeded to read that word in such a way that it would not provide additional constitutional guarantees to women. The Bradwell *case offered a striking example. Myra Bradwell had studied law with her attorney husband and founded and published the* Chicago Legal News, *the leading midwestern legal publication. An Illinois statute provided that any adult "person," of good character and having the requisite training, was eligible for admission to the bar. The Illinois Supreme Court denied her admission, however, because she was a woman. Bradwell claimed that practicing law was one of the privileges and immunities protected by the Fourteenth Amendment. The Supreme Court, by a vote of 8 to 1, disagreed, with Justice Samuel F. Miller speaking for the Court and Chief Justice Salmon P. Chase silently dissenting.*

Mr. Justice Miller delivered the opinion of the court.

The record in this case is not very perfect, but it may be fairly taken that the plaintiff asserted her right to a license on the grounds, among others, that she was a citizen of the United States, and that having been a citizen of Vermont at one time, she was, in the State of Illinois, entitled to any right granted to citizens of the latter State.

The court having overruled these claims of right founded on the clauses of the Federal Constitution before referred to, those propositions may be considered as properly before this court.

As regards the provision of the Constitution that citizens of each State shall be entitled to all the privileges and immunities of citizens in the several States, the plaintiff in her affidavit has stated very clearly a case to which it is inapplicable.

The protection designed by that clause, as has been repeatedly held, has no application to a citizen of the State whose laws are complained of. If the plaintiff was a citizen of the State of Illinois, that provision of the Constitution gave her no protection against its courts or its legislation.

The plaintiff seems to have seen this difficulty, and attempts to avoid it by stating that she was born in Vermont.

While she remained in Vermont that circumstance made her a citizen of that State. But she states, at the same time, that she is a citizen of the United States, and that she is now, and has been for many years past, a resident of Chicago, in the State of Illinois.

The fourteenth amendment declares that citizens of the United States are citizens of the State within which they reside; therefore the plaintiff was, at the time of making her application, a citizen of the United States and a citizen of the State of Illinois.

We do not here mean to say that there may not be a temporary residence in one State, with intent to return to another, which will not create citizenship in the former. But the plaintiff states nothing to take her case out of the definition of citizenship of a State as defined by the first section of the fourteenth amendment.

In regard to that amendment counsel for the plaintiff in this court truly says that there are certain privileges and immunities which belong to a citizen of the United States as such; otherwise it would be nonsense for the fourteenth amendment to prohibit a State from abridging them, and he proceeds to argue that admission to the bar of a State of a person who possesses the requisite learning and character is one of those which a State may not deny.

In this latter proposition we are not able to concur with counsel. We agree with him that there are privileges and immunities belonging to citizens of the United States, in that relation and character, and that it is these and these alone which a State is forbidden to abridge. But the right to admission to practice in the courts of a State is not one of them. This right in no sense depends on citizenship of the United States. It has not, as far as we know, ever been made in any State, or in any case, to depend on citizenship at all. Certainly many prominent and distinguished lawyers have been admitted to practice, both in the State and Federal courts, who were not citizens of the United States or of any State. But, on whatever basis this right may be placed, so far as it can have any relation to citizenship at all, it would seem that, as to the courts of a State, it would relate to citizenship of the State, and as to Federal courts, it would relate to citizenship of the United States.

The opinion just delivered in the *Slaughter-House Cases* renders elaborate argument in the present case unnecessary; for, unless we are wholly and radically mistaken in the principles on which those cases are decided, the right to control and regulate the granting of license to practice law in the courts of a State is one of those powers which are not transferred for its protection to the Federal government, and its exercise is in no manner governed or controlled by citizenship of the United States in the party seeking such license.

It is unnecessary to repeat the argument on which the judgment in those cases is founded. It is sufficient to say they are conclusive of the present case.

Minor v. Happersett
21 Wall. (88 U.S.) 162 (1875)

The United States Supreme Court also refused to recognize women as the political equals of men. In this case, Virginia Minor, a Missouri woman, claimed a Fourteenth Amendment right to vote as one of her "privileges or immunities," despite Missouri's men-only suffrage laws.

The chief justice, Morrison R. Waite, delivered the opinion of the court.

The question is presented in this case, whether, since the adoption of the fourteenth amendment, a woman, who is a citizen of the United States and of the State of Missouri, is a voter in that State, notwithstanding the provision of the constitution and laws of the State, which confine the right of suffrage to men alone.

♦ ♦ ♦

There is no doubt that women may be citizens. They are persons, and by the fourteenth amendment "all persons born or naturalized in the United States and subject to the jurisdiction thereof" are expressly declared to be "citizens of the United States and of the State wherein they reside." But, in our opinion, it did not need this amendment to give them that position. Be-fore its adoption the Constitution of the United States did not in terms prescribe who should be citizens of the United States or of the several States, yet there were necessarily such citizens without such provision. There cannot be a nation without a people. The very idea of a political community, such as a nation is, implies an association of persons for the promotion of their general welfare. Each one of the persons associated becomes a member of the nation formed by the association. He owes it allegiance and is entitled to its protection. Allegiance and protection are, in this connection, reciprocal obligations. The one is a compensation for the other; allegiance for protection and protection for allegiance.

♦ ♦ ♦

Sex has never been made one of the elements of citizenship in the United States. In this respect men have never had an advantage over women. The same laws precisely apply to both. The fourteenth amendment did not affect the citizenship of women any more than it did of men. In this particular, therefore, the rights of Mrs. Minor do not depend upon the amendment. She has always been a citizen from her birth, and entitled to all the privileges and immunities of citizenship. The amendment prohibited the State, of which she is a citizen, from abridging any of her privileges and immunities as a citizen of the United States; but it did not confer citizenship on her. That she had before its adoption.

If the right of suffrage is one of the necessary privileges of a citizen of the United States, then the constitution and laws of Missouri confining it to men are in violation of the Constitution of the United States, as amended, and consequently void. The direct question is, therefore, presented whether all citizens are necessarily voters.

The Constitution does not define the privileges and immunities of citizens. For that definition we must look elsewhere. In this case we need not determine what they are, but only whether suffrage is necessarily one of them.

◆ ◆ ◆

The amendment did not add to the privileges and immunities of a citizen. It simply furnished an additional guaranty for the protection of such as he already had. No new voters were necessarily made by it. Indirectly it may have had that effect, because it may have increased the number of citizens entitled to suffrage under the constitution and laws of the States, but it operates for this purpose, if at all, through the States and the State laws, and not directly upon the citizen.

It is clear, therefore, we think, that the Constitution has not added the right of suffrage to the privileges and immunities of citizenship as they existed at the time it was adopted. This makes it proper to inquire whether suffrage was coextensive with the citizenship of the States at the time of its adoption. If it was, then it may with force be argued that suffrage was one of the rights which belonged to citizenship, and in the enjoyment of which every citizen must be protected. But if it was not, the contrary may with propriety be assumed.

◆ ◆ ◆

In respect to suffrage in the several States it cannot for a moment be doubted that if it had been intended to make all citizens of the United States voters, the framers of the Constitution would not have left it to implication. So important a change in the condition of citizenship as it actually existed, if intended, would have been expressly declared.

◆ ◆ ◆

After the adoption of the fourteenth amendment, it was deemed necessary to adopt a fifteenth, as follows: "The right of citizens of the United States to vote shall not be denied or abridged by the United States, or by any State, on account of race, color, or previous condition of servitude." The fourteenth amendment had already provided that no State should make or enforce any law which should abridge the privileges or immunities of citizens of the United States. If suffrage was one of these privileges or immunities, why amend the Constitution to prevent its being denied on account of race, &c? Nothing is more evident than that the greater must include the less, and if all were already protected why go through with the form of amending the Constitution to protect a part?

◆ ◆ ◆

It is true that the United States guarantees to every State a republican form of government. . . . The guaranty is of a republican form of government. No particular government is designated as republican, neither is the exact form to be guaranteed, in any manner especially designated.

◆ ◆ ◆

All the citizens of the States were not invested with the right of suffrage. In all, save perhaps New Jersey, this right was only bestowed upon men and not upon all of them. Under these circumstances it is certainly now too late to contend that a government is not republican, within the meaning of this guaranty in the Constitution, because women are not made voters.

The same may be said of the other provisions just quoted. Women were excluded from suffrage in nearly all the States by the express provision of their constitutions and laws. If that had been equivalent to a bill of attainder, certainly its abrogation would not have been left to implication. Nothing less than express language would have been employed to effect so radical a change. So also of the amendment which declares that no person shall be deprived of life, liberty, or property without due process of law, adopted as it was as early as 1791. If suffrage was intended to be included within its obligations, language better adapted to express that intent would most certainly have been employed. The right of suffrage, when granted, will be protected. He who has it can only be deprived of it by due process of law, but in order to claim protection he must first show that he has the right.

♦   ♦   ♦

Certainly, if the courts can consider any question settled, this is one. For nearly ninety years the people have acted upon the idea that the Constitution, when it conferred citizenship, did not necessarily confer the right of suffrage. If uniform practice long continued can settle the construction of so important an instrument as the Constitution of the United States confessedly is, most certainly it has been done here. Our province is to decide what the law is, not to declare what it should be.

We have given this case the careful consideration its importance demands. If the law is wrong, it ought to be changed; but the power for that is not with us. The arguments addressed to us bearing upon such a view of the subject may perhaps be sufficient to induce those having the power, to make the alteration, but they ought not to be permitted to influence our judgment in determining the present rights of the parties now litigating before us. No argument as to woman's need of suffrage can be considered. We can only act upon her rights as they exist. It is not for us to look at the hardship of withholding. Our duty is at an end if we find it is within the power of a State to withhold.

Being unanimously of the opinion that the Constitution of the United States does not confer the right of suffrage upon any one, and that the constitutions and laws of the several States which commit that important trust to men alone are not necessarily void, we affirm the judgment.

Note: The Case of *United States* v. *Susan B. Anthony* (1873)

In the November 1872 presidential election, Susan B. Anthony, a leading suffragette, and thirteen other women offered their votes to the inspectors of election, claiming the right to vote as among the privileges and immunities secured to them as citizens by the Fourteenth Amendment to the Constitution of the United States. Two of the inspectors decided to receive their votes and deposit them in a ballot box. The women were arrested, held to bail, and indicted under a federal law that made it an offense to "knowingly vote without having a lawful right to vote." The three inspectors were also arrested, but only two of them were held to bail, the dissenter being discharged by the commissioner on whose warrant they were arrested. All three, however, were jointly indicted under the same statute—for having "knowingly and willfully received the votes of persons not entitled to vote."

Of the women voters, only Anthony's case was brought to trial in June 1873 in the U.S. Circuit Court for the Northern District of New York, presided over by Justice Ward Hunt of the United State Supreme Court.

The court held that the defendant had no right to vote, that she acted in the good faith belief that she could vote constituted no defense, and that there was nothing in the case for the jury to decide. Hunt directed the jury to find a verdict of guilty—refusing to submit, at the request of the defendant's counsel, any question to the jury, or to allow the clerk to ask the jurors, severally, whether they assented to the verdict that the court had directed to be entered. The verdict of guilty was entered by the clerk, as directed by the court, without any express assent or dissent on the part of the jury. A fine of $100, and costs, was imposed upon the defendant.

At her sentencing, Anthony and Judge Hunt engaged one another over the justice of her trial and the right to vote:

Judge Hunt—(Ordering the defendant to stand up), "Has the prisoner anything to say why sentence shall not be pronounced?"

Miss Anthony—Yes, your honor, I have many things to say; for in your ordered verdict of guilty, you have trampled under foot every vital principle of our government. My natural rights, my civil rights, my political rights, my judicial rights, are all alike ignored. Robbed of the fundamental privilege of citizenship, I am degraded from the status of a citizen to that of a subject; and not only myself individually, but all of my sex, are, by your honor's verdict, doomed to political subjection under this, so-called, form of government.

Judge Hunt—The Court cannot listen to a rehearsal of arguments the prisoner's counsel has already consumed three hours in presenting.

Miss Anthony—May it please your honor, I am not arguing the question, but simply stating the reasons why sentence cannot, in justice, be pronounced against me. Your denial of my citizen's right to vote, is the denial of my right of consent as one of the governed, the denial of my right of representation as one of the taxed, the denial of my right to a trial by a jury of my peers as an offender against law, therefore, the denial of my sacred rights to life, liberty, property and—

Judge Hunt—The Court cannot allow the prisoner to go on.

Miss Anthony—But your honor will not deny me this one and only poor privilege of protest against this high-handed outrage upon my citizen's rights. May it please the Court to remember that since the day of my arrest last November, this is the first time that either myself or any person of my disfranchised class has been allowed a word of defense before judge or jury—

Judge Hunt—The prisoner must sit down—the Court cannot allow it.

Miss Anthony—All of my prosecutors, from the 8th ward corner grocery politician, who entered the compliant, to the United States Marshal, Commissioner, District Attorney, District Judge, your honor on the bench, not one is my peer, but each and all are my political sovereigns; and had your honor submitted my case to the jury, as was clearly your duty, even then I should have had just cause of protest, for not one of those men was my peer; but, native or foreign born, white or black, rich or poor, educated or ignorant, awake or asleep, sober or drunk, each and every man of them was my political superior; hence, in no sense, my peer. Even, under such circumstances, a commoner of England, tried before a jury of Lords, would have far less cause to complain than should I, a woman, tried before a jury of men. Even my counsel, the Hon. Henry R. Selden, who has argued my cause so ably, so earnestly, so unanswerably before your honor, is my political sovereign. Precisely as no disfranchised person is entitled to sit upon a jury, and no woman is entitled to the franchise, so, none but a regularly admitted lawyer is allowed to practice in the courts, and no woman can gain admission to the bar—hence, jury, judge, counsel, must all be of the superior class.

Judged Hunt—The Court must insist—the prisoner has been tried according to the established forms of law.

Miss Anthony—Yes, your honor, but by forms of law all made by men, interpreted by men, administered by men, in favor of men, and against women; and hence, your honor's ordered verdict of guilty; against a United States citizen for the exercise of "that citizen's right to vote," simply because that citizen was a woman and not a man. But, yesterday, the same man made forms of law, declared it a crime punishable with $1,000 fine and six months imprisonment, for you, or me, or you of us, to give a cup of cold water, a crust of bread, or a night's shelter to a panting fugitive as he was tracking his way to Canada. And every man or woman in whose veins coursed a drop of human sympathy violated that wicked law, reckless of consequences, and was justified in so doing. As then, the slaves who got their freedom must take it over, or under, or through the unjust forms of law, precisely so, now, must women, to get their right to a voice in this government, take it; and I have taken mine, and mean to take it at every possible opportunity.

Judge Hunt—The Court orders the prisoner to sit down. It will not allow another word.

Miss Anthony—When I was brought before your honor for trial, I hoped for a broad and liberal interpretation of the Constitution and its recent amendments, that should declare all United States citizens under its protecting aegis—that should declare equality of rights the national guarantee to all persons born or naturalized in the United States. But failing to get this justice—failing, even, to get a trial by a jury not of my peers—I ask not leniency at your hands—but rather the full rigors of the law:

Judge Hunt—The Court must insist—(Here the prisoner sat down.)

Judge Hunt—The prisoner will stand up. (Here Miss Anthony arose again.) The sentence of the Court is that you pay a fine of one hundred dollars and the costs of the prosecution.

Miss Anthony—May it please your honor, I shall never pay a dollar of your unjust penalty. All the stock in trade I possess is a $10,000 debt, incurred by publishing my paper—*The Revolution*—four years ago, the sole object of which was to educate all women to do precisely as I have done, rebel against your manmade, unjust, unconstitutional forms of law, that tax, fine, imprison and hang women, while they deny them the right of representation in the government; and I shall work on with might and main to pay every dollar of that honest debt, but not a penny shall go to this unjust claim. And I shall earnestly and persistently continue to urge all women to the practical recognition of the old revolutionary maxim, that "Resistance to tyranny is obedience to God."

Judge Hunt—Madam, the Court will not order you committed until the fine is paid.

MARRIAGE AND DIVORCE

In 1800, the law of domestic relations was scattered through such diverse categories as contracts, property, and tort. By 1900, a more or less unified body of law had emerged. Economic change, the rise of companionate marriage, and the increasing assertiveness of women about their rights generated demands for legal reforms in marriage, divorce, child custody, birth control, and abortion. In most instances, greater certainty in the law was accompanied by growing state intervention in matters that had historically been left to private decision making and by increasing judicial oversight.

"The Nature of Marriage and How Defined"
1881

Joel Bishop, a Whiggish Massachusetts lawyer, dominated the law of domestic relations during the nineteenth century. He led the way in clarifying and adjusting the law of husband and wife, and his Commentaries, *which first appeared in 1852 and went through successive revisions and new editions into the twentieth century, was the standard treatise on the subject of domestic relations.*

1. Harmony and Diversities of Opinion—The universal sentiment of mankind accepts the fundamental doctrine of the law of marriage, that the sexes should not associate promiscuously as prompted by mere animal instinct, but "pair off," to use an expression applied to the birds of the air. Even where polygamy is tolerated, fidelity to and among the family of wives is enjoined, the same as is the more restricted fidelity in monogamy. In Christian countries, marriage comprehends the union of one man with one woman only, and all outside commerce of the sexes is forbidden, though, like other admitted evils, it is less severely dealt with in some countries than in others. . . .

2. Assumed by Contract—[M]arriage is entered into by contract. The meaning of which is, that those and those only who mutually agree to marry, being legally capable of intermarrying, are by the laws made husband and wife. This contract of marriage differs from the marriage itself, as the agreement to build a house differs from the completed structure, or as the egg and the incubation differ from the bird produced. It has the properties of any other ordinary contract: as, for example, the parties must be capable of contracting, and those already married cannot agree to marry others, though one who has concealed his incapacity may be sued by the other . . . ; it must be founded on a consideration, which, in the facts of most cases and in a certain sense of necessity, consists of mutual promises, the consideration must not involve what is immoral or against public policy; fraud or mistake, such as a concealed or undisclosed lack of chastity, will justify the breaking of the promise; the contract between an infant and an adult is binding on the adult but voidable by the infant; the "act of God," occurring after the contract is made, whereby one becomes physically incapable of performing the functions of marriage, will justify its breach by either of the parties; an action of damages for a breach may be maintained; and this contract, like any other, ends when performance is fully done and accepted. Actual marriage, in any form which makes the parties in law husband and wife, is performance. Nothing short is. At marriage, therefore, the contract ceases. Hence,—

3. Marriage Defined.—Marriage . . . is the civil status of one man and one woman united in law for life, for the discharge, to each other and the community, of the duties legally incumbent on those whose association is founded on the distinction of sex. . . .

Source of Marriage—Further of the Definition.—The source of marriage is the law of nature, whence it has flowed into the municipal laws of every civilized country, and into the general law of nations. And since it can exist only in pairs, and since none are compelled, but all who are capable are permitted, to assume it,—marriage may be said to proceed, as just explained, from a civil contract between one man and one woman, of the needful physical and civil capacity. While the contract remains a mere agreement to marry, it is not essentially different from other executory civil contracts; it does not superinduce the status; and, on its violation, an action may be maintained by the injured party to recover his damages of the other. But when it is executed in what the law accepts as a valid marriage, its nature as a contract is merged in the higher nature of the status. And though the new relation—that is, the status—retains some similitudes reminding us of its origin, the contract does in truth no longer exist, but the parties are governed by the law of husband and wife. In other words, the parties, when they agreed to marry, undertook only to assume the marital status; and, on its assumption, the agreement, being fully performed according to its terms, bound them no longer.

♦ ♦ ♦

4. Further of the Definition of Marriage.— We know that the foregoing definition of marriage is correct, because it accurately describes what the courts constantly decide. That marriage executed is not a contract we know, because the parties cannot mutually dissolve it, because the act of God incapacitating one to discharge its duties will not release the bond, because there is no accepted performance which will end it, because a minor of marriageable age can no more recede from it than an adult, because it is not dissolved by a failure of the original consideration, because no suit for damages will lie for the non-fulfillment of its duties, because its duties are not derived from its terms but from the law, because legislation may annul it at pleasure, and because none of its other elements are those of contract, but all are of status. Still,—

5. Continued.—Plain as this view is, and incredible as it may seem that anything contrary to it should be seriously entertained, marriage was generally in our books, prior to the present one, defined as a contract. But this definition, thus broadly stated, was so obviously inaccurate that it was commonly more or less qualified; and, by some, so much was excepted out of it as to leave little or nothing of the original. So that, if marriage was pronounced a contract, it was said also to be more than a contract, and to differ from all other contracts. A frequent question was, whether it is a civil contract, or a religious vow. The Roman Catholic Church holds it to be a sacrament; and, though Protestants do not generally so esteem it, they account it as of Divine origin, and invest it with the sanctions of religion. Therefore it has been said, that, "according to juster notions of the nature of the marriage contract, it is not merely either a civil or religious contract; and at the present time it is not to be considered as originally and simply one or the other." Yet all the decisions attest, that, however deeply the religious nature of marriage may engage the affections of the community, the law leaves this nature to the sole care of religion, and contemplates it only as a civil institution.

Wightman v. *Coates*
15 Mass. 1 (1833)

Through the first half of the nineteenth century, breach-of-promise suits were an important means by which private parties policed courtship. Marriage among the English upper class was a property transaction in which love played a minor role. Under such circumstances, courtship was like a stage in bargaining about the economic terms of wedlock, and men who jilted would-be brides were guilty of breaching a promise with often significant economic implications. As the explicit economic basis of marriage declined and the concept of companionate marriage increased in significance during the century, the underlying basis of the breach-of-promise suit changed. It increasingly rested on the assumption that women had to marry to become mothers in order to fulfill their social responsibilities.

Assumpsit on a promise to marry the plaintiff, and a breach thereof by refusal, and having married another woman.

At the trial on the general issue, at the last November term before Parker C.J. the evidence of a promise resulted from sundry letters written to the plaintiff by the defendant, and from his attentions to her for a considerable length of time.

It was objected by the defendant, that there being no direct evidence of an express promise, the action could not be maintained.

This objection was overruled by the judge; and the jury were instructed that if, from the letters of the defendant read in evidence, and the course of his conduct towards the plaintiff, they were satisfied that there was a mutual understanding and engagement between the parties to marry each other, they might find for the plaintiff, which they did.

If the said direction was right, judgment was to be rendered on the verdict: otherwise a new trial was to be granted.

Parker C.J. delivered the opinion of the court. Respectable counsel having expressed doubts upon the point reserved in this case, and having also suggested an opinion that the action was of a nature to be discountenanced rather than favored; we have given more consideration to the case, than our impression of the merits of the objections would have required.

We can conceive of no more suitable ground of application to the tribunals of justice for compensation, than that of a violated promise to enter into a contract, on the faithful performance of which the interest of all civilized countries so essentially depends. When two parties, of suitable age to contract, agree to pledge their faith to each other, and thus withdraw themselves from that intercourse with society, which might probably lead to a similar connexion with another; the affections being so far interested as to render a subsequent engagement not probable or desirable; and one of the parties wantonly and capriciously refuses to execute the contract, which is thus commenced; the injury may be serious, and circumstances may often justify a claim of pecuniary indemnification.

When the female is the injured party, there is generally more reason for a resort to the laws, then when the man is the sufferer. Both have a right of action, but the jury will discriminate and apportion the damages according to the injury sustained. A deserted female, whose prospects in life may be materially affected by the treachery of the man, to whom she has plighted her vows, will always receive from a jury the attention which her situation requires.

And it is not disreputable for one, who may have to mourn for years over lost prospects and broken vows, to seek such compensation as the laws can give her. It is also for the public interest, that conduct tending to consign a virtuous woman to celibacy, should meet with that punishment, which may prevent it from becoming common. That delicacy of the sex, which happily in this country gives the man so much advantage over the woman, in the intercourse which leads to matrimonial engagements, requires for its protection and continuance the aid of the laws. When it shall be abused by the injustice of those who would take advantage of it, moral justice as well as public policy dictate the propriety of a legal indemnity.

This is not a new doctrine. As early as the time of Lord *Holt,* it was enforced, as the common law, by that wise and learned judge and his brethren, that a breach of promise of marriage was a meritorious cause of action, and although the value of a marriage in money might have had some influence in that decision, there is no doubt that the loss sustained in other respects,—the wounded spirit, the unmerited disgrace, and the probable solitude,—which would be the consequences of desertion after a long courtship, were considered to be as legitimate claims for pecuniary compensation, as the loss of reputation by slander, or the wounded pride in slight assaults and batteries.

Nor is this English law become obsolete. It is the common law of our country, always recognized when occasions have offered; and the occasions have not been infrequent since the adoption of our constitution. . . . Several actions of this nature have been before this court, since I have been upon the bench, and I remember several when I was in practice at the bar, in which I was counsel. Indeed there is no country, in which the relative situation of the sexes, and their joint influence on society, would render such a principle of jurisprudence more useful or necessary.

As to the technical ground, upon which the objection to the verdict now rests, we entertain no doubts. The exception taken is, that there was no direct evidence of an express promise of marriage made by the defendant. The objection implies that there was indirect evidence, from which such a promise may have been inferred; and the jury were instructed that if, from the letters written by the defendant, as well as his conduct, they believed that a mutual engagement subsisted between the parties, they ought to find for the plaintiff. They made the inference, and without doubt it was justly drawn.

Is it then necessary that an express promise in direct terms should be proved? A necessity for this would imply a state of public manners by no means desirable. That young persons of different sexes, instead of having their mutual engagements inferred from a course of devoted attention, and apparently exclusive attachment, which is now the common evidence, should be obliged, before they considered themselves bound, to call witnesses, or execute instruments under hand and seal, would be destructive of that chaste and modest intercourse, which is the pride of our country; and a boldness of manners would probably succeed, by no means friendly to the character of the sex, or the interests of society.

A mutual engagement must be proved, to support this action: but it may be proved by those circumstances, which usually accompany such a connexion. No case has been cited, in support of the defendant's objection. On the contrary, it is very clear from all the *English* cases, that a promise may be inferred, and that direct proof is not necessary. In the case before referred to of *Hutton* vs. *Mansell,* Lord *Holt* says expressly, that where one has promised, and the behavior of the other is such as to countenance the belief that an engagement has taken place, this is evidence enough of a promise on the part of the person so conducting; and the same principle will apply to both the parties.

In the present case, however, the evidence on which the jury relied, was of a decisive nature; for the letters of the defendant, which were submitted to them, were couched in terms which admit only of the alternative, that he was bound in honor and conscience to marry the plaintiff, or that he was prosecuting a deeply laid scheme of fraud and deception, with a view to seduction. The jury believed the former; and in so doing, have vindicated his character from the greater stain: and he ought to be content with the damages, which they thought it reasonable to assess for the lighter injury. *Judgment on the verdict.*

Reynolds v. United States
98 U.S. 145 (1879)

Marriage also carried with it powerful cultural values. The following case involved polygamy, a practice adopted on religious grounds by the Church of Jesus Christ of Latter-Day Saints in Utah Territory. Much of the Court's decision in Reynolds *dealt with the power of the federal government to interfere with freedom of religion, but it also touched on important questions about whether the state had a responsibility to define the marriage agreement.*

[Chief Justice Waite] On the trial, the plaintiff in error, the accused, proved that at the time of his alleged second marriage he was, and for many years before had been, a member of the Church of Jesus Christ of Latter-Day Saints, commonly called the Mormon Church, and a believer in its doctrines; that it was an accepted doctrine of that church "that it was the duty of male members of said church, circumstances permitting, to practice polygamy; . . . that this duty was enjoined by different books which the members of said church believed to be of divine origin, and among others the Holy Bible, and also that the members of the church believed that the practice of polygamy was directly enjoined upon the male members thereof by the Almighty God, in a revelation to Joseph Smith, the founder and prophet of said church;

that the failing or refusing to practice polygamy by such male members of said church, when circumstances would admit, would be punished, and that the penalty for such failure and refusal would be damnation in the life to come." He also proved "that he had received permission from the recognized authorities in said church to enter into polygamous marriage; . . . " that Daniel H. Wells, one having authority in said church to perform the marriage ceremony, married the said defendant on or about the time the crime is alleged to have been committed, to some woman by the name of Schofield, and that such marriage ceremony was performed under and pursuant to the doctrines of said church.

Upon this proof he asked the court to instruct the jury that if they found from the evidence that he "was married as charged—if he was married—in pursuance of and in conformity with what he believed at the time to be a religious duty, that the verdict must be 'not guilty.'" This request was refused, and the court did charge "that there must have been a criminal intent, but that if the defendant, under the influence of a religious belief that it was right,—under an inspiration, if you please, that it was right,—deliberately married a second time, having a first wife living, the want of consciousness of evil intent—the want of understanding on his part that he was committing a crime—did not excuse him; but the law inexorably in such case implies the criminal intent."

Upon this charge and refusal to charge the question is raised, whether religious belief can be accepted as a justification of an overt act made criminal by the law of the land. The inquiry is not as to the power of Congress to prescribe criminal laws for the Territories, but as to the guilt of one who knowingly violates a law which has been properly enacted, if he entertains a religious belief that the law is wrong.

Congress cannot pass a law for the government of the Territories which shall prohibit the free exercise of religion. The first amendment to the Constitution expressly forbids such legislation. Religious freedom is guaranteed everywhere throughout the United States, so far as congressional interference is concerned. The question to be determined is, whether the

law now under consideration comes within this prohibition.

[Here Chief Justice Waite explored the history of religious freedom in America, finding that Congress had authority to control those religious actions that violated the social order.]

Polygamy has always been odious among the northern and western nations of Europe, and, until the establishment of the Mormon Church, was almost exclusively a feature of the life of Asiatic and of African people. At common law, the second marriage was always void and from the earliest history of England polygamy has been treated as an offence against society. After the establishment of the ecclesiastical courts, and until the time of James I, it was punished through the instrumentality of those tribunals, not merely because ecclesiastical rights had been violated, but because upon the separation of the ecclesiastical courts from the civil the ecclesiastical were supposed to be the most appropriate for the trial of matrimonial causes and offences against the rights of marriage, just as they were for testamentary causes and the settlement of the estates of deceased persons.

By the statute of 1 James I, the offence, if committed in England or Wales, was made punishable in the civil courts, and the penalty was death. As this statute was limited in its operation to England and Wales, it was at a very early period reenacted, generally with some modifications, in all the colonies. In connection with the case we are now considering, it is a significant fact that on the 8th of December, 1788, after the passage of the act establishing religious freedom, and after the convention of Virginia had recommended as an amendment to the Constitution of the United States the declaration in a bill of rights that "all men have an equal, natural, and unalienable right to the free exercise of religion, according to the dictates of conscience," the legislature of that State substantially enacted the statute of James I, death penalty included, because, as recited in the preamble, "it hath been doubted whether bigamy or polygamy be punishable by the laws of this Commonwealth." From that day to this we think it may safely be said there never has been a time in any State of the Union when polygamy has not been an offence against society, cognizable by the civil courts and punishable with more or less severity. In the face of all this evidence, it is impossible to believe that the constitutional guaranty of religious freedom was intended to prohibit legislation in respect to this most important feature of social life. Marriage, while from its very nature a sacred obligation, is nevertheless, in most civilized nations, a civil contract, and usually regulated by law. Upon it society may be said to be built, and out of its fruits spring social relations and social obligations and duties, with which government is necessarily required to deal. In fact, according as monogamous or polygamous marriages are allowed, do we find the principles on which the government of the people, to a greater or less extent, rests. Professor Lieber says, polygamy leads to the patriarchal principle, and which, when applied to large communities, fetters the people in stationary despotism, while that principle cannot long exist in connection with monogamy.

◆ ◆ ◆

In our opinion, the statute immediately under consideration is within the legislative power of Congress. It is constitutional and valid as prescribing a rule of action for all those residing in the Territories, and in places over which the United States have exclusive control. This being so, the only question which remains is, whether those who make polygamy a part of their religion are an exception from the operation of the statute. If they are, then those who do not make polygamy a part of their religious belief may be found guilty and punished, while those who do, must be acquitted and go free. This would be introducing a new element into criminal law. Laws are made for the government of actions, and while they cannot interfere with mere religious belief and opinions, they may with practices. Suppose one believed that human sacrifices were a necessary part of religious worship, would it be seriously contended that the civil government

under which he lived could not interfere to prevent a sacrifice? Or if a wife religiously believed it was her duty to burn herself upon the funeral pile of her dead husband, would it be beyond the power of the civil government to prevent her carrying her belief into practice?

So here, as a law of the organization of society under the exclusive dominion of the United States, it is provided that plural marriages shall not be allowed. Can a man excuse his practices to the contrary because of his religious belief? and there are pure-minded women and there are innocent children,—innocent in a sense even beyond the degree of the innocence of childhood itself. These are to be the sufferers; and as jurors fail to do their duty, and as these cases come up in the Territory of Utah, just so do these victims multiply and spread themselves over the land.

While every appeal by the court to the passions or the prejudices of a jury should be promptly rebuked, and while it is the imperative duty of a reviewing court to take care that wrong is not done in this way, we see no just cause for complaint in this case. Congress, in 1862, saw fit to make bigamy a crime in the Territories. This was done because of the evil consequences that were supposed to flow from plural marriages. All the court did was to call the attention of the jury to the peculiar character of the crime for which the accused was on trial, and to remind them of the duty they had to perform. There was no appeal to the passions, no instigation of prejudice. Upon the showing made by the accused himself, he was guilty of a violation of the law under which he had been indicted: and the effort of the court seems to have been not to withdraw the minds of the jury from the issue to be tried, but to bring them to it; not to make them partial, but to keep them impartial.

Upon a careful consideration of the whole case, we are satisfied that no error was committed by the court below.

Judgment affirmed.

Note: Divorce

Divorce had been extremely rare in colonial America. When couples divorced from "bed and board," they simply separated without legally dissolving their relationship. Although the incidence of divorce increased in the nineteenth century, the practice grew more rapidly during the last forty years of the century as industrialization took hold. Most divorces were granted to women, and most of these were based on either a husband's alleged adultery or his cruelty. By the end of the nineteenth century, a liberal view of divorce began to emerge, one that recognized the sweeping economic changes of the era and had vast implications for the marriage contract. Judicial divorce became more popular as a means of allocating property when things went sour.

Waldron v. Waldron
85 Cal. 251 (1890)

The rise of companionate marriage invited matrimonial dissolutions because the expectations of love and affection that it raised were often unattainable. Legislators set the terms for divorce; judges applied them. Adultery figured prominently in every state, but by the end of the century, cruelty was also widely accepted as grounds for divorce. What this vague term meant was another matter. The court in 1863 had rejected the idea that physical harm alone constituted cruelty. In Powelson *v.* Powelson, *22 Cal. 360, the judges concluded that any "conduct sufficiently aggravated to produce ill-health or bodily pain . . . though operating primarily upon the mind only, should be regarded as legal cruelty." The court's finding in* Waldron, *although it worked against the wife, did provide that if the indignities were sufficient, they could destroy a marriage, even if there had been no physical harm. In 1892, the California General Assembly ratified this view in legislation that made it possible to prove mental suffering even if there was no evidence of deterioration in a spouse's physical health.*

Vanclief, C.—This is an action for divorce on the ground of extreme cruelty, by the use of vile and offensive language, without any physical force or violence applied to the person of the plaintiff.

The answer of the defendant denies the cruelty and the use of the language alleged. The court found for the plaintiff, and decreed a divorce and permanent alimony of one hundred dollars per month while she shall remain unmarried, and one thousand dollars for her attorneys fees; and defendant appeals from the judgment, and from an order denying his motion for a new trial.

The material substance of the findings as to extreme cruelty is as follows:—

That, upon occasions when the defendant was intoxicated, he wrongfully and unjustly, and without sufficient provocation to justify him in so doing, called the plaintiff vile names,

once called her a "whore," and on several different occasions called her a "damned bitch," and a "damned witch from hell," in the presence and hearing of other people, and thereby inflicting upon her grievous mental suffering, but without injury to her health; that when he called her such vile names she was not without fault, and that she was not uniformly kind to him; that there is reasonable apprehension to believe that such cruel treatment will be continued if a divorce is not granted.

♦ ♦ ♦

Although the character of the ill treatment, whether it operates directly upon the body or primarily upon the mind alone, and all the attending circumstances, are to be considered for the purpose of estimating the degree of the cruelty, yet the final test of its sufficiency, as a cause of divorce, must be its actual or reasonably apprehended injurious effect upon the body or health of the complaining party. . . . This is the only practically safe rule. The grave remedy of divorce is disproportioned to the petty marital wrongs and annoyances whose injurious effect upon the body or health cannot be shown and sensibly appreciated, and it is not to be administered on the ground of cruelty, except in conservation of life or health. Many of such wrongs and annoyances, productive of more or less unhappiness, must be borne, if they cannot be justly remedied or avoided by the parties themselves.

◆ ◆ ◆

Yet the practical view of the law is, that a degree of cruelty which cannot be perceived to injure the body or the health of the body, "can be practically endured," and *must* be endured, if there is no other remedy than by divorce; because no "scale" by which to gauge the purely mental susceptibilities and sufferings has yet been invented or discovered, except such as indicate the degrees thereof by their *perceptible* effects upon the physical organization of the body.

From the foregoing considerations, it follows that the findings of fact are not sufficient to sustain the judgment. "Extreme cruelty" is not expressly found in any sense; nor does it, in the legal sense above described, follow, as a necessary inference, from the facts found. The finding of "grievous mental suffering" is, and purports to be, only an inference or conclusion from the opprobrious language found to have been used by the defendant.

◆ ◆ ◆

Plaintiff admitted that the defendant was an honest man in all his business transactions, and that he liberally supplied her and her children and niece. She complained of no unkindness when he was sober, and feared no physical violence from him when he was drunk. In their quarrels she appears to have been more than his match, though she could not descend to answer his profanity and obscenity in kind. While drunkenness was no excuse for calling her vile names under any circumstances, yet the injurious effect thereof upon her mind should not have been, and probably was not, so bad as

if he had deliberately called her by those names when he was sober. No mental suffering produced by his drunkenness, merely, can be considered, because not complained of. The mental suffering, caused by his words alone, can be considered in this case.

The finding that defendant called the plaintiff a whore and a bitch, *in the presence and hearing of other people,* should be qualified by the admitted facts that none but the niece and her caller and the colored servant heard him call out her name, and that he was not aware that even they heard what he said, or that the caller upon the niece was in the house at the time. This seems material, as tending both to modify the otherwise apparent motive of the defendant, and to mitigate the alleged painful effect upon the mind of the plaintiff, as without this qualification it would appear that the defendant intended to defame the plaintiff in public estimation, which would indicate a worse motive on his part, and produce a more painful effect upon her mind than would the mere intention privately to annoy her, or to revenge himself for the fancied wrongs of having been barred out of her room and threatened with the police.

While the defamatory, obscene, and profane language of the defendant was wholly unjustified, inexcusable, and unmanly, it may be said that the conduct of the plaintiff was at least unkind and censorious, and tended to provoke anger and harsh language on the part of the defendant. It probably resulted from her ill temper, bad judgment, and a mistaken view of the duty of a wife under the circumstances. She probably deemed it her duty, by means of censure, reproach, and scolding, to make her husband "do what was right," and it seems that she faithfully, in season and out of season, applied such means. In this I think she was mistaken. Intemperate husbands are seldom, if ever, reformed by such treatment, whereas uniform kindness may often prove effectual, and never harmful; but should kindness fail, and the intemperance of the husband become habitual, the wife will be entitled to a divorce on that ground alone.

I think the judgment should be reversed, and the court below directed to render judgment for the defendant on the findings, without costs, and that the appellant pay his own costs of the appeal.

Birth Control and Abortion

A dramatic decline in female fertility (and, hence, family size) was an important demographic feature of nineteenth-century America. By the beginning of the twentieth century, the United States had one of the lowest fertility rates in the world. Historians have debated why this decline took place and on whose initiative (husband, wife, or both). The companionate form of marriage and the greater emotional attention given to children may explain some of the decline in births. Women also seem to have viewed the practice of birth control as one way of increasing their autonomy. Yet male lawmakers grew increasingly wary of these practices and intervened, with greater and greater frequency, in an area that had been deemed exclusively private, going so far as to criminalize the dissemination of birth control information and the practice of abortion.

State v. Slagle
82 N.C. 653 (1880)

Abortion carried a far heavier moral and legal burden than did birth control. Infanticide had been a feature of colonial America, but as the fertility rate dropped and birth control practices became better and more widespread its significance also declined. However, at the beginning of the nineteenth century, abortion carried no legal penalties so long as it was performed before "quickening," the period about four or five months when the fetus begins to move in the womb. The leading American case was Commonwealth v. Bangs, *9 Mass. 369 (1812), which gave the quickening doctrine, with its long roots in English common law, a firm hold in nineteenth-century American common law. By the end of the century, however, American judges began to de-emphasize the quickening doctrine.*

Ashe, J. The indictment contained four counts; the first two charged the defendant with having *wilfully* and *feloniously* administered a poisonous drug to one Eva Bryson, with intent to kill and murder her, varying only in the description of the drug used. The last two counts charged him with having unlawfully and wickedly administered a noxious potion to the said Eva, then being quick with child, with the intent to cause and procure the miscarriage of the said Eva, and the premature birth of the said child; these two counts only differing as to the nature of the drugs employed to effect the purpose. The defendant . . . argued [t]hat the facts set forth and charged against him in said bill of indictment do not constitute an offence or crime against the laws of North Carolina.

♦ ♦ ♦

The defendant is . . . charged in the indictment with a crime under the laws of the state. And when one in this state is indicted and tried as for a felony, yet the facts averred in the indictment do not support the charge of felony, but a misdemeanor, the court may give judgment for such misdemeanor.

♦ ♦ ♦

We have no statute making it indictable to administer "drugs" to produce abortion, and there is very little to be found on the subject in either the English or American writers on criminal law, but it is held by the highest authority that it is a misdemeanor at common law. . . . And Wharton in his work on Criminal Law, 1220 says: "There is no doubt at common law the destruction of an infant unborn is a high misdemeanor and at an early period, it seems to have been murder." It has been said it is not an indictable offence to administer a drug to a woman and thereby to procure an abortion, unless the mother is quick with child, though such a distinction, it is submitted, is neither in accordance with the results of medical experience or with the principles of the common law.

♦ ♦ ♦

Per Curiam.

Note: Abortion and the Quickening Doctrine

The decision in *Slagle* marked a growing retreat by both courts and legislatures from the quickening doctrine. To some extent, this change in direction revealed the influence of an increasingly vocal and well-organized antiabortion campaign by the medical profession. The American Medical Association made an end to abortion one of its chief goals: its leaders considered abortion law reform a means by which the profession could enhance its moral influence, extend the influence of scientific medical practices against midwives, and monopolize the health-care business generally. Legislatures cooperated by adopting more comprehensive acts that imposed stiffer penalties on both the woman and the abortionist. Abortion was a risky procedure, and the states had a plausible role in saving women from death and sterility as a result of hemorrhage and infection. The Massachusetts Supreme Judicial Court in 1882 reversed its earlier holding in *Bangs* by disposing of the quickening doctrine altogether in considering whether an abortion was illegal (see *Commonwealth* v. *Taylor,* 132 Mass. 261 [1882]). But quickening did continue to play some part in determining the extent of criminal penalty. The aborting of a prequickened fetus was generally treated as a misdemeanor; that of a fully animated fetus was considered a felony.

Despite the criminalization of abortion in most states, the practice continued to flourish. Only a small percentage of those persons who performed abortions were ever convicted. Like birth control information and devices, the public demand for abortion produced its own black market, one in which women of standing and wealth had far greater access to competent treatment than did lower-class and poor women. New abortion statutes limited the discretionary rights of all women.

People v. *Sanger*
222 N.Y. 192 (1918)

Like abortion, birth control came under increased scrutiny by state government. By the end of the nineteenth century, moral reformers had made limitation of such knowledge one of their chief objectives. Margaret Sanger was a prominent advocate of birth control, and she and her sister sought to test the constitutionality of a New York State law against distributing birth control information by purposely being convicted under it.

Crane, J. Section 1142 of the Penal Law, among other things, makes it a misdemeanor for a person to sell, or give away, or to advertise or offer for sale, any instrument or article, drug or medicine, for the prevention of conception; or to give information orally stating when, where or how such an instrument, article or medicine can be purchased or obtained.

The appellant was convicted . . . for a violation of this section, and sentenced to thirty days in the workhouse. She claims that the law is unconstitutional.

Some of the reasons assigned below for the illegality of this act have now been abandoned and it is conceded to be within the police power of the legislature, for the benefit of the morals and health of the community, to make such a law as this applicable to unmarried persons. But it is argued that if this law be broad enough to prevent a duly licensed physician from giving advice and help to his married patients in a proper case, it is an unreasonable police regulation, and, therefore, unconstitutional. There are two answers to this suggestion.

In the first place, the defendant is not a physician, and the general rule applies in a criminal as well as a civil case that no one can plead the unconstitutionality of a law except the person affected thereby. . . .

Secondly, by section 1145 of the Penal Law, physicians are excepted from the provisions of this act under circumstances therein mentioned. This section reads: "An article or instrument, used or applied by physicians lawfully practicing, or by their direction or prescription, for the cure or prevention of disease, is not an article of indecent or immoral nature or use, within this article. The supplying of such articles to such physicians or by their direction or prescription, is not an offense under this article."

This exception in behalf of physicians does not permit advertisements regarding such matters, nor promiscuous advice to patients irrespective of their condition, but it is broad enough to protect the physician who in good faith gives such help or advice to a married person to cure or prevent disease. "Disease," by Webster's International Dictionary, is defined to be, "an alteration in the state of the body, or of some of its organs, interrupting or disturbing the performance of the vital functions, and causing or threatening pain and sickness; illness; sickness; disorder."

The protection thus afforded the physician would also extend to the druggist, or vendor, acting upon the physician's prescription or order.

Much of the argument presented to us by the appellant touching social conditions and sociological questions are matters for the legislature and not for the courts.

Judgment affirmed.

CRIME AND CRIMINAL JUSTICE

Criminal law involves the power of the state to deprive individuals of their liberty (through imprisonment, even death) and property (through fines and confiscations). In the American federal system, the states almost entirely created and enforced this body of law. Nineteenth-century state lawmakers did so based on the police powers—powers to provide for the morals, health, welfare, and safety of the public. Both the criminal law and the criminal justice system underwent significant change during the century, although historians disagree sharply about the causes and consequences of those changes. For example, the rate of serious crime dropped during the nineteenth century, a decline that continued well into the twentieth century. But why this decrease occurred remains uncertain (the amount of crime increased, but so did the population). The debate over the crime rate revolves around two of the most important developments of the century: industrialization and urbanization. Some scholars argue that a greater concentration of people in urban areas and the rise of an industrial market economy should have produced social dislocations sufficient to encourage crime. Others contend that capitalism and the emerging American city actually encouraged a system of discipline and order that inhibited crime. Still others insist that neither of these broad developments had much to do directly with the decline in the rate of serious crime: rather, they argue that the emergence of professional police forces, beginning in mid-century, effectively deterred crime.

Students of the era have also argued that crime was endemic in rural, frontier areas where the arm of the law failed to reach. Such a view holds that what law did exist flowed out of the barrel of a gun and that vigilantism was an everyday occurrence. Other scholars have concluded that there was far more stability and order than previously believed. John P. Reid, for example, has argued persuasively that travelers on the Overland Trail during mid-century displayed an extraordinary commitment to law and order, a commitment that they learned in the more civilized East and carried with them into the West.[1]

There is also disagreement about the nature of nineteenth-century crime. William E. Nelson, for instance, has noted that by the beginning of the century, crimes against property rather than moral crimes (adultery, fornication, and such) received greatest attention from the criminal justice system.[2] Yet by the end of the century, as some of the previous material in this chapter makes clear, social reformers turned increasingly to criminal law to control abortion, birth control, and supposedly obscene materials, such as birth control literature.

Nineteenth-century Americans also wrestled with the problem of punishing criminal offenders, and social reformers gave great attention to prison reform and the abolition of the death penalty. Perhaps the most dramatic response during the first half of the century was the discovery of the asylum. Penitentiaries, madhouses, and poorhouses were institutional responses to the problems of deviancy and dependency. Advocates of the penitentiary insisted that the causes of crime had environmental roots and that by taking offenders out of degraded surroundings and placing them in an atmosphere of discipline and order, change was possible. The quest to rehabilitate the individual, however, always clashed with persistent societal demands that retribution be meted out to wrongdoers.

By the end of the century, the rehabilitative ideal that undergirded the asylum movement came under increasing attack from proponents of biological inheritance and eugenics. There were, in short, born criminals. A bad environment, like crowded urban slums, only exacerbated the problems created by a faulty inheritance.

Conflicts over the proper method of punishment and the relationship of environment and inheritance to crime also surfaced in the growing debate over what constituted a proper legal excuse for crime. Pleas of insanity and self-defense, for example, became increasingly important in nineteenth-century homicide law.

CRIME AND PUNISHMENT

Nineteenth-century students of American crime expounded conflicting views about its causes. Some spokesmen stressed environment; others, especially as the eugenics movement gathered momentum at century's end, emphasized biological inheritance; and still others claimed that both elements explained criminal behavior. Crime, of course, is a wholly subjective designation; it is what those who control the power of the state say it is. For most of the century, however, lawmakers drew from an Enlightenment inheritance that stressed reason and environment over innate sinfulness. By the end of the century, however, a scientific explanation that derived from eugenics gained increasing currency.

CESARE BECCARIA

On Crimes and Punishments
1764

Cesare Bonesana, Marquis of Beccaria, was an Italian nobleman who founded the classical or rational school of criminology. In 1764 Beccaria published his now-famous essay On

Crimes and Punishments, *and it received wide attention in pre- and post-Revolutionary America. The first English translation in America appeared in Charleston, South Carolina, in 1777, and Thomas Jefferson's* Commonplace Book *contained twenty-six extracts from the essay. Jefferson in 1776 also drew heavily on it to formulate his proposed reforms to Virginia's penal laws.*

It is better to prevent crimes than to punish them. This is the ultimate end of every good legislation, which, to use the general terms for assessing the good and evils of life, is the art of leading men to the greatest possible happiness or to the least possible unhappiness.

♦ ♦ ♦

Do you want to prevent crimes? See to it that the laws are clear and simple and that the entire force of a nation is united in their defense, and that no part of it is employed to destroy them. See to it that the laws favor not so much classes of men as men themselves. See to it that men fear the laws and fear nothing else. For fear of the laws is salutary, but fatal and fertile for crimes is one man's fear of another. Enslaved men are more voluptuous, more depraved, more cruel than free men. These study the sciences, give thought to the interests of their country, contemplate grand objects and imitate them, while enslaved men, content with the present moment, seek in the excitement of debauchery a distraction from the emptiness of the condition in which they find themselves. Accustomed to an uncertainty of outcome in all things, the outcome of their crimes remains for them problematical, to the advantage of the passions that determine them. If uncertainty regarding the laws befalls a nation which is indolent because of climate, its indolence and stupidity are confirmed and increased; if it befalls a voluptuous but energetic nation, the result is a wasteful diffusion of energy into an infinite number of little cabals and intrigues that sow distrust in every heart, make treachery and dissimulation the foundation of prudence; if it befalls a brave and powerful nation, the uncertainty is removed finally, but only after having caused many oscillations from liberty to slavery and from slavery back to liberty.

Do you want to prevent crimes? See to it that enlightenment accompanies liberty. Knowledge breeds evils in inverse ratio to its diffusion, and benefits in direct ratio. A daring impostor, who is never a common man, is received with adoration by an ignorant people, and with hisses by an enlightened one. Knowledge, by facilitating comparisons and by multiplying points of view, brings on a mutual modification of conflicting feelings, especially when it appears that others hold the same views and face the same difficulties. In the face of enlightenment widely diffused throughout the nation, the calumnies of ignorance are silenced and authority trembles if it be not armed with reason. The vigorous force of the laws, meanwhile, remains immovable, for no enlightened person can fail to approve of the clear and useful public compacts of mutual security when he compares the inconsiderable portion of useless liberty he himself has sacrificed with the sum total of liberties sacrificed by other men, which, except for the laws, might have been turned against him. Any person of sensibility, glancing over a code of well-made laws and observing that he has lost only a baneful liberty to injure others, will feel constrained to bless the throne and its occupant.

CHARLES LORING BRACE

"The Causes of Crime"
1880

By the end of the nineteenth century, Beccaria's rational view came under attack from authorities who tied crime to biological inheritance. Cesare Lombroso, an Italian physician and the father of modern criminology, for example, pioneered the science of anthropometry, which purported to describe a set of physical characteristics, such as a low-sloping forehead and heavily massed ears, that all criminals supposedly shared. Lombroso outlined his theory in Criminal Man *(1876), and its claims that criminals were born, not made, received considerable attention in the United States. Charles Loring Brace, a leader of the New York Children's Aid Society, added yet another dimension to these arguments by borrowing ideas from both the environmental and inheritance schools. He described the existence of a "dangerous class," composed of the masses of poor, foreign-born immigrants who were filling up American cities. Brace's anti-Irish bias paralleled racial stereotypes formed of blacks, Chinese, and Native Americans. Yet Brace also believed that the city, more so than small villages and towns, was best suited to deal with the causes of crime.*

There is no question that the breaking of the ties with one's country has a bad moral effect, especially on a laboring class. The Emigrant is released from the social inspection and judgment to which he has been subjected at home, and the tie of church and priesthood is weakened. If a Roman Catholic, he is often a worse Catholic, without being a better Protestant. If a Protestant, he often becomes indifferent. Moral ties are loosened with the religious. The intervening process which occurs here, between his abandoning the old state of things and fitting himself to the new, is not favorable to morals or character.

The consequence is, that an immense proportion of our ignorant and criminal class are foreign-born; and of the dangerous classes here, a very large part, though native-born, are of foreign parentage.

♦　♦　♦

It is another marked instance of the demoralizing influence of emigration, that so large a proportion of the female criminal class should be Irish-born, though the Irish female laboring class are well known to be at home one of the most virtuous in the world.

A hopeful fact, however, begins to appear in regard to this matter; the worst effects of emigration in this country seem over. The machinery for protecting and forwarding the newly-arrived immigrants, so that they may escape the dangers and temptations of the city, has been much improved. Very few, comparatively, now remain in our sea-ports to swell the current of poverty and crime. The majority find

their way at once to the country districts. The quality, too, of the immigration has improved. More well-to-do farmers and peasantry, with small savings, arrive than formerly, and the preponderance, as to nationality, is inclining to Germany. It comparatively seldom happens now that paupers or persons absolutely without means, land in New York.

As one of the great causes of crime, Emigration will undoubtedly have a much feebler influence in the future in New York [City] than it has had in the past.

♦　♦　♦

A most powerful and continual source of crime with the young is Inheritance—the transmitted tendencies and qualities of their parents, or of several generations of ancestors.

It is well-known to those familiar with the criminal classes, that certain appetites or habits, if indulged abnormally and excessively through two or more generations, come to have an almost irresistible force, and, no doubt, modify the brain so as to constitute almost an instance condition. This is especially true of the appetite for liquor and of the sexual passion, and sometimes of the peculiar weakness, dependence, and laziness which make confirmed paupers.

The writer knows of an instance in an almshouse in Western New York, where four generations of females were paupers and prostitutes. Almost every reader who is familiar with village life will recall poor families which have had dissolute or criminal members beyond the memory of the oldest inhabitant, and who still continue to breed such characters. I have known a child of nine or ten years, given up, apparently beyond control, to licentious habits and desires, and who in all different circumstances seemed to show the same tendencies; her mother had been of similar character, and quite likely her grandmother. The "gemmules," or latent tendencies, or forces, or cells of her immediate ancestors were in her system, and working in her blood, producing irresistible effects on her brain, nerves, and mental emotions, and finally, not being met early enough by other moral, mental, and physical influences, they have modified her organization, until her will is scarcely able to control them and she gives herself up to them. All those who instruct or govern "Houses of Refuge," or "Reform Schools," or Asylums for criminal children and youths, will recall many such instances. They are much better known in the Old World than this; they are far more common here in the country than in the city.

My own experience during twenty years has been in this regard singularly hopeful. I have watched great numbers of degraded families in New York, and exceedingly few of them have transmitted new generations of paupers, criminals, or vagrants.

The causes of this encouraging state of things are not obscure. The action of the great law of "Natural Selection," in regard to the human race, is always towards temperance and virtue. That is, vice and extreme indulgence weaken the physical powers and undermine the constitution; they impair the faculties by which man struggles with adverse conditions and gets beyond the reach of poverty and want. The vicious and sensual and drunken die earlier, or they have fewer children, or their children are carried off by diseases more frequently, or they themselves are unable to resist or prevent poverty and suffering. As a consequence, in the lowest class, the more self-controlled and virtuous tend constantly to survive, and to prevail in "the struggle for existence," over the vicious and ungoverned, and to transmit their progeny. The natural drift among the poor is towards virtue. Probably no vicious organization with very extreme and abnormal tendencies is transmitted beyond the fourth generation; it ends in insanity or cretinism or the wildest crime.

The result is then, with the worst-endowed families, that the "gemmules," or latent forces of hundreds of virtuous, or at least, not vicious, generations, lie hid in their constitutions. The immediate influences of parents or grandparents are, of course, the strongest in heritance; but these may be overcome, and the latent tendencies to good, coming down from remote ancestors, be aroused and developed.

Thus is explained the extraordinary improvement of the children of crime and poverty in our Industrial Schools; and the reforms and happy changes seen in, the boys and girls of our dangerous classes when placed in kind Western homes. The change of circumstances, the improved food, the daily moral and mental influences, the effect of regular labor and discipline, and, above all, the power of Religion, awaken these hidden tendencies to good, both those coming from many generations of comparative virtue and those inherent in the soul, while they control and weaken and cause to be forgotten those diseased appetites or extreme passions which these unfortunate creatures inherit directly, and substitute a higher moral sense for the low moral instincts which they obtained from their parents. So it happens, also, that American life, as compared with European, and city life, as compared with country, produces similar results. In the United States, a boundless hope pervades all classes; it reaches down to the outcast and vagrant. There is no fixity, as is so often the fact in Europe, from the sense of despair. Every individual, at least till he is old, hopes and expects to rise out of his condition.

The daughter of the rag-picker or vagrant sees the children she knows, continually dressing better or associating with more decent people; she beholds them attending the public schools and improving in education and manners; she comes in contact with the greatest force the poor know—public opinion, which requires a certain decency and respectability among themselves. She becomes ashamed of her squalid, ragged, or drunken mother. She enters an Industrial School, or creeps into a Ward School, or "goes out" as a servant. In every place, she feels the profound forces of American life; the desire of equality, ambition to rise, the sense of self-respect and the passion for education.

These new desires overcome the low appetites in her blood, and she continually rises and improves. If Religion in any form reach her, she attains a still greater height over the sensual and filthy ways of her parents. She is in no danger of sexual degradation, or of any extreme vice. The poison in her blood has found an antidote. When she marries, it will inevitably be with a class above her own. This process goes on continually throughout the country, and breaks up criminal inheritance.

Moreover, the incessant change of our people, especially in cities, the separation of children from parents, of brothers from sisters, and of all from their former localities, destroy that continuity of influence which bad parents and grandparents exert, and do away

with those neighborhoods of crime and pauperism where vice concentrates and transmits itself with ever-increasing power. The fact that tenants must forever be "moving" in New York, is a preventive of some of the worst evils among the lower poor. The mill of American life, which grinds up so many delicate and fragile things, has its uses, when it is turned on the vicious fragments of the lower strata of society.

Villages, which are more stable and conservative, and tend to keep families together more and in the same neighborhoods, show more instances of inherited and concentrated wickedness and idleness. In New York the families are constantly broken up; some members improve, some die out, but they do not transmit a progeny of crime. There is little inherited criminality and pauperism.

Note: The Police and the Prison

Although Brace did not touch on the matter in the preceding selection, he also believed that in every major urban area an organized and professional police force contributed significantly to law and order. During the nineteenth century, the police had undergone a metamorphosis. The informal and typically nonuniformed police of the pre–Civil War years gave way after the war to an increasingly professional police order—one that took on a paramilitary style of organization including uniforms and, unlike the Metropolitan Police of London (the prototypal modern police force formed in the 1850s), arms. Until about the mid-1880s, the police were as much social welfare agents, providing temporary housing for the homeless and collecting lost children, as they were crime preventors and detectors. Thereafter, however, their role narrowed, and they became much more agents of the criminal justice system who detected and prevented crimes by the "dangerous classes" that Brace describes.

The prison also emerged during the nineteenth century as an essential element in the criminal justice systems of most states. Two major prison systems vied for acceptance—the separate and the congregate. The former was associated with the Eastern State Penitentiary in Philadelphia; the latter was represented by the Auburn State Penitentiary in Auburn, New York. These two institutions also underscored the age-old tensions that have beset prison as a form of punishment: the need to keep costs within reason (the congregate system) while designing individualized approaches (the separate system) to the treatment of criminals. Both systems, however, imbibed the rehabilitative ideal—the notion that the purpose of punishment was to return the individual to society.

THE EXCUSE OF CRIME

Nineteenth-century lawmakers responded to the threat of criminal disorder by passing more laws. Rhode Island, for example, listed only 50 criminal acts in 1822; by 1872, that number had jumped to 128. The substantive criminal law also gradually shifted in its underlying assumptions. Colonial Americans had generally equated crime with sin, but nineteenth-century lawmakers, influenced by a rising tide of scientific learning, rooted it in hereditary, environmental, and emotional conditions. More so than in the colonial era, therefore, the question of excusing criminal behavior became more complex, as the debate over insanity and self-defense reveals.

The insanity defense was a product of scientific naturalism, a body of thought that held that physical and emotional causes, rather than moral wickedness, explained human behavior. The infant discipline of psychiatry was one offshoot of scientific naturalism, but so was the eugenics movement, with its stress on inherited criminal behavior. Isaac Ray, the most famous American student of medical jurisprudence in the nineteenth century, disagreed with the latter approach. Instead, he stressed that a physical disease of the brain forced persons to act contrary to their own moral standards. Ray insisted that the traditional common-law test, which the English court had outlined in *Regina* v. *McNaghten* (1843), was needlessly narrow in considering the question of whether the defendant knew right from wrong and that it flew in the face of advancing scientific knowledge. He subscribed to the "irresistible impulse" test, but only a handful of jurisdictions agreed with him.

State v. *Felter*
25 Iowa 67 (1868)

The following is the leading case on "irresistible impulse." Its author, John Forrest Dillon, after serving as Chief Justice of the Iowa Supreme Court, became a prominent Wall Street lawyer, an authority on municipal bonds, and the president of the American Bar Association in 1892.

[Dillon, C.J.] Finally, it is insisted that the court erred in its instructions to the jury, and in its refusal to give certain instructions prayed by the defendant relative to the defense of insanity. Before noticing the assignment of error, it is proper, briefly, to refer to the circumstances of the homicide. That the defendant took the life of his wife was not disputed; and the only defense made or relied on was that species of mental unsoundness which has received the name of homicidal mania.

The testimony tends to show that the defendant was about forty years of age, and resided with his wife and a child (who was a witness on the trial), in Tama county, on a farm, about one mile distant from neighbors. He had resided in that county for over ten years, and had served in the army during the war. He had, during the forenoon of the day on which the homicide was committed, been at work in the usual manner. Shortly after dinner the neighbors, from seeing the fire, or some other reason, visited the premises of the defendant, and found the house in ashes, and the defendant's wife within a few feet of it, dead, without clothing upon her person, one of her feet burned off, her features so destroyed by fire that they could not be recognized, and her skull badly fractured, evidently in consequence of heavy blows with a club or other deadly instrument. The defendant himself was found (although he had been seen walking around by persons when approaching the premises) lying near some stacks a few rods from the dwelling-house, with his throat cut from ear to ear, and very weak from the loss of blood. His hair and whiskers were singed, and there was a blister on his nose, but no evidence of fire on any other part of his person, and his clothes were not burned.

There was but one eyewitness to the terrible occurrence—a very young daughter of the defendant, whose age is not stated in the record; and she saw only the first portion of it. The testimony in the case is very imperfectly reported, having been taken down by an unskilled person. The daughter testified, in substance, thus:

"My mother is dead—my father killed her; he struck her—I don't know with what; he was mad at her before I left; it was because she poured the buttermilk out; I left because he was going to kill me; I knew this by the way he acted; mother told me to go to Mr. P.'s (a neighbor's); it was in front of the house that father struck her, about a rod from the house; he shot the gun off by her head; my father was cross to her and did everything mean he could."

◆ ◆ ◆

There was other evidence, showing that they did not at times live happily together, and that the defendant was fault-finding and cross toward her. The physician who examined the deceased, gave it as his opinion, that the blow upon her skull would produce instant death. When Doctor Daniels afterward dressed the defendant's wound in his throat, he had a conversation with him in respect to the homicide. The defendant said, "that the reason he shot at her was, that he wanted to scare her." He said he wanted to destroy everything, so that she would not get anything, and this was the reason why he burned the house.

◆ ◆ ◆

A great number of witnesses who had known the defendant for many years, testified that they never saw anything strange in his conduct, or anything that lead them to suspect that he was of unsound mind.

The defendant stated that he cut his throat with a razor, and told where it could be found.

◆ ◆ ◆

It was admitted by the State that the defendant intended to take his own life when he cut his own throat. There were no witnesses

upon the stand who knew of or testified respecting the alleged insanity of the defendant when at home, or the alleged insanity of his father.

The medical witnesses examined on the trial, as not unfrequently happens, differed in opinion as to the defendant's sanity. Most of these witnesses, however, had given to the subject of insanity no special attention.

The court charged the jury that "if the defendant, at the time of the commission of the act (if he did commit it), was laboring under such a degree of insanity as irresistibly and uncontrollably forced him to commit the act, and if he did not at the time of the act, have reason sufficient to discriminate between right and wrong in reference to the act about to be committed by him, it is your duty to acquit wholly; in other words, if you believe from the evidence that the defendant's mind, at the time of committing the act (if he did commit it), was so insane that he did not know the nature of the crime, and did not know that *he was doing wrong in doing the act,* it is your duty to acquit him altogether."

The defendant's counsel complain of this instruction, and in their written argument make to it this objection: "The court did not state the law; only a part of it. It told the jury if the defendant had sufficient mind to discriminate between right and wrong he was responsible. This is not sufficient. He must have mind enough to know that he will be held responsible for his act."

◆ ◆ ◆

With reference to the right and wrong test referred to in the instructions given, it will be seen that the court does not adopt this criterion as a general one, that is the court does not say if the defendant has capacity to distinguish between right and wrong generally, he is criminally responsible.

But it held that if at the time and with respect to the act about to be committed, the defendant had not reason enough to discriminate between right and wrong with reference to that act, had not reason enough to know the nature of the crime, and did not *know that he was doing wrong in committing it,* he is not criminally punishable. The court in substance held that if the defendant's reason was so far gone or overwhelmed that his perception of right or wrong with respect to the comtemplated act was destroyed, if he did not rationally comprehend the character of the act he was about to commit, he should be acquitted.

◆　◆　◆

On the other hand, the right and wrong test, even when guarded as carefully as in the court's instruction, has been very vehemently opposed as incorrect and delusive, especially as a criterion of responsibility in cases of moral insanity.

In my opinion, the right and wrong test is not to be applied too strictly, and belongs more properly to intellectual than to moral insanity. Intelligent medical observers who have made insanity a special study, insist that it not unfrequently happens that persons undoubtedly insane, and who are confined on that account in asylums, are able to distinguish right from wrong, and to know the moral qualities of acts.

Perhaps the profession of law has not fully kept pace with that of medicine on the subject of insanity. And yet medical theorists have propounded doctrines respecting insanity as an excuse for criminal acts, which a due regard for the safety of the community and an enlightened public policy must prevent jurists from adopting as part of the law of the land.

If, as the court charged, the defendant committed the act from an irresistible and uncontrollable insane impulse, not knowing it was wrong, it is clear that he is not criminally responsible.

But suppose he knew it was wrong, but yet was driven to it by an uncontrollable and irresistible impulse, arising, not from natural passion, but from an insane condition of the mind, would he then be criminally responsible?

Most of the cases before cited have recognized the doctrine, that there is a responsibility for the criminal act if the accused knew at the time it was wrong; or, as it would be better expressed, if he rationally comprehended the character and consequences of the act.

But, if, from the observation and concurrent testimony of medical men who make the study of insanity a specialty, it shall be definitely established to be true, that there is an unsound condition of the mind,—that is a diseased condition of the mind, in which, though a person abstractly knows that a given act is wrong, he is yet by an *insane impulse*, that is, an impulse proceeding from a diseased intellect, irresistibly driven to commit it,—the law must modify its ancient doctrines and recognize the truth, and give to this condition, when it is satisfactorily shown to exist, its exculpatory effect.

It is not too much to say, that both medicine and law now recognize the existence of such a mental disease as homicidal insanity; the remaining question in jurisprudence being what must be shown to make it available as a defense to a charge of murder.

◆　◆　◆

If this want of power of control arose from the *insane* condition of the mind of the accused, he should not be held responsible. But if want of power to control his actions arose from violent and ungovernable passions, in a mind not diseased or unsound, he would and ought to be criminally punishable for his acts.

Without further discussion, we conclude by stating what, under the facts of this case, would be safe and proper directions to be given to the jury respecting the point under consideration. The jury, in substance, should be told that if the defendant's act in taking the life of his wife (if he did take it), was caused by mental disease or unsoundness, which dethroned his reason and judgment with respect to that act, which destroyed his power rationally to comprehend the nature and consequences of that act, and which, overpowering his will, irresistibly forced him to its commission, then he is not amenable to legal punishment. But if the jury believe from all the evidence and circumstances, that the defendant was in the possession of a rational intellect or sound mind, and allowed his passions to escape control, then, though *passion* may for the time being have driven *reason* from her seat and usurped it, and have urged the defendant with a force at the moment irresistible to desperate acts, he cannot claim for such acts the protection of insanity.

Whether *passion* or *insanity* was the ruling force and controlling agency which led to the homicide,—in other words, whether the defendant's act was the insane act of an unsound mind, or the outburst of violent, reckless and uncontrolled passion in a mind not diseased,—is the practical question which the jury should be told to determine according to their best judgment upon the evidence before them. If they believe that the homicide was the direct result or offspring of *insanity,* they should acquit; if of *passion,* unless it be an insane passion, they should convict. This is a much more practical inquiry than to direct their attention solely to the defendant's capacity at the time to distinguish right from wrong—an inquiry which must often be speculative and difficult of determination from the data possible to be laid before the jury, and which as a test or criterion of responsibility rather belongs, when applicable, to what is known as *intellectual,* as distinguished from *moral* insanity.

Note: Insanity Tests

The "irresistible impulse," or "wild beast," test meant that a person could know that he or she was doing wrong, yet still be excused from doing it because the individual was driven to do so by an insane condition of the mind. Ray approved of the test because it broadened the scope of the insanity defense in keeping with the best psychiatric learning of the day.

McNaghten was the majority test; *Felter* sketched the minority position. Chief Justice Charles Doe of the New Hampshire Supreme Court urged yet a third and even broader guideline. In *State* v. *Pike,* 49 N.H. 399 (1869), Doe held that neither delusion nor knowledge of right and wrong, as a matter of law, should be the test of mental disease. Instead, he preferred to leave the matter entirely as a fact in question to the jury to decide. This rule stood by itself in New Hampshire and was adopted nowhere else.

Felter was retried and his counsel failed to prove hereditary insanity, resulting in a conviction of manslaughter.

Bill Bell v. The State
17 Tex. Crim. 538 (1885)

Violence riddled nineteenth-century America, and nowhere was it more apparent than in the South, where the code duello persisted long after lawmakers banned it. Statistical compilations on homicide go back more than a century, and they leave little doubt that an extraordinary level of personal violence plagued the South. The reasons for this record are hotly debated among scholars, but cultural influences that stressed a strong code of honor were certainly critical. Not surprisingly, the excuse of self-defense had a particularly luxuriant growth in that region, nowhere more so than in the most violent state—Texas.

In the following case, the defendant, who drove a horse-drawn hack in Waco, Texas, stabbed to death a customer who became belligerent and refused to pay the proper fare. He was found guilty of second-degree murder and sentenced to seven years in the penitentiary.

Wilson, Judge. It cannot be questioned but that the evidence is sufficient to sustain the conviction. It is not so clear and conclusive of the defendant's guilt, however, as to exclude a lower grade of homicide than murder in the second degree, or justifiable homicide in self-defense. As we view the evidence, it demanded of the trial court to instruct the jury, 1st. Upon the law of murder in the second degree; 2nd. Upon the law of manslaughter; and, 3d. Upon the law of self-defense. In the main charge the court sufficiently, and with substantial correctness, explained to the jury the law of murder in the second degree and of manslaughter.

It omitted entirely to submit the issue of self-defense. To supply this omission, defendant's counsel requested a special instruction in the following language, viz.: "If the jury believe, from all the facts and circumstances in evidence, that, at the time of the difficulty between the deceased Moreland and the defendant Bell, and at the time Bell inflicted the injury which proved fatal (if the jury find that Bell did inflict the injury), that Bell did not intend to kill Moreland, and only intended by his acts to defend himself from an unlawful and violent attack made upon him by Moreland, and used no means in such resistance disproportioned to such attack, considering the relative disproportion in size of the combatants (if there was such disproportion), and Bell had reason to believe and did believe that such attack was likely to endanger his own life, or result in serious bodily injury to himself, then the homicide would be justifiable, and the jury will acquit." This special charge was given, and it constitutes the only charge given to the jury upon the issue of self-defense,—nor did the defendant request any additional charge upon the subject.

At the time of the trial no exceptions were taken by the defendant to the charge of the court or any portion of it, but in his motion for a new trial several objections to it are urged, which are insisted upon in this court, and among them, that "the court erred in failing to define justifiable homicide, and in failing to submit to the jury proper issues arising upon the evidence as to the law of self-defense and justifiable homicide." This objection is, we think, well taken. As far as it goes the special charge we have quoted is correct and applicable to the evidence. It does not, however, go far enough. It does not give *all* the law of self-defense demanded by the evidence. It should have stated that the de-

fendant, if unlawfully attacked by the deceased, was not bound to retreat in order to avoid the necessity of killing him. . . . This is a very material part of the law of self-defense, and is a statutory innovation upon the common law, and upon the common view of what constitutes self-defense. The common law required the assailed party to "retreat to the wall," and this requirement, while it no longer exists as the law of this State, is still believed by many who are unlearned in the law to be in force. In all cases, therefore, where the issue of self-defense arises from the evidence, the jury should be instructed that the assailed party is not bound to retreat in order to make perfect his right of self-defense. And when the evidence presents the issue of self-defense, the law, and *all* the law, applicable to that issue, as made by the evidence, should be given in charge to the jury, whether requested or not. . . . When the court omits to do this it is error, and, if excepted to at the time of the trial, the conviction would necessarily be set aside. But if the error be not excepted to, but be called to the attention of the trial court for the first time in a motion for new trial, it will not be cause for reversal unless it should appear to this court that the defendant's rights have probably been injured thereby. . . .

In the case before us, the inquiry therefore arises, did the error of the court, in failing to instruct the jury that the defendant was not bound to retreat, probably weaken his plea of self-defense, and prejudice his legal rights in respect thereto? In view of the evidence in the case, we must say that in our opinion it was calculated to have that effect. It was within the power of the defendant to have retreated, and by this means to have avoided the necessity of killing the deceased. It may have been the opinion of the jury that he should have retreated, and that, as he did not in this way avoid his assailant, he was not justified in slaying him. They should have been told by the court that the law of this State does not require retreat under any circumstances. By giving the special charge requested, the trial judge conceded, and we think correctly, that the issue of self-defense was presented by the evidence, and this special charge called his attention to that issue, and, being imperfect, it was the duty of the court to supply its defects by additional instructions. Because the charge as requested was not as full as the law required, should not, we think, be regarded as a waiver by the defendant of his right to a full and correct charge, and should not be held to relieve the court of the duty of giving such charge. Considering the evidence of this case, we think the failure of the court to give in charge article 573 of the Penal Code was material error calculated to injure the rights of the defendant, and is therefore reversible error although not excepted to at the time of the trial.

♦ ♦ ♦

But we are not prepared to say that the special charge was even abstractly correct, especially in view of the evidence in the case. It was not shown clearly that the wounds inflicted upon deceased were inflicted with a knife, and, if with a knife, that it was such a one as was calculated ordinarily to produce death or serious bodily injury, when used in the manner and under the circumstances here shown. There were but two wounds upon deceased, one in the arm, which was slight, and the other in the temple above the eye, which proved fatal. These wounds were made with some sharp pointed instrument and were small. It is quite reasonable to infer that the wounds were made with a knife, but still the testimony does not place this conclusion beyond doubt. If made with a knife, evidently it was a small one, as demonstrated by the small size of the wounds. The fatal wound was fatal because perhaps of its locality. The instrument used penetrated at the suture or lap in the skull bone, fracturing the bone to some extent, and wounding the brain, producing meningitis which caused death. Had the blow fallen on almost any other portion of the body it might not have been serious, much less mortal. Therefore, the fact that the wound produced death does not of itself warrant the deduction that the instrument used was of a character calculated ordinarily, when so used, to produce death or serious bodily injury.

It is not every *knife* that is a deadly or even a dangerous weapon, and yet with any kind of a knife it is possible, no doubt, to produce death or serious bodily injury. A small sewing needle is not an instrument that could be considered deadly or dangerous, and yet one skilled in human anatomy might, under favorable circumstances, use it with fatal effect, or it might be so used accidentally, or without any intention to kill or seriously injure. Considering the absence of any evidence, except the fatal result of the wound, to show the deadly or dangerous character of the weapon used, we are of the opinion that the special charge is not even abstractly correct when viewed with reference to the facts of this case, and that under the circumstances it was erroneous, and prejudicial to the defendant's rights. It was furthermore not in harmony with the main charge, which submitted to the jury, as a question to be determined from the evidence, whether or not, in inflicting the blows, it was the intention of the defendant to kill or inflict serious bodily injury. The special charge, in a great measure, supplied this question of fact with a presumption of the law, and that, too, without explaining that this presumption of the law was not a conclusive one, but that it might be removed by other evidence showing an absence of such criminal intent. The *intent* with which the wounds were inflicted was a most vital issue to the defendant. Upon this pivot hung his fate. In the main charge this issue was properly submitted to the jury to be determined by them from the evidence, without the aid of any presumption of law, except that the defendant should be presumed innocent until his guilt was established by competent evidence. Here, we think, upon this issue, the charge should have rested.

♦ ♦ ♦

We are of the opinion that the facts of this case are of a character which demanded of the trial court a full and correct charge upon justifiable homicide in self-defense, and also a full and correct charge upon the issue of the defendant's intent in inflicting the wounds, leaving the jury to determine that intent from the evidence in the case, without incumbering such determination with any arbitrary presumption of the law, adverse to the presumption of innocence. Believing that he has not had the benefit of such a charge, and that thereby his rights have probably been prejudiced, the judgment is reversed and the cause is remanded.

Reversed and remanded.

Note: The South and Self-Defense

The penal codes of several southern states tolerated the taking of lives in personal disputes. Texas, however, was exceptional. All other southern states (and northern ones as well) adopted the rule of "duty to retreat." Simply put, it meant that in a life-threatening situation an assailed person was required to "retreat to the wall." Only after having done so could that person claim that he had acted in self-defense. The so-called Texas rule put forth in *Bell* was strikingly different. It permitted a person under attack to "stand his ground" and kill his assailant; he had no duty to retreat.

Differences in the rules of self-defense did not predict the incidence of personal assault and homicide. For example, the Alabama Supreme Court strongly endorsed the "duty to retreat" rule, but bloodletting in that state was above the national average and close to that of Texas. Different legal rules for self-defense, along with the insanity defense, seem to have reflected cultural and moral assumptions. The "stand-one's-ground" rule merely supported the ethical etiquette of duelists.

LATE-NINETEENTH-CENTURY CRIME AND MORALITY

Colonial lawmakers had lavished great attention on regulating moral behavior by proscribing sexual practices, such as adultery and fornication. During the nineteenth century, these concerns ebbed as lawmakers shifted their attention to crimes against property. By the end of the century, however, another wave of moral purity swept the nation. For instance, several states passed legislation that regulated the production, sale, and consumption of alcoholic beverages. This new moral reform movement, as we have seen, also sought to criminalize abortion and the dissemination of birth control information in the belief that both of these practices were already fomenting moral debauchery.

People v. *Plath*
100 N.Y. 590 (1885)

Nowhere in the late nineteenth century were the ambiguities of criminal law greater and the tensions over sex roles and morality clearer than with regard to prostitution. What public authorities sought to deal with was not so much sin as sin in public. Prostitution was thoroughly illegal, but it flourished everywhere; it continued to exist by tacit agreement between brothel owners and public authorities. That understanding required, however, that prostitution remain within specific geographical limits and that owners not force or entice young girls into the world's oldest profession. A few nineteenth-century cities, most notably St. Louis and New Orleans, attempted to regulate the practice by passing ordinances defining so-called red-light districts. The punishments meted out were invariably greater for those who ran houses of prostitution or procured girls and women into the service than it was for the prostitute.

In the American West, where until the early twentieth century men greatly outnumbered women, prostitution was an important and apparently profitable business. However, in ma-

jor urban areas, prostitution was closely linked with vice and other criminal activities associated with the dangerous classes. In some cities, such as Detroit, brothel riots occurred in which local citizens, angry that authorities continued to countenance the practice, took matters into their own hands. But in most instances, an accommodation was reached. As long as prostitution remained underground and off the streets, the authorities winked at it.

Brothels became the object of special attack during the late nineteenth century as the moral purity movement swung into action. These establishments served as more than sexual pleasure domes; they were also centers of information about birth control and abortion.

The New York statute at issue in this case was typical of measures passed in most states that made the "taking" of a female under a certain age (usually sixteen) for the purposes of prostitution a crime. Legislators sought not so much to eliminate prostitution as to shield children from its scourge.

Ruger, Ch.J. The defendant was indicted and upon trial convicted of the crime of abduction, in that he "with force and arms feloniously did take one Katie Kavanaugh for the purpose of prostitution, she the said Katie Kavanaugh being then and Society and there a female under the age of sixteen years." It was essential to the support of this conviction that the people show, not only a taking by the defendant within the meaning of the statute, but also that such taking was for the purpose of prostitution. Penal Code, 282; as amended by 2 chap. 46, Laws of 1884. If the evidence establishes only a taking and fails to show that it was *for the prohibited purpose* it is insufficient to sustain the conviction, and so proof of the fact that the person of the female was used for purposes of prostitution without proof of the abduction would not bring the accused within the condemnation of the statute. It is elementary, when a specific intent is required to make an act an offense, that the doing of the act does not raise a presumption that it was done with the specific intent. . . . Neither can a conviction under this act be sustained upon the unsupported evidence of the female abducted.

◆　◆　◆

An examination of the proof in this case fails to disclose any evidence corroborating the testimony of the female alleged to have been abducted, as to the participation of the defendant in the abduction, assuming that her evidence established a taking within the meaning of the statute. We have, however, grave doubts as to the sufficiency of such evidence to establish such taking. . . . But passing over that question, we will examine the evidence which it is claimed corroborated the testimony of the abducted female.

Her evidence was to the effect that in July, 1884, the defendant kept a dance hall or concert saloon and drinking place in Chatham street, New York, and had no previous acquaintance with, or knowledge of the witness, her friends or family; that she was a young girl about fifteen years of age, of somewhat dissolute character, residing with her parents at Newark; that some time in the latter part of July, in company with a young companion, the former inmate of a house of prostitution, of her own free will, she visited New York without the consent of her parents, and in strolling about the streets came to the defendant's saloon and entered. After sitting in the bar room for awhile she saw the defendant go behind the bar, and asked him "how much it was to see the entertainment;" he replied "nothing, my little dear, come in." He then treated the girls to soda water and asked them if they came to stay, to which Kavanaugh replied that she did. He then invited the girls to go upstairs and while there offered Kavanaugh a dress which she declined. He also took indecent liberties with the persons of both girls and after remaining there about twenty minutes left them. Both girls voluntarily remained in the place several days, and the Kavanaugh girl for about one month, during which time she had intercourse with a large number of men. No evidence was furnished by the prosecution showing that the defendant knew the true name of the girl *or the place of residence of herself or family, or that he had had any previous acquaintance with her or knowledge of her family,* or their circumstances or condition. No direct proof was given to establish the existence of any fact testified to by Kavanaugh, but she was attempted to be supported by circumstances alone. Two witnesses testified that they visited defendant's saloon the latter part of August and found quite a number of women and men assembled there engaged in dancing, drinking, and sitting around together among whom was Kavanaugh. They asked defendant if he had there a girl by the name of Kavanaugh who came from Newark. Defendant denied any knowledge of such a girl, and offered to allow them to search the premises for her. While they were talking Kavanaugh disappeared. It nowhere appeared that defendant was acquainted with the true name of Kavanaugh, or that she came from Newark. The witnesses also inspected the upper rooms of the saloon and there found a number of small apartments filled with beds and bunks; they saw women intoxicated and some quarreling and fighting going on. Afterward in September, one of the witnesses saw a man and woman in bed together there, and the man stated that he was not the husband of the woman. A physical examination of the girl revealed appearances indicating that attempts at sexual intercourse with her had been made, but that in fact it never had been accomplished. Beyond this no evidence was given looking toward corroboration of the testimony of the alleged abducted female.

We are utterly unable to see how this evidence tends to prove any of the facts going to show the agency of the defendant, in inducing Kavanaugh either to come to or remain in his place, unless a presumption of criminal persuasion is always to be imputed to a person with whom a dissolute female is domiciled. That he kept a disorderly house and was engaged in a vile and reprehensible occupation is quite sufficiently demonstrated, and that the object of

Kavanaugh's residence in his house was presumably for the purpose of prostitution; but there is nothing in the corroborative proof inconsistent with the theory that her stay there was the result of her own will, uninfluenced by any persuasion, allurement or device of the defendant. The evidence does not tend to show that the influences inducting Kavanaugh to come or remain at the defendant's house were any different from those operating upon the other inmates of the place or upon females generally, who had not become inmates.

It is a lamentable fact that a life of prostitution presents attractions to some young and inexperienced females and that many are induced to enter upon it by the expectation of pleasures to be derived, wants to be supplied, or disagreeable social conditions to be escaped, and that from some or all of these causes combined, the haunts of vice and immorality are too largely supplied; but the statute in question was not intended to provide a remedy for this evil, or prescribe a punishment for those who keep such places. There is nothing in the section of the act under which defendant was convicted making the employment of a female under sixteen years of age for purposes of prostitution or sexual intercourse a criminal offense, *except where it is accompanied with a taking of her person by some active agency for such purpose.* The word "takes" seems to be used to distinguish the act prohibited, from those where the female is merely received, or permitted and allowed to follow a life of prostitution without persuasive inducement by the person accused.

The statutory age under which the consent of the female does not deprive the act of sexual intercourse of its criminal effect is fixed at ten years, but over that age the act in question does not make such intercourse a crime if effected without persuasion or device, by the free will and consent of the female. The same evidence which has been produced against the defendant in this case could doubtless be given as to every keeper of a brothel or disorderly house in New York, and it would tend to impair confidence in the administration of the law and confound the distinction in crimes made by statute to permit this conviction to be upheld upon the proof shown by the record. Every criminal, however vile, has a right to require that the elements of his offense shall be clearly defined by law and established by legal proof before he can be convicted thereof, and until then he may safely assert his immunity from punishment for any offense which is not thus defined and proved. The defendant in this case is entitled to the same presumption of innocence which prevails in other cases, and we are constrained to say that evidence has not been given here rebutting such presumption.

We think the evidence was insufficient in the absence of the proper confirmatory proof to warrant his conviction, and that the judgment of the General Term and Sessions should be reversed and a new trial granted.

All concur.

Judgment reversed.

The Federal Government, Crime, and Morality

Historically, the states had exercised their police powers to provide for the health, safety, morals, and welfare of their respective populations. However, the increasingly national character of late-nineteenth-century American society continually frustrated proponents of moral purity. They achieved some success at the state level, but they realized that only federal laws could stem what they believed to be a rush of immorality. The most important federal statute was the Comstock Act (1873), named after Anthony Comstock, a failed New York businessman and prominent moral reformer who enjoyed the support of Vice President Henry Wilson and Supreme Court Justice William Strong. Comstock personified the excesses of the moral purity movement that formed such a central part of the Victorian era. For example, he hounded Madame Restell, a wealthy operator of a New York City bordello and abortion clinic, until she committed suicide. For his efforts, Comstock was made special agent to enforce the act named for him.

Several states passed their own versions of the national legislation. In 1879, the Connecticut legislature adopted the harshest of these "little" Comstock acts. There, the great circus promoter Phineas T. Barnum successfully urged legislators to make the *use* of contraceptive materials a crime.

Ex parte Jackson
96 U.S. 727 (1877)

The Comstock Act derived its authority from the power vested in Congress to establish "post-offices and post-roads." But the act was also an opening chapter in Congress's development of a federal police power. The act chipped away at the once exclusive authority of the states to provide for the health, safety, morals, and welfare of their residents. In this case, Jackson sought a writ of habeas corpus on the grounds that he was being restrained by the United States marshal for the Southern District of New York after having been convicted of violating that provision of the Comstock Act that made it illegal to mail a circular concerning a lottery that offered prizes.

Mr. Justice Field, after stating the case, delivered the opinion of the court.

The power vested in Congress "to establish post-offices and post-roads" has been practically construed, since the foundation of the government, to authorize, not merely the designation of the routes over which the mail shall be carried, and the offices where letters and other documents shall be received to be dis-tributed or forwarded, but the carriage of the mail, and all measures necessary to secure its safe and speedy transit, and the prompt deliv-ery of its contents. The validity of legislation prescribing what should be carried, and its weight and form, and the charges to which it should be subjected, has never been questioned. What should be mailable has varied at differ-ent times, changing with the facility of trans-portation over the post-roads. At one time, only letters, newspapers, magazines, pamphlets, and other printed matter, not exceeding eight ounces in weight, were carried; afterwards books were added to the list; and now small packages of merchandise, not exceeding a prescribed weight, as well as books and printed matter of all kinds, are transported in the mail. The power possessed by Congress embraces the regulation of the entire postal system of the country. The right to designate what shall be carried neces-sarily involves the right to determine what shall be excluded. The difficulty attending the sub-ject arises, not from the want of power in Con-gress to prescribe regulations as to what shall constitute mail matter, but from the necessity of enforcing them consistently with rights re-served to the people, of far greater importance than the transportation of the mail. In their en-forcement, a distinction is to be made between different kinds of mail matter,—between what is intended to be kept free from inspection, such as letters, and sealed packages subject to letter postage; and what is open to inspection, such as newspapers, magazines, pamphlets, and other printed matter, purposely left in a condi-tion to be examined. Letters and sealed pack-ages of this kind in the mail are as fully guarded from examination and inspection, except as to their outward form and weight, as if they were retained by the parties forwarding them in their own domiciles. The constitutional guaranty of the right of the people to be secure in their pa-pers against unreasonable searches and seizures extends to their papers, thus closed against in-spection, wherever they may be. Whilst in the mail, they can only be opened and examined un-der like warrant, issued upon similar oath or af-firmation, particularly describing the thing to be seized, as is required when papers are subjected

to search in one's own household. No law of Congress can place in the hands of officials con-nected with the postal service any authority to invade the secrecy of letters and such sealed packages in the mail; and all regulations adopted as to mail matter of this kind must be in subordination to the great principle embod-ied in the fourth amendment of the Constitution.

Nor can any regulations be enforced against the transportation of printed matter in the mail, which is open to examination, so as to interfere in any manner with the freedom of the press. Liberty of circulating is as essential to that freedom as liberty of publishing; indeed, without the circulation, the publication would be of little value. If, therefore, printed matter be excluded from the mails, its transportation in any other way cannot be forbidden by Congress.

◆ ◆ ◆

In excluding various articles from the mail, the object of Congress has not been to interfere with the freedom of the press, or with any other rights of the people; but to refuse its facilities for the distribution of matter deemed injurious to the public morals. Thus, by the act of March 3, 1873, Congress declared "that no obscene, lewd, or lascivious book, pamphlet, picture, pa-per, print, or other publication of an indecent character, or any article or thing designed or in-tended for the prevention of conception or procuring of abortion, nor any article or thing intended or adapted for any indecent or immoral use or nature, nor any written or printed card, circular, book, pamphlet, advertisement, or no-tice of any kind, giving information, directly or indirectly, where, or how, or of whom, or by what means, either of the things before men-tioned may be obtained or made, nor any letter upon the envelope of which, or postal-card upon which indecent or scurrilous epithets may be written or printed, shall be carried in the mail; and any person who shall knowingly deposit, or cause to be deposited, for mailing or deliv-ery, any of the hereinbefore mentioned articles or things, . . . shall be deemed guilty of a mis-demeanor, and, on conviction thereof, shall, for every offence, be fined not less than $100, nor more than $5,000, or imprisonment at hard labor not less than one year nor more than ten years, or both, in the discretion of the judge."

All that Congress meant by this act was, that the mail should not be used to transport such corrupting publications and articles, and that any one who attempted to use it for that purpose should be punished. The same inhibition has been extended to circulars concerning lotteries,—institutions which are supposed to have a demoralizing influence upon the people. There is no question before us as to the evi-

dence upon which the conviction of the petitioner was had; nor does it appear whether the envelope in which the prohibited circular was deposited in the mail was sealed or left open for examination. The only question for our determination relates to the constitutionality of the act; and of that we have no doubt.

The commitment of the petitioner to the county jail, until his fine was paid, was within the discretion of the court under the statute.

[Motion] Denied.

Note: Morality and Free Speech

Justice Stephen J. Field's opinion in *Jackson* underscored the great tensions in late-nineteenth-century jurisprudence. On the one hand, Field and other critics of legislative action, such as Thomas M. Cooley and Christopher Tiedeman, complained that government should leave individuals alone to make their own economic choices. On the other hand, Field's opinion makes clear that he, and his brethren, believed that government had a duty to promote moral behavior, even at the expense of individual rights.

Comstock, for example, believed that "expressions of libertarian radical views about religion and sex were examples of blasphemy and obscenity that should be suppressed in the public interest." While Comstock might have argued that he sought only to suppress cultural speech, many of the works he eliminated also contained messages constituting political speech. For example, the Comstock Act allowed the federal government to prosecute anyone whose "obscene" publication was placed in the mails, or in some other way taken across state lines. To eradicate pornographic publications, the "statute created the position of special agent of the post office." To Comstock, pornography was a "death trap . . . by mail," which he sought to eliminate nationwide. In his classic book, *Traps for the Young*, Comstock wrote: "Satan is permitted to place his traps where they will do him most good and the children most harm." He described the pornographer as "a moral vulture" who "steals upon our youth . . . striking its terrible talons into their vitals, and forcibly bearing them away on hideous wings to shame and death." During his career, Comstock secured the destruction of more than 160 tons of "obscene" materials, the prosecution of hundreds of individuals, and the conviction of approximately 75 percent of those arrested. While some of the confiscated material was indeed pornography directed at children, the majority of it was directed at adults, and much of Comstock's "obscene" materials had little to do with pornography. Comstock also confiscated nonfiction produced by freelovers, freethinkers, and popularizers of medical information, much of which was both cultural and political speech.

Comstock focused on authors and publications that challenged traditional notions of family or marriage, advocated birth control or abortion (or explained how to accomplish either), or simply discussed sex. He fought against Margaret Sanger's manual for birth control, *Family Limitations*, her magazine, *Woman Rebel*, and other publications. In addition, Comstock pursued *Medical Common Sense*, a serious book containing a section on birth control; Walt Whitman's *Leaves of Grass*; Leo Tolstoy's *Kreutzer Sonata*, and hundreds of other books.

The National Defense Association (NDA) and the Free Speech League were formed in response to the Comstock Act. These organizations fought for free speech by distributing anti-Comstock literature, lobbying against expansion of the Comstock Act, and defending Comstock's victims in court. They preceded the founding of the American Civil Liberties Union (ACLU) by decades. As the scholar David Rabban has noted, the leaders of the Free Speech League tried repeatedly but unsuccessfully to convince the emerging ACLU that the defense of free speech should extend beyond the protection of dissenting political speech.

→ 6 ←

Lawyers and the Rise of the Regulatory State
1850–1920

THE LAWYER IN AMERICAN SOCIETY

The legal system has never been exempt from the forces of change. But American lawyers preferred cautious and piecemeal reform of the legal order rather than revolutionary upheaval. They were often skeptical of proposals for change, especially when such changes would have an impact on the law itself. The documents in this section first consider the lawyer's place in American society as well as the evolution of legal education. The material then presents intellectual developments that shaped legal thought in the late nineteenth century as the legal system confronted the challenges posed by industrialization.

Alexis de Tocqueville on Lawyers and Judges
1835

In 1835, the French visitor Alexis de Tocqueville offered striking observations on the actual workings of popular sovereignty, judicial power, and lawyers in the bumptious American democracy that so fascinated him. Tocqueville was astonishingly perceptive in his own time; do his remarks remain as relevant and valid for today's society?

Whenever a law that the judge holds to be unconstitutional is invoked in a tribunal of the United States, he may refuse to admit it as a rule; this power is the only one peculiar to the American magistrate, but it gives rise to immense political influence. In truth, few laws can escape the searching analysis of the judicial power for any length of time, for there are few that are not prejudicial to some private interest or other, and none that may not be brought before a court of justice by the choice of parties or by the necessity of the case. But as soon as a judge has refused to apply any given law in a case, that law immediately loses a portion of its moral force.

♦ ♦ ♦

Within these limits the power vested in the American courts of justice of pronouncing a statute to be unconstitutional forms one of the most powerful barriers that have ever been devised against the tyranny of political assemblies.

♦ ♦ ♦

When we have examined in detail the organization of the [United States] Supreme Court and the entire prerogatives which it exercises, we shall readily admit that a more imposing judicial power was never constituted by any people. The Supreme Court is placed higher than any other known tribunal, both by the nature of its rights and the class of justiciable parties which it controls.

♦ ♦ ♦

The peace, the prosperity, and the very existence of the Union are vested in the hands of the seven Federal judges [of the United States Supreme Court]. Without them the Constitution would be a dead letter: the executive appeals to them for assistance against the encroachments of the legislative power; the legislature demands their protection against the assaults of the executive; they defend the Union from the disobedience of the states, the states from the exaggerated claims of the Union, the public interest against private interests, and the conservative spirit of stability against the fickleness of the democracy. Their power is enormous, but it is the power of public opinion. They are all-powerful as long as the people respect the law; but they would be impotent against popular neglect or contempt of the law. The force of public opinion is the most intractable of agents, because its exact limits cannot be defined; and it is not less dangerous to exceed than to remain below the boundary prescribed.

♦ ♦ ♦

Democratic laws generally tend to promote the welfare of the greatest possible number; for they emanate from the majority of the citizens, who are subject to error, but who cannot have an interest opposed to their own advantage. The laws of an aristocracy tend, on the contrary, to concentrate wealth and power in the hands of the minority; because an aristocracy, by its very nature, constitutes a minority. It may therefore be asserted, as a general proposition, that the purpose of a democracy in its legislation is

more useful to humanity than that of an aristocracy. This, however, is the sum total of its advantages.

♦ ♦ ♦

No political form has hitherto been discovered that is equally favorable to the prosperity and the development of all the classes into which society is divided. These classes continue to form, as it were, so many distinct communities in the same nation; and experience has shown that it is no less dangerous to place the fate of these classes exclusively in the hands of any one of them than it is to make one people the arbiter of the destiny of another. When the rich alone govern, the interest of the poor is always endangered; and when the poor make the laws, that of the rich incurs very serious risks. The advantage of democracy does not consist, therefore, as has sometimes been asserted, in favoring the prosperity of all, but simply in contributing to the well-being of the greatest number.

The men who are entrusted with the direction of public affairs in the United States are frequently inferior, in both capacity and morality, to those whom an aristocracy would raise to power. But their interest is identified and mingled with that of the majority of their fellow citizens. They may frequently be faithless and frequently mistaken, but they will never systematically adopt a line of conduct hostile to the majority; and they cannot give a dangerous or exclusive tendency to the government.

♦ ♦ ♦

It is not always feasible to consult the whole people, either directly or indirectly, in the formation of law; but it cannot be denied that, when this is possible, the authority of law is much augmented. This popular origin which impairs the excellence and the wisdom of legislation, contributes much to increase its power. There is an amazing strength in the expression of the will of a whole people; and when it declares itself, even the imagination of those who would wish to contest it is overawed. The truth of this fact is well known by parties, and they consequently strive to make out a majority whenever they can. If they have not the greater number of voters on their side, they assert that the true majority abstained from voting; and if they are foiled even there, they have recourse to those persons who had no right to vote.

In the United States, except slaves, servants, and paupers supported by the townships, there is no class of persons who do not exercise the elective franchise and who do not indirectly contribute to make the laws. Those who wish to attack the laws must consequently either change the opinion of the nation or trample upon its decision.

A second reason, which is still more direct and weighty, may be adduced: in the United States everyone is personally interested in enforcing the obedience of the whole community to the law; for as the minority may shortly rally the majority to its principles, it is interested in professing that respect for the decrees of the legislator which it may soon have occasion to claim for its own. However irksome an enactment may be, the citizen of the United States complies with it, not only because it is the work of the majority, but because it is his own, and he regards it as a contract to which he is himself a party.

In the United States, then, that numerous and turbulent multitude does not exist who, regarding the law as their natural enemy, look upon it with fear and distrust. It is impossible, on the contrary, not to perceive that all classes display the utmost reliance upon the legislation of their country and are attached to it by a kind of parental affection.

◆　◆　◆

In visiting the Americans and studying their laws, we perceive that the authority they have entrusted to members of the legal profession, and the influence that these individuals exercise in the government, are the most powerful existing security against the excesses of democracy. This effect seems to me to result from a general cause, which it is useful to investigate, as it may be reproduced elsewhere.

Men who have made a special study of the laws derive from [that] occupation certain habits of order, a taste for formalities, and a kind of instinctive regard for the regular connection of ideas, which naturally render them very hostile to the revolutionary spirit and the unreflecting passions of the multitude.

The special information that lawyers derive from their studies ensures them a separate rank in society, and they constitute a sort of privileged body in the scale of intellect. This notion of their superiority perpetually recurs to them in the practice of their profession: they are the masters of a science which is necessary, but not very generally known; they serve as arbiters between the citizens; and the habit of directing to their purpose the blind passions of parties in litigation inspires them with a certain contempt for the judgment of the multitude. Add to this that they naturally constitute a body; not by any previous understanding, or by an agreement that directs them to a common end; but the analogy of their studies and the uniformity of their methods connect their minds as a common interest might unite their endeavors.

Some of the tastes and the habits of the aristocracy may consequently be discovered in the characters of lawyers. They participate in the same instinctive love of order and formalities; and they entertain the same repugnance to the actions of the multitude, and the same secret contempt of the government of the people. I do not mean to say that the natural propensities of lawyers are sufficiently strong to sway them irresistibly; for they, like most other men, are governed by their private interests, and especially by the interests of the moment.

◆　◆　◆

I do not, then, assert that all the members of the legal profession are at all times the friends of order and the opponents of innovation, but merely that most of them are usually so. In a community to which lawyers are allowed to occupy without opposition that high station which naturally belongs to them, their general spirit will be eminently conservative and anti-democratic. When an aristocracy excludes the leaders of that profession from its ranks, it excites enemies who are the more formidable as they are independent of the nobility by their labors and feel themselves to be their equals in intelligence though inferior in opulence and power.

◆　◆　◆

Lawyers are attached to public order beyond every other consideration, and the best security of public order is authority. It must not be forgotten, also, that if they prize freedom much, they generally value legality still more; they are less afraid of tyranny than of arbitrary power; and, provided the legislature undertakes of itself to deprive men of their independence, they are not dissatisfied.

♦ ♦ ♦

The government of democracy is favorable to the political power of lawyers; for when the wealthy, the noble, and the prince are excluded from the government, the lawyers take possession of it, in their own right, as it were, since they are the only men of information and sagacity, beyond the sphere of the people, who can be the object of the popular choice. If, then, they are led by their tastes towards the aristocracy and the prince, they are brought in contact with the people by their interests. They like the government of democracy without participating in its propensities and without imitating its weaknesses; whence they derive a two-fold authority from it and over it. The people in democratic states do not mistrust the members of the legal profession, because it is known that they are interested to serve the popular cause; and the people listen to them without irritation, because they do not attribute to them any sinister designs. The lawyers do not, indeed, wish to overthrow the institutions of democracy, but they constantly endeavor to turn it away from its real direction by means that are foreign to its nature. Lawyers belong to the people by birth and interest, and to the aristocracy by habit and taste; they may be looked upon as the connecting link between the two great classes of society.

The profession of the law is the only aristocratic element that can be amalgamated without violence with the natural elements of democracy and be advantageously and permanently combined with them. I am not ignorant of the defects inherent in the character of this body of men; but without this admixture of lawyer-like sobriety with the democratic principle, I question whether democratic institutions could long be maintained; and I cannot believe that a republic could hope to exist at the present time if the influence of lawyers in public business did not increase in proportion to the power of the people.

♦ ♦ ♦

In America there are no nobles or literary men, and the people are apt to mistrust the wealthy; lawyers consequently form the highest political class and the most cultivated portion of society. They have therefore nothing to gain by innovation, which adds a conservative interest to their natural taste for public order. If I were asked where I place the American aristocracy, I should reply without hesitation that it is not among the rich, who are united by no common tie, but that it occupies the judicial bench and the bar.

The more we reflect upon all that occurs in the United States, the more we shall be persuaded that the lawyers, as a body, form the most powerful, if not the only, counterpoise to the democratic element. In that country we easily perceive how the legal profession is qualified by its attributes, and even by its faults, to neutralize the vices inherent in popular government. When the American people are intoxicated by passion or carried away by the impetuosity of their ideas, they are checked and stopped by the almost invisible influence of their legal counselors. These secretly oppose their aristocratic propensities to the nation's democratic instincts, their superstitious attachment to what is old to its love of novelty, their narrow views to its immense designs, and their habitual procrastination to its ardent impatience.

The courts of justice are the visible organs by which the legal profession is enabled to control the democracy. The judge is a lawyer who, independently of the taste for regularity and order that he has contracted in the study of law, derives an additional love of stability from the inalienability of his own functions. His legal attainments have already raised him to a distinguished rank among his fellows; his political power completes the distinction of his station and gives him the instincts of the privileged classes.

♦ ♦ ♦

It must not be supposed, moreover, that the legal spirit is confined in the United States to the courts of justice; it extends far beyond them. As the lawyers form the only enlightened class whom the people do not mistrust, they are naturally called upon to occupy most of the public stations. They fill the legislative assemblies and are at the head of the administration; they consequently exercise a powerful influence upon the formation of the law and upon its execution. The lawyers are obliged, however, to yield to the current public opinion, which is too strong for them to resist; but it is easy to find indications of what they would do if they were free to act. The Americans, who have made so many innovations in their political laws, have introduced very sparing alterations in their civil laws, and that with great difficulty, although many of these laws are repugnant to their social condition. The reason for this is that in matters of civil law the majority are obliged to defer to the authority of the legal profession, and the American lawyers are disinclined to innovate when they are left to their own choice.

♦ ♦ ♦

The influence of legal habits extends beyond the precise limits I have pointed out.

Scarcely any political question arises in the United States that is not resolved, sooner or later, into a judicial question. Hence all parties are obliged to borrow, in their daily controversies, the ideas, and even the language, peculiar to judicial proceedings. As most public men are or have been legal practitioners, they introduce the customs and technicalities of their profession into the management of public affairs. The jury extends this habit to all classes. The language of the law thus becomes, in some measure, a vulgar tongue; the spirit of the law, which is produced in the schools and courts of justice, gradually penetrates beyond their walls into the bosom of society, where it descends to the lowest classes, so that at last the whole people contract the habits and the tastes of the judicial magistrate. The lawyers of the United States form a party which is but little feared and scarcely perceived, which has no badge peculiar to itself, which adapts itself with great flexibility to the exigencies of the time and accommodates itself without resistance to all the movements of the social body. But this party extends over the whole community and penetrates into all the classes which compose it; it acts upon the country imperceptibly, but finally fashions it to suit its own purposes.

LEGAL EDUCATION

CHRISTOPHER C. LANGDELL

A Selection of Cases on the Law of Contracts
1871

Christopher Columbus Langdell was the dean of Harvard Law School from 1870 to 1895. Best known today for developing the casebook method of law study, Langdell also had an important impact on jurisprudence. He espoused the view that law was a science, and that legal education should stress the deduction of enduring principles from leading judicial decisions. Langdell explained his approach in the preface to his pathbreaking Contracts *casebook.*

PREFACE

I entered upon the duties of my present position, a year and a half ago, with a settled conviction that law could only be taught or learned

effectively by means of cases in some form. I had entertained such an opinion ever since I knew anything of the nature of law or legal study; but it was chiefly through my experience as a learner that it was formed, as well as subsequently strengthened and confirmed. Of teaching indeed, as a business, I was entirely without experience; nor had I given much consideration to that subject, except so far as proper methods of teaching are involved in proper methods of study.

Now, however, I was called upon to consider directly the subject of teaching, not theoretically but practically, in connection with a large school with its more or less complicated organization, its daily routine, and daily duties. I was expected to take a large class of pupils, meet them regularly from day to day, and give them systematic instruction in such branches of law as had been assigned to me. To accomplish this successfully, it was necessary, first, that the efforts of the pupils should go hand in hand with mine, that is, that they should study with direct reference to my instruction; secondly, that the study thus required of them should be of the kind from which they might reap the greatest and most lasting benefit; thirdly, that the instruction should be of such a character that the pupils might at least derive a greater advantage from attending it than from devoting the same time to private study. How could this threefold object be accomplished? Only one mode occurred to me which seemed to hold out any reasonable prospect of success; and that was, to make a series of cases, carefully selected from the books of reports, the subject alike of study and instruction. But here I was met by what seemed at first to be an insuperable practical difficulty, namely, the want of books; for though it might be practicable, in case of private pupils having free access to a complete library, to refer them directly to, the books of reports, such a course was quite out of the question with a large class, all of whom would want the same books at the same time. Nor would such a course be without great drawbacks and inconveniences, even in the case of a single pupil. As he would always have to go where the books were, and could only have access to them there during certain prescribed hours, it would be impossible for him to economize his time or work to the best advantage; and he would be liable to be constantly haunted by the apprehension that he was

spending time, labor, and money in studying cases which would be inaccessible to him in after life.

It was with a view to removing these obstacles, that I was first led to inquire into the feasibility of preparing and publishing such a selection of cases as would be adapted to my purpose as a teacher. The most important element in that inquiry was the great and rapidly increasing number of reported cases in every department of law. In view of this fact, was there any satisfactory principle upon which such a selection could be made? It seemed to me that there was. Law, considered as a science, consists of certain principles or doctrines. To have such a mastery of these as to be able to apply them with constant facility and certainly to the ever-tangled skein of human affairs, is what constitutes a true lawyer; and hence to acquire that mastery should be the business of every earnest student of law. Each of these doctrines has arrived at its present state by slow degrees; in other words, it is a growth, extending in many cases through centuries. This growth is to be traced in the main through a series of cases; and much the shortest and best, if not the only way of mastering the doctrine effectually is by studying the cases in which it is embodied. But the cases which are useful and necessary for this purpose at the present day bear an exceedingly small proportion to all that have been reported. The vast majority are useless and worse than useless for any purpose of systematic study. Moreover, the number of fundamental legal doctrines is much less than is commonly supposed; the many different guises in which the same doctrine is constantly making its appearance, and the great extent to which legal treatises are a repetition of each other, being the cause of much misapprehension. If these doctrines could be so classified and arranged that each should be found in its proper place, and nowhere else, they would cease to be formidable from their number. It seemed to me, therefore, to be possible to take such a branch of the law as Contracts, for example, and, without exceeding comparatively moderate limits, to select, classify, and arrange all the cases which had contributed in any important degree to the growth, development, or establishment of any of its essential doctrines; and that such a work could not fail to be of material service to all who desire to study that branch of law systematically and in its original sources.

Note: Critics of Langdellian Assumptions

Not every legal educator endorsed Langdell's theories. One of the earliest critics was Oliver Wendell Holmes, Jr., who, reviewing the second edition (1880) of the Langdell *Contracts* casebook, charged that Langdell's

> ideal in the law, the end of all his striving, is the elegantia juris, or logical integrity of the system as a system. He is, perhaps, the greatest living legal theologian. But as a theologian he is less concerned with his postulates than to show that the conclusions from them hang together.

◆ ◆ ◆

> If Mr. Langdell could be suspected of ever having troubled himself about Hegel, we might call him a Hegelian in disguise, so entirely is he interested in the formal connection of things, or logic, as distinguished from the feelings which make the content of logic, and which have actually shaped the substance of law. The life of the law has not been logic; it has been experience. The seed of every new growth within its sphere has been a felt necessity.[1]

LEGAL THEORY IN THE LATE NINETEENTH CENTURY

THOMAS M. COOLEY

A Treatise on the Constitutional Limitations which Rest upon the Legislative Power of the States of the American Union
1868

Thomas M. Cooley towered over the legal landscape of the late nineteenth century. In influence, he had few peers, even in an age when lawyers and judges were achieving unprecedented extensions of their power to make public policy. Cooley was successively professor of law at the University of Michigan, justice of the Michigan Supreme Court, and first chairman of the Interstate Commerce Commission. But his authority cannot be measured only by the positions he held. His Treatise on the Constitutional Limitations *was canonical for constitutional interpretation well into the twentieth century. As the title of his treatise indicates, Cooley's emphasis was not on empowerment, but on its opposite— the inhibition of power. To him, the genius of the American republican experiment was that it restricted power. That axiomatic premise went far to baffle the emergence of the regulatory state.*

OF THE PROTECTION TO PROPERTY BY "THE LAW OF THE LAND"

The protection of the subject in the free enjoyment of his life, his liberty, and his property, except as they might be declared, by the judgment of his peers or the law of the land, to be forfeited, was guaranteed by the thirty-ninth chapter of Magna Charta, "which alone," says Blackstone, "would have merited the title that it bears, of the great charter." The people of the American States, holding the sovereignty in their own hands, have no occasion to exact pledges for a due observance of individual rights from anyone; but the aggressive tendency of power is such, that in framing the instruments under which their governments are to be administered by their agents, they have deemed it important to repeat the guaranty, and thereby adopted it as a principle of constitutional protection.

◆ ◆ ◆

What then is meant by "due process of law," and "the law of the land," in the constitutional provisions which we have referred to, as they are applied to the protection of rights in property, and in what cases can legislative action be annulled as not being "the law of the land," or judicial or ministerial action set aside as not being "due process of law" in the constitutional sense?

◆ ◆ ◆

When the government, through its established agencies, interferes with the title to one's property, or with his independent enjoyment of it, and its act is called in question as not in accordance with the law of the land, we are to test its validity by those principles of civil liberty and constitutional defense which have become established in our system of law, and not by any rules that pertain to forms of procedure merely. In judicial proceedings the law of the land requires a hearing before condemnation, and judgment before dispossession; but when property is appropriated by the government to public uses, or the legislature attempts to control it through remedial statutes, different considerations prevail from those which relate to controversies between man and man, different proceedings are required, and we have only to see whether the interference can be justified by the established rules applicable to the case. Due process of law in each particular case means, such an exertion of the powers of government as the settled maxims of law sanction, and under such safeguards for the protection of individual rights as those maxims prescribe for

the class of cases to which the one in question belongs.

◆ ◆ ◆

There is no rule or principle known to our system under which private property can be taken from one man and transferred to another for the private use and benefit of such other person, whether by general laws or by special enactment. The purpose must be public, and must have reference to the needs of the government. No reason of general public policy will be sufficient to protect such transfers where they operate upon existing vested rights.

◆ ◆ ◆

The doubt might also arise whether a regulation made for any one class of citizens, entirely arbitrary in its character, and restricting their rights, privileges, or legal capacities in a manner before unknown to the law, could be sustained, notwithstanding its generality. Distinctions in these respects should be based upon some reason which renders them important,— like the want of capacity in infants, and insane persons; but if the legislature should undertake to provide that persons following some specified lawful trade or employment should not have capacity to make contracts, or to receive conveyances, or to build such houses as others were allowed to erect, or in any other way to make such use of their property as was permissible to others, it can scarcely be doubted that the act would transcend the due bounds of legislative powers, even if it did not come in conflict with express constitutional provisions. The man or the class forbidden the acquisition or enjoyment of property in the manner permitted to the community at large would be deprived of liberty in particulars of primary importance to his or their "pursuit of happiness."

Equality of rights, privileges, and capacities unquestionably should be the aim of the law; and if special privileges are granted, or special burdens or restrictions imposed in any case, it must be presumed that the legislature designed to depart as little as possible from this fundamental maxim of government. The State, it is to be presumed, has no favors to bestow, and designs to inflict no arbitrary deprivation of rights. Special privileges are obnoxious and discriminations against persons or classes are still more so.

♦ ♦ ♦

[T]here are other cases where it becomes necessary for the public authorities to interfere with the control by individuals of their property, and even to destroy it, where the owners themselves have fully observed all their duties to their fellows and to the State, but where, nevertheless, some controlling public necessity demands the interference or destruction. A strong instance of this description is where it becomes necessary to take, use, or destroy the private property of individuals to prevent the spreading of a fire, the ravages of a pestilence, the advance of a hostile army, or any other great public calamity. Here the individual is in no degree in fault, but his interest must yield to that "necessity" which "knows no law." The establishment of limits within the denser portions of cities and villages, within which buildings constructed of inflammable materials shall not be erected or repaired, may also, in some cases, be equivalent to a destruction of private property; but regulations for this purpose have been sustained notwithstanding this result. Wharf lines may also be established for the general good, even though they prevent the owners of waterfronts from building out on that which constitutes private property. And, whenever the legislature deem it necessary to the protection of a harbor to forbid the removal of stones, gravel, or sand from the beach, they may establish regulations to that effect under penalties, and make them applicable to the owners of the soil equally with other persons. Such regulations are only "a just restraint of an injurious use of property, which the legislature have authority" to impose.

♦ ♦ ♦

The preservation of the public morals is peculiarly subject to legislative supervision, which may forbid the keeping, exhibition, or sale of indecent books or pictures, and cause their destruction if seized; or prohibit or regulate the places of amusement that may be resorted to for the purpose of gaming; or forbid altogether the keeping of implements of gaming for unlawful games; or prevent the keeping and exhibition of stallions in public places. And the power to provide for the compulsory observance of the first day of the week is also to be referred to the same authority.

Note: Social Tension in the 1890s

To concerned observers of American society from the 1870s to the 1890s, symptoms of social crisis abounded. Labor violence was the most conspicuous: the Molly Maguires in the mines of eastern Pennsylvania, the General Strike of 1877, the Haymarket bombing of 1886, the Homestead and the Coeur d'Alene strikes of 1892, the Pullman strike of 1894. The rise of European radical movements, such as the Marxian Socialists, the Bakuninite Anarchists, and politically oriented socialists, seemed to precede a wave of assassinations, which in turn seemed to have their American echoes: the attempted assassination of industrialist Henry Frick in connection with the Homestead strike, the assassination of President William McKinley by an anarchist in 1901.

Immigration poured masses of aliens into the country in response to the demand for unskilled labor. These "new" immigrants were largely non-Protestant: Roman Catholic, Jewish, Orthodox. Their eastern and southern European languages added a Babel to a nation only beginning to assimilate earlier waves of German and Irish immigrants. Strange in clothing and manners, they challenged what contemporaries considered to be the ethnic and religious homogeneity of an older, rural America. At a minimum, they had to be "Americanized": stripped of their languages, religions, and customs, and bent to the yoke of industrial discipline.

Urbanization seemed to validate Thomas Jefferson's vision of cities as "great sores" on the body politic, pustulating civic ulcers oozing political corruption, alien manners, and decaying public health. Mugwump political reform efforts, enfeebled by their middle-class origins and orientation, appeared inadequate to cope with the rise of the cities.

CHRISTOPHER G. TIEDEMANN

A Treatise on the Limitations of Police Power in the United States
1886

Christopher Tiedemann, a twenty-nine-year-old law professor at the time his influential treatise was first published, championed freedom of contract and was critical of most governmental involvement in the economy. He advanced a restrictive view of the exercise of the police power, maintaining that such authority should be invoked only to protect public order and punish crime. He was especially insistent that government not employ its power to benefit one social group at the expense of another.

Socialism, Communism, and Anarchism are rampant throughout the civilized world. The State is called on to protect the weak against the shrewdness of the stronger, to determine what wages a workman shall receive for his labor, and how many hours daily he shall labor. Many trades and occupations are being prohibited because some are damaged incidentally by their prosecution, and many ordinary pursuits are made government monopolies. The demands of the Socialists and Communists vary in degree and in detail, and the most extreme of them insist upon the assumption by government of the paternal character altogether, abolishing all private property in land, and making the State the sole possessor of the working capital of the nation.

Contemplating these extraordinary demands of the great army of discontents, and their apparent power, with the growth and development of universal suffrage, to enforce their views of civil polity upon the civilized world, the conservative class stand in constant fear of the advent of an absolutism more tyrannical and more unreasoning than any before experienced by man, the absolutism of a democratic majority.

The principal object of the present work is to demonstrate, by a detailed discussion of the constitutional limitations upon the police power in the United States, that under the written constitutions, Federal and State, democratic absolutism is impossible in this country, as long as the popular reverence for the constitutions, in their restrictions upon governmental activity, is nourished and sustained by a prompt avoidance by the courts of any violations of their provisions, in word or in spirit. The substantial rights of the minority are shown to be free from all lawful control or interference by the majority, except so far as such control or interference may be necessary to prevent injury to others in the enjoyment of their rights.

OLIVER WENDELL HOLMES, JR.

The Common Law
1881

Oliver Wendell Holmes, Jr., was determined to reconsider the fundamental nature of legal concepts and obligations. Influenced by the empiricism of William James and Charles Peirce, Holmes was ready to question the philosophical bases of Anglo-American common-law rules.

The following excerpts, taken from his chapters on tort law, illustrate some of the dominant themes of Holmes's work. He was determined to rid law of moral concepts, grounding it instead on views of public policy. So conceived, law would take into account only an individual's self-interest while ignoring his subjective state of mind. Law had to evolve external and objective criteria to measure liability in crimes, torts, and contracts. It also had to acknowledge the primacy of the majority's view of what is desirable as a matter of policy.

The object of this book is to present a general view of the Common Law. To accomplish the task, other tools are needed besides logic. It is something to show that the consistency of a system requires a particular result, but it is not all. The life of the law has not been logic; it has been experience. The felt necessities of the time, the prevalent moral and political theories, intuitions of public policy, avowed or unconscious, even the prejudices which judges share with their fellow-men, have had a good deal more to do than the syllogism in determining the rules by which men should be governed. The law embodies the story of a nation's development through many centuries, and it cannot be dealt with as if it contained only the axioms and corollaries of a book of mathematics. In order to know what it is, we must know what it has been, and what it tends to become. We must alternately consult history and existing theories of legislation. But the most difficult labor will be to understand the combination of the two into new products at every stage. The substance of the law at any given time pretty nearly corresponds, so far as it goes, with what is then understood to be convenient; but its form and machinery, and the degree to which it is able to work out desired results, depend very much upon its past.

OLIVER WENDELL HOLMES, JR.
"The Path of the Law"
1897

This, Holmes's best-known extrajudicial essay, carried forward themes first developed in The Common Law: *the dissociation of law and morality, the search for external criteria for legal liability, and the emphasis on policy as opposed to logic. But new emphases appeared as well, particularly a forcefully stated positivism, where Holmes defined law as a prediction of what the courts would do. Holmes's effort to strip law of moralistic concepts was now clothed in a striking metaphor: the "bad man theory" of law. The influence of Charles Darwin on Holmes's thought was evident here too. All the metaphors were biological: the law grows; it is not a machine or an equation.*

I wish, if I can, to lay down some first principles for the study of this body of dogma or systematized prediction which we call law, for men who want to use it as the instrument of their business to enable them to prophesy in their turn, and, as bearing upon the study, I wish to point out an ideal which as yet our law has not attained.

The first thing for a business-like understanding of the matter is to understand its lim-

its, and therefore I think it desirable at once to point out and dispel a confusion between morality and law, which sometimes rises to the height of conscious theory, and more often and indeed constantly is making trouble in detail without reaching the point of consciousness. You can see very plainly that a bad man has as much reason as a good one for wishing to avoid an encounter with the public force, and therefore you can see the practical importance of the distinction between morality and law. A man who cares nothing for an ethical rule which is believed and practised by his neighbors is likely nevertheless to care a good deal to avoid being made to pay money, and will want to keep out of jail if he can.

◆   ◆   ◆

If you want to know the law and nothing else, you must look at it as a bad man, who cares only for the material consequences which such knowledge enables him to predict, not a good one, who finds his reasons for conduct, whether inside the law or outside of it, in the vaguer sanctions of conscience.

The confusion with which I am dealing besets confessedly legal conceptions. Take the fundamental question, What constitutes the law? You will find some text writers telling you that it is something different from what is decided by the courts of Massachusetts or England, that it is a system of reason, that it is a deduction from principles of ethics or admitted axioms or what not, which may or may not coincide with the decisions. But if we take the view of our friend the bad man we shall find that he does not care two straws for the axioms or deductions, but that he does want to know what the Massachusetts or English courts are likely to do in fact. . . . The prophecies of what the courts will do in fact, and nothing more pretentious, are what I mean by the law.

Nowhere is the confusion between legal and moral ideas more manifest than in the law of contract. Among other things, here again the so-called primary rights and duties are invested with a mystic significance beyond what can be assigned and explained. The duty to keep a contract at common law means a prediction that you must pay damages if you do not keep it,— and nothing else. If you commit a tort, you are liable to pay a compensatory sum. If you commit a contract, you are liable to pay a compensatory sum unless the promised event comes to pass, and that is all the difference. But such a mode of looking at the matter stinks in the nostrils of those who think it advantageous to get as much ethics into the law as they can.

◆   ◆   ◆

The danger of which I speak is not the admission that the principles governing other phenomenon also govern the law, but the notion that a given system, ours, for instance, can be worked out like mathematics from some general axioms of conduct. This is the natural error of the schools, but it is not confined to them. I once heard a very eminent judge say that he never let a decision go until he was absolutely sure that it was right. So judicial dissent often is blamed, as if it meant simply that one side or the other were not doing their sums right, and, if they would take more trouble, agreement inevitably would come.

This mode of thinking is entirely natural. The training of lawyers is a training in logic. The processes of analogy, discrimination and deduction are those in which they are most at home. The language of judicial decision is mainly the language of logic. And the logical method and form flatter that longing for certainty and for repose which is in every human mind. But certainty generally is illusion, and repose is not the destiny of man. Behind the logical form lies a judgment as to the relative worth and importance of competing legislative grounds, often an inarticulate and unconscious judgment, it is true, and yet the very root and nerve of the whole proceeding. You can give any conclusion a logical form. You always can imply a condition in a contract. But why do you imply? It is because of some belief as to the practice of the community or of a class, or because of some opinion as to policy, or, in short, because of some attitude of yours upon a matter not capable of founding exact logical conclusions. Such matters really are battle grounds where the means do not exist for determinations that shall be good for all time, and where the decision can do no more than embody the preference of a given body in a given time and place. We do not realize how large a part of our law is open to reconsideration upon a slight change in the habit of the public mind.

◆   ◆   ◆

I think that the judges themselves have failed adequately to recognize their duty of weighing considerations of social advantage. The duty is inevitable, and the result of the often proclaimed judicial aversion to deal with such considerations is simply to leave the very ground and foundation of judgments inarticulate, and often unconscious, as I have said. When socialism first began to be talked about, the comfortable classes of the community were a good deal frightened. I suspect that this fear has influenced judicial action both here and in England, yet it is certain that it is not a conscious factor in the decisions to which I refer. I think that something similar has led people who no longer hope to control the legislatures to look to the courts as expounders of the Constitutions, and that in some courts now principles have been discovered outside the bodies of those instruments, which may be generalized into acceptance of the economic doctrines which prevailed about fifty years ago, and a wholesale prohibition of what a tribunal of lawyers does not think about right. I cannot but believe that if the training of lawyers led them habitually to consider more definitely and explicitly the social advantage on which the rule they lay down must be justified, they sometimes would hesitate where now they are confident, and see that really they were taking sides upon debatable and often burning questions.

THE GROWTH OF ECONOMIC REGULATION

The role of the state and federal governments changed profoundly in late-nineteenth-century America. Before the Civil War, the responsibilities of government had been distributive and promotional: states and nation conferred mostly benefits, such as charters, monopolies, patents, and land grants. The hand of government doled out opportunities to individuals; it rarely restrained or disciplined them by regulatory inhibitions. Antebellum lawyers assumed that private law was not redistributive; that is, in theory, law did not direct the force of the state to take property or money from one class of people and give it to another. In the classic *Calder* v. *Bull* (1798) formulation, a legislature could not take the property of A and give it to B. Public law could be redistributive and regula-tory, hence the protections for property and contract written into the federal and state constitutions.

The dichotomy between private law and public law began to dissolve after 1865. The wartime experience of mobilizing masses of men and materiel, of moving them by rail, barge, and ship, of outfitting soldiers and mass-producing weapons and ordnance, of coordinating communications and command, and of protecting the public health of soldiers and civilians alike convinced many Americans of the need and the usefulness of governmental regulatory control. Lessons learned during the war were applied to peacetime problems. Symbolic of such regulatory changes were the adoption of standard time and time zones (1883) and a uniform railroad track gauge (1886), necessities learned by military commanders and civilian dispatchers during the war. (The initiative for these particular innovations came from the private sector, not government.)

But while regulatory control may have appeared to some to be necessary or even valuable, it was not welcome to an individual whose dreams or greed it thwarted. Thus much of the conservative opposition to regulation was justified on pleas of retaining an older system of governance, according to which government's role was limited to distributing benefits and maintaining the peace.

Resentment at the emergence of the regulatory state was fueled by an unwelcome change in Americans' vision of themselves and their future. For the first time in their existence as a people, Americans came to see that their continent—and, by extension, their destiny—had limits. The United States and its riches were not infinite, after all. This disagreeable realization was the starting point for historian Frederick Jackson Turner's frontier hypothesis (first presented in 1893 at the Columbian Exposition in Chicago), which warned that the frontier, supposedly a safety valve for American society and the nursery of democracy, had now disappeared. Many Americans now lived in crowded cities and therefore had to accept regulation in such matters as sanitation, education, and land use. Would capitalism as it had flourished until then be able to survive in a regulated state?

Another source of the constitutional paradigm that emerged in the 1890s was a reaffirmation of traditional American concepts of liberty. The constitutional historian Michael Les Benedict has written that

> there were two related but distinct justifications for the laissez-faire principle in the later nineteenth century. The first was based directly upon classical economists' conception of the "laws" of economics. It suggested that almost any government effort to overcome or channel those laws was doomed to failure. The second was based on a concept of human liberty implicit in the principles of classical economics. It militated only against certain kinds of government interferences in the economy, not against all interference. That concept was that the power of government could not legitimately be exercised to benefit one person or group at the expense of others. It was this conviction—the notion that all government economic activity violated "immutable" economic law—that lay at the heart of laissez-faire constitutionalism. . . . Laissez-faire constitutionalism received wide support in late nineteenth-century America not because it was based on widely adhered-to economic principles, and certainly not because it protected entrenched economic privilege, but rather because it was congruent with a well-established and accepted principle of American liberty.[2]

For the most part, late-nineteenth-century businessmen were not fools. They not only bowed to the inevitable, but seized it opportunistically in order to turn it to their own ends. Thus the large-scale integrated industries of the period pioneered in the development of bureaucracies that improved the flow of information and control throughout their systems. The administrative regulatory state would not have been possible without the development of a corps of administrators—in other words, a bureaucracy. No such class existed in the United States before the Civil War. It proliferated after the war, in both the public and the private sectors, in time to serve the needs of industrializing America.

It was the states rather than the federal government that first experimented with regulatory bodies like commissions and boards. Before the Civil War, Ohio, New York, and a few other states created canal commissions to oversee the construction, maintenance, and operation of canal networks. From this came the experiment, unsuccessful before the Civil War, of railroad regulatory bodies, chiefly in New England. The judiciary provided a temporary surrogate for an administrative regulatory structure, with the Massachusetts Supreme Judicial Court under Chief Justice Lemuel Shaw creating a body of common law that provided some measure of legal control of railroads.

The Civil War proved that some forms of administrative regulation were useful and, in any event, necessary. The United States Sanitary Commission, an unofficial corps that functioned as a public-health auxiliary to the Union Army, demonstrated the value of public-health controls, first in military encampments and then in cities. The success of the Union-occupying army in controlling yellow fever in New Orleans provided a dramatic example of the benefits of administrative control.

This experience in New Orleans anticipated Massachusetts' and New York's experiments with statewide boards of health, both established shortly after the war. Antebellum pioneering efforts by Dorothea Dix on behalf of the insane and Horace Mann for public education provided the inspiration for postwar welfare services for those members of society not able to care for themselves. In a related vein, the Freedmen's Bureau worked throughout the Reconstruction South to regulate labor contracts of the freed slaves, provide minimal and temporary assistance to both races dislocated by the war, and supplement the peacekeeping operations of the army.

The emergence of professional self-consciousness after the war resulted not only in the formation of professional societies, such as the American Bar Association and its state counterparts, but also in the establishment of licensing standards and procedures for numerous occupations and professions. At the same time, some states began to supervise animals and inanimate objects to protect public health. Ohio created a body of inspectors of illuminating oils in 1867 to eradicate the practice of adulterating kerosene with naphtha, a dangerous and flammable combination. In the same period, Kansas and the U.S. Army cooperated to control the movement of cattle with Texas spotted fever across state lines.

When Americans began to experiment with regulatory administration in a serious way after the war, many assumed that coercive control was both unnecessary and undesirable. Instead, they placed their faith in two techniques: the gathering and dissemination of facts, and what in our day is called jawboning—persuading the reluctant subjects of regulation. To go beyond this and force compliance with regulatory edicts, some thought, would be incompatible with the freedoms that Americans had hitherto enjoyed. This spirit was exemplified in Charles Francis Adams, Jr., the first chairman of the Massachusetts Railroad Commission. Historian Thomas McCraw wrote of his outlook that

> above all, the Massachusetts agency must shun coercion. Legal process could not be employed merely as a matter of course. Accordingly, the board almost never instituted lawsuits on its own motion. It issued no orders that the corporations were legally bound to obey, except for orders to produce information. . . . This was to set an early precedent of voluntary, cooperative, state-sponsored negotiation. Such a design for business-government relations was particularly compelling in the early decades of industrialization, when no powerful public bureaucracies yet existed to help manage the economy and offset the political strength of corporations.[3]

Historians refer to regulatory agencies organized on such premises as "advisory" commissions.

The "strong" commissions, by contrast, appeared in the Granger states of the Middle West and South, where angry farmers and shippers demanded stringent regulatory controls on rail carriers, public utilities, and grain elevators. These strong commissions directly set rates and mandated equal access to transportation facilities. Two landmark United States Supreme Court decisions, the *Slaughterhouse Cases* of 1873 and *Munn* v. *Illinois* in 1877, ratified the exercise of these new regulatory powers.

Because of lingering antebellum assumptions about the nature of the federal Union, the national government was something of a johnny-come-lately in the new regulatory state. But pressures mounted for national regulation, and Congress responded with the Interstate Commerce Act of 1887, creating the first national regulatory agency, the Interstate Commerce Commission, and then with the Sherman Anti-Trust Act of 1890, which entrusted regulatory responsibility not to an administrative agency but to the federal courts. The real geyser of federal regulation did not spout until World War I.

The reaction of state and federal judges to the regulatory state was mixed. State courts picked up the thread of antebellum higher-law jurisprudence and developed the doctrine of substantive due process. It was generally understood that the due process norm, incorporated into the Fifth and Fourteenth Amendments, as well as state constitutions, encompassed procedural safeguards against arbitrary deprivation of the rights of individuals. Many also believed that due process encompassed substantive limits on the authority of government to abridge certain basic rights even if not specifically mentioned in the Constitution. They viewed property and contractual rights associated with the free market as fundamental aspects of the constitutional order. Accordingly, the supreme courts of the leading industrial and commercial states, particularly New York and Illinois, advanced doctrines of property and contractual relationships that sometimes stymied state regulatory efforts. The state judges were shortly abetted by their federal brethren, who expounded doctrines of liberty of contract and substantive due process that protected economic rights by limiting state and federal efforts to regulate business enterprise.

Thus the turn of the century proved to be a confusing era to contemporaries and to those who gaze back on it from later times. The nation and the states coped clumsily with unprecedented social and economic change. Their early toddling steps toward administrative regulation met first with tolerance and then with erratic hostility from judges. Out of this confused response there emerged the beginnings of the regulatory state we know today.

PROPERTY RIGHTS AND POLICE POWER

DAVID J. BREWER

"Protection to Private Property from Public Attack"
1891

The proliferation of economic controls sparked a debate over the scope of regulatory authority and the place of property and contractual rights in the constitutional order. Justice David J. Brewer was an influential member of the Supreme Court at the end of the nineteenth century and wrote a number of leading opinions upholding economic liberty. In this address he considered the constitutional protection of the rights of property owners in the face of governmental actions grounded on the police power. Not only does Brewer stress the importance of the payment of compensation to adversely impacted owners, but he recognizes that some regulations might so severely limit the use of property as to constitute a taking of property.

Private property is sacrificed at the hands of the police power in at least three ways: first, when the property itself is destroyed; second, when by regulation of charges its value is diminished; and third, when its use or some valuable use of it is forbidden. Instances of the first are these: when in the presence of a threatening conflagration a house is blown up to check the progress of the flames: when a house has been occupied by persons afflicted with small-pox or other infectious disease, and so virulent has been the disease, and so many afflicted, that the public health demands the entire destruction of the house and contents by fire to prevent the spread of that disease: when to prevent an overflow in one direction, by which large and valuable property would be destroyed, a break is made in a dyke or embankment, and the water turned elsewhere and upon less valuable property, and crops swept away in order to save buildings and lives. In these and like cases, there is an absolute destruction of the property,—the houses and crops. The individual loses for the public weal. Can there be a doubt that equity and justice demand that the burden of such loss shall not be cast upon the individual, but should be shared by those who have been protected and benefited. It may be, that at common law no action could be maintained against the State or municipality by the individual whose property has been thus destroyed. But the imperfections of the law do not militate against the demands of justice. *Salus populi suprema lex* justifies the destruction. But the equity of compensation is so clear that it has been recognized by statutes in many States, and provisions made for suit against a municipality to distribute upon the public the burden which it is inequitable that the individual should alone bear. And in enforcing such an equity, no regard is or ought to be paid to the character of, or the use to which the building or property is appropriated. It is enough, that property held by an individual under the protection of the law, is destroyed for the public welfare.

Second, under the guise of regulation, where charges for the use are so reduced as to prevent a reasonable profit on the investment. The history of this question is interesting: certain occupations have long been considered of a quasi public nature,—among these, principally, the business of carrying passengers and freight. Of the propriety of this classification, no question can be made. Without enquiring into the various reasons therefore, a common carrier is described as a quasi public servant. Private capital is invested, and the business is carried on by private persons and through private instrumentalities. Yet, it is a public service which they render, and by virtue thereof, public governmental control is warranted. The great common carriers of the country, the railroad companies, insisted that, by reason of the fact that they were built by private capital and owned by private corporations, they had the same right to fix the prices for transportation

that any individual had to fix the price at which he was willing to sell his labor or his property. They challenged the attempts of the State legislatures to regulate their tariffs. After a long and bitter struggle, the Supreme Court of the United States, in the celebrated "Granger" cases, reported in the 94 U.S., sustained the power of the public, and affirmed legislative control. The question in those cases was not as to the extent, but as to the existence of such control. Those decision, sustaining public control over the tariffs of railroads and other common carriers as a part of the police power of the State, were accompanied by the case of *Munn* vs. *Illinois*, 94 U.S., 113, putting warehouses in the same category. The scope of this decision, suggesting a far-reaching supervision over private occupations, brought vigorously up the question as to its extent. If the tariff of common carriers and warehouse-men was a matter for public control, could the public so reduce the charges that the receipts of the carrier or the warehouse-man would not only furnish no return to the owners, but also not equal the operating expenses;—so that the owner having put his property into an investment, permanent in its nature, and from which he could not at will withdraw, might be compelled to see that investment lost, and his property taken from him by an accumulation of debts from operating expenses?

On this line the struggle was again renewed and carried to the Supreme Court, which in the recent case of *Railway Company* vs. *Minnesota*, 134 U.S., 418, decided that regulation did not mean destruction; and that under the guise of legislative control over tariffs it was not possible for State or Nation to destroy the investments of private capital in such enterprises; that the individual had rights as well as the public, and rights which the public could not take from him. The opinion written in that case by Mr. Justice Blatchford, sustained as it was by the Court, will ever remain a strong and unconquerable fortress in the long struggle between individual rights and public greed. I rejoice to have been permitted to put one stone into that fortress.

The other class of cases, is where, in the exercise of the police power, some special use is stopped, and the value flowing from that use is thus wholly destroyed. In principle, there is no difference between this and the preceding cases. Property is as certainly destroyed when the use of that which is the subject of property is taken away, as if the thing itself was appropriated, for that which gives value to property, is its capacity for use. If it cannot be used, it is worth nothing; when the use is taken away, the value is gone.

◆　◆　◆

But surely authority is not needed for a proposition so clear. If one of you own a tract of land usable only for farm purposes, and the fiat of sovereign power forbids its use for such purposes, of what value is the naked title? No profit or advantage comes to you from the possession of that which you cannot use, and no one will buy that which in like manner he cannot use. So whether the thing be taken or its use stopped, the individual loses, he is deprived of his property; and if this is done in the exercise of the police power, because the public health, morals, or welfare demand, his property is sacrificed that the public may gain. When a building is destroyed that a fire may not spread, the individual's property is sacrificed for the general good. When the use of his property is forbidden because the public health or morals require such prohibition, the public gains while he loses. Equal considerations of natural justice demand that he who is thus despoiled for the public good, should not alone bear the burden, but that the public which is benefited should share with him the loss. It is unfortunate that this question came into the courts along the line of deep feeling, and in the furtherance of a lofty and noble effort to suppress the enormous evils of intemperance. I reluctantly refer to this, for having had some judicial experience in connection with it, I know how angry was the feeling, how biased the judgment, and how bitter were the denunciations. It is unfortunate, I say, that this question came into the courts along the line of such controversy, for it is a familiar staying, "hard cases make bad precedents," and it is seldom easy, under the pressing burden of a great evil, to examine questions in the calm

light of simple justice. We look back to the execution of the witches in Massachusetts by judicial decrees as a sad blot on the records of its courts. No one doubts the integrity of the judges by whom those decrees we entered, or does not feel, by way of apology, that the burden of the awful danger supposed to rest upon the community swayed the judicial mind, and bent its judgment.

When the great State of Kansas, in whose past I glory, and in whose future I believe, proclaimed by the voice of its people through constitutional amendment, that the manufacture and sale of intoxicating liquors as a beverage should cease within its borders, humanity rejoiced, and I am glad to have written the opinion of the Supreme Court of that State, affirming its validity and rightfulness. I regret to be compelled to add, that in the glory of success and the furtherance of a good cause, the State forgot to be just. There were four or five breweries, with machinery and appliances valuable only for one use, worth a few thousand dollars, a mere bagatelle in comparison with the wealth of the State, built up under the sanction of the law, owned by citizens whose convictions were different from those of the majority, and who believe the manufacture and sale of beer to be right and wise. As good citizens it was fitting that they should yield to the judgment of the majority. As honest men, it was fitting for the majority not to destroy without compensation; and to share with the few the burden of that change in public sentiment, evidence by the constitutional amendment. It will be said hereafter to the glory of the State, that she pioneered the way of temperance; to its shame, that at the same time she forgot to be honest and just, and was willing to be temperate at the expense of the individual. Had this question come to the courts along other lines, who can doubt that a different result would have followed.

◆　◆　◆

There is not only justice, with wisdom in this rule, that, when a lawful use is by statute made unlawful and forbidden, and its value destroyed, the public shall make compensation to the individual. It restrains from hasty action. It induces a small majority to hesitate in imposing upon an unwilling and large minority its notions of what is demanded by public health, or morals, or welfare. The pocket-book is a potent check on even the reformer. If this rule had been always recognized as in force, would the State of Pennsylvania have enacted that foolish law, forbidding the manufacture and sale of oleomargarine, and thus destroying a legitimate and beneficial industry? Or if it had, would the judicial eye have been so blind as not to see through the thin disguise of a pretended regard for public health, to the real purpose of the act,—the protection of another and no more deserving industry, that of the dairy?

STATE REGULATION AND THE PUBLIC INTEREST

After the Civil War, the states began to exercise their regulatory power through legislation, constitutional revision, administrative action, and judicial decision. These changes were based on the state's "police power," which Chief Justice Lemuel Shaw of the Massachusetts Supreme Judicial Court had defined in sweeping terms in *Commonwealth* v. *Alger* (1851):

> We think it is a settled principle, growing out of the nature of well ordered civil society, that every holder of property, however absolute and unqualified may be his title, holds it under the implied liability that his use of it may be so regulated, that it shall not be injurious to the equal enjoyment of others having an equal right to the enjoyment of their property, nor injurious to the rights of the community. All property in the commonwealth, as well that in the interior as that bordering on tide water, is derived directly or indirectly from the government, and held subject to those general regulations, which are necessary to the common good and general welfare. Rights of property, like all other social and conventional rights, are subject to such reasonable limitations in their enjoyment, as shall prevent them from being injurious, and to such reasonable restraints and regulations established by law, as the legislature, under the governing and controlling power vested in them by the constitution, may think necessary and expedient.[4]

The growing power of labor unions seemed to require state regulatory intervention through the exercise of the police power after the Civil War. Judges reacted with hostility to labor organization before mid-century while displaying an occasional concern for the well-being of individual industrial workers. Thus it would be a reductionist error to assume that because bar and bench were hostile to unions, they were equally hostile to workingmen and -women. Reality was more complex than that. Lawyers and judges displayed a paternalistic attitude toward workers, warily tolerating protective measures enacted by legislatures that were designed to meliorate the harshest of common-law doctrines, such as the fellow servant rule. Bench and bar did not exactly welcome legislative intervention on the side of labor when it occurred, but they displayed a surprising tolerance, even a mild sympathy, for legislative efforts to ease the lot of workers.

STATES AND LABOR LAW

Legislatures displayed some solicitude for workers who were not deemed fully capable of looking after their own interests. Children and women were the most obvious beneficiaries.

New Jersey Child Labor Act
1851

1. Be it enacted by the Senate and General Assembly of the State of New Jersey, That labor performed during a period of ten hours, on any day, in all cotton, woollen, milk, paper, glass and flax factories, and in manufactories of iron and brass, shall be considered a legal day's labor.

2. And be it enacted, That hereafter no minor engaged in any factory, shall be holden or required to work more than ten hours on any day, or sixty hours in any week; and that hereafter no minor shall be admitted as a worker under the age of ten years in any factory within this state; that if any owner of, or employer in any factory shall knowingly employ any such minor, or shall require any minor over the age of ten years to work more than ten hours on any day, or sixty hours in any week, he shall be adjudged to pay a penalty of fifty dollars.

Illinois Criminal Syndicalism Act
1887

The Chicago Haymarket riot of 1886 began when police broke up a street tumult and in doing so killed or wounded a half-dozen striking workers. The next day at a street rally called to protest the slaying, someone (who has never been identified) threw a bomb into the police line. The police opened fire, and in the aftermath, seven policemen were killed. Chicago authorities rounded up organizers of the rally as principals to the homicide. No one was ever charged with participating in the bombing or even advocating it. Nevertheless, seven anarchists were sentenced to be hanged. The punishments of two were commuted, one committed suicide, and four went to the gallows.

The long-run consequences of the Haymarket bombing and its retaliatory aftermath remain incalculable. First, the statute excerpted next was the forerunner of similar laws that were used to suppress labor organization and political radicalism through World War I. Another consequence was the delay, by at least a generation, in adoption of the eight-hour workday. Most pervasive was the confirmation in the minds of America's middle class of the stereotype of the alien bomb-throwing anarchist. Organized labor suffered severely from the association.

If any person shall, by speaking to any public or private assemblage of people, or in any public place, or shall by writing, printing or publishing, or by causing to be written, printed, published or circulated, any written or printed matter, advise, encourage, aid, abet, or incite a local revolution, or the overthrowing or destruction of the existing order of society by force or violence, or the resistance to and destruction of the lawful power and authority of the legal authorities of this State or of any of the towns, cities or counties of this State, or resistance to the same, by force and violence, or by any of the means aforesaid shall advise, abet, encourage or incite the disturbance of the public peace, and by such disturbance [an] attempt at revolution or destruction of public order or resistance to such authorities shall thereafter ensue, and human life is taken or any person is injured, or property is destroyed by any person or by any of the means employed to carry into effect the purpose so advised, encouraged, aided, abetted or incited as aforesaid: every person so aiding, advising, encouraging, abetting or inciting the same shall be deemed as having conspired with the person or persons who actually commit the crime, and shall be deemed a principal in the perpetration of the same and be punished accordingly, and it shall not be necessary for the prosecution to show that the speaking was heard or the written or printed matter aforesaid was read or communicated to the person or persons actually committing the crime, if such speaking, writing, printing or publishing is shown to have been done in a public manner within this State.

New York Worker's Compensation Act
1910

As social tensions eased at the turn of the twentieth century, state legislatures returned to policy questions involving the problems of labor. They grappled with the intertwined subjects of allocating the burdens of industrial accidents and modifying the fellow servant rule. The solution adopted in all industrial states by World War I was workers' compensation (known at the time of its origin as workmen's compensation). As it evolved, the basic policy of workers' compensation was a guaranteed recovery for death or disability and statutory abolition of the fellow servant rule, offset by a cap on liability plus abrogation of tort remedies for the injured worker. This statutory remedy replaced suits at common law by workers against their employers. Adoption of the New York statute excerpted as follows, was a milestone in the progress of workers' compensation.

An act to amend the labor law, in relation to workmen's compensation in certain dangerous employments.

Application of article. This article shall apply only to workmen engaged in manual or mechanical labor in the following employments, each of which is hereby determined to be especially dangerous, in which from the nature, conditions or means of prosecution of the work therein, extraordinary risks to the life and limb of workmen engaged therein are inherent, necessary or substantially unavoidable, and as to each of which employments it is deemed necessary to establish a new system of compensation for accidents to workmen.

[The statute then itemized eight categories of dangerous labor, including demolition, blasting, tunneling, electrical construction, and railroad operation.]

♦ ♦ ♦

Sec. 217. Basis of liability. If, in the course of any of the employments above described, personal injury by accident arising out of and in the course of the employment after this article takes effect is caused to any workman employed therein, in whole or in part, or the damage or injury caused thereby is in whole or in part contributed to by

a. A necessary risk or danger of the employment or one inherent in the nature thereof; or

b. Failure of the employer of such workman or any of his or its officers, agents or employees to exercise due care, or to comply with any law affecting such employment; then such employer shall . . . be liable to pay compensation at the rates set out in section two hundred and nineteen-a of this title; provided that the employer shall not be liable in respect of any injury which does not disable the workman for a period of at least two weeks from earning full wages at the work at which he was employed, and provided that the employer shall not be liable in respect of any injury to the workman which is caused in whole or in part by the serious and willful misconduct of the workman.

♦ ♦ ♦

Sec. 219-a. Scale of compensation. The amount of compensation shall be in case death results from injury:

a. If the workman leaves a widow or next of kin at the time of his death wholly dependent on his earnings, a sum equal to twelve hundred times the daily earnings of such workman at the rate at which he was being paid by such employer at the time of the injury subject as hereinafter provided, and in no event more than three thousand dollars. Any weekly payments made under this article shall be deducted in ascertaining such amount.

♦ ♦ ♦

2. Where total or partial incapacity for work at any gainful employment results to the workman from the injury, a weekly payment commencing at the end of the second week after the injury and continuing during such incapacity equal to fifty per centum of his average weekly earnings when at work on full time during the preceding year during which he shall have been in the employment of the same employer.

♦ ♦ ♦

In no event shall any compensation paid under this article exceed the damage suffered, nor shall any weekly payment payable under this article in any event exceed ten dollars a week or extend over more than eight years from the date of the accident.

WORKERS' COMPENSATION AND THE QUESTION OF CAUSATION

Ives v. South Buffalo Railway Co.
201 N.Y. 271 (1911)

In this opinion the New York Court of Appeals struck down the pioneering New York Worker's Compensation Act of 1910 as an impermissible deprivation of an employer's property without due process of law. The Ives *decision ignited a firestorm of criticism and did not halt the drive to overhaul the law of industrial accidents. In 1913 New York voters adopted a constitutional amendment authorizing the state legislature to enact a workers' compensation law. The Supreme Court sustained the revised New York compensation scheme in* New York Central Railroad v. White *(1917). Still,* Ives *left an imprint on the evolution of workers' compensation law. Subsequent statutes made compensation the exclusive remedy for injured employees, eliminating the option of a negligence action against the employer. To meet possible constitutional objections, lawmakers felt that there must be a benefit to employers as well as employees. Employer exemption from tort liability conferred a kind of quid pro quo that eased judicial acceptance of workers' compensation.*

The statute, judged by our common-law standards, is plainly revolutionary. Its central and controlling feature is that every employer who is engaged in any of the classified industries shall be liable for any injury to a workman arising out of and in the course of the employment by "a necessary risk or danger of the employment or one inherent in the nature thereof; . . . provided that the employer shall not be liable in respect of any injury to the workman which is caused in whole or in part by the serious and willful misconduct of the workman." This rule of liability, stated in another form, is that the employer is responsible to the employee for every accident in the course of employment, whether the employer is at fault or not, and whether the employee is at fault or not, except when the fault of the employee is so grave as to constitute serious and willful misconduct on his part. The radical character of this legislation is at once revealed by contrasting it with the rule of the common law, under which the employer is liable for injuries to his employee only when the employer is guilty of some act or acts of negligence which caused the occurrence out of which the injuries arise, and then only when the employee is shown to be free from any negligence which contributes to the occurrence.

This quoted summary of the report of the commission to the legislature, which clearly and fairly epitomizes what is more fully set forth in the body of the report, is based upon a most voluminous array of statistical tables, extracts from the works of philosophical writers and the industrial laws of many countries, all of which are designed to show that our own system of dealing with industrial accidents is economically, morally and legally unsound. Under our form of government, however, courts must regard all economic, philosophical and moral theories, attractive and desirable though they may be, as subordinate to the primary question whether they can be moulded into statutes without infringing upon the letter or spirit of our written constitutions. In that respect we are unlike any of the countries whose industrial laws are referred to as models for our guidance. Practically all of these countries are so called constitutional monarchies in which, as in England, there is no written constitution, and the Parliament or law-making body is supreme. In our country the Federal and State Constitutions are the charters which demark the extent and the limitations of legislative power; and while it is true that the rigidity of a written constitution may at times prove to be a hindrance to the march of progress, yet more often its stability protects the people against the frequent and violent fluctuations of that which, for want of a better name, we call public opinion.

◆ ◆ ◆

This legislation is challenged as void under the fourteenth amendment to the Federal Constitution and under section 6, article 1 of our State Constitution, which guarantee all persons against deprivation of life, liberty or property without due process of law.

◆ ◆ ◆

It is conceded that this is a liability unknown to the common law and we think it plainly constitutes a deprivation of liberty and property under the Federal and State Constitutions, unless its imposition can be justified under the police power which will be discussed under a separate head. In arriving at this conclusion we do not overlook the cogent economic and sociological arguments which are urged in support of the statute. There can be no doubt as to the theory of this law. It is based upon the proposition that the inherent risks of an employment should in justice be placed upon the shoulders of the employer, who can protect himself against loss by insurance and by such an addition to the price of his wares as to cast the burden ultimately upon the consumer; that indemnity to an injured employee should be as much a charge upon the business as the cost of replacing or repairing disabled or defective machinery, appliances or tools; that, under our present system, the loss falls immediately upon the employee who is almost invariably unable to bear it, and ultimately upon the community which is taxed for the support of the indigent; and that our present system is uncertain, unscientific and wasteful, and fosters a spirit of antagonism between employer and employee which it is to the interest of the state to remove. We have already admitted the strength of this appeal to a recognized and widely prevalent sentiment, but we think it is an appeal which must be made to the people and not to the courts. The right of property rests not upon philosophical or scientific speculations nor upon the commendable impulses of benevolence or charity, nor yet upon the dictates of natural justice. The right has its foundation in the fundamental law. That can be changed by the people, but not by legislatures. In a government like ours theories of public good or necessity are often so plausible or sound as to command popular approval, but courts are not permitted to forget that the law is the only chart by which the ship of state is to be guided. Law as used in this sense means the basic law and not the very act of legislation which deprives the citizen of his rights, privileges and property. Any other view would lead to the absurdity that the Constitutions protect only those rights which the legislatures do not take away. If such economic and sociologic arguments as are here advanced in support of this statute can be allowed to subvert the fundamental idea of property, then there is no private right entirely safe, because there is no limitation upon the absolute discretion of legislatures, and the guarantees of the Constitution are a mere waste of words.

In its final and simple analysis that is taking the property of A and giving it to B, and that cannot be done under our Constitutions.

◆ ◆ ◆

If we are warranted in concluding that the new statute violates private right by taking the property of one and giving it to another without due process of law, that is really the end of this case. But the auspices under which this legislation was enacted, no less than its intrinsic importance, entitle its advocates to the fullest consideration of every argument in its support, and we, therefore, take up the discussion of the police power under which this law is sought to be justified. The police power is, of course, one of the necessary attributes of civilized government. In its most comprehensive sense it embraces the whole system by which the state seeks to preserve the public order, to prevent offenses against the law, to insure to citizens in their intercourse with each other the enjoyment of their own so far as is reasonably consistent with a like enjoyment of rights by others. Under it persons and property are subjected to all kinds of restraints and burdens in order to secure the general comfort, health and prosperity of the state. But it is a power which is always subject to the Constitution, for in a constitutional government limitation is the abiding principle, exhibited in its highest form in the Constitution as the deliberative judgment of the people, which moderates every claim of right and controls every use of power.

◆ ◆ ◆

In order to sustain legislation under the police power the courts must be able to see that its operation tends in some degree to prevent some offense or evil, or to preserve public health, morals, safety and welfare. If it discloses no such purpose, but is clearly calculated to invade the liberty and property of private citizens, it is plainly the duty of the courts to declare it invalid, for legislative assumption of the right to direct the channel into which the private energies of the citizen may flow, or legislative attempt to abridge or hamper the right of the citizen to pursue, unmolested and without reasonable regulation, any lawful calling or avocation which he may choose, has always been condemned under our form of government.

Eminent Domain

Colorado Constitution
1876

Colorado, the Centennial State, was admitted to the Union in 1876. Its constitution reflected many of the trends in state constitution making that had been unleashed or accelerated by the Civil War. One of the more suggestive of these trends was the expansion of the power of eminent domain.

Before the war, eminent domain had been delegated by states to private corporations, such as canals and railroads, which were permitted to condemn private property as long as the taking conformed to the two traditional requirements of the state and federal constitutions' tak-

ings clauses: the taking had to be for a public purpose, and the taker had to provide the prop-
erty owner just compensation. In the leading case of Inhabitants of Worcester *v.* Western Railroad Co. *(1842),*[5] *Chief Justice Shaw of the Massachusetts Supreme Judicial Court sustained*
this practice by holding that although run by a private corporation, a railroad "is regarded
as a public work . . . for the public use . . . [held by the corporation] in trust for the public."
In the pell-mell industrialization of the post–Civil War era, eminent domain beckoned invit-
ingly, particularly in the new western states short of capital and avid for development, as a
substitute for or shortcut to capital formation. Many western states conferred the power of em-
inent domain upon private parties to obtain rights-of-way across the land of others for pur-
poses of mining or agriculture. The provisions of the Colorado constitution excerpted next were
typical. Apparently convinced that private property was being taken to create an overall re-
source benefit for the public, the Supreme Court upheld such measures.

ART. II—BILL OF RIGHTS

♦ ♦ ♦

Section 14. That private property shall not be taken for private use unless by consent of the owner, except for private ways of necessity, and except for reservoirs, drains, flumes or ditches on or across the lands of others, for agricultural, mining, milling, domestic or sanitary purposes.

Section 15. That private property shall not be taken or damaged, for public or private use without just compensation. Such compensation shall be ascertained by a Board of Commissioners, of not less than three freeholders, or by a jury, when required by the owner of the property, in such manner as may be prescribed by law, and until the same shall be paid to the owner, or into Court for the owner, the property shall not be needlessly disturbed, or the proprietary rights of the owner therein divested; and whenever an attempt is made to take private property for a use alleged to be public, the question whether the contemplated use be really public, shall be a judicial question, and determined as such without regard to any legislative assertion that the use is public.

♦ ♦ ♦

ART. XV—CORPORATIONS

♦ ♦ ♦

Section 8. The right of eminent domain shall never be abridged nor so construed as to prevent the General Assembly from taking the property and franchises of incorporated companies, and subjecting them to public use, the same as the property of individuals; and the police power of the State shall never be abridged or so construed as to permit corporations to conduct their business in such manner as to infringe the equal rights of individuals or the general well being of the State.

♦ ♦ ♦

ART. XVI—MINING AND IRRIGATION

♦ ♦ ♦

Section 7. All persons and corporations shall have the right of way across public, private and corporate lands for the construction of ditches, canals and flumes for the purpose of conveying water for domestic purposes, for the irrigation of agricultural land, and for mining and manufacturing purposes, and for drainage, upon payment of just compensation.

Note: The Evolution of Takings Jurisprudence

Although the "public use" limitation on the exercise of eminent domain was eroded by judicial deference to legislative determinations that a particular appropriation of property served the public interest, in other respects the Supreme Court tended to strengthen the protection afforded property owners under the takings clause of the Fifth Amendment. In the landmark case of *Chicago, Burlington and Quincy Railroad Company* v. *Chicago* (1897), the Court ruled that the payment of compensation when private property was taken for public use was an essential element of due process as guaranteed by the Fourteenth Amendment. This meant that the just compensation requirement was binding on the states. In effect, the just compensation principle became the first provision of the Bill of Rights to be applied to the states. Moreover, in *Monongahela Navigation Company* v. *United States* (1893), the justices gave an expansive reading to the right of compensation. They insisted that the determination of the amount of compensation was a judicial not a legislative function. The justices also held that the value of property was ascertained by its profitableness.

The states also took steps to strengthen the rights of property owners. Starting with Illinois in 1870, many states amended their constitutions to require compensation when property was either taken "or damaged." The purpose was to enhance the right of the owners to recover for loss when governmental actions injured their property.

In addition, as land use regulations gradually increased, courts and commentators began to wrestle with the idea that regulations might so diminish the usefulness of property as to be tantamount to an outright taking. Recall the comments of Justice Brewer at page 367. Further, in *Bent* v. *Emery* (1899), Oliver Wendell Holmes, Jr., while on the Supreme Judicial Court of Massachusetts, observed: "It would be open to argument at least that an owner might be stripped of his rights so far as to amount to a taking without any physical interference with his land."[6] These views anticipated the emergence of the modern doctrine of a regulatory taking, which was recognized by the Supreme Court in the famous decision of *Pennsylvania Coal Co.* v. *Mahon* (1922).

FEDERAL REGULATION AND THE PUBLIC INTEREST

The emergence of the regulatory state at the federal level was resisted in part because the constitutional tradition of state police power had been well established before the Civil War. No comparable tradition supported an analogous federal police power, however, lending some credence to constitutional objections that the innovation was unprecedented.

A large component of conservative difficulty with federal regulation derived from assumptions about separation of powers. The symmetry of three branches of government—legislative, executive, judicial—seemed compelling. To the traditional mind, there seemed no room for a fourth branch of government. Worse, this new branch, the administrative, blurred the separation of powers by combining executive, legislative, and judicial functions in the same body. This blurring stirred up old fears of autocratic, tyrannical government in which one branch gathered all powers into its own hands. Since the administrative agencies appeared to be predominantly executive in their origin and character, they portended one of the oldest threats to republican government: executive tyranny. This in turn might imperil judicial review and legislative autonomy.

The burden of demonstrating the constitutionality of the administrative state at the federal level lay with proponents of the innovation. This burden accounts for what otherwise appears to be willful obstructionism on the part of the United States Supreme Court, which greeted the fledgling administrative agencies in the 1890s and 1920s with cold suspicion, if not outright hostility. It was not so much that the judges thought any administrative innovation at all was unconstitutional, but that a new fourth element was being engrafted on a constitutional order that in its intrinsic character seemed to accommodate only three.

The emergence of the federal administrative structure followed state experience. Federal agencies at first had a predominantly fact-gathering mission; few in Congress believed that federal agencies should have law-enforcing or rate-setting authority. With Congress indecisive, federal judges, conservative by nature, did not rush to embrace innovation. A pattern of legislative-judicial dialogue emerged between 1890 and World War I. Congress would essay some legislative initiative, like the Interstate Commerce Act, with only vague and inconsistent suggestions about its intent in creating the new agency. Federal courts, faced with challenges to the constitutionality of the new body, would react cautiously, refusing to ascribe powers to it that congressional intent did not unambiguously support. Congress would return to the matter a few years later, restating (or articulating for the first time) its intent in setting up the new agency. If that congressional statement was sufficiently free from ambiguity, the courts would usually accept the new role being carved out for the agency.

There was also a concern for federalism running throughout federal judges' reception of the new administrative state. Some judges envisioned a constitutional order in which primary responsibility for regulating matters that affected most Americans would continue to reside with the states, not with the federal government. Thus any apparent transfer of responsibility from states to nation would be greeted suspiciously, as an innovation at best, a violation of the Constitution at worst. This was only partially offset by a slowly expanding vision of congressional power under the commerce clause or other sources of federal authority. Traditional concepts of federalism died hard, and the old order of federalism yielded slowly and reluctantly to a new configuration of federal relations.

THE INTERSTATE COMMERCE COMMISSION

Interstate Commerce Act
1887

In one way or another after the Civil War, the states tried to regulate railroads and the rates they charged. But regulation at the state level proved to be inadequate to deal with emergent problems, chief of which was the inability of a single state to control an interstate enterprise. Recognizing this, Justice Samuel Miller of the United States Supreme Court asserted in 1886 that state regulation of interstate railroad charges invaded federal authority under the commerce clause. He explained that "this species of regulation is one which must be, if established at all, of a general and national character, and cannot be safely and wisely remitted to local rules and local regulations."[7] Miller's thinly veiled hint bore fruit within a year when Congress enacted the Interstate Commerce Act of 1887.

From a railroad's point of view, the principal problem facing it was excessive and unregulated competition in a capital-intensive industry. Railroads tried to cope with that problem by organizing pooling arrangements among themselves to distribute traffic and profits in competitive routes; in a word, they created cartels. But purely private cartels were not a satisfactory long-term solution because individual participants could opt out and because the legitimacy of the cartel might be challenged by disaffected customers. What railroads needed was government sanction of cartels.

From the viewpoint of the railroads' consumers, shippers, and farmers, the situation looked altogether different. Railroad rates seemed high. In many areas railroads were what economists call natural monopolies. They offered rebates to favored customers, which were usually large enterprises with a high volume of shipments. This practice upset small business interests. Railroads also discriminated between long and short hauls in their rate structure, charging as much or more for short hauls as they did for a longer haul, a practice that made economic sense but disadvantaged certain localities.

The Interstate Commerce Act was a patchwork of ambiguous provisions. Congress was as much concerned with placating public opinion as seriously addressing what was known as "the railway problem." Not surprisingly, Congress was happy to leave unresolved policy issues to the newly created Interstate Commerce Commission and to the courts.

The provisions of this act shall apply to any common carrier or carriers engaged in the transportation of passengers or property wholly by railroad, or partly by railroad and partly by water when both are used, under a common control, management, or arrangement, for a continuous carriage or shipment, from one State or Territory of the United States, or the District of Columbia, to any other State or Territory of the United States, or the District of Columbia. . . .

All charges made for any service rendered or to be rendered in the transportation of passengers or property as aforesaid, or in connection therewith, or for the receiving, delivering, storage, or handling of such property, shall be reasonable and just; and every unjust and unreasonable charge for such service is prohibited and declared to be unlawful.

Sec. 2. That if any common carrier subject to the provisions of this act shall, directly or indirectly, by any special rate, rebate, drawback, or other device, charge, demand, collect, or receive from any person or persons a greater or less compensation for any service rendered, or to be rendered, in the transportation of passengers or property, subject to the provisions of this act, than it charges, demands, collects, or receives from any other person or persons for doing for him or them a like and contemporaneous service in the transportation of a like kind of traffic under substantially similar circumstances and conditions, such common carrier shall be deemed guilty of unjust discrimination,

which is hereby prohibited and declared to be unlawful.

Sec. 3. That it shall be unlawful for any common carrier subject to the provisions of this act to make or give any undue or unreasonable preference or advantage to any particular person, company, firm, corporation, or locality, or any particular description of traffic, in any respect whatsoever, or to subject any particular person, company, firm, corporation, or locality, or any particular description of traffic, to any undue or unreasonable prejudice or disadvantage in any respect whatsoever.

Sec. 4. That it shall be unlawful for any common carrier subject to the provisions of this act to charge or receive any greater compensation in the aggregate for the transportation of passengers or of like kind of property, under substantially similar circumstances and conditions, for a shorter than for a longer distance over the same line, in the same direction, the shorter being included within the longer distance. . . .

Sec. 5. That it shall be unlawful for any common carrier subject to the provisions of this act to enter into any contract, agreement, or combination with any other common carriers for the pooling of freights of different and competing railroads, or to divide between them the aggregate or net proceeds of the earnings of such railroads, or any portion thereof; and in any case of an agreement for the pooling of freights as aforesaid, each day of its continuance shall be deemed a separate offense.

Note: Judicial Reaction to the Interstate Commerce Commission

The Interstate Commerce Commission (ICC) was the first federal regulatory agency, and its creation heralded the rise of the administrative state during the twentieth century. The commission, however, was a feeble body in its early years. Sympathetic to private economic ordering, the Supreme Court in the 1890s narrowly construed the authority of the ICC under the act. It denied the ICC power to set rates and permitted federal courts to make fact-findings anew.[8] These decisions left the agency virtually powerless.

Congress returned to the problem in the next decade, first by prohibiting rebates in the Elkins Act of 1903—a measure supported by the railroads, which wanted to eliminate any practice that diminished their earnings. The Hepburn Act of 1906 addressed the more difficult matter of strengthening the ICC and according greater finality to its decisions. Congress empowered the ICC, upon complaint, to fix reasonable rates and limited the scope of judicial review. As shown by this Progressive Era legislation, lawmakers increasingly looked to regulatory commissions rather than competition to govern the rail industry. Railroad companies lost control of the rate-making process. This trend culminated with the Transportation Act of 1920, which further enlarged the power of the ICC and treated the rail industry as a protected cartel under tight regulation. Over the ensuing decades of the twentieth century, however, the efficacy of the ICC and railroad regulatory policy would be sharply challenged.

TRUST-BUSTING: THE STATUTORY BASIS

Sherman Anti-Trust Act
1890

Until the late nineteenth century, Congress rarely used its power to affirmatively regulate commerce between the states. Congress had two alternatives before it when it contemplated some kind of legislative action against trusts. On the one hand, it might follow the trail blazed by Charles Francis Adams, Jr., and the weak state regulatory commissions, entrusting some vaguely defined regulatory responsibility to commissions staffed by experts who might have powers of investigation and publicity. On the other hand, Congress could formulate as definite a statement of legislative policy as conflicting political pressures permitted, and then leave further articulation and enforcement of policy to courts. It chose the latter approach in the Sherman Anti-Trust Act, which sought to safeguard competition and free markets.

Sec. 1. Every contract, combination in the form of trust or otherwise, or conspiracy, in restraint of trade or commerce among the several States, or with foreign nations, is hereby declared to be illegal. Every person who shall make any such contract or engage in any such combination or conspiracy, shall be deemed guilty of a misdemeanor, and, on conviction thereof, shall be punished by fine not exceeding five thousand dollars, or by imprisonment not exceeding one year, or by both said punishments, in the discretion of the court.

Sec. 2. Every person who shall monopolize, or attempt to monopolize, or combine or conspire with any other person or persons, to monopolize any part of the trade or commerce among the several States, or with foreign nations, shall be deemed guilty of a misdemeanor, and, on conviction thereof, shall be punished by fine not exceeding five thousand dollars, or by imprisonment not exceeding one year, or by both said punishments, in the discretion of the court.

FEDERAL COMMERCE POWER

United States v. E. C. Knight & Co.
156 U.S. 1 (1895)

The extent of congressional authority over economic life has long been one of the most contentious issues in American constitutionalism. It was generally recognized in the nineteenth century that the power of Congress reached only trade among the states and did not compass all types of economic activity. This understanding of the commerce clause was consistent with the original constitutional design of a limited federal government. Implicit in cases delineating the scope of congressional power over commerce were considerations of federalism.

E. C. Knight, the first case under the Sherman Anti-Trust Act heard by the Supreme Court, involved an action against the American Sugar Refining Company. The government alleged that the company, which controlled more than 90 percent of the nation's sugar refining, was a combination in restraint of trade. Speaking for the Court, Chief Justice Melville W. Fuller ruled that manufacturing was local in nature and subject only to state control. Fuller's opinion reflects his deep commitment to state autonomy but, to modern eyes, seems to overlook the growing interdependency of production and trade. As Howard Gillman explains, the E. C. Knight decision represents "an attempt to maintain the efficacy of a traditional distinction in commerce clause jurisprudence at a time when changes in the structure of the economy were making this distinction increasingly untenable."[9]

By the purchase of the stock of the four Philadelphia refineries, with shares of its own stock, the American Sugar Refining Company acquired nearly complete control of the manufacture of refined sugar within the United States. The bill charged that the contracts under which these purchases were made constituted combinations in restraint of trade, and that in entering into them the defendants combined and conspired to restrain the trade and commerce in refined sugar among the several States and with foreign nations, contrary to the [Sherman Anti-Trust Act.]

The fundamental question is whether conceding that the existence of a monopoly in manufacture is established by the evidence, that monopoly can be directly suppressed under the act of Congress in the mode attempted by this bill.

It cannot be denied that the power of a State to protect the lives, health, and property of its citizens, and to preserve good order and the public morals, "the power to govern men and things within the limits of its dominion," is a power originally and always belonging to the States, not surrendered by them to the general government, nor directly restrained by the Constitution of the United States, and essentially exclusive.

The argument is that the power to control the manufacture of refined sugar is a monopoly over a necessary of life, to the enjoyment of which by a large part of the population of the

United States interstate commerce is indispensable, and that, therefore, the general government in the exercise of the power to regulate commerce may repress such monopoly directly and set aside the instruments which have created it. But this argument cannot be confined to necessaries of life merely, and must include all articles of general consumption. Doubtless the power to control the manufacture of a given thing involves in a certain sense the control of its disposition, but this is a secondary and not the primary sense; and although the exercise of that power may result in bringing the operation of commerce into play, it does not control it, and affects it only incidentally and indirectly. Commerce succeeds to manufacture, and is not a part of it. The power to regulate commerce is the power to prescribe the rule by which commerce shall be governed, and is a power independent of the power to suppress monopoly. But it may operate in repression of monopoly whenever that comes within the rules by which commerce is governed or whenever the transaction is itself a monopoly of commerce.

It is vital that the independence of the commercial power and of the police power, and the delimitation between them, however sometimes perplexing, should always be recognized and observed, for while the one furnishes the strongest bond of union, the other is essential to the preservation of the autonomy of the States as required by our dual form of government; and acknowledged evils, however grave and urgent they may appear to be, had better be borne, than the risk be run, in the effort to suppress them, of more serious consequences

by resort to expedients of even doubtful constitutionality.

Contracts, combinations, or conspiracies to control domestic enterprise in manufacture, agriculture, mining, production in all its forms, or to raise or lower prices or wages, might unquestionably tend to restrain external as well as domestic trade, but the restraint would be an indirect result, however inevitable and whatever its extent, and such result would not necessarily determine the object of the contract, combination, or conspiracy.

It was in the light of well-settled principles that the act of July 2, 1890, was framed. Congress did not attempt thereby to assert the power to deal with monopoly directly as such; or to limit and restrict the rights of corporations created by the States or the citizens of the States in the acquisition, control, or disposition of property; or to regulate or prescribe the price or prices at which such property or the products thereof should be sold; or to make criminal the acts of persons in the acquisition and control of property which the States of their residence or creation sanctioned or permitted. Aside from the provisions applicable where Congress might exercise municipal power, what the law struck at was combinations, contracts, and conspiracies to monopolize trade and commerce among the several States or with foreign nations; but the contracts and acts of the defendants related exclusively to the acquisition of the Philadelphia refineries and the business of sugar refining in Pennsylvania, and bore no direct relation to commerce between the States or with foreign nations.

Note: Anti-Trust Law in the Progressive Era

The decision in *E. C. Knight* defined the extent of the federal commerce power until the late 1930s, effectively preventing Congress from regulating manufacturing activity. Nonetheless, the Supreme Court sustained the application of the Sherman Anti-Trust Act in a variety of contexts where the authority of Congress was clear. In *United States* v. *Trans-Missouri Freight Association* (1897), for instance, the Court invalidated price-fixing arrangements among a number of railroad companies.

A wave of corporate mergers in the 1890s led to heightened public concern about concentrated private economic power and predatory business practices. In the early twentieth century, President Theodore Roosevelt sought to reinvigorate anti-trust enforcement by instituting a well-publicized program of "trust-busting." He prevailed in the important case of *Northern Securities Co.* v. *United States* (1904) when the Supreme Court struck down a railroad holding company that controlled three lines in the Pacific Northwest as an anticompetitive restraint of trade. The government also secured a major victory in *Standard Oil Company* v. *United States* (1911). In this case the Supreme Court ordered the dissolution of the Standard Oil Company.

In addition, the Court gingerly broadened the reach of federal anti-trust enforcement by adopting the stream of commerce doctrine. Declaring that "commerce among the States is not a technical legal conception, but a practical one, drawn from the course of business," the Court ruled in *Swift and Co.* v. *United States* (1905) that the Sherman Act could be applied to the collusive practices of local meat packers that were part of a wider current of trade among the states. This decision foreshadowed a broader reading of the federal commerce power.

Although they applied the Sherman Act in a number of cases, the justices differed as to the appropriate standard for construing the statute. Justice Edward D. White consistently objected to a literal reading of the act and urged adoption of the rule of reason. Under this approach only unreasonable restraints of trade were prohibited. Initially rejected by the Court majority, White's rule of reason interpretation was affirmed in the Standard Oil decision. This standard, of course, left a good deal of discretion in the hands of judges to determine what business practices violated the Sherman Anti-Trust Act. Progressives charged that the rule of reason weakened the anti-trust laws. In 1914 Congress attempted to strengthen the Sherman Act with passage of the Clayton Anti-Trust Act. The rule of reason, however, remains the standard mode of evaluating business practices under the anti-trust laws.

Populist Platform Adopted at St. Louis
1892

The People's Party, 1890s, better known as the Populists, provided a political expression of farmers' discontents. Its 1892 platform contained most of the prevalent proposals and nostrums for political and economic reform, including coinage of silver to inflate the currency, electoral reforms like the Australian (secret) ballot, restrictions on open immigration, an eight-hour working day, an income tax, the initiative and referendum, government ownership of railroads and telegraph companies, and opposition to subsidies to corporations. There is room to doubt that any of these proposals really addressed the root causes of agrarian discontent. Nonetheless, Populism represented the first important attempt in American history to demand that the government curb private economic power and affirmatively aid the disadvantaged. Conservatives saw portents of class warfare and expropriation of property in the Populists' program.

PREAMBLE

The conditions which surround us best justify our co-operation; we meet in the midst of a nation brought to the verge of moral, political, and material ruin. Corruption dominates the ballot-box, the Legislatures, the Congress, and touches even the ermine of the bench. The people are demoralized; most of the States have been compelled to isolate the voters at the polling places to prevent universal intimidation and bribery. The newspapers are largely subsidized or muzzled, public opinion silenced, business prostrated, homes covered with mortgages, labor impoverished, and the land concentrating in the hands of the capitalists. The urban workmen are denied the right to organize for self-protection, imported pauperized labor beats down their wages, a hireling standing army, unrecognized by our laws, is established to shoot them down, and they are rapidly degenerating into European conditions. The fruits of the toil of millions are boldly stolen to build up colossal fortunes for a few, unprecedented in the history of mankind; and the possessors of these, in turn, despise the Republic and endanger liberty. From the same prolific womb of governmental injustice we breed the two great classes—tramps and millionaires.

The national power to create money is appropriated to enrich bond-holders; a vast public debt payable in legal-tender currency has been funded into gold-bearing bonds, thereby adding millions to the burdens of the people.

Silver, which has been accepted as coin since the dawn of history, has been demonetized to add to the purchasing power of gold by decreasing the value of all forms of property as well as human labor, and the supply of currency is purposely abridged to fatten usurers, bankrupt enterprise, and enslave industry.

A vast conspiracy against mankind has been organized on two continents, and it is rapidly taking possession of the world. If not met and overthrown at once it forebodes terrible social convulsions, the destruction of civilization, or the establishment of an absolute despotism.

We have witnessed for more than a quarter of a century the struggles of the two great political parties for power and plunder, while grievous wrongs have been inflicted upon the suffering people. We charge that the controlling influences dominating both these parties have permitted the existing dreadful conditions to develop without serious effort to prevent or restrain them.

Neither do they now promise us any substantial reform. They have agreed together to ignore, in the coming campaign, every issue but one. They propose to drown the outcries of a plundered people with the uproar of a sham battle over the tariff, so that capitalists, corporations, national banks, rings, trusts, watered stock, the demonetization of silver and the oppressions of the usurer may all be lost sight of. They propose to sacrifice our homes, lives, and children on the altar of mammon; to destroy the multitude in order to secure corruption funds from the millionaires.

♦ ♦ ♦

Our country finds itself confronted by conditions for which there is no precedent in the history of the world; our annual agricultural productions amount to billions of dollars in value, which must, within a few weeks or months, be exchanged for billions of dollars' worth of commodities consumed in their production; the existing currency supply is wholly inadequate to make this exchange; the results are falling prices, the formation of combines and rings, the impoverishment of the producing class. We pledge ourselves that if given power we will labor to correct these evils by wise and reasonable legislation, in accordance with the terms of our platform.

We believe that the power of government—in other words, of the people—should be expanded (as in the case of the postal service) as rapidly and as far as the good sense of an intelligent people and the teachings of experience shall justify, to the end that oppression, injustice, and poverty shall eventually cease in the land.

TAXATION OF INCOME

One of the sharpest controversies of the late nineteenth century concerned the authority of Congress to levy an income tax. The Constitution conferred broad powers of taxation upon Congress, but restricted the imposition of direct taxes by the requirement that such taxes "shall be apportioned among the several states" according to population. The apportionment requirement rendered impractical any direct tax that could not be readily apportioned. The direct tax clause raised interpretive problems that centered on the meaning of "direct taxes." In *Springer* v. *United States* (1881) the Supreme Court upheld the Civil War income tax as applied to personal earnings against the contention that it was a direct tax that had to be apportioned according to population. The 1862 income tax, however, grew unpopular following the end of hostilities, and Congress allowed the levy to expire.

During the 1890s there was agitation, primarily in the southern and western states, to revive the income tax. The Populists proposed a graduated income tax during the presidential election of 1892. Proponents of an income tax hoped to shift the national tax burden from consumption to wealth, and to make possible a reduction in the high tariff rates. In 1894 Congress enacted the first peacetime income tax, imposing a flat tax of 2 percent on incomes over $4,000 a year and on corporate profits. It was estimated that the levy would affect less than 1 percent of the population. Most of the taxpayers were residents of the industrial Northeast. Debate over the income tax laid bare political, sectional, and class divisions in American society. Opponents charged that the levy constituted class legislation because it breached the widely accepted constitutional maxim enjoining equality of rights and duties.

In the famous case of *Pollock* v. *Farmers' Loan and Trust Co.* (1895), the Supreme Court was called upon to determine whether the levy on income was a direct tax. Implicit in this issue was a more fundamental question about the legitimacy of using governmental power to change the distribution of wealth. Speaking for a divided Court in two opinions, Chief Justice Melville W. Fuller found that the levy on income from land and from personal property constituted a direct tax that had to be apportioned. This holding rendered the entire income tax unconstitutional. Fuller saw the direct tax clause as protecting the role of the states in the federal system by limiting national taxing authority. Concurring, Justice Stephen J. Field pictured the income tax controversy in broad and dark terms: "The present assault upon capital is but the beginning. It will be but the stepping-stone to others, larger and more sweeping, till our political contests will become a war of the poor against the rich; a war constantly growing in intensity and bitterness." Not until public opinion changed markedly in the early twentieth century would the Sixteenth Amendment, adopted in 1913, effectively overrule *Pollock* and open the way for a federal tax on income.

JOSEPH H. CHOATE

Arguments for Appellant in the *Income Tax Cases* (*Pollock* v. *Farmers' Loan and Trust Co.*)
157 U.S. 429 (1895)

Joseph Choate was one of the most eminent attorneys in the United States at the close of the nineteenth century. He appeared frequently before the Supreme Court and spearheaded the legal attack on the 1894 income tax. Choate's argument suggests the emotions aroused by this controversial levy.

I look upon this case with very different eyes from those of either the Attorney General or his associate who has just closed. I believe there are private rights of property here to be pro-tected; that we have a right to come to this court and ask for their protection, and that this court has a right, without asking leave of the Attorney General or of any counsel, to hear our plea.

The act of Congress which we are impugning before you is communistic in its purposes and tendencies, and is defended here upon principles as communistic, socialistic—what shall I call them—populistic as ever have been addressed to any political assembly in the world.

I do not believe that any member of this court ever has sat or ever will sit to hear and decide a case the consequences of which will be so far-reaching as this—not even the venerable member [Justice Field] who survives from the early days of the civil war, and has sat upon every question of reconstruction, of national destiny, of state destiny that has come up during the last thirty years. No member of this court will live long enough to hear a case which will involve a question of more impor-tance than this, the preservation of the funda-mental rights of private property and equality before the law, and the ability of the people of these United States to rely upon the guaranties of the Constitution. If it be true, as my friend said in closing, that the passions of the people are aroused on this subject, if it be true that a mighty army of sixty million citizens is likely to be incensed by this decision, it is the more vital to the future welfare of this country that this court again resolutely and courageously declare, as Marshall did, that it has the power to set aside an act of Congress violative of the Constitution, and that it will not hesitate in ex-ecuting that power, no matter what the threat-ened consequences of popular or populistic wrath may be.

JUDICIAL REACTION TO THE REGULATORY STATE

So pervasive an innovation in the structure and functioning of American government as the administrative state was bound to raise constitutional questions that had to be resolved in the courts. Two themes dominate judicial reaction to regulation after the Civil War. The first was the appearance of the doctrine of substantive due process, as articulated by Thomas M. Cooley in his treatise *Constitutional Limitations*. Substantive due process provided a mod-ernized replacement for the old concept of higher law articulated in Justice Samuel Chase's opinion in *Calder* v. *Bull* (1798). The acceptance of the doctrine was followed by the emer-gence of a corollary, the doctrine of liberty of contract, which was to bedevil labor reform well into the twentieth century. Substantive due process and liberty of contract provided par-adigms of constitutional adjudication that dominated American law until the constitutional revolution of 1937.

The second theme developed out of the first. Substantive due process came into conflict with doctrines of police power at both the state and the federal levels. Out of this conflict flowed two streams of precedent, the one upholding governmental regulatory power and the other subordinating it to doctrines of individual liberty.

THE ORIGINS OF SUBSTANTIVE DUE PROCESS

Wynehamer v. *The People*
13 N.Y. 378 (1856)

There has long been disagreement as to whether the due process norm, incorporated into the Fifth and Fourteenth Amendments, imposed substantive as well as procedural constraints on governmental authority. During the antebellum era some state courts began to wrestle with substantive interpretations of due process. They concluded that due process entailed more than adherence to orderly procedure in judicial proceedings, and limited legislative actions that arbitrarily infringed upon fundamental but unwritten rights. Given the importance of property rights to the Framers of the Constitution, it is not surprising that courts initially focused on due process as a guarantee of property ownership. The due process principle found expression in the frequently repeated maxim that taking the property of A and giving it to B constituted a deprivation of property without due process. See Justice Samuel Chase in Calder v. Bull, *3 U.S. 386, 388, (1798).*

The Wynehamer *case was the most significant use of the substantive component of due process by a state court before the Civil War. In 1855 a New York prohibition statute declared alcoholic beverages to be a nuisance and made it illegal to sell liquor. This measure was justified as a step toward alleviating intemperance and pauperism. The defendant Wynehamer was convicted and fined for selling liquor in violation of the statute. At issue before the New York Court of Appeals was application of the statute to stocks of liquor already existing when the law took effect.*

When the simple question is, whether [the legislature] can confiscate and destroy property lawfully acquired by the citizen in intoxicating liquors, then we are to remember that all property is equally sacred in the view of the constitution, and therefore that speculations as to its chemical or scientific qualities, or the mischief engendered by its abuse, have very little to do with the inquiry. Property, if protected by the constitution from such legislation as that we are now considering, is protected because it is property innocently acquired under existing laws, and not upon any theory which even so much as opens the question of its utility. If intoxicating liquors are property, the constitution does not permit a legislative estimate to be made of its usefulness, with a view to its destruction. In a word, that which belongs to the citizen in the sense of property, and as such has to him commercial value, cannot be pronounced worthless or pernicious, and so destroyed or deprived of its essential attributes.

♦ ♦ ♦

In a government like ours, theories of public good or public necessity may be so plausible, or even so truthful, as to command popular majorities. But whether truthful or plausible merely, and by whatever numbers they are assented to, there are some absolute private rights beyond their reach, and among these the constitution places the right of property. It must follow that any scheme of legislation which, aiming at the destruction of this use, makes the keeping or sale of them as a beverage, in any quantity and by any person, a criminal offence—which declares them a public nuisance—which subjects them to seizure and physical destruction, and denies a legal remedy if they are taken by lawless force or robbery, must be deemed, in every beneficial sense, to deprive the owner of the enjoyment of his property.

♦ ♦ ♦

It has been urged upon us, that the power of the legislature is restricted, not only by the express provisions of the written constitution, but by limitations implied from the nature and form of our government; that, aside from all special restriction, the right to enact such laws is not among the delegated powers of the legislature, and that the act in question is void, as against the fundamental principles of liberty, and against common reason and natural rights. High authority, certainly, has been cited to show that laws which, although not specially prohibited by written constitutions are repugnant to reason, and subvert clearly vested rights, are invalid, and must so be declared by the judiciary.

I am reluctant to enter upon this field of inquiry, satisfied as I am that no rule can be laid down in terms which may not contain the germ of great mischief to society, by giving to private opinion and speculation a license to oppose themselves to the just and legitimate powers of government.

♦ ♦ ♦

I am brought, therefore to a more particular consideration of the limitations of power contained in the fundamental law: "No member of this state shall be disfranchised or deprived of any of the rights or privileges secured to any citizen thereof, unless by the law of the land of the judgment of his peers. No person shall be deprived of life, liberty or property, without due process of law; nor shall private property be taken for public use without just compensation." These provisions have been incorporated, in substance, into all our state constitutions.

No doubt, it seems to me, can be admitted of the meaning of these provisions. To say, as has been suggested, that "the law of the land," or "due process of law," may mean the very act of legislation which deprives the citizen of his rights, privileges or property, leads to a simple absurdity. The constitution would then mean, that no person shall be deprived of his property or rights, unless the legislature shall pass a law to effectuate the wrong, and this would be throwing the restraint entirely away. The true interpretation of these constitutional phrases is, that where rights are acquired by the citizen under the existing law, there is no power in any branch of the government to take them away; but where they are held contrary to the existing law, or are forfeited by its violation, then they may be taken from him—not by an act of the legislature, but in the due administration of the law itself, before the judicial tribunals of the state.

Bond Repudiation and Judicial Review

In the mid–nineteenth century many state and local governments issued bonds to encourage economic development, most often the construction of railroad lines. As certain of these projects failed or proved disappointing, public sentiment cooled and some indebted localities sought to repudiate their bonded debt. The bonds, however, had typically passed into the hands of bona fide investors. They saw debt repudiation as little more than a theft of property. The bondholders appealed to the federal courts for enforcement of these obligations.

In 1862 the Iowa Supreme Court, reversing an earlier decision, ruled that under the state constitution localities could not issue bonds to assist railroad construction. The upshot of this decision was to invalidate county bonds now held by out-of-state investors. In *Gelpcke* v. *City of Dubuque* (1864) the Supreme Court insisted that the state courts could not impair the contractual rights of bondholders by a retroactive change in the law. Apparently premised on a federal common law of commerce, the *Gelpcke* decision determined that bonds valid when issued could not be invalidated by subsequent state court rulings. *Gelpcke* curtailed state judicial authority, and has been seen by some historians as a harbinger of the Supreme Court's later affirmation of a substantive reading of the due process clause. The decision also strengthened investor confidence in the stability of municipal bonds. In the wake of *Gelpcke* the Supreme Court heard hundreds of bond repudiation cases and invariably upheld the validity of local bonds. This line of cases protected investment capital and was consistent with a policy of stimulating economic growth.

The Bradley Dissent in *Slaughterhouse*

The *Slaughterhouse Cases*
16 Wall. (83 U.S.) 36 (1873)

The origins of substantive due process in the United States Supreme Court may be traced to dissenting opinions in the Slaughterhouse Cases *of 1873. Justices Stephen J. Field and Joseph*

P. Bradley maintained that the new Civil War Amendments had fundamentally altered both the nature of the federal system and the structure of protections for the rights of individuals. They differed in their emphases, with Field finding protection for the right to pursue a calling in the new privileges-and-immunities clause of the Fourteenth Amendment exclusively. Bradley adverted to the due process clause as well, and articulated the doctrine of substantive due process. His vision would triumph within two decades.

Mr. Justice Bradley, . . . dissenting:

In my judgment, the right of any citizen to follow whatever lawful employment he chooses to adopt (submitting himself to all lawful regulations) is one of his most valuable rights, and one which the legislature of a State cannot invade, whether restrained by its own constitution or not.

The right of a State to regulate the conduct of its citizens is undoubtedly a very broad and extensive one, and not to be lightly restricted. But there are certain fundamental rights which this right of regulation cannot infringe. It may prescribe the manner of their exercise but it cannot subvert the rights themselves. I speak now of the rights of citizens of any free government.

The people of this country brought with them to its shores the rights of Englishmen; the rights, which had been wrested from English sovereigns at various periods of the nation's history. One of these fundamental rights was expressed in these words, found in Magna Charta: "No freeman shall be taken or imprisoned, or be disseized of his freehold or liberties or free customs, or be outlawed or exiled, or any otherwise destroyed; nor will we pass upon him or condemn him but by lawful judgment of his peers or by the law of the land." English constitutional writers expound this article as rendering life, liberty, and property inviolable, except by due process of law. This is the very right which the plaintiffs in error claim in this case. Another of these rights was that of habeas corpus, or the right of having any invasion of personal liberty judicially examined into, at once, by a competent judicial magistrate. Blackstone classifies these fundamental rights under three heads, as the absolute rights of individuals, to wit: the right of personal security, the right of personal liberty, and the right of private property. And of the last he says: "The third absolute right, inherent in every Eng-

lishman, is that of property, which consists in the free use, enjoyment, and disposal of all his acquisitions, without any control or diminution save only by the laws of the land."

Rights to life, liberty, and the pursuit of happiness are equivalent to the rights of life, liberty and property. These are the fundamental rights which can only be taken away by due process of law, and which can only be interfered with, or the enjoyment of which can only be modified, by lawful regulations necessary or proper for the mutual good of all; and the rights, I contend, belong to the citizens of every free government.

For the preservation, exercise, and enjoyment of these rights the individual citizen, as a necessity, must be left free to adopt such calling, profession, or trade as may seem to him most conducive to that end. Without this right he cannot be a freeman. This right to choose one's calling when chosen, is a man's property and right. Liberty and property are not protected where these rights are arbitrarily assailed.

II. The next question to be determined in this case is: Is a monopoly or exclusive right, given to one person, or corporation, to the exclusion of all others, to keep slaughterhouses in a district of nearly twelve hundred square miles, for the supply of meat for a great city, a reasonable regulation of that employment which the legislature has a right to impose?

The keeping of a slaughter-house is part of, and incidental to, the trade of a butcher—one of the ordinary occupations of human life. To compel a butcher, or rather all the butchers of a large city and an extensive district, to slaughter their cattle in another person's slaughter-house and pay him a toll therefor is such a restriction upon the trade as materially to interfere with its prosecution. It is onerous, unreasonable, arbitrary, and unjust. It has none of the qualities of a police regulation. If it were really a police regulation, it would undoubtedly be within the power of the legislature. That portion of the act which requires all slaughter-houses to be located below the city, and to be subject to inspection, &c., is clearly a police regulation. That portion which allows no one but the favored company to build, own, or have slaughter-houses is not a police regulation, and has not the faintest semblance of one. It is one of those arbitrary and unjust laws made in the interest of a few scheming individuals, by which some of the Southern States have, within the past few years, been so deplorably oppressed and impoverished. It seems to me strange that it can be viewed in any other light.

The amendment also prohibits any State from depriving any person (citizen or otherwise) of life, liberty, or property, without due process of law.

In my view, a law which prohibits a large class of citizens from adopting a lawful employment, or from following a lawful employment previously adopted, does deprive them of liberty as well as property, without due process of law. Their right of choice is a portion of their liberty; their occupation is their property. Such a law also deprives those citizens of the equal protection of the laws, contrary to the last clause of the section.

It is futile to argue that none but persons of the African race are intended to be benefited by this amendment. They may have been the primary cause of the amendment, but its language is general, embracing all citizens, and I think it was purposely so expressed.

The mischief to be remedied was not merely slavery and its incidents and consequences; but that spirit of insubordination and disloyalty to the National government which had troubled the country for so many years in some of the States, and that intolerance of free speech and free discussion which often rendered life and property insecure, and led to much unequal legislation. The amendment was an attempt to give voice to the strong National yearning for that time and that condition of things, in which American citizenship should be a sure guaranty of safety, and in which every citizen of the United States might stand erect on every portion of its soil, in the full enjoyment of every right and privilege belonging to a freeman, without fear of violence or molestation.

REAFFIRMATION OF THE POLICE POWER

Munn v. Illinois
94 U.S. 113 (1877)

Munn *upheld the constitutionality of the Illinois Granger laws, which regulated the prices charged by railroads and grain elevators. But the scope of* Munn *would soon be curtailed. Even Chief Justice Morrison R. Waite, writing for the majority here, conceded that a regulatory statute might impinge on due process constraints, thus according implicit recognition to substantive due process. Moreover, Justice Stephen J. Field, in a forceful dissenting opinion, argued that the due process norm afforded substantive protection to the right of owners to use and derive income from their property. Field's views gradually gained ascendancy.*

The question to be determined in this case is whether the general assembly of Illinois can, under the limitations upon the legislative power of the States imposed by the Constitution of the United States, fix by law the maximum of charges for the storage of grain in warehouses at Chicago and other places in the State having not less than one hundred thousand inhabitants. It is claimed that such a law is repugnant . . . to that part of amendment 14 which ordains that no State shall "deprive any person of life, liberty, or property, without due process of law, nor deny to any person within its jurisdiction the equal protection of the laws."

◆ ◆ ◆

While this provision of the amendment is new in the Constitution of the United States, as a limitation upon the powers of the States, it is old as a principle of civilized government. It is found in Magna Charta, and, in substance if not in form, in nearly or quite all the constitutions that have been from time to time adopted by the several States of the Union. By the Fifth Amendment it was introduced into the Constitution of the United States as a limitation upon the powers of the national government, and by the Fourteenth, as a guaranty against any encroachment upon the acknowledged right of citizenship by the legislatures of the states.

◆ ◆ ◆

When one becomes a member of society, he necessarily parts with some rights or privileges which, as an individual not affected by his relations to others, he might retain. "A body politic," as aptly defined in the preamble of the Constitution of Massachusetts, "is a social compact by which the whole people convenants with each citizen, and each citizen with the whole people, that all shall be governed by certain laws for the common good." This does not confer power upon the whole people to control rights which are purely and exclusively private . . . but it does authorize the establishment of laws requiring each citizen to so conduct himself, and so use his own property, as not unnecessarily to injure another. This is the very essence of government. . . . From this source came the police powers of government . . . inherent in every sovereignty, . . . that is to say, . . . the power to govern men and things. Under these powers the government regulates the conduct of its citizens one towards another, and the manner in which each shall use his own property, when such regulation becomes necessary for the public good. In their exercise it has been customary in England from time immemorial, and in this country from its first colonization, to regulate ferries, common carriers,

bakers, millers, wharfingers, innkeepers, &c., and in so doing to fix a maximum of charge to be made for services rendered, accommodations furnished, and articles sold.

◆ ◆ ◆

From this it is apparent that, down to the time of the adoption of the Fourteenth Amendment, it was not supposed that statutes regulating the use, or even the price of the use, of private property necessarily deprived an owner of his property without due process of law. Under some circumstances they may, but not under all. The amendment does not change the law in this particular: it simply prevents the States from doing that which will operate as such a deprivation.

This brings us to inquire as to the principles upon which this power of regulation rests, in order that we may determine what is within and what [is] without its operative effect. Looking, then, to the common law, from whence came the right which the Constitution protects, we find that when private property is "affected with a public interest, it ceases to be *juris privati* only." This was said by Lord Chief Justice Hale more than two hundred years ago, in his treatise *De Portibus Maris,* . . . and has been accepted without objection as an essential element in the law of property ever since. Property does become clothed with a public interest when used in a manner to make it of public consequence, and affect the community at large. When, therefore, one devotes his property to a use in which the public has an interest, he in effect, grants to the public an interest in that use, and must submit to be controlled by the public for the common good, to the extent of the interest he has thus created. He may withdraw his grant by discontinuing the use; but, so long as he maintains the use, he must submit to the control.

◆ ◆ ◆

This indicates very clearly that during the twenty years in which this peculiar business had been assuming its present "immense proportions," something had occurred which led the whole body of people to suppose that remedies such as are usually employed to prevent abuses by virtual monopolies might not be inappropriate here. For our purposes we must assume that, if a state of facts could exist that would justify such legislation, it actually did exist when the statute now under consideration was passed. For us the question is one of power, not of expediency. If no state of circumstances could exist to justify such a statute, then we may declare this one void, because in excess of the legislative power of the State. But if it could we must presume it did. Of the propriety of legislative interference within the scope of legislative power, the legislature is the exclusive judge.

Neither is it a matter of any moment that no precedent can be found for a statute precisely like this. It is conceded that the business is one of recent origin, that its growth has been rapid, and that it is already of great importance. And it must also be conceded that it is a business in which the whole public has a direct and positive interest. It presents, therefore, a case for the application of a long-known and well-established principle in social science, and this statute simply extends the law so as to meet this new development of commercial progress. There is no attempt to compel these owners to grant the public an interest in their property, but to declare their obligations if they use it in this particular manner.

◆ ◆ ◆

It is insisted, however, that the owner of property is entitled to a reasonable compensation for its use, even though it be obtained with a public interest, and that what is reasonable is a judicial and not a legislative question.

As has already been shown, the practice has been otherwise. In countries where the common law prevails, it has been customary from time immemorial for the legislature to declare what shall be a reasonable compensation under such circumstances, or, perhaps more properly speaking, to fix a maximum beyond which any charge made would be unreasonable. Undoubtedly, in mere private contracts, relating to matters in which the public has no interest, what is reasonable must be ascertained judicially. But this is because the legislature has no control over such a contract. So, too, in matters which do effect the public interest, and as to which

legislative control may be exercised, if there are no statutory regulations upon the subject, the courts must determine what is reasonable. The controlling fact is the power to regulate at all. If that exists, the right to establish the maximum of charge, as one of the means of regulation, is implied.

◆ ◆ ◆

We know that this is a power which may be abused; but that is no argument against its existence. For protection against abuses by legislatures the people must resort to the polls, not to the courts.

Justice Field, dissenting.

◆ ◆ ◆

The doctrine of the State court, that no one is deprived of his property, within the meaning of the constitutional inhibition, so long as he retains its title and possession, and the doctrine of this court, that, whenever one's property is used in such a manner as to affect the community at large, it becomes by that fact clothed with a public interest, and ceases to be *juris privati* only, appear to me to destroy, for all useful purposes, the efficacy of the constitutional guaranty. All that is beneficial in property arises from its use, and the fruits of that use; and whatever deprives a person of them deprives him of all that is desirable or valuable in the title and possession. If the constitutional guaranty extends no further than to prevent a deprivation of title and possession, and allows a deprivation of use, and the fruits of that use, it does not merit the encomiums it has received. Unless I have misread the history of the provision now incorporated into all our State constitutions, and by the Fifth and Fourteenth Amendments into our Federal Constitution, and have misunderstood the interpretation it has received, it is not thus limited in its scope, and thus impotent for good. It has a much more extended operation than either court, State, or Federal has given to it. The provision, it is to be observed, places property under the same protection as life and liberty. Except by due process of law, no State can deprive any person of either. The provision has been supposed to secure to every individual the essential conditions for the pursuit of happiness; and for that reason has not been heretofore, and should never be, construed in any narrow or restricted sense.

No State "shall deprive any person of life, liberty, or property without due process of law," says the Fourteenth Amendment to the Constitution. By the term "life," as here used, something more is meant than mere animal existence. The inhibition against its deprivation extends to all those limbs and faculties by which life is enjoyed. The provision equally prohibits the mutilation of the body by the amputation of an arm or leg, or the putting out of an eye, or the destruction of any other organ of the body through which the soul communicates with the outer world. The deprivation not only of life, but whatever God has given to every one with life, for its growth and enjoyment, is prohibited by the provision in question, if its efficacy be not frittered away by judicial decision.

By the term "liberty," as used in the provision, something more is meant than mere freedom from physical restraint or the bounds of a prison. It means freedom to go where one may choose, and to act in such manner, not inconsistent with the equal rights of others, as his judgment may dictate for the promotion of his happiness; that is, to pursue such callings and avocations as may be most suitable to develop his capacities, and give to them their highest enjoyment.

The same liberal construction which is required for the protection of life and liberty, in all particulars in which life and liberty are of any value, should be applied to the protection of private property. If the legislature of a State, under pretence of providing for the public good, or for any other reason, can determine, against the consent of the owner, the uses to which private property shall be devoted, or the prices which the owner shall receive for its uses, it can deprive him of the property as completely as by a special act for its confiscation or destruction. If, for instance, the owner is prohibited from using his building for the purposes for which it was designed, it is of little consequence that he is permitted to retain the title and possession; or, if he is compelled to take as compensation for its use less than the expenses to which he is subjected by its ownership, he is, for all practical purposes, deprived of the property, as effectually as if the legislature had ordered his forcible dispossession. If it be admitted that the legislature has any control over the compensation, the extent of that compensation becomes a mere matter of legislative discretion. The amount fixed will operate as a partial destruction of the value of the property, if it fall below the amount which the owner would obtain by contract, and, practically, as a complete destruction, if it be less than the cost of retaining its possession. There is, indeed, no protection of any value under the constitutional provision, which does not extend to the use and income of the property, as well as to its title and possession.

Note: Federal Judicial Review of State Rate Regulations

By the 1880s federal judges began to move away from the *Munn* decision and insist that state regulatory authority did not encompass the power to impose unremunerative or confiscatory rates. In *Chicago, Milwaukee and St. Paul Railway Company* v. *Minnesota* (1890), the Supreme Court ruled that unless a railroad could charge reasonable rates, it was in effect deprived of its property without due process of law. Therefore federal courts could scrutinize the reasonableness of state-imposed rates. In *Smyth* v. *Ames* (1898) the Court adopted the fair value rule as the baseline for determining the reasonableness of rates. This line of cases curtailed state regulation of railroad and utility charges, and represented endorsement by the Supreme Court of the view that the due process norm placed substantive as well as procedural limits on government.

SUBSTANTIVE DUE PROCESS IN THE STATE COURTS

In re Jacobs
98 N.Y. 98 (1885)

The New York Court of Appeals was in the forefront among the state courts in the development of due process as a safeguard for economic rights. In this opinion, Judge Robert Earl touched on all the elements of the doctrine as it would be fully developed in the next generation.

The relator Jacobs was arrested on the 14th day of May, 1884, [for violating] "An act to improve the public health by prohibiting the manufacture of cigars and preparation of tobacco in any form in tenement-houses in certain cases, and regulating the use of tenement-houses in certain cases."

♦ ♦ ♦

What does this act attempt to do? In form, it makes it a crime for a cigarmaker in New York and Brooklyn . . . to carry on a perfectly lawful trade in his own home. Whether he owns the tenement-house or has hired a room therein for the purpose of prosecuting his trade, he cannot manufacture therein his own tobacco into cigars for his own use or for sale, and he will become a criminal for doing that which is perfectly lawful outside of the two cities named—everywhere else, so far as we are able to learn, in the whole world. He must either abandon the trade by which he earns a livelihood for himself and family, or, if able, procure a room elsewhere, or hire himself out to one who has a room upon such terms as, under the fierce competition of trade and the inexorable laws of supply and demand, he may be able to obtain from his employer. He may choose to do his work where he can have the supervision of his family and their help, and such choice is denied him. He may choose to work for himself rather than for a taskmaster, and he is left without freedom of choice. He may desire the advantage of cheap production in consequence of his cheap rent and family help, and of this he is deprived. In the unceasing struggle for success and existence which pervades all societies of men, he may

be deprived of that which will enable him to maintain his hold, and to survive. . . . It is therefore, plain that this law interferes with the profitable and free use of his property by the owner or lessee of a tenement-house who is a cigarmaker, and trammels him in the application of his industry and the disposition of his labor, and thus, in a strictly legitimate sense, it arbitrarily deprives him of his property and of some portion of his personal liberty.

The constitutional guaranty that no person shall be deprived of his property without due process of law may be violated without the physical taking of property for public or private use. Property may be destroyed, or its value may be annihilated; it is owned and kept for some useful purpose and it has no value unless it can be used. Its capability for enjoyment and adaptability to some use are essential characteristics and attributes without which property cannot be conceived; and hence any law which destroys it or its value, or takes away any of its essential attributes, deprives the owner of his property.

The constitutional guaranty would be of little worth, if the legislature could, without compensation, destroy property or its value, deprive the owner of its use, deny him the right to live in his own house, or to work at any lawful trade therein. If the legislature has the power under the Constitution to prohibit the prosecution of one lawful trade in a tenement-house, then it may prevent the prosecution of all trades therein.

♦ ♦ ♦

So, too, one may be deprived of his liberty and his constitutional rights thereto violated without the actual imprisonment or restraint of his person. Liberty, in its broad sense as understood in this country, means the right, not only of freedom from actual servitude, imprisonment or restraint, but the right of one to use his faculties in all lawful ways, to live and work where he will, to earn his livelihood in any lawful calling, and to pursue any lawful trade or avocation. All laws, therefore, which impair or trammel these rights, which limit one in his choice of a trade or profession, or confine him to work or live in a specified locality, or exclude him from his own house, or restrain his otherwise lawful movements (except as such laws may be passed in the exercise by the legislature of the police power, which will be noticed later), are infringements upon his fundamental rights of liberty, which are under constitutional protection.

♦　♦　♦

But the claim is made that the legislature could pass this act in the exercise of the police power which every sovereign State possesses. That power is very broad and comprehensive, and is exercised to promote the health, comfort, safety and welfare of society. . . . Under it the conduct of an individual and the use of property may be regulated so as to interfere, to some extent, with the freedom of the one and the enjoyment of the other; and in cases of great emergency engendering overruling necessity, property may be taken or destroyed without compensation, and without what is commonly called due process of law. The limit of the power cannot be accurately defined and the courts have not been able or willing definitely to circumscribe it. But the power, however broad and extensive, is not above the Constitution.

♦　♦　♦

These citations are sufficient to show that the police power is not without limitations, and that in its exercise the legislature must respect the great fundamental rights guaranteed by the Constitution. If this were otherwise, the power of the legislature would be practically without limitation. In the assumed exercise of the police power in the interest of the health, the welfare or the safety of the public, every right of the citizen might be invaded and every constitutional barrier swept away.

Generally it is for the legislature to deter-mine what laws and regulations are needed to protect the public health and secure the public comfort and safety, and while its measures are calculated, intended, convenient and appropriate to accomplish these ends, the exercise of its discretion is not subject to review by the courts. But they must have some relation to these ends. Under the mere guise of police regulations, personal rights and private property cannot be arbitrarily invaded, and the determination of the legislature is not final or conclusive. If it passes an act ostensibly for the public health, and thereby destroys or takes away the property of a citizen, or interferes with his personal liberty, then it is for the courts to scrutinize the act and see whether it really relates to and is convenient and appropriate to promote health.

It is plain that this is not a health law, and that it has no relation whatever to the public health. Under the guise of promoting the public health the legislature might as well have banished cigarmaking from all the cities of the State, or confined it to a single city or town, or have placed under a similar ban the trade of a baker, of a tailor, of a shoemaker, of a woodcarver, or of any other of the innocuous trades carried on by artisans in their own homes. The power would have been the same, and its exercise, so far as it concerns fundamental constitutional rights, could have been justified by the same arguments. Such legislation may invade one class of rights to-day and another tomorrow, and if it can be sanctioned under the Constitution, while far removed in time we will not be far away in practical statesmanship from those ages when governmental prefects supervised the building of houses, the rearing of cattle, the sowing of seed and the reaping of grain, and governmental ordinances regulated the movements and labor of artisans, the rate of wages, the price of food, the diet and clothing of the people, and a large range of other affairs long since in all civilized lands regarded as outside of governmental functions. Such governmental interferences disturb the normal adjustments of the social fabric, and usually derange the delicate and complicated machinery of industry and cause a score of ills while attempting the removal of one.

Note: Substantive Due Process and Corporations

Before the Civil War, it was doubtful that corporations could claim the protection of the Fifth Amendment's due process clause. The United States Supreme Court had held that corporations were not "Citizens" within the meaning of the privileges and immunities clause of Article IV, Section 2. There is no evidence in the debates preceding adoption of the Fourteenth Amendment that its Framers in Congress intended its due process clause to apply to corporations, although for a time some scholars suggested that there had been a conspiracy among congressional Republicans to have it thus apply. That far-fetched notion was exploded more than a generation ago and may be consigned to the attic of defunct conspiracy theories.

In oral arguments before the Supreme Court in 1886, counsel began to make the point that corporations were now protected by the Fourteenth Amendment. Chief Justice Morrison R. Waite cut him off, stating that

> the Court does not wish to hear argument on the question whether the provision in the Fourteenth Amendment to the Constitution, which forbids a State to deny any person within its jurisdiction the equal protection of the laws, applies to these corporations. We are all of the opinion that it does.[10]

Seldom has so momentous a decision been made so offhandedly. Thereafter, corporations enjoyed the full protection of the due process and equal protection clauses. However, there was a historical irony in this. While corporations were now positioned to reap the benefits of the substantive due process era, the real beneficiaries of the Fourteenth Amendment's Section 1 (the freed black people whom Congress explicitly intended to help) were relegated to a nether region outside the bounds of the amendment's protection.

Note: The Labor Injunction

Since 1883, federal and state judges had been expanding the use of injunctions to halt strikes, despite legislative attempts to restrict the innovation. The labor injunction was an especially powerful device. It worked as follows: a United States attorney, often acting at the behest of colleagues in private practice who represented employers, would request an injunction to stop all activities in connection with a strike, including those that after World War I would be considered to be protected by the First Amendment. (In the late nineteenth century, the First Amendment had not yet assumed the prominent place that it occupies today in the protection of the freedom of speech, press, and association. If not a dead letter, it was at most dormant.) The proceedings themselves were sometimes ex parte, meaning that the union was not notified or permitted to participate. Failure to comply with an injunction was punishable as contempt of court without a jury trial.

FEDERAL POLICE POWER AND LABOR

<hr/>

In re Debs
154 U.S. 564 (1895)

The Debs *case grew out of the Pullman strike of 1894, which had halted the operations of all railroads running through Chicago. President Grover Cleveland, a conservative Demo-*

crat, sent federal troops to Chicago to break the strike, while his attorney general, Richard Olney (a railroad lawyer before he assumed public office), sought an injunction against the American Railway Union and its president, Eugene V. Debs. Debs was held in contempt for violation of the injunction, and this opinion by Justice David J. Brewer for a unanimous Court resulted from his appeal.

The Debs *opinion has sometimes been contrasted with* E. C. Knight, *excerpted earlier. Critics have charged that the Supreme Court construed federal power broadly when it served to safeguard economic rights and narrowly when congressional legislation threatened business interests. Yet the central issue in* Debs *was quite distinct from that presented in* E. C. Knight. Debs *involved the role of the judiciary with respect to railroading, a business activity clearly within the ambit of interstate commerce. In contrast,* E. C. Knight *turned upon the contested scope of congressional power over manufacturing. Constitutional historian Owen M. Fiss has aptly observed: "There was . . . ample basis in prevailing doctrine for distinguishing the exertion of federal power in* Debs *(over transportation) from the denial of federal power in* E. C. Knight *(over manufacturing)."[11] Still, the decision in* Debs *put the Supreme Court's imprimatur on the growing use of federal court injunctions in labor disputes.*

The case presented by the bill is this: The United States, finding that the interstate transportation of persons and property, as well as the carriage of the mails, is forcibly obstructed, and that a combination and conspiracy exists to subject the control of such transportation to the will of the conspirators, applied to one of their courts, sitting as a court of equity, for an injunction to restrain such obstruction and prevent carrying into effect such conspiracy. Two questions of importance are presented: First. Are the relations of the general government to interstate commerce and the transportation of the mails such as authorize a direct interference to prevent a forcible obstruction thereof? Second. If authority exists, as authority in governmental affairs implies both power and duty, has a court of equity jurisdiction to issue an injunction in aid of the performance of such duty?

First. What are the relations of the general government to interstate commerce and the transportation of the mails? They are those of direct supervision, control and management. While under the dual system which prevails with us the powers of government are distributed between the State and the Nation, and while the latter is properly styled a government of enumerated powers, yet within the limits of such enumeration it has all the attributes of sov-

ereignty, and, in the exercise of those enumerated powers, acts directly upon the citizen, and not through the intermediate agency of the State.

As, under the Constitution, power over interstate commerce and the transportation of the mails is vested in the national government, and Congress by virtue of such grant has assumed actual and direct control, it follows that the national government may prevent any unlawful and forcible interference therewith. But how shall this be accomplished? Doubtless, it is within the competency of Congress to prescribe by legislation that any interference with these matters shall be offences against the United States, and prosecuted and punished by indictment in the proper courts. But is that the only remedy? Have the vast interests of the nation in interstate commerce, and in the transportation of the mails, no other protection than lies in the possible punishment of those who interfere with it? To ask the question is to answer it.

But there is no such impotency in the national government. The entire strength of the nation may be used to enforce in any part of the land the full and free exercise of all national powers and the security of all rights entrusted by the Constitution to its care. The strong arm of the national government may be put forth to brush away all obstructions to the freedom of interstate commerce or the transportation of the mails. If the emergency arises, the army of the Nation and all its miltia, are at the service of the Nation to compel obedience to its laws.

But passing to the second question, is there no other alternative than the use of force on the part of the executive authorities whenever obstructions arise to the freedom of interstate commerce or the transportation of the mails? Is the army the only instrument by which rights of the public can be enforced and the peace of the nation preserved? Grant that any public nuisance may be forcibly abated either at the instance of the authorities, or by an individual suffering private damage therefrom, the existence of this right of forcible abatement is not inconsistent with nor does it destroy the right of appeal in an orderly way to the courts for a judicial determination, and an exercise of their powers by writ of injunction and otherwise to accomplish the same result.

So, in the case before us, the right to use force does not exclude the right of appeal to the courts for a judicial determination and for the exercise of all their powers of prevention. Indeed, it is more to the praise than to the blame of the government, that, instead of determining for itself questions of right and wrong on the part of these petitioners and their associates and enforcing that determination by the club of the policeman and the bayonet of the soldier, it submitted all those questions to the peaceful determination of judicial tribunals, and invoked their consideration and judgment as to the measure of rights and powers and the correlative obligations of those against whom it made complaint. And it is equally to the credit of the latter that the judgment of those tribunals was by the great body of them respected, and the troubles which threatened so much disaster terminated.

We have given to this case the most careful and anxious attention, for we realize that it touches closely questions of supreme importance to the people of this country. Summing up our conclusions, we hold that the government of the United States is one hav-ing jurisdiction over every foot of soil within its territory, and acting directly upon each citizen; that while it is a government of enumerated powers, it has within the limits of those powers all the attributes of sovereignty; that to it is committed power over interstate commerce and the transmission of the mail; that the powers thus conferred upon the national government are not dormant, but have been assumed and put into practical exercise by the legislation of Congress; that in the exercise of those powers it is competent for the nation to remove all obstructions upon highways, natural or artificial, to the passage of interstate commerce or the carrying of the mail; that while it may be competent for the government (through the executive branch and in the use of the entire executive power of the nation) to forcibly remove all such obstructions, it is equally within its competency to appeal to the civil courts for an inquiry and determination as to the existence and character of any alleged obstructions, and if such are found to exist, or threaten to occur, to invoke the powers of those courts to remove or restrain such obstructions; that the jurisdiction of courts to interfere in such matters by injunction is one recognized from ancient times and by indubitable authority; that such jurisdiction is not ousted by the fact that the obstructions are accompanied by or consist of acts in themselves violations of the criminal law; that the proceeding by injunction is of a civil character, and may be enforced by proceedings in contempt; that such proceedings are not in execution of the criminal laws of the land; that the penalty for a violation of injunction is no substitute for and no defense to a prosecution for any criminal offences committed in the course of such violation; that the complaint filed in this case clearly showed an existing obstruction of artificial highways for the passage of interstate commerce and the transmission of the mail—an obstruction not only temporarily existing, but threatening to continue; . . . and, finally, that, the Circuit Court, having full jurisdiction in the premises, its finding of the fact of disobedience is not open to review on habeas corpus in this or any other court.

Note: Labor and the Law

In *Loewe* v. *Lawlor* (1908) the Supreme Court, in a unanimous opinion written by Chief Justice Melville W. Fuller, ruled that the Sherman Anti-Trust Act applied to labor unions. It also held that a secondary boycott organized by a union amounted to a restraint of trade in violation of the Sherman Act. This outcome raised the possibility of damage actions against unions for boycotts. In response, unions lobbied Congress to gain an exemption from anti-trust legislation. The Clayton Anti-Trust Act of 1914 contained some ambiguous wording that could have been construed as limiting federal court labor injunctions and precluding the application of anti-trust laws to unions. In *Duplex Printing Co.* v. *Deering* (1921), however, the Supreme Court insisted that the Clayton Act did not protect unions engaged in illegal activities, such as secondary boycotts. Federal courts continued to enforce anti-trust laws against unions for another decade. Then the New Deal labor legislation of the 1930s for the most part exempted unions from the anti-trust laws. Additionally, the Norris-LaGuardia Act of 1932 largely prohibited the grant of labor injunctions by federal courts, and specifically exempted unions from injunctions based on the anti-trust laws.

LIBERTY OF CONTRACT

Allgeyer v. *Louisiana*
165 U.S. 578 (1897)

Contractual freedom played a vital role in shaping American law during the nineteenth century. Contracts were widely seen both as the cornerstone of a free economy and as a vehicle by which individuals could seek to govern their own economic prospects. Indeed, the leading legal historian J. Willard Hurst characterized the nineteenth century as "above all else, the years of contract in our law."[12]

In the landmark Allgeyer *case, Justice Rufus W. Peckham, speaking for a unanimous Supreme Court, ruled that the right of capable parties to enter contracts was part of the liberty protected by the due process clause of the Fourteenth Amendment against unreasonable state abridgement. At issue in that case was a Louisiana law prohibiting persons from obtaining insurance from companies not qualified to do business in the state. In a series of later cases the Supreme Court applied the liberty of contract doctrine to employment arrangements, hampering workplace regulations.*

The Supreme Court of Louisiana says that the act of writing within that State, the letter of notification, was an act therein done to effect an insurance on property then in the State, in a marine insurance company which had not complied with its laws, and such act was, therefore, prohibited by the statute. As so construed we think the statute is a violation of the Fourteenth Amendment of the Federal Constitution, in that it deprives the defendants of their liberty without due process of law. The statute which forbids such acts does not become due process of law, because it is inconsistent with the provisions of the Constitution of the Union. The liberty mentioned in that amendment means not only the right of the citizen to be free from the mere physical restraint of his person, as by incarceration, but the term is deemed to embrace the right of the citizen to be free in the enjoyment of all his faculties; to be free to use them in all lawful ways; to live and work where he will; to earn his livelihood by any lawful calling; to pursue any livelihood or avocation, and for that purpose to enter into all contracts which may be proper, necessary and essential to his carrying out to a successful conclusion the purposes above mentioned.

Has not a citizen of a State, under the provisions of the Federal Constitution above mentioned, a right to contract outside the State for insurance on his property—a right of which state legislation cannot deprive him?

♦ ♦ ♦

The act done within the limits of the State under the circumstances of this case and for the purpose therein mentioned, we hold a proper act, one which the defendants were at liberty to perform and which the state legislature had no right to prevent, at least with reference to the Federal Constitution. To deprive the citizen of such a right as herein described without due process of law is illegal. Such a statute as this in question is not due process of law, because it prohibits an act which under the Federal Constitution the defendants had a right to perform. This does not interfere in any way with the acknowledged right of the State to enact such legislation in the legitimate exercise of its police or other powers as to it may seem proper. In the exercise of such right, however, care must be taken not to infringe upon those other rights of the citizen which are protected by the Federal Constitution.

In the privilege of pursuing an ordinary calling or trade and of acquiring, holding and selling property must be embraced the right to make all proper contracts in relation thereto, and although it may be conceded that this right to contract in relation to persons or property or to do business within the jurisdiction of the State may be regulated and sometimes prohibited when the contracts or business conflict with the policy of the State as contained in its statutes, yet the power does not and cannot extend to prohibiting a citizen from making contracts of the nature involved in this case outside of the limits and jurisdiction of the State, and which are also to be performed outside such jurisdiction.

LIBERTY OF CONTRACT AND WORKPLACE REGULATION

Holden v. *Hardy*
169 U.S. 366 (1898)

Lawmakers in the late nineteenth century attempted to alleviate harsh working conditions by regulating the terms of employment. As demonstrated in Holden, *the Supreme Court frequently rebuffed the argument that state labor laws impaired the right of employers and employees to enter contracts. Significantly, Justice Henry Billings Brown accepted the idea that employer and employee do not stand on an equal bargaining footing.*

An examination of both these classes of cases under the Fourteenth Amendment will demonstrate that, in passing upon the validity of state legislation under that amendment, this court has not failed to recognize the fact that the law is, to a certain extent, a progressive science; that in some of the States' methods of procedure, which at the time the Constitution was adopted were deemed essential to the protection and safety of the people, or to the liberty of the citizen, have been found to be no longer necessary; that restrictions which had formerly been laid upon the conduct of individuals, or of classes of individuals, had proved detrimental to their interests; while, upon the other hand, certain other classes of persons, particularly those engaged in dangerous or unhealthful employments, have been found to be in need of additional protection.

◆   ◆   ◆

The present century has originated legal reforms of no less importance. The whole fabric of special pleading, once thought to be necessary to the culmination of the real issue between the parties, has crumbled to pieces. The ancient tenures of real estate have been largely swept away, and land is now transferred almost as easily and cheaply as personal property. Married women have been emancipated from the control of their husbands and placed upon a practical equality with them with respect to the acquisition, possession and transmission of property. Imprisonment for debt has been abolished. Exemptions from execution have been largely added to, and in most of the States homesteads are rendered incapable of seizure and sale upon forced process. [These examples] are mentioned only for the purpose of calling attention to the probability that other changes of no less importance may be made in the future, and that while the cardinal principles of justice are immutable, the methods by which justice is administered are subject to constant fluctuation, and that the Constitution of the United States, which is necessarily and to a large extent inflexible and exceedingly difficult of amendment, should not be so construed as to deprive the States of the power to so amend their laws as to make them conform to the wishes of the citizens as they may deem best for the public welfare without bringing them into conflict with the supreme law of the land.

Of course, it is impossible to forecast the character or extent of these changes, but in view of the fact that from the day Magna Charta was signed to the present moment, amendments to the structure of the law have been made with increasing frequency, it is impossible to suppose that they will not continue, and the law be forced to adapt itself to new conditions of society, and, particularly, to the new relations between employers and employees, as they arise.

◆   ◆   ◆

This right of contract, however, is itself subject to certain limitations which the State may lawfully impose in the exercise of its police powers. While this power is inherent in all governments, it has doubtless been greatly expanded in its application during the past century, owing to an enormous increase in the number of occupations which are dangerous, or so far detrimental to the health of employees as to demand special precautions for their well-being and protection, or the safety of adjacent property.

◆   ◆   ◆

But if it be within the power of a legislature to adopt such means for the protection of the lives of its citizens, it is difficult to see why precautions may not also be adopted for the protection of their health and morals. It is as much for the interest of the State that the public health should be preserved as that life should be made secure. With this end in view quarantine laws have been enacted in most if not all of the States; insane asylums, public hospitals and institutions for the care and education of the blind established; and special measures taken for the exclusion of infected cattle, rags and decayed fruit. In other States laws have been enacted limiting the hours during which women and children shall be employed in factories; and while their constitutionality, at least as applied to women, has been doubted in some of the States, they have been generally upheld.

◆   ◆   ◆

Upon the principles above stated, we think the act in question may be sustained as a valid exercise of the police power of the State. The enactment does not profess to limit the hours of all workmen, but merely those who are employed in underground mines, or in the smelting, reduction or refining of ores or metals. These employments, when too long pursued, the legislature has judged to be detrimental to the health of the employees, and, so long as there are reasonable grounds for believing that this is so, its decision upon this subject cannot be reviewed by the Federal courts.

The legislature has also recognized the fact, which the experience of legislators in

◆   ◆   ◆

many States has corroborated, that the proprietors of these establishments and their operatives do not stand upon an equality, and that their interests are, to a certain extent, conflicting. The former naturally desire to obtain as much labor as possible from their employees, while the latter are often induced by the fear of discharge to conform to regulations which their judgment, fairly exercised, would pronounce to be detrimental to their health or strength. In other words, the proprietors lay down the rules and the laborers are practically constrained to obey them. In such cases self-interest is often an unsafe guide, and the legislature may properly interpose its authority.

It may not be improper to suggest in this connection that although the prosecution in this case was against the employer of labor, who apparently under the statute is the only one liable, his defense is not so much that his right to contract has been infringed upon, but that the act works as a peculiar hardship to his employees, whose right to labor as long as they please is alleged to be thereby violated. The argument would certainly come with better grace and greater cogency from the latter class. But the fact that both parties are of full age and competent to contract does not necessarily deprive the State of the power to interfere where the parties do not stand upon an equality, or where the public health demands that one party to the contract shall be protected against himself.

We are of opinion that the act in question was a valid exercise of the police power of the State, and the judgments of the Supreme Court of Utah are, therefore,

Affirmed.

Lochner v. New York
198 U.S. 45 (1905)

Justice Rufus W. Peckham's majority opinion in Lochner *stands as the classic expression of substantive due process and liberty of contract. Justice Holmes's dissent, which contains some of his most frequently quoted aphorisms, rejected the notion of a constitutionally protected freedom of contract and insisted that it was not for judges to weigh the justifications for legislative policy making. The much-debated* Lochner *decision remains at the heart of a continuing dialogue about the appropriate role of the judiciary in the American polity.*

The indictment, it will be seen, charges that the plaintiff in error violated the one hundred and tenth section of article 8, chapter 415, of the Laws of 1897, known as the labor law of the State of New York, in that he wrongfully and unlawfully required and permitted an employee working for him to work more than sixty hours in one week.

♦ ♦ ♦

The statute necessarily interferes with the right of contract between the employer and employees, concerning the number of hours in which the latter may labor in the bakery of the employer. The general right to make a contract in relation to his business is part of the liberty of the individual protected by the Fourteenth Amendment of the Federal Constitution. Under that provision no State can deprive any person of life, liberty or property without due process of law. The right to purchase or to sell labor is part of the liberty protected by this amendment, unless there are circumstances which exclude the right. There are, however, certain powers, existing in the sovereignty of each State in the Union, somewhat vaguely termed police powers, the exact description and limitation of which have not been attempted by the courts. Those powers, broadly stated and without, at present, any attempt at a more specific limitation, relate to the safety, health, morals and general welfare of the public. Both property and liberty are held on such reasonable conditions as may be imposed by the governing power of the State in the exercise of those powers, and with such conditions the Fourteenth Amendment was not designed to interfere.

♦   ♦   ♦

Therefore, when the State, by its legislature, in the assumed exercise of its police powers, has passed an act which seriously limits the right to labor or the right of contract in regard to their means of livelihood between persons who are sui juris (both employer and employee), it becomes of great importance to determine which shall prevail—the right of the individual to labor for such time as he may choose, or the right of the State to prevent the individual from laboring or from entering into any contract to labor, beyond a certain time prescribed by the State.

♦   ♦   ♦

It must, of course, be conceded that there is a limit to the valid exercise of the police power by the State. There is no dispute concerning the general proposition. Otherwise the Fourteenth Amendment would have no efficacy and legislatures of the States would have unbounded power, and it would be enough to say that any piece of legislation was enacted to conserve the morals, the health or the safety of the people; such legislation would be valid, no matter how absolutely without foundation the claim might be. The claim of the police power would be a mere pretext—become another and delusive name for the supreme sovereignty of the State to be exercised free from constitutional restraint. This is not contended for. In every case that comes before this court, therefore, where legislation of this character is concerned and where the protection of the Federal Constitution is sought, the question necessarily arises: Is this a fair, reasonable and appropriate exercise of the police power of the State, or is it an unreasonable, unnecessary and arbitrary interference with the right of the individual to his personal liberty or to enter into those contracts in relation to labor which may seem to him appropriate or necessary for the support of himself and his family? Of course the liberty of

contract relating to labor includes both parties to it. The one has as much right to purchase as the other to sell labor.

This is not a question of substituting the judgment of the court for that of the legislature. If the act is within the power of the State it is valid, although the judgment of the court might be totally opposed to the enactment of such a law. But the question would still remain: Is it within the police power of the State? and that question must be answered by the court.

The question whether this act is valid as a labor law, pure and simple, may be dismissed in a few words. There is no reasonable ground for interfering with the liberty of person or the right of free contract, by determining the hours of labor, in the occupation of a baker. There is no contention that bakers as a class are not equal in intelligence and capacity to men in other trades or manual occupations, or that they are not able to assert their rights and care for themselves without the protecting arm of the State, interfering with their independence of judgment and of action. They are in no sense wards of the State. Viewed in the light of a purely labor law, with no reference whatever to the question of health, we think that a law like the one before us involves neither the safety, the morals nor the welfare of the public, and that the interest of the public is not in the slightest degree affected by such an act. The law must be upheld, if at all, as a law pertaining to the health of the individual engaged in the occupation of a baker. It does not affect any other portion of the public than those who are engaged in that occupation. Clean and wholesome bread does not depend upon whether the baker works but ten hours per day or only sixty hours a week. The limitation of the hours of labor does not come within the police power on that ground.

It is a question of which of two powers or rights shall prevail—the power of the State to legislate or the right of the individual to liberty of person and freedom of contract. The mere assertion that the subject relates though but in a remote degree to the public health does not necessarily render the enactment valid. The act must have a more direct relation, as a means to an end, and the end itself must be appropriate and legitimate, before an act can be held to be valid which interferes with the general right of an individual to be free in his person and in his power to contract in relation to his own labor.

◆ ◆ ◆

We think the limit of the police power has been reached and passed in this case. There is, in our judgment, no reasonable foundation for holding this to be necessary or appropriate as a health law to safeguard the public health or the health of the individuals who are following the trade of a baker. If this statute be valid, and if, therefore, a proper case is made out in which to deny the right of an individual, sui juris, as employer or employee, to make contracts for the labor of the latter under the protection of the provisions of the Federal Constitution, there would seem to be no length to which legislation of this nature might not go.

We do not believe in the soundness of the views which uphold this law. On the contrary, we think that such a law as this, although passed in the assumed exercise of the police power, and as relating to the public health, or the health of the employees named, is not within that power, and is invalid. The act is not, within any fair meaning of the term, a health law, but is an illegal interference with the rights of individuals, both employers and employees, to make contracts regarding labor upon such terms as they may think best, or which they may agree upon with the other parties to such contracts. Statutes of the nature of that under review, limiting the hours in which grown and intelligent men may labor to earn their living, are mere meddlesome interferences with the rights of the individual, and they are not saved from condemnation by the claim that they are passed in the exercise of the police power and upon the subject of the health of the individual whose rights are interfered with, unless there be some fair ground, reasonable in and of itself, to say that there is material danger to the public health or to the health of the employees, if the hours of labor are not curtailed.

◆ ◆ ◆

It is impossible for us to shut our eyes to the fact that many of the laws of this character, while passed under what is claimed to be the police power for the purpose of protecting the public health or welfare, are, in reality, passed from other motives. We are justified in saying so when, from the character of the law and the subject upon which it legislates, it is apparent that the public health or welfare bears but the most remote relation to the law. The purpose of a statute must be determined from the natural and legal effect of the language employed; and whether it is or is not repugnant to the Constitution of the United States must be determined from the natural effect of such statutes when put into operation, and not from their proclaimed purpose.

◆ ◆ ◆

It is manifest to us that the limitation of the hours of labor as provided for in this section of the statute under which the indictment was found, and the plaintiff in error convicted, has no such direct relation to and no such substantial effect upon the health of the employee, as to justify us in regarding the section as really a health law. It seems to us that the real object and purpose were simply to regulate the hours of labor between the master and his employees (all being men, sui juris), in a private business, not dangerous in any degree to morals or in any real and substantial degree, to the health of the employees. Under such circumstances the freedom of master and employe to contract with each other in relation to their employment, and in defining the same, cannot be prohibited or interfered with, without violating the Federal Constitution.

Reversed.

Mr. Justice Holmes dissenting.

I regret sincerely that I am unable to agree with the judgment in this case, and that I think it my duty to express my dissent.

This case is decided upon an economic theory which a large part of the country does not entertain. If it were a question whether I agreed with that theory, I should desire to study it further and long before making up my mind. But I do not conceive that to be my duty, because I strongly believe that my agreement or disagreement has nothing to do with the right of a majority to embody their opinions in law. It is settled by various decisions of this court that state constitutions and state laws may regulate life in many ways which we as legislators might think as injudicious or if you like as tyrannical as this, and which equally with this interfere with the liberty to contract. Sunday laws and usury laws are ancient examples. A more modem one is the prohibition of lotteries. The liberty of the citizen to do as he likes so long as he does not interfere with the liberty of others to do the same, which has been a shibboleth for some well-known writers, is interfered with by school laws, by the Post Office, by every state or municipal institution which takes his money for purposes thought desirable, whether he likes it or not. The Fourteenth Amendment does not enact Mr. Herbert Spencer's Social Statics.

◆　◆　◆

Some of these laws embody convictions or prejudices which judges are likely to share. Some may not. But a constitution is not intended to embody a particular economic theory, whether of paternalism and the organic relation of the citizen to the State or of laissez faire. It is made for people of fundamentally different views, and the accident of our finding certain opinions natural and familiar or novel and even shocking ought not to conclude our judgment upon the question whether statutes embodying them conflict with the Constitution of the United States.

General propositions do not decide concrete cases. The decision will depend on a judgment or intuition more subtle than any articulate major premise. But I think that the proposition just stated, if it is accepted, will carry us far toward the end. Every opinion tends to become a law. I think that the word liberty in the Fourteenth Amendment is perverted when it is held to prevent the natural outcome of a dominant opinion, unless it can be said that a rational and fair man necessarily would admit that the statute proposed would infringe fundamental principles as they have been understood by the traditions of our people and our law. It does not need research to show that no such sweeping condemnation can be passed upon the statute before us. A reasonable man might think it a proper measure on the score of health.

Muller v. Oregon
208 U.S. 412 (1908)

The liberty of contract doctrine, although potent, was not an absolute bar to employment regulations. As demonstrated by Justice David J. Brewer's opinion in the Muller *case, the Supreme Court sustained workplace regulations for persons not deemed capable of protecting themselves in the marketplace. The* Muller *case is also noteworthy because the Court relied in part on social science data contained in the brief of Louis D. Brandeis as a factual basis justifying different legal treatment of women. The Brandeis brief dovetailed with prevailing societal views about the appropriate place of women in society. Do these paternalistic assumptions have any continuing validity? The* Muller *decision was consistent with the liberty of contract premise of* Lochner, *but found the doctrine inapplicable in these circumstances.*

On February 19, 1903, the legislature of the State of Oregon passed an act (Session Laws, 1903, p. 148), the first section of which is in these words:

"Sec. 1. That no female (shall) be em-

ployed in any mechanical establishment, or factory, or laundry in this State more than ten hours during any one day."

◆　◆　◆

It is the law of Oregon that women, whether married or single, have equal contractual and personal rights with men.

♦ ♦ ♦

It thus appears that, putting to one side the elective franchise, in the matter of personal and contractual rights [women] stand on the same plane as the other sex. Their rights in these respects can no more be infringed than the equal rights of their brothers.

In patent cases counsel are apt to open the argument with a discussion of the state of the art. It may not be amiss, in the present case, before examining the constitutional question, to notice the course of legislation as well as expressions of opinion from other than judicial sources. In the brief filed by Mr. Louis D. Brandeis, for the defendant in error, is a very copious collection of all these matters, an epitome of which is found in the margin.

The legislation and opinions referred to in the margin may not be, technically speaking, authorities, and in them is little or no discussion of the constitutional question presented to us for determination, yet they are significant of a widespread belief that woman's physical structure, and the functions she performs in consequence thereof, justify special legislation restricting or qualifying the conditions under which she should be permitted to toil. Constitutional questions, it is true, are not settled by even a consensus of present public opinion, for it is the peculiar value of a written constitution that it places in unchanging form limitations upon legislative action, and thus gives a permanence and stability to popular government which otherwise would be lacking. At the same time, when a question of fact is debatable, and the extent to which a special constitutional limitation goes is affected by the truth in respect to that fact, a widespread and long continued belief concerning it is worthy of consideration. We take judicial cognizance of all matters of general knowledge.

It is undoubtedly true, as more than once declared by this court, that the general right to contract in relation to one's business is part of the liberty of the individual, protected by the Fourteenth Amendment to the Federal Constitution; yet it is equally well settled that this liberty is not absolute and extending to all contracts, and that a State may, without conflicting with the provisions of the Fourteenth Amendment, restrict in many respects the individual's power of contract.

♦ ♦ ♦

That woman's physical structure and the performance of maternal functions place her at a disadvantage in the struggle for subsistence is obvious. This is especially true when the burdens of motherhood are upon her. Even when they are not, by abundant testimony of the medical fraternity continuance for a long time on her feet at work, repeating this from day to day, tends to injurious effects upon the body, and as healthy mothers are essential to vigorous offspring, the physical wellbeing of woman becomes an object of public interest and care in order to preserve the strength and vigor of the race.

Still again, history discloses the fact that woman has always been dependent upon man. He established his control at the outset by superior physical strength, and this control in various forms, with diminishing intensity, has continued to the present. As minors, though not to the same extent, she has been looked upon in the courts as needing especial care that her rights may be preserved. Education was long denied her, and while now the doors of the school room are opened and her opportunities for acquiring knowledge are great, yet even with that and the consequent increase of capacity for business affairs it is still true that in the struggle for subsistence she is not an equal competitor with her brother. Though limitations upon personal and contractual rights may be removed by legislation, there is that in her disposition and habits of life which will operate against a full assertion of those rights. She will still be where some legislation to protect her seems necessary to secure a real equality of right. Doubtless there are individual exceptions, and there are many respects in which she has an advantage over him; but looking at it from the viewpoint of the effort to maintain an independent position in life, she is not upon an equality. Differentiated by these matters from the other sex, she is properly placed in a class by herself, and legislation designed for her protection may be sustained, even when like legislation is not necessary for men and could not be sustained. It is impossible to close one's eyes to the fact that she still looks to her brother and depends upon him. Even though all restrictions on political, personal and contractual rights were taken away, and she stood, so far as statutes are concerned, upon an absolutely equal plane with him, it would still be true that she is so constituted that she will rest upon and look to him for protection; that her physical structure and a proper discharge of her maternal functions—having in view not merely her own health, but the well-being of the race—justify legislation to protect her from the greed as well as the passion of man. The limitations which this statute places upon her contractual powers, upon her right to agree with her employer as to the time she shall labor, are not imposed solely for her benefit, but also largely for the benefit of all. Many words cannot make this plainer. The two sexes differ in structure of body, in the functions to be performed by each, in the amount of physical strength, in the capacity for long-continued labor, particularly when done standing, the influence of vigorous health upon the future well-being of the race, the self-reliance which enables one to assert full rights, and in the capacity to maintain the struggle for subsistence. This difference justifies a difference in legislation and upholds that which is designed to compensate for some of the burdens which rest upon her.

For these reasons, and without questioning in any respect the decision in Lochner v. New York, we are of the opinion that it cannot be adjudged that the act in question is in conflict with the Federal Constitution, so far as it respects the work of a female in a laundry, and the judgment of the Supreme Court of Oregon is

Affirmed.

TOWARD A FEDERAL POLICE POWER

Champion v. Ames
188 U.S. 321 (1903)

It was generally agreed in the nineteenth century that the federal government did not possess a police power to regulate public health, safety, and morals. Such authority was a province of the states. In the early twentieth century, however, Congress started to make unprecedented use of the commerce clause to indirectly regulate health and morals. The Supreme Court proved receptive to such legislation despite the fact that these laws infringed traditional state powers.

The case excerpted here, popularly known as the Lottery Case, was the first major decision in the twentieth century that sustained the federal police power. It was notable for Justice John M. Harlan's insistence that the power to regulate commerce included the power to prohibit entirely the shipment of an article, thus destroying commerce in it, and for his sweeping assertion that Congress could regulate for the protection of the people's morals. The practical result of Champion was to sanction the exercise of a federal police power by means of professing to regulate interstate commerce.

The appellant insists that the carrying of lottery tickets from one State to another State by an express company engaged in carrying freight and packages from State to State, although such tickets may be contained in a box or package, does not constitute, and cannot by any act of Congress be legally made to constitute, commerce among States within the meaning of the clause of the Constitution of the United States providing that Congress shall have power "to regulate commerce with foreign nations, and among the several States, and with the Indian tribes;" consequently, that Congress cannot make it an offence to cause such tickets to be carried from one State to another.

The questions presented by these opposing contentions are of great moment, and are entitled to receive, as they have received, the most careful consideration.

What is the import of the word "commerce" as used in the Constitution? It is not defined by that instrument. Undoubtedly, the carrying from one State to another by independent carriers of things or commodities that are ordinary subjects of traffic, and which have in themselves a recognized value in money, constitutes interstate commerce. But does not commerce among the several States include something more? Does not the carrying from one State to another, by independent carriers, of lottery tickets that entitle the holder to the payment of a certain amount of money therein specified also constitute commerce among States?

♦ ♦ ♦

Commerce among the States embraces navigation, intercourse, communication, traffic, the transit of persons, and the transmission of messages by telegraph. They also show that the power to regulate commerce among the several States is vested in Congress as absolutely as it would be in a single government, having in its constitution the same restrictions on the exercise or the power as are found in the Constitution of the United States; that such power is plenary, complete in itself, and may be exerted by Congress to its utmost extent, subject only to such limitations as the Constitution imposes upon the exercise of the powers granted by it; and that in determining the character of the regulations to be adopted Congress has a large discretion which is not to be controlled by the courts, simply because, in their opinion, such

regulations may not be the best or most effective that could be employed.

♦ ♦ ♦

We are of opinion that lottery tickets are subjects of traffic and therefore are subjects of commerce, and the regulation of the carrying of such tickets from State to State, at least by independent carriers, is a regulation of commerce among the several States.

♦ ♦ ♦

We have said that the carrying from State to State of lottery tickets constitutes interstate commerce, and that the regulation of such commerce is within the power of Congress under the Constitution. Are we prepared to say that a provision which in, in effect, a prohibition of the carriage of such articles from State to State is not a fit or appropriate mode for the regulation of that particular kind of commerce? If lottery traffic, carried on through interstate commerce, is a matter of which Congress may take cognizance and over which its power may be exerted, can it be possible that it must tolerate the traffic, and simply regulate the manner in which it may be carried on? Or may not Congress, for the protection of the people of all the States, and under the power to regulate interstate commerce, devise such means, within the scope of the Constitution, and not prohibited by it, as will drive that traffic out of commerce among the States?

If a State when considering legislation for the suppression of lotteries within its own limits, may properly take into view the evils that inhere in the raising of money, in that mode, why may not Congress, invested with the power to regulate commerce among the several States, provide that such commerce shall not be polluted by the carrying of lottery tickets from one State to another? In this connection it must not be forgotten that the power of Congress to regulate commerce among the States is plenary, is complete in itself, and is subject to no limitations except such as may be found in the Constitution. What provision in that instrument can be regarded as limiting the exercise of the power granted? What clause can be cited which, in any degree, countenances the suggestion that one may, of right, carry or cause to be carried from one State to another that which will harm the public morals? We cannot think of any clause of that instrument that could possibly be invoked by those who assert their right to send lottery tickets from State to State except the one providing that no person shall be deprived of his liberty without due process of law. But surely it will not be said to be a part of one's liberty, as recognized by the supreme law of the land, that he shall be allowed to introduce into commerce among the States an element that will be confessedly injurious to the public morals.

If it be said that the 1895 [act] is inconsistent with the Tenth Amendment, reserving to the States respectively or to the people the powers not delegated to the United States, the answer is that the power to regulate commerce among the States has been expressly delegated to Congress.

♦ ♦ ♦

The judgment is

Affirmed.

Mr. Chief Justice Fuller, with whom concur Mr. Justice Brewer, Mr. Justice Shiras and Mr. Justice Peckham, dissenting.

♦ ♦ ♦

The naked question is whether the prohibition by Congress of the carriage of lottery tickets from one State to another by means other than the mails is within the powers vested in that body by the Constitution of the United States. That the purpose of Congress in this enactment was the suppression of lotteries cannot reasonably be denied. That purpose is avowed in the title of the act, and is its natural and reasonable effect, and by that its validity must be tested.

The power of the State to impose restraints and burdens on persons and property in conservation and promotion of the public health, good order and prosperity is a power originally and always belonging to the States, not surrendered by them to the General Government nor directly restrained by the Constitution of the United States, and essentially exclusive, and the suppression of lotteries as a harmful business falls within this power, commonly called of police.

It is urged, however, that because Congress is empowered to regulate commerce between the several States, it, therefore, may suppress lotteries by prohibiting the carriage of lottery matter. Congress may indeed make all laws necessary and proper for carrying the powers granted to it into execution, and doubtless an act prohibiting the carriage of lottery matter would be necessary and proper to the execution of a power to suppress lotteries; but that power belongs to the States and not to Congress. To hold that Congress has general police power would be to hold that it may accomplish objects not entrusted to the General Government, and to defeat the operation of the Tenth Amendment, declaring that: "The powers not delegated to the United States by the Constitution, nor prohibited by it to the States, are reserved to the States respectively, or to the people."

Note: The Growth of Federal Police Power

Following *Champion*, Congress enacted a series of social reform laws grounded on the commerce power. For instance, the Pure Food and Drug Act of 1906 excluded adulterated and misbranded foods from interstate commerce. In 1910 Congress enacted the Mann Act, banning the transportation of women across state lines for immoral purposes. Both measures were sustained by the Supreme Court as within the authority of Congress to regulate interstate commerce.

Moreover, Congress began to utilize its power of taxation to achieve regulatory goals. In 1902 Congress levied a prohibitory tax on yellow oleomargarine. Although the obvious purpose of this tax was not to raise revenue but to assist the dairy industry by prohibiting oleomargarine, the Supreme Court in *McCray* v. *United States* (1904) affirmed this use of the tax power to indirectly regulate commerce. This understanding of the taxing authority established an additional basis for the exercise of a federal police power.

In addition, Congress had begun setting aside federal lands for national parks in 1872, with the creation of Yellowstone, and for national monuments in the Antiquities Act of 1906, later providing for the administration of these by creation of the National Park Service in 1916. In a comparable move, the Forest Reserve Act of 1891 authorized the president to set aside forest lands in the public domain. Theodore Roosevelt's conspicuous interest in conservation, signaled by the 1908 White House Conservation Conference, led to the adoption of U.S. Forester Gifford Pinchot's approach to the problem of natural resources and scenic lands. Pinchot popularized the concept of "multiple use," a policy that encouraged exploitation of national lands and was opposed to the lock-up or set-aside policies advocated by John Muir. The Newlands or National Reclamation Act of 1902 began the federal government's program of large-scale irrigation in arid lands.

Note: Child Labor

Another contested issue involved child labor. In the late nineteenth century, states began to curtail the use of child labor in factories and mines, and by 1900 a majority of states had some type of legal protection for child workers. Unions backed child labor laws because child workers undercut the wages of adult employees. Compulsory school attendance laws also did much to keep children from work in manufacturing establishments. Still, state child labor laws contained many exceptions and enforcement was spotty.

The Progressive movement took special aim at child labor. Invoking an enlarged concept of federal police power, Congress in 1916 barred from interstate commerce goods produced by child labor. Both the Supreme Court and state courts had strongly endorsed state legislation restricting child labor. The Supreme Court, however, drew the line at national regulation of child labor. In *Hammer* v. *Dagenhart* (1918) the Court struck down the federal child labor act as an invasion of the authority reserved to the states under the Tenth Amendment. Writing for the Court, Justice William R. Day explained:

> The thing intended to be accomplished by this statute is the denial of the facilities of interstate commerce to those manufacturers in the States who employ children within the prohibited ages. The act in its effect does not regulate transportation among the States, but aims to standardize the ages at which children may be employed in mining and manufacturing within the States. The goods shipped are of themselves harmless.
>
> The grant of power to Congress over the subject of interstate commerce was to enable it to regulate such commerce, and not to give it authority to control the States in their exercise of the police power over local trade and manufacture.
>
> The grant of authority over a purely federal matter was not intended to destroy the local power always existing and carefully reserved to the States in the Tenth Amendment to the Constitution.
>
> The maintenance of the authority of the States over matters purely local is as essential to the preservation of our institutions as is the conservation of the supremacy of the federal power in all matters entrusted to the Nation by the Federal Constitution.

In interpreting the Constitution it must never be forgotten that the Nation is made up of States to which are entrusted the powers of local government. And to them and to the people the powers not expressly delegated to the National Government are reserved.

Congress then placed a prohibitory tax on the products of child labor, but the Supreme Court in *Bailey* v. *Drexel Furniture Company* (1922) invalidated this measure as an attempt to circumvent the Tenth Amendment. In 1924 Congress proposed a constitutional amendment to eliminate child labor, but it failed to secure enough state ratifications.

→ 7 ←

Total War, Civil Liberties, and Civil Rights

INDIVIDUAL RIGHTS IN A CHANGING CULTURE

From 1900 to 1950, the culture, economy, and demography of the United States changed dramatically. Immigration, internal migration, industrialization, urbanization, and war altered the face of America and the nation's role in world affairs. This substantial transformation of the society affected law and legal culture. The locus of legal change shifted from the state courts to the federal courts. Similarly, political power moved from Congress to the executive branch and increasingly to the courts; the membership of the bench and bar also changed to reflect some, but not all, of the changes in the population.

Massive immigration from 1880 to 1924 altered the culture. In 1850, America was a nation largely populated by Protestants of Anglo-Saxon and northern European origin, pockets of Irish Catholics, and slaves of African origin. By World War I, the nation looked and sounded like a different place. Millions of Catholics and Jews destroyed the Protestant hegemony of an earlier age. Immigrants from eastern and southern Europe, the Middle East, and the Far East similarly undermined the dominance of northern European culture. In 1924, in a futile attempt to preserve a Protestant America that no longer existed, Congress established strict immigration quotas, virtually stopping immigration from much of the world. This law symbolized the tension between the America of the nineteenth century and the nation that had emerged in the twentieth century.

Almost as dramatic as immigration was the movement of people within the United States. The western frontier disappeared before 1900. The last two contiguous territories became states in 1912. But if the age of the western frontier was over, the age of the urban frontier had just begun. Although some western farming and mining regions were dominated by immigrants, most newcomers from Europe and Asia moved to cities. Starting with World War I, they were joined by the movement of southern blacks into cities. In 1900, the problem of race relations was confined to the South for blacks and whites, and to the West Coast for Asians and whites. The migration of blacks out of the South increased rapidly during the Depression and World War II and expanded even more rapidly after 1945.

These new people flooded into American cities, providing laborers for expanding industries. The nexus of law and economics in this period is dealt with in Chapter 6 of this

411

book. But immigration, industrialization, and urbanization also affected noneconomic aspects of legal culture. In response to these changes, radical movements emerged that rejected the social and economic order of the day. The repression of these movements during and after World War I forced lawyers and jurists to consider seriously, for the first time since the Civil War, the place of radical dissent in American legal and political culture. The changing population also affected the legal profession. The children of immigrants looked to law as a way to rise in American society; more established lawyers feared that attorneys from these new groups would alter the "club" that the bar had become. The established bar objected to the social values of lawyers from immigrant families, who more often supported labor unions, poor people, and progressive reform. They also feared the competition of the hardworking, upwardly mobile immigrants and their children. Two results of this growing antagonism were new educational requirements for admission to the bar or to law schools and attempts by the organized bar to destroy law schools that catered to immigrants and blacks. The segregation of the American Bar Association and the ABA's opposition to the nomination of Louis Brandeis, the first Jew to serve on the United States Supreme Court, symbolized the tension in the profession between the old and the new.

The two world wars had an enormous impact on society and thus on law. During the wars, Congress increasingly regulated economic activities, conscripted civilians for military service, and limited free speech while continuing to expand programs and budgets. The presidency became even more powerful as Congress gradually, and sometimes almost gleefully, relinquished power to the chief executive. The president soon came to command bloated bureaucracies, enormous resources, and gigantic armies. From 1917 to 1920, the executive branch used wartime powers to crush radicals and labor organizers under the banner of patriotism. The wartime experience revealed that liberties were easily ignored or trampled on. For these reasons, civil liberties emerged from the wartime experience as an important legal issue. More durable than the repressive statutes were the ideas set forth in dissenting opinions by United States Supreme Court Justices Louis Brandeis and Oliver Wendell Holmes, Jr. More durable than the repressive prosecutions of Attorney General A. Mitchell Palmer and New York's Lusk Committee in 1919 to 1920 was the American Civil Liberties Union (ACLU), organized to protect the political and civil liberties of all Americans, regardless of their ideology. Starting in the 1930s, the ACLU developed into one of the most important litigation-oriented organizations in the country.

The two wars, the Depression, and black migration out of the South led to heightened racial consciousness. At the beginning of this period, black rights were at their lowest point since 1866. Lynchings were common and increased dramatically during World War I. Black veterans, who fought to "make the world safe for democracy," were disinclined to accept second-class citizenship at home. When these veterans returned from France, they found an organization ready to serve their needs. The National Association for the Advancement of Colored People (NAACP), organized in 1909, took the lead in fighting for civil rights through lobbying and litigation. Victories were few at first, but gradually the organization convinced the United States Supreme Court to breathe new life into the moribund Civil War Amendments.

The NAACP began with a battery of upper-class white lawyers, inheritors of the abolitionist tradition and a sense of noblesse oblige toward blacks. Gradually black attorneys, led by Charles Hamilton Houston and William Hastie of Howard Law School and their brilliant protégé Thurgood Marshall, began to represent black litigants at the local, state, and federal levels. Just the sight of a black attorney arguing for civil rights in the rural South or before the United States Supreme Court was a victory of sorts. More substantive victories came later. When soldiers returned from the war against racism and hate in Europe and Japan, the war against segregation and prejudice at home would begin in earnest. Within a decade, the arguments of Thurgood Marshall, like Joshua's trumpets, began to destroy the walls of segregation. Unfortunately, the prejudices behind those walls proved more durable than many lawyers or judges expected.

The kinds of changes brought about by ACLU and NAACP litigation were possible because of fundamental changes in American constitutional law. At the same time, these two organizations, along with other litigators, helped change the meaning of the nation's Constitution. At the beginning of this period, the United States Supreme Court played a minor role in the development of law. Few legal issues raised federal questions. By mid-century, almost anything could raise a federal question. The states had become subordinate to the national government, and important legal changes increasingly came from the Supreme Court rather than from state courts. Legislatures at the state and federal levels also mattered less. At the national level, presidential power grew while the power of Congress diminished.

In 1900, individual rights—civil liberties, civil rights, criminal due process—were generally the domain of the states, which treated their residents and citizens pretty much as they wished. By 1950, the Supreme Court was dramatically altering the relationship between the states and the people. Supreme Court decisions in the 1930s and 1940s set the stage for a massive revolution of rights in the 1950s and 1960s, and for the intervention of federal legislation in areas that, since the end of Reconstruction, had been the domain of the states.

Technology meanwhile restructured American life and the law. Race relations changed as public transportation made internal migration easier and cheaper and as newspapers and radio made all Americans feel closer together. The concept of states' rights began to crumble as the borders between states became more artificial. Technology also meant that people could more easily lose their privacy. In criminal law, the telephone and the wiretap forced judges to rethink the concept of "search" as defined in the Bill of Rights. Telephones, high-speed printing presses, and photography made it more difficult for people—be they common or prominent—to retain their privacy.

Louis D. Brandeis and Samuel D. Warren

"The Right to Privacy"
1890

After his marriage to Mabel Bayard, the daughter of Senator Thomas Bayard, newspaper gossip columns plagued Samuel D. Warren, the former law partner of Louis D. Brandeis. This problem led to their seminal Harvard Law Review *article "The Right to Privacy." Brandeis hoped the article would "make more people see that invasions of privacy" should not be tolerated. According to the* Columbia Law Review, *this enormously influential article "enjoyed the unique distinction of having initiated and theoretically outlined a new field of jurisprudence" by setting the stage for the protection "against the use of one's personality for private gain by others, or to feed a prurient curiosity." The article also pointed the way to a second subfield of law, the tort of emotional distress, whether caused by negligence or intention.*

In addition, the article illustrates the crucial changes taking place in American society as photography, new forms of journalism, and urbanization intruded on the lives of individuals. The article helps explain the need for new legal theories to protect individual rights in the changing society of industrial America. Critical to this is Brandeis's assertion of "the right to be let alone." The articulation of this right lay the foundation for the evolution of a right to privacy in both common law and constitutional law.

That the individual shall have full protection in person and in property is a principle as old as the common law; but it has been found necessary from time to time to define anew the exact nature and extent of such protection. Political, social, and economic changes entail the recognition of new rights, and the common law, in its eternal youth, grows to meet the demands of society. Thus, in very early times, the law gave a remedy only for physical interference with life and property. . . . The "right to life" served only to protect the subject from battery in its various forms; liberty meant freedom from actual restraint; and the right to property secured to the individual his lands and his cattle. Later, there came a recognition of man's spiritual nature, of his feelings and his intellect. Gradually the scope of these legal rights broadened; and now the right to life has come to mean the right to enjoy life,—the right to be let alone; the right to liberty secures the exercise of extensive civil privileges; and the term "property" has grown to comprise every form or possession—intangible, as well as tangible.

♦ ♦ ♦

Recent inventions and business methods call attention to the next step which must be taken for the protection of the person, and for securing to the individual what Judge Cooley calls the right "to be let alone." Instantaneous photographs and newspaper enterprise have invaded the sacred precincts of private and domestic life; and numerous mechanical devices threaten to make good the prediction that "what is whispered in the closet shall be proclaimed from the house-tops." For years there has been a feeling that the law must afford some remedy for the unauthorized circulation of portraits of private persons and the evil of the invasion of privacy by the newspapers . . . and the question whether our law will recognize and protect the

right to privacy . . . must soon come before our courts for consideration.

Of the desirability—indeed of the necessity—of some such protection, there can, it is believed, be no doubt. The press is overstepping in every direction the obvious bounds of propriety and of decency. Gossip is no longer the resource of the idle and of the vicious, but has become a trade, which is pursued with industry as well as effrontery. To satisfy a prurient taste the details of sexual relations are spread broadcast in the columns of the daily papers. To occupy the indolent, column upon column is filled with idle gossip, which can only be procured by intrusion upon the domestic circle. The intensity and complexity of life, attendant upon advancing civilization, have rendered necessary some retreat from the world, and man, under the refining influence of culture, has become more sensitive to publicity, so that solitude and privacy have become more essential to the individual; but modem enterprise and invention have, through invasions upon his privacy, subjected him to mental pain and distress, far greater than could be inflicted by mere bodily injury. . . . In this, as in other branches of commerce, the supply creates the demand. Each crop of unseemly gossip, thus harvested, becomes the seed of more, and, in direct proportion to its circulation, results in a lowering of social standards and of morality. Even gossip apparently harmless, when widely and persistently circulated, is potent for evil. . . . It belittles by inverting the relative importance of things, thus dwarfing the thoughts and aspirations of a people. When personal gossip attains the dignity of print, and crowds the space available for matters of real interest to the community, what wonder that the ignorant and thoughtless mistake its relative importance. Easy of comprehension, appealing to that weak side of human nature which is never wholly cast down by the misfortunes and frailties of our neighbors, no one can be surprised that it usurps the place of interest in brains capable of other things. Triviality destroys at once robustness of thought and delicacy of feelings. No enthusiasm can flourish, no generous impulse can survive under its blighting influence.

♦   ♦   ♦

The common law secures to each individual the right of determining, ordinarily, to what extent his thoughts, sentiments, and emotions shall be communicated to others. Under our system of government, he can never be compelled to express them (except when upon the witness stand); and even if he has chosen to give them expression, he generally retains the power to fix the limits of the publicity which shall be given them. . . . [T]his right does not depend upon the particular method of expression adopted. . . . Neither does the existence of the right depend upon the nature or value of the thought or emotion, nor upon the excellence of the means of expression. The same protection is accorded to a casual letter or an entry in a diary and to the most valuable poem or essay, to a botch or daub and to a masterpiece. In every such case the individual is entitled to decide whether that which is his shall be given to the public. No other has the right to publish his productions in any form, without his consent. This right is wholly independent of the material on which, or the means by which, the thought, sentiment, or emotion is expressed. It may exist independently of any corporeal being, as in words spoken, a song sung, a drama acted. Or if expressed on any material, as a poem in writing, the author may have parted with the paper, without forfeiting any proprietary right in the composition itself. The right is lost only when the author himself communicates his production to the public—in other words, publishes it. It is entirely independent of the copyright laws, and their extension into the domain of art. The aim of those statutes is to secure to the author, composer, or artist the entire profits arising from publication; but the common-law protection enables him to control absolutely the act of publication, and in . . . his own discretion, to decide whether there shall be any publication at all. The statutory right is of no value, unless there is a publication.

What is the nature, the basis, of this right to prevent the publication of manuscripts or works of art? It is stated to be the enforcement of a right of property; and no difficulty arises in accepting this view, so long as we have only to deal with the reproduction of literary and artistic compositions. . . . But where the value of the production is found not in the right to take the profits arising from publication, but in the peace of mind or the relief afforded by the ability to prevent any publication at all, it is difficult to regard the right as one of property, in the common acceptation of that term. . . . A man writes a dozen letters to different people. No person would be permitted to publish a list of the letters written. If the letters or the contents of the diary were protected as literary compositions, the scope of the protection afforded should be the same secured to a published writing under the copyright law. But the copyright law would not prevent an enumeration of the letters, or the publication of some of the facts contained therein. The copyright of a series of paintings or etchings would prevent a reproduction of the paintings as pictures; but it would not prevent a publication of a list or even a description of them. Yet in the famous case of *Prince Albert* v. *Strange,* the court held that the common-law rule prohibited not merely the reproduction of the etchings which the plaintiff and Queen Victoria had made for their own pleasure, but also "the publishing (at least by printing or writing), though not by copy or resemblance, a description of them, whether more or less limited or summary, whether in the form of a catalogue or otherwise."

♦   ♦   ♦

These considerations lead to the conclusion that the protection afforded to thoughts, sentiments, and emotions, expressed through the medium of writing or of the arts, so far as it consists in preventing publication, is merely an instance of the enforcement of the more general right of the individual to be let alone. It is like the right not to be assaulted or beaten, the right not to be imprisoned, the right not to be maliciously prosecuted, the right not to be defamed. . . . The principle which protects personal writings and all other personal productions, not against theft and physical appropriation, but against publication in any form, is in reality not the principle of private property, but that of an inviolate personality.

If we are correct in this conclusion, the existing law affords a principle which may be invoked to protect the privacy of the individual from invasion either by the too enterprising press, the photographer, or the possessor of any other modem device for recording or reproducing scenes or sounds. For the protection afforded is not confined by the authorities to those cases where any particular medium or form of expression has been adopted, nor to products of the intellect. The same protection is afforded to emotions and sensations expressed in a musical composition or other work of art as to a literary composition; and words spoken, a pantomime acted, a sonata performed, is no less entitled to protection than if each had been reduced to writing. . . . If, then, the decisions indicate a general right to privacy for thoughts, emotions, and sensations, these should receive the same protection, whether expressed in writing, or in conduct, in conversation, in attitudes, or in facial expression.

◆ ◆ ◆

If the invasion of privacy constitutes a legal *injuria,* the elements for demanding redress exist, since already the value of mental suffering, caused by an act wrongful in itself, is recognized as a basis for compensation.

The right of one who has remained a private individual, to prevent his public portraiture, presents the simplest case for such extension; the right to protect one's self from pen portraiture, from a discussion by the press of one's private affairs, would be a more important and far-reaching one. If casual and unimportant statements in a letter, if handiwork, however inartistic and valueless, if possessions of all sorts are protected not only against reproduction, but against description and enumeration, how much more should the acts and sayings of a man in his social and domestic relations be guarded from ruthless publicity. If you may not reproduce a woman's face photo-

graphically without her consent, how much less should be tolerated the reproduction of her face, her form, and her actions, by graphic descriptions colored to suit a gross and depraved imagination.

◆ ◆ ◆

It remains to consider what are the limitations of this right to privacy. . . .

1. The right to privacy does not prohibit any publication of matter which is of public or general interest.

In determining the scope of this rule, aid would be afforded by the analogy, in the law of libel and slander, of cases which deal with the qualified privilege of comment and criticism on matters of public and general interest. . . . The design of the law must be to protect those persons with whose affairs the community has no legitimate concern, from being dragged into an undesirable and undesired publicity and to protect all persons, whatsoever; their position or station, from having matters which they may properly prefer to keep private, made public against their will. It is the unwarranted invasion of individual privacy which is reprehended, and to be, so far as possible, prevented. . . . There are persons who may reasonably claim as a right, protection from the notoriety entailed by being made the victims of journalistic enterprise. There are others who, in varying degrees, have renounced the right to live their lives screened from public observation. . . . Peculiarities of manner and person, which in the ordinary individual should be free from comment, may acquire a public importance, if found in a candidate for political office. . . . To publish of a modest and retiring individual that he suffers from an impediment in his speech or that he cannot spell correctly, is an unwarranted . . . infringement of his rights, while to state and comment on the same characteristics found in a would-be congressman could not be regarded as beyond the pale of propriety.

◆ ◆ ◆

In general, then, the matters of which the publication should be repressed may be described as those which concern the private life, habits, acts, and relations of an individual, and have no legitimate connection with his fitness for a public office which he seeks or for which he is suggested, or for any public or quasi public position which he is suggested, and have no legitimate relation to or bearing upon any act done by him in a public or quasi public capacity. . . . Some things all men alike are entitled to keep from popular curiosity, whether in public life or not, while others are only private because the persons concerned have not assumed a position which makes their doings legitimate matters of public investigation.

2. The right to privacy . . . is not invaded by any publication made in a court of justice, in legislative bodies, or the committees of those bodies; in municipal assemblies, or the committees of such assemblies, or practically by any communication made in any other public body, municipal or parochial, or in any body quasi public, like the large voluntary associations formed for almost every purpose of benevolence, business, or other general interest; and (at least in many jurisdictions) reports of any such proceedings would in some measure be accorded a like privilege.

◆ ◆ ◆

5. The truth of the matter published does not afford a defense. . . . It is not for injury to the individual's character that redress or prevention is sought, but for injury to the right of privacy. For the former, the law of slander and libel provides perhaps a sufficient safeguard. The latter implies the right not merely to prevent inaccurate portrayal of private life, but to prevent its being depicted at all.

6. The absence of "malice" in the publisher does not afford a defence.

Personal ill-will is not an ingredient of the offence, any more than in an ordinary case of trespass to person or to property. . . . The invasion of the privacy that is to be protected is equally complete and equally injurious, whether the motives by which the speaker or writer was actuated are, taken by themselves, culpable or not. . . . Viewed as a wrong to the individual, this rule is the same pervading the whole law of torts, by which one is held responsible for his intentional acts, even though they are committed with no sinister intent; and viewed as a wrong to society, it is the same principle adopted in a large category of statutory offences.

◆ ◆ ◆

[T]he protection of society must come mainly through a recognition of the rights of the individual. Each man is responsible for his own acts and omissions only. If he condones what he reprobates, with a weapon at hand equal to his defence, he is responsible for the results. If he resists, public opinion will rally to his support. Has he then such a weapon? It is believed that the common law provides him with one, forged in the slow fire of the centuries, and to-day fitly tempered to his hand. The common law has always recognized a man's house as his castle, impregnable, often, even to its own officers engaged in the execution of its commands. Shall the courts thus close the front entrance to constituted authority, and open wide the back door to idle or prurient curiosity?

WORLD WAR I AND CIVIL LIBERTIES

World War I stimulated an enormous expansion of federal power. Military procurement, the draft, and opposition to the war led to a new and unprecedented role for the federal government in the economy and to a "pattern of repression" previously unknown in American history. Out of this repression emerged modern civil liberties.

Wartime laws permanently altered the federal government's role in the economy. The war allowed the Wilson administration to "rationalize" the economy along progressive lines, affecting areas of the economy previously unregulated or ineffectively regulated by the states. Congress created numerous bureaucracies, such as the Office of Food Administration and the War Industries Board, to regulate almost all aspects of manufacturing and commerce.

The Lever Act (1917) allowed the president to regulate food and fuel prices, to seize and operate mines and factories, to limit liquor production, and to "commandeer" any "distilled spirits . . . for redistillation" and use "in the manufacture of munitions and other military and hospital supplies." The Wartime Prohibition Act (1918) temporarily stopped the sale of liquor. Another act established rent control in Washington, D.C. The prewar Army Appropriation Act (1916) allowed wartime seizure of the railroads. When these laws were challenged, the Supreme Court upheld them. Although emergency acts, these laws set the stage for more far-reaching economic regulation of the modern era.

The government also sought to regulate the ideas, thoughts, sympathies, and actions of the American people. World War I was not universally popular, and even some members of Congress opposed the declaration of war. This opposition to the war led to intense repression. One lasting result of the war was the emergence of the government's power to restrict freedom of expression through various statutes. The Espionage Act of 1917 punished spying and communicating with the enemy and allowed $10,000 fines and twenty-year jail terms for anyone who made

> false statements with intent to interfere with the operation of success of the military or naval forces of the United States or to promote the success of its enemies and who- ever . . . cause or attempt to cause insubordination, disloyalty, mutiny, or refusal of duty, in the military . . . or shall willfully obstruct the recruiting or enlisted service of the United States.

The act also allowed the post office to prohibit from the mails any publication deemed dangerous, seditious, or treasonous. Without defining these terms, postal officials banned such publications as the *New York Times* and the *Saturday Evening Post,* as well as numerous pacifist, radical, socialist, religious, and antiwar publications. The Supreme Court upheld this law in *Schenck* v. *United States* (1919).

The Sedition Act of 1918 (technically an amendment to the Espionage Act) stipulated the same punishments as the 1917 act for anyone who might

> utter, print, write or publish any disloyal profane, scurrilous, or abusive language about the form of government of the United States, or the Constitution . . . or the military or naval forces . . . or the flag . . . or the uniform of the Army or Navy . . . or any language intended to bring the form of the government of the United States . . . into contempt, scorn, contumely, or disrepute.

The law also punished anyone who

> by utterance, writing, printing, publication, or language spoken, urge, incite or ad- vocate any curtailment of production in this country of any thing or things, product or products, necessary or essential to the prosecution of the war . . . with intent to cripple or hinder the United States in the prosecution of the war, and whoever shall willfully advocate, teach, defend, or suggest the doing of any of the acts or things in this section . . . and whoever shall by word or act support or favor the cause of any country with which the United States is at war.

The law also provided for the immediate dismissal of any federal employee who "utters any unpatriotic or disloyal language, or who, in an abusive and violent manner criticizes the Army or Navy or the flag of the United States." The Supreme Court affirmed the constitutionality of this law in *Abrams* v. *United States* (1919).

THE SUPPRESSION OF DISSENT DURING WORLD WAR I

The Espionage Act and the Sedition Act helped create a climate of fear, hostility, and repression during the war. Throughout the nation, free speech was virtually impossible for those who did not support the war. At the local, state, and federal level, legislators, police, and the "people" suppressed opponents of the war. The sheer variety of repression described next by historian Paul Murphy suggests the nature of the problem of civil liberties during wartime.

PAUL MURPHY

World War I and the Origins of Civil Liberties in the United States
1979

Any empirically precise analysis of public reaction to the whole national pattern of repression is impossible. Attitudinal surveys were not carried out at the time, nor were public opinion polls taken. Impressionistic and anecdotal evidence, however, tends to suggest a number of things. By and large, the country's collective political conscience regarding civil liberties was not sufficiently well developed to make a meaningful general response. By and large the public was less likely to react to the steady expansion of the government's formal repressive policies and mechanisms than to specific episodes and outrages with which they could identify in a highly personalized way. Regrettably, for the scholar, little satisfactory documentation remains which affords any accurate contemporary group response to the wide range of nationally reported episodes which punctuated the war period. Reciting some of the more colorful, however, affords a flavor of wartime behavior. Consider the following:

- Beethoven's music was banned in Pittsburgh for the duration of the war.
- J. M. Ellis, a black Baptist preacher, was beaten by a mob at Newport, Arkansas, for alleged treasonable utterances which were regarded as unproved by a grand jury after he had been kept in jail for ninety-six days.
- Aliens were barred from holding licenses and permits to do business within the city limits of Cleveland, Ohio.

♦ ♦ ♦

- At Marysville, Nebraska, a mob broke into a school, removed all books and material either written in German or about Germany, including Bibles in German, piled them outside and burned them.
- In Detroit, Louis Rafelburge, who was said to have made unfavorable remarks about the Red Cross, was taken from his home in his night clothes, given a haircut and had his mustache trimmed by members of a mob which for a while threatened to duck him in the river.
- After being tarred and feathered, George Koetzer, a brewery worker of San Jose, California, was chained to a brass cannon in the city park. He was charged with having made pro-German remarks.
- Clarence Nesbitt, of Thetford Township, Michigan, was tarred and feathered by a group of men who were displeased because he bought only $1,500 worth of Liberty Bonds instead of the $3,000 that they thought he ought to have purchased.
- The Austrian-born violinist, Fritz Kreisler, and the famous Swiss-born conductor of the Boston Symphony, Dr. Karl Muck, were denied access to American music halls.
- In Columbus, Ohio, school teachers were required to meet after school to paste in school music books blank sheets of paper covering "The Watch on the Rhine" and "The Lorelei."

♦ ♦ ♦

- Victor Berger, Milwaukee Socialist editor, whose newspaper the *Milwaukee Leader,* was indicted for violating the Espionage Act, was denied his seat, with only one dissenting vote, following election to the House of Representatives. One congressman summarized the opposition position, "The one and only issue in this case is that of Americanism."

♦ ♦ ♦

- In Montana, Ves Hall was arrested and charged with espionage for having stated that he would not go to war, that Germany would win, that President Wilson was crooked, and that the war was being fought for the benefit of Wall Street millionaires.
- John White, an Ohio farmer, was sentenced to twenty-one months in the penitentiary for stating that soldiers in American camps "were dying off like flies" and that the "murder of innocent women and children by German soldiers was no worse than the United States' soldiers did in the Philippines."
- In Texas, three organizers of the Non-Partisan League were arrested and jailed for disloyalty. When M. M. Offut, state office manager, protested, he was seized and had his hair and beard cut off with sheep shears before he was driven out of town. The three men were taken by a mob and given a severe whipping. The *Greenville* (Texas) *Banner* stated that this was evidence that "Americanism is not to be tampered with around Mineola."
- A Minnesota man was arrested under the Minnesota Espionage Act for criticizing women knitting socks for soldiers, in stating, "No soldier ever sees these socks."

◆ ◆ ◆

- Women in charge of the Emergency Peace Federation, headquartered in Washington, D.C., were ordered by militiamen to close the office and "beat it," or they would be "raided and raped."
- Six farmers in Texas were horsewhipped because they had not subscribed to the Red Cross.
- George Maynard of Medford, Oregon, a member of the International Bible Students' Association, had an iron cross painted on his chest, and was driven out of town.
- In Baltimore, the day before Wilson's war message, rioters broke up a meeting at which David Starr Jordan, president of Stanford University, was to talk under the auspices of the American Union against Militarism, chanting "We'll hang Dave Jordan to a sour apple tree." The New York Times noted that the mob was led by "men socially prominent," including "college professors, students, bankers, and lawyers."
- The producer of a film *The Spirit of '76* which dealt exclusively with the American Revolution but showed scenes unflattering to the British army, was convicted of attempting to cause insubordination in the armed forces of the United States and sentenced to prison for ten years.
- D. T. Blodgett was sentenced to twenty years in prison for circulating a pamphlet urging the voters of Iowa not to re-elect a congressman who had voted for conscription.
- Twenty-seven South Dakota farmers were convicted for sending a petition to the government objecting to the draft quota for their county and calling the war a "capitalist's war."

CENSORSHIP DURING WORLD WAR I

Shortly after the adoption of the Espionage Act of 1917, the post office began to censor radical publications. In July, *The Masses,* a socialist monthly, sought an injunction to prevent the post office from refusing to deliver the magazine. In *Masses Publishing Co.* v. *Patten* (1917), Federal District Judge Learned Hand warned that "one may not counsel or advise others to violate the law as it stands." He recognized that

> words are not only the keys of persuasion, but the triggers of action, and those which have no purport but to counsel the violation of law cannot by any latitude of interpretation be a part of that public opinion which is the final source of government In a democratic state.

But Hand warned that suppression was acceptable only under narrow circumstances. He rejected suppression of a publication for "abuse and criticism of the existing law, or of the policies of the war." Merely "hostile criticism" that might, in some remote way, "cause" dissatisfaction with the government or the military did not justify censorship. He asserted that to "assimilate" legitimate agitation with direct incitement to violent resistance, is to disregard the tolerance of all methods of political agitation which in normal times is a safeguard of free government. The distinction is not a scholastic subterfuge, but a hard-bought acquisition in the fight for freedom. . . . If one stops short of urging upon others . . . to resist the law, it seems to me one should not be held to have attempted to cause its violation. If that be not the test, I can see no escape from the conclusion that under this section every political agitation which can be shown to be apt to create a seditious temper is illegal.

Hand held that the post office could not prohibit *The Masses* from the mails. Hand's test was whether the publication directly advocated violation of the law. Had Hand's test been applied nationally, the war might have passed with relatively few prosecutions for dissent and with much free discussion of the war and its merits. But Hand was overruled by the Court of Appeals, and in the *Schenck* case the United States Supreme Court articulated a more open-ended test of freedom of expression.

Schenck v. *United States*
249 U.S. 47 (1919)

Schenck was the first Supreme Court case to interpret the First Amendment's speech and press clauses. In upholding Socialist party General Secretary Charles Schenck's conviction under the Espionage Act for having attempted to obstruct the draft by printing, and mailing to draft-age men, 15,000 antiwar leaflets, Justice Oliver Wendell Holmes, Jr., set out the "clear and present danger test," which dominated First Amendment jurisprudence for the next half-century. Holmes developed this test through common-law reasoning, rather than relying on precedent.

The document in question upon its first printed side recited the first section of the Thirteenth Amendment, said that the idea embodied in it was violated by the Conscription Act and that a conscript is little better than a convict. In impassioned language it intimated that conscription was despotism in its worst form and a monstrous wrong against humanity in the interest of Wall Street's chosen few. It said "Do not submit to intimidation," but in form at least confined itself to peaceful measures such as a petition for the repeal of the act. The other . . . side of the sheet was headed "Assert Your Rights." It stated reasons for alleging that any one violated the Constitution when he refused to recognize "your right to assert your opposition to the draft," and went on "If you do not assert and support your rights, you are helping to deny or disparage rights which it is the solemn duty of all citizens and residents of the United States to retain." It described the arguments on the other side as coming from cunning politicians and a mercenary capitalist law as helping to support an infamous conspiracy. It denied the power to send our citizens away to foreign shores to shoot up the people of other lands, and added that words could not express the condemnation such cold-blooded ruthlessness deserves, &c., &c., winding up "You must do your share to maintain, support and uphold the rights of the people of this country." Of course the document would not have been sent unless it had been intended to have some effect, and we do not see what effect it could be expected to have upon persons subject to the draft except to influence them to obstruct the carrying of it out. The defendants do not deny that the jury might find against them on this point.

But it is said, suppose that was the tendency of this circular, it is protected by the First Amendment. . . . Two of the strongest expressions are said to be quoted respectively from well-known public men. It well may be that the prohibition of laws abridging the freedom of speech is not confined to previous restraints, although to prevent them may have been the main purpose. . . . We admit that in many places and in ordinary times the defendants in saying all that was said in the circular would have been within their constitutional rights. But the character of every act depends upon the circumstances in which it is done. The most stringent protection of free speech would not protect a man in falsely shouting fire in a theatre and causing a panic. It does not even protect a man from an injunction against uttering words that may have all the effect of force. The question in every case is whether the words used are used in such circumstances and are of such a nature as to create a clear and present danger that they will bring about the substantive evils that Congress has a right to prevent. It is a question of proximity and degree. When a nation is at war many things that might be said in time of peace are such a hindrance to its effort that their utterance will not be endured so long as men fight and that no Court could regard them as protected by any constitutional right. It seems to be admitted that if an actual obstruction of the recruiting service were proved, liability for words that produced that effect might be enforced. The statute of 1917 . . . punishes conspiracies to obstruct as well as actual obstruction. If the act, (speaking, or circulating a paper,) its tendency and the intent with which it is done are the same, we perceive no ground for saying that success alone warrants making the act a crime.

Note: *Debs* v. *United States*, 249 U.S. 211 (1919)

A week after the Court decided *Schenck,* Justice Holmes upheld the Espionage Act conviction of Eugene V. Debs. This case was particularly troublesome because as the Socialist party candidate for president in 1912, Debs had captured nearly a million votes. Debs was convicted for a speech in which he had attacked militarism, war, and the draft. At his trial, Debs bravely declared: "I have been accused of obstructing the war. I admit it. Gentlemen, I abhor war. I would oppose the war if I stood alone." Debs spent the rest of the war in federal prison. In 1920, he ran for president from prison, getting over 900,000 votes, in the face of a massive "red scare," which led to the arrest of thousands of socialists, labor organizers, and others viewed as "radical" by the Wilson administration.

Abrams et al. v. *United States*
250 U.S. 616 (1919)

Abrams and his co-defendants printed leaflets condemning American intervention in the Russian Revolution, which they "distributed" by throwing out of a window onto a New York City street. The pamphlet called President Wilson "Our Kaiser" and accused him of being "too much of a coward to come out openly and say: 'We capitalistic nations cannot afford to have a proletarian republic in Russia.'" The pamphlet urged a general strike to protest the "barbaric intervention" in the Russian Revolution. Justice John H. Clarke, writing for a 7 to 2 majority, dismissed Abrams's First Amendment claims with a swift reference to Schenck *and sustained the conviction under the Sedition Act, on the theory that "men must be held to have intended, and to be accountable for, the effects which their acts were likely to produce." Clark declared that "the obvious effect" of the leaflet "would be to persuade persons . . . not to work in ammunition factories, where their work would produce 'bullets, bayonets, cannon' and other munitions," and this would affect the war against Germany as well as the American Expeditionary Force in Russia.*

Mr. Justice Holmes dissenting.

This indictment is founded wholly upon the publication of two leaflets. . . .

The first of these leaflets says that the President's cowardly silence about the intervention in Russia reveals the hypocrisy of the plutocratic gang in Washington. It intimates that "German militarism combined with allied capitalism to crush the Russian revolution"—goes on that the tyrants of the world fight each other until they see a common enemy-working class enlightenment, when they combine to crush it; and that now militarism and capitalism combined, though not openly, to crush the Russian revolution. It says that there is only one enemy of the workers of the world and that is capitalism; that it is a crime for workers of America, &c., to fight the workers' republic of Russia, and ends "Awake! Awake, you Workers of the World! Revolutionists." A note adds "It is absurd to call us pro-German. We hate and despise German militarism more than do you hypocritical tyrants. We have more reasons for denouncing German militarism than has the coward of the White House."

The other leaflet, headed "Workers—Wake Up," with abusive language says that America together with the Allies will march for Russia to help the Czecko-Slovaks in their struggle against the Bolsheviki, and that this time the hypocrites shall not fool the Russian emigrants and friends of Russia in America. It tells the Russian emigrants that they now must spit in the face of the false military propaganda by which their sympathy and help to the prosecution of the war have been called forth and says that with the money they have lent or are going to lend "they will make bullets not only for the Germans but also for the Workers Soviets of Russia," and further, "Workers in the ammunition factories, you are producing bullets, bayonets, cannon, to murder not only the Germans, but also your dearest, best, who are in Russia and are fighting for freedom." It then appeals to the same Russian emigrants at some length not to consent to the "inquisitionary expedition to Russia," and says that the destruction of the Russian revolution is "the politics of the march to Russia." The leaflet winds up by saying "Workers, our reply to this barbaric intervention has to be a general strike!," and after a few words on the spirit of revolution, exhortations not to be afraid, and some usual tall talk ends "Woe unto those who will be in the way of progress. Let solidarity live! The Rebels."

No argument seems to me necessary to show that these pronunciamentos in no way attack the form of government of the United States. . . . [I]t seems too plain to be denied that the suggestion to workers in the ammunition factories that they are producing bullets to murder their dearest, and the further advocacy of a general strike, both in the second leaflet, do urge curtailment of production of things necessary to the prosecution of the war within the meaning of the [Espionage] Act. . . .

But to make the conduct criminal that statute requires that it should be "with intent by such curtailment to cripple or hinder the United States in the prosecution of the war." It seems to me that no such intent is proved.

♦ ♦ ♦

It seems to me that this statute must be taken to use its words in a strict and accurate sense. They would be absurd in any other. A patriot might think that we were wasting money on aeroplanes, or making more cannon of a certain kind than we needed, and might advocate curtailment with success, yet even if it turned out that the curtailment hindered and was thought by other minds to have been obviously likely to hinder the United States in the prosecution of the war, no one would hold such conduct a crime. I admit that my illustration does not answer all that might be said but it is enough to show what I think and to let me pass to a

American Legal History

more important aspect of the case. I refer to the First Amendment to the Constitution that Congress shall make no law abridging the freedom of speech.

I never have seen any reason to doubt that the questions of law that alone were before this Court in the cases of *Schenck, Frohwerk* and *Debs* were rightly decided. I do not doubt for a moment that by the same reasoning that would justify punishing persuasion to murder, the United States constitutionally may punish speech that produces or is intended to produce a clear and imminent danger that it will bring about forthwith certain substantive evils that the United States constitutionally may seek to prevent. The power undoubtedly is greater in time of war than in time of peace because war opens dangers that do not exist at other times.

But as against dangers peculiar to war, as against others, the principle of the right to free speech is always the same. It is only the present danger of immediate evil or an intent to bring it about that warrants Congress in setting a limit to the expression of opinion where private rights are not concerned. Congress certainly cannot forbid all effort to change the mind of the country. Now nobody can suppose that the surreptitious publishing of a silly leaflet by an unknown man, without more, would present any immediate danger that its opinions would hinder the success of the government arms or have any appreciable tendency to do so. . . .

I do not see how anyone can find the intent required by the statute in any of the defendants' words. The second leaflet is the only one that affords even a foundation for the charge, and there, without invoking the hatred of German militarism expressed in the former one, it is evident from the beginning to the end that the only object of the paper is to help Russia and stop American intervention there against the popular government—not to impede the United States in the war that it was carrying on. To say that two phrases taken literally might import a suggestion of conduct that would have interference with the war as an indirect and probably undesired effect seems to me by no means enough to show an attempt to produce that effect.

◆   ◆   ◆

In this case sentences of twenty years imprisonment have been imposed for the publishing of two leaflets that I believe the defendants had as much right to publish as the Government has to publish the Constitution of the United States now vainly invoked by them. Even if I am technically wrong and enough can be squeezed from these poor and puny anonymities to turn the color of legal litmus paper; I will add, even if what I think the necessary intent were shown; the most nominal punishment seems to me all that possibly could be inflicted, unless the defendants are to be made to suffer not for what the indictment alleges but for the creed that they avow—a creed that I believe to be the creed of ignorance and immaturity when honestly held, as I see no reason to doubt that it was held here, but which, although made the subject of examination at the trial, no one has a right even to consider in dealing with the charges before the Court.

Persecution for the expression of opinions seems to me perfectly logical. If you have no doubt of your premises or your power and want a certain result with all your heart you naturally express your wishes in law and sweep away all opposition. To allow opposition by speech seems to indicate that you think the speech impotent, as when a man says that he has squared the circle, or that you do not care wholeheartedly for the result, or that you doubt either your power or your premises. But when men have realized that time has upset many fighting faiths, they may come to believe even more than they believe the very foundations of their own conduct that the ultimate good desired is better reached by free trade in ideas—that the best test of truth is the power of the thought to get itself accepted in the competition of the market, and that truth is the only ground upon which their wishes safely can be carried out. That at any rate is the theory of our Constitution. It is an experiment, as all life is an experiment. Every year if not every day we have to wager our salvation upon some prophecy based upon imperfect knowledge. While that experiment is part of our system I think that we should be eternally vigilant against attempts to check the expression of opinions that we loathe and believe to be fraught with death, unless they so imminently threaten immediate interference with the lawful and pressing purposes of the law that an immediate check is required to save the country. I wholly disagree with the argument of the Government that the First Amendment left the common law as to seditious libel in force. History seems to me against the notion. I had conceived that the United States through many years had shown its repentance for the Sedition Act of 1798, by repaying fines that it imposed. Only the emergency that makes it immediately dangerous to leave the correction of evil counsels to time warrants making any

exception to the sweeping command, "Congress shall make no law . . . abridging the freedom of speech." Of course I am speaking only of expressions of opinion and exhortations, which were all that were uttered here, but I regret that I cannot put into more impressive words my belief that in their conviction upon this indictment the defendants were deprived of their rights under the Constitution of the United States.

Mr. Justice Brandeis concurs with the foregoing opinion.

Note: The *Abrams* Dissent

Justice Holmes's *Abrams* dissent was an eloquent and moving defense of free speech equal to that of Milton's *Areogpagitica*. Here Holmes laid out a theory of freedom of speech in a democracy that would eventually be adopted by the Supreme Court. Nevertheless, the change from *Schenck* to *Abrams* is puzzling. Despite his ringing defense of free speech, Holmes endorsed his *Schenck* opinion while appearing to modify his test. Is the test in *Abrams* different from that in *Schenck*? Is this a change of position or merely the application of different facts to the same test?

RADICALS AND CIVIL LIBERTIES

At the end of World War I, Americans faced rampant inflation and unemployment. Returning soldiers found it difficult to find jobs, while workers in defense-related industries were laid off or fired. Socialists saw an opportunity to increase their following. They were heartened by the Communist revolution in Russia in 1917 and by the strength of socialism in other European countries, including Germany. For many American radicals, the age of revolution seemed at hand. Most members of the old Socialist party split from that organization to form what evolved into the American Communist party.

Conservatives also thought the revolution was at hand, and they were not pleased. On January 2, 1920, United States Attorney General A. Mitchell Palmer launched a nationwide preemptive strike against radicals, arresting over 4,000 people, mostly members of the Socialist party or the Industrial Workers of the World (IWW). These raids were conducted without warrants and with little regard for due process. Thousands were incarcerated in overcrowded jails for months.

What Palmer did on the national scale, others accomplished at the state and local levels. Even before the Palmer raids began, the New York legislature, through the Lusk Committee, began to investigate radicals in that state. "Investigation" for the Lusk Committee meant police raids on the offices of radical organizations and arrests of members. The New York Assembly also refused to seat five legally elected socialists.

Most of the radicals jailed by state and federal authorities were eventually pardoned, although many were deported or died in jail. The survivors left prison with their lives shattered. For most, their only crime was believing in the wrong ideology and joining the wrong organizations.

By mid-decade, the "red scare" had run its course, leaving the IWW virtually destroyed, the Communist party decimated, and the Socialist party no longer able to garner much electoral support. Americans of the 1920s turned from mass hysteria over radicalism to the mass excesses of the Jazz Age. Prohibition, gangsters, and conspicuous consumption occupied the public's mind. While huge raids on radicals ceased, the 1920s remained a dangerous decade for Americans with radical ideas. Although the courts rarely protected civil liberties, hints of a more tolerant future could be found in the prophetic dissents of Justices Oliver Wendell Holmes, Jr., and Louis Brandeis, and in the recognition by the Supreme Court that the Fourteenth Amendment made the First Amendment applicable to the states.

Note: Civil Liberties and Fourteenth Amendment Incorporation

The Fourteenth Amendment prohibits state infringements of due process with expansive language, which the late-nineteenth-century Court had turned into a shield for business interests. From 1884 to 1908, the United States Supreme Court refused to use the due process clause of the Fourteenth Amendment to make various provisions of the Bill of Rights applicable to the states. *Hurtado* v. *California* (1884) upheld a California murder conviction without a grand jury indictment. In *Maxwell* v. *Dow* (1900), the Court upheld a Utah conviction of the bank-robbing desperado "Gunplay" Maxwell by an eight-man jury (instead of the traditional twelve-man jury). In *Twining* v. *New Jersey* (1908), the Court rejected a claim that the due process clause of the Fourteenth Amendment and the Fifth Amendment protected Twining, a corrupt bank officer, against self-incrimination in a state trial. Justice William H. Moody concluded that the protection against self-incrimination was neither a "fundamental" right nor necessary for due process. In reaching this decision, however, the Court opened the door to future applications of the Bill of Rights to the states through the Fourteenth Amendment, noting that "some of the personal rights safeguarded by the first eight Amendments against national action may also be safeguarded against state action, because a denial of them would be a denial of due process of law."

The connection between civil liberties and property continued after World War I. After the war, Nebraska prohibited teaching foreign languages to children who had not "successfully passed the eighth grade." This act was aimed at the state's large German-speaking community. In *Meyer* v. *Nebraska* (1922), the Court reversed the conviction of a German instructor at a German Lutheran parochial school. The Court held that the Nebraska law deprived citizens of their "liberty, or property, without due process of law" because the Fourteenth Amendment protected

> the right of the individual to contract, to engage in any of the common occupations of life, to acquire useful knowledge, to marry, establish a home and bring up children, to worship God according to the dictates of his own conscience, and generally to enjoy those privileges long recognized at common law as essential to the orderly pursuit of happiness of free men.

This decision did not incorporate First Amendment protections of religious liberty through the Fourteenth Amendment. Rather, it applied the conservative doctrine found in *Lochner* v. *New York* (1905) and other cases that the state "under the guise of protecting the public interest" could not interfere with the liberty of contract and the common-law rights of parents to raise their children. In *Pierce* v. *Society of the Sisters* (1925), the Court reaffirmed the doctrine in *Meyer* by striking down Oregon's prohibition on private schools. The Court found that

> the fundamental theory of liberty upon which all governments in this Union repose excludes any general power of the state to standardize its children by forcing them to accept instruction from public teachers only. The child is not the mere creature of the state; those who nurture him and direct this destiny have the right . . . to recognize and prepare him [for life].

In addition, the Court held that the Society of Sisters and other owners of private schools had a property right in their schools that the state could not arbitrarily take from them. Thus the Court permanently enjoined enforcement of the Oregon law.

Seven days after deciding *Pierce*, the Court began the incorporation of the Bill of Rights to the states in *Gitlow* v. *New York* (1925). Gitlow, a Communist party leader, had been convicted of violating New York's criminal anarchy law. On appeal, Gitlow argued that his conviction violated his First Amendment rights because he never constituted a "clear and present danger" that the state could legitimately suppress. The conservative Taft Court rejected Gitlow's arguments about the nature of free speech in a democracy, but did accept Gitlow's theoretical point: that the Fourteenth Amendment prohibited the states from abridging First Amendment rights. Casually and almost without any careful thought, the Court reversed over fifty years of precedent with a simple statement: "For present purposes we may and do assume that freedom of speech and of the press—which are protected by the First Amendment from abridgment by Congress—are among the fundamental personal rights 'liberties' protected by the due process clause of the Fourteenth Amendment from impairment by the States."

Gitlow thus became a major watershed in American legal and constitutional history. After *Gitlow,* most of the Bill of Rights would be gradually incorporated, through the Fourteenth Amendment, to apply to the states. This held both for politically sensitive cases tied to freedom of expression and for run-of-the-mill criminal cases involving search and seizure, arrest, and trial. *Gitlow* began an era when almost all public law, and a good deal of private law, would come under federal jurisdiction through the Fourteenth Amendment and the Bill of Rights.

Whitney v. *California*
274 U.S. 357 (1927)

A California court found Whitney in violation of the state's Criminal Syndicalism Act because of her membership in the Communist Labor Party of America. Because at trial Whitney failed to assert a right to freedom of speech under the First and Fourteenth Amendments, the Supreme Court unanimously held that no federal question had been properly raised. Justice Brandeis, joined by Justice Holmes, concurred in the technical result of the case with one of the most eloquent defenses of freedom of expression in American legal history.

This Court has not yet fixed the standard by which to determine when a danger shall be deemed clear; how remote the danger may be and yet be deemed present; and what degree of evil shall be deemed sufficiently substantial to justify resort to abridgment of free speech and assembly as the means of protection. To reach sound conclusions on these matters, we must bear in mind why a State is, ordinarily, denied the power to prohibit dissemination of social, economic and political doctrine which a vast majority of its citizens believes to be false and fraught with evil consequence.

Those who won our independence believed that the final end of the State was to make men free to develop their faculties; and that in its government the deliberative forces should prevail over the arbitrary. They valued liberty both as an end and a means. They believed liberty to be the secret of happiness and courage to be the secret of liberty. They believed that freedom to think as you will and to speak as you think are means indispensable to the discovery and spread of political truth; that without free speech and assembly discussion would be futile; that with them, discussion affords ordinarily adequate protection against the dissemination of noxious doctrine; that the greatest menace to freedom is an inert people; that public discussion is a political duty; and that this should be a fundamental principle of the American government. They recognized the risks to which all human institutions are subject. But they knew that order cannot be secured merely through fear of punishment for its infraction; that it is hazardous to discourage thought, hope and imagination; that fear breeds repression; that repression breeds hate; that hate menaces stable government; that the path of safety lies in the opportunity to discuss freely supposed grievances and proposed remedies; and that the fitting remedy for evil counsels is good ones. Believing in the power of reason as applied through public discussion, they eschewed silence coerced by law—the argument of force in its worst form. Recognizing the occasional tyrannies of governing majorities, they amended the Constitution so that free speech and assembly should be guaranteed.

Fear of serious injury cannot alone justify suppression of free speech and assembly. Men feared witches and burnt women. It is the function of speech to free men from the bondage of irrational fears. To justify suppression of free speech there must be reasonable ground to fear that serious evil will result if free speech is practiced. There must be reasonable ground to believe that the danger apprehended is imminent. There must be reasonable ground to believe that the evil to be prevented is a serious one. Every denunciation of existing law tends in some measure to increase the probability that there will be violation of it. Condonation of a breach enhances the probability. Expressions of approval add to the probability. Propagation of the criminal state of mind by teaching syndicalism increases it. Advocacy of lawbreaking heightens it still further. But even advocacy of violation, however reprehensible morally, is not a justification for denying free speech where the advocacy falls short of incitement and there is nothing to indicate that the advocacy would be immediately acted on. The wide difference between advocacy and incitement, between preparation and attempt, between assembling and conspiracy, must be borne in mind. In order to support a finding of clear and present danger it must be shown either that immediate serious violence was to be expected or was advocated, or that the past conduct furnished reason to believe that such advocacy was then contemplated.

Those who won our independence by revolution were not cowards. They did not fear political change. They did not exalt order at the cost of liberty. To courageous, self-reliant men, with confidence in the power of free and fearless reasoning applied through the processes of popular government, no danger flowing from speech can be deemed clear and present, unless the incidence of the evil apprehended is so imminent that it may befall before there is opportunity for full discussion. If there be time to expose through discussion the falsehood and fallacies, to avert the evil by the processes of education, the remedy to be applied is more speech, not enforced silence. Only an emergency can justify repression. Such must be the rule if authority is to be reconciled with freedom. Such, in my opinion, is the command of the Constitution. It is therefore always open to Americans by showing that there was no emergency justifying it.

Moreover, even imminent danger cannot justify resort to prohibition of these functions essential to effective democracy, unless the evil apprehended is relatively serious. Prohibition of free speech and assembly is a measure so stringent that it would be inappropriate as the means for averting a relatively trivial harm to society. A police measure may be unconstitutional merely because the remedy, although effective as means of protection, is unduly harsh or oppressive. Thus, a State might, in the exercise of its police power, make any trespass upon the land of another a crime, regardless of the results or of the intent or purpose of the trespasser. It might, also, punish an attempt, a conspiracy, or an incitement to commit the trespass. But it is hardly conceivable that this Court would hold constitutional a statute which punished as a felony the mere voluntary assembly with a society formed to teach that pedestrians had the moral right to cross unenclosed, unposted, waste lands and to advocate their doing so, even if there was imminent danger that advocacy would lead to a trespass. The fact that speech is likely to result in some violence or in destruction of property is not enough to justify its suppression. There must be the probability of serious injury to the State. Among free men, the deterrents ordinarily to be applied to prevent crime are education and punishment for violations of the law, not abridgment of the rights of free speech and assembly.

WORLD WAR II AND LEGAL DEVELOPMENTS

World War I unleashed unprecedented hysteria, undermining civil liberties in the nation. This hysteria was partly a result of the mixed feelings Americans had about the war. Many Americans opposed the war or at least doubted that a war in Europe was an American concern. The uncertain causes of the war and the weakness of support for the war partly explain the aggressive suppression of opposition to the war.

The situation was different at the beginning of World War II. In the 1930s, the United States had aided China in its war against Japan and openly sided with Britain in the war against Germany. Although isolationism had been a powerful force in the 1930s, the surprise bombing of Pearl Harbor united Americans as few events have. During this war there were, with one gigantic exception, few attacks on civil liberties. Some American fascists were tried,[1] but unlike World War I, during World War II, Americans tolerated dissent and conscientious objectors. In the flag salute cases, the Court finally recognized the importance of protecting minority rights, even during wartime.

The great exception to this trend was the forcible incarceration of approximately 112,000 Japanese Americans in what were euphemistically called "relocation centers" or "internment camps." Two-thirds of these people were American citizens of Japanese ancestry. The rest were mostly aged immigrants who had lived in the United States for decades, but, because of racist naturalization laws, were not allowed to become citizens.

THE FLAG SALUTE CASES

In 1936, school officials in Minersville, Pennsylvania, expelled Lillian and William Gobitis for refusing to salute the flag. As Jehovah's Witnesses, the Gobitis family believed that saluting a flag violated biblical injunctions against worshiping graven images. In *Minersville School District* v. *Gobitis* (1940), the Court ruled 8 to 1 (Justice Harlan Stone dissenting) in favor of the school district. Writing for the Court, Justice Felix Frankfurter argued that saluting the flag "promot[ed] . . . national cohesion," and this was "an interest inferior to none in the hierarchy of legal values." Frankfurter thought that "National unity" was "the basis of national security," and he was unwilling "to deny the legislature the right to select appropriate means for its attainment."

Frankfurter personally opposed the forced flag salute, but he thought the courts ought not interfere with the legitimate goal of instilling patriotism in children and the reasonable method of saluting the flag. He suggested that

> where all effective means of inducing political changes are left free from interference, education in the abandonment of foolish legislation is itself a training in liberty. To fight out the wise use of legislative authority in the forum of public opinion and before legislative assemblies rather than to transfer such a context to the judicial arena, serves to vindicate the self-confidence of a free people.

West Virginia State Board of Education v. Barnette
319 U.S. 624 (1943)

Immediately after Gobitis, *Jehovah's Witnesses faced widespread suppression and violence at the hands of mobs, vigilantes, and even police officials. In 1942, West Virginia's State Board of Education required that all teachers and students "participate in the salute honoring the Nation represented by the Flag." Refusal to salute the flag was considered "insubordination," which led to expulsion of the children and subjected their parents to up to $50 fines and up to thirty days in jail. The Barnette children, who were Jehovah's Witnesses, challenged the law after they were subjected to its penalties. A federal district court enjoined the enforcement of the law, and the Board of Education appealed to the United States Supreme Court, relying on* Gobitis.

Mr. Justice Jackson delivered the opinion of the Court.

◆ ◆ ◆

As the present Chief Justice [Stone] said in dissent in the *Gobitis* case, the State may "require teaching by instruction and study of all in our history and in the structure and organization of our government, including the guaranties of civil liberty, which tend to inspire patriotism and love of country." Here, however, we are dealing with a compulsion of students to declare a belief. They are not merely made acquainted with the flag salute so that they may be informed as to what it is or even what it means. The issue here is whether this slow and easily neglected route to aroused loyalties constitutionally may be short-cut by substituting compulsory salute and slogan. This issue is not prejudiced by the Court's previous holding that where a State, without compelling attendance, extends college facilities to pupils who voluntarily enroll, it may prescribe military training

as part of the course without offense to the Constitution. It was held that those who take advantage of its opportunities may not on ground of conscience refuse compliance with such conditions. *Hamilton* v. *Regents.* In the present case attendance is not optional. . . .

There is no doubt that the flag salute is a form of utterance. Symbolism is a primitive but effective way of communicating ideas. The use of an emblem or flag to symbolize some system, idea, institution, or personality, is a short cut from mind to mind. Causes and nations, political parties, lodges and ecclesiastical groups seek to knit the loyalty of their followings to a flag or banner, a color or design. The State announces rank, function, and authority through crowns and maces, uniforms and black robes; the church speaks through the Cross, the Crucifix, the altar and shrine, and clerical raiment. Symbols of State often convey political ideas just as religious symbols come to convey theological ones. Associated with many to these symbols are appropriate gestures of acceptance or respect: a salute, a bowed or bared head, a bended knee. A person gets from a symbol the meaning he puts into it, and what is one man's comfort and inspiration is another's jest and scorn.

Over a decade ago Chief Justice Hughes led this Court in holding that the display of a red flag as a symbol of opposition by peaceful and legal means to organized government was protected by the free speech guaranties of the Constitution. *Stromberg* v. *California.* Here it is the State that employs a flag as a symbol of adherence to government as presently organized. It requires the individual to communicate by word and sign his acceptance of the political ideas it thus bespeaks. Objection to this form of communication when coerced is an old one, well known to the framers of the Bill of Rights.

It is also to be noted that the compulsory flag salute and pledge requires affirmation of a belief and an attitude of mind. . . . It is now a commonplace that censorship or suppression of expression of opinion is tolerated by our Constitution only when the expression presents a clear and present danger of action of a kind the State is empowered to prevent and punish. It would seem that involuntary affirmation could be commanded only on even more immediate and urgent grounds than silence. But here the power of compulsion is invoked without any allegation that remaining passive during a flag salute ritual creates a clear and present danger that would justify an effort even to muffle expression. To sustain the compulsory flag salute we are required to say that a Bill of Rights guards the individual's right to speak his own mind, left it open to public authorities to compel him to utter what is not in his mind.

♦   ♦   ♦

The *Gobitis* decision, however, *assumed* . . . that power exists in the State to impose the flag salute discipline upon school children in general. The Court only examined and rejected a claim based on religious beliefs of immunity from an unquestioned general rule. The question which underlies the flag salute controversy is whether such a ceremony so touching matters of opinion and political attitude may be imposed upon the individual by official authority under powers committed to any political organization under our Constitution. We examine rather than assume existence of this power and . . . re-examine specific grounds assigned for the *Gobitis* decision.

1. It was said [in Frankfurter's *Gobitis* opinion] that the flag-salute controversy confronted the Court with "the problem which Lincoln cast in memorable dilemma: 'Must a government of necessity be too *strong* for the liberties of its people, or too *weak* to maintain its own existence?' and that the answer must be in favor of strength."

We think issues may be examined free of pressure or restraint growing out of such considerations.

It may be doubted whether Mr. Lincoln would have thought that the strength of government to maintain itself would be impressively vindicated by our confirming power of the State to expel a handful of children from school. Such oversimplification, so handy in political debate, often lacks the precision necessary to postulates of judicial reasoning. If validly applied to this problem, the utterance cited would resolve every issue of power in favor of those in authority and would require us to override every liberty thought to weaken or delay execution of their policies.

Government of limited power need not be anemic government. Assurance that rights are secure tends to diminish fear and jealousy of strong government, and by making us feel safe to live under it makes for its better support. Without promise of a limiting Bill of Rights it is doubtful if our Constitution could have mustered enough strength to enable its ratification. To enforce those rights today is not to choose weak government over strong government. It is only to adhere as a means of strength to individual freedom of mind in preference to officially disciplined uniformity for which history indicates a disappointing and disastrous end.

2. It was also considered in the *Gobitis* case that functions of educational officers in States, counties and school districts were such that to interfere with their authority "would in effect make us the school board for the country."

♦   ♦   ♦

Such Boards are numerous and their territorial jurisdiction often small. But small and local authority may feel less sense of responsibility to the Constitution, and agencies of publicity may be less vigilant in calling it to account. The action of Congress in making flag observance voluntary and respecting the conscience of the objector in a matter so vital as raising the Army contrasts sharply with these local regulations in matters relatively trivial to the welfare of the nation. There are village tyrants as well as village Hampdens, but none who acts under color of law is beyond reach of the Constitution.

3. The *Gobitis* opinion reasoned that this is a field "where courts possess no marked . . . competence," that it is committed to the legislatures as well as the courts to guard cherished liberties and that it is constitutionally appropriate to "fight out the wise use of legislative authority in the forum of public opinion and before legislative assemblies rather than to transfer such a contest to the judicial arena. . . .

The very purpose of a Bill of Rights was to withdraw certain subjects from the vicissitudes of political controversy, to place them beyond the reach of majorities and officials and to establish them as legal principles to be applied by the courts. One's right to life, liberty, and property, to free speech, a free press, freedom of worship and assembly, and other fundamental rights may not be submitted to vote; they depend on the outcome of no elections.

4. Lastly, and this is the very heart of the *Gobitis* opinion, it reasons that "National unity is the basis of national security," that the authorities have "the right to select appropriate means for its attainment," and hence reaches the conclusion that such compulsory measures toward "national unity" are constitutional. Upon the verity of this assumption depends our answer in this case.

◆   ◆   ◆

Struggles to coerce uniformity of sentiment in support of some end thought essential to their time and country have been waged by many good as well as by evil men. Nationalism is a relatively recent phenomenon but at other times and places the ends have been racial or territorial security, support of a dynasty or

regime, and particular plans for saving souls. As . . . moderate methods to attain unity have failed, those bent on its accomplishment must resort to an ever-increasing severity. . . . Ultimate futility of such attempts to compel coherence is the lesson of every such effort from the Roman drive to stamp out Christianity as a disturber of its pagan unity, the Inquisition, as a means to religious and dynastic unity, the Siberian exiles as a means to Russian unity, down to the fast failing efforts of our present totalitarian enemies. Those who begin coercive elimination of dissent soon find themselves exterminating dissenters. Compulsory unification of opinion achieves only the unanimity of the graveyard.

It seems trite but necessary to say that the First Amendment to our Constitution was designed to avoid these ends by avoiding these beginnings. There is no mysticism in the American concept of the State or of the nature or origin of its authority. We set up government by consent of the governed, and the Bill of Rights denies those in power any legal opportunity to coerce that consent. Authority here is to be controlled by public opinion, not public opinion by authority.

The case is made difficult not because the principles of its decision are obscure but because the flag involved is our own. Nevertheless, we apply the limitations of the Constitution with no fear that freedom to be intellectually and spiritually diverse or even contrary will disintegrate the social organization. To believe that patriotism will not flourish if patriotic ceremonies are voluntary and spontaneous instead of a compulsory routine is to make an unflattering estimate of the appeal of our institutions to free minds. We can have intellectual individualism and the rich cultural diversities that we owe to exceptional minds only at the price of occasional eccentricity and abnormal attitudes. When they are so harmless to others or to the State as those we deal with here, the price is not too great. But freedom to differ is not limited to things that do not matter much. That would be a mere shadow of freedom. The test of its substance is the right to differ as to things that touch the heart of the existing order.

If there is any fixed star in our constitutional constellation, it is that no official, high or petty, can prescribe what shall be orthodox in politics, nationalism, religion, or other matters of opinion or force citizens to confess by word or act their faith therein. If there are any circumstances which permit an exception, they do not now occur to us.

We think the action of the local authorities in compelling the flag salute and pledge transcends constitutional limitations on their power and invades the sphere of intellect and spirit which it is the purpose of the First Amendment to our Constitution to reserve from all official control.

The decision of this Court in *Minersville School District* v. *Gobitis* . . . [is] overruled, and the judgment enjoining enforcement of the West Virginia Regulation is

Affirmed.

Mr. Justice Frankfurter, dissenting:

One who belongs to the most vilified and persecuted minority in history is not likely to be insensible to the freedoms guaranteed by our Constitution. Were my purely personal attitude relevant I should wholeheartedly associate myself with the general libertarian views in the Court's opinion, representing as they do the thought and action of a lifetime. But as judges we are neither Jew nor Gentile, neither Catholic nor agnostic. We owe equal attachment to the Constitution and are equally bound by our judicial obligations whether we derive our citizenship from the earliest or the latest immigrants to these shores. As a member of this Court I am not justified in writing my private notions of policy into the Constitution, no matter how deeply I may cherish them or how mischievous I may deem their disregard. The duty of a judge who must decide which of two claims before the Court shall prevail, that of a State to enact and enforce laws within its general competence or that of an individual to refuse obedience because of the demands of his conscience, is not that of the ordinary person. It can never be emphasized too much that one's own opinion about the wisdom or evil of a law should be excluded altogether when one is doing one's duty on the bench. The only opinion of our own even looking in that direction that is material is our opinion whether legislators could in reason have enacted such a law. In the

light of all the circumstances, including the history of this question in this Court, it would require more daring than I possess to deny that reasonable legislators could have taken the action which is before us for review. Most unwillingly, therefore, I must differ from my brethren with regard to legislation like this. I cannot bring my mind to believe that the "liberty" secured by the Due Process Clause gives this Court authority to deny to the State of West Virginia the attainment of that which we all recognize as a legitimate legislative end, namely, the promotion of good citizenship, by employment of the means here chosen.

◆　◆　◆

That claims are pressed on behalf of sincere religious convictions does not of itself establish their constitutional validity. Nor does waving the banner of religious freedom relieve us from examining into the power we are asked to deny the states. Otherwise the doctrine of separation of church and state, so cardinal in the history of this nation and for the liberty of our people, would mean not the disestablishment of a state church but the establishment of all churches and of all religious groups.

The subjection of dissidents to the general requirement of saluting the flag, as a measure conducive to the training of children in good citizenship, is very far from . . . exacting obedience to general laws that have offended deep religious scruples. Compulsory vaccination . . . food inspection regulations . . . the obligation to bear arms . . . testimonial duties . . . compulsory medical treatment . . . these are but illustrations of conduct that has often been compelled in the enforcement of legislation of general applicability even though the religious consciences of particular individuals rebelled at the exaction.

Law is concerned with external behavior and not with the inner life of man. It rests in large measure upon compulsion. Socrates lives in history partly because he gave his life for the conviction that duty of obedience to secular law does not presuppose consent to its enactment or belief in its virtue. The consent upon which free government rests is the consent that comes from sharing in the process of making and unmaking laws. . . . The individual conscience may profess what faith it chooses. . . . [B]ut it cannot hereby restrict community action through political organs in matters of community concern, so long as the action is not asserted in a discriminatory way either openly or by stealth. One may have the right to practice one's religion and at the same time owe the duty of formal obedience to laws that run counter to one's beliefs.

♦ ♦ ♦

The flag salute exercise has no kinship whatever to the oath tests so odious in history. For the oath test was one of the instruments for suppressing heretical beliefs. Saluting the flag suppresses no belief nor curbs it. Children and their parents may believe what they please, avow their belief and practice it. It is not even remotely suggested that the requirement for saluting the flag involves the slightest restriction against the fullest opportunity on the part both of the children and of their parents to disavow as publicly as they choose to do so the meaning that others attach to the gesture of salute. All channels of affirmative free expression are open to both children and parents. Had we before us any act of the state putting the slightest curbs upon such free expression, I should not lag behind any member of this Court in striking down such an invasion of the right to freedom of thought and freedom of speech protected by the Constitution.

♦ ♦ ♦

One's conception of the Constitution cannot be severed from one's conception of a judge's function in applying it. . . . Our system is built on the faith that men set apart for this special function, freed from the influences of immediacy and from the deflections of worldly ambition, will become able to take a view of longer range than the period of responsibility entrusted to Congress and legislatures. We are dealing with matters as to which legislators and voters have conflicting views. Are we as judges to impose our strong convictions on where wisdom lies? That which three years ago had seemed . . . to lie within permissible areas of legislation is now outlawed by the deciding shift of opinion of two Justices. What reason is there to believe that they or their successors may not have another view a few years hence? Is that which was deemed to be of so fundamental a nature as to be written into the Constitution to endure for all times to be the sport of shifting winds of doctrine? Of course, judicial opinions, even as to questions of constitutionality, are not immutable. As has been true in the past, the Court will from time to time reverse its position. But I believe that never before these Jehovah's Witnesses cases . . . has this Court overruled decisions so as to restrict the powers of democratic government. Always heretofore, it has withdrawn narrow views of legislative authority so as to authorize what formerly it had denied.

♦ ♦ ♦

Of course patriotism can not be enforced by the flag salute. But neither can the liberal spirit be enforced by judicial invalidation of illiberal legislation. Our constant preoccupation with the constitutionality of legislation rather than with its wisdom tends to preoccupation of the American mind with a false value. The tendency of focusing attention on constitutionality is to make constitutionality synonymous with wisdom, to regard a law as all right if it is constitutional. Such an attitude is a great enemy of liberalism. Particularly in legislation affecting freedom of thought and freedom of speech much which should offend a free-spirited society is constitutional. Reliance for the most precious interests of civilization, therefore, must be found outside of their vindication in courts of law. Only a persistent positive translation of the faith of a free society into the convictions and habits and actions of a community is the ultimate reliance against unabated temptations to fetter the human spirit.

The Japanese Internment

Shortly after the attack on Pearl Harbor, General John DeWitt, head of the Western Defense Command, argued for military control of the 112,000 West Coast Japanese Americans, three-quarters of whom were citizens. His erroneous reports of sabotage in California and off-shore Japanese naval activity added to a growing hysteria. "To hell with habeas corpus," one newspaper columnist said, in arguing for "concentration camps" for Japanese Americans. Republican Congressman Leland Ford urged that any "Japanese, whether citizens or not" would prove he is "patriotic" by "permitting himself to be placed in a concentration camp."[2]

Attorney General Francis Biddle resisted any mass evacuation of American citizens on the grounds that such a procedure would violate their constitutional rights. However, Biddle was outmaneuvered by Assistant Attorney General Tom Clark, who favored an internment, and by Assistant Secretary of War John J. McCloy. When Biddle opposed military evacuation of civilians, McCloy told the attorney general, "You are putting a Wall Street lawyer in a helluva box, but if it is a question of the safety of the country [or] the constitution . . . why the constitution is just a scrap of paper to me."[3]

Note: Executive Order-No. 9066

On February 19, 1942, acting in his capacity as commander-in-chief under authority granted by the Espionage Act of 1917 and various acts passed in 1940 and 1941, President Franklin D. Roosevelt issued Executive Order-No. 9066, allowing the exclusion of civilians from "military areas." Declaring "that the successful prosecution of the war requires every possible protection against espionage and against sabotage," Roosevelt authorized

> the Secretary of War and the Military Commanders who he may from time to time designate . . . to prescribe military areas in such places and of such extent as [they] . . . may determine, from which any or all persons may be excluded and with respect to which, the right of any person to enter, remain in, or leave shall be subject to whatever restrictions the Secretary of War or the appropriate Military Commander may impose in his discretion.

Roosevelt ordered the secretary of war "to provide for residents of any such area who are excluded therefrom, such transportation, food, shelter, and other accommodations as may be necessary." All other executive departments and federal agencies were ordered to assist the secretary of war or the said military commanders in carrying out this executive order, including the furnishing of medical aid, hospitalization, food, clothing, transportation, use of land, shelter, and other supplies, equipment, utilities, facilities, and services.

In March, President Roosevelt signed Executive Order-No. 9102, creating the War Relocation Authority. On March 24, General DeWitt imposed a nighttime curfew on all persons of Japanese ancestry. On March 27, DeWitt prohibited Japanese Americans from moving away from where they lived. Starting on March 24 and continuing through May, General DeWitt issued a series of "Civilian Exclusion Orders" requiring Japanese Americans to report to civilian control centers, from which they were removed to internment camps.

Hirabayashi v. United States
320 U.S. 81 (1943)

In May 1942, Gordon Hirabayashi, an American citizen of Japanese ancestry and a senior at the University of Washington, refused to obey a curfew imposed on Japanese Americans

and to report to the civilian control station where his "presence" was "required" as "a pre-
liminary step to the exclusion from that area of persons of Japanese ancestry." Hirabayashi
believed that if he obeyed these orders, "he would be waiving his rights as an American cit-
izen." Although the Court unanimously justified the curfew as a military necessity, Justice
Frank Murphy's concurrence indicates the Court's fragile unanimity.

Mr. Chief Justice Stone delivered the Opinion
of the Court.

♦ ♦ ♦

The challenged orders were defense
measures for the avowed purpose of safeguarding the military area in question, at a
time of threatened air raids and invasion by
the Japanese forces, from the danger of sabotage and espionage. As the curfew was made
applicable to citizens residing in the area only
if they were of Japanese ancestry, our inquiry
must be whether in the light of all the facts
and circumstances there was any substantial
basis for the conclusion . . . that the curfew
as applied was a protective measure necessary to meet the threat of sabotage and espionage which would substantially affect the
war effort and which might reasonably be expected to aid a threatened enemy invasion.
The alternative which appellant insists must
be accepted is for the military authorities to
impose the curfew on all citizens within the
military area, or on none. In a case of threatened danger requiring prompt action, it is a
choice between inflicting obviously needless
hardship on the many, or sitting passive and
unresisting in the presence of the threat. We
think that constitutional government, in time
of war, is not so powerless and does not compel so hard a choice if those charged with the
responsibility of our national defense have
reasonable ground for believing that the
threat is real.

♦ ♦ ♦

But appellant insists that the exercise of the
power is inappropriate and unconstitutional because it discriminates against citizens of Japanese ancestry. . . .

Distinctions between citizens solely because of their ancestry are by their very nature
odious to a free people whose institutions are
founded upon the doctrine of equality. For that
reason, legislative classification or discrimination based on race alone has often been held to
be a denial of equal protection. . . .

We may assume that these considerations
would be controlling here were it not for the
fact that the danger of espionage and sabotage,
in time of war and of threatened invasion, calls
upon the military authorities to scrutinize every
relevant fact bearing on the loyalty of populations in the danger areas. Because racial discriminations are in most circumstances irrelevant and therefore prohibited, it by no means
follows that, in dealing with the perils of war,
Congress and the Executive are wholly precluded from taking into account those facts and
circumstances which are relevant to measures
for our national defense and for the successful
prosecution of the war, and which may in fact
place citizens of one ancestry in a different category from others. . . . The adoption by Government, in the crisis of war and of threatened
invasion, of measures for the public safety,
based upon the recognition of facts and circumstances which indicate that a group of one
national extraction may menace that safety
more than others, is not wholly beyond the limits of the Constitution and is not to be condemned merely because in other and in most
circumstances racial distinctions are irrelevant.

♦ ♦ ♦

Mr. Justice Murphy, concurring:

Distinctions based on color and ancestry
are utterly inconsistent with our traditions and
ideals. They are at variance with the principles
for which we are now waging war. We cannot
close our eyes to the fact that for centuries the
Old World has been torn by racial and religious
conflicts and has suffered the worst kind of an-

guish because of inequality of treatment for different groups. There was one law for one and a different law for another. Nothing is written more firmly into our law than the compact of the Plymouth voyagers to have just and equal laws. To say that any group cannot be assimilated is to admit that the great American experiment has failed, that our way of life has failed when confronted with the normal attachment of certain groups to the lands of their forefathers. As a nation we embrace many groups, some of them among the oldest settlements in our midst, which have isolated themselves for religious and cultural reasons.

Today is the first time, so far as I am aware, that we have sustained a substantial restriction of the personal liberty of citizens of the United States based upon the accident of race or ancestry. Under the curfew order here challenged no less than 70,000 American citizens have been placed under a special ban and deprived of their liberty because of their particular racial inheritance. In this sense it bears a melancholy resemblance to the treatment accorded to members of the Jewish race in Germany and in other parts of Europe. The result is the creation in this country of two classes of citizens for purposes of a critical and perilous hour—to sanction discrimination between groups of United States citizens on the basis of ancestry. In my opinion this goes to the very brink of constitutional power.

Korematsu v. United States
323 U.S. 214 (1944)

Fred Korematsu was a native Californian of Japanese ancestry. After the bombing of Pearl Harbor, he volunteered for the army, but was rejected for health reasons. He then studied welding and obtained a defense industry job. In May 1942, he had a good job and a Caucasian girlfriend unaffected by the relocation. He tried to avoid relocation by claiming to be of Mexican ancestry. In June he was arrested for violating the exclusion orders.

Korematsu is usually read because of Justice Hugo Black's assertion that racial restrictions are "immediately suspect" and should be given "the most rigid scrutiny." This is the only case in which the Supreme Court applied the "rigid scrutiny" test to a racial restriction and upheld the challenged law. Korematsu is also important for the dissents challenging the majority's deference to the military's handling of civilian matters.

Mr. Justice Black delivered the opinion of the Court.

♦ ♦ ♦

It should be noted, to begin with, that all legal restrictions which curtail the civil rights of a single racial group are immediately suspect. That is not to say that all such restrictions are unconstitutional. It is to say that courts must subject them to the most rigid scrutiny. Pressing public necessity may sometimes justify the existence of such restrictions; racial antagonism never can.

♦ ♦ ♦

In the light of the principles we announced in the *Hirabayashi* case, we are unable to conclude that it was beyond the war power of Congress and the Executive to exclude those of Japanese ancestry from the West Coast war area at the time they did. True, exclusion from the area in which one's home is located is a far greater deprivation than constant confinement to the home from 8:00 P.M. to 6:00 A.M. Nothing short of apprehension by the proper military authorities of the gravest imminent danger to the public safety can constitutionally justify either. But exclusion from a threatened area, no less than curfew, has a definite and close relationship to the prevention of espionage and sabotage. The military authorities, charged with the primary responsibility of defending our shores, concluded that curfew provided inadequate protection and ordered exclusion. They did so, as pointed out in our *Hirabayashi* opinion, in accordance with Congressional authority to the military to say who should, and who should not, remain in the threatened areas.

◆ ◆ ◆

Like curfew, exclusion of those of Japanese origin was deemed necessary because of the presence of an unascertained number of disloyal members of the group, most of whom we have no doubt were loyal to this country. It was because we could not reject the finding of the military authorities that it was impossible to bring about an immediate segregation of the disloyal from the loyal that we sustained the validity of the curfew order as applying to the whole group. In the instant case, temporary exclusion of the entire group was rested by the military on the same ground. The judgment that exclusion of the whole group was for the same reason a military imperative answers the contention that the exclusion was in the nature of group punishment based on antagonism to those of Japanese origin. That there were members of the group who retained loyalties to Japan has been confirmed by investigations made subsequent to the exclusion. Approximately five thousand American citizens of Japanese ancestry refused to swear unqualified allegiance to the United States and to renounce allegiance to the Japanese Emperor, and several thousand evacuees requested repatriation to Japan.

We uphold the exclusion order as of the time it was made and when the petitioner violated it. . . . In doing so, we are not unmindful of the hardships imposed by it upon a large group of American citizens. . . . But hardships are part of war, and war is an aggregation of hardships. All citizens alike, both in and out of uniform, feel the impact of war in greater or lesser measure. Citizenship has its responsibilities as well as its privileges, and in time of war the burden is always heavier. Compulsory exclusion of large groups of citizens from their homes, except under circumstances of direst

emergency and peril, is inconsistent with our basic governmental institutions. But when under conditions of modern warfare our shores are threatened by hostile forces, the power to protect must be commensurate with the threatened danger.

◆ ◆ ◆

We are . . . being asked to pass . . . upon the whole subsequent detention program in both assembly and relocation centers, although the only issues framed at the trial related to petitioner's remaining in the prohibited area in violation of the exclusion order. Had petitioner here left the prohibited area and gone to an assembly center we cannot say either as a matter of fact or law that . . . [I] would have resulted in his detention in a relocation center. Some who did report to the assembly center were not sent to relocation centers, but were released upon condition that they remain outside the prohibited zone. . . . The lawfulness of one [order] does not necessarily determine the lawfulness of the others. This is made clear when we analyze the requirements of the separate provisions of the separate orders . . . that those of Japanese ancestry (1) depart from the area; (2) report to and temporarily remain in an assembly center; (3) go under military control to a relocation center there to remain for an indeterminate period until released conditionally or unconditionally by the military authorities. Each of these requirements . . . imposed distinct duties in connection with the separate steps in a complete evacuation program.

◆ ◆ ◆

Since the petitioner has not been convicted of failing to report or to remain in an assembly or relocation center, we cannot in this case determine the validity of those separate provisions of the order. It is sufficient here for us to pass upon the order which petitioner violated. . . . It will be time enough to decide the serious constitutional issues which petitioner seeks to raise when an assembly or relocation order is applied or is certain to be applied to him, and we have its terms before us.

◆ ◆ ◆

It is said that we are dealing here with the case of imprisonment of a citizen in a concentration camp solely because of his ancestry, without evidence or inquiry concerning his loyalty and good disposition towards the United States. Our task would be simple, our duty clear, were this a case involving the imprisonment of a loyal citizen in a concentration camp because of racial prejudice. Regardless of the true nature of the assembly and relocation centers—and we deem it unjustifiable to call them concentration camps with all the ugly connotations that term implies—we are dealing specifically with nothing but an exclusion order. To cast this case into outlines of racial prejudice, without reference to the real military dangers which were presented, merely confuses the issue. Korematsu was not excluded from the Military Areas because of hostility to him or his race. He *was* excluded because we are at war with the Japanese Empire, because the properly constituted military authorities feared an invasion of our West Coast and felt constrained to take proper security measures, because they decided that the military urgency of the situation demanded that all citizens of Japanese ancestry be segregated from the West Coast temporarily, and finally, because Congress, reposing its confidence in this time of war in our military leaders—as inevitably it must—determined that they should have the power to do just this. There was evidence of disloyalty on the part of some, the military authorities considered that the need for action was great, and time was short. We cannot—by availing ourselves of the calm perspective of hindsight—now say that at that time these actions were unjustified.

Affirmed.

Mr. Justice Roberts.

I dissent. . . .

This is not a case of keeping people off the streets at night as was *Hirabayashi*. . . . On the contrary, it is the case of convicting a citizen as a punishment for not submitting to imprisonment in a concentration camp . . . solely because of his ancestry, without evidence or inquiry concerning his loyalty.

◆   ◆   ◆

The petitioner . . . according to the uncontradicted evidence, is a loyal citizen of the nation.

◆   ◆   ◆

[Here Roberts presented the chronology of events leading to Korematsu's arrest. Under DeWitt's order of March 27, Korematsu was "prohibited from leaving" Military Area 1. Under DeWitt's order of May 3, all Japanese Americans were excluded from Military Area 1 and required to report to a civil control station "for instructions to go to an Assembly Center." Roberts concluded that "the obvious purpose of the orders . . . was to drive all citizens of Japanese ancestry into Assembly Centers."]

The predicament in which the petitioner thus found himself was this: He was forbidden, by Military Order, to leave the zone in which he lived; he was forbidden, by Military Order, after a date fixed, to be found within that zone unless he were in an Assembly Center located in that zone. General DeWitt's report to the Secretary of War . . . makes it entirely clear . . . that an Assembly Center was a euphemism for a prison. No person within such a center was permitted to leave except by Military Order.

In the dilemma that he dare not remain in his home, or voluntarily leave the area, without incurring criminal penalties, and that the only way he could avoid punishment was to go to an Assembly Center and submit himself to military imprisonment, the petitioner did nothing.

◆   ◆   ◆

We cannot shut our eyes to the fact that had the petitioner attempted to . . . leave the military area in which he lived he would have been arrested and tried and convicted. . . . The two conflicting orders, one which commanded him to stay and the other which commanded him to go, were nothing but a cleverly devised trap to accomplish the real purpose of the military authority, which was to lock him up in a concentration camp. The only course by which the petitioner could avoid arrest and prosecution was to go to that camp according to instructions to be given him when he reported at a Civil Control Center. We know that is the fact.

Why should we set up a figmentary and artificial situation instead of addressing ourselves to the actualities of the case?

♦ ♦ ♦

Mr. Justice Murphy, dissenting.

This exclusion of "all persons of Japanese ancestry, both alien and non-alien," from the Pacific Coast area on a plea of military necessity in the absence of martial law ought not to be approved. Such exclusion goes over "the very brink of constitutional power" and falls into the ugly abyss of racism.

In dealing with matters relating to the prosecution and progress of a war, we must accord great respect and consideration to the judgments of the military authorities who are on the scene and who have full knowledge of the military facts. . . .

At the same time, however, it is essential that there be definite limits to military discretion, especially where martial law has not been declared. Individuals must not be left impoverished of their constitutional rights on a plea of military necessity that has neither substance nor support. Thus . . . the military claim must subject itself to the judicial process of having its reasonableness determined and its conflicts with other interests reconciled.

♦ ♦ ♦

That this forced exclusion was the result in good measure of this erroneous assumption of racial guilt rather than bona fide military necessity is evidenced by the Commanding General's Final Report on the evacuation . . . In it he refers to all individuals of Japanese descent as "subversive," as belonging to "an enemy race" whose "racial strains are undiluted," and as constituting "over 112,000 potential enemies . . . at large today". . . . In support of this blanket condemnation of all persons of Japanese descent, however, no reliable evidence is cited to show that such individuals were generally disloyal, or . . . constitute[d] a special menace to defense installations or war industries, or had otherwise by their behavior furnished reasonable ground for their exclusion as a group.

Justification for the exclusion is sought, instead, mainly upon questionable racial and so- ciological grounds not ordinarily within the realm of expert military judgment, supplemented by certain semi-military conclusions drawn from an unwarranted use of circumstantial evidence. Individuals of Japanese ancestry are condemned because they are said to be "a large, unassimilated, tightly knit racial group, bound to an enemy nation by strong ties of race, culture, custom and religion." They are claimed to be given to "emperor worshipping ceremonies" and to "dual citizenship." Japanese language schools and allegedly pro-Japanese organizations are cited as evidence of possible group disloyalty, together with facts as to certain persons being educated and residing at length in Japan. . . .

The main reasons relied upon by those responsible for the forced evacuation . . . [are] largely an accumulation of much of the misinformation, half-truths and insinuations that for years have been directed against Japanese Americans by people with racial and economic prejudices—the same people who have been among the foremost advocates of the evacuation. A military judgment based upon such racial and sociological considerations is not entitled to the great weight ordinarily given the judgments based upon strictly military considerations. Especially is this so when every charge relative to race, religion, culture, geographical location, and legal and economic status has been substantially discredited by independent studies made by experts in these matters.

No adequate reason is given for the failure to treat these Japanese Americans on an individual basis by holding investigations and hearings to separate the loyal from the disloyal, as was done in the case of persons of German and Italian ancestry. It is asserted merely that the loyalties of this group "were unknown and time was of the essence." Yet nearly four months elapsed after Pearl Harbor before the first exclusion order was issued; nearly eight months went by until the last order was issued; and the last of these "subversive" persons was not actually removed until almost eleven months had elapsed. Leisure and deliberation seem to have been more of the essence than speed. And the fact that conditions were not such as to warrant a declaration of martial law adds strength to the belief that the factors of time and military necessity were not as urgent as they have been represented to be.

Moreover, there was no adequate proof that the Federal Bureau of Investigation and the military and naval intelligence services did not have the espionage and sabotage situation well in hand during this long period. Nor is there any denial of the fact that not one person of Japanese ancestry was accused or convicted of espionage or sabotage after Pearl Harbor while they were still free, a fact which is some evidence of the loyalty of the vast majority of those individuals and of the effectiveness of the established methods of combating these evils. It seems incredible that under these circumstances it would have been impossible to hold loyalty hearings for the mere 112,000 persons involved—or at least for the 70,000 American citizens—especially when a large part of this number represented children and elderly men and women. . . .

I dissent, therefore, from this legalization of racism. Racial discrimination in any form and in any degree has no justifiable part whatever in our democratic way of life. It is unattractive in any setting but it is utterly revolting among a free people who have embraced the principles set forth in the Constitution of the United States. All residents of this nation are kin in some way by blood or culture to a foreign land. Yet they are primarily and necessarily a part of the new and distinct civilization of the United States. They must accordingly be treated at all times as the heirs of the American experiment and as entitled to all the rights and freedoms guaranteed by the Constitution.

Mr. Justice Jackson, dissenting.

Korematsu was born on our soil, of parents born in Japan. The Constitution makes him a citizen of the United States by nativity and a citizen of California by residence. No claim is made that he is not loyal to this country. There is no suggestion that apart from the matter involved here he is not law-abiding and well disposed. Korematsu, however, has been convicted of an act not commonly a crime. It consists merely of being present in the state whereof he is a citizen, near the place where he was born, and where all his life he has lived.

Even more unusual is the series of military orders which made this conduct a crime. They forbid such a one to remain, and they also forbid him to leave. They were so drawn that the only way Korematsu could avoid violation was to give himself up to the military authority. This meant submission to custody, examination, and transportation out of the territory, to be followed by indeterminate confinement in detention camps.

A citizen's presence in the locality, however, was made a crime only if his parents were of Japanese birth. Had Korematsu been one of four—the others being, say, a German alien enemy, an Italian alien enemy, and a citizen of American-born ancestors, convicted of treason but out on parole—only Korematsu's presence would have violated the order. The difference between their innocence and his crime would result, not from anything he did, said or thought, different than they, but only in that he was born of different racial stock.

Now, if any fundamental assumption underlies our system, it is that guilt is personal and not inheritable. Even if all of one's antecedents had been convicted of treason, the Constitution forbids its penalties to be visited upon him, for it provides that "no attainder of treason shall work corruption of blood, or forfeiture except during the life of the person attainted." But here is an attempt to make an otherwise innocent act a crime merely because this prisoner is the son of parents as to whom he had no choice, and belongs to a race from which there is no way to resign.

◆ ◆ ◆

[A] judicial construction of the due process clause that will sustain this order is a far more subtle blow to liberty than the promulgation of the order itself. A military order, however unconstitutional, is not apt to last longer than the military emergency. Even during that period a succeeding commander may revoke it all. But once a judicial opinion rationalizes such an order to show that it conforms to the Constitution, or rather rationalizes the Constitution to show that the Constitution sanctions such an order, the Court for all time has validated the principle of racial discrimination in criminal procedure and of transplanting American citizens. The principle then lies about like a loaded weapon ready for the hand of any authority that can bring forward a plausible claim of an urgent need. Every repetition imbeds that principle more deeply in our law and thinking and expands it to new purposes. All who observe the work of courts are familiar with what Judge Cardozo described as "the tendency of a principle to expand itself to the limit of its logic." A military commander may overstep the bounds of constitutionality, and it is an incident. But if we review and approve, that passing incident becomes the doctrine of the Constitution. There it has a generative power of its own, and all that it creates will be in its own image.

◆   ◆   ◆

I should hold that a civil court cannot be made to enforce an order which violates constitutional limitations even if it is a reasonable exercise of military authority. The courts can exercise only the judicial power, can apply only law, and must abide by the Constitution, or they cease to be civil courts and become instruments of military policy.

Of course the existence of a military power resting on force, so vagrant, so centralized, so necessarily heedless of the individual, is an inherent threat to liberty. But I would not lead people to rely on this Court for a review that seems to me wholly delusive. The military reasonableness of these orders can only be determined by military superiors. If the people ever let command of the war power fall into irresponsible and unscrupulous hands, the courts wield no power equal to its restraint. The chief restraint upon those who command the physical forces of the country, in the future as in the past, must be their responsibility to the political judgments of their contemporaries and to the moral judgments of history.

My duties as a justice as I see them do not require me to make a military judgment as to whether General DeWitt's evacuation and detention program was a reasonable military necessity. I do not suggest that the courts should have attempted to interfere with the Army in carrying out its task. But I do not think they may be asked to execute a military expedient that has no place in law under the Constitution. I would reverse the judgment and discharge the prisoner.

Note: *Ex parte Endo,* 323 U.S. 273 (1944)

On the same day it upheld Korematsu's conviction, a unanimous Court ordered the release of Mitsuye Endo from the War Relocation Center at Topaz, Utah. Endo claimed she was a "loyal and law-abiding citizen of the United States, that no charge has been made against her, and that she is being unlawfully . . . confined in the Relocation Center under armed guard and held there against her will." The government did not dispute her loyalty or claim a right to "detain citizens against whom no charges of disloyalty or subversiveness have been made for a period longer than that necessary to separate the loyal from the disloyal and to provide the necessary guidance for relocation." But the government argued that "a planned and orderly relocation was essential to the success of the evacuation program" and that an immediate release of Endo and others would lead to "a dangerously disorderly migration of unwanted people to unprepared communities," which would result in "hardship and disorder."

Speaking for a unanimous Court, Justice William O. Douglas rejected these arguments. Douglas asserted:

> Loyalty is a matter of the heart and mind, not of race, creed, or color. He who is loyal is by definition not a spy or a saboteur. When the power to detain is derived

from the power to protect the war effort against espionage and sabotage, detention which has no relationship to that objective is unauthorized.

Note: The Internment Cases a Generation Later

In *Korematsu* v. *United States*, 584 F. Supp. 1406 (N.D. Cal.) (1984), and *Hirabayashi* v. *United States*, 828 F.2d. 591 (9th Cir.) (1987), federal courts in California overturned the convictions of Korematsu and Hirabayashi, after they appealed on a rarely used writ of *coram nobis*. This writ allowed them to clear their names after they had served their sentences, on the basis of newly discovered evidence. The evidence consisted of a report written by the U.S. military commander on the West Coast, General John L. DeWitt, which undermined the credibility of the claim by the government that the Japanese Americans were a threat to the nation. The evidence showed that at the time the cases were litigated, the Department of War did not actually believe that the Japanese Americans on the West Coast posed any danger to the United States. However, the U.S. government suppressed the DeWitt report and attempted to destroy all copies of it. Many years later a researcher found a copy that had not been destroyed. The U.S. Court of Appeals, in upholding Hirabayashi's claim, noted:

> The suppressed DeWitt Report is not the only evidence which has surfaced as a result of research during this decade. There are memos, which have only recently come to light, by Justice Department lawyers [at the time of the internment] . . . relating to the War Department's suppression of the revised report, and their doubts about the accuracy of the report. . . . The discovery of these materials recently caused the District of Columbia Circuit to hold that the government's fraudulent concealment tolled the statute of limitations in cases brought by Japanese Americans for civil damages arising out of their internment.

CIVIL LIBERTIES AND CRIMINAL JUSTICE IN CRISIS TIMES

The first four decades of the twentieth century were marked by a rapid rise in crime and important changes in the criminal justice system. Millions of immigrants and their children swelled the nation's population from the 1880s to World War I and account for an absolute rise in the crime rate. As historian Mark Haller notes, crime provided a "means of social mobility for persons of marginal social and economic position in society."[4]

Reform legislation regulating prostitution, narcotics, labor, and manufacturing created new federal and state crimes. The most important "reform" to affect crime was Prohibition, which created the conditions for popular illegal behavior and the development of organized crime. It is estimated that between 1923 and 1926 in Chicago alone, over 375 people were killed by gangsters or the police. Prohibition strengthened organized crime while weakening police departments and state and local governments. Police and political corruption grew from the dollars earned through organized criminal activity. This activity soon spread to organized prostitution, gambling, extortion, and numerous other criminal activities.

Changes in constitutional law led to a rethinking of criminal law. By the end of the 1930s, the selective incorporation of the Bill of Rights had affected many of the due process and criminal procedure provisions of the Constitution. Equally important, the changing nature of crime and technological developments led to troublesome constitutional questions.

For example, *Olmstead* v. *United States* (1928) raised the question whether the Fourth Amendment prohibited a warrantless wiretap.

THE EMERGENCE OF CRIMINAL DUE PROCESS

The Fourth, Fifth, Sixth, and Eighth Amendments collectively guarantee that persons accused of crimes will have fair trials. Between World War I and World War II, a small revolution in criminal due process took place as the Supreme Court took steps to guarantee reasonably fair criminal trials in federal courts. This modern redefinition of what constituted due process began with *Weeks* v. *United States*.

Weeks v. *United States*
232 U.S. 383 (1914)

Weeks was convicted of violating a federal law prohibiting the selling of lottery tickets through the mail. He appealed, asserting that his house was searched without a warrant, his property was illegally seized, and he was arrested without a warrant. Justice William R. Day delivered the opinion of the Court.

[T]he question presented involves . . . the duty of the court with reference to the motion made by the defendant for the return of certain letters, as well as other papers, taken from his room by the United States marshal, who, without authority of process . . . visited the room of the defendant for the declared purpose of obtaining additional testimony to support the charge against the accused, and having gained admission to the house took . . . certain letters written to the defendant, tending to show his guilt. These letters were placed in the control of the District Attorney and were subsequently produced by him and offered in evidence against the accused at the trial. The defendant contends that such appropriation of his private correspondence was in violation of rights secured to him by the . . . Fourth Amendment, which provides:

"The right of the people to be secure in their persons, houses, papers, and effects, against unreasonable searches and seizures, shall not be violated, and no warrants shall issue, but upon probable cause, supported by oath or affirmation and particularly describing the place to be searched, and the persons or things to be seized."

The history of this Amendment is given with particularity in the opinion of Mr. Justice Bradley, speaking for the court in *Boyd* v. *United States* [1885]. As was there shown, it took its origin in the determination of the framers of the Amendments to the Federal Constitution to provide for that instrument a Bill of Rights, securing to the American people, among other things, those safeguards which had grown up in England to protect the people from unreasonable searches and seizures, such as were permitted under the general warrants issued under authority of the Government by which there had been invasions of the home and privacy of the citizens and the seizure of their private papers in support of charges, real or imaginary, made against them. Such practices had also received sanction under warrants and seizures under the so-called writs of assistance, issued in the American colonies. Resistance to these practices had established the principle which was enacted into the fundamental law in the Fourth Amendment, that a man's house was his castle and not to be invaded by any general authority to search and seize his goods and papers. Judge Cooley, in his *Constitutional Limitations* . . . said: "The maxim that 'every man's house is his castle,' is made a part of our constitutional law in the clauses prohibiting unreasonable searches and seizures, and has always been looked upon as of high value to the citizen." "Accordingly," says Lieber in . . . *Civil Liberty and Self-Government* . . . "no man's house can be forcibly opened, or he or his goods be carried away after it has thus been forced, except in cases of felony, and then the sheriff must be furnished with a warrant, and take great care lest he commit a trespass. This principle is jealously insisted upon." In *Ex parte Jackson* this court recognized the principle of protection as applicable to letters and sealed packages in the mail, and held that . . . such matter could only be opened and examined upon warrants issued on oath or affirmation particularly describing the thing to be seized, "as is required when papers are subjected to search in one's own household."

In the *Boyd Case* . . . Mr. Justice Bradley said:

"The principles laid down in this opinion affect the very essence of constitutional liberty and security. They reach farther than the concrete form of the case then before the court, with its adventitious circumstances; they apply to all invasions on the part of the government and its employees of the sanctity of a man's home and the privacies of life. It is not the breaking of his doors, and the rummaging of his drawers, that constitutes the essence of the offence; but it is the invasion of his indefeasible right of personal liberty and private property, where that right has never been forfeited by his conviction of some public offence,—it is the invasion of this sacred right which underlies and constitutes the essence of Lord Camden's judgment [in *Entick v. Carrington*]."

♦ ♦ ♦

The effect of the Fourth Amendment is to put the courts of the United States and Federal officials . . . under limitations and restraints as to the exercise of such power and authority, and to forever secure the people, their persons, houses, papers and effects against all unreasonable searches and seizures under the guise of law. This protection reaches all alike, whether accused of crime or not, and the duty of giving to it force and effect is obligatory upon all entrusted under our Federal system with the enforcement of the laws. The tendency of those who execute the criminal laws of the country to obtain conviction by means of unlawful seizures and enforced confessions . . . should find no sanction in the judgments of the courts which are charged at all times with the support of the Constitution and to which people of all conditions have a right to appeal for the maintenance of such fundamental rights.

♦ ♦ ♦

The case [before the Court] . . . involves the right of the court in a criminal prosecution to retain for the purposes of evidence the letters and correspondence of the accused, seized in his house in his absence and without his authority, by a United States marshal holding no warrant for his arrest and none for the search of his premises. The accused . . . made timely application to the court for an order for the return of these letters, as well as other property. This application was denied, the letters retained and put in evidence. . . . If letters and private documents can thus be seized and held and used in evidence against a citizen accused of an offense, the protection of the Fourth Amendment declaring his right to be secure against such searches and seizures is of no value, and . . . might as well be stricken from the Constitution. The efforts of the courts and their officials to bring the guilty to punishment, praiseworthy as they are, are not to be aided by the sacrifice of those great principles established by years of endeavor and suffering which have resulted in their embodiment in the fundamental law of the land. The United States Marshal could only have invaded the house of the accused when armed with a warrant issued as required by the Constitution, upon sworn information and describing with reasonable particularity the thing for which the search was to be made. Instead, he acted without sanction of law, doubtless prompted by the desire to bring further proof to the aid of the Government, and under color of his office undertook to make a seizure of private papers in direct violation of the constitutional prohibition against such action. Under such circumstances, without sworn information and particular description, not even an order of court would have justified such procedure, much less was it within the authority of the United States Marshal to thus invade the house and privacy of the accused. In *Adams* v. *New York* this court said that the Fourth Amendment was intended to secure the citizen in person and property against unlawful invasion of the sanctity of his home by officers of the law acting under legislative or judicial sanction. . . . To sanction such proceedings would be to affirm by judicial decision a manifest neglect if not an open defiance of the prohibitions of the Constitution, intended for the protection of the people against such unauthorized action.

♦ ♦ ♦

It results that the judgment of the court below must be reversed, and the case remanded for further proceedings in accordance with this opinion.

Olmstead v. United States
277 U.S. 438 (1928)

Olmstead, a Prohibition-era bootlegger in Seattle, Washington, with fifty employees and annual sales of over $2 million, was convicted on evidence "largely obtained by intercepting messages on the telephones of the conspirators by four federal prohibition officers." In upholding the conviction, Chief Justice William Howard Taft noted that the wiretaps "were made without trespass upon any property of the defendants. They were made in the basement of the large office building. The taps from house lines were made in the streets near the houses." Taft acknowledged that the "historical purpose of the Fourth Amendment . . . was to prevent the use of governmental force to search a man's house, his person, his papers and his effects; and to prevent their seizure against his will." But, Taft argued, "the Amendment does not forbid what was done here. There was no searching. There was no seizure. The evidence was secured by the use of the sense of hearing and that only. There was no entry of the houses or offices of the defendants." Taft found that "the language of the Fourth Amendment can not be extended and expanded to include telephone wires reaching to the whole world from the defendant's house or office." He argued that the wires were "not part of his house or office any more than are the highways along which they are stretched." Taft noted that wiretaps were illegal under Washington law but did not believe this barred federal agents from using them in the absence of congressional action.

Mr. Justice Louis Brandeis dissenting:

♦ ♦ ♦

The Government makes no attempt to defend the methods employed by its officers. Indeed, it concedes that if wire-tapping can be deemed a search and seizure within the Fourth Amendment, such wire-tapping . . . was an unreasonable search and seizure, and that the evidence thus obtained was inadmissible. But it relies on the language of the Amendment; and it claims that the protection given thereby can not properly be held to include a telephone conversation.

♦ ♦ ♦

When the Fourth and Fifth Amendments were adopted, "the form that evil had theretofore taken," had been necessarily simple. Force and violence were then the only means known to man by which a Government could directly effect self-incrimination. It could compel the individual to testify—a compulsion effected, if need be, by torture. It could secure possession of his papers and other articles incident to his private life—a seizure effected, if need be, by breaking and entry. Protection against such invasion of "the sanctities of a man's home and the privacies of life" was provided in the Fourth and Fifth Amendments by specific language. *Boyd* v. *United States.* But "time works changes, brings into existence new conditions and purposes." Subtler and more far-reaching means of invading privacy have become available to the Government. Discovery and invention have made it possible for the Government, by means far more effective than stretching upon the rack, to obtain disclosure in court of what is whispered in the closet.

Moreover, "in the application of a constitution, our contemplation cannot be only of what has been but of what may be." The progress of science in furnishing the Government with means of espionage is not likely to stop with wire-tapping. Ways may some day be developed by which the Government, without removing papers from secret drawers, can reproduce them in court, and by which it will be enabled to expose to a jury the most intimate occurrences of the home. Advances in the psychic and related sciences may bring means of exploring unexpressed beliefs, thoughts and emotions. "That places the liberty of every man in the hands of every petty officer" was said by James Otis of much lesser intrusions than these. To Lord Camden, a far slighter intrusion seems "subversive of all the comforts of society." Can it be that the Constitution affords no protection against such invasions of individual security.

♦ ♦ ♦

Decisions of this Court applying the principle of the *Boyd* case have settled these things. Unjustified search and seizure violates the Fourth Amendment, whatever the character of the paper; whether the paper when taken by the federal officers was in the home, in an office or elsewhere; whether the taking was effected by force, by fraud, or in the orderly process of a court's procedure. From these decisions, it follows necessarily that the Amendment is violated by the officer's reading the paper without a physical seizure, without his even touching it; and that use, in any criminal proceeding, of the contents of the paper so examined—as where they are testified to by a federal officer who thus saw the document . . . any such use constitutes a violation of the Fifth Amendment.

. . . The makers of our Constitution undertook to secure conditions favorable to the pursuit of happiness. They recognized the significance of man's spiritual nature, of his feelings and of his intellect. They knew that only a part of the pain, pleasure and satisfactions of life are to be found in the material things. They sought to protect Americans in their beliefs, their thoughts, their emotions and their sensations. They conferred, as against the Government, the right to be let alone—the most comprehensive of rights and the right most valued by civilized men. To protect that right, every unjustifiable intrusion by the Government upon the privacy of the individual, whatever the means employed, must be deemed a violation of the Fourth Amendment. And the use, as evidence in a criminal proceeding, of facts ascertained by such intrusion, must be deemed a violation of the Fifth.

Applying to the Fourth and Fifth Amendments the established rule of construction, the defendants' objections to the evidence by wiretapping must, in my opinion be sustained. It is, of course, immaterial where the physical connection with the telephone wires leading into the defendants' premises was made. And it is also immaterial that the intrusion was in aid of law enforcement. Experience should teach us to be most on our guard to protect liberty when the Government's purposes are beneficent. Men born to freedom are naturally alert to repel invasion of their liberty by evil-minded rulers. The greatest dangers to liberty lurk in insidious encroachment by men of zeal, well-meaning but without understanding.

Independently of the constitutional question, I am of opinion that the judgment should be reversed. By the laws of Washington, wiretapping is a crime. To prove its case, the Government was obliged to lay bare the crimes committed by its officers on its behalf. A federal court should not permit such a prosecution to continue.

♦ ♦ ♦

When these unlawful acts were committed, they were crimes only of the officers individually. The Government was innocent . . . for no federal official is authorized to commit a crime on its behalf. When the Government, having full knowledge, sought, through the Department of Justice, to avail itself of the fruits of these acts in order to accomplish its own ends, it assumed moral responsibility for the officers' crimes. And if this Court should permit the Government, by means of its officers' crimes, to effect its purpose of punishing the defendants, there would seem to be present all the elements of a ratification. If so, the Government itself would become a lawbreaker.

. . . The governing principle has long been settled. It is that a court will not redress a wrong when he who invokes its aid has unclean hands. The maxim of unclean hands comes from courts of equity. But the principle prevails also in courts of law. Its common application is in civil actions between private parties. Where the Government is the actor, the reasons for applying it are even more persuasive. Where the remedies invoked are those of the criminal law, the reasons are compelling.

The door of a court is not barred because the plaintiff has committed a crime. The confirmed criminal is as much entitled to redress as his most virtuous fellow citizen; no record of crime, however long, makes one an outlaw. The court's aid is denied only when he who seeks it has violated the law in connection with the very transaction as to which he seeks legal redress. Then aid is denied despite the defendant's wrong. It is denied in order to maintain respect for law; in order to promote confidence in the administration of justice; in order to preserve the judicial process from contamination. The rule is one, not of action, but of inaction. . . . A defense may be waived. It is waived when not pleaded. But the objection that the plaintiff comes with unclean hands will be taken by the court itself. It will be taken despite the wish to the contrary of all the parties to the litigation. The court protects itself.

Decency, security and liberty alike demand that government officials shall be subjected to the same rules of conduct that are commands to the citizen. In a government of laws, existence of the government will be imperilled if it fails to observe the law scrupulously. Our Government is the potent, the omnipresent teacher. For good or for ill, it teaches the whole people by its example. Crime is contagious. If the Government becomes a lawbreaker, it breeds contempt for law; it invites every man to become a law unto himself; it invites anarchy. To declare that in the administration of the criminal law the end justifies the means—to declare that the Government may commit crimes in order to secure the conviction of a private criminal—would bring terrible retribution. Against that pernicious doctrine this Court should resolutely set its face.

Note: Prohibition and the Law

Olmsted can be seen as a "Prohibition case" as well as a criminal law case. *Olmsted* reminds us of the dangers to civil liberties from the suppression of vice and other "victimless crimes." The Eighteenth Amendment prohibited the manufacture, importation, and sale of "intoxicating liquors." In *Rhode Island* v. *Palmer* (1920), New Jersey, Rhode Island, individuals, and companies argued that the amendment had not been properly passed by Congress or properly ratified, that it violated the sovereignty of the states, and that its enforcement clause ("The Congress and the several States shall have concurrent power to enforce this article") empowered the states to allow liquor within their jurisdiction. The Court rejected these contentions, but gave no rationale for its holding and offered no "opinion" as such. Instead, Justice Willis Van Devanter "announced the conclusions of the court" upholding Prohibition.

America's experiment with Prohibition was short-lived but, in terms of law enforcement, extremely costly. While per capita alcohol consumption dropped, the crime rate rose as criminal organizations expanded to satisfy the nation's thirst for drink. Prohibition's legacy includes the institutionalization of the FBI as a national police force and the entrenchment of organized crime throughout the nation.

CRIME IN THE CITIES

The rapid growth of cities after the Civil War was accompanied by an appallingly high crime rate. In the first third of the twentieth century, few people pondered the causes of crime, such as poverty, discrimination against ethnic and racial minorities, and of course Prohibition, which instantly converted millions of Americans into "criminals" when they drank a beer. Prohibition also created huge opportunities for criminals to make large profits and have the support of millions of Americans who were anxious to obtain prohibited liquor.

ROSCOE POUND AND FELIX FRANKFURTER
Criminal Justice in Cleveland
1922

Progressive reformers believed that crime might be stopped through improved training of local police, more efficient courts, and an eradication of political corruption. Illustrative of the problem of urban crime and the progressive response to it, Criminal Justice in Cleveland *was written by a team of eleven legal scholars hired by a civic foundation to thoroughly examine the criminal justice system in Cleveland.*

A cursory examination of the problem of crime in Cleveland produces some startling facts. For the year 1920 Cleveland, with approximately 800,000 population, had six times as many murders as London, with 8,000,000 population. For every robbery or assault with intent to rob committed during this same period in London there were 17 such crimes committed in Cleveland. Cleveland had as many murders during the first three months of the present year as London had during all of 1920. . . . There are more robberies and assaults to rob in Cleveland every year than in all England, Scotland, and Wales put together. In 1919 there were 2,327 automobiles stolen in Cleveland; in London there were 290; in Liverpool, 10.

Comparisons of this kind between Cleveland, on the one hand, and European cities, on the other, could be almost indefinitely extended. . . . And yet, compared with other American cities, Cleveland's record does not show to any special disadvantage. For the first quarter of 1921 there were four more murders committed in Detroit than in Cleveland, and nearly

twice as many automobiles stolen in Detroit. During the first three months of 1921 St. Louis had 481 robberies, while Cleveland had 272; for the same period complaints of burglary and housebreaking in St. Louis numbered 1,106, as compared to 565 such complaints in Cleveland. For this same period the number of murders in Buffalo, a much smaller city, equaled those in Cleveland, and burglaries, housebreakings, and larcenies were almost as numerous. In 1919 Chicago, more than three times the size of Cleveland, had 293 murders and manslaughters, compared with Cleveland's 55, so that the ratio was easily two to one in Cleveland's favor; the 1920 statistics of the two cities show an even better proportion for Cleveland.

On the other side of the scale, for the first three months of the present year Cleveland had more than twice the number of robberies and assaults to rob that Detroit had, and a similar large proportion of burglaries and housebreakings. During this period there were 296 automobiles stolen in St. Louis, as against 446 in Cleveland. Cleveland is approximately three times larger than Toledo, and yet in 1920 Cleveland had 87 murders, while Toledo had only 11.

Another basis of comparison is between the crime statistics of Cleveland in 1921 and Cleveland in former years. For the first six months of 1921, the period in which this survey was carried on, the number of murders committed in Cleveland was 15. For the same period in 1920 the number of murders was 30. . . . The following figures show the average number of complaints for the first quarter of each of the four years from 1917 to 1920 inclusive, classified according to four outstanding crimes:

Robbery and assault to rob	283
Burglary and larceny	418
Murder	17
Automobiles driven away	361

The following figures give the number of complaints of the same crimes for the first quarter of 1921:

Robbery and assault to rob	272
Burglary and larceny	265
Murder	6
Automobiles driven away	446

Obviously, there has been some improvement within the last four years.

All in all, crime conditions are no more vicious in Cleveland than they are in other American cities. . . . In this respect, therefore, Cleveland's problem is the problem of America, for the same causes that are maintaining the high crime rate of Chicago, St. Louis, New York, Detroit, and San Francisco are operating here.

What are these causes? Here we can only hint at some of the deeper social and economic causes. The lack of homogeneity in our population and its increasing instability, the absence of settled habits and traditions of order, the breakdown of the administration of criminal law in the United States, and the many avenues by which offenders can escape punishment, our easy habit of passing laws which do not represent community standards or desires, our lack of cohesive industrial organization, our distrust of experts in the management of governmental enterprises—all these are undoubtedly contributing factors.

But there is another factor, still more potent: police machinery in the United States has not kept pace with modem demands. It has developed no effective technique to master the burden which modern social and industrial conditions impose. Clinging to old traditions, bound by old practices which business and industry long ago discarded, employing a personnel poorly adapted to its purposes, it grinds away on its perfunctory task without self-criticism, without imagination, and with little initiative.

CIVIL RIGHTS AND RACIAL JUSTICE

In 1954, the Supreme Court initiated a revolution in American law and culture in *Brown* v. *Board of Education of Topeka*. Much of American legal history can be phrased in terms of pre-*Brown* and post-*Brown*. Legalized racial discrimination, which had been developing for 300 years, disappeared within 25 years after *Brown*.

Revolutionary though it was, *Brown* did not emerge full-blown from the pen of Chief Justice Earl Warren. *Brown* was the culmination of case law that had been developing throughout the century. Successful challenges to discrimination in political institutions, public education, and law enforcement laid the foundation for *Brown*. This foundation for a civil rights revolution was laid by black and white attorneys, usually working under the auspices of the NAACP Legal Defense and Education Fund and tied to initiatives taken by the faculty and students at Howard Law School. These cases suggest the way in which the Supreme Court began to reverse the long pattern of legalized discrimination in most American institutions.

The civil rights litigation from World War I to *Brown* did more than undermine segregation and set the stage for the civil rights revolution of the 1950s and 1960s. This litigation also initiated an era of legal activism, as reformers turned to the courts to gain new rights and reform society. This perhaps is the most dramatic change of the era. Before the mid-1930s, reformers generally feared courts, which tended to overturn progressive legislation. By the 1950s, reformers, led by the civil rights movement, saw the federal judiciary as an ally in battles against discrimination, unfair police methods, corrupt and old-fashioned political practices, and reactionary state legislatures. Activists, from environmental reformers to women's rights advocates, turned to the courts to change laws and protect rights. The civil rights litigation of the 1930s and 1940s thus turned out to be the harbinger of the future.

RACE AND THE FRANCHISE

The Fifteenth Amendment prohibited racial discrimination in voting, but in *United States* v. *Reese* (1876), the Supreme Court severely limited Congress's enforcement power, holding that the amendment did "not confer the right of suffrage upon anyone." In *Williams* v. *Mississippi* (1898), the Court upheld literacy tests and poll taxes for voters. Through these and other methods, the South effectively disfranchised blacks.

Literacy tests had the disadvantage of also disfranchising uneducated whites. Ingenious southern legislators solved this problem through "grandfather clauses," which allowed the direct descendants of pre-1866 voters to vote without taking literacy tests, thus permitting illiterate whites to vote while disfranchising most blacks. The first twentieth-century United States Supreme Court victory for blacks came in *Guinn* v. *United States* (1915), when the Court struck down Oklahoma's "grandfather clause." Solicitor General John W. Davis successfully argued this case. Ironically, some forty years later Davis would defend South Carolina and segregation in *Brown* v. *Board of Education* (1954).

Partly in response to *Guinn,* in 1923 Texas prohibited blacks from participating in the Democratic party primary. Blacks could still vote in the general election, but the "white primary" barred them from effective political participation because at this time the Democratic candidate invariably won the general election. In *Nixon* v. *Herndon* (1927) and *Nixon* v. *Condon* (1932), the United States Supreme Court found that the Texas laws violated the equal protection clause of the Fourteenth Amendment because the Democratic party acted under state sanction. But the "Democrats of Texas were nothing if not resourceful." A state convention called without the benefit of enabling legislation limited participation in Democratic primaries to "'all white citizens' qualified to vote under the state Constitution and laws."[5] In *Grovey* v. *Townsend* (1935), the Supreme Court upheld this version of the white primary because it did not involve "state action." Once again, black Texans were effectively barred from politics.

In *United States* v. *Classic* (1941), the Supreme Court affirmed the federal election fraud convictions of Louisiana officials who had failed to count the ballots of *whites* in a congressional primary. The Court held that a congressional primary could be regulated by Congress. The *Classic* decision, combined with the appointment of new, liberal Justices, set the stage for *Smith* v. *Allright* (1944), in which Thurgood Marshall argued against the white primary. The Texas Democratic party failed to send counsel, confident that the Court would uphold the *Grovey* precedent. Associate Justice Stanley Reed of Kentucky spoke for an 8 to 1 majority, which finally ended the white primary.

Reed relied on the earlier *Nixon* cases and the *Classic* case to overrule *Grovey*. Justice Reed concluded that:

> it may now be taken as a postulate that the right to vote in such a primary for the nomination of candidates without discrimination by the State, like the right to vote in a general election, is a right secured by the Constitution. By the terms of the Fifteenth Amendment that right may not be abridged by any State on account of race. Under our Constitution the great privilege of the ballot may not be denied a man by the State because of his color.

This decision led the Court to reevaluate its position in *Grovey* in an unusually blunt way:

> The privilege of membership in a party may be, as this Court said in *Grovey* v. *Townsend,* no concern of a State. But when, as here, that privilege is also the essential qualification for voting in a primary to select nominees for a general election, the State makes the action of the party the action of the State. In reaching this conclusion we are not unmindful of the desirability of continuity of decision in constitutional questions. However, when convinced of former error, this Court has never felt constrained to follow precedent. In constitutional questions, where correction depends upon amendment and not upon legislative action this Court throughout its history has freely exercised its power to reexamine the basis of its constitutional decisions. This has long been accepted practice, and this practice has continued to this day. This is particularly true when the decision believed erroneous is the application of a constitutional principle rather than an interpretation of the Constitution to extract the principle itself. Here we are applying, contrary to the recent decision in *Grovey* v. *Townsend,* the well-established principle of the Fifteenth Amendment, forbidding the abridgement by a State of a citizen's right to vote. *Grovey* v. *Townsend* is overruled.

RACE AND EDUCATION

In *Plessy* v. *Ferguson* (1896), the United States Supreme Court had upheld the concept of "separate but equal" in public facilities. In *Cumming* v. *Board of Education of Richmond* (1899), the Court refused to order a Georgia school district to dismantle a white high school when the district failed to provide a similar school for blacks. Since the case did not directly present the question of segregated education, the Court did not directly address it. In *Berea College* v. *Kentucky* (1908), the Court once again dodged the constitutionality of segregated schools. The Court upheld Kentucky's prohibition on integrated classes at this state-chartered private school on the grounds that the state retained the right to amend the college's corporate charter.

Gong Lum v. *Rice* (1927) was the last major Supreme Court decision to uphold segregated schools. Mississippi's 1890 Constitution provided that "separate schools shall be maintained for children of the white and colored races." Gong Lum, a Chinese American, tried to register his daughter at the only public high school in her district, which was solely for whites. Officials determined she was "colored" and rejected her. Gong Lum did not challenge the concept of segregation per se, but only its application to his daughter. In upholding the Mississippi school officials' right to assign students as they wished, Chief Justice William Howard Taft noted that they were obligated to provide schools for all children, regardless of their race. A decade later, the Court took its first tentative step toward school integration.

Missouri ex rel. Gaines v. *Canada*
305 U.S. 337 (1938)

Lloyd Gaines was denied admission to the University of Missouri School of Law solely because of his race. The state offered to pay his tuition at the public law schools in adjacent states. Gaines refused this offer, arguing that he had a constitutional right to a legal education in the state where he lived. Chief Justice Charles Evans Hughes wrote the majority opinion, vindicating Gaines's claim. After he won this case, Gaines disappeared. Some scholars speculate he was murdered by the Ku Klux Klan or other vigilantes opposed to racial equality.

In answering petitioner's contention that this discrimination constituted a denial of his constitutional right, the state court has fully recognized the obligation of the State to provide negroes with advantages for higher education substantially equal to the advantages afforded to white students. The State has sought to fulfill that obligation by furnishing equal facilities in separate schools, a method the validity of which has been sustained by our decisions. Respondents' counsel have appropriately emphasized the special solicitude of the State for the higher education of negroes as shown in the establishment of Lincoln University, a state institution well conducted on a plane with the University of Missouri so far as the offered courses are concerned. It is said that Missouri is a pioneer in that field and is the only State in the Union which has established a separate university for negroes on the same basis as the state university for white students. But, commendable as is that action, the fact remains that instruction in law for negroes is not now afforded by the State, either at Lincoln University or elsewhere within the State, and that the State excludes negroes from the advantages of the law school it has established at the University of Missouri.

It is manifest that this discrimination if not relieved . . . would constitute a denial of equal protection. . . .

The Supreme Court of Missouri in the instant case has . . . [argued] (1) that in Missouri . . . there is "a legislative declaration of a purpose to establish a law school for negroes at Lincoln whenever necessary or practical"; and

(2) that, "pending the establishment of such a school, adequate provision has been made for the legal education of negro students in recognized schools outside of this State."

As to the first ground, it appears that the policy of establishing a law school at Lincoln University has not yet ripened into an actual establishment, and it cannot be said that a mere declaration of purpose, still unfulfilled, is enough. The provision for legal education at Lincoln is at present entirely lacking. Respondents' counsel urge that if, on the date when petitioner applied for admission to the University of Missouri, he had instead applied to the curators of Lincoln University it would have been their duty to establish a law school; that this "agency of the State," to which he should have applied, was "specifically charged with mandatory duty to furnish him what he seeks."

♦ ♦ ♦

The state court has not held that it would have been the duty of the curators to establish a law school at Lincoln University for the petitioner on his application. Their duty, as the court defined it, would have been either to supply a law school at Lincoln University . . . or to furnish him the opportunity to obtain his legal training in another State. . . . Thus the law left the curators free to adopt the latter course. The state court has not ruled or intimated that their failure or refusal to establish a law school for a very few students, still less for one student, would have been an abuse of the discretion with which the curators were entrusted. . . .

The state court stresses the advantages that are afforded by the law schools of the adjacent States,—Kansas, Nebraska, Iowa and Illinois,—which admit non-resident negroes. The court considered that these were schools of high standing where one desiring to practice law in Missouri can get "as sound, comprehensive, valuable legal education" as in the University of Missouri; that the system of education in the former is the same as that in the latter and is designed to give the students a basis for the practice of law in any State where the Anglo-American system of law obtains; that the law school of the University of Missouri does not specialize in Missouri law and that the course of study and the case books used in the five schools are substantially identical. Petitioner insists that for one intending to practice in Missouri there are special advantages in attending a law school there, both in relation to the opportunities for the particular study of Missouri law and for the observation of the local courts, and also in view of the prestige of the Missouri law school among the citizens of the State, his prospective clients. . . .

We think that these matters are beside the point. The basic consideration is not as to what sort of opportunities other States provide, or whether they are as good as those in Missouri, but as to what opportunities Missouri itself furnishes to white students and denies to negroes solely upon the ground of color. The admissibility of laws separating the races in the enjoyment of privileges afforded by the State rests wholly upon the equality of the privileges which the laws give to the separated groups within the State. The question here is not of a duty of the State to supply legal training, or of the quality of the training which it does supply, but of its duty when it provides such training to furnish it to the residents of the State upon the basis of an equality of right. By the operation of the laws of Missouri a privilege has been created for white law students which is denied to negroes by reason of their race. The white resident is afforded legal education within the State; the negro resident having the same qualifications is refused it there and must go outside the State to obtain it. That is a denial of the equality of legal right to the enjoyment of the privilege which the State has set up, and the provision for the payment of tuition fees in another State does not remove the discrimination.

The equal protection of the law is "a pledge of the protection of equal laws." *Yick Wo* v. *Hopkins*. Manifestly, the obligation of the State to give the protection of equal laws can be performed only where its laws operate, that is, within its own jurisdiction. It is there that the equality of legal right must be maintained. That obligation is imposed by the Constitution upon the States severally as governmental entities,—each responsible for its own laws establishing the rights and duties of persons within its borders. It is an obligation the burden of which cannot be cast by one State upon another, and no State can be excused from performance by what another State may do or fail to do. That separate responsibility of each State within its own sphere is of the essence of statehood maintained under our dual system. We find it impossible to conclude that what otherwise would be an unconstitutional discrimination, with respect to the legal right to the enjoyment of opportunities within the State, can be justified by requiring resort to opportunities elsewhere. That resort may mitigate the inconvenience of the discrimination but cannot serve to validate it.

◆   ◆   ◆

Here, petitioner's right was a personal one. It was as an individual that he was entitled to the equal protection of the laws, and the State was bound to furnish him within its borders facilities for legal education substantially equal to those which the State there afforded for persons of the white race.

Note: Beyond *Gaines*

Gaines did not require integrated education. It left the states the option of building separate law schools and graduate schools. Not until *Sweatt* v. *Painter* (1950) would the Supreme Court hold that segregation in graduate and professional schools, such as law schools, was unconstitutional. Nevertheless, *Gaines* was a major civil rights victory because, for the first time, the United States Supreme Court required that a state actually provide "equal" facilities along with "separate" ones.

RACIAL JUSTICE AND CRIMINAL LAW

From the earliest period of American history, race and racial discrimination have been connected to the criminal justice system. Some of the very first enslaved blacks were initially runaway servants whose punishment for escaping was lifetime servitude. Throughout the antebellum period, the South maintained special criminal codes for blacks. After the Civil War, formal equality existed in criminal codes, but discrimination in enforcement was the rule. Before 1950, the vast majority of blacks lived in the South, where they faced a criminal justice system designed to keep them at the bottom of the social structure.

In the 1930s, the United States Supreme Court began to provide some due process protections for southern blacks. The worst excesses of police brutality and kangaroo-court justice were declared unconstitutional. But the dictates of the High Court filtered down slowly, if at all, to local police departments.

In addition to formal law, informal "lynch law" remained an all-too-common method of repressing blacks. It was not uncommon for police officials to aid lynchers or even take part in clandestine murders. Between 1889 and 1941, the nation recorded 3,700 lynchings. Some were politically motivated, such as radical union members lynched in the West or the German American lynched in Illinois in 1918 for "disloyal remarks." Others were against ethnic groups, such as the mob killing of eleven Italian immigrants in New Orleans in 1891 and the anti-Semitic murder of Leo Frank in Georgia in 1915. Sometimes whites were lynched for less dramatic reasons, such as horse stealing.

Although there was at least 1 lynching in all but five states between 1889 and 1918, most lynchings—over 2,900—took place in the South, where the overwhelming majority of the victims were black. Despite the myths, only 16 percent of southern black victims were accused of interracial rape or other sex-related crimes. Many black victims were accused of murder and assault, but others were lynched for "creating a disturbance," "stealing hogs," "aiding a colored man to escape," "disagreement with a white man," "writing a letter to a white woman," "miscegenation," "mistaken identity," "bad reputation," "insulting" whites, or "giving evidence" at the trials of whites. Often the cause was determined to be simply "race prejudice."[6]

Opposition from the NAACP and southern white civic organizations, such as the Commission on Interracial Cooperation and the Association of Southern Women for the Prevention of Lynching, eventually undermined public support for lynching. During World War II, the rate of lynchings dropped, but in the 1950s and 1960s lynchings and racially motivated murders became more common as some Southerners responded to the civil rights movement with extreme violence. The most infamous incident was the torture murders of three civil rights workers—two whites and a black—in Philadelphia, Mississippi, in 1964.

JAMES HARMON CHADBOURN

"Lynching and the Administration of Justice"
1933

This introductory chapter to the book Lynching and the Law *sets out some of the sociological and legal analyses of the antilynching movement. The fact that this book was written by a southern white, and published by the University of North Carolina Press, indicates that the southern establishment regarded lynching as a problem. Also significant is Chadbourn's positive reference to* Rope and Faggot, *a study of lynching written by Walter White, the head of the NAACP. Despite the antilynching attitude among many educated Southerners, senators from the South continued to oppose any federal legislation to ban lynching.*

The amount of study given today to the problem of lynching is evidence that the public conscience has been awakened by the 3,753 lynchings between 1889 and 1932. Witness, for example, the reports of the Southern Commission on the Study of Lynching; Walter White's penetrating book, *Rope and Faggot.*

♦ ♦ ♦

Thanks to the pioneer record-keeping of *The Chicago Tribune,* begun in 1889, later taken up and amplified by Tuskegee Institute and the National Association for the Advancement of Colored People, certain elemental statistics are available. These are: number of occurrences, location, race and sex of the lynched person, inciting offense or event, and the manner of killing. . . . We have been shown the proportion between the various offenses, manners of killing, men and women, Negroes and whites; the proportions of occurrences by sections of the country . . . the proportions according to total and race populations by counties, states, and sections; and finally, the proportions according to months of the year and days of the week.

We have been carried beyond the laboratory of the statistician by the findings of the Southern Commission. The basis of its information is a series of painstaking case studies of the lynchings in 1930 made by trained investigators working in the field. Common threads of economic and social factors have thus been found woven into the pattern of the typical 1930 lynching community.

It is a rural Southern county characterized in general by social and economic decadence. For example, it is below the state average in per capita tax valuation, bank deposits, income from farm and factory, income tax returns, and ownership of automobiles. Educational facilities are also below the state average. The church membership is seventy five per cent Southern

Baptist and Methodist. There is generally prevalent a supposed necessity for protecting white women against sex crimes by the Negroes. All these, plus emotional and recreational starvation and a fear of economic domination by enterprising Negroes, create the complex of "keeping the nigger in his place." Periodic lynchings are the result.

♦ ♦ ♦

Lynching is often interpreted as a protest against the inefficiency of courts as agencies for the punishment of crime. As far back as 1893, the Georgia Bar Association resolved that "the reason, or at least one great reason, why lynchings occur is because there is a distrust, and a constantly growing distrust, in the promptness and efficiency of the law." In later years the same idea has been constantly reiterated, along with its obvious corollary that "the remedy for lynching is to restore the confidence of society in the just, prompt, and efficient trial and punishment of criminals."

♦ ♦ ♦

An examination of available data from this standpoint brings forth some significant facts. In some cases a person has been lynched during the course of, or after, the completion of legal proceedings against him. While of course no amount of judicial malpractice in such cases affords a valid excuse for lynching, such cases should be examined to determine whether it was present. If it was, then one of the probable incentives for lynchings can be identified and possibly corrected.

Not judicial error, but executive clemency, seems to have occasioned most of the lynchings which occurred during or after completion of the legal process. This was true in Georgia's *cause célèbre*—the case of Leo Frank. Similar are the cases . . . in Angleton, Texas, [and] . . . Crawfordsville, Georgia. . . . A stay of execution by the Supreme Court in Mississippi had the same effect . . . and the same was true of the filing of a motion for an appeal [in] . . . Louisiana.

◆ ◆ ◆

[Here Chadbourn discussed cases in which blacks were lynched after they were paroled or had served their sentences.]

A protest against the way in which legal processes operated can perhaps be discerned in these cases. But who can say whether the pardons, the stay of execution, or the light sentences were improper?

In some cases, moreover, there is not even the suspicion of judicial malpractice. Cases are on record where lynchings have followed in the face of extreme sentences. In 1916 a Negro in Waco, Texas, killed a white woman. He was carried to Dallas for safekeeping. There an agreement was made between a part of the Waco community, the local authorities, and the Negro that he would be promptly tried, that he would waive his right to seek change of venue and to appeal, and that he would be protected from lynch law. On this agreement he was brought back. In a courtroom seating 500 there were 1500, with 2000 outside. As the jurors were called, members of the crowd yelled, "We don't need any jury!" After a hurried trial, the jury deliberated three minutes and returned a verdict of guilty. The defendant was sentenced to hang in a few hours. There was a pause of a full minute while the judge made the entry: "Jury verdict of guilty." Meanwhile the court stenographer . . . slipped back of the sheriff and out of the room. The sheriff followed him. The silence was broken as a tall Waco citizen, driver of a brewery truck, yelled to the crowd, "Get the nigger!" A gruesome burning at the stake followed.

◆ ◆ ◆

These sample cases . . . leave one in some doubt . . . that sometimes . . . lynching is an expression of distrust in the efficacy of legal processes in the given case. But whether there was some ground for the distrust, in that the particular case was mishandled, an investigator is at a loss to say. Yet this expression of distrust is not an invariable condition in all lynchings. In [many cases] . . . the lynchers could have had no ground for dissatisfaction with the operation of orderly legal processes. In a word, in the case of a person who is lynched during or after trial, the evidence of a correlation between the judicial handling of his case and the lynching is contradictory and inconclusive. It can scarcely be said . . . [that] we can identify judicial inefficiency as a major factor in these lynchings.

◆ ◆ ◆

It should be remembered, moreover, that most victims of lynching are Negroes. The evidence is convincing that Negroes who are tried for serious crimes in lynching communities are more drastically punished than are whites similarly circumstanced. Professor Brearley estimates that in South Carolina for the period 1920–1926, 64.1 percent of the Negroes charged with murder or manslaughter were found guilty, while the similar percentage for whites was 31.7. In regard to the severity of the punishment inflicted on Negroes, he says:

"Further evidence that the Negro is more severely punished than is the white person is presented by the 1910 census of prisoners. At this time Negroes constituted only 10.69 per cent of the total population of the United States but they received 56.0 per cent of the grave homicide sentences and 49.1 per cent of the lesser homicide sentences in the United States. In the South the Negroes provided 74.4 per cent of those sentenced for grave homicide during the year 1910 and 67.6 per cent of those committed for lesser homicides. During the same year the average sentence for those punished by imprisonment without fine and by definite sentences was 5.2 months for the whites and 17.4 months for the Negroes." . . .

Dr. Raper finds that. . . .

"Data secured from the superintendents of state prison systems and wardens of penitentiaries of Southern States for the eighteenth-month period ending July 1, 1931, demonstrate conclusively that Negro criminals brought before the courts are not dealt with leniently. In ten Southern States, of the eighty-one executions, thirteen were white—all convicted of murder—and sixty-eight were Negroes: fifty-seven murderers, eight rapists, and three burglars. During the same period, in twelve states, of 669 life sentences imposed, 199 were whites: 192 murders, six rapists, and one burglar; of the 470 Negroes, 425 were convicted of murder, twenty of rape, and twenty-five of burglary and other offenses. For minor offenses, too, the sentences for Negroes were often greater than for whites."

Note: Lynching and Federal Law

In the 1930s, northern Democrats and civil rights organizations worked for the passage of a federal antilynching bill. In 1937, such a bill passed the House, but filibusters led by Senators Tom Connally of Texas and Theodore K. Bilbo of Mississippi killed the bill. Although President Roosevelt expressed his support for the bill, he never worked for its passage. Some New Deal policies, especially the creation of the Civilian Conservation Corps (CCC), may have helped end lynching by removing to the CCC camps "actual and potential lynchers from the environment which favored mob violence." The military draft before and during World War II also led to a decline in lynching.

Note: Black Rights, Southern Justice, and the Supreme Court

In the 1930s and 1940s, the Supreme Court and the executive branch of the federal government began to intervene on behalf of blacks who were denied fair trials in the Deep South.

The *Scottsboro Cases*. In 1931 nine black youths, the Scottsboro Boys, were convicted of rape in Alabama on the basis of perjured testimony at a circus trial. Their convictions were overturned in *Powell* v. *Alabama* (1932) because they had been denied adequate counsel. They were retried, and in *Norris* v. *Alabama* (1935), their convictions were again reversed because of the "long continued, systematic and arbitrary exclusion of qualified negro [*sic*] citizens from service on juries." The Court forced Alabama officials to place the names of blacks on the jury rolls. All the Scottsboro Boys were subsequently convicted by all-white juries that were chosen from an integrated pool of jurors.

Brown v. *Mississippi* (1936). Ed Brown was convicted of murder based on a confession he gave after police officers "hanged him by a rope to the limb of a tree, and, having let him down, they hung him again, and when he was let down the second time, and he still protested his innocence, he was tied to a tree and whipped." Declaring that "the rack and torture chamber may not be substituted for the witness stand," the Supreme Court reversed the conviction "for want of the essential elements of due process."

Screws v. *United States* (1945). This case involved what Justice William O. Douglas described as "a shocking and revolting episode in law enforcement." After arresting Robert Hall, a black accused of theft, Claude Screws, a Georgia sheriff, and two deputies "began beating him with their fists and with a solid-bar blackjack about eight inches long and weighing two pounds." After some thirty minutes of this treatment, Hall died. Screws was convicted under a modern version of the Civil Rights Act of 1866. This law, as the dissenters noted, had been "a dead letter" since Reconstruction. A sharply divided Supreme Court upheld the constitutionality of the law and the prosecution, but ordered a new trial on narrowly technical grounds. *Screws* indicates the beginning of federal protection of the civil rights of blacks against the violence of southern law enforcement.

→ 8 ←

The Rise of Legal Liberalism, Economic Reform, and the New Deal 1900–1945

Momentous events between World Wars I and II reshaped American legal culture. The most important of these was the Great Depression, which followed the Wall Street panic of November 1929. The Depression was an economic scourge of mammoth proportions; it spread with devastating impact over not just the American but the world economy. By the late 1920s, the ups and downs of the business cycle were a routine feature of American life, but at no time in the past had the economy plunged so low and then remained there. Unemployment soared, rising to almost one-quarter of the labor force in 1933, a twentieth-century high. Banks failed in record numbers. Between 1929 and 1932, 5,000 banks closed their doors, and the life savings of millions of Americans evaporated.

The Great Depression called into question the optimistic and laissez-faire attitudes that had characterized post–Civil War America. The idea that voluntary rather than governmental regulation was best seemed debatable when so many people suffered. Moreover, the economic pall fell over not just poor blacks and whites, but also the aspiring middle class, with its faith in the idea that economic well-being flowed from personal virtue and that government had a limited role in promoting the collective social welfare. Socialist leaders, such as Norman Thomas, urged radical collectivist solutions to the problems of building economic confidence and alleviating human suffering. Others, like William Dudley Pelly, called for the restoration of democracy, Christianity, and free enterprise through an American brand of fascism.

The New Deal of President Franklin Delano Roosevelt, who swept to victory in 1932, emerged as the consensus, middle-of-the-road approach to the problems of economic collapse. Critics on both the right and the left challenged the New Deal, believing that while FDR was a decent and well-meaning man he was squandering an opportunity to fundamentally transform American life. Although the New Deal did not offer any fundamental reshuffling of American government and society, it did bring about broad changes, many of which involved the legal culture. The Great Depression, after all, was as much a legal as an economic crisis, one that was magnified by the simple fact that the American economy since

459

the Civil War had developed a national market structure that the states were increasingly unable to deal with alone. Alleviating human suffering and restoring economic confidence, therefore, required a degree of governmental involvement in the day-to-day lives of Americans that raised unprecedented questions about the protection of individual property interests, the separation of powers among the three branches, and the proper relationship between the states and the federal government. Property rights, separation of powers, social welfare, and federalism emerged as central concerns in the legal history of these years. The national programs associated with FDR's presidency became the center of these concerns, although many of the same issues were raised by "little" New Deal programs in the states.

These issues were given even greater currency since the intellectual context in which they occurred was itself rapidly developing. The mechanical legal scientism of Christopher Columbus Langdell faced new challenges, especially with the advent of social science as a legitimate method of organizing human knowledge. The social sciences relied on a scientific method that invested great credibility in empirical evidence as opposed to the supposedly immutable doctrines of Langdell. The result was a more empirical and experimental attitude toward the problems and assumptions of the learned disciplines. Psychology, economics, anthropology, and political science, for example, applied social science techniques in ways that placed human behavior within a functional social context.

The social science revolution, which was firmly connected to the Progressive legacy of efficiency and rationality in government, had important implications for the relationship between law and public policy. The Langdellian scheme of legal education stressed a priori assumptions. The genius of his "science of the law" was that it gave fixed and supposedly objective principles to guide succeeding generations. The social sciences enfeebled these basic assumptions by demonstrating that for human knowledge to be valid it had to be based on empirical evidence. That meant, as Edward A. Purcell, Jr., has argued, that all "knowledge was necessarily tentative and subject to change."[1] The implication was quite clear: the new methods administered a heavy dose of ethical relativism to a legal system that prided itself on moral certainties supported by Langdellian legal science. Social science dealt with only objective facts and was morally neutral. Thus social science could not tell civilization how it should act; it could help only in understanding the circumstances in which such judgments had to be made.

The methods of social science, the moral relativism that accompanied it, and the economic stress of the Great Depression combined to reshape the legal culture. The traditional objective notion of the late nineteenth century held that judicial decisions were based on rules and precedents defined historically and applied mechanically. When placed in the context of the Progressive theory of lawmaking by administrative agencies, the social sciences held forth new hope of adapting law to particular social exigencies. The result was a growing attention to the ways in which social science could "improve" the decisions made according to the rule of law. Two of the most important consequences of these developments were Sociological Jurisprudence, which had its roots in the Progressive era, and Legal Realism, which flourished in the 1920s and 1930s. Sociological Jurisprudence and Legal Realism increasingly conflicted with not just the legal science of Langdell, but also each other. The sociological jurisprudents, such as Roscoe Pound and Louis Brandeis, persisted in a view of law that stressed moral and ethical beliefs. Law might be flexible, but it was—and should be—value laden. At the same time, Legal Realists rejected such notions and increasingly drifted into ethical relativism.

The economic crisis of the Great Depression propelled these trends toward the formulation of legal liberalism, the dominant value of modern American legal culture. It fused the social reformist and administrative-law impulses of Progressivism, the relativism and instrumentalism of Legal Realism and Sociological Jurisprudence, and the regulatory responsibility of the state that marked the New Deal. Traditional liberalism had held the individual paramount and feared the active state. The new liberalism reversed that pattern; it emphasized that the state had a positive duty, through administrative agencies, courts, and legislatures, to promote the public interest by encouraging social and economic justice. The emphasis, however, was always on harmony and stability among contending interests; the object of the new liberal state was neither to redistribute wealth significantly nor to guarantee fully that every person should be put in the same condition as every other. Classical notions of laissez-faire, which had never fully characterized the American historical experience, withered but did not die, and in the decades after the New Deal, legal liberal culture flourished until it came under sustained attack beginning in the 1960s from both the political right and left.

SOCIOLOGICAL JURISPRUDENCE, THE AMERICAN LAW INSTITUTE, AND LEGAL REALISM

Progressive reformers during the late nineteenth and early twentieth centuries brought the institutions of American law under attack. They cast the judiciary as unresponsive to the social demands of industrialization, urbanization, and immigration; they charged that administrative and regulatory agencies were little more than tools of the regulated; and they condemned legislatures as the agencies of the wealthy. Many Progressives, for example, in pushing for the direct election of United States senators, portrayed the upper house of Congress as a millionaires' club.

Yet the generation of Americans who came into public life in the first third of the twentieth century disagreed about how law was to respond to social change, with resulting diversity in the legal culture. Sociological Jurisprudence, the American Law Institute, and Legal Realism offered their distinctive and often competing solutions to the new problems of the age.

OLIVER WENDELL HOLMES, JR.

"Law and the Court"
1913

President Theodore Roosevelt appointed Oliver Wendell Holmes, Jr., to the Supreme Court in 1902, where he served until his retirement in 1932 at age ninety. Holmes was in many ways a transitional figure between the strict legal scientism of Langdell, with whom he disagreed sharply while serving on the Harvard Law School faculty, and the Legal Realists. Holmes was a great skeptic; he believed that the common law was not "a brooding omnipresence in the sky," but the reflection of historically contingent choices. Each generation, he concluded, had to come to terms with the law. On balance, his conservative, property-oriented colleagues on the high bench had failed to do so, and they had brought public ridicule on themselves by failing to appreciate the limits of their authority. Holmes argued that once the legislature had spoken, unless an act was palpably unconstitutional, the courts should not intervene. He also insisted that new forms of learning, especially the social sciences, could illuminate legal controversies. As the essay below suggests, Holmes doubted that judges alone had the capacity to deal with the great issues of the Progressive era.

[I] turn to the Court to which for ten now accomplished years it has been my opportunity to belong. We are very quiet there, but it is the quiet of a storm centre, as we all know. Science has taught the world skepticism and has made it legitimate to put everything to the test of proof. Many beautiful and noble reverences are impaired, but in these days no one can complain if any institution, system, or belief is called on to justify its continuance in life. Of course we are not excepted and have not escaped. Doubts are expressed that go to our very being. Not only are we told that when John Marshall pronounced an Act of Congress unconstitutional in *Marbury* v. *Madison* he usurped a power that the Constitution did not give, but we are told that we are the representatives of a class—a tool of the money power. I get letters, not always anonymous, intimating that we are corrupt. Well, gentlemen, I admit that it makes my heart ache. It is very painful, when one spends all the energies of one's soul in trying to do good work, with no thought but that of solving a problem according to the rules by which one is bound, to know that many see sinister motives and would be glad of evidence that one was consciously bad. But we must take such things philosophically and try to see what we can learn from hatred and distrust and whether behind them there may not be some germ of inarticulate truth.

The attacks upon the Court are merely an expression of the unrest that seems to wonder vaguely whether law and order pay. When the ignorant are taught to doubt they do not know what they safely may believe. And it seems to me that at this time we need education in the obvious more than investigation of the obscure. I do not see so much immediate use in committees on the high cost of living and inquiries how far it is due to the increased production of gold, how far to the narrowing of cattle ranges and the growth of population, how far to the

bugaboo, as I do in bringing home to people a few social and economic truths.

♦   ♦   ♦

I should like to see it brought home to the public that the question of fair prices is due to the fact that none of us can have as much as we want of all the things we want; that as less will be produced than the public wants, the question is how much of each product it will have and how much go without; that thus the final competition is between the objects of desire, and therefore between the producers of those objects; that when we oppose labor and capital, labor means the group that is selling its product and capital all the other groups that are buying it. The hated capitalist is simply the mediator, the prophet, the adjuster according to his divination of the future desire. If you could get that believed, the body of the people would have no doubt as to the worth of law.

That is my outside thought on the present discontents. As to the truth embodied in them, in part it cannot be helped. It cannot be helped, it is as it should be, that the law is behind the times. I told a labor leader once that what they asked was favor, and if a decision was against them they called it wicked. The same might be said of their opponents. It means that the law is growing. As law embodies beliefs that have triumphed in the battle of ideas and then have translated themselves into action, while there still is doubt, while opposite convictions still keep a battle front against each other, the time for law has not come; the notion destined to prevail is not yet entitled to the field. It is a misfortune if a judge reads his conscious or unconscious sympathy with one side or the other prematurely into the law, and forgets that what seem to him to be first principles are believed by half his fellow men to be wrong. I think that we have suffered from this misfortune, in State courts at least, and that this is another and very important truth to be extracted from the popular discontent. When twenty years ago a vague terror went over the earth and the word socialism began to be heard, I thought and still think that fear was translated into doctrines that had no proper place in the Constitution or the common law. Judges are apt to be naif, simple-minded men, and they need something of Mephistopheles. We too need education in the obvious—to learn to transcend our own convictions and to leave room for much that we hold dear to be done away with short of revolution by the orderly change of law.

I have no belief in panaceas and almost none in sudden ruin. I believe with Montesquieu that if the chance of a battle—I may add, the passage of a law—has ruined a state, there was a general cause at work that made the state ready to perish by a single battle or a law. Hence I am not much interested one way or the other in the nostrums now so strenuously urged. I do not think the United States would come to an end if we lost our power to declare an Act of Congress void. I do think the Union would be imperiled if we could not make that declaration as to the laws of the several States. For one in my place sees how often a local policy prevails with those who are not trained to national views

and how often action is taken that embodies what the Commerce Clause was meant to end. But I am not aware that there is any serious desire to limit the Court's power in this regard. For most of the things that properly can be called evils in the present state of the law I think the main remedy, and for the evils of public opinion, is for us to grow more civilized.

If I am right it will be a slow business for our people to reach rational views, assuming that we are allowed to work peaceably to that end. But as I grow older I grow calm. If I feel what are perhaps an old man's apprehensions, that competition from new races will cut deeper than working men's disputes and will test whether we can hang together and can fight; if I fear that we are running through the world's resources at a pace that we cannot keep; I do not lose my hopes. I do not pin my dreams for the future to my country or even to my race. I think it probable that civilization somehow will last as long as I care to look ahead—perhaps with smaller numbers, but perhaps also bred to greatness and splendor by science. I think it not improbable that man, like the grub that prepares a chamber for the winged thing it never has seen but is to be—that man may have cosmic destinies that he does not understand. And so beyond the vision of battling.

Note: Oliver Wendell Holmes, Jr., and Judging

Holmes believed that practical considerations rooted in underlying social needs and conflicts ultimately shaped the course of the law. Hence, lawmakers could resist such trends on only a temporary basis by appealing to abstract logic and deductive reasoning, the foundation on which Langdell rested his vaunted method. Nor did Holmes assume that there were moral and social absolutes; instead, judges articulated the law based on their perceptions and sentiments. The lawyer's job was to predict their behavior and to advise clients accordingly. Thus Holmes spoke for a practical legal science, one tailored to the behavioral insights of the new social sciences.

The excerpt from Holmes also points to the growing emphasis on the commerce power as a means of uniting the island economic communities that had so characterized nineteenth-century America. The commerce clause of the Constitution had a controversial history, but it became even more important in the early twentieth century as Progressive reformers enlisted it in an attempt to impose some national order on the economy. Holmes had been at the forefront in sketching broader regulatory authority for the government under the commerce power. His famous decision in *Swift & Co.* v. *United States* (1905) enunciated the "stream of commerce doctrine," which affirmed the power of Congress to regulate commerce even in individual states as long as it was part of the broader current of national commerce.

Holmes also pushed then-current understanding of judging toward a greater sense of the individual jurist rather than the logic of the law itself. What judges did made a difference; they were not mindless, mechanical operators of an autonomous, logical body of rules. By the beginning of the twentieth century, therefore, legal reformers, most notably John Chipman Gray, a professor of law at Harvard, and Louis D. Brandeis, a Boston lawyer and future justice of the Supreme Court, argued that judges had to pay attention to the probable social results of their decisions.

LOUIS D. BRANDEIS

"Brief for the Defendant in Error,"
Muller v. *Oregon*
October Term, 1907

Louis D. Brandeis, a Boston lawyer, was known in the early twentieth century as the "people's attorney" because of his prominent role in advocating public-interest causes. Brandeis employed litigation to press his social agenda, loading his briefs with a maximum of sociological evidence and a minimum of logical argumentation. The Muller *arguments became the best known example of the "Brandeis brief." These arguments were especially important because earlier the Supreme Court had decided* Lochner v. *New York (1905) (see Chapter 6). The Justices in that case overturned a New York State law that limited the number of hours men were permitted to work in bakeries. The* Lochner *majority relied on the concept of freedom to contract, claiming that this right existed in the due process clause of the Fourteenth Amendment and "protected" employees from having state legislatures deny their "freedom" to work twelve, fourteen, or even sixteen hours a day. The Court in* Muller *was asked to consider whether an Oregon statute passed in 1903 that provided that "no female [shall] be employed in any mechanical establishment or factory or laundry . . . more than ten hours during any one day" violated the same due process provision of the Fourteenth Amendment.*

THE WORLD'S EXPERIENCE UPON WHICH THE LEGISLATION LIMITING THE HOURS OF LABOR FOR WOMEN IS BASED

I. The Dangers of Long Hours

A. Causes

(1) Physical Differences Between Men and Women

The dangers of long hours for women arise from their special physical organization taken in connection with the strain incident to factory and similar work.

Long hours of labor are dangerous for women primarily because of their special phys-

ical organization. In structure and function women are differentiated from men. Besides these anatomical and physiological differences, physicians are agreed that women are fundamentally weaker than men in all that makes for endurance: in muscular strength, in nervous energy, in the powers of persistent attention and application. Overwork, therefore, which strains endurance to the utmost, is more disastrous to the health of women than of men, and entails upon them more lasting injury.

Report of Select Committee on Shops Early Closing Bill, British House of Commons, 1895.

Dr. Percy Kidd, physician in Brompton and London Hospitals:

The most common effect I have noticed of

the long hours is general deterioration of health; very general symptoms which we medically attribute to over-action, and debility of the nervous system; that includes a great deal more than what is called nervous disease, such as indigestion, constipation, a general slackness, and a great many other indefinite symptoms.

Are those symptoms more marked in women than in men?

I think they are much more marked in women. I should say one sees a great many more women of this class than men; but I have seen precisely the same symptoms in men, I should not say in the same proportion, because one has not been able to make anything like a statistical inquiry. There are other symptoms, but I mention those as being the most common. Another symptom especially among women is anemia, bloodlessness or pallor, that I have no doubt is connected with long hours indoors.

Report of the Maine Bureau of Industrial and Labor Statistics, 1888.

Let me quote from Dr. Ely Van der Warker (1875):

Woman is badly constructed for the purposes of standing eight or ten hours upon her feet. I do not intend to bring into evidence the peculiar position and nature of the organs contained in the pelvis, but to call attention to the peculiar construction of the knee and the shallowness of the pelvis, and the delicate nature of the foot as part of a sustaining column. The knee joint of woman is a sexual characteristic. Viewed in front and extended, the joint in but a slight degree interrupts the gradual taper of the thigh into the leg. Viewed in a semi-flexed position, the joint forms a smooth ovate spheroid. The reason of this lies in the smallness of the patella in front, and the narrowness of the articular surfaces of the tibia and femur, and which in man form the lateral prominences, and thus is much more perfect as a sustaining column than that of a woman. The muscles which keep the body fixed upon the thighs in the erect position labor under the disadvantage of shortness of purchase, owing to the short distance, compared to that of man, between the crest of the ilium and the great trochanter of the femur, thus giving to man a much larger purchase in

the leverage existing between the trunk and the extremities. Comparatively the foot is less able to sustain weight than that of man, owing to its shortness and the more delicate formation of the tarsus and metatarsus.

Report of the Massachusetts Bureau of Labor Statistics, 1875.

A "lady operator," many years in the business, informed us: "I have had hundreds of lady compositors in my employ, and they all exhibited, in a marked manner, both in the way they performed their work and in its results, the difference in physical ability between themselves and men. They cannot endure the prolonged close attention and confinement which is a great part of type-setting. I have few girls with me more than two or three years at a time; they must have vacations, and they break down in health rapidly. I know no reason why a girl could not set as much type as a man, if she were as strong to endure the demand on mind and body."

Report of the Nebraska Bureau of Labor and Industrial Statistics, 1901–1902.

They (women) are unable, by reason of their physical limitations, to endure the same hours of exhaustive labor as may be endured by men without injury to their health would wreck the constitution and destroy the health of women, and render them incapable of bearing their share of the burdens of the family and the home. The State must be accorded the right to guard and protect women as a class against such a condition, and the law in question to that extent conserves the public health and welfare.

In strength as well as in rapidity and precision of movement women are inferior to men. This is not a conclusion that has ever been contested. It is in harmony with all the practical experience of life. It is perhaps also in harmony with the results of those investigators . . . who have found that, as in the blood of women, so also in their muscles, there is more water than in those of men. To a very great extent it is a certainty, a matter of difference in exercise and environment. It is probably, also, partly a matter of organic constitution.

The motor superiority of men, and to some extent of males generally, is, it can scarcely be doubted, a deep-lying fact. It is related to what is most fundamental in men and in women, and to their whole psychic organization.

There appears to be a general agreement that women are more docile and amenable to discipline; that they can do light work equally well; that they are steadier in some respects; but that, on the other hand, they are often absent on account of slight indisposition, and they break down sooner under strain.

◆ ◆ ◆

It has been estimated that out of every one hundred days women are in a semi-pathological state of health for from fourteen to sixteen days. The natural congestion of the pelvic organs during menstruation is augmented and favored by work on sewing machines and other industrial occupations necessitating the constant use of the lower part of the body. Work during these periods tends to induce chronic congestion of the uterus and appendages, and dysmenorrhea and flexion of the uterus are well known affections of working girls.

VII. Laundries

The specific prohibition in the Oregon Act of more than ten hours' work in laundries is not an arbitrary discrimination against that trade. Laundries would probably not be included under the general terms of "manufacturing" or "mechanical establishments"; and yet the special dangers of long hours in laundries, as the business is now conducted, present strong reasons for providing a legal limitation of the hours of work in that business.

DANGEROUS TRADES. THOMAS OLIVER, MEDICAL EXPERT ON DANGEROUS TRADES COMMITTEES OF THE HOME OFFICE. 1902

Chapter XLVII. Laundry Workers

It is perhaps difficult to realize that the radical change which has everywhere transformed industrial conditions has already affected this occupation (laundry work) also, and that for good or for evil the washerwoman is passing under the influences which have so profoundly modified the circumstances of her sister of the spinning-wheel and the sewing needle. When the first washing machine and ironing roller were applied to this occupation, alteration in the conditions became as much a foregone conclusion as it did in the case of the textile or the clothing manufactures, when the spinning frame, the power loom, or the sewing machine appeared.

Meanwhile, few industries afford at the present time a more interesting study. From a simple home occupation it is steadily being transformed by the application of power-driven machinery and by the division of labor into a highly organized factory industry, in which complicated labor-saving contrivances of all kinds play a prominent part. The tremendous impetus in the adoption of machinery, and the consequent modification of the system of employment so striking in the large laundries, is not greater than the less obvious but even more important development in the same direction among small laundries. Indeed the difference is rapidly becoming one of degree only. In the large laundries may be found perhaps more machinery and a greater number of the newest devices, but the fundamental change has affected all alike.

◆ ◆ ◆

D. Bad Effect upon Morals

Report of British Chief Inspector of Factories and Workshops, 1900.

One of the most unsatisfactory results of the present system of lack of working hours in laundries is the unfortunate moral effect on the women and girls. . . . Women who are employed at arduous work till far into the night are not likely to be early risers nor given to punctual attendance in the mornings, and workers who on one or two days in the week are dismissed to idleness or to other occupations, while on the remaining days they are expected to work for abnormally long hours, are not rendered methodical, industrious, or dependable workers by such an unsatisfactory training. The self-control and good habits engendered by a regular and definite period of moderate daily employment, which affords an excellent training for the young worker in all organized industries, is sadly lacking, and, instead, one finds periods of violent over-work alternating with hours of exhaustion. The result is the establishment of a kind of "vicious circle"; bad habits among workers make compliance by their employers with any regulation as to hours very difficult while a lack of loyal adherence to reasonable hours of employment by many laundry occupiers increases the difficulty for those who make the attempt in real earnestness.

THE AMERICAN LAW INSTITUTE

ELIHU ROOT

"Report of the Committee," American Law Institute
1923

Elihu Root was one of the nation's most successful early-twentieth-century Wall Street lawyers. In short, he was the establishment, and the American Law Institute (ALI), which was founded in Washington, D.C., in 1923, was the establishment's response to the flux and uncertainty in the law. Root's "Report," which was presented to the organizational meeting of the ALI, broadly outlined the institute's goal of adding greater precision to the administration of justice.

I have been requested by the Committee to make a brief statement in explanation of the proceedings which bring us to the point where we are now. Most of you know that for many years we have been talking in the American Bar Association and in many State Bar Associations about the increasing complexity and confusion of the substantive law which is applied in all our states and in the Federal courts. . . . It was apparent that the confusion, the uncertainty, was growing worse from year to year. It was apparent that the vast multitude of decisions which our practitioners are obliged to consult was reaching a magnitude which made it impossible in ordinary practice to consult them. It was apparent that whatever authority might be found for one view of the law upon any topic, other authorities could be found for a different view upon the same topic. The great number of books, the enormous amount of litigation, the struggles of the courts to avoid too strict an application of the rule of state decision, the fact that the law had become so vast and complicated that the conditions of ordinary practice and ordinary judicial duty made it impossible to make adequate examinations—all these had tended to create a situation where the law was becoming guesswork.

You will find in the paper which has been distributed the statement that a count made in 1917 showed 175,000 pages of reported decisions in the United States, as against 7,000 in Great Britain. Three years before I had a count made in the Library of Congress. . . . It showed that during the five years preceding 1914 over 62,000 statutes had been passed and included in the printed volumes of laws in the United States, and that during the same five years over 65,000 decisions of courts of last resort had been delivered and included in the printed volumes of reports. And still it goes on.

It was evident that the time would presently come, unless something were done, when courts would be forced practically to decide cases not upon authority but upon the impression of the moment, and that we should ultimately come to the law of the Turkish Kadi, where a good man decides under good impulses and a bad man decides under bad impulses, as the case may be; and that our law, as a system, would have sunk below the horizon, and the basis of our institutions would have disappeared.

The result of the conference was first to consider an attempt to secure a great meeting of representatives of the bar from all over the country, and then the suggestion was made that the meeting would have nothing to do of practical effect, because they would have nothing to work on, and that they would be driven to appoint a committee to study the subject and to report upon . . . this problem.

Accordingly, such a committee was got together. They secured funds, they employed competent and experienced assistants, and for nearly a year the work has been conducted, and the result of the work is this report. . . . The idea of the report is that if we can get a statement of the law so well done as to be generally acceptable and made the basis for judicial consideration, we will have accomplished at the outset a very great advance.

We recall the part played in judicial decisions by what Judge Story said, not only in his decisions, but in his textbooks and in his writings; the part played in judicial decision by what Chancellor Kent said in his great work. To take recent instances, take the work on equity written by John Norton Pomeroy. I have not followed the reports closely enough to know whether it still continues, but for a good many years after the publication of that work the courts quoted what he said with practically the effect with which they would have quoted a great judicial decision.

There is a work now which is playing the same part, Mr. Samuel Williston's work on contracts, which is being quoted in the same way.

Now, if you can have the law systematically, scientifically stated, the principles stated by competent men, giving their discussions of the theories upon which their statements are based, giving a presentation and discussion of all the judicial decisions upon which their statements are based, and if such a statement can be revised and criticized and tested by a competent group of lawyers of eminence, and when their work is done if their conclusions can be submitted to the bar that we have here, if that can be done when the work is completed, we will have a statement of the common law of America which will be the prima facie basis on which judicial action will rest; and any lawyer, whose interest in litigation requires him to say that a different view of the law shall be taken, will have upon his shoulders the burden to overturn the statement.

Instead of going back through ten thousand cases it will have been done for him; there will be not a conclusive presumption but a practical prima facie statement upon which, unless it is overturned, judgment may rest.

If such a thing is done it will tend to assert itself and to confirm itself and to gather authority as time goes on. Of course it cannot be final, for times are continually changing and new conditions arise, and there will have to be revision after revision; but we will have dealt with the past and will have gotten this old man of the sea off our shoulders in a great measure.

It is a great work. It is a work before which anyone might well become discouraged. Unless the work can be done greatly it is worthless. It is of no use to produce another digest, another cyclopedia. That kind of work is being done admirably. It is no use to duplicate the work of the West Publishing Company, which has done so well. It must be so done as to carry authority, as to carry conviction of impartial judgment upon the most thorough scientific investigation and tested accuracy of statement.

Can it be done? If it cannot, why we must go on through this swamp of decisions with consequences which we cannot but dread. The great work of the Roman law had imperial power behind it; Theodosius and Justinian could command and all the resources of a great empire responded. In the simpler and narrower work of the Code Napoleon, again, imperial will put motive power behind the enterprise. What have we? No legislature, no Congress can command; no individual can do the work. Men who come and go, who spend a little time from their ordinary occupations, and go, cannot accomplish it.

Means must be raised for an adequate force, for continuous application. Participation in the enterprise must be deemed highly honorable. Selection for participation must be deemed to confer distinction, it must be recognized as a great and imperative public service. How can it be done? It can be done only if the public opinion of the American democracy recognizes the need of the service, and that public opinion you here today represent and can awaken and direct.

That is why the Committee solicited your attendance here, to ask you whether you will put all that you represent behind the undertaking, so that the American democracy may be behind it.

Note: The American Law Institute and the Restatements

Since certainty in the law was the major concern of the ALI, its major contribution was the publication of restatements of the law. These restatements summarized the law in a major field (contract, tort, and such) and reorganized it along symmetrical lines. The first restatement appeared in 1932 with the publication of Samuel Williston's volumes on the law of contracts. Although the restatements never attained the level of prestige projected for them by the ALI, they were important contributions to the ongoing effort to organize knowledge about the law. The restatements foundered in part because of the Great Depression, which dried up foundation funds that had supported the research and publication effort, and forced the ALI to scrap all but a few projects. By 1945 the ALI had published only eight restatements, and those functioned more as research tools than as the sources of legal authority Root and others had envisaged.

LEGAL REALISM

JEROME FRANK

Law and the Modern Mind
1936

The most controversial stream of legal reform flowed not out of the ALI or Sociological Jurisprudence, but from Legal Realism. Composed of legal educators mostly at Yale and Columbia universities, this movement expanded on Holmes's original insight into the relationship between law and social change, took seriously the idea that judges' actions grew from their own innate personality traits, and insisted that the words of the law had always to be measured against the behavior of persons operating under them. The Realists' adoption of a behavioral perspective and their belief that not a single set of moral values could reign permanently, since society was always in flux, introduced a strong sense of ethical relativism into legal culture at the very time in which the Great Depression placed enormous demands on it for change. The following excerpt from Jerome Frank, a Yale law professor, member of the New Deal bureaucracy in Washington, and subsequently United States Court of Appeals Judge for the Second Circuit, underscores the Realists' skepticism about precedent and the powerful psychological forces that shaped a judge's decision making.

Lawyers and judges purport to make large use of precedents; that is, they purport to rely on the conduct of judges in past cases as a means of procuring analogies for action in new cases.

But since what was actually decided in the earlier cases is seldom revealed, it is impossible, in a real sense, to rely on these precedents. What the courts in fact do is to manipulate the language of former decisions. They could approximate a system of real precedents only if the judges, in rendering those former decisions, had reported with fidelity the precise steps by which they arrived at their decisions. The paradox of the situation is that, granting there is value in a system of precedents, our present use of illusory precedents makes the employment of real precedents impossible.

The decision of a judge after trying a case is the product of a unique experience. "Of the many things which have been said of the mystery of the judicial process," writes [Hessel] Yntema, "the most salient is that decision is reached after an emotive experience in which principles and logic play a secondary part. The function of juristic logic and the principles which it employs seem to be like that of language, to describe the event which has already transpired. These considerations must reveal to us the impotence of general principles to control decision. Vague because of their generality, they mean nothing save what they suggest in the organized experience of one who thinks them, and, because of their vagueness, they only remotely compel the organization of that experience. The important problem . . . is not the formulation of the rule but the ascertainment of the cases to which, and the extent to which, it applies. And this, even if we are seeking uniformity in the administration of justice, will lead us again to circumstances of the concrete case. . . . The reason why the general principle cannot control is because it does not inform. . . . It should be obvious that when we have observed a recurrent phenomenon in the decisions of the courts, we may appropriately express the classification in a rule. But the rule will be only a mnemonic device, a useful but hollow diagram of what has been. It will be intelligible only if we relive again the experience of the classifier."

The rules a judge announces when publishing his decision are, therefore, intelligible only if one can relive the judge's unique experience while he was trying the case—which, of course, cannot be done. One cannot even approximate that experience as long as opinions take the form of abstract rules applied to facts formally described. Even if it were desirable

that, despite its uniqueness, the judge's decision should be followed, as an analogy, by other judges while trying other cases, this is impossible when the manner in which the judge reached his judgment in the earlier case is most inaccurately reported, as it now is. You are not really applying his decision as a precedent in another case unless you can say, in effect, that, having relived his experience in the earlier case, you believe that he would have thought his decision applicable to the facts of the latter case. And as opinions are now written it is impossible to guess what the judge did experience in trying a case. The facts of all but the simplest controversies are complicated and unlike those of any other controversy; in the absence of a highly detailed account by the judge of how he reacted to the evidence, no other person is capable of reproducing his actual reactions. The rules announced in his opinions are therefore often insufficient to tell the reader why the judge reached his decision.

[T]he "personal bent of the judge" to some extent affects his decisions. But this "personal bent," . . . is a factor only in the selection of new rules for unprovided cases. However, in a profound sense the unique circumstances of almost any case make it an "unprovided case" where no well-established rule "authoritatively" compels a given result. The uniqueness of the facts and of the judge's reaction thereto is often concealed because the judge so states the facts that they appear to call for the application of a settled rule. But that concealment does not mean that the judge's personal bent has been inoperative or that his emotive experience is simple and reproducible.

[Herman] Oliphant has argued that the courts have been paying too much attention to the language of prior cases and that the proper use of the doctrine of following the precedents should lead courts to pay more attention to what judges in earlier cases have decided as against what they have said in their opinions. It may be true that in a limited number of simple cases we can guess what the judge believed to be the facts, and therefore can guess what facts, in any real sense, he was passing on. But usually there are so many and such diverse factors in the evidence which combine in impelling the judge's mind to a decision, that what he decided is unknown—except in the sense that he gave judgment for A, or sent B to prison for ten years, or enjoined C from interfering with D.

At any rate, that will be true while the present method of reporting and deciding cases is adhered to. If and when we have judges trained to observe their own mental processes and such judges with great particularity set forth in their opinions all the factors which they believe led to their conclusions, a judge in passing on a case may perhaps find it possible, to some considerable extent, intelligently to use as a control or guide, the opinion of another judge announced while passing on another case. But as matters stand, reliance on precedents is illusory because judges can seldom tell precisely what has been theretofore decided.

What has just been said is not intended to mean that most courts arrive at their conclusions arbitrarily or apply a process of casuistical deception in writing their opinions. The process we have been describing involves no insincerity or duplicity. The average judge sincerely believes that he is using his intellect as

"a cold logic engine" in applying rules and principles derived from the earlier cases to the objective facts of the case before him.

A satirist might indeed suggest that it is regrettable that the practice of precedent-mongering does not involve conscious deception, for it would be comparatively easy for judges entirely aware of what they were doing, to abandon such conscious deception and to report accurately how they arrived at their decisions. Unfortunately, most judges have no such awareness. Worse than that, they are not even aware that they are not aware. Judges Holmes, Cardozo, Hand, Hutcheson, Lehman and a few others have attained the enlightened state of awareness of their unawareness. A handful of legal thinkers off the bench have likewise come to the point of ignorance of all of us as to just how decisions, judicial or otherwise, are reached. Until many more lawyers and judges become willing to admit that ignorance which is the beginning of wisdom and from that beginning work forward painstakingly and consciously, we shall get little real enlightenment on that subject.

Note: Legal Realism

Frank's contribution to Legal Realism involved more than *Law and the Modern Mind,* which became the most provocative statement of the movement's position. He was also an intellectual prod to his Yale colleague Karl N. Llewellyn, who wrote "Some Realism About Realism—Responding to Dean [Roscoe] Pound," *Harvard Law Review* (1931). The essay became a landmark in twentieth-century legal thought because it succeeded in summing up the essential nature of Legal Realism while pointing to the open and dynamic legal culture that emerged from the New Deal era. Llewellyn himself was involved in the American Law Institute, and after World War II, he published under its auspices the model Uniform Commercial Code.

Realists, however, regularly quarreled with one another from the movement's beginning, a development that dissipated much of its energies in theoretical hair splitting. In the case of Llewellyn, for example, his essay took direct aim at Dean Roscoe Pound of Harvard, one of the early advocates of Sociological Jurisprudence. Llewellyn argued that the way Realists examined the law was more significant than any particular values that analysis might reveal. Truth, for the Realists, was based on empirically established facts that yielded necessarily tentative and relative hypotheses. This approach meant that the Realists had difficulty articulating a consistent ethical and moral position; instead, with each situation a different set of facts influenced the course of the law. It was this relativism against which Pound reacted. The differences within the legal community only sharpened during the late 1930s and the 1940s with the rise and ultimate defeat of Nazism. Catholic legal educators in particular reasserted the view that human reason could discover certain universal principles of justice by analyzing philosophically the nature of reality. Such an analysis, they claimed, promised to yield not only a consistent rule of law but one rooted in moral principles.

The Realists did score one impressive victory. They stressed the virtues of an instrumental as opposed to a formalistic approach to social change through law at a time when the nation reeled under the weight of the Great Depression. The pragmatism and instrumentalism of the New Deal complemented the result-oriented and behavioral approach of Legal Realism, although the specific theories of Legal Realists seldom directly influenced the conduct of New Deal policy makers. Rather, the contribution was one of tone as squads of lawyers educated in the visions of Legal Realism and Sociological Jurisprudence arrived in Washington to administer the New Deal.

THE NEW DEAL AND THE RISE OF LEGAL LIBERALISM

The Great Depression raised profound questions about the relationship of government to the economy and of the nation to the states, questions made critical in the legal culture by the Legal Realists' pronouncements about the instrumental character of law. Classical nineteenth-century liberalism stressed the passive rather than the active role of government. According to laissez-faire ideology, a government that governed least governed best. Unrestrained market forces were the fairest and most efficient means of deciding between winners and losers in life's economic race. Of course, government was never altogether passive; the states had bequeathed a rich tradition of governmental involvement in the economy that stretched back to the colonial era. These efforts had modest redistributional consequences; there was no broad consensus in favor of the idea that government at any level should provide for individual economic security. Moreover, what governmental activity did take place stressed promotion more than regulation. In the late nineteenth and early twentieth centuries, however, Progressive reformers pressed successfully for a shift from promotion to regulation. The purpose of the new regulatory state was to restore both business efficiency and economic justice by substituting administrative expertise for the traditional distributional scheme of political parties. Even big business found much to applaud in this regulatory movement, since it promised to replace cut-throat competition with predictable market relations. The Great Depression, then, merely hastened, albeit in dramatic fashion, a shift in the underlying character of liberalism.

The critical issue in the 1930s, therefore, was not whether government should intervene but the method of its intervention. During the previous decade, the direct role of the federal government in the economy declined. The Progressive insistence on an efficient and orderly economy did persist in such government-sponsored activities as the trade association movement. The administration of Republican President Herbert Hoover (1929–1933), for example, expected government to create the circumstances in which private individuals and groups would police themselves. With the Depression, however, this cheery vision of an economy founded on voluntary controls faded. In its place came the New Deal.

Democratic President Franklin D. Roosevelt, who came into office in 1933, masterminded the New Deal. One of the keystones of his program was greater involvement by the national government in the national economy. The alphabet soup of New Deal programs was controversial because it broke down the traditional scheme of federalism, raised the specter of a growing administrative state, and embraced certain social-welfare assumptions, the most significant of which was the belief that government had a positive duty to provide for the well-being of each citizen. The New Deal seems relatively benign today, in large measure because we have come to accept most of its tenets. But in the 1930s, with the nation shocked by an economic earthquake, it seemed a good deal more far-reaching, even revolutionary, to its detractors. The New Deal encountered its stiffest test before the Supreme Court, whose justices questioned the notion of emergency powers (on which much of FDR's and the Democratic Congress's actions rested), the delegation by Congress of its authority to administrative agencies, and the intervention by the national government in matters previously the domain of the states.

There were, as well, plenty of "little" New Deals in the states. There lawmakers passed a host of relief and regulatory measures that reflected, even though they seldom drew directly from, the instrumental vision of law proffered by the Legal Realists. Many of these state measures were also tested before the Supreme Court, where, like federal legislation, they came into collision with constitutional doctrines and judicial attitudes of another era.

THE STATE AND FEDERAL LEGISLATIVE RESPONSE

Economic panics and financial contractions were nothing new in American history; the Great Depression was only one more phase of the business cycle. Demands by debtors for relief had accompanied every downturn. State efforts to provide relief collided with the federal constitutional guarantee that no state could impair contracts. For example, Minnesota in 1933 passed the Mortgage Moratorium Law, which delayed foreclosures on real property, doing so with the hope that debtors might be able to regain their economic footing, repay their debts, and return to normal economic conduct. Unhappy creditors challenged such laws, arguing that protection of contracts was most important when economic conditions were most difficult.

The Minnesota law was only one of many measures passed by the states to deal with the hardships created by the Depression. New Jersey passed legislation adjusting insurance rates; Oklahoma decided to regulate the price of ice. Lawmakers in every state believed that the economic crisis warranted these measures.

Restoration of the moribund economy was the most important task before Roosevelt's administration and Congress. During his first one hundred days in office, FDR enjoyed broad support in Congress as well as in the business community, which realized that something had to be done to restore economic confidence. The President declared a four-day national bank holiday and suspended the payment of private debts in gold. He also successfully urged Congress to pass the Federal Securities Act (which required full disclosure to investors of information about new securities and established a new agency, the Securities and Exchange Commission, to oversee Wall Street) and the Glass-Steagall Act (which created the Federal Deposit Insurance Corporation to guarantee bank deposits up to $2,500), to create the Tennessee Valley Authority (an independent public corporation to produce and sell electric power and nitrogen fertilizer as a way of promoting economic development in the poverty-stricken Tennessee River Valley), and to pass the Agricultural Adjustment Act (which subsidized farmers for not growing crops on the theory that as the supply of agricultural commodities declined, their value would increase).

The National Industrial Recovery Act of 1933 was only one of several measures that FDR's administration supported, but its commitment to economic planning, based on administrative decision making, was the heart of the so-called First New Deal. The preamble read something like a lawyer's brief, making the ingenious but questionable argument that since the Great Depression had placed burdens on interstate commerce, Congress could regulate vast areas of business and labor that it had previously left untouched. The measure was also a grab bag of political offerings; everybody got something. Business received authority to draft codes that were exempt from anti-trust laws; labor received, under Section 7(a), the right to bargain collectively and to have minimum wages and maximum hours; and those out of work were promised public works. The law established the National Recovery Administration (NRA) to facilitate code drafting and granted to the president authority to impose codes on any recalcitrant industry. Once the president approved a code, it had the force of law. In sum, the measure not only broke down many of the traditional lines blocking government involvement in the economy, but also delegated significant authority from Congress to the president and through him to an administrative agency. In this way, the New Deal built on the mobilization experience of World War I and the Progressive belief in rational administration. The emerging social-welfare state envisioned in the "First New Deal," therefore, relied on authority delegated by Congress to administrative bodies.

Despite the rich harvest of legislation and the rapid growth of the new administrative network in Washington, the Great Depression persisted. The economy did revive somewhat in 1934, giving the NRA an illusion of success, but by 1935 unemployment still stood at around 20 percent. The persistence of the Depression only deepened the sense of urgency and unease with government. FDR responded to a seeming failure of the "First New Deal" by embarking on an even more aggressive legislative campaign. This "Second New Deal" involved far-reaching legislation that brought even greater penetration by the national government through administrative authority into the day-to-day lives of the citizenry. For example, the National Labor Relations Act (also known as the Wagner Act) of 1935 bolstered labor's position by guaranteeing two of its most important long-term goals: the rights to unionize and to bargain collectively. The Social Security Act of 1935 established a vast system that provided a modest cushion for most Americans against unemployment, dependency, and old age. These and many other measures permanently affected American society; they were bold (but not radical) experiments that summoned federal legal authority to reshape certain underlying economic and social relationships. Even FDR's harshest critics agree today that he continued to deal from the same deck as Theodore Roosevelt, Woodrow Wilson, and even Herbert Hoover. His New Deal adjusted the system of American business enterprise to new realities by making certain economic practices, previously considered private, matters of public oversight.

While these New Deal measures have become the essence of the modern liberal, social-welfare state, they initially stirred great constitutional controversy. Congress passed the legislation of the "First New Deal" in great haste and often with sloppy wording. FDR gave the committee charged with writing the NRA one week to overhaul the nation's business structure.

THE SUPREME COURT AND THE NEW DEAL

The Hundred Days brought enormous excitement to the nation and with it a sense of hope for economic revival. An almost electric charge existed in Washington, and the new lawyers that piled into the New Deal administrative agencies did much to revive spirits. Roosevelt attracted into government bright young lawyers from some of the nation's most prestigious law schools. Legal Realist Jerome Frank, for example, became general counsel for the Agricultural Adjustment Agency. "I am—I make no secret of it—a reformer," Frank proudly admitted.[2] William O. Douglas, who had studied law at Columbia and believed that it was more a social science than a profession, became at age thirty-six the chief enforcement officer on the newly created Securities and Exchange Commission. And so it went—bright, aggressive, young lawyers seeking to remake the constitutional order through administrative and legal posts in a government dedicated to restoring the nation's economic health.

The justices of the High Court, however, took exception to much of the legislative enthusiasm of the New Deal, as it manifested itself both in Washington and in the states—with the result that the president and the justices were at odds with one another. In *New State Ice Company* v. *Liebman* (1932), for example, the Court struck down an Oklahoma statute as a violation of the principle that a state could regulate only those businesses "affected with a public interest." The justices concluded that the Oklahoma lawmakers had improperly invoked their police powers to foster an economic monopoly.

The nearly desperate circumstances surrounding the passage of the Minnesota Mortgage Moratorium Law seem to have influenced the justices. More than one-half of the citizens of Minnesota lived on farms, and they simply could not make ends meet. In the fall and winter of 1932, for example, corn was quoted as low as 8 cents per bushel, oats at 2 cents and wheat at 29 cents per bushel, eggs at 7 cents per dozen, and butter at 10 cents per pound. Moreover, mining, the state's second most important economic activity, was left reeling. The production of iron ore fell to less than 15 percent of normal production. The justices, in *Home Building and Loan Association* v. *Blaisdell* (1934), voted 5 to 4 to sustain the Minnesota law on the grounds that it was a proper emergency act that merely extended the period of redemption between foreclosure and sale of the farm, giving farmers a greater amount of time to raise money. The law did not cancel any outstanding debt; it simply adjusted the remedy available under the law. Chief Justice Charles Evans Hughes wrote for the majority that

> [w]hile emergency does not create power, emergency may furnish the occasion for the exercise of power. . . . The constitutional question presented in the light of an emergency is whether the power possessed embraces the particular conditions.
>
> When the provisions of the Constitution, in grant or restriction, are specific, so particularized as not to admit of construction, no question is presented. . . . But where constitutional grants and limitations of power are set forth in general clauses, which afford a broad outline, the process of construction is essential to fill in the details. That is true of the contract clause. . . .
>
> But full recognition of the occasion and general purpose of the clause does not suffice to fix its precise scope. Nor does an examination of the details of prior legislation in the States yield criteria which can be considered controlling. To ascertain the scope of the constitutional prohibition we examine the course of judicial decisions in its application. These put it beyond question that the prohibition is not an absolute one and is not to be read with literal exactness like a mathematical formula.

The New Dealers ignored many traditional limits of authority between the states and the nation, extended the commerce and taxing powers in novel ways, and invoked a constitutional theory of emergency powers to rationalize what they did. They were pragmatic and determined to end the Depression, but they were often impatient with prevailing constitutional rules.

The Supreme Court was not. The result was a collision between the justices, who saw their responsibility as remaining faithful to the Constitution as they understood it, and the administration, which charged that the Court was indifferent to the plight of millions of Americans. The administration's task of defending itself legally was made all the more difficult by its limited resources and internal bickering. Attorney General Homer Cummings, for example, expected that his office would represent the administration in every proceeding brought before the Supreme Court; at the same time, the chief counsels and heads of the various New Deal agencies wanted to protect their own turf. Moreover, many of the Department of Justice lawyers, who came from a different generation than the young New Dealers, were not only hostile to their youthful and exuberant colleagues but critical of much of the New Deal legislation. Even if there had been no infighting, the novel constitutional grounds on which the New Deal rested guaranteed close scrutiny by the High Court.

That scrutiny was ensured by the composition of the Court. The conservative wing of the Court was composed of the Four Horsemen, named after the Four Horsemen of the Apocalypse. Justices Willis Van Devanter, James McReynolds, George Sutherland, and Pierce Butler consistently voted together and against the New Deal. On the other wing were three generally liberal justices: Benjamin N. Cardozo, Louis D. Brandeis, and Harlan Fiske Stone. Between these two wings, on what was a highly contentious Court, rested the swing votes of Chief Justice Charles Evans Hughes and Justice Owen J. Roberts.

Schechter v. United States
295 U.S. 495 (1935)

Initially, the Supreme Court accepted some New Deal measures. The justices gave a favorable reading to two important state Depression laws. In Home Building and Loan Association *v.* Blaisdell *(1934), they sustained the Minnesota Mortgage Moratorium Law, and in* Nebbia *v.* New York *(1934), they upheld a New York law regulating the price of milk. In both instances, the Court had split 5 to 4. But when the Court began in December 1934 to hear cases involving hastily drawn "First New Deal" legislation, the administration quickly realized that it was headed for trouble. Two of the main components of its program—the National Industrial Recovery Act (NIRA) and the Agricultural Adjustment Act—came under withering and ultimately fatal constitutional inspection. In* Schechter *v.* United States, *the so-called sick-chicken case, the Court had to determine whether the live-poultry code of the NIRA was an unconstitutional regulation of intrastate commerce and an excessive delegation of legislative power to the president.*

Mr. Chief Justice Hughes delivered the opinion of the Court.

A. L. A. Schechter Poultry Corporation and Schechter Live Poultry Market are corporations conducting wholesale poultry slaughterhouse markets in Brooklyn, New York City. Joseph Schechter operated the latter corporation and also guaranteed the credits of the former corporation which was operated by Martin,

Alex and Aaron Schechter. Defendants ordinarily purchase their live poultry from commission men at the West Washington Market in New York City or at the railroad terminals serving the City, but occasionally they purchase from commission men in Philadelphia. They buy the poultry for slaughter and resale. After the poultry is trucked to their slaughterhouse markets in Brooklyn, it is there sold, usually within twenty-four hours, to retail poultry dealers and butchers who sell directly to consumers. The poultry purchased from defendants is immediately slaughtered, prior to delivery, by Schochtim [slaughterers working under Orthodox Jewish law and ritual to provide kosher meat] in defendants' employ. Defendants do not sell poultry in interstate commerce.

The "Live Poultry Code" was promulgated under [Section] 3 of the National Industrial Recovery Act. That section . . . authorizes the President to approve "codes of fair competition." Such a code may be approved for a trade or industry, upon application by one or more trade or industrial associations or groups, if the President finds (1) that such associations or groups "impose no inequitable restrictions on admission to membership therein and are truly representative," and (2) that such codes are not designed "to promote monopolies or to eliminate or oppress small enterprises and will not operate to discriminate against them, and will tend to effectuate the policy" of Title I of the Act. Such codes "shall not permit monopolies or monopolistic practices." As a condition of his approval, the President may "impose such conditions (including requirements for the making of reports and the keeping of accounts) for the protection of consumers, competitors, employees, and others, and in furtherance of the public interest, and may provide such exceptions to and exemptions from the provisions of such code as the President in his discretion deems necessary to effectuate the policy herein declared." Where such a code has not been approved, the President may prescribe one, either on his own motion or on complaint. Violation of any provision of a code (so approved or prescribed) "in any transaction in or affecting interstate or foreign commerce" is made a misdemeanor punishable by a fine of not more than $500 for each offense, and each day the violation continues to be deemed a separate offense.

♦   ♦   ♦

First. Two preliminary points are stressed by the Government with respect to the appropriate approach to the important questions presented. We are told that the provision of the statute authorizing the adoption of codes must be viewed in the light of the grave national crisis with which Congress was confronted. Undoubtedly, the conditions to which power is addressed are always to be considered when the exercise of power is challenged. Extraordinary conditions may call for extraordinary remedies. But the argument necessarily stops short of an attempt to justify action which lies outside the sphere of constitutional authority. Extraordinary conditions do not create or enlarge constitutional power. The Constitution established a national government with powers deemed to be adequate, as they have proved to be both in war and peace, but these powers of the national government are limited by the constitutional grants. Those who act under these grants are not at liberty to transcend the imposed limits because they believe that more or different power is necessary. Such assertions of extra-constitutional authority were anticipated and precluded by the explicit terms of the Tenth Amendment,—"the powers not delegated to the United States by the Constitution, nor prohibited by it to the States, are reserved to the States respectively, or to the people."

Second. The question of the delegation of legislative power.

♦   ♦   ♦

[W]e turn to the Recovery Act to ascertain what limits have been set to the exercise of the President's discretion. First, the President, as a condition of approval, is required to find that the trade or industrial associations or groups which propose a code, "impose no inequitable restrictions on admission to membership" and are "truly representative." That condition, however, relates only to the status of the initiators of the new laws and not to the permissible scope of such laws. Second, the President is required to find that the code is not "designed to promote monopolies or to eliminate or oppress small enterprises and will not operate to discriminate against them." And, to this is added a proviso that the code "shall not permit monopolies or monopolistic practices." But these restrictions leave virtually untouched the field of policy envisaged by section one, and, in that wide field of legislative possibilities, the proponents of a code, refraining from monopolistic designs, may roam at will and the President may approve or disapprove their proposals as he may see fit. That is the precise effect of the further finding that the President is to make—that the code "will tend to effectuate the policy of this title." While this is called a finding, it is really but a statement of an opinion as to the general effect upon the promotion of trade or industry of a scheme of laws. These are the only findings which Congress has made essential in order to put into operation a legislative code having the aims described in the "Declaration of policy."

Nor is the breadth of the President's discretion left to the necessary implications of this limited requirement as to his findings. As already noted, the President in approving a code may impose his own conditions, adding to or taking from what is proposed, as "in his discretion" he thinks necessary "to effectuate the policy" declared by the Act. Of course, he has no less liberty when he prescribes a code on his own motion or on complaint, and he is free to prescribe one if a code has not been approved. The Act provides for the creation by the President of administrative agencies to assist him, but the action or reports of such agencies, or of his other assistants,—their recommendations and findings in relation to the making of codes—have no sanction beyond the will of the President, who may accept, modify or reject them as he pleases. Such recommendations or findings in no way limit the authority which 3 undertakes to vest in the President with no other conditions than those there specified. And this authority relates to a host of different trades and industries, thus extending the President's discretion to all the varieties of laws which he may deem to be beneficial in dealing with the vast array of commercial and industrial activities throughout the country.

Such a sweeping delegation of legislative power finds no support in the decisions upon which the Government especially relies.

◆ ◆ ◆

Third. The question of the application of the provisions of the Live Poultry Code to intrastate transactions. Although the validity of the codes (apart from the question of delegation) rests upon the commerce clause of the Constitution, 3(a) is not in terms limited to in-terstate and foreign commerce. From the generality of its terms, and from the argument of the Government at the bar, it would appear that 3(a) was designed to authorize codes without that limitation. But under 3(f) penalties are confined to violations of a code provision "in any transaction in or affecting interstate or foreign commerce." This aspect of the case presents the question whether the particular provisions of the Live Poultry Code, which the defendants were convicted for violating and for having conspired to violate, were within the regulating power of Congress.

These provisions relate to the hours and wages of those employed by defendants in their slaughterhouses in Brooklyn and to the sales there made to retail dealers and butchers. The undisputed facts thus afford no warrant for the argument that the poultry handled by defendants at their slaughterhouse markets was in a "current" or "flow" of interstate commerce and was thus subject to congressional regulation. . . .

Did the defendants' transactions directly "affect" interstate commerce so as to be subject to federal regulations? The power of Congress extends not only to the regulation of transactions which are part of interstate commerce, but to the protection of that commerce from injury. It matters not that the injury may be due to the conduct of those engaged in intrastate operations.

◆ ◆ ◆

In determining how far the federal government may go in controlling intrastate transactions upon the ground that they "affect" interstate commerce, there is a necessary and well-established distinction between direct and indirect effects. The precise line can be drawn only as individual cases arise, but the distinction is clear in principle. Direct effects are illustrated by the railroad cases we have cited, e.g., the effect of failure to use prescribed safety appliances on railroads which are the highways of both interstate and intrastate commerce, injury to an employee engaged in interstate transportation by the negligence of an employee engaged in an intrastate movement, the fixing of rates for intrastate transportation which unjustly discriminate against interstate commerce. But where the effect of intrastate transactions upon interstate commerce is merely indirect, such transactions remain within the domain of state power. If the commerce clause were construed to reach all enterprises and transactions which could be said to have an indirect effect upon interstate commerce, the federal authority would embrace practically all the activities of the people and the authority of the State over its domestic concerns would exist only by sufferance of the federal government. In deed, on such a theory, even the development of the State's commercial facilities would be subject to federal control.

The question of chief importance relates to the provisions of the Code as to the hours and wages of those employed in defendants' slaughterhouse markets. It is plain that these requirements are imposed in order to govern the details of defendants' management of their local business. The persons employed in slaughtering and selling in local trade are not employed in interstate commerce. Their hours and wages have no direct relation to interstate commerce. The question of how many hours these employees should work and what they should be paid differs in no essential respect from similar questions in other local businesses which handle commodities brought into a State and there dealt in as a part of its internal commerce. This appears from an examination of the considerations urged by the Government with respect to conditions in the poultry trade. Thus, the Government argues that hours and wages affect prices; that slaughterhouse men sell at a small margin above operating costs; that labor represents 50 to 60 percent of these costs; that a slaughterhouse operator paying lower wages or reducing his cost by exacting long hours of work, translates his saving into lower prices; that this results in demands for a cheaper grade of goods; and that the cutting of prices brings about a demoralization of the price structure. Similar conditions may be adduced in relation to other business.

♦ ♦ ♦

It is not the province of the Court to consider the economic advantages or disadvantages of such a centralized system. It is sufficient to say that the Federal Constitution does not provide for it. Our growth and development have called for wide use of the commerce power of the federal government in its control over the expanded activities of commerce, and in protecting that commerce from burdens, interferences, and conspiracies to restrain and monopolize it. But the authority of the federal government may not be pushed to such an extreme as to destroy the distinction, which the commerce clause itself establishes, between commerce "among the several States" and the internal concerns of a State. The same answer must be made to the contention that is based upon the serious economic situation which led to the passage of the Recovery Act,—the fall in prices, the decline in wages and employment, and the curtailment of the market for commodities. Stress is laid upon the great importance of maintaining wage distributions which would provide the necessary stimulus in starting "the cumulative forces making for expanding commercial activity." Without in any way disparaging this motive, it is enough to say that the recuperative efforts of the federal government must be made in a manner consistent with the authority granted by the Constitution.

We are of the opinion that the attempt through the provisions of the Code to fix the hours and wages of employees of defendants in their intrastate business was not a valid exercise of federal power.

United States v. Butler
297 U.S. 1 (1936)

The Agricultural Adjustment Act was designed to raise agricultural prices by limiting crop production. The AAA established a processing tax to fund crop subsidies and soil restrictions. Where the NIRA had relied on the commerce power, the AAA depended on the taxing power for its constitutional authority. Critics complained that the government had taken on the unconstitutional task of controlling agriculture and that the tax was an integral part of this unconstitutional plan. The government insisted that it could not be challenged in its taxing authority, basing its view on Frothingham v. Mellon *(1923). The Court held in* Frothingham *that taxpayers had no standing to question how the federal government spent its tax revenues. The conservatives on the Court, in a part of the decision not reprinted below, disposed of this precedent.*

Justice Roberts for the majority.

It is inaccurate and misleading to speak of the exaction from processors prescribed by the challenged act as a tax, or to say that as a tax it is subject to no infirmity. A tax, in the general understanding of the term, and as used in the Constitution, signifies an exaction for the support of the Government. The word has never been thought to connote the expropriation of money from one group for the benefit of another. . . . But manifestly no justification for it can be found unless as an integral part of such regulation. The exaction cannot be wrested out of its setting, denominated an excise for raising revenue and legalized by ignoring its purpose as a mere instrumentality for bringing about a desired end. To do this would be to shut our eyes to what all others than we can see and understand. . . .

We conclude that the act is one regulating agricultural production; that the tax is a mere incident of such regulation and that the respondents have standing to challenge the legality of the exaction.

The Government asserts that even if the respondents may question the propriety of the appropriation embodied in the statute their attack must fail because Article I, [Section] 8 of the Constitution authorizes the contemplated expenditure of the funds raised by the tax. This contention presents the great and the controlling question in the case. . . .

There should be no misunderstanding as to the function of this court in such a case. It is sometimes said that the court assumes a power to overrule or control the action of the people's representatives. This is a misconception. The Constitution is the supreme law of the land ordained and established by the people. All legislation must conform to the principles it lays down. When an act of Congress is appropriately challenged in the courts as not conforming to the constitutional mandate the judicial branch of the Government has only one duty,—to lay the article of the Constitution which is invoked beside the statute which is challenged and to decide whether the latter squares with the former. All the court does, or can do, is to announce its considered judgment upon the question. The only power it has, if such it may be called, is the power of judgment. This court neither approves nor condemns any legislative policy. Its delicate and difficult office is to ascertain and declare whether the legislation is in accordance with, or in contravention of, the provisions of the Constitution; and, having done that, its duty ends.

The clause thought to authorize the legislation,—the first,—confers upon the Congress power "to lay and collect Taxes, Duties, Imposts and Excises, to pay the Debts and provide for the common Defense and general Welfare of the United States. . . . " It is not contended that this provision grants power to regulate agricultural production upon the theory that such legislation would promote the general welfare. The Government concedes that the phrase "to provide for the general welfare" qualifies the power "to lay and collect taxes." The view that the clause grants power to provide for the general welfare, independently of the taxing power, has never been authoritatively accepted. . . . The true construction undoubtedly is that the only thing granted is the power to tax for the purpose of providing funds for payment of the nation's debts and making provision for the general welfare.

Nevertheless the Government asserts that warrant is found in this clause for the adoption of the Agricultural Adjustment Act. The argument is that Congress may appropriate and authorize the spending of moneys for the "general welfare"; that the phrase should be liberally construed to cover anything conducive to national welfare; that decision as to what will promote such welfare rests with Congress alone, and the courts may not review its determination; and finally that the appropriation under attack was in fact for the general welfare of the United States.

Since the foundation of the Nation sharp differences of opinion have persisted as to the true interpretation of the phrase. Madison asserted it amounted to no more than a reference to the other powers enumerated in the subsequent clauses of the same section; that, as the United States is a government of limited and enumerated powers, the grant of power to tax and spend for the general national welfare must be confined to the enumerated legislative fields committed to the Congress. In this view the phrase is mere tautology, for taxation and appropriation are or may be necessary incidents of the exercise of any of the enumerated legislative powers. Hamilton, on the other hand, maintained the clause confers a power separate and distinct from those later enumerated, is not restricted in meaning by the grant of them, and Congress consequently has a substantive power to tax and to appropriate, limited only by the requirement that it shall be exercised to provide for the general welfare of the United States. Each contention has' had the support of those whose views are entitled to weight. . . .

We are not now required to ascertain the scope of the phrase "general welfare of the United States" or to determine whether an appropriation in aid of agriculture falls within it. Wholly apart from that question, another principle embedded in our Constitution prohibits the enforcement of the Agricultural Adjustment Act. The act invades the reserved rights of the states. It is a salutary plan to regulate and control agricultural production, a matter beyond the powers delegated to the federal government. The tax, the appropriation of the funds raised, and the direction for their disbursement, are but parts of the plan. They are but means to an unconstitutional end.

From the accepted doctrine that the United States is a government of delegated powers, it follows that those not expressly granted, or reasonably to be implied from such as are conferred, are reserved to the states or to the people. To

forestall any suggestion to the contrary, the Tenth Amendment was adopted. The same proposition, otherwise stated, is that powers not granted are prohibited. None to regulate agricultural production is given, and therefore legislation by Congress for that purpose is forbidden.

It is an established principle that the attainment of a prohibited end may not be accomplished under the pretext of the exertion of powers which are granted.

◆   ◆   ◆

Congress could not, under the pretext of raising revenue, lay a tax on processors who refuse to pay a certain price for cotton, and exempt those who agree so to do, with the purpose of benefiting producers.

If the taxing power may not be used as the instrument to enforce a regulation of matters of state concern with respect to which the Congress has no authority to interfere, may it, as in the present case, be employed to raise the money necessary to purchase a compliance which the Congress is powerless to command?

The Government asserts that whatever might be said against the validity of the plan if compulsory, it is constitutionally sound because the end is accomplished by voluntary cooperation. There are two sufficient answers to the contention. The regulation is not in fact voluntary. The farmer, of course, may refuse to comply, but the price of such refusal is the loss of benefits. The amount offered is intended to be sufficient to exert pressure on him to agree to the proposed regulation. The power to confer or withhold unlimited benefits is the power to coerce or destroy.

Congress has no power to enforce its commands on the farmer to the ends sought by the Agricultural Adjustment Act. It must follow that it may not indirectly accomplish those ends by taxing and spending to purchase compliance. . . . It does not help to declare that local conditions throughout the nation have created a situation of national concern; for this is but to say that whenever there is a widespread similarity of local conditions, Congress may ignore constitutional limitations upon its own powers and usurp those reserved to the states. If, in lieu of compulsory regulation of subjects within the states' reserved jurisdiction, which is prohib-

ited, the Congress could invoke the taxing and
spending power as a means to accomplish the
same end, Article I would become the instrument for total subversion of the governmental
powers reserved to the individual states.

If the act before us is a proper exercise of
the federal taxing power, evidently the regulation of all industry throughout the United States
may be accomplished by similar exercises of
the same power. It would be possible to exact
money from one branch of an industry and pay
it to another branch in every field of activity
which lies within the province of the states. The
mere threat of such a procedure might well induce the surrender of rights and the compliance
with federal regulation as the price of continuance in business.

We have held in *Schechter Poultry Corp.*
v. *United States,* that Congress has no power to
regulate wages and hours of labor in a local
business. If the petitioner is right, this very end
may be accomplished by appropriating money
to be paid to employers from the federal treasury under contracts whereby they agree to comply with certain standards fixed by federal law
or by contract.

Until recently no suggestion of the existence
of any such power in the Federal Government
has been advanced. The expressions of the
framers of the Constitution, the decisions of this
court interpreting that instrument, and the writings of great commentators will be searched in
vain for any suggestion that there exists in the
clause under discussion or elsewhere in the Constitution, the authority whereby every provision
and every fair implication from that instrument
may be subverted, the independence of the individual states obliterated, and the United States
converted into a central government exercising
uncontrolled police power in every state of the
Union, superseding all local control or regulation of the affairs or concerns of the states.

Since, as we have pointed out, there was
no power in the Congress to impose the contested exaction, it could not lawfully ratify or
confirm what an executive officer had done in
that regard. Consequently the Act of 1935 does
not affect the rights of the parties.

The judgment is

Affirmed.

Mr. Justice Stone, dissenting.

I think the judgment should be reversed.

That the governmental power of the purse
is a great one is not now for the first time announced. Every student of the history of government and economics is aware of its magnitude and of its existence in every civilized
government. Both were well understood by the
framers of the Constitution when they sanctioned the grant of the spending power to the
federal government, and both were recognized
by Hamilton and Story, whose views of the
spending power as standing on a parity with the
other powers specifically granted, have hereto
been generally accepted.

The suggestion that it must now be
curtailed by judicial fiat because it may be
abused by unwise use hardly rises to the dignity of argument. So may judicial power be
abused.

A tortured construction of the Constitution
is not to be justified by recourse to extreme examples of reckless congressional spending
which might occur if courts could not prevent—expenditures which, even if they could
be thought to effect any national purpose,
would be possible only by action of a legislature lost to all sense of public responsibility.
Such suppositions are addressed to the mind
accustomed to believe that it is the business of
courts to sit in judgment on the wisdom of legislative action. Courts are not the only agency
of government that must be assumed to have
capacity to govern. Congress and the courts
both unhappy may falter or be mistaken in the
performance of their constitutional duty. But
interpretation of our great charter of government which proceeds on any assumption that
the responsibility for the preservation of our institutions is the exclusive concern of any one
of the three branches of government, or that it
alone can save them from destruction is far
more likely, in the long run, "to obliterate the
constituent members" of "an indestructible
union of indestructible states" than the frank
recognition that language, even of a constitution, may mean what it says: that the power to
tax and spend includes the power to relieve a
nationwide economic maladjustment by conditional gifts of money.

FDR's Court-Packing Plan

By the presidential election of 1936, the Supreme Court had overturned or significantly limited all the major parts of the "First New Deal," and the justices were about to tackle the new stream of laws that encompassed the "Second New Deal." Roosevelt won a landslide victory in 1936 over his Republican opponent, Alfred Landon, and he intended to start his second term by taking on his last significant adversary—the Supreme Court. Roosevelt was especially frustrated because during his first term no vacancies had occurred on the high bench. Critics complained that the justices were too old and out of touch with the times to render decisions during a period of such great national crisis. The newspaper columnists Drew Pearson and Robert S. Allen in 1936 wrote an exposé of the Court, and the public fastened its title, *The Nine Old Men,* on the justices. The description was disingenuous; the oldest member of the Court, Louis D. Brandeis, while thoroughly independent, was also a member of the Court's liberal wing.

FRANKLIN ROOSEVELT

"Fireside Chat on the 'Court-Packing' Bill"
March 9, 1937

This radio address by President Roosevelt was his strongest effort to garner public support for his "court-packing" plan. It came at a time when FDR enjoyed enormous popular support, as his victory at the polls only a few months before had demonstrated. The Judiciary Reorganization Bill, however, stirred public anxiety because it seemed to place political considerations above the rule of law. The measure also divided the Democratic party, gave conservative Republicans an issue on which they successfully attacked the president for the first time, and raised in dramatic fashion one of the most important constitutional issues of the New Deal—separation of powers.

Tonight, sitting at my desk in the White House, I make my first radio report to the people in my second term of office. . . .

In 1933 you and I knew that we must never let our economic system get completely out of joint again—that we could not afford to take the risk of another great depression.

We also become convinced that the only way to avoid a repetition of those dark days was to have a government with power to prevent and to cure the abuses and the inequalities which had thrown that system out of joint.

The American people have learned from the depression. For in the last three national elections an overwhelming majority of them voted a mandate that the Congress and the President begin the task of providing that protection—not after long years of debate, but now.

The Courts, however, have cast doubts on the ability of the elected Congress to protect us against catastrophe by meeting squarely our modern social and economic conditions.

We are at a crisis, a crisis in our ability to proceed with that protection. . . .

I want to talk with you very simply tonight about the need for present action in this crisis— the need to meet the unanswered challenge of one-third of a Nation ill-nourished, ill-clad, ill-housed.

Last Thursday I described the American form of Government as a three-horse team provided by the Constitution to the American people so that their field might be plowed. The three horses are, of course, the Congress, the Executive and the Courts. Two of the horses, the Congress and the Executive, are pulling in unison today; the third is not. Those who have intimated that the President of the United States is trying to drive that team, overlook the simple fact that the President, as Chief Executive, is himself one of the horses.

It is the American people themselves who are in the driver's seat. It is the American people themselves who want the furrow plowed.

It is the American people themselves who expect the third horse to pull in unison with the other two.

I hope that you have re-read the Constitution of the United States in these past few weeks. Like the Bible, it ought to be read again and again.

It is an easy document to understand when you remember that it was called into being because the Articles of Confederation under which the original thirteen States tried to operate after the Revolution showed the need of a National Government with power enough to handle national problems. In its Preamble, the Constitution states that it was intended to form a more perfect Union and promote the general welfare; and the powers given to the Congress to carry out those purposes can best be described by saying that they were all the powers needed to meet each and every problem which then had a national character and which could not be met by merely local action.

But the framers went further. Having in mind that in succeeding generations many other problems then undreamed of would become national problems, they gave to the Congress the ample broad powers "to levy taxes . . . and provide for the common defense and general welfare of the United States."

That, my friends, is what I honestly believe to have been the clear and underlying purpose of the patriots who wrote a Federal Constitution to create a National Government with national power, intended as they said, "to form a more perfect union . . . for ourselves and our posterity."

For nearly twenty years there was no conflict between the Congress and the Court. Then in 1803, Congress passed a statute which the Court said violated an express provision of the Constitution. The Court claimed the power to declare it unconstitutional and did so declare it.

But a little later the Court itself admitted that it was an extraordinary power to exercise and through Mr. Justice Washington laid down this limitation upon it. He said: "It is but a decent respect due to the wisdom, the integrity and the patriotism of the Legislative body, by which any law is passed, to presume in favor of its validity until its violation of the Constitution is proved beyond all reasonable doubt."

But since the rise of the modern movement for social and economic progress through legislation, the Court has more and more often and more and more boldly asserted a power to veto laws passed by the Congress and by State Legislatures in complete disregard of this original limitation, which I have just read.

In the last four years the sound rule of giving statutes the benefit of all reasonable doubt has been cast aside. The Court has been acting not as a judicial body, but as a policy-making body.

The Court, in addition to the proper use of its judicial functions, has improperly set itself up as a third House of the Congress—a super-legislature, as one of the Justices has called it—reading into the Constitution words and implications which are not there, and which were never intended to be there.

We have, therefore, reached the point as a Nation where we must take action to save the Constitution from the Court, and the Court from itself. We must find a way to take an appeal from the Supreme Court to the Constitution itself. We want a Supreme Court which will do justice under the Constitution—not over it. In our Courts we want a government of laws and not of men.

I want—as all Americans want—an independent judiciary as proposed by the framers of the Constitution. That means a Supreme Court that will enforce the Constitution as written—that will refuse to amend the Constitution by the arbitrary exercise of judicial power—amendment, in other words, by judicial say-so. It does not mean a judiciary so independent that it can deny the existence of facts which are universally recognized.

What is my proposal? It is simply this: Whenever a Judge or Justice of any Federal Court has reached the age of seventy and does not avail himself of the opportunity to retire on a pension, a new member shall be appointed by the President then in office, with the approval, as required by the Constitution, of the Senate of the United States.

That plan has two chief purposes. By bringing into the Judicial system a steady and continuing stream of new and younger blood, I hope, first, to make the administration of all Federal justice, from the bottom to the top, speedier and, therefore, less costly; secondly, to bring to the decision of social and economic problems younger men who have had personal experience and contact with modem facts and circumstances under which average men have to live and work. This plan will save our national Constitution from hardening of the judicial arteries.

♦ ♦ ♦

Those opposing this plan have sought to arouse prejudice and fear by crying that I am seeking to "pack" the Supreme Court and that a baneful precedent will be established.

What do they mean by the words "packing the Supreme Court"?

Let me answer this question with a bluntness that will end all honest misunderstanding of my purposes.

If by that phrase "packing the Court" it is charged that I wish to place on the bench spineless puppets who would disregard the law and would decide specific cases as I wished them to be decided, I make this answer—that no President fit for this office would appoint, and no Senate of honorable men fit for their office would confirm, that kind of appointees to the Supreme Court.

But if by that phrase the charge is made that I would appoint and the Senate would confirm Justices worthy to sit beside present members of the Court who understand modem con-

ditions—that I will appoint Justices who will not undertake to override the judgment of the Congress on legislative policy—that I will appoint Justices who will act as Justices and not as legislators—if the appointment of such Justices can be called "packing the Court," then I say that I, and with me the vast majority of the American people, favor doing just that thing—now.

♦ ♦ ♦

So, I now propose that we establish by law an assurance against any . . . ill-balanced Court in the future. I propose that hereafter, when a Judge reaches the age of seventy, a new and younger Judge shall be added to the Court automatically. In this way I propose to enforce a sound public policy by law instead of leaving the composition of our Federal Courts, including the highest, to be determined by chance or the personal decision of individuals.

♦ ♦ ♦

Like all lawyers, like all Americans, I regret the necessity of this controversy. But the welfare of the United States, and indeed of the Constitution itself, is what we all must think about first. Our difficulty with the Court today rises not from the Court as an institution but from human beings within it. We cannot yield our constitutional destiny to the personal judgment of a few men who, being fearful of the future, would deny us the necessary means of dealing with the present.

This plan of mine is no attack on the Court; it seeks to restore the Court to its rightful and historic place in our system of Constitutional Government and to have it resume its high task of building anew on the Constitution "a system of living law." The Court itself can best undo what the Court has done.

Note: The Fate of FDR's Court-Packing Plan

Roosevelt cloaked his court-packing scheme in the rhetoric of judicial reform. More judges were required to clear the dockets of the lower federal courts. While the dockets of the lower federal courts had expanded dramatically in the twentieth century, Chief Justice Hughes testified before Congress that more members of the High Court would only slow its work. In the final analysis, the president attempted to pull every possible lever to make his proposal, which was blatantly political, work by appealing to those interests with grievances against the courts. For example, Roosevelt and his attorney general, Homer Cummings, sought labor support by stressing that Democratic appointees to the lower courts would curtail the practice of federal judges issuing injunctions against workers engaged in strikes. To this extent, FDR's proposal for new blood on the federal courts confirmed one of the basic assumptions of the Legal Realists: judges protected the interests with which they were associated.

The Judiciary Reorganization Bill, while probably doomed from the outset, suffered from some bad luck. Senator Joseph T. Robinson, the Senate floor manager for the bill and a strong ally of the president, died during the summer debate over the measure. The Court itself also seemingly influenced the outcome; at least some historians believe that a few of the justices read the election returns.

THE RETREAT FROM ECONOMIC SUBSTANTIVE DUE PROCESS

West Coast Hotel v. *Parrish*
300 U.S. 379 (1937)

This case involved a Washington State minimum wage law that applied exclusively to women. The Court had previously dealt with such matters and had sharply limited the authority of the states and Congress to pass such legislation. As late as June 1936, for example, the justices in Morehead v. New York ex rel. Tipaldo *overturned by a 5 to 4 vote a model New York State minimum wage law. Justice George Sutherland rested his majority opinion on the leading precedent,* Adkins v. Children's Hospital *(1923). The justices in that case had invalidated a Washington, D.C., minimum wage law as a violation of the due process clause of the Fifth Amendment. The* West Coast Hotel *case involved similar concerns with substantive due process of law and freedom to contract as they arose under the Fourteenth Amendment. The decision, coming as it did on the heels of FDR's court-packing plan, also clearly signaled the Court's acceptance of the main features of the New Deal.*

Mr. Chief Justice Hughes delivered the opinion of the Court.

This case presents the question of the constitutional validity of the minimum wage law of the State of Washington.

♦ ♦ ♦

The appellant conducts a hotel. The appellee Elsie Parrish was employed as a chambermaid and (with her husband) brought this suit to recover the difference between the wages paid her and the minimum wage fixed pursuant to the state law. The minimum wage is $14.50 per week of 48 hours. The appellant challenged the act as repugnant to the due process clause of the Fourteenth Amendment of the Constitution of the United States. The Supreme Court of the State, reversing the trial court, sustained the statute and directed judgment for the plaintiffs. The case is here on appeal.

♦ ♦ ♦

The principle which must control our decision is not in doubt. The constitutional provision invoked is the due process clause of the Fourteenth Amendment governing the States, as the due process clause invoked in the *Adkins* case governed Congress. In each case the violation alleged by those attacking minimum wage regulation for women is deprivation of freedom of contract. What is this freedom? The Constitution does not speak of freedom of contract. It speaks of liberty and prohibits the deprivation of liberty without due process of law. In prohibiting that deprivation the Constitution does not recognize an absolute and uncontrollable liberty. Liberty in each of its phases has its history and connotation. But the liberty safeguarded is liberty in a social organization which requires the protection of law against the evils which menace the health, safety, morals and welfare of the people. Liberty under the Constitution is thus necessarily subject to the restraints of due process, and regulation which is reasonable in relation to its subject and is adopted in the interests of the community is due process.

This essential limitation of liberty in general governs freedom of contract in particular.

This power under the [Fourteenth Amendment to the] Constitution to restrict freedom of contract has had many illustrations. That it may be exercised in the public interest with respect to contracts between employer and employee is undeniable.

In dealing with the relation of employer and employed, the legislature has necessarily a wide field of discretion in order that there may be suitable protection of health and safety, and that peace and good order may be promoted through regulations designed to insure wholesome conditions of work and freedom from oppression.

The point that has been strongly stressed that adult employees should be deemed competent to make their own contracts was decisively met nearly forty years ago in *Holden* v. *Hardy,* supra, where we pointed out the inequality in the footing of the parties.

It is manifest that this principle is peculiarly applicable in relation to the employment of women in whose protection the State has a special interest. That phase of the subject received elaborate consideration in *Muller* v. *Oregon* (1908) where the constitutional authority of the State to limit the working hours of women was sustained.

♦ ♦ ♦

We think that the decision in the *Adkins* case was a departure from the true application of the principles governing the regulation by the State of relation of employer and employed.

With full recognition of the earnestness and vigor which characterizes the prevailing opinion in the *Adkins* case, we find it impossible to reconcile that ruling with these well-considered declarations. What can be closer to the public interest than the health of women and the protection from unscrupulous and overreaching employers? And if the protection of women is a legitimate end of the exercise of state power, how can it be said that the requirement of the payment of a minimum wage fairly fixed in order to meet the very necessities of existence is not an admissible means to that end? The legislature of the State was clearly entitled to consider the situation of women in employment, the fact that they are in the class receiving the least pay, that their bargaining power is relatively weak, and that they are the ready victims of those who would take advantage of their necessitous circumstances. The legislature was entitled to adopt measures to reduce the evils of the "sweating system," the exploiting of workers at wages so low as to be insufficient to meet the bare cost of living, thus making their very helplessness the occasion of a most injurious competition. The legislature had the right to consider that its minimum wage requirements would be an important aid in carrying out its policy of protection. The adoption of similar requirements by many States evidences a deep-seated conviction both as to the presence of the evil and as to the means adapted to check it. Legislative response to that conviction cannot be regarded as arbitrary or capricious, and that is all we have to decide. Even if the wisdom of the policy be regarded as debatable and its effects uncertain, still the legislature is entitled to its judgment.

There is an additional and compelling consideration which recent economic experience has brought into a strong light. The exploitation of a class of workers who are in an unequal position with respect to bargaining power and are thus relatively defenseless against the denial of a living wage is not only detrimental to their health and well being but casts a direct burden for their support upon the community. What these workers lose in wages the taxpayers are called upon to pay. The bare cost of living must be met. We may take judicial notice of the unparalleled demands for relief which arose during the recent period of depression and still continue to an alarming extent despite the degree of economic recovery which has been achieved. It is unnecessary to cite official statistics to establish what is of common knowledge through the length and breadth of the land. While in the instant case no factual brief has been presented, there is no reason to doubt that the State of Washington has encountered the same social problem that is present elsewhere. The community is not bound to provide what is in effect a subsidy for unconscionable employers. The community may direct its law-making power to correct the abuse which springs from their selfish disregard of the public interest. The argument that the legislation in question constitutes an arbitrary discrimination, because it does not extend to men, is unavailing. This Court has frequently held that the legislative authority, acting within its proper field, is not bound to extend its regulation to all cases which it might possibly reach. The legislature "is free to recognize degrees of harm and it may confine its restrictions to those classes of cases where the need is deemed to be clearest." If "the law presumably hits the evil where it is most felt, it is not to be overthrown because there are other instances to which it might have been applied." There is no "doctrinaire requirement" that the legislation should be couched in all embracing terms. . . . This familiar principle has repeatedly been applied to legislation which singles out women, and particular classes of women, in the exercise of the State's protective power. Their relative need in the presence of the evil, no less than the existence of the evil itself, is a matter for the legislative judgment.

Our conclusion is that the case of *Adkins* v. *Children's Hospital* should be, and it is, overruled. The judgment of the Supreme Court of the State of Washington is

Affirmed.

Mr. Justice Sutherland, dissenting:

Under our form of government, where the written Constitution, by its own terms, is the supreme law, some agency, of necessity, must have the power to say the final word as to the validity of a statute assailed as unconstitutional. The Constitution makes it clear that the power has been entrusted to this court when the question arises in a controversy within its jurisdiction; and so long as the power remains there, its exercise cannot be avoided without betrayal of the trust.

♦ ♦ ♦

It is urged that the question involved should now receive fresh consideration, among other reasons, because of the "economic conditions which have supervened"; but the meaning of the Constitution does not change with the ebb and flow of economic events. We frequently are told in more general words that the Constitution must be construed in the light of the pres-ent. If by that it is meant that the Constitution is made up of living words that apply to every new condition which they include, the statement is quite true. But to say, if that be intended, that the words of the Constitution mean today what they did not mean when written— that is, that they do not apply to a situation now to which they would have applied—then is to rob that instrument of the essential element which continues it in force as the people have made it until they, and not their official agents, have made it otherwise.

The judicial function is that of interpretation; it does not include the power of amendment under the guise of interpretation. To miss the point of difference between the two is to miss all that the phrase "supreme law of the land" stands for and to convert what was intended as inescapable and enduring mandates into mere moral reflections.

If the Constitution, intelligently and reasonably construed in the light of these principles, stands in the way of desirable legislation, the blame must rest upon that instrument, and not upon the court for enforcing it according to its terms. The remedy in that situation—and the only true remedy—is to amend the Constitution.

Note: The Decline of Substantive Due Process

Historians and observers of the Court have frequently described the decision in *West Coast Hotel* as a "switch in time that saved nine." There is no doubt that the Court changed direction, and the justices' determination to overrule their earlier holding in *Adkins* underscored their serious purpose. The Court subsequently indicated that its behavior in *West Coast Hotel* was no fluke. Two weeks later, it decided *National Labor Relations Board v. Jones & Laughlin Steel Company,* in which Chief Justice Hughes used Holmes's "stream of commerce" theory to sustain the constitutionality of the Wagner Act. On May 24, 1937, the justices upheld the Social Security Act in *Steward Machine Company* v. *Davis,* a decision that repudiated Roberts's narrow view of the taxing power in *Butler* (1936). In a companion case, *Helvering* v. *Davis* (1937), Justice Cardozo actually cited Roberts as authority to sketch an expansive view of the general welfare clause in support of the old-age tax and benefits provisions of the Social Security Act. While the justices did not formally abandon substantive due process in economic regulatory cases until *Ferguson* v. *Skrupa* (1963), there was no doubt that they had retreated from the business of trying to regulate business.

ORDERED LIBERTY, PREFERRED POSITIONS, AND SELECTIVE INCORPORATION

While the Supreme Court had removed itself from matters of economic regulation after 1937, its influence over American life grew, not diminished. Almost immediately, the justices began to build a new line of cases involving civil liberties and civil rights. To do so, the justices had to reconsider the scope of the Fourteenth Amendment as it applied to the Bill of Rights. The problem before the Court became the extent to which the Fourteenth Amendment had incorporated—that is, made a part of—the Bill of Rights guarantees. Such a matter was crucial, since the Court had historically taken the position that the Bill of Rights applied against only the national and not the state governments. The Roosevelt Court appointees (and their successors) never agreed on the matter, however; the result was a continuing debate about the power of the Court to provide national protection for civil liberties and civil rights.

Palko v. *Connecticut*
302 U.S. 219 (1937)

Palko was convicted initially of second-degree murder, after which the prosecutor took the unusual step of appealing and winning a new trial. At the second trial, Palko was convicted, this time for first-degree murder, and was sentenced to death. He claimed that the second trial amounted to double jeopardy, in violation of the Fifth Amendment, which his counsel argued applied to the states through the Fourteenth Amendment.

Mr. Justice Cardozo delivered the opinion of this Court:

We have said that in appellant's view the Fourteenth Amendment is to be taken as embodying the prohibitions of the Fifth. His thesis is even broader. Whatever would be a violation of the original bill of rights (Amendments I to VIII) if done by the federal government is now equally unlawful by force of the Fourteenth Amendment if done by a state. There is no such general rule.

The Fifth Amendment provides, among other things, that no person shall be held to answer for a capital or otherwise infamous crime unless on presentment or indictment of a grand jury. This court held that, in prosecutions by a state, presentment or indictments by a grand jury may give way to informations at the instance of a public officer.

♦ ♦ ♦

On the other hand, the due process clause of the Fourteenth Amendment may make it unlawful for a state to abridge by its statutes the freedom of speech which the First Amendment safeguards against encroachment by the Congress, or the like freedom of the press, or the free exercise of religion, or the right of peaceable assembly, without which speech would be unduly trammeled, or right of one accused of crime to the benefit of counsel. In these and other situations immunities that are valid as against the federal government by force of the specific pledges of particular amendments have been found to be implicit in the concept of ordered liberty, and thus, through the Fourteenth Amendment, become valid as against the states.

The line of division may seem to be wavering and broken if there is a hasty catalogue of the cases on the one side and the other. Reflection and analysis will induce a different view. There emerges the perception of a rationalizing principle which gives to discrete instances a proper order and coherence. The right to trial by jury and the immunity from prosecution except as the result of an indictment may have value and importance. Even so, they are not of the very essence of a scheme of ordered liberty. To abolish them is not to violate a "principle of justice so rooted in the traditions and conscience of our people as to be ranked as fundamental". . . . Few would be so narrow or provincial as to maintain that a fair and enlightened system of justice would be impossible without them. What is true of jury trials and indictments is true also, as the cases show, of the immunity from compulsory self-incrimination. . . . This too might be lost, and justice still be done. Indeed, today as in the past there are students of our penal system who look upon the immunity as a mischief rather than a benefit, and who would limit its scope, or destroy it altogether. No doubt there would remain the need to give protection against torture, physical or mental.

Justice, however, would not perish if the accused were subject to a duty to respond to orderly inquiry. The exclusion of these immunities and privileges from the privileges and immunities protected against the action of the states has not been arbitrary or casual. It has been dictated by a study and appreciation of the meaning, the essential implications, of liberty itself.

We reach a different plane of social and moral values when we pass to the privileges and immunities that have been taken over from the earlier articles of the federal bill of rights and brought within the Fourteenth Amendment by a process of absorption. These in their origin were effective against the federal government alone. If the Fourteenth Amendment has absorbed them, the process of absorption has had its source in the belief that neither liberty nor justice would exist if they were sacrificed. . . . This is true, for illustration, of freedom of thought, and speech. Of that freedom one may say that it is the matrix, the indispensable condition, of nearly every other form of freedom. With rare aberrations a pervasive recognition of that truth can be traced in our history, political and legal. So it has come about that the domain of liberty, withdrawn by the Fourteenth Amendment from encroachment by the states, has been enlarged by latter-day judgments to include liberty of the mind as well as liberty of action. The extension became, indeed, a logical imperative when once it was recognized, as long ago it was, that liberty is something more than exemption from physical restraint, and that even in the field of substantive rights and duties the legislative judgment, if oppressive and arbitrary, may be overridden by the courts. . . . Fundamental too in the concept of due process, and so in that of liberty, is the thought that condemnation shall be rendered by after trial. . . . The hearing, moreover, must be a real one, not a sham or a pretense. For that reason, ignorant defendants in a capital case [*Powell* v. *Alabama*] were held to have been condemned unlawfully when in truth, though not in form, they were refused the aid of counsel. . . . The decision did not turn upon the fact that the benefit of counsel would have been guaranteed to the defendants by the provisions of the Sixth Amendment if they had been prosecuted in a federal court. The decision turned upon the fact that in the particular situation laid before us in the evidence the benefit of counsel was essential to the substance of a hearing.

Note: *Carolene Products* and Preferred Positions

Cardozo's opinion in *Palko* was one of the most important in the history of twentieth-century civil liberties. He concluded that the Fourteenth Amendment did not automatically incorporate the entire Bill of Rights. Some parts of it were incorporated; other parts were not. The difficult question, of course, became which ones. What Cardozo said was that those rights essential to the maintenance of "ordered liberty" and "so rooted in the traditions . . . of our people as to be ranked as fundamental" were incorporated. Cardozo, therefore, adopted a doctrine of "selective incorporation" through which the Court became a powerful arbitrator of what was a fundamental right.

A year later, the Court took another decisive step in shaping the future agenda of civil liberties and civil rights. In *United States* v. *Carolene Products* (1938), Justice Harlan F. Stone seized on a minor piece of federal regulatory legislation passed well before the New Deal to make an important point about what rights the Court believed to be fundamental and to mark a new direction in the Court's agenda. Stone warned legislators that thenceforth the Court was going to devote greater attention to the operation of legislation that affected individual noneconomic rights, especially those rights necessary to the full functioning of the political process. Thus while the Court asserted a theory of judicial restraint and deference on matters of economic regulation, it indicated a willingness to become active in protecting individual rights in the political process. The social scientific rationale behind judicial restraint in matters of economic regulatory legislation was turned to support increasingly active intervention by the Court in noneconomic matters.

Footnote 4:
United States v. *Carolene Products Co.*
304 U.S. 144 (1938)

Almost ignored at the time, Justice Stone's footnote 4 became the opening constitutional wedge in the most important feature of post-1937 legal liberalism—civil rights and civil liberties.

Mr. Justice Stone delivered the opinion of the Court.

There may be narrower scope for operation of the presumption of constitutionality when legislation appears on its face to be within a specific prohibition of the Constitution, such as those of the first ten amendments, which are deemed equally specific when held to be embraced within the Fourteenth. See *Stromberg* v. *California*, 283 U.S. 359, 369–370; *Lovell* v. *Griffin*, 303 U.S. 444, 452.

It is unnecessary to consider now whether legislation which restricts those political processes which can ordinarily be expected to bring about repeal of undesirable legislation, is to be subjected to more exacting judicial scrutiny under the general prohibitions of the Fourteenth Amendment than are most other types of legislation. On restrictions upon the right to vote, see *Nixon* v. *Herndon,* 273 U.S. 536; *Nixon* v. *Condon,* 286 U.S. 73; on restraints upon the dissemination of information, see *Near* v. *Minnesota ex rel. Olson,* 283 U.S. 697, 713–714, 718–720, 722; *Grosjean* v. *American Press Co.,* 297 U.S. 233; *Lovell* v. *Griffin,* supra; on interferences with political organizations, see *Stromberg* v. *California,* supra, 369; *Fiske* v. *Kansas,* 274 U.S. 380; *Whitney* v. *California,* 274 U.S. 357, 373–378; *Herndon* v. *Lowry,* 301 U.S. 242; and see Holmes, J., in *Gitlow* v. *New York,* 268 U.S. 652, 673; as to prohibition of peaceable assembly, see *De Jonge* v. *Oregon,* 299 U.S. 353, 365.

Nor need we enquire whether similar considerations enter into the review of statutes directed at particular religious, *Pierce* v. *Society of Sisters,* 268 U.S. 510, or national, *Meyer* v. *Nebraska,* 262 U.S. 390; *Bartels* v. *Iowa,* 262 U.S. 404; *Farrington* v. *Tokushige,* 273 U.S. 484, or racial minorities, *Nixon* v. *Herndon,* supra; *Nixon* v. *Condon,* supra; whether prejudice against discrete and insular minorities may be a special condition, which tends seriously to curtail the operation of those political processes ordinarily to be relied upon to protect minorities, and which may call for a correspondingly more searching judicial inquiry. Compare *McCulloch* v. *Maryland,* 4 Wheat, 316, 428; *South Carolina* v. *Barnwell Bros.,* 303 U.S. 177, 184, n. 2, and cases cited.

THE LIMITS OF FEDERAL JUDICIAL POWER

In *Swift* v. *Tyson* (1842), Supreme Court Justice Joseph Story had developed the concept of a federal common law of commerce. Story had done so in the belief that only through a general, national law of commerce would it be possible for the nation to grow economically. The pro-business federal courts invoked Story's opinion in *Swift* where commercial cases were in diversity—that is, where citizens of different states were involved. By the 1930s, however, most states had revised their commercial law to fit national practices, since doing so was clearly to the advantage of businesses in every state. But many businesses, hoping to find a friendlier forum in the federal courts, continued to manufacture diversity cases in order to avoid the state courts. Not only did these suits add to the already clogged dockets of the federal courts, but they seriously undermined the authority of the individual states. On the Supreme Court, Justice Louis Brandeis campaigned relentlessly to overturn *Swift,* finally succeeding in securing a majority of the justices in *Erie Railroad Co.* v. *Tompkins* (1938).

Note: The Fate of *Erie*

The *Erie* decision was seemingly a turning point in the history of the federal courts, since it appeared to return to the states significant control over commercial law. But Brandeis's hopes proved wistful. For example, the same day that Brandeis gave his opinion, the Court also held in *Hinderlider* v. *La Plata River Co.* that there was a federal common law that regulated the division of water between states and that the interpretation of that law rested exclusively with the federal courts. Moreover, Brandeis had expected that state law would apply as long as a federal statute did not exist, but the Supreme Court itself in 1941 took the step of holding that federal law applied where a procedural issue was raised, while state law would apply where a substantive question was involved. But

> the line between procedural and substantive law could not always be easily determined. . . . Although *Erie* remains the law, so many exceptions and explanations have been created that . . . we have in essence adopted a neo-Swiftian doctrine under which federal courts always apply federal law unless there is a compelling reason to use state law—just the opposite of what Brandeis had hoped to accomplish.[3]

9

Rights, Liberty, and Science
in Modern America

World War II was a major turning point in American history, the consequences of which rippled through the legal culture. The United States emerged from the war as the world's greatest power, but the exercise of its economic and military might brought it into conflict with Communist powers in the Soviet Union and China. America, especially during the administrations of Presidents Harry S. Truman (1945–1953) and Dwight D. Eisenhower (1953–1961), became mired in an ideological Cold War. From time to time, however, the Cold War turned hot, as in Korea from 1950 to 1954 and in Vietnam from 1964 to 1973. The atmosphere of domestic politics became so permeated with fears of a Communist threat that much of the emergency wartime legislation passed between 1941 and 1945 remained on the books well into the 1970s. With the nation on a permanent war footing, a consensus initially emerged that the United States was a uniquely free, moral society and a political democracy. But it was more a fear of foreign political ideologies (notably Communism), the possibility of nuclear warfare, and the loss of American influence throughout the world that promoted this consensus. From a constitutional perspective, the atmosphere of fear was hostile to traditional American values, such as political dissent, freedom of association, and separation of powers.

World War II also had important economic consequences. FDR's New Deal programs had only limited success at restoring national prosperity; the four years of conflict following Pearl Harbor, however, provided the economic foundation for postwar prosperity. Technological innovations, accumulated savings from wartime wages, the GI Bill, and housing loans from the Veterans Administration fueled four decades of unparalleled economic growth. Yet the resulting economic prosperity was not evenly distributed; the top 10 percent of Americans steadily gained a larger percentage of the nation's total wealth.

The war resulted in another change. For blacks and women, wartime conditions provided a glimpse of economic opportunities that, once enjoyed, were not easily forgotten when the conflict ended. The wartime emergency generated tremendous pressures for manpower, and blacks participated in the armed services to a degree unknown since the Civil War. Blacks who stayed at home found their services much in demand as well, and they gained access to manufacturing jobs previously denied them. The wartime economy also brought women in unprecedented numbers into manufacturing, service, and supervisory roles long closed to them. The legendary "Rosie the Riveter" symbolized the heightened gender diversity of the American labor force.

World War II also had important structural implications for the American constitutional system. In order to fight the conflict, the government continued the process of greater and greater centralization of decision making and increased reliance on an ever-expanding administrative network, one that far surpassed in size and ambition anything attempted during World War I or the New Deal. Indeed, many New Deal lawyers of the 1930s went into service in the wartime federal government and then, after 1945, entered into lucrative practices in the nation's capital, where administrative and regulatory law emerged as a distinct body of authority governing such matters as labor relations, telecommunications, the environment, and transportation. The regulatory bureaucracy in Washington became a kind of fourth branch of government that in theory placed expertise ahead of partisan necessity in decision making.

The full implications of the changes wrought by the war appeared during the next four decades. The political consensus of the 1950s, for example, crumbled under the weight of the civil rights and antiwar movements of the mid-1960s and early 1970s. The nonviolent tactics developed by black leaders, such as the Reverend Martin Luther King, Jr., became part of the protest arsenal of antiwar activists. Many Americans lumped hippies, civil rights advocates, and antiwar protesters in the same lot. The so-called silent majority, while troubled by the war in Southeast Asia and lingering social inequality, also supported the traditional values of hard work, the nuclear family, good manners, and patriotism.

An underlying demographic shift further abetted social discontent. Following the end of World War II, Americans married and reproduced at levels not seen since the nineteenth century. At the height of this baby boom in the mid-1950s, the average family had more than three children. This generation not only created strong demands for education, employment, and such, but also ushered in a new crime wave. The ranks of the most crime-prone age group, those between fifteen and twenty-four, swelled by more than a million persons a year during the 1960s. And the great urban race riots from 1964 to 1968 brought increasingly strident demands for improvements in the criminal justice system. Americans were divided over whether the issues should be attacked by addressing the social pathology of crime (poverty, hunger, broken families, and such) or by implementing get-tough measures intended to deter crime and, once it occurred, mete out appropriate retributive punishments. Under such circumstances, the rights of the accused became a major public law issue.

Behind these events lay mounting pressures for change from groups previously considered to be on the margins of law, society, and politics. Minority groups became impatient with business as usual and with traditional political solutions. Blacks and feminist leaders, for example, attacked entrenched race and gender discrimination, although they did so with different degrees of success and with the realization that race and gender, as defining categories, cut quite differently across American life. They were joined by environmentalists and consumer rights advocates, both of whom denounced long-standing practices that defiled the environment and permitted dangerous goods and shoddy practices in the marketplace. While these groups differed from one another, they shared the belief that the scheme of legal liberalism forged by the New Deal offered the means by which to restore balance in the environment, the economy, and society.

These groups pursued special-interest litigation in an effort to achieve through the legal process what they had not realized through politics. As Lawrence M. Friedman has observed, their efforts symbolized the emergence in the mid-1960s of a general "expectation of justice" and an accompanying "general expectation of recompense" for wrongs of every nature.[1] The Supreme Court, with its agenda switched from the economic regulatory issues of the New Deal era to matters of civil liberties and civil rights, emerged at the center of this quest for "total justice." The justices' decisions, especially during the period from 1954 to 1969 when Earl Warren presided over the Court, became a source of continuing controversy. Political and legal conservatives believed that the Court, in its quest to give greater emphasis to equality and political openness, had usurped authority over matters, such as criminal justice, that properly belonged to the states and had set itself up as a quasi-legislative body.

The proliferation of claims of individual rights has created problems and aroused intense criticism. Conflicting assertions of rights increasingly compete for popular and judicial attention. Moreover, critics maintain that the stress on individual rights undercuts the building of a community based on the principle of majority rule. Framing contested issues in terms of individual rights in effect removes them from democratic decision making and hampers the ability of lawmakers to fashion compromises that seek to accommodate different interests. Thus, some critics picture the growing "rights consciousness" as anti-democratic because it frustrates the determination of public policy by elected legislative bodies.

The documents in this chapter deal with many of the resulting tensions over law in contemporary society. We begin with an examination of how the growing stress on rights has impacted our understanding of race relations, individual liberties, and the administration of criminal justice. We conclude with a look at the relationship between science and the formation of legal norms.

CIVIL RIGHTS

RACE

Brown v. Board of Education of Topeka, Kansas
347 U.S. 483 (1954)

Beginning in the 1940s, the NAACP's Legal Defense Fund mounted a litigation strategy designed to dislodge the separate-but-equal doctrine of Plessy v. Ferguson *(1896). The South remained a racially divided society, with blacks and whites using different public toilets, different seats in movie theaters, and different public schools. Under the leadership of Thurgood Marshall, the NAACP in 1950 decided to challenge directly the separate-but-equal doctrine.* Brown v. Board of Education *was the result. The case was actually a class action brought not only by black elementary-school children in Topeka, Kansas, but by other school-age children in South Carolina, Virginia, and Delaware. A companion case,* Bolling v. Sharpe *(1954), was also decided by the Court, although it was brought in the District of Columbia under the Fifth rather than the Fourteenth Amendment.*

Mr. Chief Justice Warren delivered the opinion of the Court.

These cases came to us from the states of Kansas, South Carolina, Virginia, and Delaware. They are premised on different facts and different local conditions, but a common legal question justifies their consideration together in this consolidated opinion.

In each of the cases, minors of the Negro race . . . seek the aid of the courts in obtaining admission to the public schools of their community on a nonsegregated basis. In each instance, they have been denied admission to schools attended by white children under laws requiring or permitting segregation according to race. This segregation was alleged to deprive the plaintiffs of the equal protection of the laws under the Fourteenth Amendment. In each of the cases other than the Delaware case, a three-judge federal district court denied relief to the plaintiffs on the so-called "separate but equal" doctrine announced by this Court in *Plessy* v. *Ferguson* (1896). . . . Under that doctrine, equality of treatment is accorded when the races are provided substantially equal facilities, even though these facilities be separate. In the Delaware case, the Supreme Court of Delaware adhered to that doctrine, but ordered that the plaintiffs be admitted to the white schools because of their superiority to the Negro schools.

The plaintiffs contend that segregated public schools are not "equal" and cannot be made "equal," and that hence they are deprived of the equal protection of the laws. Because of the obvious importance of the question presented, the Court took jurisdiction. Argument was heard in the 1952 Term, and reargument was heard this Term on certain questions propounded by the Court.

Reargument was largely devoted to the circumstances surrounding the adoption of the Fourteenth Amendment in 1868. It covered exhaustively consideration of the Amendment in Congress, ratification by the states, then existing practices in racial segregation, and the views of proponents and opponents of the Amendment. This discussion and our own investigation convince us that, although these sources cast some light, it is not enough to resolve the problem with which we are faced. At best, they are inconclusive. The most avid proponents of the post-War Amendments undoubtedly intended them to remove all legal distinctions among "all persons born or naturalized in the United States." Their opponents, just as certainly, were antagonistic to both the letter and the spirit of the Amendments and wished them to have the most limited effect. What others in Congress and the state legislatures had in mind cannot be determined with any degree of certainty.

An additional reason for the inconclusive nature of the Amendment's history, with respect to segregated schools, is the status of public education at that time. In the South, the movement toward free common schools, supported by general taxation, had not yet taken hold. Education of white children was largely in the hands of private groups. Education of Negroes was almost nonexistent, and practically all of the race were illiterate. In fact, any education of Negroes was forbidden by law in some states. Today, in contrast, many Negroes have achieved outstanding success in the arts and sciences as well as in the business and professional world. It is true that public school education at the time of the Amendment had advanced further in the North, but the effect of the Amendment on Northern States was generally ignored in the congressional debates. Even in the North, the conditions of public education did not approximate those existing today. The curriculum was usually rudimentary; ungraded schools were common in rural areas; the school term was but three months a year in many states; and compulsory school attendance was virtually unknown. As a consequence, it is not surprising that there should be so little in the history of the Fourteenth Amendment relating to its intended effect on public education.

In the first cases in this Court construing the Fourteenth Amendment, decided shortly after its adoption, the Court interpreted it as proscribing all state-imposed discriminations against the Negro race. The doctrine of "separate but equal" did not make its appearance in this Court until 1896 in the case of *Plessy* v. *Ferguson,* supra, involving not education but transportation. American courts have since labored with the doctrine for over half a century.

In this Court, there have been six cases involving the "separate but equal" doctrine in the field of public education. . . . [T]he validity of the doctrine itself was not challenged. In more recent cases, all on the graduate school level, inequality was found in that specific benefits enjoyed by white students were denied to Negro students of the same educational qualifications. In none of these cases was it necessary to reexamine the doctrine to grant relief to the Negro plaintiff. And in *Sweatt* v. *Painter,* supra, the Court expressly reserved decision on the question whether *Plessy* v. *Ferguson* should be held inapplicable to public education.

In the instant case, that question is directly presented. Here, unlike *Sweatt* v. *Painter,* there are findings below that the Negro and white schools involved have been equalized, or are being equalized, with respect to buildings, curricula, qualifications and salaries of teachers, and other "tangible" factors. Our decision, therefore, cannot turn on merely a comparison of these tangible factors in the Negro and white schools involved in each of the cases. We must look instead to the effect of segregation itself on public education.

In approaching this problem, we cannot turn the clock back to 1868 when the Amendment was adopted, or even to 1896 when *Plessy* v. *Ferguson* was written. We must consider public education in the light of its full development and its present place in American life throughout the Nation. Only in this way can it be determined if segregation in public schools deprives these plaintiffs of the equal protection of the laws.

Today, education is perhaps the most important function of state and local governments. Compulsory school attendance laws and the great expenditures for education both demonstrate our recognition of the importance of education to our democratic society. It is required in the performance of our most basic public responsibilities, even service in the armed forces. It is the very foundation of good citizenship. Today it is a principal instrument in awakening the child to cultural values, in preparing him for later professional training, and in helping him to adjust normally to his environment. In these days, it is doubtful that any child may reasonably be expected to succeed in life if he is denied the opportunity of an education. Such an opportunity, where the state has undertaken to provide it, is a right which must be made available to all on equal terms.

We come then to the question presented: Does segregation of children in public schools solely on the basis of race, even though the physical facilities and other "tangible" factors may be equal, deprive the children of the minority group of equal educational opportunities? We believe that it does.

In *Sweatt* v. *Painter* (1950), in finding that a segregated law school for Negroes could not provide them equal educational opportunities, this Court relied in large part on "those qualities which are incapable of objective measurement but which make for greatness in a law school." In *McLaurin* v. *Oklahoma State Regents* (1950), the Court, in requiring that a Negro admitted to a White graduate school be treated like all other students, again resorted to intangible considerations: "his ability to study, to engage in discussions and exchange views with other students, and, in general, to learn his profession." Such considerations apply with added force to children in grade and high schools. To separate them from others of similar age and qualifications solely because of their race generates a feeling of inferiority as to their status in the community that may affect their hearts and minds in a way unlikely ever to be undone. The effect of this separation on their educational opportunities was well stated by a finding in the Kansas case by a court which nevertheless felt compelled to rule against the Negro plaintiffs:

> Segregation of white and colored children in public schools has a detrimental effect upon the colored children. The impact is greater when it has the sanction of the law; for the policy of separating the races is usually interpreted as denoting the inferiority of the negro group. A sense of inferiority affects the motivation of a child to learn. Segregation with the sanction of law, therefore, has a tendency to [retard] the educational and mental development of Negro children and to deprive them of some of the benefits they would receive in a racial[ly] integrated school system.

Whatever may have been the extent of psychological knowledge at the time of *Plessy* v. *Ferguson,* this finding is amply supported by modern authority. Any language in *Plessy* v. *Ferguson* contrary to this finding is rejected.

We conclude that in the field of public education the doctrine of "separate but equal" has no place. Separate educational facilities are inherently unequal. Therefore, we hold that the plaintiffs and others similarly situated for whom the actions have been brought are, by reason of the segregation complained of, deprived of the equal protection of the laws guaranteed by the Fourteenth Amendment. This disposition makes unnecessary any discussion whether such segregation also violates the Due Process Clause of the Fourteenth Amendment.

Because these are class actions, because of the wide applicability of this decision, and because of the great variety of local conditions, the formulation of decrees in these cases presents problems of considerable complexity. On reargument, the consideration of appropriate relief was necessarily subordinated to the primary question—the constitutionality of segregation in public education. We have now announced that such segregation is a denial of the equal protection of the laws. In order that we may have the full assistance of the parties in formulating decrees, the cases will be restored to the docket, and the parties are requested to present further argument on Questions 4 and 5 previously propounded by the Court for the reargument this Term. The Attorney General of the United States is again invited to participate. The Attorneys General of the states requiring or permitting segregation in public education will also be permitted to appear as amici curiae upon request to do so by September 15, 1954, and submission of briefs by October 1, 1954.

It is so ordered.

"Southern Declaration on Integration"
March 12, 1956

Chief Justice Warren's opinion in Brown *ignited a firestorm of southern protest. An entire generation of white southern segregationist politicians, such as Governor George Wallace of Alabama, built their careers by claiming that the decision violated the tradition that local authorities should regulate race relations. White Citizens Councils in the South conspired to frustrate implementation of the decision, and the Ku Klux Klan, which had been moribund for a number of years, sprang back to life. The "Southern Declaration on Integration" was the initial step in what became a program of massive southern resistance to* Brown *and to the Supreme Court decisions that followed in its wake. It was signed by 101 members of Congress, including all but 3 southern senators. The manifesto set out the principal constitutional objections to* Brown.

We regard the decision of the Supreme Court in the school cases as clear abuse of judicial power. It climaxes a trend in the Federal judiciary undertaking to legislate, in derogation of the authority of Congress, and to encroach upon the reserved rights of the states and the people.

The original Constitution does not mention education. Neither does the Fourteenth Amendment nor any other amendment. The debates preceding the submission of the Fourteenth Amendment clearly show that there was no intent that it should affect the systems of education maintained by the states.

The very Congress which proposed the amendment subsequently provided for segregated schools in the District of Columbia.

When the amendment was adopted in 1868, there were thirty-seven states of the Union. Every one of the twenty-six states that had any substantial racial differences among its people either approved the operation of segregated schools already in existence or subsequently established such schools by action of the same law-making body which considered the Fourteenth Amendment.

As admitted by the Supreme Court in the public school case (*Brown* v. *Board of Education*), the doctrine of separate but equal schools "apparently originated in *Roberts* v. *City of Boston* (1849), upholding school segregation against attack as being violative of a state constitutional guarantee of equality." This constitutional doctrine began in the North—not in the South—and it was followed not only in Massachusetts but in Connecticut, New York, Illinois, Indiana, Michigan, Minnesota, New Jersey, Ohio, Pennsylvania and other northern states until they, exercising their rights as states through the constitutional processes of local self-government, changed their school systems.

In the case of *Plessy* v. *Ferguson* in 1896 the Supreme Court expressly declared that under the Fourteenth Amendment no person was denied any of his rights if the states provided separate but equal public facilities. This decision has been followed in many other cases. . . .

This interpretation, restated time and again, became a part of the life of the people of many of the states and confirmed their habits, customs, traditions, and way of life. It is founded on elemental humanity and common sense, for parents should not be deprived by Government of the right to direct the lives and education of their own children.

Though there has been no constitutional amendment or act of Congress changing this established legal principle almost a century old, the Supreme Court of the United States, with no legal basis for such action, undertook to exercise their naked judicial power and substituted their personal political and social ideas for the established law of the land.

This unwarranted exercise of power by the court, contrary to the Constitution, is creating chaos and confusion in the states principally affected. It is destroying the amicable relations between the white and Negro races that have been created through ninety years of patient effort by the good people of both races. It has planted hatred and suspicion where there has been heretofore friendship and understanding.

Without regard to the consent of the governed, outside agitators are threatening immediate and revolutionary changes in our public school systems. If done, this is certain to destroy the system of public education in some of the states.

With the gravest concern for the explosive and dangerous condition created by this decision and inflamed by outside meddlers:

We reaffirm our reliance on the Constitution as the fundamental law of the land.

We decry the Supreme Court's encroachments on rights reserved to the states and to the people, contrary to established law and to the Constitution.

We commend the motives of those states which have declared the intention to resist forced integration by any lawful means.

We appeal to the states and people who are not directly affected by these decisions to consider the constitutional principles involved against the time when they too, on issues vital to them, may be the victims of judicial encroachment.

Even though we constitute a minority in the present Congress, we have full faith that a majority of the American people believe in the dual system of government which has enabled us to achieve our greatness and will in time demand that the reserved rights of the states and of the people be made secure against judicial usurpation.

We pledge ourselves to use all lawful means to bring about a reversal of this decision which is contrary to the Constitution and to prevent the use of force in its implementation.

In this trying period, as we all seek to right this wrong, we appeal to our people not to be provoked by the agitators and troublemakers invading our states and to scrupulously refrain from disorder and lawless acts.

Note: Race and the Constitution

Brown v. *Board of Education* was certainly one of the most important decisions in the entire history of the Supreme Court. The justices did not overturn *Plessy* v. *Ferguson;* instead, they abolished the separate-but-equal doctrine in public schools and, by implication, in all public facilities. Although two more decades of difficult litigation lay ahead, the *Brown* decision equipped the NAACP with a precedent that allowed it to attack de jure segregation throughout the nation. The decision did not mean that segregation came to an end, however; it persisted (and still persists today) on a de facto basis throughout the nation, largely as a result of residential housing patterns.

Chief Justice Earl Warren's opinion, which was the first of his tenure on the Court, owed as much to principles of equity as to strict constitutional law. The justices had originally hoped to find some guidance in either the history of the Fourteenth Amendment or the social sciences to clarify the issues. In the end, however, both avenues of inquiry proved unavailing, and Chief Justice Warren resorted to principles of equity.

The decision in *Brown I* stated only the broad principles behind the Court's decision. It did not provide a specific remedy. The Court ordered the parties to reappear at the next term to argue what action should be taken to implement the decision. In *Brown II*, 349 U.S. 294 (1955), the Court ordered lower federal courts to require "defendants [to] make a prompt and reasonable start toward full compliance" by ensuring that the "parties to these cases" were admitted "to public schools on a racially nondiscriminatory basis with all deliberate speed." The wording was an invitation to delay that white southern segregationists readily accepted.

Change in the racial composition of public schools in the South was glacial, and school boards there openly flaunted the High Court's mandate. In 1957, for example, President Dwight D. Eisenhower called out federal troops to restore order in Little Rock, Arkansas, and to integrate Little Rock Central High School. The Court, in *Cooper* v. *Aaron* (1958), took the same occasion to assert that it alone could conclusively interpret the meaning of the Constitution. Even after Little Rock, the movement toward integrated public schools staggered along, with white opponents adopting a variety of techniques, going so far in some instances as to close the public schools altogether.

Part of the difficulty in achieving racial integration in public schools was the prevalence of residential segregation. To overcome this problem, some federal judges in the 1970s directed the busing of children between different schools to bring about a mix of white and black students. Busing proved to be the most controversial remedy fashioned to end school segregation, and critics charged that it accelerated white flight from urban to suburban schools.

In *Swann* v. *Charlotte-Mecklenburg Board of Education* (1971), Chief Justice Warren Burger, speaking for a unanimous Court, approved a lower federal court plan calling for busing of schoolchildren in order to achieve certain mathematical ratios between black and white students in each school. On the other hand, the Supreme Court made clear in *Milliken* v. *Bradley*, 418 U.S. 717 (1974), that federal judges could not order busing across school district lines absent unusual circumstances. In that case the justices, by a 5 to 4 vote, rejected a plan to consolidate the predominately black Detroit city schools with adjacent suburban school districts. As a practical matter, the *Milliken* decision confined the busing remedy to urban school districts with high concentrations of minority students and left largely white suburban schools untouched.

The evidence suggests that despite tremendous efforts to bring about greater racial balance in public schools, de facto segregation persists. While the number of interracial schools has increased since 1954, many schools remain predominately white or black. Indeed, decades after *Brown,* education is still largely divided along racial lines. And the busing scheme adopted in *Swann* remains a source of controversy, so much so that in many communities school boards have adopted magnet-school programs as a substitute. These programs encourage the crossing of racial lines by offering different programs of study in schools, many of whose students must be bused in order to attend. Moreover, the emergence of Hispanics after 2000 as the nation's largest minority group has further complicated the quest for school integration.

MARTIN LUTHER KING, JR.

"Letter from Birmingham City Jail"
1963

While imprisoned in the Birmingham, Alabama, jail in 1963 for failing to file an Alabama tax return, Martin Luther King, Jr., responded to critics who complained that his tactics of civil disobedience against white racism were not only illegal but also immoral. King was particularly stung by the attack made on him by white clergymen, to whom this letter was addressed, who charged that his tactics of resistance were fomenting civil discord and bloodshed. They urged a cautious and lawful approach. Like the abolitionists of the 1840s and 1850s, King had no time to wait, and he argued as well that nonviolent civil disobedience was a proper response to the immorality of southern race relations. King wrote the letter on bits and pieces of newspapers that were smuggled out by a black jail attendant.

You express a great deal of anxiety over our willingness to break laws. This is certainly a legitimate concern. Since we so diligently urge people to obey the Supreme Court's decision of 1954 outlawing segregation in the public schools, it is rather strange and paradoxical to find us consciously breaking laws. One may well ask, "How can you advocate breaking some laws and obeying others?" The answer is found in the fact that there are two types of laws: There are *just* laws and there are *unjust* laws. I would be the first to advocate obeying just laws. One has not only a legal but moral responsibility to obey just laws. Conversely, one has a moral responsibility to disobey unjust laws. I would agree with Saint Augustine that "An unjust law is no law at all."

Now what is the difference between the two? How does one determine when a law is just or unjust? A just law is a man-made code that squares with the moral law or the law of God. An unjust law is a code that is out of harmony with the moral law. To put in the terms of Saint Thomas Aquinas, an unjust law is a human law that is not rooted in eternal and natural laws. Any law that uplifts human personality is just. Any law that degrades human personality is unjust. All segregation statutes are unjust because segregation distorts the soul and damages the personality. It gives the segregator a false sense of superiority and the segregated a false sense of inferiority. To use the words of Martin Buber, the great Jewish philosopher, segregation substitutes an "I—it" relationship for the "I—thou" relationship, and ends up relegating persons to the status of things. So segregation is not only politically, economically, and sociologically unsound, but it is morally wrong and sinful. Paul Tillich has said that sin is separation. Isn't segregation an existential expression of man's tragic separation, an expression of his awful estrangement, his terrible sinfulness? So I can urge men to obey the 1954 decision of the Supreme Court because it is morally right, and I can urge them to disobey segregation ordinances because they are morally wrong.

Let us turn to a more concrete example of just and unjust laws. An unjust law is a code that a majority inflicts on a minority that is not binding on itself. This is *difference* made legal. On the other hand a just law is a code that a majority compels a minority to follow that it is willing to follow itself. This is *sameness* made legal.

Let me give another explanation. An unjust law is a code inflicted upon a minority which that minority had no part in enacting or creating because they did not have the unhampered right to vote. Who can say the legislature of Alabama which set up the segregation laws was democratically elected? Throughout the state of Alabama all types of conniving methods are used to prevent Negroes from becoming registered voters and there are some counties without a single Negro registered to vote despite the fact that the Negro constitutes a majority of the population. Can any law set up in such a state be considered democratically structured?

These are just a few examples of just and unjust laws. There are some instances when a law is just on its face but unjust in its application. For instance, I was arrested Friday on a charge of parading without a permit. Now there is nothing wrong with an ordinance which requires a permit for a parade, but when the ordinance is used to preserve segregation and to deny citizens the First Amendment privilege of peaceful assembly and peaceful protest, then it becomes unjust.

I hope you can see the distinction I am trying to point out. In no sense do I advocate evading or defying the law as the rabid segregationist would do. This would lead to anarchy. One who breaks an unjust law must do it *openly, lovingly* (not hatefully as the white mothers did in New Orleans when they were seen on television screaming "nigger, nigger, nigger") and with a willingness to accept the penalty. I submit that an individual who breaks a law that conscience tells him is unjust, and willingly accepts the penalty by staying in jail to arouse the conscience of the community over its injustice, is in reality expressing the very highest respect for the law.

CIVIL RIGHTS ACT OF 1964

As the conflict over racial segregation grew in the 1960s, Congress passed the far-reaching Civil Rights Act of 1964. It covered a variety of civil rights issues. One of the most significant provisions (Title II) banned discrimination based on "race, color, religion, or national origin" in any public accommodations if its operations affected commerce or if discrimination was "supported by State action." Equally important were provisions prohibiting discrimination in federally assisted programs (Title VI) and in employment (Title VII). Armed with this enlarged statutory authority, the federal government moved forcefully to attack segregated facilities in the South and to change the workplace more nationally. The constitutionality of the public accommodations section was sustained by the Supreme Court in *Heart of Atlanta Motel* v. *United States*, 379 U.S. 241 (1964).

AFFIRMATIVE ACTION

The most contentious issues in civil rights law today concern affirmative action programs designed to surmount past discrimination based on race and gender. Dissenting in *Plessy* v. *Ferguson* (1896), Justice John Marshall Harlan had declared: "Our Constitution is colorblind and neither knows nor tolerates classes among citizens." Yet by the 1960s some observers had concluded that it was insufficient to remove prior legal barriers for racial minorities. They insisted that affirmative steps must be taken to remedy the effects of a long history of racial discrimination and to ensure greater educational and employment opportunities for minorities. President Lyndon B. Johnson articulated this view in an address at Howard University in 1965:

But freedom is not enough. You do not wipe away the scars of centuries by saying: Now you are free to go where you want, and do as you desire, and choose the leaders you please.

You do not take a person who, for years, has been hobbled by chains and liberate him, bring him up to the starting line of a race and then say, "you are free to compete with all the others," and still justly believe that you have been completely fair.

Thus it is not enough just to open the gates of opportunity. All out citizens must have the ability to walk through those gates.

This is the next and the more profound stage of the battle for civil rights. We seek not just freedom but opportunity. We seek not just legal equity but human ability, not just equality as a right and a theory but equality as a fact and equality as a result.

For the task is to give 20 million Negroes the same chance as every other American to learn and grow, to work and share in society, to develop their abilities—physical, mental and spiritual, and to pursue their individual happiness.

To this end equal opportunity is essential, but not enough, not enough. Men and women of all races are born with the same range of abilities. But ability is not just the product of birth. Ability is stretched or stunted by the family that you live with, and the neighborhood you live in—by the school you go to and the poverty or the richness of your surroundings. It is the product of a hundred unseen forces playing upon the little infant, the child, and finally the man.

Originally envisioned as a response to a pattern of discrimination against disadvantaged racial minorities, affirmative action programs were subsequently extended to women.

At the heart of affirmative action are governmental policies that award public contracts, jobs, admission to higher education, and other social goods on the basis of membership in designated groups seen as victims of discrimination. Moreover, private employers, in order to comply with the requirements of Title VII of the Civil Rights Act of 1964, began to implement affirmative action plans that entail race- and gender-conscious hiring and promotion. At root, affirmative action is premised on the idea of group rather than individual rights, and emphasizes equality of results instead of equality of opportunity. The racial and gender preferences inherent in affirmative action have been repeatedly challenged as a deprivation of equal protection by individuals, often white males, who are not members of protected groups. Critics picture affirmative action as a retreat from the goal of a color-blind society in which each individual should be judged on his or her merit. They maintain that any classifications based on race or gender violate the equal protection clause. The Supreme Court has addressed the legitimacy of affirmative action in a series of cases. A sharply divided Court has accepted affirmative action programs but has pursued a checkered course and placed some limits on such schemes.

Regents of the University of California v. *Bakke*
438 U.S. 265 (1978)

The Supreme Court first considered affirmative action in the context of professional and graduate education. At issue was a preferential admissions program at the University of California at Davis Medical School, which annually reserved a number of spaces in the enter-

ing class for racial minorities. As a practical matter, Davis conducted two admissions programs, one for regular applicants and one for a smaller pool of minority candidates with lower criteria. Allan Bakke, a white male, was rejected three times even though his grades and MCAT scores were higher than many of those admitted as part of the affirmative action program. He sued in the California state courts, alleging that he had been denied his right to equal protection under the Fourteenth Amendment. The California Supreme Court declared that the special admissions program was unlawful and barred any consideration of race in the admissions process. Justice Lewis Powell, speaking for a fragmented Court, authored an influential opinion that opened the door for carefully tailored affirmative action programs. Powell invalidated the Davis plan as an illegal quota, but he stopped short of banning any use of race in the admissions process. He ruled that the university could utilize race as one element in seeking to achieve a diverse student body. In effect Powell provided an alternative rationale for affirmative action that did not rest upon a showing of prior discrimination and allowed universities considerable latitude in fashioning admissions policies. Thereafter, race-conscious admissions programs were increasingly justified in terms of the need for diversity.

Mr. Justice Powell announced the judgment of the Court.

This case presents a challenge to the special admissions program of the petitioner, the Medical School of the University of California at Davis, which is designed to assure the admission of a specified number of students from certain minority groups. The Supreme Court of California affirmed those portions of the trial court's judgment declaring the special admissions program unlawful and enjoining petitioner from considering the race of any applicant. It modified that portion of the judgment denying respondent's requested injunction and directed the trial court to order his admission.

For the reasons stated in the following opinion, I believe that so much of the judgment of the California court as holds petitioner's special admissions program unlawful and directs that respondent be admitted to the Medical School must be affirmed. For the reasons expressed in a separate opinion, my Brothers The Chief Justice, Mr. Justice Stewart, Mr. Justice Rehnquist, and Mr. Justice Stevens concur in this judgment.

I also conclude for the reasons stated in the following opinion that the portion of the court's judgment enjoining petitioner from according any consideration to race in its admissions process must be reversed. For reasons expressed in separate opinions, my Brothers Mr. Justice Brennan, Mr. Justice White, Mr. Justice Marshall, and Mr. Justice Blackmun concur in this judgment.

♦   ♦   ♦

Because the special admissions program involved a racial classification, the Supreme Court [of California] held itself bound to apply strict scrutiny. It then turned to the goals the University presented as justifying the special program. Although the court agreed that the goals of integrating the medical profession and increasing the number of physicians willing to serve members of minority groups were compelling state interests, it concluded that the special admissions program was not the least intrusive means of achieving those goals. Without passing on the state constitutional or the federal statutory grounds cited in the trial court's judgment, the California court held that the Equal Protection Clause of the Fourteenth Amendment required that "no applicant may be rejected because of his race, in favor of other who is less qualified, as measured by standards applied without regard to race."

♦   ♦   ♦

The parties do disagree as to the level of judicial scrutiny to be applied to the special admissions program.

♦   ♦   ♦

En route to this crucial battle over the scope of judicial review, the parties fight a sharp preliminary action over the proper characterization of the special admissions program. Petitioner prefers to view it as establishing a "goal" of minority representation in the Medical School. Respondent, echoing the courts below, labels it a racial quota.

This semantic distinction is beside the point: The special admissions program is undeniably a classification based on race and ethnic background. To the extent that there existed a pool of at least minimally qualified minority applicants to fill the 16 special admissions seats, white applicants could compete only for 84 seats in the entering class, rather than the 100 open to minority applicants. Whether this limitation is described as a quota or a goal, it is a line drawn on the basis of race and ethnic status.

The guarantees of the Fourteenth Amendment extend to all persons. Its language is explicit: "No State shall . . . deny to any person within its jurisdiction the equal protection of the laws." It is settled beyond question that the rights created by the first section of the Fourteenth Amendment are, by its terms, guaranteed to the individual. The rights established are personal rights. The guarantee of equal protection cannot mean one thing when applied to one individual and something else when applied to a person of another color. If both are not accorded the same protection, then it is not equal.

Nevertheless, petitioner argues that the court below erred in applying strict scrutiny to the special admissions program because white males, such as respondent, are not a "discrete and insular minority" requiring extraordinary protection from the majoritarian political process. This rationale, however, has never been invoked in our decisions as a prerequisite to subjecting racial or ethnic distinctions to strict scrutiny. Nor has this Court held that discreteness and insularity constitute necessary preconditions to a holding that a particular classification is invidious. Racial and ethnic classifications, however, are subject to stringent examination without regard to these additional characteristics.

♦   ♦   ♦

Racial and ethnic distinctions of any sort are inherently suspect and thus call for the most exacting judicial examination.

♦   ♦   ♦

Over the past 30 years, this Court has embarked upon the crucial mission of interpreting the Equal Protection Clause with the view of assuring to all persons "the protection of equal laws," in a Nation confronting a legacy of slavery and racial discrimination. Because the landmark decisions in this area arose in response to the continued exclusion of Negroes from the mainstream of American society, they could be characterized as involving discrimination by the "majority" white race against the Negro minority. But they need not be read as depending upon that characterization for their results. It suffices to say that "[o]ver the years, this Court has consistently repudiated '[d]istinctions between citizens solely because of their ancestry' as being 'odious to a free people whose institutions are founded upon the doctrine of equality.'"

Petitioner urges us to adopt for the first time a more restrictive view of the Equal Protection Clause and hold that discrimination against members of the white "majority" cannot be suspect if its purpose can be characterized as "benign." The clock of our liberties, however, cannot be turned back to 1868. It is far too late to argue that the guarantee of equal protection to *all* persons permits the recognition of special wards entitled to a degree of protection greater than that accorded others. "The Fourteenth Amendment is not directed solely against discrimination due to a 'two-class theory'—that is, based upon differences between 'white' and Negro."

Once the artificial line of a "two-class theory" of the Fourteenth Amendment is put aside, the difficulties entailed in varying the level of judicial review according to a perceived "referred" status of a particular racial or ethnic minority are intractable. The concepts of "majority" and "minority" necessarily reflect temporary arrangements and political judgments. As observed above, the white "majority" itself is composed of various minority groups, most of which can lay claim to a history of prior discrimination at the hands of the State and private individuals. Not all of these groups can receive preferential treatment and corresponding judicial tolerance of distinctions drawn in terms of race and nationality, for then the only "majority" left would be a new minority of white Anglo-Saxon Protestants. There is no principled basis for deciding which groups would merit "heightened judicial solicitude" and which would not. Courts would be asked to evaluate the extent of the prejudice and consequent harm suffered by various minority groups. Those whose societal injury is thought to exceed some arbitrary level of tolerability then would be entitled to preferential classifications at the expense of individuals belonging to other groups. Those classifications would be free from exacting judicial scrutiny. As these preferences began to have their desired effect, and the consequences of past discrimination were undone, new judicial rankings would be necessary. The kind of variable sociological and political analysis necessary to produce such rankings simply does not lie within the judicial competence—even if they otherwise were politically feasible and socially desirable.

Moreover, there are serious problems of justice connected with the idea of preference itself. First, it may not always be clear that a so-called preference is in fact benign. Courts may be asked to validate burdens imposed upon individual members of a particular group in order to advance the group's general interest. Nothing in the Constitution supports the notion that individuals may be asked to suffer otherwise impermissible burdens in order to enhance the societal standing of their ethnic groups. Second, preferential programs may only reinforce common stereotypes holding that certain groups are unable to achieve success without special protection based on a factor having no relationship to individual worth. Third, there is a measure of inequity in forcing innocent persons in respondent's position to bear the burdens of redressing grievances not of their making.

By hitching the meaning of the Equal Protection Clause to these transitory considerations, we would be holding as a constitutional principle, that judicial scrutiny of classifications touching on racial and ethnic background may vary with the ebb and flow of political forces. Disparate constitutional tolerance of such classifications well may serve to exacerbate racial and ethnic antagonisms rather than alleviate them. Also, the mutability of a constitutional principle, based upon shifting political and social judgments, undermines the chances for consistent application of the Constitution from one generation to the next, a critical feature of its coherent interpretation.

♦   ♦   ♦

If it is the individual who is entitled to judicial protection against classifications based upon his racial or ethnic background because such distinctions impinge upon personal rights, rather than the individual only because of his membership in a particular group, then constitutional standards may be applied consistently. Political judgments regarding the necessity for the particular classification may be weighed in the constitutional balance, but the standards of justification will remain constant. This is as it should be, since those political judgments are the product of rough compromise struck by contending groups within the democratic process. When they touch upon an individual's race or ethnic background, he is entitled to a judicial determination that the burden he is asked to bear on that basis is precisely tailored to serve a compelling governmental interest. The Constitution guarantees that right to every person regardless of his background.

♦   ♦   ♦

IV

We have held that in "order to justify the use of a suspect classification, a State must show that its purpose or interest is both constitutionally permissible and substantial, and that its use of the classification is 'necessary . . . to the accomplishment' of its purposes or the safeguarding of its interest." The special admissions program purports to serve the purposes of: (i) "reducing the historic deficit of traditionally disfavored minorities in medical schools and in the medical profession," (ii) countering the effects of societal discrimination; (iii) increasing the number of physicians who will practice in communities currently underserved; and (iv) obtaining the educational benefits that flow from an ethnically diverse student body. It is necessary to decide which, if any, of these purposes is substantial enough to support the use of a suspect classification.

A

If petitioner's purpose is to assure within its student body some specified percentage of a particular group merely because of its race or ethnic origin, such a preferential purpose must be rejected not as insubstantial but as facially invalid. Preferring member of any one group for no reason other than race or ethnic origin is discrimination for its own sake. This the Constitution forbids.

B

The State certainly has a legitimate and substantial interest in ameliorating, or eliminating where feasible, the disabling effects of identified discrimination. The line of school desegregation cases, commencing with *Brown*, attests to the importance of this state goal and the commitment of the judiciary to affirm all lawful means toward its attainment. In the school cases, the States were required by court order to redress the wrongs worked by specific instances of racial discrimination. That goal was far more focused than the remedying of the effects of "societal discrimination," an amorphous concept of injury that may be ageless in its reach into the past.

We have never approved a classification that aids persons perceived as members of relatively victimized groups at the expense of other innocent individuals in the absence of judicial, legislative, or administrative findings of constitutional or statutory violations.

◆ ◆ ◆

C

Petitioner identifies, as another purpose of its program, improving the delivery of health-care services to communities currently underserved. It may be assumed that in some situations a State's interest in facilitating the health care of its citizens is sufficiently compelling to support the use of a suspect classification. But there is virtually no evidence in the record indicating that petitioner's special admissions program is either needed or geared to promote that goal.

◆ ◆ ◆

Petitioner simply has not carried its burden of demonstrating that it must prefer members of particular ethnic groups over all other individuals in order to promote better health-care delivery to deprived citizens. Indeed, petitioner has not shown that its preferential classification is likely to have any significant effect on the problem.

D

The fourth goal asserted by petitioner is the attainment of a diverse student body. This clearly is a constitutionally permissible goal for an institution of higher education. Academic freedom, though not a specifically enumerated constitutional right, long has been viewed as a special concern of the First Amendment. The freedom of a university to make its own judgments as to education includes the selection of its student body.

◆ ◆ ◆

Thus, in arguing that its universities must be accorded the right to select those students who will contribute the most to the "robust exchange of ideas," petitioner invokes a countervailing constitutional interest, that of the First Amendment. In this light, petitioner must be viewed as seeking to achieve a goal that is of paramount importance in the fulfillment of its mission.

It may be argued that there is greater force to these views at the undergraduate level than in a medical school where the training is centered primarily on professional competency. But even at the graduate level, our tradition and experience lend support to the view that the contribution of diversity is substantial.

◆ ◆ ◆

Physicians serve a heterogeneous population. An otherwise qualified medical student with a particular background—whether it be ethnic, geographic, culturally advantaged or disadvantaged—may bring to a professional school of medicine experiences, outlooks, and ideas that enrich the training of its student body and better equip its graduates to render with understanding their vital service to humanity.

Ethnic diversity, however, is only one element in a range of factors a university properly may consider in attaining the goal of a heterogeneous student body. Although a university must have wide discretion in making the sensitive judgments as to who should be admitted, constitutional limitations protecting individual rights may not be disregarded. Respondent urges—and the courts below have held—that petitioner's dual admissions program is a racial classification that impermissibly infringes his rights under the Fourteenth Amendment. As the interest of diversity is compelling in the context of a university's admissions program, the question remains whether the program's racial classification is necessary to promote this interest.

V

A

It may be assumed that the reservation of a specified number of seats in each class for individuals from the preferred ethnic groups would contribute to the attainment of considerably ethnic diversity in the student body. But petitioner's argument that this is the only effective means of serving the interest of diversity is seriously flawed. In a most fundamental sense the argument misconceives the nature of the state interest that would justify consideration of race or ethnic background. It is not an interest in simple ethnic diversity, in which a specified percentage of the student body is in effect guaranteed to be members of selected ethnic groups, with the remaining percentage an undifferentiated aggregation of students. The diversity that furthers a compelling state interest encompasses a far broader array of qualifications and characteristics of which racial or ethnic origin is but a single though important element. Petitioner's special admissions pro-

gram, focused *solely* on ethnic diversity, would hinder rather than further attainment of genuine diversity.

♦ ♦ ♦

The experience of other university admissions programs, which take race into account in achieving the educational diversity valued by the First Amendment, demonstrates that the assignment of a fixed number of places to a minority group is not a necessary means toward that end.

♦ ♦ ♦

In such an admissions program, race or ethnic background may be deemed a "plus" in a particular applicant's file, yet it does not insulate the individual from comparison with all other candidates for the available seats. The file of a particular black applicant may be examined for his potential contribution to diversity without the factor of race being decisive when compared, for example, with that of an applicant identified as an Italian-American if the latter is thought to exhibit qualities more likely to promote beneficial educational pluralism. Such qualities could include exceptional personal talents, unique work or service experience, leadership potential, maturity, demonstrated compassion, a history of overcoming disadvantage, ability to communicate with the poor, or other qualifications deemed important. In short, an admissions program operated in this way is flexible enough to consider all pertinent elements of diversity in light of the particular qualifications of each applicant, and to place them on the same footing for consideration, although not necessarily according them the same weight. Indeed, the weight attributed to a particular quality may vary from year to year depending upon the "mix" both of the student body and the applicants for the incoming class.

♦ ♦ ♦

B

In summary, it is evident that the Davis special admissions program involves the use of an explicit racial classification never before countenanced by this Court. It tells applicants who are not Negro, Asian, or Chicano that they are to-tally excluded from a specific percentage of the seats in an entering class. No matter how strong their qualifications, quantitative and extracur-ricular, including their own potential for con-tribution to educational diversity, they are never afforded the chance to compete with applicants from the preferred groups for the special ad-missions seats. At the same time, the preferred applicants have the opportunity to compete for every seat in the class.

The fatal flaw in petitioner's preferential program is its disregard of individual rights as guaranteed by the Fourteenth Amendment. Such rights are not absolute. But when a State's distribution of benefits or imposition of burdens hinges on ancestry or the color of a person's skin, that individual is entitled to a demonstra-tion that the challenged classification is neces-sary to promote a substantial state interest. Pe-titioner has failed to carry this burden. For this reason, that portion of the California court's judgment holding petitioner's special admis-sions program invalid under the Fourteenth Amendment must be affirmed.

C

In enjoining petitioner from ever considering the race of any applicant, however, the courts below failed to recognize that the State has a substantial interest that legitimately may be served by a properly devised admissions program involving the competitive consider-ation of race and ethnic origin. For this rea-son, so much of the California court's judg-ment as enjoins petitioner from any consideration of the race of any applicant must be reversed.

VI

With respect to respondent's entitlement to an injunction directing his admission to the Med-ical School, petitioner has conceded that it could not carry its burden of proving that, but for the existence of its unlawful special admis-sions program, respondent still would not have been admitted. Hence, respondent is entitled to the injunction, and that portion of the judgment must be affirmed.

Note: The Future of Affirmative Action in Education

Following *Bakke* many institutions of higher education instituted programs giving preference in the admissions process to blacks and Hispanics. Criticism of such arrangements mounted in the 1990s. California and Washington, by popular vote, adopted state constitutional amend-ments eliminating preferential treatment based on race or sex in government hiring and school admissions. Conservative activists and some white students hoped to overturn *Bakke* and achieved some success in halting affirmative action in the lower federal courts.

The Supreme Court reconsidered affirmative action in 2003 in a pair of cases arising from admissions policies at the University of Michigan. In *Grutter* v. *Bollinger* the Court upheld the University of Michigan Law School's use of race, along with other factors, in at-tempting to obtain a diverse educational environment. Justice Sandra Day O'Connor, speak-ing for a 5 to 4 majority, endorsed the diversity rationale first set forth by Justice Powell in *Bakke*. She concluded that "the Equal Protection Clause does not prohibit the Law School's narrowly tailored use of race in admissions decisions to further a compelling interest in ob-taining the educational benefits that flow from a diverse student body." In reaching this re-sult Justice O'Connor stressed that "universities occupy a special niche in our constitutional tradition" adopted a deferential approach to the academic decisions of universities. She also maintained that fixed racial quotas would be unconstitutional and pointed out that "racial classifications, however compelling their goals, are potentially so dangerous" that race-conscious admissions policies must be limited in duration. O'Connor expressed the hope that racial preferences would no longer be necessary in twenty-five years. The four dissenting justices charged that the ostensibly flexible admissions program was in practice a carefully managed scheme to admit less qualified applicants from selected minority groups in violation of the equal protection clause.

In the companion case of *Gratz* v. *Bollinger* the Supreme Court placed some limits on the use of affirmative action in education. The justices, by a vote of 6 to 3, struck down the University of Michigan's use of racial preferences in undergraduate admissions. At issue was a policy under which a number of points were automatically added to the selection index of every applicant from an "underrepresented" racial or ethnic minority group. Writing for the majority, Chief Justice Rehnquist ruled that such a blanket racial preference was "not narrowly tailored" to achieve the asserted interest in diversity and thus ran afoul of the equal protection clause.

The two Michigan decisions appear to allow universities to give weight to an applicant's membership in a racial minority in the context of an individualized admissions determination, but not as part of arbitrary formulas or quotas. Yet these rulings are unlikely to halt the controversy over affirmative action in higher education. Further litigation is almost a certainty. Among the unresolved issues are which racial or ethnic groups qualify for affirmative action in the name of diversity and the status of minority-only scholarships and campus housing.

City of Richmond v. *J. A. Croson Company*
488 U.S. 469 (1989)

Affirmation action programs have also had a significant impact on public employment and contracting. In 1969 the presidential administration of Richard M. Nixon developed the Philadelphia Plan, which required contractors on federally supported projects to set minority hiring goals. Congress has adopted preferential hiring for racial minorities and mandated that a percentage of federally funded projects be reserved for minority-owned enterprise. Many state and local governments have enacted similar schemes. In this setting affirmative action is essentially a means of redistributing economic benefits in favor of historically disadvantaged groups. The Supreme Court was initially sympathetic to such arrangements. For example, in Fullilove v. *Klutznick, 448 U.S. 448 (1980), the justices sustained a federal law that set aside at least 10 percent of contracts on public works projects for minority contractors. Subsequently, however, the Court has looked more skeptically at set-aside programs.*

At issue in Croson *was the validity of a city ordinance, passed by a black-majority city council in Richmond, Virginia, that established a set-aside plan for municipal contracts. The Croson Company was the winning bidder for renovations at the city jail, but was unable to locate a minority business subcontractor. The city decided to rebid the contract, and Croson challenged the constitutionality of the ordinance. Justice Sandra Day O'Connor wrote the opinion of the Court.*

In this case, we confront once again the tension between the Fourteenth Amendment's guarantee of equal treatment to all citizens, and the use of race-based measures to ameliorate the effects of past discrimination on the opportunities enjoyed by members of minority groups in our society. In *Fullilove* v. *Klutznick*, 448 U.S. 448 (1980), we held that a congressional program requiring that 10% of certain federal construction grants be awarded to minority contractors did not violate the equal protection principles embodied in the Due Process Clause of the Fifth Amendment. Relying largely on our decision in *Fullilove*, some lower federal courts have applied a similar standard of review in assessing the constitutionality of state and local minority set-aside provisions under the Equal Protection Clause of the Fourteenth Amendment. Since our decision two Terms ago in *Wygant* v. *Jackson Board of Education*, 476 U.S. 267 (1986), the lower federal courts have attempted to apply its standards in evaluating the constitutionality of state and local programs which allocate a portion of public contracting opportunities exclusively to minority-owned businesses. We noted probable jurisdiction in this case to consider the applicability of our decision in *Wygant* to a minority set-aside program adopted by the city of Richmond, Virginia.

On April 11, 1983, the Richmond City Council adopted the Minority Business Utilization Plan (the Plan). The Plan required prime contractors to whom the city awarded construction contracts to subcontract at least 30% of the dollar amount of the contract to one or more Minority Business Enterprises (MBE's). The 30% set-aside did not apply to city contracts awarded to minority-owned prime contractors.

The Plan defined an MBE as "[a] business at least fifty-one (51) percent of which is owned and controlled . . . by minority group members." "Minority group members" were defined as "[c]itizens of the United States who are Blacks, Spanish-speaking, Orientals, Indians, Eskimos, or Aleuts." There was no geographic limit to the Plan; an otherwise qualified MBE from anywhere in the United States could avail itself of the 30% set-aside. The Plan declared that it was "remedial" in nature, and enacted "for the purpose of promoting wider participation by minority business enterprises in the construction of public projects." The Plan expired on June 30, 1988, and was in effect for approximately five years.

The Plan authorized the Director of the Department of General Services to promulgate rules which "shall allow waivers in those individual situations where a contractor can prove to the satisfaction of the director that the requirements herein cannot be achieved." To this end, the Director promulgated Contract Clauses, Minority Business Utilization Plan (Contract Clauses).

♦ ♦ ♦

Opponents of the ordinance questioned both its wisdom and its legality. They argued that a disparity between minorities in the population of Richmond and the number of prime contracts awarded to MBE's had little probative value in establishing discrimination in the construction industry. Representatives of various contractors' associations questioned whether there were enough MBE's in the Richmond area to satisfy the 30% set-aside requirement. Mr. Murphy noted that only 4.7% of all construction firms in the United States were minority owned and that 41% of these were located in California, New York, Illinois, Florida, and Hawaii. He predicted that the ordinance would thus lead to a windfall for the few minority firms in Richmond.

♦ ♦ ♦

The parties and their supporting amici fight an initial battle over the scope of the city's power to adopt legislation designed to address the effects of past discrimination. Relying on our decision in *Wygant*, appellee argues that the city must limit any race-based remedial efforts to eradicating the effects of its own prior discrimination. This is essentially the position taken by the Court of Appeals below. Appellant argues that our decision in *Fullilove* is controlling, and that as a result the city of Richmond enjoys sweeping legislative power to define and attack the effects of prior discrimination in its local construction industry. We find that neither of these two rather start alternatives can withstand analysis.

In *Fullilove*, we upheld the minority set-aside contained in the Public Works Employment Act of 1977, against a challenge based on the equal protection component of the Due Process Clause. The Act authorized a $4 billion appropriation for federal grants to state and local governments for use in public works projects. The primary purpose of the Act was to give the national economy a quick boost in a recessionary period; funds had to be committed to state or local grantees by September 30, 1977. The Act also contained the following requirement: " 'Except to the extent the Secretary determines otherwise, no grant shall be made under this Act . . . unless the applicant gives satisfactory assurance to the Secretary that at least 10 per centum of the amount of each grant shall be expended for minority business enterprises.' " MBE's were defined as businesses effectively controlled by "citizens of the United States who are Negroes, Spanish-speaking, Orientals, Indians, Eskimos, and Aleuts."

The principal opinion in *Fullilove*, written by Chief Justice Burger, did not employ "strict scrutiny" or any other traditional standard of equal protection review. The Chief Justice noted at the outset that although racial classifications call for close examination, the Court was at the same time "bound to approach [its] task with appropriate deference to the Congress, a co-equal branch charged by the Constitution with the power to 'provide for the . . . general Welfare of the United States' and 'to enforce by appropriate legislation,' the equal protection guarantees of the Fourteenth Amendment."

◆ ◆ ◆

Appellant and its supporting amici rely heavily on *Fullilove* for the proposition that a city council, like Congress, need not make specific findings of discrimination to engage in race-conscious relief. Thus, appellant argues "[it] would be a perversion of federalism to hold that the federal government has a compelling interest in remedying the effects of racial discrimination in its own public works program, but a city government does not."

What appellant ignores is that Congress, unlike any State or political subdivision, has a specific constitutional mandate to enforce the dictates of the Fourteenth Amendment. The power to "enforce" may at times also include

the power to define situations which *Congress* determines threaten principles of equality and to adopt prophylactic rules to deal with those situations. The Civil War Amendments themselves worked a dramatic change in the balance between congressional and state power over matters of race. Speaking of the Thirteenth and Fourteenth Amendments in *Ex parte Virginia*, 100 U.S. 339, 345 (1880), the Court stated: "They were intended to be, what they really are, limitations of the powers of the States and enlargements of the power of Congress."

That Congress may identify and redress the effects of society-wide discrimination does not mean that, a fortiori, the States and their political subdivisions are free to decide that such remedies are appropriate. Section 1 of the Fourteenth Amendment is an explicit *constraint* on state power, and the States must undertake any remedial efforts in accordance with that provision. To hold otherwise would be to cede control over the content of the Equal Protection Clause to the 50 state legislatures and their myriad political subdivisions. The mere recitation of a benign or compensatory purpose for the use of a racial classification would essentially entitle the States to exercise the full power of Congress under § 5 of the Fourteenth Amendment and insulate any racial classification from judicial scrutiny under § 1. We believe that such a result would be contrary to the intentions of the Framers of the Fourteenth Amendment, who desired to place clear limits on the States' use of race as a criterion for legislative action, and to have the federal courts enforce those limitations.

◆ ◆ ◆

The Equal Protection Clause of the Fourteenth Amendment provides that "[n]o State shall . . . deny to *any person* within its jurisdiction the equal protection of the laws." (Emphasis added.) As this Court has noted in the past, the "rights created by the first section of the Fourteenth Amendment are, by its terms, guaranteed to the individual. The rights established are personal rights." The Richmond Plan denies certain citizens the opportunity to compete for a fixed percentage of public contracts based solely upon their race. To whatever racial group these citizens belong, their "personal rights" to be treated with equal dignity and respect are implicated by a rigid rule erecting race as the sole criterion in an aspect of public decisionmaking.

Absent searching judicial inquiry into the justification for such race-based measures, there is simply no way of determining what classifications are "benign" or "remedial" and what classifications are in fact motivated by illegitimate notions of racial inferiority or simple racial politics. Indeed, the purpose of strict scrutiny is to "smoke out" illegitimate uses of race by assuring that the legislative body is pursuing a goal important enough to warrant use of a highly suspect tool. The test also ensures that the means chosen "fit" this compelling goal so closely that there is little or no possibility that the motive for the classification was illegitimate racial prejudice or stereotype.

Classifications based on race carry a danger of stigmatic harm. Unless they are strictly reserved for remedial settings, they may in fact promote notions of racial inferiority and lead to a politics of racial hostility. See *University of California Regents* v. *Bakke*, 438 U.S., at 298 (opinion of Powell, J.) ("[P]referential programs may only reinforce common stereotypes holding that certain groups are unable to achieve success without special protection based on a factor having no relation to individual worth"). We thus reaffirm the view expressed by the plurality in *Wygant* that the standard of review under the Equal Protection Clause is not dependent on the race of those burdened or benefited by a particular classification.

♦ ♦ ♦

Appellant argues that it is attempting to remedy various forms of past discrimination that are alleged to be responsible for the small number of minority businesses in the local contracting industry. Among these the city cites the exclusion of blacks from skilled construction trade unions and training programs. This past discrimination has prevented them "from following the traditional path from laborer to entrepreneur." The city also lists a host of nonracial factors which would seem to face a member of any racial group attempting to establish a new business enterprise, such as deficiencies in working capital, inability to meet bonding requirements, unfamiliarity with bidding procedures, and disability caused by an inadequate track record.

While there is no doubt that the sorry history of both private and public discrimination in this country has contributed to a lack of opportunities for black entrepreneurs, this observation, standing alone, cannot justify a rigid racial quota in the awarding of public contracts in Richmond, Virginia. Like the claim that discrimination in primary and secondary schooling justifies a rigid racial preference in medical school admissions, an amorphous claim that there has been past discrimination in a particular industry cannot justify the use of an unyielding racial quota.

It is sheer speculation how many minority firms there would be in Richmond absent past societal discrimination, just as it was sheer speculation how many minority medical students would have been admitted to the medical school at Davis absent past discrimination in educational opportunities. Defining these sorts of injuries as "identified discrimination" would give local governments license to create a patchwork of racial preferences based on statistical generalizations about any particular field of endeavor.

♦ ♦ ♦

Reliance on the disparity between the number of prime contracts awarded to minority firms and the minority population of the city of Richmond is similarly misplaced. There is no doubt that "[w]here gross statistical disparities can be shown, they alone in a proper case may constitute prima facie proof of a pattern or practice of discrimination" under Title VII. But it is equally clear that "[w]hen special qualifications are required to fill particular jobs, comparisons to the general population (rather than to the smaller group of individuals who possess the necessary qualifications) may have little probative value."

In the employment context, we have recognized that for certain entry level positions or positions requiring minimal training, statistical comparisons of the racial composition of an employer's work force to the racial composition of the relevant population may be probative of a pattern of discrimination. But where special qualifications are necessary, the relevant statistical pool for purposes of demonstrating discriminatory exclusion must be the number of minorities qualified to undertake the particular task.

In this case, the city does not even know how many MBE's in the relevant market are qualified to undertake prime or subcontracting work in public construction projects. Nor does the city know what percentage of total city construction dollars minority firms now receive as subcontractors on prime contracts let by the city.

To a large extent, the set-aside of subcontracting dollars seems to rest on the unsupported assumption that white prime contractors simply will not hire minority firms. Indeed, there is evidence in this record that overall minority participation in city contracts in Richmond is 7 to 8%, and that minority contractor participation in Community Block Development Grant *construction* projects is 17 to 22%. Without any information on minority participation in subcontracting, it is quite simply impossible to evaluate overall minority representation in the city's construction expenditures.

◆ ◆ ◆

In sum, none of the evidence presented by the city points to any identified discrimination in the Richmond construction industry. We, therefore, hold that the city has failed to demonstrate a compelling interest in apportioning public contracting opportunities on the basis of race. To accept Richmond's claim that past societal discrimination alone can serve as the basis for rigid racial preferences would be to open the door to competing claims for "remedial relief" for every

disadvantaged group. The dream of a Nation of equal citizens in a society where race is irrelevant to personal opportunity and achievement would be lost in a mosaic of shifting preferences based on inherently unmeasurable claims of past wrongs. "Courts would be asked to evaluate the extent of the prejudice and consequent harm suffered by various minority groups. Those whose societal injury is thought to exceed some arbitrary level of tolerability then would be entitled to preferential classifications . . . ." *Bakke*, 438 U.S., at 296–297 (Powell, J.). We think such a result would be contrary to both the letter and spirit of a constitutional provision whose central command is equality.

The foregoing analysis applies only to the inclusion of blacks within the Richmond set-aside program. There is *absolutely no evidence* of past discrimination against Spanish-speaking, Oriental, Indian, Eskimo, or Aleut persons in any aspect of the Richmond construction industry. The District Court took judicial notice of the fact that the vast majority of "minority" persons in Richmond were black. It may well be that Richmond has never had an Aleut or Eskimo citizen. The random inclusion of racial groups that, as a practical matter, may never have suffered from discrimination in the construction industry in Richmond suggests that perhaps the city's purpose was not in fact to remedy past discrimination.

◆ ◆ ◆

Because the city of Richmond has failed to identify the need for remedial action in the awarding of its public construction contracts, its treatment of its citizens on a racial basis violates the dictates of the Equal Protection Clause. Accordingly, the judgment of the Court of Appeals for the Fourth Circuit is

Affirmed.

Note: The Aftermath of *Croson*

Following *Croson,* state and local government affirmative action programs began to wither. In *Adarand Constructors* v. *Peña*, 515 U.S. 200 (1995), the Supreme Court held that all governmental racial classifications by federal as well as state agencies were subject to strict scrutiny. It also emphasized that the equal protection guarantees in the Constitution protected persons not groups. The upshot of *Adarand* was to restrict, but not to absolutely prohibit, the power of the federal government to adopt set-aside programs to assist minority contractors.

GENDER

Women learned from the civil rights movement's fight against race-based discrimination. Since the mid–nineteenth century, women had fought to achieve political and economic equality. During the early twentieth century, Alice Paul, a leader of the National Woman's party, had urged the adoption of an equal rights amendment to the federal Constitution, but her efforts came to naught.

By the 1960s, women's roles had changed dramatically, both in the home and in the job market. As the incidence of two-wage-earner families increased, so did the demands of women for greater recognition. The Civil Rights Act of 1964 was particularly important because, as a result of last-minute maneuvering in Congress, that measure included a provision banning discrimination in employment based on gender. Activists relied on the act to press for greater rights for women. Part of their energy was also expended in an ultimately unsuccessful effort to pass the equal rights amendment to the Constitution. Activists, however, understood that even without such authority, the federal courts offered an ideal forum in which to enhance the rights of women. The outcome has been additional guarantees for women, although the Supreme Court has refused to impose the same level of scrutiny on gender-based legislation as it has on race-based measures. These developments are particularly clear in three areas: privacy and procreation, sex as a suspect classification, and employment discrimination.

Griswold v. *Connecticut*
381 U.S. 479 (1965)

Estelle Griswold was the executive director of the Planned Parenthood League of Connecticut. She was arrested in November 1961 for giving information to married persons about available contraceptive devices and was fined $100 under a Connecticut law prohibiting the distribution of birth control devices or birth control information. Connecticut courts had twice upheld the decision. When it reached the Supreme Court, the justices had to consider whether there was a constitutional basis for a right to privacy, since no such right was explicitly enumerated in the Constitution.

Mr. Justice Douglas delivered the opinion of the Court.

Coming to the merits, we are met with a wide range of questions that implicate the Due Process Clause of the Fourteenth Amendment. Overtones of some arguments suggest that *Lochner* v. *New York* (1905) should be our guide. But we decline that invitation. . . . We do not sit as a super-legislature to determine the wisdom, need, and propriety of laws that touch economic problems, business affairs, or social conditions. This law, however, operates directly on an intimate relation of husband and wife and their physician's role in one aspect of that relation.

The association of people is not mentioned in the Constitution nor in the Bill of Rights. The right to educate a child in a school of the parents' choice—whether public or private or parochial—is also not mentioned. Nor is the right to study any particular subject or any foreign language. Yet the First Amendment has been construed to include certain of these rights.

By *Pierce* v. *Society of Sisters* (1920), the right to educate one's children as one chooses is made applicable to the States by the force of the First and Fourteenth Amendments. By *Meyer* v. *Nebraska* (1925), the same dignity is given the right to study the German language in a private school. In other words, the State may not, consistently with the spirit of the First Amendment, contract the spectrum of available knowledge. The right of freedom of speech and press includes not only the right to utter or to print, but the right to distribute, the right to receive, the right to read . . . and freedom of inquiry, freedom of thought, and freedom to teach . . . indeed the freedom of the entire university community. . . . Without those peripheral rights the specific rights would be less secure. And so we reaffirm the principle of the *Pierce* and the *Meyer* cases.

In *NAACP* v. *Alabama* (1962), we protected the "freedom to associate and privacy in one's associations," noting that freedom of association was a peripheral First Amendment right. Disclosure of membership lists of a constitutionally valid association, we held, was invalid "as entailing the likelihood of a substantial restraint upon the exercise by petitioner's members of their right to freedom of association." In other words, the First Amendment has a penumbra where privacy is protected from governmental intrusion. In like context, we have protected forms of "association" that are not political in the customary sense but pertain to the social, legal, and economic benefit of the members. . . .

Those cases involved more than the "right of assembly"—a right that extends to all irrespective of their race or ideology. . . . The right of "association" like the right of belief is more than the right to attend a meeting; it includes the right to express one's attitudes or philosophies by membership in a group or by affiliation with it or by other lawful means. Association in that context is a form of expression of opinion; and while it is not expressly included

in the First Amendment its existence is necessary in making the express guarantees fully meaningful.

◆ ◆ ◆

The foregoing cases suggest that specific guarantees in the Bill of Rights have penumbras, formed by emanations from those guarantees that help give them life and substance. . . . Various guarantees create zones of privacy. The right of association contained in the penumbra of the First Amendment is one, as we have seen. The Third Amendment in its prohibition against the quartering of soldiers "in any house" in time of peace without the consent of the owner is another facet of that privacy. The Fourth Amendment explicitly affirms the "right of the people to be secure in their persons, houses, papers, and effects, against unreasonable searches and seizures." The Fifth Amendment in its Self-Incrimination Clause enables the citizen to create a zone of privacy which government may not force him to surrender to his detriment. The Ninth Amendment provides: "The enumeration in the Constitution, of certain rights, shall not be construed to deny or disparage others retained by the people."

The present case, then, concerns a relationship lying within the zone of privacy created by several fundamental constitutional guarantees. And it concerns a law which, in forbidding the *use* of contraceptives rather than regulating their manufacture or sale, seeks to achieve its goals by means having a maximum destructive impact upon that relationship. Such a law cannot stand in light of the familiar principle, so often applied by this Court, that a "governmental purpose to control or prevent activities constitutionally subject to state regulation may not be achieved by means which sweep unnecessarily broadly and thereby invade the area of protected freedoms" *NAACP* v. *Alabama* (1958). Would we allow the police to search the sacred precincts of marital bedrooms for telltale signs of the use of contraceptives? The very idea is repulsive to the notions of privacy surrounding the marriage relationship.

We deal with a right of privacy older than the Bill of Rights—older than our political parties, older than our school system. Marriage is a coming together for better or for worse, hopefully enduring, and intimate to the degree of being sacred. It is an association that promotes a way of life, not causes; a harmony in living, not political faiths; a bilateral loyalty, not commercial or social projects. Yet it is an association for as noble a purpose as any involved in our prior decisions.

Reversed.

Note: The Debate in *Griswold*

The justices divided sharply over where to locate the new constitutional right of privacy. Some members of the Court (John Marshall Harlan and Byron White) believed it was rooted in the due process clause; another faction (Douglas and Tom Clark) thought it was covered by one of the "penumbras" of the Ninth Amendment; and still a third group (Arthur Goldberg, Earl Warren, and William Brennan) agreed with both groups, concluding that the Ninth Amendment provided the source of authority to infer unwritten rights into the Constitution.

The *Griswold* case also reopened the debate over substantive due process. This concept had been largely abandoned in matters of economic regulation in the late 1930s, but remained a viable doctrine to safeguard individual liberty interests. *Griswold* was a landmark decision in which a majority of the Court relied on substantive due process to protect a right of privacy not mentioned in the Constitution. Douglas, as his opinion makes clear, explicitly disavowed such a course of action, as did Justice Hugo Black, who wrote a strong dissenting opinion. *Griswold* has been sharply criticized for its judicial activism and hailed as a creative defense of individual liberty. What do you think?

Roe v. *Wade*
410 U.S. 113 (1973)

Jane Roe was an unmarried pregnant woman who wanted an abortion. Texas law, which was like most other abortion statutes in the United States, forbade this procedure unless the life of the mother was at risk. Roe began her lawsuit in March 1970, although when the case reached the Supreme Court she had already had her child and given it up for adoption. Critics of this decision, of which there are many, claim that the Court should never have heard it because the issue that it raised had been mooted by the birth of the child. This case has implications not only for the rights of women, but for the ways in which the Supreme Court uses its powers.

Mr. Justice Blackmun delivered the opinion of the Court.

The principal thrust of appellant's attack on the Texas statutes is that they improperly invade a right, said to be possessed by the pregnant woman, to choose to terminate her pregnancy. Appellant would discover this right in the concept of personal "liberty" embodied in the Fourteenth Amendment's Due Process Clause; or in personal, marital, familial, and sexual privacy said to be protected by the Bill of Rights or its penumbras . . . ; or among those rights reserved to the people by the Ninth Amendment. . . . Before addressing this claim, we feel it desirable briefly to survey, in several aspects, the history of abortion, for such insight as that history may afford us, and then to examine the state purposes and interests behind the criminal abortion laws.

It perhaps is not generally appreciated that the restrictive criminal abortion laws in effect in a majority of States today are of relatively recent vintage. Those laws, generally proscribing abortion or its attempt at any time during pregnancy except when necessary to preserve that pregnant woman's life, are not of ancient or even of common-law origin. Instead, they derive from statutory changes effected, for the most part, in the latter half of the nineteenth century.

◆ ◆ ◆

It is thus apparent that at common law, at the time of the adoption of our Constitution, and throughout the major portion of the nineteenth century, abortion was viewed with less disfavor than under most American statutes currently in effect. Phrasing it in another way, a woman enjoyed a substantially broader right to terminate a pregnancy than she does in most States today. At least with respect to the early stage of pregnancy, and very possibly without such a limitation, the opportunity to make this choice was present in this country well into the nineteenth century. Even later, the law continued for some time to treat less punitively an abortion procured in early pregnancy.

◆ ◆ ◆

Three reasons have been advanced to explain historically the enactment of criminal abortion laws in the nineteenth century and to justify their continued existence.

It has been argued occasionally that these laws were the product of a Victorian social concern to discourage illicit sexual conduct. Texas, however, does not advance this justification in the present case. . . .

A second reason is concerned with abortion as a medical procedure. When most criminal abortion laws were first enacted, the procedure was a hazardous one for the woman. This was particularly true prior to the development of antisepsis. . . .

Modern medical techniques have altered this situation. Appellants and various amici refer to medical data indicating that abortion in early pregnancy, that is, prior to the end of the first trimester, although not without its risk, is now relatively safe. Mortality rates for women undergoing early abortions, where the procedure is legal, appear to be as low or lower than the rates for normal childbirth. Consequently, any interest of the State in protecting the woman from an inherently hazardous procedure, except when it would be equally dangerous for her to forgo it, has largely disappeared. Of course, important state interests in the areas of health and medical standards do remain. The State has a legitimate interest in seeing to it that abortion, like any other medical procedure, is performed under circumstances that insure maximum safety for the patient. This interest obviously extends at least to the performing physician and his staff, to the facilities involved, to the availability of after-care, and to adequate provision for any complication or emergency that might arise. . . . Moreover, the risk to the woman increases as her pregnancy continues. Thus, the State retains a definite interest in protecting the woman's own health and safety when an abortion is proposed at a late stage of pregnancy.

The third reason is the State's interest—some phrase it in terms of duty—in protecting prenatal life. Some of the arguments for this justification rests on the theory that a new human life is present from the moment of conception. The State's interest and general obligation to protect life then extends, it is argued, to prenatal life. Only when the life of the pregnant mother herself is at stake, balanced against the life she carried within her, should the interest of the embryo or fetus not prevail. Logically, of course, a legitimate state interest in this area need not stand or fall on acceptance of the belief that life begins at conception or at some other point prior to live birth. In assessing the State's interest, recognition may be given to the less rigid claim that as long as at least *potential* life is involved, the State may assert interests beyond the protection of the pregnant woman alone.

Parties challenging state abortion laws have sharply disputed in some courts the contention that a purpose of these laws, when enacted, was to protect prenatal life . . . [and] they claim that most state laws were designed solely to protect the woman. Because medical advances have lessened this concern, at least with respect to abortion in early pregnancy, they argue that with respect to such abortions the laws can no longer be justified by any state interest. There is some scholarly support for this view of original purpose. The few state courts called upon to interpret their laws in the late nineteenth and early twentieth centuries did focus on the State's interest in protecting the woman's health rather than in preserving the embryo and fetus. Proponents of this view point out that in many States, including Texas, by statute or judicial interpretation, the pregnant woman herself could not be prosecuted for self-abortion or for cooperating in an abortion performed upon her by another. They claim that adoption of the "quickening" distinction through received common law and state statutes tacitly recognizes the greater health hazards inherent in the late abortion and impliedly repudiates the theory that life begins at conception. . . .

The Constitution does not explicitly mention any right of privacy. In a line of decisions, however, . . . the Court has recognized that a right of personal privacy, or a guarantee of certain areas or zones of privacy, does exist under the Constitution. In varying contexts, the Court or individual Justices have, indeed, found at least the roots of that right.

♦ ♦ ♦

This right of privacy, whether it be founded in the Fourteenth Amendment's concept of personal liberty and restrictions upon state action, as we feel it is, or, as the District Court determined, in the Ninth Amendment's reservation of rights to the people, is broad enough to encompass a woman's decision whether or not to terminate her pregnancy. The detriment that the State would impose upon the pregnant woman by denying this choice altogether is apparent. Specific and direct harm medically diagnosable even in early pregnancy may be involved. Maternity, or additional offspring, may force upon the woman a distressful life and future. Psychological harm may be imminent. Mental and physical health may be taxed by child care. There is also the distress, for all concerned, associated with the unwanted

child, and there is the problem of bringing a child into a family already unable, psychologically and otherwise, to care for it. In other cases, as in this one, the additional difficulties and continuing stigma of unwed motherhood may be involved. All these are factors the woman and her responsible physician necessarily will consider in consultation.

On the basis of elements such as these, appellant and some amici argue that the woman's right is absolute and that she is entitled to terminate her pregnancy at whatever time, in whatever way, and for whatever reason she alone chooses. With this we do not agree. Appellant's arguments that Texas either has no valid interest at all in regulating the abortion decision, or no interest strong enough to support any limitation upon the woman's sole determination, are unpersuasive. The Court's decisions recognizing a right of privacy also acknowledge that some regulation in areas protected by that right is appropriate. As noted above, a State may properly assert important interests in safeguarding health, in maintaining medical standards, and in protecting potential life. At some point in pregnancy, these respective interests become sufficiently compelling to sustain regulation of the factors that govern the abortion decision. The privacy right involved, therefore, cannot be said to be absolute. In fact, it is not clear to us that the claim asserted by some amici that one has an unlimited right to do with one's body as one pleases bears a close relationship to the right of privacy previously articulated in the Court's decisions. The Court has refused to recognize an unlimited right of this kind in the past. . . .

We, therefore, conclude that the right of personal privacy includes the abortion decision, but that this right is not unqualified and must be considered against important state interests in regulation. . . . [This] right, nonetheless, is not absolute and is subject to some limitations; and . . . at some point the state interests as to protection of health, medical standards, and prenatal life, become dominant. . . .

While certain "fundamental rights" are involved, the Court has held that regulation limiting these rights may be justified only by a "compelling state interest" . . . and that legislative enactments must be narrowly drawn to express only the legitimate state interests at stake. . . .

In the recent abortion cases, . . . courts have recognized these principles. Those striking down state laws have generally scrutinized the State's interests in protecting health and potential life, and have concluded that neither interest justified broad limitations on the reasons for which a physician and his pregnant patient might decide that she should have an abortion in the early stages of pregnancy. Courts sustaining state laws have held that the State's determinations to protect health or prenatal life are dominant and constitutionally justifiable.

◆ ◆ ◆

The appellee and certain amici argue that the fetus is a "person" within the language and meaning of the Fourteenth Amendment. In support of this, they outline at length and in detail the well-known facts of fetal development. If this suggestion of personhood is established, the appellant's case, of course, collapses, for the fetus' right to life would then be guaranteed specifically by the Amendment . . . [but] no case [can] be cited that holds that a fetus is a person within the meaning of the Fourteenth Amendment.

The Constitution does not define "person" in so many words. Section 1 of the Fourteenth Amendment contains three references to "person." The first, in defining "citizens," speaks of "persons born or naturalized in the United States." . . . "Person" is used in other places in the Constitution. . . . But in nearly all these instances, the use of the word is such that it has application only postnatally. None indicates, with any assurance, that it has any possible prenatal application.

All this, together with our observation . . . that throughout the major portion of the nineteenth century prevailing legal abortion practices were far freer than they are today, persuades us that the word "person," as used in the Fourteenth Amendment, does not include the unborn. This is in accord with the results reached in those few cases where the issue has been squarely presented.

The pregnant woman cannot be isolated in her privacy. She carries an embryo and, later, a fetus. . . . The situation therefore is inherently different from marital intimacy, or bedroom possession of obscene material, or marriage, or procreation, or education. . . . As we have intimated above, it is reasonable and appropriate for a State to decide that at some point in time another interest, that of health of the mother or that of potential human life, becomes significantly involved. The woman's privacy is no longer sole and any right of privacy she possesses must be measured accordingly.

Texas urged that, apart from the Fourteenth Amendment, life begins at conception and is present throughout pregnancy, and that, therefore, the State has a compelling interest in protecting that life from and after conception. We need not resolve the difficult question of when life begins. When those trained in the respective disciplines of medicine, philosophy, and theology are unable to arrive at any consensus, the judiciary, at this point in the development of man's knowledge, is not in a position to speculate as to the answer.

It should be sufficient to note briefly the wide divergence of thinking on this most sensitive and difficult question. There has always been strong support for the view that life does not begin until live birth. . . . Substantial problems for precise definition of this view are posed, however, by new embryological data that purpose to indicate that conception is a "process" over time, rather than an event, and by new medial techniques such as menstrual extraction, the "morning-after" pill, implantation of embryos, artificial insemination, and even artificial wombs.

◆ ◆ ◆

In view of all this, we do not agree that, by adopting one theory of life, Texas may override the rights of the pregnant woman that are at stake. We repeat, however, that the State does have an important and legitimate interest in preserving and protecting the health of the pregnant woman, whether she be a resident of the State or a nonresident who seeks medical consultation and treatment there, and that it has still *another* important and legitimate interest in protecting the potentiality of human life. These interests are separate and distinct. Each grows in substantiality as the woman approaches term and, at a point during pregnancy, each becomes "compelling."

With respect to the State's important and legitimate interest in the health of the mother, the "compelling" point, in the light of present medical knowledge, is at approximately the end of the first trimester. This is so because of the now-established medical fact, referred to above, that until the end of the first trimester mortality in abortion may be less than mortality in normal childbirth. It follows that, from and after this point, a State may regulate the abortion procedure to the extent that the regulation reasonably relates to the preservation and protection of maternal health. Examples of permissible state regulation in this area are requirements as to the qualifications of the person who is to perform the abortion; as to the licensure of that person; as to the facility in which the procedure is to be performed, that is, whether it must be a hospital or may be a clinic or some other place of less-than-hospital status; as to the licensing of the facility; and the like.

This means, on the other hand, that, for the period of pregnancy prior to this "compelling" point, the attending physician, in consultation with his patient, is free to determine, without regulation by the State, that, in his medical judgment, the patient's pregnancy should be terminated. If that decision is reached, the judgment may be effectuated by an abortion free of interference by the State.

With respect to the State's important and legitimate interest in potential life, the "compelling" point is at viability. This is so because the fetus then presumably has the capability of meaningful life outside the mother's womb. State regulation protective of fetal life after viability thus has both logical and biological justifications. If the State is interested in protecting fetal life after viability, it may go so far as to proscribe abortion during that period, except when it is necessary to preserve the life or health of the mother.

Measured against these standards, Article 1196 of the Texas Penal Code, in restricting legal abortions to those "procured or attempted by medical advice for the purpose of saving the life of the mother," sweeps too broadly. The statute made no distinction between abortions performed early in pregnancy and those performed later, and it limits to a single reason, "saving" the mother's life, the legal justification for the procedure. The statute, therefore, cannot survive the constitutional attack made upon it here.

Note: The Future of *Roe*

The Supreme Court has reaffirmed its *Roe* holding in several subsequent cases, most notably *Planned Parenthood of Southeastern Pennsylvania* v. *Casey* (1992). Yet the justices reached their position only after indicating that they had substantial misgivings about the original *Roe* holding. Thus, in *Webster* v. *Reproductive Health Services* (1989), for example, a closely divided Court concluded that a statutory ban placed by the state of Missouri on the use of public employees and facilities for performance or assistance of nontherapeutic abortions did not contravene the Constitution.

Johnson v. *Transportation Agency, Santa Clara County*
480 U.S. 616 (1987)

Affirmative action programs remain the most controversial aspects of the drive for equal rights. Such programs offer remedies meant to counter past racial and gender discrimination, but they face serious constitutional and political objections.

This case began when Paul Johnson was passed over for promotion to road dispatcher for Santa Clara County, California. Instead, Diane Joyce was awarded that position, one that no female had previously occupied. Her promotion was based on a voluntary affirmative action plan adopted by the county with the purpose of bringing women into traditionally male-dominated positions. Joyce was selected even though the review committee had determined that Johnson was the more worthy candidate.

Justice Brennan delivered the opinion of the court.

The first issue is therefore whether consideration of the sex of applicants for skilled craft jobs was justified by the existence of a "manifest imbalance" that reflected underrepresentation of women in "traditionally segregated job categories" [*United Steelworkers* v. *Weber* (1979)]. In determining whether an imbalance exists that would justify taking sex or race into account, a comparison of the percentage of minorities or women in the employer's work force with the percentage in the area labor market or general population is appropriate in analyzing jobs that require no special expertise, or training programs designed to provide expertise. . . . Where a job requires special training, however, the comparison should be with those in the labor force who possess the relevant qualifications. . . . The requirement that the "manifest imbalance" relate to a "traditionally segregated job category" provides assurance both that sex or race will be taken into account in a manner consistent with Title VII's purpose of eliminating the effects of employment discrimination, and that the interests of those employees not benefiting from the plan will not be unduly infringed.

A manifest imbalance need not be such that it would support a prima facie case against the employer, . . . since we do not regard as identical the constraints of Title VII and the federal constitution on voluntarily adopted affirmative action plans. Application of the "prima facie" standard in Title VII cases would be inconsistent with *Weber*'s focus on statistical imbalance, and could inappropriately create a significant disincentive for employers to adopt an affirmative action plan. . . . A corporation concerned with maximizing return on investment, for instance, is hardly likely to adopt a plan if in order to do so it must compile evidence that

could be used to subject it to a colorable Title VII suit.

It is clear that the decision to hire Joyce was made pursuant to an Agency plan that directed that sex or race be taken into account for the purpose of remedying underrepresentation. The Agency Plan acknowledged the "limited opportunities that have existed in the past," App. 57, for women to find employment in certain job classifications "where women have not been traditionally employed in significant numbers." As a result, observed the Plan, women were concentrated in traditionally female jobs in the Agency, and represented a lower percentage in other job classifications than would be expected if such traditional segregation had not occurred. Specifically, 9 of the 10 Para-Professionals and 110 of the 145 Office and Clerical Workers were women. By contrast, women were only 2 of the 28 Officials and Administrators, 5 of the 58 Professionals, 12 of the 124 Technicians, none of the Skilled Craft Workers, and 1—who was Joyce—of the 110 Road Maintenance Workers. The Plan sought to remedy these imbalances through "hiring, training and promotion of . . . women throughout the Agency in all major job classifications where they are underrepresented."

♦   ♦   ♦

As the Agency Plan recognized, women were most egregiously underrepresented in the Skilled Craft job category, since none of the 238 positions was occupied by a woman. In mid-1980, when Joyce was selected for the road dispatcher position, the Agency was still in the process of refining its short-term goals for Skilled Craft Workers in accordance with the directive of the Plan. This process did not reach fruition until 1982, when the Agency established a short-term goal for that year of three women for the 55 expected openings in that job category—a modest goal of about 6% for that category.

We reject petitioner's argument that, since only the long-term goal was in place for Skilled Craft positions at the time of Joyce's promotion, it was inappropriate for the Director to take into account affirmative action considerations in filling the road dispatcher position. The Agency's Plan emphasized that the long-term goals were not to be taken as guides for actual hiring decisions, but that supervisors were to consider a host of practical factors in seeking to meet affirmative action objectives, including the fact that in some job categories women were not qualified in numbers comparable to their representation in the labor force.

By contrast, had the Plan simply calculated imbalances in all categories according to the proportion of women in the area labor pool, and then directed that hiring be governed solely by those figures, its validity fairly could be called into question. This is because analysis of a more specialized labor pool normally is necessary in determining underrepresentation in some positions. If a plan failed to take distinctions in qualifications into account in providing guidance for actual employment decisions, it would dictate mere blind hiring by the numbers, for it would hold supervisors to "achievement of a particular percentage of minority employment or membership . . . regardless of circumstances such as economic conditions or the number of qualified minority applicants. . . . "

Justice Scalia dissenting:

Today's decision does more, however, than merely reaffirm *Weber,* and more than merely extend it to public actors. It is impossible not to be aware that the practical effect of our holding is to accomplish de facto what the law-in language even plainer than that ignored in *Weber* . . . —forbids anyone from accomplishing de jure: in many contexts it effectively *requires* employers, public as well as private, to engage in intentional discrimination on the basis of race or sex. This Court's prior interpretations of Title VII, especially the decision in *Griggs* v. *Duke Power Co.* (1971), subject employers to a potential Title VII suit whenever there is a noticeable imbalance in the representation of minorities or women in the employer's work force. Even the employer who is confident of ultimately prevailing in such a suit must contemplate the expense and adverse publicity of a trial, because the extent of the imbalance, and the "job relatedness" of his selection criteria, are questions of fact to be explored through rebuttal and counter-rebuttal of a "prima facie case" consisting of no more than the showing that the employer's selection process "selects those from the protected class at a 'significantly' lesser rate than their counterparts." . . . If, however, employers are free to discriminate through affirmative action, without fear of "reverse discrimination" suits by their nonminority or male victims, they are offered a threshold defense against Title VII liability premised on numerical disparities. Thus, after today's decision the *failure* to engage in reverse discrimination is economic folly, and arguably a breach of duty to shareholders or taxpayers, wherever the cost of anticipated Title VII litigation exceeds the cost of hiring less capable (though still minimally capable) workers. (This situation is more likely to obtain, of course, with respect to the least skilled jobs—perversely creating an incentive to discriminate against precisely those members of the nonfavored groups least likely to have profited from societal discrimination in the past.) It is predictable, moreover, that this incentive will be greatly magnified by economic pressures brought to bear by government contracting agencies upon employers who refuse to discriminate in the fashion we have now approved. A statute designed to establish a color-blind and gender-blind work place has thus been converted into a powerful engine of racism and sexism, not merely *permitting* intentional race- and sex-based discrimination, but often making it, through operation of the legal system, practically compelled.

It is unlikely that today's result will be displeasing to politically elected officials, to whom it provides the means of quickly accommodating the demands of organized groups to achieve concrete, numerical improvement in the economic status of particular constituencies. Nor will it displease the world of corporate and governmental employers (many of whom have filed briefs as amici in the present case, all on the side of Santa Clara) for whom the cost of hiring less qualified workers is often substantially less—and infinitely more predictable—than the cost of litigating Title VII cases and of seeking to convince federal agencies by nonnumerical means that no discrimination exists. In fact, the only losers in the process are the Johnsons of the country, for whom Title VII has been not merely repealed but actually inverted. The irony is that these individuals—predominantly unknown, unaffluent, unorganized—suffer this injustice at the hands of a Court fond of thinking itself the champion of the politically impotent. I dissent.

Note: Affirmative Action and Sexual Harassment

The Court in *Johnson* attempted to come to terms with affirmative action, or, as its critics term it, reverse discrimination. Proponents of these measures argue that they are necessary to overcome long-standing discriminatory practices, as a way of essentially providing damages to a class of persons that had been injured by previous governmental and private policies. The defenders also insist that there are certain social groups in America that have suffered discrimination and that the traditional emphasis on rights of the individual should be extended to these groups. In essence, they urge a group rather than an individual approach to matters of discrimination. Critics of affirmative action programs complain that such programs not only break with traditional constitutional values, but seriously weaken the principle of individual rights. Such class legislation, they argue, will have the long-term effect of rewarding incompetence instead of rewarding ability and talent.

The *Johnson* case is of interest as well because it treated the issue of gender discrimination. Another important case has been *Meritor Savings* v. *Vinson,* 477 U.S. 57 (1986). Mechelle Vinson had accused her supervisor of demanding sexual favors (including fondling and sexual intercourse) as a requirement for keeping her job. The supervisor and the bank denied this charge, and a federal district court found no violation of the law. The Supreme Court, however, concluded that Title VII of the Civil Rights Act of 1964 made sexual harassment a form of discrimination and that women could, under the law, press claims in federal courts based on the concept that an employer had created a "hostile environment."

SEXUAL ORIENTATION

Sodomy among consenting adults was long a criminal offense in every state. Such statutes provided a basis for state and federal governmental agencies as well as private employers to treat homosexuals differently from heterosexuals in a variety of ways unrelated to criminal law. By the late twentieth century, public attitudes about homosexuality began to change. Prosecutions under sodomy laws were rare. Half of the states eliminated by legislative action the criminal penalties for sodomy by consenting adults. Moreover, a number of state courts struck down their state sodomy laws on various state constitutional grounds. The Supreme Court initially rejected a constitutional challenge to sodomy laws in *Bowers* v. *Hardwick* (1986). The Court declined to extend the privacy rights recognized for heterosexuals in *Griswold* v. *Connecticut* (1965) to homosexuals.

In *Lawrence* v. *Texas* (2003) the Supreme Court, in an opinion by Justice Anthony M. Kennedy, overruled *Bowers* and held that the substantive reach of liberty protected by the due process clause of the Fourteenth Amendment encompasses private homosexual conduct among consenting adults. Speaking for five justices, he invoked "an emerging awareness that liberty gives substantial protection to adult persons in deciding how to conduct their private lives in matters pertaining to sex." Kennedy struck down the Texas sodomy statute as a violation of due process, declaring:

> The case does involve two adults who, with full and mutual consent from each other, engaged in sexual practices common to a homosexual lifestyle. The petitioners are entitled to respect for their private lives. The State cannot demean their existence or control their destiny by making their private sexual conduct a crime. Their right to liberty under the Due Process Clause gives them the full right to engage in their conduct without intervention of the government. "It is a promise of the Constitution that there is a realm of personal liberty which the government may not enter." The Texas statute furthers no legitimate state interest which can justify its intrusion into the personal and private life of the individual.

The dissenters argued, among other things, that this matter should appropriately be governed by the democratic process rather than through "the invention" of new constitutional rights by the Supreme Court. The *Lawrence* decision underscores the continuing importance of substantive due process as a vehicle to safeguard certain noneconomic liberties.

Thinking about homosexuality, moreover, has continued to evolve with respect to an array of areas outside criminal law. The drive for homosexual rights accelerated in the 1990s, raising a number of unresolved issues.

Romer v. Evans
517 U.S. 620 (1996)

States and cities started to pass laws banning discrimination based on sexual orientation in housing, employment, education, and public accommodations. In Colorado opponents of such legislation proposed a constitutional referendum forbidding state and local governments from protecting the status of persons based on their "homosexual, lesbian or bisexual orientation, conduct, practices or relationships." Adopted by the voters in 1992, the referendum was promptly challenged. The Supreme Court struck down the referendum as a violation of the equal protection clause of the Fourteenth Amendment. This decision prompted a vigorous dissent by Justice Antonin Scalia.

Justice Kennedy delivered the opinion of the Court.

One century ago, the first Justice Harlan admonished this Court that the Constitution "neither knows nor tolerates classes among citizens." *Plessy* v. *Ferguson* (1896)(dissenting opinion). Unheeded then, those words now are understood to state a commitment to the law's neutrality where the rights of persons are at stake. The Equal Protection Clause enforces this principle and today requires us to hold invalid a provision of Colorado's Constitution.

The enactment challenged in this case is an amendment to the Constitution of the State of Colorado, adopted in a 1992 statewide referendum. The parties and the state courts refer to it as "Amendment 2," its designation when submitted to the voters. The impetus for the amendment and the contentious campaign that preceded its adoption came in large part from ordinances that had been passed in various Colorado municipalities. . . . What gave rise to the statewide controversy was the protection the ordinances afforded to persons discriminated against by reason of their sexual orientation. Amendment 2 repeals these ordinances to the extent they prohibit discrimination on the basis of "homosexual, lesbian or bisexual orientation, conduct, practices or relationships." Colo. Const., Art. II, § 30b.

Yet Amendment 2, in explicit terms, does more than repeal or rescind these provisions. It prohibits all legislative, executive or judicial action at any level of state or local government designed to protect the named class, a class we shall refer to as homosexual persons or gays and lesbians. The amendment reads:

No Protected Status Based on Homosexual, Lesbian or Bisexual Orientation. Neither the State of Colorado, through any of its branches or departments, nor any of its agencies, political subdivisions, municipalities or school districts, shall enact, adopt or enforce any statute, regulation, ordinance or policy whereby homosexual, lesbian or bisexual orientation, conduct, practices or relationships shall constitute or otherwise be the basis of or entitle any person or class of persons to have or claim any minority status, quota preferences, protected status or claim of discrimination. This Section of the Constitution shall be in all respects self-executing. Ibid.

◆ ◆ ◆

The State's principal argument in defense of Amendment 2 is that it puts gays and lesbians in the same position as all other persons. So, the State says, the measure does no more than deny homosexuals special rights. This reading of the amendment's language is implausible. We rely not upon our own interpretation of the amendment but upon the authoritative construction of Colorado's Supreme Court. The state court, deeming it unnecessary to determine the full extent of the amendment's reach, found it invalid even on a modest reading of its implications.

◆ ◆ ◆

Sweeping and comprehensive is the change in legal status effected by this law. So much is evident from the ordinances the Colorado Supreme Court declared would be void by operation of Amendment 2. Homosexuals, by state decree, are put in a solitary class with

respect to transactions and relations in both the private and governmental spheres. The amendment withdraws from homosexuals, but no others, specific legal protection from the injuries caused by discrimination, and it forbids reinstatement of these laws and policies.

◆ ◆ ◆

Amendment 2 bars homosexuals from securing protection against the injuries that these public-accommodations laws address. That in itself is a severe consequence, but there is more. Amendment 2, in addition, nullifies specific legal protections for this targeted class in all transactions in housing, sale of real estate, insurance, health and welfare services, private education, and employment.

◆ ◆ ◆

Amendment 2's reach may not be limited to specific laws passed for the benefit of gays and lesbians. It is a fair, if not necessary, inference from the broad language of the amendment that it deprives gays and lesbians even of the protection of general laws and policies that prohibit arbitrary discrimination in governmental and private settings.

◆ ◆ ◆

If this consequence follows from Amendment 2, as its broad language suggests, it would compound the constitutional difficulties the law creates. The state court did not decide whether the amendment has this effect, however, and neither need we.

◆ ◆ ◆

In any event, even if, as we doubt, homosexuals could find some safe harbor in laws of general application, we cannot accept the view that Amendment 2's prohibition on specific legal protections does no more than deprive homosexuals of special rights. To the contrary, the amendment imposes a special disability upon those persons alone. Homosexuals are forbidden the safeguards that others enjoy or may seek without constraint. They can obtain specific protection against discrimination only by enlisting the citizenry of Colorado to amend the State Constitution or perhaps, on the State's view, by trying to pass helpful laws of general applicability. This is so no matter how local or discrete the harm, no matter how public and widespread the injury. We find nothing special in the protections Amendment 2 withholds. These are protections taken for granted by most people either because they already have them or do not need them; these are protections against exclusion from an almost limitless number of transactions and endeavors that constitute ordinary civic life in a free society.

The Fourteenth Amendment's promise that no person shall be denied the equal protection of the laws must coexist with the practical necessity that most legislation classifies for one purpose or another, with resulting disadvantage to various groups or persons. We have attempted to reconcile the principle with the reality by stating that, if a law neither burdens a fundamental right nor targets a suspect class, we will uphold the legislative classification so long as it bears a rational relation to some legitimate end.

Amendment 2 fails, indeed defies, even this conventional inquiry. First, the amendment has the peculiar property of imposing a broad and undifferentiated disability on a single named group, an exceptional and, as we shall explain, invalid form of legislation. Second, its sheer breadth is so discontinuous with the reasons offered for it that the amendment seems inexplicable by anything but animus toward the class it affects; it lacks a rational relationship to legitimate state interests.

Taking the first point, even in the ordinary equal protection case calling for the most deferential of standards, we insist on knowing the relation between the classification adopted and the object to be attained. The search for the link between classification and objective gives substance to the Equal Protection Clause; it provides guidance and discipline for the legislative, which is entitled to know what sorts of laws it can pass; and it marks the limits of our own authority. In the ordinary case, a law will be sustained if it can be said to advance a legitimate government interest, even if the law seems unwise or works to the disadvantage of a particular group, or if the rational for it seems tenuous.

♦ ♦ ♦

Amendment 2 confounds this normal process of judicial review. It is at once too narrow and too broad. It identifies persons by a single trait and then denies them protection across the board. The resulting disqualification of a class of persons from the right to seek specific protection from the law is unprecedented in our jurisprudence. The absence of precedent for Amendment 2 is itself instructive; "[d]iscriminations of an unusual character especially suggest careful consideration to determine whether they are obnoxious to the constitutional provision."

It is not within our constitutional tradition to enact laws of this sort. Central both to the idea of the rule of law and to our own Constitution's guarantee of equal protection is the principle that government and each of its parts remain open on impartial terms to all who seek its assistance. "Equal protection of the laws is not achieved through indiscriminate imposition of inequalities." Respect for this principle explains why laws signaling out a certain class of citizens for disfavored legal status or general hardships are rare. A law declaring that in general it shall be more difficult for one group of citizens than for all others to seek aid from the government is itself a denial of equal protection of the laws in the most literal sense. "The guaranty of 'equal protection of the laws is a pledge of the protection of equal laws.'"

♦ ♦ ♦

A second and related point is that laws of the kind now before us raise the inevitable inference that the disadvantage imposed is born of animosity toward the class of persons affected. "[I]f the constitutional conception of 'equal protection of the laws' means anything, it must at the very least mean that a bare . . . desire to harm a politically unpopular group cannot constitute a *legitimate* governmental interest." Even laws enacted for broad and ambitious purposes often can be explained by reference to legitimate public policies which justify the incidental disadvantages they impose on certain persons. Amendment 2, however, in making a general announcement that gays and lesbians shall not have any particular protections from the law, inflicts on them immediate, continuing, and real injuries that outrun and belie any legitimate justifications that may be claimed for it. We conclude that, in addition to the far-reaching deficiencies of Amendment 2 that we have noted, the principles it offends, in another sense, are conventional and venerable; a law must bear a rational relationship to a legitimate governmental purpose, and Amendment 2 does not.

The primary rationale the State offers for Amendment 2 is respect for other citizens' freedom of association, and in particular the liberties of landlords or employers who have personal or religious objections to homosexuality. Colorado also cites its interest in conserving resources to fight discrimination against other groups. The breadth of the amendment is so far removed from these particular justifications that we find it impossible to credit them. We cannot say that Amendment 2 is directed to any identifiable legitimate purpose or discrete objective. It is a status-based enactment divorced from any factual context from which we could discern a relationship to legitimate state interests; it is a classification of persons undertaken for its own sake, something the Equal Protection Clause does not permit. "[C]lass legislation . . . [is] obnoxious to the prohibitions of the Fourteenth Amendment. . . ."

We must conclude that Amendment 2 classifies homosexuals not to further a proper legislative end but to make them unequal to everyone else. This Colorado cannot do. A State cannot so deem a class of persons a stranger to its laws. Amendment 2 violates the Equal Protection Clause and the judgment of the Supreme Court of Colorado is affirmed.

Justice Scalia, with whom the Chief Justice and Justice Thomas join, dissenting.

The Court has mistaken a Kulturkampf for a fit of spite. The constitutional amendment before us here is not the manifestation of a " 'bare . . . desire to harm' " homosexuals, but is rather a modest attempt by seemingly tolerant Coloradans to preserve traditional sexual mores against the efforts of a politically powerful minority to revise those mores through use of the laws. That objective, and the means chosen to achieve it, are not only unimpeachable under any constitutional doctrine hitherto pronounced (hence the opinion's heavy reliance upon principles of righteousness rather than judicial holdings); they have been specifically approved by the Congress of the United States and by this Court.

In holding that homosexuality cannot be singled out for disfavorable treatment, the Court contradicts a decision, unchallenged here, pronounced only 10 years ago, see *Bowers* v. *Hardwick*, (1986), and places the prestige of this institution behind the proposition that opposition to homosexuality is as reprehensible as racial or religious bias. Whether it is or not is *precisely* the cultural debate that gave rise to the Colorado constitutional amendment (and to the preferential laws against which the amendment was directed). Since the Constitution of the United States says nothing about this subject, it is left to be resolved by normal democratic means, including the democratic adoption of provisions in state constitutions. This Court has no business imposing upon all Americans the resolution favored by the elite class from which the Members of this institution are selected, pronouncing that "animosity" toward homosexuality is evil. I vigorously dissent.

♦   ♦   ♦

Despite all of its hand wringing about the potential effect of Amendment 2 on general anti-discrimination laws, the Court's opinion ultimately does not dispute all this, but assumes it to be true. The only denial of equal treatment it contends homosexuals have suffered is this: They may not obtain *preferential* treatment without amending the State Constitution. That is to say, the principle underlying the Court's opinion is that one who is accorded equal treatment under the laws, but cannot as readily as other obtain *preferential* treatment under the laws, has been denied equal protection of the laws. If merely stating this alleged "equal protection" violation does not suffice to refute it, our constitutional jurisprudence has achieved terminal silliness.

The central thesis of the Court's reasoning is that any group is denied equal protection when, to obtain advantage (or, presumably, to avoid disadvantage), it must have recourse to a more general and hence more difficult level of political decisionmaking than others. The world has never head of such a principle, which is why the Court's opinion is so long on emotive utterance and so short on relevant legal citation. And it seems to me most unlikely that any multilevel democracy can function under such a principle. For *whenever* a disadvantage is imposed, or conferral of a benefit is prohibited, at one of the higher levels of democratic decisionmaking (i.e., by the state legislature rather than local government, or by the people at large in the state constitution rather than the legislature), the affected group has (under this theory) been denied equal protection. To take the simplest of examples, consider a state law prohibiting the award of municipal contracts to relatives of mayors or city councilmen. Once such a law is passed, the group composed of such relatives must, in order to get the benefit of city contracts, persuade the state legislature—unlike all other citizens, who need only persuade the municipality. It is ridiculous to consider this a denial of equal protection, which is why the Court's theory is unheard of.

◆ ◆ ◆

I turn next to whether there was a legitimate rational basis for the substance of the constitutional amendment—for the prohibition of special protection for homosexuals. It is unsurprising that the Court avoids discussion of this question, since the answer is so obviously yes. The case most relevant to the issue before today is not even mentioned in the Court's opinion: In *Bowers* v. *Hardwick* (1986), we held that the Constitution does not prohibit what virtually all States had done from the founding of the Republic until very recent years—making homosexual conduct a crime. That holding is unassailable, except by those who think that the Constitution changes to suit current fashions. . . . If it is constitutionally permissible for a State to make homosexual conduct criminal, surely it is constitutionally permissible for a State to enact other laws merely *disfavoring* homosexual conduct.

◆ ◆ ◆

When the Court takes sides in the culture wars, it tends to be with the knights rather than the villeins—and more specifically with the Templars, reflecting the views and values of the lawyer class from which the Court's Members are drawn. How that class feels about homosexuality will be evident to anyone who wishes to interview job applicants at virtually any of the Nation's law schools. The interviewer may refuse to offer a job because the applicant is Republican; because he is an adulterer; because he went to the wrong prep school or belongs to the wrong country club; because he eats snails; because he is a womanizer; because she wears real-animal fur; or even because he hates the Chicago Cubs. But if the interviewer should wish not to be an associate or partner of an applicant because he disapproves of the applicant's homosexuality, *then* he will have violated the pledge which the Association of American Law Schools requires all its member schools to exact from job interviewers: "assurance of the employer's willingness" to hire homosexuals. This law-school view of what "prejudices" must be stamped out may be contrasted with the more plebeian attitudes that apparently still prevail in the United States Congress, which has been unresponsive to repeated attempts to extend to homosexuals the protections of federal civil rights laws.

◆ ◆ ◆

Today's opinion has no foundation in American constitutional law, and barely pretends to. The people of Colorado have adopted an entirely reasonable provision which does not even disfavor homosexuals in any substantive sense, but merely denies them preferential treatment. Amendment 2 is designed to prevent piecemeal deterioration of the sexual morality favored by a majority of Coloradans, and is not only an appropriate means to that legitimate end, but a means that Americans have employed before. Striking it down is an act, not of judicial judgment, but of political will. I dissent.

SAME-SEX MARRIAGES

By the early twenty-first century, gay and lesbian activists began to demand that some form of same-sex marriage be recognized by states. Such a move would entail a redefinition of traditional marriage as a union between a man and a woman, and that alarmed many. Although Ontario, Canada, Belgium, and the Netherlands have allowed same-sex marriages, no state in the United States has yet taken this step. Prodded by the state supreme court, however, Vermont legislators have provided for civil unions for homosexual couples. California has enacted similar legislation.

In *Goodridge* v. *Department of Public Health* (2003), the Supreme Judicial Court of Massachusetts, by a vote of 4 to 3, ruled that denying gays and lesbians the right to marry violated equal protection guarantees of the Massachusetts Constitution. Defining marriage as an "evolving paradigm," the majority concluded that there was no "constitutionally adequate reason for denying civil marriage to same-sex couples." The court stayed the effect of its decision for 180 days to permit the legislature to take "appropriate" action. The dissenters maintained that marriage has long been understood as a union of a man and a woman, and the regulation of marriage was a legislative not a judicial task. The *Goodridge* decision ignited a firestorm, and the response of Massachusetts lawmakers is uncertain at this writing. The debate over same-sex marriage demonstrates the way that states remain laboratories for legal change.

Baker v. *State*
170 Vt. 194, 744 A. 2d 864 (1999)

Several same-sex couples applied for marriage licenses. When these applications were denied, they sought a declaratory judgment that the refusal to issue them marriage licenses violated the Vermont Constitution. The state defended the denial of marriage licenses to same-sex couples as a means to strengthen the link between procreation and child rearing. Rejecting this argument, the Vermont Supreme Court considered whether the exclusion of same-sex couples from the benefits available to married persons violated the state constitution.

Amestoy, C.J.

May the State of Vermont exclude same-sex couples from the benefits and protections that its laws provide to opposite-sex married couples? That is the fundamental question we address in this appeal, a question that the Court well knows arouses deeply felt religious, moral and political beliefs. Our constitutional responsibility to consider the legal merits of issues properly before us provides no exception for the controversial case. The issue before the Court, moreover, does not turn on the religious or moral debate over intimate same-sex relationships, but rather on the statutory and constitutional basis for the exclusion of same-sex couples from the secular benefits and protections offered married couples.

We conclude that under the Common Benefits Clause of the Vermont Constitution, which, in pertinent part, reads,

> That government is, or ought to be, instituted for the common benefit, protection, and security of the people, nation, or community, and not for the particular emolument or advantage of any single person, family, or set of persons, who are a part only of that community. . . .

Vt. Const. ch. I, art. 7., plaintiffs may not be deprived of the statutory benefits and protections afforded persons of the opposite sex who choose to marry. We hold that the State is constitutionally required to extend to same-sex couples the common benefits and protections that flow from marriage under Vermont law. Whether this ultimately takes the form of inclusion within the marriage laws themselves or a parallel "domestic partnership" system or some equivalent statutory alternative, rests with the legislature. Whatever system is chosen, however, must conform with the constitutional imperative to afford all Vermonters the common benefit, protection, and security of the law.

◆ ◆ ◆

II. THE CONSTITUTIONAL CLAIM

Assuming that the marriage statutes preclude their eligibility for a marriage license, plaintiffs contend that the exclusion violates their right to the common benefit and protection of the law guaranteed by Chapter I, Article 7 of the Vermont Constitution. They note that in denying them access to a civil marriage license, the law effectively excludes them from a broad array of legal benefits and protections incident to the marital relation, including access to a spouse's medical, life, and disability insurance, hospital visitation and other medical decisionmaking privileges, spousal support, intestate succession, homestead protections, and many other statutory protections. They claim the trial court erred in upholding the law on the basis that it reasonably served the State's interest in promoting the "link between procreation and childrearing." They argue that the large number of married couples without children, and the increasing incidence of same-sex couples with children, undermines the State's rationale. They note that Vermont law affirmatively guarantees the right to adopt and raise children regardless of the sex of the parents, see 15A V.S.A. § 1-102, and challenge the logic of a legislative scheme that recognizes the rights of same-sex partners as parents, yet denies them—and their children—the same security as spouses.

In considering this issue, it is important to emphasize at the outset that it is the Common Benefits Clause of the Vermont Constitution we are construing, rather than its counterpart, the Equal Protection Clause of the Fourteenth Amendment to the United States Constitution. It is altogether fitting and proper that we do so. Vermont's constitutional commitment to equal rights was the product of the successful effort to create an independent republic and a fundamental charter of government, the Constitution of 1777, both of which preceded the adoption of the Fourteenth Amendment by nearly a century. As we explained in *State* v. *Badger*, 141 Vt. 430, 448–49, 450 A.2d 336, 347 (1982), "our constitution is not a mere reflection of the federal charter. Historically and textually, it differs from the United States Constitution. It predates the federal counterpart, as it extends back to Vermont's days as an independent republic. It is an independent authority, and Vermont's fundamental law."

◆ ◆ ◆

The powerful movement for "social equivalence" unleashed by the revolution ultimately found its most complete expression in the first state constitutions adopted in the early years of the rebellion. In Pennsylvania, where social antagonisms were most acute, the result was a fundamental charter that has been described as "the most radical constitution of the Revolution." Yet the Pennsylvania Constitution's egalitarianism was arguably eclipsed the following year by the Vermont Constitution of 1777. In addition to the commitment to government for the "common benefit, protection, and security," it contained novel provisions abolishing slavery, eliminating property qualifications for voting, and calling for the governor, lieutenant governor, and twelve councilors to be elected by the people rather than appointed by the legislature. These and other provisions have led one historian to observe that Vermont's first charter was the "most democratic constitution produced by any of the American states."

The historical origins of the Vermont Constitution thus reveal that the framers, although enlightened for their day, were not principally concerned with civil rights for African-Americans and other minorities, but with equal access to public benefits and protections for the community as a whole. The concept of equality at the core of the Common Benefits Clause was not the eradication of racial or class distinctions, but rather the elimination of artificial governmental preferments and advantages. The Vermont Constitution would ensure that the law uniformly afforded every Vermonter its benefit, protection, and security so that social and political preeminence would reflect differences of capacity, disposition, and virtue, rather than governmental favor and privilege.

Thus, viewed in the light of history, logic, and experience, we conclude that none of the interests asserted by the State provides a reasonable and just basis for the continued exclusion of same-sex couples from the benefits incident to a civil marriage license under Vermont law. Accordingly, in the faith that a case beyond the imagining of the framers of our Constitution may, nevertheless, be safely anchored in the values that infused it, we find a constitutional obligation to extend to plaintiffs the common benefit, protection, and security that Vermont provides opposite-sex married couples. It remains only to determine the appropriate means and scope of relief compelled by this constitutional mandate.

F. Remedy

It is important to state clearly the parameters of today's ruling. Although plaintiffs sought in-

junctive and declaratory relief designed to secure a marriage license, their claims and arguments here have focused primarily upon the consequences of official exclusion from the statutory benefits, protections, and security incident to marriage under Vermont law. While some future case may attempt to establish that—notwithstanding equal benefits and protections under Vermont law—the denial of a marriage license operates per se to deny constitutionally-protected rights, that is not the claim we address today.

We hold only that plaintiffs are entitled under Chapter I, Article 7, of the Vermont Constitution to obtain the same benefits and protections afforded by Vermont law to married opposite-sex couples. We do not purport to infringe upon the prerogatives of the Legislature to craft an appropriate means of addressing this constitutional mandate, other than to note that the record here refers to a number of potentially constitutional statutory schemes from other jurisdictions. These include what are typically referred to as "domestic partnership" or "registered partnership" acts, which generally establish an alternative legal status to marriage for same-sex couples, impose similar formal requirements and limitations, create a parallel licensing or registration scheme, and extend all or most of the same rights and obligations provided by the law to married partners.

Vermont Civil Union Act
2000

(a) The purpose of this act is to respond to the constitutional violation found by the Vermont Supreme Court in *Baker* v. *State*, and to provide eligible same-sex couples the opportunity to "obtain the same benefits and protections afforded by Vermont law to married opposite-sex couples" as required by Chapter I, Article 7th of the Vermont Constitution.

(b) This act also provides eligible blood-relatives and relatives related by adoption the opportunity to establish a reciprocal benefici-

aries relationship so they may receive certain benefits and protections and be subject to certain responsibilities that are granted to spouses.

The General Assembly finds that:

(1) Civil marriage under Vermont's marriage statutes consists of a union between a man and a woman. This interpretation of the state's marriage laws was upheld by the Supreme Court in *Baker* v. *State*.

(2) Vermont's history as an independent republic and as a state is one of equal treatment and respect for all Vermonters. This tradition is embodied in the Common Benefits Clause of the Vermont Constitution, Chapter I, Article 7th.

◆　◆　◆

(3) The state's interest in civil marriage is to encourage close and caring families, and to protect all family members from the economic and social consequences of abandonment and divorce, focusing on those who have been especially at risk.

(4) Legal recognition of civil marriage by the state is the primary and, in a number of instances, the exclusive source of numerous benefits, responsibilities and protections under the laws of the state for married persons and their children.

(5) Based on the state's tradition of equality under the law and strong families, for at least 25 years, Vermont Probate Courts have qualified gay and lesbian individuals as adoptive parents.

(6) Vermont was one of the first states to adopt comprehensive legislation prohibiting discrimination on the basis of sexual orientation (Act. No. 135 of 1992).

(7) The state has a strong interest in promoting stable and lasting families, including families based upon a same-sex couple.

(8) Without the legal protections, benefits and responsibilities associated with civil marriage, same-sex couples suffer numerous obstacles and hardships.

(9) Despite longstanding social and economic discrimination, many gay and lesbian Vermonters have formed lasting, committed, caring and faithful relationships with persons of their same sex. These couples live together, participate in their communities together, and some raise children and care for family members together, just as do couples who are married under Vermont law.

(10) While a system of civil unions does not bestow the status of civil marriage, it does satisfy the requirements of the Common Benefits Clause. Changes in the way significant legal relationships are established under the constitution should be approached carefully, combining respect for the community and cul-

tural institutions most affected with a commitment to the constitutional rights involved. Granting benefits and protections to same-sex couples through a system of civil unions will provide due respect for tradition and longstanding social institutions, and will permit adjustment as unanticipated consequences or unmet needs arise.

(11) The constitutional principle of equality embodied in the Common Benefits Clause is compatible with the freedom of religious belief and worship guaranteed in Chapter I, Article 3rd of the state constitution. Extending the benefits and protections of marriage to same-sex couples through a system of civil unions preserves the fundamental constitutional right of each of the multitude of religious faiths in Vermont to choose freely and without state interference to whom to grant the religious status, sacrament or blessing of marriage under the rules, practices or traditions of such faith.

◆　◆　◆

§ 1204 BENEFITS, PROTECTIONS AND RESPONSIBILITIES OF PARTIES TO A CIVIL UNION

(a) Parties to a civil union shall have all the same benefits, protections and responsibilities under law, whether they derive from statute, administrative or court rule, policy, common law or any other source of civil law, as are granted to spouses in a marriage.

(b) A party to a civil union shall be included to any definition or use of the terms "spouse," "family," "immediate family," "dependent," "next of kin," and other terms that denote the spousal relationship as those terms are used throughout the law.

(c) Parties to a civil union shall be responsible for the support of one another to the same degree and in the same manner as prescribed under law for married persons.

(d) The law of domestic relations, including annulment, separation and divorce, child custody and support, and property division and maintenance shall apply to parties to a civil union.

(e) The following is a nonexclusive list of legal benefits protections and responsibilities of spouses, which shall apply in like manner to parties to a civil union:

(1) laws relating to title, tenure, descent and distribution, intestate succession, waiver of will, survivorship, and other incidents of the acquisition, ownership, or transfer, inter vivos or at death, of real or personal property, including eligibility to hold real and personal property as tenants by the entirety (parties to a civil union meet the common law unity of person qualification for purposes of a tenancy by the entirety);

(2) causes of action related to or dependent upon spousal status, including an action for wrongful death, emotional distress, loss of consortium, dramshop, or other torts or actions under contracts reciting, related to, or dependent upon spousal status;

(3) probate law and procedure, including nonprobate transfer.

(4) adoption law and procedure;

(5) group insurance for state employees under 3 V.S.A. § 631, and continuing care contracts under 8 V.S.A. § 8005;

(6) spouse abuse programs under 3 V.S.A. § 18;

(7) prohibitions against discrimination based upon marital status;

(8) victim's compensation rights under 13 V.S.A. § 5351;

(9) workers' compensation benefits;

(10) laws relating to emergency and nonemergency medical care and treatment, hospital visitation and notification, including the Patient's Bill of Rights under 18 V.S.A. chapter 42 and the Nursing Home Residents' Bill of Rights under 33 V.S.A. chapter 73;

(11) terminal care documents under 18 V.S.A. chapter 111, and durable power of attorney for health care execution and revocation under 14 V.S.A. chapter 121;

(12) family leave benefits under 21 V.S.A. chapter 5, subchapter 4A;

(13) public assistance benefits under state law;

(14) laws relating to taxes imposed by the state or a municipality;

(15) laws relating to immunity from compelled testimony and the marital communication privilege;

(16) the homestead rights of a surviving spouse under 27 V.S.A. § 105 and homestead property tax allowance under 32 V.S.A. § 6062;

(17) laws relating to loans to veterans under 8 V.S.A. § 1849;

(18) the definition of family farmer under 10 V.S.A. § 272;

(19) laws relating to the making, revoking and objecting to anatomical gifts by others under 18 V.S.A. § 5240.

(20) state pay for military service under 20 V.S.A. § 1544;

(21) application for early voter absentee ballot under 17 V.S.A. § 2532;

(22) family landowner rights to fish and hunt under 10 V.S.A. § 4253;

(23) legal requirements for assignment of wages under 8 V.S.A. § 2235; and

(24) affirmance of relationship under 15 V.S.A. § 7.

(f) The rights of parties to a civil union, with respect to a child of whom either becomes the natural parent during the term of the civil union, shall be the same as those of a married couple, with respect to a child of whom either spouse becomes the natural parent during the marriage.

DEFENSE OF MARRIAGE ACT

The agitation for states to recognize same-sex marriages has upset social and religious conservatives. They fear that such a step would undermine the institution of marriage and have adverse consequences for society. Responding to these concerns, Congress passed the Defense of Marriage Act in 1996. The act stipulated that no state "shall be required to give effect to any public act" of another state "respecting a relationship between persons of the same sex that is treated as a marriage under the laws of such other State." This provision represents an effort by Congress to limit a state's obligation under the full faith and credit clause of the Constitution to give legal effect to same-sex marriages recognized in another state. Moreover, the act defined marriage as meaning "only a legal union between one man and one woman as husband and wife" in the interpretation of federal statutes. Marital status is a factor in determining access to numerous federal programs, such as Social Security, and military and veterans' benefits. Congress clearly intends to confine eligibility to such benefits to spouses in a traditional marriage. The exact scope of the Defense of Marriage Act remains uncertain, as courts have not construed it. More than half of the states have enacted laws or constitutional provisions declaring that marriage is a relationship between one man and one woman. In addition, President George W. Bush has proposed amending the federal Constitution to prohibit same-sex marriage.

CIVIL LIBERTIES

The pre-twentieth-century Supreme Court seldom addressed issues of civil liberties. State high court judges, relying on state constitutions, considered questions of freedom of speech, press, association, and religion—when they were addressed at all. Only during the crisis over the Alien and Sedition Acts of the late 1790s did the federal courts become significantly involved in settling the constitutional boundaries of civil liberties. During the first half of the twentieth century, however, the Court heard an increasing number of cases involving these issues. This development, as with civil rights, was part of the long-term process of intensifying centralization within the American federal system. Growing ethnic diversity and the entry of the United States into both world wars generated social tensions over the proper scope of governmental authority with regard to basic freedoms. Special-interest groups, most notably the American Civil Liberties Union, which was born in 1914 to support opponents of World War I, pressed issues of individual liberty in the federal courts as had never been done before. Moreover, following the constitutional revolution of 1937 and the demise of judicial oversight of economic regulation, the justices of the Supreme Court increasingly filled their dockets with civil liberties cases.

Throughout the post–World War II era, the Court has continually struggled with the tension between individual liberty and governmental authority. Much of that tension can be traced to pressures for political and social consensus stimulated by the Cold War. National security interests, for example, were regularly cited in the early 1950s and during the protests over the war in Vietnam as a legitimate basis for curtailing political dissent. The limits of individual liberty were also tested by minority religious groups, such as the Jehovah's Witnesses.

The following materials provide only a sampling of the broad and rich contemporary history of civil liberties. As with the section on civil rights, the following cases speak eloquently to the Supreme Court's role in seeking a balance between the rights of the individual and the authority of government. Not surprisingly, the justices' role in settling disputes over civil liberties was as controversial as it was in the area of civil rights.

Dennis et al. v. *United States*
341 U.S. 494 (1951)

Fear of Communist subversion in the United States dated to the Russian Revolution of 1917. This worry intensified during the early 1950s. Growing antagonism between the United States and the Soviet Union, the threat of nuclear war, and the Communist revolution in mainland China ushered in the darker spirits of American politics. Senator Joseph McCarthy of Wisconsin, for example, boosted his political fortunes by claiming that hundreds of Soviet agents had infiltrated the Pentagon. Eugene Dennis was the head of the American Communist party, and following a spectacular trial in New York City in 1949, he and several other party members were found guilty under the Smith Act of advocating the overthrow of the government of the United States. There was no proof that they had actually engaged in such activity; instead, the evidence indicated that they had only advocated such a result. In previous First Amendment cases, the Court had held that mere advocacy was not a sufficient basis to restrict individual liberty.

Mr. Chief Justice Vinson announced the judgment of the Court.

The obvious purpose of the [Smith Act] is to protect existing Government, not from change by peaceable, lawful and constitutional means, but from change by violence, revolution and terrorism. That it is within the *power* of the Congress to protect the Government of the United States from armed rebellion is a proposition which requires little discussion. Whatever theoretical merit there may be to the argument that there is a "right" to rebellion against dictatorial governments is without force where the existing structure of the government provides for peaceful and orderly change. We reject any principle of governmental helplessness in the face of preparation for revolution, which principle, carried to its logical conclusion, must lead to anarchy. No one could conceive that it is not within the power of Congress to prohibit acts intended to overthrow the Government by force and violence. The question with which we are concerned here is not whether Congress has such *power,* but whether the *means* which it has employed conflict with the First and Fifth Amendments to the Constitution.

One of the bases for the contention that the means which Congress has employed are invalid takes the form of an attack on the face of the statute on the grounds that by its terms it prohibits academic discussion of the merits of Marxism-Leninism, that it stifles ideas and is contrary to all concepts of a free speech and a free press.

◆ ◆ ◆

The very language of the Smith Act negates the interpretation which petitioners would have us impose on that Act. It is directed at advocacy, not discussion. Thus, the trial judge properly charged the jury that they could not convict if they found that petitioners did "no more than pursue peaceful studies and discussions or teaching and advocacy in the realm of ideas." He further charged that it was not unlawful "to conduct in an American college or university a course explaining the philosophical theories set forth in the books which have been placed in evidence." Such a charge is in strict accord with the statutory language, and illustrates the meaning to be placed on those words. Congress did not intend to eradicate the free discussion of political theories, to destroy the traditional rights of Americans to discuss and evaluate ideas without fear of governmental sanction. Rather Congress was concerned with the very kind of activity in which the evidence showed these petitioners engaged.

◆ ◆ ◆

In this case we are squarely presented with the application of the "clear and present danger" test, and must decide what that phrase imports.

◆ ◆ ◆

Obviously, the words cannot mean that before the Government may act, it must wait until the putsch is about to be executed, the plans have been laid and the signal is awaited. If Government is aware that a group aiming at its overthrow is attempting to indoctrinate its members and to commit them to a course whereby they will strike when the leaders feel the circumstances permit, action by the Government is required. The argument that there is no need for Government to concern itself, for Government is strong, it possesses ample powers to put down a rebellion, it may defeat the revolution with ease needs no answer. For that is not the question. Certainly an attempt to overthrow the Government by force, even though doomed from the outset because of inadequate numbers or power of the revolutionists, is a sufficient evil for Congress to prevent. The damage which such attempts create both physically and politically to a nation makes it impossible to measure the validity in terms of the probability of success, or the immediacy of a successful attempt. In the instant case the trial judge charged the jury that they could not convict unless they found that petitioners intended to overthrow the Government "as speedily as circumstances would permit." This does not mean, and could not properly mean, that they would not strike until there was certainty of success. What was meant was that the revolutionists would strike when they thought the time was ripe. We must therefore reject the contention that success or probability of success is the criterion.

♦   ♦   ♦

Chief Judge Learned Hand, writing for the majority below, interpreted the phrase as follows: "In each case [courts] must ask whether the gravity of the 'evil,' discounted by its improbability, justifies such invasion of free speech as is necessary to avoid the danger." 183 F2d at 212. We adopt this statement of the rule. As articulated by Chief Judge Hand, it is as succinct and inclusive as any other we might devise at this time. It takes into consideration those factors which we deem relevant, and relates their significances. More we cannot expect from words.

The mere fact that from the period 1945 to 1948 petitioners' activities did not result in an attempt to overthrow the Government by force and violence is of course no answer to the fact that there was a group that was ready to make the attempt. The formation by petitioners of such a highly organized conspiracy, with rigidly disciplined members subject to call when the

leaders, these petitioners, felt that the time had come for action, coupled with the inflammable nature of world conditions, similar uprisings in other countries, and the touch-and-go nature of our relations with countries with whom petitioners were in the very least ideologically attuned, convince us that their convictions were justified on this score. And this analysis disposes of the contention that a conspiracy to advocate, as distinguished from the advocacy itself, cannot be constitutionally restrained, because it comprises only the preparation. It is the existence of the conspiracy which creates the danger. . . . If the ingredients of the reaction are present, we cannot bind the Government to wait until the catalyst is added.

♦   ♦   ♦

We hold that sections 2(a) (1), 2(a) (3) and 3 of the Smith Act do not inherently, or as construed or applied in the instant case, violate the First Amendment and other provisions of the Bill of Rights, or the First and Fifth Amendments because of indefiniteness. Petitioners intended to overthrow the Government of the United States as speedily as the circumstances would permit. Their conspiracy to organize the Communist Party and to teach and advocate the overthrow of the Government of the United States by force and violence created a "clear and present danger" of an attempt to overthrow the Government by force and violence. They were properly and constitutionally convicted for violation of the Smith Act. The judgments of conviction are upheld.

♦   ♦   ♦

Mr. Justice Black, dissenting.

♦   ♦   ♦

At the outset I want to emphasize what the crime involved in this case is, and what it is not. These petitioners were not charged with an attempt to overthrow the Government. They were not charged with overt acts of any kind designed to overthrow the Government. They were not even charged with saying anything or writing anything designed to overthrow the Government. The charge was that they agreed to assemble and to talk and publish certain ideas at a later date: The indictment is that they conspired to organize the Communist Party and to use speech or newspapers and other publications in the future to teach and advocate the forcible overthrow of the Government. No matter how it is worded, this is a virulent form of prior censorship of speech and press, which I believe the First Amendment forbids. I would hold section 3 of the Smith Act authorizing this prior restraint unconstitutional on its face and as applied.

But let us assume, contrary to all constitutional ideas of fair criminal procedure, that petitioners although not indicted for the crime of actual advocacy, may be punished for it. Even on this radical assumption, the other opinions in this case show that the only way to affirm these convictions is to repudiate directly or indirectly the established "clear and present danger" rule. This the Court does in a way which greatly restricts the protections afforded by the First Amendment. The opinions for affirmance indicate that the chief reason for jettisoning the rule is the expressed fear that advocacy of Communist doctrine endangers the safety of the Republic. Undoubtedly, a governmental policy of unfettered communication of ideas does entail dangers. To the Founders of this Nation, however, the benefits derived from free expression were worth the risk. They embodied this philosophy in the First Amendment's command that "Congress shall make no law . . . abridg-

ing the freedom of speech, or of the press. . . .
" I have always believed that the First Amendment is the keystone of our Government, that the freedoms it guarantees provide the best insurance against destruction of all freedom. At least as to speech in the realm of public matters, I believe that the "clear and present danger" test does not "mark the furthermost constitutional boundaries of protected expression" but does "no more than recognize a minimum compulsion of the Bill of Rights."

So long as this Court exercises the power of judicial review of legislation, I cannot agree that the First Amendment permits us to sustain laws suppressing freedom of speech and press on the basis of Congress' or our own notions of mere "reasonableness." Such a doctrine waters down the First Amendment so that it amounts to little more than an admonition to Congress. The Amendment as so construed is not likely to protect any but those "safe" or orthodox views which rarely need its protection. . . .

◆ ◆ ◆

Public opinion being what it now is, few will protest the conviction of these Communist petitioners. There is hope, however, that in calmer times, when present pressures, passions and fears subside, this or some later Court will restore the First Amendment liberties to the high preferred place where they belong in a free society.

Note: Free Speech and Internal Security

Chief Justice Fred Vinson's opinion in *Dennis* modified the "clear and present danger" test earlier crafted by Oliver Wendell Holmes, Jr. Until *Dennis,* the Court had generally given a liberal interpretation to that test, but the Cold War climate undermined it. The Court did so by modifying the test to provide that offenders could be punished under the Smith Act for conspiring to teach and advocate revolution against the government of the United States. They did not have to take any direct, forcible action.

The federal government relied on *Dennis* to prosecute Communist party members. Over the next six years, the government obtained 128 indictments against party leaders and members, and of these more than 100 were convicted. By the early 1960s, however, as the Cold War climate eased, the Court reevaluated its position with regard to internal security and the First Amendment. First in *Yates* v. *United States* (1957) and then in *Scales* v. *United States* (1961), the justices sustained key provisions of the Smith Act but adopted much tougher evidentiary requirements to prove that an actual threat existed. The Court went even further in *Albertson* v. *S.A.C.B.* (1965), when it made virtually unenforceable a provision of the McCarran Internal Security Act of 1950 that required Communist party members to register with the government. Since being a member of the Communist party was illegal, the McCarran Act registration requirement violated the self-incrimination provision of the Fifth Amendment. In *Brandenburg* v. *Ohio,* 395 U.S. 444 (1969), the Court went still further by declaring an Ohio criminal syndicalism law unconstitutional because it inevitably punished advocacy and assembly.

New York Times v. Sullivan
376 U.S. 254 (1964)

Actions for libel and slander, designed to protect the reputation of individuals from defamatory falsehoods, were traditionally governed by state common law. Classed as abuses of free speech, libel and slander were long seen as unprotected by the First Amendment. The landmark case of New York Times *v.* Sullivan *arose out of the civil rights struggle in the South. In December of 1960 a group placed an advertisement in the* New York Times *protesting "an unprecedented wave of terror" against blacks engaged in nonviolent demonstrations. Sullivan, the commissioner of public affairs in Montgomery, Alabama, sued the* Times *and some of the ad's sponsors for libel, alleging that the advertisement contained false statements and had injured his reputation. A local jury awarded Sullivan $500,000 in damages. The* New York Times *appealed on grounds that the Alabama libel law as applied in this case abridged the freedom of speech and press.*

In this opinion the Supreme Court enlarged the reach of the First Amendment by severely limiting the protection against libel available to public officials for comments relating to their official conduct.

Mr. Justice Brennan delivered the opinion of the Court.

We are required in this case to determine for the first time the extent to which the constitutional protections for speech and press limit a State's power to award damages in a libel action brought by a public official against critics of his official conduct.

♦ ♦ ♦

II.

Under Alabama law as applied in this case, a publication is "libelous per se" if the words "tend to injure a person . . . in his reputation" or to "bring [him] into public contempt"; the trial court stated that the standard was met if the words are such as to "injure him in his public office, or impute misconduct to him in his office, or want of official integrity, or want of fidelity to a public trust. . . . " The jury must find that the words were published "of and concerning" the plaintiff, but where the plaintiff is a public official his place in the governmental hierarchy is sufficient evidence to support a finding that his reputation has been affected by statements that reflect upon the agency of which he is in charge. Once "libel per se" has been established, the defendant has no defense as to stated facts unless he can persuade the jury that they were true in all their particulars.

♦ ♦ ♦

Unless he can discharge the burden of proving truth, general damages are presumed, and may be awarded without proof of pecuniary injury.

◆ ◆ ◆

The question before us is whether this rule of liability, as applied to an action brought by a public official against critics of his official conduct, abridges the freedom of speech and of the press that is guaranteed by the First and Fourteenth Amendments.

. . . The Alabama courts [rely] on statements of this Court to the effect that the Constitution does not protect libelous publications. Those statements do not foreclose our inquiry here. None of the cases sustained the use of libel laws to impose sanctions upon expression critical of the official conduct of public officials.

◆ ◆ ◆

Like insurrection, contempt, advocacy of unlawful acts, breach of the peace, obscenity, solicitation of legal business, and the various other formulae for the repression of expression that have been challenged in this Court, libel can claim no talismanic immunity from constitutional limitations. It must be measured by standards that satisfy the First Amendment.

◆ ◆ ◆

Thus we consider this case against the background of a profound national commitment to the principle that debate on public issues should be uninhibited, robust, and wide-open, and that it may well include vehement, caustic, and sometimes unpleasantly sharp attacks on government and public officials.

The present advertisement as an expression of grievance and protest on one of the major public issues of our time, would seem clearly to qualify for the constitutional protection. The question is whether it forfeits that protection by the falsity of some of its factual statements and by its alleged defamation of respondent.

Authoritative interpretations of the First Amendment guarantees have consistently refused to recognize an exception for any test of truth—whether administered by judges, juries, or administrative officials—and especially one

that puts the burden of proving truth on the speaker. The constitutional protection does not turn upon "the truth, popularity, or social utility of the ideas and beliefs which are offered."

◆ ◆ ◆

Injury to official reputation affords no more warrant for repressing speech that would otherwise be free than does factual error.

◆ ◆ ◆

Criticism of their official conduct does not lose its constitutional protection merely because it is effective criticism and hence diminishes their official reputations.

If neither factual error nor defamatory content suffices to remove the constitutional shield from criticism of official conduct, the combination of the two elements is no less inadequate. This is the lesson to be drawn from the great controversy over the Sedition Act of 1798, which first crystallized a national awareness of the central meaning of the First Amendment.

◆ ◆ ◆

Although the Sedition Act was never tested in this Court, the attack upon its validity has carried the day in the court of history. Fines levied in its prosecution were repaid by Act of Congress on the ground that it was unconstitutional. Jefferson, as President, pardoned those who had been convicted and sentenced under the Act and remitted their fines. These views reflect a broad consensus that the Act, because of the restraint it imposed upon criticism of government and public officials, was inconsistent with the First Amendment.

◆ ◆ ◆

The state rule of law is not saved by its allowance of the defense of truth. A defense for erroneous statements honestly made is no less essential here than was the requirement of proof of guilty knowledge which we held indispensable to a valid conviction of a bookseller for possessing obscene writings for sale.

◆ ◆ ◆

A rule compelling the critic of official conduct to guarantee the truth of all his factual assertions—and to do so on pain of libel judgments virtually unlimited in amount—leads to a comparable "self-censorship." Allowance of the defense of truth, with the burden of proving it on the defendant, does not mean that only false speech will be deterred. . . . Under such a rule, would-be critics of official conduct may be deterred from voicing their criticism, even though it is believed to be true and even though it is in fact true, because of doubt whether it can be proved in court or fear of the expense of having to do so. . . . The rule thus dampens the vigor and limits the variety of public debate. It is inconsistent with the First and Fourteenth Amendments.

The constitutional guarantees require, we think, a federal rule that prohibits a public official from recovering damages for a defamatory falsehood relating to his official conduct unless he proves that the statement was made with "actual malice"— that is, with knowledge that it was false or with reckless disregard of whether it was false or not.

OFFENSIVE SPEECH

During the twentieth century, strong protection of free speech emerged as the cardinal constitutional principle. Yet the drive for equal rights, promoted in part by the federal judiciary, soon came into conflict with an expansive reading of the First Amendment. By the 1980s and 1990s, pornography and racially motivated speech presented new challenges to First Amendment jurisprudence.

Feminists, for example, charged that sexually explicit material tended to demean women. The Supreme Court, however, summarily rejected this theory as a basis for censorship in 1986.

In the same vein, civil rights activists expressed alarm about words that targeted persons because of race, gender, or sexual orientation. They view such language, sometimes termed "hate speech," as having a hurtful and exclusionary impact on its victims. States, localities, and educational institutions started to adopt laws and rules prohibiting "hate speech." To justify these restrictions, lawmakers and educators pointed to *Chaplinsky* v. *New Hampshire*, 315 U.S. 568 (1942), in which the Supreme Court ruled that abusive or "fighting words" were not protected by the First Amendment. The attempt to curtail "hate speech" presented a quandary for many liberals, who saw themselves as defenders of free speech as well as civil rights. Liberals divided on this issue, with some insisting that preventing hurt to minorities should outweigh the commitment to free speech. This argument has not prevailed. In *R.A.V.* v. *City of St. Paul*, 505 U.S. 377 (1992), the Supreme Court invalidated a municipal ordinance that outlawed the display of a symbol that "arouses anger, alarm or resentment in others on the basis of race, color, creed, religion or gender." The justices found that the ordinance unconstitutionally silenced speech based on its content. The decision indicates that the Court will not allow suppression of speech offensive to minorities or look favorably on efforts to legislate politically correct discourse. Thereafter, a number of public university speech codes were held to violate the First Amendment's guarantee of freedom of expression. Still, in *Virginia* v. *Black* (2003), the Court determined that a state may punish persons who burn crosses in order to intimidate particular individuals, but not cross burnings as a means of political expression.

Engel v. Vitale
370 U.S. 421 (1962)

The Supreme Court rewrote much First Amendment law, especially in the area of religious freedom, following World War II. The religion clause cases, of which Engel *was the most controversial, also revealed the tremendous nationalizing effect that the justices had on American culture. Traditionally, local government and officials had been left to regulate matters such as school prayer. But in* Engel, *the justices reviewed the requirement by New York State school officials that students in the public schools recite daily a nondenominational prayer.*

Mr. Justice Black delivered the opinion of the Court.

The respondent Board of Education of Union Free School District No. 9, New Hyde Park, New York, acting in its official capacity under state law, directed the School District's principal to cause the following prayer to be said aloud by each class in the presence of a teacher at the beginning of each school day:

"Almighty God, we acknowledge our dependence upon Thee, and we beg Thy blessings upon us, our parents, our teachers and our Country."

This daily procedure was adopted on the recommendation of the State Board of Regents. . . . These state officials composed the prayer which they recommended and published as a part of their "Statement on Moral and Spiritual Training in the Schools," saying: "We believe that this Statement will be subscribed to by all men and women of good will, and we call upon all of them to aid in giving life to our program."

Shortly after the practice of reciting the Regents' prayer was adopted by the School District, the parents of ten pupils brought this action in a New York State Court insisting that use of this official prayer in the public schools was contrary to the beliefs, religions, or religious practices of both themselves and their children. Among other things, these parents challenged the constitutionality of both the state law authorizing the School District to direct the use of prayer in public schools and the School District's regulation ordering the recitation of this particular prayer on the ground that these actions of official governmental agencies violate that part of the First Amendment of the Federal Constitution which commands that "Congress shall make no law respecting an establishment of religion"—a command which was "made applicable to the State of New York by the Fourteenth Amendment of the said Constitution. . . . "

We think that by using its public school system to encourage recitation of the Regents' prayer, the State of New York has adopted a practice wholly inconsistent with the Establishment Clause. There can, of course, be no doubt that New York's program of daily classroom invocation of God's blessings as prescribed in the Regents' prayer is a religious activity. It is a solemn avowal of divine faith and supplication for the blessings of the Almighty. The nature of such a prayer has always been religious, none of the respondents has denied this and the trial court expressly so found.

♦   ♦   ♦

The petitioners contend among other things that the state laws requiring or permitting use of the Regents' prayer must be struck down as a violation of the Establishment Clause because that prayer was composed by governmental officials as a part of a governmental program to further religious beliefs. For this reason, petitioners argue, the State's use of the Regents' prayer in its public school system breaches the constitutional wall of separation between Church and State. We agree with that contention since we think, that the constitutional prohibition against laws respecting an establishment of religion must at least mean that in this country it is no part of the business of government to compose official prayers for any group of the American people to recite as a part of a religious program carried on by government.

It is a matter of history that this very practice of establishing governmentally composed prayers for religious services was one of the reasons which caused many of our early colonists to leave England and seek religious freedom in America.

♦ ♦ ♦

The First Amendment was added to the Constitution to stand as a guarantee that neither the power nor the prestige of the Federal Government would be used to control support or influence the kinds of prayer the American people can say—that the people's religions must not be subjected to the pressures of government for change each time a new political administration is elected to office. Under that Amendment's prohibition against governmental establishment of religion, as reinforced by the provisions of the Fourteenth Amendment, government in this country, be it state or federal, is without power to prescribe by law any particular form of prayer which is to be used as an official prayer in carrying on any program of governmentally sponsored religious activity.

There can be no doubt that New York's state prayer program officially establishes the religious beliefs embodied in the Regents' prayer. The respondents' argument to the contrary, which is largely based upon the contention that the Regents' prayer is "nondenominational" and the fact that the program, as modified and approved by state courts, does not require all pupils to recite the prayer but permits those who wish to do so to remain silent or be excused from the room, ignores the essential nature of the program's constitutional defects. Neither the fact that the prayer may be denominationally neutral nor the fact that its observance on the part of the students is voluntary can serve to free it from the limitations of the Establishment Clause, as it might from the Free Exercise Clause, of the First Amendment, both of which are operative against the States by virtue of the Fourteenth Amendment. Although these two clauses may in certain instances overlap, they forbid two quite different

kinds of governmental encroachment upon religious freedom. The Establishment Clause, unlike the Free Exercise Clause, does not depend upon any showing of direct governmental compulsion and is violated by the enactment of laws which establish an official religion whether those laws operate directly to coerce nonobserving individuals or not. This is not to say, of course, that laws officially prescribing a particular form of religious worship do not involve coercion of such individuals. When the power, prestige and financial support of government is placed behind a particular religious belief, the indirect coercive pressure upon religious minorities to conform to the prevailing officially approved religion is plain. But the purposes underlying the Establishment Clause go much further than that. Its first and most immediate purpose rested on the belief that a union of government and religion tends to destroy government and to degrade religion. The history of governmentally established religion both in England and in this country showed that whenever government had allied itself with one particular form of religion, the inevitable result had been that it had incurred the hatred, disrespect and even contempt of those who held contrary beliefs. That same history showed that many people had lost their respect for any religion that had relied upon the support of government to spread its faith. The Establishment Clause thus stands as an expression of principle on the part of the Founders of our Constitution that religion is too personal, too sacred, too holy, to permit its "unhallowed perversion" by a civil magistrate. Another purpose of the Establishment Clause rested upon an awareness of the historical fact that governmentally established religions and religious persecutions go hand in hand.

♦ ♦ ♦

It has been argued that to apply the Constitution in such a way as to prohibit state laws respecting an establishment of religious services in public schools is to indicate a hostility toward religion or toward prayer. Nothing, of course, could be more wrong. The history of man is inseparable from the history of religion. And perhaps it is not too much to say that since the beginning of that history many people have devoutly believed that "More things are wrought by prayer than this world dreams of." It was doubtless largely due to men who believed this that there grew up a sentiment that caused men to leave the cross-currents of officially established state religions and religious persecution in Europe and come to this country filled with the hope that they could find a place in which they could pray when they pleased to the God of their faith in the language they chose. And there were men of this same faith in the power of prayer who led the fight for adoption of our Constitution and also for our Bill of Rights with the very guarantees of religious freedom that forbid the sort of governmental activity which New York has attempted here. These men knew that the First Amendment, which tried to put an end to governmental control of religion and of prayer, was not written to destroy either. They knew rather that it was written to quiet well-justified fears which nearly all of them felt arising out of an awareness that governments of the past had shackled men's tongues to make them speak only the religious thoughts that government wanted them to speak and to pray only to the God that government wanted them to pray to. It is neither sacrilegious nor antireligious to say that each separate government in this country should stay out of the business of writing or sanctioning official prayers and leave that purely religious function to the people themselves and to those the people choose to look to for religious guidance.

◆   ◆   ◆

The judgment of the Court of Appeals of New York is reversed and the cause remanded for further proceedings not inconsistent with this opinion.

Reversed and remanded.

◆   ◆   ◆

Mr. Justice Stewart, dissenting.

With all respect, I think the Court has misapplied a great constitutional principle. I cannot see how an "official religion" is established by letting those who want to say a prayer say it. On the contrary, I think that to deny the wish of these school children to join in reciting this prayer is to deny them the opportunity of sharing in the spiritual heritage of our Nation.

◆   ◆   ◆

At the opening of each day's Session of this Court we stand, while one of our officials invokes the protection of God. Since the days of John Marshall our Crier has said, "God save the United States and this Honorable Court." Both the Senate and the House of Representatives open their daily Sessions with prayer. Each of our Presidents, from George Washington to John F. Kennedy, has upon assuming his Office asked the protection and help of God.

The Court today says that the state and federal governments are without constitutional power to prescribe any particular form of words to be recited by any group of the American people on any subject touching religion. One of the stanzas of "The Star-Spangled Banner," made our National Anthem by Act of Congress in 1931, contains [the verse]:

"And this be our motto 'In God is our Trust.'" In 1954 Congress added a phrase to the Pledge of Allegiance to the Flag so that it now contains the words "one Nation *under* God, indivisible, with liberty and justice for all." In 1952 Congress enacted legislation calling upon the President each year to proclaim a National Day of Prayer. Since 1865 the words "In God We Trust" have been impressed on our coins.

I do not believe that this Court, or the Congress, or the President has by the actions and practices I have mentioned established an "official religion" in violation of the Constitution. And I do not believe the State of New York has done so in this case. What each has done has been to recognize and to follow the deeply entrenched and highly cherished spiritual traditions of our Nation—traditions which come down to us from those who almost two hundred years ago avowed their "firm Reliance on the Protection of divine Providence" when they proclaimed the freedom and independence of this brave new world.

I dissent.

Employment Division, Department of Human Resources of Oregon v. Smith
494 U.S. 872 (1990)

Laws of general application, such as compulsory school attendance or eligibility for unemployment insurance, may adversely impact particular religious groups. Starting with Sherbert v. Verner, *374 U.S. 398 (1963), the Supreme Court had determined that government could burden the free exercise of religion only if it was necessary to protect a compelling interest. The Court insisted that government must make reasonable accommodation to the religious practices of citizens. In* Smith, *however, the Court took a more narrow view of the free exercise clause of the First Amendment and effectively abandoned the* Sherbert *doctrine. It reaffirmed the power of government to regulate religiously motivated conduct. In that case the Court held that two Native Americans who lost their jobs after they violated Oregon criminal law by using peyote as part of religious ceremonies could be denied unemployment benefits.*

Justice Scalia delivered the opinion of the Court.

This case requires us to decide whether the Free Exercise Clause of the First Amendment permits the State of Oregon to include religiously inspired peyote use within the reach of its general criminal prohibition on use of that drug, and thus permits the State to deny unemployment benefits to persons dismissed from their jobs because of such religiously inspired use.

I

Oregon law prohibits the knowing or intentional possession of a "controlled substance" unless the substance has been prescribed by a medical practitioner. The law defines "controlled substance" as a drug classified in Schedules I through V of the Federal Controlled Substances Act. Persons who violate this provision by possessing a controlled substance listed on Schedule I are "guilty of a Class B felony." As compiled by the State Board of Pharmacy under its statutory authority, Schedule I contains the drug peyote, a hallucinogen derived from the plant *Lophophora williamsii Lemaire*.

Respondents Alfred Smith and Galen Black (hereinafter respondents) were fired from their jobs with a private drug rehabilitation organization because they ingested peyote for sacramental purposes at a ceremony of the Native American Church, of which both are members. When respondents applied to petitioner Employment Division (hereinafter petitioner) for unemployment compensation, they were determined to be ineligible for benefits because they had been discharged for work-related "misconduct."

♦ ♦ ♦

We have never held that an individual's religious beliefs excuse him from compliance with an otherwise valid law prohibiting conduct that the State is free to regulate. On the contrary, the record of more than a century of our free exercise jurisprudence contradicts that proposition. As described succinctly by Justice Frankfurter in *Minersville School Dist. Bd. of Ed. v. Gobitis*, 310 U.S. 586, 594–595 (1940): "Conscientious scruples have not, in the course of the long struggle for religious toleration, relieved the individual from obedience to a general law not aimed at the promotion or restriction of religious beliefs. The mere possession of religious convictions which contradict the relevant concerns of a political society does not relieve the citizen from discharge of political responsibilities." We first had occasion to assert that principle in *Reynolds* v. *United States*, 98 U.S. 145 (1879), where we rejected the claim that criminal laws against polygamy could not be constitutionally applied to those whose religion commanded the practice. "Laws," we said, "are made for the government of actions, and while they cannot interfere with mere religious belief and opinions, they may with practices. . . . Can a man excuse his practices to the contrary because of his religious belief? To permit this would be to make the professed doctrines of religious belief superior to the law of the land, and in effect to permit every citizen to become a law unto himself."

♦ ♦ ♦

Our most recent decision involving a neutral, generally applicable regulatory law that compelled activity forbidden by an individual's religion was *United States* v. *Lee*, 455 U.S., at 258–261. There, an Amish employer, on behalf of himself and his employees, sought exemption from collection and payment of Social Security taxes on the ground that the Amish faith prohibited participation in governmental support programs. We rejected the claim that an exemption was constitutionally required. There would be no way, we observed, to distinguish The Amish believer's objection to Social Security taxes from the religious objections that others might have to the collection or use of other taxes. "If, for example, a religious adherent believes war is a sin, and if a certain percentage of the federal budget can be identified as devoted to war-related activities, such individuals would have a similarly valid claim to be exempt from paying that percentage of the income tax. The tax system could not function if denominations were allowed to challenge the tax system because tax payments were spent in a manner that violates their religious belief."

♦ ♦ ♦

Respondents' claim for relief rests on our decision in *Sherbert* v. *Verner*, in which we held that a State could not condition the availability of unemployment insurance on an individual's willingness to forgo conduct required by his religion. . . . [H]owever, the conduct at issue in those cases was not prohibited by law.

♦ ♦ ♦

The free exercise of religion means, first and foremost, the right to believe and profess whatever religious doctrine one desires. Thus, the First Amendment obviously excludes all "governmental regulation of religious *beliefs* as such."

♦ ♦ ♦

But the "exercise of religion" often involves not only belief and profession but the performance of (or abstention from) physical acts: assembling with others for a worship service, participating in sacramental use of bread and wine, proselytizing, abstaining from certain foods or certain modes of transportation. It would be true, we think (though no case of ours has involved the point), that a State would be "prohibiting the free exercise [of religion]" if it sought to ban such acts or abstentions only when they are engaged in for religious reasons, or only because of the religious belief that they display. It would doubtless be unconstitutional, for example, to ban the casting of "statues that are to be used for worship purposes," or to prohibit bowing down before a golden calf.

♦ ♦ ♦

Respondents argue that even though exemption from generally applicable criminal laws need not automatically be extended to religiously motivated actors, at least the claim for a religious exemption must be evaluated under the balancing test set forth in *Sherbert* v. *Verner* (1963). Under the *Sherbert* test, governmental actions that substantially burden a religious practice must be justified by a compelling governmental interest.

♦ ♦ ♦

We have never invalidated any governmental action on the basis of the *Sherbert* test except the denial of unemployment compensation.

♦ ♦ ♦

In recent years we have abstained from applying the *Sherbert* test (outside the unemployment compensation field) at all.

♦ ♦ ♦

Even if we were inclined to breathe into *Sherbert* some life beyond the unemployment compensation field, we would not apply it to require exemptions from a generally applicable criminal law.

♦ ♦ ♦

Nor is it possible to limit the impact of respondents' proposal by requiring a "compelling state interest" only when the conduct prohibited is "central" to the individual's religion. It is no more appropriate for judges to determine the "centrality" of religious beliefs before applying a "compelling interest" test in the free exercise field, than it would be for them to determine the "importance" of ideas before applying the "compelling interest" test in the free speech field. What principle of law or logic can be brought to bear to contradict a believer's assertion that a particular act is "central" to his personal faith? Judging the centrality of different religious practices is akin to the unacceptable "business of evaluating the relative merits of differing religious claims." As we affirmed only last Term, "[i]t is not within the judicial ken to question the centrality of particular beliefs or practices to a faith, or the validity of particular litigants' interpretations of those creeds."

♦ ♦ ♦

Values that are protected against government interference through enshrinement in the Bill of Rights are not thereby banished from the political process. Just as a society that believes in the negative protection according to the press by the First Amendment is likely to enact laws that affirmatively foster the dissemination of the printed word, so also a society that believes in the negative protection accorded to religious belief can be expected to be solicitous of that value in its legislation as well. It is therefore not surprising that a number of States have made an exception to their drug laws for sacramental peyote use. See, e.g., Ariz. Rev. Stat. Ann. §§ 13-3402(B)(1)-(3) (1989); Colo. Rev. Stat. § 12-22-317(3) (1985); N.M. Stat. Ann. § 30-31-6(D) (Supp. 1989). But to say that a nondiscriminatory religious-practice exemption is permitted, or even that it is desirable, is not to say that it is constitutionally required, and that

the appropriate occasions for its creation can be discerned by the courts. It may fairly be said that leaving accommodation to the political process will place at a relative disadvantage those religious practices that are not widely engaged in; but that unavoidable consequence of democratic government must be preferred to a system in which each conscience is a law unto itself or in which judges weigh the social importance of all laws against the centrality of all religious beliefs.

♦ ♦ ♦

Because respondents' ingestion of peyote was prohibited under Oregon law, and because that prohibition is constitutional, Oregon may, consistent with the Free Exercise Clause, deny respondents unemployment compensation when their dismissal results from use of the drug. The decision of the Oregon Supreme Court is accordingly reversed.

Justice O'Connor, with whom Justice Brennan, Justice Marshall, and Justice Blackmun join, concurring in the judgment.

Although I agree with the result the Court reaches in this case, I cannot join its opinion. In my view, today's holding dramatically departs from well-settled First Amendment jurisprudence, appears unnecessary to resolve the question presented, and is incompatible with our Nation's fundamental commitment to individual religious liberty.

♦ ♦ ♦

[R]espondents invoke our traditional compelling interest test to argue that the Free Exercise Clause requires the State to grant them a limited exemption from its general criminal prohibition against the possession of peyote. The Court today, however, denies them even the opportunity to make that argument, concluding that "the sounder approach, and the approach in accord with the vast majority of our precedents, is to hold the [compelling interest] test inapplicable to" challenges to general criminal prohibitions.

In my view, however, the essence of a free exercise claim is a relief from a burden imposed by government on religious practices or beliefs, whether the burden is imposed directly through laws that prohibit or compel specific religious practices, or indirectly through laws that, in effect, make abandonment of one's own religion or conformity to the religious beliefs of others the prices of an equal place in the civil community.

◆ ◆ ◆

A State that makes criminal an individual's religiously motivated conduct burdens that individual's free exercise of religion in the severest manner possible, for it "results in the choice to the individual of either abandoning his religious principle or facing criminal prosecution." I would have thought it beyond argument that such laws implicate free exercise concerns.

◆ ◆ ◆

Given the range of conduct that a State might legitimately make criminal, we cannot assume, merely because a law carries criminal sanctions and is generally applicable, that the First Amendment *never* requires the State to grant a limited exemption for religiously motivated conduct.

Moreover, we have not "rejected" or "declined to apply" the compelling interest test in our recent cases. Recent cases have instead affirmed that test as a fundamental part of our First Amendment doctrine.

◆ ◆ ◆

There is no dispute that Oregon's criminal prohibition of peyote places a severe burden on the ability of respondents to freely exercise their religion. Peyote is a sacrament of the Native American Church and is regarded as vital to respondents' ability to practice their religion.

◆ ◆ ◆

Under Oregon law, as construed by that State's highest court, members of the Native American Church must choose between carrying out the ritual embodying their religious beliefs and avoidance of criminal prosecution. That choice is, in my view, more than sufficient to trigger First American scrutiny.

◆ ◆ ◆

Thus, the critical question in this case is whether exempting respondents from the State's general criminal prohibition "will unduly interfere with fulfillment of the governmental interest."

◆ ◆ ◆

I believe that granting a selective exemption in this case would seriously impair Oregon's compelling interest in prohibiting possession of peyote by its citizens. Under such circumstances, the Free Exercise Clause does not require the State to accommodate respondents' religiously motivated conduct.

Note: Religious Freedom Restoration Act of 1993

In response to the *Smith* decision, Congress in 1993 passed the Religious Freedom Restoration Act. This measure was an attempt to in effect overrule *Smith* and bring about a substantive change in the constitutional protection afforded practices based on religious belief. The act sought to restore the compelling interest test set forth in *Sherbert* and to compel its application in all cases where religious exercise was burdened by general laws. In *City of Boerne* v. *Flores*, 521 U.S. 507 (1997), the Supreme Court struck down the act as beyond the power of Congress. Stressing the separation of powers doctrine, the Court pointed out that Congress could not invade the Court's authority to interpret the Constitution. The role of religion also figures significantly in the debates over and the response to terrorism. To explore these matters, we have included *Zelman* v. *Simmons-Harris*, 536 U.S. 639 (2002), in Chapter 11.

CRIMINAL JUSTICE

The Supreme Court under Chief Justice Earl Warren also nationalized the rights of the accused. Since colonial times, local authorities had administered criminal justice. The federal

Bill of Rights protections for the accused (the Fourth, Fifth, and Sixth Amendments) applied against the federal and not state and local governments. The Warren Court's constitutional revolution, however, carried over into this area as well, with the justices incorporating the protections of these amendments against the states through the Fourteenth Amendment. In *Mapp* v. *Ohio* (1961), the Court extended the exclusionary rule to the states. This rule provided that evidence seized in an illegal search could not be used in court against the accused. In *Gideon* v. *Wainwright* (1963), the Warren Court nationalized the right to counsel provided for in the Sixth Amendment, when it held that the failure to provide Clarence Earl Gideon, a small-time Florida thief, with counsel in a felony proceeding was unconstitutional. These and other cases were decided at the same time that the crime rate surged as children of the post—World War II baby boom swelled the ranks of sixteen- to twenty-seven year olds— the age cohort most prone to criminal activity. Thus when the Court provided more protection for criminals, the crime rate shot up. In this climate, law-and-order politicians attacked the Court and demanded get-tough measures, including restoration of the death penalty in several states.

Miranda v. *Arizona*
384 U.S. 436 (1966)

The Miranda *decision was the most visible and controversial of the criminal procedural rulings by the Warren Court. In it, a 5 to 4 majority of the justices extended the line of reasoning developed in* Gideon *and addressed as well in* Escobedo v. Illinois *(1964), where the justices had reversed a state murder conviction because the accused had been denied the right to counsel during interrogation and because the arresting officers had failed to advise him of his constitutional right to remain silent. In* Miranda, *the Court established, for the first time, guidelines for police officials that were designed to protect suspects against self-incrimination.*

Mr. Chief Justice Warren delivered the opinion of the Court.

♦ ♦ ♦

On March 13, 1963, petitioner, Ernesto Miranda, was arrested at his home and taken in custody to a Phoenix police station. He was there identified by the complaining witness. The police then took him to "Interrogation Room No. 2" of the detective bureau. There he was questioned by two police officers. The officers admitted at trial that Miranda was not advised that he had a right to have an attorney present. Two hours later, the officers emerged from the interrogation room with a written confession signed by Miranda. At the top of the statement was a typed paragraph stating that the con-

fession was made voluntarily, without threats or promises of immunity and "with full knowledge of my legal rights, understanding any statement I make may be used against me."

At his trial before a jury, the written confession was admitted into evidence over the objection of defense counsel, and the officers testified to the prior oral confession made by Miranda during the interrogation. Miranda was found guilty of kidnapping and rape. He was sentenced to 20 to 30 years' imprisonment on each count, the sentences to run concurrently. On appeal, the Supreme Court of Arizona held that Miranda's constitutional rights were not violated in obtaining the confession and affirmed the conviction. . . . In reaching its decision the court emphasized heavily the fact that Miranda did not specifically request counsel.

◆ ◆ ◆

An understanding of the nature and setting of . . . in-custody interrogation is essential to our decisions today. The difficulty in depicting what transpires at such interrogations stems from the fact that in this country they have largely taken place incommunicado. From extensive factual studies undertaken in the early 1930's, including the famous Wickersham Report to Congress by a Presidential Commission, it is clear that police violence and the "third degree" flourished at that time. In a series of cases decided by this Court long after these studies, the police resorted to physical brutality—beating, hanging, whipping—and to sustained and protracted questioning incommunicado in order to extort confessions. The Commission on Civil Rights in 1961 found much evidence to indicate that "some policemen still resort to physical force to obtain confessions." . . . The use of physical brutality and violence is not, unfortunately, relegated to the past or to any part of the country. Only recently in Kings County, New York, the police brutally beat, kicked and placed lighted cigarette butts on the back of a potential witness under interrogation for the purpose of securing a statement incriminating a third party.

◆ ◆ ◆

[W]e stress that the modern practice of in-custody interrogation is psychologically rather than physically oriented. . . . To be alone with the subject is essential to prevent distraction and to deprive him of any outside support. The aura of confidence in his guilt undermines his will to resist. He merely confirms the preconceived story the police seek to have him describe. Patience and persistence, at times relentless questioning, are employed. To obtain a confession, the interrogator must "patiently maneuver himself or his quarry into a position from which the desired objective may be attained." When normal procedures fail to produce the needed result, the police may resort to deceptive stratagems such as giving false legal advice. It is important to keep the subject off balance, for

example, by trading on his insecurity about himself or his surroundings. The police then persuade, trick, or cajole him out of exercising his constitutional rights.

◆ ◆ ◆

At the outset, if a person in custody is to be subjected to interrogation, he must first be informed in clear and unequivocal terms that he has the right to remain silent. For those unaware of the privilege, the warning is needed simply to make them aware of it—the threshold requirement for an intelligent decision as to its exercise. More important, such a warning is an absolute prerequisite in overcoming the inherent pressures of the interrogation atmosphere. It is not just the subnormal or woefully ignorant who succumb to an interrogator's imprecations, whether implied or expressly stated, that the interrogation will continue until a confession is obtained or that silence in the face of accusation is itself damning and will bode ill when presented to a jury. Further, the warning will show the individual that his interrogators are prepared to recognize his privilege should he choose to exercise it.

The Fifth Amendment privilege is so fundamental to our system of constitutional rule and the expedient of giving an adequate warning as to the availability of the privilege so simple, we will not pause to inquire in individual cases whether the defendant was aware of his rights without a warning being given. Assessments of the knowledge the defendant possessed, based on information as to his age, education, intelligence, or prior contact with authorities, can never be more than speculation; a warning is a clearcut fact. More important, whatever the background of the person interrogated, a warning at the time of the interrogation is indispensable to overcome its pressures and to insure that the individual knows he is free to exercise the privilege at that point in time.

The warning of the right to remain silent must be accompanied by the explanation that anything said can and will be used against the individual in court. This warning is needed in order to make him aware not only of the privilege, but also of the consequences of forgoing it. It is only through an awareness of these consequences that there can be any assurance of real understanding and intelligent exercise of the privilege. Moreover, this warning may serve to make the individual more acutely aware that he is faced with a phase of the adversary system—that he is not in the presence of persons acting solely in his interest.

The circumstances surrounding in-custody interrogation can operate very quickly to overbear the will of one merely made aware of his privilege by his interrogators. Therefore, the right to have counsel present at the interrogation is indispensable to the protection of the Fifth Amendment privilege under the system we delineate today. Our aim is to assure that the individual's right to choose between silence and speech remains unfettered throughout the interrogation process. A once-stated warning, delivered by those who will conduct the interrogation, cannot itself suffice to that end among those who most require knowledge of their rights. A mere warning given by the interrogators is not alone sufficient to accomplish that end. Prosecutors themselves claim that the admonishment of the right to remain silent without more "will benefit only the recidivist and the professional." . . . Even preliminary advice given to the accused by his own attorney can be swiftly overcome by the secret interrogation process. . . . Thus, the need for counsel to protect the Fifth Amendment privilege comprehends not merely a right to consult with counsel prior to questioning, but also to have counsel present during any questioning if the defendant so desires.

The presence of counsel at the interrogation may serve several significant subsidiary functions as well. If the accused decides to talk to his interrogators, the assistance of counsel can mitigate the dangers of untrustworthiness. With a lawyer present the likelihood that the police will practice coercion is reduced, and if coercion is nevertheless exercised the lawyer can testify to it in court. The presence of a lawyer can also help to guarantee that the accused gives a fully accurate statement to the police and that the statement is rightly reported by the prosecution at trial. . . .

An individual need not make a pre-interrogation request for a lawyer. While such request affirmatively secures his right to have one, his failure to ask for a lawyer does not constitute a waiver. No effective waiver of the right to counsel during interrogation can be recognized unless specifically made after the warnings we here delineate have been given. The accused who does not know his rights and therefore does not make a request may be the person who most needs counsel.

◆　◆　◆

Accordingly we hold that an individual held for interrogation must be clearly informed that he has the right to consult with a lawyer and to have the lawyer with him during interrogation under the system for protecting the privilege we delineate today. As with the warnings of the right to remain silent and that anything stated can be used in evidence against him, this warning is an absolute prerequisite to interrogation. No amount of circumstantial evidence that the person may have been aware of this right will suffice to stand in its stead. Only through such a warning is there ascertainable assurance that the accused was aware of this right.

◆　◆　◆

Once warnings have been given, the subsequent procedure is clear. If the individual indicates in any manner, at any time prior to or during questioning, that he wishes to remain silent, the interrogation must cease. At this point he has shown that he intends to exercise his Fifth Amendment privilege; any statement taken after the person invokes his privilege cannot be other than the product of compulsion, subtle or otherwise. Without the right to cut off questioning, the setting of in-custody interrogation operates on the individual to overcome free choice in producing a statement after the privilege has been once invoked. If the individual states that he wants an attorney, the interrogation must cease until an attorney is present. At that time, the individual must have an opportunity to confer with the attorney and to have him present during any subsequent questioning. If the individual cannot obtain an attorney and he indicates that he wants one before speaking to police, they must respect his decision to remain silent.

◆ ◆ ◆

Our decision is not intended to hamper the traditional function of police officers in investigating crime. When an individual is in custody on probable cause, the police may, of course, seek out evidence in the field to be used at trial against him. Such investigation may include inquiry of persons not under restraint. General on-the-scene questioning as to facts surrounding a crime or other general questioning of citizens in the fact-finding process is not affected by our holding. It is an act of responsible citizenship for individuals to give whatever information they may have to aid in law enforcement. In such situations the compelling atmosphere inherent in the process of in-custody interrogation is not necessarily present.

In dealing with statements obtained through interrogation, we do not purport to find all confessions inadmissible. Confessions remain a proper element in law enforcement. Any statement given freely and voluntarily without any compelling influences is, of course, admissible in evidence. The fundamental import of the privilege while an individual is in custody is not whether he is allowed to talk to the police without the benefit of warnings and counsel, but whether he can be interrogated. There is no requirement that police stop a person who enters a police station and states that he wishes to confess to a crime, or a person who calls the police to offer a confession or any other statement he desires to make. Volunteered statements of any kind are not barred by the Fifth Amendment and their admissibility is not affected by our holding today.

Note: The Supreme Court and Criminal Justice

The Supreme Court was sharply divided over Chief Justice Warren's *Miranda* opinion, in part because the justices, especially John Marshall Harlan, believed that the new procedures weighted the criminal justice process in favor of the criminal and against the public. Harlan also argued in dissent that it was unnecessary to incorporate the self-incrimination provisions of the Fifth Amendment into the Fourteenth, since, in his view, the due process clause of the Fourteenth Amendment provided all the protection necessary against coerced confessions by police officials.

The *Miranda* warning subsequently became a standard part of police practice. Studies have shown that the warning system, contrary to fears at the time, has actually benefited police arrest and conviction records because it has forced a higher standard of conduct on police officials. In fact, the effect of *Miranda* on the rate of confessions has been minimal. Indeed, some liberals charge that *Miranda* has done little to curb police abuse during custodial interrogations. Even though Presidents Nixon and Reagan blasted the decision and promised to appoint law-and-order justices to the bench who would be tough on crime, the Supreme Court has carved out only minor exceptions to this milestone ruling. In the wake of the *Miranda* decision, Congress enacted a statute that in essence made the admissibility of a confession in criminal prosecutions in federal courts turn solely upon whether such statement was voluntary. The statute clearly conflicted with *Miranda* and was probably intended to overrule that decision. In *Dickerson* v. *United States*, 530 U.S. 428 (2000), however, the Supreme Court, by a 7 to 2 vote, pointed out that Congress cannot by legislation supersede Court decisions interpreting the Constitution. More significantly, the justices reaffirmed *Miranda*. Chief Justice William Rehnquist tellingly observed:

Whether or not we would agree with *Miranda*'s reasoning and its resulting rule, were we addressing the issue in the first instance, the principles of stare decisis weigh heavily against overruling it now.

◆ ◆ ◆

We do not think there is such justification for overruling *Miranda. Miranda* has become embedded in routine police practice to the point where the warnings have become part of our national culture. While we have overruled our precedents when subsequent cases have undermined their doctrinal underpinnings, we do not believe that this has happened to the *Miranda* decision. If anything, our subsequent cases have reduced the impact of the *Miranda* rule on legitimate law enforcement while reaffirming the decision's core ruling that unwarned statements may not be used as evidence in the prosecution's case in chief.

The disadvantage of the *Miranda* rule is that statements which may be by no means involuntary, made by a defendant who is aware of his "rights," may nonetheless be excluded and a guilty defendant go free as a result. But experience suggests that the totality-of-the-circumstances test which § 3501 seeks to revive is more difficult than *Miranda* for law enforcement officers to conform to, and for courts to apply in a consistent manner.

At the same time, the Court under Chief Justice Rehnquist has refused to further expand the rights of the accused and has generally sided with law enforcement officials. Many of the highest appellate courts of the states, however, have continued to chart new and innovative paths in this and other areas of civil liberties and civil rights by invoking the authority of Bill of Rights provisions contained in their own state constitutions.

Renewed enthusiasm for the death penalty in capital crimes was one response to the crime wave of the 1960s and early 1970s. Historically, that penalty had fallen most often on blacks and poor persons, a finding that raised serious questions about whether the law was being equally applied. The NAACP Legal Defense Fund challenged a host of state laws mandating the death penalty for crimes ranging from rape to murder. They were joined by other critics, notably the ACLU, that argued that capital punishment was contrary to the prohibition against "cruel and unusual" punishment contained in the Eighth Amendment. In *Furman* v. *Georgia* (1972), the closely divided justices held that the Georgia death penalty was unconstitutional because it was capriciously imposed, but only two of the justices found that it violated per se the Eighth Amendment. In the wake of *Furman,* the vast majority of states redrew their death penalty statutes to make them comply with the Court's direction that they be rationally applied. Amid strong public support for capital punishment, Justice Potter Stewart, in *Gregg* v. *Georgia* (1976), announced the Court's new position upholding the revised Georgia statute.

Note: Surge in Incarceration

Reflecting public support for a get-tough approach to crime, the number of inmates held in federal and state prisons has surged since the 1970s. By 2002 the nation's prison and jail population exceeded 2 million inmates. In fact, the United States had the highest incarceration rate in the world. The Federal Bureau of Prisons operated the largest prison system, followed by the states of California and Texas. The characteristics of prison and jail inmates are also noteworthy. Men are far more likely to be incarcerated than women. Black and Hispanic males are imprisoned at a higher rate than other groups.

SCIENCE AND LAW

Law and science have become closely linked, and scientific knowledge often informs legal decision making. Reliance on scientific knowledge poses a fundamental question as to how far legal norms should be shaped by the views of scientists. The steady advance of scientific research has raised novel and difficult issues that implicate a number of areas of law, including criminal justice, torts, environmental regulation, and family relations. Yet law is often slow to react to the rapid advance of science and to fashion rules that minimize risk of abuse. A recurring theme in this section is how the legal system responds to and is molded by science.

The use of scientific evidence in the legal system has been a source of continuing debate. For example, in the important case of *Daubert* v. *Merrell Dow Pharmaceuticals, Inc.,* 509 U.S. 579 (1993), the United States Supreme Court addressed the question of the admissibility of expert scientific evidence in civil trials. Two minor children and their parents alleged that the children's serious birth defects had been caused by the mothers' prenatal ingestion of Bendectin, a prescription drug marketed by Merrell Dow Pharmaceuticals. A federal district court granted summary judgment to Merrell Dow based on a well-credentialed expert's affidavit concluding, upon reviewing the extensive published scientific literature on the subject, that maternal use of Bendectin has not been shown to be a risk factor for human birth defects. Daubert had responded with the testimony of eight well-credentialed experts who concluded, based on animal studies and previously published human statistical studies, that Bendectin can cause birth defects. The Supreme Court, however, found in favor of Merrell Dow and sustained the principle that expert opinion based on a scientific technique is inadmissible unless the technique is "generally accepted" as reliable in the relevant scientific community. In light of the growing use of science in the courtroom, this decision has broad ramifications for the future of the legal system.

DEFINITION OF DEATH

In re Quinlan
70 N.J. 10, 355 A.2d 647 (1976)

The ability of medical science to continue respiration by artificial means has obfuscated the traditional definition of death. Some of the legal issues raised by this development were explored in the tragic case of Karen Quinlan. Suffering severe brain damage, Quinlan lapsed into a chronic vegetative state and survived only with the assistance of a respirator. There was no treatment that could improve her condition. Under these circumstances, Quinlan's father sought appointment as guardian with the express power to authorize the discontinuance of medical procedures sustaining her life. Asserting its interest in the preservation of life according to prevailing medical standards, the state challenged the grant of such au-

thorization. Chief Justice Richard J. Hughes ruled that the constitutional right of privacy encompassed the right to terminate medical treatment, and addressed the relationship between law and the professional judgment of doctors.

It is the issue of the constitutional right of privacy that has given us most concern, in the exceptional circumstances of this case. Here a loving parent, *qua* parent and raising the rights of his incompetent and profoundly damaged daughter, probably irreversibly doomed to no more than a biologically vegetative remnant of life, is before the court. He seeks authorization to abandon specialized technological procedures which can only maintain for a time a body having no potential for resumption or continuance of other than a "vegetative" existence.

We have no doubt, in these unhappy circumstances, that if Karen were herself miraculously lucid for an interval (not altering the existing prognosis of the condition to which she would soon return) and perceptive of her irreversible condition, she could effectively decide upon discontinuance of the life support apparatus, even if it meant the prospect of natural death. To this extent we may distinguish Heston, supra, which concerned a severely injured woman (Delores Heston), whose life depended on surgery and blood transfusion; and who was in such extreme shock that she was unable to express an informed choice (although the Court apparently considered the case as if the patient's own religious decision to resist transfusion were at stake), but most importantly a patient apparently salvable to long life and vibrant health;—a situation not at all like the present case.

We have no hesitancy in deciding, in the instant diametrically opposite case, that no external compelling interest of the State could compel Karen to endure the unendurable, only to vegetate a few measurable months with no realistic possibility of returning to any semblance of cognitive or sapient life. We perceive no thread of logic distinguishing between such a choice on Karen's part and a similar choice which, under the evidence in this case, could be made by a competent patient terminally ill, riddled by cancer and suffering great pain; such a patient would not be resuscitated or put on a respirator . . . , and a fortiori would not be kept against his will on a respirator.

◆　◆　◆

The claimed interests of the State in this case are essentially the preservation and sanctity of human life and defense of the right of the physician to administer medical treatment according to his best judgment. In this case the doctors say that removing Karen from the respirator will conflict with their professional judgment. The plaintiff answers that Karen's present treatment serves only a maintenance function; that the respirator cannot cure or improve her condition but at best can only prolong her inevitable slow deterioration and death; and that the interests of the patient, as seen by her surrogate, the guardian, must be evaluated by the court as predominant, even in the face of an opinion *contra* by the present attending physicians. Plaintiff's distinction is significant. The nature of Karen's care and the realistic chances of her recovery are quite unlike those of the patients discussed in many of the cases where treatments were ordered. In many of those cases the medical procedure required (usually a transfusion) constituted a minimal bodily invasion and the chances of recovery and return to functioning life were very good. We think that the State's interest *contra* weakens and the individual's right to privacy grows as the degree of bodily invasion increases and the prognosis dims. Ultimately there comes a point at which the individual's rights overcome the State interest. It is for that reason that we believe Karen's choice, if she were competent to make it, would be vindicated by the law. Her prognosis is extremely poor,—she will never resume cognitive life. And the bodily invasion is very great,—she requires 24 hour intensive nursing care, antibiotics, the assistance of a respirator, a catheter and feeding tube.

Our affirmation of Karen's independent right of choice, however, would ordinarily be based upon her competency to assert it. The sad truth, however, is that she is grossly incompetent and we cannot discern her supposed choice based on the testimony of her previous conversations with friends, where such testimony is without sufficient probative weight. Nevertheless we have concluded that Karen's right of privacy may be asserted on her behalf by her guardian under the peculiar circumstances here present.

If a putative decision by Karen to permit this non-cognitive, vegetative existence to terminate by natural forces is regarded as a valuable incident of her right of privacy, as we believe it to be, then it should not be discarded solely on the basis that her condition prevents her conscious exercise of the choice. The only practical way to prevent destruction of the right is to permit the guardian and family of Karen to render their best judgment, subject to the qualifications hereinafter stated, as to whether she would exercise it in these circumstances. If their conclusion is in the affirmative this decision should be accepted by a society the overwhelming majority of whose members would, we think, in similar circumstances, exercise such a choice in the same way for themselves or for those closest to them. It is for this reason that we determine that Karen's right of privacy may be asserted in her behalf, in this respect, by her guardian and family under the particular circumstances presented by this record.

◆ ◆ ◆

IV. THE MEDICAL FACTOR

Having declared the substantive legal basis upon which plaintiff's rights as representative of Karen must be deemed predicated, we face and respond to the assertion on behalf of defendants that our premise unwarrantably offends prevailing medical standards. We thus turn to consideration of the medical decision supporting the determination made below, conscious of the paucity of pre-existing legislative and judicial guidance as to the rights and liabilities therein involved.

A significant problem in any discussion of sensitive medical-legal issues is the marked, perhaps unconscious, tendency of many to distort what the law is, in pursuit of an exposition of what they would like the law to be. Nowhere is this barrier to the intelligent resolution of legal controversies more obstructive than in the debate over patient rights at the end of life. Judicial refusals to order lifesaving treatment in the face of contrary claims of bodily self-determination or free religious exercise are too often cited in support of a preconceived "right to die," even though the patients, wanting to live, have claimed no such right. Conversely, the assertion of a religious or other objection to lifesaving treatment is at times condemned as attempted suicide, even though suicide means something quite different in the law. (Byrn, "Compulsory Lifesaving Treatment for the Competent Adult," 44 *Fordham L. Rev.* 1 [1975]).

Perhaps the confusion there adverted to stems from mention by some courts of statutory or common law condemnation of suicide as demonstrating the state's interest in the preservation of life. We would see, however, a real distinction between the self-infliction of deadly harm and a self-determination against artificial life support or radical surgery, for instance, in the face of irreversible, painful and certain imminent death. The contrasting situations mentioned are analogous to those continually faced by the medical profession. When does the institution of life-sustaining procedures, ordinarily mandatory, become the subject of medical discretion in the context of administration to persons In extremis? And when does the withdrawal of such procedures, from such persons already supported by them, come within the orbit of medical discretion? When does a determination as to either of the foregoing contingencies court the hazard of civil or criminal liability on the part of the physician or institution involved?

The existence and nature of the medical dilemma need hardly be discussed at length, portrayed as it is in the present case and complicated as it has recently come to be in view of the dramatic advance of medical technology. The dilemma is there, it is real, it is constantly resolved in accepted medical practice without attention in the courts, it pervades the issues in the very case we here examine.

♦ ♦ ♦

Such notions as to the distribution of responsibility, heretofore generally entertained, should however neither impede this Court in deciding matters clearly justifiable nor preclude a reexamination by the Court as to underlying human values and rights. Determinations as to these must, in the ultimate, be responsive not only to the concepts of medicine but also to the common moral judgment of the community at large. In the latter respect the Court has a nondelegable judicial responsibility.

Put in another way, the law, equity and justice must not themselves quail and be helpless in the face of modern technological marvels presenting questions hitherto unthought of. Where a Karen Quinlan, or a parent, or a doctor, or a hospital, or a State seeks the process and response of a court, it must answer with its most informed conception of justice in the previously unexplored circumstances presented to it. That is its obligation and we are here fulfilling it, for the actors and those having an interest in the matter should not go without remedy.

Courts in the exercise of their *parens patriae* responsibility to protect those under disability have sometimes implemented medical decisions and authorized their carrying out under the doctrine of "substituted judgment."

♦ ♦ ♦

We glean from the record here that physicians distinguish between curing the ill and comforting and easing the dying; that they refuse to treat the curable as if they were dying or ought to die, and that they have sometimes refused to treat the hopeless and dying as if they were curable. In this sense, as we were reminded by the testimony of Drs. Korein and Diamond, many of

them have refused to inflict an undesired prolongation of the process of dying on a patient in irreversible condition when it is clear that such "therapy" offers neither human or humane benefit. We think these attitudes represent a balanced implementation of a profoundly realistic perspective on the meaning of life and death and that they respect the whole Judeo-Christian tradition of regard for human life. No less would they seem consistent with the moral matrix of medicine, "to heal," very much in the sense of the endless mission of the law, "to do justice."

Yet this balance, we feel, is particularly difficult to perceive and apply in the context of the development by advanced technology of sophisticated and artificial life-sustaining devices. For those possibly curable, such devices are of great value, and, as ordinary medical procedures, are essential. Consequently, as pointed out by Dr. Diamond, they are necessary because of the ethic of medical practice. But in light of the situation in the present case (while the record here is somewhat hazy in distinguishing between "ordinary" and "extraordinary" measures), one would have to think that the use of the same respirator or like support could be considered "ordinary" in the context of the possibly curable patient but "extraordinary" in the context of the forced sustaining by cardio-respiratory processes of an irreversibly doomed patient. And this dilemma is sharpened in the face of the malpractice and criminal action threat which we have mentioned.

♦ ♦ ♦

In summary of the present Point of this opinion, we conclude that the state of the pertinent medical standards and practices which guided the attending physicians in this matter is not such as would justify this Court in deeming itself bound or controlled thereby in responding to the case for declaratory relief established by the parties on the record before us.

Note: Right to Die

The increasing power of science to prolong the life of persons suffering from a terminal illness has sparked a vigorous debate over whether sick individuals have a constitutional right to refuse medical care and thus control the manner of their death. The Supreme Court has wrestled with this difficult question but failed to provide clear answers. In *Cruzan* v. *Director, Missouri Department of Health*, 497 U.S. 261 (1990), Chief Justice William Rehnquist, speaking for the Court, insisted that a competent person has a liberty interest, protected by the due process clause of the Fourteenth Amendment, to refuse medical treatment, such as artificial nutrition or respiration. Yet Rehnquist also determined that a state could require clear and convincing evidence of the patient's decision to cease medical treatment. This evidentiary standard might well hamper guardians in carrying out the wishes of an incompetent patient.

The Supreme Court also made clear that the right to refuse medical treatment did not support an asserted right to commit suicide. In *Washington* v. *Glucksberg*, 521 U.S. 702 (1997) it sustained the validity of a state law banning assistance in committing suicide. The Court held that the due process clause did not protect a claimed right to assisted suicide, and suggested that state legislatures were free to evaluate the emerging issue of assisted suicide and to experiment with solutions.

There has been considerable legislative action concerning the right to refuse medical treatment. A growing number of states have enacted statutes which authorize an individual to designate a health care proxy to make medical treatment decisions and carry out the patient's instructions in the event that the patient should become incompetent. Many states also recognize living wills, a document that expresses the patient's wishes with respect to life-prolonging medical procedures. Moreover, in 1994 Oregon voters enacted, through ballot initiative, a Death with Dignity Act, which legalized physician-assisted suicide for competent, terminally ill adults. When both a constitutional challenge and voter initiative to repeal it failed, the act finally went into effect in October 1997. In 2001 Attorney General John Ashcroft asserted that the use of controlled drugs to assist suicides violated the Controlled Substances Act. He authorized adverse actions against doctors who prescribed lethal drugs for terminally ill patients. Characterizing the Ashcroft directive as a move to nullify the Oregon assisted suicide law, a federal district court enjoined enforcement of the order.

SURROGATE PARENTING

In re Baby M
109 N.J. 396, 537 A.2d 1227 (1988)

New reproduction biotechnology has created both great promise and the potential for conflict. Some couples are unable to conceive a child naturally. A number of such couples have turned to alternative means of reproduction in order to have a family. Medical science has developed a process of in vitro fertilization whereby a fertilized embryo is placed in the wife's womb for gestation. This technique has also made possible surrogate parenting. Under such an arrangement, a woman, acting as surrogate, would be artificially implanted with an egg fertilized by a sperm donor, commonly another woman's husband. The surrogate mother would carry the child to term and after delivery relinquish all parental rights to the natural father, who was the sperm donor. The wife of the biological father might then adopt the child.

Surrogacy arrangements, however, can give rise to unfortunate human situations and unprecedented legal questions. In Baby M *a husband entered into a surrogacy contract with a woman recommended by an infertility clinic. Following artificial insemination the woman became pregnant and gave birth to a baby girl. When the surrogate mother refused to relinquish the child, the husband brought suit to enforce the contract. After a sweeping review of surrogacy arrangements, Chief Justice Robert N. Wilentz invalidated the contract as contrary to public policy and affirmed the surrogate's status as the mother of the child.*

This is the sale of a child, or, at the very least, the sale of a mother's right to her child, the only mitigating factor being that one of the purchasers is the father. Almost every evil that prompted the prohibition on the payment of money in connection with adoptions exists here.

The differences between adoption and a surrogacy contract should be noted, since it is asserted that the use of money in connection with surrogacy does not pose the risks found where money buys adoption.

First, and perhaps most important, all parties concede that it is unlikely that surrogacy will survive without money. Despite the alleged selfless motivation of surrogate mothers, if there is no payment, there will be no surrogates, or very few. That conclusion contrasts with adoption; for obvious reasons, there remains a steady supply, albeit insufficient, despite the prohibitions against payment. The adoption itself, relieving the natural mother of the financial burden of supporting an infant, is in some sense the equivalent of payment.

Second, the use of money in adoptions does not produce the problem—conception occurs, and usually the birth itself, before illicit funds are offered. With surrogacy, the "problem," if one views it as such, consisting of the purchase of a woman's procreative capacity, at the risk of her life, is caused by and originates with the offer of money.

Third, with the law prohibiting the use of money in connection with adoptions, the built-in financial pressure of the unwanted pregnancy and the consequent support obligation do not lead the mother to the highest paying, ill-suited, adoptive parents. She is just as well-off surrendering the child to an approved agency. In surrogacy, the highest bidders will presumably become the adoptive parents regardless of suitability, so long as payment of money is permitted.

Fourth, the mother's consent to surrender her child in adoptions is revocable, even after surrender of the child, unless it be to an approved agency, where by regulation there are protections against an ill-advised surrender. In surrogacy, consent occurs so early that no amount of advice would satisfy the potential mother's need, yet the consent is irrevocable.

The main difference, that the unwanted pregnancy is unintended while the situation of the surrogate mother is voluntary and intended, is really not significant. Initially, it produces stronger reactions of sympathy for the mother whose pregnancy was unwanted than for the surrogate mother, who "went into this with her eyes wide open." On reflection, however, it appears that the essential evil is the same, taking advantage of a woman's circumstances (the unwanted pregnancy or the need for money) in order to take away her child, the difference being one of degree.

In the scheme contemplated by the surrogacy contract in this case, a middle man, propelled by profit, promotes the sale. Whatever idealism may have motivated any of the participants, the profit motive predominates, permeates, and ultimately governs the transaction. The demand for children is great and the supply small. The availability of contraception, abortion, and the greater willingness of single mothers to bring up their children has led to a shortage of babies offered for adoption. The situation is ripe for the entry of the middleman who will bring some equilibrium into the market by increasing the supply through the use of money.

Intimated, but disputed, is the assertion that surrogacy will be used for the benefit of the rich at the expense of the poor. . . . Nevertheless, it is clear to us that it is unlikely that surrogate mothers will be as proportionately numerous among those women in the top twenty percent income bracket as among those in the bottom twenty percent. Put differently, we doubt that infertile couples in the low-income bracket will find upper income surrogates.

♦ ♦ ♦

The point is made that [the surrogate mother] agreed to the surrogacy arrangement, supposedly fully understanding the consequences. Putting aside the issue of how compelling her need for money may have been, and how significant her understanding of the consequences, we suggest that her consent is irrelevant. There are, in a civilized society, some things that money cannot buy. In America, we decided long ago that merely because conduct purchased by money was "voluntary" did not mean that it was good or beyond regulation and prohibition.

♦ ♦ ♦

There are, in short, values that society deems more important than granting to wealth whatever it can buy, be it labor, love, or life. Whether this principle recommends prohibition of surrogacy, which presumably sometimes results in great satisfaction to all of the parties, is not for us to say. We note here only that, under existing law, the fact that [the surrogate mother] "agreed" to the arrangement is not dispositive.

The long-term effects of surrogacy contracts are not known, but feared—the impact on the child who learns her life was bought, that she is the offspring of someone who gave birth to her only to obtain money; the impact on the natural mother as the full weight of her isolation is felt along with the full reality of the sale of her body and her child; the impact on the natural father and adoptive mother once they realize the consequences of their conduct. Literature in related areas suggests these are substantial considerations, although, given the newness of surrogacy, there is little information.

The surrogacy contract is based on principles that are directly contrary to the objectives of our laws. It guarantees the separation of a child from its mother; it looks to adoption regardless of suitability; it totally ignores the child; it takes the child from the mother regardless of her wishes and her maternal fitness; and it does all of this, it accomplishes all of its goals, through the use of money.

♦ ♦ ♦

Beyond that is the potential degradation of some women that may result from this arrangement. In many cases, of course, surrogacy may bring satisfaction, not only to the infertile couple, but to the surrogate mother herself. The fact, however, that many women may not perceive surrogacy negatively but rather see it as an opportunity does not diminish its potential for devastation to other women.

In sum, the harmful consequences of this surrogacy arrangement appear to us all too palpable. In New Jersey the surrogate mother's agreement to sell her child is void. Its irrevocability infects the entire contract, as does the money that purports to buy it.

THE CHALLENGE OF DNA

DNA, the common abbreviation for deoxyribonucleic acid, is the genetic material present in the cells of all living organisms. No two people have the same DNA. The emergence of DNA profiling has dramatically impacted the administration of criminal justice. DNA testing can determine whether biological matter, such as blood, saliva, skin cells, or semen left at the scene of a crime, match the DNA collected from a particular suspect. Such DNA samples can also be compared with that of persons in growing data banks. Given its high degree of reliability, DNA profiling has become both an investigative tool and a compelling type of forensic evidence. It is routinely admitted in criminal trials. The importance of scientific evidence in criminal cases will likely grow in the future, prompting calls for improved laboratory facilities to handle DNA testing and evaluation. Some have even proposed creation of a national data bank to improve the criminal justice system. It has also been suggested that the federal government should be empowered to collect DNA samples by reasonably necessary means from suspected terrorists.

DNA testing has also raised troublesome questions about the adequacy of trial procedures and other forms of evidence, particularly eyewitness identification. An increasing number of convicted felons have been exonerated as the result of postconviction DNA tests. The number of death sentences overturned on the basis of DNA reports has intensified the debate over capital punishment. Concerned that thirteen death penalty sentences had been overturned in Illinois since 1977 after the condemned were found innocent and pointing out that some of these exonerations were based on DNA, Governor George Ryan in January 2003 commuted the sentences of all death row inmates in that state.

SCIENCE AND ENVIRONMENTAL LAW

TVA v. Hill
437 U.S. 153 (1978)

Scientific research is essential to the development and implementation of environmental regulations. Yet the reliability of scientific findings is often in doubt. There have even been allegations of political manipulation of scientific research to reach predetermined conclusions. One recurring problem is the formulation of regulations based on limited and uncertain data.

In 1973 Congress passed the Endangered Species Act, the most significant piece of legislation for protecting biodiversity. Some of the issues posed by this law were addressed in the leading case of TVA v. Hill *in which the Supreme Court affirmed the broad safeguards that this measure affords to endangered or threatened species. Note that the justices refused to weigh the costs and benefits of halting the dam project.*

Mr. Chief Justice Burger delivered the opinion of the Court.

The questions presented in this case are (a) whether the Endangered Species Act of 1973 requires a court to enjoin the operation of a virtually completed federal dam—which had been authorized prior to 1973—when, pursuant to authority vested in him by Congress, the Secretary of the Interior has determined that operation of the dam would eradicate an endangered species; and (b) whether continued congressional appropriations for the dam after 1973 constituted an implied repeal of the Endangered Species Act, at least as to the particular dam.

♦ ♦ ♦

In this area of the Little Tennessee River the Tennessee Valley Authority, a wholly owned public corporation of the United States, began constructing the Tellico Dam and Reservoir Project in 1967, shortly after Congress appropriated initial funds for its development. Tellico is a multipurpose regional development project designed principally to stimulate shoreline development, generate sufficient electric current to heat 20,000 homes, and provide flatwater recreation and flood control, as well as improve economic conditions in "an area characterized by underutilization of human resources and outmigration of young people." Of particular relevance to this case is one aspect of the project, a dam which TVA determined to place on the Little Tennessee, a short distance from where the river's waters meet with the Big Tennessee. When fully operational, the dam would impound water covering some 16,500 acres—much of which represents valuable and productive farmland—thereby converting the river's shallow, fast-flowing waters into a deep reservoir over 30 miles in length.

The Tellico Dam has never opened, however, despite the fact that construction has been virtually completed and the dam is essentially ready for operation. Although Congress has appropriated monies for Tellico every year since 1967, progress was delayed, and ultimately stopped, by a tangle of lawsuits and administrative proceedings. After unsuccessfully urging TVA to consider alternatives to damming the Little Tennessee, local citizens and national conservation groups brought suit in the District Court, claiming that the project did not conform to the requirements of the National Environmental Policy Act of 1969 (NEPA). After finding TVA to be in violation of NEPA, the District Court enjoined the dam's completion pending the filing of an appropriate environmental impact statement. The injunction remained in effect until late 1973, when the District Court concluded that TVA's final environmental impact statement for Tellico was in compliance with the law.

A few months prior to the District Court's decision dissolving the NEPA injunction, a discovery was made in the waters of the Little Tennessee which would profoundly affect the Tellico Project. Exploring the area around Coytee Springs, which is about seven miles from the mouth of the river, a University of Tennessee ichthyologist, Dr. David A. Etnier, found a previously unknown species of perch, the snail darter, or *Percina (Imostoma) tanasi*. This three-inch, tannish-colored fish, whose numbers are estimated to be in the range of 10,000 to 15,000, would soon engage the attention of environmentalists, the TVA, the Department of the Interior, the Congress of the United States, and ultimately the federal courts, as a new and additional basis to halt construction of the dam.

Until recently the finding of a new species of animal life would hardly generate a cause

célèbre. This is particularly so in the case of darters, of which there are approximately 130 known species, 8 to 10 of these having been identified only in the last five years. The moving force behind the snail darter's sudden fame came some four months after its discovery, when the Congress passed the Endangered Species Act of 1973. This legislation, among other things, authorizes the Secretary of the Interior to declare species of animal life "endangered" and to identify the "critical habitat" of these creatures.

◆ ◆ ◆

In January 1975, the respondents in this case and others petitioned the Secretary of the Interior to list the snail darter as an endangered species. After receiving comments from various interested parties, including TVA and the State of Tennessee, the Secretary formally listed the snail darter as an endangered species on October 8, 1975. In so acting, it was noted that "the snail darter is a living entity which is genetically distinct and reproductively isolated from other fishes." More important for the purposes of this case, the Secretary determined that the snail darter apparently lives only in that portion of the Little Tennessee River which would be completely inundated by the reservoir created as a consequence of the Tellico Dam's completion. The Secretary went on to explain the significance of the dam to the habitat of the snail darter:

> [T]he snail darter occurs only in the swifter portions of shoals over clean gravel substrate in cool, low-turbidity water. Food of the snail darter is almost exclusively snails which require a clean gravel substrate for their survival. *The proposed impoundment of water behind the proposed Tellico Dam would result in total destruction of the snail darter's habitat.* Ibid. (emphasis added).

Subsequent to this determination, the Secretary declared the area of the Little Tennessee which would be affected by the Tellico Dam to be the "critical habitat" of the snail darter. Using these determinations as a predicate, and notwithstanding the near completion of the dam, the

Secretary declared that pursuant to § 7 of the Act, "all Federal agencies must take such action as is necessary to insure that actions authorized, funded, or carried out by them do not result in the destruction or modification of this critical habitat area." This notice, of course, was pointedly directed at TVA and clearly aimed at halting completion or operation of the dam.

◆ ◆ ◆

In February 1976, pursuant to § 11 (g) of the Endangered Species Act, respondents filed the case now under review, seeking to enjoin completion of the dam and impoundment of the reservoir on the ground that those actions would violate the Act by directly causing the extinction of the species *Percina (Imostoma) tanasi*. The District Court denied respondents' request for a preliminary injunction and set the matter for trial.

◆ ◆ ◆

Trial was held in the District Court on April 29 and 30, 1976, and on May 25, 1976, the court entered its memorandum opinion and order denying respondents their requested relief and dismissing the complaint. The District Court found that closure of the dam and the consequent impoundment of the reservoir would "result in the adverse modification, if not complete destruction, of the snail darter's critical habitat," making it "highly probably" that "the continued existence of the snail darter" would be "jeopardize[d]." Despite these findings, the District Court declined to embrace the plaintiffs' position on the merits: that once a federal project was shown to jeopardize an endangered species, a court of equity is compelled to issue an injunction restraining violation of the Endangered Species Act.

In reaching this result, the District Court stressed that the entire project was then about 80% complete and, based on available evidence, "there [were] no alternatives to impoundment of the reservoir, short of scrapping the entire project."

◆ ◆ ◆

Thereafter, in the Court of Appeals, respondents argued that the District Court had

abused its discretion by not issuing an injunction in the face of "a blatant statutory violation." The Court of Appeals agreed, and on January 31, 1977, it reversed remanding "with instructions that a permanent injunction issue halting all activities incident to the Tellico Project which may destroy or modify the critical habitat of the snail darter." The Court of Appeals directed that the injunction "remain in effect until Congress, by appropriate legislation, exempts Tellico from compliance with the Act or the snail darter has been deleted from the list of endangered species or its critical habitat materially redefined."

◆ ◆ ◆

One would be hard pressed to find a statutory provision whose terms were any plainer than those in § 7 of the Endangered Species Act. Its very words affirmatively command all federal agencies "to *insure* that actions *authorized, funded,* or *carried out* by them do not *jeopardize* the continued existence" of an endangered species or "*result* in the destruction or modification of habitat of such species . . . " (emphasis added). This language admits of no exception. Nonetheless, petitioner urges, as do the dissenters, that the Act cannot reasonably be interpreted as applying to a federal project which was well under way when Congress passed the Endangered Species Act of 1973. To sustain that position, however, we would be forced to ignore the ordinary meaning of plain language. It has not been shown, for example, how TVA can close the gates of the Tellico Dam without "carrying out" an action that has been "authorized" and "funded" by a federal agency. Nor can we understand how such action will "insure" that the snail darter's habitat is not disrupted. Accepting the Secretary's determinations, as we must, it is clear that TVA's proposed operation of the dam will have precisely the opposite effect, namely the *eradication* of an endangered species.

Concededly, this view of the Act will produce results requiring the sacrifice of the anticipated benefits of the project and of many millions of dollars in public funds. But examination of the language, history, and structure of the legislation under review here indicates beyond doubt that Congress intended endangered species to be afforded the highest of priorities.

♦ ♦ ♦

The legislative proceedings in 1973 are, in fact, replete with expressions of concern over the risk that might lie in the loss of *any* endangered species.

♦ ♦ ♦

The plain intent of Congress in enacting this statute was to halt and reverse the trend toward species extinction, whatever the cost. This is reflected not only in the stated policies of the Act, but in literally every section of the statute. All persons, including federal agencies, are specifically instructed not to "take" endangered species, meaning that no one is "to harass, harm, pursue, hunt, shoot, wound, kill, trap, capture, or collect" such life forms. Agencies in particular are directed by §§ 2 (c) and 3(2) of the Act to "use . . . *all methods* and procedures which are necessary" to preserve endangered species (emphasis added). In addition, the legislative history undergirding § 7 reveals an explicit congressional decision to require agencies to afford first priority to the declared national policy of saving endangered species. The pointed omission of the type of qualifying language previously included in endangered species legislation reveals a conscious decision by Congress to give endangered species priority over the "primary missions" of federal agencies.

♦ ♦ ♦

One might dispute the applicability of these examples to the Tellico Dam by saying that in this case the burden on the public through the loss of millions of unrecoverable dollars would greatly outweigh the loss of the snail darter. But neither the Endangered Species Act nor Art. III of the Constitution provides federal courts with authority to make such fine utilitarian calculations. On the contrary, the plain language of the Act, buttressed by its legislative history, shows clearly that Congress viewed the value of endangered species as "incalculable." Quite obviously, it would be difficult for a court to balance the loss of a sum

certain—even $100 million—against a congressionally declared "incalculable" value, even assuming we had the power to engage in such a weighing process, which we emphatically do not.

♦ ♦ ♦

Having determined that there is an irreconcilable conflict between operation of the Tellico Dam and the explicit provisions of § 7 of the Endangered Species Act, we must now consider what remedy, if any, is appropriate. It is correct, of course, that a federal judge sitting as a chancellor is not mechanically obligated to grant an injunction for every violation of law. This Court made plain in *Hecht Co.* v. *Bowles*, 321 U.S. 321, 329 (1944), that "[a] grant of *jurisdiction* to issue compliance orders hardly suggests and absolute duty to do so under any and all circumstances." As a general matter it may be said that "[s]ince all or almost all equitable remedies are discretionary, the balancing of equities and hardships is appropriate in almost any case as a guide to the chancellor's discretion." D. Dobbs, Remedies 52 (1973).

♦ ♦ ♦

But these principles take a court only so far. Our system of government is, after all, a tripartite one, with each branch having certain defined functions delegated to it by the Constitution. While "[i]t is emphatically the province and duty of the judicial department to say what the law is," *Marbury* v. *Madison,* 1 Cranch 137, 177 (1803), it is equally—and emphatically— the exclusive province of the Congress not only to formulate legislative policies and mandate programs and projects, but also to establish their relative priority for the Nation. Once Congress, exercising its delegated powers, has decided the order of priorities in a given area, it is for the Executive to administer the laws and for the courts to enforce them when enforcement is sought.

Here we are urged to view the Endangered Species Act "reasonably," and hence shape a remedy "that accords with some modicum of common sense and the public weal." *Post,* at 196. But is that our function? We have no expert knowledge on the subject of endangered species, much less do we have a mandate from the people to strike a balance of equities on the side of the Tellico Dam. Congress has spoken in the plainest of words, making it abundantly clear that the balance has been struck in favor of affording endangered species the highest of priorities, thereby adopting a policy which it described as "institutionalize caution."

Our individual appraisal of the wisdom or unwisdom of a particular course consciously selected by the Congress is to be put aside in the process of interpreting a statute. Once the meaning of an enactment is discerned and its constitutionality determined, the judicial process comes to an end. We do not sit as a committee of review, nor are we vested with the power of veto.

Note: The Fate of *Hill*

Following the Supreme Court's decision, Congress in 1979 expressly authorized completion of the Tellico Dam by exempting the project from the Endangered Species Act. Congress has also exempted other projects from compliance with the act.

As the *Hill* case demonstrates, the decision to list a species as endangered is the key to the entire act. The listing of species is often hotly contested and rests ultimately on the conclusions one draws from the scientific data. As it turned out, the snail darter had other habitats and was not extinguished by eventual completion of the dam. Critics cite this result as showing the danger of triggering regulatory controls on the basis of partial or skewed findings.

CYBERSPACE

The emergence of the Internet has greatly enlarged opportunities for communications. This new technology has also given rise to a host of novel issues pertaining to intellectual property, freedom of expression, control of obscenity available to minors, invasion of privacy, and computer crime. The Internet has facilitated the creation of new types of intellectual property and presented novel difficulties in enforcing the laws designed to protect such property. Rules that evolved to deal with more traditional modes of communication may not be sufficient to handle the challenge of cyberspace. As the Supreme Court of California has observed, "The so-called Internet revolution has spawned a host of new legal issues as courts struggle to apply traditional legal frameworks to this new communication medium" (*Pavlovich* v. *Superior Court*, 29 Cal. 4th 262, 266 [2002]). These developments have stimulated a growing interest in cyber law.

The exercise of free speech in cyberspace has engendered a number of concerns. The amount of sexually explicit and offensive material has grown exponentially. But the Supreme Court made clear in *Reno* v. *ACLU*, 521 U.S. 844 (1997), that the First Amendment protects the right to receive information on the Internet. It struck down much of the Communications Decency Act, passed by Congress in 1996, which sought to ban posting "indecent" material on the Internet that would be available to children. A related problem has been the ability of public libraries to control access to information on their computer systems. In *United States* v. *American Library Association* (2003), the Supreme Court ruled that Congress could require libraries that receive federal funds to use computer filters that block access to pornography on the Internet.

Unsolicited commercial bulk e-mail, popularly known as spam, has grown rapidly and proven costly to business. Spamming has been both the target of litigation and the subject of legislation. In 2003 Congress, hoping to stem the tide of spam, enacted legislation imposing civil and criminal penalties on Internet marketers who ignore consumer requests to stop spamming. Moreover, owners of computer systems insist that they have a right to prevent others from using their property.

Intel v. Hamidi
30 Cal.4th 1342, 71 P.3d 296 (2003)

Unwanted noncommercial use of the Internet has presented vexing questions. In this case Intel brought suit to enjoin a disgruntled former employee from sending mass distribution e-mails to Intel employees over its computer network. The company invoked the common-law doctrine of trespass to chattels, which allows redress for interference with the possession of personal property. A splintered California Supreme Court, in an opinion by Chief Justice Ronald M. George, refused to grant the requested injunction. The various opinions focus on the application of common-law tort principles, but implicit in the discussion is the underlying need to balance the rights of free speech and property ownership.

Intel Corporation (Intel) maintains an electronic mail system, connected to the Internet, through which messages between employees and those outside the company can be sent and received, and permits its employees to make reasonable nonbusiness use of this system. On six occasions over almost two years, Kourosh Kenneth Hamidi, a former Intel employee, sent e-mails criticizing Intel's employment practices to numerous current employees on Intel's electronic mail system. Hamidi breached no computer security barriers in order to communicate with Intel employees. He offered to, and did, remove from his mailing list any recipient who so wished. Hamidi's communications to individual Intel employees caused neither physical damage nor functional disruption to the company's computers, not did they at any time deprive Intel the use of its computers. The contents of the messages, however, caused discussion among employees and managers.

On these facts, Intel brought suit, claiming that by communicating with its employees over the company's e-mail system Hamidi committed the tort of trespass to chattels. The trial court granted Intel's motion for summary judgment and enjoined Hamidi from any further mailings. A divided Court of Appeal affirmed.

After reviewing the decisions analyzing unauthorized electronic contact with computer systems as potential trespasses to chattels, we conclude that under California law the tort does not encompass, and should not be extended to encompass, an electronic communication that neither damages the recipient computer system nor impairs its functioning. Such an electronic communication does not constitute an actionable trespass to personal property, i.e., the computer system, because it does not interfere with the possessor's use or possession of, or any other legally protected interest in, the personal property itself. The consequential economic damage Intel claims to have suffered, i.e., loss of productivity caused by employees reading and reacting to Hamidi's messages and company efforts to block the messages, is not an injury to the company's interest in its computers—which worked as intended and were unharmed by the communications—any more than the personal distress caused by reading an unpleasant letter would be an injury to the recipient's mailbox, or the loss of privacy caused by an intrusive telephone call would be an injury to the recipient's telephone equipment.

Our conclusion does not rest on any special immunity for communications by electronic mail; we do not hold that messages transmitted through the Internet are exempt from the ordinary rules of tort liability. To the contrary, e-mail, like other forms of communication, may in some circumstances cause legally cognizable injury to the recipient or to third parties and may be actionable under various common law or statutory theories. Indeed, on facts somewhat similar to those here, a company or its employees might be able to plead causes of action for interference with prospective economic relations, interference with contract, or intentional infliction of emotional distress. And, of course, as with any other means of publication, third party subjects of e-mail communications may under appropriate facts make claims for defamation, publication of private facts, or other speech-based torts. Intel's claim fails not because e-mail transmitted through the Internet enjoys unique immunity, but because the trespass to chattels tort—unlike the causes of action just mentioned—may not, in California, be proved without evidence of an injury to the plaintiff's personal property or legal interest therein.

Nor does our holding affect the legal remedies of Internet service providers (ISP's) against senders of unsolicited commercial bulk e-mail (UCE), also known as "spam." A series of federal district court decisions, has approved the use of trespass to chattels as a theory of spammers' liability to ISP's, based upon evidence that the vast quantities of mail sent by spammers both overburdened the ISP's own computers and made the entire computer system harder to use for recipients, the ISP's customers. In those cases, discussed in greater detail below, the underlying complaint was that the extraordinary *quantity* of UCE impaired the computer system's functioning. In the present case, the claimed injury is located in the disruption or distraction caused to recipients by the *contents* of the e-mail messages, an injury entirely separate from, and not directly affecting, the possession or value of personal property.

FACTUAL AND PROCEDURAL BACKGROUND

◆　◆　◆

Hamidi, a former Intel engineer, together with others, formed an organization named Former and Current Employees of Intel (FACE-Intel) to disseminate information and views critical of Intel's employment and personnel policies and practices. FACE-Intel maintained a Web site (which identified Hamidi as Webmaster and as the organization's spokesperson) containing such material. In addition, over a 21-month period Hamidi, on behalf of FACE-Intel, sent six mass e-mails to employee addresses on Intel's electronic mail system. The messages criticized Intel's employment practices, warned employees of the dangers those practices posed to their careers, suggested employees consider moving to other companies, solicited employees' participation in FACE-Intel, and urged employees to inform themselves further by visiting FACE-Intel's Web site. The messages stated that recipients could, by notifying the sender of their wishes, be removed from FACE-Intel's mailing list; Hamidi did not subsequently send messages to anyone who requested removal.

Each message was sent to thousands of addresses (as many as 35,000 according to FACE-Intel's Web site), though some messages were blocked by Intel before reaching employees. Intel's attempt to block internal transmission of the messages succeeded only in part; Hamidi later admitted he evaded blocking efforts by using different sending computers. When Intel, in March 1998, demanded in writing that Hamidi and FACE-Intel stop sending e-mails to Intel's computer system, Hamidi asserted the organization had a right to communicate with willing Intel employees; he sent a new mass mailing in September 1998.

The summary judgment record contains no evidence Hamidi breached Intel's computer security in order to obtain the recipient addresses for his messages; indeed, internal Intel memoranda show the company's management concluded no security breach had occurred. Hamidi stated he created the recipient address list using an Intel directory on a floppy disk anonymously sent to him. Nor is there any evidence that the receipt or internal distribution of Hamidi's electronic messages damaged Intel's computer system or slowed or impaired its functioning. Intel did present uncontradicted evidence, however, that many employee recipients asked a company official to stop the messages and that staff time was consumed in attempts to block further messages from FACE-Intel. According to the FACE-Intel Web site, moreover, the messages had prompted discussions between "[e]xcited and nervous managers" and the company's human resources department.

Intel sued Hamidi and FACE-Intel, pleading causes of action for trespass to chattels and nuisance, and seeking both actual damages and an injunction against further e-mail messages. Intel later voluntarily dismissed its nuisance claim and waived its demand for damages. The trial court entered default against FACE-Intel upon that organization's failure to answer. The court then granted Intel's motion for summary judgment, permanently enjoining Hamidi, FACE-Intel, and their agents "from sending unsolicited e-mail to addresses on Intel's computer systems." Hamidi appealed; FACE-Intel did not.

The Court of Appeal, with one justice dissenting, affirmed the grant of injunctive relief. The majority took the view that the use of or intermeddling with another's personal property is actionable as a trespass to chattels without proof of any actual injury to the personal property; even if Intel could not show any damages resulting from Hamidi's sending of messages, "it showed he was disrupting its business by using its property and therefore is entitled to injunctive relief based on a theory of trespass to chattels." The dissenting justice warned that the majority's application of the trespass to chattels tort to "unsolicited electronic mail that causes no harm to the private computer system that receives it" would "expand the tort of trespass to chattel in untold ways and to unanticipated circumstances."

♦   ♦   ♦

We discuss this debate among the amici curiae and academic writers only to note its existence and contours, not to attempt its resolution. Creating an absolute property right to exclude undesired communications from one's e-mail and Web servers might help force spammers to internalize the costs they impose on ISP's and their customers. But such a property rule might also create substantial new costs, to e-mail and e-commerce users and to society generally, in lost ease and openness of communication and in lost network benefits. In light of the unresolved controversy, we would be acting rashly to adopt a rule treating computer servers as real property for purposes of trespass law.

The Legislature has already adopted detailed regulations governing UCE. (Bus. & Prof. Code, §§ 17538.4,17538.45) It may see fit in the future also to regulate noncommercial e-mail, such as that sent by Hamidi, or other kinds of unwanted contact between computers on the Internet, ... But we are not persuaded that these perceived problems call at present for judicial creation of a rigid property rule of computer server inviolability. We therefore decline to create an exception, covering Hamidi's unwanted electronic messages to Intel employees, to the general rule that a trespass to chattels is not actionable if it does not involve actual or threatened injury to the personal property or to the possessor's legally protected interest in the personal property. No such injury having been shown on the undisputed facts, Intel was not entitled to summary judgment in its favor.

Concurring Opinion by Kennard, J.

I concur.

Does a person commit the tort of trespass to chattels by making occasional personal calls to a mobile phone despite the stated objection of the person who owns the mobile phone and pays for the mobile phone service? Does it matter that the calls are not made to the mobile phone's owner, but to another person who ordinarily uses that phone? Does it matter that the person to whom the calls are made has not objected to them? Does it matter that the calls do not damage the mobile phone or reduce in any significant way its availability or usefulness?

The majority concludes, and I agree, that using another's equipment to communicate with a third person who is an authorized user of the equipment and who does not object to the communication is trespass to chattels only if the communications damage the equipment or in some significant way impair its usefulness or availability.

Intel has my sympathy. Unsolicited and unwanted bulk e-mail, most of it commercial, is a serious annoyance and inconvenience for persons who communicate electronically through the Internet, and bulk e-mail that distracts employees in the workplace can adversely affect overall productivity. But, as the majority persuasively explains, to establish the tort of trespass to chattels in California, the plaintiff must prove either damage to the plaintiff's personal property or actual or threatened impairment of the plaintiff's ability to use that property. Because plaintiff Intel has not shown that defendant Hamidi's occasional bulk e-mail messages to Intel's employees have damaged Intel's computer system or impaired its functioning in any significant way, Intel has not established the tort of trespass to chattels.

This is not to say that Intel is helpless either practically or legally. As a practical matter, Intel need only instruct its employees to delete messages from Hamidi without reading them and to notify Hamidi to remove their workplace email addresses from his mailing lists. Hamidi's messages promised to remove recipients from the mailing list on request, and there is no evidence that Hamidi has ever failed to do so. From a legal perspective, a tort theory other than trespass to chattels may provide Intel with an effective remedy if Hamidi's messages are defamatory or wrongfully interfere with Intel's economic interests. Additionally, the Legislature continues to study the problems caused by bulk e-mails and other dubious uses of modern communication technologies and may craft legislation that accommodates the competing concerns in these sensitive and highly complex areas.

Accordingly, I join the majority in reversing the Court of Appeal's judgment.

Dissenting Opinion of Brown, J.

♦ ♦ ♦

Intel has invested millions of dollars to develop and maintain a computer system. It did this not to act as a public forum but to enhance the productivity of its employees. Kourosh Kenneth Hamidi sent as many as 200,000 e-

mail messages to Intel employees. The time required to review and delete Hamidi's messages diverted employees from productive tasks and undermined the utility of the computer system. "There may . . . be situations in which the value to the owner of a particular type of chattel may be impaired by dealing with it in a manner that does not affect its physical condition." (Rest.2d Torts, § 218, com. h, p. 422.) This is such a case.

The majority repeatedly asserts that Intel objected to the hundreds of thousands of messages solely due to their content, and proposes that Intel seek relief by pleading content-based speech torts. This proposal misses the point that Intel's objection is directed not toward Hamidi's message but his use of Intel's property to display his message. Intel has not sought to prevent Hamidi from expressing his ideas on his Web site, through private mail (paper or electronic) to employees' homes, or through any other means like picketing or billboards. But as counsel for Intel explained during oral argument, the company objects to Hamidi's using Intel's property to advance his message.

Of course, Intel deserves an injunction even if its objections are based entirely on the e-mail's content. Intel is entitled, for example, to allow employees use of the Internet to check stock market tables or weather forecasts without incurring any concomitant obligation to allow access to pornographic Web sites. A private property owner may choose to exclude unwanted mail for any reason, including its content.

♦ ♦ ♦

As in those cases in which courts have granted injunctions to prevent the delivery of unwanted mail, paper or electronic, Intel is not attempting to *profit* from its trespass action by receiving nominal damages. Rather, it seeks an injunction to *prevent* further trespass. Moreover, Intel suffered the requisite injury by losing a great deal of work product, a harm properly related to the property itself, as well as the money it spent in maintaining the system, which Hamidi wrongfully expropriated.

CONCLUSION

Those who have contempt for grubby commerce and reverence for the rarified heights of intellectual discourse may applaud today's decision, but even the flow of ideas will be curtailed if the right to exclude is denied. As the Napster controversy revealed, creative individuals will be less inclined to develop intellectual property if they cannot limit the terms of its transmission. Similarly, if online newspapers cannot charge for access, they will be unable to pay the journalists and editorialists who generate ideas for public consumption.

This connection between the property right to objects and the property right to ideas and speech is not novel. James Madison observed, "a man's land, or merchandize, or money is called his property." (Madison, *Property,* Nat. Gazette (Mar. 27, 1792), reprinted in *The Papers of James Madison* (Robert A. Rutland et al. edits. 1983) p. 266.

Likewise, "a man has a property in his opinions and the free communication of them." Accordingly, "freedom of speech and property rights were seen simply as different aspects of an indivisible concept of liberty."

The principles of both personal liberty and social utility should counsel us to usher the common law of property into the digital age.

→ 10 ←

Law and the Economy
in Modern America

For decades following World War II, the liberal legal culture that emerged from the New Deal held sway and profoundly influenced both public and private law. The dominant political ideology supported the growth of a powerful regulatory state and looked for governmental solutions to economic and social problems. Federal courts broadly deferred to regulatory bodies based on their supposed expertise and experience in dealing with specialized subjects. Business enterprises came to terms with the regulatory state and sought to shape the regulatory environment to suit their ends. There remained, of course, sharp differences over the precise role of government in managing the economy and over what administrative agencies should do. Labor relations, for example, were a contested area. In 1947 Congress passed the Taft-Hartley Act, which made the National Labor Relations Board more receptive to employer concerns, over union opposition. But there was no wholesale assault on the value of regulation. Consequently, both state and federal governments steadily mushroomed in size, playing a large role in supervising nearly every aspect of the economy and pursuing the goal of full employment.

The growth of entitlement programs was another important legacy of the New Deal. For decades after World War II, the welfare state steadily expanded. Federal and state governments provided an increasingly wide array of social benefits. Some took the form of direct payments, such as Social Security, unemployment compensation, and welfare payments. Entitlements also included contracts with government, public employment, and licenses to engage in certain professions or trades. These entitlements became a major source of wealth and gave rise to a sharp debate over whether they represented property interests that should receive judicial protection.

During the tenure of Chief Justice Earl Warren (1953–1969), the Supreme Court was largely preoccupied with civil rights, the rights of criminal defendants, and civil liberties. It demonstrated little interest in the rights of property owners and consistently sustained the validity of economic regulations. In *Williamson* v. *Lee Optical Co.*, 348 U.S. 438 (1955), and *Ferguson* v. *Skrupa*, 372 U.S. 726 (1963), the Court indicated that the due process clause of the Fourteenth Amendment imposed no meaningful limit on state regulation of business enterprise. The Warren Court also favored a strong national government and gave a broad reading to congressional power. This judicial climate helped to foster the growth of the regulatory state.

In the late 1960s and early 1970s, consumer groups and advocates for the environment scored major legislative victories, which enlarged the scope of the regulatory state. The Auto Safety Act of 1966 set federal safety standards for automobiles. Congress imposed regulations on the workplace with the Occupational Safety and Health Act of 1970. In addition, Congress enacted a series of sweeping environmental measures. The National Environmental Policy Act of 1969 mandated that agency regulators consider the environmental impact of their actions. President Richard M. Nixon created the Environmental Protection Agency by executive order in 1970. Congress then strengthened the enforcement powers of the Environmental Protection Agency and required it to supervise the reduction of exhaust emissions by automobile manufacturers.

Paradoxically, support for the regulatory state began to fade even as Congress enacted new regulations. Administrative agencies were attacked from all sides. Consumer advocates, spearheaded by Ralph Nader, charged that agencies had largely become allies of regulated businesses and failed to protect the public. The business community, on the other hand, maintained that regulatory bodies imposed unworkable and costly rules, which raised the expense of goods and services. Many observers, for example, partly attributed the decline of the railroad industry in the 1950s and 1960s to a suffocating regulatory straitjacket. In the 1970s the federal courts moved away from their deferential approach and started to review administrative decision making more closely. They insisted that regulatory bodies must adhere to due process norms in deciding cases and in making rules.

By the late 1970s, a powerful deregulation movement took shape. This reassessment of the regulatory state was prompted by a rise in inflation, a decline in industrial production, and the loss of market share by U.S. companies to foreign competition. In response, Congress enacted legislation that overhauled the governance of transportation, the first industry to be heavily regulated. The Airline Deregulation Act of 1978 provided for a gradual end to fare controls and to entry barriers for new carriers. Similarly, the landmark Staggers Act of 1980 embraced deregulation as a means to revitalize the nation's railroads. It substantially eliminated rate regulation and eased entry requirements to facilitate the creation of new railroads. Congress also reduced rate controls on trucking with the Motor Carrier Reform Act of 1980. The same year Congress abolished interest rate ceilings on savings deposits.

The deregulation movement was reinforced by the election of Ronald Reagan as president in 1980. A skeptic about governmental intervention in the economy, Reagan named administrators and federal judges who shared his views. But Reagan could not bring about any fundamental change in the regulatory state. Agencies such as the Securities and Exchange Commission, the Federal Reserve Board, and the Federal Trade Commission continue to play a key role in governing the economy. Proposals to modify environmental controls aroused heated opposition and provoked Congress to enact more detailed environmental statutes. Attacks on big government and calls for further deregulation coexist uneasily with the far-ranging administrative regulations that touch many aspects of life.

In addition to the deregulation movement, other long-term trends impacted legal norms. Economic policy after 1980 stressed opportunity and growth rather than egalitarian objectives. To this end, Congress reduced income and estate taxes. Moreover, the United States economy was increasingly exposed to international competition, making it difficult to sustain the generous benefits associated with the welfare state.

There were also new currents in constitutional thought. By the 1980s the political and intellectual hegemony of the New Deal began to unravel, with significant implications for the legal culture. Conservatives charged that the Supreme Court after 1937 had inappropriately abandoned its historic role of harnessing the power of the federal government. They sought to revitalize the tenets of pre–New Deal constitutionalism—evocatively termed the "constitution in exile" by some observers—which stressed a limited federal government, state sovereignty, and respect for the rights of property owners. The Supreme Court under Chief Justice William Rehnquist (1986–) has displayed intermittent interest in bringing a new life to these once powerful constitutional principles. On the other hand, scholars on the political left, many of them associated with the Critical Legal Studies movement, also increasingly reject the New Deal settlement. They complain that New Deal constitutionalism failed to bring about any fundamental change in the economic structure of the United States, and maintain that government has an affirmative obligation to alleviate inequality. Emphasizing the importance of communitarianism rather than individual rights, such scholars have especially sought to promote constitutionally mandated social welfare rights.

Private law, governing such fields as contracts, torts, and property, were influenced by the same trends that shaped public law. Legislative activism emerged as one of the significant new features of the post–World War II legal order. A single fat volume of statutes in the early nineteenth century could encompass all the laws of a state. By the early twenty-first century, a whole bookshelf was often necessary. In this new "age of statutes," legislators intervened in relationships that common-law judges had historically regulated. More legislation also meant that the task of judges increasingly become one of construing statutes and administrative regulations and not just elaborating on common-law doctrines. But the character of disputes raised through the common law also changed. In the trial courts, a pronounced shift occurred from civil to criminal matters, and on the civil side there was a smaller proportion of cases that involved market transactions (e.g., contract, property, debt collection) and a greater number of cases concerning tort and family issues. The traditional lines that demarcated private law categories blurred, leading to the creation of bodies of new law, such as administrative law and products liability, that gave judges extensive new policy-making authority.

The materials in this chapter explore the tensions between individual and community interests, the appropriate role of the government in the economy, the place of property rights in the constitutional order, and the reemergence of federalism. These tensions have unsettled both public and private law and at the same time have blurred the distinction between these traditional legal categories.

REGULATORY STATE
DEREGULATION

The Staggers Act
1980

The first industry to be subjected to strict federal regulation, railroads entered an era of economic decline after World War II. The railroads steadily lost freight and passenger traffic to trucks and airlines. By the 1970s many carriers were on the verge of bankruptcy, and it was clear that a fundamental change in railroad policy was essential if the United States was to retain privately owned rail service. Critics blamed a fossilized regulatory regime, enacted to meet the problems of an earlier day, for stifling innovation, hampering rail competition with other modes of transportation, and adding to transit costs. Congress began to reduce governmental regulation of railroads in the 1970s. This trend culminated with the landmark Staggers Act of 1980, in which Congress embraced deregulation as a means to restore the financial health of the rail industry. Among other changes, the Staggers Act substantially eliminated rate regulation and expedited the procedures for abandoning unprofitable lines. In 1995 Congress abolished the Interstate Commerce Commission, the nation's first regulatory body, and transferred its remaining functions to the newly created Surface Transportation Board.

FINDINGS

Sec. 2. The Congress hereby finds that—

(1) historically, railroads were the essential factor in the national transportation system;

(2) the enactment of the Interstate Commerce Act was essential to prevent an abuse of monopoly power by railroads and to establish and maintain a national railroad network;

(3) today, most transportation within the United States is competitive;

(4) many of the Government regulations affecting railroads have become unnecessary and inefficient;

(5) nearly two-thirds of the Nation's intercity freight is transported by modes of transportation other than railroads;

(6) earnings by the railroad industry are the lowest of any transportation mode and are insufficient to generate funds for necessary capital improvements;

(7) by 1985, there will be a capital shortfall within the railroad industry of between $16,000,000,000 and $20,000,000,000;

(8) failure to achieve increased earnings within the railroad industry will result in either further deterioration of the rail system or the necessity for additional Federal subsidy; and

(9) modernization of economic regulation for the railroad industry with a greater reliance on the marketplace is essential in order to achieve maximum utilization of railroads to save energy and combat inflation.

GOALS

Sec. 3. The purpose of this Act is to provide for the restoration, maintenance, and improvement of the physical facilities and financial stability of the rail system of the United States. In order to achieve this purpose, it is hereby declared that the goals of this Act are—

(1) to assist the railroads of the Nation in rehabilitating the rail system in order to meet the demands of interstate commerce and the national defense;

(2) to reform Federal regulatory policy so as to preserve a safe, adequate, economical, efficient, and financially stable rail system;

(3) to assist the rail system to remain viable in the private sector of the economy;

(4) to provide a regulatory process that balances the needs of carriers, shippers, and the public; and

(5) to assist in the rehabilitation and financing of the rail system.

THE CONTOURS OF ENVIRONMENTAL REGULATION

The direction of environmental regulation has been at the center of an intense debate since the 1980s. Environmental laws have generally imposed command and control requirements aimed at industrial sources of pollution by proscribing certain conduct. Such laws are enforced by agency regulators who seek to develop effective control strategies to prevent environmental injury. As a broad proposition, the regulatory focus has been upon strict pollution controls rather than a balance between regulatory costs and benefits. Some critics of the current system, however, maintain that environmental standards are often inefficient, costly, and unproductive. They urge an overhaul of the regulatory regime to emphasize market incentives as an alternative means to encourage the attainment of desired goals. Others insist that the existing level of regulation is insufficient to protect the environment.

While this debate continues, policy makers are confronting a new situation that complicates the task of environmental regulation. As industrial pollution has been reduced, agricultural practices and individual behavior have been identified as large sources of environmental harm. Yet Congress has shown little enthusiasm for imposing environmental regulations directly on farmers or individual citizens.

The following documents examine the conflict over contemporary environmental law and highlight contrasting modes of regulation.

HOWARD LATIN

"Ideal Versus Real Regulatory Efficiency: Implementation of Uniform Standards and 'Fine-Tuning' Regulatory Reforms"
1985

Howard Latin, a professor at Rutgers University School of Law at Newark, is a leading advocate of the command and control approach to environmental regulation. As this excerpt makes clear, he strongly defends the present system against proposals to rely on economic incentives as regulatory alternatives.

Many environmental, public health, and safety statutes place primary emphasis on the implementation of uniform regulatory standards. In return for benefits that are often difficult to assess, "command-and-control" standards promulgated under such statutes as the Clean Air Act (CAA), Occupational Safety and Health Act (OSH Act), and Federal Water Pollution Control Act (FWPCA) impose billions of dollars in annual compliance costs on society and also entail significant indirect costs including decreases in productivity, technological innovation, and market competition. As these costs have become increasingly evident, prominent legal scholars such as Bruce Ackerman, Steven Breyer, and Richard Stewart have concluded that command-and-control regulation is inefficient and should be replaced by more flexible strategies. Their principal criticisms may be summarized as follows: Uniform standards do not reflect the opportunity costs of environ-

mental protection, they disregard the individual circumstances of diverse conflicts, they do not achieve environmental protection on a "lowest-cost" basis, and they fail to provide adequate incentives for improved performance.

In response to these alleged deficiencies in the present system, advocates of "regulatory reform" argue that environmental controls should be tailored to particularized ecological and economic circumstances, regulatory benefits weighed against the costs of environmental protection, and increased reliance placed on economic incentive mechanisms, such as taxes on environmentally destructive activities or transferable pollution rights. Professor Stewart, for example, recently advocated "a more individualized or 'fine-tuning' approach to regulation." Critics of command-and-control standards differ on suggested "fine-tuning" prescriptions, but there is widespread agreement that *some* alternative must be preferable to the current regulatory system.

[T]he academic literature on "regulatory reform" reflects an excessive preoccupation with theoretical efficiency, while it places inadequate emphasis on actual decision-making costs and implementation constraints. Any system for environmental regulation must function despite the presence of pervasive uncertainty, high decisionmaking costs, and manipulative strategic behavior resulting from conflicting private and public interests. Under these conditions, the indisputable fact that uniform standards are inefficient does not prove that any other approach would necessarily perform better. In a "second-best" world, the critical issue is not which regulatory system aspires to ideal "efficiency" but which is most likely to prove effective.

In recognition of severe implementation constraints on environmental regulation, this article identifies numerous advantages of uniform standards in comparison with more particular-ized and flexible regulatory strategies. These advantages include decreased information collection and evaluation costs, greater consistency and predictability of results, greater accessibility of decisions to public scrutiny and participation, increased likelihood that regulations will withstand judicial review, reduced opportunities for manipulative behavior by agencies in response to political or bureaucratic pressures, reduced opportunities for obstructive behavior by regulated parties, and decreased likelihood of social dislocation and "forum shopping" resulting from competitive disadvantages between geographical regions or between firms in regulated industries. A realistic implementation analysis indicates that "fine-tuning" would prove infeasible in many important environmental contexts; indeed, the effectiveness of environmental regulation could often be improved by reducing even the degree of "fine-tuning" that is currently attempted.

BRUCE A. ACKERMAN AND RICHARD B. STEWART

"Reforming Environmental Law"
1985

Bruce A. Ackerman of Yale University Law School and Richard B. Stewart of New York University Law School have sharply criticized the present system of environmental regulation. In the following selection they summarize their views and call for a market-oriented approach to achieve environmental objectives.

In 1971, Ezra Mishan brilliantly satirized the views of a Dr. Pangloss, who argued that a world of largely unregulated pollution was "optimal" because cleanup would involve enormous transactions costs. Less than 15 years later, Professor Latin uses the same Panglossian argument to rationalize the current regulatory status quo. He not only accepts but endorses our extraordinarily crude, costly, litigious and counterproductive system of technology-based environmental controls. Like Mishan's Pangloss, he seems to believe that if it were possible to have a better world, it would exist. Since it does not, the transaction costs involved in regulatory improvements must exceed the benefits. Proposals for basic change accordingly are dismissed as naïve utopianism.

What explains this celebration of the regulatory status quo? As critics of the present system, we believe this question to be of more than academic interest. The present regulatory system wastes tens of billions of dollars every year, misdirects resources, stifles innovation, and spawns massive and often counterproductive litigation. There is a variety of fundamental but practical changes that could be made to improve its environmental and economic performance. Why have such changes not been adopted? Powerful organized interests have a vested state in the status quo. The congressional committees, government bureaucracies, and industry and environmental groups that have helped to shape the present system want to see it perpetuated. But the current system is also bolstered by an often inarticulate sense that, however cumbersome, it "works," and that complexity and limited information make major improvements infeasible.

Professor Latin has performed an important service in providing an articulate, informed, and sophisticated exposition of this view. By developing and making transparent the arguments that might justify the status quo, he has made it easier to assess their merits. If, as we believe, those arguments lack merit, his sophisticated defense of status quo may ultimately serve to hasten its demise.

We will not respond to all of the groundless charges that Professor Latin levels at the critics of the current system, ourselves included. We focus instead on the major flaws in his defense of existing law and policy. First, Latin's view is based on a Panglossian interpretation of the status quo. The current system does not in fact "work" and its malfunctions, like those of Soviet-style central planning, will become progressively more serious as the economy grows and changes and our knowledge of environmental problems develops.

Second, Latin mistakenly treats economic incentive systems as a form of regulatory "fine-tuning," rather than the recognizing them as fundamental alternatives to our current reliance on centralized regulatory commands to implement environmental goals. Moreover, he completely ignores experience showing that economic incentive systems are feasible and effective.

Third, Latin ignores the increasingly urgent need to improve the process by which Congress, the agencies, and the courts set environmental goals. He is mesmerized by decisionmaking costs, ignoring the great social benefits flowing from a more intelligent and democratically accountable dialogue on environmental policy. We deal with each of these points in turn.

I. THE EXISTING SYSTEM

The existing system of pollution regulation, which is the focus of Latin's defense, is primarily based on a Best Available Technology (BAT) strategy. If an industrial process or product generates some nontrivial risk, the responsible plant or industry must install whatever technology is available to reduce or eliminate this risk, so long as the costs of doing so will not cause a shut-down of the plant or industry. BAT requirements are largely determined through uniform federal regulations. Under the Clean Water Act's BAT strategy, the EPA adapts nationally uniform effluent limitations for some 500 different industries. A similar BAT strategy is deployed under the Clean Air Act for new industrial sources of air pollution, new automobiles, and industrial sources of toxic air pollutants. BAT strategies are also widely used in many fields of environmental regulation other than air and water pollution, which are the focus of Latin's analysis.

BAT was embraced by Congress and administrators in the early 1970s in order to impose immediate, readily enforceable federal controls on a relatively few widespread pollutants, while avoiding widespread industrial shutdowns. Subsequent experience and analysis has demonstrated:

1. Uniform BAT requirements waste many billions of dollars annually by ignoring variations among plants and industries in the cost of reducing pollution and by ignoring geographic variations in pollution effects. A more cost-effective strategy of risk reduction could free enormous resources for additional pollution reduction or other purposes.

2. BAT controls, and the litigation they provoke, impose disproportionate penalties on new products and processes. A BAT strategy typically imposes far more stringent controls on new sources because there is no risk of shutdown. Also, new plants and products must run the gauntlet of lengthy regulatory and legal proceedings to win approval; the resulting uncertainty and delay discourage new investment. By contrast, existing sources can use the delays and costs of the legal process to burden regulators and postpone or "water-down" compliance. BAT strategies also impose disproportionate burdens on more productive and profitable industries because these industries can "afford" more stringent controls. This "soak the rich" approach penalizes growth and international competitiveness.

3. BAT controls can ensure that established control technologies are installed. They do not, however, provide strong incentives for the development of new, environmentally superior strategies, and may actually discourage their development. Such innovations are essential for maintaining long-term economic growth without simultaneously increasing pollution and other forms of environmental degradation.

4. BAT involves the centralized determination of complex scientific, engineering, and economic issues regarding the feasibility of controls on hundreds of thousands of pollution sources. Such determinations impose massive information-gathering burdens on administrators, and provide a fertile ground for complex litigation in the form of massive adversary rule-making proceedings and protracted judicial review. Given the high costs of regulatory compliance and the potential gains from litigation brought to defeat or delay regulatory requirements, it is often more cost-effective for industry to "invest" in such litigation rather than to comply.

5. A BAT strategy is inconsistent with intelligent priority setting. Simply regulating to the hilt whatever pollutants happen to get on the regulatory agenda may preclude an agency from dealing adequately with more serious problems that come to scientific attention later. BAT also tends to reinforce regulatory inertia. Foreseeing that "all or nothing" regulation of a given substance under BAT will involve large administrative and compliance costs, and recognizing that resources are limited, agencies often seek to limit sharply the number of substances on the agenda for regulatory action.

◆   ◆   ◆

Our basic reform would respond to these deficiencies by allowing polluters to buy and sell each other's permits—thereby creating a powerful financial incentive for those who can clean up most cheaply to sell their permits to those whose treatment costs are highest. This reform will, at one stroke, cure many of the basic flaws of the existing command-and-control regulatory systems discussed earlier.

A system of tradeable rights will tend to bring about a least-cost allocation of control

burdens, saving many billions of dollars annually. It will eliminate the disproportionate burdens that BAT imposes on new and more productive industries by treating all sources of the same pollutant on the same basis. It will provide positive economic rewards for polluters who develop environmentally superior products and processes. It will, as we show below, reduce the incentives for litigation, simplify the issues in controversy, and facilitate more intelligent setting of priorities.

◆   ◆   ◆

The marketable permit system would also provide much stronger incentives for effective monitoring and enforcement. If polluters did not expect rigorous enforcement during the term of their permits, this fact would show up at the auction in dramatically lower bids: Why pay a lot for the right to pollute legally when one can pollute illegally without serious risk of detection? Under a marketable permit approach, this problem would be at the center of bureaucratic attention. For if, as we envisage, the size of the budget available to the EPA and state agencies would depend on total auction revenues, the bureaucracy's failure to invest adequately in enforcement would soon show up in a potentially dramatic drop in auction income available for the next budgetary period. This is not a prospect that top EPA administrators will take lightly. Monitoring and enforcement will become agency priorities of the first importance. Moreover, permit holders may themselves support strong enforcement in order to ensure that cheating by others does not depreciate the value of the permit holders' investments.

A system of marketable permits, then, not only promises to save Americans many billions of dollars a year, to reward innovative improvements in existing clean-up techniques, and to eliminate the BAT system's penalty on new, productive investment. It also offers formidable administrative advantages. It relieves agencies of the enormous information-processing burdens that overwhelm them under the BAT system; it greatly reduces litigation and delay; it offers a rich source of budgetary revenue in a period of general budgetary stringency; and it forces agencies to give new importance to the critical business of enforcing the law in a way that America's polluters will take seriously.

Executive Order 12866
1993

Anxious to make environmental regulations more efficient and to balance regulatory objectives with economic growth, President William J. Clinton issued this executive order to guide the regulatory process. The order refines a regulatory oversight process developed in earlier presidential administrations. Of particular significance was the directive that agencies should consider the costs and benefits of proposed regulations and should assess market incentives as a vehicle to secure desired behavior.

REGULATORY PLANNING AND REVIEW

The American people deserve a regulatory system that works for them, not against them: a regulatory system that protects and improves their health, safety, environment, and well-being and improves the performance of the economy without imposing unacceptable or unreasonable costs on society; regulatory policies that recognize that the private sector and private markets are the best engine for economic growth; regulatory approaches that respect the role of State, local, and tribal governments; and regulations that are effective, consistent, sensible, and understandable. We do not have such a regulatory system today.

With this Executive order, the Federal Government begins a program to reform and make more efficient the regulatory process. The objectives of this Executive order are to enhance planning and coordination with respect to both new and existing regulations; to reaffirm the primacy of Federal agencies in the regulatory decision-making process; to restore the integrity and legitimacy of regulatory review and oversight; and to make the process more accessible and open to the public. In pursuing these objectives, the regulatory process shall be conducted so as to meet applicable statutory requirements and with due regard to the discretion that has been entrusted to the Federal agencies.

Accordingly, by the authority vested in me as President by the Constitution and the laws of the United States of America, it is hereby ordered as follows:

Section 1. Statement of Regulatory Philosophy and Principles

(a) *The Regulatory Philosophy.* Federal agencies should promulgate only such regulations as are required by law, are necessary to interpret the law, or are made necessary by compelling public need, such as material failures of private markets to protect or improve the health and safety of the public, the environment, or the well being of the American people. In deciding whether and how to regulate, agencies should assess all costs and benefits of available regulatory alternatives, including the alternative of not regulating. Costs and benefits shall be understood to include both quantifiable measures (to the fullest extent that these can be usefully estimated) and qualitative measures of costs and benefits that are difficult to quantify, but nevertheless essential to consider. Further, in choosing among alternative regulatory approaches, agencies should select those approaches that maximize net benefits (including potential economic, environmental, public health and safety, and other advantages; distributive impacts; and equity), unless a statute requires another regulatory approach.

(b) *The Principles of Regulation.* To ensure that the agencies' regulatory programs are consistent with the philosophy set forth above, agencies should adhere to the following principles, to the extent permitted by law and where applicable:

(1) Each agency shall identify the problem that it intends to addressing (including, where applicable, the failures of private markets or public institutions that warrant new agency action) as well as assess the significance of that problem.

(2) Each agency shall examine whether existing regulations (or other law) have created, or contributed to, the problem that a new regulation is intended to correct and whether those regulations (or other law) should be modified to achieve the intended goal of regulation more effectively.

(3) Each agency shall identify and assess available alternatives to direct regulation, including providing economic incentives to encourage the desired behavior, such as user fees or marketable permits, or providing information upon which choices can be made by the public.

(4) In setting regulatory priorities, each agency shall consider, to the extent reasonable, the degree and nature of the risks posed by various substances or activities within its jurisdiction.

(5) When an agency determines that a regulation is the best available method of achieving the regulatory objective, it shall design its regulations in the most cost-effective manner to achieve the regulatory objective. In doing so, each agency shall consider incentives for innovation, consistency, predictability, the costs of enforcement and compliance (to the government, regulated entities, and the public), flexibility, distributive impacts, and equity.

(6) Each agency shall assess both the costs and the benefits of the intended regulation and, recognizing that some costs and benefits are difficult to quantify, propose or adopt a regulation only upon a reasoned determination that the benefits of the intended regulation justify its costs.

(7) Each agency shall base its decisions on the best reasonably obtainable scientific, technical, economic, and other information concerning the need for, and consequences of, the intended regulation.

(8) Each agency shall identify and assess alternative forms of regulation and shall, to the extent feasible, specify performance objectives, rather than specifying the behavior or manner of compliance that regulated entities must adopt.

(9) Wherever feasible, agencies shall seek views of appropriate State, local, and tribal officials before imposing regulatory requirements that might significantly or uniquely affect those governmental entities. Each agency shall assess the effects of Federal regulations on State, local, and tribal governments, including specifically the availability of resources to carry out those mandates, and seek to minimize those burdens that uniquely or significantly affect such governmental entities, consistent with achieving regulatory objectives. In addition, as appropriate, agencies shall seek to harmonize Federal regulatory actions with related State, local, and tribal regulatory and other governmental functions.

(10) Each agency shall avoid regulations that are inconsistent, incompatible, or duplicative with its other regulations or those of other Federal agencies.

(11) Each agency shall tailor its regulations to impose the least burden on society, including individuals, businesses of differing sizes, and other entities (including small communities and governmental entities), consistent with obtaining the regulatory objectives, taking into account, among other things, and to the extent practicable, the costs of cumulative regulations.

(12) Each agency shall draft its regulations to be simple and easy to understand, with the goal of minimizing the potential for uncertainty and litigation arising from such uncertainty.

ANTI-TRUST POLICY

During the early decades of the twentieth century, many reformers were hostile to concentrations of private economic power and sought to overhaul the structure of capitalism by means of anti-trust policy. This was reflected in periods of intense enforcement of the anti-trust laws to curb anti-competitive and monopolistic behavior by business enterprises. After World War II, however, the public grew more comfortable with large-scale business enterprise and anti-monopoly sentiment waned. By the 1970s, moreover, the law and economics movement associated with the University of Chicago began dramatically to influence anti-trust doctrine and enforcement policy. The emerging view stressed economic efficiency and asserted that markets would generally remain competitive without governmental intervention. In reviewing mergers, for instance, both enforcement agencies and judges have given greater emphasis to the potential economic gains of merger activity. The Supreme Court has also tightened the criteria for establishing predatory pricing and made the prosecution of private anti-trust actions more difficult.

In the Progressive Era, anti-trust cases such as the 1911 *Standard Oil* decision were highly visible. Today most anti-trust cases raise largely technical issues that arouse little public interest. Still, a few modern anti-trust cases have received a good deal of public attention. In 1982 the federal government settled its monopolization suit against American Telephone and Telegraph Company, which resulted in the divestiture of the company's long-distance service from its local operating companies. In a case that highlighted the application of anti-trust laws to the "new economy" of high-technology firms, the federal government and several states charged that Microsoft, the world's largest software company, had engaged in a variety of practices to frustrate competition in operating systems for personal computers. In 2001 a federal appeals court found that Microsoft had violated the anti-trust laws, but declined to order that Microsoft be divided into two companies. Later that year Microsoft and the Justice Department entered a settlement agreement under which Microsoft would make portions of its software available to competitors. Two states, however, refused to join the settlement and continue to seek stiffer penalties for Microsoft.

ECONOMIC ACTIVITY

CONTRACT

In the nineteenth century, contract became the most important category of private law because it stressed such "classical" elements as the importance of caveat emptor, consideration, and mutuality of bargaining. But in the twentieth century, the weight of the Legal Realist movement combined with the rise of a mass consumer economy to undermine the once dominant role of contract. The attack on the entire idea of contract became so ferocious that Yale Law School professor Grant Gilmore in 1974 proclaimed its demise in a widely discussed book, *The Death of Contract*. Gilmore argued that expansive concepts of tort law had rendered contract ideals meaningless.

Gilmore's obituary for contract law was premature, since contract continues to have vitality in sustaining important social and economic relationships. Yet legal commentators, judges, and legislators have significantly reshaped it. They have done so by promoting two concepts: reliance and unconscionability. Together, these concepts have circumscribed unrestrained bargaining among private parties.

Williams v. Walker-Thomas Furniture Company
350 F.2d 445 (1965)

This case involved the question of whether an equitable doctrine of unconscionability covered by Section 2-302 of the Uniform Commercial Code, as adopted by Congress for the District of Columbia, should prevail over a traditional commitment to a meeting of minds between bargaining parties. The case pitted paternalism against individual autonomy as represented by freedom of contract. It also raised a number of social and economic permutations as well. For example, should ghetto merchants be given greater leeway, in view of their customer base, to protect their property interests through tougher contract terms than would be the case in an affluent suburb? What impact might the Williams *decision be expected to have on the availability and prices of consumer goods in poor urban neighborhoods? Indeed, should judges take such matters into consideration?*

Williams *represents a notable application of the UCC's unconscionability doctrine. As later decisions make clear, courts usually invoke the doctrine of unconscionability to protect consumers. They have been reluctant to use the doctrine in cases involving contracts between legally sophisticated business enterprises. Moreover, courts rarely pass upon the fairness of price terms and usually focus on other terms of the contract to determine unconscionability.*

J. Skelly Wright, Circuit Judge:

Appellee, Walker-Thomas Furniture Company, operates a retail furniture store in the District of Columbia. During the period from 1957 to 1962 each appellant in these cases purchased a number of household items from Walker-Thomas, for which payment was to be made in installments. The terms of each purchase were contained in a printed form contract, which set forth the value of the purchased item and purported to lease the item to appellant for a stipulated monthly rent payment. The contract then provided, in substance, that title would remain in Walker-Thomas until the total of all the monthly payments made equated the stated value of the item, at which time appellants could take title. In the event of a default in the payment of any monthly installment, Walker-Thomas could repossess the item.

The contract further provided that "the amount of each periodical installment payment to be made by [purchaser] to the Company under this present lease shall be inclusive of and not in addition to the amount of each installment payment to be made by [purchaser] under

such prior leases, bills or accounts; *and all payments now and hereafter made by [purchaser] shall be credited pro rata on all outstanding leases, bills and accounts* due the Company by [purchaser] at the time each such payment is made." [Emphasis added.] The effect of this rather obscure provision was to keep a balance due on every item purchased until the balance due on all items, whenever purchased, was liquidated. As a result, the debt incurred at the time of purchase of each item was secured by the right to repossess all the items previously purchased by the same purchaser, and each new item purchased automatically became subject to a security interest arising out of the previous dealings.

On May 12, 1962, appellant purchased an item described as Daveno, three tables, and two lamps, having a total stated value of $391.10. Shortly thereafter, she defaulted on her monthly payments and appellee sought to replevy all the items purchased since the first transaction in 1958. Similarly, on April 17, 1962, appellant Williams bought a stereo set of stated value of $514.95. She too defaulted shortly thereafter, and appellee sought to replevy all the items purchased since December, 1957. . . .

Appellants' principal contention, rejected by both the trial and the appellate courts below, is that these contracts, or at least some of them, are unconscionable and, hence, not enforceable. In its opinion . . . the District of Columbia Court of Appeals reject[ed] this contention.

♦ ♦ ♦

We do not agree that the court lacked the power to refuse enforcement to contracts found to be unconscionable. In other jurisdictions, it has been held as a matter of common law that unconscionable contracts are not enforceable. While no decision of this court so holding has been found, the notion that an unconscionable bargain should not be given full enforcement is by no means novel. Since we have never adopted or rejected such a rule, the question here presented is actually one of the first impressions.

Congress has recently enacted the Uniform Commercial Code, which specifically provides that the court may refuse to enforce a contract, which it finds to be unconscionable at the time it was made. The enactment of this section, which occurred subsequent to the contracts here in suit, does not mean that the common law of the District of Columbia was otherwise at the time of enactment, nor does it preclude the court from adopting a similar rule in the exercise of its powers to develop the common law for the District of Columbia. In fact, in view of the absence of prior authority on the point, we consider the congressional adoption of section 2–302 persuasive authority for following the rationale of the cases from which the section is explicitly derived. Accordingly, we hold that where the element of unconscionability is present at the time a contract is made, the contract should not be enforced.

Unconscionability has generally been recognized to include an absence of meaningful choice on the part of one of the parties together with contract terms, which are unreasonably favorable to the other party. Whether a meaningful choice is present in a particular case can only be determined by consideration of all the cir-cumstances surrounding the transaction. In many cases the meaningfulness of the choice is negated by a gross inequality of bargaining power. The manner in which the contract was entered into is also relevant to this consideration. Did each party to the contract, considering his obvious education or lack of it, have a reasonable opportunity to understand the terms of the contract, or were the important terms hidden in a maze of fine print and minimized by deceptive sales practices? Ordinarily, one who signs an agreement without full knowledge of its terms might be held to assume the risk that he has entered a one-sided bargain. But when a party of little bargaining power, and hence little real choice, signs a commercially unreasonable contract with little or no knowledge of its terms, it is hardly likely that his consent, or even an objective manifestation of his consent, was ever given to all the terms. In such a case the usual rule that the terms of the agreement are not to be questioned should be abandoned and the court should consider whether the terms of the contract are so unfair that enforcement should be withheld.

In determining reasonableness or fairness, the primary concern must be with the terms of the contract considered in light of the circumstances existing when the contract was made. The test is not simple, nor can it be mechanically applied. The terms are to be considered "in light of the general commercial background and the commercial needs of the particular trade or case." Corbin suggests the test as being whether the terms are "so extreme as to appear unconscionable according to the mores and business practices of the time and place." . . . We think this formulation correctly states the test to be applied in those cases where no meaningful choice was exercised upon entering the contract.

Because the trial court and the appellate court did not feel that enforcement could be refused, no findings were made on the possible unconscionability of the contracts in these cases. Since the record is not sufficient for our deciding the issue as a matter of law, the cases must be remanded to the trial court for further proceedings.

So ordered.

Torts

In the nineteenth century, tort law emphasized fault and the establishment of blameworthiness; in the twentieth century, especially in the post–World War II era, it began to stress compensation for injured persons. This shift in tort law has tended to place the costs of accidents and their prevention on the party to whom it was most bearable. Legal scholars, however, have differed radically on the wisdom of this development. Richard Posner and Richard Epstein, both associated with the Law and Economics movement, have protested that placing the costs of accidents on those businesses and persons with the deepest pockets only drives up the cost of goods and services without providing any significant deterrent against future recklessness. Yale Law School professor Guido Calabresi, on the contrary, insists that spreading the costs of accidents over those best able to pay makes good moral sense.

As a matter of historical development, modern tort law would be unthinkable without liability insurance. Through premiums paid by many policyholders, insurance companies spread the costs of accidents while making a profit. Insurance has social utility in another way because it permits businesses to develop and individuals to use new, complex technologies under a protective umbrella. The modern transportation system depends on automobile insurance.

Yet an extraordinary degree of controversy has plagued both modern tort law and liability insurance. The rising costs of all kinds of liability insurance sparked demands for reform of the system in the late twentieth century. The most prominent of these legislatively imposed reforms has been "no-fault" insurance (in which the insured person's company rather than that of the party at fault pays the bills), caps on damages in medical malpractice suits, and comparative negligence (in which responsibility for an accident is apportioned among those involved in it). Taken together, these developments have turned what was once an almost exclusively private branch of law into one that is more and more controlled by public policy concerns.

Nowhere is the unique character of modern tort law clearer than in the broadened application of strict liability standards. In the nineteenth century, the concept applied with a very few exceptions to ultrahazardous activities, but in the twentieth century judges increasingly applied it to a variety of consumer-related goods. Products liability rests on the assumption that with the spread of new technologies and the growing remoteness of producers from consumers, strict liability standards encourage manufacturers to give close attention to matters of safety. Posner, Epstein, and other Law and Economics scholars hotly dispute such assumptions, once again.

Greenman v. Yuba Power Products, Inc.
59 Cal. 2d 57 (1962)

Perhaps nowhere was the so-called death of contract more evident than in cases in which the traditional rule requiring privity between buyer and seller was set aside. This line of development began with McPherson v. Buick Motor Co. *(N.Y., 1916), a case that involved an injury caused by a defective automobile wheel. Judge Benjamin Cardozo's opinion established the notion of third-party liability when privity of contract did not exist. In* Greenman, *the California Supreme Court, which was the most important court for establishing modern tort law, further extended this doctrine. The court was asked to consider whether a manufacturer's liability for defective products was governed by the law of contract warranties or by the law of strict liability. Judge Roger Traynor, who wrote the opinion in this case, was, like Cardozo, one of the great twentieth-century state judges. The* Greenman *decision was a key milestone in establishing the doctrine of strict products liability.*

Traynor, Justice.

Plaintiff brought this action for damages against the retailer and the manufacturer of a Shopsmith, a combination power tool that could be used as a saw, drill, and wood lathe. He saw a Shopsmith demonstrated by the retailer and studied a brochure prepared by the manufacturer. He decided he wanted a Shopsmith for his home workshop, and his wife bought and gave him one for Christmas in 1955. In 1957 he bought the necessary attachments to use the Shopsmith as a lathe for turning a large piece of wood he wished to make into a chalice. After he had worked on the piece of wood several times without difficulty, it suddenly flew out of the machine and struck him on the forehead, inflicting serious injuries. About ten and a half months later, he gave the retailer and the manufacturer written notice of claimed breaches of warranties and filed a complaint against them alleging such breaches and negligence.

After a trial before a jury, the court . . . submitted to the jury only the cause of action alleging breach of implied warranties against the retailer and the causes of action alleging negligence and breach of express warranties against the manufacturer. The jury returned a verdict for the retailer against plaintiff and for plaintiff against the manufacturer in the amount of $65,000. The trial court denied the manufacturer's motion for a new trial and entered judgment on the verdict. The manufacturer . . . appeal[s].

Plaintiff introduced substantial evidence that his injuries were caused by defective design and construction of the Shopsmith. His expert witnesses testified that inadequate set screws were used to hold parts of the machine together so that normal vibration caused the tailstock of the lathe to move away from the piece of wood being turned permitting it to fly out of the lathe. They also testified that there

were other more positive ways of fastening the parts of the machine together, the use of which would have prevented the accident. The jury could therefore reasonably have concluded that the manufacturer negligently constructed the Shopsmith. The jury could also reasonably have concluded that statements in the manufacturer's brochure were untrue, that they constituted express warranties, and that plaintiff's injuries were caused by their breach.

◆ ◆ ◆

A manufacturer is strictly liable in tort when an article he places on the market knowing that it is to be used without inspection for defects, proves to have a defect that causes injury to a human being. Recognized first in the case of unwholesome food products, such liability has now been extended to a variety of other products that create as great or greater hazards if defective. . . .

Although . . . strict liability has usually been based on the theory of an express or implied warranty running from the manufacturer to the plaintiff, the abandonment of the requirement of a contract between them, the recognition that the liability is not assumed by agreement but imposed by law . . . , and the refusal to permit the manufacturer to define the scope of its own responsibility for defective products . . . , make clear that the liability is not one governed by the law of contract warranties but by the law of strict liability in tort.

We need not recanvass the reasons for imposing strict liability on the manufacturer. . . . The purpose of such liability is to insure that the costs of injuries resulting from defective products are borne by the manufacturers that put such products on the market rather than by the injured persons who are powerless to protect themselves. Sales warranties serve this purpose fitfully at best. . . . In the present case, for example, plaintiff was able to plead and prove an express warranty only because he read and relied on the representations of the Shopsmith's ruggedness contained in the manufacturer's brochure. Implicit in the machine's presence on the market, however, was a representation that it would safely do the jobs for which it was built. Under these circumstances, it should not be controlling whether plaintiff selected the machine because of the statements in the brochure, or because of the machine's own appearance of excellence that belied the defect lurking beneath the surface, or because he merely assumed that it would safely do the jobs it was built to do. It should not be controlling whether the details of the sales from manufacturer to retailer and from retailer to plaintiff's wife were such that one or more of the implied warranties of the sales act arose. . . . To establish the manufacturer's liability it was sufficient that plaintiff proved that he was injured while using the Shopsmith in a way it was intended to be used as a result of a defect in design and manufacture of which plaintiff was not aware that made the Shopsmith unsafe for its intended use. The judgment is affirmed.

Fassoulas v. Ramey
450 So. 2d 822 (Fla. 1984)

Medical malpractice suits have been one of the most visible and controversial aspects of modern tort law. Nowhere else has the general expectation of justice and the idea of recompense for wrongs of every nature been more evident. In cases such as this one, issues of emotional suffering and not just physical injury add a new dimension to the meaning of damages in modern tort law.

Per Curiam . . .

Plaintiffs, Edith and John Fassoulas, were married and had two children, both of whom had been born with severe congenital abnormalities. After much consideration, they decided not to have any more children due to the fear of having another physically deformed child and the attendant high cost of medical care. They then decided that John would undergo a vasectomy. Defendant, Dr. Ramey, performed this medical procedure in January 1974. However, due to the negligence of the defendant in performing the operation, in giving medical advice concerning residual pockets of sperm, and in examining and judging the viability of sperm samples, Edith twice became pregnant and gave birth to two children. The first of these, Maria, was born in November 1974 and had many congenital deformities. Roussi, the second of the post-vasectomy children and the fourth Fassoulas child, was born in September 1976 with a slight physical deformity which was corrected at birth; he is now a normal, healthy child.

The plaintiffs sued Dr. Ramey and his clinic in tort based on medical malpractice for the two "wrongful births." They sought as damages Edith's past and future lost wages, her anguish and emotional distress at twice becoming pregnant, her loss of the society, companionship and consortium of her husband, John's mental anguish and emotional distress, his loss of the society, companionship and consortium of his wife, medical and hospital expenses and the expenses for the care and upbringing of the two new children until the age of twenty-one.

At trial, the jury found in favor of the plaintiffs, finding the defendant 100% negligent with reference to Maria and 50% negligent with reference to Roussi. The plaintiffs were found to be comparatively negligent as to the birth of Roussi. Damages were assessed in the amount of $250,000 for the birth of Maria and $100,000 for the birth of Roussi, the latter sum being reduced to $50,000 because of the plaintiff's comparative negligence. . . .

The rule in Florida is that "a parent cannot be said to have been damaged by the birth and rearing of a normal, healthy child." "[I]t has been imbedded in our law for centuries that the father and now both parents or legal guardians of a child have the sole obligation of providing the necessaries in raising the child, whether the child be wanted or unwanted." "The child is still the child of the parents, not the physician, and it is the parents' legal obligation, not the physician's, to support the child." For public policy reasons, we decline to allow rearing damages for the birth of a healthy child.

The same reasoning forcefully and correctly applies to the ordinary, everyday expenses associated with the care and upbringing of a physically or mentally deformed child. We likewise hold as a matter of law that ordinary rearing expenses for a defective child are not recoverable as damages in Florida.

We agree with the district court below that an exception exists in the case of special upbringing expenses associated with a deformed child. Special medical and educational expenses, beyond normal rearing costs, are often staggering and quite debilitating to a family's financial and social health; "indeed the financial and emotional drain associated with raising such a child is often overwhelming to the affected parents." There is no valid policy argument against parents being recompensed for these costs of extraordinary care in raising a deformed child to majority. We hold these special upbringing costs associated with a deformed child to be recoverable.

[The court allowed only the extraordinary rearing costs associated with Maria; it permitted nothing for the birth of Roussi.]

Note: Legislative Reform of the Tort System

The operation of the tort system has become one of the most controversial issues in modern law. Spurred by businesses, insurance companies, and doctors, the tort reform movement gained momentum in the 1970s. Proponents of reform argued that courts and juries disregarded a finding of fault before imposing liability and awarded excessive monetary damages. They maintained that the threat of tort liability raised the cost of goods and services, discouraged product innovation, and undercut personal responsibility for careless conduct on the part of injured claimants. In contrast, supporters of the tort system insist that it has enhanced public safety, driven dangerous products off the market, and deterred negligent conduct by holding wrongdoers liable for harms they caused. The debate over tort law continues, but advocates of reform have convinced a number of state legislatures to revamp tort doctrine and to limit damages for noneconomic loss.

Medical malpractice has been an area of particular concern to legislators. The spiraling cost of medical malpractice insurance has negatively impacted the availability of health-care providers in some jurisdictions. Lawmakers have responded with a variety of measures designed to hold down the amounts paid in malpractice claims. Some states, such as Virginia, simply impose a cap on the damages that can be awarded in medical malpractice actions. Others have mandated presuit investigations in order to eliminate frivolous claims.

Some doctors also pushed for no-fault malpractice insurance as a means of stemming the rising costs of practice in certain particularly hazardous areas, such as obstetrics, neurosurgery, and orthopedics. While this proposal has made little headway, the no-fault concept has had much greater success in automobile-related torts. In 1970 Massachusetts became the first state to adopt a no-fault automobile insurance law, and by the end of the twentieth century a number of other states had embraced similar schemes. At the time, Massachusetts had the highest automobile premiums in the nation, and consumer action groups sought to curtail these expenses by eliminating the need to determine fault in an accident. As the Massachusetts statute provided, however, the plan was a modified no-fault scheme, since it permitted victims, in serious cases, to still bring suits to recover for high medical costs and other expenses. In fact, during the 1990s some state legislatures concluded that no-fault automobile insurance failed to reduce the amount of accident litigation and did not result in lower insurance premiums. They repealed no-fault schemes.

BMW of North America, Inc. v. Gore
517 U.S. 559 (1996)

Since 1980 the award of punitive damages has become a highly controversial topic. Such damages are awarded to a plaintiff in addition to compensatory or nominal damages. Punitive damages are intended to punish or deter serious misconduct, coupled with a malicious or reckless disregard for others. Despite being a windfall to the plaintiff, punitive damages are justified as a means of vindicating the public good. It is widely perceived that both the frequency and size of punitive damage awards has markedly increased in the past twenty years. There is debate over whether this perception is accurate, and some scholars maintain that punitive damages are awarded in relatively few cases. Nonetheless, legislatures in a number of states have enacted laws to either place a cap on the amount of primitive damages, or to leave the decision to allow such damages to judges rather than juries. As shown in Gore, *there have also been constitutional challenges to punitive damages. In this case the Supreme Court, by a 5 to 4 vote, struck down an Alabama punitive damage award as grossly excessive in violation of the due process clause of the Fourteenth Amendment.*

Justice Stevens delivered the opinion of the Court.

The Due Process Clause of the Fourteenth Amendment prohibits a State from imposing a " 'grossly excessive' " punishment on a tortfeasor. The wrongdoing involved in this case was the decision by a national distributor of automobiles not to advise its dealers, and hence their customers, of predelivery damage to new cars when the cost of repair amounted to less than 3 percent of the car's suggested retail price. The question presented is whether a $2 million punitive damages award to the purchaser of one of these cars exceeds the constitutional limit.

In January 1990, Dr. Ira Gore, Jr. (respondent), purchased a black BMW sports sedan for $40,750.88 from an authorized BMW dealer in Birmingham, Alabama. After driving the car for approximately nine months, and without noticing any flaws in its appearance, Dr. Gore took

the car to "Slick Finish," an independent detailer, to make it look " 'snazzier than it normally would appear.' " Mr. Slick, the proprietor, detected evidence that the car had been repainted. Convinced that he had been cheated, Dr. Gore brought suit against petitioner BMW of North America (BMW), the American distributor of BMW automobiles. Dr. Gore alleged, inter alia, that the failure to disclose that the car had been repainted constituted suppression of a material fact. The complaint prayed for $500,000 in compensatory and punitive damages, and costs.

At trial, BMW acknowledged that it had adopted a nationwide policy in 1983 concerning cars that were damaged in the course of manufacture or transportation. If the cost of repairing the damage exceeded 3 percent of the car's suggested retail price, the car was placed in company service for a period of time and then sold as used. If the repair costs did not exceed 3 percent of the suggested retail price, however, the car was sold as new without advising the dealer that any repairs had been made. Because the $601.37 cost of repainting Dr. Gore's car was only 1.5 percent of its suggested retail price, BMW did not disclose the damage or repair to the Birmingham dealer.

Dr. Gore asserted that his repainted car was worth less than a car that had not been refinished. To prove his actual damages of $4,000, he relied on the testimony of a former BMW dealer, who estimated that the value of a repainted BMW was approximately 10 percent less than the value of a new car that had not been damaged and repaired. To support his claim for punitive damages, Dr. Gore introduced evidence that since 1983 BMW had sold 983 refinished cars as new, including 14 in Alabama, without disclosing that the cars had been repainted before sale at a cost of more than $300 per vehicle. Using the actual damage estimate of $4,000 per vehicle, Dr. Gore argued that a punitive award of $4 million would provide an appropriate penalty for selling approximately 1,000 cars for more than they were worth.

In defense of its disclosure policy, BMW argued that it was under no obligation to disclose repairs of minor damage to new cars and that Dr. Gore's car was as good as a car with the original factory finish. It disputed Dr. Gore's assertion that the value of the car was impaired by the repainting and argued that this good-faith belief made a punitive award inappropriate. BMW also maintained that transactions in jurisdictions other than Alabama had no relevance to Dr. Gore's claim.

The jury returned a verdict finding BMW liable for compensatory damages of $4,000. In addition, the jury assessed $4 million in punitive damages, based on a determination that the nondisclosure policy constituted "gross, oppressive or malicious" fraud.

BMW filed a post-trial motion to set aside the punitive damages award. The company introduced evidence to establish that its nondisclosure policy was consistent with the laws of roughly 25 States defining the disclosure obligations of automobile manufacturers, distributors, and dealers. The most stringent of these

statutes required disclosure of repairs costing more than 3 percent of the suggested retail price; none mandated disclosure of less costly repairs. Relying on these statutes, BMW contended that its conduct was lawful in these States and therefore could not provide the basis for an award of punitive damages.

BMW also drew the court's attention to the fact that its nondisclosure policy had never been adjudged unlawful before this action was filed. Just months before Dr. Gore's case went to trial, the jury in a similar lawsuit filed by another Alabama BMW purchaser found that BMW's failure to disclose paint repair constituted fraud. Before the judgment in this case, BMW changed its policy by taking steps to avoid the sale of any refinished vehicles in Alabama and two other States. When the $4 million verdict was returned in this case, BMW promptly instituted a nationwide policy of full disclosure of all repairs, no matter how minor.

In response to BMW's arguments, Dr. Gore asserted that the policy change demonstrated the efficacy of the punitive damages award. He noted that while no jury had held the policy unlawful, BMW had received a number of customer complaints relating to undisclosed repairs and had settled some lawsuits. Finally, he maintained that the disclosure statutes of other States were irrelevant because BMW had failed to offer any evidence that the disclosure statutes supplanted, rather than supplemented, existing causes of action for common-law fraud.

◆　◆　◆

The Alabama Supreme Court . . . rejected BMW's claim that the award exceeded the constitutionally permissible amount.

◆　◆　◆

The Alabama Supreme Court did, however, rule in BMW's favor on one critical point: The court found that the jury improperly computed the amount of punitive damages by multiplying Dr. Gore's compensatory damages by the number of similar sales in other jurisdictions. Having found the verdict tainted, the court held that "a constitutionally reasonable punitive damages award in this case is

$2,000,000," and therefore ordered a remittitur in that amount.

♦ ♦ ♦

Punitive damages may properly be imposed to further a State's legitimate interests in punishing unlawful conduct and deterring its repetition. In our federal system, States necessarily have considerable flexibility in determining the level of punitive damages that they will allow in different classes of cases and in any particular case. Most States that authorize exemplary damages afford the jury similar latitude, requiring only that the damages awarded be reasonably necessary to vindicate the State's legitimate interests in punishment and deterrence. Only when an award can fairly be categorized as "grossly excessive" in relation to these interests does it enter the zone of arbitrariness that violates the Due Process Clause of the Fourteenth Amendment. For that reason, the federal excessiveness inquiry appropriately begins with an identification of the state interests that a punitive award is designed to serve. We therefore focus our attention first on the scope of Alabama's legitimate interests in punishing BMW and deterring it from future misconduct.

No one doubts that a State may protect its citizens by prohibiting deceptive trade practices and by requiring automobile distributors to disclose presale repairs that affect the value of a new car. But the States need not, and in fact do not, provide such protection in a uniform manner. Some States rely on the judicial process to formulate and enforce an appropriate disclosure requirement by applying principles of contract and tort law. Other States have enacted various forms of legislation that define the disclosure obligations of automobile manufacturers, distributors, and dealers. The result is a patchwork of rules representing the diverse policy judgments of lawmakers in 50 States.

That diversity demonstrates that reasonable people may disagree about the value of a full disclosure requirement. Some legislatures may conclude that affirmative disclosure requirements are unnecessary because the self-interest of those involved in the automobile trade in developing and maintaining the good-will of their customers will motivate them to make voluntary disclosures or to refrain from selling cars that do not comply with self-imposed standards. Those legislatures that do adopt affirmative disclosure obligations may take into account the cost of government regulation, choosing to draw a line exempting minor repairs from such a requirement. In formulating a disclosure standard, States may also consider other goals, such as providing a "safe harbor" for automobile manufacturers, distributors, and dealers against lawsuits over minor repairs.

We may assume, *arguendo*, that it would be wise for every State to adopt Dr. Gore's preferred rule, requiring full disclosure of every presale repair to a car, no matter how trivial and regardless of its actual impact on the value of the car. But while we do not doubt that Congress has ample authority to enact such a policy for the entire Nation, it is clear that no single State could do so, or even impose its own policy choice in neighboring States. Similarly, one State's power to impose burdens on the interstate market for automobiles is not only subordinate to the federal power over interstate commerce, but is also constrained by the need to respect the interests of other States.

We think it follows from these principles of state sovereignty and comity that a State may not impose economic sanctions on violators of its laws with the intent of changing the tortfeasors' lawful conduct in other States. Before this Court Dr. Gore argued that the large punitive damages award was necessary to induce BMW to change the nationwide policy that it adopted in 1983. But by attempting to alter BMW's nationwide policy, Alabama would be infringing on the policy choices of other States. To avoid such encroachment, the economic penalties that a State such as Alabama inflicts on those who transgress its laws, whether the penalties take the form of legislatively authorized fines or judicially imposed punitive damages, must be supported by the State's interest in protecting its own consumers and its own economy. Alabama may insist that BMW adhere to a particular disclosure policy in that State. Alabama does not have the power, however, to punish BMW for conduct that was lawful where it occurred and that had no impact on Alabama or its residents. Nor may Alabama impose sanctions on BMW in order to deter conduct that is lawful in other jurisdictions.

In this case, we accept the Alabama Supreme Court's interpretation of the jury verdict as reflecting a computation of the amount of punitive damages "based in large part on conduct that happened in other jurisdictions." As the Alabama Supreme Court noted, neither the jury nor the trial court was presented with evidence that any of BMW's out-of-state conduct was unlawful. "The only testimony touching the issue showed that approximately 60% of the vehicles that were refinished were sold in states where failure to disclose the repair was not an unfair trade practice." The Alabama Supreme Court therefore properly eschewed reliance on BMW's out-of-state conduct, and based its remitted award solely on conduct that occurred within Alabama. The award must be analyzed in the light of the same conduct, with consideration given only to the interests of Alabama consumers, rather than those of the entire Nation. When the scope of the interest in punishment and deterrence that an Alabama court may appropriately consider is properly limited, it is apparent—for reasons we shall now address—that this award is grossly excessive.

Elementary notions of fairness enshrined in our constitutional jurisprudence dictate that a person receive fair notice not only of the conduct that will subject him to punishment, but also of the severity of the penalty that a State may impose. Three guideposts, each of which indicates that BMW did not receive adequate notice of the magnitude of the sanction that Alabama might impose for adhering to the nondisclosure policy adopted in 1983, lead us to the conclusion that the $2 million award against BMW is grossly excessive: the degree of reprehensibility of the nondisclosure; the disparity between the harm or potential harm suffered by Dr. Gore and his punitive damages award; and the difference between this remedy and the civil penalties authorized or imposed in comparable cases. We discuss these considerations in turn.

DEGREE OF REPREHENSIBILITY

Perhaps the most important indicium of the reasonableness of a punitive damages award is the degree of reprehensibility of the defendant's conduct. As the Court stated nearly 150 years ago, exemplary damages imposed on a defendant should reflect "the enormity of his offense." This principle reflects the accepted view that some wrongs are more blameworthy than others. Thus, we have said, "nonviolent crimes are less serious than crimes marked by violence or the threat of violence." Similarly, "trickery and deceit," are more reprehensible than negligence. . . .

In this case, none of the aggravating factors associated with particularly reprehensible conduct is present. The harm BMW inflicted on Dr. Gore was purely economic in nature. The presale refinishing of the car had no effect on its performance or safety features, or even its appearance for at least nine months after his purchase. BMW's conduct evinced no indifference to or reckless disregard for the health and safety of others. To be sure, infliction of economic injury, especially when done intentionally through affirmative acts of misconduct, or when the target is financially vulnerable, can warrant a substantial penalty. But this observation does not convert all acts that cause economic harm into torts that are sufficiently reprehensible to justify a significant sanction in addition to compensatory damages.

♦ ♦ ♦

Finally, the record in this case discloses no deliberate false statements, acts of affirmative misconduct, or concealment of evidence of improper motive. We accept, of course, the jury's finding that BMW suppressed a material fact, which Alabama law obligated it to communicate to prospective purchasers of repainted cars in that State. But the omission of a material fact may be less reprehensible than a deliberate false statement, particularly when there is a good-faith basis for believing that no duty to disclose exists.

That conduct is sufficiently reprehensible to give rise to tort liability, and even a modest award of exemplary damages does not establish the high degree of culpability that warrants a substantial punitive damages award. Because this case exhibits none of the circumstances ordinarily associated with egregiously improper conduct, we are persuaded that BMW's conduct was not sufficiently reprehensible to warrant imposition of a $2 million exemplary damages award.

have been difficult to determine. It is appropriate, therefore, to reiterate our rejection of a categorical approach. . . . In most cases, the ratio will be within a constitutionally acceptable range, and remittitur will not be justified on this basis. When the ratio is a breathtaking 500 to 1, however, the award must surely "raise a suspicious judicial eyebrow."

RATIO

The second and perhaps most commonly cited indicium of an unreasonable or excessive punitive damages award is its ratio to the actual harm inflicted on the plaintiff. The principle that exemplary damages must bear a "reasonable relationship" to compensatory damages has a long pedigree. Scholars have identified a number of early English statutes authorizing the award of multiple damages for particular wrongs. Some 65 different enactments during the period between 1275 and 1753 provided for double, treble, or quadruple damages. Our decisions in [two earlier cases] endorsed the proposition that a comparison between the compensatory award and the punitive award is significant.

◆ ◆ ◆

The $2 million in punitive damages awarded to Dr. Gore by the Alabama Supreme Court is 500 times the amount of his actual harm as determined by the jury. Moreover, there is no suggestion that Dr. Gore or any other BMW purchaser was threatened with any additional potential harm by BMW's nondisclosure policy. . . .

Of course, we have consistently rejected the notion that the constitutional line is marked by a simple mathematical formula, even one that compares actual *and potential* damages to the punitive award. Indeed, low awards of compensatory damages may properly support a higher ratio than high compensatory awards, if, for example, a particularly egregious act has resulted in only a small amount of economic damages. A higher ratio may also be justified in cases in which the injury is hard to detect or the monetary value of noneconomic harm might

SANCTIONS FOR COMPARABLE MISCONDUCT

Comparing the punitive damages award and the civil or criminal penalties that could be imposed for comparable misconduct provides a third indicium of excessiveness. As Justice O'Connor has correctly observed, a reviewing court engaged in determining whether an award of punitive damages is excessive should "accord 'substantial deference' to legislative judgments concerning appropriate sanctions for the conduct at issue." . . . In this case the $2 million economic sanction imposed on BMW is substantially greater than the statutory fines available in Alabama and elsewhere for similar malfeasance.

The maximum civil penalty authorized by the Alabama Legislature for a violation of its Deceptive Trade Practices Act is $2,000; other States authorize more severe sanctions, with the maxima ranging from $5,000 to $10,000. Significantly, some statutes draw a distinction between first offenders and recidivists; thus, in New York the penalty is $50 for a first offense and $250 for subsequent offenses. None of these statutes would provide an out-of-state distributor with fair notice that the first violation—or, indeed the first 14 violations—of its provisions might subject an offender to a multimillion-dollar penalty. Moreover, at the time BMW's policy was first challenged, there does not appear to have been any judicial decision in Alabama or elsewhere indicating that application of that policy might give rise to such severe punishment.

The sanction imposed in this case cannot be justified on the ground that it was necessary to deter future misconduct without considering whether less drastic remedies could be expected to achieve that goal. The fact that a multimillion-dollar penalty prompted a change in policy sheds no light on the question whether a lesser deterrent would have adequately protected the interests of Alabama consumers. In the absence of a history of noncompliance with known statutory requirements, there is no basis for assuming that a more modest sanction would not have been sufficient to motivate full compliance with the disclosure requirement imposed by the Alabama Supreme Court in this case.

♦ ♦ ♦

[W]e are not prepared to draw a bright line marking the limits of a constitutionally acceptable punitive damages award. [H]owever, we are fully convinced that the grossly excessive award imposed in this case transcends the constitutional limit. Whether the appropriate remedy requires a new trial or merely an independent determination by the Alabama Supreme Court of the award necessary to vindicate the economic interests of Alabama consumers is a matter that should be addressed by the state court in the first instance.

The judgment is reversed, and the case is remanded for further proceedings not inconsistent with this opinion.

It is so ordered.

♦ ♦ ♦

Justice Scalia, with whom Justice Thomas joins, dissenting.

Today we see the latest manifestation of this Court's recent and increasingly insistent "concern about punitive damages that 'run wild.'" Since the Constitution does not make that concern any of our business, the Court's activities in this area are an unjustified incursion into the province of state governments.

In earlier cases that were the prelude to this decision, I set forth my view that a state trial procedure that commits the decision whether to impose punitive damages, and the amount, to the discretion of the jury, subject to some judicial review for "reasonableness," furnishes a defendant with all the process that is "due." I do not regard the Fourteenth Amendment's Due Process Clause as a secret repository of substantive guarantees against "unfairness"—neither the unfairness of an excessive civil compensatory award, nor the unfairness of an "unreasonable" punitive award. What the Fourteenth Amendment's procedural guarantee assures is an opportunity to contest the reasonableness of a damages judgment in state court; but there is no federal guarantee a damages award actually *be* reasonable.

Note: Beyond *Gore*

Although the Supreme Court had previously raised the possibility that punitive damage awards might violate due process norms, *Gore* was the first instance in which the justices invalidated a state court punitive damage assessment as excessive. In *State Farm Mutual Automobile Insurance Co.* v. *Campbell*, 538 U.S. 408 (2003), the Court, by a 6 to 3 vote, struck down a state court award of $145 million in punitive damages, where the compensatory damages were $1 million, as excessive and in violation of the due process clause of the Fourteenth Amendment. Amplifying the guidelines set forth in *Gore* for reviewing punitive damages, the Court put particular stress upon the ratio between punitive damages and the amount of compensatory damages. The Court declared: "Our jurisprudence and the principles it has now established demonstrate, however, that, in practice, few awards exceeding a single-digit ration between punitive and compensatory damages, to a significant degree, will satisfy due process." In these cases the Supreme Court appears to recognize a substantive right to be protected against unreasonable awards of punitive damages.

Note: Tobacco Litigation

Starting in the 1950s, litigation against tobacco manufacturers has been premised on a variety of grounds. In an early wave of lawsuits, individual smokers sued cigarette companies in tort to recover damages for personal injuries caused by smoking-related diseases. This line of cases reached a climax in *Cipollone* v. *Liggett Group, Inc.,* 505 U.S. 504 (1992), in which the Supreme Court found that the warnings on cigarette packages, imposed by the Cigarette Label Act of 1965 as amended, precluded suits based on the failure to warn about health hazards. The Court ruled, however, that the federal act did not bar claims for fraudulent misrepresentation and concealment.

A second phase of tobacco litigation focused on allegations that smoking was addictive and that cigarette companies fraudulently concealed health risks. Several state court actions grounded on such arguments have resulted in sizable compensatory and punitive damage awards against tobacco manufacturers. Yet in 2003 a Florida appellate court reversed the largest punitive damage award in American history against the industry. Although a number of suits proceeding on the fraud and concealment theory are pending at this time, it should be noted that juries in several cases have returned verdicts in favor of the cigarette companies. The juries evidently reasoned that the plaintiffs knew that cigarettes were injurious and assumed the health risk by continuing to smoke.

Another chapter in the ongoing tobacco litigation involves lawsuits by state governments to recover from cigarette manufacturers Medicare expenses for treating patients with smoking-related illnesses. These state suits produced a master settlement in 1998 under which all major tobacco companies agreed to pay $240 billion to state governments through 2025. In addition to defraying state health-care expenses, it was thought that the increase in cigarette prices to finance the payments would discourage future smoking. The master settlement also limits certain forms of tobacco advertising.

Observers have been sharply divided over the desirability and likely outcome of the tobacco litigation. Some maintain that the lawsuits have revealed industry misconduct and compelled the companies to shoulder the costs that cigarettes impose upon public health. Others are more critical. They point out that the tobacco payments constitute in effect an indirect tax on smokers. They also question whether the use of tort law in lieu of regulation as a means to penalize industry wrongdoing will prove effective to curb the health risks of smoking. At root the tobacco litigation raises the fundamental question of whether the tort system should stress compensation for injury or hold persons responsible for the adverse consequences of their own actions.

PROPERTY

Broad changes took place in many areas of property law in the post–World War II era. Public regulation of land use grew more intense and generated tension between the needs of the community and the rights of individuals to enjoy their property. Increased governmental involvement in property law has been a source of controversy. This has been especially true with respect to the law governing zoning, eminent domain, environmental controls, and landlord-tenant relations, as the following materials indicate.

Lionshead Lake, Inc. v. Wayne Tp.
10 N.J. 165 (1952)

Zoning laws after World War II went hand in hand with suburban development. The auto-mobile opened the countryside; low land values put housing within the reach of many peo-ple; and the suburbs offered prosperous middle-class and well-to-do persons a refuge from the social problems of the inner city. City and county officials quickly learned that through zoning regulations they could enhance the value of their communities by restricting the ac-cess of undesirable persons. This celebrated case deals with one such "snob"-zoning zon-ing ordinance in New Jersey.

The opinion of the court was delivered by Van-derbilt, C.J.

The plaintiff, the owner and developer of a large tract of land in the defendant township, commenced this action . . . challenging the va-lidity of the defendant's zoning ordinance in fixing the minimum size of dwellings and in placing certain of its properties in a residential district. . . .

The Township of Wayne is the most ex-tensive municipality in Passaic County. It cov-ers 25.34 square miles in comparison with the 23.57 square miles of Newark. It has a popula-tion of 11,815 in comparison with Newark's 437,857. Only 12% of the total area of the town-ship has been built up. Included within its bor-ders are several sizable lakes . . . and as a re-sult a considerable number of its residences have been built for summer occupancy only. Al-though a political entity it is in fact a compos-ite of about a dozen widely scattered residen-tial communities, varying from developments like the plaintiff's where the average home costs less than $10,000, to more expensive sec-tions where the homes cost from $35,000 to $75,000. It has but little business or industry.

On July 12, 1949, four years after the plain-tiff had commenced the development of its Li-onshead Lake properties and after over a hun-dred houses had been constructed there, the defendant adopted a revised zoning ordinance dividing the entire township into four districts; resident districts A and B, a business district and an industrial district, the last two compris-ing but a very small proportion of the town-ship's total area. In section 3 of the ordinance pertaining to residence A districts it was pro-vided that:

(d) Minimum Size of Dwellings:
    Every dwelling hereafter erected or placed in a Residence A District shall have a living-floor space, as herein defined.
    of not less than 768 square feet for a one story dwelling:
    of not less than 1000 square feet for a two story dwelling having an attached garage;
    of not less than 1200 square feet for a two story dwelling not having an attached garage.

These minimum size requirements for dwellings were made applicable . . . through-out the entire township.

Within the entire township only about 70% of all the existing dwellings meet the minimum requirements of the ordinance; in some sections of the township as few as 20% of the existing dwellings comply with the ordinance require-ments, in others (among them the plaintiff's Li-onshead Lake development) only about 50% are above the prescribed minimum, while in other areas the percentage of compliance is far greater, reaching 100% in some of the more ex-clusive sections. The low percentage of com-pliance in certain areas is not particularly sig-nificant, however, for the reason that the township is as yet substantially undeveloped. [This court] has held that so long as the zoning ordinance was reasonably designed, by what-ever means, to further the advancement of a community as a social, economic, and political unit, it is in the general welfare and therefore a proper exercise of the zoning power. The underlying question before us is whether in the light of these constitutional and legislative provisions the zoning ordinance of the defendant township is arbitrary and unreasonable. That question, moreover, must be answered in the light of the facts of this particular case. We must bear in mind, finally, that a zoning ordinance is not like the law of the Medes and Persians; variances may be permitted, the zoning ordinance may be amended, and if the ordinance proves unreasonable in operation it may be set-aside at any time.

◆ ◆ ◆

The Township of Wayne is still for the most part a sparsely settled countryside with great natural attractions in its lakes, hills and streams, but obviously it lies in the path of the next onward wave of suburban development. Whether that development shall be "with a view of conserving the value of property and encouraging the most appropriate use of land throughout such municipality" and whether it will "prevent the overcrowding of land or buildings" and "avoid undue concentration of population" depends in large measure on the wisdom of the governing body of the municipality as expressed in its zoning ordinance. It requires as much official watchfulness to anticipate and prevent suburban blight as it does to eradicate city slums.

Has a municipality the right to impose minimum floor area requirements in the exercise of its zoning powers? Much of the proof adduced by the defendant township was devoted to showing that the mental and emotional health of its inhabitants depended on the proper size of their homes. We may take notice without formal proof that there are minimums in housing below which one may not go without risk of impairing the health of those who dwell therein. One does not need extensive experience in matrimonial causes to become aware of the adverse effect of over-crowding on the well being of our most important institution, the home. Moreover, people who move into the country rightly expect more land, more living room, indoors and out, and more freedom in their scale of liv-

ing than is generally possible in the city. City standards of housing are not adaptable to suburban areas and especially to the upbringing of children. But quite apart from these considerations of public health which cannot be overlooked, minimum floor-area standards are justified on the ground that they promote the general welfare of the community and, as we have seen in *Schmidt* v. *Board of Adjustment of the City of Newark,* the courts in conformance with the constitutional provisions and the statutes hereinbefore cited take a broad view of what constitutes general welfare. The size of the dwellings in any community inevitably affects the character of the community and does much to determine whether or not it is a desirable place in which to live. It is the prevailing view in municipalities throughout the State that such minimum floor-area standards are necessary to protect the character of the community. In the light of the Constitution and of the enabling statutes, the right of a municipality to impose minimum floor-area requirements is beyond controversy.

◆ ◆ ◆

The zoning powers of municipalities have been extended by Art. IV, Sec. VI, par. 2 of the Constitution of 1947:

The Legislature may enact general laws under which municipalities, other than counties, may adopt zoning ordinances limiting and restricting to specified districts and regulating therein, buildings and structures, according to their construction, and the nature and extent of their use, *and the nature and extent of the uses of land,* and the exercise of such authority shall be deemed to be within the police power of the State. Such laws shall be subject to repeal or alteration by the Legislature.

◆ ◆ ◆

When the enabling zoning statutes . . . are read in the light of the constitutional mandate to construe them liberally, there can be no doubt that a municipality has the power by a suitable zoning ordinance to impose minimum living-floor space requirements for dwellings.

◆ ◆ ◆

Thus not only has the Constitution conferred on the Legislature very broad powers to pass enabling acts with respect to zoning but the Legislature in a like effort to make effective its constitutional power in this respect has given the municipalities similar broad powers expressed in considerably greater detail than in the Constitution. To the traditional presumption with respect to the validity of every legislative act there has been added, moreover, the constitutional mandate to construe such legislation liberally in favor of the municipalities.

◆　◆　◆

We are bound by these changes in our organic law and . . . in the light of all of the surrounding circumstances the minimum floor-area requirements are reasonable. . . . If some such requirements were not imposed there would be grave danger in certain parts of the township, particularly around the lakes which attract summer visitors, of the erection of shanties which would deteriorate land values generally to the great detriment of the increasing number of people who live in Wayne Township the year round. The minimum floor area requirements imposed by the ordinance are not large for a family of normal size. Without some such restrictions there is always the danger that after some homes have been erected giving a character to a neighborhood others might follow which would fail to live up to the standards thus voluntarily set. This has been the experience in many communities and it is against this that the township has sought to safeguard itself within limits which seem to us to be altogether reasonable. . . .

The judgment on the first count of the plaintiff's complaint is reversed.

Oliphant, J. (dissenting)

I find I must dissent from the philosophy and the result arrived at in the majority opinion. Zoning has its purposes, but as I conceive the effect of the majority opinion precludes individuals in those income brackets who could not pay between $8,500 and $12,000 for the erection of a house on a lot from ever establishing a residence in this community as long

as the 768 square feet of living space is the minimum requirement in the zoning ordinance. A zoning provision that can produce this effect certainly runs afoul of the fundamental principles of our form of government. It places an unnecessary and severe restriction upon the alienation of real estate. It is not necessary; it seems to me, in order to meet any possible threat to the general health and welfare of the community.

◆　◆　◆

While zoning regulations may legitimately be imposed in the district to serve the general welfare by "conserving the value of property and encouraging the most appropriate uses of land," such regulations are wholly unreasonable and beyond the zoning power and an unwarranted interference with private property rights if they are designed or operate to change completely, for better or for worse, the very character of the district. Any regulation imposed must bear a reasonable relation to the particular area subject thereto. Insofar as the minimum living floor space requirements of the ordinance under review apply to the entire community and to the plaintiff's properties in particular, they are clearly arbitrary and capricious and were very properly set aside by the trial court as an abuse of the zoning power.

My views on this particular phase of zoning do not prohibit minimum floor space in a house in particular districts or a proper correlation of minimum floor space in the house and the area of the lot or lots in question, but I cannot agree with the majority when they state with respect to this minimum square footage requirements that "whether it will 'prevent the overcrowding of land or buildings' and 'avoid undue concentration of population' depends in large measure on the wisdom of the governing body of the municipality." This is clearly indicative of a lack of standard with respect to this particular phase of zoning in the Zoning Act itself and it assumes that the discretion of the zoning board or governing body of a municipality amounts to wisdom.

Note: Zoning

The authority to zone, derived from the police powers of the states, is typically delegated to municipalities. New York City passed the first comprehensive zoning plan in 1916, and it subsequently became a model for the rest of the nation. The Supreme Court a decade later, in *Village of Euclid* v. *Ambler Realty Co.* (1926), upheld local zoning control as a rational extension of traditional public-nuisance law. Justice George Sutherland, speaking for the Court, made the point that zoning laws had the added advantage of alerting all owners before the fact of what they could and could not do with their property.

Zoning rested on the police power to protect the health, safety, and welfare of the public. After years of hesitation, by the 1980s most state courts adopted the position that land use controls could be based upon aesthetic considerations alone. They reasoned that a community's desire to enhance scenic beauty might protect property values, indirectly promote public health and safety, and preserve community character. Reliance on aesthetic considerations, however, means that local government must resolve subjective questions about beauty and unsightliness. Moreover, regulations that prohibit the display of signs raise free speech concerns.

Proponents of the Law and Economics school insist that zoning and, more generally, most forms of property regulation are economically inefficient because public officials are far less likely than rationally acting private individuals to maximize the use and derive the greatest wealth from land. The impact of this theory on land use planning is uncertain, but some courts have become more protective of the rights of landowners. In *Nollan* v. *California Coastal Commission,* 483 U.S. 825 (1987), for example, the Supreme Court indicated that it will give increased scrutiny to takings carried out by *regulatory* bodies. In that case, Justice Antonin Scalia's opinion for the Court held that the California Coastal Commission could not, without paying compensation, condition the grant of permission to rebuild a property owner's house on the transfer to the public of an easement across beachfront property that would allow the public access to the beach. The justices strengthened the constitutional restraints on governmentally imposed building conditions in *Dolan* v. *City of Tigard,* 512 U.S. 374 (1994). The Court insisted that a condition must be "roughly proportional" to the need that the proposed land development would cause. It struck down a requirement that the owner of a plumbing supply store dedicate an easement over her land to the city for use as a floodplain and a bicycle pathway as a condition to obtain a permit to expand her store.

EMINENT DOMAIN

Eminent domain is the power of government to compel an owner of real or personal property to transfer it to the government for public use. The Constitution does not expressly confer eminent domain authority, but the existence of such power has long been regarded as an inherent aspect of governmental sovereignty. As discussed in earlier chapters, state and federal governments in the nineteenth century started to delegate the power of eminent domain to private corporations, such as railroads and utilities, thought to carry out quasi-public functions. The takings clause of the Fifth Amendment, and similar provisions in state constitutions, restricts the exercise of eminent domain in two significant respects. It requires that private property be taken for "public use" and mandates that "just compensation" be paid to the owners of such property. Thus, the Fifth Amendment sought to strike a balance between the rights of property owners and societal needs.

Hawaii Housing Authority v. Midkiff
467 U.S. 229 (1984)

During the nineteenth century, both federal and state courts agreed that eminent domain could only be employed to acquire property for "public use." In other words, eminent domain did not empower government to take the property of one individual and transfer it to another, even with the payment of compensation. However, courts tended to adopt an open-ended definition of "public use" and to defer to legislative findings that a particular appropriation of property served the public interest. Hence, the "public use" limitation was gradually weakened as restraint on the exercise of eminent domain. Following World War II both federal and state governments utilized eminent domain on a more extensive scale for urban renewal and business development projects. Although many of those projects entailed the transfer of land to a private corporation or redevelopment agency, the Supreme Court broadly upheld such schemes in Berman v. Parker, 348 U.S. 26 (1954). *In* Midkiff *the justices went a step further, sustaining a Hawaii land reform statute that allowed tenants under long-term leases to acquire by eminent domain their landlord's title to the land. In so doing the justices reaffirmed the policy of judicial deference to the judgment of lawmakers as to what constitutes public use.*

Justice O'Connor delivered the opinion of the Court.

The Fifth Amendment of the United States Constitution provides, in pertinent part, that "private property [shall not] be taken for public use, without just compensation." These cases present the question whether the Public Use Clause of that Amendment, made applicable to the States through the Fourteenth Amendment, prohibits the State of Hawaii from taking, with just compensation, title in real property from lessors and transferring it to lessees in order to reduce the concentration of ownership of fees simple in the State. We conclude that it does not.

I

A

The Hawaiian Islands were originally settled by Polynesian immigrants from the western Pacific. These settlers developed an economy around a feudal land tenure system in which one island high chief, the ali'i nui, controlled the land and assigned it for development to certain subchiefs. The subchiefs would then reassign the land to other lower ranking chiefs, who would administer the land and govern the farmers and other tenants working it. All land was held at the will of the ali'i nui and eventually had to be returned to his trust. There was no private ownership of land.

Beginning in the early 1800's, Hawaiian leaders and American settlers repeatedly attempted to divide the lands of the kingdom among the crown, the chiefs, and the common people. These efforts proved largely unsuccessful, however, and the land remained in the hands of a few. In the mid-1960's, after extensive hearings, the Hawaii Legislature discovered that, while the State and Federal Governments owned almost 49% of the State's land, another 47% was in the hands of only 72 private landowners. The legislature further found that 18 landholders, with tracts of 21,000 acres or more, owned more than 40% of this land and that on Oahu, the most urbanized of the islands, 22 landowners owned 72.5% of the fee simple titles. The legislature concluded that concentrated land ownership was responsible for skewing the State's residential fee simple market, inflating land prices, and injuring the public tranquility and welfare.

To redress these problems, the legislature decided to compel the large landowners to break up their estates. The legislature considered requiring large landowners to sell lands, which they were leasing, to homeowners. However, the landowners strongly resisted this scheme, pointing out the significant federal tax liabilities they would incur. Indeed, the landowners claimed that the federal tax laws were the primary reason they previously had chosen to lease, and not sell, their lands. Therefore, to accommodate the needs of both lessors and lessees, the Hawaii Legislature enacted the Land Reform Act of 1967 (Act) which created a mechanism for condemning residential tracts and for transferring ownership of the condemned fees simple to existing lessees. By condemning the land in question, the Hawaii legislature intended to make the land sales involuntary, thereby making the federal tax consequences less severe while still facilitating the redistribution of fees simple.

Under the Act's condemnation scheme, tenants living on single-family residential lots within developmental tracts at least five acres in size are entitled to ask the Hawaii Housing Authority (HHA) to condemn the property on which they live. When 25 eligible tenants, or tenants on half the lots in the tract, whichever is less, file appropriate applications, the Act authorizes HHA to hold a public hearing to determine whether acquisition by the State of all or part of the tract will "effectuate the public purposes" of the Act. If HHA finds that these public purposes will be served, it is authorized to designate some or all of the lots in the tract for acquisition. It then acquires, at prices set either by condemnation trial or by negotiation between lessors and lessees, the former fee owners' full "right, title, and interest" in the land.

After compensation has been set, HHA may sell the land titles to tenants who have applied for fee simple ownership. HHA is authorized to lend these tenants up to 90% of the purchase price, and it may condition final transfer on a right of first refusal for the first 10 years following sale. If HHA does not sell the lot to the tenant residing there, it may lease the lot or sell it to someone else, provided that public notice has been given. However, HHA may not sell to any one purchaser, or lease to any one tenant, more than one lot, and it may not operate for profit. In practice, funds to satisfy the condemnation awards have been supplied entirely by lessees. While the Act authorizes HHA to issue bonds and appropriate funds for acquisition, no bonds have issued and HHA has not supplied any funds for condemned lots.

B

In April 1977, HHA held a public hearing concerning the proposed acquisition of some of appellees' lands. HHA made the statutorily required finding that acquisition of appellees' lands would effectuate the public purposes of the Act. Then, in October 1978, it directed appellees to negotiate with certain lessees concerning the sale of the designated properties. These negotiations failed, and HHA subsequently ordered appellees to submit to compulsory arbitration.

Rather than comply with the compulsory arbitration order, appellees filed suit, in February 1979, in United States District Court, asking that the Act be declared unconstitutional and that its enforcement be enjoined. The District Court temporarily restrained the State from proceeding against appellees' estates. Three months later, while declaring the compulsory arbitration and compensation formulae provisions of the Act unconstitutional, the District Court refused preliminarily to enjoin appellants from conducting the statutory designation and condemnation proceedings. Finally, in December 1979, it granted partial summary judgment to appellants, holding the remaining portion of the Act constitutional under the Public Use Clause. The District Court found that the Act's goals were within the bounds of the State's police powers and that the means the legislature had chosen to serve these goals were not arbitrary, capricious, or selected in bad faith.

The Court of Appeals for the Ninth Circuit reversed. First, the Court of Appeals decided that the District Court had permissibly chosen not to abstain from the exercise of its jurisdiction. Then, the Court of Appeals determined that the Act could not pass the requisite judicial scrutiny of the Public Use Clause. It found that the transfers contemplated by the Act were unlike those of takings previously held to constitute "public uses" by this Court. The court further determined that the public purposes offered by the Hawaii Legislature were not deserving of judicial deference. The court concluded that the Act was simply "a naked attempt on the part of the state of Hawaii to take the private property of A and transfer it to B solely for B's private use and benefit." One judge dissented.

On applications of HHA and certain private appellants who had intervened below, this Court noted probably jurisdiction. We now reverse.

◆ ◆ ◆

III

The majority of the Court of Appeals . . . determined that the Act violates the "public use" requirement of the Fifth and Fourteenth Amendments. On this argument, however, we find ourselves in agreement with the dissenting judge in the Court of Appeals.

A

The starting point for our analysis of the Act's constitutionality is the Court's decision in *Berman* v. *Parker*, 348 U.S. 26 (1954). In *Berman*, the Court held constitutional the District of Columbia Redevelopment Act of 1945. That Act provided both for the comprehensive use of the eminent domain power to redevelop slum areas and for the possible sale or lease of the condemned lands to private interests. In discussing whether the takings authorized by that Act were for a "public use," the Court stated:

We deal, in other words, with what traditionally has been known as the police power. An attempt to define its reach or trace its outer limits is fruitless, for each case must turn on its own facts. The definition is essentially the product of legislative determinations addressed to the purposes of government, purposes neither abstractly nor historically capable of complete definition. Subject to specific constitutional limitations, when the legislature has

spoken, the public interest has been declared in terms well-high conclusive. In such cases the legislature, not the judiciary, is the main guardian of the public needs to be served by social legislation, whether it be Congress legislating concerning the District of Columbia . . . or the States legislating concerning local affairs. . . . This principle admits of no exception merely because the power of eminent domain is involved. . . .

The Court explicitly recognized the breadth of the principle it was announcing, noting:

Once the object is within the authority of Congress, the right to realize it through the exercise of eminent domain is clear. For the power of eminent domain is merely the means to the end. . . . Once the object is within the authority of Congress, the means by which it will be attained is also for Congress to determine. Here one of the means chosen is the use of private enterprise for redevelopment of the area. Appellants argue that this makes the project a taking from one businessman for the benefit of another businessman. But the means of executing the project are for Congress and Congress alone to determine, once the public purpose has been established.

The "public use" requirement is thus coterminous with the scope of a sovereign's police powers.

There is, of course, a role for courts to play in reviewing a legislature's judgment of what constitutes a public use, even when the eminent domain power is equated with the police power. But the Court in *Berman* made clear that it is an "extremely narrow" one. The Court in *Berman* cited with approval the Court's decision in *Old Dominion Co.* v. *United States*, 269 U.S. 55, 66 (1925), which held that deference to the legislature's "public use" determination is required "until it is shown to involve an impossibility." The *Berman* Court also cited to *United States ex rel. TVA* v. *Welch*, 327 U.S. 546, 552 (1946), which emphasized that "[a]ny departure from this judicial restraint would result in courts deciding on what is and is not a governmental function and in their invalidating legislation on the basis of their view on that question at the moment of decision, a practice which has proved impracticable in other fields." In short, the Court has made clear that it will not substitute its judgment for a legislature's judgment as to what constitutes a public use "unless the use be palpably without reasonable foundation." *United States* v. *Gettysburg Electric R. Co.,* 160 U.S. 668, 680 (1896).

To be sure, the Court's cases have repeatedly stated that "one person's property" may not be taken for the benefit of another private person without a justifying public purpose, even though compensation be paid." Thus, in *Missouri Pacific R. Co.* v. *Nebraska,* 164 U.S. 403 (1896), where the "order in question was not, *and was not claimed to be,* . . . a taking of private property for a public use under the right of eminent domain," (emphasis added), the Court invalidated a compensated taking of property for lack of a justifying public purpose. But where the exercise of the eminent domain power is rationally related to a conceivable public purpose, the Court has never held a compensated taking to be proscribed by the Public Use Clause.

On this basis, we have no trouble concluding that the Hawaii Act is constitutional. The people of Hawaii have attempted, much as the settlers of the original 13 Colonies did, to reduce the perceived social and economic evils of a land oligopoly traceable to their monarchs. The land oligopoly has, according to the Hawaii Legislature, created artificial deterrents to the normal functioning of the State's residential land market and forced thousands of individual homeowners to lease, rather than buy, the land underneath their homes. Regulating oligopoly and the evils associated with it is a classic exercise of a State's police powers. We cannot disapprove of Hawaii's exercise of this power.

Nor can we condemn as irrational the Act's approach to correcting the land oligopoly problem. The Act presumes that when a sufficiently large number of persons declare that they are willing but unable to buy lots at fair prices the land market is malfunctioning. When such a malfunction is signaled, the Act authorizes HHA to condemn lots in the relevant tract. The Act limits the number of lots any one tenant can

purchase and authorizes HHA to use public funds to ensure that the market dilution goals will be achieved. This is a comprehensive and rational approach to identifying and correcting market failure.

Of course, this Act, like any other, may not be successful in achieving its intended goals. But "whether *in fact* the provision will accomplish its objectives is not the question: the [constitutional requirement] is satisfied if . . . the . . . [state] Legislature *rationally could have believed* that the [Act] would promote its objective." *Western & Southern Life Ins. Co.* v. *State Bd. of Equalization,* 451 U.S. 648, 671-672 (1981). When the legislature's purpose is legitimate and its means are not irrational, our cases make clear that empirical debates over the wisdom of takings—no less than debates over the wisdom of other kinds of socioeconomic legislation—are not to be carried out in the federal courts. Redistribution of fees simple to correct deficiencies in the market determined by the state legislature to be attributable to land oligopoly is a rational exercise of the eminent domain power. Therefore, the Hawaii statute must pass the scrutiny of the Public Use Clause.

B

The Court of Appeals read our cases to stand for a much narrower proposition. First, it read our "public use" cases, especially *Berman*, as requiring that government possess and use property at some point during a taking. Since Hawaiian lessees retain possession of the property for private use throughout the condemnation process, the court found that the Act exacted takings for private use. Second, it determined that these cases involved only "the review of . . . *congressional* determination[s] that there was a public use, *not* the review of . . . state legislative determination[s]," (emphasis in original). Because state legislative determinations are involved in the instant cases, the Court of Appeals decided that more rigorous judicial scrutiny of the public use determinations was appropriate. The court concluded that the Hawaii Legislature's professed purposes were mere "statutory rationalizations." We disagree with the Court of Appeals' analysis.

The mere fact that property taken outright by eminent domain is transferred in the first instance to private beneficiaries does not condemn that taking as having only a private purpose. The Court long ago rejected any literal requirement that condemned property be put into use for the general public. "It is not essential that the entire community, nor even any considerable portion, . . . directly enjoy or participate in any improvement in order [for it] to constitute a public use." *Rindge Co. v. Los Angeles,* 262 U.S., at 707. "[W]hat in its immediate aspect [is] only a private transaction may . . . be raised by its class or character to a public affair." *Block v. Hirsh,* 256 U.S., at 155. As the unique way titles were held in Hawaii skewed the land market, exercise of the power of eminent domain was justified. The Act advances its purposes without the State's taking actual possession of the land. In such cases, government does not itself have to use property to legitimate the taking; it is only the taking's purpose, and not its mechanics, that must pass scrutiny under the Public Use Clause.

Similarly, the fact that a state legislature, and not the Congress, made the public use determination does not mean that judicial deference is less appropriate. Judicial deference is required because, in our system of government, legislatures are better able to assess what public purposes should be advanced by an exercise of the taking power. State legislatures are as capable as Congress of making such determinations within their respective spheres of authority. Thus, if a legislature, state or federal, determines there are substantial reasons for an exercise of the taking power, courts must defer to its determination that the taking will serve a public use.

IV

The State of Hawaii has never denied that the Constitution forbids even a compensated taking of property when executed for no reason other than to confer a private benefit on a particular private party. A purely private taking could not withstand the scrutiny of the public use requirement; it would serve no legitimate purpose of government and would thus be void. But no purely private taking is involved in these cases. The Hawaii Legislature enacted its Land Reform Act not to benefit a particular class of identifiable individuals but to attack certain perceived evils of concentrated property ownership in Hawaii—a legitimate public purpose. Use of the condemnation power to achieve this purpose is not irrational. Since we assume for purposes of these appeals that the weighty demand of just compensation has been met, the requirements of the Fifth and Fourteenth Amendments have been satisfied. Accordingly, we reverse the judgment of the Court of Appeals, and remand these cases for further proceedings in conformity with this opinion.

It is so ordered.

Note: Eminent Domain Beyond *Midkiff*

With its decision in *Midkiff* the Supreme Court virtually eliminated the "public use" requirement of the Fifth Amendment as a check on the power of government to appropriate private property by means of eminent domain. Some state courts, however, have adopted a less deferential attitude toward the question of public use than that followed by the federal courts. They have invalidated the exercise of eminent domain when undertaken primarily for private use, with only incidental public benefit. In *Southwestern Illinois Development Authority v. National City Environmental, LLC,* 199 Ill.2d 225, 768 N.E.2d 1 (2002), for example, the Supreme Court of Illinois struck down the exercise of eminent domain to transfer land from one private party to another on grounds that such taking did not serve a public purpose. The court added: "The power of eminent domain is to be exercised with restraint, not abandon."

REGULATORY TAKINGS

In addition to the acquisition of private property under the power of eminent domain, government may also regulate the use of privately owned land under the police power. Whether a particular governmental action is a taking or a regulation is often contested. The Fifth Amendment provides in part: "nor shall private property be taken for public use without just compensation." As Justice Hugo Black explained in *Armstrong* v. *United States,* 364 U.S. 40, 49 (1960), the takings clause "was designed to bar Government from forcing some people alone to bear public burdens which, in all fairness and justice, should be borne by the public as a whole." Although sometimes shrouded in technical doctrine, jurisprudence under the takings clause raises a fundamental question for a free society: should individual owners or the general public pay the expense of providing social goods?

A critical inquiry is whether property has been "taken" by the government. One vexing problem is the extent to which governmental action, short of outright acquisition of title, constitutes a taking for which compensation must be paid. As Justice Oliver Wendell Holmes formulated the question in *Pennsylvania Coal Co.* v. *Mahon,* 260 U.S. 393, 415 (1922): "The general rule at least is, while property may be regulated to a certain extent, if regulation goes too far it will be recognized as a taking." A regulatory taking, then, is not an actual acquisition or physical invasion by government but an excessive restriction on an owner's right to use land in certain ways. Although the Supreme Court upheld the constitutionality of zoning as a land control device, the doctrine of a regulatory taking represents a potential check on the exercise of governmental authority. Starting in the 1980s the Supreme Court began to put some teeth into the regulatory takings doctrine.

Lucas v. South Carolina Coastal Council
505 U.S. 1003 (1992)

Most traditional land use controls do not have the effect of preventing all economically beneficial use of land. Environmental regulations, however, particularly with respect to beaches and wetlands, have grown progressively more stringent. Regulations that ban development and require that land remain in a natural state have been challenged as a regulatory taking of property. The underlying question is whether a limited number of landowners can fairly be required to bear the burden of protecting the environment. In Lucas *the Supreme Court, by a margin of 6 to 3, ruled that land use controls that deprived an owner of "all economically beneficial or productive use of land" were the practical equivalent of a physical appropriation and amounted to a per se taking of property.*

Justice Scalia delivered the opinion of the court.

In 1986, petitioner David H. Lucas paid $975,000 for two residential lots on the Isle of Palms in Charleston County, South Carolina, on which he intended to build single-family homes. In 1988, however, the South Carolina legislature enacted the Beachfront Management Act, (Act), which had the direct effect of barring petitioner from erecting any permanent habitable structures on his two parcels. A state trial court found that this prohibition rendered Lucas's parcels "valueless." This case requires us to decide whether the Act's dramatic effect on the economic value of Lucas's lots accomplished a taking of private property under the Fifth and Fourteenth Amendments requiring the payment of "just compensation."

I

A

South Carolina's expressed interest in intensively managing development activities in the so-called "coastal zone" dates from 1977 when, in the aftermath of Congress's passage of the federal Coastal Zone Management Act of 1972, the legislature enacted a Coastal Zone Management Act of its own. In its original form, the South Carolina Act required owners of coastal zone land that qualified as a "critical area" (defined in the legislation to include beaches and immediately adjacent sand dunes) to obtain a permit from the newly created South Carolina Coastal Council (respondent here) prior to committing the land to a "use other than the use the critical area was devoted to on [September 28, 1977]."

In the late 1970's, Lucas and others began extensive residential development of the Isle of Palms, a barrier island situated eastward of the City of Charleston. Toward the close of the development cycle for one residential subdivision known as "Beachwood East," Lucas in 1986 purchased the two lots at issue in this litigation for his own account. No portion of the lots, which were located approximately 300 feet from the beach, qualified as a "critical area" under the 1977 Act; accordingly, at the time Lucas acquired these parcels, he was not legally obliged to obtain a permit from the Council in advance of any development activity. His intention with respect to the lots was to do what the owners of the immediately adjacent parcels had already done: erect single-family residences. He commissioned architectural drawings for this purpose.

The Beachfront Management Act brought Lucas's plans to an abrupt end. Under that 1988 legislation, the Council was directed to establish a "baseline" connecting the landward most "point[s] of erosion . . . during the past forty years" in the region of the Isle of Palms that includes Lucas's lots. In action not challenged here, the Council fixed this baseline landward of Lucas's parcels. That was significant, for under the Act construction of occupiable improvement was flatly prohibited seaward of a line drawn 20 feet landward of, and parallel to, the baseline. The Act provided no exceptions.

B

Lucas promptly filed suit in the South Carolina Court of Common Pleas, contending that the Beachfront Management Act's construction bar effected a taking of his property without just compensation. Lucas did not take issue with the validity of the Act as a lawful exercise of South Carolina's police power, but contended that the Act's complete extinguishment of his property's value entitled him to compensation regardless of whether the legislature had acted in furtherance of legitimate police power objectives. Following a bench trial, the court agreed. Among its factual determinations was the finding that "at the time Lucas purchased the two lots, both were zoned for single-family residential construction and . . . there were no restrictions imposed upon such use of the property by either the State of South Carolina, the County of Charleston, or the Town of the Isle of Palms." The trial court further found that the Beachfront Management Act decreed a permanent ban on construction insofar as Lucas's lots were concerned, and that this prohibition "deprive[d] Lucas of any reasonable economic use of the lots, . . . eliminated the unrestricted rights of use, and render[ed] them valueless." The court thus concluded that Lucas's properties had been "taken" by operation of the Act, and it ordered respondent to pay "just compensation" in the amount of $1,232,387.50.

The Supreme Court of South Carolina reversed.

◆ ◆ ◆

We granted certiorari.

Prior to Justice Holmes' exposition in *Pennsylvania Coal Co.* v. *Mahon,* 260 U.S. 393 (1922), it was generally thought that the Takings Clause reached only a "direct appropriation" of property, Legal Tender Cases, 12 Wall. 457, 551

(1871), or the functional equivalent of a "practical ouster of [the owner's] possession." *Transportation Co. v. Chicago*, 99 U.S. 635, 642 (1879). Justice Holmes recognized in *Mahon*, however, that if the protection against physical appropriations of private property was to be meaningfully enforced, the government's power to redefine the range of interests included in the ownership of property was necessarily constrained by constitutional limits. If, instead, the uses of private property were subject to unbridled, uncompensated qualification under the police power, "the natural tendency of human nature [would be] to extend the qualification more and more until at last private property disappear[ed]." These considerations gave birth in that case to the oft-cited maxim that, "while property may be regulated to a certain extent, if regulation goes too far it will be recognized as a taking."

Nevertheless, our decision in *Mahon* offered little insight into when, and under what circumstances, a given regulation would be seen as going "too far" for purposes of the Fifth Amendment. In 70-odd years of succeeding "regulatory takings" jurisprudence, we have generally eschewed any " 'set formula' " for determining how far is too far, preferring to "engag[e] in . . . essentially ad hoc, factual inquiries." We have, however, described at least two discrete categories of regulatory action as compensable without case-specific inquiry into the public interest advanced in support of the restraint. The first encompasses regulations that compel the property owner to suffer a physical "invasion" of his property. In general (at least with regard to permanent invasions), no matter how minute the intrusion, and no matter how weighty the public purpose behind it, we have required compensation. For example, in *Loretto v. Teleprompter Manhattan CATV Corp.*, 458 U.S. 419 (1982), we determined that New York's law requiring landlords to allow television cable companies to emplace cable facilities in their apartment buildings constituted a taking, even though the facilities occupied at most $1^1/_2$ cubic feet of the landlords' property.

The second situation in which we have found categorical treatment appropriate is where regulation denies all economically ben-

eficial or productive use of land. As we have said on numerous occasions, the Fifth Amendment is violated when land-use regulation "does not substantially advance legitimate state interests *or denies an owner economically viable use of his land.*"

We have never set forth the justification for this rule. Perhaps it is simply . . . that total deprivation of beneficial use is, from the landowner's point of view, the equivalent of a physical appropriation. "[F]or what is the land but the profits thereof[?]" 1 E. Coke, Institutes, ch. 1, § 1 (1st Am. Ed. 1812). Surely, at least, in the extraordinary circumstance when *no* productive or economically beneficial use of land is permitted, it is less realistic to indulge our usual assumption that the legislature is simply "adjusting the benefits and burdens of economic life," in a manner that secures an "average reciprocity of advantage," to everyone concerned. And the *functional* basis for permitting the government, by regulation, to affect property values without compensation—that "Government hardly could go on if to some extent values incident to property could not be diminished without paying for every such change in the general law,"—does not apply to the relatively rare situations where the government has deprived a landowner of all economically beneficial uses.

On the other side of the balance, affirmatively supporting a compensation requirement, is the fact that regulations that leave the owner of land without economically beneficial or productive options for its use—typically, as here, by requiring land to be left substantially in its natural state—carry with them a heightened risk that private property is being pressed into some form of public service under the guise of mitigating serious public harm. As Justice Brennan explained: "From the government's point of view, the benefits flowing to the public from preservation of open space through regulation may be equally great as from creating a wildlife refuge through formal condemnation or increasing electricity production through a dam project that floods private property." The many statutes on the books, both state and federal, that provide for the use of eminent domain to impose servitudes on private scenic lands preventing developmental uses, or to acquire such lands altogether, suggest the practical equivalence in this setting of negative regulation and appropriation.

We think, in short, that there are good reasons for our frequently expressed belief that when the owner of real property has been called upon to sacrifice *all* economically beneficial uses in the name of the common good, that is, to leave his property economically idle, he has suffered a taking.

The trial court found Lucas's two beachfront lots to have been rendered valueless by respondent's enforcement of the coastal-zone construction ban. Under Lucas's theory of the case, which rested upon our "no economically viable use" statements, that finding entitled him to compensation. Lucas believed it unnecessary to take issue with either the purposes behind the Beachfront Management Act, or the means chosen by the South Carolina Legislature to effectuate those purposes. The South Carolina Supreme Court, however, thought otherwise. In its view, the Beachfront Management Act was no ordinary enactment, but involved an exercise of South Carolina's "police powers" to mitigate the harm to the public interest that petitioner's use of his land might occasion. By neglecting to dispute the findings enumerated in the Act or otherwise to challenge the legislature's purposes, petitioner "concede[d] that the beach/dune area of South Carolina's shores is an extremely valuable public resource; that the erection of new construction, inter alia, contributes to the erosion and destruction of this public resource; and that discouraging new construction in close proximity to the beach/dune area is necessary to prevent a great public harm." . . .

It is correct that many of our prior opinions have suggested that "harmful or noxious uses" of property may be proscribed by government regulation without the requirement of compensation. For a number of reasons, however, we think the South Carolina Supreme Court was too quick to conclude that that principle decides the present case. The "harmful or noxious uses" principle was the Court's early attempt to describe in theoretical terms why government may, consistent with the Takings Clause, affect property values by regulation without incurring an obligation to compensate—a reality we nowadays acknowledge explicitly with respect to the full scope of the State's police power. . . .

The transition from our early focus on control of "noxious" uses to our contemporary understanding of the broad realm within which government may regulate without compensation was an easy one, since the distinction between "harm-preventing" and "benefit-conferring" regulation is often in the eye of the beholder. It is quite possible, for example, to describe in *either* fashion the ecological, economic, and aesthetic concerns that inspired the South Carolina legislature in the present case. One could say that imposing servitude on Lucas's land is necessary in order to prevent this use of it from "harming" South Carolina's ecological resources; or, instead, in order to achieve the "benefits" of an ecological preserve. Whether one or the other of the competing characterizations will come to one's lips in a particular case depends primarily upon one's evaluation of the worth of competing uses of real estate. A given restraint will be seen as mitigating "harm" to the adjacent parcels or securing a "benefit" for them, depending upon the observer's evaluation of the relative importance of the use that the restraint favors. Whether Lucas's construction of single-family residences on his parcels should be described as bringing "harm" to South Carolina's adjacent ecological resources thus depends principally upon whether the describer believes that the State's use interest in nurturing those resources is so important that *any* competing adjacent use must yield.

When it is understood that "prevention of harmful use" was merely our early formulation of the police power justification necessary to sustain (without compensation) *any* regulatory diminution in value; and that the distinction between regulation that "prevents harmful use" and that which "confers benefits" is difficult, if not impossible, to discern on an objective, value-free basis; it becomes self-evident that noxious-use logic cannot serve as a touchstone to distinguish regulatory "takings"—which require compensation—from regulatory depriva-

tions that do not require compensation. A fortiori the legislature's recitation of a noxious-use
justification cannot be the basis for departing
from our categorical rule that total regulatory
takings must be compensated. If it were, departure would virtually always be allowed. The
South Carolina Supreme Court's approach
would essentially nullify *Mahon's* affirmation
of limits to the noncompensable exercise of the
police power. Our cases provide no support for
this: None of them that employed the logic of
"harmful use" prevention to sustain a regulation involved an allegation that the regulation
wholly eliminated the value of the claimant's
land.

Where the State seeks to sustain regulation
that deprives land of all economically beneficial use, we think it may resist compensation
only if the logically antecedent inquiry into the
nature of the owner's estate shows that the proscribed use interests were not part of his title to
begin with. This accords, we think, with our
"takings" jurisprudence, which has traditionally
been guided by the understandings of our citizens regarding the content of, and the State's
power over, the "bundle of rights" that they acquire when they obtain title to property. It
seems to us that the property owner necessarily expects the uses of his property to be restricted, from time to time, by various measures
newly enacted by the State in legitimate exercise of its police powers; "[a]s long recognized,
some values are enjoyed under an implied limitation and must yield to the police power."
Pennsylvania Coal Co. v. *Mahon,* 260 U.S., at
413. . . . In the case of land, however, we think
the notion pressed by the Council that title is
somehow held subject to the "implied limitation" that the State may subsequently eliminate
all economically valuable use is inconsistent
with the historical compact recorded in the Takings Clause that has become part of our constitutional culture.

Where "permanent physical occupation"
of land is concerned, we have refused to allow
the government to decree it anew (without compensation) no matter how weighty the asserted
"public interests" involved, though we assuredly *would* permit the government to assert
a permanent easement that was a pre-existing

limitation upon the landowner's title. We believe similar treatment must be accorded confiscatory regulations, i.e., regulations that prohibit all economically beneficial use of land:
Any limitation so severe cannot be newly legislated or decreed (without compensation), but
must inhere in the title itself, in the restrictions
that background principles of the State's law of
property and nuisance already place upon land
ownership. A law or decree with such an effect
must, in other words, do no more than duplicate the result that could have been achieved in
the courts—by adjacent landowners (or other
uniquely affected persons) under the State's law
of private nuisance, or by the State under its
complementary power to abate nuisances that
affect the public generally, or otherwise.

On this analysis, the owner of a lake bed,
for example, would not be entitled to compensation when he is denied the requisite permit to engage in a landfilling operation that
would have the effect of flooding others' land.
Nor the corporate owner of a nuclear generat-
ing plant, when it is directed to remove all improvements from its land upon discovery that
the plant sits astride an earthquake fault. Such
regulatory action may well have the effect of
eliminating the land's only economically productive use, but it does not proscribe a productive use that was previously permissible
under relevant property and nuisance principles. The use of these properties for what are
now expressly prohibited purposes was *always*
unlawful, and (subject to other constitutional
limitations), it was open to the State at any
point to make the implication of those background principles of nuisance and property
law explicit. In light of our traditional resort
to "existing rules or understandings that stem
from an independent source such as state law"
to define the range of interests that qualify for
protection as "property" under the Fifth (and
Fourteenth) amendments, this recognition that
the Takings Clause does not require compensation when an owner is barred from putting
land to a use that is proscribed by those "existing rules or understandings" is surely unex-
ceptional. When, however, a regulation that
declares "off-limits" all economically productive or beneficial uses of land goes beyond

what the relevant background principles would dictate, compensation must be paid to sustain it.

The "total taking" inquiry we require today will ordinarily entail (as the application of state nuisance law ordinarily entails) analysis of, among other things, the degree of harm to public lands and resources, or adjacent private property, posed by the claimant's proposed activities, the social value of the claimant's activities and their suitability to the locality in question, and the relative ease with which the alleged harm can be avoided through measures taken by the claimant and the government (or adjacent private landowners) alike. The fact that a particular use has long been engaged in by similarly situated owners ordinarily imports a lack of any common-law prohibition (though changed circumstances or new knowledge may make what was previously permissible no longer so[)]. So also does the fact that other landowners, similarly situated, are permitted to continue the use denied to the claimant.

It seems unlikely that common-law principles would have prevented the erection of any habitable or productive improvements on petitioner's land; they rarely support prohibi-

tion of the "essential use" of land. The question, however, is one of state law to be dealt with on remand. We emphasize that to win its case South Carolina must do more than proffer the legislature's declaration that the uses Lucas desires are inconsistent with the public interest, or the conclusory assertion that they violate a common-law maxim such as *sic utere tuo ut alienum non laedas.* As we have said, a "State, by *ipse dixit,* may not transform private property into public property without compensation . . . ." *Webb's Fabulous Pharmacies, Inc.* v. *Beckwith,* 449 U.S. 155, 164 (1980). Instead, as it would be required to do if it sought to restrain Lucas in a common-law action for public nuisance, South Carolina must identify background principles of nuisance and property law that prohibit the uses he now intends in the circumstances in which the property is presently found. Only on this showing can the State fairly claim that, in proscribing all such beneficial uses, the Beachfront Management Act is taking nothing.

The judgment is reversed and the cause remanded for proceedings not inconsistent with this opinion

So ordered.

RESIDENTIAL LEASES

During the 1960s and 1970s, courts rejected common-law doctrines favorable to landlords and recognized new substantive and procedural rights for residential tenants. Motivated in part by a belief that landlords possessed greater economic power, these changes had the effect of trumping written agreements between the parties by altering lease terms. Among other steps, courts imposed procedural safeguards against evictions to retaliate against a tenant who complained about housing conditions, and curtailed the landlord's use of self-help evictions. Following some path-breaking judicial decisions, legislatures in many states enacted comprehensive laws that overhauled residential landlord-tenant relationships. Governmental regulation of residential lease agreements is a prime example of how policy-driven law reform can impact traditional property laws. An even more far-reaching assault on the common law of landlord and tenant was the imposition of residential rent controls in a number of localities. Highly controversial, rent controls speak to the larger debate over the legitimate extent of governmental regulation of private property. It should be emphasized, however, that both courts and lawmakers have distinguished between residential and commercial leases in devising rules. As a general proposition, agreements struck in the marketplace and common-law doctrines continue to govern commercial leases.

Javins v. *First National Realty Corporation*
428 F.2d 1071 (D.C. Cir. 1970)

In this landmark decision the court rejected application of common-law principles and ruled that a residential landlord had an affirmative duty based on housing codes to maintain leased premises in a habitable condition. It also found that tenants were obligated to pay rent only when the premises were habitable and concluded that tenants need not vacate the property before asserting the right to refuse to pay rent based on the landlord's failure to make necessary repairs. In the wake of Javins, *virtually all states, by either judicial decision or legislative action, have imposed a warranty of habitability on residential leases.*

J. Skelly Wright, Circuit Judge:

These cases present the question whether housing code violations which arise during the term of a lease have any effect upon the tenant's obligation to pay rent. The Landlord and Tenant Branch of the District of Columbia Court of General Sessions ruled proof of such violations inadmissible when proffered as a defense to an eviction action for nonpayment of rent. The District of Columbia Court of Appeals upheld this ruling.

Because of the importance of the question presented, we granted appellants' petitions for leave to appeal. We now reverse and hold that a warranty of habitability, measured by the standards set out in the Housing Regulations for the District of Columbia, is implied by operation of law into leases of urban dwelling units covered by those Regulations and that breach of this warranty gives rise to the usual remedies for breach of contract.

I

The facts revealed by the record are simple. By separate written leases, each of the appellants rented an apartment in a three-building apartment complex in Northwest Washington known as Clifton Terrace. The landlord, First National Realty Corporation, filed separate actions in the Landlord and Tenant Branch of the Court of General Sessions on April 8, 1966, seeking possession on the ground that each of the appellants had defaulted in the payment of rent due for the month of April. The tenants, appellants here, admitted that they had not paid the landlord any rent for April. However, they alleged numerous violations of the Housing Regulations as "an equitable defense or [a] claim by way of recoupment or set-off in an amount equal to the rent claim," as provided in the rules of the Court of General Sessions. They offered to prove

[t]hat there are approximately 1500 violations of the Housing Regulations of the District of Columbia in the building at Clifton Terrace, where Defendant resides[,] some affecting the premises of this Defendant directly, others indirectly, and all tending to establish a course of conduct of violation of the Housing Regulations to the damage of Defendants. . . .

Settled Statement of Proceedings and Evidence, p. 2 (1966). Appellants conceded at trial, however, that this offer of proof reached only violations which had arisen since the term of the lease had commenced. The Court of General Sessions refused appellants' offer of proof and entered judgment for the landlord. The District of Columbia Court of Appeals affirmed, rejecting the argument made by appellants that the landlord was under a contractual duty to maintain the premises in compliance with the Housing Regulations.

II

Since, in traditional analysis, a lease was the conveyance of an interest in land, courts have usually utilized the special rules governing real property transactions to resolve controversies involving leases. However, as the Supreme Court has noted in another context, "the body of private property law . . . , more than almost any other branch of law, has been shaped by distinctions whose validity is largely historical." Courts have a duty to reappraise old doctrines in the light of the facts and values of contemporary life—particularly old common law doctrines which the courts themselves created and developed. As we have said before, "[T]he continued vitality of the common law . . . depends upon its ability to reflect contemporary community values and ethics."

The assumption of landlord-tenant law, derived from feudal property law, that a lease primarily conveyed to the tenant an interest in land may have been reasonable in a rural, agrarian society; it may continue to be reasonable in some leases involving farming or commercial land. In these cases, the value of the lease to the tenant is the land itself. But in the case of the modern apartment dweller, the value of the lease is that it gives him a place to live. The city dweller who seeks to lease an apartment on the third floor of a tenement has little interest in the land 30 or 40 feet below, or even in the bare right to possession within the four walls of his apartment. When American city dwellers, both rich and poor, seek "shelter" today, they seek a well known package of goods and services—a package which includes not merely walls and ceilings, but also adequate heat, light and ventilation, serviceable plumbing facilities, secure windows and doors, proper sanitation, and proper maintenance.

Professor Powell summarizes the present state of the law:

> . . . The complexities of city life, and the pro-liferated problems of modern society in general, have created new problems for lessors and lessees and these have been commonly handled by specific clauses inserted in leases. This growth in the number and detail of specific lease covenants has reintroduced into the law of estates for years a predominantly contractual ingredient. In practice, the law today concerning estates for years consists chiefly of rules determining the construction and effect of lease covenants. . . .

Ironically, however, the rules governing the construction and interpretation of "predominantly contractual" obligations in leases have too often remained rooted in old property law.

Some courts have realized that certain of the old rules of property law governing leases are inappropriate for today's transactions. In order to reach results more in accord with the legitimate expectations of the parties and the standards of the community, courts have been gradually introducing more modern precepts of contract law in interpreting leases. Proceeding piecemeal has, however, led to confusion where "decisions are frequently conflicting, not because of a healthy disagreement on social policy, but because of the lingering impact of rules whose policies are long since dead."

In our judgment the trend toward treating leases as contracts is wise and well considered. Our holding in this case reflects a belief that leases of urban dwelling units should be interpreted and construed like any other contract.

III

Modern contract law has recognized that the buyer of goods and services in an industrialized society must rely upon the skill and honesty of the supplier to assure that goods and services purchased are of adequate quality. In interpreting most contracts, courts have sought to protect the legitimate expectations of the buyer and have steadily widened the seller's responsibility for the quality of goods and services through implied warranties of fitness and merchantability. Thus without any special agreement a merchant will be held to warrant that his goods are fit for the ordinary purposes for which such goods are used and that they are at least of reasonably average quality. Moreover, if the supplier has been notified that goods are required for a specific purpose, he will be held to warrant that any goods sold are fit for that purpose. These implied warranties have become widely accepted and well established features of the common law, supported by the overwhelming body of case law. Today most states as well as the District of Columbia have codified and enacted these warranties into statute, as to the sale of goods, in the Uniform Commercial Code.

Implied warranties of quality have not been limited to cases involving sales. The consumer renting a chattel, paying for services, or buying a combination of goods and services must rely upon the skill and honesty of the supplier to at least the same extent as a purchaser of goods. Courts have not hesitated to find implied warranties of fitness and merchantability in such situations. In most areas product liability law has moved far beyond "mere" implied warranties running between two parties in privity with each other.

The rigid doctrines of real property law have tended to inhibit the application of implied warranties to transactions involving real estate. Now, however, courts have begun to hold sellers and developers of real property responsible for the quality of their product. For example, builders of new homes have recently been held liable to purchasers for improper construction on the ground that the builders have breached an implied warranty of fitness. In other cases courts have held builders of new homes liable for breach of an implied warranty that all local building regulations had been complied with. And following the developments in other areas, very recent decisions and commentary suggest the possible extension of liability to parties other than the immediate seller for improper construction of residential real estate.

Despite this trend in the sale of real estate, many courts have been unwilling to imply warranties of quality, specifically a warranty of habitability, into leases of apartments. Recent decisions have offered no convincing explanation for their refusal; rather they have relied without discussion upon the old common law rule that the lessor is not obligated to repair unless he covenants to do so in the written lease contract. However, the Supreme Courts of at least two states, in recent and well reasoned opinions, have held landlords to implied warranties of quality if housing leases. *Lemle* v. *Breeden,* S.Ct. Hawaii, 462 P.2d 470 (1969); *Reste Realty Corp.* v. *Cooper,* 53 N.J. 444, 251 A.2d 268 (1969). *See also Pines* v. *Perssion,* 14 Wis.2d 590, 111 N.W.2d 409 (1961). In our

judgment, the old no-repair rule cannot coexist with the obligations imposed on the landlord by a typical modern housing code, and must be abandoned in favor of an implied warranty of habitability. In the District of Columbia, the standards of this warranty are set out in the Housing Regulations.

IV

A

In our judgment the common law itself must recognize the landlord's obligation to keep his premises in a habitable condition. This conclusion is compelled by three separate considerations. First, we believe that the old rule was based on certain factual assumptions which are not longer true; on its own terms, it can no longer be justified. Second, we believe that the consumer protection cases discussed above require that the old rule be abandoned in order to bring residential landlord-tenant law into harmony with the principles on which those cases rest. Third, we think that the nature of today's urban housing market also dictates abandonment of the old rule.

The common law rule absolving the lessor of all obligation to repair originated in the early Middle Ages. Such a rule was perhaps well suited to an agrarian economy; the land was more important than whatever small living structure was included in the leasehold, and the tenant farmer was fully capable of making repairs himself. These historical facts were the basis on which the common law constructed its rule; they also provided the necessary prerequisites for its application.

Court decisions in the late 1800's began to recognize that the factual assumptions of the common law were no longer accurate in some cases. For example, the common law, since it assumed that the land was the most important part of the leasehold, required a tenant to pay rent even if any building on the land was destroyed. Faced with such a rule and the ludicrous results it produced, in 1863 the New York Court of Appeals declined to hold that an upper story tenant was obliged to continue paying rent after his apartment building burned down. The court simply pointed out that the urban tenant had no interest in the land, only in the attached building.

Another line of cases created an exception to the no-repair rule for short term leases of furnished dwellings. The Massachusetts Supreme Judicial Court, a court not know for its willingness to department from the common law, supported this exception, pointing out:

... [A] different rule should apply to one who hires a furnished room or a furnished house, for a few days, or a few weeks or months. Its fitness for immediate use of a particular kind, as indicated by its appointments, is a far more important element entering into the contract than when there is a mere lease of real estate. One who lets for a short term a house provided with all furnishings and appointments for immediate residence may be supposed to contract in reference to a well-understood purpose of the hirer to use it as a habitation. . . . It would be unreasonable to hold, under such circumstances, that the landlord does not impliedly agree that what he is letting is a house suitable for occupation in its condition at the time. . . .

These as well as other similar cases demonstrate that some courts began some time ago to question the common law's assumptions that the land was the most important feature of a leasehold and that the tenant could feasibly make any necessary repairs himself. Where those assumptions no longer reflect contemporary housing patterns, the courts have created exceptions to the general rule that landlords have no duty to keep their premises in repair.

It is overdue for courts to admit that these assumptions are no longer true with regard to all urban housing. Today's urban tenants, the vast majority of whom live in multiple dwelling houses, are interested, not in the land, but solely in "a house suitable for occupation." Furthermore, today's city dweller usually has a single, specialized skill unrelated to maintenance work; he is unable to make repairs like the "jack-of-all-trades" farmer who was the common law's model of the lessee. Further, unlike his agrarian predecessor who often remained on one piece of land for his entire life, urban tenants today are more mobile than ever before. A tenant's tenure in a specific apartment will often not be sufficient to justify efforts at repairs. In addition, the increasing complexity of today's dwellings renders them much more difficult to repair than the structures of earlier times. In a multiple dwelling, repair may require access to equipment and areas in the control of the landlord. Low and middle income tenants, even if they were interested in making repairs, would be unable to obtain any financing for major repairs since they have no long-term interest in the property.

Our approach to the common law of landlord and tenant ought to be aided by principles derived from the consumer protection cases referred to above. In a lease contract, a tenant seeks to purchase from his landlord shelter for a specified period of time. The landlord sells housing as a commercial businessman and has much greater opportunity, incentive and capacity to inspect and maintain the condition of his building. Moreover, the tenant must rely upon the skill and bona fides of his landlord at least as much as a car buyer must rely upon the car manufacturer. In dealing with major problems, such as heating, plumbing, electrical or structural defects, the tenant's position corresponds precisely with "the ordinary consumer who cannot be expected to have the knowledge or capacity or even the opportunity to make adequate inspection of mechanical instrumentalities, like automobiles, and to decide for himself whether they are reasonably fit for the designed purpose." *Henningsen* v. *Bloomfield Motors, Inc.,* 32 N.J. 358, 375, 161 A.2d 69, 78 (1960).

Since a lease contract specifies a particular period of time during which the tenant has a right to use his apartment for shelter, he may legitimately expect that the apartment will be fit for habitation for the time period for which it is rented. We point out that in the present cases there is no allegation that appellants' apartments were in poor condition or in violation of the housing code at the commencement of the leases. Since the lessees continue to pay the same rent, they were entitled to expect that the landlord would continue to keep the premises in their beginning condition during the lease term. It is precisely such expectations that the law now recognizes as deserving of formal, legal protection.

Even beyond the rationale of traditional products liability law, the relationship of landlord and tenant suggests further compelling reasons for the law's protection of the tenants' legitimate expectations of quality. The inequality in bargaining power between landlord and tenant has been well documented. Tenants have very little leverage to enforce demands for better housing. Various impediments to competition in the rental housing market, such as racial and class discrimination and standardized form leases, mean that landlords place tenants in a take it or leave it situation. The increasingly severe shortage of adequate housing further increases the landlord's bargaining power and escalates the need for maintaining and improving the existing stock. Finally, the findings by various studies of the social impact of bad housing has led to the realization that poor housing is detrimental to the whole society, not merely to the unlucky ones who must suffer the daily indignity of living in a slum.

Thus we are led by our inspection of the relevant legal principles and precedents to the conclusion that the old common law rule imposing an obligation upon the lessee to repair during the lease term was really never intended to apply to residential urban leaseholds. Contract principles established in other areas of the law provide a more rational framework for the apportionment of landlord-tenant responsibilities; they strongly suggest that a warranty of habitability be implied into all contracts for urban dwellings.

B

We believe, in any event, that the District's housing code requires that a warranty of habitability be implied in the leases of all housing that it covers. The housing code—formally designated the Housing Regulations of the District of Columbia—was established and authorized by the Commissioners of the District of Columbia on August 11, 1955. Since that time, the code has been updated by numerous orders of the Commissioners. The 75 pages of the Regulations provide a comprehensive regulatory scheme setting forth in some detail: (a) the standards which housing in the District of Columbia must meet; (b) which party, the lessor or the lessee, must meet each standard; and (c) a system of inspections, notifications and criminal penalties. The Regulations themselves are silent on the question of private remedies.

Two previous decisions of this court, however, have held that the Housing Regulations create legal rights and duties enforceable in tort by private parties. In *Whetzel* v. *Jess Fisher Management Co.,* 108 U.S.App.D.C. 385, 282 F.2d 943 (1960), we followed the leading case of *Altz* v. *Lieberson,* 233 N.Y. 16, 134 N.E. 703 (1922), in holding (1) that the housing code altered the common law rule and imposed a duty to repair upon the landlord, and (2) that a right of action accrued to a tenant injured by the landlord's breach of this duty. As Judge Cardozo wrote in *Lieberson:*

> . . . We may be sure that the framers of this statute, when regulating tenement life, had uppermost in thought the care of those who are unable to care for themselves. The Legislature must have known that unless repairs in the rooms of the poor were made by the landlord, they would not be made by any one. The duty imposed became commensurate with the need. The right to seek redress is not limited to the city or its officers. The right extends to all whom there was a purpose to protect. . . .

134 N.E. at 704. Recently, in *Kanelos* v. *Kettler,* 132 U.S.App.D.C. 133, 136, 406 F.2d 951, 953 (1968), we reaffirmed our position in *Whetzel,* holding that "the Housing Regulations did impose maintenance obligations upon appellee [landlord] which he was not free to ignore."

The District of Columbia Court of Appeals gave further effect to the Housing Regulations in *Brown* v. *Southall Realty Co.,* 237 A.2d 834 (1968). There the landlord knew at the time the lease was signed that housing code violations existed which rendered the apartment "unsafe and unsanitary." Viewing the lease as a contract, the District of Columbia Court of Appeals held that the premises were let in violation of Sections 2304 and 2501 of the Regulations and that the lease, therefore, was void as an illegal contract. In the light of *Brown,* it is clear not only that the housing code creates privately enforceable duties as held in *Whetzel,* but that the basic validity of every housing contract depends upon substantial compliance with the housing code at the beginning of the lease term. The *Brown* court relied particularly upon Section 2501 of the Regulations which provides:

Every premises accommodating one or more habitations shall be maintained and kept in repair so as to provide decent living accommodations for the occupants. This part of this Code contemplates more than mere basic repairs and maintenance to keep out the elements; its purpose is to include repairs and maintenance designed to make a premises or neighborhood healthy and safe.

By its terms, this section applies to maintenance and repair during the least term. Under the *Brown* holding, serious failure to comply with this section before the lease term begins renders the contract void. We think it untenable to find that this section has no effect on the contract after it had been signed. To the contrary, by signing the lease the landlord has undertaken a continuing obligation to the tenant to maintain the premises in accordance with all applicable law.

This principle of implied warranty is well established. Courts often imply relevant law into contracts to provide a remedy for any damage caused by one party's illegal conduct. In a case closely analogous to the present ones, the Illinois Supreme Court held that a builder who constructed a house in violation of the Chicago building code had breached his contract with the buyer:

. . . [T]he law existing at the time and place of the making of the contract is deemed a part of the contract, as though expressly referred to or incorporated in it. . . .

The rationale for this rule is that the parties to the contract would have expressed that which the law implies "had they not supposed that it was unnecessary to speak of it because the law provided for it." . . . Consequently, the courts, in construing the existing law as part of the express contract, are not reading into the contract provisions different from those expressed and intended by the parties, as defendants contend, but are merely construing the contract in accordance with the intent of the parties.

We follow the Illinois court in holding that the housing code must be read into housing contracts—a holding also required by the purposes and the structure of the code itself. The duties imposed by the Housing Regulations may not be waived or shifted by agreement if the Regulations specifically place the duty upon the lessor. Criminal penalties are provided if these duties are ignored. This regulatory structure was established by the Commissioners because, in their judgment, the grave conditions in the housing market required serious action. Yet official enforcement of the housing code has been far from uniformly effective. Innumerable studies have documented the desperate condition of rental housing in the District of Columbia and in the nation. In view of these circumstances, we think the conclusion reached by the Supreme Court of Wisconsin as to the effect of a housing code on the old common law rule cannot be avoided:

. . . [T]he legislature has made a policy judgment—that it is socially (and politically) desirable to impose these duties on a property owner—which has rendered the old common law rule obsolete. To follow the old rule of no implied warranty of habitability in leases would, in our opinion, be inconsistent with the current legislative policy concerning housing standards. . . .

We would therefore hold that the Housing Regulations imply a warranty of habitability, measured by the standards which they set out, into leases of all housing that they cover.

V

In the present cases, the landlord sued for possession for nonpayment of rent. Under contract principles, however, the tenant's obligation to pay rent is dependent upon the landlord's performance of his obligations, including his warranty to maintain the premises in habitable condition. In order to determine whether any rent is owed to the landlord, the tenants must be given an opportunity to prove the housing code violations alleged as breach of the landlord's warranty.

At trial, the finder of fact must make two findings: (1) whether the alleged violations existed during the period for which past due rent is claimed, and (2) what portion, if any or all, of the tenant's obligation to pay rent was suspended by the landlord's breach. If no part of the tenant's rental obligation is found to have been suspended, then a judgment for possession may issue forthwith. On the other hand, if the jury determines that the entire rental obligation has been extinguished by the landlord's total breach, then the action for possession on the ground of nonpayment must fail.

The jury may find that part of the tenant's rental obligation has been suspended but that part of the unpaid back rent is indeed owed to the landlord. In these circumstances, no judgment for possession should issue if the tenant agrees to pay the partial rent found to be due. If the tenant refuses to pay the partial amount, a judgment for possession may then be entered.

The judgment of the District of Columbia Court of Appeals is reversed and the cases are remanded for further proceedings consistent with this opinion.

Entitlements and "New Property"

The New Deal ushered in the welfare state, which included the concept of entitlement. An entitlement is a claim that a person has on some benefit distributed by the government, such as a parent's claim to payments under the federal Aid to Families with Dependent Children program. Considered as a property concept, it differs from traditional kinds of property in that the claimant ("owner") does not have legal "title" to a tangible or an intangible object of real or personal property; instead, he or she has a claim against a benefit program. Thus the federal government particularly, but also state governments, became sources of wealth. This so-called new property was invariably legislatively created in the form, for example, of Social Security, unemployment, and welfare benefits, but it also included licenses and franchises given by the government to private individuals. Administrative bureaucracies typically regulated the distribution of this new property, although in the 1960s and 1970s aggrieved plaintiffs frequently asked the courts to overturn administrative decisions on the grounds that this new property should be as securely protected as had been the traditional concept of property. This contention was somewhat ironic because since the New Deal era the federal courts had afforded little protection to traditional forms of property. Nonetheless, liberal public-interest lawyers claimed that the Court should shield the recipients of these entitlements from the capricious activities of the bureaucratic state by granting certain of them (the poor, veterans, unwed mothers, dependent children) constitutional protections. The government, however, insisted that such entitlements were mere grants made at the discretion of the government and that entitlements required no new special constitutional protections. Moreover, critics charged that the notion of "new property" was simply a subterfuge to constitutionalize the welfare state and protect the economic interests of groups allied with political liberals.

The Supreme Court in *Dandridge* v. *Williams*, 397 U.S. 471 (1969), refused to adopt the position that entitlements were matters of rights. It concluded that the administration of public welfare assistance was just a type of economic regulation, and that officials had wide latitude in allocating public funds among potential recipients. While the Court has accepted greater judicial intervention to examine the conduct of bureaucratic and regulatory officials, it has also permitted them significant discretion in deciding whether particular individuals can receive certain benefits. Hence, at the same time that public officials have made inroads on the enjoyment of traditional private property, they have withstood challenges to their authority to distribute the so-called new property. The Supreme Court, however, held in *Goldberg* v. *Kelly*, 397 U.S. 254 (1970), that state welfare agencies could not terminate welfare benefits without affording the recipient a prior hearing. Failure to conduct such a hearing was deemed a violation of procedural due process as guaranteed by the Fourteenth Amendment.

NEW FEDERALISM

One of the most conspicuous themes of the Supreme Court under Chief Justice William Rehnquist has been the revival of a high regard for state autonomy. This trend, termed the "new federalism," has been reflected in a line of cases, which have restricted congressional power under the commerce clause and revitalized the Tenth and Eleventh Amendments. For decades following the New Deal era and the constitutional revolution of 1937, the Supreme Court regularly upheld broad exercises of congressional authority and gave little heed to claims of states' rights. The Court treated the commerce clause as a blanket justification for Congress to govern whatever activity it wished. It was always difficult, however, to square plenary congressional authority over all aspects of the economy with the original constitutional design of a limited federal government of enumerated powers.

The emergence of the new federalism was foreshadowed by *National League of Cities* v. *Usery*, 426 U.S. 833 (1976), in which the Court struck down a federal statute that applied the maximum hours and minimum wage provisions of the Fair Labor Standards Act to state and municipal employees. The Court held that the act interfered with an essential "attribute of sovereignty attaching to every state government" and ran afoul of the Tenth Amendment. This decision was the first time since the New Deal era that the Supreme Court had invoked the Tenth Amendment to limit congressional power. *National League of Cities* did not have a long life. It was overruled in *Garcia* v. *San Antonio Metropolitan Transit Authority*, 469 U.S. 528 (1985). Still, *National League of Cities* represented a symbolic gesture in favor of federalism. Not until the 1990s would the Rehnquist Court's commitment to federalism emerge forcefully.

The new federalism has stirred a lively debate among constitutional scholars, and it remains uncertain how far the Supreme Court is prepared to stress states' rights over federal power. It should be noted, moreover, that the Court has not curtailed congressional power in situations that have practical consequences for most people.

United States v. *Lopez*
514 U.S. 549 (1995)

In 1990 Congress passed the Gun-Free School Zones Act, which made it a federal crime for an individual to possess a firearm in a school zone. A high school student in San Antonio was arrested when he came to school with a concealed handgun. The student was initially charged under a Texas law, but the state charges were dismissed when federal officials charged the student with violating the Gun-Free School Zones Act. For the first time since

1937, the Supreme Court, speaking through Chief Justice Rehnquist, found that a federal statute exceeded the power of Congress under the commerce clause. Of particular interest is the concurring opinion by Justice Clarence Thomas, in which he argues that the Court's commerce clause jurisprudence has wandered far from the original understanding of that clause.

We start with first principles. The Constitution creates a Federal Government of enumerated powers. As James Madison wrote: "The powers delegated by the proposed Constitution to the federal government are few and defined. Those which are to remain in the State governments are numerous and indefinite." The Federalist No. 45. This constitutionally mandated division of authority "was adopted by the Framers to ensure protection of our fundamental liberties." "Just as the separation and independence of the coordinate branches of the Federal Government serve to prevent the accumulation of excessive power in any one branch, a healthy balance of power between the States and the Federal Government will reduce the risk of tyranny and abuse from either front."

The Constitution delegates to Congress the power "[t]o regulate Commerce with foreign Nations, and among the several states, and with the Indian Tribes." The Court, through Chief Justice Marshall, first defined the nature of Congress' commerce power in *Gibbons* v. *Ogden* (1824).

Commerce, undoubtedly, is traffic, but it is something more: it is intercourse. It describes the commercial intercourse between nations, and parts of nations, in all its branches, and is regulated by prescribing rules for carrying on that intercourse.

The commerce power "is the power to regulate; that is, to prescribe the rule by which commerce is to be governed. This power, like all others vested in congress, is complete in itself, may be exercised to its utmost extent, and acknowledges no limitations, other than are prescribed in the constitution." The *Gibbons* Court, however, acknowledged that limitations on the commerce power are inherent in the very language of the Commerce Clause.

It is not intended to say that these words comprehend that commerce, which is completely internal, which is carried on between man and man in a State, or between different parts of the same State, and which does not extend to or affect other States. Such a power would be inconvenient, and is certainly unnecessary.

Comprehensive as the word "among" is, it may very properly be restricted to that commerce which concerns more States than one. . . . The enumeration presupposes something not enumerated; and that something, if we regard the language, or the subject of the sentence, must be the exclusively internal commerce of a State.

For nearly a century thereafter, the Court's Commerce Clause decisions dealt but rarely with the extent of Congress' power, and almost entirely with the Commerce Clause as a limit on state legislation that discriminated against interstate commerce.

♦ ♦ ♦

[A series of cases decided during the New Deal period] ushered in an era of Commerce Clause jurisprudence that greatly expanded the previously defined authority of Congress under that Clause. In part, this was recognition of the great changes that had occurred in the way business was carried on in this country. Enterprises that had once been local or at most regional in nature had become national in scope. But the doctrinal change also reflected a view that earlier Commerce Clause cases artificially had constrained the authority of Congress to regulate interstate commerce.

But even these modern-era precedents which have expanded congressional power under the Commerce Clause confirm that this power is subject to outer limits. . . .

Consistent with this structure, we have identified three broad categories of activity that Congress may regulate under its commerce power. First, Congress may regulate the use of the channels of interstate commerce. Second, Congress is empowered to regulate and protect the instrumentalities of interstate commerce, or persons or things in interstate commerce, even though the threat may come only from intrastate activities. Finally, Congress' commerce authority includes the power to regulate those activities having a substantial relation to interstate commerce, i.e., those activities that substantially affect interstate commerce.

Within this final category, admittedly, our case law has not been clear whether an activity must "affect," or "substantially affect" interstate commerce in order to be within Congress' power to regulate it under the Commerce Clause. We conclude, consistent with the great weight of our case law, that the proper test requires an analysis of whether the regulated activity "substantially affects" interstate commerce.

We now turn to consider the power of Congress, in the light of this framework, to enact § 922(q). The first two categories of authority may be quickly disposed of: § 922(q) is not a regulation of the use of the channels of interstate commerce, nor is it an attempt to prohibit the interstate transportation of a commodity through the channels of commerce; nor can § 922(q) be justified as a regulation by which Congress has sought to protect an instrumentality of interstate commerce or a thing in interstate commerce. Thus, if § 922(q) is to be sustained, it must be under the third category as a regulation of an activity that substantially affects interstate commerce.

♦ ♦ ♦

Section 922(q) is a criminal statute that by its terms has nothing to do with "commerce" or any sort of economic enterprise, however broadly one might define those terms. Section 922(q) is not an essential part of a larger regulation of economic activity, in which the regulatory scheme could be undercut unless the intrastate activities were regulated. It cannot, therefore, be sustained under our cases upholding regulations of activities that arise out of or are connected with a commercial transaction, which viewed in the aggregate, substantially affects interstate commerce.

Second, § 922(q) contains no jurisdictional element, which would ensure, through case-by-case inquiry, that the firearm possession in question affects interstate commerce.

♦ ♦ ♦

The Government's essential contention, *in fine*, is that we may determine here that § 922(q) is valid because possession of a firearm in the local school zone does indeed substantially affect interstate commerce. The Government argues that possession of a firearm in a school zone may result in violent crime and that violent crime can be expected to affect the functioning of the national economy in two ways. First, the costs of violent crime are substantial, and through the mechanism of insurance, those costs are spread throughout the population. Second, violent crime reduces the willingness of individuals to travel to areas within the country that are perceived to be unsafe. The Government also argues that the presence of guns in schools poses a substantial threat to the educational process by threatening the learning environment. A handicapped educational process, in turn, will result in a less productive citizenry. That, in turn, would have an adverse effect on the Nation's economic well being. As a result, the Government argues that Congress could rationally have concluded that § 922(q) substantially affects interstate commerce.

We pause to consider the implications of the Government's arguments. The Government admits, under its "costs of crime" reasoning, that Congress could regulate not only all violent crime, but all activities that might lead to violent crime, regardless of how tenuously they related to interstate commerce. Similarly, under the Government's "national productivity" reasoning, Congress could regulate any activity that it found was related to the economic productivity of individual citizens: family (including marriage, divorce, and child custody), for example. Under the theories that the Government presents in support of § 922(q), it is difficult to perceive any limitation on federal power, even in areas such as criminal law enforcement or education where States historically have been sovereign. Thus, if we were to accept the Government's arguments, we are hard pressed to posit any activity by an individual that Congress is without power to regulate.

Although Justice Breyer argues that acceptance of the Government's rationales would not authorize a general federal police power, he is unable to identify any activity that the States may regulate but Congress may not.

♦ ♦ ♦

For instance, if Congress can, pursuant to its Commerce Clause power, regulate activities that adversely affect the learning environment, then, a fortiori, it also can regulate the educational process directly. Congress could determine that a school's curriculum has a "significant" effect on the extent of classroom learning. As a result, Congress could mandate a federal curriculum for local elementary and secondary schools because what is taught in local schools has a significant "effect on classroom learning," and that, in turn, has a substantial effect on interstate commerce.

♦ ♦ ♦

Admittedly, a determination whether an intrastate activity is commercial or noncommercial may in some cases result in legal uncertainty. But, so long as Congress' authority is limited to those powers enumerated in the Constitution, and so long as those enumerated powers are interpreted as having judicially enforceable outer limits, congressional legislation under the Commerce Clause always will engender "legal uncertainty."

♦ ♦ ♦

The possession of a gun in a local school zone is in no sense an economic activity that might, through repetition elsewhere, substantially affect any sort of interstate commerce. Respondent was a local student at a local school; there is no indication that he had recently moved in interstate commerce, and there is no requirement that his possession of the firearm have any concrete tie to interstate commerce.

To uphold the Government's contentions here, we would have to pile inference upon inference in a manner that would bid fair to convert congressional authority under the Commerce Clause to a general police power of the sort retained by the States. Admittedly, some of our prior cases have taken long steps down that road, giving great deference to congressional action. The broad language in these opinions has suggested the possibility of additional expansion, but we decline here to proceed any further. To do so would require us to conclude that the Constitution's enumeration of powers does not presuppose something not enumerated, and that there never will be a distinction between what is truly national and what is truly local. This we are unwilling to do.

For the foregoing reasons the judgment of the Court of Appeals is

Affirmed.

Justice Thomas, concurring.

The Court today properly concludes that the Commerce Clause does not grant Congress the authority to prohibit gun possession within 1,000 feet of a school, as it attempted to do in the Gun-Free School Zones Act of 1990. Although I join the majority, I write separately to observe that our case law has drifted far from the original understanding of the Commerce Clause. In a future case, we ought to temper our Commerce Clause jurisprudence in a manner that both makes sense of our more recent case law and is more faithful to the original understanding of that Clause.

♦ ♦ ♦

In an appropriate case, I believe that we must further reconsider our "substantial effects" test with an eye toward constructing a standard that reflects the text and history of the Commerce Clause without totally rejecting our more recent Commerce Clause jurisprudence.

♦ ♦ ♦

I am aware of no cases prior to the New Deal that characterized the power flowing from the Commerce Clause as sweepingly as does our substantial effects test. My review of the case law indicates that the substantial effects test is but an innovation of the 20th century.

◆　◆　◆

Apart from its recent vintage and its corresponding lack of any grounding in the original understanding of the Constitution, the substantial effects test suffers from the further flaw that it appears to grant Congress a police power over the Nation. When asked at oral argument if there were *any* limits to the Commerce Clause, the Government was at a loss for words. Likewise, the principal dissent insists that there are limits, but it cannot muster even one example. Indeed, the dissent implicitly concedes that its reading has no limits when it criticizes the Court for "threaten[ing] legal uncertainty in an area of law that . . . seemed reasonably well settled." The one advantage of the dissent's standard is certainty: It is certain that under its analysis everything may be regulated under the guise of the Commerce Clause.

The substantial effects test suffers from this flaw, in part, because of its "aggregation principle." Under so-called "class of activities" statutes, Congress can regulate whole categories of activities that are not themselves either "interstate" or "commerce." In applying the effects test, we ask whether the class of activities *as a whole* substantially affects interstate commerce, not whether any specific activity within the class has such effects when considered in isolation.

The aggregation principle is clever, but has no stopping point. Suppose all would agree that gun possession within 1,000 feet of a school does not substantially affect commerce, but that possession of weapons generally (knives, brass knuckles, nunchakus, etc.) does. Under our substantial effects doctrine, even though Congress cannot single out gun possession, it can prohibit weapon possession generally. But one *always* can draw the circle broadly enough to cover an activity that, when taken in isolation, would not have substantial effects on commerce. Under our jurisprudence, if Congress passed an omnibus "substantially affects interstate commerce" statute, purporting to regulate every aspect of human existence, the Act apparently would be constitutional. Even though particular sections may govern only trivial activities, the statute in the aggregate regulates matters that substantially affect commerce.

This extended discussion of the original understanding and our first century and a half of case law does not necessarily require a wholesale abandonment of our more recent opinions. It simply reveals that our substantial effects test is far removed from both the Constitution and from our early case law and that the Court's opinion should not be viewed as "radical" or another "wrong turn" that must be corrected in the future. The analysis also suggests that we ought to temper our Commerce Clause jurisprudence.

Justice Breyer, with whom Justice Stevens, Justice Souter, and Justice Ginsburg join, dissenting.

The issue in this case is whether the Commerce Clause authorizes Congress to enact a statute that makes it a crime to possess a gun in, or near, a school. In my view, the statute falls well within the scope of the commerce power, as this Court has understood that power over the last half century.

In reaching this conclusion, I apply three basic principles of Commerce Clause interpretation. First, the power to "regulate Commerce . . . among the several States," encompasses the power to regulate local activities insofar as they significantly affect interstate commerce.

◆　◆　◆

Second, in determining whether a local activity will likely have a significant effect upon interstate commerce, a court must consider, not the effect of an individual act (a single instance of gun possession), but rather the cumulative effect of all similar instances (i.e., the effect of all guns possessed in or near schools). . . .

Third, the Constitution requires us to judge the connection between a regulated activity and interstate commerce, not directly, but at one remove. Courts must give Congress a degree of leeway in determining the existence of a significant factual connection between the regulated activity and interstate commerce—both because the Constitution delegates the commerce power directly to Congress and because the determination requires an empirical judgment of a kind that a legislature is more likely than a court to make with accuracy. The traditional words "rational basis" capture this leeway. Thus, the specific question before us, as the Court recognizes, is not whether the "regulated activity sufficiently affected interstate commerce," but, rather, whether Congress could have had *"a rational basis"* for so concluding.

◆ ◆ ◆

Applying these principles to the case at hand, we must ask whether Congress could have had a *rational basis* for finding a significant (or substantial) connection between gun-related school violence and interstate commerce. Or, to put the question in the language of the *explicit* finding that Congress made when it amended this law in 1994: Could Congress rationally have found that "violent crime in school zones," through its effect on the "quality of education," significantly (or substantially) affects "interstate" or "foreign commerce"? . . . [T]he answer to this question must be yes. Numerous reports and studies—generated both inside and outside government—make clear that Congress could reasonably have found the empirical connection that its law, implicitly and explicitly, asserts. . . .

For one thing, reports, hearings, and other readily available literature make clear that the problem of guns in and around schools is widespread and extremely serious. [These materials] report that this widespread violence in schools throughout the Nation significantly interferes with the quality of education in those schools. Based on reports such as these, Congress obviously could have thought that guns and learning are mutually exclusive. Congress could therefore have found a substantial educational problem—teachers unable to teach, students unable to learn—and concluded that guns near schools contribute substantially to the size and scope of that problem.

Having found that guns in schools significantly undermine the quality of education in our Nation's classrooms, Congress could also have found, given the effect of education upon interstate and foreign commerce, that gun-related violence in and around schools is a commercial, as well as a human, problem. Education, although far more than a matter of economics, has long been inextricably intertwined with the Nation's economy.

◆ ◆ ◆

In recent years the link between secondary education and business has strengthened, becoming both more direct and more important. Scholars on the subject report that technological changes and innovations in management techniques have altered the nature of the workplace so that more jobs now demand greater educational skills.

◆ ◆ ◆

Increasingly global competition also has made primary and secondary education economically more important. The portion of the American economy attributable to international trade nearly tripled between 1950 and 1980, and more than 70 percent of American-made goods now compete with imports.

◆ ◆ ◆

The economic links I have just sketched seem fairly obvious. Why then is it not equally obvious, in light of those links, that a widespread, serious, and substantial physical threat to teaching and learning *also* substantially threatens the commerce to which that teaching and learning is inextricably tied?

◆ ◆ ◆

Upholding this legislation would do no more than simply recognize that Congress had a "rational basis" for finding a significant connection between guns in or near schools and (through their effect on education) the interstate and foreign commerce they threaten. For these reasons, I would reverse the judgment of the Court of Appeals. Respectfully, I dissent.

Note: New Directions in Commerce Clause Jurisprudence

Following *Lopez*, the Supreme Court overturned a number of federal statutes on grounds that Congress had exceeded its authority under the commerce clause. In *United States* v. *Morrison*, 529 U.S. 598 (2000), for example, the justices, voting 5 to 4, voided part of the Violence Against Women Act of 1994, which provided a federal civil remedy for the victims of gender-motivated violence. The Court majority ruled that Congress cannot control noneconomic violent crime based solely on such conduct's aggregate effect on interstate commerce. Likewise, the Court invalidated attempts by Congress, based on the commerce power, to abrogate the Eleventh Amendment's immunity of states from suit in federal court. See *Seminole Tribe* v. *Florida*, 517 U.S. 44 (1996). Moreover, the justices have narrowly construed other federal statutes in order to avoid what otherwise might have been serious commerce clause questions.

On the other hand, the Supreme Court held in *Nevada Department of Human Resources* v. *Hibbs*, 538 U.S. 721 (2003), that Congress could abrogate state immunity from suits in federal court under the Eleventh Amendment if such action was a valid exercise of its power under section 5 of the Fourteenth Amendment. Accordingly, the Court determined that state employees could recover monetary damages in federal court if the state failed to comply with the Family and Medical Leave Act.

Printz v. *United States*
521 U.S. 898 (1997)

Another aspect of the new federalism has been a move by the Supreme Court under Chief Justice Rehnquist to revive the Tenth Amendment as a check on national power. The Brady Handgun Violence Prevention Act of 1993 required the attorney general to create a national system for instantly checking the background of prospective gun purchasers. Until the national system was in place, the act mandated that local chief law enforcement officers (CLEOs) conduct such checks on an interim basis. This provision raised the question of whether Congress could command state officials to enforce a federal law. A sheriff in Montana and another in Arizona challenged the constitutionality of this feature of the Brady Act. The Court struck down the interim provision by a 5 to 4 vote. Justice Antonin Scalia, writing for the majority, stressed that states retained a residual sovereignty.

Justice Scalia delivered the opinion of the Court.

The question presented in these cases is whether certain interim provisions of the Brady Handgun Violence Prevention Act commanding state and local law enforcement officers to conduct background checks on prospective handgun purchasers and to perform certain related tasks, violate the Constitution.

♦ ♦ ♦

From the description set forth above, it is apparent that the Brady Act purports to direct state law enforcement officers to participate, albeit only temporarily, in the administration of a federally enacted regulatory scheme. Regulated firearms dealers are required to forward Brady Forms not to a federal officer or employee, but to the CLEOs, whose obligation to accept those forms is implicit in the duty imposed upon them to make "reasonable efforts" within five days to determine whether the sales reflected in the forms are lawful.

♦ ♦ ♦

Petitioners here object to being pressed into federal service, and contend that congressional action compelling state officers to execute federal laws is unconstitutional. Because there is no constitutional text speaking to this precise question, the answer to the CLEOs' challenge must be sought in historical understanding and practice, in the structure of the Constitution, and in the jurisprudence of this Court. We treat those three sources, in that order, in this and the next two sections of this opinion.

Petitioners contend that compelled enlistment of state executive officers for the administration of federal programs is, until very recent years at least, unprecedented. The Government contends, to the contrary, that "the earliest Congresses enacted statutes that required the participation of state officials in the implementation of federal laws."

♦ ♦ ♦

These early laws establish, at most, that the Constitution was originally understood to permit imposition of an obligation on state *judges* to enforce federal prescriptions, insofar as those prescriptions related to matters appropriate for the judicial power.

♦ ♦ ♦

For these reasons, we do not think the early statutes imposing obligations on state courts imply a power of Congress to impress the state executive into its service. . . . In addition to early legislation, the Government also appeals to other sources we have usually regarded as indicative of the original understanding of the Constitution. It points to portions of The Federalist. . . . But none of these statements necessarily implies—what is the critical point here—that Congress could impose these responsibilities *without the consent of the States.* They appear to rest on the natural assumption that the States would consent to allowing their officials to assist the Federal Government, an

assumption proved correct by the extensive mutual assistance the States and Federal Government voluntarily provided one another in the early days of the Republic.

♦ ♦ ♦

To complete the historical record, we must note that there is not only an absence of executive-commandeering statutes in the early Congresses, but there is an absence of them in our late history as well, at least until very recent years.

♦ ♦ ♦

The Government points to a number of federal statutes enacted within the past few decades that require the participation of state or local officials in implementing federal regulatory schemes. Some of these are connected to federal funding measures, and can perhaps be more accurately described as conditions upon the grant of federal funding than as mandates to the States; others, which require only the provision of information to the Federal Government, do not involve the precise issue before us here, which is the forced participation of the State's executive in the actual administration of a federal program. We of course do not address these or other currently operative enactments that are not before us; it will be time enough to do so if and when their validity is challenged in a proper case. For deciding the issue before us here, they are of little relevance. Even assuming they represent assertion of the very same congressional power challenged here, they are of such recent vintage that they are no more probative than the statute before us of a constitutional tradition that lends meaning to the text. Their persuasive force is far outweighed by almost two centuries of apparent congressional avoidance of the practice. . . .

The constitutional practice we have examined above tends to negate the existence of the congressional power asserted here, but is not conclusive. We turn next to consideration of the structure of the Constitution, to see if we can discern among its "essential postulate[s]," a principle that controls the present cases.

It is incontestable that the Constitution established a system of "dual sovereignty." Although the States surrendered many of their powers to the new Federal Government, they retained "a residuary and inviolable sovereignty." This is reflected throughout the Constitution's text. . . . Residual state sovereignty was also implicit, of course, in the Constitution's conferral upon Congress of not all governmental powers, but only discrete, enumerated ones, Art. I, § 8, which implication was rendered express by the Tenth Amendment's assertion that "[t]he powers not delegated to the United States by the Constitution, nor prohibited by it to the States, are reserved to the States respectively, or to the people."

The Framers' experience under the Articles of Confederation had persuaded them that using the States as the instruments of federal governance was both ineffectual and provocative of federal-state conflict. Preservation of the States as independent political entities being the price of union, and "[t]he practicality of making laws, with coercive sanctions, for the States as political bodies" having been, in Madison's words, "exploded on all hands," the Framers rejected the concept of a central government that would act upon and through the States, and instead designed a system in which the State and Federal Governments would exercise concurrent authority over the people—who were, in Hamilton's words, "the only proper objects of government."

◆ ◆ ◆

It suffices to repeat the conclusion: "the Framers explicitly chose a Constitution that confers upon Congress the power to regulate individuals, not States." The great innovation of this design was that "our citizens would have two political capacities, one state and one federal, each protected from incursion by the other"—"a legal system unprecedented in form and design, establishing two orders of government, each with its own direct relationship, its own privity, its own set of mutual rights and obligations to the people who sustain it and are governed by it." The Constitution thus contemplates that a State's government will represent and remain accountable to its own citizens.

◆ ◆ ◆

This separation of the two spheres is one of the Constitution's structural protections of liberty. "Just as the separation and independence of the coordinate branches of the Federal Government serve to prevent the accumulation of excessive power in any one branch, a healthy balance of power between the States and the Federal Government will reduce the risk of tyranny and abuse from either front." To quote Madison once again:

> In the compound republic of America, the power surrendered by the people is first divided between two distinct governments, and then the portion allotted to each subdivided among distinct and separate departments. Hence a double security arises to the rights of the people. The different governments will control each other, at the same time that each will be controlled by itself.

The power of the Federal government would be augmented immeasurably if it were able to impress into its service—and at no cost to itself—the police officers of the 50 States.

◆ ◆ ◆

Finally, and most conclusively in the present litigation, we turn to the prior jurisprudence of this Court. Federal commandeering of state governments is such a novel phenomenon that this Court's first experience with it did not occur until the 1970's, when the Environmental Protection Agency promulgated regulations requiring States to prescribe auto emissions testing, monitoring and retrofit programs, and to designate preferential bus and carpool lanes. . . .

Although we had no occasion to pass upon the subject in [the EPA cases], later opinions of ours have made clear that the Federal Government may not compel the States to implement, by legislation or executive action, federal regulatory programs.

◆ ◆ ◆

When we were at last confronted squarely with a federal statute that unambiguously required the States to enact or administer a federal regulatory program, our decision should have come as no surprise. At issue in *New York v. United States*, 505 U.S. 144 (1992), were the so-called "take title" provisions of the Low-Level Radioactive Waste Policy Amendments Act of 1985, which required States either to enact legislation providing for the disposal of radioactive waste generated within their borders, or to take title to, and possession of, the waste—effectively requiring the States either to legislate pursuant to Congress's directions, or to implement an administrative solution. We concluded that Congress could constitutionally require the States to do neither. "The Federal Government," we held, "may not compel the States to enact or administer a federal regulatory program."

◆ ◆ ◆

Even assuming, moreover, that the Brady Act leaves no "policymaking" discretion with the States, we fail to see how that improves rather than worsens the intrusion upon state sovereignty. Preservation of the States as independent and autonomous political entities is arguably less undermined by requiring them to make policy in certain fields than (as Judge Sneed aptly described it over two decades ago) by "reduce[ing] [them] to puppets of a ventriloquist Congress." It is an essential attribute of the States' retained sovereignty that they remain independent and autonomous within their proper sphere of authority. It is no more compatible with this independence and autonomy that their officers be "dragooned" into administering federal law, than it would be compatible with the independence and autonomy of the United States that its officers be impressed into service for the execution of state laws.

◆ ◆ ◆

The Government also maintains that requiring state officers to perform discrete, ministerial tasks specified by Congress does not violate the principle of *New York* because it does not diminish the accountability of state or federal officials. This argument fails even on its own terms. By forcing state governments to absorb the financial burden of implementing a federal regulatory program, Members of Congress can take credit for "solving" problems without having to ask their constituents to pay for the solutions with higher federal taxes. And even when the States are not forced to absorb the costs of implementing a federal program, they are still put in the position of taking the blame for its burdensomeness and for its defects. Under the present law, for example, it will be the CLEO and not some federal official who stands between the gun purchaser and immediate possession of his gun. And it will likely be the CLEO, not some federal official who will be blamed for any error (even one in the designated federal database) that causes a purchaser to be mistakenly rejected.

◆ ◆ ◆

Finally, the Government puts forward a cluster of arguments that can be grouped under the heading: "The Brady Act serves very important purposes, is most efficiently administered by CLEOs during the interim period, and places a minimal and only temporary burden upon state officers." There is considerable disagreement over the extent of the burden, but we need not pause over that detail. Assuming *all* the mentioned factors were true, they might be relevant if we were evaluating whether the incidental application to the States of a federal law of general applicability excessively interfered with the functioning of state governments. But where, as here, it is the whole *object* of the law to direct the functioning of the state executive, and hence to compromise the structural framework of dual sovereignty, such a "balancing" analysis is inappropriate. It is the very *principle* of separate state sovereignty that such a law offends, and no comparative assessment of the various interests can overcome that fundamental defect.

◆ ◆ ◆

We adhere to that principle today, and conclude categorically, as we concluded categorically in *New York:* "The Federal Government may not compel the States to enact or administer a federal regulatory program." The mandatory obligation imposed on CLEOs to perform background checks on prospective handgun purchasers plainly runs afoul of that rule.

◆   ◆   ◆

Justice Stevens, with whom Justice Souter, Justice Ginsburg, and Justice Breyer join, dissenting.

When Congress exercises the powers delegated to it by the Constitution, it may impose affirmative obligations on executive and judicial officers of state and local governments as well as ordinary citizens. This conclusion is firmly supported by the text of the Constitution, the early history of the Nation, decisions of this Court, and a correct understanding of the basic structure of the Federal Government.

These cases do not implicate the more difficult questions associated with congressional coercion of state legislatures addressed in *New York* v. *United States*, 505 U.S. 144 (1992). Nor need we consider the wisdom of relying on local officials rather than federal agents to carry out aspects of a federal program, or even the question whether such officials may be required to perform a federal function on a permanent basis. The question is whether Congress, acting on behalf of the people of the entire Nation, may require local law enforcement officers to perform certain duties during the interim needed for the development of a federal gun control program.

⇢ 11 ⇠

Law, Politics, and Terror

Generations of Americans have viewed the government as more a master than a servant. Suspicion of government, therefore, has been a persistent theme in American thinking about how to adapt individual interests and personal liberties to the collective good. Although there is little evidence that Americans ever really believed in the value of what Thomas Jefferson called the "night watchman state," in which government played only a housekeeping role, Americans have viewed government and its handmaiden, politics, with a mixture of suspicion, fear, and even cynicism. As a result, generations of Americans have set on such schemes as term limits, balanced budget amendments to state constitutions, and strong separation of powers to keep government in check.

Americans have had a love-hate relationship with their government and the various and shifting political majorities of which they are a part. If the revolutionary generation treasured individual liberty, and it surely did, that same generation also found strength in collective action and in the value of government to organize their mutual fortunes, notably securing the nation against foreign threats. The presidency was a uniquely American institution, one designed to not only bolster separation of powers but also energize the new national government. As a result, the executive has enjoyed a prominent role in reconciling matters of individual and collective well-being, whether as a result of the powerful dislocations associated with the rise of a market economy in the nineteenth century, the emergence of a post-industrial society in the last half of the twentieth century, or more recently the specter of terror raised by the attacks of September 11, 2001, on the World Trade Center and the Pentagon. Many Americans, frustrated and in some instances fearful about the future, have turned to government not just for support but for direction and intervention on their behalf. As the historian Lawrence Friedman has observed, "Weak Presidents are still possible, but a weak Presidency is not."[1]

In recent American history, then, the presidency has emerged as a singularly important institution, one through which the historic tension between law and politics has become palpable. The result has been a series of profound constitutional collisions between the executive and legislative branches, with the courts frequently mediating the differences and being asked to sustain the rule of law. First Richard Nixon, then Bill Clinton, and most recently George W. Bush have overseen some of the most eventful moments in the history of the Republic. The first two faced impeachment charges, the third was asked to lead an unprecedented effort to protect American national interests against a new and elusive threat—international terrorism. The result has been more than three decades of sustained constitutional conflict over the scope of presidential powers, the nature of the rule of law, the role of the courts, and the maintenance of individual liberty in the shadow of terror.

In this context, then, as scholar Amitai Etzioni has explained, the events that have flowed from the 9/11 attacks have exacerbated the fragile and, in some instances, fractured nature of the relationship between law and politics, between individual rights and public safety, and between the requirement for a strong presidency and a democratic constitutional system. The question is, as it has always been in American history, whether the actions of the national government in general and the president in particular in addressing these issues amounts to coming to the rescue or pouring more fuel on a bonfire that threatens to consume liberty. At each step in the process, the judiciary has often played the decisive role in setting the meaning of the rule of law.

THE MODERN PRESIDENCY AND SEPARATION OF POWERS

New York Times Company v. *United States*
United States v. *Washington Post Company*
403 U.S. 713 (1971)

In 1971, President Richard M. Nixon was seeking to extricate the United States from the Vietnam War through secret talks with the North Vietnamese government. Daniel Ellsberg, a former Department of Defense employee, copied a highly classified report, "History of U.S. Decision-Making Process on Viet Nam Policy," and gave parts of it to the New York Times and the Washington Post. When the newspapers began to publish these so-called Pentagon Papers, Nixon ordered government attorneys, on national security grounds, to gain a lower federal court injunction against further publication. A majority of the Court resisted this argument, holding in a per curiam decision that prior restraint on publication carried an extremely heavy burden of proof. The government's lawyers failed to meet this burden. At the same time, some of the justices objected that they were rushed to decide the case and that, under certain circumstances, such as war plans, they would embrace the government's position. These two cases, which were consolidated before the Court, presented the classic question of whether the government could exercise prior restraint over the press. They also demonstrated the extraordinary view that President Nixon held of his powers, a perspective that would become even more dramatic in his response to the Watergate break-in.

Per Curiam.

   Mr. Justice Black, with whom Mr. Justice Douglas joins, concurring.

◆ ◆ ◆

   In seeking injunctions against these newspapers and in its presentation to the Court, the Executive Branch seems to have forgotten the essential purpose and history of the First Amendment. When the Constitution was adopted, many people strongly opposed it because the document contained no Bill of Rights to safeguard certain basic freedoms. They especially feared that the new powers granted to a central government might be interpreted to permit the government to curtail freedom of religion, press, assembly, and speech. In response to an overwhelming public clamor, James Madison offered a series of amendments to satisfy citizens that these great liberties would remain safe and beyond the power of government to abridge. Madison proposed what later became the First Amendment in three parts, two of which are set out below, and one of which proclaimed: "The people shall not be deprived or abridged of their right to speak, to write, or to publish their sentiments; *and the freedom of the press, as one of the great bulwarks of liberty, shall be inviolable.*" The amendments were offered to curtail and restrict the general powers granted to the Executive, Legislative, and Judicial Branches two years before in the original Constitution. The Bill of Rights changed the original Constitution into a new charter under which no branch of government could abridge the people's freedoms of press, speech, religion, and assembly. Yet the Solicitor General argues and some members of the Court appear to agree that the general powers of the Government adopted in the original Constitution should be interpreted to limit and restrict the specific and emphatic guarantees of the Bill of Rights adopted later. I can imagine no greater perversion of history. Madison and the other Framers of the First Amendment, able men that they were, wrote in language they earnestly believed could never be misunderstood: "Congress shall make no law . . . abridging the freedom . . . of the press. . . . " Both the history and language of the First Amendment support the view that the press must be left free to publish news, whatever the source, without censorship, injunctions, or prior restraints.

In the First Amendment the Founding Fathers gave the free press the protection it must have to fulfill its essential role in our democracy. The press was to serve the governed, not the governors. The Government's power to censor the press was abolished so that the press would remain forever free to censure the Government. The press was protected so that it could bare the secrets of government and inform the people. Only a free and unrestrained press can effectively expose deception in gov-

ernment. And paramount among the responsibilities of a free press is the duty to prevent any part of the government from deceiving the people and sending them off to distant lands to die of foreign fevers and foreign shot and shell. In my view, far from deserving condemnation for their courageous reporting, the *New York Times,* the *Washington Post,* and other newspapers should be commended for serving the purpose that the Founding Fathers saw so clearly. In revealing the workings of government that led to the Vietnam war, the newspapers nobly did precisely that which the Founders hoped and trusted they would do.

The Government's case here is based on premises entirely different from those that guided the Framers of the First Amendment. . . .

[W]e are asked to hold that despite the First Amendment's emphatic command, the Executive Branch, the Congress, and the Judiciary can make laws enjoining publication of current news and abridging freedom of the press in the name of "national security." The Government does not even attempt to rely on any act of Congress. Instead it makes the bold and dangerously far-reaching contention that the courts should take it upon themselves to "make" a law abridging freedom of the press in the name of equity, presidential power and national security, even when the representatives of the people in Congress have adhered to the command of the First Amendment and refused to make such a law. . . . To find that the President has "inherent power" to halt the publication of news by resort to the courts would wipe out the First Amendment and destroy the fundamental liberty and security of the very people the Government hopes to make "secure." No one can read the history of the adoption of the First Amendment without being convinced beyond any doubt that it was injunctions like those sought here that Madison and his collaborators intended to outlaw in this Nation for all time.

The word "security" is a broad, vague generality whose contours should not be invoked to abrogate the fundamental law embodied in the First Amendment. The guarding of military and diplomatic secrets at the expense of informed representative government provides no real security for our Republic. The Framers of the First Amendment, fully aware of both the need to defend a new nation and the abuses of the English and Colonial Governments, sought to give this new society strength and security by providing that freedom of speech, press, religion, and assembly should not be abridged.

Note: The Modern Presidency

One of the main features of American legal and constitutional development during the post–World War II period has been the growing power of the federal government through the movement of authority from the periphery of the states to the core in Washington, D.C. Both Congress and the Supreme Court have been beneficiaries of and contributors to this development. This same pattern has also characterized the presidency. The growing strength of the presidential office resulted from the need for decisive leadership in protecting American national security interests in first the Cold War and more recently the age of terror.

Throughout American history, presidential power has expanded especially rapidly during wartime. The emergency conditions associated with World Wars I and II, for example, offered Presidents Woodrow Wilson and Franklin D. Roosevelt the opportunity to stretch the constitutional boundaries of their offices. In a few instances, the Court resisted. In *Youngstown Sheet & Tube, et al.* v. *Sawyer* (1952), the justices held by a vote of 6 to 3 that President Harry Truman had unconstitutionally usurped legislative power when he directed that strike-bound steel mills remain open during the undeclared Korean War. Most of the time, however, the Court has left Congress and the president to struggle between themselves over the scope of their wartime authority.

The result has been a cyclical pattern of Congress acceding, in the early phases of emergencies, to presidential initiatives and then attempting later on to recapture lost authority. Consider the Vietnam conflict. Presidents Lyndon B. Johnson and Richard M. Nixon believed that their office commanded sufficient constitutional authority to conduct military operations in Vietnam without a formal declaration of war. In the early years of the conflict, President Johnson wrested from a compliant Congress the Gulf of Tonkin Resolution of August 7, 1964. The resolution approved and supported "the determination of the President, as Commander in Chief, to take all necessary measures to repel any armed attack against the forces of the United States" and "to take all necessary steps, including the use of armed force, to assist any member . . . of the Southeast Asian Collective Defense Treaty requesting assistance in defense of its freedom."[2] The resolution, however, was predicated on an apparently erroneous report that two American destroyers in the Gulf of Tonkin had been fired on by North Vietnamese gunboats.

President Richard M. Nixon also claimed the Tonkin Gulf Resolution as his authority to take actions necessary to end the war in Vietnam. Nixon's progress in securing a negotiated settlement contributed to his landslide victory over liberal Democrat George McGovern in 1972. With the war winding down, Congress began the process of attempting to rein in presidential power both domestically and internationally. Its boldest measure was the War Powers Act of 1973, which placed certain restraints on presidential military actions when Congress had not declared war. Nixon vetoed the measure, but Congress overrode it. Ultimately, however, the greatest blow to the prestige of the presidential office came from the actions of Nixon and his political operatives in domestic matters.

United States v. Nixon
418 U.S. 683 (1974)

*During the 1972 presidential campaign, supporters of President Richard M. Nixon, includ-
ing Attorney General John Mitchell, authorized a break-in at Democratic party headquar-
ters in the Watergate office complex in Washington, D.C. The burglars were caught, but instead of bringing the participation of his staff and Republican party officials to light, President
Nixon chose to cover up their role. Nixon, however, had tape-recorded his conversations
with various persons about the cover-up, and he refused to provide the tapes either to Special Prosecutor Leon Jaworski, who had been appointed to investigate the affair, to the congressional committee investigating the affair, or to federal District Court Judge John Sirica,
who subpoenaed them. Nixon claimed that as president he had an absolute privilege to control materials generated in his office. The justices by a vote of 8 to 0, with Justice William
H. Rehnquist, a former attorney general in Nixon's administration, not participating, concluded otherwise. The president was not above the law.*

Mr. Chief Justice Burger delivered the opinion
of the Court.

◆ ◆ ◆

In the performance of assigned constitutional duties each branch of the Government
must initially interpret the Constitution, and the
interpretation of its powers by any branch is due
great respect from the others. The President's
counsel . . . reads the Constitution as providing
an absolute privilege of confidentiality for all
Presidential communications. Many decisions
of this Court, however, have unequivocally
reaffirmed the holding of *Marbury* v. *Madison*
(1803), that "[i]t is emphatically the province
and duty of the judicial department to say what
the law is."

◆ ◆ ◆

Our system of government "requires that
federal courts on occasion interpret the Constitution in a manner at variance with the construction given the document by another
branch. . . . " Notwithstanding the deference
each branch must accord the others, the "judicial Power of the United States" vested in the
federal courts by Art. III, Section 1, of the Constitution can no more be shared with the Executive Branch than the Chief Executive, for example, can share with the Judiciary the veto
power, or the Congress share with the Judiciary

the power to override a Presidential veto. Any
other conclusion would be contrary to the basic concept of separation of powers and the
checks and balances that flow from the scheme
of a tripartite government. . . .

The second ground asserted by the President's counsel in support of the claim of absolute privilege rests on the doctrine of separation of powers. Here it is argued that the
independence of the Executive Branch within
its own sphere . . . insulates a President from a
judicial subpoena in an ongoing criminal prosecution, and thereby protects confidential Presidential communications.

However, neither the doctrine of separation of powers, nor the need for confidentiality
of high-level communications, without more,
can sustain an absolute, unqualified Presidential privilege of immunity from judicial process
under all circumstances. The President's need
for complete candor and objectivity from advisers calls for great deference from the courts.
However, when the privilege depends solely on
the broad, undifferentiated claim of public interest in the confidentiality of such conversations, a confrontation with other values arises.
Absent a claim of need to protect military,
diplomatic, or sensitive national security secrets, we find it difficult to accept the argument
that even the very important interest in confidentiality of Presidential communications is

significantly diminished by production of such material for in camera inspection with all the protection that a district court will be obliged to provide.

The impediment that an absolute, unqualified privilege would place in the way of the primary constitutional duty of the Judicial Branch to do justice in criminal prosecutions would plainly conflict with the function of the courts under Art. III. In designing the structure of our Government and dividing and allocating the sovereign power among three co-equal branches, the Framers of the Constitution sought to provide a comprehensive system, but the separate powers were not intended to operate with absolute independence.

♦ ♦ ♦

To read the Art. II powers of the President as providing an absolute privilege as against a subpoena essential to enforcement of criminal statutes on no more than a generalized claim of the public interest in confidentiality of nonmilitary and non-diplomatic discussions would upset the constitutional balance of "a workable government" and gravely impair the role of the courts under Art. III.

Since we conclude that the legitimate needs of the judicial process may out-weigh Presidential privilege, it is necessary to resolve those competing interests in a manner that preserves the essential functions of each branch. The right and indeed the duty to resolve that question does not free the Judiciary from according high respect to the representations made on behalf of the President. . . .

The expectation of a President to the confidentiality of his conversations and correspondence, like the claim of confidentiality of judicial deliberations, for example, has all the values to which we accord deference for the privacy of all citizens and, added to those values, is the necessity for protection of the public interest in candid, objective, and even blunt or harsh opinions in Presidential decision-making. A President and those who assist him must be free to explore alternatives in the process of shaping policies and making decisions and to do so in a way many would be unwilling to express except privately. These are the consider-

ations justifying a presumptive privilege for Presidential communications. The privilege is fundamental to the operation of Government and inextricably rooted in the separation of powers under the Constitution. . . . We agree with Mr. Chief Justice Marshall's observation, therefore, that "[i]n no case of this kind would a court be required to proceed against the president as against an ordinary individual."

But this presumptive privilege must be considered in light of our historic commitment to the rule of law. This is nowhere more profoundly manifest than in our view that "the twofold aim [of criminal justice] is that guilt shall not escape or innocence suffer." . . . We have elected to employ an adversary system of criminal justice in which the parties contest all issues before a court of law. The need to develop all relevant facts in the adversary system is both fundamental and comprehensive. The ends of criminal justice would be defeated if judgments were to be founded on a partial or speculative presentation of the facts. The very integrity of the judicial system and public confidence in the system depend on full disclosure of all the facts, within the framework of the rules of evidence. To ensure that justice is done, it is imperative to the function of courts that compulsory process be available for the production of evidence needed either by the prosecution or by the defense.

♦ ♦ ♦

In this case the President challenges a subpoena served on him as a third party requiring the production of materials for use in a criminal prosecution; he does so on the claim that he has a privilege against disclosure of confidential communications. He does not place his claim of privilege on the ground they are military or diplomatic secrets. As to these areas of Art. II duties the courts have traditionally shown the utmost deference to Presidential responsibilities.

♦ ♦ ♦

No case of the Court, however, has extended this high degree of deference to a President's generalized interest in confidentiality. Nowhere in the Constitution . . . is there any explicit reference to a privilege of confidentiality, yet to the extent this interest relates to the effective discharge of a President's powers, it is constitutionally based.

The right to the production of all evidence at a criminal trial similarly has constitutional dimensions. The Sixth Amendment explicitly confers upon every defendant in a criminal trial the right "to be confronted with the witnesses against him" and "to have compulsory process for obtaining witnesses in his favor." Moreover, the Fifth Amendment also guarantees that no person shall be deprived of liberty without due process of law. It is the manifest duty of the courts to vindicate those guarantees, and to accomplish that it is essential that all relevant and admissible evidence be produced.

In this case we must weigh the importance of the general privilege of confidentiality of Presidential communications in performance of the President's responsibilities against the inroads of such a privilege on the fair administration of criminal justice. The interest in preserving confidentiality is weighty indeed and entitled to great respect. However, we cannot conclude that advisers will be moved to temper the candor of their remarks by the infrequent occasions of disclosure because of the possibility that such conversations will be called for in the context of a criminal prosecution.

On the other hand, the allowance of the privilege to withhold evidence that is demonstrably relevant in a criminal trial would cut deeply into the guarantee of due process of law and gravely impair the basic function of the courts. A President's acknowledged need for confidentiality in the communications of his office is general in nature, whereas the constitutional need for production of relevant evidence in a criminal proceeding is specific and central to the fair adjudication of a particular criminal case in the administration of justice. Without access to specific facts a criminal prosecution may be totally frustrated. The President's broad interest in confidentiality of communications will not be vitiated by disclosure of a limited number of conversations preliminarily shown to have some bearing on the pending criminal cases.

We conclude that when the ground for asserting privilege as to subpoenaed materials sought for use in a criminal trial is based only on the generalized interest in confidentiality, it cannot prevail over the fundamental demands of due process of law in the fair administration of criminal justice. The generalized assertion of privilege must yield to the demonstrated, specific need for evidence in a pending criminal trial.

Note: The Resignation of Richard Nixon

Chief Justice Warren Burger's opinion was a powerful blow to the concept of absolute presidential privilege. Nixon clearly hoped to use the privilege as a basis for keeping the tapes that would reveal his complicity in the Watergate break-in out of the hands of prosecutors and thus enable him to maintain his office. But with the Court's decision, Nixon was faced with either repudiating the federal courts by refusing to surrender the materials or giving the materials and facing certain impeachment by the House of Representatives.

After Nixon's counsel reviewed the tape of June 23, 1972, there was no doubt of his early complicity in an effort to cover up the affair. In it, the president ordered his staff to use the Central Intelligence Agency to abort the Watergate investigation, clear evidence of the crime of obstruction of justice.

In the meantime, the House Committee on the Judiciary was preparing to impeach the president. The House committee voted three articles of impeachment against the president, doing so on the theory that Nixon had abused his constitutional power. The House Committee on the Judiciary rejected two other proposed articles of impeachment: the bombing of Cambodia and corruption in the president's personal and partisan finances. Whether the committee had adopted a proper constitutional view of the impeachment power was a matter of sharp debate, but its behavior was moot in any case because Nixon was vulnerable to impeachment by the full House and conviction before a trial in the Senate on the basis of his criminal wrongdoing. Faced with that reality, the president resigned from office on August 8, 1974.

THE IMPEACHMENT OF BILL CLINTON

Compared with the Nixon crisis, the impeachment of President Bill Clinton, a Democrat, was far less clear-cut. Throughout his presidency, Clinton had been dogged first by an investigation into land dealings made by him and his wife, Hillary, while he was governor of Arkansas, then by a lawsuit brought by Paula Jones, a former Arkansas state employee, alleging sexual harassment, and finally, in September 1998 with charges that he had a relationship with a White House intern, Monica Lewinsky, who had provided the president with oral and phone sex. Clinton's evasive approach to these latter charges, which ranged from an outright denial to a poorly stated mea culpa, were made to friends, the public, and under oath before Special Prosecutor Kenneth Starr. Even more troubling were charges that the president had attempted to lead Lewinsky and key witnesses into giving false testimony about the affair. Unlike Nixon's case, however, the House impeachment proceedings and the Senate trial, over which Chief Justice William H. Rehnquist presided, were marked by bitter partisan disagreements over the standards to be used to measure both the president's private conduct and the application of the meaning of the term "high crimes and misdemeanors" in the Constitution. In the end, the congressional debate about Clinton never reached the fundamental issues of executive power and democratic accountability, in large measure because politics got in the way of sustained constitutional debate.

HOUSE COMMITTEE ON THE JUDICIARY

Resolutions of Impeachment Against William Jefferson Clinton, President of the United States, for High Crimes and Misdemeanors
December 19, 1998

Bill Clinton was the second president to be impeached and the first elected president to be impeached and forced to stand trial before the Senate. (President Andrew Johnson, who succeeded to the presidency on the assassination of Abraham Lincoln, never had a popular mandate to hold the office.) In the House, the majority Republicans approved the first article of impeachment. It alleged that Clinton committed perjury before Independent Counsel Kenneth Starr's grand jury in August when asked about his relationship with Monica Lewinsky. The vote was 228 to 206 in favor of impeachment. Five Democrats sided with Republicans and five GOP lawmakers backed the president.

In rapid-fire order, the other three articles were voted on, all of them stemming from Starr's eight-month investigation and the politically drenched House impeachment inquiry that followed. The second article, alleging that Clinton lied in a deposition in the Paula Jones sexual harassment case, was rejected, 229 to 205. More than two dozen Republicans joined Democrats in voting it down, and some of them expressed concern about voting to impeach a president for actions in a civil case that has since been dismissed. The third article, al-

*leging obstruction of justice, cleared narrowly, 221 to 212, and needed the votes of five Dem-
ocrats to pass. It cited Clinton for efforts to influence grand jury testimony by Ms. Lewinsky and Betty Currie, his secretary, as well as other actions. The fourth article fell, 285 to
148, on a bipartisan rejection. It would have impeached Clinton for abuse of his office in
lying to Congress in written responses to eighty-one questions that the House Judiciary Committee posed to him as part of its impeachment inquiry.*

Resolved, that William Jefferson Clinton, President of the United States, is impeached for high crimes and misdemeanors, and that the following articles of impeachment be exhibited to the United States Senate:

Articles of impeachment exhibited by the House of Representatives of the United States of America in the name of itself and of the people of the United States of America, against William Jefferson Clinton, President of the United States of America, in maintenance and support of its impeachment against him for high crimes and misdemeanors.

ARTICLE I

In his conduct while President of the United States, William Jefferson Clinton, in violation of his constitutional oath faithfully to execute the office of President of the United States and, to the best of his ability, preserve, protect, and defend the Constitution of the United States, and in violation of his constitutional duty to take care that the laws be faithfully executed, has willfully corrupted and manipulated the judicial process of the United States for his personal gain and exoneration, impeding the administration of justice, in that:

On August 17, 1998, William Jefferson Clinton swore to tell the truth, the whole truth, and nothing but the truth before a Federal grand jury of the United States. Contrary to that oath, William Jefferson Clinton willfully provided perjurious, false and misleading testimony to the grand jury concerning one or more of the following: (1) the nature and details of his relationship with a subordinate Government employee; (2) prior perjurious, false and misleading testimony he gave in a Federal civil rights action brought against him; (3) prior false and misleading statements he allowed his attorney

to make to a Federal judge in that civil rights action; and (4) his corrupt efforts to influence the testimony of witnesses and to impede the discovery of evidence in that civil rights action.

In doing this, William Jefferson Clinton has undermined the integrity of his office, has brought disrepute on the Presidency, has betrayed his trust as President, and has acted in a manner subversive of the rule of law and justice, to the manifest injury of the people of the United States.

Wherefore, William Jefferson Clinton, by such conduct, warrants impeachment and trial, and removal from office and disqualification to hold and enjoy any office of honor, trust or profit under the United States.

ARTICLE II

In his conduct while President of the United States, William Jefferson Clinton, in violation of his constitutional oath faithfully to execute the office of President of the United States and, to the best of his ability, preserve, protect, and defend the Constitution of the United States, and in violation of his constitutional duty to take care that the laws be faithfully executed, has willfully corrupted and manipulated the judicial process of the United States for his personal gain and exoneration, impeding the administration of justice, in that:

(1) On December 23, 1997, William Jefferson Clinton, in sworn answers to written questions asked as part of a Federal civil rights action brought against him, willfully provided perjurious, false and misleading testimony in response to questions deemed relevant by a Federal judge concerning conduct and proposed conduct with subordinate employees.

(2) On January 17, 1998, William Jefferson Clinton swore under oath to tell the truth,

the whole truth, and nothing but the truth in a deposition given as part of a Federal civil rights action brought against him. Contrary to that oath, William Jefferson Clinton willfully provided perjurious, false and misleading testimony in response to questions deemed relevant by a Federal judge concerning the nature and details of his relationship with a subordinate Government employee, his knowledge of that employee's involvement and participation in the civil rights action brought against him, and his corrupt efforts to influence the testimony of that employee.

In all of this, William Jefferson Clinton has undermined the integrity of his office, has brought disrepute on the Presidency, has betrayed his trust as President, and has acted in a manner subversive of the rule of law and justice, to the manifest injury of the people of the United States.

Wherefore, William Jefferson Clinton, by such conduct, warrants impeachment and trial, and removal from office and disqualification to hold and enjoy any office of honor, trust or profit under the United States.

ARTICLE III

In his conduct while President of the United States, William Jefferson Clinton, in violation of his constitutional oath faithfully to execute the office of President of the United States and, to the best of his ability, preserve, protect, and defend the Constitution of the United States, and in violation of his constitutional duty to take care that the laws be faithfully executed, has prevented, obstructed, and impeded the administration of justice, and has to that end engaged personally, and through his subordinates and agents, in a course of conduct or scheme designed to delay, impede, cover up, and conceal the existence of evidence and testimony related to a Federal civil rights action brought against him in a duly instituted judicial proceeding.

The means used to implement this course of conduct or scheme included one or more of the following acts:

(1) On or about December 17, 1997, William Jefferson Clinton corruptly encour-

aged a witness in a Federal civil rights action brought against him to execute a sworn affidavit in that proceeding that he knew to be perjurious, false and misleading.

(2) On or about December 17, 1997, William Jefferson Clinton corruptly encouraged a witness in a Federal civil rights action brought against him to give perjurious, false and misleading testimony if and when called to testify personally in that proceeding.

(3) On or about December 28, 1997, William Jefferson Clinton corruptly engaged in, encouraged, or supported a scheme to conceal evidence that had been subpoenaed in a Federal civil rights action brought against him.

(4) Beginning on or about December 7, 1997, and continuing through and including January 14, 1998, William Jefferson Clinton intensified and succeeded in an effort to secure job assistance to a witness in a Federal civil rights action brought against him in order to corruptly prevent the truthful testimony of that witness in that proceeding at a time when the truthful testimony of that witness would have been harmful to him.

(5) On January 17, 1998, at his deposition in a Federal civil rights action brought against him, William Jefferson Clinton corruptly allowed his attorney to make false and misleading statements to a Federal judge characterizing an affidavit, in order to prevent questioning deemed relevant by the judge. Such false and misleading statements were subsequently acknowledged by his attorney in a communication to that judge.

(6) On or about January 18 and January 20–21, 1998, William Jefferson Clinton related a false and misleading account of events relevant to a Federal civil rights action brought against him to a potential witness in that proceeding, in order to corruptly influence the testimony of that witness.

(7) On or about January 21, 23 and 26, 1998, William Jefferson Clinton made false and misleading statements to potential witnesses in a Federal grand jury proceeding in order to corruptly influence the testimony of those witnesses. The false and misleading statements made by William Jefferson Clinton were repeated by the witnesses to the grand jury, caus-

ing the grand jury to receive false and misleading information.

In all of this, William Jefferson Clinton has undermined the integrity of his office, has brought disrepute on the Presidency, has betrayed his trust as President, and has acted in a manner subversive of the rule of law and justice, to the manifest injury of the people of the United States.

Wherefore, William Jefferson Clinton, by such conduct, warrants impeachment and trial, and removal from office and disqualification to hold and enjoy any office of honor, trust or profit under the United States.

ARTICLE IV

Using the powers and influence of the office of President of the United States, William Jefferson Clinton, in violation of his constitutional oath faithfully to execute the office of President of the United States and, to the best of his ability, preserve, protect, and defend the Constitution of the United States, and in disregard of his constitutional duty to take care that the laws be faithfully executed, has engaged in conduct that resulted in misuse and abuse of his high office, impaired the due and proper administration of justice and the conduct of lawful inquiries, and contravened the authority of the legislative branch and the truth-seeking purpose of a coordinate investigative proceeding in that, as President, William Jefferson Clinton, refused and failed to respond to certain written requests for admission and willfully made perjurious, false and misleading sworn statements in response to certain written requests for admission propounded to him as part of the impeachment inquiry authorized by the House of Representatives of the Congress of the United States.

William Jefferson Clinton, in refusing and failing to respond, and in making perjurious, false and misleading statements, assumed to himself functions and judgments necessary to the exercise of the sole power of impeachment vested by the Constitution in the House of Representatives and exhibited contempt for the inquiry.

In doing this, William Jefferson Clinton has undermined the integrity of his office, has brought disrepute on the Presidency, has betrayed his trust as President, and has acted in a manner subversive of the rule of law and justice, to the manifest injury of the people of the United States.

Wherefore, William Jefferson Clinton, by such conduct, warrants impeachment and trial, and removal from office and disqualification to hold and enjoy any office of honor, trust or profit under the United States.

TRANSCRIPT: HOUSE DEBATE ON IMPEACHMENT (OCTOBER 8, 1998)

Mr. Hyde, Chairman of the House Judiciary Committee: Today, we will vote on a historic resolution to begin an inquiry into whether the president has committed impeachable offenses. All of us are pulled in many directions by our political parties, by philosophy and friendships. We're pulled by many competing forces. But mostly, we're moved by our consciences.

We must listen to that still small voice that whispers in our ear—duty, duty, duty.

Some years ago, Douglas MacArthur in a famous speech at West Point asserted the idea of our military forces as duty, honor and country. You don't have to be a soldier in a far-off land to feel the force of those words. They are our ideal here today as well.

We have another ideal here—to attain justice through the rule of law. Justice is always and everywhere under assault. And our duty is to vindicate the rule of law as the surest protector of that fragile justice. And so here today, having received the referral and 17 cartons of supportive material from the independent counsel, the question asks itself: Shall we look further or shall we look away?

I respectfully suggest we must look further by voting for this resolution and thus commencing an inquiry into whether or not the president has committed impeachable acts.

We don't make any judgments. We don't make any charges. We simply begin a search for truth.

You will hear from our opponents that yes, we need to look further, but do it our way.

Their way imposes artificial time limits, limits our inquiry to the Lewinsky matter, and requires us to establish standards for impeachment that have never been established before—certainly, not in the Nixon impeachment proceedings, which we're trying to follow to the letter.

◆ ◆ ◆

Hyde: Many raise concerns about that proposition. Let me speak directly to those concerns.

Some suggest the process to date has been partisan. Yet every member of the Judiciary Committee voted for an inquiry in some form. We differ over the procedural details, not the fundamental question of whether we should go forward.

Many on the other side of the aisle worry that this inquiry will become an excuse for an open-ended attack on this administration. I understand that worry.

During times when Republicans controlled the executive branch and I was in the minority, I lived where you're living now. With that personal experience, I pledge to you the fairest and most expeditious search for the truth that I can muster.

I do not expect that I will agree with my Democratic friends at each step along the way, but I know that to date we have agreed on many things. In fact, we have agreed on many more things than is generally known. I hope, at the end of this long day, we will agree on the result.

I'm determined we will continue to look every day for common ground and to agree where we can. When we must disagree, we will do everything we can to minimize those disagreements. At all times, civility must be the watchword for members on both sides of the aisle. Too much hangs in the balance for us not to rise above partisan politics.

I will use all my strength to ensure that this inquiry does not become a fishing expedition. Rather, I'm determined that it will be a fair and expeditious search for truth.

We have plenty enough to do now. We don't need to search for new material. How-ever, I can't say that we will never address other subjects, nor would it be responsible to do so. I don't know what the future holds. If substantial and credible evidence of other impeachable offenses comes to us, as the independent counsel hinted or suggested in a letter we received only yesterday, the Constitution will demand that we do our duty.

Like each of you, I took an oath to answer that call. I intend to do so and I hope you will join with me, if that day comes. I don't think we want to settle for less than the whole truth.

Some are concerned about timing. Believe me, nobody wants to end this any sooner than I do. But the Constitution demands that we take the amount of time necessary to do the right thing in the right way. A rush to judgment doesn't serve anybody's interest, certainly not the public's interest.

As I've said publicly, my fervent hope and prayer is we can end this process by the end of the year. That's my New Year's resolution.

However, to agree to an artificial deadline would be irresponsible. It would only invite delay and discourage cooperation. For those who worry about the timing, I urge you to do everything possible to encourage cooperation.

No one likes to have their behavior questioned.

The best way to end the questions is to answer them in a timely and truthful manner. Thorough and thoughtful cooperation will do more than anything to put this matter behind us.

◆ ◆ ◆

U.S. Representative Rick Boucher (D-VA): . . . While we would have preferred that Democrats have a normal opportunity to present our resolution as an amendment, the procedure that is being used by the House today does not make a Democratic amendment in regular course in order. The motion to recommit with instructions does, however, give us an opportunity to have the House adopt the Democratic plan.

The Democratic amendment is a resolution for a full and complete review by the Judiciary Committee of the material that has been presented to the House by the Office of Independent Counsel.

The Republican resolution also provides for that full and complete review. The difference between the Democratic and the Republican approaches is only over the scope of the review, only over the time that the review will take, and only over our insistence that the Judiciary Committee, in conducting its process, pay deference and become aware of the historical constitutional standard for impeachment that has evolved to us over the centuries, and was recognized most recently by the Judiciary Committee in 1974, and then recognized by the full House of Representatives.

The public interest requires a fair and deliberate inquiry in this matter. Our resolution provides for that fair and deliberate inquiry. But the public interest also requires an appropriate boundary on the scope of the inquiry.

♦ ♦ ♦

U.S. Representative James Sensenbrenner (R-WI): Mr. Speaker, I rise in support of the resolution of inquiry. At Monday's meeting of the Judiciary Committee, investigative counsel David Schippers informed the committee that the material received to date shows that the president may have committed 15 felonies. These alleged felonies were in the course of the president successfully defeating Paula Jones' civil rights lawsuit—claims the Supreme Court in a nine-to-nothing decision said that she had the right to pursue.

The president denies all these allegations.

Obviously, someone is telling the truth and someone is lying. The Judiciary Committee must be given the power to decide this issue.

What's at stake here is the rule of law. Even the president of the United States has no right to break the law.

If the House votes down this inquiry, in effect it will say that even if President Clinton committed as many as 15 felonies, nothing will happen. The result will be a return to the imperial presidency of the Nixon era, where the White House felt that the laws did not apply to them since they never would be punished. That would be a national tragedy of immense consequences.

Vote for the resolution. Let the Judiciary Committee try to find the truth.

♦ ♦ ♦

U.S. Representative Charles Schumer (D-NY): . . . Mr. Speaker, this is a serious and solemn day. And after a careful reading of the Starr report and other material submitted by the office of the independent counsel, as well as a study of the origins and history of the impeachment clause of the Constitution, I have come to the conclusion that given the evidence before us, while the president deserves significant punishment, there is no basis for impeachment of the president, and it is time to move on and solve the problems facing the American people—like health care, education, and protecting seniors' retirement.

To me, Mr. Speaker, it is clear that the president lied when he testified before the grand jury—not to cover a crime, but to cover embarrassing personal behavior. While it is true that in ordinary circumstances and in most instances an ordinary person would not be punished for lying about an extramarital affair, the president has to be held to a higher standard and must be held accountable.

But high crimes and misdemeanors as defined in the Constitution and as amplified by the "Federalist Papers" and Justice Story (ph) have always been intended to apply to public actions relating to or affecting the operation of the government, not to personal or private conduct.

That said, the punishment for lying about an improper sexual relationship should fit the crime. Censure or rebuke is the appropriate punishment. Impeachment is not.

It is time to move forward, and not have the Congress and American people enjoy the specter of what could be a year-long focus on a tawdry, but not impeachable affair.

Today, the world economy is in crisis and cries out for American leadership, without which worldwide turmoil is a grave possibility.

The American people cry out for us to solve the problems facing them.

This investigation, now in its fifth year, has run its course. It is time to move on.

♦ ♦ ♦

U.S. Representative Paul McHale (D-PA): Mr. Speaker, (off-mike) that the presidency is preeminently a place of moral leadership. I want my strong criticism of President Clinton to be placed in context.

I voted for President Clinton in 1992 and 1996. I believed him to be the man from Hope as he was depicted in his 1992 campaign video.

I have voted for more than three-fourths of the president's legislative agenda, and I would do so again.

My blunt criticism of the president has nothing to do with policy. Moreover, the president has always treated me with courtesy and respect, and he has been more than responsive to the concerns of my constituents.

Unfortunately, the president's misconduct has now made immaterial my past support or agreement with him on issues.

Last January 17th, the president of the United States attempted to cover up a sordid and irresponsible relationship by repeated deceit under oath in a federal civil rights suit.

Contrary to his later public statements, his answers were not legally accurate. They were intentionally and blatantly false.

He allowed his lawyer to make arguments to the court based on an affidavit the president knew to be false.

The president later deceived the American people and belatedly admitted the truth only when confronted some seven months later by a mountain of irrefutable evidence. I am convinced that the president would otherwise have allowed his false testimony to stand in perpetuity.

What is at stake is really the rule of law. When the president took an oath to tell the truth, he was no different at that point from any other citizen—both as a matter of morality and as a matter of legal obligation.

We cannot excuse that kind of misconduct because we happen to belong to the same party as the president or agree with him on issues or feel tragically that the removal of the president from office would be enormously painful for the United States of America.

The question is whether or not we will say to all of our citizens, including the president of the United States, when you take an oath, you must keep it. Having deliberately provided false testimony under oath, the president, in my judgment, forfeited his right to office.

It was with a deep sense of sadness that I called for his resignation. By his own misconduct, the president displayed his character and he defined it badly.

His actions were not inappropriate. They were predatory, reckless, breathtakingly arrogant for a man already a defendant in a sexual harassment suit—whether or not that suit was politically motivated.

And if in disgust or dismay we were to sweep aside the president's immoral and illegal conduct, what dangerous precedent would we set for the abuse of power by some future president of the United States?

We cannot define the president's character, but we must define the nation's. I urge an affirmative vote on the resolution.

♦ ♦ ♦

U.S. Representative Jerrold Nadler (D-NY): Thank you, Mr. Speaker.

The issue in a potential impeachment is whether to overturn the results of a national election, the free expression of the popular will of the American people.

It's an enormous responsibility and an extraordinary power. It's not one that should be exercised lightly. It certainly is not one which should be exercised in a manner which is or would be perceived to be unfair or partisan.

The work of this House during the Nixon impeachment investigation commanded the respect and support of the American people. A broad consensus that President Nixon had to go was developed precisely because the process was seen to be fair and deliberate.

If our conduct in this matter does not earn the confidence of the American people, then any action we take, especially if we seek to overturn the results of a free election, will be viewed with great suspicion and could divide a nation for years to come.

We do not need another who-lost-China debate. We do not need a decade of candidates running for office accusing each other of railroading a democratically elected president out of office or participating in a thinly veiled coup d'état.

This issue has the potential to be the most divisive issue in American public life since the Vietnam War.

The process by which we arrive at our decision must be seen to be both nonpartisan and fair. The legitimacy of American political institutions must not be called into question.

I do not believe personally that all the allegations in this—in this Starr report, if proven true, describe impeachable offenses. We need to remember that the framers of the Constitution did not intend impeachment as a punishment for wrongdoing, but as a protection of constitutional liberties and of the structure of government they were establishing against the president who might seek to become a tyrant.

The president's acts, if proven true, may be crimes, calling for prosecution or other punishment, but not impeachment. So I do not believe we need a formal impeachment inquiry.

But if we are to have an inquiry, it must be fair. So far, it has been anything but fair.

The president was not given the Starr report before it was made public, a violation of all the precedents. No debate on the committee occurred on the merits whatsoever. We spent the month on deciding what should be released and what should be kept in private. And then we heard the report of the two counsels, and then we discussed procedure—but not a minute of debate on the merits, on the evidence, on the standard of impeachment, on anything.

And now, the supreme insult to the American people, an hour of debate on the House floor on whether to start for the third time in the American history a formal impeachment proceeding. We debated two resolutions to name post offices yesterday for an hour and a half. An hour debate on this momentous decision—an insult to the American people and another sign that this is not going to be fair.

◆　◆　◆

U.S. Representative Charles Canady (R-FL): Thank you, Mr. Speaker.

I rise today to support the Judiciary Committee's impeachment inquiry resolution—a resolution which ensures that we expeditiously deal with the serious charges against the president in a process that is fair, thoughtful and deliberative.

In this resolution, we follow the pattern and procedures established in the Nixon impeachment inquiry. This model served the House well in the Nixon case. It has stood the test of time, and there is no reason that we should abandon this model now.

The House should reject the unprecedented Democratic alternative with its unwise, arbitrary, and unrealistic limitations and restrictions on the ability of the Judiciary Committee to do its job. We must recognize that the Democratic alternative sets up a process that has never—not once—been followed in the more than 200-year history of impeachment under our Constitution. It is totally without precedent.

Now, some have claimed that the charges against the president do not amount to high crimes and misdemeanors. But the very report cited by the president's lawyers, which was prepared by the impeachment inquiry staff in the Nixon case, recognizes that conduct of the president which—and I quote—"undermines the integrity of office" is impeachable.

The unavoidable consequence of perjury and obstruction of justice by a president would be to erode respect for the office of the president. Such acts inevitably subvert the respect for the law, which is essential to the well-being of our constitutional system.

If perjury and obstruction of justice do not undermine the integrity of office, what offenses would?

Not long after the Constitution was adopted, one of the framers wrote: "If it were to be asked what is the most sacred duty and the greatest source of security in a republic, the answer would be an inviolable respect for the Constitution and laws. Those therefore who set examples which undermine or subvert the authority of the laws lead us from freedom to slavery. They incapacitate us for a government of laws."

Today, as members of this House, it is our solemn responsibility under the Constitution to move forward with this inquiry and to set an example that strengthens the authority of the laws and preserves the liberty with which we have been blessed as Americans.

◆ ◆ ◆

U.S. Representative Robert Wexler (D-FL): Mr. Speaker, God help this nation if today we become a Congress of endless investigation— accomplices to this un-American inquisition that would destroy the presidency over an extramarital affair.

The global economy is crumbling, and we're talking about Monica Lewinsky. Saddam Hussein hides weapons, and we're talking about Monica Lewinsky. Genocide wracks Kosovo, and we're talking about Monica Lewinsky.

Children cram into packed classrooms, and we're talking about Monica Lewinsky. Families can't pay their medical bills, and we're talking about Monica Lewinsky.

God help this nation if we trivialize the Constitution of the United States and reject the conviction of our founding fathers that impeachment is about no less than the subversion of the government.

The president betrayed his wife. He did not betray the country. God help this nation if we fail to recognize the difference.

◆ ◆ ◆

U.S. Representative Asa Hutchinson (R-AR): Mr. Speaker, today we are considering a resolution of inquire in the conduct of the president of the United States. It is not about a person, but it is about the rule of law.

Each of us took a simple oath to uphold the Constitution of the United States. The Constitution provides a path to follow in these circumstances. The path may not be well-worn, but it is well-marked. And we would be wise to follow it rather than to concoct our own ideas on how to proceed.

The gentleman from New York indicated that—concluded that the president has lied under oath, that he should be punished, but he should not be impeached.

The gentleman is way ahead in his conclusion of where this process should be and where I am.

I would say that this process is not about punishment. The purpose of this process is to examine the public trust, and if it is breached, to repair it.

We have been referred serious charges of perjury, obstruction of justice and abuse of power. The president and his lawyers have denied each of these charges as is his right to do. Our response should be that we need to examine these facts to determine the truth and to weigh the evidence. And it is our highest duty today to vote for this inquiry so that if the result is there are no impeachable offenses we can move on, but if there is more to be done, then we can assure that the rule of law will not be suspended or ignored by this Congress.

The Watergate model was chosen because that was what was demanded by my friends from across the aisle. This resolution does not direct the committee to go into any additional areas. But it does give the committee the authority to carry out its responsibility and to bring this matter to a conclusion without further delay.

It is my firm commitment as an Arkansan, as an American and as someone who has tried to work my colleagues from both sides of the aisle to be fair in every way in its search for truth.

Did the president participate in a scheme to obstruct justice? Did the president commit perjury? Do these allegations, if proven, constitute impeachable offenses? We can answer these questions in a fair and bipartisan manner, and that is my commitment.

People say this is not Watergate. That's true. Every case is different. But the rule of law and our obligation to it does not change.

They do not change because of position, personalities or power. The rule of law and justice depends on this truth. I ask my colleagues to support the resolution.

◆ ◆ ◆

U.S. Representative David Dreier (R-CA): . . . Mr. Speaker, this is obviously a very difficult time for every member of this House. I think it was said first by Henry Hyde—duty, duty, duty. The gentleman from Wisconsin, Mr. Barrett, just talked about duty.

But I think over and above our duty, I think it's important for us to recognize the words of the gentleman from Pennsylvania, Mr. McHale, who talked about the importance of the rule of law.

That really is why we're here. And over the past several weeks and months, a number of us have dusted off our copies of the Federalist Papers, John Jay, Alexander Hamilton and James Madison—James Madison being the author, the father of the Constitution.

Toward the end of the 51st Federalist, James Madison puts it perfectly as we look at the challenge that we face today. He said: "Justice is the end of government. It is the end of civil society. It ever has been and ever will be pursued until it be obtained or until liberty be lost in the pursuit."

◆   ◆   ◆

Conyers: Twenty-four years ago, as an idealistic young student, I worked on the staff of a member of the committee, and I saw the committee, and I saw this Congress do a very hard thing: come together, become nonpartisan, and do a tough job for America. And I am very concerned that instead of rising to this occasion today, we are falling down and lowering ourselves and America with it.

Note: The Senate Vote on President Clinton

The Senate, over which Chief Justice William H. Rehnquist presided, ultimately acquitted President Clinton. His conviction, like that of Andrew Johnson, failed because the Senate could not muster the two-thirds majority required by the Constitution. In the end, while many Democratic senators were unhappy with Clinton, they refused to join their Republican colleagues in a bipartisan vote against the president. The Senate concluded that the allegations did not begin to satisfy the stringent showing required by the Founding Fathers to remove a duly elected president from office, either as a matter of fact or law.

POLITICAL QUESTIONS, THE PRESIDENTIAL ELECTION OF 2000, AND THE SUPREME COURT

The presidential election of 2000 came down to an unusually close vote in one state, Florida. Vice President Al Gore, the Democratic nominee, trailed his Republican challenger, George W. Bush, by a few hundred votes. Gore, in fact, had won the popular national contest by more than 500,000 votes. Gore, who had been a strong supporter of President Bill Clinton during the latter's impeachment, trailed, however, in the electoral college. Gore therefore requested a hand recount of disputed ballots in four Florida counties where voting machines were considered suspect. Bush, on the other hand, resisted the recount with every resource available to him, political and legal. After the Florida Supreme Court ruled that state law required a statewide manual recount of all ballots, the Supreme Court, in response to demands from Bush, issued an injunction blocking the recount. The result was *Bush* v. *Gore*, a landmark in not just the constitutional law of the country but the intervention by the High Court in the nation's political business.

Bush v. *Gore*
531 U.S. 98 (2000)

On December 11, 2000, the justices heard oral arguments and later the next day, December 12, 2000, a clearly divided court issued its opinion. Under different circumstances, the justices might have remanded the case back to the Florida Supreme Court in order that a more explicit counting standard could be created. The five-justice majority announced their belief that Florida intended to resolve the disputed ballot questions by December 12 in order that the state would benefit from a federal law that ensured that its electoral college votes would not be contested in Congress. Under the majority's decision, then, there was no time left to count votes in Florida. The Court's conservative majority, all Republican appointees, for all practical purposes gave the election to Bush. Gore conceded the following day.

Per Curiam.

On December 8, 2000, the Supreme Court of Florida ordered that the Circuit Court of Leon County tabulate by hand 9,000 ballots in Miami-Dade County. It also ordered the inclusion in the certified vote totals of 215 votes identified in Palm Beach County and 168 votes identified in Miami-Dade County for Vice President Albert Gore, Jr., and Senator Joseph Lieberman, Democratic Candidates for President and Vice President. The Supreme Court noted that petitioner, Governor George W. Bush asserted that the net gain for Vice President Gore in Palm Beach County was 176 votes, and directed the Circuit Court to resolve that dispute on remand. 772 So. 2d, at 1243 (slip op., at 4, n. 6). The court further held that relief would require manual recounts in all Florida counties where so-called "undervotes" had not been subject to manual tabulation. The court ordered all manual recounts to begin at once. Governor Bush and Richard Cheney, Republican Candidates for the Presidency and Vice Presidency, filed an emergency application for a stay of this mandate. On December 9, we granted the application, treated the application as a petition for a writ of certiorari, and granted certiorari. *Post,* p. ____.

The proceedings leading to the present controversy are discussed in some detail in our opinion in Bush v. *Palm Beach County Canvassing Bd., ante,* p. ____ *(per curiam) (Bush I).* On November 8, 2000, the day following the Presidential election, the Florida Division of Elections reported that petitioner, Governor Bush, had received 2,909,135 votes, and respondent, Vice President Gore, had received 2,907,351 votes, a margin of 1,784 for Governor Bush. Because Governor Bush's margin of victory was less than "one-half of a percent . . . of the votes

cast," an automatic machine recount was conducted under § 102.141(4) of the election code, the results of which showed Governor Bush still winning the race but by a diminished margin. Vice President Gore then sought manual recounts in Volusia, Palm Beach, Broward, and Miami-Dade Counties, pursuant to Florida's election protest provisions. Fla. Stat. § 102.166 (2000). A dispute arose concerning the deadline for local county canvassing boards to submit their returns to the Secretary of State (Secretary). The Secretary declined to waive the November 14 deadline imposed by statute. §§ 102.111, 102.112. The Florida Supreme Court, however, set the deadline at November 26. We granted certiorari and vacated the Florida Supreme Court's decision, finding considerable uncertainty as to the grounds on which it was based. . . . On November 26, the Florida Elections Canvassing Commission certified the results of the election and declared Governor Bush the winner of Florida's 25 electoral votes. On November 27, Vice President Gore, pursuant to Florida's contest provisions, filed a complaint in Leon County Circuit Court contesting the certification. Fla. Stat. § 102.168 (2000). He sought relief pursuant to § 102.168(3)(c), which provides that "[r]eceipt of a number of illegal votes or rejection of a number of legal votes sufficient to change or place in doubt the result of the election" shall be grounds for a contest. The Circuit Court denied relief, stating that Vice President Gore failed to meet his burden of proof. He appealed to the First District Court of Appeal, which certified the matter to the Florida Supreme Court.

Accepting jurisdiction, the Florida Supreme Court affirmed in part and reversed in part. *Gore* v. *Harris,* 779 So. 2d. 270 (2000). The court held that the Circuit Court had been correct to reject Vice President Gore's challenge to the results certified in Nassau County and his challenge to the Palm Beach County Canvassing Board''s determination that 3,300 ballots cast in that county were not, in the statutory phrase, "legal votes."

The Supreme Court held that Vice President Gore had satisfied his burden of proof under § 102.168(3)(c) with respect to his challenge to Miami-Dade County's failure to tabulate, by manual count, 9,000 ballots on which the machines had failed to detect a vote for President ("undervotes"). . . . Noting the closeness of the election, the Court explained that "[o]n this record, there can be no question that there are legal votes within the 9,000 uncounted votes sufficient to place the results of this election in doubt." A "legal vote," as determined by the Supreme Court, is "one in which there is a 'clear indication of the intent of the voter.'" The court therefore ordered a hand recount of the 9,000 ballots in Miami-Dade County. Observing that the contest provisions vest broad discretion in the circuit judge to "provide any relief appropriate under such circumstances," The Supreme Court further held that the Circuit Court could order "the Supervisor of Elections and the Canvassing Boards, as well as the necessary public officials, in all counties that have not conducted a manual recount or tabulation of the undervotes . . . to do so forthwith, said tabulation to take place in the individual counties where the ballots are located."

The Supreme Court also determined that both Palm Beach County and Miami-Dade County, in their earlier manual recounts, had identified a net gain of 215 and 168 legal votes for Vice President Gore. Rejecting the Circuit Court's conclusion that Palm Beach County lacked the authority to include the 215 net votes submitted past the November 26 deadline, the Supreme Court explained that the deadline was not intended to exclude votes identified after that date through ongoing manual recounts. As to Miami-Dade County, the Court concluded that although the 168 votes identified were the result of a partial recount, they were "legal votes [that] could change the outcome of the election." The Supreme Court therefore directed the Circuit Court to include those totals in the certified results, subject to resolution of the actual vote total from the Miami-Dade partial recount.

The petition presents the following questions: whether the Florida Supreme Court established new standards for resolving Presidential election contests, thereby violating Art. II, § 1, cl. 2, of the United States Constitution and failing to comply with 3 U.S.C. § 5 and whether the use of standardless manual recounts violates the Equal Protection and Due Process Clauses. With respect to the equal protection question, we find a violation of the Equal Protection Clause.

II

A

The closeness of this election, and the multitude of legal challenges which have followed in its wake, have brought into sharp focus a common, if heretofore unnoticed, phenomenon. Nationwide statistics reveal that an estimated 2% of ballots cast do not register a vote for President for whatever reason, including deliberately choosing no candidate at all or some voter error, such as voting for two candidates or insufficiently marking a ballot. . . . In certifying election results, the votes eligible for inclusion in the certification are the votes meeting the properly established legal requirements.

This case has shown that punch card balloting machines can produce an unfortunate number of ballots which are not punched in a clean, complete way by the voter. After the current counting, it is likely legislative bodies nationwide will examine ways to improve the mechanisms and machinery for voting.

B

The individual citizen has no federal constitutional right to vote for electors for the President of the United States unless and until the state legislature chooses a statewide election as the means to implement its power to appoint members of the Electoral College. U.S. Const., Art. II, § 1. This is the source for the statement in *McPherson* v. *Blacker* (1892), that the State legislature's power to select the manner for appointing electors is plenary; it may, if it so chooses, select the electors itself, which indeed was the manner used by State legislatures in several States for many years after the Framing of our Constitution. History has now favored the voter, and in each of the several States the citizens themselves vote for Presidential electors. When the state legislature vests the right to vote for President in its people, the right to vote as the legislature has prescribed is fundamental; and one source of its fundamental nature lies in the equal weight accorded to each vote and the equal dignity owed to each voter. The State, of course, after granting the franchise in the special context of Article II, can take back the power to appoint electors. ("[T]here is no doubt of the right of the legislature to resume the power at any time, for it can neither be taken away nor abdicated")

The right to vote is protected in more than the initial allocation of the franchise. Equal protection applies as well to the manner of its exercise. Having once granted the right to vote on equal terms, the State may not, by later arbitrary and disparate treatment, value one person's vote over that of another. See, e.g., *Harper* v. *Virginia Bd. of Elections* (1966) ("[O]nce the franchise is granted to the electorate, lines may not be drawn which are inconsistent with the Equal Protection Clause of the Fourteenth Amendment"). It must be remembered that "the right of suffrage can be denied by a debasement or dilution of the weight of a citizen's vote just as effectively as by wholly prohibiting the free exercise of the franchise." *Reynolds* v. *Sims* (1964).

There is no difference between the two sides of the present controversy on these basic propositions. Respondents say that the very purpose of vindicating the right to vote justifies the recount procedures now at issue. The question before us, however, is whether the recount procedures the Florida Supreme

Court has adopted are consistent with its obligation to avoid arbitrary and disparate treatment of the members of its electorate.

Much of the controversy seems to revolve around ballot cards designed to be perforated by a stylus but which, either through error or deliberate omission, have not been perforated with sufficient precision for a machine to count them. In some cases a piece of the card—a chad—is hanging, say by two corners. In other cases there is no separation at all, just an indentation.

The Florida Supreme Court has ordered that the intent of the voter be discerned from such ballots. For purposes of resolving the equal protection challenge, it is not necessary to decide whether the Florida Supreme Court had the authority under the legislative scheme for resolving election disputes to define what a legal vote is and to mandate a manual recount implementing that definition. The recount mechanisms implemented in response to the decisions of the Florida Supreme Court do not satisfy the minimum requirement for non-arbitrary treatment of voters necessary to secure the fundamental right. Florida's basic command for the count of legally cast votes is to consider the "intent of the voter." *Gore* v. *Harris*, 779 So. 2d, at 270. This is unobjectionable as an abstract proposition and a starting principle. The problem inheres in the absence of specific standards to ensure its equal application. The formulation of uniform rules to determine intent based on these recurring circumstances is practicable and, we conclude, necessary.

The law does not refrain from searching for the intent of the actor in a multitude of circumstances; and in some cases the general command to ascertain intent is not susceptible to much further refinement. In this instance, however, the question is not whether to believe a witness but how to interpret the marks or holes or scratches on an inanimate object, a piece of cardboard or paper which, it is said, might not have registered as a vote during the machine count. The factfinder confronts a thing, not a person. The search for intent can be confined by specific rules designed to ensure uniform treatment.

The want of those rules here has led to unequal evaluation of ballots in various respects. See *Gore* v. *Harris,* 779 So. 2d, at 270 (Wells, J., dissenting) ("Should a county canvassing board count or not count a 'dimpled chad' where the voter is able to successfully dislodge the chad in every other contest on that ballot? Here, the county canvassing boards disagree"). As seems to have been acknowledged at oral argument, the standards for accepting or rejecting contested ballots might vary not only from county to county but indeed within a single county from one recount team to another.

The record provides some examples. A monitor in Miami-Dade County testified at trial that he observed that three members of the county canvassing board applied different standards in defining a legal vote. 3 Tr. 497, 499 (Dec. 3, 2000). And testimony at trial also revealed that at least one county changed its evaluative standards during the counting process. Palm Beach County, for example, began the process with a 1990 guideline which precluded counting completely attached chads, switched to a rule that considered a vote to be legal if any light could be seen through a chad, changed back to the 1990 rule, and then abandoned any pretense of a per se rule, only to have a court order that the county consider dimpled chads legal. This is not a process with sufficient guarantees of equal treatment.

An early case in our one person, one vote jurisprudence arose when a State accorded arbitrary and disparate treatment to voters in its different counties. *Gray* v. *Sanders* (1963). The Court found a constitutional violation. We relied on these principles in the context of the Presidential selection process in *Moore* v. *Ogilvie* (1969), where we invalidated a county-based procedure that diluted the influence of citizens in larger counties in the nominating process. There we observed that "[t]he idea that one group can be granted greater voting strength than another is hostile to the one man, one vote basis of our representative government."

The State Supreme Court ratified this uneven treatment. It mandated that the recount totals from two counties, Miami-Dade and Palm Beach, be included in the certified total. The court also appeared to hold *sub silentio* that the recount totals from Broward County, which were not completed until after the original November 14 certification by the Secretary of State, were to be considered part of the new certified vote totals even though the county certification was not contested by Vice President Gore. Yet each of the counties used varying standards to determine what was a legal vote. Broward County used a more forgiving standard than Palm Beach County, and uncovered almost three times as many new votes, a result markedly disproportionate to the difference in population between the counties.

In addition, the recounts in these three counties were not limited to so-called undervotes but extended to all of the ballots. The distinction has real consequences. A manual recount of all ballots identifies not only those ballots which show no vote but also those which contain more than one, the so-called overvotes. Neither category will be counted by the machine. This is not a trivial concern. At oral argument, respondents estimated there are as many as 110,000 overvotes statewide. As a result, the citizen whose ballot was not read by a machine because he failed to vote for a candidate in a way readable by a machine may still have his vote counted in a manual recount; on the other hand, the citizen who marks two candidates in a way discernable by the machine will not have the same opportunity to have his vote count, even if a manual examination of the ballot would reveal the requisite indicia of intent. Furthermore, the citizen who marks two candidates, only one of which is discernable by the machine, will have his vote counted even though it should have been read as an invalid ballot. The State Supreme Court's inclusion of vote counts based on these variant standards exemplifies concerns with the remedial processes that were under way.

That brings the analysis to yet a further equal protection problem. The votes certified by the court included a partial total from one county, Miami-Dade. The Florida Supreme Court's decision thus gives no assurance that the recounts included in a final certification must be complete. Indeed, it is respondent's submission that it would be consistent with the rules of the recount procedures to include whatever partial counts are done by the time of final certification, and we interpret the Florida Supreme Court's decision to permit this. See 779 So. 2d, at 270, n. 21 (noting "practical difficulties" may control outcome of election, but certifying partial Miami-Dade total nonetheless). This accommodation no doubt results from the truncated contest period established by the Florida Supreme Court in *Bush I*, at respondents' own urging. The press of time does not diminish the constitutional concern. A desire for speed is not a general excuse for ignoring equal protection guarantees.

In addition to these difficulties the actual process by which the votes were to be counted under the Florida Supreme Court's decision raises further concerns. That order did not specify who would recount the ballots. The county canvassing boards were forced to pull together ad hoc teams comprised of judges from various Circuits who had no previous training in handling and interpreting ballots. Furthermore, while others were permitted to observe, they were prohibited from objecting during the recount.

The recount process, in its features here described, is inconsistent with the minimum procedures necessary to protect the funda-

mental right of each voter in the special instance of a statewide recount under the authority of a single state judicial officer. Our consideration is limited to the present circumstances, for the problem of equal protection in election processes generally presents many complexities.

The question before the Court is not whether local entities, in the exercise of their expertise, may develop different systems for implementing elections. Instead, we are presented with a situation where a state court with the power to assure uniformity has ordered a statewide recount with minimal procedural safeguards. When a court orders a statewide remedy, there must be at least some assurance that the rudimentary requirements of equal treatment and fundamental fairness are satisfied.

Given the Court's assessment that the recount process underway was probably being conducted in an unconstitutional manner, the Court stayed the order directing the recount so it could hear this case and render an expedited decision. The contest provision, as it was mandated by the State Supreme Court, is not well calculated to sustain the confidence that all citizens must have in the outcome of elections. The State has not shown that its procedures include the necessary safeguards. The problem, for instance, of the estimated 110,000 overvotes has not been addressed, although Chief Justice Wells called attention to the concern in his dissenting opinion. See 779 So. 2d, at 270, n. 26 (slip op., at 45, n. 26).

Upon due consideration of the difficulties identified to this point, it is obvious that the recount cannot be conducted in compliance with the requirements of equal protection and due process without substantial additional work. It would require not only the adoption (after opportunity for argument) of adequate statewide standards for determining what is a legal vote, and practicable procedures to implement them, but also orderly judicial review of any disputed matters that might arise. In addition, the Secretary of State has advised that the recount of only a portion of the ballots requires that the vote tabulation equipment be used to screen out undervotes, a function for which the machines were not designed. If a recount of overvotes were also required, perhaps even a second screening would be necessary. Use of the equipment for this purpose, and any new software developed for it, would have to be evaluated for accuracy by the Secretary of State, as required by Fla. Stat. § 101.015 (2000).

The Supreme Court of Florida has said that the legislature intended the State's electors to "participat[e] fully in the federal electoral process," as provided in 3 U.S.C. § 5. 779 So. 2d, at 270. That statute, in turn, requires that any controversy or contest that is designed to lead to a conclusive selection of electors be completed by December 12. That date is upon us, and there is no recount procedure in place under the State Supreme Court's order that comports with minimal constitutional standards. Because it is evident that any recount seeking to meet the December 12 date will be unconstitutional for the reasons we have discussed, we reverse the judgment of the Supreme Court of Florida ordering a recount to proceed.

Seven Justices of the Court agree that there are constitutional problems with the recount ordered by the Florida Supreme Court that demand a remedy. See post, at 6 (Souter, J., dissenting); *post*, at 2, 15 (Breyer, J., dissenting). The only disagreement is as to the remedy. Because the Florida Supreme Court has said that the Florida Legislature intended to obtain the safe-harbor benefits of 3 U.S.C. § 5 Justice Breyer's proposed remedy—remanding to the Florida Supreme Court for its ordering of a constitutionally proper contest until December 18—contemplates action in violation of the Florida election code, and hence could not be part of an "appropriate"

order authorized by Fla. Stat. § 102.168(8) (2000).

♦　♦　♦

None are more conscious of the vital limits on judicial authority than are the members of this Court, and none stand more in admiration of the Constitution's design to leave the selection of the President to the people, through their legislatures, and to the political sphere. When contending parties invoke the process of the courts, however, it becomes our unsought responsibility to resolve the federal and constitutional issues the judicial system has been forced to confront.

The judgment of the Supreme Court of Florida is reversed, and the case is remanded for further proceedings not inconsistent with this opinion.

Pursuant to this Court's Rule 45.2, the Clerk is directed to issue the mandate in this case forthwith.

It is so ordered.

Justice Stevens, with whom Justice Ginsburg and Justice Breyer join, dissenting.

The Constitution assigns to the States the primary responsibility for determining the manner of selecting the Presidential electors. See Art. II, § 1, cl. 2. When questions arise about the meaning of state laws, including election laws, it is our settled practice to accept the opinions of the highest courts of the States as providing the final answers. On rare occasions, however, either federal statutes or the Federal Constitution may require federal judicial intervention in state elections. This is not such an occasion.

The federal questions that ultimately emerged in this case are not substantial. Article II provides that "[e]ach *State* shall appoint, in such Manner as the Legislature *thereof* may direct, a Number of Electors." Ibid. (emphasis added). It does not create state legislatures out of whole cloth, but rather takes them as they come—as creatures born of, and constrained by, their state constitutions. Lest there be any doubt, we stated over 100 years ago in *McPherson* v. *Blacker* (1892), that "[w]hat is forbidden or required to be done by a State" in the Article II context "is forbidden or required of the legislative power under state constitutions as they exist." In the same vein, we also observed that "[t]he [State's] legislative power is the supreme authority except as limited by the constitution of the State." Ibid. . . . The legislative power in Florida is subject to judicial review pursuant to Article V of the Florida Constitution, and nothing in Article II of the Federal Constitution frees the state legislature from the constraints in the state constitution that created it. Moreover, the Florida Legislature's own decision to employ a unitary code for all elections indicates that it intended the Florida Supreme Court to play the same role in Presidential elections that it has historically played in resolving electoral disputes. The Florida Supreme Court's exercise of appellate jurisdiction therefore was wholly consistent with, and indeed contemplated by, the grant of authority in Article II.

It hardly needs stating that Congress, pursuant to 3 U.S.C. § 5, did not impose any affirmative duties upon the States that their governmental branches could "violate." Rather, § 5 provides a safe harbor for States to select electors in contested elections "by judicial or other methods" established by laws prior to the election day. Section 5, like Article II, assumes the involvement of the state judiciary in interpreting state election laws and resolving election disputes under those laws. Neither § 5 nor Article II grants federal judges any special authority to substitute their views for those of the state judiciary on matters of state law.

Nor are petitioners correct in asserting that the failure of the Florida Supreme Court to specify in detail the precise manner in which the "intent of the voter," Fla. Stat. § 101.5614(5) (Supp. 2001), is to be determined rises to the level of a constitutional violation. We found such a violation when individual votes within the same State were weighted unequally, see, e.g., *Reynolds* v. *Sims* (1964), but we have never before called into question the substantive standard by which a State determines that a vote has been legally cast. And there is no reason to think that the guidance provided to the factfinders, specifically the various canvassing boards, by the "intent of the voter" standard is any less sufficient—or will lead to results any less uniform—than, for example, the

"beyond a reasonable doubt" standard employed everyday by ordinary citizens in courtrooms across this country.

Admittedly, the use of differing substandards for determining voter intent in different counties employing similar voting systems may raise serious concerns. Those concerns are alleviated—if not eliminated—by the fact that a single impartial magistrate will ultimately adjudicate all objections arising from the recount process. Of course, as a general matter, "[t]he interpretation of constitutional principles must not be too literal. We must remember that the machinery of government would not work if it were not allowed a little play in its joints." *Bain Peanut Co. of Tex.* v. *Pinson* (1931) (Holmes, J.). If it were otherwise, Florida's decision to leave to each county the determination of what balloting system to employ—despite enormous differences in accuracy—might run afoul of equal protection. So, too, might the similar decisions of the vast majority of state legislatures to delegate to local authorities certain decisions with respect to voting systems and ballot design.

Even assuming that aspects of the remedial scheme might ultimately be found to violate the Equal Protection Clause, I could not subscribe to the majority's disposition of the case. As the majority explicitly holds, once a state legislature determines to select electors through a popular vote, the right to have one's vote counted is of constitutional stature. As the majority further acknowledges, Florida law holds that all ballots that reveal the intent of the voter constitute valid votes. Recognizing these principles, the majority nonetheless orders the termination of the contest proceeding before all such votes have been tabulated. Under their own reasoning, the appropriate course of action would be to remand to allow more specific procedures for implementing the legislature's uniform general standard to be established.

In the interest of finality, however, the majority effectively orders the disenfranchisement of an unknown number of voters whose ballots reveal their intent—and are therefore legal votes under state law—but were for some reason rejected by ballot-counting machines. It does so on the basis of the deadlines set forth in Title 3 of the United States Code. But, as I have already noted, those provisions merely provide rules of decision for Congress to follow when selecting among conflicting slates of electors. They do not prohibit a State from counting what the majority concedes to be legal votes until a bona fide winner is determined. Indeed, in 1960, Hawaii appointed two slates of electors and Congress chose to count the one appointed on January 4, 1961, well after the Title 3 deadlines. Thus, nothing prevents the majority, even if it properly found an equal protection violation, from ordering relief appropriate to remedy that violation without depriving Florida voters of their right to have their votes counted. As the majority notes, "[a] desire for speed is not a general excuse for ignoring equal protection guarantees."

Finally, neither in this case, nor in its earlier opinion in *Palm Beach County Canvassing Bd.* v. *Harris* (Fla., Nov. 21, 2000), did the Florida Supreme Court make any substantive change in Florida electoral law. Its decisions were rooted in long-established precedent and were consistent with the relevant statutory provisions, taken as a whole. It did what courts do—it decided the case before it in light of the legislature's intent to leave no legally cast vote uncounted. In so doing, it relied on the sufficiency of the general "intent of the voter" standard articulated by the state legislature, coupled with a procedure for ultimate review by an impartial judge, to resolve the concern about disparate evaluations of contested ballots. If we assume—as I do—that the members of that court and the judges who would have carried out its mandate are impartial, its decision does not even raise a colorable federal question.

What must underlie petitioners' entire federal assault on the Florida election procedures is an unstated lack of confidence in the impartiality and capacity of the state judges who would make the critical decisions if the vote count were to proceed. Otherwise, their position is wholly without merit. The endorsement of that position by the majority of this Court can only lend credence to the most cynical appraisal of the work of judges throughout the land. It is confidence in the men and women who administer the judicial system that is the true backbone of the rule of law. Time will one day heal the wound to that confidence that will be inflicted by today's decision. One thing, however, is certain. Although we may never know with complete certainty the identity of the winner of this year's Presidential election, the identity of the loser is perfectly clear. It is the Nation's confidence in the judge as an impartial guardian of the rule of law.

I respectfully dissent.

Note: The Supreme Court and the Political Process

Commentators have disagreed sharply about the appropriateness of the High Court's action in *Bush* v. *Gore*. Harvard Law Professor Lawrence Tribe, for example, insisted that the case presented a political question that most likely never should have been decided by a federal court. Properly applied, according to Tribe, justiciability is inextricably linked both with the institutional context in which judicial intervention is sought and with the substantive constitutional principles that undergird the allegedly "political" question at issue. Tribe concluded that unless the political and administrative processes were so structured that the political branches could not be trusted to make a decision, then the case for judicial intervention in the political process was unacceptable. Others insisted, however, that the Court's actions saved the nation from a drawn-out debate and backroom politicking in Congress over who should be president. Whatever the perspective, the Court's intervention in the 2000 election ran counter to a long although uneven tradition of the justices refusing to intervene directly in the political process when they knew that their actions would produce a direct political result—the selection of the next president. The concern that the Court acted politically rather than legally was only heightened by Justice Antonin Scalia's remark, with which Chief Justice Rehnquist and Justice Clarence Thomas associated themselves, that the review of the ballots proposed by Gore threatened "irreparable harm to [Bush], and to the country, by casting a cloud upon what he claims to be the legitimacy of his elections." Justice Stevens and the three other dissenters, of course, concluded that merely counting every legally cast vote could never result in irreparable harm in a democracy.

President-Elect George W. Bush Addresses the Nation
December 13, 2000

Thank you all. (APPLAUSE)

Thank you very much. Good evening, my fellow Americans. I appreciate so very much the opportunity to speak with you tonight.

Mr. Speaker, Lieutenant Governor, friends, distinguished guests, our country has been through a long and trying period, with the outcome of the presidential election not finalized for longer than any of us could ever imagine.

Vice President Gore and I put our hearts and hopes into our campaigns. We both gave it our all. We shared similar emotions, so I understand how difficult this moment must be for Vice President Gore and his family.

He has a distinguished record of service to our country as a congressman, a senator and a vice president.

This evening I received a gracious call from the vice president. We agreed to meet early next week in Washington and we agreed to do our best to heal our country after this hard-fought contest.

Tonight I want to thank all the thousands of volunteers and campaign workers who worked so hard on my behalf.

I also salute the vice president and his supporters for waging a spirited campaign. And I thank him for a call that I know was difficult to make. Laura and I wish the vice president and Senator Lieberman and their families the very best.

I have a lot to be thankful for tonight. I'm thankful for America and thankful that we were able to resolve our electoral differences in a peaceful way.

I'm thankful to the American people for the great privilege of being able to serve as your next president.

I want to thank my wife and our daughters for their love. Laura's active involvement as first lady has made Texas a better place, and she will be a wonderful first lady of America. (APPLAUSE)

I am proud to have Dick Cheney by my side, and America will be proud to have him as our next vice president. (APPLAUSE)

Tonight I chose to speak from the chamber of the Texas House of Representatives because it has been a home to bipartisan cooperation. Here in a place where Democrats have the majority, Republicans and Democrats have worked together to do what is right for the people we represent.

We've had spirited disagreements. And in the end, we found constructive consensus. It is an experience I will always carry with me, an example I will always follow.

I want to thank my friend, House Speaker Pete Laney, a Democrat, who introduced me today. I want to thank the legislators from both political parties with whom I've worked.

Across the hall in our Texas capitol is the state Senate. And I cannot help but think of our mutual friend, the former Democrat lieutenant governor, Bob Bullock. His love for Texas and his ability to work in a bipartisan way continue to be a model for all of us. (APPLAUSE)

The spirit of cooperation I have seen in this hall is what is needed in Washington, D.C. It is the challenge of our moment. After a difficult election, we must put politics behind us and work together to make the promise of America available for every one of our citizens.

I am optimistic that we can change the tone in Washington, D.C.

I believe things happen for a reason, and I hope the long wait of the last five weeks will heighten a desire to move beyond the bitterness and partisanship of the recent past.

Our nation must rise above a house divided. Americans share hopes and goals and values far more important than any political disagreements.

Republicans want the best for our nation, and so do Democrats. Our votes may differ, but not our hopes.

I know America wants reconciliation and unity. I know Americans want progress. And we must seize this moment and deliver.

Together, guided by a spirit of common sense, common courtesy and common goals, we can unite and inspire the American citizens.

Together, we will work to make all our public schools excellent, teaching every student of every background and every accent, so that no child is left behind.

Together we will save Social Security and renew its promise of a secure retirement for generations to come.

Together we will strengthen Medicare and offer prescription drug coverage to all of our seniors.

Together we will give Americans the broad, fair and fiscally responsible tax relief they deserve.

Together we'll have a bipartisan foreign policy true to our values and true to our friends, and we will have a military equal to every challenge and superior to every adversary.

Together we will address some of society's deepest problems one person at a time, by encouraging and empowering the good hearts and good works of the American people.

This is the essence of compassionate conservatism and it will be a foundation of my administration.

These priorities are not merely Republican concerns or Democratic concerns; they are American responsibilities.

During the fall campaign, we differed about the details of these proposals, but there was remarkable consensus about the important issues before us: excellent schools, retirement and health security, tax relief, a strong military, a more civil society.

We have discussed our differences. Now it is time to find common ground and build consensus to make America a beacon of opportunity in the 21st century.

I'm optimistic this can happen. Our future demands it and our history proves it. Two hundred years ago, in the election of 1800, America faced another close presidential election. A tie in the Electoral College put the outcome into the hands of Congress.

After six days of voting and 36 ballots, the House of Representatives elected Thomas Jefferson the third president of the United States. That election brought the first transfer of power from one party to another in our new democracy.

Shortly after the election, Jefferson, in a letter titled "Reconciliation and Reform," wrote this. "The steady character of our countrymen is a rock to which we may safely moor; unequivocal in principle, reasonable in manner. We should be able to hope to do a great deal of good to the cause of freedom and harmony."

Two hundred years have only strengthened the steady character of America. And so as we begin the work of healing our nation, tonight I call upon that character: respect for each other, respect for our differences, generosity of spirit, and a willingness to work hard and work together to solve any problem.

I have something else to ask you, to ask every American. I ask for you to pray for this great nation. I ask for your prayers for leaders from both parties. I thank you for your prayers for me and my family, and I ask you pray for Vice President Gore and his family.

I have faith that with God's help we as a nation will move forward together as one nation, indivisible. And together we will create an America that is open, so every citizen has access to the American dream; an America that is educated, so every child has the keys to realize that dream; and an America that is united in our diversity and our shared American values that are larger than race or party.

I was not elected to serve one party, but to serve one nation.

The president of the United States is the president of every single American, of every race and every background.

Whether you voted for me or not, I will do my best to serve your interests and I will work to earn your respect.

I will be guided by President Jefferson's sense of purpose, to stand for principle, to be reasonable in manner, and above all, to do great good for the cause of freedom and harmony.

The presidency is more than an honor. It is more than an office. It is a charge to keep, and I will give it my all. Thank you very much and God bless America. (APPLAUSE)

TERROR, LIBERTY, AND THE PRESIDENCY

The events of September 11, 2001, ushered in a new chapter for America, although the themes it contained were perhaps not nearly as novel as some commentators imagined. There is no doubt that the hijacking of four airliners and the destruction at the World Trade Center in New York and the Pentagon in Washington, D.C., were seared into the minds of all Americans just as much as Pearl Harbor. The attacks took some 3,000 lives and caused vast economic damage. They also vividly demonstrated that the nation was unprepared for terrorist activity and changed assumptions about the nature of the threat to national security. The war on terror, however, had been coming for years, although the responses to it gained significant momentum following 9/11. The question quickly became: what was the main threat to American liberty? Was it the terrorists or was it the public officials attempting to deal with them? But Americans have historically had to address these same issues, albeit formed as a more visible and therefore manageable threat. Where to strike the balance between the individual's rights and the public's requirement to be secure? Can there be liberty without security, both for the individual and for the nation?

President Bush and his administration, who came to power in perhaps the nation's most contested election and without the support of a popular majority, had to find a way to move forward. Ironically, to do so they had to shed some of their traditional conservative rhetoric, which insisted that individual liberty was to be prized and that the Constitution was a changeless document, in favor of a far more active state and a Constitution susceptible to being adapted to the changing needs of the times. Because the new war on terror depended so heavily on intelligence and because maintaining the secrecy of the sources, methods, and results of that intelligence was so essential to the nation's security, the presidency was strengthened and the person holding the office grew more powerful. Hence, President Bush committed the nation to a doctrine of preemptive war abroad and a vast new security and self-defense apparatus to defend the homeland.

Note: The USA PATRIOT Act of 2001, Public Law No: 107-56

On October 26, 2001, President Bush signed the USA PATRIOT Act into law. USA PATRIOT is an acronym for Uniting and Strengthening America by Providing Appropriate Tools Required to Intercept and Obstruct Terrorism. Attorney General John Ashcroft played a decisive role in shaping the legislation, which gave sweeping new powers to both domestic law enforcement and international intelligence agencies and eliminated the checks and balances that previously gave courts the opportunity to ensure that such powers were not abused. Most of these checks and balances were put into place after previous misuse of surveillance powers by these agencies were uncovered, including the revelation in 1974 that the

FBI and foreign intelligence agencies had spied on over 10,000 U.S. citizens, including Martin Luther King, Jr.

The act is 342 pages long and made changes, some large and some small, to over fifteen different statutes, including those relating to online activities and surveillance, money laundering, immigration, and provisions for the victims of terrorism. This large and complex law was created in five weeks. Congress did not carefully study the vast majority of the sections included, nor was sufficient time taken to debate the act or to hear testimony from experts outside of law enforcement in the fields where it makes major changes. Several key procedural processes applicable to any other proposed laws, including interagency review, the normal committee and hearing processes, and thorough voting, were suspended for this bill.

The act granted additional surveillance authority to federal law enforcement officials, eliminated legal barriers to information sharing between law enforcement and intelligence agencies, sought to disrupt terrorist financial networks by requiring banks to report suspicious transactions, and increased the authority of the attorney general to detain and deport aliens suspected of having terrorist links. Of particular note was the authorization of roving wiretaps, which permit the surveillance of any communications device that a suspect may utilize, rather than a particular phone. This provision was dictated largely by the growing use of cellular telephones, which suspects may change often to escape detection. The USA PATRIOT Act passed both houses of Congress by an overwhelming margin, but there was concern that the measure might abridge civil liberties. Consequently, Congress stipulated that many sections of the act will sunset on December 31, 2005. This requirement ensured a continuing role for congressional oversight. The state legislatures of Alaska, Hawaii, and Vermont, as well as a number of local governments, have adopted resolutions expressing concern that the USA PATRIOT Act poses a threat to civil liberties and urging Congress to amend the measure.

The Uniting and Strengthening America by Providing Appropriate Tools Required to Intercept and Obstruct Terrorism (USA PATRIOT) Act of 2001, H.R. 3162, Section-by-Section Analysis

TITLE I—ENHANCING DOMESTIC SECURITY AGAINST TERRORISM

Sec. 101. Counterterrorism fund. Establish a counterterrorism fund in the Treasury of the United States, without affecting prior appropriations, to reimburse Department of Justice components for costs incurred in connection with terrorism and terrorism prevention, rebuild any Justice Department component damaged or destroyed as a result of a terrorism incident, pay terrorism-related rewards, conduct terrorism threat assessments, and reimburse Federal agencies for costs incurred in connection with detaining suspected terrorists in foreign countries.

Sec. 102. Sense of Congress condemning discrimination against Arab and Muslim Americans. Both the House and Senate bills included this provision to condemn acts of violence and discrimination against Arab Americans, American Muslims, and Americans from South Asia, and to declare that every effort must be taken to protect their safety.

Sec. 103. Increased funding for the technical support center at the Federal Bureau of Investigation. Both the House and Senate bills included this provision to authorize $200,000,000 per year for fiscal years 2002, 2003 and 2004 for the Technical Support Center established in section 811 of the Antiterrorism and Effective Death Penalty Act of 1996 to help meet the demands of activities to combat terrorism and enhance the technical support and tactical operations of the FBI.

Sec. 104. Requests for Military Assistance to Enforce Prohibition in Certain Emergencies. Authorizes the Attorney General to request military assistance in support of Department of Justice activities relating to the enforcement of 18 U.S.C. § 2332a during an emergency situation involving a weapon of mass destruction. Current law references a statute that was repealed in 1998, relating to chemical weapons.

Sec. 105. Expansion of National Electronic Crime Task Force Initiative. This provision allows the Secret Service to develop a national network of electronic crime task forces, based on the highly successful New York Electronic Crimes Task Force model, for the purpose of preventing, detecting, and investigating various forms of electronic crimes, including potential terrorist attacks against critical infrastructure and financial payment systems.

Sec. 106. Presidential authority. Authorizes the President, in limited circumstances involving armed hostilities or attacks against the United States, to confiscate and vest in the United States the property of enemies of the United States during times of national emergency, which was permitted by the Trading with the Enemy Act, 50 app. U.S.C. § 5(b), until 1977, when the International Economic Emergency Act was passed. The provision permits the President, when the United States is engaged in military hostilities or has been subject to attack, to confiscate property of any foreign country, person or organization involved in hostilities or attacks on the United States. This section also permits courts, when reviewing determinations made by the executive branch, to consider classified evidence ex parte and in camera.

TITLE II—ENHANCED SURVEILLANCE PROCEDURES

Sec. 201. Authority to intercept wire, oral, and electronic communications relating to terror-

ism. This provision adds criminal violations relating to terrorism to the list of predicate statutes in the criminal procedures for interception of communications under chapter 119 of title 18, United States Code.

Sec. 202. Authority to intercept wire, oral, and electronic communications relating to computer fraud and abuse offenses. . . .

Sec. 203. Authority to share criminal investigative information. Includes provisions amending the criminal procedures for interception of communications under chapter 119 of title 18, United States Code, and the grand jury procedures under Rule 6(e) of the Federal Rules of Criminal Procedures to authorize disclosure of foreign intelligence information obtained by such interception or by a grand jury to any Federal law enforcement, intelligence, national security, national defense, protective or immigration personnel to assist the official receiving that information in the performance of his official duties. Section 203(a) requires that within a reasonable time after disclosure of any grand jury information, an attorney for the government notify the court of such disclosure and the departments, agencies or entities to which disclosure was made. Section 203(b) pertains to foreign intelligence information obtained by intercepting communications pursuant to a court-ordered wiretap. Section 203(c) also authorizes such disclosure of information obtained as part of a criminal investigation notwithstanding any other law.

The information must meet statutory definitions of foreign intelligence or counterintelligence or foreign intelligence information. Recipients may use that information only as necessary for their official duties, and use of the information outside those limits remains subject to applicable penalties, such as penalties for unauthorized disclosure under chapter 119, contempt penalties under Rule 6(e) and the Privacy Act. The Attorney General must establish procedures for disclosure of information that identifies a United States person, such as the current procedures established under Executive Order 12333 for the intelligence community. In case of grand jury information, limited proposal to require notification to court after disclosure.

◆　◆　◆

Sec. 206. Roving surveillance authority under the Foreign Intelligence Surveillance Act of 1978. Includes a provision that modifies the Foreign Intelligence Surveillance Act ("FISA") to allow surveillance to follow a person who uses multiple communications devices or locations, a modification which conforms FISA to the parallel criminal procedure for electronic surveillance in 18 U.S.C. § 2518(11)(b). The court order need not specify the person whose assistance to the surveillance is required (such as a particular communications common carrier), where the court finds that the actions of the target may have the effect of thwarting the identification of a specified person.

Sec. 207. Duration of FISA surveillance of non-United States persons who are agents of foreign power. Includes a provision to change the initial period of a FISA order for a surveillance or physical search targeted against an agent of a foreign power from 90 to 120 days, and changes the period for extensions from 90 days to one year. One-year extensions for physical searches are subject to the requirement in current law that the judge find "probable cause to believe that no property of any United States person will be acquired during the period." Section 207 also changes the ordinary period for physical searches under FISA from 45 to 90 days.

◆ ◆ ◆

Sec. 209. Seizure of voice-mail messages pursuant to warrants. This section authorizes government access to voice mails with a court order supported by probable cause in the same way e-mails currently may be accessed, and authorizes nationwide service with a single search warrant for voice mails. Current law, 18 U.S.C. § 2510(1), defines "wire communication" to include "any electronic storage of such communication," with the result that the government must apply for a Title III wiretap order before it may obtain unopened voice mail messages held by a service provider. This section amends the definition of "wire communication" so that it no longer includes stored communications. It also amends 18 U.S.C. § 2703 to specify that

the government may use a search warrant (instead of a wiretap order) to compel the production of unopened voicemail, thus harmonizing the rules applicable to stored voice and non-voice (e.g., e-mail) communications.

Sec. 210. Scope of subpoenas for records of electronic communications. This provision broadens the types of records that law enforcement may obtain, pursuant to a subpoena, from electronic communications service providers by requiring providers to disclose the means and source of payment, including any bank account or credit card numbers. Current law allows the government to use a subpoena to compel communications providers to disclose a small class of records that pertain to electronic communications, limited to such records as the customer's name, address, and length of service. Investigators may not use a subpoena to obtain such records as credit card number or other form of payment and must use a court order. In many cases, users register with Internet service providers using false names, making the form of payment critical to determining the user's true identity.

Sec. 211. Clarification of scope. Amends the Cable Communications Policy Act to clarify that when a cable company acts as a telephone company or an Internet service provider, it must comply with the same laws governing the interception and disclosure of wire and electronic communications that apply to any other telephone company or Internet service provider.

Sec. 212. Emergency disclosure of electronic communications to protect life and limb. Amends 18 U.S.C. § 2702 to authorize providers of electronic communications services to disclose the communications (or records of such communications) of their subscribers if the provider reasonably believes that an emergency involving immediate danger of death or serious physical injury to any person requires the disclosure of the information without delay. This section also corrects an anomaly in the current law by clearly permitting a provider to disclose non-content records (such as a subscriber's log-in records) as well as the contents of the customer's communications to protect their computer systems.

Sec. 213. Authority for delaying notice of the execution of a warrant. . . . First, delayed notice is authorized only in cases where the government has demonstrated reasonable cause to believe that providing immediate notice would have an adverse result as defined in 18 U.S.C. § 2705. Second, the provision prohibits the government from seizing any tangible property or any wire or electronic communication or stored wire or electronic communication unless it makes a showing of reasonable necessity for the seizure. Third, the warrant must require the giving of notice within a reasonable time of the execution of the search.

Sec. 214. Pen register and trap and trace authority [wiretapping] under FISA. This provision modifies FISA provisions for pen register and trap and trace to eliminate the requirement to show to the court that the target is in contact with an "agent of a foreign power."

Sec. 215. Access to records and other items under the FISA. This provision removes the "agent of a foreign power" standard for court-ordered access to certain business records under FISA and expands the scope of court orders to include access to other records and tangible items. The authority may be used for an investigation to protect against international terrorism or clandestine intelligence activities or to obtain foreign intelligence information not concerning U.S. persons. An investigation of a United States person may not be based solely on activities protected by the First Amendment.

Sec. 216. Modification of authorities relating to use of pen registers and trap and trace [wiretapping] devices. Authorizes courts to grant pen register and trap and trace orders that are valid anywhere in the nation. It also ensures that the pen register and trap and trace provisions apply to facilities other than telephone lines (e.g., the Internet). It specifically provides, however, that the grant of authority to capture "routing" and "addressing" information for Internet users does not authorize the interception of the content of any such communications. It further requires the government to use the latest available technology to insure that a pen register or trap and trace device does not intercept the content of any communications. Finally, it

provides for a report to the court on each use of "Carnivore"-like devices on packet-switched data networks.

Sec. 217. Interception of computer trespasser communications. This provision allows computer service providers who are victims of attacks by computer trespassers to authorize persons acting under color of law to monitor trespassers on their computer systems in a narrow class of cases. A computer trespasser is defined as a person who accesses a protected computer without authorization and thus has no reasonable expectation of privacy in any communications transmitted to, through, or from the protected computer. However, it does not include a person known by the owner or operator of the protected computer to have an existing contractual relationship with the owner or operator for access to all or part of the protected computer.

◆ ◆ ◆

Sec. 219. Single-jurisdiction search warrants for terrorism. Amends Federal Rule of Criminal Procedure 41(a) to provide that warrants relating to the investigation of terrorist activities may be obtained in any district in which the activities related to the terrorism may have occurred, regardless of where the warrants will be executed.

Sec. 220. Nationwide service of search warrants for electronic surveillance. Amends 18 U.S.C. § 2703(a) to authorize courts with jurisdiction over the offense to issue search warrants for electronic communications in electronic storage anywhere in the United States, without requiring the intervention of their counterparts in the districts where Internet service providers are located.

Sec. 221. Trade sanctions. Authorizes the President unilaterally to restrict exports of agricultural products, medicine or medical devices to the Taliban or the territory of Afghanistan controlled by the Taliban.

◆ ◆ ◆

Sec. 223. Civil liability for certain unauthorized disclosures. This provision creates civil liability for violations, including unauthorized disclosures, by law enforcement authorities of the electronic surveillance procedures set forth in title 18, United States Code (e.g., unauthorized disclosure of pen trap, wiretap, stored communications), or FISA information. Also requires administrative discipline of officials who engage in such unauthorized disclosures.

Sec. 224. Sunset. Includes a provision to sunset certain amendments made by this title in 3 to 5 years. H.R. 3162 provides a 4-year sunset for sections 206, 201, 202, 203(b), 204, 206, 207, 209, 210, 212, 214, 215, 217, 218, 220, 223—at the end of December 31, 2005, with the authorities "grandfathered" as to particular investigations based on offenses occurring prior to sunset.

◆ ◆ ◆

TITLE III—INTERNATIONAL MONEY LAUNDERING ABATEMENT AND ANTI-TERRORIST FINANCING ACT OF 2001

[In sections 301 to 377 of the PATRIOT Act, Congress sought to disrupt terrorist financial networks by tightening requirements on financial institutions to detect and report money laundering. It also created new regulations governing counterfeiting.]

◆ ◆ ◆

TITLE IV—PROTECTING THE BORDER

Subtitle A. Protecting the Northern Border

◆ ◆ ◆

Sec. 402. Northern border personnel. Authorizes additional appropriations to allow for a tripling in personnel for the Border Patrol, INS Inspectors, and the US Customs Service in each State along the northern border, and an additional $50 million each to the INS and the US Customs Service to improve technology and acquire additional equipment for use at the northern border.

Sec. 403. Access by the Department of State and the INS to certain identifying information in the criminal history records of visa applicants and applicants for admission to the United States. Gives the State Department and INS access to the criminal history record information contained in the National Crime Information Center's Interstate Identification Index, Wanted Persons File, and any other information mutually agreed upon between the Attorney General and the agency receiving access.

◆ ◆ ◆

Sec. 405. Report on the integrated automated fingerprint identification system for points of entry and overseas consular posts. Requires the Attorney General to report to Congress on the feasibility of enhancing the FBI's Integrated Automated Fingerprint Identification System or other identification systems to identify foreign passport and visa holders who may be wanted in connection with a criminal investigation in the United States or abroad before issuing a visa to that person or their entry or exist from the United States.

Subtitle B. Enhanced Immigration Provisions

Sec. 411. Definitions relating to terrorism. Amends the definition of "engage in terrorist activity" to clarify that an alien who solicits funds or membership or provides material support to a certified terrorist organization is inadmissible and removable. Aliens who solicit funds or membership or provide material support to organizations not designated as terrorist organizations have the opportunity to show that they did not know and should not have known that their actions would further terrorist activity. This section also creates a definition of "terrorist organization," which is not defined under current law, for purposes of making an alien inadmissible or removable. It defines a terrorist organization as one that is (1) designated by the Secretary of State as a terrorist organization under the process supplied by current law; (2) designated by the Secretary of State as a terrorist organization for immigration purposes; or (3) a group of two or more individuals that commits terrorist activities or plans or prepares to commit (including locating targets for) terrorist activities. The changes made by this section will apply to actions taken by an alien before enactment with respect to any group that was at that time certified by the Secretary of State.

♦ ♦ ♦

Sec. 412. Mandatory detention of suspected terrorists; habeas corpus; judicial review. Grants the Attorney General the authority to certify that an alien meets the criteria of the terrorism grounds of the Immigration and Nationality Act, or is engaged in any other activity that endangers the national security of the United States, upon a "reasonable grounds to believe" standard, and take such aliens into custody. This authority is delegable only to the Deputy Attorney General. The Attorney General must either begin removal proceedings against such aliens or bring criminal charges within seven days, or release them from custody. An alien who is charged but ultimately found not to be removable is to be released from custody. An alien who is found to be removable but has not been removed, and whose removal is unlikely in the reasonably foreseeable future, may be detained if the Attorney General demonstrates that release of the alien will adversely affect national security or the safety of the community or any person. Judicial review of any action taken under this section, including review of the merits of the certification, is available through habeas corpus proceedings, with appeal to the U.S. Court of Appeals for the D.C. Circuit. The Attorney General shall review his certification of an alien every six months.

Sec. 413. Multilateral cooperation against terrorists. Provides new exceptions to the laws regarding disclosure of information from State Department records pertaining to the issuance of or refusal to issue visas to enter the U.S., and allows the sharing of this information with a foreign government on a case-by-case basis for the purpose of preventing, investigating, or punishing acts of terrorism.

Sec. 414. Visa integrity and security. . . . Particular focus should be given to the utilization of biometric technology and the development of tamper-resistant documents.

Sec. 415. Participation of Office of Homeland Security on Entry-Exit Task Force. This section includes the new Office of Homeland Security as a participant in the Entry and Exit Task Force established by the Immigration and Naturalization Service Data Management Improvement Act of 2000.

Sec. 416. Foreign student monitoring program. This section seeks to implement the foreign student monitoring program created in 1996 by temporarily supplanting the collection of user fees mandated by the statute with an appropriation of $36,800,000 for the express purpose of fully and effectively implementing the program through January 2003. Thereafter, the program would be funded by user fees. Currently, all institutions of higher education that enroll foreign students or exchange visitors are required to participate in the monitoring program. This section expands the list of institutions to include air flight schools, language training schools, and vocational schools.

♦ ♦ ♦

Subtitle C. Preservation of Immigration Benefits for Victims of Terrorism

[Note: It is certain that some aliens fell victim to the terrorist attacks on the United States on September 11. For many families, these tragedies will be compounded by the trauma of husbands, wives, and children losing their immigration status due to the death or serious injury of a family member. These family members are facing deportation because they are out of status: they no longer qualify for their current immigration status or are no longer eligible to complete the application process because their loved one was killed or injured in the September 11 terrorist attack. Others are threatened with the loss of their immigration status, through no fault of their own, due to the disruption of communication and transportation that has resulted directly from the terrorist attacks. Because of these disruptions, people have been and will be unable to meet important deadlines, which will mean the loss of eligibility for certain benefits and the inability to maintain lawful status, unless the law is changed. Modifies the immigration laws to provide the humanitarian relief to these victims and their family members in preserving their immigration status.]

◆ ◆ ◆

Title V—Removing Obstacles to Investigating Terrorism

Sec. 501. Attorney General's authority to pay rewards to combat terrorism. Authorizes the Attorney General to offer rewards—payments to individuals who offer information pursuant to a public advertisement—to gather information to combat terrorism and defend the nation against terrorist acts without any dollar limitation (Current law limits rewards to $2 million). Rewards of $250,000 or more require the personal approval of the Attorney General or President and notice to Congress.

Sec. 502. Secretary of State's authority to pay rewards. Authorizes the Secretary of State to offer rewards—payments to individuals who offer information pursuant to a public advertisement—to gather information to combat terrorism and defend the nation against terrorist acts without any dollar limitation (Current law limits rewards to $5 million). Rewards of $100,000 or more require the personal approval of the Secretary of State and notice to Congress.

Sec. 503. DNA identification of terrorists and other violent offenders. Authorizes the collection of DNA samples from any person convicted of certain terrorism-related offenses and other crimes of violence, for inclusion in the national DNA database.

Sec. 504. Coordination with law enforcement. Authorizes consultation between FISA officers and law enforcement officers to coordinate efforts to investigate or protect against international terrorism, clandestine intelligence activities, or other grave hostile acts of a foreign power or an agent of a foreign power.

Sec. 505. Miscellaneous national security authorities. Modifies current statutory provisions on access to telephone, bank, and credit records in counterintelligence investigations to remove the "agent of a foreign power" standard. The authority may be used only for investigations to protect against international terrorism or clandestine intelligence activities, and an investigation of a United States person may not be based solely on activities protected by the First Amendment.

◆ ◆ ◆

Sec. 507. Disclosure of educational records. Requires application to a court to obtain educational records in the possession of an educational agency or institution if it is determined by the Attorney General or Secretary of Education (or their designee) that doing so could reasonably be expected to assist in investigating or preventing a federal terrorism offense or domestic or international terrorism. Limited immunity is given to persons producing such information acting in good faith, and the Attorney General is directed to issue guidelines to protect confidentiality.

◆ ◆ ◆

Title VI—Providing for Victims of Terrorism, Public Safety Officers, and Their Families

Subtitle A. Aid for Families of Public Safety Officers

Sec. 611. Expedited payment for public safety officers involved in the prevention, investigation, rescue, or recovery efforts related to a terrorist attack. Streamlines the Public Safety Officers Benefits Program application process for family members of law enforcement officers, firefighters, and emergency personnel who perished or suffered serious injury in connection with prevention, investigation, rescue or recovery efforts related to a terrorist attack. The Public Safety Officers Benefits Program provides benefits for each of the families of law enforcement officers, fire fighters, emergency response squad members, ambulance crew members who are killed or permanently and totally disabled in the line of duty ($151,635 in FY 2001). Previous regulations, however, required the families of public safety officers who have fallen in the line of duty to go through a cumbersome and time-consuming application process.

♦ ♦ ♦

Sec. 624. Victims of terrorism. Conforms VOCA's domestic terrorism section to the international terrorism section, giving OVC the flexibility to deliver timely and critically-needed assistance to victims of terrorism and mass violence occurring within the United States. It also makes a technical correction to recent legislation that inadvertently reversed the existing exclusion under VOCA of individuals eligible for other Federal compensation under the Omnibus Diplomatic Security and Antiterrorism Act of 1986.

TITLE VII—INCREASED INFORMATION SHARING FOR CRITICAL INFRASTRUCTURE PROTECTION

Sec. 711. Expansion of regional information sharing system to facilitate Federal-State-local law enforcement response related to terrorist attacks. Expands the Department of Justice Regional Information Sharing Systems (RISS) Program to facilitate information sharing among Federal, State and local law enforcement agencies to investigate and prosecute terrorist conspiracies and activities and doubles its authorized funding for FY2002 and FY2003. Currently, 5,700 Federal, State and local law enforcement agencies participate in the RISS Program.

TITLE VIII—STRENGTHENING THE CRIMINAL LAWS AGAINST TERRORISM

Sec. 801. Terrorist attacks and other acts of violence against mass transportation systems. Creates a new statute (to be codified at 18 U.S.C. §1993) to make punishable acts of terrorism and other violence against mass transportation vehicles, systems, facilities, employees and passengers; the reporting of false

information about such activities; and attempts and conspiracies to commit such offenses. Violations are punishable by a fine and term imprisonment of 20 years; however, if the mass transportation vehicle was carrying a passenger at the time of the attack, or if death resulted from the offense, the maximum term of imprisonment is increased to life.

Sec. 802. Definition of domestic terrorism. Defines the term "domestic terrorism" as a counterpart to the current definition of "international terrorism" in 18 U.S.C. § 2331. The new definition for "domestic terrorism" is for the limited purpose of providing investigative authorities (i.e., court orders, warrants, etc.) for acts of terrorism within the territorial jurisdiction of the United States. Such offenses are those that are "(1) dangerous to human life and violate the criminal laws of the United States or any state; and (2) appear to be intended (or have the effect)—to intimidate a civilian population; influence government policy intimidation or coercion; or affect government conduct by mass destruction, assassination, or kidnapping (or a threat of)."

Sec. 803. Prohibition against harboring terrorists. Establishes a new criminal prohibition against harboring terrorists, similar to the current prohibition in 18 U.S.C. §792 against harboring spies, and makes it an offense when someone harbors or conceals another they know or should have known had engaged in or was about to engage in federal terrorism offenses.

Sec. 804. Jurisdiction over crimes committed at U.S. facilities abroad. Extends the special maritime and territorial jurisdiction of the United States to cover, with respect to offenses committed by or against a U.S. national, U.S. diplomatic, consular and military missions, and residences used by U.S. personnel assigned to such missions.

Sec. 805. Material support for terrorism. Amends 18 U.S.C. § 2339A, which prohibits providing material support to terrorists, in four respects. First, it adds three terrorism-related offenses. . . . Second, it provides that violations may be prosecuted in any Federal judicial district in which the predicate offense was committed. Third, it clarifies that monetary instruments, like currency and other financial securities, may constitute "material support or resources." . . . Fourth, it explicitly prohibits providing terrorists with "expert advice or assistance," such as flight training, knowing or intending that it will be used to prepare for or carry out an act of terrorism.

Sec. 806. Assets of terrorists organizations. Provides that the assets of individuals and organizations engaged in planning or perpetrating acts of terrorism against the United States, as well as the proceeds and instrumentalities of such acts, are subject to civil forfeiture.

♦ ♦ ♦

Sec. 809. No statute of limitation for certain terrorism offenses. Eliminates the statute of limitations for certain terrorism-related offenses, if the commission of such offense resulted in, or created a foreseeable risk of, death or serious bodily injury to another person.

Sec. 810. Alternative maximum penalties for terrorism offenses. Raises the maximum prison terms to 15 or 20 years or, if death results, life, in the following criminal statutes: (a) arson within the special maritime and territorial jurisdiction of the United States); (b) (destruction of an energy facility); . . . (d) (provision of material support to terrorists and terrorist organizations); (e) (destruction of national-defense materials); (f) (sabotage of nuclear facilities or fuel); (g) (killings on aircraft); (h) (destruction of interstate gas or hazardous liquid pipeline facility).

Sec. 811. Penalties for terrorist conspiracies. Ensures adequate penalties for certain terrorism-related conspiracies by adding conspiracy provisions to the following criminal statutes: (arson within the special maritime and territorial jurisdiction of the United States); (killings in Federal facilities); (destruction of communications lines, stations, or systems); (destruction of property within the special maritime and territorial jurisdiction of the United States (wrecking trains); (material support to terrorists); (torture); (sabotage of nuclear facilities or fuel); (interference with flight crews); (carrying weapons or explosives on aircraft); (destruction of interstate gas or hazardous liquid pipeline facility).

♦ ♦ ♦

Sec. 813. Inclusion of acts of terrorism as racketeering activity. Amends the RICO statute to include certain terrorism-related offenses within the definition of "racketeering activity," thus allowing multiple acts of terrorism to be charged as a pattern of racketeering for RICO purposes. This section expands the ability of prosecutors to prosecute members of established, ongoing terrorist organizations that present the threat of continuity that the RICO statute was designed to permit prosecutors to combat.

Sec. 814. Deterrence and prevention of cyberterrorism. Clarifies the criminal statute prohibiting computer hacking, 18 U.S.C. § 1030, to cover computers located outside the United States when used in a manner that affects the interstate commerce or communications of this country, update the definition of "loss" to ensure full costs to victims of hacking offenses are counted, clarify the scope of civil liability and eliminate the current mandatory minimum sentence applicable in some cases.

♦ ♦ ♦

Sec. 817. Expansion of the biological weapons statute. Amends the definition of "for use as a weapon" in the current biological weapons statute, 18 U.S.C. § 175, to include all situations in which it can be proven that the defendant had any purpose other than a prophylactic, protective, or peaceful purpose. This section also creates a new criminal statute, 18 U.S.C. § 175b, which generally makes it an offense for certain restricted persons, including non-resident foreign nationals of countries that support international terrorism, to possess a listed biological agent or toxin.

TITLE IX—IMPROVED INTELLIGENCE

Sec. 901. Responsibilities of Director of Central Intelligence regarding foreign intelligence collected under the Foreign Intelligence Surveillance Act of 1978. Clarifies the role of the Director of Central Intelligence ("DCI") with respect to the overall management of collection goals, analysis and dissemination of foreign intelligence gathered pursuant to the Foreign Intelligence Surveillance Act, in order to ensure that FISA is properly and efficiently used for foreign intelligence purposes. It requires the DCI to assist the Attorney General in ensuring that FISA efforts are consistent with constitutional and statutory civil liberties. The DCI will have no operational authority with respect to implementation of FISA, which will continue to reside with the FBI.

Sec. 902. Inclusion of international terrorism activities within scope of foreign intelligence under National Security Act of 1947. Revises the National Security Act definitions section to include "international terrorism" as a subset of "foreign intelligence." This change will clarify the DCI's responsibility for collecting foreign intelligence related to international terrorism.

♦ ♦ ♦

Sec. 905. Disclosure to Director of Central Intelligence of foreign intelligence-related information with respect to criminal investigations. Creates a responsibility for law enforcement agencies to notify the Intelligence Community when a criminal investigation reveals information of intelligence value. Regularizes existing ad hoc notification, and makes clear that constitutional and statutory prohibitions of certain types of information sharing apply.

Sec. 906. Foreign Terrorist Asset Tracking Center. Regularizes the existing Foreign Terrorist Asset Tracking Center by creating an element within the Department of Treasury designed to review all-source intelligence in support of both intelligence and law enforcement efforts to counter terrorist financial support networks.

Sec. 907. National Virtual Translation Center. Directs the submission of a report on the feasibility of establishing a virtual translation capability, making use of cutting-edge communications technology to link securely translation capabilities on a nationwide basis.

Sec. 908. Training of government officials regarding identification and use of foreign intelligence. Directs the Attorney General, in consultation with the DCI, to establish a training program for Federal, State and local officials on the recognition and appropriate handling of intelligence information discovered in the normal course of their duties.

TITLE X—MISCELLANEOUS

Sec. 1001. Review of the Department of Justice. Authorizes the Inspector General of the Department of Justice to designate one official to review information and receive complaints alleging abuses of civil rights and civil liberties by employees and officials of the Department of Justice.

Sec. 1002. Sense of Congress. This provision condemns discrimination and acts of violence against Sikh-Americans.

Sec. 1003. Definition of "electronic surveillance." This provision authorizes the use of the new computer trespass authority under FISA.

♦ ♦ ♦

Sec. 1006. Inadmissibility of aliens engaged in money laundering. This provision makes inadmissible to the United States any alien who a consular officer or the Attorney General knows, or has reason to believe, is involved in a Federal money laundering offense.

Sec. 1007. Authorization of funds for DEA police training in South and Central Asia. This provision authorizes money for anti-drug training in the Republic of Turkey, and for increased precursor chemical control efforts in the South and Central Asia region.

Sec. 1008. Feasibility study on use of biometric identifier scanning system with access to the FBI Integrated automated fingerprint identification system at overseas consular posts and points of entry to the United States. This provision directs the Attorney General to report to Congress on the feasibility of using a biometric identifier (fingerprint) scanning system, with access to the FBI fingerprint database, at consular offices abroad and at points of entry into the United States.

Sec. 1009. Study of access. This provision directs the FBI to report to Congress on the feasibility of providing airlines with computer access to the names of suspected terrorists.

♦ ♦ ♦

Sec. 1011. Crimes against charitable Americans. This provision amends the Telemarketing and Consumer Fraud and Abuse Prevention Act to require any person engaged in telemarketing for the solicitation of charitable contributions to disclose to the person receiving the call that the purpose of the call is to solicit charitable contributions, and to make such other disclosures as the FTC considers appropriate.

Sec. 1012. Limitation on issuance of hazmat licenses. This provision allows the Department of Transportation to obtain background records checks for any individual applying for a license to transport hazardous materials in interstate commerce.

Sec. 1013. Expressing the sense of the Senate concerning the provision of funding for bioterrorism preparedness and response. This provision expresses the sense of the Senate that the United States should make a substantial new investment this year toward improving State and local preparedness to respond to potential bioterrorism attacks.

Sec. 1014. Grant program for State and local domestic preparedness support. This pro-

vision authorizes an appropriated Department of Justice program to provide grants to States to prepare for and respond to terrorist acts including but not limited to events of terrorism involving weapons of mass destruction and biological, nuclear, radiological, incendiary, chemical, and explosive devices. The authorization revises this grant program to provide: (1) additional flexibility to purchase needed equipment; (2) training and technical assistance to State and local first responders; and (3) a more equitable allocation of funds to all States.

◆ ◆ ◆

Sec. 1016. Critical infrastructures protection. This provision establishes a National Infrastructure Simulation and Analysis Center (NISAC) to address critical infrastructure protection and continuity through support for activities related to counterterrorism, threat assessment, and risk mitigation.

THE USA PATRIOT ACT: FOR AND AGAINST

Much like the Alien and Sedition Acts, the USA PATRIOT Act has evoked significantly different reactions. Even more divisive debate has arisen about another part of the Bush administration's anti-terrorism program—the proposal to try suspected terrorists who are not American citizens before military tribunals rather than in civil courts. What is clear, however, is that the act has significantly enhanced the authority of the executive branch of the federal government, clothing it with new and extensive powers to investigate not only suspected terrorists but all Americans. Indeed, proposals by the Bush administration to enact an even more aggressive version of the law, the so-called USA PATRIOT Act II, have been met with a chorus of concern from both the right and the left.

The USA PATRIOT Act: Preserving Life and Liberty
January 3, 2004

This defense of the USA PATRIOT Act comes from Attorney General John Ashcroft's Department of Justice website at www.lifeandliberty.gov/.

The Department of Justice's first priority is to prevent future terrorist attacks. Since its passage following the September 11, 2001 attacks, the Patriot Act has played a key part—and of-

ten the leading role—in a number of successful operations to protect innocent Americans from the deadly plans of terrorists dedicated to destroying America and our way of life.

While the results have been important, in passing the Patriot Act, Congress provided for only modest, incremental changes in the law. Congress simply took existing legal principles and retrofitted them to preserve the lives and liberty of the American people from the challenges posed by a global terrorist network.

Congress enacted the Patriot Act by overwhelming, bipartisan margins, arming law enforcement with new tools to detect and prevent terrorism: The USA Patriot Act was passed nearly unanimously by the Senate 98–1, and 357–66 in the House, with the support of members from across the political spectrum.

The Act Improves Our Counter-Terrorism Efforts in Several Significant Ways:

1. The Patriot Act allows investigators to use the tools that were already available to investigate organized crime and drug trafficking. Many of the tools the Act provides to law enforcement to fight terrorism have been used for decades to fight organized crime and drug dealers, and have been reviewed and approved by the courts. As Sen. Joe Biden (D-DE) explained during the floor debate about the Act, "the FBI could get a wiretap to investigate the mafia, but they could not get one to investigate terrorists. To put it bluntly, that was crazy! What's good for the mob should be good for terrorists." (Cong. Rec., 10/25/01)

- Allows law enforcement to use surveillance against more crimes of terror. Before the Patriot Act, courts could permit law enforcement to conduct electronic surveillance to investigate many ordinary, non-terrorism crimes, such as drug crimes, mail fraud, and passport fraud. Agents also could obtain wiretaps to investigate some, but not all, of the crimes that terrorists often commit. The Act enabled investigators to gather information when looking into the full range of terrorism-related crimes, including: chemical-weapons offenses, the use of weapons of mass destruction, killing Americans abroad, and terrorism financing.
- Allows federal agents to follow sophisticated terrorists trained to evade detection. For years, law enforcement has been able to use "roving wiretaps" to investigate ordinary crimes, including drug offenses and racketeering. A roving wiretap can be authorized by a federal judge to apply to a particular suspect, rather than a particular phone or communications device. Because international terrorists are sophisticated and trained to thwart surveillance by rapidly changing locations and communication devices such as cell phones, the Act authorized agents to seek court permission to use the same techniques in national security investigations to track terrorists.
- Allows law enforcement to conduct investigations without tipping off terrorists. In some cases if criminals are tipped off too early to an investigation, they might flee, destroy evidence, intimidate or kill witnesses, cut off contact with associates, or take other action to evade arrest. Therefore, federal courts in narrow circumstances long have allowed law enforcement to delay for a limited time when the subject is told that a judicially-approved search warrant has been executed. Notice is always provided, but the reasonable delay gives law enforcement time to identify the criminal's associates, eliminate immediate threats to our communities, and coordinate the arrests of multiple individuals without tipping them off beforehand. These delayed notification search warrants have been used for decades, have proven crucial in drug and organized crime cases, and have been upheld by courts as fully constitutional.
- Allows federal agents to ask a court for an order to obtain business records in national security terrorism cases. Examining business records often provides the key that investigators are looking for to solve a wide range of crimes. Investigators might seek select records from hardware stores or chemical plants, for example, to find out who bought materials to make a bomb, or bank records to see who's sending money to terrorists. Law enforcement authorities have always been able to obtain business records in criminal cases through grand jury subpoenas, and continue to do so in national security cases where appropriate. These records were sought in criminal cases such as the investigation of the Zodiac gunman, where police suspected the gunman was inspired by a Scottish occult poet, and wanted to learn who had checked the poet's books out of the library. In national security cases where use of the grand jury process was not appropriate, investigators previously had limited tools at their disposal to obtain certain business records. Under the Patriot Act, the government can now ask a federal court (the For-

eign Intelligence Surveillance Court), if needed to aid an investigation, to order production of the same type of records available through grand jury subpoenas. This federal court, however, can issue these orders only after the government demonstrates the records concerned are sought for an authorized investigation to obtain foreign intelligence information not concerning a U.S. person or to protect against international terrorism or clandestine intelligence activities, provided that such investigation of a U.S. person is not conducted solely on the basis of activities protected by the First Amendment.

2. The Patriot Act facilitated information sharing and cooperation among government agencies so that they can better "connect the dots." The Act removed the major legal barriers that prevented the law enforcement, intelligence, and national defense communities from talking and coordinating their work to protect the American people and our national security. The government's prevention efforts should not be restricted by boxes on an organizational chart. Now police officers, FBI agents, federal prosecutors and intelligence officials can protect our communities by "connecting the dots" to uncover terrorist plots before they are completed. As Sen. John Edwards (D-N.C.) said about the Patriot Act, "we simply cannot prevail in the battle against terrorism if the right hand of our government has no idea what the left hand is doing." (Press release, 10/26/01)

- Prosecutors can now share evidence obtained through grand juries with intelligence officials— and intelligence information can now be shared more easily with federal prosecutors. Such sharing of information leads to concrete results. For example, a federal grand jury recently indicted an individual in Florida, Sami al-Arian, for allegedly being the U.S. leader of the Palestinian Islamic Jihad, one of the world's most violent terrorist outfits. Palestinian Islamic Jihad is responsible for murdering more than 100 innocent people, including a young American named Alisa Flatow who was killed in a tragic bus bombing in Gaza. The Patriot Act assisted us in obtaining the indictment by enabling the full sharing of information and advice about the case among prosecutors and investigators. Alisa's father, Steven Flatow, has said, "When you know the resources of your

government are committed to right the wrongs committed against your daughter, that instills you with a sense of awe. As a father you can't ask for anything more."

3. The Patriot Act updated the law to reflect new technologies and new threats. The Act brought the law up to date with current technology, so we no longer have to fight a digital-age battle with antique weapons—legal authorities leftover from the era of rotary telephones. When investigating the murder of *Wall Street Journal* reporter Daniel Pearl, for example, law enforcement used one of the Act's new authorities to use high-tech means to identify and locate some of the killers.

- Allows law enforcement officials to obtain a search warrant anywhere a terrorist-related activity occurred. Before the Patriot Act, law enforcement personnel were required to obtain a search warrant in the district where they intended to conduct a search. However, modern terrorism investigations often span a number of districts, and officers therefore had to obtain multiple warrants in multiple jurisdictions, creating unnecessary delays. The Act provides that warrants can be obtained in any district in which terrorism-related activities occurred, regardless of where they will be executed. This provision does not change the standards governing the availability of a search warrant, but streamlines the search-warrant process.
- Allows victims of computer hacking to request law enforcement assistance in monitoring the "trespassers" on their computers. This change made the law technology-neutral; it placed electronic trespassers on the same footing as physical trespassers. Now, hacking victims can seek law enforcement assistance to combat hackers, just as burglary victims have been able to invite officers into their homes to catch burglars.

4. The Patriot Act increased the penalties for those who commit terrorist crimes. Americans are threatened as much by the terrorist who pays for a bomb as by the one who pushes the button. That's why the Patriot Act imposed tough new penalties on those who commit and support terrorist operations, both at home and abroad. In particular, the Act:

- Prohibits the harboring of terrorists. The Act created a new offense that prohibits knowingly harboring persons who have committed or are about to commit a variety of terrorist offenses, such as: destruction of aircraft; use of nuclear, chemical, or biological weapons; use of weapons of mass destruction; bombing of government property; sabotage of nuclear facilities; and aircraft piracy.
- Enhanced the inadequate maximum penalties for various crimes likely to be committed by terrorists: including arson, destruction of energy facilities, material support to terrorists and terrorist organizations, and destruction of national-defense materials.
- Enhanced a number of conspiracy penalties, including for arson, killings in federal facilities, attacking communications systems, material support to terrorists, sabotage of nuclear facilities, and interference with flight crew members. Under previous law, many terrorism statutes did

not specifically prohibit engaging in conspiracies to commit the underlying offenses. In such cases, the government could only bring prosecutions under the general federal conspiracy provision, which carries a maximum penalty of only five years in prison.
- Punishes terrorist attacks on mass transit systems.
- Punishes bioterrorists.
- Eliminates the statutes of limitations for certain terrorism crimes and lengthens them for other terrorist crimes.

The government's success in preventing another catastrophic attack on the American homeland since September 11, 2001, would have been much more difficult, if not impossible, without the USA Patriot Act. The authorities Congress provided have substantially enhanced our ability to prevent, investigate, and prosecute acts of terror.

AMERICAN CIVIL LIBERTIES UNION

"The USA PATRIOT Act and Government Actions That Threaten Our Civil Liberties"
January 3, 2004

The American Civil Liberties Union has provided steady and determined opposition to the USA PATRIOT Act from its passage. The following document has been used to stir opposition to the act by, among other strategies, urging city and town governments to pass resolutions condemning the act.

With great haste and secrecy and in the name of the "war on terrorism," Congress passed legislation that gives the Executive Branch sweeping new powers that undermine the Bill of Rights and are unnecessary to keep us safe. This 342-page USA PATRIOT Act was passed on October 26, 2001, with little debate by Members of Congress, most of whom did not even read the bill. The Administration then initiated a flurry of executive orders, regulations, and policies and practices that also threatened our rights.

THE USA PATRIOT ACT:

Expands terrorism laws to include "domestic terrorism" which could subject political organizations to surveillance, wiretapping, harass-

ment, and criminal action for political advocacy.

Expands the ability of law enforcement to conduct secret searches, gives them wide powers of phone and Internet surveillance, and access to highly personal medical, financial, mental health, and student records with minimal judicial oversight.

Allows FBI Agents to investigate American citizens for criminal matters without probable cause of crime if they say it is for "intelligence purposes."

Permits non-citizens to be jailed based on mere suspicion and to be denied re-admission to the US for engaging in free speech. Suspects convicted of no crime may be detained indefinitely in six month increments without meaningful judicial review.

WHAT RIGHTS ARE BEING THREATENED?

First Amendment—Freedom of religion, speech, assembly, and the press.

Fourth Amendment—Freedom from unreasonable searches and seizures.

Fifth Amendment—No person to be deprived of life, liberty or property without due process of law.

Sixth Amendment—Right to a speedy public trial by an impartial jury, right to be informed of the facts of the accusation, right to confront witnesses and have the assistance of counsel.

Eighth Amendment—No excessive bail or cruel and unusual punishment shall be imposed.

Fourteenth Amendment—All persons (citizens and noncitizens) within the US are entitled to due process and the equal protection of the laws.

NEW FEDERAL EXECUTIVE BRANCH ACTIONS

- 8,000 Arab and South Asian immigrants have been interrogated because of their religion or ethnic background, not because of actual wrongdoing.
- Thousands of men, mostly of Arab and South Asian origin, have been held in secretive federal custody for weeks and months, sometimes without any charges filed against them. The government has refused to publish their names and whereabouts, even when ordered to do so by the courts.
- The press and the public have been barred from immigration court hearings of those detained after September 11th and the courts are ordered to keep secret even that the hearings are taking place.
- The government is allowed to monitor communications between federal detainees and their lawyers, destroying the attorney-client privilege and threatening the right to counsel.
- New Attorney General Guidelines allow FBI spying on religious and political organizations and individuals without having evidence of wrongdoing.
- President Bush has ordered military commissions to be set up to try suspected terrorists who are not citizens. They can convict based on hearsay and secret evidence by only two-thirds vote.
- American citizens suspected of terrorism are being held indefinitely in military custody without being charged and without access to lawyers.

WHAT CAN BE DONE?

This lack of due process and accountability violates the rights extended to all persons, citizens and non-citizens, by the Bill of Rights. It resurrects the illegal COINTELPRO-type programs of the '50's, '60's, and '70's, where the FBI sought to disrupt and discredit thousands of individuals and groups engaged in legitimate political activity.

The American Civil Liberties Union, along with thousands of organizations and individuals concerned with protecting our civil rights and civil liberties, is campaigning to ensure that our rights are not a casualty of the war on terrorism.

Join us in this effort to regain our hard-won freedoms.

- Support a resolution in your city rejecting the USA PATRIOT Act, joining your city with others across the country in upholding the Bill of Rights.
- Contact your elected representatives and the President to express your opposition to the USA PATRIOT Act.
- Send letters to local newspapers. Organize discussions in your schools, organizations and religious institutions.

NEWT GINGRICH

"The Policies of War: Refocus the Mission"
San Francisco Chronicle
November 11, 2003

Newt Gingrich served as Speaker of the U.S. House of Representatives during much of the 1990s and led the successful impeachment effort against President Bill Clinton. Gingrich was also viewed as a spokesperson for conservative political values, including significantly limiting the role of the federal government. He was also the chief architect of the Contract for America, a document that played a significant role in rallying conservative political forces in the 1994 congressional elections. Gingrich had insisted that the national government had become an engine of entitlement for certain groups rather than an agent by which to provide equal opportunity for all. For example, he argued that so-called welfare queens had benefited at the cost of hardworking Americans whose tax dollars were squandered on the lazy.

We must ensure that the legal tools provided are not abused, and indeed, that they do not undermine the very foundation our country was built upon.

I strongly believe the Patriot Act was not created to be used in crimes unrelated to terrorism.

Recent reports, including one from the General Accounting Office, however indicate that the Patriot Act has been employed in investigations unconnected to terrorism or national security.

In our battle against those that detest our free and prosperous society, we cannot sacrifice any of the pillars our nation stands upon, namely respect for the Constitution and the rule of law. Our enemies in the war against terrorism abuse the Islamic law known as the Sharia that they claim to value. It is perversely used as justification for their horrific and wanton acts of violence.

We must demonstrate to the world that America is the best example of what a solid Constitution with properly enforced laws can bring to those who desire freedom and safety. If we become hypocrites about our own legal system, how can we sell it abroad or question legal systems different than our own?

I strongly believe Congress must act now to rein in the Patriot Act, limit its use to national security concerns and prevent it from developing "mission creep" into areas outside of national security.

Similarly, if prosecutors lack the necessary legislation to combat other serious domestic crimes, crimes not connected to terrorism, then lawmakers should seek to give prosecutors separate legislation to provide them the tools they need, but again not at the expense of civil rights. But in no case should prosecutors of domestic crimes seek to use tools intended for national security purposes.

This war against terrorism requires Americans and American institutions to have the "courage to be safe," this courage must include keeping to the American principles that have made this country great for more than 200 years.

Zelman v. *Simmons-Harris*
536 U.S. 639 (2002)

The issues of religion and education offer an interesting perspective on the war on terrorism. The troubled circumstances and poor academic record of many urban public schools have prompted a variety of reform proposals. Among the most controversial has been the voucher program. In brief, this program provides scholarships from public funds to students from low-income families to pay the tuition of private schools. Typically, most of the students enrolled in the voucher program attend religious schools. Opponents have challenged such schemes as a diversion of government aid to religious institutions in violation of the establishment clause of the First Amendment. In Zelman *the Supreme Court voted 5 to 4 to sustain Ohio's pilot voucher program in Cleveland. But in reaching that decision, the justices also addressed the question of religious belief and individual liberty, issues lurking below the surface of the war on terrorism.*

Chief Justice Rehnquist delivered the opinion of the Court.

The State of Ohio has established a pilot program designed to provide educational choices to families with children who reside in the Cleveland City School District. The question presented is whether this program offends the Establishment Clause of the United States Constitution. We hold that it does not.

There are more than 75,000 children enrolled in the Cleveland City School District. The majority of these children are from low-income and minority families. Few of these families enjoy the means to send their children to any school other than an inner-city public school. For more than a generation, however, Cleveland's public schools have been among the worst performing public schools in the Nation. In 1995, a Federal District Court declared a "crisis of magnitude" and placed the entire Cleveland school district under state control. Shortly thereafter, the state auditor found that Cleveland's public schools were in the midst of a "crisis that is perhaps unprecedented in the history of American education." The district had failed to meet any of the 18 state standards for minimal acceptable performance. Only 1 in 10 ninth graders could pass a basic proficiency examination, and students at all levels performed at a dismal rate compared with students in other Ohio public schools. More than two-thirds of high school students either dropped or failed out before graduation. Of those students who managed to reach their senior year, one of every four still failed to graduate. Of those students who did graduate, few could read, write, or compute at levels comparable to their counterparts in other cities.

It is against this backdrop that Ohio enacted, among other initiatives, its Pilot Project Scholarship Program. The program provides financial assistance to families in any Ohio school district that is or has been "under federal court order requiring supervision and operational management of the district by the state superintendent." Cleveland is the only Ohio school district to fall within that category.

The program provides two basic kinds of assistance to parents of children in a covered district. First, the program provides tuition aid for students in kindergarten through third grade, expanding each year through eighth grade, to attend a participating public or private school of their parent's choosing. Second, the program provides tutorial aid for students who choose to remain enrolled in public school.

♦   ♦   ♦

The Establishment Clause of the First Amendment, applied to the States through the Fourteenth Amendment, prevents a State from enacting laws that have the "purpose" or "effect" of advancing or inhibiting religion. There is no dispute that the program challenged here was enacted for the valid secular purpose of providing educational assistance to poor children in a demonstrably failing public school system. Thus, the question presented is whether the Ohio program nonetheless has the forbidden "effect" of advancing or inhibiting religion.

To answer that question, our decisions have drawn a consistent distinction between government programs that provide aid directly to religious schools, and programs of true private choice, in which government aid reaches religious schools only as a result of the genuine and independent choices of private individuals. While our jurisprudence with respect to the constitutionality of direct aid programs has "changed significantly" over the past two decades, our jurisprudence with respect to true private choice programs has remained consistent and unbroken.

♦   ♦   ♦

We believe that the program challenged here is a program of true private choice, and thus constitutional. As was true in those cases, the Ohio program is neutral in all respects toward religion. It is part of a general and multifaceted undertaking by the State of Ohio to provide educational opportunities to the children of a failed school district. It confers educational assistance directly to a broad class of individuals defined without reference to religion, i.e., any parent of a school-age child who resides in the Cleveland City School District. The program permits the participation of *all* schools within the district, religious or nonreligious. Adjacent public schools also may participate and have a financial incentive to do so. Program benefits are available to participating families on neutral terms, with no reference to religion. The only preference stated anywhere in the program is a preference for low-income families, who receive greater assistance and are given priority for admission at participating schools.

♦ ♦ ♦

There also is no evidence that the program fails to provide genuine opportunities for Cleveland parents to select secular educational options for their school-age children. Cleveland schoolchildren enjoy a range of educational choices: They may remain in public school as before, remain in public school with publicly funded tutoring aid, obtain a scholarship and choose a religious school, obtain a scholarship and choose a nonreligious private school, enroll in a community school, or enroll in a magnet school. That 46 of the 56 private schools now participating in the program are religious schools does not condemn it as a violation of the Establishment Clause. The Establishment Clause question is whether Ohio is coercing parents into sending their children to religious schools, and that question must be answered by evaluating *all* options Ohio provides Cleveland schoolchildren, only one of which is to obtain a program scholarship and then choose a religious school.

♦ ♦ ♦

In sum, the Ohio program is entirely neutral with respect to religion. It provides benefits directly to a wide spectrum of individuals, defined only by financial need and residence in a particular school district. It permits such individuals to exercise genuine choice among options public and private, secular and religious.

The program is therefore a program of true private choice. In keeping with an unbroken line of decisions rejecting challenges to similar programs, we hold that the program does not offend the Establishment Clause.

The judgment of the Court of Appeals is reversed.

It is so ordered.

♦ ♦ ♦

Justice Breyer, with whom Justice Stevens and Justice Souter join, dissenting.

I join Justice Souter's opinion, and I agree substantially with Justice Stevens. I write separately, however, to emphasize the risk that publicly financed voucher programs pose in terms of religiously based social conflict. I do so because I believe that the Establishment Clause concern for protecting the Nation's social fabric from religious conflict poses an overriding obstacle to the implementation of this well-intentioned school voucher program. And by explaining the nature of the concern, I hope to demonstrate why, in my view, "parental choice" cannot significantly alleviate the constitutional problem.

♦ ♦ ♦

The upshot is the development of constitutional doctrine that reads the Establishment Clause as avoiding religious strife, *not* by providing every religion with an *equal opportunity* (say, to secure state funding or to pray in the public schools), but by drawing fairly clear lines of *separation* between church and state—at least where the heartland of religious belief, such as primary religious education, is at issue.

II

The principle underlying these cases—avoiding religiously based social conflict—remains of great concern. As religiously diverse as America had become when the Court decided its major 20th-century Establishment Clause cases, we are exponentially more diverse today. America boasts more than 55 different religious groups and subgroups with a significant number of members. Major religions include, among others, Protestants, Catholics, Jews, Muslims, Buddhists, Hindus, and Sikhs. And several of these major religions contain different subsidiary sects with different religious beliefs. New Christian immigrant groups are "expressing their Christianity in languages, customs, and independent churches that are barely recognizable, and often controversial, for European-ancestry Catholics and Protestants."

Under these modern-day circumstances, how is the "equal opportunity" principle to work—without risking the "struggle of sect against sect" against which Justice Rutledge warned? School voucher programs finance the religious education of the young. And, if widely adopted, they may well provide billions of dollars that will do so. Why will different religions not become concerned about, and seek to influence, the criteria used to channel this money to religious schools? Why will they not want to examine the implementation of the programs that provide this money—to determine, for example, whether implementation has biased a program toward or against particular sects, or whether recipient religious schools are adequately fulfilling a program's criteria? If so, just how is the State to resolve the resulting controversies without provoking legitimate fears of the kinds of religious favoritism that, in so religiously diverse a Nation, threaten social dissension?

◆   ◆   ◆

IV

I do not believe that the "parental choice" aspect of the voucher program sufficiently offsets the concerns I have mentioned. Parental choice cannot help the taxpayer who does not want to finance the religious education of children. It will not always help the parent who may see little real choice between inadequate nonsectarian public education and adequate education at a school whose religious teachings are contrary to his own. It will not satisfy religious minorities unable to participate because they are too few in number to support the creation of their own private schools. It will not satisfy groups whose religious beliefs preclude them from participating in a government-sponsored program, and who may well feel ignored as government funds primarily support the education of children in the doctrines of the dominant religions. And it does little to ameliorate the entanglement problems or the related problems of social division that Part II, supra, describes. Consequently, the fact that the parent may choose which school can cash the government's voucher check does not alleviate the Establishment Clause concerns associated with voucher programs.

V

The Court, in effect, turns the clock back. It adopts, under the name of "neutrality," an interpretation of the Establishment Clause that this Court rejected more than half a century ago. In its view, the parental choice that offers each religious group a kind of equal opportunity to secure government funding overcomes the Establishment Clause concern for social concord. An earlier Court found that "equal opportunity" principle insufficient; it read the Clause as insisting upon greater separation of church and state, at least in respect to primary education. See *Nyquist*, 413 U.S., at 783. In a society composed of many different religious creeds, I fear that this present departure from the Court's earlier understanding risks creating a form of religiously based conflict potentially harmful to the Nation's social fabric. Because I believe the Establishment Clause was written in part to avoid this kind of conflict, and for reasons set forth by Justice Souter and Justice Stevens, I respectfully dissent.

Note: Homeland Security Act

In November of 2002 Congress passed the Homeland Security Act, which created the Department of Homeland Security. The new department was designed to help combat terrorism and to safeguard the nation's borders, airports, and infrastructure from attack. This action entailed a massive reorganization of the federal bureaucracy into a more logical arrangement. Some twenty-two federal agencies, ranging from the Coast Guard to the Secret Service, were transferred to the new department. Congress intended to bring the domestic security functions of diverse and often rival agencies under one roof. Better intelligence was seen by many observers as essential to preventing future terrorist attacks. Although intelligence-gathering bodies, such as the FBI and the CIA, remained outside the authority of the new department, the Homeland Security Act established an information analysis division within the department. The division is expected to serve as a clearinghouse to receive and assess terrorism intelligence from other agencies. The Homeland Security Act became effective in January of 2003. As of this writing, it is too early to determine its effectiveness in enhancing national security.

✦ Appendix ✦

The Constitution of
the United States

WE THE PEOPLE OF THE UNITED STATES, in order to form a more perfect Union, establish Justice, insure domestic Tranquility, provide for the common defence, promote the general Welfare, and secure the Blessings of Liberty to ourselves and our Posterity, do ordain and establish this Constitution for the United States of America.

ARTICLE I

Section 1. All legislative Powers herein granted shall be vested in a Congress of the United States, which shall consist of a Senate and House of Representatives.

Section 2. The House of Representatives shall be composed of Members chosen every second Year by the People of the several States, and the Electors in each State shall have the Qualifications requisite for Electors of the most numerous Branch of the State Legislature.

No Person shall be a Representative who shall not have attained to the Age of twenty five Years, and been seven Years a Citizen of the United States, and who shall not, when elected, be an Inhabitant of that State in which he shall be chosen.

Representatives and direct Taxes shall be apportioned among the several States which may be included within this Union, according to their respective Numbers, which shall be determined by adding to the whole Number of free Persons, including those bound to Service for a Term of Years, and excluding Indians not taxed, three fifths of all other Persons. The actual Enumeration shall be made within three Years after the first Meeting of the Congress of the United States, and within every subsequent Term of ten Years, in such Manner as they shall by Law direct. The Number of Representatives shall not exceed one for every thirty Thousand, but each State shall have at Least one Representative; and until such enumeration shall be made, the State of New Hampshire shall be entitled to chuse three, Massachusetts eight, Rhode-Island and Providence Plantations one, Connecticut five, New-York six, New Jersey four, Pennsylvania eight, Delaware one, Maryland six, Virginia ten, North Carolina five, South Carolina five, and Georgia three.

When vacancies happen in the Representation from any State, the Executive Authority thereof shall issue Writs of Election to fill such Vacancies.

The House of Representatives shall chuse their Speaker and other Officers; and shall have the sole Power of Impeachment.

Section 3. The Senate of the United States shall be composed of two Senators from each State, chosen by the Legislature thereof, for six Years; and each Senator shall have one Vote.

Immediately after they shall be assembled in Consequence of the first Election, they shall be divided as equally as may be into three Classes. The Seats of the Senators of the first Class shall be vacated at the Expiration of the second Year, of the second Class at the Expiration of the fourth Year, and of the third Class at the Expiration of the sixth Year, so that one third may be chosen every second Year; and if Vacancies happen by Resignation, or otherwise, during the Recess of the Legislature of any State, the Executive thereof may make temporary Appointments until the next Meeting of the Legislature, which shall then fill such Vacancies.

No Person shall be a Senator who shall not have attained to the Age of thirty Years, and been nine Years a Citizen of the United States, and who shall not, when elected, be an Inhabitant of that State for which he shall be chosen.

The Vice President of the United States shall be President of the Senate, but shall have no Vote, unless they be equally divided.

The Senate shall chuse their other Officers, and also a President pro tempore, in the Absence of the Vice President, or when he shall exercise the Office of President of the United States.

The Senate shall have the sole Power to try all Impeachments. When sitting for that Purpose, they shall be on Oath or Affirmation. When the President of the United States is tried, the Chief Justice shall preside: And no Person shall be convicted without the Concurrence of two thirds of the Members present.

Judgment in Cases of Impeachment shall not extend further than to removal from Office, and disqualification to hold and enjoy any Office of honor, Trust or Profit under the United States: but the Party convicted shall nevertheless be liable and subject to Indictment, Trial, Judgment and Punishment, according to Law.

Section 4. The Times, Places and Manner of holding Elections for Senators and Representatives, shall be prescribed in each State by the Legislature thereof, but the Congress may at any time by Law make or alter such Regulations, except as to the Places of chusing Senators.

The Congress shall assemble at least once in every Year, and such Meeting shall be on the first Monday in December, unless they shall by Law appoint a different Day.

Section 5. Each House shall be the Judge of the Elections, Returns and Qualifications of its own Members, and Majority of each shall constitute a Quorum to do Business; but a smaller Number may adjourn from day to day, and may be authorized to compel the Attendance of absent Members, in such Manner, and under such Penalties as each House may provide.

Each House may determine the Rules of its Proceedings, punish its Members for disorderly Behaviour, and, with the Concurrence of two thirds, expel a Member.

Each House shall keep a Journal of its Proceedings, and from time to time publish the same, excepting such Parts as may in their Judgment require Secrecy; and the Yeas and Nays of the Members of either House on any question shall, at the Desire of one fifth of those Present, be entered on the Journal.

Neither House, during the Session of Congress, shall, without the Consent of the other, adjourn for more than three days, nor to any other Place than that in which the two Houses shall be sitting.

Section 6. The Senators and Representatives shall receive a Compensation for their Services, to be ascertained by Law, and paid out of the Treasury of the United States. They shall in all Cases, except Treason, Felony and Breach of the Peace, be privileged from Arrest during their Attendance at the Session of their respective Houses, and in going to and returning from the same; and for any Speech or Debate in either House, they shall not be questioned in any other Place.

No Senator or Representative shall, during the Time for which he was elected, be appointed to any civil Office under the Authority of the United States, which shall have been created, or the Emoluments whereof shall have been encreased during such time; and no Person holding any Office under the United States, shall be a Member of either House during his Continuance in Office.

Section 7. All Bills for raising Revenue shall originate in the House of Representatives; but the Senate may propose or concur with Amendments as on other Bills.

Every Bill which shall have passed the House of Representatives and the Senate shall, before it become a Law, be presented to the President of the United States; If he approve he shall sign it, but if not he shall return it, with his Objections to that House in which it shall have originated, who shall enter the Objections at large on their Journal, and proceed to reconsider it. If after such Reconsideration two thirds of that House shall agree to pass the Bill, it shall be sent, together with the Objections, to the other House, by which it shall likewise be reconsidered, and if approved by two thirds of that House, it shall become a Law. But in all such Cases the Votes of both Houses shall be determined by yeas and Nays, and the Names of the Persons voting for and against the Bill shall be entered on the Journal of each House respectively. If any Bill shall not be returned by the President within ten Days (Sundays excepted) after it shall have been presented to him, the Same shall be a Law, in like Manner as if he had signed it, unless the Congress by their Adjournment prevent its Return, in which Case it shall not be a Law.

Every Order, Resolution, or Vote to which the Concurrence of the Senate and House of Representatives may be necessary (except on a question of Adjournment) shall be presented to the President of the United States; and before the Same shall take Effect, shall be approved by him, or being disapproved by him, shall be repassed by two thirds of the Senate and House or Representatives, according to the Rules and Limitations prescribed in the Case of a Bill.

Section 8. The Congress shall have Power To lay and collect Taxes, Duties, Imposts and Excises, to pay the Debts and provide for the common Defence and general Welfare of the United States; but all Duties, Imposts and Excises shall be uniform throughout the United States.

To borrow Money on the credit of the United States;

To regulate Commerce with foreign Nations, and among the several States, and with the Indian Tribes;

To establish an uniform Rule of Naturalization, and uniform Laws on the subject of Bankruptcies throughout the United States;

To coin Money, regulate the Value thereof, and of foreign Coin, and fix the Standard of Weights and Measures;

To provide for the Punishment of counterfeiting the Securities and current Coin of the United States;

To establish Post Offices and Post Roads;

To promote the Progress of Science and useful Arts, by securing for limited Times to Authors and Inventors the exclusive Right to their respective Writings and Discoveries;

To constitute Tribunals inferior to the supreme Court;

To define and punish Piracies and Felonies committed on the high Seas, and Offences against the Law of Nations;

To declare War, grant Letters of Marque and Reprisal, and make Rules concerning Captures on Land and Water;

To raise and support Armies, but no Appropriation of Money to that Use shall be for a longer Term than two Years;

To provide and maintain a Navy;

To make Rules for the Government and Regulation of the land and naval Forces;

To provide for calling forth the Militia to execute the Laws of the Union, suppress Insurrections and repel Invasions;

To provide for organizing, arming, and disciplining, the Militia, and for governing such Part of them as may be employed in the Service of the United States, reserving to the States respectively, the Appointment of the Officers, and the Authority of training the Militia according to the discipline prescribed by Congress;

To exercise exclusive Legislation in all Cases whatsoever, over such District (not exceeding ten Miles square) as may, by Cession of particular States, and the Acceptance of Congress, become the Seat of the Government of the United States, and to exercise like Authority over all Places purchased by the Consent of the Legislature of the State in which the Same shall be, for the Erection of Forts, Magazines, Arsenals, dock-Yards, and other needful Buildings;—And

To make all Laws which shall be necessary and proper for carrying into Execution the foregoing Powers, and all other Powers vested by this Constitution in the Government of the United States, or in any Department or Officer thereof.

Section 9. The Migration or Importation of such Persons as any of the States now existing shall think proper to admit, shall not be prohibited by the Congress prior to the Year one thousand eight hundred and eight, but a Tax or duty may be imposed on such Importation, not exceeding ten dollars for each Person.

The Privilege of the Writ of Habeas Corpus shall not be suspended, unless when in Cases of Rebellion or Invasion the public Safety may require it.

No Bill of Attainder or ex post facto Law shall be passed.

No Capitation, or other direct, Tax shall be laid, unless in Proportion to the Census or Enumeration herein before directed to be taken.

No Tax or Duty shall be laid on Articles exported from any State.

No Preference shall be given by any Regulation of Commerce or Revenue to the Ports of one State over those of another: nor shall Vessels bound to, or from, one State, be obliged to enter, clear, or pay Duties in another.

No Money shall be drawn from the Treasury, but in Consequence of Appropriations made by Law, and a regular Statement and Account of the Receipts and Expenditures of all public Money shall be published from time to time.

No Title of Nobility shall be granted by the United States: And no Person holding any Office of Profit or trust under them, shall, without the Consent of the Congress, accept of any present, Emolument, Office, or Title, of any kind whatever, from any King, Prince, or foreign State.

Section 10. No State shall enter into any Treaty, Alliance, or Confederation; grant Letters of Marque and Reprisal; coin Money; emit Bills of Credit; make any Thing but gold and silver Coin a Tender in Payment of Debts; pass any Bill of Attainder, ex post facto Law, or Law impairing the Obligation of Contracts, or grant any Title of Nobility.

No State shall, without the Consent of the Congress, lay any Imposts or Duties on Imports or Exports, except what may be absolutely necessary for executing it's inspection Laws: and the net Produce of all Duties and Imposts, laid by any State on Imports or Exports, shall be for the Use of the Treasury of the United States; and all such Laws shall be subject to the Revision and Controul of the Congress.

No State shall, without the Consent of Congress, lay any Duty of Tonnage, keep Troops, or Ships of War in time of Peace, enter into any Agreement or Compact with another State, or with a foreign Power, or engage in War, unless actually invaded, or in such imminent Danger as will not admit of delay.

ARTICLE II

Section 1. The executive Power shall be vested in a President of the United States of America. He shall hold his Office during the term of four Years, and, together with the Vice President, chosen for the same Term, be elected, as follows:

Each State shall appoint, in such Manner as the Legislature thereof may direct, a Number of Electors, equal to the whole Number of Senators and Representatives to which the State may be entitled in the Congress: but no Senator or Representative, or Person holding an Office of Trust or Profit under the United States, shall be appointed an Elector.

The Electors shall meet in their respective States, and vote by Ballot for two Persons, of whom one at least shall not be an Inhabitant of the same State with themselves. And they shall make a List of all the Persons voted for, and of the Number of Votes for each; which List they shall sign and certify, and transmit sealed to the Seat of the Government of the United States, directed to the President of the Senate. The President of the Senate shall, in the Presence of the Senate and House of Representatives, open all the Certificates, and the Votes shall then be counted. The Person having the greatest Number of Votes shall be the President, if such Number be a Majority of the whole Number of Electors appointed; and if there be more than one who have such Majority, and have an equal Number of Votes, then the House of Representatives shall immediately chuse by Ballot one of them for President; and if no Person have a Majority, then from the five highest on the List the said House shall in like Manner chuse the President. But in chusing the President, the Votes shall be taken by States, the Representation from each State having one Vote; A quorum for this Purpose shall consist of a Member or Members from two thirds of the States, and a Majority all the States shall be necessary to a Choice. In every Case, after the Choice of the President, the Person having the greatest Number of Votes of the Electors shall be the Vice President. But if there should remain two or more who have equal Votes, the Senate shall chuse from them by Ballot the Vice President.

The Congress may determine the Time of chusing the Electors, and the Day on which they shall give their Votes; which Day shall be the same throughout the United States.

No Person except a natural born Citizen, or a Citizen of the United States, at the time of the Adoption of this Constitution, shall be eligible to the Office of President, neither shall any Person be eligible to that Office who shall not have attained the Age of thirty five Years, and been fourteen Years a Resident within the United States.

In Case of the Removal of the President from Office, or of his Death, Resignation, or Inability to discharge the Powers and Duties of the said Office, the Same shall devolve on the Vice President, and the Congress may by Law provide for the Case of Removal, Death, Resignation or Inability, both of the President and Vice President, declaring what Officer shall then act as President, and such Officer shall act accordingly, until the Disability be removed, or a President shall be elected.

The President shall, at stated Times, receive for his Services, a Compensation, which shall neither be encreased or diminished during the Period for which he shall have been elected, and he shall not receive within that Period any other Emolument from the United States, or any of them.

Before he enters on the Execution of his Office, he shall take the following Oath or Affirmation:—"I do solemnly swear (or affirm) that I will faithfully execute the Office of President of the United States, and will to the best of my Ability, preserve, protect and defend the Constitution of the United States."

Section 2. The President shall be Commander in Chief of the Army and Navy of the United States, and of the Militia of the several States, when called into the actual Service of the United States; he may require the Opinion, in writing, of the principal Officer in each of the executive Departments, upon any Subject relating to the Duties of their respective Offices, and he shall have Power to grant Reprieves and Pardons for Offences against the United States, except in Cases of Impeachment.

He shall have Power, by and with the Advice and Consent of the Senate, to make Treaties, provided two thirds of the Senators present concur; and he shall nominate, and by and with the Advice and Consent of the Senate, shall appoint Ambassadors, other public Ministers and Consuls, Judges of the supreme Court, and all other Officers of the United States, whose Appointments are not herein otherwise provided for, and which shall be established by Law; but the Congress may by Law vest the Appointment of such inferior Officers, as they think proper, in the President alone, in the Courts of Law, or in the Heads of Departments.

The President shall have Power to fill up all Vacancies that may happen during the Recess of the Senate, by granting Commissions which shall expire at the End of their next Session.

Section 3. He shall from time to time give to the Congress Information of the State of the Union, and recommend to their Consideration such Measures as he shall judge necessary and expedient; he may, on extraordinary Occasions, convene both Houses, or either of them, and in Case of Disagreement between them, with Respect to the Time of Adjournment, he may adjourn them to such Time as he shall think proper; he shall receive Ambassadors and other public Ministers; he shall take Care that the Laws be faithfully executed, and shall Commission all the Officers of the United States.

Section 4. The President, Vice President and all civil Officers of the United States, shall be removed from Office on Impeachment for, and Conviction of, Treason, Bribery, or other high Crimes and Misdemeanors.

ARTICLE III

Section 1. The judicial Power of the United States, shall be vested in one supreme Court, and in such inferior Courts as the Congress may from time to time ordain and establish. The Judges, both of the supreme and inferior Courts, shall hold their Offices during good Behaviour, and shall, at stated Times, receive for their Services, a Compensation, which shall not be diminished during their Continuance in Office.

Section 2. The judicial Power shall extend to all Cases, in Law and Equity, arising under this Constitution, the Laws of the United States, and Treaties made, or which shall be made, under their Authority;—to all Cases affecting Ambassadors, other public Ministers and Consuls;—to all Cases of admiralty and maritime Jurisdiction;—to Controversies to which the United States shall be a Party;—to Controversies between two or more States;—between a State and Citizens of another State;—between Citizens of different States,—between Citizens of the same State claiming Lands under Grants of different States, and between a State, or the Citizens thereof, and foreign States, Citizens of Subjects.

In all cases affecting Ambassadors, other public Ministers and Consuls, and those in which a State shall be Party, the supreme Court shall have original Jurisdiction. In all the other Cases before mentioned, the supreme Court shall have appellate Jurisdiction, both as to Law and Fact, with such Exceptions, and under such Regulations as the Congress shall make.

The Trial of all Crimes, except in Cases of Impeachment, shall be by Jury; and such Trial shall be held in the State where the said Crimes shall have been committed; but when not committed within any State, the Trial shall be at such Place or Places as the Congress may by Law have directed.

Section 3. Treason against the United States, shall consist only in levying War against them, or in adhering to their Enemies, giving them Aid and Comfort. No Person shall be convicted of Treason unless on the Testimony of two Witnesses to the same overt Act, or on Confession in open Court.

The Congress shall have Power to declare the Punishment of Treason, but no Attainder of Treason shall work Corruption of Blood, or Forfeiture except during the Life of the Person attainted.

ARTICLE IV

Section 1. Full Faith and Credit shall by given in each State to the public Acts, Records, and judicial Proceedings of every other State. And the Congress may be general Laws prescribe the Manner in which such Acts, Records and Proceedings shall be proved, and the Effect thereof.

Section 2. The Citizens of each State shall be entitled to all Privileges and Immunities of Citizens in the several States.

A Person charged in any State with Treason, Felony, or other Crime, who shall flee from Justice, and be found in another State, shall on Demand of the executive Authority of the State from which he fled, be delivered up, to be removed to the State having Jurisdiction of the Crime.

No Person held to Service or Labour in one State, under the Laws thereof, escaping into another, shall, in Consequence of any Law or Regulation therein, be discharged from such Service or Labour, but shall be delivered up on Claim of the Party to whom such Service or Labour may be due.

Section 3. New States may be admitted by the Congress into this Union; but no new State shall be formed or erected within the Jurisdiction of any other State; nor any State be formed by the Junction of two or more States, or Parts of States, without the consent of the Legislatures of the States concerned as well as of the Congress.

The Congress shall have Power to dispose of and make all needful Rules and Regulations respecting the Territory or other Property belonging to the United States; and nothing in this Constitution shall be so construed as to Prejudice any Claims of the United States, or of any particular States.

Section 4. The United States shall guarantee to every State in this Union a Republican Form of Government, and shall protect each of them against Invasion; and on Application of the Legislature, or of the Executive (when the Legislature cannot be convened) against domestic Violence.

ARTICLE V

The Congress, whenever two thirds of both Houses shall deem it necessary, shall propose Amendments to this Constitution, or, on the Application of the Legislatures of two thirds of the several States shall call a Convention for proposing Amendments, which, in either Case, shall be valid to all Intents and Purposes, as Part of this Constitution, when ratified by the Legislatures of three fourths of the several States, or by Conventions in three fourths thereof, as the one or the other Mode of Ratification may be proposed by the Congress; Provided that no Amendment which may be made prior to the Year One thousand eight hundred and eight shall in any Manner affect the first and fourth Clauses in the Ninth Section of the first Article; and that no State, without its Consent, shall be deprived of it's equal Suffrage in the Senate.

ARTICLE VI

All Debts contracted and Engagements entered into, before the Adoption of this Constitution, shall be as valid against the United States under this Constitution, as under the Confederation.

This Constitution, and the Laws of the United States which shall be made in Pursuance thereof; and all Treaties made, or which shall be made, under the Authority of the United States, shall be the supreme Law of the Land; and the Judges in every State shall be bound thereby, any Thing in the Constitution or Laws of any State to the Contrary notwithstanding.

The Senators and Representatives before mentioned, and the Members of the several State Legislatures, and all executive and judicial Officers, both of the United States and of the several States, shall be bound by Oath or Affirmation, to support this Constitution; but no religious Test shall ever be required as a Qualification to any Office or public Trust under the United States.

ARTICLE VII

The Ratification of the Conventions of nine States, shall be sufficient for the Establishment of this Constitution between the States so ratifying the Same.

Done in Convention by the Unanimous Consent of the States present the Seventeenth Day of September in the Year of our Lord one thousand seven hundred and Eighty seven and of the Independence of the United States of America the Twelfth. In witness thereof We have hereunto subscribed our Names,

G°: WASHINGTON—Presid^t
and deputy from Virginia

New Hampshire
- John Langdon
- Nicholas Gilman

Massachusetts
- Nathaniel Gorham
- Rufus King

Connecticut
- Wm Saml Johnson
- Roger Sherman

New York
- Alexander Hamilton

New Jersey
- Wil: Livingston
- David A. Brearley.
- Wm Paterson.
- Jona: Dayton

Pennsylvania
- B. Franklin
- Thomas Mifflin
- Robt Morris
- Geo. Clymer
- Thos. FitzSimons
- Jared Ingersoll
- James Wilson
- Gouv Morris

Delaware
- Geo: Read
- Gunning Bedford jun
- John Dickinson
- Richard Bassett
- Jaco: Broom

Maryland
- James McHenry
- Dan of St Thos Jenifer
- Danl Carroll

Virginia
- James Blair—
- James Madison Jr.

North Carolina
- W^m. Blount
- Richd Dobbs Spaight.
- Hu Williamson

South Carolina
- J. Rutledge
- Charles Cotesworth Pinckney
- Charles Pinckney
- Pierce Butler.

Georgia
- William Few
- Abr Baldwin

AMENDMENTS TO THE CONSTITUTION

ARTICLES IN ADDITION TO, and Amendment of the Constitution of the United States of America, proposed by Congress, and ratified by the Legislatures of the several States, pursuant to the fifth Article of the original Constitution.

ARTICLE I

Congress shall make no law respecting an establishment of religion, or prohibiting the free exercise thereof; or abridging the freedom of speech, or of the press; or the right of the people peaceably to assemble, and to petition the Government for a redress of grievances.

ARTICLE II

A well regulated Militia, being necessary to the security of a free State, the right of the people to keep and bear Arms, shall not be infringed.

ARTICLE III

No Soldier shall, in time of peace be quartered in any house, without the consent of the Owner, nor in time of war, but in a manner to be prescribed by law.

ARTICLE IV

The right of the people to be secure in their persons, houses, papers, and effects, against unreasonable searches and seizures, shall not be violated, and no Warrants shall issue, but upon probable cause, supported by Oath or affirmation, and particularly describing the place to be searched, and the persons or things to be seized.

ARTICLE V

No person shall be held to answer for a capital, or otherwise infamous crime, unless on a presentment or indictment of a Grand Jury, except in cases arising in the land or naval forces, or in the Militia, when in actual service in time of War or public danger; nor shall any person be subject for the same offence to be twice put in jeopardy of life or limb; nor shall be compelled in any criminal case to be a witness against himself, nor be deprived of life, liberty, or property, without due process of law; nor shall private property be taken for public use, without just compensation.

ARTICLE VI

In all criminal prosecutions, the accused shall enjoy the right to a speedy and public trial, by an impartial jury of the State and district wherein the crime shall have been committed, which district shall have been previously ascertained by law, and to be informed of the nature and cause of the accusation; so be confronted with the witnesses against him; to have compulsory process for obtaining witnesses in his favor, and to have the Assistance of Counsel for his defence.

ARTICLE VII

In Suits at common law, where the value in controversy shall exceed twenty dollars, the right of trial by jury shall be preserved, and no fact tried by a jury, shall be otherwise re-examined in any Court of the United States, than according to the rules of the common law.

ARTICLE VIII

Excessive bail shall not be required, nor excessive fines imposed, nor cruel and unusual punishments inflicted.

ARTICLE IX

The enumeration in the Constitution, of certain rights, shall not be construed to deny or disparage others retained by the people.

ARTICLE X

The powers not delegated to the United States by the Constitution, nor prohibited by it to the States, are reserved to the States respectively, or to the people. [The first ten amendments went into effect December 15, 1791.]

ARTICLE XI

The Judicial power of the United States shall not be construed to extend to any suit in law or equity, commenced or prosecuted against one of the United States by Citizens of another State, or by Citizens or Subjects of any Foreign State. [January 8, 1798]

ARTICLE XII

The Electors shall meet in their respective states, and vote by ballot for President and Vice-President, one of whom, at least, shall not be an inhabitant of the same state with themselves; they shall name in their ballots the person voted for as President, and in distinct ballots the person voted for as Vice-President, and they shall make distinct lists of all persons voted for as President, and of all persons voted for as Vice-President, and of the number of votes for each, which lists they shall sign and certify, and transmit sealed to the seat of the government of the United States, directed to the President of the Senate;—The President of the Senate shall, in the presence of the Senate and House of Representatives, open all the certificates and the votes shall then be counted;—The person having the greatest number of votes for President, shall be the President, if such number be a majority of the whole number of Electors appointed; and if no person have such majority, then from the persons having the highest numbers not exceeding three on the list of those voted for as President, the House of Representatives shall choose immediately, by ballot, the President. But in choosing the President, the votes shall be taken by states, the representation from each state having one vote; a quorum for this purpose shall consist of a member or members from two-thirds of the states, and a majority of all the states shall be necessary to a choice. And if the House of Representatives shall not choose a President whenever the right of choice shall devolve upon them, before the fourth day of March next following, then the Vice-President shall act as President, as in the case of the death or other constitutional disability of the President.— The person having the greatest number of votes as Vice-President, shall be the Vice-President, if such number be a majority of the whole number of Electors appointed, and if no person have a majority, then from the two highest numbers on the list, the Senate shall choose the Vice-President; a quorum for the purpose shall consist of two-thirds of the whole number of Senators, and a majority of the whole number shall be necessary to a choice. But no person constitutionally ineligible to the office of President shall be eligible to that of Vice-President of the United States. [September 25, 1804]

ARTICLE XIII

Section 1. Neither slavery nor involuntary servitude, except as a punishment for crime whereof the party shall have been duly convicted, shall exist within the United States, or any place subject to their jurisdiction.

Section 2. Congress shall have power to enforce this article by appropriate legislation. [December 18, 1865]

ARTICLE XIV

Section 1. All persons born or naturalized in the United States, and subject to the jurisdiction thereof, are citizens of the United States and of the State wherein they reside. No State shall make or enforce any law which shall abridge the privileges or immunities of citizens of the United States; nor shall any State deprive any person of life, liberty, or property, without due process of law; nor deny to any person within its jurisdiction the equal protection of the laws.

Section 2. Representatives shall be apportioned among the several States according to their respective numbers, counting the whole number of persons in each State, excluding Indians not taxed. But when the right to vote at any election for the choice of electors for President and Vice President of the United States, Representatives in Congress, the Executive and Judicial officers of a State, or the members of the Legislature thereof, is denied to any of the male inhabitants of such State, being twenty-one years of age, and citizens of the United States, or in any way abridged, except for participation in rebellion, or other crime, the basis of representation therein shall be reduced in the proportion which the number of such male citizens shall bear to the whole number of male citizens twenty-one years of age in such State.

Section 3. No person shall be a Senator or Representative in Congress, or elector of President and Vice President, or hold any office, civil or military, under the United States, or under any State, who, having previously taken an oath, as a member of Congress, or as an officer of the United States, or as a member of any State legislature, or as an executive or judicial officer of any State, to support the Constitution of the United States, shall have engaged in insurrection or rebellion against the same, or given aid or comfort to the enemies thereof. But Congress may by a vote of two-thirds of each House, remove such disability.

Section 4. The validity of the public debt of the United States, authorized by law, including debts incurred for payment of pensions and bounties for services in suppressing insurrection or rebellion, shall not be questioned. But neither the United States nor any State shall assume or pay any debt or obligation incurred in aid of insurrection or rebellion against the United States, or any claim for the loss or emancipation of any slave; but all such debts, obligations and claims shall be held illegal and void.

Section 5. The Congress shall have power to enforce, by appropriate legislation, the provisions of this article. [July 28, 1868]

ARTICLE XV

Section 1. The right of citizens of the United States to vote shall not be denied or abridged by the United States or by any State on account of race, color, or previous condition of servitude—

Section 2. The Congress shall have power to enforce this article by appropriate legislation.—[March 30, 1870]

ARTICLE XVI

The Congress shall have power to lay and collect taxes on incomes, from whatever source derived, without apportionment among the several States, and without regard to any census or enumeration. [February 25, 1913]

ARTICLE XVII

The Senate of the United States shall be composed of two senators from each State, elected by the people thereof, for six years; and each Senator shall have one vote. The electors in each State shall have the qualifications requisite for electors of the most numerous branch of the State legislature.

When vacancies happen in the representation of any State in the Senate, the executive authority of such State shall issue writs of election to fill such vacancies: *Provided,* That the legislature of any State may empower the executive thereof to make temporary appointments until the people fill the vacancies by election as the legislature may direct.

This amendment shall not be so construed as to affect the election or term of any senator chosen before it becomes valid as part of the Constitution. [May 31, 1913]

ARTICLE XVIII

After one year from the ratification of this article, the manufacture, sale, or transportation of intoxicating liquors within, the importation thereof into, or the exportation thereof from the United States and all territory subject to the jurisdiction thereof for beverage purposes is hereby prohibited.

The Congress and the several States shall have concurrent power to enforce this article by appropriate legislation.

This article shall be inoperative unless it shall have been ratified as an amendment to the Constitution by the legislatures of the several States, as provided in the Constitution, within seven years from the date of the submission thereof to the States by Congress. [January 29, 1919]

ARTICLE XIX

The right of citizens of the United States to vote shall not be denied or abridged by the United States or by any State on account of sex.

The Congress shall have power by appropriate legislation to enforce the provisions of this article. [August 26, 1920]

ARTICLE XX

Section 1. The terms of the President and Vice-President shall end at noon on the twentieth day of January, and the terms of Senators and Representatives at noon on the third day of January, of the years in which such terms would have ended if this article had not been ratified; and the terms of their successors shall then begin.

Section 2. The Congress shall assemble at least once in every year, and such meeting shall begin at noon on the third day of January, unless they shall by law appoint a different day.

Section 3. If, at the time fixed for the beginning of the term of the President, the President-elect shall have died, the Vice-President-elect shall become President. If a President shall not have been chosen before the time fixed for the beginning of his term, or if the President-elect shall have failed to qualify, then the Vice-President-elect shall act as President until a President shall have qualified; and the Congress may by law provide for the case wherein neither a President-elect nor a Vice-President-elect shall have qualified, declaring who shall then act as President, or the manner in which one who is to act shall be selected, and such person shall act accordingly until a President or Vice-President shall have qualified.

Section 4. The Congress may by law provide for the case of the death of any of the persons from whom the House of Representatives may choose a President whenever the right of choice shall have devolved upon them, and for the case of the death of any of the persons from whom the Senate may choose a Vice-President whenever the right of choice shall have devolved upon them.

Section 5. Sections 1 and 2 shall take effect on the 15th day of October following the ratification of this article.

Section 6. This article shall be inoperative unless it shall have been ratified as an amendment to the Constitution by the legislatures of three-fourths of the several States within seven years from the date of its submission. [February 6, 1933]

ARTICLE XXI

Section 1. The eighteenth article of amendment to the Constitution of the United States is hereby repealed.

Section 2. The transportation or importation into any State, Territory or possession of the United States for delivery or use therein of intoxicating liquors, in violation of the laws thereof, is hereby prohibited.

Section 3. The article shall be inoperative unless it shall have been ratified as an amendment to the Constitution by convention in the several States, as provided in the Constitution, within seven years from the date of the submission thereof to the States by the Congress. [December 5, 1933]

ARTICLE **XXII**

Section 1. No person shall be elected to the office of the President more than twice, and no person who has held the office of President, or acted as President, for more than two years of a term to which some other person was elected President shall be elected to the office of the President more than once. But this Article shall not apply to any person holding the office of President when this Article was proposed by the Congress, and shall not prevent any person who may be holding the office of President, or acting as President, during the term within which this Article becomes operative from holding the office of President or acting as President during the remainder of such term.

Section 2. This article shall be inoperative unless it shall have been ratified as an amendment to the Constitution by the legislatures of three-fourths of the several States within seven years from the date of its submission to the States by the Congress. [February 27, 1951]

ARTICLE **XXIII**

Section 1. The District constituting the seat of government of the United States shall appoint in such manner as the Congress may direct:

A number of electors of President and Vice-President equal to the whole number of Senators and Representatives in Congress to which the District would be entitled if it were a State, but in no event more than the least populous State; they shall be in addition to those appointed by the States, but they shall be considered, for the purposes of the election of President and Vice-President, to be electors appointed by a State; and they shall meet in the District and perform such duties as provided by the twelfth article of amendment.

Section 2. The Congress shall have the power to enforce this article by appropriate legislation. [March 29, 1961]

ARTICLE **XXIV**

Section 1. The right of citizens of the United States to vote in any primary or other election for President or Vice President, for electors for President or Vice President, or for Senator or Representative in Congress, shall not be denied or abridged by the United States or any State by reason of failure to pay any poll tax or other tax.

Section 2. The Congress shall have power to enforce this article by appropriate legislation. [January 23, 1964]

ARTICLE **XXV**

Section 1. In case of the removal of the President from office or of his death or resignation, the Vice President shall become President.

Section 2. Whenever there is a vacancy in the office of Vice President, the President shall nominate a Vice President who shall take office upon confirmation by a majority vote of both Houses of Congress.

Section 3. Whenever the President transmits to the President pro tempore of the Senate and the Speaker of the House of Representatives his written declaration that he is unable to discharge the powers and duties of his office, and until he transmits to them a written declaration to the contrary, such powers and duties shall be discharged by the Vice President as Acting President.

Section 4. Whenever the Vice President and a majority of either the principal officers of the executive departments or of such other body as Congress may by law provide, transmit to the President pro tempore of the Senate and the Speaker of the House of Representatives their written declaration that the President is unable to discharge the powers and duties of his office, the Vice President shall immediately assume the powers and duties of the office as Acting President.

Thereafter, when the President transmits to the President pro tempore of the Senate and the Speaker of the House of Representatives his written declaration that no inability exists, he shall resume the powers and duties of his office unless the Vice President and a majority of either the principal officers of the executive departments or of such other body as Congress may by law provide, transmit within four days to the President pro tempore of the Senate and the Speaker of the House of Representatives their written declaration that the President is unable to discharge the powers and duties of his office. Thereupon Congress shall decide the issue, assembling within forty-eight hours for that purpose if not in session. If the Congress, within twenty-one days after receipt of the latter written declaration, or, if Congress is not in session, within twenty-one days after Congress is required to assemble, determines by two-thirds vote of both Houses that the President is unable to discharge the powers and duties of his office, the Vice President shall continue to discharge the same as Acting President; otherwise, the President shall resume the powers and duties of his office. [February 10, 1967]

ARTICLE **XXVI**

Section 1. The right of citizens of the United States, who are eighteen years of age or older, to vote shall not be denied or abridged by the United States or by any State on account of age.

Section 2. The Congress shall have power to enforce this article by appropriate legislation. [June 30, 1971]

ARTICLE **XXVII**

No law varying the compensation for the services of the Senators or Representatives, shall take effect, until an election of Representatives shall have intervened. [May 12, 1992]

Notes

Chapter 1

1. Reprinted in William F. Swindler, comp., *Sources and Documents of United States Constitutions* (New York: Oceana, 1975), 8:364.

2. Joseph Story, *Commentaries on the Constitution* (Boston: Little, Brown, 1833), sec. 148.

3. Arthur Bestor, "The American Civil War as a Constitutional Crisis," *American Historical Review* 69 (1964): 327–352.

4. Susan M. Kingsbury, ed., *Records of the Virginia Company*, 3:27–28, quoted in Wesley Frank Craven, *The Southern Colonies in the Seventeenth Century, 1607–1689* (Baton Rouge: Louisiana State University Press, 1949), 105.

5. Edmund Morgan, *American Slavery, American Freedom: The Ordeal of Colonial Virginia* (New York: W. W. Norton, 1975), 80.

6. George Percy, quoted in ibid., 74.

7. Julius Goebel, Jr., "King's Law and Local Custom in Seventeenth Century New England," 31 *Colum. L. Rev.* 416 (1931), at 420.

8. Daniel J. Boorstin, *The Americans,* vol. 1, *The Colonial Experience* (New York: Random House, 1958), 27.

9. Quoted in Stephen Botein, *Early American Law and Society* (New York: Knopf, 1983), 14.

10. [John Winthrop] *Winthrop's Journal: History of New England, 1630–1649* (New York, 1908), 2:352.

11. 1678 Remonstrance, in *Records of the Governor and Company of Massachusetts Bay in New England,* comp. Nathaniel Shurtleff (Boston: W. White, 1853–1854), 200–201.

12. John Adams, "Novanglus," in *Works of John Adams,* ed. Charles Francis Adams (Boston: Little, Brown, 1851), 4:122.

13. "Charter of Massachusetts Bay—1629," in Francis Newton Thorpe, ed., *The Federal and State Constitutions, Colonial Charters and Other Organic Laws* (Washington: Government Printing Office, 1909) 3:1853, 1857.

14. "Charter of the Colony of New Plymouth Granted to William Bradford and His Associates— 1629," in Thorpe, *The Federal and State Constitutions, Colonial Charters and Other Organic Law*, 3:1844.

15. "The Charter of Maryland—1632," in Thorpe, *The Federal and State Constitutions, Colonial Charters and Other Organic Law*, 3:1681.

16. McIlwaine 155 (Oct. 11, 1627); 212 (April 21, 1670); 477 (Oct. 17, 1640).

17. Richard B. Morris, *Studies in the History of American Law, with Special Reference to the Seventeenth and Eighteenth Centuries* (New York, 1930), 126–127.

18. Marylynn Salmon, *Women and the Law of Property in Early America* (Chapel Hill: University of North Carolina Press, 1986), xv.

19. Pennsylvania Act of 1718, chap. 30, in *The General Laws of Pennsylvania from 1700–1849,* comp. James Dunlop (Philadelphia, 1849), 65.

20. Letter to editor of *New York Journal,* January 21, 1733, in Morris, *Studies in the History of American Law,* 133–134.

21. 43 Eliz. 1, ch. 20.

22. *In re Wootton and Bradye* (Oct. 13, 1640), in H. R. McIlwaine, ed., Minutes of the Council and General Court of Colonial Virginia, 1622–1632, 1670–1676, Notes and Excerpts from Original Council and General Court Records, into 1683, Now Lost. 467 (Richmond, Va., 1924).

23. *In re Sir Henry Maneringe,* McIlwaine 33 (November 30, 1624).

24. McIlwaine, Minutes of the Council and General Court of Colonial Virginia.

25. William Waller Hening, ed., *The Statutes at Large; Being a Collection of all the Laws of Virginia from the First Session of the Legislature, In the Year 1619* (13 vols.; Richmond, Va.: Samuel Pleasants, Jr., Printer to the Commonwealth, 1809–1823).

26. Richard B. Morris, *Government and Labor in Early America* (New York: Columbia University Press, 1946), 386.

27. Shurtleff, *Records of Massachusetts Bay,* 2:180 (spelling has been slightly modernized by the editors).

28. Reprinted in Perry Miller, ed., *The American Puritans: Their Prose and Poetry* (Garden City, N.Y.: Doubleday, 1956), 79.

29. Quoted in Haskins, *Law and Authority in Early Massachusetts,* 102.

30. Shurtleff, *Records of Massachusetts Bay,* 1:111.

31. Shurtleff, *Records of Massachusetts Bay,* 5:63.

32. Shurtleff, *Records of Massachusetts Bay,* 3:243–244; "Apparrel," in *The Laws and Liberties of Massachusetts, 1641–1691,* ed. John D. Cushing (Wilmington, Del.: Scholarly Resources, 1976), 2:73.

33. Shurtleff, *Records of Massachusetts Bay,* 1:126, 274–275.

34. *Records and Files of the Quarterly Courts of Essex County, Massachusetts* (Salem, Mass.: Essex Institute, 1911), 1:303.

35. Order of 1619, in *Journals of the House of Burgesses of Virginia, 1619–1776,* ed. H. R. McIlwaine (Richmond, Va., 1905–1915), 1:10.

36. George Webb, *The Office and Authority of a Justice of the Peace* (Williamsburg, Va., 1736), 165.

37. David H. Flaherty, *Privacy in Colonial New England* (Charlottesville: University Press of Virginia, 1972), 185–186, 211.

38. Thomas Cooper and David J. McCord, eds., *The Statutes at Large of South Carolina* (Columbia, S.C., 1836–1841), 7:412.

39. Kai T. Erikson, *Wayward Puritans: A Study in the Sociology of Deviance* (New York: Macmillan, 1966), 12.

Chapter 3

1. Daniel J. Boorstin, *The Americans,* vol. 3, *The National Experience* (New York: Random House, 1965), 35.

2. R. Kent Newmyer, *Supreme Court Justice Joseph Story: Statesman of the Old Republic* (Chapel Hill: University of North Carolina Press, 1985), 204.

3. James Willard Hurst, *Law and the Conditions of Freedom in the Nineteenth Century United States* (Madison: University of Wisconsin Press, 1956), 5; Morton J. Horwitz, *The Transformation of*

American Law, 1780–1860 (Cambridge, Mass.: Harvard University Press, 1977), 1, 2; Peter Karsten *Heart Versus Head: Judge-Made Law in Nineteenth Century America* (Chapel Hill: University of North Carolina Press, 1996); William J. Novak, *The People's Welfare: Law and Regulation in Nineteenth-Century America* (Chapel Hill: University of North Carolina Press, 1996), 2.

4. William Blackstone, *Commentaries on the Laws of England*, 4 vols., ed. A. W. Brian Simpson (Oxford: Clarendon Press, 1765–1769; reprint, Chicago: University of Chicago Press, 1979), 1:455.

5. Hurst, *Law and the Conditions of Freedom in the Nineteenth Century United States*, 3–32.

6. Tapping Reeve, *The Law of Baron and Femme, of Parent and Child, Guardian and Ward, Master and Servant, and of the Powers of Courts of Chancery*, 2nd ed., ed. L. Chittenden (Burlington, Vt.: Chauncery Goodrich, 1846), 358.

7. Leonard W. Levy, *The Law of the Commonwealth and Chief Justice Shaw* (Cambridge, Mass.: Harvard University Press, 1957), 183.

8. Blackstone, *Commentaries on the Laws of England*, 2:258, 400–401.

9. Simpson, "Introduction" to Blackstone, *Commentaries on the Laws of England*, 2:v–vi.

10. Quoted in ibid., 2:x.

11. Lawrence M. Friedman, *A History of American Law*, 2nd ed. (New York: Simon and Schuster, 1985), 275.

12. William Wetmore Story, *A Treatise on the Law of Contracts Not Under Seal* (Boston: Little, Brown, 1844), 73–74.

13. Ibid.

14. Horwitz, *Transformation of American Law*, 160.

15. Ibid., 210.

16. John Langbein, "Introduction" to Blackstone, *Commentaries on the Laws of England*, 3:iii.

17. G. Edward White, "The Intellectual Origins of Torts in America," 86 *Yale L.J.* 671 (1977) [reprinted in Kermit Hall, ed., *Tort Law in American History* (New York: Garland, 1987), 576].

18. Ibid., 678 [Hall at 583].

19. Horwitz, *Transformation of American Law*, 86.

20. Charles O. Gregory, "Trespass to Nuisance to Absolute Liability," 37 *Va. L. Rev.* 359–397 at 365 (1951) [reprinted in Hall, *Tort Law in American History*, 203–241]; Horwitz, *Transformation of American Law*, 89–90.

21. Karsten, *Heart Versus Head*, 285.

22. Levy, *Law of the Commonwealth and Chief Justice Shaw*, 162; Robert A. Silverman, *Law and Urban Growth: Civil Litigation in the Boston Trial Courts, 1880–1900* (Princeton, N.J.: Princeton University Press, 1981), 107.

23. Lawrence M. Friedman, *American Law in the Twentieth Century* (New Haven, Conn.: Yale University Press, 2002), 352.

Chapter 4

1. The complicated question of who actually owned Dred Scott is dealt with in Paul Finkelman, *Dred Scott v. Sandford: A Brief History* (Boston: Bedford Books, 1995), and Don Fehrenbacher, *The Dred Scott Case: Its Significance in American Law and Politics* (New York: Oxford University Press, 1978), 267–276.

2. Ibid., 3.

3. Harold M. Hyman and William M. Wiecek, *Equal Justice Under Law: Constitutional Development, 1835–1875* (New York: Harper & Row, 1982), 390.

4. Rayford Logan, *The Betrayal of the Negro*, rev. ed. (New York: Collier Books, 1965).

5. Michael Les Benedict, *The Impeachment of Andrew Johnson* (New York: W. W. Norton, 1973), 49.

6. Herman Belz, *Emancipation and Equal Rights* (New York: W.W. Norton, 1978), 110, 114.

7. Hyman and Wiecek, *Equal Justice Under Law,* 477.

8. C. Vann Woodward, *The Strange Career of Jim Crow,* 3rd ed. (New York: Oxford University Press, 1974), 67–68.

Chapter 5

1. John P. Reid, *Law for the Elephant: Property and Social Behavior on the Overland Trail* (San Marino, Calif.: Henry E. Huntington Library, 1980), 359, 363–364.

2. William E. Nelson, *The Americanization of the Common Law: The Impact of Legal Change on Massachusetts Society, 1760–1830* (Cambridge, Mass.: Harvard University Press, 1975), 117–120.

Chapter 6

1. [Oliver Wendell Holmes, Jr.] Book review, 14 *Am. L. Rev.* 233 (1880) (reviewing the second edition of Langdell, *Contracts* casebook).

2. Michael Les Benedict, "Laissez Faire and Liberty: A Re-evaluation of the Origins of Laissez-Faire Constitutionalism," 3 *Law & Hist. Rev.* 293 (1985), at 298.

3. Thomas K. McCraw, *Prophets of Regulation: Charles Francis Adams, Louis D. Brandeis, James M. Landis, Alfred E. Kahn* (Cambridge, Mass.: Harvard University Press, 1984), 23.

4. 7 Cush. (61 Mass.) 53 (1851).

5. 4 Met. (45 Mass.) 564 at 566.

6. 173 Mass. 495, 496, 53 N.E. 910, 911 (1899).

7. *Wabash, St. Louis and Pacific Ry. Co.* v. *Illinois,* 118 U.S. 557 (1886) at 577.

8. *Cincinnati, New Orleans and Texas Pacific Ry. Co.* v. *I.C.C.,* 162 U.S. 184 (1896), and *I.C.C.* v. *Alabama Midlands Ry.,* 168 U.S. 144 (1897), respectively.

9. Howard Gillman, "More on the Origins of the Fuller Court's Jurisprudence: Reexamining the Scope of Federal Power Over Commerce and Manufacturing in Nineteenth-Century Constitutional Law," 49 *Political Science Quarterly* 415, 431 (1996).

10. *Santa Clara County* v. *Southern Pacific R.R. Co.,* 118 U.S. 394 (1886).

11. Owen M. Fiss, *History of the Supreme Court of the United States,* vol. 8, *Troubled Beginnings of the Modern State, 1888–1910* (New York: Macmillan, 1993), 113.

12. J. Willard Hurst, *Law and the Conditions of Freedom in the Nineteenth-Century United States* (Madison: University of Wisconsin Press, 1956), 18.

Chapter 7

1. The case, *United States* v. *McWilliams,* 54 F. Supp. (1944), which ended in a mistrial, is discussed in Leo Ribuffo, "*United States* v. *McWilliams:* The Roosevelt Administration and the Far Right," in *American Political Trials,* ed. Michal R. Belknap (Westport, Conn.: Greenwood Press, 1981), 201–232.

2. Quotations in Roger Daniels, *The Decision to Relocate the Japanese-Americans* (Philadelphia: Lippincott, 1975), 12–29, 47.

3. Ibid., 87.

4. Mark Haller, "Urban Crime and Criminal Justice: The Chicago Case," in *American Law and the Constitutional Order: Historical Perspectives,* ed. Lawrence M. Friedman and Harry N. Scheiber (Cambridge, Mass.: Harvard University Press, 1978), 305.

5. Richard Kluger, *Simple Justice* (New York: Knopf, 1976), 138.

6. National Association for the Advancement of Colored People, *Thirty Years of Lynchings in the United States, 1889–1919* (New York: NAACP, 1919), 41–105.

Chapter 8

1. Edward A. Purcell, Jr., "American Jurisprudence Between the Wars: Legal Realism and the Crisis of Democratic Theory," in *American Law and the Constitutional Order: Historical Perspectives,* ed. Lawrence M. Friedman and Harry N. Scheiber (Cambridge, Mass.: Harvard University Press, 1978), 360.

2. Quoted in Peter H. Irons, *The New Deal Lawyers* (Princeton, N.J.: Princeton University Press, 1982), 120.

3. Melvin I. Urofsky, *A March of Liberty: A Constitutional History of the United States* (New York: Knopf, 1988), 698–699.

Chapter 9

1. Lawrence M. Friedman, *Total Justice* (New York: Russell Sage Foundation, 1985), 5.

Chapter 11

1. Lawrence M. Friedman, *A History of American Law,* 2nd ed. (New York: Simon and Schuster, 1985), 656.

2. Gulf of Tonkin Resolution (1964), Public Law 88-408, August 10, 1964.

Sources and Credits

Chapter 1

p. 3, Carl Stephenson and Frederick George Marcham, eds., *Sources of English Constitutional History* (New York, 1972), 1:121; **7**, Articles, laws, and orders, divine, politic, and martial for the colony in Virginia, first established by Sir Thomas Gates, Know, Lieutenant-General, the 24th of May, 1610; exemplified and approved by the right honorable Sir Thomas West, Knight, Lord Lawair, Lord Governor and Captain-General, the 12 of June, 1610. Again exemplified and enlarged by Sir Thomas Dale, Knight, Marshall and Deputy-Governor, the 22nd of June, 1611 (London, 1612); **13**, William F. Swindler, ed., *Sources and Documents of United States Constitutions* (New York, 1975), 5:15; **14**, Perry Miller, ed., *The American Puritans: Their Prose and Poetry* (Garden City, N.Y., 1956), 79–83; **16**, *The Complete Writings of Roger Williams*, ed. Samuel L. Caldwell (New York, 1963), 3:3–4, 247–250 (italics omitted); **17**, Roger Williams, Letter to the Town of Providence, [Providence, January 1655], first published in Narragansett Club, Publications, VI, 278–279, reprinted in Edmund S. Morgan, ed., *Puritan Political Ideas, 1558–1794* (Indianapolis, 1965), 222–223; **18**, Max Farrand, ed., *The Laws and Liberties of Massachusetts* (1648; rpt., Cambridge, Mass., 1929) (italics omitted); **26**, William F. Swindler, ed., *Sources and Documents of United States Constitutions* (New York, 1979), 8:359–361; **28**, Mattie E. E. Parker, ed., *The Colonial Records of North Carolina: North Carolina Charters and Constitutions, 1578–1698* (Raleigh, N.C., 1963), 165–183; **30**, William F. Swindler, ed., *Sources and Documents of United States Constitutions* (New York, 1979), 8:253, 254; **31**, *The Colonial Laws of New York from 1664–1719* (Albany, N.Y., 1894), 1:111–116; **34**, William F. Swindler, ed., *Sources and Documents of United States Constitutions*, 2nd ser. (London, 1982), 1:133–134, 137; **35**, John Locke, *Two Treatises of Government*, ed. Peter Laslett (Cambridge, 1967), 341–388 (italics omitted); **39**, William Blackstone, *Commentaries on the Laws of England* (Oxford, 1765), 1:106–108; **40**, Mark D. Howe, ed., *Readings in American Legal History* (Cambridge, Mass., 1949), 233–235; **42**, William Bradford, *A History of Plymouth Plantation* (Boston, 1856), reprinted in William Bradford, *Of Plymouth Plantation* (New York, 1981), 355–358; **44**, William Blackstone, *Commentaries on the Laws of England* (Oxford, 1765), 1:430–434; **47**, William W. Hening, comp., *Virginia Statutes at Large, 1619–1660* (New York, 1823), 1:336–337; **48**, *The Book of the General Laws of . . . New Plimouth (1685)*, reprinted in facsimile in *The Laws of the Pilgrims*, ed. John D. Cushing (Wilmington, Del., 1977), 12–13 (original pagination); **49**, H. R. McIlwaine, ed., *Minutes of the Council and General Court of Colonial Virginia, 1662–1632, 1670–1676, Notes and Excerpt from Original Council and General Court Records, into 1683, Now Lost* (Richmond, Va., 1924), 467; **51–52**, H. R. McIlwaine, ed., *Minutes of the Council and General Court of Colonial Virginia, 1662–1632, 1670–1676, Notes and Excerpt from Original Council and General Court Records, into 1683, Now Lost* (Richmond, Va., 1924); **53–54**, William Waller Hening, ed., *The Statutes at Large; Being a Collection of all the Laws* *of Virginia from the First Session of the Legislature, In the Year 1619* (Richmond, Va., 1809–1823); **55**, Henry Steele Commager, ed., *Documents of American History*, 9th ed. (Englewood Cliffs, N.J., 1973), 37–38; **56**, John D. Cushing, comp., *The First Laws of the State of South Carolina* (Wilmington, Del., 1981), 163–175; **59**, [Daniel Horsmanden], *A Journal of . . . the Conspiracy Formed by Some White People, in Conjunction with Negro and Other Slaves, for Burning the City of New-York in America, and Murdering the Inhabitants,* ed. Thomas J. Davis (1744; rpt., Boston, 1971), 37–43; **61**, John D. Cushing, ed. *The Earliest Printed Laws of Delaware, 1704–1741* (Wilmington, Del., 1978), 216–223; **64**, *The Diary of Samuel Sewall,* ed. Thomas M. Halsey (New York, 1973), 1:533–534; **65**, Max Farrand, ed., *The Laws and Liberties of Massachusetts* (1648; rpt., Cambridge, Mass., 1929); **66**, Nicholas Trott, comp., *The Laws of the Province of South Carolina* (Charleston, S.C., 1734), reprinted in facsimile in *The Earliest Printed Laws of South Carolina, 1692–1794,* ed. John D. Cushing (Wilmington, Del., 1978), 1:287–288; **67**, W. Elliot Woodward, ed., *Records of the Salem Witchcraft Copied from the Original Documents* (Roxbury, Mass., 1864), 1:109–126; **69**, Reprinted in Cotton Mather, *The Wonders of the Invisible World* (London, 1862); **73**, Samuel G. Drake, ed., *The Witchcraft Delusion in New England* (1866; rpt., New York, 1970), 1:35–42; **75**, Stanley N. Katz, ed., *A Brief Narrative of the Case and Trial of John Peter Zenger* (Cambridge, Mass., 1972), 65, 67–68, 69–70, 74–75, 78–79, 99.

Chapter 2

p. 81, John Wingate Thornton, ed., *The Pulpit of the American Revolution: or the Political Sermons of the Period of 1776* (Boston, 1860), 78–79; **82**, Bernard Bailyn, ed., *Pamphlets of the American Revolution, 1750–1776* (Cambridge, Mass., 1965), 1:424–425, 438–439, 442–446, 448, 454–470; **84**, William Blackstone, *Commentaries on the Laws of England* (Oxford, 1765), 1:106–109, 160–162; **85**, William F. Swindler, ed., *Sources and Documents of United States Constitutions,* 2nd ser. (London, 1982), 1:234–235; **86**, William F. Swindler, ed., *Sources and Documents of United States Constitutions,* 2nd ser. (London, 1982), 1:292–295; **87**, *The Complete Writings of Thomas Paine,* ed. Philip S. Foner (New York, 1945), 1:13–16, 29; **88**, William F. Swindler, ed., *Sources and Documents of United States Constitutions,* 2nd ser. (London, 1982), 1:321–322; **92**, William F. Swindler, ed., *Sources and Documents of United States Constitutions* (New York, 1979), 10:48–50; **93**, Jack P. Greene, ed., *Colonies to Nation, 1763–1789: A Documentary History of the American Revolution* (New York, 1967), 2:325–328, 331–332; **97**, John P. Cushing, ed., *The First Laws of the Commonwealth of Pennsylvania* (Wilmington, Del., 1984), 282–287; **98**, Francis Newton Thorpe, *The Federal and State Constitutions, Colonial Charters and Other Organic Laws* (Washington, D.C., 1909), 3:1888; **99**, William Waller Hening, ed., *The Statutes at Large; Being a Collection of all the Laws of Virginia from the First Session of the Legislature, In the Year 1619* (Richmond, Va., 1809–1823), 11:39; **99**, *Laws of North Carolina, 1791,* ch. IV; **100**, Thomas P. Abernathy, ed. (rpt., New York, 1964), 111–115, 131–143; **103**, William W. Hening, ed., *The Statutes at Large of Virginia* (Richmond, Va., 1823), 12:84–86; **104**, Francis Newton Thorpe, *The Federal and State Constitutions, Colonial Charters and Other Organic Laws* (Washington, D.C., 1909), 4:2453; **105**, Thomas P. Abernathy, ed. (rpt., New York, 1964), 111–115, 131–143; **108**, William F. Swindler, ed., *Sources and Documents of United States Constitutions,* 2nd ser. (London, 1982), 1:335–336, 337, 338, 339, 342, 343; **109**, Max Farrand, ed., *The Records of the Federal Convention of 1787* (1911; rpt., New Haven, Conn., 1937), 1:18–23, 132–136, 250–255, 446–448; **116**, Herbert J. Storing, ed., *The Complete Antifederalist* (Chicago, 1981), 2:6–8; **117**, **120**, *The Federalist,* ed. Jacob E. Cooke (Cleveland, 1961); **123**, William F. Swindler, ed., *Sources and Documents of United States Constitutions,* 2nd ser. (London, 1982), 1:384, 385, 387–388, 389–390; **126**, *National Gazette,* March 29, 1792; **127**, *The Papers of Alexander Hamilton,* ed. Howard C. Syrett (New York, 1969), 15:38–39; *The Papers of James Madison,* ed. Thomas Mason et al. (Charlottesville, Va., 1985), 15:67, 68–69; **129**, James D. Richardson, comp., *A Compilation of the Messages and Papers of the Presidents* (New York, 1897–1917), 1:205–216; **130**, Sedition Act of 1798, ch. 74, 1 Stat. 596; **131**, Philip B. Kurland and Ralph Lerner, eds., *The Founders' Constitution* (Chicago, 1987),

5:131–136; **134**, Davis N. Lott, ed., *The Presidents Speak: The Inaugural Addresses of the American Presidents from Washington to Kennedy* (New York, 1961), 15–17; **136**, Judiciary Act of 1789, ch. 20, secs. 25, 34, 1 Stat. 73; **137**, Thomas Jefferson, "Opinion on the Constitutionality of the Bill for Establishing a National Bank," in *The Papers of Thomas Jefferson*, ed. Julian Boyd (Princeton, N.J., 1974), 19:275–281; Alexander Hamilton, "Opinion on the Constitutionality of an Act to Establish a Bank," in *The Papers of Alexander Hamilton*, ed. Harold C. Syrett (New York, 1964), 8:97–134.

Chapter 3

p. 161, James D. Richardson, comp., *A Compilation of the Messages and Papers of the Presidents* (Washington, D.C., 1897), 1139–1154; **189**, Joseph Angell, *A Treatise on the Law of Watercourses*, 5th ed. (Boston, 1854), 531–565; **193**, Walter Prescott Webb, *The Great Plains* (Boston, 1931), 431–434.

Chapter 4

p. 218, Thomas R. R. Cobb, *An Inquiry into the Law of Negro Slavery* (Savannah, Ga., 1858), 17, 21–28, 35–37, 67–70, 84–85; **240**, Paul M. Angle, *Created Equal? The Complete Lincoln–Douglas Debates of 1858* (Chicago, 1958), 1–9; **244**, James D. Richardson, ed., *A Compilation of the Messages and Papers of the Presidents* (New York, 1897), 3:1203; **250**, Reprinted in Melvin I. Urofsky and Paul Finkelman, *Documents of American Constitutional and Legal History, Volume I, From the Founding Through the Age of Industrialization*, 2nd ed. (New York, 2002), 399; **252**, *The Collected Works of Abraham Lincoln*, ed. Roy B. Basler (New Brunswick, N.J., 1953), 4:262–271; **256**, *The Collected Works of Abraham Lincoln*, ed. Roy B. Basler (New Brunswick, N.J., 1953), 6:28–30; **257**, *The Collected Works of Abraham Lincoln*, ed. Roy B. Basler (New Brunswick, N.J., 1953), 8:332; **260**, James D. Richardson, comp., *The Messages and Papers of the Presidents of the United States* (Washington, D.C., 1897), 3907–3916; **263**, Laws of Mississippi (1865), 83–86, 90–93; **265**, Act of April 9, 1866, 14 Stat. 27 (1866); **282**, *Charleston News and Courier, 1898*, quoted in C. Vann Woodward, *The Strange Career of Jim Crow* (New York, 1955), 67–68.

Chapter 5

p. 312, Elizabeth Cady Stanton, Susan B. Anthony, and Matilda Joslyn Gage, eds., *History of Woman Suffrage*, 2nd ed. (Rochester, N.Y., 1889), 1:70–73; **322**, Joel P. Bishop, *Commentaries on the Law of Marriage and Divorce* (Boston, 1881), 1–5; **333**, Cesare Beccaria, *On Crimes and Punishments*, trans. Henry Paolucci (1764; rpt., New York, 1986), 66–67, 93–95; **334**, Charles Loring Brace, *The Dangerous Classes of New York and Twenty Years Work Among Them* (New York, 1880), 25, 35–37, 42–47.

Chapter 6

p. 351, Alexis de Tocqueville, *Democracy in America*, trans. Henry Reeve (New York, 1945), 1:104–107, 118–119, 155–157, 247–249, 255–257, 283–286, 288–290; **355**, Christopher C. Langdell, *A Selection of Cases on the Law of Contracts* (Boston, 1871); **357**, Thomas M. Cooley, *A Treatise on the Constitutional Limitations which Rest upon the Legislative Power of the States of the American Union* (1868; rpt., New York, 1972), 351–357, 393, 594–596; **360**, Christopher G. Tiedemann, *A Treatise on the Limitations of Police Power in the United States* (St. Louis, 1886), vi–viii; **360**, Oliver Wendell Holmes, Jr., *The Common Law* (1881; rpt., Cambridge, Mass., 1963); **361**, Julius J. Marke, ed., *The Holmes Reader* (Dobbs Ferry, N.Y., 1964), 41–56; **366**, on file with *Albany Law Review*; **370**, New Jersey Laws (1851), 321–322; **370**, Illinois Laws (1887), ch. 168; **371**, Laws of New York (1910), ch. 674, secs. 215, 217, 219; **374**, *Proceedings of the Constitutional Convention . . . of 1875–1876 . . . for the State of Colorado* (Denver, 1907), 665, 698, 700; **377**, Interstate Commerce Act, ch. 104, secs. 1–5, 24 Stat. 379; **379**, Sherman Anti-Trust Act of 1890, ch. 647, secs. 1–2, 26 Stat. 209; **382**, Kirk H. Porter and Donald B. Johnson, eds., *National Party Platforms, 1840–1960* (Urbana, Ill., 1961), 89–91.

Chapter 7

p. 413, Louis D. Brandeis and Samuel D. Warren, "The Right to Privacy," 4 *Harv. L. Rev.* 193 (1890); **419**, Reprinted from *World War I and the Origins of Civil Liberties in the United States* by Paul L. Murphy, 127–132, by permission of W. W. Norton & Company, Inc. Copyright 1979 by W. W. Norton & Company, Inc.; **449**, Roscoe Pound and Felix Frankfurter, *Criminal Justice in Cleveland* (Cleveland, 1922), 3–5; **455**, From *Lynching and the Law* by James H. Chadbourn, 1–12. Copyright 1933 by The University of North Carolina Press. Reprinted by permission.

Chapter 8

p. 461, Oliver Wendell Holmes, *Collected Legal Papers* (New York, 1920), 291–297; **464**, Phillip B. Kurland and Gerhard Casper, eds., *Landmark Briefs and Arguments of the Supreme Court of the United States: Constitutional Law* (Arlington, Va., 1975), 16:18–20, 22–23, 104–106, 110–111; **467**, *Proceedings of the American Law Institute* (Philadelphia, 1923), 1:48–52; **469**, *Law and the Modern Mind* by Jerome Frank, 148–153. Copyright 1930 by Brentano's, Inc.. Copyright 1930, 1933, 1949 by Coward-McCann, Inc. Copyright renewed in 1958 by Florence K. Frank. Excerpts from Anchor Books Edition, 1963. Reprinted by arrangement with the estate of Barbara Frank Kristein; **483**, *Franklin D. Roosevelt: Selected Speeches, Messages, Press Conferences, and Letters*, ed. Basil Rauch (New York: 1957), 170–181.

Chapter 9

p. 498, Reprinted in Melvin I. Urofsky and Paul Finkelman, *Documents of American Constitutional Legal History, Volume II, From the Age of Industrialization to the Present*, 2nd ed. (New York, 2002), 735. Originally published in the *New York Times*, March 12, 1956; **501**, Excerpt from "Letter from Birmingham Jail" from *Why We Can't Wait* by Martin Luther King, Jr., 84–86. Copyright 1963, 1964 by Martin Luther King, Jr. Reprinted by permission of HarperCollins Publishers; **532**, 15 Vermont Statutes Annotated, ch. 23.

Chapter 10

p. 575, 37 *Stanford Law Review* 1267 (1985); **576**, 37 *Stanford Law Review* 1333 (1985).

Chapter 11

p. 635, United States. Congress. House. Committee on the Judiciary. Title: Impeachment of William Jefferson Clinton, President of the United States: report of the Committee on the Judiciary, House of Representatives, together with additional, minority, and dissenting views, to accompany H. Res. 611.1998; **653**, http://www.megalaw.com/election2000/bushaddress.php; **669**, http://www.aclu.org/SafeandFree/SafeandFree.cfm?ID=12263&c=206; **670**, *San Francisco Chronicle*, November 13, 2003, reprinted by permission.

Index of Cases